A Semicha aid for learning:
The laws of Shabbos-Volume 2

An English compilation of the laws of Shabbos from the Alter Rebbe's Shulchan Aruch, in accordance to topic.

Shulchan Aruch Chapters 313-317; 319-321

This Volume includes the Laws of:

Building
Cutting and Tearing
Smearing
Ohel
Trapping/Killing
Tying
Borer
Winnowing
Squeezing
Melting
Molid Reiach
Dyeing
Salting
Grinding
Kneading

Includes summaries and hundreds of practical Q&A.

Compiled by Rabbi Yaakov Goldstein

A Semicha aid for learning the Laws of Shabbos Vol. 2

Second Edition
Published and copyrighted © by
Yaakov Goldstein
Bar Yochaiy Safed, Israel
For orders, questions, comments, contact:
Tel: 050-695-2866
E-mail: rabbiygoldstein@gmail.com
www.shulchanaruchharav.com
Available on Amazon.com

5781 • 2021

ISBN: 1475032269

HEBREW STATE-OF-THE-ART SHIURIM BY RABBI GOLDSTEIN ON THE LAWS OF SHABBOS

*Deep, clear, & comprehensive **Hebrew** language classes on the laws of Shabbos, corresponding to this Sefer [volume 2] are available for purchase.*

⠿ 📄	סימן רנב' - מלאכה בערב שבת		✓	⋮
⠿ 📎	שבוע א-מראי מקומות pdf.		✓	⋮
⠿ 📎	הקדמה-Hakdama 1 mp3.		✓	⋮
⠿ 📎	רנב-2 mp3.		✓	⋮
⠿ 📎	רנב 3 mp3.		✓	⋮
⠿ 📎	רנב 4 mp3.		✓	⋮
⠿ 📎	רנב 5 mp3.		✓	⋮

Includes over 130 Hebrew classes.

The classes originally featured as part of a renowned college course in Talmudic and Halachic studies which attracted thousands of students, including many renowned scholars who have all sung the praise of the clear and comprehensive lessons given by Rabbi Goldstein.

Access to the classes is available through download, for all annual subscribers to our website, or through individual purchase. See this link for details: https://shulchanaruchharav.com/store/

ABOUT THE AUTHOR

Rabbi Yaakov Goldstein currently lives with his wife Shayna, and eleven children K"H, in Tzfas, Israel. Rabbi Goldstein received Semicha from Rabbi Schneur Zalman Labkowski of the Tomchei Temimim headquarters in 2005 and served as a chaplain in the Lotar/Kalatz and K9 unit of the IDF from years 2005-2008. He is also a certified Shochet, and has performed Hashgacha work in slaughterhouses. Rabbi Goldstein is the director of Shulchanaruchharav.com, the world's leading web-based Halacha database, and is the director of the Home Study Semicha Program, a self-study web-based Semicha program. He is a prolific author of over 30 Sefarim studied by a wide range of readers throughout the world, which is used regularly in Semicha programs around the globe. He is a world renowned Posek, answering questions to a web-based market, and serves as a local Posek, Rav, and Lecturer, in the Tzemach Tzedek community Shul in Tzefas, Israel. His many classes can be heard both from his website, Vimeo and YouTube channel. Students can join live to classes given in the Tzemach Tzedek Shul, through the " בית חבד צפת Chabad Tsfat" YouTube channel.

Other works by the Author

The present author has written books on various subjects in Shulchan Aruch. Some of these sections are not yet available to the public in a published format although all currently available **free of charge** on our website Shulchanaruchharav.com. In order for these subjects to become available on the bookshelf, and in order to add more subjects to the website, we are in need of funding. If you or anyone you know would like to sponsor a Halachic section to become available in print or on the web, please contact the author and the merit of spreading Halacha, and the merit of the Alter Rebbe, will certainly stand in your favor!

The following is a list of other subjects currently available in print:

    *All books are available for purchase on Shulchanaruchharav.com & Amazon.com

1. *The Chassidishe Parsha-Torah Or-Likkutei Torah*
2. *The Weekly Parsha Summary*
3. *The Tanach summary series-Sefer Yehoshua-Shoftim*
4. *Topics in Practical Halacha Vol. 1*
5. *Topics in Practical Halacha Vol. 2*
6. *Topics in Practical Halacha Vol. 3*
7. *Topics in Practical Halacha Vol. 4*
8. *Awaking like a Jew*
9. *The Laws of Tzitzis*
10. *The Laws of Tefillin*
11. *The Laws of Tefillin-Summary Edition*
12. *The Laws & Customs of Kerias Hatorah*
13. *Kedushas Habayis-A comprehensive guide on Siman Reish Mem*
14. *The laws & Customs of Rosh Chodesh*
15. *The laws & Customs of Pesach*
16. *The Pesach Seder*
17. *The Pesach Seder--Summary Edition*
18. *Between Pesach & Shavuos*
19. *The laws & Customs of Shavuos*
20. *The Laws & Customs of the Three Weeks*
21. *The Laws of Rosh Hashanah*
22. *The Laws & Customs of Yom Kippur*
23. *The Laws of Sukkos-Summary edition*
24. *The Laws & Customs of Chanukah*
25. *The Laws of Purim*
26. *A Semicha Aid for Learning the Laws of Shabbos Vol. 1*
27. *A Semicha Aid for Learning the Laws of Shabbos Vol. 2*
28. *The Laws of Shabbos Volume 3*
29. *The Practical Laws of Meat & Milk*
30. *The Laws and Customs of Erev Shabbos and Motzei Shabbos*
    a. *The laws of Shabbos-Workbook*
31. *A Semicha aid for learning the laws of Basar Bechalav*
    a. *Basar Bechalav-Workbook*
32. *A Semicha aid for learning the laws of Taaruvos*
    a. *Taaruvos-Workbook*
33. *A Semicha aid for learning the laws of Melicha*
    a. *Melicha-Workbook*
34. *The Laws & Customs of Mourning Vol. 1*
35. *The Laws & Customs of Mourning Vol. 2*
36. *The Laws & Customs of Mourning-Summary Edition*

Daily Halacha Subscription:
To subscribe to our websites mailing list please visit www.shulchanaruchharav.com **on your desktop** or tablet [not available on phone webpage] and look for the subscription bar on the right side of the page to enter your email to subscribe.

The subscription is free and includes a daily Halacha topic sent to you via email and/or WhatsApp, and a weekly Parsha email with a Parsha summary, Chassidic insights, and more. Likewise, you will be kept updated on all of our future publications.

Table of Contents

TABLE OF CONTENTS

BONEH VESOSER: THE LAWS OF BUILDING, DESTROYING, ASSEMBLING AND DISASSEMBLING ITEMS ON SHABBOS

Based on Shulchan Aruch Chapter 313 and 314

Translation
Shulchan Aruch Chapters 313-314

CHAPTER 313 TRANSLATION
Laws of moving doors, windows and locks on Shabbos
25 Halachos

Introduction:
The following chapter will discuss the laws that involve inserting and removing doors, windows and other parts into and out of houses and vessels on Shabbos. It will also discuss the laws of inserting locks onto ones door. At times doing the above transgresses the building prohibition, as well as the Muktzah prohibition.

Part 1: Inserting a shutter or windowpane into a window

Halacha 1
May one insert the frame and glass of a window into a window or skylight on Shabbos?

The inserts for a window[51], such as a board or any other item with which one seals off a window, even if it is something that does not have the status of a vessel at all, and was also never used before as an insert during the week, and one [now] wants[52] to insert it for its first time on Shabbos, then if he had in mind from before Shabbos to insert it (on Shabbos or he thought about it that it be prepared and designated to be inserted into a window, even though he did not think about [using it] on Shabbos explicitly,) then it is allowed [to be inserted on Shabbos].

The reason for this is: because through this thought [that the person had before Shabbos, the insert] received the status of a vessel and has thus become permitted to be moved just like all other vessel (as is written in chapter 308 [Halachas 50-51] that one's thought helps [to give a status of a vessel] for an item which is common to be designated towards [the purpose that one thought of].)

If it was used one time before Shabbos: (As well if one inserted it one time before Shabbos, even if he did not think about inserting it on Shabbos, it [also] receives the status of a vessel as a result of this insertion since it is an item that is common to be designated for this use, as explained there [in Halacha 51].)

Sealing off a skylight with an insert: Even the skylight[53] of a roof is permitted to be sealed off with an insert that is permitted to be moved, even if it was not tied and hanging from [the roof] before Shabbos.

The reason that this does not contain the Ohel prohibition: Doing [the above] does not transgress the [prohibition of] putting up a tent on Shabbos because through doing so one is only adding to the [already existing] tent [meaning the roof], and [even] this addition is only temporary being that [the insert] is not meant to stay in there for very long being that [a sky roof] is meant to be constantly opened. [It is thus permitted to be inserted, as] adding a temporary tent [to an already established tent] is permitted [on Shabbos], and it was only forbidden to build an entire temporary tent, as will be explained in chapter 315 [Halacha 2].

Inserting a board or the like for it to remain there for long periods of time: For this reason, if this insert is not meant to be opened regularly, but rather [only occasionally] after long periods of time, then it is forbidden to insert it even into a window that is in the wall as this is like adding a permanent structure into the wall [which carries with it the building prohibition].

---

[51] Back then the term window referred to the opening in the wall and not to the actual glass frame placed inside the opening. Thus the following laws equally apply with regards to placing the frame of one's window into his window on Shabbos. However to note that this law only refers to items that are a) not placed into sockets [see Halacha 17] and B) placed for a short period of time [end of this Halacha]. Otherwise, it is forbidden.
[52] Lit. comes
[53] Lit. Chimney

Part 2: Inserting a lock onto ones door

Halacha 2
Barricading ones door with a wooden rod:
No need to tie the rod to the door before Shabbos: A rod which one has made to be used as a lock, [through] inserting it by the wall near the door[54], does not need to be tied to the door before Shabbos. As even if it were not to be tied and hung there from before Shabbos, and one inserts it there on Shabbos, [nevertheless] this is not considered building on Shabbos since he is not nullifying it there, and rather it is meant to be removed and inserted constantly.[55]

Must modify the rod in a way that it is evident that it is meant for locking with: Nevertheless [locking with a rod] is a bit more similar to [the prohibition of] building then is the sealing of a window and skylight [through an insert], therefore even if one thought before Shabbos to use it to lock with on Shabbos, and even if one designated it for this purpose forever, and even if one had used to lock with many times during the week and it was designated for this use, nevertheless it is forbidden to use it to lock with on Shabbos unless one modified it and did an action to it and prepared it [to be used for] this, in a way that the modification shows on it that it is designated for this [use]. (As in such a case it is readily evident that the rod has not been nullified [to permanently] stay there, but rather is meant to remove and reinsert regularly, as his action of modification proves this, as through this action of modification it gives it the status of a vessel, and it is not usual to insert a vessel into a building and annul it there forever.)

The status of the rod once a modification has been done: [If one does this modification] it is allowed to lock with it even if one had never locked with it before hand, before [this] Shabbos.

As well it is permitted to move it even not for the sake of using it and [using] its space, as is the law by all other vessels which are designated for a permitted use.

However, if [the lock] is made in a way that it is forbidden to lock with it on Shabbos, then even though it is designated to lock with during the week, [nevertheless] it is forbidden to move it unless [doing so in order] to use it [for a permitted purpose] or [to use] its space, as is the law of a vessel which is designated for forbidden usage.

Halacha 3
Locking ones door with placing a peg in the doorstep behind the door:
A Nagar which is a peg that is inserted into the hole that is by the doorstep [behind the door] in order to lock the door, since it is inserted below into the doorstep it appears more like building than the insertion of the rod into the wall from the side [of the door]. [Therefore] one may not lock with it despite it being designated for this purpose and even if one mended it in a way that shows on it that it is designated for [locking, it may not be used].[56] Rather it must be tied to the [door] from before Shabbos, (in which case it is then permitted to lock with it even if it had never been locked with beforehand and even if it had not been designated for this) as since it is tied and attached to there from before Shabbos it does not appear like one is building on Shabbos.

Halacha 4
How does one tie the peg?
By a peg that has a bolted head: If its head has a bolt, meaning that its head is thick and is fit to be used to crush and grind peppers, then since it is similar to a vessel it does not appear so much as one is building [when inserting it into the lock], as it is unusual to insert a vessel into a

---

[54] Such as a wooden barricade placed behind a door, which is hung on hooks that protrude from the walls that are horizontal to the door.

[55] However, if it is inserted into holes made in the walls which are vertical to the door, and thus prevents the door from being pushed open, then it has different laws, as will be explained in Halacha 7.

[56] However, see Halacha 7, based on Beis Yosef and Rif, that if one placed on it a handle, then it may be inserted under all circumstances even if it is not tied, and even if it makes a hole in the ground.

44

building [and] nullify it there[57]. Therefore it does not need to be tied on strongly and rather even if it is attached with a thin rope in which case [the peg] is not fit to be taken with it, [meaning] that if one were to want to take the [peg out] from [the lock] and move it using this rope then [the rope] would immediately tear [from the peg], [nevertheless] this suffices even if it is not tied onto the door itself but to the latch of the door (or to the doorpost. As even though it is not so recognizable that it was tied to there before Shabbos to serve as a lock for the door being that it is not tied to the door itself as well as that it is not tied strongly, nevertheless it does not appear like building on Shabbos since it appears like a vessel)

[Furthermore] even if the rope is long and thus the peg is not hanging at all in the air when it is removed from the hole in the doorstep[58], but rather is entirely resting on the ground, [nevertheless] this poses no problem since it was tied to there from before Shabbos through a rope.

Halacha 5
By a peg that does not have a bolted head[59] but is attached to the door: If the peg does not have a bolted head then if it is tied to the door itself, even if it is tied with a thin string which is not fit to [remove the peg from the lock], it suffices. (As it is well recognizable that it was tied there before Shabbos for the sake of locking the door, being that it is tied to the door itself, even though the knot is not strong, and thus [inserting this peg into the lock] no longer appears like building on Shabbos). [As well this suffices] even if the entire [peg] rests on the floor when it is removed from the hole[60].

If the non-bolted peg is not attached to the door: However if it is not attached to the door itself, but rather to the latch (or doorpost) then the knot must be strong enough that [the peg] is able to be removed [from its hole] through [pulling at the rope], (as when [the peg] is well tied with a strong rope it is recognizable that it is designated to be used for locking the door, even though it is not tied to the door itself, and thus [inserting it into the lock] no longer appears like building on Shabbos). [This applies] even if the entire [peg] rests on the floor when it is removed from the hole that is in the doorstep[61].

Halacha 6
A peg that inserts into the ground:
However, all the above [is only allowed] if the doorstep is elevated [from the ground to the point that] its hole [in which the peg is inserted in] does not reach the ground. However, if the hole goes beyond the bottom of [the doorpost] and reaches the ground in a way that when the peg is inserted into the hole, the peg punctures a hole under [the doorpost] into the ground, then it appears like building and is forbidden to be locked with in any circumstance, [including] even if it has a bolted head and is tied to the door with a strong rope.

If there is a set hole in the ground into which the peg is inserted: However, this only applies if the peg constantly punctures a new hole into the ground. However, if to begin with one made a hole in the ground large enough for the head[62] of the peg to be inserted into, and thus the peg no longer adds to the hole already made in the ground, then it does not appear like building, and is permitted to be locked within the ways explained above [regarding tying the peg].

---

[57] Meaning leaving it there permanently without ever planning to take it out.
[58] From here it seems that in the typical scenario the rope is not long enough when hanging to have the peg reach the ground and is thus pulled at and stretched in the process of placing the peg in the ground.
[59] Such as a regular large nail and the like.
[60] Meaning that the rope is so long that it reaches the floor and thus has the peg rest on the floor.
[61] Meaning that the rope is so long that it reaches the floor and thus has the peg rest on the floor.
[62] Seemingly the Alter Rebbe is saying that only if the head of the peg is placed in, as in such a case it does not make a larger hole, is it allowed, however, to place in the pointy end of the peg which can make a deeper hole, then it is not allowed.

Halacha 7
Locking with a peg which had a handle inserted into it
A peg which had a handle inserted into its middle, and is thus similar to a mallet[63] which is a vessel, is permitted to lock with even if it punctures a hole in the ground, and even if it is not tied on at all, as it does not appear like building being that it is readily apparent that it is a vessel. This is not similar to [a peg] that has a bolted head which is also similar to a vessel but must nevertheless be tied and may not puncture the ground, as here one has done an action with his hands by inserting the handle into [the peg] and through doing so has turned it into a vessel, as opposed to by the bolted peg where no action was done with one's hands to give it the status of a vessel.

A bolt which has a handle:
The same applies by a bolt[64] that is inserted one end into the hole in the wall of one side of the door and the other end into the hole [in the wall] of the other side of the door, if it has a ring in its middle with which one holds onto when removing and inserting [the bolt] and uses it to pull the bolt [into or out of its hole], then [the ring] is [considered] a handle to the bolt and it is permitted to use it to lock with even if it is not tied.

Part 3: Inserting a door into an opening/doorway
Introduction:
The following laws will discuss when it is allowed to place a door into a doorway or entrance on Shabbos and when it is allowed to be removed from the doorway and entrance. The issue here is regarding whether or not doing so is considered like one is building on Shabbos.
If the door was placed before Shabbos onto its hinges and thus revolves around them, then it is always allowed to be opened and closed in all circumstances.

Halacha 8
Openings that are only sporadically used for entering and exiting:
Doors with hinges: All openings which are not made to be constantly entered and exited from but rather only sporadically, such as for example ones backyard which one does not constantly enter and exit, then if one made for its opening a door that does not spin on a hinge (the definition of a hinge is a piece of sharp wood which protrudes from the door to be inserted into the hole in the sill[65] in order so that the door move back and forth) and rather when one wants to close [the opening] with [this door], one stands [the door] upright over the opening of the doorway in order to close it, then whether this door is made of beams or whether it's made of mats of bamboo which one hung and placed upright [to be used] as a door, or [another example of the above type of door, if one had] a crack [in ones fence of his] garden or courtyard which one closed up with thorns in a way similar to a door, and at times one sporadically opens this door and enters and exits through its crack [in the fence] and then goes back and locks it, then [in all the above cases] if there are hinges on these doors or even if currently there aren't hinges on them but in the past it had hinges which were broken off it and it is still recognizable [that there once were hinges on it], then one is allowed to close them on Shabbos. [The reason for this is] because due to the detection of the hinges it is recognizable that they were doors made for opening and closing and it [thus] does not appear like [one is] building [by placing these doors by the doorway].
Not to enter the hinges into the sockets: However, one must beware that if they have hinges that one not return the hinge to their sockets as will be explained [in Halacha 17].
Doors that have no remnant of having had hinges: However, if [these doors] do not have any

---

[63] A mallet is a smaller sized sledgehammer.
[64] Vetzaruch Iyun how this case [of a bolt] is any different than the case of a rod, explained above [in Halacha 2]. [Alter Rebbe]
[65] Seemingly this refers to the bottom panel of the door frame, and not the doorpost as is done by most modern doors today.

remnant of having had hinges in the past, then it is forbidden to close them on Shabbos[66], as since they are only meant to be opened sporadically, they thus appear when being used to close [up an opening] like [one is] building a permanent wall, so long as they are not recognizable as doors.

Halacha 9
Tying the door to the opening: Even when [the doors] have hinges, [the Sages] only permitted to close them if they were tied and hung [by that opening] from before Shabbos in order to lock with. In such a case the case [the Sages] allow one to lock with it, even if when [the door] is opened it drags on the ground and when it is closed one lifts it up and stands it upright on the doorstep, as since they are tied and attached to there from before Shabbos [closing them] does not appear like building on Shabbos.

If the door was strongly tied then it is allowed to be closed it even if it never had hinges: If one tied and established [the door] there in a way that even when they are opened, they do not drag on the ground, then even if they are only elevated from the ground a threads worth, they are allowed to be closed even if they do not have the remnant of a hinge. [The reason for this is] because it does not appear like building through closing it being that even when they are opened, they are well attached and established there [to the point that they] do not drag on the ground [when opened or closed].

Halacha 10
Openings that are constantly used for entering and exiting:
An opening which is made for constant entrance and exit is permitted to be closed even with a door that does not have remnant of a hinge and drags on the ground when opened, or even if it is completely removed [from the opening] when one comes to open it due to it not being tied to there at all.

The reason for this is: because since [this opening] is made to be constantly opened up it, therefore by closing it one is not making a permanent wall but rather a temporary [one], and there is no prohibition in making a temporary wall on Shabbos unless made in ways to be explained in chapter 315 [Halacha 3].

Halacha 11
Inserting doors into openings that do not have a threshold:
All the above refers to a door[way] that has a lower threshold that one stands [the door] up on, as this threshold shows that the door is made for locking purposes and not for building [a wall].

However, if it does not have a threshold and when one locks with it one places it down on the earth and when one opens it one removes and uproots it, then since [this opening] does not have the form of a doorway, one is not allowed to close it even if [the door] has a hinge, so long as [the door is not inserted in its socket and thus] does not spin around on its hinge.

This applies even if [one tied the door in a way that] it is elevated off the ground, and even if the opening is meant for constant entering and exiting.

Other Opinions: [However] there are opinions which permit [placing a door] by an [opening that does not have a threshold if the] opening is made for constant entering and exiting.

The Final Ruling: One may be lenient in a [dispute over a] Rabbinical command, [and thus may place a door by even an opening that lacks a threshold if the opening is made for constant entering and exiting].

---

[66] However, see next Halacha regarding their law if they are tied strongly to the opening.

Halacha 12
Placing a door made of a single plank of wood into a doorway
The same law [that one may not place the door on Shabbos] applies for a door that is made of a single board [of wood and the like] which when opened one removes [the entire board] and uproots it [from the doorway], as since it is not similar to other doors one is not allowed to close it even if it has a hinge, so long as it does not revolve on its hinge. [This applies] even if [the door is tied in a way that it is completely] elevated from the ground, and even if its [opening] has a threshold, and even if it is made for constant entering and exiting.

The reason for this is: because [placing such a door by the opening] appears like one is building and placing a beam into the wall [so it become an extension of the wall].

Other Opinions: [However] there are opinions which permit [placing this door] by an opening that is made for constant entering and exiting.

The Final Ruling: One may be lenient in a [dispute over a] Rabbinical prohibition, [and thus may place this type of door by an opening made for constant entering and exiting].

Halacha 13
The law by a door made of many beams:
However, a door which is made from many beams and [its opening has] a threshold is permitted to be closed according to all opinions if the opening is made for constant entering and exiting, even if upon opening [this door] one completely removes it and uproots it, being that it is not tied at all to the opening, and even if it does not have any remnant of a hinge as explained above [in Halacha 10].

Using many individual beams to close the opening: The same law applies in a case that one closes up [an opening] using many individual beams by inserting the beams into an engraved [line worth of space] by the top and bottom [of the doorframe], as since the door is closed using many beams, they are all considered like a single door which is made of many beams, and it is [thus] permitted to close with it even if one completely removes it upon opening it, and even if it has no remnant of any hinges, as long as its opening is made for constant entrance and exit.

Part 4: The rules of when the prohibition of building and destroying apply in assembling and disassembling a vessel on Shabbos

Inserting the door of a vessel back into its hinges on Shabbos
Halacha 14
By doors that have hinges on their top and bottom as opposed to their side:
If the entire hinge came out of the socket: All doors of vessels, such as for example [the doors of] a drawer, a box or a portable tower, that have doors on their sides and have two hinges, meaning that they have two heads protruding out from the door, one on its top which enters into a socket that is in the top of the door frame and one on its bottom which goes into a socket that is in the threshold[67], then if [on Shabbos] the bottom hinge became completely dislocated from its [socket], then it is forbidden to reinsert it. [The reason for this is due] to a decree that one may come to [properly] fix it, meaning that one [may] strongly insert it [into the socket] using a mallet and hatchet in a way that one will no longer be able to take it out from there, and [one thus] will become liable for [transgressing the] building [prohibition] as will be explained, or [he will transgress the] "final blow' [prohibition] as will be explained in chapter 314 [Halacha 17].[68]

---

[67] Meaning that the case here is not discussing the classical hinges of a door which are positioned on the side of the door, but rather that the hinges are on the top and bottom of the door.

[68] Vetzaruch Iyun why here Admur leaves in doubt whether one transgresses the building prohibition or the Fixing prohibition, while in many other cases he rules plainly that attaching detached parts transgresses the building prohibition [see 313:20 or here 5A]. Perhaps though one can explain that Admur here is referring to the dispute brought later on in 314:17 that some opinions hold that one is never liable by building even complete structures for building but rather for Makeh Bepatish, and thus here he leaves it open to both

If only part of the bottom hinge came out of its socket: However, if only part [of the bottom hinge] came out [of its socket] then one may press on it until it returns back into its place. [The Sages in this case] were not worried that one may come to [properly] fix it [with tools] because [such a strong insertion] is not so necessary [in this case] being that [the hinge] did not completely come out of its socket [and thus does not require much action to secure it back into its socket].

If part of the upper hinge came out of its socket: However, if even [only] part of the upper hinge came out it is forbidden to push it and return it back into its place, due to a decree that one may come to [properly] fix it.

The reason for this decree by the upper hinge is because: the upper [hinge] is required to be inserted more strongly than the lower [hinge], being that the lower [hinge] is consequently secured within its socket when the upper [hinge] is in its place [correctly, thus by the upper hinge there is a suspicion that one may come to strongly insert it and thus transgress the building prohibition].

Halacha 15
By doors with a hinge on their side:
Even a door that does not have a hinge on its top or bottom, but rather on its side, meaning that on its side there is one bolt that protrudes which has a hole opposite it within the doorpost, into which one inserts the bolt into this hole when he closes the door, and when one opens the door he removes it out from the hole, in which case here there is [thus] no suspicion that one may come to [strongly] insert [the bolt into its hole] being that the door is made for constant opening and closing [and thus one will purposely not place the bolt too strongly into the hole], nevertheless it is forbidden to return this hinge into its hole on Shabbos due to a decree [that if one were to be allowed to do so then he may come to also insert] a hinge which is not on the side of the door, [in which there is suspicion that one may insert it strongly].

Its law on Yom Tov: However, on Yom Tov it is allowed [to insert this type of hinge into its socket, when done] for the sake of the joy of Yom Tov, [such as to get into ones food storage house to get food for Yom Tov], as will be explained in chapter 519 [Halacha 1].

Removing doors off their hinges

Halacha 16
By vessels that are not attached to the ground:
If the hinges are only loosely placed in their sockets: All the above discussion was with regards to returning the door [back into its sockets], however, to remove the doors from vessels is allowed in all scenarios that the hinge has not been strongly affixed into them.

The reason that this is allowed: This does not involve the [prohibition] of destroying [an item on Shabbos] because by vessels [as opposed to buildings attached to the ground] there is no [prohibition] against building and destroying.

If the hinges are strongly placed into their sockets: However, if they are strongly affixed [into their sockets] then taking it apart involves [the prohibition of] destroying as will be explained [in Halacha 22].

---

opinions. However, Tzaruch Iyun why specifically in this case did Admur choose to not finalize like whom we rule while in other cases he rules plainly that it has a building prohibition.

Halacha 17
By vessels that are attached to the ground:
Removing the door of a house or pit: However the door of a house and of a *Bor* pit and *Dus* pit[69] or of vessels which are attached to the ground, such as for example a chicken coop which is a vessel and is attached to the ground, it is forbidden to either remove or return [these doors into or out of their sockets even if they are placed in loosely], as anything attached to the ground has the [prohibition] of building [it] and destroying [it][70].[see note[71]]

Removing the window frame from the window of the house: Thus that which is accustomed to be done by large [festive] meals [on Shabbos], to remove the windows through a gentile[72], is not proper to be done being that this removal carries with it the liability to bring a Chatas offering if it were to be done by a Jew, being that he is destroying[73] [the window] in order to build it [again latter][74], as one plans to eventually return [the window] afterwards [back to its opening]. Therefore, when one tells a gentile [to do so] this [telling him] is a total Rabbinical prohibition and is not [within the category of] a Rabbinical decree on a Rabbinical decree which was permitted in order to prevent pain, as was explained in chapter 307 [Halacha 12].

Other opinions: [However] according to those that say that destroying in order to rebuild is only [Biblically] liable if one had intention that the rebuilding of it will make it better than the way it was originally, as explained in chapter 278 [Halacha 2], then the removal of the windows is only a Rabbinical prohibition [as here the eventual reinsertion of the window is done in no better a way then the way the window was before it was removed], and [thus it is permitted] to tell a gentile [to remove the windows in the above scenario as it] is a Rabbinical decree upon a Rabbinical decree which is allowed to be done in a distressful situation [such as here that it is too hot in the house and one needs to remove the windows for a breeze].

The Final Ruling: [Due to the above existing opinion one] therefore does not need to reprimand people who are lenient [to ask a gentile to do so] being that they have upon whom to rely. However, every person should be stringent upon himself like the first opinion, which is the main [Halachic] opinion.

As well one needs to warn the masses that stumble [and transgress] by removing a quarter of the windowpane from the window[75] unknowingly that this contains a great prohibition.

Halacha 18
By vessels that are large enough to hold 40 Seah:
Even vessels that are not attached to the ground, if they are large enough to hold 40 *seah*, meaning that their size is one cubit by one cubit [19x19 inches] with a height of three cubits [59 inches] including the walls [in its circumference[76]] [but] without [including] the thickness of the

---

[69] A dus pit is a pit that has a wall surrounding it, while a Bor pit does not have anything surrounding it, and is rather just a hole in the ground. [See Baba Basra 64a and Rashi there] In Chapter 587:1 the Alter Rebbe explains that a Dus is any building which majority of its space is underground level. However, if only minority of it is above ground level, then it has the same law as a house.

[70] This Biblical prohibition applies even if the door was only semi-firmly placed into its sockets. [Ketzos Hashulchan 119 note 4]

[71] However, by a door of a vessel attached to the ground this is only a Rabbinical prohibition and thus it is permitted to remove the covering of an item attached to the ground if it is meant to be constantly opened and closed and if it is not attached onto hinges, as explained in chapter 259 Halacha 7 and in 314 Halacha 19.

[72] Back then the windows were not move in a frame or revolve against hinges, and thus to open the window meant to remove it entirely from the opening in the wall.

[73] Seemingly the case here is discussing a window that is set into sockets in the wall as otherwise it would have the same law as the law in Halacha 1 that it was permitted to place an insert to the window on Shabbos. [So seems to learn also the Ketzos Hashulchan in 119 Halacha 15]

[74] Whenever one destroys in order to rebuild it carries with it the Biblical prohibition of destroying by vessels attached to the ground. However, to destroy and not plan to rebuild is only a Rabbinical prohibition.

[75] Evidently this refers to a window frame made of many removal parts.

[76] Meaning that one measures the 1x1 cubits from the outside of the vessel, and thus even if within the volume that is inside the vessel there is not 1x1 cubits, nevertheless it is included in the above law.

feet[77] and the crown[78] [within its height], then they are considered like a tent and carry with them the building and destroying [prohibition], and therefore it is forbidden to remove their doors from them.

Halacha 19
Removing and placing doors into and out of its hinges by non-sturdy vessels:
[The Sages] only said that [the Biblical prohibition of] building and destroying does not apply by vessels, if the vessel being built or destroyed is not sturdy. Such as for example removing the door from [the socket of] a vessel and returning it [to its socket], that returning it is not [considered] a sturdy [form of] building being that [the door] is still [in truth] detached from the vessel as it was not strongly inserted and thus can be easily removed from it, and therefore also when removing it one is not considered to be destroying a sturdy structure.

Assembling and disassembling the parts of a vessel on Shabbos:
Inserting and removing when the parts are loose: The same applies for all vessels that are put together through [inserting] individual parts [into sockets], that if the parts are not strongly affixed, then taking it apart is not considered destroying a sturdy structure and reassembling it is not considered [Biblically] building a sturdy structure.

To initially make a vessel: However, to initially makes a vessel[79] [on Shabbos] is [considered building] a sturdy structure and one is thus liable for building. [As well as] if one breaks a complete structure [not made of parts], then this is [considered] destroying a sturdy structure and is thus liable for destroying.

To strongly insert a handle into a vessel: As well one who inserts the wood into the ax to serve as a handle is liable for building. Similarly, anyone who inserts wood into wood, whether one inserts it with nails or whether into the wood itself, to the point that they became unified [meaning sturdy], then this is an offshoot of [the] building [prohibition] and one is thus liable.

[Consequently] anyone who removes wood that is inserted [into other wood and the like] is liable for destroying just like one who destroys a sturdy structure.

Halacha 20
Assembling parts together firmly for permanent basis:
[Furthermore] even by a vessel made of individual parts[80], if one strongly inserts the pieces, meaning that one strongly secured them together in a way that requires strength and professionalism, then this is [considered] a sturdy structure and one is [Biblically] liable for building if it was built to last a long time.

Assembling for temporary basis: However, if it was not made to last a long time then it is considered a temporary building and is [only] Rabbinically forbidden unless it is not made to last at all [in which case it is even initially permitted to be done for a Shabbos need[81]] as will be explained [in the next Halacha].[82]

---

[77] Meaning it does not include the thickness of the bottom panel of the vessel, and thus must be three cubits high measuring from the inside of the vessel.

[78] This refers to a decoration that extends above the surface of the vessel, such as a crowning which surrounds the top of a box and the like. Thus, it is saying that this decoration is not included in the 3 cubit height measurement.

[79] Seemingly this refers to making a vessel out of a single material, as opposed to assembling many pieces together, such as to make a clay pot and the like. The novelty here is that the rule of "there is no destroying and building by vessels" was not said in such a case.

[80] Vetzaruch Iyun what the novelty is in saying this, after having already mentioned in the previous Halacha regarding putting together a handle on an ax. Is that not a case of assembling parts together?

[81] The Ketzos Hashulchan [119 note 34] writes that this is only allowed to be done for a Shabbos need.

[82] The Ketzos Hashulchan [119 note 34] writes that this is only allowed to be done for a Shabbos need.

Halacha 21
Assembling the parts together semi-firmly:

For the above reason [that strongly inserting the parts of a vessel is a Biblical transgression], all vessels made [through assembling] individual parts [into sockets] which got displaced the Sages forbade to return [the part] on Shabbos even if one only slightly strengthens it inside [its socket] in a way that it is semi-loose[83], due to a decree that [if one were to be allowed to do so then] one may come to firmly insert it [into its socket].[84]

Assembling the parts completely loose: However, if one does not insert it at all, and rather leaves it there completely loose, then it is allowed [to be done] as long as it is usual for the vessel to be left loose [like this] forever. However, if it is usual for it to be secured and strongly inserted, then even if now one wants to place it in loosely, [nevertheless] it is forbidden to return it due to a decree that one may come to affix it strongly.

Assembling a cup together semi-firmly-First Opinion: A cup made of individual parts, some opinions say that even though it is usual for it to be assembled together semi-firmly, [nevertheless] it is permitted to reassemble it semi-firmly as we do not suspect that one may come to insert [the parts] firmly [into each other] being that it is not usual at all for a cup to be so strongly assembled to the extent that one would be liable for building. [Thus, it is permitted to be done semi-firmly as] it was only [made] forbidden [by the Sages] to assemble [a vessel] even slightly firmly by a bed made of individual parts and other similar items in which there can be suspicion that one may come to assemble [the parts] together in a strong way.

Other Opinions: [However] there are opinions that say that there is no difference between a cup and other vessels, and [it is thus] forbidden to reassemble the cup unless [the parts are] assembled completely loosely.

The Final Ruling: One should be stringent like the latter opinion unless it is a very pressing situation in which case one may then rely on the lenient [opinion] if it is not usual at all for the cup to be assembled firmly.

Cups that are made to be assembled firmly: However cups that are made with incisions along their circumference [in which one] inserts [the parts] firmly, then according to all it is forbidden to reassemble them even if one wants to place [the parts in] completely loosely.

Attaching a cover to a vessel: Nevertheless, the covers of vessels which are made with incisions along their circumference, even though they are inserted onto the mouth of the vessel very strongly, doing so contains no prohibition, neither of destroying when removing [the cover] nor of building when placing it back on.

The reason for this is: because the [inserted cover] is not meant to last at all but rather [is meant] to be constantly opened and closed also on Shabbos itself, and [the Sages] only prohibited building a temporary structure and destroying it if it was not made with intent to destroy it on Shabbos itself, as will be explained in chapter 314 [Halacha 19].

Halacha 22
Disassembling vessels that are only semi-firm within their sockets

All vessels made of assembled parts which are firmly attached to the point that if this insertion were to be done on Shabbos one would be liable, then it is forbidden to disassemble it on Shabbos due to [it carrying the] destroying prohibition.

However, if [the parts were only] slightly secured [into their sockets] to the point that there is no [Biblical] prohibition in this assembly [and it is only prohibited] due to a decree that one may come assemble it firmly then it does not [carry with it the prohibition of] destroying and one may

---

[83] Lit "Loose [but] not [too] loose"

[84] However, by all vessels attached to the ground it is a Biblical prohibition even if the parts are only semi-firmly placed into its sockets. [Ketzos Hashulchan 119 note 4]

thus [even] initially disassemble it [on Shabbos]. [see note[85]]

Halacha 23
Placing an item to support the beam of a roof that is caving inwards:
Using a vessel as support: A beam from the roof of a house which has broken [and has begun to cave into the house] is allowed to be supported by a bench or on the long beams[86] of a bed, [being] that they are a vessel. [However, they may] not [be placed there] in order to lift up [the beam back into the roof] as this is [considered] building, rather [it may only be placed] in order to prevent the [beam] from falling down any further.

Using a non-vessel as support: However, it is forbidden to use an item which is not a vessel to support the beam from under, even if it had been prepared to be moved [from before Shabbos, and is thus not Muktzah], because [doing so] is similar to building. This is in contrast to [supporting the beam with] a vessel which [is not similar to building being that] it is not usual to nullify it to a building, as explained above [in Halacha 4].

Placing the vessel in loosely: The vessel needs to be slightly loose under the beam in a way that it may be removed whenever one wishes to do so. However, if it is inserted [under the beam] strongly in a way that one cannot remove it from there anymore, then it is forbidden [to be done] because [doing so] nullifies the vessel from what it was prepared to do [beforehand]. [The laws of] a bench which had one of its legs become detached was explained in chapter 308 [Halacha 47].

Halacha 24
Leveling the floor and the ground:
One who levels the floor of the house or of a courtyard, such as for example he leveled a mound or filled up a ditch or valley, then this is [considered] building and he is [Biblically] liable.

Leveling the ground of a courtyard unintentionally: Therefore, a courtyard that [its floor] became ruined[87] during the rainy season, one may bring hay and throw it [over the floor] being that the straw will not be nullified [to permanently stay] there, as it is fit to be animal fodder or [to be used] for cement, and therefore there is no building [prohibition involved in doing so].

However, one may not throw something there which will get nullified [to stay] there [permanently] because this appears like one is [doing so] intentionally to level the floor and since it will be nullified there it is a permanent form of building. However, this restriction only applies by a courtyard that got ruined, as since one is coming to fix the courtyard it appears like one is also intending to level its ground, however in a different scenario [where it is not apparent that one needs to level his ground then] one is allowed to throw there even something that will be nullified there being that he has no intent to level the ground [by doing so].

Halacha 25
How to spread the hay on the ground of a ruined floor:
When one spreads the straw on a ruined courtyard, one may not throw it with a basket or a box, but rather with the bottom of the box. [Meaning that] one turns over [the box upside down] and places the straw on the bottom [part of the box that is now facing upwards]. [This is done] in order to change [the way one spreads out the straw] from the way that it is normally done during the week. However, it is forbidden to spread [the hay out] with one's hand.

---

[85] See Ketzos Hashulchan 119 note 18 that this is allowed to be done even not for a Shabbos need, as since the vessel can be easily put back together it is not considered destroying at all.
[86] Tosafos Yom Tov on Shabbos chapter 23 Mishneh 5
[87] Seemingly this refers to that the courtyard became muddy and very difficult to walk on due to the rain, and thus one wants to place material over the ground so he be able to properly walk on it, having no intention to level the ground in doing so.

CHAPTER 314: TRANSLATION
Matters forbidden [to do] because of [the prohibition of] building and destroying on Shabbos.
21 Halachas

The laws of breaking a vessel on Shabbos

Introduction:
The laws of destroying a vessel mentioned in the previous chapter were only with regards to disassembling vessels that are made of assembled parts. The following laws will discuss destroying a vessel that is not made up of individual parts, such as destroying a clay pot and the like.

Halacha 1
Breaking vessels on Shabbos:
Breaking an incomplete [non-sturdy] vessel on Shabbos: It was already explained that there is no building or destroying [prohibition] by vessels which are not large enough to hold 40 *seah* and are not sturdy structures. Based on this if an earthenware barrel which does not hold the measurement of 40 *seah* shattered [before Shabbos] and then had its pieces glued back together with tar, it is permitted to break this vessel on Shabbos, whether using one's hand or whether using a vessel, in order to remove its content.
Why breaking the above vessel is not considered destroying: Doing so does not involve [the] destroying [prohibition] because [the barrel] is no longer [considered] a complete structure [since it broke and was glued back together].
The prohibition in intending to make an elegant opening for the vessel: [However this lack of the building prohibition is only] as long as that [upon breaking into the barrel] one does not intend to puncture it into a nice hole so that it be an elegant [looking] opening for [the barrel], as if one does do so then he has fixed the vessel [on Shabbos] and is liable for [the] "Making a Finishing Touch[88]" [prohibition] as will be explained [in Halacha 17]. However, if one does not intend [upon puncturing the barrel to make a nice hole] then he is allowed [to puncture it].
The reason it is permitted when there is no intent to make an elegant opening: No decree was made against doing so [even if one has no intent] due that one may come to intend to do so, because a barrel which is broken and glued back together with tar is degrading in one's eyes and one [thus] does not think about making a nice hole in it when he returns [after gluing it back together] and punctures it.
The prohibition to break a complete/sturdy vessel on Shabbos: However, if [the barrel] is whole [meaning it never broke to begin with] then it is forbidden to break it even in a way that one is not making for it a nice opening, because breaking a complete structure is forbidden even by vessels. Furthermore [another reason] is due to a decree that one may come to intend to puncture in it a nice hole in order that it contains an elegant opening.

---
[88] Lit. "Hitting with a hammer". This refers to any finishing touch that one does to a vessel.

Introduction:

The previous law dealt with breaking a vessel to remove its content.[89] The following laws will discuss making a hole in one's wall, in a vessel, as well as removing the stopper of a hole and the like. When a hole is made in a structure attached to the ground, such as a wall it involves the "Building" prohibition, and when done to a vessel involves the "Finishing touch" prohibition.

Halacha 2
The Biblical Prohibition to hammer a hole in the wall for building purposes:

One who hammers a peg into the wall in order to hang vessels and the like on it, is liable for [the] building [prohibition]. [Furthermore] even if one did not [yet] hammer the peg [into the wall] but drilled a hole in the wall in which the peg will be inserted into, he is liable for [the] building [prohibition] on this hole [that he drilled] since this hole is an accessory for the building, which is the inserting the peg.

Similarly, one who makes a hole in the floor of his house to drain out the water is liable for [the] building [prohibition].

The Biblical prohibition in Making a hole for entering and exiting in an item detached from the ground: However, one who makes a hole in an item that is detached [from the ground] he is not liable, unless the hole was made in order to have items entered through it and taken out from it. For example, the hole that is made in a chicken coop which is not attached to the ground, which is made in order to enter light and let out air, this hole is a complete opening, and one is liable in making it for the "Fixing a vessel" [prohibition] which is an offshoot of the "Finishing Touch" prohibition, as explained in chapter 302 [Halacha 5].

Whether one made a hole in [a plank of] wood or metal[90] or in a vessel, he is liable on doing so for [the] "Finishing Touch" [prohibition], if the hole is made in order to enter things through it and to take things out from it.

Halacha 3
The Rabbinical prohibition in making a hole for entering or exiting: [The above was only with regards to the Biblical prohibition, however] the Sages decreed [against making] any hole [on Shabbos] even if it is made only for removing items from it or only for entering items into it. [The reason for this is] because [if this were to be allowed] one may come to make a [type] hole that he is liable on [which means a hole that is meant for entering and exiting].

Due to this [decree] one may not puncture a new hole in a barrel for the wine to flow from [this hole]. [Furthermore] even if it already has a hole and one [simply] wants to add to it and slightly widen it, it is forbidden.

Doing an action which inevitably causes a hole to be made unintentionally, such as removing a knife from a barrel: [However in this case it is only forbidden] when one intends to widen the hole, however if there was a knife jammed in the wooden barrel from before Shabbos in order for the wine to flow from the hole that is formed upon removing the knife then it is permitted to remove it and reinsert it on Shabbos.

The reason this is allowed: [Now], although it is impossible to avoid the hole from widening upon removing it, [nevertheless] this does not pose any [Halachic] problem since one has no intent to widen the hole. Now, although it is inevitable [for this widening to be avoided, and thus it should be prohibited even if one does not intend to widen it] nevertheless since even one who makes a new similar hole intentionally only transgresses a Rabbinical prohibition, being that [the hole] is only made removing [the wine] out from it [as opposed to also entering wine into it],

---

[89] and seemingly throw out the vessel.
[90] Vetzaruch Iyun from Halacha 14 that when such a hole is made on the cover a barrel one is not Biblically liable because it can be removed. Perhaps however this refers to making a hole in them for purposes of keeping items inside the hole and for removing them.

therefore [the Sages] were not so stringent on this to prohibit even adding to [this type of] hole unintentionally.

Other Opinions: [However] there are opinions that argue and say that [the Sages] did not permit to remove the knife from the barrel on Shabbos unless one has already removed it once from before Shabbos. [The reason removing it one time before Shabbos suffices is] as then it is no longer inevitable to avoid widening the hole through removing it on Shabbos, and rather it is possible that [removing] it will not add [to the hole] at all, in which case even if it did [happen to] add [to the hole when removed on Shabbos] it poses no [Halachic] problem being that one did not intend to do so.

The Final Ruling: The main [Halachic] opinion is like the former opinion, although in a situation that there is not much need for one to remove the knife, it is proper[91] to suspect for the latter opinion.

Halacha 4
Removing a knife from a wall:

The custom in a case that a hole will inevitably be widened in a wall, such as when removing a knife jammed in a wooden wall: However, a knife which was inserted into a wooden wall before Shabbos, then if it has been somewhat firmly inserted, the custom is to forbid removing it on Shabbos unless one had removed it already one time before Shabbos, as in such a case it is no longer inevitable to avoid widening the hole. However, when one has never yet removed the knife out from this hole it is impossible to avoid widening the hole upon removing it on Shabbos, being that it was somewhat firmly inserted into the wall.

The reason for the above custom: [Now, although this hole is widened unintentionally, nevertheless the Sages] only permitted to widen [a hole] unintentionally by a barrel, being that even to initially make a hole intentionally [in a barrel] only involves a Rabbinical prohibition. However [since] one who makes a hole in a wall with intention is at times liable for a Chatas Offering, such as if he punctured it in order to insert a peg into [the wall], and even one who widens this hole the tiniest amount with intention is [also] liable, therefore it should receive the stringency not to add to [the hole] even if he has no intention in doing so, if it is inevitable to avoid.

The reason that from the letter of the law the above is allowed: This is the reason behind the [above] custom. However from the letter of the law this is not a clear prohibition being that even if one were to initially make a new hole in the wall in the exact same scenario as above when one widens the hole through removing the knife, which is done not for the sake of inserting a peg into, then doing so would not involve a Biblical prohibition being that [a)] it is an action which is not done for its use, as well as [b)] that he is damaging the wall, as well as [c)] that the widening of the hole made through removing the knife is an irregular way of making [a hole], and all [actions done] irregularly do not at all carry any Biblical prohibition even by a complete [form of forbidden] action [and certainly here that the action itself is not a complete prohibition due to reason a) and b)]. Therefore, it should not be prohibited to widen [the hole] unintentionally just like it was not prohibited by a barrel in accordance to what was explained there that the main opinion is like those that permit doing so.

Must one be stringent like the custom: Nevertheless, one may not be lenient against [following] this custom.

---

[91] Lit. Tov

Halacha 5
Removing a knife from a bench and the like:

If the vessel cannot hold 40 Seah: However, a knife which is jammed into a bench or another detached item, is permitted to be removed on Shabbos [according to all opinions] even if it had never been removed beforehand.

The reason for this is: because making a hole in a detached item never carries with it the prohibition of building but rather [can be forbidden] only because of a decree [that one may come to] "fix a vessel" if he makes an opening that is meant for entering or exiting. However, when one is not making an opening at all for entering or exiting but rather it [just happens to] consequently be formed through removing the knife, then there is no prohibition at all in doing so. [This is opposed to the case of a barrel that the making of a hole serves that the wine flow from it, and therefore in that case there are opinions which prohibit one to remove the knife if it will inevitably widen the hole.]

If the vessel is large enough to hold 40 seah: [However] if [the knife] is jammed into a large barrel or other large vessels which hold 40 *seah* [and thus] carry with them the building and destroying [prohibition], then it has the same law as if it were jammed stuck in a wall [in which the custom is not to remove on Shabbos unless it had been previously removed before Shabbos].

Halacha 6
Unplugging the hole of a barrel of wine:

A barrel [of wine] which had a hole that was plugged up, even if it was plugged with one's hands[92], [or] with wood or another item, it is permitted to open it on Shabbos.

However, this is only allowed when [the hole in the barrel] is above the [area of the] sediment [which lies on the bottom of the barrel], however if it is parallel to the sediment then it is forbidden to open it, (unless it is meant to be constantly opened and closed as is the case with the tap of a barrel).

The reason for this is because: since the [hole] is so low [in the barrel] all the weight of the wine rests on it, and one [thus] needs to plug it up well, [and] therefore when one opens it, it is considered like one is opening a new hole. However, when [the hole] is above the sediment in which case one does not need to plug it well, it is not considered as if one is opening it for the first time.

Halacha 7
Using a tool to drill a hole through a plugged up hole:

In [any] situation that it is allowed to open the plug of an old hole it is [also] allowed to puncture it [i.e. the plug] even with a [non-electric[93]] drill. For example, if the tap of the barrel broke and one is not able to remove it, one may puncture it with a [non-electric] drill. It goes without saying that one is allowed to take another tap and bang it into the tap that is stuck [thus pushing in the broken tap and entering a new tap at the same time].

[The above however is only allowed to be done] if one wants to drink wine [from this barrel] on Shabbos, and only as long as that the tap is not parallel to the sediment, as was explained [in the previous Halacha].

Halacha 8
Unplugging the hole of a wooden barrel: There are opinions which say that [the Sages] only permitted to unplug an old hole by an earthenware barrel being that the plugs [of such material] are not well firmed into the hole, however by a wooden barrel in which the hole is well firmed

---

[92] Meaning that one intentionally did so.

[93] Meaning that one may not plug in the drill, however he may use it while it is not plugged in being that it has the status of Muktzah Machmas Issur, which is allowed to be moved in order to use.

with the wood used to plug it and one [also] cuts the protruding part[94] of [the wooden plug] with intent so it not be removed, then [removing or drilling through this plug] certainly appears like [making] a new hole and it is [thus] forbidden.

Other Opinions: [However] there are opinions that argue on this [and rather permit this to be done even by a wooden barrel].

The Final Ruling: One may rely on the latter opinion in a case of great need, to be lenient regarding a [disputed] Rabbinical prohibition.

Halacha 9
Inserting a tap into the hole of a barrel on Shabbos:
It is permitted to insert a hollow rod or other [form of] tabs into a [previously made hole that is in a] barrel, in order to remove wine from it, even if it had never before been placed in the barrel and one [thus] does not know at all whether [the tab] will fit the size of the hole of this barrel.

We do not suspect that perhaps it will not fit into [the hole, being that the tab is too large] and one will [then come to] cut and grate down [the] circumference [of the tab] until it reaches the size [of the hole], and thus be liable for the cutting prohibition as will be explained [in Halacha 16].

Halacha 10
Inserting a drainpipe into the barrel:
Made from a myrtle leaf: However, it is forbidden to insert a myrtle leaf[95] into the hole of a barrel in order to prevent the wine from flowing onto the walls of the barrel, and rather have it flow on the leaf which has been folded to form something similar to a drainpipe, due to a decree that one may come to affix a drainpipe[96] for his wine so that the wine flow into it and travel a distance.

The reason this decree does not apply by a tap: The reason that this decree was not made against inserting a hollow rod [into the barrel] is because the rod has no modification done to it [when coming to place it in the hole] and is rather just [simply] inserted into the hole [the way it is], therefore [the Sages] did not decree [against doing so] due to suspicion that one may come to do a modification to connect a drainpipe to his wine. However, by the leaf, in which a modification has been done to it being that he takes it and folds it like a drainpipe, since it appears like making a drainpipe the [Sages] decreed against it due to that one may come to attach an actual drainpipe to his wine.

Halacha 11
Another opinion regarding why it is forbidden to attach a leaf to help drain the wine: However there are opinions which say that also by a leaf there was no decree made [that one may come to affix] a drainpipe, but rather it was decreed [against] because the leaf may get damaged and one will then come to pluck another leaf from the detached[97] branch in order to place it into the hole of the barrel, and this removal [of the new leaf] is prohibited due to [the prohibition of] "fixing a vessel". As any item which is altered on Shabbos so it be fit to be used for a given purpose carries with it [the prohibition of] "fixing a vessel" as will be explained in chapter 340 [Halacha 17].

The reason for why this is forbidden even if the leaf can be used for animal fodder: Even if the leaf is soft and is [thus] fit to be eaten by animals, nevertheless it is prohibited to pluck it due to "fixing a vessel". As [the Sages] only said that [modifying] animal fodder [into a vessel] does not carry with it the prohibition of "fixing a vessel" being that they are soft and do not last, as will be

---

[94] Lit. Its head
[95] The case here is discussing even a leaf which is not Muktzah, such as that it was plucked off the tree before Shabbos to be used to smell.
[96] Meaning he may come to attach a pipe which will carry the wine to a further area.
[97] Meaning we do not suspect that one will come to pluck a leaf from a tree, however from a branch that had been previously cut off, we do suspect.

explained in chapter 322 [Halacha 4[98]], in a case that one modifies the food to become an independent vessel, such as cutting a piece of straw to use as a toothpick in which case it is not considered like one is fixing a vessel being that it is not at all common to initially make a vessel out of food, due to the fact that it does not last long. However, it is common to [use food] to modify through it a vessel that is already made, such as to place the leaf in the hole of the barrel which is already made. Therefore, when one plucks [the leaf out from the detached branch] for this purpose this removal carries with it [the prohibition of] "fixing a vessel".

The practical ramifications of this opinion-It may be done if one has many leaves available: According to this opinion that it is only prohibited to insert a leaf into the hole of the barrel because one may come to pluck off [another leaf], [the Sages] did not prohibit [doing so] in a scenario that one has many leaves which had been plucked from before Shabbos, as in this case there is no need to worry that that one may come to pluck a leaf [from a branch] as even if one or two [leaves] were to ruin he still has more and we do not suspect that perhaps all his leaves will ruin.

The Final Ruling: By a dispute over a Rabbinical prohibition, one may follow the lenient opinion.

Halacha 12
Tearing the covering off of a bottle:
A person may tear the hide which [seals] the opening of a barrel of wine or other liquids, if he does so for the need of Shabbos. He need not worry [about any tearing prohibition involved in doing so], because tearing a detached item is allowed to be done even initially as will be explained [in Halacha 16].

[However, this is only allowed] as long as one does not intend to make something similar to a drainpipe out of the torn skin [i.e. a funnel] being that doing so is considered like fixing a vessel.

Halacha 13
Chopping off the top of a barrel:
A person may present a barrel of wine before his guests, and cut off its head (the definition of the head of the barrel is the area of the lid which is the [most] elevated area of the barrel when [the barrel] is resting [on its bottom] in which the surrounding area slants downwards from all sides) with a sword from underneath its lid. Meaning that one cuts the surrounding opening of [the barrel] together with the lid that is covering it.[99]

The reason the above is allowed: Now although through doing this one makes a new opening in the barrel, [nevertheless] this does not pose a problem because for certain one has no intent to make a new opening [by doing so], being that it is not at all usual to make [an opening] this way, to chop off the head of the barrel in order to make an opening. Rather one intends [in doing so] to look good, to show off his generosity before the guests, by him widening for them the area that the wine can be taken from.

Restrictions on the above allowance: [However] this is [only allowed] if the barrel was broken and then glued back together with tar and also does not hold 40 *seah*, in which case doing so does not carry with it the destroying [prohibition] as explained above [in Halacha 1].

The prohibition to make a hole in the side of the barrel: However, it is forbidden to make a hole in the body of the barrel even with a spear in which one makes a large hole that is not similar to an opening, because nevertheless he is for certain intending to make a hole [by doing so]. Meaning that since he does not want to open the lid on a constant basis for whatever reason that he has, therefore he has made this hole to remove the wine with at all times that he does not wish

[98] Of the Michaber. This chapter of the Alter Rebbe's Shulchan Aruch did not make it to print.
[99] Meaning the following: The lid is made in a way that it inserts within the top of the barrel, and is thus surrounded by the top area of the barrel. One then cuts off the entire lid by cutting the barrel from under the lid, thus consequently also cutting with it the top edge of the barrel that surrounded the lid.

to open the lid, in which case this is a complete opening which is made for exiting purposes which the Sages prohibited.

The reason why here we do not say that he is doing so to show his generosity is because: if he had intended to [make the hole in order to] make himself look good then he should have opened the lid, being that through there one can take out a lot more wine then is able to be taken out through the hole that he made.

Halacha 14
Making a hole in the lid of a barrel:

Making a hole on the top of the lid: However, it is permitted to make a hole in the lid from above in order to take out wine through it, even if the barrel is whole [meaning was never broken and then glued back together].

The reason for this is: because it is not usual at all to make an opening in the lid from above, [as one] rather just takes off the lid. Therefore, this hole which is on top is not apparent and is not considered to be an opening at all. Thus the [Sages] did not prohibit [making a hole] within the lid, as since even if one were to make a complete hole [in the lid,] [meaning that the hole was made] for entering wine into and to remove wine from it, one is [nevertheless] not Biblically liable as [opposed to the the law] for one who makes [such a hole] in the barrel itself [in which case he is liable]. [The reason for why one is not Biblically liable by a hole made in the lid is] because the lid is not considered attached to the barrel even when it is placed on the opening [of the barrel], rather it is an individual item. Therefore the hole [which is made in it] is not considered made to enter and remove [wine] through it, as when one removes and enters [wine] through this hole it is as if he is removing and entering it through the mouth of the barrel alone [without the lid being attached to it], as this hole in the lid] does not at all help one in removing and entering [wine into the barrel] being that even without this [hole] one would be able to enter and remove [the wine] through the mouth of the barrel. Now, although the mouth is sealed with the lid [nevertheless] this is not considered a complete sealing since the lid is not considered attached to the barrel [and thus we do not consider the hole in the lid to be of any real help]. Thus [being that making a hole in the lid is never Biblically prohibited even when made to enter and exit through] therefore [the Sages] were not overly strict to forbid even making a hole which is only made to remove [wine] from it, when made in an area that it is not common to make an opening from which [by a barrel refers to the area that] is above on its top.[100]

Making a hole on the side of the lid: However, it is forbidden to make a hole on the side [of the lid], meaning in the area where the barrel slants downwards.

The reason for this is: because it is common to occasionally make an opening on its side, such as when one wants the barrel to be open to constantly be able to remove wine from it and he does not want to remove the lid [permanently for this purpose] in order so dust or waste not fall in the wine, and he therefore makes an opening on its side.

Halacha 15
Making a hole on the top of the actual barrel:

However to make a hole in the actual barrel[101] is forbidden even on its top, even though it is not common to make an opening there, as since if [this hole] were to be made to enter and remove [wine] through it then he would be Biblically liable even though it was made on its top, therefore even when the hole is only made to remove [wine] through it, it is Rabbinically forbidden even

---

[100] This implies that it was only permitted due to a joint of two reasons: a) that one would never be Biblically obligated on such a hole, and b) that it is unusual to make a hole in such an area. However, if one of the above is lacking then it remains Rabbinically prohibited.
[101] Such as if it does not have a lid and rather is completely sealed on top and bottom, or if it has a lid and one wants to make a hole on its bottom side which is part of the barrel.

when made in its top.

The prohibition of cutting an item to a required size, cutting an item to small pieces, and destroying vessels

Halacha 16
The principal prohibition: One who cuts hide and is particular to cut it to the exact size that he needs, such as for example he is cutting it for straps and for sandals, this is a principal form of forbidden work, being that in the [process of building the] Tabernacle they would cut the skin of rams or *techashim* to an exact size to be made a cover for the tent.

The offshoot prohibition: Anyone who cuts any given item which is detached [from the ground] and is particular to cut it to a specific size, is [doing an action which is] an offshoot of [the primary] cutting [prohibition].

Examples: For example, one who cuts off the head of a feather, which is thin and soft and is [thus] fit to be used [to cushion] a pillow or a blanket with, then he is liable if he intends to [use it for this] being that one is particular to cut it to the exact size that is fit for him.

Similarly, one who sands down the head of a wooden pole so that it is smooth and sharp, is liable for [the] cutting [prohibition].

The prohibition to cut an item into small pieces: [Furthermore] even if he is not meticulous on the sizes, if he cuts [wood] into very thin pieces in order to light the fire [with them], he is liable for [the] grinding [prohibition].

The prohibition of doing a mundane act even if no actual prohibited work is involved: However, one who cuts [the wood] into big pieces and is not meticulous about their size, then it only contains a Rabbinical prohibition [which was prohibited] because it is a mundane action and [thus] disgraces the Shabbos. [This is prohibited even] when doing so does not contain the [prohibition of] moving Muktzah, such as by wood which was designated for a use and is [thus] prepared to be moved.

The conditions needed to be allowed to cut an item on Shabbos: However other detached items which cutting is not considered a mundane action are allowed [to be cut] as long as one does not have intent to cut them to a specific size and does not cut them into very small pieces, as well as that it is an item that does not contain [the prohibition of] fixing a vessel in cutting it as will be explained in chapter 340 [Halacha 17][102].

Cutting the strings wrapped around food: Based on this it is permitted to cut the knots of a spit which are tied around a lamb or chicken that are roasting on it. Similarly, stuffed chickens which are sewed shut one is allowed to cut the string of the sewing.

Halacha 17
Breaking the rope that secures the cover to its vessel: Similarly, seals that are on vessels, such as a chest of drawers, box and portable tower which have their covering tied to them with a rope, it is permitted to cut the rope even with a knife or undo [the rope even] through taking apart its threads[103], in order to open [the box] to remove its content.

Undoing its knot: It goes without saying that it is allowed to undo the knot as it is not a permanent knot being that it is meant to be constantly removed.

The reason that this does not contain a destroying prohibition: Now, although the rope is made to attach the cover to the vessel, and thus when one cuts it or undoes it he is destroying this attachment, [nevertheless] this does not contain the [prohibition of] destroying, as the rope [only gives the cover] a weak attachment [to the vessel] being that it is not that strong, and thus when one destroys it one is destroying an incomplete [non-sturdy] vessel [which is allowed as the] destroying [prohibition] only applies by vessels when destroying a complete [sturdy] vessel.

---
[102] See also chapter 308 Halacha 54 and 55
[103] As opposed to untying the actual knot, which will explained below.

The prohibition to break a lock on Shabbos: Based on the above [that a rope is only allowed to be cut because it is considered to give an non-sturdy attachment] it is thus only permitted to cut and undo a rope and the like, however locks made of wood and metal, which are strong [materials], are forbidden to be undone and broken [even] if one lost the key being that this is a complete destruction [meaning a destruction of a sturdy structure] which is forbidden even by vessels.

The prohibition to remove the door off its hinges on Shabbos: Similarly, it is forbidden to remove the hinges that are behind the box (this refers to the pegs which attach the cover of the box to its walls behind it. [This is made by] inserting a peg into the small holes of the two parallel metal [bolts], one [bolt] being set on the cover and one by the wall, and through the peg that is inserted into both of them together they are attached and merge with each other. This peg has one head that is a little thick and its second head has a hole in which one inserts into it [another] small peg.[104])

The reason for this is: because the [pegs] are strongly inserted and [thus removing them] is a complete form of destruction.

The prohibition to remove the metal panels of a barrel: Similarly, it is forbidden to remove the metal panels of a wooden barrel that is made of many beams of wood which are attached [to each other] through the metal panels that are on them, as when one removes these panels it is a complete form of destruction.

The allowance to ask a gentile to break a sturdy/complete vessel on Shabbos: Nevertheless, through a gentile one may be lenient to [ask him] whether to break the locks and whether to remove the hinges and metal panels.

The reason for this allowance is: because there are opinions which say that there is no building and destroying [prohibition] by vessels including even to build a sturdy [complete] structure and to destroy a complete [sturdy] structure. [According to this opinion] it was only said that one who reassembles a chest of drawers and a box and portable tower in a strong way, and similarly that one who reassembles a vessel made up of individual parts in a strong way, that he is liable for a sin offering, because he has fixed a vessel and is [thus] obligated [for the offering] because [he has transgressed the prohibition of] "Making a finishing touch", [and not because of the building prohibition]. Thus, when one destroys an item that is firmly assembled, and even if he destroys and breaks a vessel made completely of a single part, this does not contain any prohibition when done for the sake of Shabbos, and one may rely on this opinion regarding asking a gentile to do so when needed to be done for a Shabbos need.

Halacha 18
Breaking through woven palm leaf baskets in order to get the food inside:
Baskets that are used for figs and dates, which are vessels that are made from palm leaves and have placed in them figs or dates that have not [yet] ripened in the sun in order so they completely ripen in there [in the basket], then if the cover is tied to them with a rope, it is permitted to unravel the rope or cut it as explained [in the] above [Halacha].

[Furthermore] even the actual body of these vessels are permitted to be unraveled and cut, as the structure of these vessels which are made of palm leaves are a week structure which is not made to last long, and [thus] when breaking it, it is only considered as if one is breaking hazelnuts and almonds in order to get the food that is in them.

Halacha 19
Breaking the ropes that tie a door to a pit:
Seals that are on the ground, such as the door of a pit which is tied to it with a rope is permitted to be untied being that the knot was not made to last long, as it is meant to be constantly untied.

---

[104] The idea here is that the cover is not attached to the wall through nails which are hammered into it and the like, but rather through the insertion of the pegs. Thus, the novelty here is that even in such a case one may not remove the pegs.

However, if one is unable to undo the knot then it is forbidden to undo the threads of the rope or to cut it due to [the] destroying [prohibition], as every item attached to the ground has [a] building and destroying [prohibition] even if it is not a complete [sturdy] vessel.

The law by a door not made to last: However, this only applies by a door that is made to last [on the pit] and not be removed on Shabbos, and thus when one wants to open the pit he unties the rope and opens the door [and then replaces it] and does not totally remove the door from there, as it is set to be there for some time. However, if [the door] is not made to last at all then there is no destroying [prohibition] involved neither in unraveling the rope or cutting it, and not even in removing the actual door from it, unless it is a case that the door revolves on hinges and [to remove it] one must remove the hinge from its socket as explained in chapter 313 [Halacha 17].

Breaking the opening of the oven on Shabbos: For this reason, it is permitted for one to remove the board that is placed in front of the oven and is plastered with clay from before Shabbos as written in chapter 259 [Halacha 7] being that it is not made to last at all but rather with intent to remove it on Shabbos. [However, see there that the custom is to be stringent even in this case, and do so only through a gentile or child or with an irregularity.]

The prohibition of plugging a hole on Shabbos

Halacha 20

The law: Just like it is forbidden to puncture any hole due to the decree of fixing a vessel as was explained above [in Halacha 3], so too it is forbidden to plug any hole being that this is similar to fixing a vessel.

Plugging it with wax, cloth, and a non-Muktzah rock: Therefore, it is forbidden to plug the hole of a barrel even with a material that does not smear[105] and that does not involve one coming to [transgress the] squeeze [prohibition][106], such as for example plugging it with a pebble or pieces of wood which was prepared for this use from before Shabbos and is thus not forbidden to be moved [i.e. is not Muktzah].

Plugging it with food and the like: However, if one places a given food or anything of the like into the hole in order to hide it there, and this consequently also plugs up the hole, it is allowed.

Cunningly stuffing the hole with food: [Furthermore] it is allowed for a Torah Scholar to connive and use this loophole to plug the hole with a given food or anything of the like, and then tell to anyone he sees do this that he only intends to hide [the food in the hole].

The reason why a Torah Scholar may do this is: because even if he would do this in a non-conniving way [meaning that] he would tell them [his true intentions that] he is doing so to plug it, [nevertheless] this would [still] only be a Rabbinical prohibition [and thus we do not prohibit him to connive in doing so].

As well [in addition to the above it is allowed] because being he is a Torah Scholar [allowing him to connive in doing this] will not lead him to [eventually] do it in a non-conniving way.

May an ignoramus also cunningly stuff with food? However, by an ignoramus [the Sages] did not allow him to connive [in doing this] because he may come to do so even in a non-conniving way, [meaning that] he will not say at all that he is doing so in order to hide [the food], but rather in order to stuff the hole.

Other Opinions: [However] there are opinions which allow this to be done even by an ignoramus.

The Final Ruling: One may rely on the latter opinion to be lenient by Torah Scholars, to allow them to connive in doing this even in today's times that we no longer have people that are categorized as [true] Torah Scholars with regards to other issues.

Plugging a hole with a commonly used material: All the above is with regards to stuffing the hole with an item which is not common to stuff with, however it is permitted to plug it with [a type of] wood that is commonly used as a plug, such as to plug a tap into the hole made to take out wine

---

[105] Such as soft wax and the like

[106] Meaning that it is not an absorbing material such as is a cloth, and thus it has no worry that one may come to squeeze it.

through, even if it is not made to be opened and closed regularly but rather only on distant occasions.

The reason for this is: because it does not appear like one is fixing a vessel with this stuffing since it is always commonly stuffed with this wood.

However, an item which has not been made into a tap is forbidden to plug the hole which is made to remove the wine through [even] if the tap got lost, unless one is a Torah Scholar which is cunningly doing so as was explained.

Halacha 21
The smearing prohibition:

One who smears a poultice[107], which means that he smoothens and levels the grooves that are in it, as well as one who smears wax or tar and anything of the like which is a material that can be smeared down until he smoothens its surface, then this is an offshoot of [the] "smoothing of hide" [prohibition], which is [a prohibition against] scraping the wool or the hair off the hide until its surface is smooth, which is a primary prohibited action being that this was done in the Tabernacle as explained in chapter 302 [Halacha 15].

Plugging a hole with wax: Therefore, one may not seal a hole with wax or similar things even if one does not enter the wax into the hole but rather only places it onto the opening of the hole in which case it does not appear like one is fixing a vessel with this stuffing being that the stuffing is not entering into the thickness of the walls of the vessel of the hole area and rather is only on the opening of the vessel on its back. Furthermore, even if this wax is not prohibited to be moved such as in a case that it was prepared to be used from before Shabbos, nevertheless it is forbidden to seal with it due to a decree that one may come to smear the wax to attach it to the walls of the vessel which surround the hole to the point that he smoothens its surface there and will then be liable for "smoothening".

Plugging a hole with fat or congealed oil: Even with fat or congealed oil it is forbidden to seal with due to a decree [that one may come to seal with] wax.

It is forbidden to connive here to [plug with the fat and congealed oil and tell others that] he only intends to hide [the fat in the hole] even if he is a Torah Scholar, as since with wax it is very easily possible for one to come to be liable for a sin offering, [meaning that it is very possible] that he will forget and will smear it in the way it is done usually during the week, in order so that the sealing be well firm, therefore [the Sages] also prohibited [sealing] with fat and oil due to a decree [that one may come to smear with] wax and the like.

---

[107] A poultice is any ointment or dressing that is placed on a wound. It commonly is dressed onto a bandage which is then placed onto the wound.

Supplement to the smearing prohibition
Rama Chapter 321 Halacha 19[108]

It is permitted to smoothen food on Shabbos and doing so does not contain the smearing prohibition because it is possible to eat [the food] without [spreading it].

Nevertheless, one who is stringent regarding foods made of apples and the like of which is common to [smear] will be blessed. [However, to spread foods on bread, as well as butter and fat is definable permitted.[109]]

[However, if one cannot eat the food without spreading it then it contains a Rabbinical smearing prohibition, just like foods contain a Rabbinical salting prohibition.

---

[108] The end of this chapter does not appear in the Alter Rebbe's Shulchan Aruch and we have thus brought the rulings of the Rama and Mishneh Berurah as a supplement for those omissions.
[109] Mishneh Berurah 82

Compilation of Halachas, Summaries and Q&A

CHAPTER 1: MAKEH BEPATISH-TIKKUN KELI: FIXING OR BUILDING AN ITEM ON SHABBOS

Important Note:
Building or fixing an item on Shabbos contains two possible prohibitions. The Makeh Bepatish prohibition and the Building prohibition. In Chapter 1 we will deal with the Makeh Bepatish prohibition, its definition and cases of application. In Chapter 2 the laws relevant to the building and destroying prohibition will be discussed. It is incumbent for the reader to read through both chapters prior to deducing permissible forms of fixing and building. When explained in the summaries and Q&A below that something is allowed, all the possible prohibitions were taken into account, and thus may be relied upon in actuality.

---

1. The definition of the prohibition:[110]
The principal Prohibition:[111] It is the common way for craftsmen who make a metal vessel to strike the vessel with a hammer after it is completed, in order to smooth out any bumps through this striking. This striking is the final work done to this vessel and is a principal form of labor which existed with the vessels[112] of the Tabernacle.

The offshoot of the above prohibition:[113] [Thus] anyone who does an action which is the finishing work of the vessel and of its fixing, this completion is considered a Melacha and is an offshoot of [the principal prohibition of] "Hitting with a hammer" which existed in the Tabernacle. [This applies even if the fixing is done by an amateur and does not require a professional's work.[114]]

For example-Making a design on a vessel:[115] For example one who designs a [picture of a] figure on a vessel which is waiting to be designed on, even if he only designed part of the figure, he has done part of the finishing touch of the vessel and is liable [for a sin offering]. As although the figure on its own is not considered a [Biblically] forbidden form of work[116], nevertheless now that the vessel is complete and fixed through his action it is considered [a Biblically forbidden form of] work.

---

[110] Admur 302:5
[111] Admur ibid; Mishneh Shabbos 73a and Rashi there; Mishneh 102b
[112] Admur ibid; Tosafus Shabbos 102b
Other opinions: Rashi ibid writes that the Av Melacha of Makeh Bepatish was that in the Mishkan they would break the stones off the mountain to use for building. Tosafus ibid However, negates this explanation stating that this Melacha of honing stones from mountains was not found in the Mishkan. See also Rashi 73a that writes like Tosafus.
[113] Admur ibid; Taz 302:1; M"B 302:9
[114] Is the Biblical prohibition of Makeh Bepatish only if one does a Melacha needed by professionals, or even by a Melacha that can be done by amateurs? Some Rishonim say it must be done by professionals. [Ramban; Ritva] However, from the fact that one is liable if he uses a vessel to cut twigs to use as a toothpick, as well as many other examples given, proves that we do not rule this way and therefore even a fixing that can be done by any amateur is liable for Makeh Pepatish.
[115] Admur ibid; Shabbos 75; Rambam 10:16
[116] Perhaps this is referring to an incomplete figure, in which case there is no writing prohibition involved as explained in chapter 340:8, or perhaps this is referring to the building prohibition, that in it of itself it does not apply to a drawing. However, the writing prohibition does apply to a complete drawing as explained in chapter 340:10; Alternatively, some suggest that there is no writing or erasing prohibition involved in **engraved pictures** [See Tehila Ledavid 340:3 in his initial understanding of Rambam-See Koveitz Ohalei Torah 1083 p. 108] Now, although Admur 340:6 explicitly rules that one may not engrave into ash, perhaps that refers only to letters and not pictures. Now, although the Poskim do not differentiate between pictures and letters and rather rule that making a drawing is a Tolda of writing [See Admur 340:10; M"A 340:6; Rambam Shabbos 11:17; Degul Merivava 340; Tehila Ledavid 340:3] perhaps Admur holds that when it comes to pictures, there is a difference between writing and engraving. See Admur 340:10 who writes "One who makes marks and designs on a document and the like, in the way that the artists design, is liable due to an offshoot of the writing prohibition. The same applies for one who erases it." Admur does not simply write that pictures have the same status as writing, and qualifies the case with "**on a document..in the way that artists design..**" This extra wording of Admur seems to imply that there are cases that the writing prohibition does not apply to making a picture, and perhaps an engraved drawing is one of those cases.

Fixing a vessel:[117] Similarly, anyone who [intentionally[118]] does any fixing to a vessel, [whether to a new vessel that will now enter its first use, or a vessel that broke and now requires fixing[119]] this fixing is considered a [Biblically forbidden form of] work, and one is [thus] liable [for a sin offering]. [Furthermore, even if the fixing was done unintentionally but one intends to now receive benefit from the item that was fixed, then it is forbidden to be done, as will be explained below.]

Building a vessel from scratch:[120] It goes without saying that one who makes a vessel from scratch is liable for the "hitting with a hammer" prohibition, even if it is done in a way that does not contain the building prohibition, as will be explained in chapter 314 [Halacha 17[121]] and 322 [Michaber Halacha 4[122]]. [Vetzaruch Iyun if it is done in a way that one is liable for Boneh, according to the stringent opinion in 314/17, is one also liable for Makeh Bepatish.[123]]

Unintentionally fixing a vessel-Plucking the grapes off a Hadas:[124] It is forbidden to pluck the grapes off an invalid Hadas branch on Yom Tov of Sukkos if one is doing so in order to validate the branch. Furthermore, even if one is not doing so in order to validate the branch, but rather in order to eat the grapes, but this is the only branch one has to fulfill the Mitzvah, then nevertheless it is forbidden to do so. This prohibition is due to Tikkun Keli, of which it is forbidden to be done even if one has no intent to do so, [being that one does plan to benefit from the vessel that his action created].[125] If However, one does need to use this Hadas for the Mitzvah, being he has other valid Hadassim available, then it is permitted to pluck the grapes from the Hadas for the purpose of eating being one is not fixing anything, as he has no use for it.[126]

Summary:
It is Biblically forbidden to perform any act of fixing to a vessel on Shabbos. It goes without saying that it is forbidden to initially make a vessel. It is Biblically forbidden to perform any part of the finishing touch of a vessel.

---

[117] Admur ibid; Rambam 23:4; Smak 280; However, see Rashi 73a that "One is only liable on the Gemar Melacha"
<u>Fixed only partially and needs to be fixed more</u>: From various sources it is implied that there is no transgression of Makeh Bepatish involved in only partially fixing a vessel in a way that it still can't be used [i.e. entering one leg into a table board], or fixing it in a way that will not last, although it would be forbidden due to Boneh according to those who hold there is Boneh by Keilim. [See Rashi in Shabbos 146 and Dirshu 314 Hakdama]
[118] <u>Fixed vessel without intent</u>: If one did an action which consequentially ended up fixing a vessel, then one does not transgress any prohibition if a) he did not intentionally do the action in order to consequentially fix the item and b) he does not plan on using the item for the new use that was created. [**Regarding A**: Implied from Admur 340:17; M"B 340:13; and so rules explicitly Maggid Mishneh brought in Magen Avraham 318:36-37; Sheivet Haleivi 8:57; Shabbos Kehalacha Vol. 1 p. 27. Meaning that although in general we rule that whenever something inevitably occurs it remains Biblically forbidden, nevertheless, here all agree that intent is needed to make it a Biblical Melacha, and thus without intent it remains a Rabbinical prohibition, and is allowed when the inevitable act is not wanted. [Maggid Mishneh brought in Magen Avraham ibid]. **Regarding B**: See Admur 646:13 that we do say Pesik Reishei by Tikkun Keli even if one does not have intent to do so, thus one may not Kasher the Hadaas by removing the grapes from it even if he intends to eat the grapes, as it is inevitable that the Hadas will become Kosher. Nevertheless, in 646:14 Admur explains that in truth this Issur only applies if one needs this Hadas for the Mitzvah, while if he doesn't then there is no Tikkun involved at all.]
[119] <u>Fixing a vessel that broke-when is it forbidden</u>: Fixing a vessel that broke is considered Tikkun Keli, as proven from a number of examples such as the prohibition to return a leg to a couch [is Boneh or Tikkun Keli], straightening a bent needle is Tikkun Keli. However, when it comes to fixing a vessel that was already in use, we are more lenient in certain cases, as can be seen from the fact that we allow returning the stuffing of a pillow. Seemingly, when it comes to making a vessel from scratch, any act of fixing no matter how light it is, is considered under the prohibition, while an item that is already in use and now broke, is not considered under the fixing prohibition unless the fixing is done in a way that it will last, as opposed to simply stuffing a pillow in which case the feathers can fall out once again being that they are not attached at all. See Q&A!
[120] Admur ibid; Rambam 23:4; Smak 280; However, see Rashi 73a that "One is only liable on the Gemar Melacha"
[121] There it is explained that according to some opinions [Rashi Shabbos 47a] there is no building prohibition applicable to vessels which are not attached to the ground. However, nevertheless even such vessels are forbidden to be built due to the "Hitting with a hammer" prohibition.
[122] There it is explained that one who breaks a twig to use as a toothpick transgresses the "Makeh Bepatich" prohibition despite not transgressing the building prohibition.
[123] From the wording of Admur it is implied that he is liable for both, Vetzaruch Iyun.
[124] Admur 646:12-13; See Michaber 646:11; M"A 646:2
[125] Admur 646:12
[126] Admur 646:13

Q&A
Is placing the company wrapper over the company's product considered Tikkun Keli?
- Example: Wrapping the coke symbol on the coke bottles?

Seemingly doing so is Biblically forbidden due to the "Fixing a vessel" prohibition, as it is similar to making a drawing on a vessel which is Biblically forbidden as brought above. This would be in addition to the sewing prohibition which is involved in taping or gluing the wrapper to the bottle.

May one replace the falling sticker of a soda bottle?
Seemingly, there is no prohibition **of Tikkun Keli** to simply replace the sticker of a soda bottle, just like there is no prohibition to return the stuffing to a pillow. Nonetheless, this would in any event be prohibited due to the sewing prohibition which applies anytime one sticks an item onto another item using glue or tape.

Does the prohibition of Tikkun Keli apply even after the vessel has been completed and now has broken in a way that needs fixing?
Yes.[127] However, if this fixing is very easily done, without force, and can be easily become undone on its own, then it is permitted, as fixing without force is not called fixing, being that it will anyways not last.[128] However, when being done for the first time, then it is under the prohibition of Tikkun Keli even if the action can be easily done without force.[129]

---

2. Examples of fixing that involve Tikkun Keli:
A. Removing cloth balls and straw from one's clothing:[130]
In order to beautify the clothing: One who gathers cloth balls which are on clothing, such as the cloth balls that are found on wool clothing, which remain from [after] the weaving, as well as straw and thin twigs which were woven into the clothing unintentionally, one who removes them after the weaving is liable for [the] "Hitting with a hammer" prohibition, if he is particular about them. This means that he removes them intentionally in order to beautify the clothing. [This is forbidden to be done] as [in such a case] this beautification is considered the completing work of the clothing and its fixing, as he is particular about them that they be removed.
Out of mere casualty: However, if one is not particular about them [being removed] and he only removes them out of mere casualty, then he is exempt [from Biblical liability]. However, it is Rabbinically forbidden to do so.
Removing the "Shelal" threads of the tailor:[131] The "שלל"which the tailors make, which refers to [the following]; in the beginning of their sewing they attach with threads the upper part of the clothing with what they are sewing under it, and after they are finished sewing they remove these threads from the clothing, it is questionable whether one who removes them on Shabbos is liable for [the] "Hitting with a hammer" prohibition if he is particular regarding them [to have them removed], and [as well it is questionable] whether it is Rabbinically forbidden if one is not particular [to have them removed and rather just does so casually].
The final ruling:[132] One is to be stringent.

---

[127] So is proven from all the following cases in which we rule that there is a prohibition of Tikkun Keli involved: Straightening a bent needle; Returning a leg to its socket
[128] So is proven from the allowance to return laces to a shoe, and return pillow stuffing to a pillow.
[129] So is proven from the prohibition against placing stuffing into the pillow for its first time even though once it has already been done, the stuffing may be returned on Shabbat if it falls out.
[130] Admur 302:6; Michaber 302:2
[131] Admur 302:7
[132] Admur 302:7

Summary:
It is forbidden to remove from clothing cloth balls or protruding pieces of straw and items of the like which remained from the weaving.[133]

Q&A

May one remove cloth balls from clothing if they came as a result of laundering the clothing?
Seemingly this would be Biblically forbidden. However, this requires further analysis as perhaps this is similar to returning the stuffing of a pillow, which is allowed as will be explained.

May one remove plastic threads that come out of the clothing?
No.

May one remove dirt etc from his clothing?
Doing so does not pose a prohibition of "Tikkun Keli." It, However, may pose a laundering prohibition, as explained in Chapter 302.

Fixing a smashed hat:
It is permitted to fix a smashed hat Permitted as is Tikkun Kal that will not last and is after Gemar Melacha.

May one remove a tag from a shirt or pants?
Seemingly this would be Biblically forbidden due to Tikkun Keli if it was placed onto the clothing prior to its completion, while if it was placed on after its completion, then it would be permitted, as explained in Halacha 4F regarding opening a tailor's knot.[134] However, some Poskim[135] rule that it is always permitted to break these tags off the garment even if it was attached prior to the completion of the garment as the tags created no physical impediment against wearing the garment, and hence since the garment remains fully wearable even with these tags, therefore it is not considered Tikkun Keli to remove them on Shabbos.

May one cut the string attaching two new shoes, or gloves, or socks etc on Shabbos?
This follows the same law, and distinction and opinion of leniency, as the previous Q&A.

B. Making a design on a vessel:
See above Halacha 1!

C. Placing stuffing into a pillow:[136]
Mochin [which is a general term for any soft material such as cotton and strings [made] of soft wool of an animal, and the scrapes of worn-out clothing[137]] which fell out from a pillow are permitted to be returned.[138] However, they are forbidden to be initially inserted [into the pillow]

---

[133] To remove them intentionally to beautify the clothing is Biblically forbidden. To remove it casually without any particular intent is Rabbinically forbidden.

[134] See Admur 302:6 and 317:6

[135] See Tehila Ledavid 317:9; Ritva Shabbos 48b; M"B 317:23; Chazon Ish 52:17; Rav SZ"A in SSH"K 15 footnote 223; Lehoros Nasan 10:37; Piskeiy Teshuvos 317:8

[136] Admur 340:14; Michaber 340:8

[137] 257:5

[138] The reason: This is no different than replacing a Keli Shel Perakim loosely together, or inserting laces easily into the shoe, which is permitted on Shabbos. Seemingly the reason for this is because its only considered Tikkun Keli when a) The vessel has never yet reached Gemar Melacha or b) The vessel has reached Gemar Melacha but is now broken in a way that needs force to be fixed. If,

on Shabbos due to that by doing so he is now turning it into a vessel. See Halacha E brought next.[139]

Summary:
It is Biblically forbidden to initially place stuffing into a pillow. However, to return stuffing into a pillow that it fell out from is allowed.

May one return a different stuffing to the pillow?
Some Poskim[140] rule one may not do so.[141] Other Poskim[142] rule one may do so, and so is implied from Admur.

D. Fixing a needle:[143]
A needle which has bent even slightly is forbidden to be straightened.
The reason for this is: (due to [the prohibition of] fixing a vessel.)
Fixing a skewer on Yom Tov: See Admur 509:1

Q&A

May one straighten a bent Yarmulke pin/clip on Shabbos?
No.

May one straighten a bent safety pin?
No.

May one bend a plastic cup into shape?
Yes, as the bending is not sturdy.

May one bend back into shape an indented Kiddush cup?
No. However, Tzaruch Iyun regarding if one is able to bend the metal back with his finger.

May one bend, open or close, the rim of a disposable baking pan?
Yes, as it is meant for constant opening and closing and is not meant to last at all.

---

however, it has already reached Gemar Melacah and now something in it needs to be fixed, then if this fixing is very easily done, without force, it is permitted, as fixing without force is not called fixing. Seemingly the reason for this is because a unforceful fixing will easily get undone and is hence not considered fixing at all.
[139] There it is explained that it is forbidden to place a lace permanently through a hole [even if wide] when being done for its first time due to that doing so is considered fixing a vessel.
[140] Kaf Hachaim 340:70 in name of Ritva; See also M"B 317:18 in name of Elya Raba 317:7
[141] The reason: As from the perspective of this pillow its as if you are now finishing its Gemra Melacha.
[142] Ketzos Hashulchan 146 footnote 3
[143] Admur 340:18; M"A 340:11; See also 509:1

E. Inserting straps into clothing:[144]

Inserting the straps of a shoe and sandal into its hole:[145] If the straps of shoes and sandals have come out [of the hole that they were fastened into] it is permitted to return them to their place as long as one does not make a knot at the end of the strap, so it does not escape from the hole, being that [such a knot] is a permanent knot.

However, [even this] only [is allowed] in places that it is not common to tie such a knot [at the end of the strap]. However, those places that are accustomed to make this knot then it is forbidden [for them] to even reinsert [the straps] due to a decree that they may come to tie it.

To do this for the first time on Shabbos:[146] Furthermore, even in those places that are not accustomed [to make such knots] it was only permitted to reinsert [the straps after having come out of their hole], However, a new shoe [which never yet had its straps fastened] is forbidden for one to insert the strap on Shabbos being that doing so is fixing a vessel.

To reinsert into a narrow hole:[147] Furthermore, even reinserting the strap was only permitted by a wide hole which it can be inserted into without effort, However, if the hole is narrow to the point that one needs effort to enter the strap into it then it is not considered like he is reinserting it but rather like he is doing so for the first time and is [thus] forbidden due to that it is fixing a vessel.

Inserting straps into pants:[148] The same applies by the straps of pants. However, belts are allowed to be initially inserted into pants on Shabbos being that he does not nullify it there as it is made to constantly insert and remove, [and] therefore it does not pose a problem of fixing a vessel. However, it is forbidden to enter a string into the [pants] being that he nullifies it there.

Summary
Inserting laces and the like into sandals and pants:[149]
It is forbidden to insert laces in the following cases:
1) It is the first time that the laces are being inserted into the shoe or clothing and one intends to permanently leave the lace there.
2) It is not the first time, but the holes are small, and it is thus difficult to enter the lace into the hole.
3) It is not the first time and the holes are wide, but the custom is to make a permanent knot at the end of the lace that is inserted so it does not come out of the hole.

Thus, it is only permitted to insert a lace if it is placed there temporarily, or is placed permanently but it is not being placed there for the first time and is not difficult to insert and it is not common to make a knot by its end.

Q&A
May one attach the wool lining of a coat on Shabbos?
Some opinions[150] rule it is forbidden to do so when one intends to leave the lining in the coat for a long period of time, as this is similar to fixing a vessel, as well as that doing so resembles sewing.[151] Others[152] However, rule it is allowed.

---

[144] Admur 317:5; Michaber 317:2
[145] Admur ibid; Michaber ibid
[146] Admur ibid; M"A 317:7; M"B 317:16
[147] Admur ibid; Rama ibid
[148] Admur ibid; M"A 317:7; M"B 317:20
[149] Halacha 5
[150] Chelkas Yaakov 4:24; Sheivet Halevy 3:51
[151] Sheivet Halevy ibid
[152] Beir Moshe and SS"K chapter 15 Halacha 74 based on a ruling of Rav Shlomo Zalman Aurbauch, as this is the normal use of the clothing

May one insert shoelaces into his shoes on Shabbos?[153]

<u>Inserting shoelaces into a used shoe</u>: It is forbidden to insert shoelaces if the holes are small and it is thus difficult to insert the shoelace. This applies even if one already inserted shoelaces into these shoes in the past. Nevertheless, if one does so in a way that will force him to have to remove the laces after Shabbos, such as he places laces that are bright unusual colors for such shoes, then it is allowed even if the holes are small. Similarly, if he places the laces only on the front two holes [the holes closer to one's ankle] then it is allowed.[154]

<u>Inserting shoelaces into a new shoe</u>: It is forbidden to insert shoelaces into a new pair of shoes for the first time on Shabbos. However, some Poskim[155] rule that by shoes today this is permitted to be done provided that the holes of the shoes are wide and hence it is easily attainable to insert the laces.[156] However, seemingly according to the ruling of Admur this allowance does not apply even by today shoes.[157] Nevertheless, if one does so in a way that will force him to have to remove the laces after Shabbos, such as he places laces that are a bright unusual color for such shoes, it is allowed. Similarly, if he places the laces only on the front two holes [the holes closer to one's ankle] it is allowed.[158]

<u>If the shoelaces were already partially inserted before Shabbos</u>: If the shoelaces were already inserted in some of the holes from before Shabbos, one may insert them in the remaining holes.

<u>Army Shoes</u>: Seemingly it is forbidden to insert a lace into army shoes, as a knot is commonly made at the end of the string by the first hole.

May one place a string into a sweatshirt hood, or sweatpants?
No.

May one place new shoelaces into old shoes?
Some Poskim[159] rule one may not do so.[160] Other Poskim[161] rule one may do so, and so is implied from Admur.

---

[153] Piskeiy Teshuvos 117

[154] Based on Ketzos Hashulchan chapter 146:3 which rules there since one will definitely remove the laces after Shabbos there is no prohibition of Tikkun Keli, as rules Admur above regarding the strap of pants. Now although the allowance in Ketzos Hashulchan is only in reference to new shoes, this likewise applies to small holes, as the entire prohibition of inserting into small holes is likewise due to Tikkun Keli as writes Admur above. This is unlike the ruling of other Poskim [See Beir Moshe 6:60] which understand the prohibition against inserting into small holes due to it being a Tircha. According to them there would be no allowance to enter the shoelaces in the above way into small holes.

[155] Beir Moshe 6:60

[156] As the concept of Tikkun Keli by shoes only applied in shoes of the old days in which case without the laces they were unusable. However, today that shoes are useable even without laces no concept of Tikkun Keli applies with their insertion. [ibid]

[157] As Admur [308:45] already brings and recognizes the difference between the old and new sandal which do not need laces to make them useable, and hence in the Laws of Muktzah he novelizes a change in a previously accepted Halacha, due to the change of shoe. However, in 317 where the prohibition of entering laces for the first time are mentioned he makes no mention of any change in Halacha due to the change of shoe style. This shows that the change of shoe style has no repercussion on the Tikkun Keli prohibition of entering new laces.

Perhaps the explanation to this is because nevertheless, even if a shoe is useable without laces the final touch for all normal shoes are to insert laces. Hence it is considered that one has done Tikkun Keli.

[158] Ketzos Hashulchan chapter 146:3

[159] Elya Raba 317:7; M"B 317:19; See also Kaf Hachaim 340:70 in name of Ritva

[160] <u>The reason</u>: As from the perspective of this new shoelace it's as if you are now finishing its Gemar Melacha.

[161] Ketzos Hashulchan 146 footnote 3

F. Inserting a door into vessels that do not hold 40 Seah and are not attached to the ground:

By doors that have hinges on their top and bottom as opposed to their side:[162] All doors of vessels, such as for example [the doors of] a drawer, a box or a portable tower, that have doors on their sides and have two hinges, meaning that they have two heads protruding out from the door, one on its top which enters into a socket that is in the top of the door frame and one on its bottom which goes into a socket that is in the threshold[163], then if [on Shabbos] the bottom hinge became completely dislocated from its [socket], then it is forbidden to reinsert it.

The reason for this is: [due] to a decree that one may come to [properly] fix it, meaning that one [may] strongly insert it [into the socket] using a mallet and hatchet in a way that one will no longer be able to take it out from there, and [one thus] will become liable for [transgressing the] building [prohibition] as will be explained, **or [he will transgress the] "final blow' [prohibition] as will be explained in chapter 314.**

Practical Q&A

May one inflate a ball, tire, or mattress with air on Shabbos?

Opinion 1: Some opinions[164] hold that this is forbidden in all cases, whether it was already previously filled with air or is being filled now for the first time, due to that it is considered like he is fixing a vessel and is thus a possible Biblical prohibition of Makeh Bepatish.

Opinion 2: Other opinions[165] hold that items which have been previously filled with air and are occasionally deflated and then re-inflated, such as air mattresses and the like, then it is permitted to add air to it on Shabbos. However, by other items it is forbidden due to that it is considered one is fixing the item.

Opinion 3: Other Opinions[166] hold that it is permitted to inflate all items which have been previously inflated once before, as this is similar to the case of returning the fallen stuffing of a pillow which is allowed.

Opinion 4: Other Opinions[167] hold it is permitted to inflate items in all cases even if it had never yet before been inflated, as since the air will eventually dissipate it is not an everlasting form of fixing and is thus not similar to adding stuffing to a pillow for the first time which is forbidden.

May one inflate a balloon?[168]

It is allowed to be done according to the lenient [4th] opinion mentioned above, even if the balloon contains pictures[169]. However, in accordance to the first three opinions it would be forbidden, and so practically rule some Poskim[170]. According to all, it is forbidden to tie the top of the balloon.[171]

May one inflate using a mechanical pump?[172]

It is permitted to use a mechanical pump in those cases that it is permitted to inflate the object

---

[162] Admur 313:14

[163] Meaning that the case here is not discussing the classical hinges of a door which are positioned on the side of the door, but rather that the hinges are on the top and bottom of the door.

[164] Ketzos Hashulchan 110 footnote 16; Minchas Yitzchak 6:30; Chelkas Yaakov 3:159; Piskeiy Teshuvos 1:55

[165] Rav Poalim 1:25

[166] Yesod Yeshurun 4 page 270

[167] Betzeil Hachachmah 4:92; Beir Moshe 2:20

[168] Piskeiy Teshuvos 340:23

[169] So rules Beir Moshe 2:20; 6:23 that it is allowed.

[170] Sheivet Halevy 9:78

[171] Beir Moshe ibid; As this is considered similar to double knot as one is making a single knot on a single end, as explained in "The Laws of Tying".

[172] Piskeiy Teshuvos 340:23; SSH"K 34 footnote 92

with air, based on all the different opinions mentioned above.

May one make a necklace or bracelet by entering items into a string?[173]
This is forbidden due to the "fixing a vessel" prohibition[174], and according to others[175] also due to the "Meameir" prohibition. Some[176] However, permit it to be done, as they say that the Meameir prohibition only applies by gathering items that grow from the ground, and they do not mention that doing so involves the fixing prohibition.[177]
Toy necklaces and bracelets:[178] Toy necklaces and bracelets which are not made to last, but rather to have the pieces inserted, removed and reinserted constantly, do not pose an Issur of Tikkun Keli.

May one use earplugs on Shabbos?[179]
See "The Laws of Mimacheik/Smearing" Q&A for the full details of this subject! In Short:
Wax earplugs: If they are required to be shaped to fit into one's ear some Poskim rule they may not be inserted as this may be forbidden due to the smearing prohibition[180] as well as possibly the "Makeh Bepatish" prohibition.
Foam earplugs: Are permitted to be used.

Compilation-May one wear a Covid mask on Shabbos and adjust the metal strip around one's nose?

Background: It is forbidden to fix things on Shabbos due to the prohibition of Tikkun Keli.[181] Thus, it is forbidden to even simply bend a needle back in shape due to the prohibition of Tikkun Keli.[182] The question is thus asked as to whether due to this law it would likewise be forbidden to adjust the metal strip of a face mask to fit one's nose on Shabbos.
The law: While bending the metal strip within the mask seems similar to bending the metal needle into shape, and therefore should be forbidden, in truth it is not similar at all. The prohibition of Tikkun Keli only applies when fixing an item from a broken state or at least enhancing it into a state that it will now permanently remain in. For this reason, bending a needle back into shape is forbidden, as when it is out of shape it is unusable, and its bending into shape is meant to be a permanent fix. However, the metal strip within the mask is not considered broken in its current state, and is meant to be bent back and forth as needed. Its adjusted state is also not necessarily permanent and can easily bend back and need readjusting. Thus, in conclusion it is permitted to wear a mask on Shabbos and adjust the metal strip around the nose. Just as it is permitted to adjust the cloth onto the face, so too the metal strip. This is similar to the allowance to bend the brim of a hat back into shape if it folded upwards on Shabbos, and doing so is not considered under Tikkun Keli, as it is meant to be adjusted to various directions and is not considered broken in its prior state. A similar idea can be found in the Poskim[183] regarding the allowance to reinsert feathers that came out of a pillow, back into the pillow on Shabbos, and doing so does not transgress Tikkun Keli.

---

[173] Ketzos Hashulchan 146 footnote 49-25; Piskeiy Teshuvos 340:26
[174] Ketzos Hashulchan 146 footnote 49-25
[175] Orchos Chayim 13
[176] Shevisas Hashabbos Meameir
[177] According to all it does not involve the writing prohibition as there is no prohibition in forming a word as explained above.
[178] Beir Moshe 6:36
[179] SSH"K 14:39
[180] Admur 314:20
[181] Admur 302:5; Rambam 23:4; Smak 280; However, see Rashi 73a that "One is only liable on the Gemar Melacha"
[182] Admur 340:18; M"A 340:11; See also 509:1
[183] Admur 340:14; Michaber 340:8

Summary:
It is permitted to wear a mask on Shabbos and adjust the metal strip to fit one's nose and doing so does not transgress Tikkun Keli.

---

3. Cutting, tearing, or breaking an item in order to make a use with it:

Important Note: There are several prohibitions that can be involved in cutting an item on Shabbos. These are: Destroying, Fixing a vessel, Tearing, Grinding, Erasing. Below we will deal with only the aspect of Tikkun Keli-fixing- involved in cutting. For the full details, final rulings, and practical Q&A on this subject please refer to "The Laws of Cutting and Tearing an item on Shabbos"!

Cutting an item with a knife to make a use with it:[184] Although cutting items detached [from the ground] is initially permitted when one is not particular to cut it in a specific measurement, as explained in chapter 314 [Halacha 16[185]] nevertheless if through doing so one fixes the item to be used for a certain use, then he is liable for [the] "fixing a vessel" [prohibition] if he cut it using a knife, as was explained in chapter 322 [Michaber Halacha 4] regarding the cutting of a twig.[186]

Tearing it with ones hands to make a use of it:[187] If it was done without a knife then one is exempt [from Biblical liability], although it is [Rabbinically] forbidden.

Breaking earthenware and tearing paper for a use:[188] Therefore one may not break earthenware and may not tear paper which is permitted to move [i.e. is not Muktzah] in order to use the [torn or broken piece] for a use due to that doing so is similar to him fixing a vessel. See Chapter 508 [Halacha 2[189]]

May one break a piece of material off a broken vessel in order to use it for a purpose on Shabbos?[190] A vessel which has become damaged [and is thus no longer in use] one may not detach from it a piece of earthenware to use to cover something with or to place something on, being that doing so is like making a vessel, as any item which one fixes on Shabbos for it to be useable for any use transgresses the prohibition of "Tikun Keli" [making a vessel on Shabbos].

Summary of cutting an item to make it fit for a use:
Is forbidden to be done whether using a knife [in which case it is Biblically forbidden] or one's hands [in which case it is Rabbinically forbidden[191]]. It is thus forbidden to break off a piece of earthenware or a piece of paper in order to make it fit for a use.

Q&A

If one tears a piece of paper to a larger size than one needs, does it still contain the fixing prohibition?
Yes.[192]

---

[184] Admur 340:17; See Michaber 340:13; M"B 322:13
[185] There it is explained that cutting wood to a desired measurement is Biblically forbidden.
[186] This will be brought below in Halacha 4
[187] Admur 340:17; See Michaber 340:13; M"B 322:13
[188] Admur 340:17
[189] There Admur brings different cases that tearing or breaking an item is forbidden due to one making it now fit for a use.
[190] Admur 308:82
[191] Accordingly, one must say that all the other cases discussing Tikkun Keli when tearing something [earthenware/leaf for drainpipe] must be referring to when one does so with a knife, as only then is he liable, or perhaps even with one's hands and Admur means to say it is Rabbinically forbidden. Vetzaruch Iyun as if it is common to cut something with one's hands versus a knife, such as plucking a leaf, should this not be Biblically forbidden?
[192] Pashut! See Admur 308/54 that if shorten is Tikkun Keli. However, see Tzitz Eliezer 13/45 that when one does not care of the size of the cut then it is not Tikkun Keli

---

May one cut toilet paper?
No, as explained above.

---

4. Examples of cutting and breaking which involve Tikkun Keli:

A. Tearing an item in the process of barbecuing fish on Yom Tov:[193]

Tearing a piece of paper to place under the fish: One who roasts fish over a grill is not to cut a piece of paper in order to soak it in water and then place it under the fish over the grill in order to prevent the fish from burning.

Breaking a piece of earthenware to place under the fish: Similarly, one may not break a piece of earthenware in order to place it under the fish.

Breaking open a cane to place its sheath under the fish: Similarly, one may not break open a cane in order to place its sheath under the fish.

Making the cane into a skewer: As well, one may not break open the cane to make it into a figure like skewer to roast with.

The reason for all the above restrictions is: because in all cases that one makes and fixes an item to be fit for a use, it is like he has fixed a vessel on Yom Tov.

B. Cutting a vine to fit a use:[194]

Using a vine as a rope to help draw water with: A [detached] vine which has its head split like a fork and is [thus] fit to [use to] hang a bucket on and to [thus use to] draw [water] with [such as to place it down a well to draw water, using the vine as a rope to place it down and bring it back up], then even if one thought about this from before Shabbos to use the [vine] to [help] draw [water] with on Shabbos, then [nevertheless] it is forbidden to use it to draw with, unless the vine was tied to the bucket from before Shabbos.

The reason for this is: due to a decree that perhaps the vine will be too long for him, and one will cut it, being that it is soft and easy to be cut, and will thus end up [transgressing the prohibition of] fixing a vessel on Shabbos.

C. May one remove a reed from one's broom?[195]

It is forbidden to remove a reed[196] from a broom which is used to clean the house, being that through removing it he is fixing it for the use that he wishes to use it for, which is for hitting the children with, and [the law is that] any item that one fixes to be used for any use is included in the prohibition of fixing vessels. [Furthermore] even through a gentile it is forbidden to remove it, meaning [to even have him] detach it and remove it out from under the binding area[197] of the broom, and it goes without saying that it is forbidden to [ask a gentile to] break the reed off from the broom, as by breaking it there is an additional prohibition [being transgressed which is] breaking a vessel, as will be explained in chapter 337 [Halacha 3]. However, when one removes out an entire reed [from the broom] there is no [prohibition involved] of destroying a vessel, as this is similar to a vessel assembled by placing many pieces together, which does not contain [the prohibition of] destroying [a vessel] when taking it apart, unless the [attached pieces] were inserted [in their sockets] strongly and professionally.

---

[193] Admur 508:2
[194] Admur 308:54
[195] Admur 308:55
[196] Lit. a branch
[197] Meaning out from the area where all the reeds have been fixed into.

Summary:
It is forbidden to break a reed off a broom[198], or even detach a reed from its setting in a broom, in order to make a use of it. It is forbidden to do so even through a gentile.

D. Using a twig as a toothpick:[199]
A twig which is not animal food, even to take it in order to pick at his teeth is forbidden [due to it being Muktzah, and to cut a piece off is forbidden also due to the prohibition of "fixing a vessel"[200]].

E. Plucking a leaf from a branch to use as a funnel:
Is forbidden. See below Halacha 5 "Tikkun Keli by foods"

F. Cutting a knot:[201]
Cutting the sewing and knot of a tailor: [Furthermore] even if the collar had already been opened [after being made] but a professional [tailor] returned and sewed [the two sides of the collar] together in the way done by professionals, or if the professional tied it [in a way] that one is unable to untie it, then it is forbidden to cut the strings.
However, this [prohibition to cut an un-openable knot] only refers to a knot tied by the professional prior to having finished making the clothing, being that then the cutting of the strings of this knot involves the [prohibition of doing a] "Finishing touch", as this finalizes the work needed to be done to the clothing being that through doing so the clothing is now fit to be worn, while until this was done it was never yet fit to be worn, [and it is thus forbidden as] any [action] done which is the finishing stroke [of the making of the vessel] contains [the prohibition of] "Finishing Touch" as was explained in chapter 302 [Halacha 5]
Cutting the knot of the launderer: See "The laws of Cutting and Tearing" Prohibition #2 Halacha 3E for the full details of this subject. See summary below for a summary what is explained there!

Summary-Cutting the strings of a knot:[202]
Anytime it is permitted to open a knot on Shabbos one is likewise permitted to cut it. However, one may not be lenient to cut it in front of an ignoramus, and rather should do it privately. [As well in a case that the knot attaches an item to the ground then the rope may not be torn even if one is allowed to untie the knot being that doing so involves the destroying prohibition.][203]
Anytime that the knot is forbidden to be undone, it is likewise forbidden to be cut.
Q&A
May one open a new shirt or pants on Shabbos, and remove its parts?
Seemingly to remove the plastics and needles is permitted, as its merely external. However, to cut the tags is seemingly forbidden due to Tikkun Keli, as explained above

---

[198] When breaking it off for a use it contains two prohibitions, destroying and Tikkun Keli. When simply detaching it from its setting, then if loose, it only contains the Tikkun Keli prohibition.
[199] Michaber 322:4
[200] If done with one's hand it is Rabbinically forbidden, and if done with a vessel is Biblically forbidden. [M"B 322:13]
[201] Admur 317:6; Michaber 317:3
[202] Admur 317: 6
[203] Chapter 314 Halacha 19

G. Cutting and tearing sewn threads:[204]
See "The Laws of cutting and Tearing" Prohibition #1 Halacha 4!

H. Tearing the cover off of a bottle:[205]
A person may tear the hide which [seals] the opening of the barrel of wine or other liquids if he is doing so for the need of Shabbos. He need not worry [about any tearing prohibition involved in doing so], because tearing a detached item is allowed to be done even initially. [However, this is only allowed] as long as one does not intend to make something similar to a drainpipe out of the torn skin [i.e. a funnel] being that doing so is considered like fixing a vessel.

Summary:
Is permitted to tear the leather covering of a bottle for a Shabbos need so long as one does not form it into a drain [and it is a single entity like a piece of leather as opposed to a cloth[206]].

Q&A
Why is tearing the cover off a bottle not considered Tikkun Keli, that one is fixing the barrel?[207]
As a cover of a bottle is not considered a complete attachment, and hence is considered as if it is not on the bottle.

If the cover has letters or designs may it be torn?
One may only tear it open around the letters.

Q&A
May one separate plastic ware which is attached together, such as two plastic spoons which are attached or two yogurts which are attached?[208]
No. This is forbidden due to the fixing a vessel prohibition. [Seemingly, However, according to those opinions who permit opening disposable cans likewise here it would be permitted to separate the above disposable items. See Chapter 2 Halacha 9 Q&A!]

May one separate a two-part ices[209]?
No. This is forbidden due to the fixing a vessel prohibition. [Seemingly, However, according to those opinions who permit opening disposable cans likewise here it would be permitted to separate the above disposable items. See Chapter 2 Halacha 9 Q&A!]

May one tear garbage bags or tablecloths that are attached to each other?
No.[210]

---

[204] Admur 317:7
[205] Admur 314:12; M"A 314:14
[206] See "The Laws of Cutting and Tearing" Halacha 2
[207] See Chazon Ish Shabbos 51:11
[208] Piskeiy Teshuvos 314:3
[209] This refers to a long plastic tube which contains sweet frozen ices inside. The tube is split into two parts with a narrow area in the middle that connects them. It is customary during the week to cut the tube down the middle and give out one ices to each child. The question is can this be done on Shabbos. Although foods do not contain a Tikun Keli prohibition, the plastic which holds the ices perhaps does.
[210] Tearing with a Shinuiy in time of need: Seemingly is only Rabbinical with Shinuiy which is mutar in time of need. See 307/12. However, tzaruch iyun on definition of time of need.

Compilation-Cutting items on Shabbos, such as a table cloth, garbage bag, paper towel, piece of tinfoil, and toilet paper?

It is Biblically forbidden to perform an action on Shabbos which prepares an item for a use. The principal Melacha of this prohibition is called "Makeh Bepatish," while its offshoot is known as Tikkun Keli.[211] Accordingly, it is forbidden to cut or tear an item on Shabbos for the sake of making a use out of the cut piece. If one cuts the item with a vessel, such as a scissor or knife, it is Biblically forbidden. If one tears it with his hands, it is Rabbinically forbidden.[212] In addition to the above prohibition of Tikkun Keli, cutting or tearing an item on Shabbos [even not for a use] may also transgress other Biblical or Rabbinical prohibitions, including: Koreiah/Tearing[213]; Michateich[214]; Tochein[215]; Soseir/destroying; Erasing letters.

Based on the above prohibition of Tikkun Keli, it is forbidden to cut or tear the following items on Shabbos and they are all to be prepared, and pre-cut, before Shabbos:[216]

- Tablecloth: It is forbidden to cut a tablecloth roll for the sake of using the cut piece to cover one's table [or other usage]. This applies whether or not one cuts the tablecloth on the pre-serrated lines. It is forbidden to do so even with one's hands, and certainly with a knife.

- Garbage bags: It is forbidden to cut a garbage bag from a garbage bag roll on Shabbos.

- Plastic sandwich bags: A pack of sandwich bags in which each bag is slightly attached to the bag under it, and needs to be torn off, is forbidden to be used on Shabbos. This applies whether or not one cuts the tissues on the pre-serrated lines.

- Tinfoil: It is forbidden to cut a piece of tinfoil from a roll, on Shabbos, whether with one's hands or using a knife.

- Paper towel: It is forbidden to cut a piece of paper towel from a roll, on Shabbos, whether with one's hands or using a knife. This applies whether or not one cuts the paper towel on the pre-serrated lines.

---

[211] Admur 302:5 *"It is the common way for craftsmen who make a metal vessel to strike the vessel with a hammer after it is completed, in order to smooth out any bumps through this striking. This striking is the final work done to this vessel and is a principal form of labor which existed with the vessels[211] of the Tabernacle. [Thus] anyone who does an action which is the finishing work of the vessel and of its fixing, this completion is considered a Melacha and is an offshoot of [the principal prohibition of] "Hitting with a hammer" which existed in the Tabernacle. **Similarly, anyone who does any fixing to a vessel, this fixing is considered a [Biblically forbidden form of] work, and one is [thus] liable [for a sin offering].*; Mishneh Shabbos 73a and Rashi there; Mishneh 102b; Rambam 23:4; Smak 280; Taz 302:1; M"B 302:9

[212] Admur 340:17; 308:54; 82; 314:12; 508:2; See Michaber 340:13; M"B 322:13

[213] See Admur 302:4; 278:1-3; 317:7; 340:17; Mishneh Berurah 340 Biur Halacha "Eiyn Shovrin"; Piskeiy Teshuvos 340:34

[214] See Admur 314:16; Aruch Hashulchan 321:40; Az Nidbaru 1:79

[215] Admur 314:16; M"A 314:14; M"B 31441

[216] Piskeiy Teshuvos 340:34

Does the Koreiah prohibition apply in the cases listed below? The Koreiah prohibition only applies if the item is made of several fabrics or pieces which are being torn apart. Accordingly, the Koreiah prohibition would not apply in the cases listed below in which the item is a single solid material. [See Admur ibid;] However, Tzaruch Iyun, as perhaps the beads of plastic which are melted to form the plastic sheet would be considered "several fabrics" which would transgress the Koreia prohibition. Likewise, paper which is made from ground wood may also be defined as "several fabrics" and transgress the prohibition. [See Piskeiy Teshuvos]

Does the Biblical Tikkun Keli prohibition apply in the cases below? As stated above, if one cuts the item with a scissor or knife, it is a Biblical prohibition, while if he tears it with his hand, it is a Rabbinical prohibition. This is unlike Piskeiy Teshuvos 340:34 footnote 308 who writes that according to Admur there is no Biblical prohibition, as in truth, while there is no Biblical prohibition of Koreia according to Admur, there is a Biblical prohibition of Tikkun Keli if cut with a vessel. However, see there based on Maor Hashannos 4 that the Biblical prohibition of Tikkun Keli does not apply being that the vessel is able to be used in a time of need even without cutting and thus the simple act of cutting is not considered a complete fixing. However, in the case of the garbage bags or plastic bags, since the cutting turns it into a useable bag, then it is a Biblical prohibition of Tikkun Keli [if done with a vessel]. The practical ramification is regarding Amira Lenachri and if we can consider it Shevus Deshvus to cut it even with a knife.

Does the Michateich prohibition apply in the cases below? For the most part, the Michateich prohibition does not apply in the below mentioned cases even if one cuts it by the dotted lines as one has no intent to truly cut it to a specific measurement. [See Admur 314:16; Piskeiy Teshuvos 340:34 footnote 308] However, see Aruch Hashulchan 321:40 and Az Nidbaru 1:79 who rules that one who tears paper for a use transgresses Michateich. Vetzaruch Iyun.

- Toilet paper: It is forbidden to cut a piece of toilet paper from a roll, on Shabbos, whether with one's hands or using a knife. This applies whether or not one cuts the paper towel on the pre-serrated lines.
- Tissues: A pack of tissues in which each tissue is slightly attached to the tissue below it, and needs to be torn off, is forbidden to be used on Shabbos. This applies whether or not one cuts the tissues on the pre-serrated lines.

Q&A

Are the above items Muktzah on Shabbos?[217]
All the above items that may not be cut on Shabbos receive the status of Keli Shemilachto Li'issur, of which the ruling is that it may not be moved to save from damage, but may be moved for the sake of using it, or to free up its space.[218] If practically the item is not useable due to one's inability to cut it, then it may be judged under the higher status of Muktzah called Muktzha Machams Chisaron Kis, or Muktzah Machamas Gufo, of which the ruling is that it may not be moved for any purpose.[219] If, However, one would not abstain from using the item without cutting it [i.e. placing the entire garbage roll in the garbage can and opening the one on top, or placing the plastic tablecloth on the table and resting the roll on a chair at the edge] then seemingly its status would be of Keli Shemilachto Li'issur.

In the above cases, does it help to cut the above items to a larger quantity then necessary to avoid the above prohibition of Tikkun Keli?[220]
The prohibition applies even in such a case, as any cutting which further assists one in achieving his use of the vessel is forbidden due to Tikkun Keli.

In the above cases, does it make a difference if one cuts the item with one's hands versus a knife?
The prohibition applies whether it is cut with a knife or torn with one's hands, although the level of prohibition, and whether it is Biblical or Rabbinical does change if it was cut with one's hands versus a knife and the like, as explained above.

Does it make a difference if one cuts the above items on the serrated lines, or elsewhere?[221]
No. The prohibition of Tikkun Keli applies wherever one cuts it. Likewise, cutting it by the dotted lines does not necessarily transgress the additional Michateich prohibition[222], and hence there is no Halachic difference regarding where one intends to cut it.

May one ask a gentile to cut the above items on Shabbos?
No, as is always the rule regarding Amira Lenachri. However, in a case of great need, or for the sake of a Mitzvah, one may ask the gentile to cut it for him using his hands, without mentioning the use of a scissor or knife.[223]

---

[217] See Piskeiy Teshuvos 340:34 footnote 309
[218] See Admur 308:2, 12; M"A 308:5; M"B 308:10
[219] See regarding blank paper that it becomes both MMCK and MMG: Admur 308:6; M"A 308:10 in name of Shiltei Giborim 8; M"B 308:3
[220] See Admur 308:54 regarding shortening the length of a vine" due to it being too long for him"; However, see Tzitz Eliezer 13:45 that when one does not care of the size of the cut then it is not Tikkun Keli
[221] Piskeiy Teshuvos 340:34
[222] See footnotes above where this matter was explained.
[223] See Admur 307:12, 16; Piskeiy Teshuvos 340:34 footnote 310

5. Tikkun Keli by foods:[224]

A. For the sake of using as a vessel:

Animal food [which includes all foods which are edible to animals[225]] does not contain within it [the prohibition of] fixing a vessel [and is permitted to be moved being that it is edible[226]].[227]

The reason:[228] As animal fodder is soft and do not last, as will be explained in chapter 322 [Halacha 4[229]], in a case that one modifies the food to become an independent vessel, being that it is not at all common to initially make a vessel out of food, due to the fact that it does not last long.

Using straw or hay as a toothpick: Therefore, it is permitted to cut even with a knife [even into a particular measurement[230]] straw or hay and [use it] to pick his teeth [i.e. to use as a toothpick].

Using a twig as a toothpick: However, a twig which is not animal food, even to take it in order to pick his teeth is forbidden [due to it being Muktzah, and to cut a piece off is forbidden also due to the fixing a vessel prohibition[231]].

Plucking a leaf from a branch to use as a funnel:[232] Plucking a leaf from a detached[233] branch in order to place it into the hole of the barrel, is prohibited due to [the prohibition of] "fixing a vessel", as any item which is altered on Shabbos, so it be fit to be used for a given purpose carries with it [the prohibition of] "fixing a vessel".

The reason for why this is forbidden even if the leaf can be used for animal fodder:[234] Even if the leaf is soft and is [thus] fit to be eaten by animals, nevertheless it is prohibited to pluck it due to "fixing a vessel". As [the Sages] only said that [modifying] animal fodder [into a vessel] does not carry with it the prohibition of "fixing a vessel" being that they are soft and do not last, as will be explained in chapter 322 [Halacha 4[235]], in a case that one modifies the food to become an independent vessel, such as cutting a piece of straw to use as a toothpick in which case it is not considered like one is fixing a vessel being that it is not at all common to initially make a vessel out of food, due to the fact that it does not last long. However, it is common to [use food] to modify through it a vessel that is already made, such as to place the leaf in the hole of the barrel which is already made. Therefore, when one plucks [the leaf out from the detached branch] for this purpose this removal carries with it [the Biblical[236] prohibition of] "fixing a vessel".

B. For the sake of a Mitzvah:

Plucking the grapes off a Hadas:[237] It is forbidden to pluck the grapes off an invalid Hadas branch on Yom Tov of Sukkos if one is doing so in order to validate the branch. Furthermore, even if one is not doing so in order to validate the branch, but rather in order to eat the grapes, but this is the only branch one has to fulfill the Mitzvah, then nevertheless it is forbidden to do so. This prohibition is due to Tikkun Keli, of which it is forbidden to be done even if one has no intent to do so, [being that one does plan to benefit from the vessel that his action created].[238] If However, one does need to use this Hadas for the Mitzvah, being he has other valid Hadassim

---

[224] Michaber 322:4
[225] M"B 322:9
[226] M"B 322:10
[227] Michaber ibid; Mishneh Beitza 33b
[228] Admur 314:11; Ran Beitza 19
[229] Of the Michaber. This chapter of the Alter Rebbe's Shulchan Aruch did not make it to print.
[230] In which case it would normally contain the cutting prohibition, although here it is allowed being that it is a food, and by foods the cutting prohibition is not applicable. [M"B 322:12]
[231] If done with one's hand it is Rabbinically forbidden, and if done with a vessel is Biblically forbidden. [M"B 13]
[232] Admur 314:11; See Michaber 314:5
[233] Meaning we do not suspect that one will come to pluck a leaf from a tree, However, from a branch that had been previously cut off, we do suspect.
[234] Admur 314:11; M"A 314:6; Ran ibid; M"B 322:11 in name of Ran; Chayeh Adam
[235] Of the Michaber. This chapter of the Alter Rebbe's Shulchan Aruch did not make it to print.
[236] So is implied from Admur ibid and so rules M"B 322:11 in name of Nishmas Adam
[237] Admur 646:12-13; See Michaber 646:11; M"A 646:2
[238] Admur 646:12

available, then it is permitted to pluck the grapes from the Hadas for the purpose of eating being one is not fixing anything he has no use for it.[239]

C. For the sake of eating:
There is no prohibition of Makeh Bepatish/Tikkun Keli in fixing foods for the sake of eating.[240] One may thus do any permitted action to a food even if that action makes it edible, such as to pour cold water on salted fish[241], or to rub animal fodder and make it edible.[242] However, there are other prohibitions relevant to fixing foods such as Boneh[243], Memacheik, Borer, and Bishul.

D. Boneh by foods:
See Chapter 2 Halacha 1E

E. Example-Hanging the Matzah of Afikoman came from a hole:[244]
Some are accustomed to make a hole inside of the Matzah for the sake of hanging it. It is permitted to do so even on [Shabbos or] Yom Tov, and it is not forbidden due to Tikkun Keli.[245] [Practically, it is not the Chabad custom to do so.]

Summary of Tikkun Keli by foods:
All foods that are edible for animals do not contain the Tikkun Keli prohibition and may thus be cut for the purpose of making a use out of the torn piece, so long as one does not attach the piece to a vessel.

---

[239] Admur 646:13

[240] Admur 318:11; 324:4; M"B 318 in Biur Halacha "Hadachasan"; Ketzos Hashulchan 130 pp. 21-31; Igros Moshe 3:52; Malbushei Yom Tov 318:9; Avnei Nezer 419; See Shabbos Kehalacha 3 p. 296-303!
Other opinions: Some Poskim rule that the prohibition of Tikkun Keli does apply to making foods edible. [Levush 318:4; Peri Megadim 318 A"A 16 [brought in Biur Halacha ibid]; Shevisas Hashabbos; Chayeh Adam 20:5; Rav Poalim 16; Maharshag 51; Shevet Halevi 8:54] The Biur Halacha ibid negates their opinion stating "it is a "Davar Chadash" that is not found in previous Poskim and there are many contradictions to this assertion and hence one is not to be stringent at all". See Shabbos Kehalacha 3 p. 296-303!

[241] Admur 318:11; Taz 318:5; Mishneh Berurah 318:36; Ketzos Hashulchan 124:24
Other opinions: See above!

[242] Admur 324:4
Other opinions: See above!

[243] See Admur 319:26; See Kitzur Shulchan Aruch 80:25 who learns this from the Magen Avraham 340:17 which rules that pressing figs together and smoothening them down to beautify their appearance involves the Building prohibition. Other Poskim However, [Cheishev Haeiphod 2:77; Daas Torah 321, and so is apparently the opinion of the M"B and Ketzos Hashulchan [146 p. 12] which do not mention this prohibition in their summary and commentary of the above Halacha in the Rama] rule that this prohibition of building stated by the Magen Avraham only applies by pressing hard items together and making them into one unit. However, to spread something nicely does not resemble in any way the building prohibition but is rather only proper to avoid due to the smoothening prohibition as rules the Rama.

[244] Admur 477:11 [See Admur 500:11]; M"A 500:7; Chok Yaakov 476:3

[245] The reason: Making a hole inside of the Matzah does not consist of a prohibition of making a hole on Yom Tov, as even on Shabbos This prohibition is not applicable to foods but rather to wood stones and metals and the like (of items which are fit to make vessels out of them. See chapter 314:2). [Admur ibid]

Q&A
May one fix a vessel through using food parts, such as to carve a piece of vegetable to be fit to be used as a funnel for a barrel?[246]
No, doing so may be Biblically forbidden.

May one cut a medicine in half [for one who may take medicine on Shabbos], such as to achieve a smaller dose for a child and the like?[247]
Yes. The prohibition of Tikkun Keli does not apply by medicine just as it does not apply towards food, and hence one may cut it to a small size for Shabbos use.[248]
Suppository: There is no prohibition in cutting a suppository in half on Shabbos.[249]

Other topics of prohibitions due to Tikkun Keli:
1. Tikkun keli by folding clothing
2. Tikkun keli by immersing things in a mikveh
3. Tikkun keli by bathing in mikveh

6. The laws of puncturing a hole into a vessel on Shabbos [Halachas 6-10]
Important note 1: The following laws only relate to a hole which one intends to make in a vessel that he plans on continuing to use, and is thus fixing the vessel by doing so. However, if his intent is to break through the vessel to remove that which it contains then its laws will be discussed in Chapter 2 Halacha 1 under the laws of destroying.
Important Note 2: The following laws brought below [Halacha 6-10] is only with regards to vessels that do not hold 40 Seah and are not attached to the ground. If a vessel holds 40 Seah [or is attached to the ground] then it has the same laws as making a hole in a wall for all matters[250] which will be discussed in Chapter 2 Halacha 7 under the building prohibition-see there!

A. The Biblical prohibition:[251]
Making a hole in the walls or floor of one's house:[252] One who hammers a peg into the wall in order to hang vessels and the like on it, is liable for [the] building [prohibition]. [Furthermore] even if one did not [yet] hammer the peg [into the wall] but drilled a hole in the wall in which the peg will be inserted into, he is liable for [the] building [prohibition] on this hole [that he drilled] since this hole is an accessory for the building which is the inserting the peg. Similarly, one who makes a hole in the floor of his house to drain out the water is liable for [the] building [prohibition].[253]
Making a hole for entering and exiting in an item detached from the ground:[254] However, one

---

[246] M"B 322:11
[247] SSH"K 33 footnote 36 in name of Rav SZ"A; Piskeiy Teshuvos 328:39; 322 footnote 20 [New]
[248] See Michaber 322:4 "Animal food does not contain within it [the prohibition of] fixing a vessel."; Admur 314:11 " As animal fodder is soft and does not last, as will be explained in chapter 322 [Halacha 4], in a case that one modifies the food to become an independent vessel, **being that it is not at all common to initially make a vessel out of food**, due to the fact that it does not last long."
[249] The reason: Being that this is similar to food which does not contain a cutting prohibition. [SSH"K ibid]
[250] See 314:5 and 313:17-18
[251] Admur 314:2
[252] Admur ibid; Taz 314:2; Terumos Hadeshen 64; Based on Rav in Shabbos 103 and Rashi there; See Michaber 314:12
Other opinions: Some write one transgresses the prohibition of Makeh Bepatish by hammering a nail into the wall. [M"B 314:8 based on Shmuel in Shabbos ibid] However, see M"B 314:11 and 52 that making a hole in a wall is prohibited due to Boneh.
[253] Admur ibid; M"A 314:3 in name of Rashdam 4; M"B 314:8
[254] Admur ibid; M"A 314:3 in name of Rambam 23:1; Raba in Shabbos 146a; M"B 314:8
The reason: Some say this is because it is not the common practice to make a hole in only one direction, and hence if it is common practice then even one direction would be a Biblcial prohibition. [Shaar Hatziyon 314:9] However, Admur writes the reason is

who makes a hole in an item that is detached [from the ground] he is not liable, unless the hole was made in order to have items entered through it and taken out from it. For example, the hole that is made in a chicken coop which is not attached to the ground, which is made in order to enter light and let out air, this hole is a complete opening, and one is liable in making it for the "Fixing a vessel" [prohibition] which is an offshoot of the "Makeh Bepatish" prohibition, as explained in chapter 302 [Halacha 5]. Whether one made a hole in [a plank of] wood or metal[255] or in a vessel, he is liable on doing so for [the] "Finishing Touch" [prohibition], if the hole is made in order to enter things through it and to take things out from.

The prohibition to intentionally make an elegant opening for the vessel:[256] [However, this stipulation by a vessel which is detached from the ground, that it is only Biblically prohibited to make a hole if the hole is meant for inserting and removing is only] as long as that [upon making the hole] one does not intend to puncture it into a nice hole so that it be an elegant [looking] opening for [the barrel].[257] However, if one does do so then he has fixed the vessel [on Shabbos] and is liable for [the] "Making a Finishing Touch[258]" [prohibition].[259]

Making a hole in a vessel which can hold 40 Seah:[260] A large barrel or other large vessels which hold 40 *seah* carry with them the building and destroying [prohibition], and has the same law as ....a wall.

B. The Rabbinical prohibition in making a hole for entering or exiting:[261]

[The above was only with regards to the Biblical prohibition, However,] the Sages decreed [against making] any hole [on Shabbos] even if it is made only for removing items from it or only for entering items into it. [The reason for this is] because [if this were to be allowed] one may come to make a [type of] hole that he is liable on [which means a hole that is meant for entering and exiting]. Due to this [decree] one may not puncture a new hole in a barrel for the wine to flow from [this hole]. [Furthermore] even if it already has a hole and one [simply] wants to add to it and slightly widen it, it is forbidden.

Making a hole in order to remove the content of the item and then throw out the item[262]: It is allowed to break an un-sturdy vessel in order to remove its content so long as one does not intend to make a nice hole. However, by a sturdy vessel it is forbidden to break it even in a way that one is not making for it a nice opening, because breaking a complete structure is forbidden even by vessels that are not attached to the ground. Furthermore [another reason it is forbidden to make a hole in a sturdy vessel] is due to a decree that one may come to intend to puncture in it a nice hole in order so that it have an elegant opening. **See Chapter 2 Halacha 13 "The laws of destroying vessels" for the full details of this subject.**

---

because it is not considered a complete opening, Vetzaruch Iyun as in 302:5 Admur rules that even a partial fixing is considered a Biblical prohibition of Makeh Bepatish. Thus, one must say that this only applies when one is doing the partial fixing of a full job of fixing. If, however, the partial fixing is faulty then it is similar to a shinuiy and one is not Chayav.

[255] Vetzaruch Iyun from Halacha 14 that when such a hole is made on the cover a barrel one is not Biblically liable because it can be removed. Perhaps However, this refers to making a hole in them for purposes of keeping items inside the hole and for removing them.

[256] Admur 314:1; Michaber 314:1; Mishneh Shabbos 146a and Rashi there; Beitza 33

[257] See Shabbos Kehalacha Vol. 3 17 footnote 131 that the definition is any specific form of hole that benefits the person. Vetzaruch Iyun from the added words of Admur "so that it be an elegant [looking] opening for it [the barrel]" which implies that only if the opening makes the vessel look elegant is it forbidden.

[258] Lit. "Hitting with a hammer". This refers to any finishing touch that one does to a vessel.

[259] Admur ibid; P"M 314 M"Z 1

Other opinions: Some Poskim rule that one is only Biblically liable by a nice hole if it is made to enter and exit. [Taz 314:1; M"B 314:10]

[260] Admur 314:5; as well as 313:18, brought below in Chapter 2 Halacha 2B; Rama 314:1; Terumos Hadeshen 64; M"B 314:2

[261] Admur 314:3; M"A 314:3 in name of Rambam 23:1; Raba in Shabbos 146a; M"B 314:8

[262] Admur 314:1

Summary-Making a hole in a vessel not attached to the ground which does not hold 40 Seah:

Important Note: See note 1&2 above

Biblically: Is Biblically forbidden due to the prohibition of fixing a vessel when made for both entering and removing items through it[263], or when intentionally made into an elegant hole[264]. It never carries with it the building prohibition.[265]

Rabbinically: Is Rabbinically forbidden when made for only entering items into, or for only removing items through it[266].

May one widen an already existing hole? It carries the same laws as one who initially makes the hole on Shabbos both by walls and vessels.[267]

Permitted:

It is permitted to make a hole in a vessel if all the following conditions are fulfilled:

1. One plans to throw out the vessel after removing its content, rather than fix a hole in the vessel for permanent use.[268]
2. One does not intend to make a nice hole.[269]
3. The vessel is defined as an un-sturdy structure. [270]

Q&A

May one ask a gentile to make a hole inside a vessel on Shabbos?

If he does not plan on throwing out the vessel then it is forbidden. See Chapter 2 Summary of "The laws of destroying vessels" [Halacha 13-16] and Q&A there!

---

7. Making a hole in a barrel:

A. Chopping off the top of a barrel:[271]

A person may present a barrel of wine before his guests, and cut off its head (the definition of the head of the barrel is the area of the lid which is the [most] elevated area of the barrel when [the barrel] is resting [on its bottom] in which the surrounding area slants downwards from all sides) with a sword from underneath its lid. Meaning that one cuts the surrounding opening of [the barrel] together with the lid that is covering it.[272]

The reason the above is allowed:[273] Now although through doing this one makes a new opening in the barrel, [nevertheless] this does not pose a problem because for certain one has no intent to make a new opening [by doing so], being that it is not at all usual to make [an opening] this way, to chop off the head of the barrel in order to make an opening. Rather one intends [in doing so] to look good, to show his generosity before the guests by him widening for them the area that the wine can be taken from.

Restrictions on the above allowance:[274] [However,] this is [only allowed] if the barrel was broken and then glued back together with tar and also does not hold 40 *seah,* in which case doing so does

---

[263] Admur 314:2
[264] Admur 314:1
[265] Admur 314:5
[266] Admur 314:3
[267] Admur 314:2 and 3
[268] Otherwise this is a problem of Tikkun Keli .
[269] Otherwise this is a problem of Tikkun Keli .
[270] Otherwise, this is a problem of Soser/Destroying.
[271] Admur 314:13; Michaber 314:6; Braisa Shabbos 146a
[272] Meaning the following: The lid is made in a way that it inserts within the top of the barrel, and is thus surrounded by the top area of the barrel. One then cuts off the entire lid by cutting the barrel from under the lid, thus consequently also cutting with it the top edge of the barrel that surrounded the lid.
[273] Admur ibid; Gemara ibid and Mefarshim there; M"B 314:23 in name of Rambam and Rashal; See Shaar Hatziyon 314:25
[274] Admur ibid; M"A 314:7; M"B 314:23

not carry with it the destroying [prohibition] as explained above.

B. The prohibition to make a hole in the side of the barrel:[275]
[Although chopping off the top of the barrel is allowed if it is an un-sturdy structure and does not hold 40 Seah,] nevertheless it is forbidden to make a hole in the body of the barrel even with a spear, in which one makes a large hole that is not similar to an opening, because nevertheless he is for certain intending to make a hole [by doing so]. Meaning that since he does not want to open the lid on a constant basis for whatever reason that he has, therefore he has made this hole to remove the wine with at all times that he does not wish to open the lid, in which case this is a complete opening which is made for exiting purposes which the Sages prohibited.[276]
The reason why here we do not say that he is doing so to show his generosity is because:[277] If he had intended to [make the hole in order to] make himself look good then he should have opened the lid, being that through there one can take out a lot more wine then is able to be taken out through the hole that he made.

C. Making a hole in the lid of a barrel:[278]
Making a hole on the top of the lid: However, it is permitted to make a hole in the lid from above in order to take out wine through it even if the barrel is whole[279] [i.e. meaning was never broken and then glued back together].
The reason for this is:[280] because it is not usual at all to make an opening in the lid from above, [as one] rather just takes off the lid. Therefore, this hole which is on top does not appear and is not considered to be an opening at all. Thus the [Sages] did not prohibit [making a hole] within the lid, as since even if one were to make a complete hole [in the lid,] [meaning that the hole was made] for entering wine into and to remove wine from it, one is [nevertheless] not Biblically liable as [opposed to the law] for one who makes [such a hole] in the barrel itself [in which case he is liable]. [The reason for why one is not Biblically liable by a hole made in the lid is] because the lid is not considered attached to the barrel even when it is placed on the opening [of the barrel], rather it is an individual item. Therefore the hole [which is made in it] is not considered made to enter and remove [wine] through it, as when one removes and enters [wine] through this hole it is as if he is removing and entering it through the mouth of the barrel alone [without the lid being attached to it], as this hole in the lid does not at all help one in removing and entering [wine into the barrel] being that even without this [hole] one would be able to enter and remove [the wine] through the mouth of the barrel. Now, although the mouth is sealed with the lid [nevertheless] this is not considered a complete sealing since the lid is not considered attached to the barrel [and thus we do not consider the hole in the lid to be of any real help]. Thus [being that making a hole in the lid is never Biblically prohibited even when made to enter and exit through] therefore [the Sages] were not overly strict to forbid even making a hole which is only made to remove [wine] from it, when made in an area that it is not common to make an opening from which [by a barrel refers to the area that] is above on its top.[281]
Making a hole on the side of the lid:[282] However, it is forbidden to make a hole on the side [of the lid], meaning in the area where the barrel slants downwards.

---

[275] Admur 314:13; Michaber 314:6
[276] Admur ibid; Taz 314:4
[277] Admur ibid; Gemara ibid; M"B 314:27
[278] Admur 314:14; Michaber 314:6
[279] Admur ibid; M"A 308:8; M"B 314:28
[280] Admur ibid; M"A 314:
[281] This implies that it was only permitted due to a joint of three reasons: a) that one would never be Biblically obligated on such a hole even if made to enter and exit, and b) that it is unusual to make a hole in such an area and c) That one is making the hole only for exiting. However, if one of the above is lacking then it remains Rabbinically prohibited.
[282] Admur 31414; Michaber 3146

The reason for this is:[283] because it is common to occasionally make an opening on its side, such as when one wants the barrel to be open to constantly be able to remove wine from it and he does not want to remove the lid [permanently for this purpose] in order so dust or waste not fall in the wine, and he therefore makes an opening on its side.

Making a hole on the top of the actual barrel:[284] However, to make a hole in the actual barrel[285] is forbidden even on its top, even though it is not common to make an opening there, as since if [this hole] were to be made to enter and remove [wine] through it then he would be Biblically liable even though it was made on its top, therefore even when the hole is only made to remove [wine], it is Rabbinically forbidden even when made in its top.

Summary:
One may chop off the top of an un-sturdy structured barrel [i.e. an earthenware barrel which has been broken and re-glued together] which does not hold 40 Seah in order to show benevolence to his guests. One may also make a hole on a removable lid of a barrel even if the barrel is considered a sturdy structure. One may not However, make a hole on the side of the lid or on the side of the barrel. If the barrel is completely closed and does not contain a removable lid, it is forbidden to make a hole in any part of the barrel including its top.

If a barrel holds 40 seah or is a sturdy structure making a hole in the actual barrel is forbidden in any situation due to the destroying prohibition.

In summary: One can only make a hole in a barrel in one of two cases:
1. Chop off the top of an un-sturdy barrel.
2. Make a hole on the lid of even a sturdy vessel, for the sake of exiting or entering alone.

Q&A
May one make a hole in the cover of a vessel?[286]
It is permitted if the cover is removable and for whatever reason one would rather remove the content through making a hole, and it is not common to make a hole in such an area, and the hole is only being made for use in one direction, either for exiting or entering, but not both.

May a corivon cork opener be used on Shabbos?
It should only be used if one does not press the air into the wine.[287]

---

8. *Doing an action which causes a hole to be made unintentionally:*
A. Removing a knife from a barrel:[288]
Due to the [Rabbinical decree against performing any hole in a vessel, whether for entering or exiting] one may not puncture a new hole in a barrel for the wine to flow from [this hole]. [Furthermore] even if it already has a hole and one [simply] wants to add to it and slightly widen it, it is forbidden.[289] [However, in this case it is only forbidden] when one intends to widen the

---

[283] Admur ibid based on Rashi ibid
[284] Admur 314:15; M"A 3148
[285] Such as if it does not have a lid and rather is completely sealed on top and bottom, or if it has a lid and one wants to make a hole on its bottom side which is part of the barrel.
[286] Halacha 14
[287] The reason: As it is permitted to make a hole in a cover. However, this only applies if it goes one way, such as to remove the wine. However, here that it is made also to enter gas, seemingly it should be forbidden. However, seemingly if your intent in entering the gas is only to remove the wine, then it would remain permitted, as its like sticking a hand through the hole to get the item. However, if one's intent is to leave the gas there for preservation, then seemingly it would not be allowed, Rabbinically, as it is made for exit and entrance.
[288] Admur 314:3; Michaber/Rama 314:1
[289] Admur ibid; Michaber ibid

hole, However, if there was a knife jammed in the wooden barrel from before Shabbos in order for the wine to flow from the hole that is formed upon removing the knife, then it is permitted to remove it and reinsert it on Shabbos.[290]

The reason this is allowed:[291] [Now], although it is impossible to avoid the hole from widening upon removing it, [nevertheless] this does not pose any [Halachic] problem since one has no intent to widen the hole. Now, although it is inevitable [for this widening to be avoided, and thus it should be prohibited even if one does not intend to widen it] nevertheless since even one who makes a new similar hole intentionally only transgresses a Rabbinical prohibition, being that [the hole] is only made removing [the wine] out from it [as opposed to also entering wine into it], therefore [the Sages] were not so stringent on this to prohibit even adding to [this type of] hole unintentionally. [This opinion holds that we do not apply the prohibition of Pesik Reishei by an Issur Derabanan.]

Other Opinions:[292] [However,] there are opinions[293] that argue and say that [the Sages] did not permit to remove the knife from the barrel on Shabbos unless one has already removed it once from before Shabbos. [The reason removing it one time before Shabbos suffices is] as then it is no longer inevitable to avoid widening the hole through removing it on Shabbos, and rather it is possible that [removing] it will not add [to the hole] at all, in which case even if it did [happen to] add [to the hole when removed on Shabbos] it poses no [Halachic] problem being that one did not intend to do so.

The Final Ruling:[294] The main [Halachic] opinion is like the former opinion, although in a situation that there is not much need for one to remove the knife, it is proper[295] to suspect for the latter opinion.

B. Removing a knife from a bench and the like:[296]

If the vessel cannot hold 40 Seah: However, a knife which is jammed into a bench or another detached item, is permitted to be removed on Shabbos [according to all opinions] even if it had never been removed beforehand.

The reason for this is: because making a hole in a detached item never carries with it the prohibition of building but rather [can be forbidden] only because of a decree [that one may come to] "fix a vessel" if he makes an opening that is meant for entering or exiting. However, when one is not making an opening at all for entering or exiting but rather it [just happens to] consequently be formed through removing the knife, then there is no prohibition at all in doing so. [This is opposed to the case of a barrel that the making of a hole serves that the wine flow from it, and therefore in that case there are opinions which prohibit one to remove the knife if it will inevitably widen the hole.]

C. Removing a knife from a vessel which is large enough to hold 40 seah:[297]

If [a knife] is jammed into a large barrel or other large vessels which hold 40 seah [and thus] carry with them the building and destroying [prohibition], then it has the same law as if it were jammed stuck in a wall [in which the custom is not to remove on Shabbos unless it had been

---

[290] Admur ibid; Rama ibid in accordance to opinion of Michaber, as rules the Ravaya and Mordechai [See M"B 314:10]
[291] Admur ibid; Taz 314:2; M"B 314:11
Opinion of Michaber by Pesik Resihei of Derabana: From this Halacha we see the Michaber rules there is no prohibition of Pesik Resihei by a Rabbinical prohibition. Vetzaruch Iyun as in 320:18 the Michaber argues on the Aruch and rules by a Rabbinical case that one may not do a Pesik Resihei even if Nicha Lei. Vetzaruch Iyun Gadol!
[292] Admur ibid; Opinion of Rama ibid
[293] Terumos Hadeshen 64
[294] Admur ibid; Taz 314:2; M"B 314:11; To note that according to those Poskim that rule in 314:4 that even by a wall there is no prohibition to remove the knife, then certainly here there is no prohibition involved. See M"B ibid]
[295] Lit. Tov
[296] Admur 314:5; Michaber 314:12
[297] Admur 314:5; M"B 314:11

Summary-May one remove a knife from a vessel which does not hold 40 Seah?
If the knife had been removed one time before Shabbos, then it is permitted to remove it. If not, then if this hole could be used to remove items through it, then it is proper to avoid removing the knife in a case of no need.[298] If the hole would not serve one any purpose, such as a knife that is jammed in a bench that does not hold 40 seah [and is not attached to the ground[299]] then it is always allowed.[300]

---

9. Unplugging the hole of a barrel of wine:[301]

A barrel [of wine] which had a hole that was plugged up, even if it was plugged with one's hands[302], [or] with wood or another item, it is permitted to open it on Shabbos. However, this is only allowed when [the hole in the barrel] is above the [area of the] sediment [which lies on the bottom of the barrel], However, if it is parallel to the sediment then it is forbidden to open it, (unless it is meant to be constantly opened and closed as is the case with the tap of a barrel).
The reason for this is because:[303] since the [hole] is so low [in the barrel] all the weight of the wine rests on it, and one [thus] needs to plug it up well, [and] therefore when one opens it, it is considered like one is opening a new hole. However, when [the hole] is above the sediment in which case one does not need to plug it well, it is not considered as if one is opening it for the first time.
Unplugging the hole of a wooden barrel:[304] There are opinions[305] which say that [the Sages] only permitted to unplug an old hole by an earthenware barrel being that the plugs [of such material] are not well firmed into the hole, However, by a wooden barrel in which the hole is well firmed with the wood used to plug it and one [also] cuts the protruding part[306] of [the wooden plug] with intent so it not be removed, then [removing or drilling through this plug] certainly appears like [making] a new hole and it is [thus] forbidden.
Other Opinions:[307] [However,] there are opinions that argue on this [and rather permit this to be done even by a wooden barrel].
The Final Ruling:[308] One may rely on the latter opinion in a case of great need, to be lenient regarding a [disputed] Rabbinical prohibition.

Summary-May one unplug a hole of vessel, such as the stuffing of the hole of a barrel?
It is always permitted if the plug is meant to constantly be removed and returned.
If not, then by a barrel of wine and the like, if the hole reaches within the area of the sediment on the bottom of the barrel, it may not be removed.[309] Even when the hole is above the

---

[298] Admur 314:2
[299] Admur 313:17; as well as 314:19
[300] Admur 314:5
[301] Admur 314:6; Michaber 314:2
[302] Meaning that one intentionally did so.
[303] Admur ibid; Michaber ibid
[304] Admur 314:8; Michaber 314:3
[305] Kol Bo
[306] Lit. Its head
[307] Admur 314:8; Elya Raba 314:4; M"B 314:19
[308] Admur 314:8; See M"B ibid in name of P"M and Chayeh Adam
[309] Admur 314:6

sediment area if the barrel is made of wood then it may not be removed unless in a case of very great need.[310]

10. Using a tool to drill a hole through a plugged up hole of a vessel:[311]

In [any] situation that it is allowed to open the plug of an old hole it is [also] allowed to puncture it [i.e. the plug] even with a [non-electric[312]] drill. For example, if the tap of the barrel broke and one is not able to remove it, one may puncture it with a [non-electric] drill. It goes without saying that one is allowed to take another tap and bang it into the tap that is stuck [thus pushing in the broken tap and entering a new tap at the same time].

[The above However, is only allowed to be done] if one wants to drink wine [from this barrel] on Shabbos, and only as long as that the tap is not parallel to the sediment, as was explained [in the previous Halacha].

Summary-May one make a hole in the plug that is stopping up the hole?
In any case that it is permitted to unplug the hole [see previous Halacha] then one may also puncture a hole into the plug if one desires to use the content on Shabbos.[313]

Q&A
May one use a corkscrew to remove the cork of a bottle?[314]
Yes.

---

11. May one unplug a drainage pipe on Shabbos?[315]

It is forbidden to unplug a stuffed drainage pipe on Shabbos unless lack of doing so will cause flooding to one's house, in which case one may discreetly[316] press on the blockage of the pipe with an irregularity.[317] [It is However, forbidden to remove the items causing the blockage from the pipe.[318]]

Example: If one's rain pipes on his roof became stuffed with dirt and twigs and is causing flooding in one's house, one may use his feet to press down the blockage, allowing the water to flow freely.

---

[310] Admur 314:8

[311] Admur 314:7; Michaber 314:3

[312] Meaning that one may not plug in the drill, However, he may use it while it is not plugged in being that it has the status of Muktzah Machmas Issur, which is allowed to be moved in order to use.

[313] Halacha 7

[314] Chayeh Adam 41; Ketzos Hashulchan 119 note 7 based on Admur and Michaber ibid

Other opinions: There are opinions which say this should not be used because it appears like a mundane activity. [Tiferes Yisrael Kalkeles Shabbos, brought in Ketzos Haashulchan ibid] However, based on the ruling in 314:7 it appears that it is allowed without restriction. [ibid]

[315] Admur 336:15; Michaber 336:9; Kesubos 60a

[316] Admur ibid and Michaber ibid rule it may only be done "Betzina" in discreet.

Other opinions: Some Poskim rule it may be done even in public if necessary. [Beis Yosef in name of Ran; See Biur Halacha 336:9 "Betzina"]

[317] As since this case involves loss, the Sages did not decree against fixing the pipes in an irregular way. [ibid]

[318] M"B 336:47

Summary:
It is permitted to undo a blocked drain if all the conditions apply:
1. It will cause damage to one's property.
2. One uses an irregularity to free the blockage, such as one steps on it with one's feet.
3. One does not remove the blockage from the drain.
4. One does so discreetly.

Q&A

May one unplug a stuffed toilet or sink?
Yes.[319] One may even use a plunger or "snake" to do so.[320] However, some Poskim[321] limit this allowance to only if it is a common occurrence and if it is not completely stuffed.[322] Others[323] allow it without difference. If easily available it is best to do so through a gentile.[324] If However, the blockage is so strong that it requires the work of a professional, then one may not do so on Shabbos, unless he fulfills all the conditions mentioned above.[325]

12. The prohibition of plugging a hole on Shabbos:[326]

The law: Just like it is forbidden to puncture any hole due to the decree of fixing a vessel as was explained above [in Halacha 3], so too it is forbidden to plug any hole being that this is similar to fixing a vessel.

Plugging it with wax, cloth, and a non-Muktzah rock:[327] Therefore it is forbidden to plug the hole of a barrel even with a material that does not smear[328] and that does not involve one coming to [transgress the] squeezing [prohibition][329], such as for example plugging it with a pebble or pieces of wood which was prepared for this use from before Shabbos and is thus not forbidden to be moved [i.e. is not Muktzah].

Plugging it with food and the like in order to hide the food in the hole: However, if one places a given food or anything of the like into the hole in order to hide it there, and this consequently also plugs up the hole, then it is allowed.

Cunningly stuffing the hole with food: [Furthermore] it is allowed for a Torah Scholar to connive and use this loophole to plug the hole with a given food or anything of the like, and then tell to anyone who sees him doing this that he only intends to hide [the food in the hole].

The reason for why a Torah Scholar may do is: because even if he would do this in a non-

---

[319] Beir Moshe 1:29; Minchas Yitzchak 5:75; 7:19

The reason: As this is not a true blockage, as certainly some water goes through and it is very easy to open, as is seen that with a mere push of air the entire blockage is freed. It is thus not similar to the case in 336:15 where the drainpipe was blocked with twigs, as in that case the blockage formed a complete block. It is rather similar to 314:6 by the plug of a barrel of wine that is above the sediment, which is permitted to remove. In addition to all the above, by a toilet there is a lot more room to be lenient as it is a case of Kavod Habriyos, and thus one may be lenient just as the Sages were lenient in many matters of using the bathroom in chapter 312. [Beir Moshe ibid; Minchas Yitzchak ibid]

[320] ibid

[321] Igros Moshe 4:40

[322] As only then is it not considered Tikkun Keli, as explained in 314:6 and 336:15; Seemingly the Igros Moshe does not accept the differentiations brought in the Beir Moshe and Minchas Yitzchak above.

[323] Bier Moshe and Minchas Yitzchak ibid

[324] Minchas Yitzchak 5:75; 7:19

[325] So is implied from Beir Moshe ibid; Minchas Yitzchak ibid as then it is exactly similar to the case

[326] Admur 314:20; Michaber 314:11

[327] Admur ibid; Rambam 23:3; Bach; Poskim in M"B 314:47

Other opinions: The Michaber ibid rules that one may always stuff the hole which is above the wine, and hence wine does not leek through. Vetzaruch Iyun in Admur which at first rules like the Rambam which forbids all types of holes without differentiation, and then in the end of the Halacha writes that it is forbidden to stuff the hole which wine leaves through, hence implying that by other holes it is allowed.

[328] Such as soft wax and the like

[329] Meaning that it is not an absorbing material such as is a cloth, and thus it has no worry that one may come to squeeze it.

conniving way [meaning that] he would tell them [his true intentions that] he is doing so to plug it, [nevertheless] this would [still] only be a Rabbinical prohibition [and thus we do not prohibit him to connive in doing so].

As well [in addition to the above it is allowed] because being he is a Torah Scholar [allowing him to connive in doing this] will not lead him to [eventually] do it in a non-conniving way.

May an ignoramus also cunningly stuff with food? However, by an ignoramus [the Sages] did not allow him to connive [in doing this] because he may come to do so even in a non-conniving way, [meaning that] he will not say at all that he is doing so in order to hide [the food], but rather in order to stuff the hole.

Other Opinions: [However,] there are opinions which allow this to be done even by an ignoramus.

The Final Ruling: One may rely on the latter opinion to be lenient by Torah Scholars, to allow them to connive in doing this even in today's times that we no longer have people that are categorized as [true] Torah Scholars with regards to other issues.

Plugging a hole with a commonly used material:[330] All the above is with regards to stuffing the hole with an item which is not common to stuff with, However, it is permitted to plug it with [a type of] wood that is commonly used as a plug, such as to plug a tap into the hole made to take out wine through, even if it is not made to be opened and closed regularly but rather only on distant occasions.[331]

The reason for this is: because it does not appear like one is fixing a vessel with this stuffing since it is always commonly stuffed with this wood. However, an item which has not been made into a tap is forbidden to plug the hole which is made to remove the wine through[332] [even] if the tap got lost, unless one is a Torah Scholar which is cunningly doing so as was explained.

Regarding plugging a hole using wax, fat or other smear able materials-See "The Laws of Mimacheik-Smearing"

Summary-May one plug up the hole of a vessel on Shabbos?[333]
<u>With items not commonly used for plugs</u>: Is forbidden to be done with uncommon plugging materials due to it being similar to fixing a vessel. However, it is permitted for one to place food [other than fat and congealed oil[334]] and other items of the like into the hole if one's intention is to conceal the items rather than stuff the hole. A Torah scholar may even enter the above items with intention to stuff the hole as long as he lets others know that his intention is to conceal the item.
<u>With items that are commonly used as plugs:</u> Is permitted to plug a hole with a commonly used plug even if one plans to leave it there for some time.

---

[330] Admur ibid; M"A 314:15; M"B 314:48
[331] Nevertheless, the above allowance is only to insert the tap semi-firmly, and only if the barrel does not hold 40 Seah. [M"B 314:20; Tehila Ledavid 314:15-16 See next!]
[332] Vetzaruch Iyun as this implies that by other holes it is allowed in which the wine does not leave through this is allowed. This follows the Michaber ibid. Now, in the beginning of this Halacha Admur rules like the Rambam which forbids all types of holes without differentiation. Vetzaruch Iyun!
[333] Halacha 20
[334] Halacha 21

13. Inserting a tap into the hole of a barrel on Shabbos:

A hollow rod:[335] It is permitted to insert a hollow rod or other [forms of] taps into a [previously made hole that is in a] barrel, in order to remove wine from it, even if it had never before been placed in the barrel and one [thus] does not know at all whether [the tab] will fit the size of the hole of this barrel. We do not suspect that perhaps it will not fit into [the hole, being that the tab is too large] and one will [then come to] cut and grate down [the] circumference [of the tab] until it reaches the size [of the hole], and thus be liable for the cutting prohibition.

[Nevertheless, the above allowance is only to insert the tap semi-firmly, and only if the barrel does not hold 40 Seah.[336] It is However, forbidden to firmly insert the tap, or if the barrel holds 40 Seah to even semi-firmly insert the tap, due to the prohibition of Tikkun Keli. If, however, the tap is meant to be constantly inserted and removed it is allowed in all cases.[337]][338]

Inserting a myrtle leaf and drain pipe into the barrel:[339] However, it is forbidden to insert a myrtle leaf[340] into the hole of a barrel in order to prevent the wine from flowing onto the walls of the barrel, and rather have it flow on the leaf which has been folded to form something similar to a drainpipe, due to a decree that one may come to affix a drainpipe for his wine so that the wine flow into it and travel a distance.[341]

The reason this decree does not apply by a tap:[342] The reason that this decree was not made against inserting a hollow rod [into the barrel] is because the rod has no modification done to it [when coming to place it in the hole] and is rather just [simply] inserted into the hole [the way it is], therefore [the Sages] did not decree [against doing so] due to suspicion that one may come to do a modification to connect a drainpipe to his wine. However, by the leaf, in which a modification has been done to it being that he takes it and folds it like a drainpipe, since it appears like making a drainpipe the [Sages] decreed against it due to that one may come to attach an actual drainpipe to his wine.

Another opinion regarding why it is forbidden to attach a leaf to help drain the wine:[343] However, there are opinions which say that also by a leaf there was no decree made [that one may come to affix] a drainpipe, but rather it was decreed [against] because the leaf may get damaged and one will then come to pluck another leaf from the detached[344] branch in order to place it into the hole of the barrel, and this removal [of the new leaf] is prohibited due to [the prohibition of] "fixing a vessel". As any item which is altered on Shabbos, so it be fit to be used for a given purpose carries with it [the prohibition of] "fixing a vessel".

The reason for why this is forbidden even if the leaf can be used for animal fodder:[345] See above Halacha 5

The practical ramifications of this opinion-It may be done if one has many leaves available:[346] According to this opinion that it is only prohibited to insert a leaf into the hole of the barrel

---

[335] Admur 314:9; Michaber 314:5

[336] As by vessels that do not hold 40 seah it is only Rabbinically forbidden to enter items semi-firmly, and if it is not common to ever enter it firmly, then according to some opinions is permitted. [see Tehilah Ledavid ibid] Vetzaruch Iyun as why here is it not considered the common way to enter it firmly, and should hence be Rabbinically forbidden even when done not semi firmly?!!! Perhaps, however, this is because here it refers to a case that the tap is meant to be eventually removed, and hence has two leniencies involved.

[337] As rules Admur in 314:7

[338] The above addition is from Tehilah Ledavid 314:15-16 and is a forced conclusion based on the other rulings of Admur. See also M"B 314:20 that limits the allowance to if the tap is not strongly inserted.

[339] Admur 314:10; Michaber 314:5

[340] The case here is discussing even a leaf which is not Muktzah, such as that it was plucked off the tree before Shabbos to be used to smell.

[341] Meaning he may come to attach a pipe which will carry the wine to a further area.

[342] Admur 314:10; Michaber 314:5

[343] Admur 314:11; Rama 314:11; Rosh 22:8

[344] Meaning we do not suspect that one will come to pluck a leaf from a tree, However, from a branch that had been previously cut off, we do suspect.

[345] Admur 314:11

[346] Admur 314:11

because one may come to pluck off [another leaf], [the Sages] did not prohibit [doing so] in a scenario that one has many leaves which had been plucked from before Shabbos, as in this case there is no need to worry that that one may come to pluck a leaf [from a branch] as even if one or two [leaves] were to ruin he still has more and we do not suspect that perhaps all his leaves will ruin.

The Final Ruling: [347] By a dispute over a Rabbinical prohibition one may follow the lenient opinion.

May one insert a tap into the hole of a vessel?
Yes[348], However, only if no modification is done to the tab that is inserted.[349] [Nevertheless, the above allowance is only to insert the tap semi-firmly, and only if the barrel does not hold 40 Seah.[350] It is However, forbidden to firmly insert the tap, or if the barrel holds 40 Seah to even semi-firmly insert the tap, due to the prohibition of Tikkun Keli. If However, the tap is meant to be constantly inserted and removed it is allowed in all cases.[351]][352]

May one enter a tap into a beer keg on Shabbos?[353]
If the tap is securely fastened into the keg, then it is Biblically forbidden to do so. If the tap is semi loosely found within the keg then it is permitted to do so if this is the common way of attachment, or if one plans to eventually remove the tap.

---

[347] Admur 314:11
[348] Admur 314:9
[349] Admur 314:10
[350] As by vessels that do not hold 40 seah it is only Rabbinically forbidden to enter items semi-firmly, and if it is not common to ever enter it firmly, then according to some opinions is permitted. [see Tehilah Ledavid ibid]
[351] As rules Admur in 314:7
[352] Above addition is from Tehilah Ledavid 314:15-16 and is a forced conclusion based on the other rulings of Admur. See also M"B 314:20 that limits the allowance to if the tap is not strongly inserted.
[353] Based on Tehila Ledavid ibid

CHAPTER 2: THE BUILDING AND DESTROYING PROHIBITION:

1. The general rules of the prohibition:
A. Items attached to the ground:[354]
Any item attached to the ground [including vessels, even if they are not sturdy[355]] contain the [prohibition] of building and destroying, [even if one plans to build them semi-loosely or take them apart when they only semi-loosely attached.[356] This prohibition applies even if the item that is attached to the ground is only meant to last temporarily.[357]]

Not made to last at all:[358] However, this only applies by a door that is made to last [on the pit] and not be removed on Shabbos, and thus when one wants to open the pit he unties the rope and opens the door [and then replaces it] and does not totally remove the door from there, as it is set to be there for some time. **However, if [the door] is not made to last at all then there is no destroying [prohibition] involved neither in unraveling the rope or cutting it, and not even in removing the actual door from it, unless it is a case that the door revolves on hinges and [to remove it] one must remove the hinge from its socket** as explained.

Q&A
May one reinsert a toilet seat that came out of its hinges?
Seemingly one may not do so even loosely as the toilet is attached to the ground.

May one remove or attach the toilet paper roller that is removed from the socket for the sake of placing on a new role?
Seemingly it is forbidden to do so.[359]

If a tether ball fell off its string that is attached to the pole, may one reattach it?
Seemingly one may not do so even loosely as it is attached to the ground.

May one attach a hammock to a fence on Shabbos?
If it is meant to remain there for some time doing so is forbidden. If it is meant to be constantly placed and removed as needed, then it is permitted.

May one attach a wall hanger or hook to his wall or door on Shabbos?[360]
This is forbidden, whether using glue, tape, or a suction item, due to the building prohibition.

If a Mezuzah fell on Shabbos may one insert it back onto the doorpost?[361]
The Mezuzah fell together with its case: A Mezuzah which fell together with its case may never be replaced on Shabbos to the door being that doing so involves nailing or taping the Mezuzah to the doorpost which contains a Building prohibition.[362]

---

[354] Admur 313:17; as well as 314:19; Michaber 308:9; 314:10
[355] Admur 314:17
[356] Admur 314:17, Ketzos Hashulchan 119 footnote 4
[357] See Admur 314:19 in next case that only if it is made not to last at all is it permitted; Ketzos Hashulchan 119 footnote 4 [rules that if is temporary and not Mivatlo Sham and not meant to be there is permitted, otherwise is forbidden] Vetzaruch Iyun if placing it there temporarly is a Biblical prohibition or Rabbinical prohibition. From Admur ibid it seems that the prohibition is Biblcial. However, from Ketzos Hashulchan ibid it is implied that it is only Rabbinical. Vetzaruch Iyun.
[358] Admur 314:19; Michaber 314:10
[359] In dirshu they bring a dispute without sources
[360] Az Nidbaru 3:23
[361] See Daas Kedoshim 289:2; Tzitz Eliezer 13:53
[362] However, see Daas Kedoshim ibid which writes that one may ask a child [even above the age of Chinuch] to attach the Mezuzah in a temporary method [Kevius Aray] as in such a case it is a Shvus Deshvus which is overridden by the Mitzvah of Mezuzah.

If a Mezuzah fell out of its case: If a Mezuzah slid out of its case, and its case has remained on the doorpost, then some Poskim[363] allow one to return the Mezuzah into its case on Shabbos.[364] Others[365] However, rule that one may not do so being that it is similar to fixing a vessel.[366] Practically, seemingly one may be lenient[367] so long as it does not involve a building prohibition.[368]

From the Rav's Desk

Question:
During our meal, the Mezuzah [with its case] fell off from the door of the dining room. What do we do? Can we replace it on Shabbos? Must we leave the room to a different room in order not to be in a room without a Mezuzah?

Answer:
Forbidden to replace. One may remain in the room.

The explanation: One may not replace the Mezuzah on Shabbos due to the building prohibition. The only time it would be permitted to replace a Mezuzah is if the Mezuzah parchment slid out of the case, in which case one may enter it back into the case. However, to tape, or nail, or glue etc the Mezuzah back on is forbidden. Nonetheless, one is not required to leave the room being that some Poskim rule that there is no prohibition against living in a home without a Mezuzah, and even according to the stringent opinion who prohibits one can argue that on Shabbos there is no prohibition, as since he is unable to erect the Mezuzos on Shabbos, he is therefore exempt from the Mitzvah, and it is as if he living in a room that is not obligated in a Mezuzah. Nonetheless, some Poskim conclude that even on Shabbos if another room is available then one must switch rooms. However, regarding the above case that the Mezuzah fell from the dining room, being that relocating the meal would take much time, seemingly even the stringent approach would be lenient to define it as if another room is not available at that time, and hence it would be permitted to remain there according to all. To note that if the above occurred on Sukkos, such as if the Mezuzah of the backdoor from which one enters into the Sukkah fell off, there would be an even greater leniency if based on Heker Tzir the Mezuzah is placed towards the direction of entering the Sukkah, as a Sukkah is exempt from Mezuzah during the seven days of Sukkos.

Sources: See M"A 13:8 [no prohibition to enter home without Mezuzah]; P"M 38 A"A 15 [must move out of room on Shabbos if other room is available]; Pischeiy Teshuvah Y.D. 285:1; Daas Kedoshim 289:2; Sdei Chemed Mareches 40:115 [main opinion follows that there is no prohibition to live in home without Mezuzah]; Tzitz Eliezer 13:53; Shevet Halevi 4:143

[Vetzaruch Iyun as he himself sides that a Katan is invalid for placing a Mezuzah even during the week. Furthermore attaching something to a building even loosely is Biblically forbidden, thus how is this matter a mere Shvus. Vetzaruch Iyun]

[363] Tzitz Eliezer 13:53

[364] This does not appear like Tikkun Keli even according to the opinion which rules one may not live in a house without a Mezuzah, as this is an obligation on the person and not on the house.

[365] Sdei Chemed Mareches 40:115

[366] The Sdei Chemed brings that this matter is subject to the same dispute as is immersing vessels in a Mikveh. As according to those which rule one may not live in a house without a Mezuzah, placing the Mezuzah fixes the house for living in. According to those which hold one may live in a house without a Mezuzah, there is fixing occurring to the house by placing the Mezuzah back.

[367] As even regarding immersing a vessel a dispute is brought, and certainly here that it is unclear if even according to the stringent opinion there is an issue of Tikkun Keli, one may be lenient.

[368] Meaning the use of tape, as taping something to the ground is like building. Hence the allowance only applies if one is able to simply slide the Mezuzah back into the case without use of any item to attach it there.

B. Vessels that are not attached to the ground but are large enough to hold 40 Seah:[369]

Even vessels that are not attached to the ground, if they are large enough to hold 40 *seah*, meaning that their size is one cubit by one cubit [19x19 inches] with a height of three cubits [59 inches] including the walls [in its circumference[370]] [but] without [including] the thickness of the feet[371] and the crown[372] [within its height][373], then they are considered like a tent[374] and carry with them the building and destroying [prohibition], and therefore it is forbidden to remove their doors from them. [Thus, it is forbidden to attach even semi loosely, and it is forbidden to build and destroy even a un-sturdy structure of this built, as explained next.]

The prohibition by an unsturdy structure:[375] It was already explained that there is no building or destroying [prohibition] by vessels which are not large enough to hold 40 *seah* and are not sturdy structures. Based on this if an earthenware barrel which does not hold the measurement of 40 *seah* shattered [before Shabbos] and then had its pieces glued back together with tar, then it is permitted to break this vessel on Shabbos, whether using one's hand or whether using a vessel, in order to remove its content.

Summary:
Vessels that are not attached to the ground but are large enough to hold 40 Seah have the same law as an item attached to the ground.

Q&A

May one replace the door of a regular fridge on Shabbos if it fell out of its socket?
No.[376]

May one remove or replace the pole of the Aron Kodesh?
This matter requires further analysis.

May one insert a metal pin holder onto the Bima in order to fasten Bimah cover?
The insert constantly falls off: Seemingly this is allowed to be done.[377]
The insert stays put for a while: Seemingly this would be forbidden.[378]

May one remove the panel of a bookcase if it is resting on hooks?
Some write that if the bookcase holds 40 Seah then doing so is forbidden.[379] However, perhaps it should be viewed as permitted, similar to how it is allowed to hang an item on a hook even permanently on Shabbos. Vetzaruch Iyun.

---

[369] Admur 313:18; See also 314:1; 314:5; Rama 314:1; Terumos Hadeshen 64; M"B 314:2

[370] Meaning that one measures the 1x1 cubits from the outside of the vessel, and thus even if within the volume that is inside the vessel there is not 1x1 cubits, nevertheless it is included in the above law.

[371] Meaning it does not include the thickness of the bottom panel of the vessel, and thus must be three cubits high measuring from the inside of the vessel.

[372] This refers to a decoration that extends above the surface of the vessel, such as a crowning which surrounds the top of a box and the like. Thus it is saying that this decoration is not included in the 3 cubit height measurement.

[373] Admur ibid; M"A 314:1-2

[374] Admur ibid; M"B 314:2

[375] Admur 314:1; M"B 314:2
Other opinions: However, see Biur Halacha 3141 "Sheiyno" that according to the Rashba brought in Elya Raba it is not forbidden to destroy an unsturdy structure even if it hodls 40 Seah.

[376] As it holds 40 Seah and is normally inserted strongly. Thus, even if one were to weekly insert it, it would be forbidden.

[377] As rules the Ashel Avraham regarding inserting a door handle which constantly falls off.

[378] As a Bima can hold 40 Seah, and hence attaching anything to it, even loosely, is forbidden.

[379] Dirshu

C. Vessels that are not attached to the ground and are not large enough to hold 40 Seah:

To initially make a vessel:[380] To initially make a vessel[381] [on Shabbos] is [considered to be building] a sturdy structure and is thus liable for building.

To destroy a complete structure:[382] [As well as] if one breaks a complete structure [not made of parts], then this is [considered] destroying a sturdy structure and is thus liable for destroying.

Other opinions regarding if we apply Boneh and Soser by vessels:[383] There are opinions[384] which say that there is no building and destroying [prohibition] by vessels including even to build a sturdy [complete] structure and to destroy a complete [sturdy] structure. [According to this opinion] it was only said that one who reassembles a chest of drawers and a box and portable tower in a strong way, and similarly that one who reassembles a vessel made up of individual parts in a strong way, that he is liable for a sin offering, because he has fixed a vessel and is [thus] obligated [for the offering] because [he has transgressed the prohibition of] "Making a finishing touch", [and not because of the building prohibition]. Thus, when one destroys an item that is firmly assembled, and even if he destroys and breaks a vessel made completely of a single part, this does not contain any prohibition when done for the sake of Shabbos, and one may rely on this opinion regarding asking a gentile to do so when needed to be done for a Shabbos need.

Tikkun Keli and Boneh when Fixing a vessel, and building a vessel from scratch:[385] Similarly, anyone who does any fixing to a vessel, this fixing is considered a [Biblically forbidden form of] work, and one is [thus] liable [for a sin offering]. It goes without saying that one who makes a vessel from scratch is liable for the "hitting with a hammer" prohibition, even if it is done in a way that does not contain the building prohibition, as will be explained in chapter 314 [Halacha 17[386]] and 322 [Michaber Halacha 4[387]]. [Vetzaruch Iyun if it is done in a way that one is liable for Boneh, according to the stringent opinion in 314/17, is one also liable for Makeh Bepatish.[388]]

Tikkun Keli and Boneh when returning a hinge back into its socket:[389] All doors of vessels, such as for example [the doors of] a drawer, a box or a portable tower, that have doors on their sides and have two hinges, meaning that they have two heads protruding out from the door, one on its top which enters into a socket that is in the top of the door frame and one on its bottom which goes into a socket that is in the threshold[390], then if [on Shabbos] the bottom hinge became completely dislocated from its [socket], then it is forbidden to reinsert it. The reason for this is [due] to a decree that one may come to [properly] fix it, meaning that one [may] strongly insert it [into the socket] using a mallet and hatchet in a way that one will no longer be able to take it out from there, and [one thus] will become liable for [transgressing the] building [prohibition] as will be explained, or [he will transgress the] "final blow' [prohibition] as will be explained in chapter

---

[380] Admur 313:19; However, see 302:5 that doing so is forbidden due to Tikkun Keli. See other opinions below
So rules: Rambam 10:13; Tosafus Shabbos 102b; Rosh Eiruvin 3:5; Rashba; Michaber 314:1; See M"B 313:41; 314:7
Other Poskim: Some Poskim rule there is never a prohibition of Boneh and Soser by vessels, and rather one only transgresses Makeh Bepatish. [Rashi Shabbos 47a; Gr"a in M"B 314:7; mentioned in Admur 314:17 and 302:5 that doing so is forbidden due to Tikkun Keli]
[381] Seemingly this refers to making a vessel out of a single material, as opposed to assembling many pieces together, such as to make a clay pot and the like. The novelty here is that the rule of "there is no destroying and building by vessels" was not said in such a case.
[382] Admur 313:19; Michaber 314:1
[383] Admur 314:17; See also 302:5 that doing so is forbidden due to Tikkun Keli; Michaber 314:7
[384] Hagahos Maimanis 23:1 in name of Reim; Yireim; Rashi Shabbos 47a; Gr"a in M"B 314:7
[385] Admur ibid; Rambam 23:4; Smak 280; However, see Rashi 73a that "One is only liable on the Gemar Melacha"
[386] There it is explained that according to some opinions [Rashi 47a] there is no building prohibition applicable to vessels which are not attached to the ground. However, nevertheless even such vessels are forbidden to be built due to the "Hitting with a hammer" prohibition.
[387] There it is explained that one who breaks a twig to use as a toothpick transgresses the "Makeh Bepatich" prohibition despite not transgressing the building prohibition.
[388] From the wording of Admur it is implied that he is liable for both, Vetzaruch Iyun.
[389] Admur 313:14
[390] Meaning that the case here is not discussing the classical hinges of a door which are positioned on the side of the door, but rather that the hinges are on the top and bottom of the door.

314 [Halacha 17].[391]

To strongly insert a handle into a vessel:[392] As well one who inserts the wood into the ax to serve as a handle is liable for building. Similarly, anyone who inserts wood into wood, whether one inserts it with nails or whether into the wood itself, to the point that they became unified [meaning sturdy], then this is an offshoot of [the] building [prohibition] and one is thus liable.

Removing the strongly inserted part:[393] [Consequently] anyone who removes wood that is inserted [into other wood and the like] is liable for destroying just like one who destroys a sturdy structure.

To take apart Un-sturdy vessels:[394] To remove the doors from vessels [which are not attached to the ground and do not hold 40 seah] is allowed in all scenarios that the hinge has not been strongly affixed into them, as by vessels there is no [Biblical prohibition] against building and destroying [when they are un-sturdy vessels]. [Regarding building such vessels However, in many cases it is Rabbinically forbidden as will be explained in Halacha 5]

To take apart a sturdy vessel:[395] However, if they are strongly affixed then taking it apart involves [the prohibition of] destroying [and building them contains the building prohibition].

The reason for this is because:[396] [The Sages] only said that [the Biblical prohibition of] building and destroying does not apply by vessels, if the vessel being built or destroyed is not sturdy.

Summary:
Un-sturdy vessels: Do not retain a [Biblical prohibition] against building and destroying [when they are un-sturdy vessels], and thus their doors may be removed.
By sturdy vessels: Retain fully the Biblical building and destroying prohibition.

D. Destroying not for the sake of building a better building:

First Opinion-Destroying with intent for improvement:[397] [According to the opinion which exempts one from work done not for the sake of its body this not only applies when he has no intent at all to do the work for the body of the item but furthermore] one who destroys a building with intent to return and build it, or one who tears with intent to return and sew, is not Biblically liable unless his intent is that the latter building be greater than the former, and so too in sewing the [torn] cloth [his intent must be that it get improved more than it was originally prior to the tearing]. As without this destroying and tearing, it is completely impossible to fix the building and cloth in order to improve it.

The Rabbinical prohibition:[398] It is However, a Rabbinical prohibition to extinguish, build or tear [even when not done in order to improve].

Asking a gentile to extinguish, destroy or tear in a time of need:[399] Based on the above that destroying without intent to better an item is only Rabbinically forbidden it is [thus permitted] to

---

[391] Vetzaruch Iyun why here Admur leaves in doubt whether one transgresses the building prohibition or the Fixing prohibition, while in many other cases he rules plainly that attaching detached parts transgresses the building prohibition [see 313:20 or here 5A]. Perhaps though one can explain that Admur here is referring to the dispute brought later on in 314:17 that some opinions hold that one is never liable by building even complete structures for building but rather for Makeh Bepatish, and thus here he leaves it open to both opinions. However, Tzaruch Iyun why specifically in this case did Admur choose to not finalize like whom we rule while in other cases he rules plainly that it has a building prohibition.

[392] Admur 313:19; Michaber 313:9
[393] Admur 313:19
[394] Admur 313:16
[395] Admur 313:16
[396] Admur 313:19
[397] Admur 278:2; So rules Tosafus Shabbos 94a
[398] Admur 313:17
[399] Admur 313:17

tell a gentile to do so in a distressful situation, as it is a Rabbinical decree upon a Rabbinical decree which is allowed to be done in a distressful situation.

Other Opinions-Even by destroying no need for improvement:[400] There are opinions which say that even by actions of destruction it is not necessary that the rebuilding be better than the way it was originally.

Other Opinions-One is liable for work even if not done for use of its body:[401] All the above is in accordance to those which say that an action which is not done for the need of its body one is exempt for and is only Rabbinically forbidden. However, there are opinions which argue on this and say that even work which is not done for the need of its body one is Biblically liable for. [According to this opinion, if one destroys for any intent of fixing, even an external fixing, such as out of anger in order to sooth his anger, or in order to take out food from a jar, one is liable.[402] If, However, one destroys simply for the sake of destroying without any benefit, one is exempt according to all opinions. See appendix!]

The Final Ruling:[403] [Due to the above lenient opinion one] therefore does not need to reprimand people who are lenient [to ask a gentile in a time of distress to destroy an item when they do not plan to rebuild it in a better way] being that they have upon whom to rely. However, every person should be stringent upon himself like the stringent opinion which is the main [Halachic] opinion.

Summary:
Some rule one is only liable for destroying if he does so in order to rebuild it in a better way. Others rule he is liable if he plans to rebuild it even if he rebuilds it to the same state it was in when destroyed. Others rule he is always liable even if he does not plan to rebuild it. One of the ramifications is, may one ask a gentile to destroy an item in a case of great need if one plans to rebuild it after Shabbos to the same state. Practically one is to be stringent against doing so, although those that are lenient do not need to be protested.

General Summary:
Building: Is only Biblically forbidden by an item attached to the ground, or an item that holds 40 Seah, or when building a firm and sturdy structure.
Destroying: Is only Biblically forbidden when the item is attached to the ground, or holds 40 Seah, or is a sturdy structure, and as well only if one's intent is to rebuild it, and according to some only if he rebuilds it better than it was originally.

E. Boneh by foods:
There is no prohibition of Makeh Bepatish/Tikkun Keli in fixing foods for the sake of eating.[404] One may thus do any permitted action to a food even if that action makes it edible, such as to

---

[400] Admur 278:2; so rules Rashi Shabbos 31
[401] Admur 278:3; So rules Rebbe Yehuda and Rambam
[402] Peri Chadash Yoreh Deah 118:18; Minchas Yitzchak; Peri Megadim
[403] Admur 313:17
Other opinions: Some Poskim rule one must protest against those that are lenient to ask a gentile to remove the window. [Taz 313:5; M"B 308:38]
[404] Admur 318:11; 324:4; M"B 318 in Biur Halacha "Hadachasan"; Ketzos Hashulchan 130 pp. 21-31; Igros Moshe 3:52; Malbushei Yom Tov 318:9; Avnei Nezer 419; See Shabbos Kehalacha 3 p. 296-303!
Other opinions: Some Poskim rule that the prohibition of Tikkun Keli does apply to making foods edible. [Levush 318:4; Peri Megadim 318 A"A 16 [brought in Biur Halacha ibid]; Shevisas Hashabbos; Chayeh Adam 20:5; Rav Poalim 16; Maharshag 51; Shevet Halevi 8:54] The Biur Halacha ibid negates their opinion stating "it is a "Davar Chadash" that is not found in previous Poskim and there are many contradictions to this assertion and hence one is not to be stringent at all". See Shabbos Kehalacha 3 p. 296-303!

pour cold water on salted fish[405], or to rub animal fodder and make it edible.[406] However, there are other prohibitions relevant to fixing foods such as Boneh[407], Memacheik; Borer, and Bishul.
Making hard cheese:[408] If one solidified [curd] and turned it into cheese he is liable for building. *The reason for this is:*[409] because anyone who gathers parts [of an item] to each other and bonds them together until they become a single substance has [transgressed] an offshoot of [the] building [prohibition].

Halachas 2-5: The laws of Assembling and Disassembling the parts of a vessel:
2. Inserting or removing the door of a vessel attached to the ground or which hold 40 seah:
Note: The laws of inserting or removing the doors, windows and locks of a house are elaborated in Chapter 3-See there!

A. Returning or removing the door of a pit, or of a vessel attached to the ground, to or from its hinges:[410]
[Although it is permitted to remove the door of a vessel which is only semi-loosely attached[411],] nevertheless the door of a house and of a Bor pit and Dus pit[412] or of vessels which are attached to the ground, such as for example a chicken coop which is a vessel and is attached to the ground, it is forbidden to either remove or return [the hinges of these doors into or out of their sockets[413] even if they are placed in loosely[414]], as anything attached to the ground has the [Biblical prohibition] of building [it] and destroying [it] [even if it is only semi-firmly attached[415]].[see note[416]] **See however Halacha D that removing the door of a pit is only Rabbinical!**

B. Removing the doors of vessels which hold 40 seah:[417]
Even vessels that are not attached to the ground, if they are large enough to hold 40 seah, meaning that their size is one cubit by one cubit [19x19 inches] with a height of three cubits [59 inches] including the walls [in its circumference[418]] [but] without [including] the thickness of the

---

[405] Admur 318:11; Taz 318:5; Mishneh Berurah 318:36; Ketzos Hashulchan 124:24
Other opinions: See above!
[406] Admur 324:4
Other opinions: See above!
[407] See Admur 319:26; See Kitzur Shulchan Aruch 80:25 who learns this from the Magen Avraham 340:17 which rules that pressing figs together and smoothening them down to beautify their appearance involves the Building prohibition. Other Poskim However, [Cheishev Haeiphod 2:77; Daas Torah 321, and so is apparently the opinion of the M"B and Ketzos Hashulchan [146 p. 12] which do not mention this prohibition in their summary and commentary of the above Halacha in the Rama] rule that this prohibition of building stated by the Magen Avraham only applies by pressing hard items together and making them into one unit. However, to spread something nicely does not resemble in any way the building prohibition but is rather only proper to avoid due to the smoothening prohibition as rules the Rama.
[408] Admur 319:26; M"A 319:18; M"B 319:63
[409] Admur 319:26
[410] Admur 313:17; see also 313:8: "However, one must beware that if they have hinges that one not return the hinge to their sockets as will be explained [in Halacha 17]."; Michaber 308:9
[411] Admur 313:16
[412] A dus pit is a pit that has a wall surrounding it, while a Bor pit does not have anything surrounding it, and is rather just a hole in the ground. [See Baba Basra 64a and Rashi there] In Chapter 587:1 the Alter Rebbe explains that a Dus is any building which majority of its space is underground level. However, if only minority of it is above ground level, then it has the same law as a house.
[413] Admur 313:8
[414] Admur So is clearly evident from Admur, as this Halacha is a continuation of the previous Halacha where semi-loosely is allowed, and here Admur is coming to contrast that ruling. So rules also Ketzos Hashulchan 119 footnote 4.
[415] This Biblical prohibition applies even if the door was only semi-firmly placed into its sockets. [Ketzos Hashulchan 119 note 4]
[416] However, by a **door** of a vessel attached to the ground this is only a Rabbinical prohibition and thus it is permitted to remove the covering of an item attached to the ground if it is meant to be constantly opened and closed and if it is not attached onto hinges, as will be explained in C.
[417] Admur 313:18
[418] Meaning that one measures the 1x1 cubits from the outside of the vessel, and thus even if within the volume that is inside the vessel there is not 1x1 cubits, nevertheless it is included in the above law.

feet[419] and the crown[420] [within its height], then they are considered like a tent and carry with them the building and destroying [prohibition], and therefore it is forbidden to remove their doors from them.

C. Removing the door of a pit which is not on hinges:[421]
Seals that are on the ground, such as the door of a pit which is tied to it with a rope is permitted to be untied being that the knot was not made to last long, as it is meant to be constantly untied. However, if one is unable to undo the knot then it is forbidden to undo the threads of the rope or to cut it due to [the] destroying [prohibition], as every item attached to the ground has [a] building and destroying [prohibition] even if it is not a complete [sturdy] vessel.

The law by a door not made to last: However, this only applies by a door that is made to last [on the pit] and not be removed on Shabbos, and thus when one wants to open the pit he unties the rope and opens the door [and then replaces it] and does not totally remove the door from there, as it is set to be there for some time. **However, if [the door] is not made to last at all then there is no destroying [prohibition] involved neither in unraveling the rope or cutting it, and not even in removing the actual door from it, unless it is a case that the door revolves on hinges and [to remove it] one must remove the hinge from its socket** as explained.

D. Breaking the opening of the oven which has been plastered shut:[422]
An oven which one places the hot food in for Shabbos and closes its opening with a sheet of wood, which is then sealed with clay, is permitted to [be opened on Shabbos and remove the wooden board[423] even though that by doing so one needs to] break through the plastering on Shabbos, in order to remove the hot food that is in it.

The reason for the above leniency: Now, although the oven is attached to the ground, and it is forbidden to break a structure that is attached to the ground, nevertheless [here it is permitted], **since Biblically it is only forbidden to break the body of the structure and not to break its opening**, and it is only that the Sages made a decree that one may not destroy the doors of a structure which is attached to the ground. Even this decree only applies when [destroying] a door made to be there permanently for some time, and thus one did not have in mind to make it on condition to break through it on Shabbos, [as in such a case] it appears like [the prohibition] of destroying [a permanent object]. However, the plastering of the [opening of the] oven which was not made at all to be there permanently, but rather to just temporarily retain the heat, and to then be removed the next day, the Sages never decreed against breaking it.

The Stringent Opinion: There are those which are stringent to not break the plaster through a Jew if it is possible to have it done through a gentile. Similarly [when there is no gentile available] if it is possible to do it through a child then it should not be done through an adult, and if this is not possible then the adult should do it in a slightly irregular way.

Do we follow the stringent opinion? The custom is like the stringent opinion.

---

[419] Meaning it does not include the thickness of the bottom panel of the vessel, and thus must be three cubits high measuring from the **inside** of the vessel.
[420] This refers to a decoration that extends above the surface of the vessel, such as a crowning which surrounds the top of a box and the like. Thus it is saying that this decoration is not included in the 3 cubit height measurement.
[421] Admur 314:19; Michaber 314:10
[422] Admur 259:7; see also 314:17: "It is permitted for one to remove the board that is placed in front of the oven and is plastered with clay from before Shabbos as written in chapter 259 [Halacha 7] being that it is not made to last at all but rather with intent to remove it on Shabbos. [However, see there that the custom is to be stringent even in this case, and do so only through a gentile or child or with an irregularity.]; Michaber 314
[423] Admur 314:17

Summary of inserting or removing the door of a building or a vessel attached to the ground or of a vessel that is large enough to hold 40 Seah:

It is never allowed to have doors, or any part inserted into the above items even semi-loosely due to the Biblical building prohibition. Similarly, it is prohibited to remove a door or any part from the above items even if they are only loosely in their sockets due to the destroying prohibition.[424] However, by a door or other opening of a vessel attached to the ground which is not resting in hinges, it is only a Rabbinical prohibition to be removed, and is thus allowed to be removed if the non-hinged door is meant for constant removal and insertion.[425]

Q&A

May one insert or remove the door of one's house into or from its hinge?

This is Biblically forbidden even if the door was or will be placed loosely in its hinge. This prohibition applies even if the door is already partially on its hinges and one is merely pushing it in further.[426]

One's front door: If one's front door has somehow fallen out of its socket, it nevertheless remains forbidden to replace it in the socket, even if he fears from robbers.[427]

May one insert or remove the handle of the door of a room or window?

See the compilation brought next!

No, doing so is Biblically forbidden, and the handle is thus completely Muktzah [MM"G].[428]

If, however, this is the common way one opens and closes the door, meaning that he leaves the handle out of the door and when he desires to open it or close it, he inserts it, then it is allowed to be inserted or removed as it is similar to a key.[429]

Regarding a handle which constantly falls off, and thus when one reinserts it, he knows it will not last long, some Poskim[430] rule that it is permitted to have it reinserted[431], although it is best to do so through a child, and if needed the adult can then fully insert the rest of the handle. It requires further analysis if in other cases one may enter the handle with intent to remove it immediately after opening the door.

What is one to do in a case that it is forbidden to return the handle? If one is locked in the room then another item, such as a screw driver, may be entered into the socket to close and open the door.[432] If this is not possible, then if a baby is stuck in the room one may even enter the handle into the socket.[433] If an ill person or elderly man is stuck in the room, then if there is danger involved if the door were to not be opened, one is to go ahead and do so.[434]

May one ask a gentile to open the door: Seemingly it is forbidden to ask the gentile to reinsert the handle.[435] However, if there is a great need to open the door, or not doing so will

---

[424] Admur 313:17 and 18.
When one removes the above for the sake of destroying the item, without intention to rebuild it, then it is only a Rabbinical prohibition. However, when done with intention to rebuild then it is a Biblical prohibition [Ketzos Hashulchan 119 note 8]
[425] Admur 314:19
[426] So is implied from 313:14 that by items attached to the ground it is forbidden in all cases,
[427] See 316:10 that one may not close his windows or door even to protect from robbers if doing so will trap an animal or bird within his house, and there the trapping is only Rabbinical. Thus certainly here it would be forbidden.
[428] As any item attached to the ground is forbidden to attach even loosely. Vetzaruch Iyun as to why the handle is not considered a Shevus as is the door of a pit that is only a shevus
[429] SSH"K 23:32; Piskeiy Teshuvos ibid
[430] Ashel Avraham Butshetch 313; See Orchos Chayim 313:3 which says that in such a case it is more lenient. SSH"K 20:43 However, leaves this matter un-ruled.
[431] As seemingly this is similar to a door of a pit which is not made to last, which does not contain the destroying prohibition.
[432] Piskeiy Teshuvos 308:12
[433] As one may even destroy the door in order to get to a baby out [328:15]
[434] Piskeiy Teshuvos ibid
[435] As then this is a case of actual Shvus [building through a gentile], which even the Ashel Avraham did not permit.

cause a nullification of Oneg Shabbos, such as he will not be able to eat the Shabbos meals, then one may be lenient to ask the gentile to break open the lock or break the door.[436] However, if possible it is best to have a child ask the gentile to do so.[437] Regarding asking the gentile to remove the door from its sockets, seemingly according to Admur[438] this should be avoided, However, there are Poskim[439] which rule that it is permitted.

If one leaves a key constantly in his door may he remove it on Shabbos?
Yes.[440]

May a pit in a public area be covered?[441]
If it poses a public safety hazard, then one may move an item to cover the pit [by walking less than 4 cubits at a time]. If, possible, one should only cover it partially in order to avoid the building prohibition. If, however, leaving it partially open still poses a hazard then it may be fully covered.

May one remove the drain cover of one's floor on Shabbos?[442]
If the cover has a handle, or indentation which forms a handle area, then it is permitted to be removed.[443] If there is no handle at all then it is forbidden and is Muktzah.

---

[436] As in such a case it is Shvus Deshvus, as destroying without intent to rebuild is only Rabbinically forbidden.

[437] Ashel Avraham Butshesh 314. See also 313:17. Now, although there Admur concludes to be stringent, that is because one intends to replace the window back, and it is thus done with intent to rebuild, just not in a better way. Here However, it is being destroyed without any intent whatsoever to rebuild.

[438] Admur 313:17 as one intends to return the door to its socket, and it is thus a mere Shvus and not Shvus Deshvus.

[439] Ashel Avraham ibid. as the gentile himself does not have intent to return it.

[440] Admur 313:21, as it is not meant to last at all in the door.

[441] Sheivet Halevy 5:40

[442] Piskeiy Teshuvos 308:13; SSH"K 23 footnote 28

[443] Vetzaruch Iyun as why this is not forbidden being that the cover is attached to the ground and is only removed infrequently. Perhaps However, since it is meant for constant removal and insertion it is permitted to be removed, even though one does not constantly remove it.

Compilation-Placing door handles into a door on Shabbos?[444]

> ➤ *Case example: The handle fell off my door and I have no way of opening it, or closing and then opening it, unless the handle is reinserted. may I do so on Shabbos?*

A. Introduction:

Building or fixing an item on Shabbos enters into the question of the Biblical prohibition of building [i.e. Boneh] and/or fixing [i.e. Makeh Bepatish, or Tikkun Keli].[445] In some circumstances, fixing an item is prohibited under Biblical law, while in other circumstances it is forbidden only due to Rabbinical law, and in other circumstances is permitted to be done and is not viewed as a prohibited form of fixing at all. The general law is as follows: Assembling parts together in a firm and professional way for the sake of permanently fixing or building an item, is under the Biblical building prohibition.[446] Assembling parts together in a loose way, or for only temporary attachment, is merely under Rabbinical prohibition if the item is not attached to the ground[447], while if it is attached to the ground then it is under Biblical prohibition even if the attachment his loose.[448] Assembling parts together very loosely is even initially allowed if this is the common way of how it is assembled.[449] Likewise, if the assembled parts are only meant to last a very short while, as they are made to be constantly removed and replaced within that same day, then it is even initially permitted to be assembled on Shabbos.[450] This applies even by items attached to the ground.[451]

B. The law:[452]

In general, it is Biblically forbidden to insert a door handle into the socket of a door on Shabbos.[453] Accordingly, if a handle fell out of the door on Shabbos, it is forbidden to be

---

[444] See Ashel Avraham Butchach 313; SSH"K 20:45; 23:37 [new]; Piskeiy Teshuvos 308:12 [old]; 313:3 [new]

[445] See Admur 302:5; Mishneh Shabbos 73a; Shulchan Aruch Chapters 313-314;
Which prohibition is transgressed upon building/fixing an item, the building prohibition or fixing prohibition? In general, the building prohibition relates to building or fixing items that are attached to the ground, while the fixing prohibition relates to moveable items. [See Admur 314:17; Rashi Shabbos 47a] Nonetheless, we find that even by movable items the act of fixing them can be considered under the building prohibition and not the fixing prohibition. [See Admur 302:5 that fixing an item falls under the fixing of vessel prohibition. However, see Admur 313:19-20 that it transgresses the building prohibition; Admur 313:14 regarding returning doors of a moveable vessel to hinges that one is *"liable for [transgressing the] building [prohibition], or [the] "final blow' [prohibition]"*] Practically, this matter is debated amongst the Poskim, with some ruling that fixing or building an item consists of the building prohibition with others ruling that it consists of the fixing of a vessel prohibition. [See Admur 314:17] According to the former approach, it requires further clarity to understand what consists of the fixing vessel prohibition according to their opinion.

[446] Admur 313:19-20; Michaber 313:6 and 9; M"A 313:11; Yerushalmi Shabbos 12:1; Rashi 47a

[447] So rule regarding assembling in a semi loose method that it is Rabbinical: Admur 313:19 and 21; Michaber and Rama 313:6 as explained in M"B 313:43 and 46; M"A 313:12 in name of Beis Yosef; M"B 313:43; So rule regarding assembling even very loosely if the common way is to assemble it strongly that it is nevertheless Rabbinically forbidden: Admur 313:21; Rama 313:6; So rule regarding assembling even strongly but for a temporary basis that it is only Rabbinically forbidden: Admur 313:20; Beitza 32; See Minchas Yitzchak 4:122
Other opinions: The Chazon Ish argues on the ruling of the Rama/Admur and rules that if it's weakly attached then it's always allowed to assemble it even if it is common to attach it strongly. The Sheivet Halevy 6:32 argues on the Chazon Ish and answers his questions on the Rama's ruling. [See Piskeiy Teshuvos 313:1]

[448] Admur 314:17, Ketzos Hashulchan 119 footnote 4

[449] Admur 313:21; Rama 313:6
Other opinions: The Chazon Ish argues on this ruling of the Rama/Admur and rules that if it's weakly attached then it's always allowed to attach it. The Sheivet Halevy 6:32 argues on the Chazon Ish and answers his questions on the Rama's ruling. [See Piskeiy Teshuvos 313:1]

[450] Admur 313:21; see also 314:19; M"A 313:12; Taz 313:7; M"B 313:45; Aruch Hashulchan 313:31; Minchas Yitzchak 4:122
Other opinions: Some Poskim rule that to strongly assemble parts together is forbidden even if it is meant not to last at all. [Tehila Ledavid; Chazon Ish]

[451] See Admur 314:19

[452] See Ashel Avraham Butchach 313; SSH"K 20:45; 23:37 [new]; Piskeiy Teshuvos 308:12 [old]; 313:3 [new]

[453] If it is strongly inserted, similar to how it is inserted when initially built, then it is under a Biblical building prohibition. Furthermore, even if it is inserted only slightly firmly, it would still be under the Biblical building prohibition, being that the door is attached to the ground. [See Admur 314:17, Ketzos Hashulchan 119 footnote 4] However, see Admur 259:7 who rules at the door of an item attached to the ground is only under rabbinical prohibition, enhance perhaps likewise replacing the door handle in a semi loose way would only be under a Rabbinical prohibition. Vetzaruch Iyun! Practically, the Piskeiy Teshuvos 313:3 concludes that if it is

replaced. In such a case, the handle becomes completely Muktzah [Muktzah Machmas Gufo], and may not be moved for any purpose in its regular method [excluding a Shinuiy].[454] Nonetheless, in the following cases, and in the following methods, there is room for leniency:

1. Using a knife, screwdriver or other tool to open the door:[455] It is permitted to enter a screwdriver[456], knife, or other tool, into the socket of the door handle for the sake of opening the door.[457]

2. If one commonly removes and reinsert the handle whenever he opens/closes the door:[458] A door handle that is made in a recognizable way then it is meant to be constantly removed and reinserted to open and close the door, then it is allowed to be inserted or removed on Shabbos, as it is similar to a key, and is not made to last at all as a permanent fixture of the door. [If, However, it is a regular looking door handle and the common way that one chooses to open and close his door is by removing and reinserting it, then it is subject to the same discussion as a loose handle which constantly falls off, as brought next.]

3. A loose handle which constantly falls off: If the handle is only loosely fit into the door, and hence constantly falls off, then some Poskim[459] suggest that it is permitted to have it reinserted on Shabbos.[460] Nonetheless, they conclude that it is best to have it initially inserted at least partially by a child, and if needed, the adult can then fully insert the rest of the handle.[461] [Practically, it is best in such a case not to reinsert the handle on Shabbos if it is not necessary, and to rather use a screwdriver and the like to open the door.[462] Nonetheless, those who are lenient in the above case have upon whom to rely.]

4. If one inserts the handle with intent to immediately remove: It is forbidden to reinsert the handle even with intent to immediately remove it after opening the door.[463] Practically, this is not to be done and rather one is to use a screwdriver and the like to open the door.

---

returned in only a weak way, without strengthening it inside the socket, then it is only Rabbinically forbidden, while if it is inserted strongly and screwed in with its screw then it is biblically forbidden.

[454] SSH"K 20:45; 23:37; Piskeiy Teshuvos 313:3; So rule regarding if the door of a home fell out of its hinges and the same would apply regarding a door handle: Admur 308:35; Shabbos ibid; M"A 308:38; M"B 308:35 [See SSH"K 20 footnote 167 who writes that it is Muktzah for this reason as it is no different than the door. However, see Piskeiy Teshuvos ibid footnote 13 and 308:24 who learns that it is only Muktzah being that it is forbidden to be fixed. Vetzaruch Iyun on his understanding.]

[455] SSH"K 23:37 in gloss; Piskeiy Teshuvos 308:12

[456] As it is permitted to use a Keli Shemilachto Lissur for a permitted purpose on Shabbos.

[457] The reason: As this item is not meant to last at all within the door and his hand similar to entering a key into a door for the sake of opening and closing it. [See Admur 314:19]

[458] SSH"K 23:32 [37 in new]; Piskeiy Teshuvos ibid and ibid

[459] Ashel Avraham Butchach 313; See Orchos Chayim 313:3 who says that in such a case it is more lenient; SSH"K 20:43 However, leaves this matter un-ruled.

[460] The reason: As seemingly this is similar to a door of a pit which is not made to last at all, which does not contain the destroying prohibition. [Admur 314:19] and thus here too since he knows that his re-insertion will not last at all, then it would be permitted to be done. On the other hand, perhaps we rule that since the handle is meant to remain by a door on a permanent basis it appears like one is building even in a case that it is made to be constantly removed and replaced, similar to the ruling against placing a peg by a door, brought in Admur 313:3. [See Ashel Avraham ibid; Piskeiy Teshuvos 313:3 footnote 15]

[461] Ashel Avraham ibid; Piskeiy Teshuvos ibid

[462] Piskeiy Teshuvos ibid concludes that one should be stringent

[463] On the one hand one can argue that since it will not last at all inside of the door then it does not consist of any building prohibition, as rules Admur 314:19. On the other hand one can argue that since this is an item that is meant to remain attached for a while onto the door, it is therefore Rabbinically forbidden to be done less one come to leave it in the handle and transgress. [See Admur 313:21 for a similar decree against inserting semi loosely] In addition, the handle is Muktzah and hence may not be lifted and inserted irrelevant of the building prohibition. Practically, I have not seen this possible allowance recorded in any of the Poskim, hence lending to the notion that it is forbidden. See Piskeiy Teshuvos 313 footnote 13 that it may only be inserted in an irregular manner
Inserting the handle in a irregular manner: Some Poskim rule that if the handle is not easily fixable for it to remain there in a permanent way, then it is permitted to insert the handle in an irregular manner in order to open the door, such as by putting it in upside down, or only inserting it to the very tip of the socket, As there is no chance that it will remain there on a permanent basis. [Piskeiy Teshuvos 313 footnote 13-14, based on his understanding that the handle is only considered Muktzah if it is easily fixable.] Practically, However, this is not to be done being at the handle is considered Muktzah, as we have explained. [See previous footnotes that it has the status of a door of a house, and hence is not dependent on whether or not it is easily fixable.]

Summary:
It is forbidden to insert a door handle into a door on Shabbos, with exception to the following cases:

1. If the common way one opens and closes his door is by removing and reinserting the door handle.
2. If the handle is only loosely fit into the door, and hence constantly falls off, then some Poskim are lenient.

Using a screwdriver or other tool to open the door: It is permitted to enter a screwdriver, or other tool, into the socket of the door handle for the sake of opening the door.

Q&A

What is one to do in a case that it is forbidden to return the handle and there is someone locked inside?

If a person is locked in the room, then a tool, such as a screw driver, is to be entered into the socket to open the door.[464] If this is not possible, then if a baby is stuck in the room, one may even enter the handle into the socket.[465] If an ill person or elderly man is stuck in the room, then if there could be potential danger of life involved if the door is not opened, then one is to do so.[466] If there is no danger of life apparent for the person to remain in the room, the handle is not to be inserted.

May one ask a gentile to return the handle to the door for the sake of opening it?

Seemingly it is forbidden to ask the gentile to reinsert the handle.[467] However, if there is a great need to open the door, or not doing so will cause a nullification of Oneg Shabbos, such as he will not be able to eat the Shabbos meals, then one may be lenient to ask the gentile to break open the lock or break the door.[468] However, if possible it is best to have a child ask the gentile to do so.[469] Regarding asking the gentile to remove the door from its sockets, seemingly according to Admur[470] this should be avoided, However, there are Poskim[471] who rule that it is permitted.

---

[464] Piskeiy Teshuvos 308:12

[465] The reason: As one may even destroy the door in order to get to a baby out, as this is considered Sakana. [Admur 328:15]

[466] Piskeiy Teshuvos ibid

[467] As then this is a case of actual Shvus [building through a gentile], which even the Ashel Avraham did not permit. Vetzaruch Iyun why the handle is not considered a Shevus even for a Jew, similar to the door of a pit which is only a shevus, as rules Admur in 259:7.

[468] As in such a case it is Shvus Deshvus, as destroying without intent to rebuild is only Rabbinically forbidden.

[469] Ashel Avraham Butshesh 314. See also 313:17. Now, although there Admur concludes to be stringent, that is because one intends to replace the window back, and it is thus done with intent to rebuild, just not in a better way. Here However, it is being destroyed without any intent whatsoever to rebuild.

[470] Admur 313:17 as one intends to return the door to its socket, and it is thus a mere Shvus and not Shvus Deshvus.

[471] Ashel Avraham ibid. as the gentile himself does not have intent to return it.

3. Inserting a door into vessels that do not hold 40 Seah and are not attached to the ground:

A. By doors that have hinges on their top and bottom as opposed to their side:[472]

If the entire hinge came out of the socket: All doors of vessels, such as for example [the doors of] a drawer, a box or a portable tower, that have doors on their sides and have two hinges, meaning that they have two heads protruding out from the door, one on its top which enters into a socket that is in the top of the door frame and one on its bottom which goes into a socket that is in the threshold[473], then if [on Shabbos] the bottom hinge became completely dislocated from its [socket], then it is forbidden to reinsert it.

The reason for this is: [due] to a decree that one may come to [properly] fix it, meaning that one [may] strongly insert it [into the socket] using a mallet and hatchet in a way that one will no longer be able to take it out from there, and [one thus] will become liable for [transgressing the] building [prohibition] as will be explained, or [he will transgress the] "final blow' [prohibition] as will be explained in chapter 314 [Halacha 17].[474]

If only part of the bottom hinge came out of its socket: However, if only part [of the bottom hinge] came out [of its socket] then one may press on it until it returns back into its place. [The Sages in this case] were not worried that one may come to [properly] fix it [with tools] because [such a strong insertion] is not so necessary [in this case] being that [the hinge] did not completely come out of its socket [and thus does not require much action to secure it back into its socket].

If part of the upper hinge came out of its socket: However, if even [only] part of the upper hinge came out it is forbidden to push it and return it back into its place, due to a decree that one may come to [properly] fix it.

The reason for this decree by the upper hinge is because: the upper [hinge] is required to be inserted more strongly than the lower [hinge], being that the lower [hinge] is consequently secured within its socket when the upper [hinge] is in its place [correctly, thus by the upper hinge there is a suspicion that one may come to strongly insert it and thus transgress the building prohibition].

B. By doors with a hinge on their side:[475]

Even a door that does not have a hinge on its top or bottom, but rather on its side, meaning that on its side there is one bolt that protrudes which has a hole opposite it within the doorpost, into which one inserts the bolt into this hole when he closes the door, and when one opens the door he removes it out from the hole, in which case here there is [thus] no suspicion that one may come to [strongly] insert [the bolt into its hole] being that the door is made for constant opening and closing [and thus one will purposely not place the bolt too strongly into the hole], nevertheless it is forbidden to return this hinge into its hole on Shabbos due to a decree [that if one were to be allowed to do so then he may come to also insert] a hinge which is not on the side of the door, [in which there is suspicion that one may insert it strongly].

Its law on Yom Tov: However, on Yom Tov it is allowed [to insert this type of hinge into its socket, when done] for the sake of the joy of Yom Tov, [such as to get into one's food storage house to get food for Yom Tov], as will be explained in chapter 519 [Halacha 1].

---

[472] Admur 313:14

[473] Meaning that the case here is not discussing the classical hinges of a door which are positioned on the side of the door, but rather that the hinges are on the top and bottom of the door.

[474] Vetzaruch Iyun why here Admur leaves in doubt whether one transgresses the building prohibition or the Fixing prohibition, while in many other cases he rules plainly that attaching detached parts transgresses the building prohibition [see 313:20 or here 5A]. Perhaps though one can explain that Admur here is referring to the dispute brought later on in 314:17 that some opinions hold that one is never liable by building even complete structures for building but rather for Makeh Bepatish, and thus here he leaves it open to both opinions. However, Tzaruch Iyun why specifically in this case did Admur choose to not finalize like whom we rule while in other cases he rules plainly that it has a building prohibition.

[475] Admur 313:15

Summary of inserting doors into vessels that are not attached to the ground and are not large enough to contain 40 seah:

It is never allowed to initially enter the hinges of a door into its sockets on Shabbos. If one inserts it very strongly one is liable for the Building prohibition. If he inserts it weakly it is Rabbinically forbidden.[476]

Inserting a hinge which is already partially in its socket: Even if the hinge is already partially in its socket it is forbidden to further hammer it in on Shabbos. This is with exception to a door that has a top and bottom hinge [meaning a hinge attached to the top and bottom of the door as opposed to the side] in which case it is allowed to bang in the bottom hinge if it only partially came out, as longs as the top hinge [that is on the top of the door] is fully set inside of its hinge.[477]

On Yom Tov: In cases of need one is allowed to remove and replace a door with a bolt on its side [which is entered into a hole in the doorpost] back into its socket as will be explained in Chapter 519.[478]

To remove a door from its socket: See next Halacha.

Q&A

May one insert a door into a toy house?
This is forbidden even if less than 40 Seah.

May one insert a drawer onto its railing on Shabbos?
If cabinet/table holds 40 Seah: Seemingly this is forbidden. [Vetzaruch Iyun why no mention of this is made in Poskim which deal with this question- See The Laws of Ohel Halacha 2 Q&A!]
If does not hold 40 Seah: See The Laws of Ohel Halacha 2 Q&A!

___

4. Removing doors from vessels that are not attached to the ground and do not hold 40 Seah:[479]

If the hinges were only loosely placed in their sockets: The above discussion [in Halacha 3] was with regards to returning the door [back into its sockets], However, to remove the doors from vessels is allowed in all scenarios that the hinge has not been strongly affixed into them.

If the hinges are strongly placed into their sockets: However, if they are strongly affixed [into their sockets] then taking it apart involves [the prohibition of] destroying as will be explained.

The reason that this is allowed when placed loosely: This does not involve the [prohibition] of destroying [an item on Shabbos] because by vessels [as opposed to buildings attached to the ground] there is no [prohibition] against building and destroying.[480] However, [the Sages] only said that [the Biblical prohibition of] building and destroying does not apply by vessels, if the vessel being built or destroyed is not sturdy. Such as for example removing the door from [the socket of] a vessel and returning it [to its socket], that returning it is not [considered] a sturdy [form of] building being that [the door] is still [in truth] detached from the vessel as it was not strongly inserted and thus can be easily removed from it. Therefore, when removing it one is not considered to be destroying a sturdy structure.[481]

___

[476] Admur 313:14-15
[477] Admur 313:14
[478] Admur 313:15
[479] Admur 313:16; see also 313:19; Michaber 308:9
[480] Admur 313:16
[481] Admur 313:19

Summary:
It is permitted to remove the door of a vessel which is not attached to the ground and does not hold 40 seah if the door is not strongly affixed to its socket. If it is strongly affixed to its socket, then it is forbidden.

Q&A

May one remove the door of a toy house?
If it is strongly attached to its socket, then it is forbidden. If loosely attached then it is allowed, so long as it is not attached to the ground and does not hold 40 seah.

5. Assembling and disassembling vessels [that do not hold 40 Seah and are not attached to the ground]:[482]

A. Assembling parts firmly:

To strongly insert a handle into a vessel:[483] As well one who inserts the wood into the ax to serve as a handle is liable for building. Similarly, anyone who inserts wood into wood, whether one inserts it with nails or whether into the wood itself, to the point that they became unified [meaning sturdy], then this is an offshoot of [the] building [prohibition] and one is thus liable.

How strongly must the items be inserted?[484] [Furthermore] even by a vessel made of individual parts[485], if one strongly inserts the pieces, meaning that one strongly secured them together in a way that requires strength and professionalism, then this is [considered] a sturdy structure and one is [Biblically] liable for building.

Assembling a vessel made of individual parts for permanent basis:[486] [Furthermore] even by a vessel made of individual parts[487], if one strongly inserts the pieces, meaning that one strongly secured them together in a way that requires strength and professionalism, then this is [considered] a sturdy structure and one is [Biblically] liable for building, if it was built to last a long time.

Assembling firmly for temporary basis:[488] However, if it was not made to last a long time then it is considered a temporary building and is [only] Rabbinically forbidden unless it is not made to last at all[489] [in which case it is even initially permitted to be done firmly, even not for a Shabbos necessity[490]] as will be explained [next]. **[See Q&A]**

Attaching a cover to a vessel:[491] [Thus] the covers of vessels which are made with incisions along their circumference, even though they are inserted onto the mouth of the vessel very strongly, this contains no prohibition, neither of destroying when removing [the cover] nor of building when placing it back on.

The reason for this is:[492] because the [inserted cover] is not meant to last at all but rather [is

---

[482] See Michaber 313:6 regarding a Mita shel Perakim, omitted by Admur
[483] Admur 313:19; Michaber 313:6 and 9
[484] Admur 313:20; Michaber 313:6; M"A 313:11
[485] Vetzaruch Iyun what the novelty is in saying this, after having already mentioned in the previous Halacha regarding putting together a handle on an ax. Is that not a case of assembling parts together?
[486] Admur 313:20; Yerushalmi 12:1; Rashi 47a
[487] Vetzaruch Iyun what the novelty is in saying this, after having already mentioned in the previous Halacha regarding putting together a handle on an ax. Is that not a case of assembling parts together?
[488] Admur 313:20; Beitza 32; See Minchas Yitzchak 4:122
[489] This is based on the law by a cover of vessels explained next, and the opinions there.
[490] The Ketzos Hashulchan 119 footnote 34 rules based on Admur 314:1 and other Poskim that destroying a Binyan Garua can only be done for a Shabbos need. Now although in this case it is a Binyan Gamur, as it is attached very strongly, nevertheless since it can easily be put back together, and so is its normal intended usage, therefore it is similar to ruling of the Ketzos Hashulchan in 119 footnote 18 that by Keli Shel Perakim that loosely attached it is permitted to be done even if it is not a Shabbos need.
[491] Admur 313:21; M"A 313:12; Taz 313:7; M"B 313:45
[492] Admur 313:21; see also 314:19; Aruch Hashulchan 313:31; Minchas Yitzchak 4:122

meant] to be constantly opened and closed also on Shabbos itself, and [the Sages] only prohibited building a temporary structure and destroying it if it was not made with intent to destroy it on Shabbos itself.

B. Disassembling parts that are firmly attached:[493]
All vessels made of assembled parts which are firmly attached to the point that if this insertion were to be done on Shabbos one would be liable, then it is forbidden to disassemble it on Shabbos due to [it carrying the] destroying prohibition.
Removing the strongly inserted part:[494] [Consequently] anyone who removes wood that is inserted [into other wood and the like] is liable for destroying just like one who destroys a sturdy structure.

C. Assembling parts together semi-firmly:[495]
No Biblical prohibition:[496] [The Sages] only said that [the Biblical prohibition of] building and destroying does not apply by vessels, if the vessel being built or destroyed is not sturdy. Such as for example removing the door from [the socket of] a vessel and returning it [to its socket], that returning it is not [considered] a sturdy [form of] building being that [the door] is still [in truth] detached from the vessel as it was not strongly inserted and thus can be easily removed from it, and therefore also when removing it one is not considered to be destroying a sturdy structure. The same applies for all vessels that are put together through [inserting] individual parts [into sockets], that if the parts are not strongly affixed, then taking it apart is not considered destroying a sturdy structure and reassembling it is not considered [Biblically] building a sturdy structure.
Rabbinically:[497] However, due to that which was explained above [in A, that strongly inserting the parts of a vessel is a Biblical transgression], all vessels made [through assembling] individual parts [into sockets] which got displaced the Sages forbade to return [the part] on Shabbos even if one only slightly strengthens it inside [its socket] in a way that it is semi-loose, due to a decree that [if one were to be allowed to do so then] one may come to firmly insert it [into its socket].[498]
Assembling a cup together semi-firmly-First Opinion:[499] A cup made of individual parts, some opinions say that even though it is usual for it to be assembled together semi-firmly, [nevertheless] it is permitted to reassemble it semi-firmly as we do not suspect that one may come to insert [the parts] firmly [into each other] being that it is not usual at all for a cup to be so strongly assembled to the extent that one would be liable for building. [Thus it is permitted to be done semi-firmly as] it was only [made] forbidden [by the Sages] to assemble [a vessel] even slightly firmly by a bed made of individual parts and other similar items in which there can be suspicion that one may come to assemble [the parts] together in a strong way.
Other Opinions:[500] [However,] there are opinions that say that there is no difference between a cup and other vessels, and [it is thus] forbidden to reassemble the cup unless [the parts are]

Background: The Magen Avraham and Taz are the source of this ruling as they allow one to insert a cover tightly, and Admur deduced from here that it is permitted to do so in all cases that the attachment is not meant to last at all. So learns also the Aruch Hashulchan [313:31]
Other opinions: The Tehila Ledavid and Chazon Ish However, learn that only regarding the cover of a vessel was the above allowance given to attach it tightly when it is not meant to last at all, as it is a mere cover and is not part of the vessel. However, to attach two parts and create one vessel strongly was never allowed even if it is not meant to last at all. The Tehila Ledavid ibid concludes with a Tzaruch Iyun based on Admur ibid. The Minchas Yitzchak [4:122] sides with Admur in this ruling, and brings different.
[493] Admur 313:22; 313:19
[494] Admur 313:19; Rambam; M"B 313:54
[495] Admur 313:21; Michaber 313:6
[496] Admur 313:19
[497] Admur 313:21; Rama 313:6 as explained in M"B 313:43 and 46; M"A 313:12 in name of Beis Yosef; M"B 313:43
[498] However, by all vessels attached to the ground it is a Biblical prohibition even if the parts are only semi-firmly placed into its sockets. [Ketzos Hashulchan 119 note 4]
[499] Admur 313:21; first opinion in Michaber ibid as explained in M"A 313:12; Tur and Rabbeinu Yerucham
[500] Admur ibid; Second opinion in Michaber ibid as explained in M"A 313:12; Tur in name of Maharam Merothenberg and Kol Bo

assembled completely loosely.

The Final Ruling:[501] One should be stringent like the latter opinion unless it is a very pressing situation in which case one may then rely on the lenient [opinion] if it is not usual at all for the cup to be assembled firmly.

Cups that are made to be assembled firmly: However, cups that are made with grooves along their circumference [in which one] inserts [the parts] firmly, then according to all it is forbidden to reassemble them even if one wants to place [the parts in] completely loosely.

D. Disassembling parts that are semi-firmly attached:[502]

All vessels made of assembled parts….. which are [merely] slightly secured [into their sockets as opposed to firmly] to the point that there is no [Biblical] prohibition in this assembly [and it is only prohibited] due to a decree that one may come assemble it firmly [as explained above in C], then it does not [carry with it the prohibition of] destroying and one may thus [even] initially disassemble it [on Shabbos even not for Shabbos necessity[503]].

E. Assembling the parts completely loose:[504]

All vessels made [through assembling] individual parts [into sockets] which got displaced the Sages forbade to return [the part] on Shabbos even if one only slightly strengthens it inside [its socket] in a way semi-loose, due to a decree that [if one were to be allowed to do so then] one may come to firmly insert it [into its socket]. However, if one does not insert it at all, and rather leaves it there completely loose, then it is allowed [to be done] as long as it is usual for the vessel to be left loose [like this] forever. However, if it is usual for it to be secured and strongly inserted, then even if now one wants to place it in loosely, [nevertheless] it is forbidden to return it due to a decree that one may come to affix it strongly. [However, if it is common to only be attached semi-firmly, then all agree it is permitted to place it in completely loosely.[505]]

F. Muktzah decrees made due to prohibition to reinsert firmly:[506]

An oven which had one of its legs detached: A Kirah oven which had one of its legs detached from it, meaning its pegs which are similar to legs, then it is forbidden to move it in order to use it, due to a decree that [if one were allowed to use it then] he may come to replace the leg and will insert it there strongly and will thus be liable for [transgressing the prohibition of] building.

A bench which had one of its legs detached: Similarly a long bench which one of its legs became detached, and certainly if two legs [became detached] is forbidden to move and to place it onto another bench and to then sit on it, even if the leg fell off from before Shabbos, unless one already sat on the bench in this way one time before Shabbos without having replaced its leg, in which case we do not suspect that one will change his mind to return [the leg] and insert it on Shabbos.

May one reinsert the leg loosely into the bench? It is forbidden to reinsert the leg into it on Shabbos even loosely, due to a decree that one may come to insert it strongly, unless it is common for the leg to be loose inside the bench.

---

[501] Admur ibid; Taz 313:7; M"B 313:46 rules like Taz However, is lenient in a case of "Shabbos need"

[502] Admur 313:22; Taz 314:7; So is also evident from Michaber 308:9 that allows detaching the doors of a vessel; M"B 519:10

[503] See Ketzos Hashulchan 119 note 18 that this is allowed to be done even not for a Shabbos need, as since the vessel can be easily put back together it is not considered destroying at all.

[504] Admur 313:21; Rama 313:6

Other opinions: The Chazon Ish argues on this ruling of the Rama/Admur and rules that if it's weakly attached then it's always allowed to attach it. The Sheivet Halevy 6:32 argues on the Chazon Ish and answers his questions on the Rama's ruling. [Piskeiy Teshuvos 313:1]

[505] So rules Admur clearly in 313:21 and so rules Chazon Ish 50:10; However, the M"B 313:45 explains this matter differently saying that even a very loose attachment is forbidden if it is meant to be attached even semi firmly according to the stringent opinion. See Shaar Hatziyon 313:30

[506] Admur 308:47; See also Admur 308:35; Michaber 308:8; M"B 313:45

What is the law if the leg actually broke? All the above is referring only to when the leg has become detached [from its socket and thus only needs to be inserted back in]. However, if it [actually] broke[507], then one is permitted to move the bench and place it on top of another bench, and sit on it, even if one did not sit on it in this way from before Shabbos, as in this situation there is no suspicion that one may come to return [the leg] and insert it strongly, as the top part of the leg has remained inside the bench [and thus fixing it in this method is not relevant].

For summary and full details see "The Laws of Muktzah"!

Summary of assembling and disassembling vessels that are not attached to the ground and do not hold 40 Seah:

Assembling vessels on Shabbos:

A. It is a Biblical prohibition to assemble the vessels if:

A. It assembles in a strong and durable way that requires strength and professionalism.[508]
And

B. It is meant to remain assembled permanently.[509]

B. It is a Rabbinical prohibition to assemble vessels when:

A. It is assembled strongly for temporary use.[510]
or

B. It is assembled in a semi firm way [unless this is the common way of assembling it and it is a time of great need[511]].[512]
Or

C. Is assembled completely loosely but the vessel is meant to be assembled in a totally firm way.[513]

C. It is allowed to assemble a vessel on Shabbos if either:

A. The pieces are placed in very loosely, and the vessel being assembled is a type of vessel that always has its pieces loosely or semi loosely[514] placed in it.[515]
Or

B. If the assembled vessel or piece of the vessel is not meant to last even temporarily, **[See Q&A for definition]** such as the cap of a bottle, then it may be placed on it even very strongly[516], [even not for a Shabbos necessity[517]].[518]

---

[507] Meaning that part of it still remains in the socket, as it cracked in half.
[508] Admur 313:19-20
[509] Admur 313:20
[510] Admur 313:20-21
[511] As rules Admur in his final ruling regarding the dispute if one may assemble cups semi-firmly.
[512] Admur 313:21
[513] Admur 313:21.
Other opinions: To note that the Chazon Ish argues on this ruling of the Rama/Admur and rules that if it's weekly attached then it's always allowed to attach it. The Sheivet Halevy 6:32 argues on the Chazon Ish and answers his questions on the Rama's ruling. [Piskeiy Teshuvos 313:1]
[514] So is proven from the stringent opinion in the cup case which says: "[However,] there are opinions that say that there is no difference between a cup and other vessels, and [it is thus] forbidden to reassemble the cup unless [the parts are] **assembled completely loosely**." Thus, we see that despite the cups being commonly inserted semi-firmly, it may be inserted completely loosely. So is also evident from the conclusion of that Halacha by Admur that: "However, if it is usual for it to be **secured and strongly inserted**, then even if now one wants to place it in loosely, [nevertheless] it is forbidden to return it due to a decree that one may come to **affix it strongly**."
[515] Halacha 21
[516] Halacha 20 and 21
[517] The Ketzos Hashulchan 119 footnote 34 rules based on Admur 314:1 and other Poskim that destroying a Binyan Garua can only be done for a Shabbos need. Now although in this case it is a Binyan Gamur, as it is attached very strongly, nevertheless since it can

> Or
>
> C. If it is a time of great need one may be lenient to semi firmly assemble a vessel that is always common for it to be assembled only semi-firmly.
>
> *To disassemble vessels on Shabbos*
>
> **A. Is Biblically forbidden:**
>
> If the assembled parts of the vessel were strongly affixed into their socket one who disassembles it on Shabbos is liable for the Biblical destroying prohibition[519] if he did so with intention to rebuild. However, when he disassembles the vessel for the sake of destroying the item, without intention to rebuild it, then it is only a Rabbinical prohibition, even if it was strongly inserted into its socket.[520]
>
> **B. Is allowed in all scenarios that:**
>
> 1. The parts are not strongly affixed into the vessel to the point that if it were to be assembled in this way on Shabbos then he would be exempt from Biblically liability of building. Thus, if it is only semi firmed into the socket, the parts may be removed [even not for Shabbos necessity[521]].[522]
>   or
> 2. If the vessel is not meant to last even temporarily, then it may be taken apart even if the pieces were assembled strongly,[523] [even not for a Shabbos necessity[524]].
>
> **C. Examples of forms of building that are prohibited to be done based on the above laws:**
>
> 1. To place a handle into a vessel[525], such as to attach a shaft to a knife, or a broom stick to a broom or mop, whether attached with a screw or glue or just jammed in.
> 2. To tighten the screw of any vessel.[526] Thus one may not tighten the screws of his glasses.
>
> **D. Examples of forms of destruction that are forbidden to be done:**
>
> To remove the handle of an ax[527], knife, broom, or mop.
>
> ***Practical Q&A***
> **What is the definition of a vessel "not made to last even temporarily?"**
> The Ketzos Hashulchan[528] brings in the name of the Peri Megadim that if the vessel is meant to

---

easily be put back together, and so is its normal intended usage, therefore it is similar to ruling of the Ketzos Hashulchan in 119 footnote 18 that by Keli Shel Perakim that are loosely attached it is permitted to be done even if it is not a Shabbos need.

[518] The Magen Avraham and Taz are the source of this ruling as they allow one to insert a cover tightly, and Admur deduced from here that it is permitted to do so in all cases that the attachment is not meant to last at all. So learns also the Aruch Hashulchan [313:31]
The Chazon Ish However, learns that only regarding the cover of a vessel was the above allowance given to attach it tightly when it is not meant to last at all. However, to attach two parts and create one vessel strongly was never allowed even if it is not meant to last at all.
The Minchas Yitzchak [4:122] sides with Admur in this ruling.
[519] Admur 313:16 and 22
[520] Ketzos Hashulchan 119 note 8
[521] See Ketzos Hashulchan 119 note 18 that this is allowed to be done even not for a Shabbos need, as since the vessel can be easily put back together it is not considered destroying at all.
[522] Admur 313:22
[523] Admur 313:20
[524] The Ketzos Hashulchan 119 footnote 34 rules based on Admur 314:1 and other Poskim that destroying a Binyan Garua can only be done for a Shabbos need. Now although in this case it is a Binyan Gamur, as it is attached very strongly, nevertheless since it can easily be put back together, and so is its normal intended usage, therefore it is similar to ruling of the Ketzos Hashulchan in 119 footnote 18 that by Keli Shel Perakim that are loosely attached it is permitted to be done even if it is not a Shabbos need.
[525] Admur 313:19
[526] Ketzos Hashulchan 119 note 12
[527] Admur 313:19
[528] 119 note 7

be disassembled within two days of it being built, then it is considered a not even temporary vessel. However, if it is made to last two days or more then it is considered a temporary vessel which is Rabbinically forbidden to destroy if it is a sturdy structure.[529]

What is the law if it is meant to be attached only temporarily and is not firmly attached, may one initially attach it on Shabbos?
This matter requires further analysis.[530]

May one detach the parts if they are strongly attached but only meant to last temporarily?
This matter requires further analysis.

May one attach together the pieces of a disposable vessel?
- Example 1: May one insert the parts of a disposable "spork" found in tradition soups?
- Example 2: May one enter a disposable needle into its socket?

If the pieces attach even slightly firmly: Some Poskim[531] rule that doing so is forbidden. Others[532] rule that it is allowed to be done, as throwing out an item is equivalent to disassembling it, and it is hence not meant to last at all. According to all it is only allowed if one plans to throw it out within the day, or at the very least within 2 days' time. However, if he plans to keep it longer it is forbidden to originally assemble it on Shabbos.
If the pieces are attached very loosely: Is permitted.

Disposable aluminum pan:
Lifting and closing the metal piece. Is permitted as is not lasting and is easily done, just like allowance to lift brim of hat and put down.

May one enter a tap into a beer keg on Shabbos?
See Chapter 1 Halacha 13!

May one adjust the height of a shtender on Shabbos?[533]
Yes. This may be done even if it involves loosening and tightening screws, as it is not made to last even temporarily.[534] However, some Poskim[535] are stringent to forbid doing so being that at times one does leave the Shtender in the adjusted position temporarily for a few days.

May one open or close a folding chair, table, bed, stroller, and crib on Shabbos?[536]
Yes. Doing so involves neither a building nor "Ohel" prohibition, as explained in "The Laws of making an Ohel" Halacha 3. See there!

---

[529] Vetzaruch Iyun as Admur 313:21 states: "because the [inserted cover] is not meant to last at all but rather [is meant] to be constantly opened and closed also on Shabbos itself, and [the Sages] only prohibited building a temporary structure and **destroying it if it was not made with intent to destroy it on Shabbos itself! So rules Admur also in 259:7**

[530] See the case of inserting a tap to a keg, which implies this may be done. Vetzaruch Iyun!

[531] Rav SZ"A brought in Piskeiy Teshuvos 317 footnote 24. However, in Minchas Yitzchak 8:27 he brings that Rav SZ"A ruled to him that when the item is thrown out it is considered destroyed, and thus should be allowed. However, it can be implied from Admur 651:6 which considers the knot of a Lulav that it is made to never be undone, even though after Sukkos it has no use, that throwing out an item is not considered like destroying. However, see Tzitz Eliezer 15:17 which explains that possibly one keeps a Lulav to inherit to his children. Vetzaruch Iyun.

[532] Minchas Yitzchak 8:27

[533] Piskeiy Teshuvos 9:38

[534] So rules Az Nidbaru 14:11 and Sheivet Halevy 6:32; Shulchan Shlomo 313:7

[535] Minchas Yitzchak 9:38

[536] Piskeiy Teshuvos 315:7

May one attach a table extender to his table on Shabbos?[537]

Yes. It may even be inserted into its sockets which are found in the table for this purpose. [See footnote[538]]

May a child play building games such as Lego and the like?[539]

Some Poskim[540] allow this in all cases[541], as the built structures are not meant to last at all, as they are assembled and disassembled constantly.[542] However, other Poskim[543] forbid playing with Lego and other building games of the like which involve attaching pieces strongly together. Others forbid it only in cases where the structure forms a roofing [due to the Ohel prohibition][544] or an actual vessel like a ship and the like.[545]

Assembling structures which are meant to last:[546] According to all opinions those building games which are meant to be left intact [in their built state] for a while are forbidden to be assembled on Shabbos.

Regarding adults playing with the above games: It is not in the spirit of Shabbos[547], although it is not forbidden due to it not being a Shabbos necessity.[548]

May one form a ship, plane and the like from [non-Muktzah] paper?[549]

Some opinions[550] allow this to be done. Others[551] are stringent.

May one make napkin designs for the Shabbos table setting?[552]

Some opinions[553] allow this to be done. Others[554] are stringent.

May one blow bubbles on Shabbos?[555]

Blowing bubbles on Shabbos enters into the question of whether it transgresses the Molid prohibition due to it changing the form of the water into foam. Practically, the mainstream

---

[537] Piskeiy Teshuvos 315:7; SSH"K 24:23

[538] Does this apply even if one plans to leave the attachment in for a long time, or only if he plans to remove it after Shabbos? May it be inserted strongly into its sockets? May one close a clamp over it?
Seemingly if it is only meant to be left there over Shabbos and then removed it is permitted even if it is strongly attached. However, perhaps we say that this allowance only applies by attachments that are not common at all to last even temporarily However, attachments which are common to be left attached temporarily and it is just that the owner does not plan to do so, then perhaps the allowance does not apply.

[539] Piskeiy Teshuvos 313:4

[540] Beir Moshe 6:25; Tztitz Eliezer 13:30

[541] Even to build ships and vessels of the like.

[542] As well for a child it is considered a Shabbos need and thus fulfills all the conditions required by a not even temporary vessel.

[543] Shalmei Yehuda 85:1

[544] Michzei Eliyahu 69

[545] SSH"K 16:20

[546] SSH"K 16:20

[547] Beir Moshe 6:24

[548] The Ketzos Hashulchan 119 footnote 34 rules based on Admur 314:1 and other Poskim that destroying a Binyan Garua can only be done for a Shabbos need. Now although in this case it is a Binyan Gamur, as it is attached very strongly, nevertheless since it can easily be put back together, and so is its normal intended usage, therefore it is similar to ruling of the Ketzos Hashulchan in 119 footnote 18 that by Keli Shel Perakim that are loosely attached it is permitted to be done even if it is not a Shabbos need.

[549] Piskeiy Teshuvos 313:4

[550] Beir Moshe 6:102

[551] SSH"K 16:20; Sheivet Halevy 5:35

[552] Piskeiy Teshuvos 302:5

[553] Beir Moshe 6:102

[554] SSH"K 16:20; Sheivet Halevy 5:35

[555] See SSH"K 16:30; Shabbos Kehalacha Vol. 3 17:79; Piskeiy Teshuvos 326:13 footnote 161

approach follows that it does not contain a Molid prohibition, and therefore children may blow bubbles on Shabbos.[556] However, it is best for adults to abstain from doing so.[557] Furthermore, some Poskim[558] rule that even children who have reached the age of Chinuch are to avoid blowing bubbles on Shabbos.[559]

May one make snowballs and snow men?
The Boneh prohibition: Some Poskim[560] rule that making snowballs carries a Boneh prohibition. Other Poskim[561] However, rule it does not carry a Boneh prohibition.
The Molid prohibition: Making snowballs on Shabbos does not transgress the Molid prohibition.[562] Nevertheless, some Poskim[563] rule it is forbidden to make snow balls on Shabbos due to the Molid prohibition.
Children: Some Poskim[564] rule that by children below nine years old one may be lenient to allow them to make snowballs in an area where there is an Eiruv. If, however, there is no Eiruv then every child above Chinuch is forbidden to throw snowballs. Other Poskim[565] rule it is proper to refrain all children [which have reached the age of Chinuch] from making snowballs on Shabbos.
Snow man:[566] In all cases it is forbidden for even children [above the age of Chinuch] to make snowmen and the like.

May one adjust the focus of binoculars?[567]
Yes.

---

[556] Evident from Ketzos Hashulchan 146:32; SSH"K ibid in name of Rav SH"Z Aurbauch; Shabbos Kehalacha ibid; Piskeiy Teshuvos ibid although writes that initially one should not instruct children to do so and it is just that if they do so they do not have to be protested
The reason: Although it is forbidden on Shabbos to change the form of an item, such as to turn ice into water, due to the Molid/Nolad prohibition, nevertheless the Poskim rule that the formation of foam/bubbles that becomes created when using soap to wash hands/dishes does not fall under this prohibition as the foam has no real substance, and does not last at all. [So rules Ketzos Hashulchan 146 footnote 32; Tzitz Eliezer 6:34; -14; in length; Beir Moshe 8:247; SSH"K ibid in name of Rav SZ"A; Piskeiy Teshuvos ibid; However, some are stringent in this: See Ginas Veradim [Halevi] O.C. Klall 3:14 regarding hard soap; Shevisas Hashabbos Dash 61; Az Nidbaru 10:16] For this reason, also the placing of toothpaste on one's teeth [without a tooth brush] does not consist of a Nolad prohibition, even though it creates foam in the process, as the foam has no substance. [Ketzos Hashulchan 138 footnote 31]. Accordingly, it would be permitted here as well to blow bubbles, being that the bubbles hold no substance and do not last. However, Tzaruch Iyun, as in the case of blowing bubbles one has intent to create the foam and it is thus unlike the case discussed above in the Poskim regarding soap bubbles, in which case one has no intent for them to be made. [see Shabbos Kehalacha ibid; Piskeiy Teshuvos ibid] Nevertheless, it is clear that the Ketzos Hashulchan 146 footnote 32 learns it is permitted even a case that one intends to make the bubbles, as he also explains that it is permitted to make seltzer for this reason, even though one certainly has intent to create the bubbles.
[557] SSH"K ibid; Shabbos Kehalacha ibid
The reason: As one intends to make the bubble and it is hence unlike the case discussed regarding soap bubbles in which case one has no intent for them to be made. [SSH"K ibid; Piskeiy Teshuvos ibid]
[558] Shraga Hameir 7:44; Koveitz Mibeiys Halevy 6:44 in name of Rav Shmuel Wozner and Nishmas Shabbos 250, brought in Shabbos Kehalacha ibid footnote 192
[559] The reason: As nevertheless, one has intent to make the bubbles and it is hence similar to Molid Davar Chadash. [ibid]
[560] Makor Chaim [Chavos Yair] 320:9; SSH"K 16:44
[561] Beir Moshe 6:30
[562] Shabbos Kehalacha ibid; Nishmas Shabbos 320:249
The reason: As all the reasons for permitting breaking ice on Shabbos is likewise relevant here.
[563] Beir Moshe 6:30 concludes that it is nevertheless forbidden being that doing so causes snow to melt, which is forbidden. Vetzaruch Iyun Gadol as from Admur [320:16 -18] which writes that the prohibition is only when one intends to use the melted water, while by a snow ball there is no intent for it to melt at all. Furthermore, the source of the Beir Moshe from 320:19 itself is dealing with crushing snow together within water when washing, and one thus certainly cares about having more melted water.
[564] Beir Moshe ibid
[565] Shabbos Kehalacha ibid; In footnote 167 he writes that in truth there seems to be no reason to prohibit making snow balls, However, he nullifies his opinion in face of the Makor Chaim which explicitly chastises those that make lads that make snowballs on Shabbos and throw them at each other.
[566] Beir Moshe ibid; Shabbos Kehalacha ibid
[567] Ketzos Hashulchan 119 footnote 12

May one fix broken glasses?

Lens came out: Is forbidden to be reinserted even loosely.[568] Is the lens and frame Muktzah? The lens itself is never Muktzah[569] unless it shattered or the glasses have broken to the point they are no longer useable.[570] The frames However, are Muktzah[571] unless 1) one had worn it like this before Shabbos, or 2) the lens has shattered and thus can no longer be fixed[572] or 3) It is very difficult to reinsert the lens, such as if one lost the screw or if the screw broke and cases of the like.[573]

Plastic glasses: If the lens popped out it is forbidden to reinsert it even though it can be done easily.[574] However, there are Poskim[575] which are lenient if this had occurred once before Shabbos and one reinserted it. Furthermore, there are Poskim[576] which allow it in all cases being that they do not consider this a proper fastening of parts being that the parts are very easily attached.

The handle which rests on the ears came out: It is forbidden to reinsert the screw even lightly. As well one may not fasten it using a safety pin, twist tie and the like, unless he plans to undo it immediately after Shabbos.[577] Are the glasses Muktzah? The handle that dislocated is not Muktzah[578]. However, the glasses, some Poskim[579] say it is Muktzah[580] while others[581] say that if only one ear handle became disconnected it is not Muktzah. According to all if 1) One had worn it in its broken state before Shabbos, or 2) the ear handle has broken and thus can no longer be reattached[582] or 3) It is very difficult to reinsert the handle, such as if one lost the screw or if the screw broke and cases of the like, then the glasses are not Muktzah.[583]

Bending the glasses back into shape: Is forbidden due to Tikkun Keli.[584]

If the nose piece broke: If the nose piece falls off then both the glasses and the nose piece are not Muktzah since this doesn't diminish the use of the glasses in any way.

May one fix a baby stroller?

A detached wheel: Is forbidden to be reinserted even lightly.[585] Is it Muktzah? The weal is not

---

[568] Due to a Rabbinical decree that one may come to insert it firmly and transgress a Biblical prohibition of Building:Tikkun Keli. [Based on ruling of Admur: Rama in summary above, and so rules Ashel Avraham Mahdurah Tinyana; Betzeil Hachachmah 6:123, Az Nidbaru 8:33; Imreiy Yosher 1:202; SSH"K 15:77]
Other opinions: However, according to the Chazon Ish [mentioned above by the summary] it is permitted to put it in loosely, and so rules Tzitz Eliezer 9:28; Cheilek Leivi 101; Beis Yisrael Landau 12 that one may loosely put it in without tightening the screw.

[569] Regarding the lens in a case that both the frame and lens are intact, it would appear it does not become Muktzah, being similar to the case of doors that have detached which are not Muktzah, and so rules Imrei Yosher 1:202

[570] Regarding the lens of glasses that have completely broken to the point they cannot be used unless fixed, it would appear that they would be Muktzah. This is not similar to the door case, being that the object that the doors were attached to are still usable even on Shabbos. Here However, neither the lens or the glasses have a use. Despite this However, one can also say that since they can be re-fixed they are not Muktzah and that is the reason for permitting to move the door of vessels. צ"ע

[571] Since it if forbidden to fix it on Shabbos this would seemingly make the glasses be Muktzah (at least to use-see above) out of fear that one may come to fix it. So rules also Piskeiy Teshuvos 313:5

[572] As in such a case it is similar to the case that the leg broke as opposed to simply became disassembled.

[573] So rules Piskeiy Teshuvos 313:5 and so seems pashut from Admur.

[574] So rules Shraga Hameir 3:43, and so seems pashut from Admur.

[575] Betzeil Hachachmah 6:123

[576] Tzitz Eliezer 9:28; Az Nidbaru 8:33

[577] Some write that it is allowed to enter a safety pin to attach the handle to the glasses, although not a twist tie. [Shulchan Shlomo 314:11-; M"B Dirshu in 308:9]

[578] As explained above regarding a popped lens

[579] Kanah Bosem 1:19

[580] As it is difficult to wear the glasses in such a way and thus is no different than a lens which has popped out.

[581] Az Nidbaru 8:33

[582] As in such a case it is similar to the case of the bench which broke a leg as opposed to simply having a leg become disassembled.

[583] So rules Piskeiy Teshuvos 313:5 and so seems pashut from Admur.

[584] Piskeiy Teshuvos ibid, Upashut.

[585] Due to a Rabbinical decree that one may come to insert it firmly and transgress a Biblical prohibition of Building:Tikkun Keli. [Based on ruling of Admur:Rama in summary above, and so rules Ashel Avraham Mahdurah Tinyana; Betzeil Hachachmah 6:123,

Muktzah. If the carriage is not currently useable, it is Muktzah. If the carriage is still useable, it is disputed whether it is Muktzah.[586] According to all if it was used before Shabbos in its broken state it is not Muktzah.

<u>Replacing a bassinet with a regular stroller seat or vice versa</u>: Those strollers which can also be converted to a basinet through removing the seat and fastening a bassinet in the place of the seat, are forbidden to be converted on Shabbos through the use of screws. However, if they are attached through axes or hooks it is allowed.[587] If the bassinet clicks in then seemingly it is forbidden to do so on Shabbos because such an attachment is considered semi-firm.

May one attach a hood to baby stroller?
This may involve a building prohibition in attaching it, as well as an Ohel prohibition in opening the attachment.
<u>Regarding the Building prohibition in attaching it</u>: If it is attached through screws then it is forbidden to be done. If it is attached through hinges, then it is allowed to be attached.
<u>Regarding if one may open the hood once it is attached</u>: It is forbidden to be opened[588]. However, there are Poskim[589] which are lenient[590]. See "The laws of making an Ohel" for further details.

May one insert or remove the seat of a baby walker?[591]
Yes, as it is meant to be constantly removed and inserted.

May one oil the squeaky hinges of an item?[592]
This is forbidden due to Tikkun Keli.

May one screw in the rod of a broom into a broom?[593]
No. It is forbidden to insert a broom onto a broomstick even if it does not involve using any screws. It is likewise forbidden to tighten the attachment while it is already attached.

From the Rav's Desk

Question:
Hi. Is it permitted on Shabbos to make seltzer using SodaStream with the non-electric model?

Answer:
While this matter is under debate amongst the Poskim with some claiming that it transgresses the rabbinical Nolad prohibition, as well as other possible prohibitions [i.e. Tikkun Keli] especially if one needs to assemble the cylinder to it on Shabbos. Practically, the vast majority of Poskim rule that is permitted to be used on Shabbos to make soda water and many even permit attaching the cylinder to it on Shabbos [being that it is made for constant entrance and removal and is thus similar to the cover of a bottle]. Nonetheless, I would suggest that the best thing is to make it before Shabbos and certainly not to attach the cylinder on Shabbos. Although if the cylinder is already attached and one forgot to make the soda water before

---

Az Nidbaru 8:33; Imreiy Yosher 1:202; SSH"K 15:77] However, according to the Chazon Ish [mentioned above by the summary] it is permitted to put it in loosely
[586] Az Nidbaru 8:33 rules it is not Muktzah. Kana Bosem 1:19; SSH"K 28 footnote 105 rule it is Muktzah.
[587] SSH"K 28:44
[588] SSH"K 24:13
[589] Az Nidbaru 3:24
[590] Seemingly they hold that once it is attached it is considered like a door and is thus allowed to be opened.
[591] SSH"K 28:46
[592] SSH"K 28:47
[593] SSH"K 23:1

Shabbos than he may be lenient to make it on Shabbos, and those who even attach a new cylinder to it on Shabbos have upon whom to rely, although those who are stringent not to attach a new cylinder and not to even make soda water on Shabbos, are blessed.

Sources: See Ketzos Hashulchan 130 footnote 12 and 146 footnote 32; Minchas Yitzchak 4:122 although it is best to do so from before Shabbos [9:33]; SSH"K 11:35 in name of Rav SZ"A; Yabia Omer 3:21 who also permits the attaching of the cylinder; See Maharsham 3:140; 6:33; Bris Olam Ofeh 91; Chelkas Yaakov 3:168; Tzitz Eliezer 7:24; 20:13; See list of all Poskim who are stringent and lenient in Piskeiy Teshuvos 320:15 footnote 163 and 313 footnote 99 regarding attaching the cylinder

Question:

Is opening a climbing scaffold allowed on Shabbos? One can fasten two bolts/screws with one's hand without needing a screwdriver or other tool. It needs to be fastened hard so that it doesn't fall apart, and we might forget to close it after Shabbat.

Answer:

The fact you can use your hands and tighten the screws and don't need a screwdriver is completely irrelevant. The only way that it would be permitted on Shabbos to screw or unscrew it is if it is meant to not last even temporarily meaning not more than that days' worth and at the very least not more than 48 hours. This would depend on how you use the item. Practically, what I would resolve in this case is that you do not do so unless the common way of you using this vessel during the week is in a way that the screws do not last for that day and you constantly put them in and out. If the latter is correct, then even if by mistake you forgot to remove the screws after Shabbos or one time during the week it doesn't affect the allowance, as it nonetheless retains the status of being meant for constant opening and closing and not to last at all.

Sources: See Admur 313:14; 20-21; 259:7; Ketzos Hashulchan 119 note 12

Question:

May one put together a folding table on Shabbos by inserting the legs into the table surface? I own a folding table which is made in the following way: The legs and frame on which the table rests are taken apart from the table and then put back together. There are pieces that protrude from under the table onto which one inserts the leg frame to lock it in and secure it. Is the attachment of the leg frame into the socket under the table prohibited due to the building prohibition and is taking it apart prohibited due to the destroying prohibition?

Answer:

Indeed, there are certain cases in which the above can be permitted and certain cases in which it would be prohibited, it all depends on the tightness and firmness of the legs when they sit inside the socket under the table, as well as on the amount of time that the table is meant to last in this erect position. If the table is not meant to last even 24 hours in this position as it is only opened for the use of guests and then immediately taken apart after Shabbos, then indeed it is permitted to be inserted and removed even on Shabbos itself, even if it is inserted very strongly in its sockets and even if one may come to forget to take it apart right away in 24 hours. If, However, the table is meant to last for some time in this position, then it depends on the firmness of the attachment of the legs into the sockets. If it is a very weak attachment, in which the sockets are wider than the legs and the legs actually jiggle inside the socket being loosely inside, then it is permitted to erect and take apart on Shabbos without limitation even if it is meant to last a long time in this position. If, however, the sockets are narrow to the size of the legs and thus grasp the legs in a way that the legs cannot jiggle inside the socket, then if it is a very firm and strong attachment that requires very strong effort to insert and remove then it may not be put together or taken apart on Shabbos being that it is meant to last more than 24 hours. However, if it is not a very firm attachment and requires only light effort to inserted and remove it, then it is disputed whether it may be attached on Shabbos and practically we are stringent unless it is a time of great need, although it is permitted even initially to take it apart on Shabbos.

Bottom line, after further verification of the facts of the case, it was determined that the above said table in question may be taken apart on Shabbos being that it effortlessly can fit inside of its socket, although it may not be erected on Shabbos being that they are accustomed to leave it erect throughout the week, and it is not a very loose fit inside the socket. However, in a time of great need, such as that there are not enough tables for guests, then one may be lenient to put it together on Shabbos.

Sources: See Admur 313, 19-22; 314:19; Michaber and Rama 313:6 and 9; M"A 313:12; Taz 313:7; M"B 313:45; Aruch Hashulchan 313:31; Ketzos Hashulchan 119 note 7; Chazon Ish 50:10; Minchas Yitzchak 4:122; 9:38; Nonetheless it's possible to argue, that since the entire intent of the manufacturing of this table is for it to be folded and have his legs removed whenever necessary then perhaps it is never deemed similar to a regular vessel that contains assembled parts, and is rather similar to the cover of the bottle which may be screwed back onto the bottle even if he does not plan on opening it for another month being that it is made for constant removal and insertion. Thus, so too, here since this table was made for constant insertion and removal of its legs, one's intent on leaving it there for a long time is irrelevant. On the other hand, one can argue that in truth the cover of a vessel is a unique case being that it is not possible to use the vessel without opening it and hence its function requires the ability to constantly be able to remove the cover. However, by the table, it is perfectly okay if one decides to leave it erect forever just like a regular table and hence if one does decide to leave it for more than 24 hours it would be subject to all the regular rules of a vessel that contains assembled parts. Practically, one can deduct from the ruling of the Minchas Yitzchak regarding using a screw to adjust the height of a standing Shtender that it is forbidden being that at times last more than a few days, that the same would apply here regarding a folding table, and it is hence forbidden to be done as we concluded.

Halachas 6-9: The laws of breaking a vessel on Shabbos[594]

Introduction:
The laws of destroying a vessel dealt with in Halachas 2-5 were only with regards to disassembling vessels that are made with assembled parts. The following law will discuss the laws of destroying a one-piece vessel, such as destroying a clay pot and the like.

Important Note:
The below laws only relate to breaking an item in order to remove its contents and then throw out the item. Breaking an item in order to make a use of the broken piece, as well as making a hole in an item which one plans to keep is forbidden due to Tikkun Keli. See above Chapter 1 Halacha 3-6!
Regarding tearing or cutting an item on Shabbos-See "The Laws of cutting and Tearing items and Shabbos"

---

6. Breaking vessels that are attached to the ground:

A. Breaking the ropes that tie a door to a pit:[595]

Seals that are on the ground, such as the door of a pit which is tied with a rope is permitted to be untied being that the knot was not made to last long, as it is meant to be constantly untied. However, if one is unable to undo the knot then it is forbidden to undo the threads of the rope or to cut it due to [the] destroying [prohibition], as every item attached to the ground has [a] building and destroying [prohibition] even if it is not a complete [sturdy] vessel.

The law by a door not made to last: However, this only applies by a door that is made to last [on the pit] and not be removed on Shabbos, and thus when one wants to open the pit he unties the rope and opens the door [and then replaces it] and does not totally remove the door from there, as it is set to be there for some time. However, if [the door] is not made to last at all then there is no destroying [prohibition] involved neither in unraveling the rope or cutting it.

Breaking the opening of the oven on Shabbos: For this reason, it is permitted for one to remove the board that is placed in front of the oven and is plastered with clay from before Shabbos as will be explained next.

B. Breaking the clay off from the opening of the oven which has been plastered shut:[596]

An oven which one places the hot food in for Shabbos and closes its opening with a sheet of wood, which is then sealed with clay, is permitted to [be opened on Shabbos and remove the wooden board[597] even though that by doing so one needs to] break through the plastering on Shabbos, in order to remove the hot food that is in it.

The reason for the above leniency: Now, although the oven is attached to the ground, and it is forbidden to break a structure that is attached to the ground, nevertheless [here it is permitted], since Biblically it is only forbidden to break the body of the structure and not to break its opening, and it is only that the Sages made a decree that one may not destroy the doors of a structure which is attached to the ground. Even this decree only applies when [destroying] a door made to be there permanently for some time, and thus one did not have in mind to make it on

---

[594] Regarding the laws of Soser on Yom Tov: See Admur 519:6 that one may tear open an envelope on Yom Tov. See Halacha 10
[595] Admur 314:19
[596] Admur 259:7; see also 314:17: "It is permitted for one to remove the board that is placed in front of the oven and is plastered with clay from before Shabbos as written in chapter 259 [Halacha 7] being that it is not made to last at all but rather with intent to remove it on Shabbos. [However, see there that the custom is to be stringent even in this case, and do so only through a gentile or child or with an irregularity.]
[597] Admur 314:17

condition to break through it on Shabbos, [as in such a case] it appears like [the prohibition] of destroying [a permanent object]. However, the plastering of the [opening of the] oven which was not made at all to be there permanently, but rather to just temporarily retain the heat, and to then be removed the next day, the Sages never decreed against breaking it.

The Stringent Opinion: There are those which are stringent to not break the plaster through a Jew if it is possible to have it done through a gentile. Similarly [when there is no gentile available] if it is possible to do it through a child then it should not be done through an adult, and if this is not possible then the adult should do it in a slightly irregular way.

Do we follow the stringent opinion? The custom is like the stringent opinion.

7. Destroying not for the sake of building a better building:

First Opinion:[598] [According to the opinion which exempts one from work done not for the sake of its body this not only applies when he has no intent at all to do the work for the body of the item but furthermore] one who destroys a building with intent to return and build it, or one who tears with intent to return and sew, is not Biblically liable unless his intent is that the latter building be greater than the former, and so too in sewing the [torn] cloth [his intent must be that it get improved more than it was originally prior to the tearing]. As without this destroying and tearing, it is completely impossible to fix the building and cloth in order to improve it.

The Rabbinical prohibition:[599] It is However, a Rabbinical prohibition to extinguish, build or tear [even when not done in order to improve].

Asking a gentile to extinguish, destroy or tear in a time of need:[600] Based on the above that destroying without intent to better an item is only Rabbinically forbidden it is [thus permitted] to tell a gentile to do so in a distressful situation, as it is a Rabbinical decree upon a Rabbinical decree which is allowed to be done in a distressful situation

Other Opinions-Even by destroying no need for improvement:[601] There are opinions which say that even by actions of destruction it is not necessary that the rebuilding be better than the way it was originally.

Other Opinions-One is liable for work even if not done for use of its body:[602] All the above is in accordance to those which say that an action which is not done for the need of its body one is exempt for and is only Rabbinically forbidden. However, there are opinions which argue on this and say that even work which is not done for the need of its body one is Biblically liable for.

The Final Ruling:[603] [Due to the above lenient opinion one] therefore does not need to reprimand people who are lenient [to ask a gentile in a time of distress to destroy an item when they do not plan to rebuild it in a better way] being that they have upon whom to rely. However, every person should be stringent upon himself like the stringent opinion which is the main [Halachic] opinion.

Summary:
Some rule one is only liable for destroying if he does so in order to rebuild it in a better way. Others rule he is liable if he plans to rebuild it even if he rebuilds it to the same state it was in when destroyed. Others rule he is always liable even if he does not plan to rebuild it. One of the ramifications is, may one ask a gentile to destroy an item in a case of great need if one plans to rebuild it after Shabbos to the same state. Practically, one is to be stringent against

---

[598] Admur 278:2; So rules Tosafus Shabbos 94a
[599] Admur 313:17
[600] Admur 313:17
[601] Admur 278:2; so rules Rashi Shabbos 31
[602] Admur 278:3; So rules Rebbe Yehuda and Rambam
[603] Admur 313:17
Other opinions: Some Poskim rule one must protest against those that are lenient to ask a gentile to remove the window. [Taz 313:5; M"B 308:38]

doing so, although those that are lenient do not need to be protested.

8. The prohibition to break a complete/sturdy vessel on Shabbos:[604]

If [a barrel] is whole [meaning it never broke and was then refurbished] it is forbidden to break it even in a way that one is not making for it a nice opening, because breaking a complete structure is forbidden even by vessels. Furthermore [another reason] is due to a decree that one may come to intend to puncture in it a nice hole in order that it contains an elegant opening.

The allowance to ask a gentile to break a sturdy/complete vessel on Shabbos:[605] Nevertheless through a gentile one may be lenient to [ask him for the purpose of a Shabbos need] whether to break the locks and whether to remove the hinges and metal panels.

The reason for this allowance is:[606] because there are opinions[607] who say that there is no building and destroying [prohibition] by vessels including even to build a sturdy [complete] structure and to destroy a complete [sturdy] structure. [According to this opinion] it was only said that one who reassembles a chest of drawers and a box and portable tower in a strong way, and similarly that one who reassembles a vessel made up of individual parts in a strong way, that he is liable for a sin offering, because he has fixed a vessel and is [thus] obligated [for the offering] because [he has transgressed the prohibition of] "Making a finishing touch", [and not because of the building prohibition]. Thus when one destroys an item that is firmly assembled, and even if he destroys and breaks a vessel made completely of a single part, this does not contain any prohibition when done for the sake of Shabbos, and one may rely on this opinion regarding asking a gentile to do so when needed to be done for a Shabbos need.[608] [Likewise, one may ask a gentile to destroy it in a case of great need, even if it does not contain a Shabbos need.[609]]

Q&A

May one ask a gentile to make a hole inside a vessel on Shabbos?[610]

The allowance to ask a gentile to destroy a vessel is only if the vessel is being damaged through the gentile's actions. However, if the vessel is benefiting. Such as to make a hole into a barrel, then according to all opinions it would be forbidden. [Although seemingly it would be permitted in a case of great need, or need of a Mitzvah, if the hole is only being made for entering or exiting as is always the rule by Shevus Deshvus.]

May one ask a gentile to fix a vessel on Shabbos?[611]
No.

What is the definition of a Shabbos need?[612]

It is only permitted to destroy an un-sturdy structure if one needs to remove something from within the item in order to use that content for Shabbos. For example, if an un-sturdy vessel

---

[604] Admur 314:1; 313:19: [As well as] if one breaks a complete structure [not made of parts], then this is [considered] destroying a sturdy structure and is thus liable for destroying.

[605] Admur 314:17; Michaber 314:7

[606] Admur 314:17

[607] Hagahos Maimanis 23:1 in name of Reim; Yireim; Rashi Shabbos 47a; Gr"a in M"B 314:7

[608] Admur ibid; See Q&A for the definition of a Shabbos need.

Other opinions: Some Poskim rule one may only be lenient to ask a gentile to break the vessel if it is a case of great loss, or the need of a Mitzvah. [M"A 314:11 in name of Rashal; M"B 314:37]

[609] M"B ibid; and so rules Admur in 307:12 being that it is a Shvus Deshvus in place of a great need, as it is Soser Shelo Al Menas Letaken.

[610] Ketzos Hashulchan 119 footnote 7; See M"B 314:34 in name of Chayeh Adam

[611] M"B 314:34 in name of Chayeh Adam; Ketzos Hashulchan 119 footnote 7

[612] Ketzos Hashulchan 119 footnote 18

contains food, one may break through it in order to eat food that is in it. However, to destroy it in order to hide something in it is forbidden even by a non-sturdy structure.

9. Breaking an incomplete [non-sturdy] vessel on Shabbos "Mustaki":[613]

It was already explained that there is no building or destroying [prohibition] by vessels which are not large enough to hold 40 *seah* and are not sturdy structures. Based on this if an earthenware barrel which does not hold the measurement of 40 *seah* shattered [before Shabbos] and then had its pieces glued back together with tar, then it is permitted to break this vessel on Shabbos, whether using one's hand or whether using a vessel, in order to remove its content. [This means that the allowance to break even such an item is only if one is doing so for a Shabbos need, top use its content.[614]]

Why breaking the above vessel is not considered destroying: Doing so does not involve [the] destroying [prohibition] because [the barrel] is no longer [considered] a complete structure [since it broke and has been glued back together].

The prohibition in intending to make an elegant opening for the vessel: [However, this lack of the building prohibition is only] as long as that [upon breaking into the barrel] one does not intend to puncture a nice hole so that it be an elegant [looking] opening for [the barrel], as if one does do so then he has fixed the vessel [on Shabbos] and is liable for [the] "Making a Finishing Touch[615]" [prohibition] as will be explained [in Halacha 17]. However, if one does not intend [upon puncturing the barrel to make a nice hole] then he is allowed [to puncture it]

The reason it is permitted when there is no intent to make an elegant opening:[616] No decree was made against making a hole [even when one does not intend to make an elegant opening] due that one may come to intend to do so, because a barrel which is broken and glued back together with tar is degrading in one's eyes and one [thus] does not think about making a nice hole in it when he returns [after gluing it back together] and punctures it.

What is the definition of a Shabbos need?[617]
It is only permitted to destroy an un-sturdy structure if one needs to remove something from within the item in order to use that content for Shabbos. For example, if an un-sturdy vessel contains food, one may break through it in order to eat food that is in it. However, to destroy it in order to hide something in it is forbidden even by a non-sturdy structure.

---

10. Examples:

Tearing the covering off of a bottle:[618] A person may tear the hide which [seals] the opening of a barrel of wine or other liquids, if he does so for the need of Shabbos. He need not worry [about any tearing prohibition involved in doing so], because tearing a detached item is allowed to be done even initially as will be explained [in Halacha 16].

[However, this is only allowed] as long as one does not intend to make something similar to a drainpipe out of the torn skin [i.e. a funnel] being that doing so is considered like fixing a vessel.

Cutting the strings wrapped around food:[619] Based on the above it is permitted to cut the knots of a spit which are tied around a lamb or chicken that are roasting on it. Similarly, stuffed chickens

---

[613] Admur 314:1; Michaber 314:1; Beitza 33b; Mishneh Shabbos 146a
[614] Levush; Peri Megadim; Ketzos Hashulchan 119 note 18
[615] Lit. "Hitting with a hammer." This refers to any finishing touch that one does to a vessel.
[616] Admur ibid; Tosafus Shabbos 146a
[617] Ketzos Hashulchan 119 footnote 18
[618] Admur 314:12; M"A 314:14 in name of Beis Yosef; Michaber 314:
[619] Admur 314:16; Michaber 314:9

which are sewed shut one is allowed to cut the string of the sewing.

Breaking the rope that secures the cover to its vessel:[620] Similarly seals that are on vessels, such as a chest of drawers, box and portable tower which have their covering tied to them with a rope, it is permitted to cut the rope even with a knife or undo [the rope even] through taking apart its threads[621], in order to open [the box] to remove its content. It goes without saying that it is allowed to undo the knot as it is not a permanent knot being that it is meant to be constantly removed.

The reason that this does not contain a destroying prohibition:[622] Now, although the rope is made to attach the cover to the vessel, and thus when one cuts it or undoes it he is destroying this attachment, [nevertheless] this does not contain the [prohibition of] destroying as the rope [only gives the cover] a weak attachment [to the vessel] being that it is not that strong, and thus when one destroys it one is destroying an incomplete [non-sturdy] vessel [which is allowed as the] destroying [prohibition] only applies by vessels when destroying a complete [sturdy] vessel.

The prohibition to break a lock on Shabbos:[623] Based on the above [that a rope is only allowed to be cut because it is considered to give an non-sturdy attachment] it is thus only permitted to cut and undo a rope and the like, However, locks made of wood and metal, which are strong [materials], are forbidden to be undone and broken [even] if one lost the key being that this is a complete destruction [meaning a destruction of a sturdy structure] which is forbidden even by vessels.

The prohibition to remove the door off its hinges on Shabbos:[624] Similarly it is forbidden to remove the hinges that are behind the box (this refers to the pegs which attach the cover of the box to its walls behind it. [This is made by] inserting a peg into the small holes of the two parallel metal [bolts], one [bolt] being set on the cover and one by the wall, and through the peg that is inserted into both of them together they are attached and merge with each other. This peg has one head that is a little thick and its second head has a hole in which one inserts into it [another] small peg.[625])

The reason for this is:[626] because the [pegs] are strongly inserted and [thus removing them] is a complete form of destruction.

The prohibition to remove the metal panels of a barrel:[627] Similarly it is forbidden to remove the metal panels of a wooden barrel that is made of many beams of wood which are attached [to each other] through the metal panels that are on them, as when one removes these panels it is a complete form of destruction.

Breaking through woven palm leaf baskets in order to get the food inside:[628] Baskets that are used for figs and dates, which are vessels that are made from palm leaves [i.e. wicker baskets] and have placed in them figs or dates that have not [yet] ripened in the sun in order so they completely ripen in there [in the basket], then if the cover is tied to them with a rope, then it is permitted to unravel the rope or cut it as explained [in the] above [Halacha]. [Furthermore] even the actual body of these vessels are permitted to be unraveled and cut, as the structure of these vessels which are made of palm leaves are a weak structure [Binyan Garua] which is not made to

---

[620] Admur 314:17; Michaber 314:7
[621] As opposed to untying the actual knot, which will explained below.
[622] Admur 314:17; M"B 314:31
[623] Admur 314:17; Michaber 314:7
[624] Admur 314:17; First opinion in Michaber 314:7; 1st opinion in Mordechai

Other opinions: Some Poskim rule one may take apart the hinges from the vessel if the key is lost. [2nd opinion in Michaber ibid; 2nd opinion in Mordechai] The reason for this is because one has not truly broken the vessel by doing so. [M"B 314:34] Vetzaruch Iyun iof according to this opinion it is permitted to take apart anyt strongly attached item. This would contradict the palin ruling brought in the previous Halacha regarding disassembling vessels on Shabbos.

[625] The idea here is that the cover is not attached to the wall through nails which are hammered into it and the like, but rather through the insertion of the pegs. Thus the novelty here is that even in such a case one may not remove the pegs.
[626] Admur 314:17
[627] Admur 314:17; M"A 314:14
[628] Admur 314:18; Michaber 314:8; Shabbos 146a

last long[629], and [thus] when breaking it, it is only considered as if one is breaking hazelnuts and almonds in order to get the food that is in them.[630] [See Q&A]

Stepping on pieces of earthenware thus causing them to break:[631] Broken pieces of an earthenware vessel which [has broken in a way that it no longer is fit for any use and thus] is forbidden to move, is forbidden to remove [from ones table or area that people walk, as earthenware pieces are not hazardous]. [Now] even though that [if they are not removed] people will walk on them and break them [even more, and thus we should remove them in order so they not transgress the prohibition of breaking things on Shabbos, nevertheless it may not be removed as in truth] there is no problem in breaking it more, as the prohibition of breaking earthenware only applies when intentionally breaks it so that it be fit for [another type of] use[632], in which case it is prohibited because by doing so he is creating[633] a vessel.

May one open an envelope in order to remove its letter?[634]

It is forbidden to open an envelope on Shabbos.[635] [This applies even in a case of great need.[636] However, some Poskim[637] rule one may do so in a time of great need, if he destroys the envelope in the process.]

Asking a gentile:[638] One may not ask a gentile directly to open the letter. However, it is permitted to tell the gentile mail man that he cannot read the letter until it is opened, and have the mailman understand that he wants him to open it.[639] [This allowance applies only for the mailman who delivered the letter, and not to another gentile, in which case one must protest if he sees him opening the letter.[640] Likewise some Poskim[641] rule this allowance only applies if one personally asked the mailman to deliver the letter, and not by the state appointed mailman. However, in a time of great need one may ask the gentile to open it.[642]]

On Yom Tov:[643] One may tear open an envelope on Yom Tov. [According to those who hold that opening cans on Shabbos is forbidden due to Tikkun Keli, it is to be opened in a destructive

---

[629] Admur ibid seemingly in explanation of the M"A 314:13 [as brings M"B 314:40] and so explains Tehila Ledavid 314:12
Understanding of Admur/M"A ibid: The M"A ibid states that the allowance to break the vessel is because it is not a complete structure, and if it is a complete structure then it is forbidden. Seemingly Admur here is clarifying that the reason why the baskets are not considered a complete structure is not because they are not made to last, as in truth a complete structure may never be broken, even if it is not made to last. Rather the reason these baskets are permitted to be broken is because their structure is built weak, and the reason why their structure is built weak is because in any event they are not meant to last. If, however, it were to be built strongly, then even it is not meant to last, it would be forbidden to destroy. [so explains Tehila Ledavid ibid in M"A]
Other opinions: Some Poskim rule that even a sturdy vessel which is strong may be broken if its entire purpose is simply to guard the food. [Kneses Hagedola; Simple understanding of the Michaber ibid and Kol Bo; see Tehila Ledavid ibid; Igros Moshe 40]
[630] Admur ibid; Michaber ibid based on Kol Bo;
[631] Admur 308:28
[632] Seemingly this is referring to breaking a broken piece of earthenware as in such a case it is considered a non-sturdy vessel, However, to break a sturdy vessel of earthenware would be forbidden due to the destroying prohibition. Vetzaruch Iyun as it is not implied this way from the wording.
[633] Lit. Fixing
[634] Admur 307:7; 519:6; So also rules: M"A 307:20 based on Aguda; Peri Chadash Y.D. 118:18 [brought in Biur Halacha 340:13 "Haneyar"]; Chacham Tzvi 39; M"B 340:41 forbids according to all opinions, see Biur Halacha "Haniyar"; Ketzos Hashulchan 119 note 34; SSH"K 28:4; See Piskeiy Teshuvos 340:29
[635] The reason: This is due to a Rabbinical prohibition of Soser/destroying. [Admur 519:6] The reason for this is because although the envelope is considered an un-sturdy structure, nevertheless since there is no Shabbos need involved in opening it, meaning that reading the letter is not a Shabbos necessity, therefore it is forbidden, as destroying a non-sturdy vessel was only allowed in order to remove what is inside for a Shabbos need, as explained in 314:1. [Ketzos Hashulchan ibid]
Other reasons: Some Poskim rule that it contains a Biblical prohibition of Soser being one is tearing the envelope with intent to fix a certain matter, which is the reading of the letter. [Peri Chadash ibid] Others maintain that it contains a Rabbinical prohibition. [Admur ibid; Chacham Tzvi ibid, brought in Biur Halacha ibid; Igros Moshe 1:122 argues on the Peri Chadash]
[636] Ketzos Hashulchan ibid; M"B ibid
[637] Bris Olam Koreia 7; based on Chazon Ish 61:2, and so leans to rule Rav SZ"A in SSH"K 28 footnote 15, Shut Even Yisrael 16
[638] Admur 307:7; M"A 307:20 based on Aguda; M"B ibid
[639] The reason: As the gentile is doing so to simply complete the job he was paid to perform by delivering the letter, and hence one is not required to protest against him doing so. [Admur ibid in parentheses; See Ketzos Hashulchan ibid]
[640] Ketzos Hashulchan ibid
[641] Ketzos Hashulchan ibid based on Admur ibid that states the reason for the allowance is because he is doing so to complete
[642] M"B ibid as explained in Biur Halacha ibid; Ketzos Hashulchan ibid
[643] Admur 519:6

manner, just as they rule by cans.[644] However, according to those who hold that cans may be opened in a non-destructive manner then seemingly it is permitted to open an envelope even in the area of the glue, by separating the two parts.[645]]

Summary of Destroying vessels-Halachas 6-9

One may only destroy a vessel [as opposed to disassemble[646]] if all the conditions are fulfilled:

   A. It is not attached to the ground
     And
   B. It cannot hold 40 Seah
     And
   C. It is considered a non-sturdy vessel [or is sturdy but one asks a gentile to break it as will be explained]
     And
   D. One does not intend to make a nice looking opening
     And
   E. One needs to destroy it for a Shabbos need.[647] [See Q&A]
     And
   F. It does not involve a prohibition of Tikkun Keli. See important note brought above!
     And
   G. One is not tearing apart two objects that were attached.

Regarding tearing or cutting an item on Shabbos-See "The Laws of cutting and tearing items on Shabbos"

Examples:
One may not destroy the lock of a vessel even if he has lost the key as it is considered a sturdy vessel.[648]
One may cut the following items in order to take out the food or objects that are within them:
- A piece of leather that is serving as the cap of a bottle.[649]
- Strings that are tied around food, such as by a stuffed turkey[650], or that are tied around the cover of vessels in order to secure them onto the vessel.[651]
- A basket made of weak material which is not made to last long and has food inside.[652]

---

[644] See Piskeiy Teshuvos ibid; Bris Olam Koreia 7; based on Chazon Ish 61:2; SSH"K 28 footnote 14-15
[645] Ketzos Hashulchan ibid
The reason: Although on the onset it seems that doing so should be forbidden due to Koreia, as it is forbidden to separate glued items, as written in 340:17, nevertheless in truth one can argue that in this case it is permitted to do so as a) the prohibition only applies by two entities that are glued together as opposed to a single entity, and b) It was sealed with intent to be opened, and is hence a temporary sealing. [Ketzos Hashulchan ibid]
[646] Its laws were explained in Halacha 5 above. The only difference between this case and a vessel made up of individual parts is with regards to that the latter is allowed to be destroyed even not for a Shabbos need. [See Ketzos Hashulchan 119 note 18]
[647] The only difference between this case and a vessel made up of individual parts is with regards to that the latter is allowed to be destroyed even not for a Shabbos need. [See Ketzos Hashulchan 119 note 18]
[648] Admur 314:17
[649] Admur 314:9
[650] Admur 314:16
[651] Admur 314:19
[652] Admur 314:18

May one ask a gentile to break a sturdy vessel for him on Shabbos?[653]
A vessel which is not attached to the ground and does not hold 40 seah may be broken by a gentile, even if it is a sturdy vessel, as long as one needs to do so for a Shabbos use.[654]

Breaking the rope of the door of a vessel attached to the ground:
Is only allowed to be cut or unraveled if it is meant for constant removal and insertion.[655]

Breaking the clay mold of the opening of an oven attached to the ground:
One is to ask a gentile to break it. If a gentile is not available then it is allowed to ask a child to remove it, and if even a child is not available then it may be removed by oneself irregularly.[656]

Q&A
May one ask a gentile to make a hole inside a vessel on Shabbos?[657]
The allowance to ask a gentile to destroy a vessel is only if the vessel is being damaged through the gentile's actions. However, if the vessel is benefiting. Such as to make a hole into a barrel, then according to all opinions it would be forbidden. [Although seemingly it would be permitted in a case of great need, or need of a Mitzvah, if the hole is only being made for entering or exiting as is always the rule by Shevus Deshvus.]

May one ask a gentile to fix a vessel on Shabbos?[658]
No.

What is the definition of a Shabbos need?[659]
It is only permitted to destroy an unsturdy structure if one needs to remove something from within the item in order to use that content for Shabbos. For example, if an unsturdy vessel contains food, one may break through it in order to eat food that is in it. However, to destroy it in order to hide something in it is forbidden even by a non-sturdy structure.

May one open the Chametz closets on Shabbos which follows the last day of Pesach in Eretz Yisrael?
It is permitted to open on Shabbos all Chametz closets and rooms that do not require the destruction of the lock, rope, or tape, such as if it was locked with a padlock and the like which is opened with a key or by combination. However, one may not tear, or break, any ropes, tape, or other locking devices for the sake of opening the closets, unless the closet is portable [not attached to the ground] and is not large enough to hold 40 Seah.[660] Thus, typical kitchen cabinets which are sealed with tape or string may not be cut or torn open.

---

[653] Admur 314:17
[654] Admur 314:17
[655] Admur 314:19
[656] Admur 259:7 and chapter 314:19
[657] Ketzos Hashulchan 119 footnote 7; See M"B 314:34 in name of Chayeh Adam
[658] M"B 314:34 in name of Chayeh Adam; Ketzos Hashulchan 119 footnote 7
[659] Ketzos Hashulchan 119 footnote 18
[660] See Admur 314:19, regarding the prohibition of tearing the rope of the door of a pit, being that it is attached to the ground, and it is only permitted to do so if the door/lock is not meant to last at all, not even one day. See also Admur 259:7, 314:17. Now, since the locks and tape are meant to last throughout the seven days of Pesach, therefore it carries with it the destroying prohibition if it is attached to the ground.

Practical Q&A relating to destroying items:

May one open cans of food on Shabbos?[661]
> **Examples: Tuna; Sardine; corn; chickpea; tomato sauce; canned fruit**

- If one plans to still use the can after its content is consumed, such as to use as a permanent container, then it is forbidden to open the can on Shabbos according to all opinions.[662]
- If one intends to make a nice opening in the can, it is forbidden to open it according to all.[663]
- If one plans to throw the can out after its content has been removed then this matter is disputed amongst Poskim:[664]

First Opinion: Some Poskim[665] rule that it is forbidden to open cans in all cases, even if one destroys the can in the process and immediately removes its content.[666]

Second Opinion: Many other Poskim[667] rule it is permitted to open cans if one opens it in an apparent destructive form, avoiding making a nice opening, and does not reuse the can after its content has been consumed.[668] [However, there is no need to immediately remove all the content and throw out the can[669]].

Third Opinion: Other Poskim[670] rule cans may be opened in an even non-destructive form, so long as one does not make a nice opening and does not plan to reuse the can after its content is finished.[671]

---

[661] Piskeiy Teshuvos 313:1. To note he does not make mention of the Third opinion. Upeleh!

[662] Ketzos Hashulchan 119 footnote 7; Upashut as this is the classic case of making a hole in an item and intending to use it which is forbidden.

[663] Admur 314:1

[664] According to some [Chazon Ish 51:11] there is no destroying prohibition involved as a closed item is not considered a vessel. The question is regarding "Tikkun Keli", as by opening it he now turns the can into a vessel. Others However, [Ketzos Hashulchan ibid] do learn that the closed can has a vessel status and opening it is a question of the destroying prohibition, being that cans are considered strong and sturdy vessels.

[665] Tehila Ledavid 314:12; Chazon Ish 51:11 as is understood by Az Nidbaru 11:12
Background of ruling of Chazon Ish:
The Chazon Ish states that it is forbidden to open cans due to that one is making a hole in a vessel which one plans on using [which is Rabbinically forbidden due to Tikkun Keli]. Furthermore, he adds even if one intends to throw out the can it should be forbidden as we have only find the allowance to break an item which already has an opening. However, a completely closed item, giving it any opening, even to remove its content and throw out the vessel, is considered a nice opening and forbidden due to Tikkun Keli. The Az Nidbaru thus understands the Chazon Ish that it is never permitted even when done in a way which destroys the item. However, see next footnote that SSH"K learns that even according to the Chazon Ish when opened in a destructive fashion there is no problem of either forms of Tikkun Keli.
Other opinions who agree with above: Rav Farkash notes in Koveitz Habracha 8 that it is very difficult to allow opening cans on Shabbos in any which way although those which are lenient like the Shiyuirei Kneses Hagedola and Ketzos Hashulchan have upon whom to rely. His reason of stringency is because the cans are considered a complete and sturdy vessel even when closed [as learns Ketzos Hashulchan ibid] and thus destroying them is forbidden. This is based on the Tehila Ledavid [314:12] who explains in the M"A that the allowance to destroy the vessel of figs is because the vessel itself is made of unsturdy material. If, however, it is made of sturdy material then destroying it is forbidden.
Rav Zalman Shimon Dworkon, the noted previous Rav of Crown Heights records [Koveitz Zalman Shimon p. 63] that majority of Poskim [Tehila Ledavid; Chazon Ish] forbid opening cans on Shabbos due to that opening it turns it into a vessel.

[666] As the moment he makes the first opening of the can, he has deemed it a vessel. The fact that he later destroys it does not change this fact.

[667] Or Letziyon 24; Minchas Yitzchak 1:77; 6:27; Chelkas Yaakov 3:8; Cheishev Haeifod 3:118; Lehoros Nasan 3:16; 7:19; Igros Moshe 4:78; SSH"K 9:3 which says that this is true even in accordance to the Chazon Ish [the stringent opinion]! Beir Moshe 3:89 in cases that one is accustomed to reuse the can.
The reason it's not allowed without destruction: Tikkun Keli as writes Chazon Ish [due to that one plans to continue using it or due to that it does not have an opening yet]. And due to the tearing prohibition, which applies when done in a non-destructive form. [Minchas Yitzchak ibid] However, according to Admur by a single entity there is no tearing prohibition that would apply.

[668] As then it has the status of an item which is not made to serve as a vessel but rather just to preserve the food that is in it which is allowed to be destroyed on Shabbos as explained 314:18.

[669] So rules explicitly Ketzos Hashulchan, Beir Moshe ibid

[670] Ketzos Hashulchan 119 footnote 7; Rav SZ"A in SSH"K 9 footnote 10; SSH"K 9:3 in their lenient opinion; Beir Moshe ibid regarding cans that are not commonly reused. He only requires the destructive form by opening items that are at times reused. Nevertheless he himself writes that it is best to do so in a destructive form even by cans that are not reused.

[671] Ketzos Hashulchan ibid writes that the custom of the world is to be lenient and allow opening cans on Shabbos. He first suggests the reason for allowance being that the can is meant to be opened at any moment and it is hence similar to the plaster covering of an

According to the stringent opinion above, may one ask a gentile to open a can on Shabbos?

According to the Poskim[672] above who rule that opening a can is forbidden due to Tikkun Keli, then it is likewise forbidden to ask a gentile. However, according to those Poskim[673] who rule it is forbidden due to Soser, one may ask a gentile.[674]

May one open a can using its easy open lid?

Some Poskim[675] rule it is forbidden to open a can through an easy open lid [even according to those which are generally lenient in opening cans] as by doing so one intentionally[676] creates a nice hole which is forbidden due to the Tikkun Keli prohibition.[677] However, one may open the other side of the can and remove the content that is inside. Likewise [according to those that are lenient to open cans on Shabbos] one may open the easy open lid halfway. Other Poskim[678] rule it is permitted to open even such lids, as one has no intent to create a nice opening.

May one open a can of soda?[679]

It is forbidden to open it regularly through the cap [even according to those which are generally lenient], as by doing so one intentionally[680] creates a nice hole which is forbidden due to the Tikkun Keli prohibition. One may However, cut through the soda can [avoiding the cutting of pictures or letters] and remove the content that is inside. Likewise [according to those that are lenient to open cans on Shabbos] one may open the cap half way and drink it.

May one break open packages which contain food, such as a sealed bag or box, in order to remove its content?[681]

Note: The following only relates to single closed entities. Regarding opening the sealed cover of a cup, such as a yogurt, coffee and the like-see next question.

Plastic bags and cardboard boxes: Some Poskim[682] learn that by these weak structures which are glued together it is permitted according to all to open them regularly on Shabbos. Others[683] rule as follows: This has the same ruling as does opening cans, and is thus forbidden according to all to be done with intent to reuse the bag after emptying its contents. If one intends to throw it out after finishing its contents, then it is subject to the same dispute mentioned by cans, and thus according to the first opinion is forbidden to ever be opened on Shabbos[684]; according to the second opinion it may only be opened in a way of destruction.[685]

---

oven which may also be broken on Shabbos. He However, asks on this and concludes that if people would throw out the can after its content became finished, it would be permitted to open it on Shabbos.

[672] Chazon ish ibid
[673] Tehila Ledavid ibid
[674] As rules Admur in 314:17
[675] Piskeiy Teshuvos 314 footnote 3; See Or Letziyon 1:26; 2:27-6
[676] One certainly intends here to make a nice hole as he desires to open the cap fully rather than half way and hence receive the nice opening that the company originally formed on the can.
[677] Vetzaruch Iyun how this hole is any different than the hole created in a can that is opened with a can opener?
[678] Rav SZ"A in new SSH"K 9 footnote ?
[679] Piskeiy Teshuvos 313 footnote 1; Oar Letziyon 1:26; 2:27-6
[680] One certainly intends here to make a nice hole as he desires to open the cap fully rather than halfway and hence receive the nice opening that the company originally formed on the can.
[681] Piskeiy Teshuvos 314:1
[682] Rav SZ"A in SSH"K 9 footnote 11 and 12, as it is considered already a vessel even according to the Chazon Ish and is similar to the sealing of a bottle, and it is a unsturdy vessel even according to the Tehila Ledavid.
[683] Piskeiy Teshuvos 314:1; SSH"K 9:3
[684] Vetzaruch Iyun Gadol as seemingly here by wrappers according to all they are considered a weak structure and it is exactly similar to the case of a woven basket of which the Shulchan Aruch rules that it is allowed to be opened. Furthermore see SSH"K 9 footnote 12 that learns perhaps even according to the Chazon Ish it is considered here an actual vessel even beforehand. To note that the Chazon Ish does allow tearing paper wrappings of foods, comparing it to the woven baskets. Although perhaps he learns that plastic or tinfoil

It may thus not be opened according to this opinion by separating the top ends which were glued shut as doing so makes it into a useable item rather than destroying it.[686] According to the third opinion mentioned above, if one intends to throw the wrapping or bag out after its content is removed, it may be opened in an even non-destructive way, although one may not form a nice opening upon opening it. However, possibly it may not be opened in the glued area.[687] However, some Poskim[688] rule that it may be opened even in the glued areas.[689]

Paper wrapping:[690] Is permitted to be torn according to all opinions even in a non-destructive way.

In all cases it is forbidden to tear letters or pictures while opening the item!

May one open a bag of chips from the top area which attaches the sides together?
According to those who hold that opening cans on Shabbos is forbidden due to Tikkun Keli, it is to be opened in a destructive manner, just as they rule by cans.[691] However, according to those who hold that cans may be opened in a non-destructive manner then seemingly it is permitted to open an envelope even in the area of the glue, by separating the two parts.[692]

May one open a milk bag on Shabbos?
One should not do so using a scissor due to it making a nice opening. Likewise, one may not use the set razor placed into a milk carton to open it.

May one open an "Igloo" [popsicle in plastic wrapper] on Shabbos?[693]
Some Poskim[694] rule that the hole in the ices is to be torn with one's mouth and not with a vessel.[695] One must be careful not to tear it in an area that contains letters or pictures.

---

is considered a sturdy structure as opposed to paper. However, see Minchas Yitzchak 1:77 which seems to learn it does contain a destroying prohibition.

[685] Such as by tearing it in a way that makes it unusable afterwards, or making in it a very small hole which is not useable to enter things through.
The reason: Due to the tearing prohibition, which applies when done in a non-destructive form. [Minchas Yitzchak ibid] However, according to Admur by a single entity there is no tearing prohibition that would apply.

[686] Az Nidbaru 4:33. However, regarding the tearing prohibition seemingly it does not apply being that it only applies when two independent items are attached and thus being separated while here the bag itself is one single item which has been glued to itself [one end to the other end]. This is besides for the debate of whether a temporary glued item receives the tearing restrictions.

[687] SSH"K 9 footnote 11 due to Koreia, separating glued papers, which is forbidden in 340:17; However, see in footnote 12, 19 and 36 that Rav SZ"A allows opening it in the glued area

[688] Ketzos Hashulchan 119 footnote 34

[689] The reason: Although on the onset it seems that doing so should be forbidden due to Koreia, as it is forbidden to separate glued items, as written in 340:17, nevertheless in truth one can argue that in this case it is permitted to do so as a) the prohibition only applies by two entities that are glued together as opposed to a single entity, and b) It was sealed with intent to be opened, and is hence a temporary sealing. [Ketzos Hashulchan ibid]

[690] SSH"K 9 footnote 11; Piskeiy Teshuvos 314:4 in name of Chazon Ish; Minchas Yitzchak, Tzitz Eliezer as this case is exactly similar to the case of the woven basket of which the Shulchan Aruch rules that it is allowed to be opened.

[691] See Piskeiy Teshuvos ibid; Bris Olam Koreia 7; based on Chazon Ish 61:2; SSH"K 28 footnote 14-15

[692] Ketzos Hashulchan ibid; See SSH"K 9 footnote 11; However, see in footnote 12, 19 and 36 that Rav SZ"A allows opening it in the glued area
The reason: Although on the onset it seems that doing so should be forbidden due to Koreia, as it is forbidden to separate glued items, as written in 340:17, nevertheless in truth one can argue that in this case it is permitted to do so as a) the prohibition only applies by two entities that are glued together as opposed to a single entity, and b) It was sealed with intent to be opened, and is hence a temporary sealing. [Ketzos Hashulchan ibid]

[693] See Shabbos Kehalacha Vol. 3 17:52-55

[694] Shabbos Kehalacha 17 footnote 131; See Meor Hashabbos 13 footnote 105

[695] As perhaps since the size and form of the hole made is of benefit to the eater, perhaps it is considered a "nice hole" which is forbidden due to Tikkun Keli. [314:1]

May one remove or make a hole in the covering of an item such as yogurt, and the like?[696]

Yes.[697] It is permitted according to all to remove the cover of an item even if it is glued closed over that item[698], as is done with yogurts and the like. [It, however, requires further clarification if one may peel off the covering, separating it from the glued area or if he must make a hole in the covering, as perhaps separating the glued area carries the tearing prohibition.[699]] Thus one may remove or puncture a hole in the cover of a yogurt, Materna, coffee jar cover, cream cheese, and the like.

In all cases it is forbidden to tear letters or pictures while opening the item, and it is forbidden to form the item into a funnel and the like of any useable item.

May one open the cap of a bottle, such as soda or wine bottle, for the first time on Shabbos?[700]

Metal caps such as of a wine bottle: Some Poskim[701] rule it is forbidden to open such caps on Shabbos.[702] Other Poskim[703] rule that this is permitted being that the cap so easily removable from its ring that it is considered already detached and thus does not contain any fixing prohibition.

Plastic caps such as soda bottles: Some opinions[704] say that by plastic caps it is completely permitted to be opened even according to the stringent opinion mentioned above by metal caps.[705]

Puncturing a hole in the cap:[706] According to all it is permitted to puncture the metal or plastic cap and remove the contents through it.

Opening the cap with intent to throw out right away, or making a hole in the cap and then opening with intent to throw out right away: Seemingly it is permitted to do so, as one has no intent to save the cap and is hence not turning it into any use even temporarily, and by Tikkun Keli we always follow the intent.

May one remove the metal/plastic strip of the cover of a container or bottle, to thus be able to open it?

This has the same ruling as opening the metal cap of a bottle which is disputed whether it is allowed or not.

May one destroy the baskets that are sold in stores today?

Even if the basket is made of weak material, such as palm leaves, if made to last for a long time then it is a complete vessel and thus may not be destroyed.[707]

---

[696] Piskeiy Teshuvos 314:3 in name of Az Nidbaru 4:17

[697] As this is exactly similar to the case mentioned in Shulchan Aruch regarding tearing the leather cover of a bottle of wine, which is allowed.

[698] Sharreiy Teshuvah 314:4

[699] See SSH"K 9 footnote 36; Ketzos Hashulchan 119 footnote 34 that if it is not meant to last it does not contain a tearing prohibition!

[700] Piskeiy Teshuvos 314:5

[701] RSZ"A in Minchas Shlomo 91:12; Divrei Moshe [Rav Moshe Halbershtam] 12-13; Minchas Yitzchak [see Divrei Moshe there]; Rav Moshe Feinstein [brought in Revivos Efrayim 4:96]; Az Nidbaru 3:40

[702] This is forbidden being that the opening breaks the cap from the ring and fixes the cap to be a useable cover. This is thus forbidden due to the "Makeh Bepatish" prohibition.

[703] Chazon Ish 51:11; Kinyan Torah 5:34; Beir Moshe 3:90; Even Yisrael; Cheishev Haeifod 3:93; Mishneh Halachos 7:47; Dvar Yehoshua 2:45; Tzitz Eliezer 14:45; Lehoros Nasan 7:21

[704] RSZ"A in SSH"K 9 footnote 61; Yeshuos Moshe 3:27

[705] Being that the plastic caps are already made prior to them being attached to the bottle in contrast to the metal caps which are formed on the bottle itself, as well as that it is possible to open the plastic caps without detaching it from its plastic ring as opposed to metal caps which cannot, and it is thus no longer subject to the fixing prohibition.

[706] Az Nidbaru ibid

[707] Ketzos Hashulchan 119 note 22

May one break the top of a bottle if he is not able to remove the cap?[708]
Bottles which are discarded to the trash after their use, seemingly they have the same law as do cans. However, if they are usually kept or recycled then they may not be broken as they have the status of a complete vessel that is made to last.

May one pop bubble wrap on Shabbos?
No, as doing so has no Shabbos need.

May one crush disposable pans and plates on Shabbos?[709]
Seemingly, this is subject to the same dispute as opening a can on Shabbos, vis a vis whether it contains a destroying prohibition. Those who allow opening cans on Shabbos due to it being a disposable item which loses its status of a vessel seemingly would be lenient here as well.

From the Rav's Desk

Question:
My child was playing with plastic straps used for tying Sukkos, also known as plastic handcuffs, and closed it over her wrist. It is loose enough to not be of danger but I can't slide it off. May I cut it on Shabbos?

Answer:
Yes.

The reason: In general, plastic is viewed as a non-sturdy material which may be destroyed on Shabbos for a Shabbos need. Now, although this material is strong and can last a long time, nevertheless sit is viewed as temporary and disposable and is usually used for short term purposes. Thus, it would fall under the above allowance to break on Shabbos.

Sources: See Admur 314:1; 16-18; Piskeiy Teshuvos 317 footnote 135 [permits]; Meishiv Nefesh p. 90 [leaves with Tzaruch Iyun]

---

[708] See Ketzos Hashulchan 119 note 7. There he mentions that there are people which are accustomed to be lenient in this, based on the opinion that rules that it is always permitted to destroy even sturdy vessels. However, according to the Alter Rebbe's ruling this would be forbidden.
[709] See Piskeiy Teshuvos 314 footnote 109

11. The Biblical Prohibition to make a hole in a wall, floor, or vessel which holds 40 Seah:[710]

A. The general rule:

A wall or floor:[711] One who hammers a peg into the wall in order to hang vessels and the like on it, is liable for [the] building [prohibition]. [Furthermore] even if one did not [yet] hammer the peg [into the wall] but drilled a hole in the wall in which the peg will be inserted into, he is liable for [the] building [prohibition] on this hole [that he drilled] since this hole is an accessory for the building, which is the inserting the peg. Similarly one who makes a hole in the floor of his house to drain out the water is liable for [the] building [prohibition].

Making a hole in a vessel which holds 40 Seah:[712] A large barrel or other large vessels which hold 40 *seah* carry with them the building and destroying [prohibition], and has the same law as ....a wall.

Regarding making holes in vessels which do not hold 40 Seah[713] –See above Chapter 1 Halacha 6C for the full details of this subject.

B. Removing a knife from a wall:[714]

The custom in a case that a hole will inevitably be widened in a wall, such as when removing a knife jammed in a wooden wall: [Although the Sages allowed one to remove a knife that was inserted into a vessel detached from the ground, as explained above in Chapter 1 Halacha 6C] nevertheless a knife which was inserted into a wooden wall before Shabbos, if it has been somewhat firmly inserted, the custom is to forbid removing it on Shabbos unless one had removed it already one time before Shabbos, as in such a case it is no longer inevitable to avoid widening the hole. However, when one has never yet removed the knife from this hole it is impossible to avoid widening the hole upon removing it on Shabbos, being that it was somewhat firmly inserted into the wall.

The reason for the above custom: [Now, although this hole is widened unintentionally, nevertheless the Sages] only permitted to widen [a hole] unintentionally by a barrel, being that even to initially make a hole intentionally [in a barrel] only involves a Rabbinical prohibition. However, [since] one who makes a hole in a wall with intention is at times liable for a Chatas Offering, such as if he punctured it in order to insert a peg into [the wall], and even one who widens this hole the tiniest amount with intention is [also] liable, therefore it should receive the stringency not to add to [the hole] even if he has no intention in doing so, if it is inevitable to avoid.

The reason that from the letter of the law the above is allowed: This is the reason behind the [above] custom. However, from the letter of the law this is not a clear prohibition being that even if one were to initially make a new hole in the wall in the exact same scenario as above when one widens the hole through removing the knife, which is done not for the sake of inserting a peg into, then doing so would not involve a Biblical prohibition being that [a)] it is an action which is not done for its use, as well as [b)] that he is damaging the wall, as well as [c)] that the widening of the hole made through removing the knife is an irregular way of making [a hole], and all [actions done] irregularly do not at all carry any Biblical prohibition even by a complete [form of forbidden] action [and certainly here that the action itself is not a complete prohibition due to reason a) and b)]. Therefore, it should not be prohibited to widen [the hole] unintentionally just like it was not prohibited by a barrel in accordance to what was explained there that the main

---

[710] Admur 314:2
[711] Admur 314:2
[712] Admur 314:5; as well as 313:18, brought above in Chapter 2 Halacha 2B
[713] which falls under the Makeh Bepatish prohibition as opposed to the building prohibition
[714] Admur 314:4; Michaber 314:12; M"A 314:5; Taz 314:2; M"B 314:11

opinion is like those that permit doing so.
Must one be stringent like the custom:[715] Nevertheless one may not be lenient against [following] this custom.

Summary:
Making a hole in the wall of a building [or vessel that holds 40 seah or is attached to the ground]: Is prohibited due to that it is considered building. If one does so with intention to insert a nail and the like into the wall then this is Biblically prohibited.[716] If, however, it is not done with intent to stick anything in it, then it is only Rabbinically prohibited.[717]
May one remove a knife from a wall on Shabbos?[718] If the knife had been removed once before Shabbos and then reinserted, it may be removed on Shabbos. If it has never been removed before then the custom is to not allow to remove it on Shabbos because it inevitably widens the hole
May one widen an already existing hole? It carries the same laws as one who initially makes the hole on Shabbos both by walls and vessels.[719]

Q&A
May one enter a nail or other item into an already existing hole?[720]
Any item which is commonly firmly attached to a wall, such as a nail or hook, may not be placed even loosely into a pre-existing hole on Shabbos, even if the hole is wider than the item.[721] However, an item which is not meant to be firmly attached to the wall, such as a key and the like, may be inserted even semi-firmly into a hole in the wall, as long as he does not widen the hole in the process.

May one attach a wall hanger or hook to his wall or door on Shabbos?[722]
This is forbidden, whether attaching it using glue, tape, or a suction item, due to the building prohibition.

---

12. Placing an item to support the beam of a roof that is caving inwards:[723]
Using a vessel as a support: A beam from the roof of a house which has broken [and has begun to cave into the house] is allowed to be supported by a bench or on the long beams[724] of a bed, [being] that they are a vessel. [However, they may] not [be placed there] in order to lift up [the beam back into the roof] as this is [considered] building, rather [it may only be placed] in order to prevent the [beam] from falling down any further.
Using a non-vessel as support: However, it is forbidden to use an item which is not a vessel to support the beam from under, even if it had been prepared to be moved [from before Shabbos, and is thus not Muktzah], because [doing so] is similar to building. This is in contrast to [supporting the beam with] a vessel which [is not similar to building being that] it is not usual to nullify it to a building.

---

[715] Admur ibid; M"A ibid; Taz ibid; M"B ibid
[716] Admur 314:2
[717] Admur 314:4
[718] Halacha 4
[719] Halacha 2 and 3
[720] Ketzos Hashulchan 119 footnote 4 Vetzaruch Iyun from chapter 313 Halacha 21 that one should not reassemble cups even if never done in a firm way.
[721] This is forbidden due to suspicion that one may come to insert the nail firmly or even semi-firmly into the hole and be liable for building.
[722] Az Nidbaru 3:23
[723] Admur 313:23
[724] Tosafos Yom Tov on Shabbos chapter 23 Mishneh 5

Placing the vessel in loosely: The vessel needs to be slightly loose under the beam in a way that it may be removed whenever one wishes to do so. However, if it is inserted [under the beam] strongly in a way that one cannot remove it from there anymore, then it is forbidden [to be done] because [doing so] nullifies the vessel from what it was prepared to do [beforehand].

Summary:
May only be done if:
- A. One uses a **vessel** to give the support, such as a bench or table as opposed to a mere plank of wood [even if not Muktzah].
  And
- B. It is placed in a way that it simply prevents the roof beam from caving in any further and does not lift it back up into its roofing position.
  And
- C. The vessel of support is placed loosely, in a way that it can easily be removed from there.

What is one to do if the roof of his Sukkah is caving in?
Based on the above, one can place a bench loosely under the Sechach to prevent it from falling any further down.

---

13. Placing an item to support the broken leg of a couch or bench and the like:
[The laws of] a bench which had one of its legs become detached was explained in "The Laws of Muktzah"! See above Halacha 5F!

14. Leveling the floor and the ground:[725]
One who levels the floor of the house or of a courtyard, such as for example he leveled a mound or filled up a ditch or valley, then this is [considered] building and he is [Biblically] liable.
Leveling the ground of a courtyard unintentionally: Therefore, a courtyard that [its floor] became ruined[726] during the rainy season, one may bring hay and throw it [over the floor] being that the straw will not be nullified [to permanently stay] there, as it is fit to be animal fodder or [to be used] for cement, and therefore there is no building [prohibition involved in doing so].
However, one may not throw something there which will get nullified [to stay] there [permanently] because this appears like one is [doing so] intentionally to level the floor and since it will be nullified there it is a permanent form of building.
However, this restriction only applies by a courtyard that got ruined, as since one is coming to fix the courtyard it appears like one is also intending to level its ground, However, in a different scenario [where it is not apparent that one needs to level his ground then] one is allowed to throw there even something that will be nullified there being that he has no intent to level the ground [by doing so].
How to spread the hay on the ground of a ruined floor:[727] When one spreads the straw on a ruined courtyard, one may not throw it with a basket or a box, but rather with the bottom of the box. [Meaning that] one turns over [the box upside down] and places the straw on the bottom [part of the box that is now facing upwards]. [This is done] in order to change [the way one spreads out the straw] from the way that it is normally done during the week. However, it is forbidden to

---

[725] Admur 313:24
[726] Seemingly this refers to that the courtyard became muddy and very difficult to walk on due to the rain, and thus one wants to place material over the ground so he be able to properly walk on it, having no intention to level the ground in doing so.
[727] Admur 313:25

spread [the hay out] with one's hand.

Summary of leveling a floor:
It is Biblically forbidden due to the building prohibition to level a floor either by filling one of its holes with dirt and the like or by smoothening down a mound which it contains.[728]

Placing items on one's floor when there is no intent to level the ground: If ones front yard ruined due to rain it is forbidden to cover its ground using something which can become permanently nullified there. Other materials, such as hay, may be placed there using an irregularity. In other scenarios it is permitted to place even permanent material on a floor when one has no intent to level it.

Q&A

May one cover a hole in the ground with an item?
No.

If a tile came out from one's floor may one enter it back into his floor?
No.

May one place a plank of wood over a puddle on Shabbos?
Seemingly yes, as a) One will not nullify it there, and b) One is not filling up the hole, but rather hovering something over it. It is similar to returning the cover of a pit to a pit if it has a handle.

---

15. The laws of smearing saliva on the ground:[729]

Rubbing it into the ground: One may not rub saliva with his feet onto an earth floor.

The reason for this is because: by doing so one is leveling the holes in the earth.

Walking over it: However, it is permitted to casually step over the saliva [if the saliva is in ones walking direction. In such a case one may slightly rub the saliva as he is walking.[730] However, it is forbidden to purposely walk to the saliva area in order to step on it.[731] However, some Poskim[732] rule one may even purposely walk in that direction and then step on it.]

The reason for this is because: as by doing so one has no intent to smear[733] [the saliva] and smooth the surface holes. Now, although this smoothening occurs inevitably[734], since he has no intent to do so it is [therefore] permitted due to it being repulsive [to have the saliva remain on the ground].

---

[728] Admur 313:24

[729] Michaber 316:11; Shabbos 121b; This law is omitted in Admur; See Ketzos Hashulchan 146:30 and footnots there for a lengthy discussion of all the opinions of Poskim on this issue
The reason why this Halacha is brought in 316: As in the Gemara ibid the two Halachas of rubbing spit while walking and killing an animal while walking are brought together, and they thus share the common denominator of being permitted "Lefi Tumo". [Levushei Serud 316:9]

[730] M"A 316:25; M"B 316:51; Ketzos Hashulchan 146:30; See there footnote 6 on page 137 that some Poskim [Derisha] rule one may even completely rub it while walking

[731] M"B 316:51 in name of Derisha

[732] Ketzos Hashulchan ibid footnote 10 argues on the M"B and explains that in truth the Derisha does not support his opinion

[733] The M"B 316:80 explains this to mean that one is only allowed to rub it slightly while walking if he ahs no intent to even rub the saliva. However, the Ketzos Hashulchan 146:30 footnote 10 explains that one may have intent to rub the saliva so long as he does not have intent to smoothen the ground

[734] So is simple meaning of Michaber and so learns Taz 316:10
The reason: As it is a mere matter of Misaseik [which is only Rabbiniclaly forbidden according to all] and is a Melacha Sheiyon Tzericha Legufo [and is hence only Rabbinical] and therefore in a case of repulsiveness, the Sages were lenient. [P"M 316 M"Z 10]
Other opinions: Others explain that it only at times gets smoothened upon stepping over it and that nevertheless we would forbid it if not for it being repulsive due to that one may onetime forget and actually intentionally rub it. However, if in truth it was always inevitable then it would not be permitted. [M"B 316:50 in name of Peri Megadim, Olas Shabbos, Tosefes Shabbos,]

May one stand on the saliva? [735] One is allowed to stand on the saliva as long as he does not rub it.

Does the above law apply today when saliva is no longer viewed as very repulsive? [736] Today that we are not so particular about the repulsiveness of saliva one is to be careful not rub on it at all while stepping over it. [However, he may nevertheless step on it if he is careful not to rub it at all. [737] Furthermore, some Poskim [738] rule that if one views the Saliva as repulsive, then he may rub on it while walking even today.] However, mucus is considered repulsive and may be stepped over [regularly while walking despite that some of it gets smoothened by doing so. [739] As well in a Synagogue one may step even on saliva while walking due to that it's not honorable. As well, on a tiled floor one need not be stringent to not step over saliva any more than he is by mucus. [740] However, as will be explained next there are Poskim which are completely lenient today by tiled floors to even allow initial rubbing.]

May one smear saliva on a tiled floor? [741] It is implied from the Michaber that this is dependent on the dispute between the Rama and Michaber regarding if one may sweep a tiled floor. Thus, according to the Michaber it is allowed [742] while according to the Rama it is forbidden. [743] [However, there are Poskim [744] which rule that by tiled floors one may be lenient to rub saliva even according to those which follow the Rama. Furthermore, if majority of the city houses have tiled floors, it is permitted according to all to rub saliva on all tiled or wooden floors. [745] Furthermore, based on this it is even permitted to rub saliva on a public earth floor, such as on a dirt road, so long as one does not intend to smooth the gaps. However, by a dirt floor which one owns it remains forbidden to rub the saliva. [746]]

May one smear saliva on a bench? [747] It is permitted according to all to rub saliva on a bench.

Why is smearing saliva not forbidden due to the smearing prohibition? [748] It requires analysis why this matter is not forbidden due to the smearing prohibition. One can However, say that the smearing prohibition only applies when one's intent is to smear one item on to another, However, here that his intent is that it become completely absorbed into the ground [and not remain at all over the ground] it thus does not contain the smearing prohibition. [**See footnote for other opinions [749]**]

---

[735] M"A 316:24, Levushei Serud on M"A; M"B 316:51

[736] M"A 316:25; brought in M"B 316:51

[737] M"B 316:51

[738] Ketzos Hashulchan 146:30 page 140 in name of Elya Raba and other Poskim

[739] Levushei Serud; M"B 316:51

[740] M"B 316:51

[741] M"A 316:24, Machatzis Hashekel:Levushei Serud on M"A; M"B 316:49

[742] M"A

[743] Levushei Serud; M"B.

[744] Ketzos Hashulchan 146:65; The P"M 316 A"A 24 question whether the prohibition applies to a tiled floor, even according to the Rama ibid, as this is a decree upon a decree.

[745] Ketzos Hashulchan 146:65; Az Nidbaru 6:24; Piskeiy Teshuvos 316:7; See also 337 Biur Halacha "Veyeish Machmirim"

[746] Ketzos Hashulchan 146 footnote 63-13

[747] M"A 316:24, Levushei Serud on M"A; M"B 316:49

[748] M"A 316:24, Levushei Serud on M"A; M"B 49

[749] The Elyah Raba 316:35 learns that according to Rashi:Ran:Tur there is a smearing prohibition involved. The Daas Torah concludes that one may certainly be lenient like the Magen Avraham in a case that one is smearing saliva for one who is sick. To note that this dissenting opinion of the Elyah Raba is not recorded by the M"B.

May one rub saliva into the ground/floor/bench on Shabbos:
A. Earth floor:[750]
One may not rub saliva or mucus into the earth/ground due to the "Building" prohibition.[751] [However, some Poskim[752] rule that if majority of the city houses have tiled floors [as opposed to earth floors], it is permitted to rub saliva on a public earth floor, such as on a dirt road, so long as one does not intend to smoothen the gaps. However, by a dirt floor which one owns it remains forbidden to rub in the saliva according to all.[753]]

Standing on the saliva without rubbing on a dirt floor:[754] In all cases, one may stand on the saliva until it gets absorbed into the floor.

Walking over the saliva on a dirt floor: It is permitted to casually step over the saliva [if the saliva is in ones walking direction].[755] In such a case one may slightly rub the saliva as he is walking[756], if the saliva is repulsiveness to him.[757] [However, it is forbidden to purposely walk to the saliva area in order to step on it.[758] However, some Poskim[759] rule one may even purposely walk in that direction and then step on it.]

B. Tiled floor:
One may not rub saliva or mucus onto even a tiled floor due to a decree that one may come to do so on an earth floor.[760] However, some Poskim[761] rule that by tiled floors one may be lenient to rub saliva. Furthermore, if majority of the city houses have tiled floors [as opposed to earth floors], it is permitted according to all to rub saliva on all tiled or wooden floors.[762]

Summary-May one rub saliva into the ground/floor/bench:
One may not rub saliva or mucus into the ground or onto a tiled floor[763] due to the "Building" prohibition.[764] [However, there are Poskim[765] which rule that by tiled floors one may be

---

[750] Michaber 316:11; Shabbos 121b; This law is omitted in Admur; See Ketzos Hashulchan 146:30 and footnotes there for a lengthy discussion of all the opinions of Poskim on this issue
The reason why this Halacha is brought in 316: As in the Gemara ibid the two Halachas of rubbing spit while walking and killing an animal while walking are brought together, and they thus share the common denominator of being permitted "Lefi Tumo". [Levushei Serud 316:9]

[751] The reason: The reason for this is because by doing so one is leveling the holes in the earth and transgresses the building prohibition. [ibid]

[752] Ketzos Hashulchan 146:65

[753] Ketzos Hashulchan 146 footnote 63-13

[754] M"A 316:24, Levushei Serud on M"A; M"B 316:51

[755] The reason: The reason for this is because by doing so one has no intent to smear [the saliva] and smooth the surface holes. Now, although this smoothening occurs inevitably, since he has no intent to do so it is [therefore] permitted due to it being repulsive [to have the saliva remain on the ground]. [Michaber ibid] The simple meaning of Michaber, and so learns Taz 316:10, is that the above applies even if the smoothening is inevitable. The reason: As it is a mere matter of Misaseik [which is only Rabbinically forbidden according to all] and is a Melacha Sheiyon Tzericha Legufo [and is hence only Rabbinical] and therefore in a case of repulsiveness, the Sages were lenient. [P"M 316 M"Z 10]
Other opinions: Others explain that it only at times gets smoothened upon stepping over it and that nevertheless we would forbid it if not for it being repulsive due to that one may onetime forget and actually intentionally rub it. However, if in truth it was always inevitable then it would not be permitted. [M"B 316:50 in name of Peri Megadim, Olas Shabbos, Tosefes Shabbos,]

[756] M"A 316:25; M"B 316:51; Ketzos Hashulchan 146:30; See there footnote 6 on page 137 that some Poskim [Derisha] rule one may even completely rub it while walking
May one have intent to do so? The M"B 316:80 explains this to mean that one is only allowed to rub it slightly while walking if he has no intent to even rub the saliva. However, the Ketzos Hashulchan 146:30 footnote 10 explains that one may have intent to rub the saliva so long as he does not have intent to smoothen the ground.

[757] See M"A 316:25; brought in M"B 316:51; Ketzos Hashulchan 146:30 page 140 in name of Elya Raba and other Poskim

[758] M"B 316:51 in name of Derisha

[759] Ketzos Hashulchan ibid footnote 10 argues on the M"B and explains that in truth the Derisha does not support his opinion

[760] Regarding a tiled floor this is a matter of dispute between the Michaber and Rama. Our custom is to be stringent like the Rama. [Mishneh Berurah 316:49]

[761] Ketzos Hashulchan 146:65 that the applie even according to those which follow the Rama

[762] Ketzos Hashulchan 146:65; Az Nidbaru 6:24; Piskeiy Teshuvos 316:7; See also 337 Biur Halacha "Veyeish Machmirim"

[763] Regarding a tiled floor this is a matter of dispute between the Michaber and Rama. Our custom is to be stringent like the Rama. [Mishneh Berurah 316:49]

lenient to rub saliva even according to those which follow the Rama. **Furthermore, if majority of the city houses have tiled floors [as opposed to earth floors], it is permitted according to all to rub saliva on all tiled or wooden floors.**[766] Furthermore, based on this it is even permitted to rub saliva on a public earth floor, such as on a dirt road, so long as one does not intend to smoothen the gaps. However, by a dirt floor which one owns it remains forbidden to rub in the saliva according to all.[767]] In all cases one may stand on the saliva until it gets absorbed into the floor, and may walk over it if it is in his path while walking. However, by saliva that is found on an earth floor one is to beware not to rub the saliva at all while walking over it. One may rub saliva into a bench.

Q&A
Practically, when spitting upon saying Aleinu in Shul may one rub the saliva?[768]
Yes. It is permitted to rub the saliva as he does during the week if one is spitting on a tiled floor.[769] [Those which desire to be stringent must at least step on the saliva until it disappears.] It is forbidden to rub the saliva when spitting on an earth floor, and one is rather to simply step on it until it disappears.[770]

16. May one gather non-Muktzah rocks and use it to build a temporary structure:
For insulating food on Yom Tov for the sake of Shabbos:[771] When Yom Tov which falls out on Erev Shabbos, it is forbidden to insulate hot food for Shabbos with stones, as it is forbidden to gather stones on Yom Tov, as this is similar to [the prohibition against] building [on Shabbos and Yom Tov].

However, if one has nothing else [available] to insulate with other than the stones, then it is permitted for him to insulate with them, as [by doing so] he is not making a permanent structure, but rather a temporary one, which is only Rabbinically forbidden to be done, and due to the [Mitzvah of] honoring Shabbos the Sages did not decree [in this situation, against using the stones to insulate], being that [in this case] it's not possible for him to insulate in any other way.

Making oneself a toilet out from stones:[772] Large stones which are organized to create a seat with a hole which one sits on in fields by the area designated to be used as a bathroom, is permitted to be organized on Shabbos, being that [doing so] is a temporary structure that is not made to last, and a temporary structure is only prohibited to [be made] Rabbinically, and due to respect of humanity they did not apply their decree [in this case].[773]

Nevertheless, to make a form of a tent with a roof is forbidden even though it is only a temporary.

---

[764] As by doing so he is smoothening out the floor.
[765] Ketzos Hashulchan 146:65
[766] Ketzos Hashulchan 146:65; Az Nidbaru 6:24; Piskeiy Teshuvos 316:7; See also 337 Biur Halacha "Veyeish Machmirim"
[767] Ketzos Hashulchan 146 footnote 63-13
[768] Ketzos Hashulchan 146:65; Az Nidbaru 6:24; Piskeiy Teshuvos 316:7; See also 337 Biur Halacha "Veyeish Machmirim"
[769] The reason: Being that today majority of houses are tiled, and thus according to all the decree against tiled floors do not apply.
[770] Michaber 316:11; Shabbos 121b; However, some Poskim rule that if majority of the city houses have tiled floors [as opposed to earth floors], it is permitted to rub saliva on a public earth floor, such as on a dirt road, so long as one does not intend to smoothen the gaps. However, by a dirt floor which one owns it remains forbidden to rub in the saliva according to all. [Ketzos Hashulchan 146 footnote 63-13]
[771] Admur 259:6
[772] Admur 312:15
[773] Regarding the problem of Muktzah there are opinions that say that this is only referring to stones that have been designated before Shabbos to be used for this purpose. However, others learn that even if not predestinated the Sages allowed one to move it. [Mishneh Berurah 25] [It seems from the Alter Rebbe like the latter as a) Why didn't the Alter Rebbe mention the case is referring to designated stones, and b) if the stones were designated for this, then the structure made out from them is permanent not temporary.

Summary-May one gather non-Muktzah rocks and use it to build a temporary structure?[774]

This is forbidden due that it appears like building, However, if one is doing so for the sake of a Mitzvah or in order to relive his bowels then it is allowed.

---

[774] Chapter 259 Halacha 6

CHAPTER 3: LAWS WHICH RELATE TO INSERTING OR REMOVING WINDOWS, SHUTTERS, DOORS AND LOCKS ON SHABBOS

> **Introduction:**
> The following chapter will discuss the laws that involve inserting and removing doors, windows and other parts into and out of houses on Shabbos. It will also discuss the laws of inserting locks onto ones doors. At times doing the above transgresses the prohibition against building an item on Shabbos, as well as the Muktzah prohibition.

1. Inserting a shutter, windowpane or screen into a window:[775]

May one insert the frame and glass of a window into a window or skylight on Shabbos? The inserts for a window[776], such as a board or any other item with which one seals off a window with, even if it is something that does not have the status of a vessel at all, and was also never used before as an insert during the week, and one [now] wants[777] to insert it for its first time on Shabbos, then if he had in mind before Shabbos to insert it (on Shabbos or he thought about it that it be prepared and designated to be inserted into a window, even though he did not think about [using it] on Shabbos explicitly,) then it is allowed [to be inserted on Shabbos].

The reason for this is: because through this thought [that the person had before Shabbos, the insert] received the status of a vessel and has thus become permitted to be moved just like all other vessel (as is written in chapter 308 [Halachas 50-51] that one's thought helps [to give a status of a vessel] for an item which is common to be designated towards [the purpose that one thought of].)

If it was used one time before Shabbos: (As well if one inserted it one time before Shabbos, even if he did not think about inserting it on Shabbos, it [also] receives the status of a vessel as a result of this insertion since it is an item that is common to be designated for this use.)

Sealing off a skylight with an insert: Even the skylight[778] of a roof is permitted to be sealed off with an insert that is permitted to be moved, even if it was not tied and hanging from [the roof] from before Shabbos.

The reason that this does not contain the Ohel prohibition: Doing [the above] does not transgress the [prohibition of] putting up a tent on Shabbos because through doing this one is only adding to the [already existing] tent [meaning the roof], and [even] this addition is only temporary being that [the insert] is not meant to stay in there for very long being that [a sky roof] is meant to be constantly opened. [It is thus permitted to be inserted, as] adding a temporary tent [to an already established tent] is permitted [on Shabbos], and it was only forbidden to build an entire temporary tent, as is explained in "The Laws of Making an Ohel".

Inserting a board or the like for it to remain there for long periods of time: For this reason, if this insert is not meant to be reopened regularly, but rather [only occasionally] after long periods of time, then it is forbidden to insert it even into a window that is in the wall as this is like adding a permanent structure into the wall [which carries with it the building prohibition].

---

[775] Admur 313:1

[776] Back then the term window referred to the opening in the wall and not to the actual glass frame placed inside the opening. Thus, the following laws equally apply with regards to placing the frame of one's window into his window on Shabbos. However, to note that this law only refers to items that are a) not placed into sockets [see 313:17] and B) placed for a short period of time [end of this Halacha]. Otherwise, it is forbidden.

[777] Lit. comes

[778] Lit. Chimney

Summary of when its allowed to insert a frame or glass window into a window opening or skylight:

It is only permitted to insert a windowpane, frame or anything of the like into ones window or skylight if both:

1. The item being inserted is not Muktzah. Meaning that if it does not have the status of a vessel then it needs to be either designated before Shabbos to be used as an insert, or placed in one time before Shabbos.
   And

2. That there is no building prohibition involved. Thus, it is only allowed to be inserted if it is meant to constantly be removed and replaced. [Such as is the case with a shutter, or the like, that it is only meant to temporarily cover the window.] However, if one intends to leave it there for a long period of time, [which is usually the case regarding windowpanes, frames and screens], then this is not allowed as it transgresses the building prohibition.
   And

3. Furthermore, if the window frame has hinges, it may not be inserted into a socket [as is evident from 313/17]

Q&A

May one insert a screen into his window on Shabbos for the first time?

Based on the above if it is done to be left there for a long period of time, which is usually the case, it is forbidden. However, if for some reason one only puts up the screen for so many hours and then removes it, then it is allowed.

If a screen or window came out of its sockets, as is common by sliding screens, may it be reinserted?[779]

It is forbidden to return a screen or window to its setting on Shabbos, and they are considered Muktzah, just like a detached door of a house. Thus, a sliding screen which became removed from its socket is Muktzah. This applies even if the screen or window is only loosely attached to its socket and may thus be easily removed.[780] However, if one's screen or window is not attached well and constantly comes out upon moving it, then it may be reinserted if it comes out.[781]

May one remove the window/insert on Shabbos?

If the insert is not meant to be constantly removed and reinserted, then it may not be removed. See next Halacha regarding if one may ask a gentile to remove the window in a case that one is very hot and needs a breeze.

---

[779] Piskeiy Teshuvos 308:12
[780] Kitzur SHU"A 80:72
[781] Kaneh Bosem 1:20; Ashel Avraham Butchach 313

2. Removing the window frame from the window of the house:[782]

The door of a house and of a *Bor* pit and *Dus* pit[783] or of vessels which are attached to the ground, such as for example a chicken coop which is a vessel and is attached to the ground, it is forbidden to either remove or return [these doors into or out of their sockets even if they are placed in loosely], as anything attached to the ground has the [prohibition] of building [it] and destroying [it][784].[see note[785]]

Thus that which is accustomed to be done by large [festive] meals [on Shabbos], to remove the windows through a gentile[786], is not proper to be done being that this removal carries with it the liability to bring a Chatas offering if it were to be done by a Jew, being that he is destroying[787] [the window] in order to build it [again latter][788], as one plans to eventually return [the window] afterwards [back to its opening]. Therefore, when one tells a gentile [to do so] this [telling him] is a total Rabbinical prohibition and is not [within the category of] a Rabbinical decree on a Rabbinical decree which was permitted in order to prevent pain, as was explained in chapter 307 [Halacha 12].

Other opinions: [However,] according to those that say that destroying in order to rebuild is only [Biblically] liable if one had intention that the rebuilding of it will make it better than the way it was originally, as explained in chapter 278 [Halacha 2], then the removal of the windows is only a Rabbinical prohibition [as here the eventual reinsertion of the window is done in no better a way then the way the window was before it was removed], and [thus it is permitted] to tell a gentile [to remove the windows in the above scenario as it] is a Rabbinical decree upon a Rabbinical decree which is allowed to be done in a distressful situation [such as here that it is too hot in the house and one needs to remove the windows for a breeze].

The Final Ruling:[789] [Due to the above existing opinion one] therefore does not need to reprimand people who are lenient [to ask a gentile to do so] being that they have upon whom to rely. However, every person should be stringent upon himself like the first opinion which is the main [Halachic] opinion.

As well one needs to warn the masses that stumble [and transgress] by removing a quarter of the windowpane from the window[790] unknowingly that this contains a great prohibition.

---

[782] Admur 313:17;

[783] A dus pit is a pit that has a wall surrounding it, while a Bor pit does not have anything surrounding it, and is rather just a hole in the ground. [See Baba Basra 64a and Rashi there] In Chapter 587:1 the Alter Rebbe explains that a Dus is any building which majority of its space is underground level. However, if only minority of it is above ground level, then it has the same law as a house.

[784] This Biblical prohibition applies even if the door was only semi-firmly placed into its sockets. [Ketzos Hashulchan 119 note 4]

[785] However, by a door of a vessel attached to the ground this is only a Rabbinical prohibition and thus it is permitted to remove the covering of an item attached to the ground if it is meant to be constantly opened and closed and if it is not attached onto hinges, as explained in chapter 259 Halacha 7 and in 314 Halacha 19.

[786] Back then the windows were not move in a frame or revolve against hinges, and thus to open the window meant to remove it entirely from the opening in the wall.

[787] Seemingly the case here is discussing a window that is set into sockets in the wall as otherwise it would have the same law as the law in Halacha 1 that it was permitted to place an insert to the window on Shabbos. [So seems to learn also the Ketzos Hashulchan in 119 Halacha 15]

[788] Whenever one destroys in order to rebuild it carries with it the Biblical prohibition of destroying by vessels attached to the ground. However, to destroy and not plan to rebuild is only a Rabbinical prohibition.

[789] Admur ibid

Other opinions: Some Poskim rule one must protest against those that are lenient to ask a gentile to remove the window. [Taz 313:5; M"B 308:38]

[790] Evidently this refers to a window frame made of many removal parts.

May one ask a gentile to remove a windowpane from the window of a house on Shabbos?
Even if one does not plan to have the windowpane placed back in any better a form then it originally was in, one should not ask a gentile to remove it, although those that are lenient to do so do not need to be rebuked.[791] [See footnote for other opinions[792]]
Regarding asking a gentile to break or take apart a vessel, see the previous chapter.

Inserting or removing a door into or from an opening/doorway

Introduction:
The following laws will discuss when it is allowed to place a door into a doorway or entrance on Shabbos and when it is allowed to be removed from the doorway and entrance. The issue here is regarding whether or not doing so is considered like one is building on Shabbos. If the door was placed before Shabbos onto its hinges and thus revolves around them, then it is always allowed to be opened and closed in all circumstances.

3. Returning or removing a door into or from its hinges:
Removing the door of a house or pit:[793] The door of a house and of a *Bor* pit and *Dus* pit[794] or of vessels which are attached to the ground, such as for example a chicken coop which is a vessel and is attached to the ground, it is forbidden to either remove or return [the hinges of these doors into or out of their sockets[795] even if they are placed in loosely], as anything attached to the ground has the [prohibition] of building [it] and destroying [it][796].[see note[797]]
By doors with a hinge on their side:[798] Even a door that does not have a hinge on its top or bottom, but rather on its side, meaning that on its side there is one bolt that protrudes which has a hole opposite it within the doorpost, into which one inserts the bolt into this hole when he closes the door, and when one opens the door he removes it out from the hole, in which case here there is [thus] no suspicion that one may come to [strongly] insert [the bolt into its hole] being that the door is made for constant opening and closing [and thus one will purposely not place the bolt too strongly into the hole], nevertheless it is forbidden to return this hinge into its hole on Shabbos due to a decree [that if one were to be allowed to do so then he may come to also insert] a hinge which is not on the side of the door, [in which there is suspicion that one may insert it strongly].
Its law on Yom Tov:[799] However, on Yom Tov it is allowed [to insert this type of hinge into its socket, when done] for the sake of the joy of Yom Tov, [such as to get into ones food storage house to get food for Yom Tov], as will be explained in chapter 519 [Halacha 1].

---

[791] Admur 313:17
[792] There are Poskim [Ashel Avraham 314] which rule that it is permitted in a case of need to ask a gentile to remove a door from its setting as the gentile himself does not have intent to return it.
[793] Admur 313:17; see also 313:8: "However, one must beware that if they have hinges that one not return the hinge to their sockets as will be explained [in Halacha 17]."
[794] A dus pit is a pit that has a wall surrounding it, while a Bor pit does not have anything surrounding it, and is rather just a hole in the ground. [See Baba Basra 64a and Rashi there] In Chapter 587:1 the Alter Rebbe explains that a Dus is any building which majority of its space is underground level. However, if only minority of it is above ground level, then it has the same law as a house.
[795] Admur 313:8
[796] This Biblical prohibition applies even if the door was only semi-firmly placed into its sockets. [Ketzos Hashulchan 119 note 4]
[797] However, by a door of a vessel attached to the ground this is only a Rabbinical prohibition and thus it is permitted to remove the covering of an item attached to the ground if it is meant to be constantly opened and closed and if it is not attached onto hinges, as explained in chapter 259 Halacha 7 and in 314 Halacha 19.
[798] Admur 313:15
[799] Admur 313:15

Summary:
It is never allowed to place a door onto its hinges or remove it from its hinges on Shabbos.

Q&A

If a sliding door or screen came out of its sockets may it be reinserted?[800]
It is forbidden to return a screen or door to its setting on Shabbos, and they are considered Muktzah, just like a detached door of a house. Thus, a sliding screen or glass door which became removes from its sockets is Muktzah. This applies even if the screen or door is only loosely attached to its socket and may thus be easily removed.[801]
However, if one's screen or door is not attached well and constantly comes out upon moving it, then it may be reinserted if it comes out.[802]

4. Placing a door by an opening without placing it on hinges:
A. Openings that are only sporadically used for entering and exiting from:

-*By Doors with hinges:*[803] All openings which are not made to be constantly entered and exited from but rather only sporadically, such as for example ones backyard which one does not constantly enter and exit, then if one made for its opening a door that does not spin on a hinge (the definition of a hinge is a piece of sharp wood which protrudes from the door to be inserted into the hole in the sill[804] in order so that the door move back and forth) and rather when one wants to close [the opening] with [this door], one stands [the door] upright over the opening of the doorway in order to close it, then whether this door is made of beams or whether it's made of mats of bamboo which one hung and placed upright [to be used] as a door, or [another example of the above type of door, if one had] a break [in ones fence of his] garden or courtyard which one closed up with thorns in a way similar to a door, and at times one sporadically opens this door and enters and exits through its break [in the fence] and then goes back and locks it, then [in all the above cases], if there are hinges on these doors or even if currently there aren't hinges on them but in the past it had hinges which were broken off it and it is still recognizable [that there once were hinges on it], then one is allowed to close them on Shabbos. [The reason for this is] because through the detection of the hinges it is recognizable that they were doors made for opening and closing and it [thus] does not appear like [one is] building [by placing these doors by the doorway].[805] However, one must beware that if they have hinges that one not return the hinge to their sockets as was explained above in Halacha 1.[806]
Tying the door to the opening:[807] Even when [the doors] have hinges, [the Sages] only permitted to close them if they were tied and hung [by that opening] from before Shabbos in order to lock with. In such a case [the Sages] allow one to lock with it, even if when [the door] is opened it drags on the ground and when it is closed one lifts it up and stands it upright on the doorstep, as since they are tied and attached to there from before Shabbos [closing them] does not appear like building on Shabbos.
-*By Doors that have no remnant of having had hinges:*[808] However, if [these doors] do not have any remnant of having had hinges in the past, then it is forbidden to close them on Shabbos[809], as since they are only meant to be opened sporadically, they thus appear when being used to close

---

[800] Piskeiy Teshuvos 308:12
[801] Kitzur SHU"A 80:72
[802] Kaneh Bosem 1:20; Ashel Avraham Butshesh 313
[803] Admur 313:8; Michaber 313:3; Mishneh Eruvin 101a
[804] Seemingly this refers to the bottom panel of the door frame, and not the doorpost as is done by most modern doors today.
[805] Admur ibid; Michaber ibid; M"B 313:26 in name of Admur
[806] Admur ibid; Rama 313:3
[807] Admur 313:9; Michaber 313:3
[808] Admur 313:8; Michaber 313:2
[809] However, see next Halacha regarding their law if they are tied strongly to the opening.

[up an opening] like building a permanent wall so long as they are not recognizable as doors.[810]

If the door was strongly tied then it is allowed to be closed it even if it never had hinges:[811] If one tied and established [the door] there in a way that even when they are opened they do not drag on the ground, then even if they are only elevated from the ground a threads worth, they are allowed to be closed even if they do not have the remnant of a hinge. [The reason for this is] because it does not appear like building through closing it being that even when they are opened they are well attached and established there [to the point that they] do not drag on the ground [when opened or closed].[812]

-In all cases, the above allowance does not apply by doors without a threshold or by single plank doors-See below C-D!

B. Openings that are constantly used for entering and exiting:[813]

An opening which is made for constant entrance and exit is permitted to be closed even with a door that does not have remnant of a hinge and drags on the ground when opened[814], or even if it is completely removed [from the opening] when one comes to open it due to it not being tied to there at all.[815]

The reason for this is:[816] because since [this opening] is made to be constantly opened up, it therefore by closing it one is not making a permanent wall but rather a temporary [one], and there is no prohibition in making a temporary wall on Shabbos unless made in ways to be explained in "The Laws of Making an Ohel."

Regarding if this allowance applies even if the door does not have a threshold and even if it is made of a single plank-See below C-D.

C. Inserting doors into openings that do not have a threshold:[817]

All the above refers to a door[way] that has a lower threshold that one stands [the door] on, as this threshold shows that the door is made for locking purposes and not for building [a wall]. However, if it does not have a threshold and when one locks with it one places it down on the earth and when one opens it one removes and uproots it[818], then since [this opening] does not have the form of a doorway, one is not allowed to close it even if [the door] has a hinge, so long as [the door is not inserted in its socket and thus] does not spin around on its hinge. This applies

---

[810] Admur ibid; Rashi Gemara ibid; M"B 313:23
[811] Admur 313:9; Michaber 313:3; Mishneh ibid
[812] Admur ibid; M"B 313:27
[813] Admur 313:10; Michaber 313:3
[814] Admur ibid; implication of Michaber ibid as explains Gr"a and M"B 313:29 and 33
[815] Admur ibid, based on Rama 313:4, as explained in Gra ibid and M"B ibid
Other opinions: Some Poskim rule that according to the Michaber ibid it is forbidden to be closed or opened if it is not tied, even if it is meant for constant opening and closing, due to a building prohibition. [Gra ibid; M"B ibid] seemingly this is because in such a case it is considered actual Boneh, or Michzi Keboneh. [see next footnote] The M"B himself rules one may be lenient.
[816] Admur ibid
Other opinions: Some Poskim write the reason is because a door meant for contents opening and closing does not appear like one is building. [M"B 313:28 in name of Levush and so wrote Admur in 313:8-9 in explanation of why a Tzir and tying is required] Seemingly this explanation only suffices for the opinion the Michaber ibid, which implies that the door must nevertheless be tied for this to be allowed, and hence there is never a question of Boneh involved and rather it is Maaras Ayin of Boneh, which is not relevant when the door is meant for constant opening and closing. However, according to the ruling of Admur ibid, based on Rama ibid, that even if the door is not tied, and does not contain any hinges, it is allowed to be opened if it is meant for constant opening, more than just explaining why it does not appear like building one must also explain why it is not essentially a prohibition of building, irrelevant of what it looks like. [See Rashi on Mishneh 101a which explicitly implies as above that there are two prohibitions involved, one of Boneh if the door is not attached, and one of Michzi Keboneh when it is attached.]
[817] 313:11; Michaber 313:4
[818] This seems to imply like the Girsa of the Rif in the Gemara ibid which writes "Ein Nigreres", which implies, as explained in Gr"a and M"B 313:32, Shaar Hatziyon 313:23, that if it is attached then it does not need to fulfill these conditions of a threshold, and being made of more than one board. However, from later in Admur where he says "is above the ground" it implies that even if it is tied very hard it applies. Veztaruch Iyun as to how truly Admur is ruling according to the Rif. In any event, either way this Heter of being tied only applies by a door mmade for constant opening, of which we are anywayts lenient even if it is not tied at all, as explained in Admur below.

even if [one tied the door in a way that] it is elevated off the ground, and even if the opening is meant for constant entering and exiting.[819]

Other Opinions:[820] [However,] there are opinions which permit [placing a door] by an [opening that does not have a threshold if the] opening is made for constant entering and exiting.

The Final Ruling:[821] One may be lenient in a [dispute over a] Rabbinical command, [and thus may place a door by even an opening that lacks a threshold if the opening is made for constant entering and exiting].

D. Placing a door made of a single plank of wood into a doorway:[822]

The same law [that one may not place the door on Shabbos] applies for a door that is made of a single board [of wood and the like] which when opened one removes [the entire board] and uproots it [from the doorway], as since it is not similar to other doors one is not allowed to close it even if it has a hinge, so long as it does not revolve on its hinge. [This applies] even if [the door is tied in a way that it is completely] elevated from the ground, and even if its [opening] has a threshold, and even if it is made for constant entering and exiting.[823]

The reason for this is: because [placing such a door by the opening] appears like one is building and placing a beam into the wall [so it become an extension of the wall].

Other Opinions:[824] [However,] there are opinions which permit [placing this door] by an opening that is made for constant entering and exiting.

The Final Ruling:[825] One may be lenient in a [dispute over a] Rabbinical prohibition, [and thus may place this type of door by an opening made for constant entering and exiting].

The law by a door made of many beams:[826] However, a door which is made from many beams and [its opening has] a threshold is permitted to be closed according to all opinions if the opening is made for constant entering and exiting, even if upon opening [this door] one completely removes it and uproots it, being that it is not tied at all to the opening[827], and even if it does not have any remnant of a hinge as explained above.

Using many individual beams to close the opening:[828] The same law applies in a case that one closes up [an opening] using many individual beams by inserting the beams into an engraved [line worth of space] by the top and bottom [of the doorframe], as since the door is closed using many beams, they are all considered like a single door which is made of many beams, and it is [thus] permitted to close with even if one completely removes it upon opening it, and even if it has no remnant of any hinges, as long as its opening is made for constant entrance and exit.

---

[819] First opinion in Admur ibid; ruling of Michaber ibid as explained in Beis Yosef; M"B 313:30

[820] Second opinion in Admur ibid; M"A 313:8 in name of Bach

[821] Admur ibid; based on his understanding of M"A ibid; Tosafus brought in machatzis Hashekel ibid

Other opinions: Some Poskim rule one may only be lenient by a door made for constant opening, if the door does not have a threshold, if the door is made of one plank, as explained next. If, however, it also is made up of a single plank, one may not be lenient. [Rambam, brought in M"A ibid; and so rules M"B in his understanding of M"A ibid; and so explains Levushei Serud and Machatzis Hashekel in M"A ibid]

[822] 313:12; Michaber 313:4

[823] First opinion in Admur ibid; ruling of Michaber ibid as explained in Beis Yosef; M"B 313:30

[824] Second opinion in Admur ibid; M"A 313:8 in name of Bach

[825] Admur ibid; based on his understanding of M"A ibid; Tosafus brought in Machatzis Hashekel ibid

Other opinions: Some Poskim rule one may only be lenient by a door made for constant opening, if the door does is made of one plank, if the door also has a threshold, as explained next. If, however, it also does not have a threshold, one may not be lenient. [Rambam, brought in M"A ibid; and so rules M"B in his understanding of M"A ibid; and so explains Levushei Serud and Machatzis Hashekel in M"A ibid]

[826] Admur 313:13; Rama 313:4

[827] Admur ibid; Rama ibid

Other opinions: Some Poskim rule that according to the Michaber ibid it is forbidden to be closed or opened if it is not tied, even if it is meant for constant opening and closing, due to a building prohibition. [Gra ibid; M"B ibid] Seemingly this is because in such a case it is considered actual Boneh, or Michzi Keboneh. [see next footnote] The M"B himself rules one may be lenient.

[828] Admur 313:13

Summary of when it is permitted to place a door on Shabbos into an entrance

Note: The following laws only relate to placing a door by an entrance <u>without placing it into its hinges</u>. It is never allowed to place a door into its hinges on Shabbos as will be discussed in the next set of laws.

An opening that is made for sporadic entering and exiting:
A door that does not revolve on its hinges may only be placed into an entrance or removed from an entrance if:

1. <u>The door was tied to the entrance from before Shabbos.</u> If the door has hinges, or a remnant of hinges which had broken off it suffices even if it is loosely tied to the entrance, and thus when one opens the door it drags on the ground. However, if the door does not have any remnant of hinges then it must be tied strong enough to the entrance that when opened and closed it remains completely above the ground.[829]

And

2. <u>The doorway has a threshold.</u> If it does not have a threshold then the door may never be lifted off or placed there on Shabbos.[830]

And

3. The door is made of more than one board.[831]

An opening that is made for constant entering and exiting:
It is always allowed to place a door into such an entrance or remove it from there, even if the door had not been tied to the entrance from before Shabbos, and even if it does not have any remnant of hinges[832], and may be lenient even if its entrance does not have a threshold[833], and even if the door is made of a single plank of wood.[834]

A door that was placed on its hinges from before Shabbos:
May be revolved on its hinges [opened and closed but not removed] under all circumstances.[835]

---

[829] Admur 313:8-9
[830] Admur 313:11
[831] Admur 313:12
[832] Admur 313:10
[833] Admur 313:11
[834] Admur 313:12
[835] Admur 313:8, 11, and 12

5. Barricading ones door using a bolt or rod:

A. Barricading one's door with a wooden rod:[836]

No need to tie the rod to the door before Shabbos: A rod which one has made to be used as a lock, [through] inserting it by the wall near the door[837], does not need to be tied to the door before Shabbos. As even if it were not to be tied and hung there from before Shabbos, and one inserts it there on Shabbos, [nevertheless] this is not considered building on Shabbos since he is not nullifying it there, as it is meant to be removed and inserted constantly.[838]

Must modify the rod in a way that it is evident that it is meant for locking with: Nevertheless [locking with a rod] is a bit more similar to [the prohibition of] building then is the sealing of a window and skylight [through an insert], therefore even if one thought before Shabbos to use it to lock with on Shabbos, and even if one designated it for this purpose forever, and even if one had used to lock with many times during the week and it was designated for this use, nevertheless it is forbidden to use it to lock with on Shabbos unless one modified it and did an action to it and prepared it [to be used for] this, in a way that the modification shows on it that it is designated for this [use]. (As in such a case it is readily evident that the rod has not been nullified [to permanently] stay there, but rather is meant to remove and reinsert regularly, as his action of modification proves this, as through this action of modification it gives it the status of a vessel, and it is not usual to insert a vessel into a building and annul it there forever.)

The status of the rod once a modification has been done: [If one does this modification] it is allowed to lock with it even if one had never locked with it before hand, before [this] Shabbos.

As well it is permitted to move it even not for the sake of using it and [using] its space, as is the law by all other vessel which are designated for a permitted use.

However, if [the lock] is made in a way that it is forbidden to lock with it on Shabbos, then even though it is designated to lock with during the week, [nevertheless] it is forbidden to move it unless [doing so in order] to use it [for a permitted purpose] or [to use] its space, as is the law of a vessel which is designated for forbidden usage.

B. Barricading ones door using a bolt which has a handle:[839]

The same applies by a bolt[840] that is inserted one end into the hole in the wall of one side of the door and the other end into the hole [in the wall] of the other side of the door, [then] if it has a ring in its middle with which one holds onto when removing and inserting [the bolt] and uses it to pull the bolt [into or out of its hole], then [the ring] is [considered] a handle to the bolt and it is permitted to use to lock with even if it is not tied.

---

[836] Admur 313:2
[837] Such as a wooden barricade placed behind a door, which is hung on hooks that protrude from the walls that are horizontal to the door.
[838] However, if it is inserted into holes made in the walls which are vertical to the door, and thus prevents the door from being pushed open, then it has different laws, as will be explained.
[839] Admur 313:7
[840] Vetzaruch Iyun how this case [of a bolt] is any different than the case of a rod, explained above [in Halacha 2]. [Alter Rebbe]

Summary-Barricading ones door using a bolt or rod:
It may only be placed on Shabbos even if it is not Muktzah if:
  A. It is meant to be constantly removed and reinserted.[841]
  And
  B. If a **rod** is placed against the door [such as by hanging it on hooks that protrude from the wall] then it must have some modification done to it that shows that it is meant to be used as a lock.[842]
  or
  C. If a **bolt** is placed inside holes within the walls that are next to the door then it is not enough for a modification to be done, but rather the bolt must have a handle made on it with which one removes and inserts it into the holes.[843]

---

6. Locking ones door with placing a peg in the doorstep behind the door:

A. The law by a peg without a handle:[844]

A Nagar which is a peg that is inserted into the hole that is by the doorstep [behind the door] in order to lock the door, since it is inserted below into the doorstep it appears more like building than the insertion of the rod into the wall from the side [of the door]. [Therefore] one may not lock with it despite it being designated for this purpose, and even if one mended it in a way that shows on it that it is designated for [locking, it may not be used].[845] Rather it must be tied to the [door] from before Shabbos, (in which case it is then permitted to lock with it even if it had never been locked with beforehand and even if it had not been designated for this) as since it is tied and attached to there from before Shabbos it does not appear like one is building on Shabbos.
See below B-D regarding how it is to be tied and the law regarding if the inserting of the peg will create a new hole and the law regarding if the peg has a handle!

B. How does one tie the peg?

By a peg that has a bolted head:[846] If its head has a bolt, meaning that its head is thick and is fit to be used to crush and grind peppers, then since it is similar to a vessel it does not appear so much as one is building [when inserting it into the lock], as it is unusual to insert a vessel into a building [and] nullify it there[847]. Therefore it does not need to be tied on strongly and rather even if it is attached with a thin rope in which case [the peg] is not fit to be taken with it, [meaning] that if one were to want to take the [peg out] from [the lock] and move it using this rope then [the rope] would immediately tear [from the peg], [nevertheless] this suffices even if it is not tied onto the door itself but to the latch of the door (or to the doorpost. As even though it is not so recognizable that it was tied to there before Shabbos to serve as a lock for the door being that it is not tied to the door itself as well as that it is not tied strongly, nevertheless it does not appear like building on Shabbos since it appears like a vessel).
[Furthermore] even if the rope is long and thus the peg is not hanging at all in the air when it is removed from the hole in the doorstep[848], but rather is entirely resting on the ground, [nevertheless] this poses no problem since it was tied to there from before Shabbos through a

---

[841] Halacha 2
[842] Halacha 2
[843] Halacha 7
[844] Admur 313:3
[845] However, if one placed on it a handle, then it may be inserted under all circumstances even if it is not tied, and even if it makes a hole in the ground.
[846] Admur 313:4
[847] Meaning leaving it there permanently without ever planning to take it out.
[848] From here it seems that in the typical scenario the rope is not long enough when hanging to have the peg reach the ground and is thus pulled at and stretched in the process of placing the peg in the ground.

rope.

By a peg that does not have a bolted head[849] but is attached to the door:[850] If the peg does not have a bolted head then if it is tied to the door itself, even if it is tied with a thin string which is not fit to [remove the peg from the lock], it suffices. (As it is well recognizable that it was tied there before Shabbos for the sake of locking the door, being that it is tied to the door itself, even though the knot is not strong, and thus [inserting this peg into the lock] no longer appears like building on Shabbos). [As well this suffices] even if the entire [peg] rests on the floor when it is removed from the hole[851].

If the non-bolted peg is not attached to the door: [852] However, if it is not attached to the door itself, but rather to the latch (or doorpost) then the knot must be strong enough that [the peg] is able to be removed [from its hole] through [pulling at the rope], (as when [the peg] is well tied with a strong rope it is recognizable that it is designated to be used for locking the door, even though it is not tied to the door itself, and thus [inserting it into the lock] no longer appears like building on Shabbos). [This applies] even if the entire [peg] rests on the floor when it is removed from the hole that is in the doorstep[853].

C. A peg that inserts into the ground:[854]

However, all the above [is only allowed] if the doorstep is elevated [from the ground to the point that] its hole [in which the peg is inserted in] does not reach the ground. However, if the hole goes beyond the bottom of [the doorpost] and reaches the ground in a way that when the peg is inserted into the hole, the peg punctures a hole under [the doorpost] into the ground, then it appears like building and is forbidden to be locked with in any circumstance, [including] even if it has a bolted head and is tied to the door with a strong rope.

If there is a set hole in the ground to which it is inserted into: However, this only applies if the peg constantly punctures a new hole into the ground. However, if to begin with one made a hole in the ground large enough for the head[855] of the peg to be inserted into, and thus the peg no longer adds to the hole already made in the ground, then it does not appear like building, and is permitted to be locked with, in the ways explained above [regarding tying the peg].

D. Locking with a peg which had a handle inserted into it:[856]

A peg which had a handle inserted into its middle, and is thus similar to a mallet[857] which is a vessel, is permitted to lock with even if it punctures a hole in the ground, and even if it is not tied on at all, as it does not appear like building being that it is readily apparent that it is a vessel. This is not similar to [a peg] that has a bolted head which is also similar to a vessel but must nevertheless be tied and may not puncture the ground, as here one has done an action with his hands by inserting the handle into [the peg] and through doing so has turned it into a vessel, as opposed to by the bolted peg where no action was done with ones hands to give it the status of a vessel.

---

[849] Such as a regular large nail and the like.
[850] Admur 313:5
[851] Meaning that the rope is so long that it reaches the floor and thus has the peg rest on the floor.
[852] Admur 313:5
[853] Meaning that the rope is so long that it reaches the floor and thus has the peg rest on the floor.
[854] Admur 313:6
[855] Seemingly the Alter Rebbe is saying that only if the head of the peg is placed in, as in such a case it does not make a larger hole, is it allowed, However, to place in the pointy end of the peg which can make a deeper hole, then it is not allowed.
[856] Admur 313:7
[857] A mallet is a smaller sized sledgehammer.

A bolt which has a handle:

The same applies by a bolt[858] that is inserted one end into the hole in the wall of one side of the door and the other end into the hole [in the wall] of the other side of the door, [then] if it has a ring in its middle with which one holds onto when removing and inserting [the bolt] and uses it to pull the bolt [into or out of its hole], then [the ring] is [considered] a handle to the bolt and it is permitted to use it to lock with even if it is not tied.

Summary-Locking ones door using a peg:
A peg may only be placed on Shabbos behind ones door in order to lock it, even if the peg is not Muktzah, if:
  A. It is meant to be constantly removed and reinserted.[859]

And

  B. The peg has a handle that was specifically inserted into it, in which case it is allowed to be inserted even if was not tied to the door before Shabbos, and even if it punctures a hole in the earth.[860]

or

  If condition b is not fulfilled [no handle] then it is only allowed if one fulfills condition c and d.

  C. If the peg reaches into the actual earth when stuck into its hole, then it is only allowed if it enters into a previously made hole. However, to make a new hole by inserting it is forbidden in all cases that the peg does not have a handle.[861]

And

  D. If the peg does not have an inserted handle then it must be tied to the door from before Shabbos[862]. When tied to the door itself it suffices even if it is a weak knot which does not have the ability to lift up the peg out from the hole. However, when tied to the doorpost then if the peg does not have a bolted head it must be tied strong enough to be able to pull the peg out of its hole using the cord.[863]

Q&A

One who has a bolt lock screwed onto his door which is made for pressing into a hole that has been drilled into the threshold, as is common in many two door entrances, may one lock it or open it on Shabbos if it is meant to be constantly locked?
This matter requires further analysis.[864] However, practically, it would seem that it is permitted to do so, as once something is built and modified for the sake of constant opening and closing as one chooses, it by definition can no longer be considered a part of the structure and transgress the Boneh and Soser prohibition. Thus, even if a window has been left closed for over 24 hours, or even for over a year, is permitted to open it on Shabbos, as it is clearly evident that it is meant for constant opening and closing, and that it is not part of the structure. The same would apply to a door that has been left closed for a long time that it may be opened on Shabbos, and the same would apply for a peg that closes the door, that if the peg is attached to the door and modified for the purpose of opening and closing then by definition it cannot be

---

[858] Vetzaruch Iyun how this case [of a bolt] is any different than the case of a rod, explained above [in Halacha 2]. [Alter Rebbe]
[859] similar to the law by a rod in 313:2 [Brought above in Halacha 1a]
[860] Admur 313:7
[861] Admur 313:6
[862] Admur 313:3
[863] Admur 313:4-5
[864] The Chayeh Adam Klal 39:10, brought in Mishneh Berura 313:13, writes that when the peg is attached to the door and is pulled up to open and down to close, then according to all it may be opened and closed on Shabbos. However, Tzaruch Iyun what the ruling would be regarding a door that is not meant for constant opening and closing, as from the ruling of Admur by the bolt locks [313:2] it seems that it must be not left there for a long time for it to be allowed to lock with.

considered under a building or destroying prohibition, and hence may be opened on Shabbos even if it has been left closed for a long time.

MICHATEICH & KOREIA: CUTTING AND TEARING ITEMS ON SHABBOS

Based on Shulchan Aruch Chapter 313 and 340

Important Note:
Cutting or tearing an item may involve any of the following Biblical and Rabbinical prohibitions: Cutting, Fixing, Tearing, erasing letters, destroying a vessel, grinding, and doing a mundane act. Below the details of when each prohibition applies will be explained. One is only allowed to tear or cut something on Shabbos if none of these prohibitions are applicable. It is thus incumbent for the reader to read through the entire section prior to deducing permissible forms of tearing and cutting. When explained in the summaries and Q&A below that something is allowed, all the possible prohibitions were taken into account, and thus may be relied upon in actuality.

PROHIBITION #1: THE/KOREAH/TEARING PROHIBITION
The laws of Tearing sewn items and separating glued items on Shabbos

1. The rules of the prohibition and when it applies:
A. The Principal prohibition-Tearing with intent to re-sew:[865]
One who tears [an item] with intent to re-sew it, in the way to be explained below in B, is liable [to bring a sin offering] being that [doing so] is amongst the principal Shabbos prohibitions. As in the Tabernacle a skin curtain which a worm had fallen on and drilled into it a small round hole, [then[866]] in order to sew it one would need to tear the hole from above and below in order so the sewing not be made in overlaps. Thus, one who tears without intent to sew is exempt [from Biblical liability of the sewing prohibition[867]] although doing so is Rabbinically forbidden [as will be explained][868].

B. Tearing without intent to re-sew:[869]
Although one who tears is not liable unless done on condition to re-sew it [afterwards] nevertheless it is Rabbinically forbidden in all scenarios [even when destroyed without intent to re-sew].

C. Tearing with intent to sew but not in a better way than done originally:[870]
One who destroys a building with intent to return and build it, or one who tears with intent to return and sew, is not Biblically liable unless his intent is that the latter building be greater than the former, and by sewing that the [torn] cloth [be re-sewn to a better result than it was originally prior to the tearing]. As without the destroying and tearing it is completely impossible to fix the building and cloth that they be improved.
Other Opinions-Even by destroying no need for improvement:[871] There are opinions which say that even by actions of destruction it is not necessary that the improvement be better than the way it was originally.
Other Opinions-One is liable for work even if not done for use of its body[872]: All the above is in accordance with those who say that an action which is not done for the need of its body one is exempt on and is only Rabbinically forbidden. However, there are opinions which argue on this and say that even work which is not done for the need of its body one is Biblically liable for.

---

[865] Admur 302:4
[866] Lit. and
[867] Admur 317:7: One is not liable for [the] tearing [prohibition] unless he [tears it] with intent to re-sew.
[868] Seemingly, there is no Koreia prohibition by skin tapestries as it is a single entity.
[869] Admur 302:4; 317:7
[870] Admur 278:1
[871] Admur 278:2
[872] Admur 278:3

The Final Ruling:[873] [Due to the above lenient opinion one] therefore does not need to reprimand people who are lenient [to ask a gentile in a time of distress to destroy an item when they do not plan to rebuild it in a better] being that they have upon whom to rely. However, every person should be stringent upon himself like the first opinion which is the main [Halachic] opinion.

D. Prohibition only applies by tearing apart many entities:[874]
(Regarding [the] tearing [prohibition] there is only a prohibition [involved] when one tears and separates many entities which have [become] attached, such as one who tears a garment woven from many threads. However, paper which is a single entity does not contain within tearing it or cutting it the tearing prohibition.[875]) **For other opinions see footnote.[876]**

May one separate the glued areas of a sealed bag or box?
According to those who hold that opening cans on Shabbos is forbidden due to Tikkun Keli, it is to be opened in a destructive manner, just as they rule by cans.[877] However, according to those who hold that cans may be opened in a non-destructive manner then seemingly it is permitted to open an envelope even in the area of the glue, by separating the two parts.[878]

What is the definition of a single entity?
This matter requires further analysis as to its exact definition [i.e. is a modern piece of paper made of dust of wood considered a single entity?]

E. The law if the sewing was only meant to last temporarily:[879]
If a launderer sewed the collar [of a shirt together], or [in a case that] a pair of shoes have been sewed together in the way that is done by professionals, then it is forbidden to cut them or to tear them from each other.
The reason for this is: because by sewing there is no difference whether it was made to last or not to last, and destroying the sewing always contains [the] tearing [prohibition]. Now, although one who tears is not liable unless done on condition to re-sew it [afterwards] nevertheless it is Rabbinically forbidden in all scenarios [even when destroyed without intent to re-sew].
Other Opinions: [However,] there are opinions which allow tearing or cutting stitches that was not made to last.
The Final Ruling: The main Halachic opinion is like the latter opinion, although nevertheless one

---

[873] Admur 313
[874] Admur 340:17
[875] This answers a question raised on the Michaber 340:13 [brought in Peri Megadim and Biur Halacha Ein Shivrim] which writes that if one tears paper, he is liable for Tikkun Keli, and thus the question is asked why one is not liable for also tearing. Thus, Admur suggests that by a single entity it does not apply. However, see next footnote.
[876] The Mishneh Berurah in 340 Biur Halacha "Eiyn Shovrin" argues on Admur and says that the prohibition applies even when tearing a single entity. He suggests answering the question mentioned in the above footnote that the tearing prohibition only applies when there is benefit to both sides being torn, as opposed to by paper that one is tearing it to simply use the torn piece and thus the other side does not benefit. He concludes with a Tzaruch Iyun. To note that there are Poskim [Minchas Yitzchak 1:77] which have learned from this Biur Halacha then when tearing in a way of destruction it is completely permitted. The Tzitz Eliezer seems to side with Admur's ruling, as is evident from his leniency by cotton balls. [see Q&A]
[877] See Piskeiy Teshuvos ibid; Bris Olam Koreia 7; based on Chazon Ish 61:2; SSH"K 28 footnote 14-15
[878] Ketzos Hashulchan ibid
The reason: Although on the onset it seems that doing so should be forbidden due to Koreia, as it is forbidden to separate glued items, as written in 340:17, nevertheless in truth one can argue that in this case it is permitted to do so as a) the prohibition only applies by two entities that are glued together as opposed to a single entity, and b) It was sealed with intent to be opened, and is hence a temporary sealing. [Ketzos Hashulchan ibid]
[879] Admur 317:7

should not be lenient in front of an ignoramus.[880]

Summary: Cutting and tearing sewn threads:
The tearing prohibition applies when one tears or separates two entities from each other, even if one does not intend to reattach them[881], if the attachment was meant to last. The tearing prohibition does not apply by tearing a single entity. If the sewn items were meant to be eventually torn then it may be torn, However, not in the presence of an ignoramus.

❖ *In all cases that there is no tearing prohibition involved in tearing an item one must verify that there is as well no cutting and fixing prohibition involved in doing so.*

Why did the Alter Rebbe bring the first opinion as a Stam to only then not rule like it?
This matter requires further analysis.

---

2. Tearing leather:[882]

It is permitted [for a person[883]] to tear leather that covers the mouth of a barrel of wine [or other liquids[884]] as explained in chapter 314 [Halacha 12], [when done for a Shabbos need. One need not worry (about any tearing prohibition involved in doing so)[885]]

The reason and avoiding the cutting prohibition-340/17: Being that the leather is a single entity, [thus] the tearing prohibition is not applicable to it, but rather only the prohibition to cut it if he is particular to cut it to a specific measurement as explained there [in chapter 314/16].)

The reason- 314/12: A person may tear the hide which [seals] the opening of the barrel of wine when done for ones needs of Shabbos because tearing a detached item is allowed to be done even initially. [If done for no need at all, then it contains a destroying prohibition.]

Avoiding the fixing prohibition: [However, this is only allowed] as long as one does not intend to make something similar to a drainpipe out of the torn skin [i.e. a funnel] being that doing so is considered like fixing a vessel.

Summary:
A piece of leather may be torn if one does not tear it into any specific measurement and does not make it into a new use through tearing it. It is thus permitted to tear the leather cover of a barrel in order to pour from the bottle.

---

3. Separating papers and other items that are glued together:[886]

One who separates attached papers is [liable for doing] an offshoot of [the] tearing [prohibition], as one who attaches papers or skins with glue of the scribes and the like is [doing] an offshoot of the sewing [prohibition] and he is liable [and the tearing prohibition applies to all cases that the sewing prohibition applies].

---

[880] Perhaps from here we can learn a Heter to take apart the bottle caps as the ring was attached for temporary purpose, and hence there is no Tikkun Keli
[881] In such a case it is Rabbinically forbidden. It is Biblically forbidden if torn with intent to re-sew, and according to some only if one has intent to re-sew in a better way than it was originally.
[882] Admur 340:17
[883] Admur 314:12
[884] Admur 314:12
[885] Admur 314:12
[886] Admur 340:17

Separating items which were accidently attached: However, this only applies when the attachment was done for it to last, However, pages of books which have been attached to each other through wax [which fell on them] or at the time of their binding, are permitted to be opened on Shabbos [if one will not be tearing any letters in the process].

The reason for this is: as since [this attachment] was not made to last and furthermore it was done on its own without intent, therefore it is not at all similar to sewing, and it does not contain [the] tearing [prohibition].

Summary-Separating glued items:
It is forbidden to separate glued items if the items were glued to be permanently attached. If they are not meant to be attached and were accidently glued on their own, as occurs during book binding that glue or wax attaches pages together, then they may be separated on Shabbos.

Q&A
May one separate items that were intentionally glued for temporary use?[887]
This may be done, However, not in the presence of an ignoramus as rules Admur regarding tearing a temporary stitch.

May one cut attached pages of a new book which were forgotten to be cut during the binding?[888]
No, [as doing so involves the prohibition of fixing a vessel].

May one tear glued pages of a book if doing so will tear some of the letters or the paper?[889]
Will tear letters: It is forbidden to be done due to the erasing prohibition.
Will tear part of the paper: Some[890] have written against doing so [even according to Admur which holds there is no tearing prohibition in tearing a single entity] due to that it is fixing a vessel.

May one place a band-aid on a wound on Shabbos?[891]
See Practical Q&A below

May one use diapers on Shabbos which are fastened using a piece of tape or Velcro which is attached to the diaper?
See Practical Q&A below!

---

[887] Minchas Yitzchak 8:31
[888] Piskeiy Teshuvos 340:31
[889] SSH"K 28:1 footnote 4; Piskeiy Teshuvos 340:31
[890] SSH"K 28 footnote 5 in name of Rav SZ"A; Piskeiy Teshuvos 340:31. There they write that it contains a tearing prohibition [according to the M"B in contrast to Admur] and a "fixing a vessel" prohibition.
[891] Piskeiy Teshuvos 328:21

Examples [Halacha 4-6]

4. Cutting and tearing threads sewn in for temporary use, such as to attach a pair of shoes together:[892]

See above 1E!

Summary: Cutting and tearing sewn threads:
Threads which were sewn for temporary usage and are meant to be eventually torn may be torn on Shabbos so long as one does not do so in the presence of an ignoramus.

---

5. Removing entangled clothing from thorns:[893]

One whose clothing became tangled in thorns is to remove it *in private*[894] [**see footnote**] and [carefully by] taking his time [to remove it], in order so it not tear. And if it [nevertheless] tears [despite ones being careful] then this is [Halachically] meaningless being that one had no intent to do so and it was not an inevitable occurrence, as since he [was careful to] slowly remove it, it was possible for it not to tear.

6. Breaking an almond using a cloth:[895]

It is permitted to break an almond with a cloth, and we do not suspect that perhaps it will tear, as will be explained in chapter 508 [Halacha 3].

PROHIBITION # 2: TIKKUN KELI-FIXING AN ITEM FOR A USAGE IN THE PROCESS OF CUTTING IT

1. Cutting an item to make a use for it:[896]

Cutting an item with a knife to make a use with it: Although cutting items detached [from the ground] is initially permitted when one is not particular to cut it in a specific measurement, as explained in chapter 314 [Halacha 16[897]] nevertheless if through doing so one fixes the item to be used for a certain use, then he is liable for [the] "fixing a vessel" [prohibition] if he cut it using a knife as was explained in chapter 322 [Michaber Halacha 4] regarding the cutting of a twig[898].
Tearing it with ones hands to make a use of it: If it was done without a knife then one is exempt [from Biblical liability], although it is [Rabbinically] forbidden.

Summary of cutting an item to make it fit for a use:
Is forbidden to be done whether using a knife [in which case it is Biblically forbidden] or one's hands [in which case it is Rabbinically forbidden].

---

[892] Admur 317:7
[893] Admur 302:4
[894] So explains the Karban Haeidah on Yerushalmi 7:2. The reason for this is so it does not appear to others like he is fixing a vessel. However, the Pnei Moshe explains that it means that the case is referring to that thorns got stuck onto his clothing and have penetrated inside [Tzina-private-here means inside] and he desires to remove them to prevent the thorns from causing him pain. Vetzaruch Iyun as to which commentary Admur agrees with.
[895] Admur 302:4
[896] Admur 340:17
[897] There it is explained that cutting wood to a desired measurement is Biblically forbidden.
[898] This will be brought below in Halacha 4

167

2. Breaking earthenware and tearing paper for a use:[899]
Due to the above one may not break earthenware and may not tear paper which is permitted to move [i.e. is not Muktzah] in order to use the [torn or broken piece] for a use due to that doing so is similar to him fixing a vessel. See Chapter 508 [Halacha 2[900]]

> **Summary:**
> It is forbidden to break off a piece of earthenware or a piece of paper in order to make it fit for a use.

3. Cutting a hole into a vessel:
See "The Laws of Building and Destroying" Chapter 1 Halacha 6!

> **Making a hole in a vessel:**
> <u>Is Biblically forbidden</u> when made for both entering and removing items through the hole[901], or when intentionally made into elegant hole[902], due to the prohibition of fixing a vessel. It never carries with it the building prohibition.[903]
> <u>Is Rabbinically forbidden</u> when made for only entering items through the hole, or for only removing items through it.[904]
> <u>Is totally permitted</u> when it is not intended to be made for either entering or removing items through it, and is rather consequently made due to an action that one does.[905]
> <u>May one widen an already existing hole?</u> It carries the same laws as one who initially makes the hole on Shabbos.[906]

4. Examples of cases which involve fixing a vessel:
A. **Tearing an item in the process of barbecuing fish on Yom Tov:**[907]
Tearing a piece of paper to place under the fish: One who roasts fish over a grill is not to cut a piece of paper in order to soak it in water and then place it under the fish over the grill in order to prevent the fish from burning.
Breaking a piece of earthenware to place under the fish: Similarly, one may not break a piece of earthenware in order to place it under the fish.
Breaking open cane to place its sheath under the fish: Similarly, one may not break open a cane in order to place its sheath under the fish.
Making the cane into a skewer: As well, one may not break open the cane to make it into a figure like skewer to roast with.
The reason for all the above restrictions is: because in all cases that one makes and fixes an item to be fit for a use, then it is like he has fixed a vessel on Yom Tov.

---

[899] Admur 340:17
[900] There Admur brings different cases that tearing or breaking an item is forbidden due to one making it now fit for a use.
[901] Admur 314:2
[902] Admur 314:1
[903] Admur 314:5
[904] Admur 314:3
[905] Admur 314:5
[906] Admur 314:2 and 3
[907] Admur 508:2

B. Cutting a vine to fit a use:[908]

Using a vine as a rope to help draw water with: A [detached] vine which has its head split like a fork and is [thus] fit to [use to] hang a bucket on and [use to] draw [water] with [such as to place it down a well to draw water, using the vine as a rope to place it down and bring it back up], then even if one thought about this from before Shabbos to use the [vine] to [help] draw [water] with on Shabbos, [nevertheless] it is forbidden to use it to draw with, unless the vine was tied to the bucket from before Shabbos.

The reason for this is: due to a decree that perhaps the vine will be too long for him, and one will cut it, being that it is soft and easy to be cut, and will thus end up [transgressing the prohibition of] fixing a vessel on Shabbos.

C. May one remove a reed from one's broom?[909]

It is forbidden to remove a reed[910] from a broom which is used to clean the house, being that through removing it he is fixing it for the use that he wishes to use it for, which is for hitting the children with, and [the law is that] any item that one fixes to be used for any use is included in the prohibition of fixing vessels. [Furthermore] even through a gentile it is forbidden to remove it, meaning [to even have him] detach it and remove it out from under the binding area[911] of the broom, and it goes without saying that it is forbidden to [ask a gentile to] break the reed off from the broom, as by breaking it there is an additional prohibition [being transgressed which is] breaking a vessel, as will be explained in chapter 337 [Halacha 3]. However, when one removes out an entire reed [from the broom] there is no [additional prohibition involved] of destroying a vessel, as this is similar to a vessel assembled by placing many pieces together, which does not contain [the prohibition of] destroying [a vessel] when taking it apart, unless the [attached pieces] were inserted [in their sockets] strongly and professionally.

D. Using a twig as a toothpick:[912]

A twig which is not animal food, even to take it in order to pick his teeth is forbidden [due to it being Muktzah, and to cut a piece off is forbidden also due to the fixing a vessel prohibition[913]].

E. Cutting a knot:[914]

Cutting the sewing and knot of a tailor: If the collar of a shirt had already been opened [after being made] but a professional [tailor] returned and sewed [the two sides of the collar] together in the way done by professionals, or if the professional tied it [in a way] that one is unable to untie it, then it is forbidden to cut the strings.

However, this [prohibition to cut an undoable knot] only refers to a knot tied by the professional prior to having finished making the clothing, being that then the cutting of the strings of this knot involves the [prohibition of doing a] "Finishing touch", as this finalizes the work needed to be done to the clothing being that through doing so the clothing is now fit to be worn, while until this was done it was never yet fit to be worn, [and it is thus forbidden as] any [action] done which is the finishing stroke [of the making of the vessel] contains [the prohibition of] "Finishing Touch" as was explained in chapter 302 [Halacha 5]

Cutting the knot of the launderer: However, other knots which were tied after the clothing had finished having its work done to it, such as the knots of the laundering or the strings of a cloak which have been tied and one is not able to undo, [then] it is permitted to cut them.

---

[908] Admur 308:54
[909] Admur 308:55
[910] Lit. a branch
[911] Meaning out from the area where all the reeds have been fixed into.
[912] Michaber 322:4
[913] If done with one's hand it is Rabbinically forbidden, and if done with a vessel is Biblically forbidden. [M"B 13]
[914] Admur 317:6

Nevertheless, even so one may not be lenient [to cut it] in front of an ignoramus, and rather should do it privately.

By a knot made to last 7 days: If one is accustomed to only cut the strings [of the collar knot] upon changing the cloak from Shabbos to Shabbos, then it is forbidden to cut [the strings of the knot] just like it is forbidden to undo it [as will be explained in "The Laws of Tying and Untying on Shabbos"].

Summary: Cutting the strings of a knot:[915]

Anytime it is permitted to open a knot on Shabbos one is likewise permitted to cut it. However, one may not be lenient to cut it in front of an ignoramus, and rather should do it privately. [As well in a case that the knot attaches an item to the ground then the rope may not be torn even if one is allowed to untie the knot being that doing so involves the destroying prohibition.][916] Anytime that the knot is forbidden to be undone, it is likewise forbidden to be cut.

---

5. *Tikkun Keli by foods:*[917]

Animal food [which includes all foods which are edible to animals[918]] does not contain within it [the prohibition of] fixing a vessel [and is permitted to be moved being that it is edible[919]].

Using straw or hay as a toothpick: Therefore, it is permitted to cut even with a knife [even into a particular measurement[920]] straw or hay and [use it] to pick at his teeth [i.e. to use as a toothpick].

Using a twig as a toothpick: However, a twig which is not animal food, even to take it in order to pick at his teeth is forbidden [due to it being Muktzah, and to cut a piece off is forbidden also due to the fixing a vessel prohibition[921]].

Plucking a leaf from a branch to use as a funnel:[922] Plucking a leaf from a detached[923] branch in order to place it into the hole of the barrel, is prohibited due to [the prohibition of] "fixing a vessel", as any item which is altered on Shabbos so it be fit to be used for a given purpose carries with it [the prohibition of] "fixing a vessel".

The reason for why this is forbidden even if the leaf can be used for animal fodder: [924] Even if the leaf is soft and is [thus] fit to be eaten by animals, nevertheless it is prohibited to pluck it due to "fixing a vessel". As [the Sages] only said that [modifying] animal fodder [into a vessel] does not carry with it the prohibition of "fixing a vessel" being that they are soft and do not last, as will be explained in chapter 322 [Halacha 4[925]], in a case that one modifies the food to become an independent vessel, such as cutting a piece of straw to use as a toothpick in which case it is not considered like one is fixing a vessel being that it is not at all common to initially make a vessel out of food, due to the fact that it does not last long. However, it is common to [use food] to modify through it a vessel that is already made, such as to place the leaf in the hole of the barrel which is already made. Therefore, when one plucks [the leaf out from the detached branch] for this purpose this removal carries with it [the prohibition of] "fixing a vessel".

---

[915] Admur 317:6
[916] Admur 314:19
[917] Michaber 322:4
[918] M"B 322:9
[919] M"B 322:10
[920] In which case it would normally contain the cutting prohibition, although here it is allowed being that it is a food, and by foods the cutting prohibition is not applicable. [M"B 322:12]
[921] If done with one's hand it is Rabbinically forbidden, and if done with a vessel is Biblically forbidden. [M"B 322:13]
[922] Admur 314:11
[923] Meaning we do not suspect that one will come to pluck a leaf from a tree, however from a branch that had been previously cut off, we do suspect.
[924] Admur 314:11
[925] Of the Michaber. This chapter of the Alter Rebbe's Shulchan Aruch did not make it to print.

Summary of Tikkun Keli by foods:
All foods that are edible for animals do not contain the Tikkun Keli prohibition and may thus be cut for the purpose of making a use out of the torn piece. It However, may not be cut for the purpose of attaching the food to a vessel.

Q&A

May one fix a vessel through using food parts, such as to carve a piece of vegetable to be fit to be used as a funnel for a barrel?[926]
No, doing so may be Biblically forbidden.

PROHIBITION # 3: MICHATEICH-THE PROHIBITION OF CUTTING AN ITEM TO A REQUIRED SIZE

1. The principal prohibition:[927]
One who cuts hide and is particular to cut it to the exact size that he needs, such as for example he is cutting it for straps and for sandals, this is a principal form of forbidden work, being that in the [process of building the] Tabernacle they would cut the skin of rams or *techashim* to an exact size to be made a cover for the tent.

2. The offshoot prohibition:[928]
Anyone who cuts any given item which is detached [from the ground] and is particular to cut it to a specific size, is [doing an action which is] an offshoot of [the primary] cutting [prohibition].

3. Examples:[929]
Cutting a feather to a specific size: For example, one who cuts off the head of a feather, which is thin and soft and is [thus] fit to be used [to cushion] a pillow or a blanket with, then he is liable if he intends to [use it for this] being that one is particular to cut it to the exact size that is fit for him.

Sanding down a pole: Similarly, one who sands down the head of a wooden pole so that it is smooth and sharp, is liable for [the] cutting [prohibition].

Summary:
It is forbidden to cut an item to a specific measurement due to the Mechateich prohibition.

Does one transgress Michateich if he cuts an item by the dotted line?[930]
No, unless one intentionally desires an exact size.

---

[926] M"B 322:11
[927] Admur 314:16
[928] Admur 314:16
[929] Admur 314:16
[930] See Admur 314:16; Piskeiy Teshuvos 340:34 footnote 308]

PROHIBITION # 4: THE PROHIBITION OF CUTTING AN ITEM TO SMALL PIECES

1. The prohibition to cut an item into small pieces:[931]
By wood: [Furthermore] even if one is not meticulous on the sizes, if he cuts [wood] into very thin pieces in order to light fire [with them], then he is liable for [the] grinding [prohibition].
By Other items: [As well] other detached items ....are only allowed [to be cut] .... if one does not cut them into very small pieces [and only if none of the other explained prohibitions apply].

Summary:
It is forbidden to cut wood or other items to small pieces due to the Grinding prohibition.

Does tearing a piece of paper into small pieces transgress the grinding prohibition?
Seemingly not being that today's papers manufactured from wood dust and there is no prohibition of grinding after grinding. Nonetheless, this would be forbidden due to Muktzah, and perhaps the destroying prohibition.

PROHIBITION # 5: THE PROHIBITION OF DOING A MUNDANE ACT
1. The prohibition of doing a mundane act even if no actual prohibited work is involved:[932]
However, one who cuts [the wood] into big pieces and is not meticulous about their size, then it only contains a Rabbinical prohibition [which was prohibited] because it is a mundane action and [thus] disgraces the Shabbos. [This is prohibited even] when doing so does not contain the [prohibition of] moving Muktzah, such as by wood which was designated for a use and is [thus] prepared to be moved.

Does tearing a piece of paper into large pieces transgress the mundane act prohibition?
This matter requires further analysis. Nonetheless, this would be forbidden due to Muktzah, and perhaps the destroying prohibition.

PROHIBITION #6: THE DESTROYING PROHIBITION
See "The laws of Building and destroying on Shabbos" Chapter 2 Halacha 16 for the full details of this prohibition. The following is its summary:

[931] Admur 314:16; M"A 314:14; M"B 31441
[932] Admur 314:16

One may only destroy a vessel [as opposed to disassemble[933]] if:

    A. It is not attached to the ground

And

    B. It cannot hold 40 Seah

And

    C. It is considered a non-sturdy vessel [or is sturdy but one asks a gentile to break it as will be explained]

And

    D. One does not intend to make a nice-looking opening.

And

    E. One needs to destroy it for a Shabbos need.[934]

PROHIBITION # 7: THE PROHIBITION AGAINST ERASING LETTERS

One may never cut or tear an item with lettering or pictures in a way that the letters or pictures become ruined. For the full details of this subject and its relevant Q&A See "The laws of Writing and Erasing on Shabbos."[935]

CASES OF TEARING WHICH DO NOT CONTAIN ANY PROHIBITION:

1. The conditions needed to be allowed to cut an item on Shabbos:[936]

[Although cutting wood even to big pieces is forbidden due to it being a mundane act, nevertheless] other detached items which cutting is 1) not considered a mundane action are allowed [to be cut] as long as 2) one does not have intent to cut them to a specific size and 3) does not cut them into very small pieces, as well as 4) that it is an item that does not contain [the prohibition of] fixing a vessel in cutting it as will be explained in chapter 340 [Halacha 17][937], [as well as 5) It does not contain the tearing prohibition, as well as 6) It does not contain a destroying prohibition, as well as 7) it does not contain an erasing prohibition].

2. Cutting the strings wrapped or sewed around food:[938]

The string wrapping around a chunk of meat: Based on this it is permitted to cut the knots of a spit which are tied around a lamb or chicken that are roasting on it.

Sewing of stuffed chicken: Similarly, stuffed chickens which are sewed shut one is allowed to cut the string of the sewing.

3. Breaking the rope that secures a cover to its vessel:[939]

Seals that are on vessels, such as a chest of drawers, box and portable tower which have their covering tied to them with a rope, it is permitted to cut the rope even with a knife or undo [the rope even] through taking apart its threads[940], in order to open [the box] to remove its content.

Undoing its knot: It goes without saying that it is allowed to undo the knot as it is not a permanent knot being that it is meant to be constantly removed.

---

[933] Its laws were explained in Halacha 5 above. The only difference between this case and a vessel made up of individual parts is with regards to that the latter is allowed to be destroyed even not for a Shabbos need. [See Ketzos Hashulchan 119 note 18]

[934] The only difference between this case and a vessel made up of individual parts is with regards to that the latter is allowed to be destroyed even not for a Shabbos need. [See Ketzos Hashulchan 119 note 18]

[935] To be available IY"H in Volume 3

[936] Admur 314:16

[937] See also chapter 308 Halacha 54 and 55

[938] Admur 314:16

[939] Admur 314:17

[940] As opposed to untying the actual knot, which will explained below.

The reason that this does not contain a destroying prohibition: Now, although the rope is made to attach the cover to the vessel, and thus when one cuts it or undoes it he is destroying this attachment, [nevertheless] this does not contain the [prohibition of] destroying as the rope [only gives the cover] a weak attachment [to the vessel] being that it is not that strong, and thus when one destroys it one is destroying an incomplete [non-sturdy] vessel [which is allowed as the] destroying [prohibition] only applies by vessels when destroying a complete [sturdy] vessel.

4. The prohibition to break a lock on Shabbos: [941]
See "The Laws of Building and Destroying" Chapter 2 Halacha 16

5. Breaking through woven palm leaf baskets in order to get the food inside: [942]
Baskets that are used for figs and dates, which are vessels that are made from palm leaves and have placed in them figs or dates that have not [yet] ripened in the sun in order so they completely ripen [in the basket], then if the cover is tied to them with a rope, it is permitted to unravel the rope or cut it as explained [in the] above [Halacha].
[Furthermore] even the actual body of these vessels are permitted to be unraveled and cut, as the structure of these vessels which are made of palm leaves are a week structure which is not made to last long, and [thus] when breaking it, it is only considered as if one is breaking hazelnuts and almonds in order to get the food that is in them.

6. Breaking the ropes that tie a door to a pit: [943]
Seals that are on the ground, such as the door of a pit which is tied to it with a rope is permitted to be untied being that the knot was not made to last long, as it is meant to be constantly untied. However, if one is unable to undo the knot then it is forbidden to undo the threads of the rope or to cut it due to [the] destroying [prohibition], as every item attached to the ground has [a] building and destroying [prohibition] even if it is not a complete [sturdy] vessel.
The law by a door not made to last: However, this only applies by a door that is made to last [on the pit] and not be removed on Shabbos, and thus when one wants to open the pit he unties the rope and opens the door [and then replaces it] and does not totally remove the door from there, as it is set to be there for some time. However, if [the door] is not made to last at all then there is no destroying [prohibition] involved neither in unraveling the rope or cutting it, and not even in removing the actual door from it, unless it is a case that the door revolves on hinges and [to remove it] one must remove the hinge from its socket as will be explained.

---

[941] Admur 314:17
[942] Admur 314:18
[943] Admur 314:19

Final Summary

May one cut an item on Shabbos?

It is only permitted to cut an item if **all** of the following conditions are fulfilled:

1. It is a single entity, such as a piece of leather or [non-Muktzah] wood, as opposed to a cloth. Thus, one may not separate two pieces of paper or plastic that has been intentionally glued or sewn together [even not to last[944]].[945]
2. One is not cutting it to a specific measurement.[946]
3. Doing so is not making it useable now for a new use.[947]
4. One does not cut it to very small pieces.[948]
5. One does not break apart any letters in doing so.[949]
6. The item is not considered a sturdy or complete vessel[950], or is but is not meant to last at all[951].
7. Does not contain a mundane act which is a disgrace to Shabbos.[952]
8. One is doing so for a Shabbos need.[953]

Examples:

One may cut the following items in order to take out the food or objects that are within them:

A. A piece of leather that is serving as the cap of a bottle.[954]
B. Strings that are tied around food, such as by a stuffed turkey[955], or that are tied around the cover of vessels in order to secure them onto the vessel.[956]
C. A basket made of weak material which is not made to last long and has food inside.[957]

Practical Q&A

May one cut a tablecloth or garbage bag from a role?

No.[958] See the compilation above in chapter 1 under the section of building and destroying.

May one cut a piece of tinfoil?

No. See the compilation above in chapter 1 under the section of building and destroying.

May one tear a piece of cotton from a cotton ball or cotton sheet?

Doing so is forbidden due to the prohibition of "fixing a vessel" [see footnote regarding the tearing prohibition[959]], and if one is particular to cut it to specific measurements then it is

---

[944] However, if they were sewn not to last, then they may be torn when not in the presence of an ignoramus.
[945] Otherwise, this is a problem of tearing as explained in Chapter 340 Halacha 17
[946] Otherwise, is a prohibition of "Cutting". Halacha 16
[947] Otherwise, it is a prohibition of Fixing a vessel. Halacha 16 here and chapter 340 Halacha 17
[948] Otherwise, it is a prohibition of "Grinding"- Halacha 16
[949] Otherwise, is a prohibition of "Erasing" Chapter 340 Halacha 4
[950] Otherwise, it is a prohibition of "Destroying" Halacha 17
[951] Admur 314:19
[952] Otherwise, it is Rabbinically forbidden. Halacha 16
[953] Otherwise, its problematic due to the destroying prohibition. See Ketzos Hashulchan 119 note 34.
[954] Admur 314:9
[955] Admur 314:16
[956] Admur 314:19
[957] Admur 314:18
[958] The reason: This is forbidden due to the prohibition of Tikkun Keli.
[959] According to the M"B and others [in contrast to Admur] it is also forbidden due to the tearing prohibition. [Minchas Yitzchak 4:45; Tzur Yaakov 152]

also forbidden due to the cutting prohibition.[960] However, there are Poskim[961] who rule that if one is not particular in how large to cut it[962] then it is completely permitted to be done.

May one tear toilet paper?[963]
Doing so is forbidden due to the tearing prohibition [even according to Admur[964]] [as well as the fixing a vessel prohibition[965]], and if it is cut by the perforated lines then it also possibly contains the cutting prohibition.[966] If one has nothing else available, then he should use writing paper [even if Muktzah] to wipe with.[967] If this too is not available, then some Poskim[968] allow one to cut [a larger than needed piece of[969]] toilet paper not on the perforated lines using an **irregularity**. Others[970] say that one is to wipe with it and without tearing it, place it into the toilet and then flush.

May one separate plastic ware which is attached together, such as two plastic spoons which are attached or two yogurts which are attached?[971]
No. This is forbidden due to the fixing a vessel prohibition. [Seemingly However, according to those opinions that permit opening disposable cans likewise here it would be permitted to separate the above disposable items. See "The Laws of Building and Destroying" Chapter 2 Halacha 9 Q&A!]

May one separate a two-part ices?
No. This is forbidden due to the fixing prohibition. [Seemingly However, according to those opinions that permit opening disposable cans likewise here it would be permitted to separate the above disposable items. See "The Laws of Building and Destroying" Chapter 2 Halacha 9 Q&A!]

May one open an envelope?[972]
It is forbidden to open an envelope on Shabbos.[973] Although there are opinions[974] which allow one to do so in a time of great need if he destroys the envelope in the process. It is permitted according to all to tell a gentile that he cannot read the letter until it is opened and have the gentile understand that he wants him to open it.[975]

---

[960] So rules that it is forbidden: Minchas Yitzchak 4:45; Tzur Yaakov 152
[961] Tzitz Eliezer 13:45; Rav Shlomo Zalman Aurbauch in SSH"K 35 footnote 48
[962] So writes Tzitz Eliezer ibid. As otherwise this would be forbidden to be done due to the fixing a vessel and cutting prohibition. Vetzaruch Iyun from Piskeiy Teshuvos and SSH"K in footnote ibid which do not mention how one is to avoid the Tikkun Keli prohibition, and it seems they learn it never applies to begin with. Vetzaruch Iyun Gadol.
[963] Piskeiy Teshuvos 340:28
[964] As the toilet paper is made up of many different pieces. [Nishmas Adam, Az Nidbaru 2:31, as opposed to Chelkas Yaakov 3:123 which stated that according to Admur there is no tearing prohibition involved with paper.]
[965] Pashut
[966] Chelkas Yaakov ibid; Sheivet Halevy 1:115
[967] SSH"K 23:16; Piskeiy Teshuvos 340:28
[968] Chelkas Yaakov ibid; SSH"K 23:16
[969] To avoid the fixing a vessel prohibition. [See Tzitz Eliezer ibid]
[970] Az Nidbaru 2:79
[971] Piskeiy Teshuvos 314:3
[972] Piskeiy Teshuvos 340:29
[973] Ketzos Hashulchan 119 note 34 as although the envelope is considered an un-sturdy structure, nevertheless since there is no Shabbos need involved in opening it, meaning that reading the letter is not a Shabbos necessity, therefore it is forbidden, as destroying a non-sturdy vessel was only allowed in order to remove what is inside for a Shabbos need, as explained in 314:1. So rules M"B 340:41 in name of different Poskim. The Peri Chadash holds that it contains a Biblical prohibition while the Chacham Tzevi maintains that it contains a Rabbinical prohibition.
[974] Chazon Ish, and so leans to rule Rav SZ"A in SSH"K 28 footnote 15; Shut Even Yisrael 16
[975] So rules M"B ibid

May one place a band-aid on a wound on Shabbos?[976]

Doing so may involve the tearing prohibition when opening it and the sewing prohibition when applying it.

Opening the band-aid: Some Poskim[977] rule that the band-aid must have its wrapping as well as its white plastic sheet which covers over the tape, removed from before Shabbos. Removing it on Shabbos involves the tearing prohibition. However, other Poskim[978] hold that the band-aid may even be opened on Shabbos, and doing so involves no suspicion at all of a prohibition. [Seemingly according to Admur it must be removed from before Shabbos.]

Applying the band-aid to the wound: May be done if both sides of the band-aid are fastened to one's skin[979] as opposed to one's clothing or to the other end of the band-aid.[980]

May one use diapers on Shabbos which are fastened using a piece of tape or Velcro which is attached to the diaper?

Velcro diapers: May be used in all cases.

Adhesive tape: This matter is disputed amongst Poskim in whether it is allowed. Some are stringent to prohibit using it even if one opened the tape from before Shabbos. Others are lenient even if he forgot to open it from before Shabbos.

Below is a full analysis on the subject:

The following "Sewing" and "Tearing" related questions apply by diapers which are attached using tape: **1)** Opening up the tape which involves removing the tape from the plastic covering. **2)** Placing the tape onto the diaper when fastening it onto the child. **3)** Removing the tape from the fastened diaper upon changing it. The following is the Halachic rulings in the above.

❖ ***Removing the protective covering from the tape:*** Many Poskim[981] hold that opening the tape is forbidden due to the tearing prohibition[982] and thus may only be done if one had previously opened it before Shabbos. Other Poskim[983] hold that if this was not done then it is allowed to open it on Shabbos.[984]

❖ ***Attaching the diaper to the child:*** Some Poskim[985] hold that placing the tape on the diaper to fasten it is forbidden due to sewing.[986] Many others[987] However, rule that this is allowed being that it is not made to last at all.

❖ ***Removing the Diaper from the child:*** Some Poskim[988] hold that removing the tape

---

[976] Piskeiy Teshuvos 328:21

[977] Minchas Yitzchak 5:39

[978] Beir Moshe 1:36; See Beir Moshe 2:29:2 that it only applies when a third item is sticking two items together.

[979] As there is no sewing prohibition relevant to sticking something to ones skin.

[980] Beir Moshe 1:36

[981] Tzitz Eliezer 16:6; see Minchas Yitzchak 5:39 regarding removing the plastic cover from a band aid in which he rules it is forbidden; Shemiras Shabbos K'hilchoso 15:81; Az Nidberu 13:25; Sheivet Ha'Levi 5:78; Yechaveh Da'as 6:24; Machzei Eliyahu 71; Be'er Moshe 6:14; Chut Shuni Shabbos 1:17 page 137

[982] As it is meant to be attached to the plastic part so long as it is not used. It is thus an attachment that is meant to last some time.

[983] Az Nidbaru 7:34; Yechaveh Daas 6:25

[984] As they hold that if one were to buy the diaper that day then it would be meant to be opened that same day, and thus the attachment of the tape to the plastic part is not really meant to last.

[985] Minchas Yitzchak 8:31; 9:41; Mishneh Halachos 8:60; Kinyan Torah 5:26; Lehoros Nasan brought in Piskeiy Teshuvos 340 footnote 101

[986] As a) The attachment is at the very least considered temporary which is also forbidden in the laws of sewing. [Minchas Yitzchak ibid]. b) Because the tape never gets removed from the diaper as it tears part of the diaper off with it upon opening the tape, and thus regarding that part which gets removed with the tape it is considered a permanent attachment. [Lehoros Nasan, and so ruled to me Rav Asher Lemel Kohen]

[987] Sheivet Halevy 5:31; Az Nidbaru 6:31; Yechaveh Daas 6:25, Tzitz Eliezer 16:6; Beir Moshe 6:14; SSH"K 15:81

[988] Minchas Yitzchak ibid

from the diaper in the process of changing the baby may only be done in private and not in the presence of an ignoramus.[989] Other Poskim[990] rule that one may remove the tape without restriction. According to all one is to avoid re-taping the diaper up after having removed it and then throw it out as is commonly done during the week.

May one cut a piece of tape?[991]

Even according to those which permit in times of need the use of tape to attach a bandage to ones wound, this only applies if the piece of tape was cut from before Shabbos, as cutting it on Shabbos poses a "Cutting" prohibition.[992] [However, the tape may be cut on Shabbos to a larger size than needed, in a case of need, such as for a wound.]

May one cut or tear a bandage to make it a better fit?[993]

Doing so is forbidden due to the "Make Bepatish" prohibition.

May one tear a plastic tablecloth as is accustomed for people to do by a plastic tablecloth when they are bored?

No, due to the destroying prohibition.

For Q&A relating to opening and closing pages of books which have stuck together-See above "Prohibition # 1 Halacha 3

---

[989] As rules Rama and Admur in 317 regarding tearing the sewn stitches of the collar done by the laundry mat to keep it temporarily in place.
[990] Sheivet Halevy 5:31; Az Nidbaru 6:31; Yechaveh Daas 6:25; Tzitz Eliezer 16:6; Beir Moshe 6:14; SSH"K 15:81
[991] Piskeiy Teshuvos 328:21
[992] Tzitz Eliezer 8:15-14-6
[993] Piskeiy Teshuvos 328:21

THE LAWS OF MIMACHEIK/SMEARING

The smearing prohibition "Mimacheik"

1. The general law:[994]

One who smears a poultice[995], which means that he smoothes and levels the grooves that are in it, as well as one who smears wax or tar and anything of the like which is a material that can be smeared down until it smoothens its surface, then this is an offshoot of [the] "smoothing of hide" [prohibition], which is [a prohibition against] scraping the wool or the hair off the hide until its surface is smooth, which is a primary prohibited action being that this was done in the Tabernacle as explained in chapter 302 [Halacha 15].

Plugging a hole with wax: Therefore, one may not seal a hole with wax or similar things even if one does not enter the wax into the hole but rather only places it onto the opening of the hole in which case it does not appear like one is fixing a vessel with this stuffing being that the stuffing is not entering into the thickness of the walls of the vessel of the hole area and rather is only on the opening of the vessel on its back. Furthermore, even if this wax is not prohibited to be moved such as in a case that it was prepared to be used from before Shabbos, nevertheless it is forbidden to seal with it due to a decree that one may come to smear the wax to attach it to the walls of the vessel which surround the hole to the point that he smoothens its surface there and will then be liable for "smoothening".

Plugging a hole with fat or congealed oil: Even with fat or congealed oil it is forbidden to seal with due to a decree [that one may come to seal with] wax. It is forbidden to connive here to [plug with the fat and congealed oil and tell others that] he only intends to hide [the fat in the hole] even if he is a Torah Scholar, as since with wax it is very easily possible for one to come to be liable for a sin offering, [meaning that it is very possible] that he will forget and will smear it in the way it is done usually during the week, in order so that the sealing be well firm, therefore [the Sages] also prohibited [sealing] with fat and oil due to a decree [that one may come to smear with] wax and the like.

2. Spreading and smoothening foods on Shabbos:[996]

The act of spreading and smoothening a food on Shabbos touches upon two different sets of prohibitions; Mimacheik and Boneh. The concept of Mimacheik applies when one smoothens an item and the concept of Boneh applies when one presses an item together.

A. The general law:[997]

It is permitted to smoothen foods on Shabbos and doing so does not contain the Smoothening prohibition.[998] [It likewise does not contain the Boneh prohibition.]

B. Smoothening a food in order to beautify it:

As stated above, from the letter of the law it is permitted to smoothen foods on Shabbos [even for beauty purposes]. Nevertheless, one who is stringent to not smoothen an apple dish [or potatoes[999]] and foods of the like which are commonly[1000] smoothened [in order to better their

---

[994] Admur 314:21
[995] A poultice is any ointment or dressing that is placed on a wound. It commonly is dressed onto a bandage which is then placed onto the wound.
[996] Rama 321:19
[997] Rama 321:19; Mordechai Klal Gadol
[998] The reason: The reason for this is because it is anyways possible to eat the food in its current state [without having smoothened it]. [Rama ibid] Thus it is not relevant to the smoothening prohibition, as the smoothening prohibition only applies in a case that the smoothening fixes the item, similar to that which was done in the Mishkan.
[999] M"B in Biur Halacha "Bemachal"; Ketzos Hashulchan 146 footnote 11.

appearance[1001]] will be blessed.[1002] [However, according to some opinions[1003] this is forbidden from the letter of the law due to the building prohibition.[1004] Practically, we do not rule like this opinion.[1005]]

<u>Foods which are not commonly smoothened</u>:[1006] The above law which states that "one who is stringent is blessed" only applies to commonly spread foods. However, those foods which are not commonly spread are permitted in all circumstances to be spread, even for beauty purposes.[1007]

C. Foods that cannot be eaten without being spread onto another food:[1008]

If the food cannot be eaten without it being spread then it is forbidden to spread this food on Shabbos [for beauty purposes[1009], as explained next].[1010] [This refers to all foods that are generally only eaten as a spread and are not eaten plain, even though they are physically edible even plain. This includes butter, margarine, cream, chocolate spread and the like.[1011]]

D. Spreading for non-beauty purposes:[1012]

It is permitted to spread all foods if there is no beauty intent involved in the spreading. This applies even to foods that are commonly smoothened for beauty.[1013] [This applies even to spreads that are not eaten plain.[1014]]

[1000] Ketzos Hashulchan 146 footnote 11 learns that the "one who is stringent" only applies to commonly spread foods. However, those foods which are not commonly spread are permitted in all circumstances to be spread. See also Shabbos Kehalacha Vol. 3 20:59

[1001] Biur Halacha 321:19 "Bemachal"; Ketzos Hashulchan 146 footnote 11.

[1002] <u>The reason</u>: The reason for this is because when spread to decorate the food then it resembles the smoothening prohibition which is learned from the smoothening of the skins of animals which is done in order to beautify the skin. [Ketzos Hashulchan 146 footnote 11] It is thus forbidden due to appearing like "Mimacheik". [Biur Halacha 321:19 "Bemachol"]

[1003] Kitzur Shulchan Aruch 80:25 regarding egg with onion salad, based on Magen Avraham 340:17; Chayeh Adam 39:1; Minchas Shabbos 80:99

<u>A single food?</u> The above stringency of the above Poskim was written regarding smoothening and beutifying two different foods that have been pressed together and unified to one entity. It is however unclear whether they would hold that smoothening a single food [such as Chumus] would likewise contain a building prohibition in their opinion. Practically, some Melaktim write that it does not apply by a single food according to their opinion. [Shabbos Kehalacha 20:68; Nishmas Shabbos 321:323] Others however write that it applies even in such a case. [Shevet Halevi 6:29; brought in Piskeiy Teshuvos 321:32]

[1004] <u>The reason</u>: As the Magen Avraham 340:17 rules that pressing figs together and smoothening them down to beautify their appearance involves the Building prohibition.

[1005] Daas Torah 321; Shevisas Hashabbos Meameir 12; Cheishev Haeiphod 2:77; Tzitz Eliezer 6:34; Sheilas Shaul 1:58; implication of the opinion of the M"B and Ketzos Hashulchan [146 p. 12] which do not mention this prohibition in their summary and commentary of the above Halacha in the Rama

<u>The reason</u>: As this prohibition of building stated by the Magen Avraham only applies by pressing hard items together and making them into one unit. However, to spread something nicely does not resemble in any way the building prohibition but is rather only proper to avoid due to the smoothening prohibition as rules the Rama. [ibid]

[1006] Implication of Rama ibid; Biur Halacha 321:19 "Bemaachol"; Ketzos Hashulchan 146 footnote 11; Piskeiy Teshuvos 321:31; Shabbos Kehalacha 20:59

[1007] <u>The reason</u>: As in such a case it does not appear like the smoothening prohibition. [Biur Halacha 321:19 "Bemaachaol"] As the entire prohibition of Mimacheik only applies when one is doing so for beauty purposes, as only then is it similar to the smoothening of the hides which was also done for beauty purposes. If, however, it is not done for beauty purposes then it has no similarity to the Mimacheik prohibition done to the hides. Thus, by those foods that it is not common at all to smoothen for beauty purposes, the prohibition of Mimacheik is not applicable even if he intends to do so for beauty purposes. [Ketzos Hashulchan 146 footnote 11]

[1008] Magen Avraham 321:29; Hagahos Smak; Implication of Rama ibid; M"B 321:81; Shabbos Kehalacha Vol. 3 20:59

[1009] See Ketzos Hashulchan 146 footnote 12; Piskeiy Teshuvos 321:31

[1010] <u>The reason</u>: If the food cannot be eaten without the spread then spreading this food contains a Rabbinical "Smoothening" prohibition, and is forbidden to be done even right before the meal, as just as there is a Rabbinical slating prohibition applicable to foods, similary there is a Rabbinical smoothening prohibition applicable to foods. [Peri Megadim 321 A"A 29; M"B ibid] The reason why this prohibition specifically applies in a case that the food cannot be eaten without the smoothening is because in such a case one is fixing the food similar to the fixing that was done to the hides in the Mishkan. [See Ketzos Hashulchan 146 footnote 11]

[1011] Implication of Ketzos Hashulchan 146 footnote 12 which prohibits spreading butter for beauty; Piskeiy Teshuvos 321:31

[1012] Based on Magen Avraham 321:29; M"B 321:82; Ketzos Hashulchan 146 footnote 11 that rule cooked apples may be spread on bread despite the Rama's ruling of "one who is stringent is blessed"

[1013] <u>The reason</u>: As the Tikkun that was done to the skins through the Melacha of Mimacheik was to beautify the skins, and hence if one does not intend to beautify it is not relevant to the prohibition. [Ketzos Hashulchan ibid]

[1014] See Ketzos Hashulchan 146 footnote 12; Piskeiy Teshuvos 321:31 based on M"B ibid allows spreading fat and butter even though they are not eaten plain [Vetzaruch Iyun on Biur Halacha 321:19 "Tavo Alav Bracha" that depends this allowance on whether the food can be eaten without spreading it, hence implying that if it is not eaten without spreading it then in truth it would be forbidden due to Mimacheik.

E. Pressing foods together:

The Boneh prohibition applies likewise to foods.[1015] Gathering foods together and pressing them into a shape in order to beautify them is forbidden due to the Boneh prohibition.[1016] If, however, one does not intend to beautify the food then it is not forbidden due to Boneh.[1017] [Based on this, some opinions[1018] rule that it is forbidden due to the building prohibition to smear foods in order to beautify them.[1019] Others[1020] however argue that this prohibition does not apply to foods that one plans to eat right away and does not apply to single entity foods. It is unclear if the stringent opinions rule stringently even regarding a single entity food.[1021]

Summary:

It is permitted to spread and smear foods on Shabbos if one does not intend to do so in order to beautify the food. If one does intend to beautify the food through spreading it then it is proper to be avoided if it is common to spread this food. [If it is not common to spread the food it is always permitted to spread it.[1022]] If the food is not commonly eaten without it being spread then it is forbidden to spread this food on Shabbos for beauty purposes. This includes butter, margarine, cream, chocolate spread and the like.

Q&A

May one smoothen the top of a dip such as Chumus, Tehina, Chatzilim, mashed eggs, mashed potatoes?[1023]

One may do so for non-beauty purposes. If, however one is doing so for beauty purposes, such as in order for the dip to look fancy, then it is proper to be stringent.

May one smoothen and spread cooked apples onto bread?[1024]

Yes, as one is not doing so for purposes of beauty.

May one spread butter onto his bread?

Yes. One may spread butter throughout the entire slice of bread in order to eat it.[1025] However

---

[1015] Admur 319:26; M"A 319:18; M"B 319:63; Shabbos 95b

[1016] Magen Avraham 340:17; See regarding cheese: Admur 319:26; M"A 319:18; M"B 319:63; Shabbos 95b

[1017] Magen Avraham 340:17

[1018] Kitzur Shulchan Aruch 80:25 regarding egg with onion salad, based on Magen Avraham 340:17; Chayeh Adam 39:1; Minchas Shabbos 80:99

A single food? The above stringency of the above Poskim was written regarding smoothening and beautifying two different foods that have been pressed together and unified to one entity. It is however unclear whether they would hold that smoothening a single food [such as Chumus] would likewise contain a building prohibition in their opinion. Practically, some Melaktim write that it does not apply by a single food according to their opinion. [Shabbos Kehalacha 20:68; Nishmas Shabbos 321:323] Others however write that it applies even in such a case. [Shevet Halevi 6:29; brought in Piskeiy Teshuvos 321:32]

[1019] The reason: As the Magen Avraham 340:17 rules that pressing figs together and smoothening them down to beautify their appearance involves the Building prohibition.

[1020] Daas Torah 321; Shevisas Hashabbos Meameir 12; Cheishev Haeiphod 2:77; Tzitz Eliezer 6:34; Sheilas Shaul 1:58; implication of the opinion of the M"B and Ketzos Hashulchan [146 p. 12] which do not mention this prohibition in their summary and commentary of the above Halacha in the Rama

The reason: As this prohibition of building stated by the Magen Avraham only applies by pressing hard items together and making them into one unit. However, to spread something nicely does not resemble in any way the building prohibition but is rather only proper to avoid due to the smoothening prohibition as rules the Rama. [ibid]

[1021] The above stringency of the above Poskim was written regarding smoothening and beautifying two different foods that have been pressed together and unified to one entity. It is however unclear whether they would hold that smoothening a single food [such as Chumus] would likewise contain a building prohibition in their opinion. Practically, some Melaktim write that it does not apply by a single food according to their opinion. [Shabbos Kehalacha 20:68; Nishmas Shabbos 321:323] Others however write that it applies even in such a case. [Shevet Halevi 6:29; brought in Piskeiy Teshuvos 321:32]

[1022] Ketzos Hashulchan 146 footnote 11; Shabbos Kehalacha Vol. 3 20:59

[1023] Shabbos Kehalacha Vol. 3 20:61; Piskeiy Teshuvos 321:31

[1024] Magen Avraham 321:29, brought in M"B 321:82 and Ketzos Hashulchan ibid

[1025] M"B 321:82

it is forbidden to do so in order to make the bread look fancy.[1026]

May one smear icing onto cake on Shabbos?
Yes. One may smear icing throughout the entire cake in order to sweeten it. However, one is to refrain from further spreading the icing in order to make the cake look fancy.

May one spread cream on a cake using an icing tip to form designs?
Some[1027] have written doing so is forbidden due to the smearing prohibition. This ruling seems puzzling.[1028] Seemingly, to use a plane tip that carries no shape is fine, while to use a shaped tip is proper to be avoided.

May one use a round shaped spoon to take out watermelon or ice cream?
Yes.[1029] However some Poskim[1030] are stringent in this matter.

May one cut fruits and vegetables into shapes such as a circle, square, star etc?
One may cut the items into simple shapes, such as a circle or square. One may not however cut them into more complex shapes such as a star and the like due to the writing prohibition.

---

3. Smearing fat and oil:
<u>Smearing oil:[1031]</u> It is permitted to smear [oil] [**See "The Laws of Smearing Oil" regarding using scented oils**] ....with ones hand over ones entire body for pleasure. [Thus, doing so does not contain the smoothening prohibition.]
<u>Smearing fat:[1032]</u> However one may not smear it with fat because it [causes it to] melt[1033] and is forbidden for the reason explained in chapter 326 [Halacha 10]

4. The laws of smearing saliva on the ground:[1034]
Regarding smearing the saliva on the floor-See "The Laws of Building and Destroying" Chapter 2 Halacha 14!
May one smear saliva on a bench?[1035] It is permitted according to all.
Why is smearing saliva not forbidden due to the smearing prohibition?[1036] It requires analysis why this matter is not forbidden due to the smearing prohibition. One can however say that the smearing prohibition only applies when one's intent is to smear one item on to another, however here that his intent is that it become completely absorbed into the ground [and not remain at all

---

[1026] Ketzos Hashulchan 146 footnote 12; Piskeiy Teshuvos 321:31
<u>The reason:</u> As the M"A ibid rules that foods that cannot be eaten plain are forbidden to be spread, and furthermore, even according to the Rama ibid if done to look fancy and this is commonly done with this food then it is proper for one to be stringent, as stated above that foods which are commonly spread for fanciness one who is stringent to refrain from doing so is blessed, as it appears like smoothening.
[1027] Piskeiy Teshuvos 321:15
[1028] As one is not smearing the icing using a knife and hence how is it similar to Mimacheik or Mimareiach? Is squeezing cream from a tube considered Mimacheik? No, hence the allowance to dab cream for pleasure on one's body.
[1029] Nishmas Shabbos 321:323-324; Piskeiy Teshuvos 321:32; Shabbos Kehalacha Vol. 3 20:68
[1030] Shevet Halevi 6:29 as perhaps it contains the Boneh prohibition according to the Kitzur ibid
[1031] Admur 327:1
[1032] Admur 328:28
[1033] As for why it is not forbidden due to the smoothening prohibition-See "The Laws of melting..." Q&A there where the Ketzos Hashulchan explains why there is no Mimacheik prohibition by soap.
[1034] SHU"A of Michaber 316:11. In Admur these laws are not found.
[1035] M"A 316:24, Levushei Serud on M"A; M"B 316:49
[1036] M"A 316:24, Levushei Serud on M"A; M"B 316:49

over the ground] it thus does not contain the smearing prohibition. [**See footnote for other opinions[1037]**]

General Summary-The Smearing prohibition:[1038]
It is a Biblical prohibition to smear and consequently smoothen wax and material of the like. It is thus forbidden to cover a hole with wax or even congealed oil and fat due to a Rabbinical decree.

Food:[1039] Food does not contain a smoothening prohibition, unless it is impossible to eat without doing so in which case it is Rabbinically forbidden. However, one who is stringent by foods which are commonly smoothened is blessed. This does not apply to spreading spreads on bread.

Q&A
May one squeeze cream out of a tube on Shabbos?
Yes. The squeezing, and consequent smoothening of the tube does not consist of Mimachek as the prohibition only applies when one smoothens one item onto another item, or one removes items from on top of the items in order to smooth it, or one smoothens an item into itself with intent to beautify it. However, if indeed one intends to smoothen then tube in order to beautify it then perhaps it would be forbidden.

Does washing one's hands with a bar of soap contain the smoothening prohibition [Mimacheik]?[1040]
Regarding the smoothening prohibition some Poskim[1041] rule by soft soap it applies and thus would be forbidden to use according to all opinions. Others[1042] hold that it only applies if there is a visible amount of soap left one one's body. If, however, the soap is absorbed into one's skin then the smoothening prohibition does not apply. The Ketzos Hashulchan[1043] however, as well as other Poskim[1044] argue that there is no smoothening prohibition applicable in such a case for variety of reasons [see footnote[1045]]. In any event the custom is not to wash at all with a bar of soap being we are stringent like the opinion which holds that doing so involves a Nolad prohibition.

[1037] However the Elyah Raba learns that according to Rashi:Ran:Tur there is a smearing prohibition involved. The Daas Torah concludes that one may certainly be lenient like the Magen Avraham in a case that one is smearing saliva for one who is sick. To note that this dissenting opinion of the Elyah Raba is not recorded by the M"B.

[1038] Admur 314:21

[1039] Rama 321:19

[1040] Based on mainly Ketzos Hashulchan 146 footnote 32

[1041] M"B in name of Tiferes Yisrael, brought in Ketzos Hashulchan 127 footnote 13. Vetzaruch Iyun from his later ruling brought in footnote below. One must say that he retracted his ruling. See as well Daas Torah brought next.

[1042] Daas Torah 326:26 brought in Minchas Yitzchak 7:20

[1043] 146 footnote 32

[1044] SSH"K 14 footnote 49, in name of RSZ"A and others.

[1045] A) It's a Melacha which is not needed for itself [Eino Tzarich Legufa] being that the source of the Memacheik prohibition is by smoothening the skin of an animal which benefits the skin. This is opposed to here where the smoothening of the soap does not benefit the soap but rather is done for the person to use the dissolved layer. B) Since the inevitable smoothening of the soap serves no benefit, as it makes no difference to oneself whether it is smooth or not, it is therefore allowed to be done even Rabbinically, as by Mimacheik if one has no intent to benefit the item from the smoothening than it is not considered a Melacha at all, similar to the ruling regarding pouring cold water into a plastic cup [brought in "The Laws of Cooking Halacha 1 Q&A there!] C) It is done in a way of its normal use, and just like we say regarding food prohibitions that when done in its way of eating it is allowed, the same applies by soap when used in the midst of bathing.
Vetzaruch Iyun based on this why we needed the Magen Avrahams explanation for why smearing saliva is permitted, as reasons a/b as well apply by saliva and thus it should be permitted without needing the Magen Avrahams explanation.

May one smear a cream onto one's skin[1046]?[1047]

This may only be done to a child [not older than age 9[1048]] or to one who is bedridden or ill[1049], **and** only if it is a type of cream which needs to be rubbed completely into the skin and it is not meant to leave any visible cream on the skin.[1050] If the cream is common to be left visibly on the skin then it is forbidden to be smeared. [However, see Beir Moshe[1051] which rules that one should not smear the cream even in a case that it is meant to be absorbed into the skin and rather is only to be dabbed.]

May one smear oil or gel on the skin on Shabbos for purposes of lubrication?[1052]

Oil:[1053] It is permitted to smear oil on one's skin on Shabbos. Thus, one may use oil, such as baby oil as a lubricant, without restriction. [Unlike a common misconception, there indeed is no smearing prohibition at all involved in rubbing liquid oil on one's body, as this prohibition is limited only to thick substances that need to be evened when on top of a surface, such as melted wax, lard, and various creams.]

Gel: It is Rabbinically forbidden to smear gels or creams on the skin on Shabbos due to the smearing prohibition.[1054] Thus, one may not use a lubricant gel on Shabbos. One is not to even dab it onto the skin, even if he does not plan on smearing it with his hands.[1055] [In the event that one does not have any oil available, and is in need for lubricant to facilitate

---

[1046] Doing so may involve a smearing prohibition, as well as a taking medicine prohibition. Due to the medicine prohibition, it may never be done to one who is not defined as bed ridden or weak in his entire body.

[1047] Minchas Yitzchak 7:20; Piskeiy Teshuvos 328:18; Vetzaruch Iyun from Piskeiy Teshuvos 327:1 which contradicts this ruling here and rules that it is always forbidden.

[1048] Regarding all the opinions in the age of the child-See "The Laws of taking Medicine" Chapter 2 Halacha 6

[1049] This applies even if the cream is not a medical lotion and thus does not contain any healing prohibition when placed, as there are opinions which hold that the smoothening prohibition applies even in a case that the cream is completely absorbed, and it is only in a case of an ill person that the Daas Torah said one may be lenient like the Magen Avraham [see Minchas Yitzchak 7:20]. [Seemingly however according to the Magen Avraham and those Poskim which rule likewise, such as the Mishneh Berurah, one may absorb non medical cream onto a healthy person.]

[1050] As in such a case there is no smoothening prohibition, as is proven from the fact that no smoothening prohibition was mentioned regarding soap, or by saliva, as explains the Magen Avraham ibid. [Daas Torah brought in Minchas Yitzchak ibid]. However see above that some Poskim hold that there is no smoothening prohibition at all by soap and that is the reason that no prohibition was mentioned. [However according to Ketzos Hashulchan ibid which argues that there is no smoothening prohibition by soap, seemingly here too it would be allowed even if the cream is visible, if one is bedridden or for a child, while by a cream placed for pleasure it would allowed in all cases.]

[1051] 1:36-4 and 2:29-3

[1052] See Sheyikadesh Atzmo 12:9

[1053] Admur 327:1-2; Michaber 327:1-2; 328:22; Mishneh Shabbos 111a and 134b and 147a

[1054] Admur 314:21 regarding thick fat and the same applies to a gel;
Regarding a cream or gel that is meant to be completed absorbed within the skin, some Poskim are lenient: See Minchas Yitzchak 7:20 in name of Daas Torah; Piskeiy Teshuvos 328:18. This allowance, however, would not apply in this case of lubrication for purposes of intimacy, in which one desires it to not become absorbed in the skin.

[1055] Admur ibid regarding wax that may not even dab in the opening of the hole and the implication is that the same applies to thick oil or fat, that it too may not be even placed on, thus implying that one may never dab a gel due to that on e may come to smear it [However, Tzaruch Iyun from Admur 328:27 who omits this prohibition, and thus perhaps one can conclude according to Admur that in general dabbing the gel is permitted, and it is only in the specific case where wax is commonly used that we prohibit even gel. Nonetheless, in this case it should be forbidden evena ccoirdng to Admur, as he ends up smearing the gel with his body, as explained below]; Implication of Michaber 314:11; Rosh Shabbos 33 and M"B 252:38 [forbids placing thick Kilor on eye because may come to smear]; M"B 314:46; Hilchos Shabbos Beshabbos 3:169; Avnei Yashpei 2:32; Piskeiy Teshuvos 314:11; Shevet Halevi 4:33 in his conclusion is only lenient in time of need;
The reason: As if one dabs it he may come to smear it as he usually does. [Admur ibid regarding wax; M"B ibid and ibid] Furthermore, the intercourse causes the gel to become smeared, and one intends for this to happen in order to benefit from the lubricant.
Other opinions: Some Poskim rule that one may dab gel on the skin on Shabbos without smearing it. [Implication of Admur 328:27 who omits reason of Rosh and M"B ibid that one may come to smear; Chazon Ish O.C. 52:16; Shevet Halevi 4:33 in his initial ruling permits dabbing using tube as it's a Shinuiy, and concludes that for the sake of healing Choleh Sheiyn Bo Sakana one may be lenient and also in a time of great need; SSH"K 33:14; Piskeiy Teshuvos 328:20; Beir Moshe 1:36-4; 2:59; 3:155] However, seemingly in this case one should be stringent according to all, as one intends for the dabbed product to be smeared when he penetrates her, and hence smearing will intentionally occur one way or the other.

intimacy, then one may simply water down the gel inside of a cup of water, and then spread the watered-down substance on the skin.[1056]]

May one dab a cream on one's body without smearing it?[1057]
See compilation at the end of this chapter!
When done for medical treatment [such as treating dryness] then when using a medical cream[1058] this may only be done to a child [not older than age 9[1059]] or to one who is bedridden or ill. Thus, Vaseline may not be dabbed on dry lips.

May one apply Vaseline to dry lips on Shabbos?
Vaseline may not be applied onto dry lips even if one will merely dab it on as opposed to smearing it, due to the healing prohibition. However, some Poskim[1060] rule that it may be dabbed on fresh skin or lips for mere pleasure. It may not be smeared due to a possible smearing prohibition.[1061] *See compilation at the end of this chapter!*

May one brush his teeth on Shabbos?[1062]
One may place a creamy toothpaste on his hand and then smear it on his teeth[1063], although it is forbidden to place it directly on a toothbrush and then smear it, as doing so is a mundane act. However, the custom is not to brush at all one's teeth on Shabbos.

May one remove wax blotches [as well as other forms of blotches] from letters of a Sefer Torah and does it invalidate the Torah?
> *First Opinion:[1064]*
> If there is wax [or other blotch] on a letter and the letter is not recognizable due to this then the sefer is invalid and another Sefer Torah must be taken out.[1065] However if the wax is dry enough that folding the parchment between the wax will cause the wax to flick off, then this may be done, and one may continue reading from it.[1066] One may not remove the wax with his hands due to the Mimacheik/smoothening prohibition.[1067]
> *Second Opinion:[1068]*
> One should not remove the wax in any case and should rather read that letter orally and continue with the reading.

[1056] Or Letziyon 2:36-6
[1057] Piskeiy Teshuvos 328:20 in name of Chazon Ish, SSH"K 33:14; Beir Moshe 1:36-4
[1058] As opposed to a cream which is commonly used for pleasure, such as body lotion, in which case since its medical treatment is not recognizable it may be dabbed even if it contains healing powers. [See "The Laws of medicine" chapter 2 Halacha 7]
[1059] Regarding all the opinions in the age of the child-See "The Laws of taking Medicine" Chapter 2 Halacha 6
[1060] Beir Moshe 1:36-4; 2:29-3
[1061] See Beir Moshe [1:36-4] where he discusses reasons for why it should be permitted to smear vaseline being that it is too soft of an item to contain the smearing prohibition as well as that its main intent is to be absorbed within the skin. However in his conclusion he rules not to be lenient to smear it and rather may only dab it. See also Beir Moshe 2:29-3. Vetzaruch Iyun from Ketzos Hashulchan ibid regarding if this really contains smearing.
[1062] Ketzos Hashulchan 138 footnote 31; See Piskeiy Teshuvah 326/3 for all details
[1063] Doing so is not a problem of smearing being that the prohibition only applies if one smoothens out the bumps of which there is no concern regarding ones teeth. However a thick toothpaste is forbidden due to Nolad as it becomes liquidly when placed in the mouth.
Other Poskim: Some Poskim rule it is forbidden to smear toothpaste on one's teeth due to the smearing prohibition. [Igros Moshe 1:112]
[1064] Shvus Yaakov 2:4; Ketzos Hashulchan 144 footnote 1; Sharreiy Efrayim; Kitzur Shulchan Aruch.
[1065] So rules Ketzos Hashulchan ibid in name of Shaareiy Efrayim and Rav Akiva Eiger.
[1066] As this proves that the wax never really covered the letter, as explains Shvus Yaakov in his Teshuvah there.
[1067] Shvus Yaakov ibid and Ketzos Hashulchan ibid [Vetzaruch Iyun based on this as to why is cleaning dishes or cleaning eyeglasses not forbidden due to Mimachek!]; However, Rav Akivah Eiger writes that the reason is because of Tikkun Keli. See Ketzos Hashulchan ibid which argues that in this case there is no problem of Tikkun Keli. Why
[1068] M"B 10

May one remove glue from one's skin on Shabbos?[1069]

Yes.[1070] However there are those which are stringent in this just as they are in regard to removing ink blotches.

May one enter ear plugs into his ears on Shabbos?[1071]

➤ *Sponge:*[1072]

Yes. There is no resemblance of a prohibition in doing so.[1073]

➤ *Wax:*[1074]

Some opinions[1075] forbid doing so due to the smearing prohibition as well as a possible fixing a vessel prohibition, being that he has to form the wax around his ear and in the hole for it to properly close out the noise. Others[1076] permit doing so if it was prepared before Shabbos for the measurement of one's ear hole, as in such a case there is very minute smearing that must be done, and such a minute amount is insignificant.

May one play with play dough and the like on Shabbos?[1077]

No. It is forbidden even for children to play with play dough and the like due to the smearing prohibition. It is thus Muktzah.

Compilation-May one dab gel or cream on the skin on Shabbos?[1078]

May one dab cream on a baby's red bottom on Shabbos? May one dab Vaseline on dried lips on Shabbos?

A. Introduction:

Placing a cream or gel on one's skin on Shabbos touches upon two possible Shabbos prohibitions, one being the Biblical smearing prohibition and the second being the Rabbinical medicine prohibition. The following are the general details of each these prohibitions:

Smearing prohibition: It is Rabbinically forbidden to smear gels or creams on the skin on Shabbos due to the smearing prohibition.[1079] The question however is asked regarding dabbing the cream or gel on the body and as to whether this is considered similar to smearing or not, as will be explained in B.

The medicine prohibition: It is forbidden to apply medicine to one's body on Shabbos, if it is

---

[1069] Piskeiy Teshuvos 140:3

[1070] Doing so does not contain the Mimacheik prohibition, as it does not apply to one's skin.

[1071] Piskeiy Teshuvos 314:6. It is a wonderment that he does not make mention of the ruling of the SSH"K regarding the wax ear plugs!

[1072]

[1073] Pashut and so rules Piskeiy Teshuvah 314:6 footnote 22.

[1074]

[1075] SSH"K 14:39

[1076] Shraga Hameir 5:23

[1077] SSH"K 16:13; Piskeiy Teshuvos 314:6

[1078] See Piskeiy Teshuvos 314:11; 328:45; Sheyikadesh Atzmo 12:9

[1079] Admur 314:21 regarding thick fat and the same applies to a gel

Regarding a cream or gel that is meant to be completed absorbed within the skin, some Poskim are lenient: See M"A 316:24; Daas Torah 328"26; Minchas Shabbos 92:30; Minchas Yitzchak 7:20 in name of Daas Torah; Nefesh Chayah 327; Maor Hashabbos 4Michtav RSZ"A 52; SSH"K 33 footnote 64; Piskeiy Teshuvos 328:18 [45 in new edition]. This allowance, however, would not apply if the cream is common to be left visibly on the skin then it is forbidden to be placed.

recognizable that one is doing so for the medicinal purposes.[1080] Accordingly, it is forbidden to place medicinal cream or gel on one's body due to the medicine prohibition, even if one simply dabs it on and does not smear it, and we follow the approach that dabbing medicine does not consist of a smearing prohibition.[1081] However, if the person is defined as a Choleh Sheiyn Bo Sakana [i.e. bedridden, or weak in his entire body, or dangerous wound] then it is permitted for such a person to take medicine on Shabbos, and hence there is no medicine prohibition involved in dabbing medicinal cream onto the body in such a case.[1082] However, nonetheless, it may involve the smearing prohibition as stated above, and as will now be clarified.

B. The law:

Some Poskim[1083] rule that it is permitted to dab a cream or gel on the body, without smearing it, if it is not being done for medicinal purposes. If, however, it is being done for medicinal purposes, then it is only permitted to be done if the person is defined as a Choleh Sheiyn Bo Sakana [as explained above in A]. Other Poskim[1084], however, rule that it is Rabbinically forbidden to even dab a gel or cream onto the skin due to the smearing prohibition, and it is thus forbidden to be done even for non-medicinal purposes.[1085] Practically, one is not to even dab gels or creams onto his body due to a possible smearing prohibition, and if done for medicinal purposes then due to the medicine prohibition, even if he does not plan on smearing it with his hands. However, in a time of great need, such as a person who is sick for whom the medicine prohibition is suspended, then one may be lenient to dab the cream or gel on the body.[1086] [One may dab it on directly from the tube, or through placing it on the finger or cue tip and then dab it.[1087]]

Dabbing gel or cream on a baby: All babies are defined in Halacha as a Choleh Sheiyn Bo Sakana, to which the medicine prohibition does not apply.[1088] Accordingly, it is permitted to dab medicinal cream or gel onto a baby's red bottom, or other skin ailment.[1089] This applies even if the cream ends up getting smeared when one closes the diaper.[1090] Some Poskim[1091] rule that one may be lenient in this regard for all children until age nine.

[1080] Admur 327:1 and 328:28; Michaber 327:1; Mishneh Shabbos 111a
[1081] See Minchas Yitzchak 7:20; Piskeiy Teshuvos 328:18
[1082] Admur 328:19
[1083] Possible implication of Admur 328:27 who omits reason of Rosh and M"B ibid that one may come to smear; Chazon Ish O.C. 52:16; Shevet Halevi 4:33 in his initial ruling permits dabbing using tube as it's a Shinuiy, and concludes that for the sake of healing Choleh Sheiyn Bo Sakana one may be lenient and also in a time of great need; SSH"K 33:14; Piskeiy Teshuvos 328:20; Beir Moshe 1:36-4; 2:59; 3:155
[1084] Possible implication of Admur 314:21 regarding wax that may not even dab in the opening of the hole and the implication is that the same applies to thick oil or fat, that it too may not be even placed on, thus implying that one may never dab a gel due to that one may come to smear it [However, Tzaruch Iyun from Admur 328:27 who omits this prohibition, and thus perhaps one can conclude according to Admur that in general dabbing the gel is permitted, and it is only in the specific case where wax is commonly used that we prohibit even gel]; Implication of Michaber 314:11; Rosh Shabbos 33 and M"B 252:38 [forbids placing thick Kilor on eye because may come to smear]; M"B 314:46; Hilchos Shabbos Beshabbos 3:169; Avnei Yashpei 2:32; Piskeiy Teshuvos 314:11; Shevet Halevi 4:33 in his conclusion is only lenient in time of need;
[1085] The reason: As if one dabs it he may come to smear it as he usually does. [Admur ibid regarding wax; M"B ibid and ibid]
[1086] All Poskim ibid in lenient opinion; Shevet Halevi ibid; Piskeiy Teshuvos 328:45 [see there footnote 367 in name of Beir Moshe 2:30 that this includes for the need of Onah-Vetzaruch Iyun!]; See Admur 328:19 that one may do a Rabbinical prohibition with a Shinuiy for the sake of a Choleh Sheiyn Bo Sakana and Shevet Halevi ibid that dabbing it on is considered a Shinuiy.
[1087] Beir Moshe 2:30; Orchos Rabbeinu 1:158; Piskeiy Teshuvos 328:45 footnote 368; Accordingly, in order to facilitate a full Shinuiy that will not accidentally cause smearing, one should dab it on directly from the tube.
[1088] Admur 328:22
[1089] See Beir Moshe 1:36, brought in Piskeiy Teshuvos 327:1; Minchas Yitzchak 7:20; Piskeiy Teshuvos 328:18
[1090] See Piskeiy Teshuvos 328:45 footnote 370
[1091] Minchas Yitzchak 1:78; SSH"K; See Shabbos Kehalacha Vol. 1 p. 214
Other opinions: Some Poskim say that it is dependent on if he still needs to be fed foods by his mother. Thus, once the child begins eating like an adult [on his own] then he is no longer considered like one who is ill. [Ketzos Hashulchan 134 footnote 18; Aruch Hashulchan 328:20] Other Poskim rule that the child is only considered like an ill person until the age of 2-3. [Sheivit Halevy, Chazon Ish, Rav SZ"A] Other Poskim rule that the child is only considered like an ill person until the age of 6. [Tzitz Eliezer 8:15-12]

<u>Dabbing Vaseline on lips</u>: Vaseline may not be applied onto dry lips even if one will merely dab it on as opposed to smearing it, due to the healing prohibition. It certainly may not be smeared due to a possible smearing prohibition.[1092]

<u>Dabbing medicinal cream on a wound</u>: Any open wound that is prone to infection may have antiseptic ointment dabbed on it on Shabbos.

Summary:
One may dab a cream or gel onto the skin if it is being done one behalf of a child under age nine, or for one who is sick or weak in his entire body, or on behalf of a potentially dangerous wound. One may not dab a cream or gel on the body for other medicinal purposes, such as chapped lips and the like. One is to be stringent not to dab the cream or gel for even non-medicinal purposes.

Good advice-Water down the gel:[1093]
In all cases that dabbing gel or cream on the body is avoided even for non-medicinal purposes due to the potential smearing prohibition, one may simply water down the gel inside of a cup of water, and then spread the watered-down substance on the skin, if it is not being done for medicinal purposes.

[1092] See Beir Moshe [1:36-4] where he discusses reasons for why it should be permitted to smear Vaseline being that it is too soft of an item to contain the smearing prohibition as well as that its main intent is to be absorbed within the skin. However, in his conclusion he rules not to be lenient to smear it and rather may only dab it. See also Beir Moshe 2:29-3. Vetzaruch Iyun from Ketzos Hashulchan ibid regarding if this really contains smearing.

[1093] Or Letziyon 2:36-6

OHEL-THE LAWS OF MAKING AN OHEL

Setting up and dismantling tents, tables, makeshift walls, curtains, and all other forms of a hovering or divider on Shabbos

Based on Shulchan Aruch Chapter 315

Translation
Shulchan Aruch Chapter 315

TRANSLATION-CHAPTER 315
Matters forbidden due to building a tent on Shabbos.
20 Halachas

Introduction:
The following chapter will discuss the laws of setting up dividers and roofing's on Shabbos. A roofing is defined as any item which hovers over a surface, such as an umbrella, or a tent, or a table. The problem involved in setting up the above items on Shabbos is because it is a subcategory of the building prohibition[1]. At times it is Biblically forbidden at others only Rabbinically and at others it is even initially allowed to be done. These details will be discussed in this chapter.

Putting up a roofing for protection purposes

Halacha 1
The law: It is forbidden to make a tent, which refers to [any] roofing which hovers over a person in order to guard him from a given matter, such as [to protect him] from the sun or from the rain or from another given matter.

The prohibition applies even by a temporary tent which has no walls: [This applies] even if [the roof] is temporary [meaning] that it is not made to last and even if there are not any walls under it, such as is the case with one who spreads a mat over four poles. Nevertheless, since it is made in order to tent and protect it is [therefore considered] a complete tent and the Sages prohibited it even though it is [only] temporary due to a decree [that one may come to make] a permanent tent which is an offshoot of [the] building [prohibition].

Halacha 2
Adding to a temporary tent that was made before Shabbos: The [Sages] only forbade to initially [make a tent] on Shabbos, however if a temporary tent had been made from before Shabbos then it is permitted to add to it on Shabbos, such as for example if the mat was spread out from before Shabbos a handbreadths worth, which is the measurement required for [a roofing item to be] considered a tent, then it is permitted to open it completely on Shabbos and to add more mats to it, as all this is only adding to the handbreadth tent which was made the day before. [Furthermore] even to spread it over walls is allowed in this case.

Is the rolled up material included in the handbreadth? This measurement of a handbreadth that was mentioned does not include the rolled material, meaning that even if it was rolled up and placed [on walls] from before Shabbos and there is in the thickness of the circumference of the rolled material the amount of a handbreadth and more, nevertheless there needs to be coming out of [this roll] a handbreadths worth of material spread out for tenting.

The reason for this is: because the circumference of the rolled material does not appear like a tent at all.

Setting up dividers [makeshift walls] on Shabbos:

Halacha 3
When done for shade, privacy, to prevent cold and similar purposes it is permitted: All the above refers to making a tent which is a roof, however it is permitted to initially make temporary dividers on Shabbos. [Furthermore] even if one makes it in order to protect himself from the sun or the cold it is not considered like a tent because of this. Similarly [it is allowed even] if one made it in order to prevent the candles from extinguishing in the wind. It goes without saying that it is allowed to make a divider for mere privacy [purposes, such as] so that one not sit in a revealed area, or such as the dividers which are made during speeches to separate between the men and women, and so too for anything similar to this.

Using dividers to separate domains and thus remove a prohibition: There is never be a case that [making] a temporary divider would be forbidden with exception to if made in order to Halachically legalize the status of a Sukkah as will be explained in chapter 630 [Halacha 12 in Michaber/Rama] or [when done] to

---

[1] Halacha 1

permit carrying [an object in an otherwise public domain] in the way explained in chapter 362[2] [Halacha 13] or [when done] to remove other prohibitions [from being effective] such as for example one who places a divider the height of ten handbreadths [80 cm] in front of Torah books, [such as] by spreading out a sheet or mat, in order to be allowed to have marital relations in that room or in order to go to the bathroom there, then it is forbidden to make these dividers on Shabbos.

The reason for this restriction is: because in every situation that a divider permits [one to do something] [it is because] it divides that area into its own separate domain, such as [in the case that] it permits one to carry [in the surrounded area] it is because it turns that area into a private domain and separates it from the public domain or Karmalis which encompasses. Similarly, regarding a room with Torah books, [the dividers] divide [the room] into two domains [as] the holy books are [now] in one domain and his marital relations or bathroom use is [being done] in another domain. Thus, since one is making it in order to divide [that area] into its own separate domain, [therefore] this is considered like he is making a tent.

Placing up dividers which separate domains in a case that one does not need to do so in order to remove the prohibition: However, if one does not need [the dividers] to separate the [area] into its own domain then its allowed to initially make it on Shabbos, even if it [consequently] removes a prohibition.

For example, one who positions a divider in front of a light in order so he be permitted to have marital relations, [then since] it is not necessary [here] to have separate domains [to permit intercourse] and rather as long as the separation extends above the light in a way that one cannot see the light from the area that he will have intercourse and as long that [the divider] is slightly thick to the point that the light cannot be well seen through the separation, then it is allowed to have intercourse even if [the divider] is not the height of ten handbreadths and thus does not separate [that area] at all into its own domain.[3] Furthermore [one is allowed to have intercourse even] if [the separation] is not tied on well enough to the point that the wind will not be able to move it, as is required when making a separation in order to separate domains, such as [when having relations in the same room as] Holy Books as was explained in chapter 240 [Halacha 6 in Michaber/Rama]. [Therefore] since one does not need [the dividers] to make a separate domain it is permitted to make it even in a way that it separates the domain, as is the case when [the divider] is higher than ten handbreadths and is tied well.

Halacha 4
Scenario in which it is allowed to place a divider by the Torah books in one's room:
The same applies with [making a separation in one's room that contains] Torah Books, that if one hangs the separation across from all the Holy Books in a way that [the books] are not revealed at all[4], in which case one does not need to make [that area into] a separate domain if one has another cover over the Torah books aside from this separation, and thus even if this divider is not ten handbreadth high and is also not tied well and thus does not separate [the area of books into its own] domain at all, nevertheless [it is valid] as this [divider] is no worse than [having] a mere covering [over the books]. It is thus permitted for one to use the bathroom there or even have intercourse if there is another cover on the Torah Books besides for the divider, as there are here two covers [over the books] and it is like a vessel within a vessel. Therefore, it is allowed to place this divider on Shabbos even in a way that will separate [that area into its own] domain since one does not need it to separate the domains. It thus goes without saying that it is allowed to cover the Torah Books with two coverings of clothing being that there is no divider here at all.

Halacha 5
Adding to an already existing divider
In all scenarios that it is forbidden to initially place a separation over the Torah Books and the like, it is nevertheless permitted to add to a separation that was placed before Shabbos: [Furthermore] even if the

---

[2] There it explains regarding carrying on Shabbos in a public property that one may not make dividers surrounding him in order to give the surrounded area a status of a Private domain and thus be allowed to carry there.

[3] As a divider only has the power to make a domain if it is 10 handbreadths tall and is sturdy enough to not be moved in the wind.

[4] Meaning that although it does not actually touch the books it nevertheless blocks one from seeing any of them.

books are revealed from above the divider in which case the divider is not considered a covering, or [if it is but] there is no other covering on the books and one wants to have intercourse and thus needs the separation to be a height of ten handbreadths and be tied as Halachically required in order to make that area into a separate domain, and similarly in any scenario that one wants to make a separation in order to create a separate domain, then it is prohibited to initially do so on Shabbos. However, if it was [already] made from before Shabbos the measurement of a handbreadth then it is allowed to extend it on Shabbos being that adding to a temporary tent is permitted.

[This applies] whether the handbreadth [of the divider] is from top to bottom, such as mats which are wrapped on a [horizontal] bar from before Shabbos and the amount of a handbreadth [of the mat] extends beneath it from before Shabbos, then it is permitted roll it all down on Shabbos and tie it as is Halachically required. [Similarly, this also applies] whether this handbreadth [extends] from the side, such as if a divider from the side extended in front of the books the width of a handbreadth then it is allowed to hang sheets if front of [the books] on Shabbos being that the sheets are an addition to a temporary tent. Now, although the divider that extends [to the side] is permanent, [nevertheless] this does not pose a problem as explained in chapter 313 [Halacha 1] that there is only a prohibition [in adding to a tent] when the addition is permanent.

Halacha 6
The prohibition to make a permanent divider:
All the above [allowances in putting up dividers] is only with regards to temporary dividers, however a permanent divider is forbidden in any scenario even if one only does so for mere privacy. [Furthermore] even to add on to [an already existing divider or tent] a permanent addition is forbidden in all scenarios.
Placing up decorative sheets: Nevertheless, it is permitted to hang decorative sheets even though that they [will be] permanently [placed there] being that they are not meant to serve as separations.

Halacha 7
Hanging sheets and other items that move in the wind as a separation:
Placing door curtains in doorways on Shabbos: Door curtains which [are sheets that are] hung in front of a doorway in substitute for a door, then even though they hang there permanently it is allowed to hang it on Shabbos, as since it moves and swings with a common breeze and also does not prevent people from walking through it[5], therefore it is not considered a permanent separation but rather a temporary separation and thus has no prohibition [in being made] when it is not made to remove [a prohibition].

For this reason, the curtain [Paroches] which is in front of the Holy Ark is allowed to be hung there on Shabbos even if the ark does not have a door and the curtain is thus a fourth divider for the ark, as [the curtain] is a temporary separation and is only made for modesty.
Taking caution to not make a tent in the process: [However the above is only allowed] as long as one is careful when he hangs the curtain and material of the like that it not be folded in a way that it extends a handbreadth towards its width[6] at the time that it is being hung, as [if this occurs then] it comes out that one has made a handbreadth of the roof of a tent.[7]
Hanging a large curtain: Therefore if [one wants to hang] a large curtain it needs to be hung by two people so that it be able to be hung all at once in a way that it won't fold [in the process], however for one [person to hang it alone] is forbidden.

[As well] a canopy which has a roof extension sewn and hung around it like [material which surrounds] the rim [of an item], is forbidden to be hung at all on Shabbos, even with ten [people] being that it is impossible to avoid lifting up the rim a little and thus make a temporary tent.[8]

---

[5] Lit. those that go and pass and return through that way
[6] Meaning that it should not be put up in a way that the curtain will hover a handbreadths worth over the floor, as this is similar to making a tent.
[7] Regarding why this should be prohibited even though one has no intention to do so, the Mishneh Berurah, in Shareiy Tziyon 315:53 explained it's because it's a Psik Reisha, or alternatively because this ruling follows the opinion that even if one does not intend to do a prohibition it is forbidden. See there
[8] Seemingly the rim of the canopy inevitably folds upon lifting up the canopy and thus causes a roof to be made for that moment.

Halacha 8

Placing mats over the frames of a roof: Wood [rods] which have one end inserted into the wall of a ship and its other end is bent into a dome form until it reaches the other wall [of the ship], and it then has mats spread over them to provide protection from the sun or rain, then if the wood [rods] have a width of a handbreadth, even in only one of the rods[9] then it is permitted to spread mats over them on Shabbos being that by doing so one is only adding on to a temporary tent which was made before Shabbos.

Spreading a roof over rods that are within three handbreadths of each other: Furthermore, even if none of [the rods] have a one handbreadth width, if they are within three handbreadths of each other then they are considered a tent, as [all items] within three handbreadths [of each other] are considered connected, and it is thus permitted to spread on them mats on Shabbos.

Spreading a sheet over a baby's crib: Similarly, a baby's crib which has metal panels [over its top] and one [wants] to spread sheets over it to protect [the child] from flies, then if the panels are positioned as explained [meaning are a Tefach wide, or are within three handbreadths of each other] then it is allowed to spread a sheet on them on Shabbos. [However] if [it is] not [positioned this way] then it is forbidden.

Halacha 9

Placing an item in an area that consequently causes a roof to be formed:

If there are no walls under the roofing item: A temporary roof which one does not intend in making it for it to be a tent to hover over what is underneath it, but rather only in order to use [this roof] for a certain use, such as for example placing the board of a table on its legs, then even though in doing so one makes a temporary roof this does not pose a problem being that one has no intent to make a tent.

If there are walls/boards under the roofing item: Nevertheless, if one also places temporary walls under this roof, then this is similar to a tent and is forbidden to be done in its normal form which is [starting] from below to above, and rather [must be done from] above to below [which is] an irregular form.

Pacing a mattress over a bed shaped like a box: For example, a bed [made in the following manner] that its legs are made out of boards which are attached [to each other] like the walls of a box and on them one spreads [a mattress, such as] leather or places on them a board from on top to sleep on, then one may not first set up the legs and then place the hide or the board on them in the way that is done during the week, because this is similar to making a tent. Rather one is to first grasp the hide or the board in the air and afterwards places the legs underneath it, as this is not similar to making a tent being that it is not common to build [starting] from top to bottom.

Halacha 10

If the top of the bed is barred with rope: If this bed does not have placed on it leather or boards but is rather barred with ropes from above, then if there are three handbreadths between each rope, in which case we do not consider the ropes to be all attached, then it is forbidden to initially spread a sheet over it on Shabbos or place a pillow or blanket on it being that this is similar to making a tent. Similarly, it is forbidden to remove the lower cloth that is on it being that this is similar to destroying a tent.

If the top was partially covered from before Shabbos: [However] if it had a pillow or blanket or clothing spread on it from before Shabbos the amount of a handbreadth, then it is permitted to spread [it] on Shabbos over the entire bed being that doing so is simply adding to a temporary tent.

Halacha 11

Beds with regular legs: All the above [restrictions] only apply to the type of bed that has walls, meaning that its legs are like the walls of a box, even if it does not have four walls but rather only two which are parallel to each other. However, by our beds which their legs are not given the status of walls, it is permitted to initially set up [the legs] and afterwards place a beam on them. [Similarly] if it is [a bed that

---

[9] Meaning that at least two rods were placed in this position on the boat in order to spread the sheets over them thus forming a tent. Thus, if one of these rods had a handbreadths worth, then it is allowed.

is] barred with ropes then it is allowed to initially spread a sheet over them on Shabbos even if there are three handbreadths between each rope.

The reason: This does not involve [the prohibition of] making a tent because such a form of temporary tent which one has no intent in making a tent out of, the Sages did not prohibit unless it has walls under it which reach the ground, as then it is similar to a tent.

If the walls of the bed are within three handbreadths of the ground: Regarding if the walls [of the bed] reach within three handbreadths of the ground, this will be explained in chapter 502 [in Magen Avraham Halacha 9][10].

Halacha 12
The above restriction only applies if one has a use for the space being formed:

Setting up barrels: When setting up barrels on top of each other, one [barrel] being placed on top of two, he is to hold in his hand the upper [barrel] and set up the lower ones under it. However, he may not set up the lower barrels first and then place the upper one on them because the space that is created between [the two lower barrels] is similar to a tent which has two walls and a roof. Therefore, it must be made in an irregular way from above to below.

Setting up books: However, it is permitted to stand two books parallel to each other and place a book over them even though that this forms a handbreadths worth of space under them.

The reason for why by books it is permitted is because: since one has no use for the space between them it is thus not at all similar to a tent which has its space used. However, by barrels [it is forbidden because] one requires the space between the two barrels in order so the barrels not mold, as it is for this reason that he set them up in this way [that one barrel stands on two as opposed to on one].

Similarly by a bed, even if it only has two [legs which are] boards parallel to each other, [since] one has use for the space between them [such as] to use it to store ones footwear and the like, and it goes without saying if it has four [legs made of] boards like a box in which one can conceal his items just like in a box, [therefore one may not place the board on them regularly].

Halacha 13
The above restriction only applies if the roofing was not attached to the walls from before Shabbos

The law: Any temporary tent which one has no intention into making into a tent [the Sages] only prohibited spreading over walls which one [had already] set up under it on Shabbos if the roofing had not been attached on its walls from before Shabbos. However, if [the roofing] had already been attached to them from before Shabbos but it was placed there folded, then it is permitted to spread it out and set it up on Shabbos.

Examples: For example, a chair made from individual parts and when one wants to sit on it one opens it and spreads and stretches the leather [seating] and when one removes [the seat] he closes it up and has the leather fold up, then it is permitted to initially open it on Shabbos even if it has walls under it.

The reason for this is: because it is not similar to making a tent since one is not doing anything as the roofing was already set up and prepared together with the walls from before Shabbos and it's just that one unfolds it on Shabbos and sits on it.

Setting up a wedding canopy: For this reason, it is allowed to set up a canopy [that from before Shabbos was already attached to its poles] and to close it up.

Opening and closing a shelf: Similarly [it is allowed to open and close] a shelf which is attached to the wall[11] which has books placed on it even if it has walls under it.

---

[10] There the Magen Avraham brings that the Beis Yosef and Rama [in Yorah Deah 371:4] rule that we do not say the concept of "levud" for a stringency. However, the Magen Avraham himself questions this ruling and concludes that one should be stringent.
[11] Meaning that one does not remove it from the wall but simply lifts it up or down, similar to the top of a chest which opens from its hinges.

Halacha 14
Setting up a strainer:

A strainer that has dregs in it: A strainer which is hung to hold the dregs to filter it [from liquids such as wine], in which one stretches its borders to all sides, this is considered like making a tent and is thus forbidden to move it and stretch it if it was hung with the dregs from before Shabbos.

The reason: Now even though that making a roofing without walls [under it] does not have the tent prohibition [when done without intent to form a tent, as explained in Halacha 9], nevertheless here it was forbade in order so one not do so in the same way that he does during the week, as this is a belittlement of Shabbos.

Setting it up to place fruits on it or filter clean water: However, it is permitted to move it and stretch it in order to place fruits on it or other matters, or even in order to filter with it clear wine and water, which is permitted to filter on Shabbos and does not contain any belittlement of Shabbos at all.

Mantling an angled roofing on Shabbos

Halacha 15
The law:

If it has a handbreadths width on its top: [Regarding] a tent which is angled, if it has on its top a consecutive[12] roof the width of one handbreadth [which is not slanted at all throughout that handbreadth], or even if it does not have a handbreadth on its top but it contains the width of a handbreadth within less than three handbreadths near its head, being that [all items] less than three handbreadths [apart from each other] are considered attached and it is thus considered as if it has on its top a roofing that is a handbreadth wide, then this is considered a permanent tent if it was made to last and one who sets it up on Shabbos is liable for building and one who dismantles it is liable for destroying just like [one who] destroys a complete building.

If it does not have a handbreadths width on its top: However if it's top does not have a roof [the width of a] handbreadth and [as well] does not have within three handbreadths near its top the width of a handbreadth, then this is considered a temporary tent and one who initially makes this [tent] on Shabbos is exempt [from the Biblical prohibition] although it is Rabbinically forbidden whether to mantle or dismantle it, even if it is not made to last at all.

Halacha 16
An example of a tent and its subsequent laws if it has pulling strings attached to it:

Spreading a sheet and the like over a bar: [Thus] For example, a folded sheet which is folded over a [horizontal] bar, meaning that half of it is hanging from one side of the bar and half from the other side and both of its ends touch the ground and one enters and sleeps in the shade [that has been formed] between the two ends, then it is forbidden to initially hang it on Shabbos even though it does not have a roof [the width of a] handbreadth and does not have within three handbreadths near its top the width of a handbreadth.

If the material has strings attached which when pulled spread open the tent: [However] if it was wrapped on the bar from before Shabbos and it has on its rim strings that are hanging which one pulls at while on the bar in order to spread the sheet to both sides [of the bar], then it is permitted to pull at these strings on Shabbos. [The reason for this is] because since these strings are hanging on it from before Shabbos in order to be pulled at to spread [the sheet], therefore they help [to allow one to be spread it on Shabbos] just like as if it were spread the width of one handbreadth from before Shabbos, in which case by doing so on Shabbos one is only adding to a temporary tent [which is allowed].

Dismantling a tent which was legally mantled on Shabbos: It is likewise permitted to dismantle it from this bar as any tent which is allowed to be mantled and [thus] does not involve [the] building [prohibition], then it likewise does not involve [the] destroying [prohibition] and is [thus] permitted to be

---

[12] Meaning that it is a single piece of material that is a handbreadth in width, as will be explained from the second scenario to come.

dismantled.

[However, this is] with exception to when one adds onto a tent that was [the width of] a handbreadth from before Shabbos, in which case it is only permitted to dismantle the material that was added [on Shabbos] however not the part of the tent that was [already] built from before Shabbos. Despite this, nevertheless it is allowed here [by the sheet case above] to remove the sheet from the bar [on Shabbos] being that here there was never actually a tent the width of a handbreadth from before Shabbos and its only that the strings help [to allow to spread it] just like does having the width of a handbreadth [from before Shabbos].

Halacha 17
The allowance to add a temporary roofing to an already existing roof only applies if it is not common to set it there permanently:

Spreading the sheets in a case that the bar is a handbreadth wide: The above [allowance to pull at the strings to spread the sheets] however only applies if it does not have a roof [the width of a] handbreadth and does not have within three handbreadths near its top the width of a handbreadth. However, if it does have a roof [the width of a] handbreadth or within three handbreadths near its top the width of a handbreadth, in which case it is a permanent tent, then the strings do not help at all as even to add to a permanent tent is forbidden. [Furthermore] even if this sheet is not meant to last over here as he intends to dismantle it, nevertheless since it is mantled in the same way as a permanent tent, [therefore] the Sages were not lenient by it at all.

The reason for this is because: [The Sages suspected that] one may change his mind and decide to permanently have the sheets remain spread this way, and it thus ends up that he has added a permanent tent [on Shabbos]. They were only lenient to allow one to add to a temporary tent in a case that it is not usual at all to permanently leave it the way that it has been spread, such as by spreading mats over poles or on the ship as written above [in Halacha 2 and 8] as [by these cases] it is not usual at all to permanently leave the mats there the way they have been spread on Shabbos, and the same applies for all similar cases [that it is not usual to permanently spread a roofing there that it is permitted to be added to on Shabbos].

Halacha 18
Making an angled tent by an item that is designated for this purpose:

The bed canopy of a groom[13] which its roof[14] does not have a roof [the width of a] handbreadth and does not have within three handbreadths near its top the width of a handbreadth, since it is prepared for this purpose it is permitted to mantle [the canopy sheet over the rod] and to dismantle it on Shabbos, as long as it does not droop the length of a handbreadth below the [walls of the] bed.

The reason for why it may not droop a handbreadth below the bed is: because the canopy is meant to protect one from the sun or from other matters and thus has the status of a roofing on it although [that in actuality it is] without a roof. Thus, [when] it droops the length of a handbreadth below the bed, the bed serves as a roof for the one handbreadth wall [canopy] which now surrounds the bed. Now, although the bed is not made to protect and is thus not considered under the status of a roofing, nevertheless since the one handbreadth wall has the status of a roofing being that it is a part of the canopy which is meant for protection, it thus comes out that there is here a tent with a roof.

The permission to have sheets and tablecloths droop below their surface: However a bed which does not have a canopy, then even though that its sheet which is spread on it droops one handbreadth below the [walls of the] bed on all its sides, [nevertheless] this does not pose a problem, as although that the bed has become a roofing for this one handbreadth wall, [since] there is no Halachic status of a roofing here at all neither on the handbreadth or on the bed.

For this reason, it is [likewise] permitted to spread a tablecloth over a table initially on Shabbos even if it droops one handbreadth below the table on all its sides.

---

[13] This refers to a canopy which hangs over a single rod that is supported by a pole in the middle of each end of the bed, similar to a tent. Other bed canopies are supported by four vertical poles which stand on the four corners of the bed. [Rashi Shabbos 138b]

[14] Meaning the horizontal rod that is placed above the bed in order to have the canopy drooped over, forming a tent over the bed.

Halacha 19

A cloth which is spread on the mouth of a barrel in order to cover it should not be spread fully across its mouth as [doing so is making a] tent. Rather part of its mouth must be left uncovered.

If the barrel is full to the top: [However] this only applies if the barrel is not full to the top and is rather lacking [at least] a handbreadth [worth of liquid in] as in such a case when one spreads the cloth over its entire mouth it is similar to making a tent over the space of a handbreadth.

However, if [it is full to the point that] it does not lack a handbreadth [worth of liquid] then it does not have the status of a tent, as any tent which does not have the space of a handbreadth [under it] is not considered a tent at all.

The reason why it is forbidden when not filled to the top: However, when it has the space of a handbreadth under it, then although the walls that surround this space, which are the walls of the barrel, were already set up from before Shabbos, and thus [one would think that] it should not be prohibited due to the tent [prohibition] [to spread a cover fully over it]. As just like it is permitted to place a pot on the mouth of a Kirah oven on Shabbos, as explained in chapter 353 [Halacha 14], and this carries no "Tent" prohibition in [roofing] the space [within] the Kirah due to that the walls of the Kirah were made and set up already from before Shabbos [and thus is permitted because] the [Sages] did not prohibit making a temporary tent when it is done without intention to form a tent with exception to when one places walls below it on Shabbos as explained above, [and thus based on this case so too here it should be allowed as] the cover placed on the mouth of the barrel is also not intended to be done in order to form a tent but rather for a mere covering. Nevertheless, it is not similar to a pot placed on [the mouth of] a Kirah because the mouth of the barrels that existed back then was a lot wider than the mouth of the Kirah, and thus when one covers its mouth it is similar to making a tent even though that its walls have already been made from before Shabbos.

Removing the cloth covering from the barrel: The same law applies [regarding removing the cloth from the barrel] that it is forbidden to remove [a cloth] covering which covers its entire mouth if it lacks a handbreadth worth of liquid, because it is similar to destroying a tent.

The reason for why removing the cap of a barrel is nevertheless always allowed: This [cloth covering] is not similar to the cap [of a barrel] which is permitted to remove and replace [on Shabbos] as explained in chapter 314 [Halacha 14] being that the cap is modified for this use and its modification reflects on it that it is designated for this use, [and] therefore it does not appear like a tent. However, when it is covered with a cloth then even if the cloth is designated for this [use], nevertheless [since] it has no modification which displays that it is designated for this [therefore it is similar to a tent].

The law by the covers of other vessels: This law applies as well for the cover of [all] other vessels which are very wide to the point of the wideness of the mouth of the barrels of those days.

Halacha 20

Other Opinions: [However] there are opinions which say that the above was never prohibited by a barrel and the like but rather by a tub and the like which are much too wide.

The Final Ruling: One is to be stringent like the first opinion, although those that are lenient like the latter opinion are not to be rebuked being that there are opinions which say that the covering of vessels does not involve [the] tent [prohibition] at all even by vessels which are very wide.

Compilation of Halachas Summaries and Q&A

COMPILATION OF HALACHAS SUMMARIES AND Q&A

Introduction:
The following chapter will discuss the laws of setting up dividers and roofing's on Shabbos. A roofing is defined as any item which hovers over a surface, such as an umbrella, or a tent, or a table. The problem involved in setting up the above items on Shabbos is because it is a subcategory of the building prohibition.[1] At times it is Biblically forbidden at others only Rabbinically and at others it is even initially allowed to be done. These details will be discussed in this chapter.

1. Putting up a roofing/hovering for protection purposes
Important Note: The following law only relates to a flat roofing/hovering.[2] It does not relate to making a slanted roofing, such as a tent, which its law will be discussed in Halacha 3!

A. To initially open a hovering on Shabbos:[3]
The law:[4] It is forbidden to make a tent, which refers to [any] roofing which hovers over a person in order to guard him from a given matter, such as [to protect him] from the sun or from the rain or from another given matter [such as flies[5], or wind[6]]. [This prohibition applies on both Shabbos and Yom Tov.[7]]
The prohibition applies even by a temporary tent which has no walls: [This applies] even if [the roof] is temporary [meaning] that it is not made to last[8] and even if there are not any walls under it[9], such as is the case with one who spreads a mat over four poles. Nevertheless, since it is made in order to tent and protect it is [therefore considered] a complete tent and the Sages prohibited it even though it is [only] temporary due to a decree [that one may come to make] a permanent tent which is an offshoot of [the] building [prohibition].[10]
What is the minimum amount of space that a roofing must hover over to be prohibited?[11] Any tent which does not have the space of a handbreadth [under it, i.e. 8 centimeters] is not considered a tent at all [and is thus permitted to be made].
How wide must the Ohel be to be forbidden? Any tent that does not have a handbreadths worth[12] [i.e. 8 centimeters] is not a tent, as a Tefach is the measurement required for [a roofing item to be] considered a tent.[13]
Making a tent to prevent pain:[14] The [Sages] permitted to make a temporary tent [in an irregular manner[15], if needed in order to reduce] the pain of a live person and not for the pain of corpse.

---

[1] Halacha 1
[2] Such as a wedding canopy.
[3] Admur 315:1; Michaber 315:1; Shabbos 125b
[4] Admur ibid; M"B 315:17
[5] Admur 301:48
[6] Admur 640:10
[7] Michaber 315:1; Admur 502:5; 626:20; 640:10 Vetzaruch Iyun why Admur omitted in 315:1 the word Yom Tov.
[8] Admur ibid; Michaber 315:1
[9] Admur ibid; M"B 315:17 and 20; Rashi ibid; So is proven from Sugya of Shabbos 138b and Michaber 301:40 regarding hats; See Ketzos Hashulchan 120 footnote 1
Other opinions: Some Poskim rule a temporary tent is permitted if it does not have walls under it. [Avnei Nezer 222] See however Ketzos Hashulchan ibid that completely negates his claim.
[10] Admur ibid; M"B ibid; Rambam 22:27; Yerushalmi 20:1
[11] Admur 315:19; 315:12; 640:10; Michaber 315:13; Rambam 22:23
[12] Admur 315:2; Michaber 315:2; Eiruvin 102a
[13] Admur ibid; Rashi on Gemara ibid
[14] Admur 311:11
[15] However even this only applies when one is making the tent with an irregularity, such as by holding it up with ones hands as says here, as opposed to supporting it on something. [Ketzos Hashulchan 120 footnote 1]

Q&A
Is an Ohel made to protect objects from the sun considered an Ohel?[16]

No, unless the item is larger than the size of a barrel, as explained in Halacha 2D.[17] However, some Poskim[18] are stringent in this matter.

If one places a Ohel for non-protection purposes but for the purpose of doing an action under it, is it considered under the laws of an Ohel made for protection, or under the laws of an Ohel not made for protection?

Some Poskim[19] rule it is considered like an Ohel made for protection. However, from Admur there is implication that it is permitted like an Ohel made for non-protection purposes.[20] Thus, if one makes a hovering for privacy purposes, it would seemingly be forbidden according to the above Poskim, but perhaps be permitted according to Admur. However, if the hovering is meant for placing items on top of it, such as a table, then according to all it is not considered an Ohel even if one also benefits from using the space under it.

May one roll open a bed canopy that is attached to the wall or poles of a bed?

If this is done for purposes of privacy, then seemingly it would be subject to the above debate and be prohibited according to the above Poskim, as it is considered done for protection purposes. Accordingly, it would make no difference if it was attached to the bed or wall before Shabbos, as this matter of attachment only helps for opening for non-protection purposes. It is likewise not similar to the allowance of Kilas Chasanim being that there there is no Gag Tefach, as opposed to here. However, some write that according to Admur it is permitted in such a case.[21]

May one wear a plastic hat rain cover on a hat or Sheital on Shabbos?

It is permitted to put on a rain cover onto one's hat on Shabbos and doing so does not pose an Ohel prohibition.[22] This applies whether the cover is a specially manufactured hat rain cover, or one is using a plastic bag. However, it is disputed if this may be done in an area without an Eiruv due to the carrying prohibition.[23]

---

[16] See Piskeiy Teshuvos 315:15

[17] See Admur 315:1 and 9 and 11 and 15-19; Michaber 315:13; P"M 315 A"A 8

Background: See Michaber 315:13 that one may cover a barrel of wine with its lid even if there is a Tefach of space in-between. Admur 315:19 permits covering a vessel of food even with a cloth; See also wording of Admur 315:1; P"M 315 A"A 8

[18] See Tehila Ledavid 315:10; Minchas Shabbos 80:225; Ben Ish Chaiy Shemos 1:12; Kaf Hachaim 315:45; Chazon Ish 52:7; Piskeiy Teshuvos 315:15 and footnote 156

[19] M"B 315:20; Shaar Hatziyon 315:26; implied from M"A 315:7 which prohibits closing up the chiminey, even though it is not done for protection.

[20] From Admur 315:1 it is implied that only when the Ohel is made for actual protection is it considered an Ohel, however from 315:9 it is implied from the words "to hover over something under it" that even if not for protection it is considered an Ohel. See also Admur 315:3 *"[Furthermore] even if one makes it in order to protect himself from the sun or the cold it is not considered like a tent because of this. Similarly [it is allowed even] if one made it in order to prevent the candles from extinguishing in the wind. **It goes without saying that it is allowed to make a divider for mere privacy** [purposes, such as] so that one not sit in a revealed area, or such as the dividers which are made during speeches to separate between the men and women, and so too for anything similar to this."* This implies that mere privacy is not considered an Ohel for protection, and so learns Chochmas Shlomo 626 that making a tent for "Tzenius Bealma" is not considered an Ohel "as explained in 315"; See Sheyikadesh Atzmo 44 footnote 2

[21] See Sheyikadesh Atzmo 44 footnote 2 in length

[22] The reason: As the Ohel prohibition does not apply in a case that there is not a Tefach of space between the cover and the hat. [Admur 315:19; 315:12; 640:10; Michaber 315:13; Rambam 22:23] B) A hovering made to protect an item [in contrast to a human] does not have the status of an Ohel when covering an item less than the size of a barrel. [See Admur 315:19 regarding a barrel]

[23] See Piskeiy Teshuvos 301:6 [old] 301:20 [new]

From the Rav's Desk

Question:

Is it permitted to cover chairs that are outside with a plastic tablecloth to prevent them from getting wet in the rain? Basically, what happened was is that Friday night we noticed that it would be raining and all the chairs by our outside Minyan would get wet and may not be dry by the next morning for Shabbos Shacharis. So, what I wondered if I can do is to take disposable plastic tablecloths to use to cover each chair individually to prevent them from getting wet. By doing so I will be in essence creating a tent over the chairs. Is this permitted or not on Shabbos?

Answer:

Yes, you may do so by covering each chair with an individual tablecloth even though it creates hovering over the chair. Nonetheless, some are stringent to do so with two people, having one first open the tablecloth and then place the chair under it. Practically, in my opinion there is no need to be stringent in this. In my opinion, however, you should not cover multiple chairs under the same tablecloth, although it is possible that this too is allowed, especially if done in the above way doing with two people as explained above.

The explanation: On Shabbos there is a prohibition of Ohel to create a hovering for the sake of protection, such as to protect from rain. However, this restriction is primarily against creating a protection for humans, and not for creating a protection items such as a chair. Nonetheless, even making a hovering over an item contains some restrictions, such as that if under the hovering there are two walls/Mechitzas one must first put the hovering over the ground and then slide the walls under it. Even in the case that the walls were already established there before Shabbos, one may not place a hovering over an area that is larger than the size of a barrel, unless certain conditions are fulfilled. Thus, based on all this, it would seem that while there is no restriction against hovering individual tablecloths over each chair [as the chair is not the size of a barrel, and there is no protection of human taking place, and the chair was already opened before Shabbos, and in any event does not contain walls under it and rather simply stands on legs] nonetheless, one should not place the hovering over multiple chairs which would reach the size of a barrel. Vetzaruch Iyun, as perhaps this restriction only applies to a barrel and the like which contains surrounding walls. Nonetheless, all the above only applies according to the approach, which is the main approach in Halacha, that there is no prohibition to create a tented hovering for non-human protection purposes. However, there are opinions who rule that one may not create a roofing that has walls attached to it, such as a tent which has a top and its sides which serve as its walls, and according to this opinion then indeed would be problematic to cover chairs with a tablecloth to protect them from the rain. However, in my opinion according to the main approach this would be permitted, and hence we ruled above that it may be done.

Sources: See Michaber 315:13; Admur 315:1 and 9 and 11 and 15-19; P"M 315 A"A 8; Tehila Ledavid 315:10; Minchas Shabbos 80:225; Ben Ish Chaiy Shemos 1:12; Kaf Hachaim 315:45; Chazon Ish 52:7; Maor Hashabbos 4 letter 10 of Rav Fisher; Piskeiy Teshuvos 315:15 and footnote 156

Question:

We have a table outside with an open summer umbrella and was wondering if it is permitted for me to move it on Shabbos, such as if the table is in one area of our yard where there is currently no sun and would like to move into a different area of our yard where we are currently sitting and where the sun is shining. I guess my question is regarding whether the prohibition of making on Shabbos is specifically against opening up the umbrella an Ohel, or even against moving it to an area in order to give shade from the sun if it was open from before Shabbos?

Answer:

You may move the table with its open umbrella to any area that you desire, whether to or from the sun.

<u>The reason</u>: As the rabbinical prohibition against making an Ohel on Shabbos is specifically against opening it or closing it on Shabbos. However, to simply move it from one area to another we find no mention of a prohibition. Furthermore, from the fact that in the discussion of using an umbrella on Shabbos that was already open from beforehand, no mention is made of the fact that you are moving it from one area to another as an argument to prohibited, proves that this argument is not legitimate as in truth moving it alone is not prohibited. Likewise, if this were to be prohibited, then there would be no allowance to use a stroller on Shabbos with its open hood, even if one opened the hood from before Shabbos. In truth, all Poskim agree that if the hood was open from before Shabbos then the stroller may be used on Shabbos even though one is going with it from inside the house where there is no sun to outside the house where there is sun, and the entire discussion in the Poskim is only regarding if you can open it on Shabbos. Thus, it is clear without doubt once a table sun umbrella has been open from before Shabbos there is no additional Ohel prohibition to move it to a different location on Shabbos. Nonetheless the use of a rain or sun umbrella that one walks with while holding his hand is prohibited on Shabbos due to other reasons, even if it was open before Shabbos and is thus free of the Ohel prohibition.

As for the reason the prohibition applies only to initially erecting the hovering, such as to initially open the table umbrella on Shabbos, and not to moving it, that this is because the entire decree of the sages was against making the structure of the hovering and not against moving it even though by doing so one accomplishes the giving of shade, the creation of shade that the sages prohibited but rather the creation of a structure that gives shade.

<u>*Sources*</u>*: Maor Hashabbos 4 letter 9 of Rav Fisher; Piskeiy Teshuvos 315:2; See regarding umbrella the following sources: Nodeh Beyehuda Tenyana; Tehila Ledavid 315:8; M"B in Biur Halacha 315:8; "Tefach"; Mamar Mordechai; Chayeh Adam, Sharreiy Teshuvah 302:?; Ketzos Hashulchan 120:13; SSH"K 24:15; Chasam Sofer 72; Chazon Ish 52:6; see regarding a stroller: M"B 315:12; Ketzos Hashulchan 120 footnote 8*

B. To further open a hovering that was opened from before Shabbos:[24]

Adding to a temporary tent that was made before Shabbos: The [Sages] only forbade to initially [make a tent] on Shabbos, however if a temporary[25] tent had been made from before Shabbos then it is permitted to add to it on Shabbos, such as for example if the mat was spread out from before Shabbos a handbreadths worth[26], which is the measurement required for [a roofing item to be] considered a tent[27], then it is permitted to open it completely on Shabbos and to add more mats to it, as all this is only adding to the handbreadth tent which was made the day before. [Furthermore] even to spread it over walls is allowed in this case.[28]

Is the rolled-up material included in the handbreadth?[29] This measurement of a handbreadth that was mentioned does not include the rolled material, meaning that even if it was rolled up and placed [on walls] from before Shabbos and there is in the thickness of the circumference of the rolled material the amount of a handbreadth and more, nevertheless there needs to be coming out of [this roll] a handbreadths worth of material spread out for tenting.

The reason for this is: because the circumference of the rolled material does not appear like a tent at all.

Panels of a hovering within three handbreadths of each other:[30] [A hovering which had its panels set up before Shabbos then] even if none of [the rods] have a one handbreadth width, if they are within three handbreadths of each other then they are considered a tent, as [all items] within three handbreadths [24 centimeters of each other] are considered connected, and it is thus permitted to spread on them mats on Shabbos. [**See Q&A**]

The allowance to add a temporary roofing to an already existing roof only applies if it is not common to set it there permanently:[31] The Sages were only lenient to allow one to add to a temporary tent in a case that it is not usual at all to permanently leave it the way that it has been spread, such as by spreading mats over poles or on the ship as written above [in Halacha 2 and 8] as [by these cases] it is not usual at all to permanently leave the mats there the way they have been spread on Shabbos, and the same applies for all similar cases [that it is not usual to permanently spread a roofing there that it is permitted to be added to on Shabbos].

Adding to a permanent tent: It is forbidden to add a permanent hovering at all on Shabbos in any circumstance.[32] It is permitted to add a temporary hovering to a permanent hovering, if it is not common to leave it there permanently.[33]

> **Within how much space vertical and horizontal of the already established material must the hovering be?**
>
> This matter requires further analysis!

---

[24] Admur 315:2; Michaber 315:2; Chachamim in Shabbos 125b

[25] From here it is implied that only if the tent is temporary may one add to it on Shabbos. If, however the tent is permanent then one may not add to it on Shabbos, even if the addition is temporary, and so is implied from 315:17. However in truth one cannot say this, as in 313:1 Admur permits adding a temporary window to a permanent ceiling. Likewise, in 315:17 he himself permits to add the sails to the poles, and the poles are permanent. Hence, we see the main thing is not the item being added to but the state of the addition, as to whether the addition is temporary or not. Vetzaruch Iyun.

[26] Admur ibid; Michaber ibid; Eiruvin 102a

[27] Admur ibid; Rashi on Gemara ibid

[28] Admur ibid; Tosafus 36b based on Eiruvin 102a

[29] Admur ibid; Michaber ibid; Ritva

[30] Admur 315:8; Michaber 15:2; Eiruvin 102a

[31] Admur 315:17

[32] Admur 313:1; 315:17; M"A 315:1; Biur Halacha 313:1 "Velo Amrinan"

[33] Admur 315:5 regarding dividers; From 315:2 it is implied that only if the tent is temporary may one add to it on Shabbos. If however the tent is permanent then one may not add to it on Shabbos, even if the addition is temporary, and so is implied from 315:17. However in truth one cannot say this, as in 313:1 Admur permits adding a temporary window to a permanent ceiling. Likewise, in 315:17 he himself permits to add the sails to the poles, and the poles are permanent. Hence we see the main thing is not the item being added to but the state of the addition, as to whether the addition is temporary or not, and so rules Admur explicitly in 315:5 "Now, although the divider that extends [to the side] is permanent, [nevertheless] this does not pose a problem as explained in chapter 313 [Halacha 1] that there is only a prohibition [in adding to a tent] when the addition is permanent." Vetzaruch Iyun.

C. Examples:

❖ *Placing mats over the frames of a roof:³⁴*

Wood [rods] which have one end inserted into the wall of a ship and its other end is bent into a dome form until it reaches the other wall [of the ship], and it then has mats spread over them to provide protection from the sun or rain, then if the wood [rods] have a width of a handbreadth, even in only one of the rods³⁵ then it is permitted to spread mats over them on Shabbos being that by doing so one is only adding on to a temporary tent which was made before Shabbos.

Spreading a roof over rods that are within three handbreadths of each other: Furthermore, even if none of [the rods] have a one handbreadth width, if they are within three handbreadths of each other then they are considered a tent, as [all items] within three handbreadths [of each other] are considered connected, and it is thus permitted to spread on them mats on Shabbos.

❖ *Spreading a sheet over a baby's crib:³⁶*

Similarly, a baby's crib which has metal panels [over its top] and one [wants] to spread sheets over it to protect [the child] from flies, then if the panels are positioned as explained [meaning are a Tefach wide, or are within three handbreadths of each other] then it is allowed to spread a sheet on them on Shabbos. [However] if [it is] not [positioned this way] then it is forbidden. [**See Q&A regarding spreading a netting over a crib**]

❖ *Making a tent over the corpse to protect it from the sun:³⁷*

A corpse which is in the sun and there is no other place to be move it to, or [there is but] they do not want to move it from its place, then it is permitted to build over it a temporary tent through deception [initially making it seem that it is being done] for the need of the living.

How it may be done: This is done as follows: Two people come along and sit on the two sides [of the corpse, one on each side], on top of the ground. [When it gets] hot for them below [on the ground] due to the heat of the ground that the sun heated, then [in a private domain] each person brings his bed there and sits on it³⁸. [When] it gets hot for them above, each one brings a mat and spreads it over the bed for shade³⁹. [Afterwards, they both may depart], each one overturns their beds, and removes them⁴⁰. In this manner, the division [needed for shade] is created on its own accord, [as it were], for the two mats are back-to-back near each other and their two ends are located on the ground on either side of the corpse⁴¹.

The reason why one may not initially spread the mat over the body is because: The [Sages only] permitted to make a temporary tent [if needed in order to reduce] the pain of a live person and not for the pain of corpse⁴². Therefore, they required [people] to initially come sit [by either side of the corpse] until they are [too] hot below [sitting on the ground], in which case they may then bring beds to sit on.

[Now], even though the beds have no use at all in making the tent, [nevertheless they are brought] so that it appear that the spreading of the mats are not being done in order to make a tent over the corpse by attaching both [mats] together⁴³, but rather [the mats are being brought] in order so each one spread it over himself to shield him from the sun, [as by bringing out the beds one makes it evident that they are bothered by the heat] as [people see] that also when it was [too] hot for them from below [while on the ground] each one brought his bed and sat on them [so they say that the same applies here].

---

³⁴ Admur 315:8

³⁵ Meaning that at least two rods were placed in this position on the boat in order to spread the sheets over them thus forming a tent. Thus, if one of these rods had a handbreadths worth, then it is allowed.

³⁶ Admur 315:8; M"A 315:4; M"B 315:12

³⁷ Admur 311:11; Michaber 315:6

³⁸ Lit. This one brings his bed and sits on it, and this one brings his bed and sits on it

³⁹ Lit. This one brings his mat and spreads it on the bed, and this one brings his mat and spreads it on the bed

⁴⁰ Lit. This one brings overturns his bed and removes it, and this one overturns his bed and removes it.

⁴¹ Thus, forming a miniature tepee over the corpse.

⁴² However even this only applies when one is making the tent with an irregularity, such as by holding it up with one's hands as says here, as opposed to supporting it on something. [Ketzos Hashulchan 120 footnote 1]

⁴³ Meaning by having them touch each other and form a tepee.

For this reason [too] they need to overturn and remove their beds from there and [thus consequently] position the spreading of the mats [over the floor] so that also here it should appear that the spreading of the mats was not done for the sake of the corpse but rather to shield themselves from the sun, as when it was [too] hot for them below they brought a bed and sat on it, and now when they have gotten up [and are ready to leave], they overturned it and brought it back.

❖ *Making oneself a toilet out from stones:*[44]

Large stones which are organized to create a seat with a hole which one sits on in fields by the area designated to be used as a bathroom, is permitted to be organized on Shabbos, being that [doing so] is a temporary structure that is not made to last, and a temporary structure is only prohibited to [be made] Rabbinically, and due to respect of humanity they did not apply their decree [in this case].[45] Nevertheless, to make a form of a tent with a roof is forbidden even though it is only a temporary tent.

❖ *May one open or close the roofing of a Sukkah?*[46]

If this [roof] door [i.e. the removable roofing of the Sukkah] has hinges with which it is opened and closed, then it is like a complete opening and is permitted to open and close it on Shabbos and Yom Tov and doing so does not contain the Building or destroying prohibition.[47] [However, if there is a Tefach between the roofing and the Sechach then it is forbidden due to the Ohel prohibition.[48]]
Spreading a sheet on top of the Schach: 640/10

Summary: Hovering's made for protection

To initially set up:
It is always forbidden to initially set up a roofing on Shabbos for protection purposes even if there are no walls under the roofing. If the roofing is made for permanent use, then it is Biblically prohibited. If made for only temporary use, then it is Rabbinically forbidden.

Examples: One may not initially spread a sheet over a baby carriage.[49]

What is the minimum amount of space that a roofing must hover over to be prohibited?[50] One handbreadth. If it does not have a handbreadth of empty space under it then it is completely permitted.

How wide must the Ohel be to be forbidden? Any tent that does not have a handbreadths worth[51] is

---

[44] Admur 312:15

[45] Regarding the problem of Muktzah there are opinions that say that this is only referring to stones that have been designated before Shabbos to be used for this purpose. However, others learn that even if not predestinated the Sages allowed one to move it. [Mishneh Berurah 25] [It seems from the Alter Rebbe like the latter as a) Why didn't the Alter Rebbe mention the case is referring to designated stones, and b) if the stones were designated for this, then the structure made out from them is permanent not temporary.]

[46] Admur 626:20; Rama 626:3

[47] Why the closing of the awning does not pose an Ohel prohibition: It requires further analysis why one is allowed to open and close the awning of the Sukkah. Why does this action not contain a prohibition of Ohel? The Chazon Ish 52:6 rules the reason this scenario does not pose a prohibition of Ohel is because the hovering is attached to hinges and is it is thus considered like one is opening a folding chair. See also Shaar Hatizyon 315:35 that implies like Chazon Ish; however, see Biur Halacha 315:8 "Tefach" regarding the prohibition against using an umbrella that implies like Admur. However, this explanation is not acceptable according to Admur, as explained in Ketzos Hashulchan 120 footnote 8 based on Admur 315:13, that Admur rules even hovering that are attached to hinges may not be opened due to the Ohel prohibition. One can answer that the case here is discussing that there is not a Tefach of space between the awning and the Sechach and hence it is not considered an Ohel [as rules Admur in 640:10]. However, it requires further analysis why Admur did not stipulate this into the case. Alternatively, the reason why this specific Halacha does not discuss the Ohel prohibition is because it is discussing a case that the Sukkah was made inside a house and part of the ceiling has a window which is opened so the Schach be directly under the heavens. Opening this window does not pose an Ohel prohibition as one is allowed to add a temporary Ohel to an Ohel which was already extended a Tefach before Yom Tov/Shabbos, and in this case when one closes the window, he is simply adding that hovering to the already existing ceiling. In conclusion the result of the above explanation in Admur is that if one built a Sukkah outside of his home and built an awning over it, this awning may only be opened and closed on Shabbos if there is not a Tefach of space between the awning and the Schach.

[48] See previous footnote.

[49] Admur 315:8

[50] Admur 315:19

[51] Admur 315:2; Michaber 315:2; Eiruvin 102a

not a tent, as a Tefach is the measurement required for [a roofing item to be] considered a tent.[52]

May one set up a temporary roofing in order to prevent pain? "The Sages permitted to make a temporary tent if needed in order to reduce the pain of a live person".[53] However this only applies when one is making the tent with an irregularity, such as by holding it up with one's hands as opposed to supporting it on something.[54]

To add on to an already existing roofing:
One is allowed to add on to a previously made roofing on Shabbos if all the following conditions are fulfilled:

A. The previously made roofing extends at least the width of a handbreadth from the area that the roofing is rolled up, or does not but the roofing has two bars within three handbreadths of each other set up before Shabbos, and they are the length of a handbreadth from one to the other.

B. The currently added roofing is only being placed for temporary use.

C. It is not common at all to have the added roofing remain there permanently.[55]

Regarding placing a sheet over a bar and the like to form a slanted roofing such as a tent-See Halacha 2!

Examples:
Making a tent over a corpse:[56] One is allowed to set up a tent over the corpse in order to shade it from the sun in the following way: Two people, each sitting on the side of the corpse after feeling hot on their bottom brings a bed and lays on it, then when they feel hot on their top they bring mats and place it over them, and then depart and move the beds, having the mats slip over the corpse, leaning on each other by their top, thus forming a tent over the corpse.

May one open or close the roofing of a Sukkah?[57] This may be done if the roofing is resting within hinges and is thus opened and closed similar to a door, [and only if there is not a Tefach space between the roofing and the Sechach].

Q&A
How many days must an Ohel last to consider it permanent and hence forbidden even to add on Shabbos?
Some Poskim rule that if the addition will last eight days it is considered a permanent tent.

May one make an Ohel that is less than one Tefach wide?[58]
Yes.

May one open and close a folded Ohel that is attached to the walls?
No.[59]

[52] Admur ibid; Rashi on Gemara ibid
[53] Admur 311:11
[54] Ketzos Hashulchan 120 footnote 1
[55] Admur 315:17
[56] Admur 311:11
[57] Admur 626:20
[58] See Admur 315:2; 302
[59] Admur 315:13; Tehila Ledavid 315:8; Ketzos Hashulchan 120 footnote 8; Igros Moshe 4:105; Sheivet Halevy 3:54; Minchas Yitzchak 10:26 leaves this matter in question although leans to be lenient in a case that the hood also forms side walls when opened.
Other opinions: Some Poskim rule one may open and close an Ohel that is attached to hinges. [Chazon Ish 52:6; Bris Olam 14; Shraga Hameir 3:37; Beir Moshe 6:87 based on Chazon Ish; SSH"K 24:13]

May one hold up a hovering using his hands?[60]

Some opinions[61] rule that in all cases that making a tent is forbidden, it is forbidden to do so even when holding it up with one's hands, unless it is a case of pain as explained above. However other opinions[62] hold that a hovering may be held up with one's hands if it has no walls underneath it. *See coming Q&A regarding the law of an umbrella!*

Does a roof netting have the same law as does a sheet?[63]

No. A netting which has more open space than actual cloth within the parameters of the netting is not considered a roofing and thus does not contain the Tent prohibition.[64]

May one on Shabbos set up non-Muktzah panels within three handbreadths of each other?[65]

If done without intent to spread a covering over them: Is allowed[66] but is questionable whether one is allowed to spread a sheet over them if he later changes his mind.[67]

If done with intent to spread a covering over them:[68] Is forbidden, and if one went ahead and did so it remains prohibited to spread a covering over them.

May one place rolled material that is one Tefach wide to hover over an item, as an Ohel?[69]

Some Poskim[70] rule one may not do so. Other Poskim[71] rule one may do so.

Practical Q&A

May people hold open a sheet or a Tallis to grant shade or protection from rain?[72]

Some opinions[73] rule that it is forbidden to do so. However other opinions[74] hold that a hovering may be held up with one's hands if it has no walls underneath it. Nevertheless, in a case of pain one may be lenient according to all.[75] *See coming Q&A regarding the law of an umbrella!*

On Simchas Torah may people spread open a Tallis over the Chasan Torah and children by Kol Nearim?[76]

Yes. In this case it is permitted according to all opinions being that its intent is not protection but rather a sign of respect.[77]

---

[60] Piskeiy Teshuvos 315:8
[61] Ketzos Hashulchan 120 footnote 1 based on Taz 319:1; P"M 315 M"Z 7
[62] Avnei Nezer 222; Tehilah Ledavid 315:9; Minchas Shabbos 80:224; Chazon Ish 54:60
[63] Piskeiy Teshuvos 315:1
[64] So rules Beir Moshe 6:97 and SSH"K 24:11 in name of Rav SZ"A.
[65] Piskeiy Teshuvos 315:4
[66] Rav Akivah Eiger being that we do not say Levud Lehachmir.
Vetzaruch Iyun Gadol from Admur 626:14: *"Even if the supports are within three handbreadths within each other, nevertheless we do not say the concept of Lavud, and therefore one may eat under the Kosher Schach. The reason that we do not say the concept of Lavud here is because this status is only given when there is no interval between the two items that are in proximity of three handbreadths. **Thus here since the Schach intervenes the concept of Lavud does not apply."*** This implies that if not for the kosher Schach having been there, we would say Levud even Lehachmir
[67] So rules Rav SZ"A in SSH"K 24 footnote 40
[68] Ketzos Hashulchan 120 footnote 11
[69] See M"B 315:16 and Shaar Hatziyon 20; Piskeiy Teshuvos 315 footnote 78
[70] Taz 315:3 based on Rashi; Tosefes Shabbos; Mamar Mordechai; Conclusion of M"B in Shaar Hatziyon ibid; Ben Ish Chaiy Shemos 2:1; Kaf Hachaim 315:27; Chazon ish 52:8
[71] Elya Raba 315:5 as rules Bach; Gr"a
[72] Piskeiy Teshuvos 315:8
[73] Ketzos Hashulchan 120 footnote 1 based on Taz 319:1; P"M 315 M"Z 7
[74] Avnei Nezer 222; Tehilah Ledavid 315:9; Minchas Shabbos 80:224; Chazon Ish 54:60
[75] Keztos Hashulchan 120 footnote1 based on Admur 311:11
[76] Piskeiy Teshuvos 315:8
[77] Ketzos Hashulchan 120 footnote 1

May one open or close a rain umbrella on Shabbos?[78]

No. This matter is discussed extensively in the Poskim of previous generations.[79] The final ruling of this issue is that doing so is forbidden due to the Ohel prohibition[80], as well as due to it being a mundane act.[81] *See above regarding the dispute of holding an Ohel in one's hand!*

May one use an umbrella that was opened from before Shabbos?[82]

It is forbidden[83] to use an umbrella on Shabbos even if it was opened from before Shabbos, and even in an area which has an eruv.

May one open a sun umbrella?[84]

Not attached to the ground: Is forbidden just like a rain umbrella.

Attached to the ground: Some Poskim[85] rule that it is permitted to be opened and closed, while others[86] prohibit this. It is implied from Admur[87] like the stringent opinion!

May one open or close a sunroof or roof window?[88]

Yes. One may do so according to all opinions.[89]

May one open or close an awning or overhang which extends past the roof of a building?[90]

Some Poskim rule that this may be done, and perhaps this applies according to all opinions.[91]

---

[78] SSH"K 24:15

[79] Opinions which prohibit it: Nodeh Beyehuda Tenyana 30 [he says it could be Biblically forbidden]; Tehila Ledavid 315:8; M"B in Biur Halacha 315:8; "Tefach"; Mamar Mordechai; Chayeh Adam, Sharreiy Teshuvah 302; Ketzos Hashulchan 120:13; SSH"K 24:15.

Opinions which permit it: Chasam Sofer 72 rules that it involves no prohibition at all, and he rules that one may be lenient to have it opened by a gentile. Chazon Ish 52:6 rules it does not contain an Ohel prohibition but is not to be done because it is Uvdin Dechol. The reason behind those which claim that it does not contain an Ohel prohibition is because they say it is similar to a folding chair which was allowed. [Chazon Ish ibid; Noda Beyehudah ibid in name of Chacham Hamatir]

Opinion of Admur: Seemingly, according to Admur it is clear that that it is forbidden to open or close an umbrella as all matters made for protection may not be spread due to the Ohel prohibition even if a) it hovers over a person and is moving [as we see clearly from Admur's ruling by the hat case] and even if b) it was attached before Shabbos and only needs to be extended [as Admur depends the allowance of opening the folding chair because it is not made for protection]. Hence all the reasons of allowance brought by the questioner in Teshuvas Nodah Beyehudah are rejected by Admur, as does the Noda Beyehudah himself.

[80] All Poskim mention above rule it is forbidden due to creating an Ohel.

[81] Chazon Ish ibid

[82] Ketzos Hashulchan 120:13; So rules also Chazon Ish 52:6 [brought in SSH"K 24:15] that it should not be done due to it being a belittling of Shabbos.

[83] From SSH"K 24:15 it is implied that it should not be done but is not such a clear prohibition.

[84] SSH"K 24:15

[85] SSH"K 24:15 based on Chazon Ish 52:6

[86] See below "May one open the hood of a baby carriage on Shabbos" for the different opinions there and seemingly this dispute would apply here as well.

[87] 315:13 : "*Any temporary tent which* **one has no intention into making into a tent** *[the Sages] only prohibited spreading over walls which one [had already] set up under it on Shabbos if the roofing had not been attached on its walls from before Shabbos. However if [the roofing] had already been attached to them from before Shabbos but it was placed there folded, then it is permitted to spread it out and set it up on Shabbos.*"

[88] SSH"K 24:15

[89] As it is similar to a door which opens and closes on its hinges. [Admur 626:20, see above example regarding roof of Sukkah]. As well one is merely adding an extension to an already existing roof, which is allowed according to all when done for temporary use.

[90] SSH"K 24:15

[91] As one is merely adding an extension to an already existing roof, which is allowed according to all when done for temporary use.

May one place a netting over a crib or one's bed to protect it from insects?[92]
If the netting has more open space than actual cloth within its parameters, then it is allowed.

Q&A on strollers
May one open the hood of a baby carriage on Shabbos? [93]
If the hood was not attached to the carriage from before Shabbos:[94] Then even in cases that it is permitted to attach the hood, it is forbidden to be opened[95]. However, there are Poskim[96] which are lenient[97].

If the hood was not opened a handbreadths width before Shabbos: Some Poskim[98] rule it is permitted to open and close the hood of a stroller on Shabbos in all cases, even if the hood was folded from before Shabbos.[99] Many other Poskim[100] however rule that it is forbidden to open or close the hood of a stroller for purposes of protection from the sun or rain and the like, if it was not opened a handbreadth [8 cm] before Shabbos, excluding the folded area.[101] **According to Admur[102] we rule like the stringent opinion.[103]**

If the hood was opened a handbreadth [8 cm] before Shabbos:[104] If the hood of the stroller was opened 8 cm before Shabbos [excluding the folded area] then is permitted to further open it on Shabbos and to close the part which was further opened.

May one open or close the hood of a baby carriage if there is no person inside?
> *Example: One is bringing from home a large amount of food in a stroller/carriage towards the Shul's Kiddush. May he open the hood to protect food from the rain or sun?*

Yes. [105] The prohibition of Ohel for protection only applies towards people and not towards items, as was explained in Halacha 1 in the Q&A. Furthermore, even according to the stringent opinion mentioned there, one may spread a sheet over the carriage if there will not be a Tefach of space between the sheet and the food. However, one may not spread a sheet over a large baby carriage unless a) there will not be a Tefach of space between the sheet and the food or b) One does not fully

---

[92] See above!
[93] See Piskeiy Teshuvos 315:6
[94] SSH"K 24:13
[95] SSH"K 24:13, as rules Ketzos Hashulchan regarding question brought earlier if one may set up on Shabbos panels within 3 handbreadths of each other, in which case he rules that it is forbidden.
[96] Az Nidbaru 3:24
[97] Seemingly they hold that once it is attached it is considered like a door and is thus allowed to be opened.
[98] Chazon Ish 52:6; Bris Olam 14; Shraga Hameir 3:37; Beir Moshe 6:87 based on Chazon Ish; SSH"K 24:13; See also Shaar Hatizyon 315:35 that implies like Chazon Ish, however see Biur Halacha 315:8 "Tefach" regarding the prohibition against using an umbrella that implies like Admur.
[99] The reason: As since the hood was already connected to the stroller from before Shabbos, it is no different than opening a door on its hinges, or a folding chair. [ibid]
[100] Ketzos Hashulchan 120 footnote 8; Igros Moshe 4:105; Sheivet Halevy 3:54; Minchas Yitzchak 10:26 leaves this matter in question although leans to be lenient in a case that the hood also forms side walls when opened.
[101] The reason: Even though the hood was attached from before Shabbos it is forbidden to open or close it being that in this case ones intent is in truth for a roofing protection, in contrast to a folding chair and the like. [ibid]
[102] Admur 315:13 : "*Any temporary tent which **one has no intention into making into a tent** [the Sages] only prohibited spreading over walls which one [had already] set up under it on Shabbos if the roofing had not been attached on its walls from before Shabbos. However, if [the roofing] had already been attached to them from before Shabbos but it was placed there folded, then it is permitted to spread it out and set it up on Shabbos.*"
[103] See Ketzos Hashulchan ibid
[104] Ketzos Hashulchan ibid
[105] The reason: This may be done as the prohibition of making an Ohel only applies when it is made for the sake of protecting people and not when it is made for the sake of protecting items, such as food or other purpose. Now, although it is forbidden on Shabbos to set up a tent with walls for even non-protective purposes, in its normal way, nonetheless here the walls are set up before Shabbos, it is permitted, similar to placing a cover on a vessel to protect the food. [See Michaber 315:13 that one may cover a barrel of wine with its lid even if there is a Tefach of space in-between. Admur 315:19 permits covering a vessel of food even with a cloth; See also wording of Admur 315:1; P"M 315 A"A 8] Furthermore, being that the hood was already attached to the stroller before Shabbos, it is similar to the allowance to open a folding chair, in which all agree is allowed when performed for non-protecting purposes. Now, although it is possible to argue that since in general a hood is meant to serve as protection for a child, therefore it should not be allowed to be opened at all on Shabbos, even for non-protective purposes, in truth, we do not find such a precedence of differentiation, and the matter is solely dependent on whether one's intent is for protection or not.

cover the carriage, as explained in Halacha 2D.

May one spread a sun or rain cover over a baby carriage on Shabbos?
If the hood was not opened a handbreadths width from before Shabbos: Some Poskim[106] allow one to open the hood of the carriage and then add to it the covering as this is similar to adding to already made roofing. Many other Poskim[107] however rule that it is forbidden to open the hood and thus according to them it would remain prohibited to place over the carriage a sun or rain cover.
If the hood was opened a handbreadth from before Shabbos: Then it is permitted to add a cover to it.

May one open an umbrella that is attached to a stroller from before Shabbos?[108]
Some opinions[109] hold that this matter is subject to the same dispute mentioned earlier regarding opening the hood of a stroller on Shabbos. Others[110] hold that in this case it would be forbidden even according to the previously mentioned lenient opinions.

May one form the plastic stroller covering into a tent over the floor from before Shabbos and place it on his stroller on Shabbos if need be?
Yes, however one must take caution not to fold the plastic on Shabbos after removing it. Rather he is to place it back into the tent position.[111]

Q&A on Sukkah
If it is raining on Yom Tov may one place a sheet or the like over or under the Sechach?[112]
Yes, as long as the sheet is not distanced more than a Tefach from the Sechach in order so one not transgress the prohibition of making an Ohel on Yom Tov.

If on Shabbos or Yom Tov the Sechach blew off due to wind may it be replaced?[113]
No. It is forbidden for a Jew to replace the Sechach. This applies even if only part of the Sechach blew off or folded over, one may nevertheless not spread it back onto the Sukkah.[114] If, however, there is no other Sukkah available, one may ask a gentile to replace the Sechach for him.

---

[106] Rav SZ"A in SSH"K 24 footnote 46
[107] Ketzos Hashulchan 120 footnote 8; Igros Moshe 4:105; Sheivet Halevy 3:54; Minchas Yitzchak 10:26 leaves this matter in question although leans to be lenient in a case that the hood also forms side walls when opened.
[108] Piskeiy Teshuvos 315:6
[109] Az Nidbaru 11:24
[110] Beir Moshe 6:108
[111] So writes Piskeiy Teshuvos 315 footnote 22, as a moveable tent is still called a tent. Vetzaruch Iyun Gadol as according to this it should be permitted also to wear a baseball cap for sun protection being that it was already a tent from before Shabbos.
[112] Piskeiy Teshuvos 326:6; See Admur 640:10
[113] M"B 637:1 in name of Shoel Umeishiv; Piskeiy Teshuvos 626:10; See however Bikurei Yaakov who is lenient; Vetzaruch Iyun if one can place invalid Sechach over the blown area of Sechach in order to validate it as a Dofen Akuma
[114] This is unlike Nitei Gavriel 18:8 that rules it is permitted to do so.

Compilation-May one open or close the hood of a baby carriage on Shabbos?

A. Background:[115]

It is a Biblical prohibition to build or destroy a permanent tent, or hovering on Shabbos. Due to this, it is Rabbinically forbidden to build/open or take down or close any hovering on Shabbos, even temporary, lest one make or destroy a permanent hovering. This prohibition is known as "Issur Ohel." Nonetheless, under certain conditions, extending, or taking down, a temporary hovering is permitted. These include: a) If the hovering was already opened one Tefach before Shabbos, then one may extend the hovering, or close the extension, on Shabbos.[116] This measurement of a handbreadth does not include any rolled up material.[117] b) If the purpose of the hovering is not for the sake of human protection from sun, rain, insects and the like, and it does not contain walls under it, then it may be opened and closed without restriction on Shabbos.[118] c) If the hovering is already attached to an item and simply needs to be opened or closed, it is permitted to be opened or closed on Shabbos even if it contains walls under it.[119] Nevertheless, it is debated amongst the Poskim[120] as to whether it may be opened or closed for all purposes, or only for purposes that do not involve human protection. All these factors are taken into account in the discussion of whether the opening the hood of a stroller is permitted on Shabbos. The following is the ruling on this subject:

B. The law:[121]

If the hood was opened a handbreadth [8 cm] before Shabbos:[122] If the hood of the stroller was opened at least one Tefach [8 cm] before Shabbos [excluding the folded area[123]] then it is permitted according to all to further open it on Shabbos. [This allowance applies even if further opening the hood will form a tent like hovering of a roof and walls.[124]] Likewise, according to all, one may close the section that was further

---

[115] See Admur 315:1; Michaber 315:1; Rambam 22:27; Shabbos 125b; Yerushalmi 20:1; M"B 315:17

[116] Admur 315:2; Michaber 315:2; Chachamim in Shabbos 125b

[117] Admur ibid; Michaber ibid; Ritva

The reason: The reason for this is because the circumference of the rolled material does not appear like a tent at all. [Admur ibid]

[118] Admur 315:1 "It is forbidden to make a tent, which refers to [any] roofing which hovers over a person **in order to guard him from a given matter**, such as [to protect him] from the sun or from the rain or from another given matter." And Admur 315:9 "A temporary roof which one does not intend in making it for it to be a tent to hover over what is underneath it, but rather only in order to use [this roof] for a certain use, such as for example placing the board of a table on its legs, then even though in doing so one makes a temporary roof this does not pose a problem being that one has no intent to make a tent. Nevertheless, if one also places temporary walls under this roof, then this is similar to a tent and is forbidden to be done in its normal form which is [starting] from below to above, and rather [must be done from] above to below [which is] an irregular form."; Michaber 315:3 as explained in M"A 315:7; M"B 315:17-19

[119] Admur 315:13 "Any temporary tent which one has no intention into making into a tent [the Sages] only prohibited spreading over walls which one [had already] set up under it on Shabbos if the roofing had not been attached on its walls from before Shabbos. However, if [the roofing] had already been attached to them from before Shabbos but it was placed there folded, then it is permitted to spread it out and set it up on Shabbos. For example a chair made from individual parts and when one wants to sit on it one opens it and spreads and stretches the leather [seating] and when one removes [the seat] he closes it up and has the leather fold, then it is permitted to initially open it on Shabbos even if it has walls under it."; Michaber 315:5; Tur 315; Shabbos 138a as explains Tosafus; Piskeiy Teshuvos 315:7 [old] 11 [new]; Biur Halacha 315:5 "Kisei" regarding a folding bed; So rule also regarding opening a Chuppah canopy: Admur 315:13; M"A 315:8 ; M"B 315:27

[120] The dispute is based on how to interpret the above sources of allowance, as well as in how to understand the allowance to open a Chuppah canopy on Shabbos, as brought in M"A 315:8 and to close a Sukkah awning due to rain, as explained in Rama 626:3; See Poskim in following footnotes!

[121] See Piskeiy Teshuvos 315:6 [old] 315:9 [new]

[122] Sources above in condition A; M"B 315:12; Ketzos Hashulchan 120 footnote 8

[123] Admur 315:2; Michaber 315:2

Other opinions: Some Poskim suggest that by a stroller, even the folded area can count as part of the Tefach, as it is made for protection and is recognizable as such. [See Or Letziyon 2:28-2; Piskeiy Teshuvos 315 footnote 98 and 101]

[124] Minchas Yitzchak 10:26; See Piskeiy Teshuvos 315 footnote 100

Background regarding if doing so is similar to making a tent and should hence be forbidden due to the tent prohibition: The Poskim rule that it is forbidden to make a tent on Shabbos for protection purposes by placing the material over a surface and having the material then dangle from the two sides, hence making a tent in between. [Admur 315:15-18; Michaber 315:8; Shabbos 138] Accordingly, it should remain forbidden to ever place a rain covering over a stroller, as by doing so one is making a tent. [See Piskeiy Teshuvos 315 footnote 99 who implies that indeed if the plastic covering will form a slant of one Tefach within three Tefachim, then it is forbidden] However, in truth, since the open hood of a stroller is recognizably there for protection purposes, therefore, adding the plastic material and having it form walls like a tent is simply like adding a temporary hovering to an already established Tefach hovering which is allowed, and hence we don't care if the material now forms a Tefach hovering. [See Tosefes Shabbos 315:18 "Before Shabbos the tent needs to have a Tefach opened before Shabbos"; Kaf Hachaim 315:61; Piskeiy Teshuvos 315:18]

opened on Shabbos.[125] [However, according to the stringent opinion brought next, one may not close the section that was opened already from before Shabbos.[126]]

If the hood was not opened a handbreadth [8 cm] before Shabbos: Some Poskim[127] rule it is permitted to open and close the hood of a stroller on Shabbos without restriction, even if the stroller or hood was folded from before Shabbos.[128] This applies irrelevant of the reason for why one desires to open the hood, whether it is to protect the baby from the sun or rain, or simply to place items on the roofing, and applies whether or not the hood was partially opened already before Shabbos. However, other Poskim[129] rule that

---

[125] Admur 315:16

[126] Admur 315:16 *"When one adds onto a tent that was [the width of] a handbreadth from before Shabbos, it is only permitted to dismantle the material that was added [on Shabbos] however not the part of the tent that was [already] built from before Shabbos."* Piskeiy Teshuvos 315:9 footnote 101 and 315:8; See Avnei Nezer 211:34 and Ketzos Hashulchan 120 footnote 17 regarding if one may close it up until the Tefach area, if it was open more than a Tfeach from before Shabbos
Other opinions: Some Poskim rule that the entire roofing may be dismantled. [Chazon Ish 52:7; SSH"K 24 footnote 31 allows this to be done in stages]

[127] Implication of all the following Poskim who understand M"A ibid to rule that one may open a Chuppah even for protection purposes if it was attached before Shabbos: P"M 315 A"A 8; Tosefes Shabbos 315:14; Beis Meir 315:1; Chasam Sofer 72; Machaneh Mayim 3:23; Shevilei David 315; Shaar Hatizyon 315:35; The following Poskim explicitly rule this way: Chazon Ish 52:6 based on Michaber 315:5 and Shabbos 138a regarding allowance of folding chair and Rama 626:3 regarding allowance of Sukkah awning and M"A 315:8 regarding allowance of Chuppah *"From here it is learned that the hoods of the baby stroller which are folded may be folded and closed on Shabbos even though one intends to make a roof [for protection of the baby]"*; Bris Olam 14; Shraga Hameir 3:37; Beir Moshe 6:87 based on Chazon Ish ibid *"It is permitted to open and close them on Shabbos"*; SSH"K 24:13; Ateres Moshe 1:87; Migdanos Eliyahu 2:78; Piskeiy Teshuvos ibid footnote 96 in name of many Milaktei Doreinu
Ruling of Mishneh Berurah: See Shaar Hatizyon 315:35 which implies like Chazon Ish ibid that one may always open a folded hovering even for protection purposes, however, see Biur Halacha 315:8 "Tefach" regarding the prohibition against using an umbrella, which implies like Admur that one may never open even a folded hovering for protection purposes. See Piskeiy Teshuvos 315 footnote 135

[128] The reason: As since the hood was already connected to the stroller from before Shabbos, it is no different than opening/closing a door on its hinges by the Sechach of a Sukkah [as rules Rama ibid], or opening a folding chair [as rules Michaber 315:5 and Shabbos 138a] or opening a Chuppah canopy [as rules M"A ibid]. From these sources we learn that all pre-attached hovering's may be opened and closed on Shabbos without restriction, even if they are being opened for protection purposes, as is the case regarding the Chuppah canopy, as explains Shaar Hatizyon 315:35, and as is clearly the case regarding the Sukkah awning which is being closed to protect from rain. The reason there is no decree against opening it in these cases is because the hovering was pre-attached before Shabbos, and its opening is simply "Derech Tashmisho" and not in a way of building. [Chazon Ish and Poskim ibid]

[129] Implication of Admur 315:13 [explained below]; Implication of all the following Poskim who understand M"A ibid to rule that one may only open a Chuppah for non-protection purposes even if it was attached before Shabbos: Noda Beyehuda Tinyana 30; Menorah Hatehorah 315:14; Shoel Umeishiv Gimel 2:43; Tiferes Yisrael Kalkeles Shabbos Boneh 3; Aruch Hashulchan 315:10 and 12; Daas Torah 315; Tehila Ledavid 315:8; Kaf Hachaim 315:44; The following Poskim explicitly rule this way: Ketzos Hashulchan 120 footnote 8 *"Regarding the hood of strollers, it is obvious that it is forbidden to be opened on Shabbos even though it is attached to the stroller...One must warn the public regarding this."*; Igros Moshe 4:105; Sheivet Halevy 3:54; Or Letziyon 2:28-2; Halichos Olam 2:1; Minchas Yitzchak 10:26 leaves this matter in question although leans to be lenient in a case that the hood also forms side walls when opened.
The ruling of Admur: Admur 315:13 rules: *"Any temporary tent which **one has no intention into making into a tent** [the Sages] only prohibited spreading over walls which one [had already] set up under it on Shabbos if the roofing had not been attached on its walls from before Shabbos. However, if [the roofing] had already been attached to them from before Shabbos but it was placed there folded, then it is permitted to spread it out and set it up on Shabbos."* Thus, Admur clearly learns that the Talmudic allowance of a folding chair is limited to a case that the intent of the hovering is not for protection purposes, and hence here that the purpose of the stroller hood is to protect the child, it is forbidden to be opened or closed.
Contradiction from the ruling regarding the Chuppah canopy: The Poskim rule that it is permitted to open a Chuppah canopy on Shabbos being that it is pre-attached [to its poles]. [Admur 315:13; M"A 315:8; M"B 315:27] This seems to imply that the allowance of a pre-attached item applies even when the item is opened for protection purposes, as if the intent of the above canopy is not for protection purposes, it should permitted be regardless, being that it does not have walls, and so learns the Shaar Hatziyon 315:35 and Chazon Ish ibid that the intent of the canopy is for protection purposes. This directly contradicts the ruling of the Poskim ibid. However, in truth it is possible to explain the case to be referring to opening the canopy for non-protection purposes, such as for Kavod Chasan Vekallah, and the novelty is that even if the canopy contains walls, it may be opened, being that it was pre-attached before Shabbos. [So explains Tehila Ledavid 315:8]
Contradiction from the ruling regarding the awning of a Sukkah: Admur 626:20 rules *"If this [roof] door [i.e. the removable roofing of the Sukkah] has hinges with which it is opened and closed, then it is like a complete opening and is permitted to open and close it on Shabbos and Yom Tov and doing so does not contain the Building or destroying prohibition."* This follows the ruling of the Rama 626:3. At first glance, this ruling seems to contradict the ruling of the Poskim ibid, as certainly the Sechach door is being closed for protection purposes, and it is nevertheless allowed, thus proving the approach of the Chazon Ish ibid. However, in truth the reason why a Ohel prohibition does not apply in this case is not because it was pre-attached before Shabbot, but rather because it is discussing a case that the Sukkah was made inside a house and part of the ceiling has a window which is opened so the Sechach be directly under the heavens. Opening this window does not pose an Ohel prohibition as one is allowed to add a temporary Ohel to an Ohel which was already extended a Tefach before Yom Tov/Shabbos, and in this case when one closes the window, he is simply adding that hovering to the already existing ceiling. [See Minchas Yitzchak 10:27, brought in Piskeiy Teshuvos 315 footnote 141, for a similar answer] Alternatively, one can answer that the case here is discussing that there is not a Tefach of space between the awning and the Sechach and hence it is not considered an Ohel [as rules Admur in 640:10]. [So answers Or Letziyon 2:28-1] In conclusion, the result of the above explanation in Admur is that if one built a Sukkah outside of his home and built an awning over it, this awning may only be opened and closed on Shabbos if there is not a Tefach of space between the awning and the Schach. See however, Noda Beyehuda

it is forbidden to open or close the hood of a stroller for purposes of protection for the baby [i.e. shade from the sun or rain and the like] in all cases that it was not opened a handbreadth [8 cm] from before Shabbos [in addition to the folded area of the hood].[130] Practically, the ruling of Admur[131] follows the stringent opinion, and it is thus forbidden for Chabad Chassidim, and all those who have accepted his rulings, to open or close the hood of a baby stroller unless it was opened a Tefach from before Shabbos, [in which case it may be further opened on Shabbos, and may be closed up until the area that was already open before Shabbos, as stated above].[132] However, amongst other sects of Jewry, many are accustomed to be lenient like the former opinion, and those who do so have upon whom to rely.[133] Nonetheless, even amongst those who are lenient, the advised approach is to open the hood of the stroller at least one Tefach every Erev Shabbos, and thus be allowed to further open it according to all.[134]

Summary:

Was opened one Tefach before Shabbos: If the hood of the stroller was opened at least one Tefach [8 cm] before Shabbos [excluding the folded area] then it is permitted according to all to further open it on Shabbos.

Was not opened one Tefach before Shabbos: It is disputed amongst Poskim whether one may open the hood of stroller on Shabbos for the sake of giving sun or rain protection, if it was not opened one Tefach before Shabbos. Admur follows the stringent opinion, and it is thus forbidden for Chabad Chassidim, and all those who have accepted his rulings, to open or close the hood of a baby stroller unless it was opened a Tefach from before Shabbos, [in which case it may be further opened on Shabbos, and may be closed up until the area that was already open before Shabbos, as stated above]. However, amongst other sects of Jewry, many are accustomed to being lenient like the former opinion, and those who do so have upon whom to rely. Nonetheless, even amongst those who are lenient, the advised approach is to open the hood of the stroller at least one Tefach every Erev Shabbos, and thus be allowed to further open it according to all.

Q&A

May one open or close the hood of a baby carriage if there is no person inside?

➤ Example: One is bringing from home a large amount of food in a stroller/carriage on behalf of the Shul's Kiddush. May he open the hood to protect the food from the rain or sun? May he open the hood for the sake of putting stuff on top?

Seemingly, even according to the stringent opinion above, one may open the hood of a baby carriage for a purpose that does not involve human protection, such as to carry item on top of it, or for the sake of giving shade to foods that are inside.[135] However, one may not spread a sheet over the

---

Tinayan 30 who answers that building awnings are an exception and may be opened being they are built into the house and considered part of it. See also Piskeiy Teshuvos 315:13 footnote 136 and 141

[130] The reason: As although the hood was attached to the stroller from before Shabbos, and is thus similar to the case of a folding chair, nevertheless, this attachment only permits one to open and close it without restriction for non-protection purposes, as is the original Talmudic example with the folding chair, which is opened and closed for non-protection purposes. However, to open or close a hovering for protection purposes is always forbidden even if the hovering as pre-attached before Shabbos, and there exists no precedent in the Poskim and in the above folding chair example, to permit it. [Ketzos Hashulchan ibid; Poskim ibid]

[131] See previous footnotes!

[132] See Ketzos Hashulchan ibid

[133] See Migdanos Eliyahu 2:78 that the custom is to be lenient and the defense of the custom

[134] Piskeiy Teshuvos 315:9 and footnote 102 that although the widespread custom is to be lenient, nevertheless it is proper to do as above and avoid the disputes

[135] The reason: This may be done as the prohibition of making an Ohel only applies when it is made for the sake of protecting people and not when it is made for the sake of protecting items, such as food or other purpose. Now, although it is forbidden on Shabbos to set up a tent with walls for even non-protective purposes, in its normal way, nonetheless here that the walls are set up before Shabbos, it is permitted, similar to placing a cover on a vessel to protect the food. [See Michaber 315:13 that one may cover a barrel of wine with its lid even if there is a Tefach of space in-between. Admur 315:19 permits covering a vessel of food even with a cloth; See also wording of Admur 315:1; P"M 315 A"A 8] Furthermore, being that the hood was already attached to the stroller before Shabbos, it is similar to the allowance to open a folding chair, in which all agree is allowed when performed for non-protecting purposes. Now, although it is possible to argue that since in general a hood is

carriage unless a) there will not be a Tefach of space between the sheet and the food or b) One does not fully cover the carriage.[136]

According to the lenient opinion, may one attach the hood on Shabbos and then open it?[137]
Even according to the lenient opinion, it is only permitted to open and extend the hood of the stroller, if the hood was attached to the stroller before Shabbos. If, however, it was not attached before Shabbos, then even in cases that it is permitted to attach the hood to the stroller on Shabbos[138], it remains forbidden to open the hood even according to the lenient opinion above.[139] Accordingly, even if the hood is permitted to be attached on Shabbos as explained in the footnote above, it is considered under the Muktzah category of Keli Shemilachto Lissur being that it cannot be opened any further.[140] [However, some Poskim[141] are lenient even in such a case, and rule may even initially attach the hood on Shabbos in a permitted way, and then open it according to the lenient opinion above.[142] Practically, one is to be stringent.]

May one spread a sun or rain cover over a baby carriage on Shabbos?
If the hood was opened a handbreadth from before Shabbos:[143] If the hood of the stroller was opened one Tefach [8 cm] before Shabbos [excluding the folded area[144]] then is permitted according to all to further add a sun/rain cover on top of it [even though it will form a tent like hovering of a roof and walls[145]]. [This applies even if the plastic cover is not on top of, or directly adjacent to the hood, so

---

meant to serve as protection for a child, therefore it should not be allowed to be opened at all on Shabbos, even for non-protective purposes, in truth, we do not find such a precedence of differentiation, and the matter is solely dependent on whether one's intent is for protection or not.

[136] See Admur 315:19 regarding covering a barrel, or a vessel the size of a barrel, and the same applies here

[137] All Poskim who forbid Tosefes Ohel unless it was set up before Shabbos, as explained in the reason below; SSH"K 24:13; Piskeiy Teshuvos 315:9 that in such a case it is forbidden according to all; Rav Y.Y. Fisher in letter printed in Maor Hashabbos 4:7

[138] Avoiding the Tikkun Keli Prohibition: One may only attach the attach the hood to the stroller on Shabbos if it avoids the Tikkun Keli prohibition, such as if the hood hangs on hooks and the like, in which the attachment is loose, and is meant to always remain loose. However, to attach it strongly using snatches, inserts, screws, or snaps and the like, is forbidden due to Tikkun Keli, unless one is always accustomed to attach and detach the hood constantly every day after its use. Practically, by most strollers, it is forbidden to attach the hood, as the attachment is strong and is commonly left on for more than 48 hours. [See Admur 313:19-21; Michaber 313:6 and 9; Rama 313:6; Ketzos Hashulchan 119 footnote 7; Piskeiy Teshuvos ibid footnote 103; 313:4]
Avoiding the Ohel prohibition: In addition to avoiding the Tikkun Keli prohibition, one may only attach the attach the hood to the stroller on Shabbos if it avoids the Ohel prohibition, such as if it does not hover a Tefach over the child, even when folded. [See M"B 315:16 and Shaar Hatziyon 20; Piskeiy Teshuvos 315 footnote 78 and 105] Likewise, it may be attached even if it extends one Tefach if one's intent is not to use it as protection for the child, but simply to put things on top of it, or under it, and the like.

[139] The reason: As it is forbidden on Shabbos to add a Tosefes Ohel Araiy unless the original panel was already set up before Shabbos. [Admur 315:8 "such as for example if the mat was spread out from before Shabbos a handbreadths worth... as all this is only adding to the handbreadth tent which was made the day before"; Rama 315:1; Levush 315:2; M"B 315:12; Chazon Ish 52:8; Piskeiy Teshuvos 315:7 footnote 72] Accordingly, it is forbidden on Shabbos to set up on Shabbos panels within 3 handbreadths of each other with intent to then spread a sheet over it on the basis of Tosefes Ohel Araiy. [Ketzos Hashulchan 120 footnote 11] Accordingly, here too it is forbidden to initially attach the hood on Shabbos for the sake of then opening it on the basis of the lenient opinions allowance. [SSH"K and Piskeiy Teshuvos ibid]

[140] Piskeiy Teshuvos 315:9 footnote 105

[141] Az Nidbaru 3:24; Bris Olam Boneh 14; 9:19; All Poskim who permit Tosefes Ohel even if it was set up on Shabbos: Tosefes Shabbos 315:7; Ateres Chachamim of Rav Baruch Taam 6 leaves this matter in question; See Piskeiy Teshuvos 315:7 footnote 72

[142] The reason: As some Poskim hold that one may add Tosefes Ohel even if the Ohel was set up on Shabbos, as stated in previous footnote, and perhaps in this case everyone would agree [according to the lenient opinion] that it is allowed being that it is considered similar to a door of a vessel which is allowed to be opened and closed on Shabbos when attached in a permitted way.

[143] Sources above in condition A; M"B 315:12; Piskeiy Teshuvos 315:9

[144] See Admur 315:2; Michaber 315:2; Ritva
Other opinions: Some Poskim rule that even though one may not open the rolled area of an Ohel on Shabbos, if it was not pre-opened to a Tefach's length before Shabbos, nevertheless, one may add to it another material of hovering. [Chazon Ish 52:8; Or Letziyon 2:28-2; Piskeiy Teshuvos 315 footnote 78; See Ketzos Hashulchan 120 footnote 8] Accordingly, one may place the plastic stroller cover over the hood even if it remained rolled up into Shabbos, even according to those who prohibit opening the stroller hood on Shabbos. [Or Letziyon ibid; Piskeiy Teshuvos 315 footnote 98]

[145] Background regarding if doing so is similar to making a tent and should hence be forbidden due to the tent prohibition: The Poskim rule that it is forbidden to make a tent on Shabbos for protection purposes by placing the material over a surface and having the material then dangle from the two sides, hence making a tent in between. [Admur 315:15-18; Michaber 315:8; Shabbos 138] Accordingly, it should remain forbidden to ever place a rain covering over a stroller, as by doing so one is making a tent. [See Piskeiy Teshuvos 315 footnote 99 who implies that indeed if the plastic covering will form a slant of one Tefach within three Tefachim, then it is forbidden] However, in truth, since the open hood of a stroller is recognizably there for protection purposes, therefore, adding the plastic material and having it form walls like a tent is simply like adding a temporary hovering to an already established Tefach hovering which is allowed, and hence we don't care if the material now forms a

long as it is within three Tefachim/24 cm from it.[146]]

<u>If the hood was not opened a handbreadths width from before Shabbos:</u>[147] According to the stringent opinion above who prohibits opening the hood of a stroller on Shabbos, it goes without saying that it is also forbidden to place the plastic rain/sun cover over the stroller on Shabbos, if it was not opened one handbreadth from before Shabbos.[148] However, according to the lenient opinion above who allows opening the hood of a stroller on Shabbos, some Poskim[149] rule that it is likewise permitted for one to add the plastic covering to the hood, after opening the hood one Tefach worth on Shabbos.[150] However, other Poskim[151] rule that in such a case it is forbidden according to all to place the plastic sun/rain cover over the stroller on the basis of the Tefach wide open hood which he opened on Shabbos for this purpose.[152] However, in the event that the open hood fully covers the top of the stroller, then it is permitted according to all to place the plastic covering over it to form protecting walls on the sides of the stroller, even if one followed the lenient opinion to open the hood on Shabbos.[153]

<u>Forming the plastic stroller covering into a tent before Shabbos:</u> If one formed the plastic stroller covering into a tent from before Shabbos, some Poskim[154] write that it is then permitted to place it on the stroller on Shabbos even if the hood of the stroller was not opened before Shabbos. However, one must take precaution not to fold the plastic on Shabbos after removing it and rather it must retain its tent position. Practically, however, one is not to rely on this, and is rather to open the hood of the stroller one Tefach before Shabbos, as stated above, in order to then be allowed to add the plastic covering to it according to all.[155]

May one open a stroller umbrella, or wheelchair umbrella, on Shabbos?[156]
Some strollers come built in with a side umbrella which is opened to protect the child from the sun/rain and the question is raised regarding if it may be opened on Shabbos. Some Poskim[157] rule that this matter is subject to the same dispute mentioned above regarding opening the hood of a stroller on Shabbos, in which some Poskim allow it to be done. [This, however, only applies to a specially manufactured stroller umbrella, and not towards a typical umbrella that one attached on his own to the stroller or wheelchair.[158]] Other Poskim[159], however, rule that this case is not subject to the debate mentioned above regarding opening the hood of the stroller, and it is thus forbidden according to all opinions to open the stroller umbrella.

Tefach hovering. [See Tosefes Shabbos 315:18 "Before Shabbos the tent needs to have a Tefach opened before Shabbos"; Kaf Hachaim 315:61; Piskeiy Teshuvos 315:8]
[146] Piskeiy Teshuvos 315 footnote 99
[147] See Piskeiy Teshuvos 315 footnote 97
[148] See however other opinions in previous footnote.
[149] Rav SZ"A in SSH"K 24 footnote 48; Beir Moshe 6:97; Rav Y.Y. Fisher in Meor Hashabbos 4:7; See Meshivas Nafesh 1:7-4; Piskeiy Teshuvos ibid
[150] <u>The reason:</u> As this is similar to adding a hovering to an already made roofing of one Tefach, and what difference does it make if the Tefach was opened on Shabbos or before Shabbos, so long as it was opened prior to adding to it. However, it is forbidden according to all [excluding the other opinions in previous footnotes] to add the plastic cover to the stroller prior to opening up the hood of the stroller to at least one Tefach.
[151] Sheivet Halevy 3:54 based on Chazon Ish 52:8; Az Nidbaru 1:79-136;
[152] <u>The reason:</u> As the allowance to add to an already made roofing of one Tefach, only applies if it was set up before Shabbos. [Chazon Ish ibid]
[153] Piskeiy Teshuvos 315 footnote 99 as there is no prohibition to make a Mechitza for protection purposes; See previous footnotes regarding why doing so does not pose a tent making prohibition
[154] Piskeiy Teshuvos 315 footnote 22 [old] footnote 99 [new], as a moveable tent is still called a tent. Se also Piskeiy Teshuvos 315:2 and Maor Hashabbos 4 in letters of Rav Y.Y. Fisher
[155] As one can argue that a tent is not considered a tent unless it was <u>recognizably</u> spread open for protection purposes, as otherwise, it should be permitted according to all to wear a baseball cap for sun protection being that it was already a tent from before Shabbos. So is also proven from the ruling in Poskim that a one by one Tefach item may not be used as a hovering for protection on Shabbos even it maintained this size from before Shabbos, as its intended use for protection was never made recognizable before Shabbos. [See Taz 215:3; M"B 315:16; Ben Ish Chaiy Shemos 2:1; Kaf Hachaim 315:27; Chazon Ish 52:8; Ketzos Hashulchan 120 footnote 8] Accordingly, perhaps having the hovering over the floor is not a recognizable hovering for protection, and hence may not be used on Shabbos.
[156] Piskeiy Teshuvos 315:6 [old] 315:9 [new] footnote 95
[157] Az Nidbaru 11:23; SSH"K 24:13; Chut Hashanai 36:10
[158] Piskeiy Teshuvos 315 footnote 95
[159] Beir Moshe 6:108

2. Making a roofing for non protection purposes:
A. If there are no walls under the roofing item:[160]

A temporary roof which one does not intend in making it for it to be a tent to hover over what is underneath it, but rather only in order to use [this roof] for a certain use, such as for example placing the board of a table on its legs, then even though in doing so one makes a temporary roof this does not pose a problem being that one has no intent to make a tent. [This applies even if one has use for the space under it.[161]]

Setting up a strainer with dregs: See Examples!

B. If there are walls/boards under the roofing item:

Definition of legs versus walls: A wall is defined as a board that reaches until the ground.[162] Practically, we are stringent to consider it a wall even if it reaches within three Tefach to the ground.[163] [It is considered a wall even if it does not reach a height of ten Tefach.[164]] If the Ohel hovering contains at least two of these types of walls, it is considered a walled hovering, and follows the laws explained in C. If, however, the hovering contains only one such wall, and is thus supported by legs in the other directions, then it is not considered a walled hovering and follows the laws explained above.[165]

Placing or removing a covering from walls which were set up from before Shabbos, such as a typical vessel: See D below.

Setting up walls on Shabbos and then placing a hovering over it:[166] If one also places temporary walls under this roof [even if it only has two legs which are boards parallel to each other[167]], then this is similar to a tent and is forbidden to be done in its normal form which is [starting] from below to above, and rather [must be done from] above to below [which is] an irregular form.

The above restriction only applies if one has a use for the space being formed:[168] When setting up barrels on top of each other, one [barrel] being placed on top of two,.... then he may not set up the lower barrels first and then place the upper one on them because the space that is created between [the two lower barrels] is similar to a tent which has two walls and a roof. Therefore, it must be made in an irregular way from above to below. However, it is permitted to stand two books parallel to each other and place a book over them even though that this forms a handbreadths worth of space under them, as since one has no use for the space between them it is thus not at all similar to a tent which has its space used. However, by [setting up] barrels [it is forbidden, because] one requires the space between the two barrels in order so the barrels not mold, as it is for this reason that he set them up in this way [that one barrel stands on two as opposed to on one]. Similarly by a bed [as will be explained in the examples], even if it only has two [legs which are] boards parallel to each other, [since] one has use for the space between them [such as] to use it to store ones footwear and the like, and it goes without saying if it has four [legs made of] boards

---

[160] Admur 315:9; Michaber 315:3 as explained in M"A 315:7; M"B 315:17
[161] So is clearly evident from Michaber 315:3; Admur ibid
Other opinions: See Biur Halacha 315:3 "Mitos" that there are Rishonim [Rashba] that rule that if one needs the air under the table, then it is considered an actual Ohel and is forbidden even without walls under it. This implies that they would rule that even if one does not need the space under it, if it has walls under, one must change from the normal way of setting it up. The Biur Halacha concludes that one should be initially stringent like their opinion unless it is a case of need.
[162] Admur 315:11; M"B 315:21
[163] M"A 502:9; M"B 315:21; see Admur in Kuntrus Achron 248:2
[164] Biur Halacha 3153 "Dapim Mechubarim"; and so is proven from Admur and all other Poskim who make no mention of such a condition, and so is proven from the fact that the only reason one may make a bridge using Sefarim is because one has no use for the space under and not because they do not reach ten Tefach. [ibid]
Other opinions: Some Poskim rule the Mechitzos must be 10 Tefach heigh to be defined as a wall. [Tosefes Shabbos brought in Biur Halacha ibid]
[165] Admur 315:11; Taz 315:4; M"B 315:22
[166] Admur 315:9; Michaber 315:3; M"B 315:19
[167] Admur 315:11; Taz 315:4; M"B 315:22
[168] Admur 315:12; Rama 315:7; M"B 315:17 "Some Poskim rule" however in 315:22 he plainly rules like their opinions.
Other opinions: See Biur Halacha 315:3 "Mitos" that there are Rishonim [Rashba] that rule that if one needs the air under the table, then it is considered an actual Ohel and is forbidden even without walls under it. This implies that they would rule that even if one does not need the space under it, if it has walls under, one must change from the normal way of setting it up. The Biur Halacha concludes that one should be initially stringent like their opinion unless it is a case of need.

like a box in which one can conceal his items just like in a box, [therefore one may not place the board on them regularly].

The above restriction only applies if the roofing was not attached to the walls from before Shabbos:[169] Any temporary tent which one has no intention into making into a tent[170] [the Sages] only prohibited spreading over walls which one [had already] set up under it on Shabbos if the roofing had not been attached on its walls from before Shabbos. However, if [the roofing] had already been attached to them from before Shabbos but it was placed there folded, then it is permitted to spread it out and set it up on Shabbos.

The reason for this is: because it is not similar to making a tent since one is not doing anything as the roofing was already set up and prepared together with the walls from before Shabbos and it is just that one unfolds it on Shabbos and sits on it.

The law if the walls are meant to serve as an Ohel for protection: See Halacha 3D that if the Mechitzos/walls are there as part of an Ohel of protection then placing a hovering under [or over] the walls even not for protection is forbidden. [Thus, if one placed Mechitzos to block the sun then one may not place a sheet over the Mechitzos even for non-protection purposes.]

Attaching the hovering board to the legs:[171]
In all cases that it is permitted to set up an Ohel on Shabbos, this is provided that one will not attach the Ohel hovering to its legs or walls, and will rather simply rest the Ohel hovering on the legs. In the event that one will attach the hovering to the legs or walls, then this may transgress the building prohibition, as discussed in chapters 313-314.

C. Examples:
❖ **Placing a board, sheet or mattress on top of a bed frame:**
Bed with walls/boards:[172] A bed [made in the following manner] that its legs are made out of boards which are attached [to each other] like the walls of a box and on them one spreads [a mattress, such as] leather or places on them a board from on top to sleep on, then one may not first set up the legs and then place the hide or the board on them in the way that is done during the week, because this is similar to making a tent. Rather one is to first grasp the hide or the board in the air and afterwards places the legs underneath it, as this is not similar to making a tent being that it is not common to build [starting] from top to bottom. [This law applies even if the walls of the bed were set up before Shabbos, nevertheless one must set it up with the mattress in the above order.[173]]

A bed of only two wall legs:[174] Similarly by a bed, even if it only has two [legs which are] boards parallel to each other, [one may not place the board on them regularly]. [This is very common today by beds

---

[169] Admur 315:13
[170] Admur 315:13 and so rules: Tehila Ledavid 315:8; Ketzos Hashulchan 120 footnote 8; Igros Moshe 4:105; Sheivet Halevy 3:54; Minchas Yitzchak 10:26 leaves this matter in question although leans to be lenient in a case that the hood also forms side walls when opened.
Other opinions: Some Poskim rule one may open and close an Ohel that is attached to hinges even for the sake of Ohel. [Chazon Ish 52:6; Bris Olam 14; Shraga Hameir 3:37; Beir Moshe 6:87 based on Chazon Ish; SSH"K 24:13; See also Shaar Hatizyon 315:35 that implies like Chazon Ish; however see Biur Halacha 315:8 "Tefach" regarding the prohibition against using an umbrella that implies like Admur]
[171] M"B 315:23
[172] Admur 315:9; Michaber 315:3; Shabbos 138
[173] Even if the walls of the bed, were set up from before Shabbos, nevertheless this condition would need to be met being that the hole which the mattress is placed on bed is as large as a tub. So is implied from Michaber 315:4 and Admur 315:11, that they are referring to a bed that was already set up before Shabbos "However if it had a pillow or blanket or clothing spread on it **from before Shabbos** the amount of a handbreadth, then it is permitted to spread [it] on Shabbos over the entire bed being that doing so is simply adding to a temporary tent."
Other opinions: Some Poskim rule that if the bed was set up before Shabbos, then there are no restrictions involved. [Shaar Hatziyon 315:31]
[174] Admur 315:11-12; Taz 315:4; M"B 315:22

which have a headboard and a backboard that reach within three Tefach to the ground.[175] It certainly applies by beds that are formed like a box, in which case they have all four walls reaching the ground[176], or within three Tefach of the ground.[177]]

The reason for why an irregularity is needed is:[178] [since] one has use for the space between the [two boards, such as] to use it to store ones footwear and the like, and it goes without saying if it has four [legs made of] boards like a box in which one can conceal his items just like in a box, [therefore one may not place the board on them regularly].

If the top of the bed is barred with rope:[179] If this bed [with walled legs] does not have placed on it leather or boards but is rather barred with ropes from above, then if there are three handbreadths between each rope, in which case we do not consider the ropes to be all attached, then it is forbidden to initially spread a sheet over it on Shabbos or place a pillow or blanket on it being that this is similar to making a tent. Similarly, it is forbidden to remove the lower cloth that is on it being that this is similar to destroying a tent. [However, it is permitted to have one person spread the sheet and another move the bed under the sheet, thus having the roof set up before the walled legs.[180]]

If the top was partially covered from before Shabbos:[181] [However] if it had a pillow or blanket or clothing spread on it from before Shabbos the amount of a handbreadth, then it is permitted to spread [it] on Shabbos over the entire bed being that doing so is simply adding to a temporary tent.

Beds with regular legs:[182] All the above [restrictions] only apply to the type of bed that has walls, meaning that its legs are like the walls of a box, even if it does not have four walls but rather only two which are parallel to each other. However, by our beds which their legs are not given the status of walls, it is permitted to initially set up [the legs] and afterwards place a beam on them. [Similarly] if it is [a bed that is] barred with ropes then it is allowed to initially spread a sheet over them on Shabbos even if there are three handbreadths between each rope.

The reason:[183] This does not involve [the prohibition of] making a tent because such a form of temporary tent which one has no intent in making a tent out of, the Sages did not prohibit unless it has walls under it which reach the ground, as then it is similar to a tent.

If the walls of the bed are within three handbreadths of the ground:[184] Regarding if the walls [of the bed] reach within three handbreadths of the ground, this will be explained in chapter 502 [in Magen Avraham Halacha 9].[185]

---

[175] Biur Halacha 315:5 "Lechatchila"

176

177

[178] Admur 315:12; Taz ibid; Rashba 138a

[179] Admur 315:10; Michaber 315:4

[180] Biur Halacha 315 "Mitah"; Ketzos Hashulchan 120 footnote 13. Vetzaruch Iyun why this option was not mentioned by Admur.

[181] Admur 315:10; Michaber 315:4

[182] Admur 315:11; Michaber 315:3; Taz 315:4;

[183] Admur 315:11; Taz ibid; M"B 315:17 and 20

[184] Admur 315:11

[185] There the Magen Avraham 502:9brings that the Beis Yosef and Rama [in Yorah Deah 371:4] rule that we do not say the concept of "levud" for a stringency. However, the Magen Avraham himself questions this ruling and concludes that one should be stringent. So rules also M"B 315:21; see Admur in Kuntrus Achron 248:2 that sides like the M"A ibid to be stringent

> **Summary-May one place a mattress over his bed on Shabbos?**[186]
> Yes. However, if the bed has two "leg walls" which reach three Tefachim to the ground then it may only be done if there is a board lying in the area the mattress is to be placed on, or its surface is lined with metal or wood panels or springs which are within three handbreadths of each other.[187] Otherwise one must first place the mattress over the area and then move the bed under it.[188]
>
> ### *Practical Q&A*
> **May one open or close a folding bed on Shabbos?**[189]
> Yes.[190] If, however, the bed does not contain a mattress or board, and does not contain panels within three Tefach from each other, then one may only set it up in the opposite order as explained above.[191]
>
> **May one open or close the top of a bed which contains storage underneath?**[192]
> Yes.[193]

❖ *Setting up barrels:*[194]

When setting up barrels on top of each other, one [barrel] being placed on top of two, he is to hold in his hand the upper [barrel] and set up the lower ones under it. However, he may not set up the lower barrels first and then place the upper one on them because the space that is created between [the two lower barrels] is similar to a tent which has two walls and a roof. Therefore, it must be made in an irregular way from above to below.

The Reason for this is because:[195] by [setting up] barrels one requires the space between the two barrels in order so the barrels not mold, as it is for this reason that he set them up in this way [that one barrel stands on two as opposed to on one].

❖ *Setting up books:*[196]

It is permitted to stand two books parallel to each other and place a book over them even though that this forms a handbreadths worth of space under them,

The Reason for this is: since one has no use for the space between them it is thus not at all similar to a tent which has its space used.

Placing a Sefer that one is learning from on top of another Sefer:

Some Poskim[197] rule one may not move a Sefer and use it as support to lean on it another Sefer that one is learning from.[198] This prohibition applies even if there is a Sefer already sitting on the table, nevertheless

---

[186] See above 3C, and Piskeiy Teshuvos 315:7

[187] Even if the walls of the bed, were set up from before Shabbos, nevertheless this condition would need to be met being that the hole which the mattress is placed on bed is as large as a tub.
Vetzaruch Iyun why in Piskeiy Teshuvos he depends the allowance of placing a mattress on the fact that its boards are within 3 handbreadths of each other when in truth this is only need by walled legs.

[188] Biur Halacha 315 "Mitah"; Ketzos Hashulchan 120 footnote 13. Vetzaruch Iyun why this option was not mentioned by Admur or Michaber

[189] Biur Halacha 315:5 "Kisei" and "Lechatchila"; Piskeiy Teshuvos 315:7

[190] Pashut, as explained in Halacha 3C in the example of folding chairs.

[191] Biur Halacha 315:5 "Lechatchila"

[192]

[193] As the board is connected to the walls of the bed and is hence similar to the allowance of opening a folding chair.

[194] Admur 315:12; Michaber 315:6

[195] Admur ibid; Taz 315:5; M"B 315:29

[196] Admur 315:12; Michaber 315:7; Rashba Beitza 33a

[197] Taz Yoreh Deah 282:13; Orach Chaim 315:6; Aruch Hashulchan 282:23; brought in M"B 315:30

one may not move it in order to use it as a support. However, if one does not move the Sefer from its place then it is permitted to rest another Sefer on it as support. As well, the above prohibition of moving a Sefer to use as a support only applies if one does not plan to also learn from the lower Sefer. If, however, one plans to also learn from the lower Sefer during this learning session then it may be brought to the table and be used to elevate the current Sefer that he is learning from.[199] Other Poskim[200] however rule it is permitted to place a Sefer as support under a Sefer that one is learning. Vetzaruch Iyun on the opinion of Admur based on above.

❖ *Setting up a table on its walled legs:*[201]
If one does not need the space [formed under an item] then it is not at all similar to making a tent, and it is thus permitted to set up the upper [item] over the lower [item which is the legs]. It is therefore permitted to set up the plank of a table on its legs despite it having walled legs which reach the ground from all four sides being that one does not need the space that is between them. [In the event however that one does use the space created under the table, then one would only be allowed to set it up in the opposite way, and even if the walled legs of the table was already set up before Shabbos one may only place the table on its walled legs in the opposite order, if the table hovers over the size of a barrel.[202]]

Practical Q&A
May one open or close a folding table or folding chair on Shabbos?[203]
Yes.
Background and details of ruling: It is forbidden on Shabbos to create a roofing or hovering due to the Ohel prohibition.[204] Nevertheless, the extremity of this prohibition is only in a case that the intent of the hovering is to protect a person from a certain matter, such as to protect from rain or from the sun and light, and the like.[205] If, however, the intent of the hovering is not to give protection for people under it, then it may be made on Shabbos under certain conditions, such as if it was pre-attached to its legs/walls before Shabbos, or does not have any walls under it, or is made with an irregularity.[206] Practically, due to these reasons, it is permitted on Shabbos to open and close a folding chair and folding table without restriction, and doing so does not pose a prohibition of Ohel, or any other prohibition.[207] This applies to

---

[198] The reason: Doing so is belittling to the Sefer, as one is using it like a piece of wood or stone, to support a Sefer. [ibid]
[199] Taz ibid
[200] M"A 254:14; Chayeh Adam 31:48; M"B 154:31 and 315:30
[201] Admur 502:6 based on Rama 502:1; brought in M"B 315:22; See however Admur 315:9 "such as for example placing the board of a table on its legs, then even though in doing so one makes a temporary roof this does not pose a problem being that one has no intent to make a tent."
Other opinions: Some Poskim rule it is forbidden to set up a table with walls in the regular method, being one does use the air that is created under the table. [Implication of Michaber 315:3; Taz 315:4; P"M 315 M"Z 4; M"B 315:22]
[202] See M"B 315:48 that states this law regarding setting up a table on a barrel, and the same should apply here; However see M"B 315:22 that says in such a case it is permitted to set it up regularly. Vetzaruch Iyun.
[203] Piskeiy Teshuvos 315:7; Biur Halacha 315:5 "Kisei" regarding a folding bed
[204] Admur 315:1; Michaber 315:1; Shabbos 125b
[205] Admur ibid "It is forbidden to make a tent, which refers to [any] roofing which hovers over a person **in order to guard him from a given matter**, such as [to protect him] from the sun or from the rain or from another given matter."
[206] Admur 315:9 "A temporary roof which one does not intend in making it for it to be a tent to hover over what is underneath it, but rather only in order to use [this roof] for a certain use, such as for example placing the board of a table on its legs, then even though in doing so one makes a temporary roof this does not pose a problem being that one has no intent to make a tent. Nevertheless, if one also places temporary walls under this roof, then this is similar to a tent and is forbidden to be done in its normal form which is [starting] from below to above, and rather [must be done from] above to below [which is] an irregular form."; Michaber 315:3 as explained in M"A 315:7; M"B 315:17-19
[207] Admur 315:13 "Any temporary tent which one has no intention into making into a tent [the Sages] only prohibited spreading over walls which one [had already] set up under it on Shabbos if the roofing had not been attached on its walls from before Shabbos. However, if [the roofing] had already been attached to them from before Shabbos but it was placed there folded, then it is permitted to spread it out and set it up on Shabbos. For example a chair made from individual parts and when one wants to sit on it one opens it and spreads and stretches the leather [seating] and when one removes [the seat] he closes it up and has the leather fold, then it is permitted to initially open it on Shabbos even if it has walls under it."; Michaber 315:5; Tur 315; Shabbos 138a as explains Tosafus; Piskeiy Teshuvos 315:7 [old] 11 [new]; Biur Halacha 315:5 "Kisei" regarding a folding bed
The reason: The reason for this is because it is not similar to making a tent, as one is not doing anything, as the roofing was already set up and prepared together with the walls from before Shabbos and it's just that one unfolds it on Shabbos and sits on it. [Admur ibid; M"A 315:8]

all forms of folding tables and chairs, even if they form a wall [i.e. box] under them.[208]

If the table/chair surface is not attached to its legs:[209] In the event that the table surface is not attached to the leg frame, and one needs to open the legs and then rest the table on it, then the following is the law: It is permitted to be done on Shabbos without restriction so long as the legs do not form into walls, and one does not actually attach the table surface to the frame using sockets and the like, but simply rests it upon the frame.[210] The same applies if the cushion area of a chair came off, it is nevertheless permitted to rest it onto the leg frame so long as one does not fasten it to the frame.[211] In all these cases, one may likewise remove the table and cushion from the leg frame so long as it is not firmly attached.

May one add an extension to one's table on Shabbos?[212]
Yes. It may be inserted even into its sockets which are found in the table for this purpose.[213]

❖ *A folding chair:[214]*
For example, a chair made from individual parts and when one wants to sit on it one opens it and spreads and stretches the leather [seating] and when one removes [the seat] he closes it up and has the leather fold, then it is permitted to initially open it on Shabbos even if it has walls under it. [This applies even if one has use for the space under it.[215]]

The reason for this is: As any temporary tent which one has no intention into making into a tent [the Sages] only prohibited spreading over walls which one [had already] set up under it on Shabbos if the roofing had not been attached on its walls from before Shabbos. However, if [the roofing] had already been attached to them from before Shabbos but it was placed there folded, then it is permitted to spread it out and set it up on Shabbos. The reason for this is because it is not similar to making a tent since one is not doing anything as the roofing was already set up and prepared together with the walls from before Shabbos and it's just that one unfolds it on Shabbos and sits on it.

Furthermore, typical folding chairs and tables do not contain actual walls under their roofing and hence are permitted to be set up on Shabbos, even if they are not reattached

[208] See Admur ibid in previous footnote

[209] See Admur 315:9 brought in previous footnotes that if there are no walls under the table, there is no Ohel prohibition to place the table surface onto it; Piskeiy Teshuvos 315:11

[210] This is due to the prohibition of Tikkun Keli.

[211] Piskeiy Teshuvos 315:11

[212] Piskeiy Teshuvos 315:7; SSH"K 24:23

[213] Does this apply even if one plans to leave the attachment in for a long time, or only if he plans to remove it after Shabbos? May it be inserted strongly into its sockets? May one close a clamp over it?
Seemingly if it is only meant to be left there over Shabbos and then removed it is permitted even if it gets strongly attached. However perhaps we say that this allowance only applies by attachments that are not common at all to last even temporarily however attachments which are common to be left attached temporarily and it's just that the owner does not plan to do so, then perhaps the allowance does not apply.

[214] Admur 315:13; Michaber 315:5; Shabbos 138a

[215] So is clearly evident from Admur 315:9 and 13 [regarding a canopy] and Michaber 315:3; Piskeiy Teshuvos 315:11
Other opinions: See Biur Halacha 315:3 "Mitos" that there are Rishonim [Rashba] that rule that if one needs the air under the table, then it is considered an actual Ohel and is forbidden even without walls under it. This implies that they would rule that even if one does not need the space under it, if it has walls under, one must change from the normal way of setting it up. The Biur Halacha concludes that one should be initially stringent like their opinion unless it is a case of need. Menoras Hamaor 315:14 leaves this matter with a tzaruch Iyun; See Noda Beyehuda Tinyana 30; Piskeiy Teshuvos 315 footnote 129]

❖ **Setting up a canopy:²¹⁶**

For the above-mentioned reason²¹⁷, it is allowed to set up a canopy [that from before Shabbos was already attached to its poles²¹⁸] and to close it up [even if it contains walls²¹⁹].

Practical Q&A
May one undo a wedding canopy that was left open from before Shabbos?
Yes²²⁰, unless the canopy is meant to be a permanent structure and remains there on permanent basis.

❖ **Opening and closing a shelf: ²²¹**

Similarly [for the above-mentioned reason, it is allowed to open and close] a shelf which is attached to the wall²²² which has books placed on it even if it has walls under it.

Practical Q&A
May one insert/remove a drawer into/from a desk or table?²²³
The question involved in doing so is that in the process one forms a hovering over the space in the drawer. The following is the ruling:

Some Poskim²²⁴ rule that it is forbidden to do so if the space in the drawer is one handbreadth deep, being that one is making a roofing through doing so. Other Poskim²²⁵ however rule that it is permitted, as the drawer is a recognizable insert to the table, and is thus similar to the allowance to cover a barrel with a recognizable cover. As well there is no prohibition in placing walls under a roofing [as will be explained in Halacha 5]. **According to Admur it is completely permitted due to the above-mentioned reasons.²²⁶**

If cabinet/table holds 40 Seah:²²⁷ Seemingly in such a case it is forbidden to enter the drawer. [Vetzaruch Iyun why no mention of this is made in Poskim which deal with this question! From their lack of mention, it seems that it is allowed in all cases in their opinion.]

---

²¹⁶ Admur 315:13; M"A 315:8 ; M"B 315:27

²¹⁷ The novelty of this ruling: Vetzaruch Iyun as to the novelty of this ruling of the Poskim ibid. Some Poskim indeed understand the M"A ibid to rule that one may open a Chuppah even for protection purposes if it was attached before Shabbos, and that this is the novelty of the ruling. [P"M 315 A"A 8; Tosefes Shabbos 315:14; Beis Meir 315:1; Chasam Sofer 72; Machaneh Mayim 3:23; Shevilei David 315; Shaar Hatizyon 315:35 [however see Biur Halacha 315:8 "Tefach"]; Chazon Ish 52:6; Bris Olam 14; Shraga Hameir 3:37; Beir Moshe 6:87 based on Chazon Ish ibid; SSH"K 24:13; Ateres Moshe 1:87; Migdanos Eliyahu 2:78; Piskeiy Teshuvos ibid footnote 96 in name of many Milaktei Doreinu; See Piskeiy Teshuvos 315 footnote 135.] However, other Poskim understand the M"A ibid to rule that one may only open a Chuppah for non-protection purposes even if it was attached before Shabbos [Noda Beyehuda Tinyana 30; Menorah Hatehorah 315:14; Shoel Umeishiv Gimel 2:43; Tiferes Yisrael Kalkeles Shabbos Boneh 3; Aruch Hashulchan 315:10 and 12; Daas Torah 315; Tehila Ledavid 315:8; Kaf Hachaim 315:44; Ketzos Hashulchan 120 footnote 8; Igros Moshe 4:105; Sheivet Halevy 3:54; Minchas Yitzchak 10:26] and so is the ruling of Admur, as in the beginning of the Halacha Admur emphasizes the Heter to be only if doing so not for protection, and hence the novelty of this ruling according to Admur is not understood, as if one is not doing so for protection, then why should it be forbidden to set up even initially on Shabbos, even if not attached before Shabbos, as it contains no walls. However, one can say that this case refers to a canopy that contains walls. An example of the above would be a wedding canopy that was set up before Shabbos and was not removed, may be taken down. [Conclusion of Tehila Ledavid 315:8 after above analysis]

²¹⁸ Shaareiy Tziyon 315:34 and so is implied from Admur

²¹⁹ Tehila Ledavid 315:8; See previous footnotes

²²⁰ As it is not made for protection and is thus not considered an Ohel.

²²¹ Admur 315:13; M"A 315:8; M"B 315:27

²²² Meaning that one does not remove it from the wall but simply lifts it up or down, similar to the top of a chest which opens from its hinges.

²²³ Piskeiy Teshuvah 315:9

²²⁴ Chayeh Adam brought in M"B 315:48. The M"B himself suspects for this opinion although brings that one who is lenient is not to be protested as they have upon whom to rely. SSH"K 24:24 rules like the stringent opinion.

²²⁵ Ketzos Hashulchan 120 footnote 21; Kitzur Shulchan Aruch brought in Shaar Hatziyon 315:56

²²⁶ Ketzos Hashulchan ibid

²²⁷ See Chazon Ish 52:14; Shulchan Shlomo 315 that discuss the issue of Tikkun Keli with drawers but make no mention of 40 Seah

---

May one place a shelf on a bookcase?
Yes[228], one may do so if it does not involve actually attaching the shelf to the walls of the bookcase, and he is simply resting the shelf on the hooks that protrude.

❖ *Setting up a strainer:*[229]
A strainer that has dregs in it: A strainer which is hung to hold the dregs to filter it [from liquids such as wine], in which one stretches its borders to all sides, this is considered like making a tent and is thus forbidden to move it and stretch it if it was hung with the dregs from before Shabbos.
The reason:[230] Now even though that making a roofing without walls [under it] does not have the tent prohibition [when done without intent to form a tent, as explained in Halacha 9], nevertheless here it was prohibited in order so one not do so in the same way that he does during the week, as this is a belittlement of Shabbos.
Setting it up to place fruits on it or filter clean water: However, it is permitted to move it and stretch it in order to place fruits on it or other matters, or even in order to filter with it clear wine and water, which is permitted to filter on Shabbos and does not contain any belittlement of Shabbos at all.

❖ *Examples which relate to setting up fireplaces on Yom Tov:*[231]
Setting up a bon fire in a way that one does not transgress the Ohel prohibition: It is the common practice when making a large bon fire to make four rows of wood [each corresponding] to the four directions, similar to the four walls of a box, and they then place on the [walls of wood] wood above and it is similar to [making] a tent [which is forbidden]. Therefore, one who desires to make [such a bonfire setup] on Yom Tov is not to first make the walls and then make over them the roof being that this is the way of building, and even a temporary building is forbidden on Yom Tov. Rather one person is to hold up in his hands in the air the upper woods which are to be used for the roof and then arrange the walls under them in order to change from the normal way done during the week.
Setting up a table in a way that one does not transgress the Ohel Prohibition: Similarly, if one is setting up a wood like roof over two stones which are made like a wall, then he is to hold the wood with his hands in the air and afterwards arrange the stones under it [in order so he not make a temporary tent without an irregularity].
Setting up a pot in a way that one will not transgress the Ohel prohibition: Similarly, one who places a pot over two stones is to hold the pot with his hands in the air and afterwards arrange the stones under it in order so he not make a temporary tent without an irregularity.
Roasting eggs in a way that one will not transgress the Ohel prohibitions: Similarly, when one is roasting eggs [in their shell] and places one egg over two eggs and the fire is between the two eggs, then he is to hold the upper [egg] in his hand and place the lower [eggs] under it.
If one does not need the space under the bottom items:[232] However the above only applies when one places fire between the lower [items] as in such a case one requires the space between them, and it is thus

---

[228] The reason: As the Mechitzos were already standing before Shabbos. Furthermore, even if the space created is as wide as a barrel, seemingly it is permitted being that it is recognizable as belonging to the bookcase, similar to the allowance of a drawer.
[229] Admur 315:14; Michaber 315:9; Mishneh Shabbos 137b
Is there a prohibition of Ohel in covering a vessel with a strainer on Shabbos? No. [See Admur Admur 315:19-20; Piskeiy Teshuvos ibid footnote 274] Now, although Admur 315:14 and Michaber 315:9 rules it is forbidden to set up a strainer on Shabbos due to the Ohel prohibition, this only applies to a strainer that contains wine dregs inside of it, being that it is forbidden to strain it on Shabbos, and hence one who sets it up on Shabbos is doing a mundane act and belittling Shabbos. However, if the strainer does not contain wine dregs, then it is permitted to set it up on Shabbos [Admur 315:14; M"A 319:18] even over a vessel, so long as it is not the size of a barrel. [Admur 315:19]. See however Taz 315:9 "It is forbidden due to the vessel under it." who implies the prohibition would apply to ever placing it over a vessel due to Ohel. Vetzaruch Iyun
[230] Admur ibid; M"A 315:11; Rambam in 21:17
Other opinions: Some Poskim rule the entire prohibition of a strainer is due to Ohel. [Michaber ibid; Tur 315; Rashi on Gemera ibid] Hence there is never a prohibition to set up a strainer in the air, as it does not have any walls and is hence not prohibited due to Ohel. It is only forbidden when one attaches it to a vessel, and hence the vessel acts as its walls. [Taz 315:9; M"B 315:36]
[231] Admur 502:5; Michaber 502:1; Beitza 33a

similar to a tent of which too he needs the space that is under it. However, if he does not need the space that is between them then it is not at all similar to making a tent, and it is thus permitted to set up the upper [item] over the lower [items].

It is permitted to initially set up a roofing when one has no intention to place it there for protection in the following cases:

A. Temporary: In all cases it is forbidden to make a permanent hovering even if one does not intend on doing so for protection purposes. The below allowances only apply when one does so temporarily.

And

B. It has less than two walls that reach the ground: If there aren't two walls under the roofing then it may be set up in any which way.[233]

Or

C. If it has two walls or more that reach the ground, then it is permitted if any of the following apply:
   A. If one first hovers the roofing over the floor and then slides the walls under it.[234]
   B. The roofing was already attached to the walls from before Shabbos, like a folding chair or table.[235]
   C. It may be set up normally even with walls if there is absolutely no use for the space which the roofing is hovering over, such as forming a small tent with placing a horizontal book over two vertical books.[236]
   D. If the walls had already been set up from before Shabbos, and the hole being covered is not as wide as the hole of a barrel.[237] –See D below!

Examples: It is permitted to:
   1. Unfold a folding chair or table.
   2. Fold or unfold a wedding canopy that was attached to its poles before Shabbos
   3. To place a table on its legs even if the legs are not formed as walls.
   4. Place a book horizontally over two books which are standing.
   5. Open and close a shelf which is attached to the wall

D. Making a roofing on walls which were set up from before Shabbos-Such as placing and removing the cover of a vessel:[238]

❖ *Items with a hole less wide than the size of the top of a barrel:[239]*

It is permitted to place a pot on the mouth of a Kira oven on Shabbos, as explained in chapter 253 [Halacha 14], and this carries no "Tent" prohibition in [roofing] the space [within] the Kira due to that the walls of the Kira were made and set up already from before Shabbos [and thus is permitted because] the [Sages] did not prohibit making a temporary tent when it is done without intention to form a tent with exception to when one places walls below it on Shabbos as explained above. However, this only applies to a pot placed on [the mouth of] a Kira [and the like which is small], however the [law by the] mouth of a barrel that existed back which was a lot wider than the mouth of the Kira will be explained next.

---

[232] Admur 502:6; Rama 502:1
[233] Admur 315:9 and 11
[234] Admur 315:9
[235] Admur 315:13
[236] Halacha 12
[237] M"B 315:28; Halacha 19 Vetzaruch Iyun Gadol from the case of the bed.
[238] Admur 315:19; Michaber 314:13; Shabbos 139b
[239] Admur ibid; M"A 315:21; Tosafus Beitza 32b; M"B 315:48

❖ *Items with a hole as wide as the top of a barrel:*
First Opinion:[240]
A cloth which is spread on the mouth of a barrel in order to cover it should not be spread fully across its mouth as [doing so is making a] tent. Rather part of its mouth must be left uncovered.

If the barrel is full to the top: [However] this only applies if the barrel is not full to the top and is rather lacking [at least] a handbreadth [worth of liquid in] as in such a case when one spreads the cloth over its entire mouth it is similar to making a tent over the space of a handbreadth. However, if [it is full to the point that] it does not lack a handbreadth [worth of liquid] then it does not have the status of a tent, as any tent which does not have the space of a handbreadth [under it] is not considered a tent at all.

The reason why it is forbidden when not filled to the top:[241] However when it has the space of a handbreadth under it, then although the walls that surround this space, which are the walls of the barrel, were already set up from before Shabbos, and thus [one would think that] it should not be prohibited due to the tent [prohibition] [to spread a cover fully over it], just like it is permitted to place a pot on the mouth of a Kira oven on Shabbos [as explained above], ...nevertheless it is not similar to a pot placed on [the mouth of] a Kira because the mouth of the barrels that existed back then was a lot wider than the mouth of the Kira, and thus when one covers its mouth it is similar to making a tent even though that its walls have already been made from before Shabbos.

Removing the cloth covering from the barrel:[242] The same law applies [regarding removing the cloth from the barrel] that it is forbidden to remove [a cloth] covering which covers its entire mouth if it lacks a handbreadth [length] worth of liquid, because it is similar to destroying a tent.

The reason for why removing the cap of a barrel is nevertheless always allowed:[243] This [cloth covering] is not similar to the cap [of a barrel] which is permitted to remove and replace [on Shabbos] as explained in chapter 314 [Halacha 14] being that the cap is modified for this use and its modification reflects on it that it is designated for this use, [and] therefore it does not appear like a tent. However, when it is covered with a cloth then even if the cloth is designated for this [use], nevertheless [since] it has no modification which displays that it is designated for this [therefore it is similar to a tent].

The law by the covers of other vessels: This law applies as well for the cover of [all] other vessels which are very wide to the point of the wideness of the mouth of the barrels of those days.

Second Opinion:[244]
There are opinions[245] which say that the above was never prohibited by a barrel and the like but rather by a tub and the like which are much too wide.

The Final Ruling: [246]
One is to be stringent like the first opinion, although those who are lenient like the latter opinion are not to be rebuked being that there are opinions[247] which say that the covering of vessels does not involve [the] tent [prohibition] at all even by vessels which are very wide.

---

[240] Admur ibid; Michaber ibid; Rashba; Ran; Rashi; Rambam 22:33; Many Rishonim as brought in M"B 315:49
[241] Admur ibid; M"A 315:21; Tosafus Beitza 32b; M"B 315:48
[242] Admur ibid; Taz 315:11
[243] Admur ibid; Taz 315:11
[244] Admur 315:20
[245] Tosafus; Rashi and Ran which mention a Gigis and not a barrel; Levush 315:13
[246] Admur 315:20
[247] Rashba in name of Raavad; Bach, brought in M"B 315:48-19

Summary:
It is only a problem to completely cover a vessel or remove its covering which completely covers it if:
A. The vessel has an opening the size of a wide barrel.
And
B. The cover is a material which is not self-evident that it has been designated for covering with, such as a cloth.
And
C. The vessel has at least a handbreadth worth of empty space below the cover. [Meaning that it is not filled beyond there.]
It is never prohibited to cover a vessel only partially, or to remove the cover of a vessel which is not fully covered.

If the walls of the hovering were set up before Shabbos, may one place the hovering onto its walls on Shabbos?[248]
Hovering covers area that is less than the size of a barrel: It is permitted to regularly place the beam on top of its walls if the walls were set up before Shabbos and the hovering does not cover the size of a barrel[249], as the Sages only required a change in the order of attachment in a case that also the walls are being made on Shabbos.[250] This applies even if the hovering contains four walls under it that were set up before Shabbos. This however only applies if the hovering is not meant for protection of items under it and is simply meant for placing things on top of the hovering.
Hovering covers area that is more than the size of a barrel: One is not to cover the entire space. However, some are lenient.
May one move the walls to a different area and then place the hovering on top of it?[251] No. In the event that one desires to move the walls it follows the same law as one who sets up the walls on Shabbos, in which case a change of order must be done if one makes use of the space under the hovering, as explained above. This applies irrelevant to how large or small the space under the hovering will be.

May one move a vessel and then place a covering over it?
Recognized vessel covering: Yes.
Towel and the like:[252] One may do so if there isn't a Tefach of empty space between the cover and the food. If there is a Tefach of space, he may only do so if he does not fully cover the vessel, or he first hovers the towel and then moves the vessel under it.

Q&A
May one turn over a vessel, such as a pot, in order to cover a certain food?[253]
Yes.[254] However some Poskim[255] question whether this is allowed if the vessel holds 40 Seah.

---

[248] based on Michaber 315:13 [that only prohibit covering a barrel, and not something of less

[249] Michaber

[250] Admur 315:19 "the [Sages] did not prohibit making a temporary tent when it is done without intention to form a tent with exception to when one places walls below it on Shabbos as explained above."; M"A 315:21; M"B 315:17-18; 22; 48

[251] P"M 315 M"Z 11; M"B 315:22 and 48

[252] Based on P"M 315 M"Z 11; M"B 315:22 and 48

[253] Biur Halacha 315:5 "Kisei"

[254] As it is similar to a folding chair of which the walls and hovering are attached, and is hence permitted to be opened for non-Ohel purposes.

[255] P"M 315 A"A 8 brought in Biur Halacha ibid

May one open or close a pool cover?²⁵⁶
It is forbidden to completely close a pool with its cover, or undo its cover if it was completely covered, if there is a Tefach of space between the cover and the water.²⁵⁷ If, however, it is clearly evident to all that the pool cover is modified for this use then it is allowed.

May one cover a garbage can or remove its cover on Shabbos?
Yes.²⁵⁸ This applies even if the can is very wide. This however only applies by the regular cover of the garbage can. If, however, one is using something else as a cover, which is not recognizably a garbage can cover such as a towel, then if the opening is as wide as a barrel one is not to cover it completely, or remove its covering completely.

May one open and close the cover of a Bench Shtender?
Yes.²⁵⁹ This applies even if the cover is not attached to hinges and even if it forms a Tefach space under it and is as wide as a barrel.

Practical Q&A
May one open or close a folding chair, table, bed, stroller, and crib on Shabbos?²⁶⁰
Yes.²⁶¹

May one insert or remove a ceiling tile on Shabbos?
Doing so is forbidden.²⁶²

May one leave keys under a ceiling tile [drop ceiling tile] by lifting the ceiling tile and placing it under?
This matter requires further analysis. Vetzaruch Iyun also regarding Muktzah. Seemingly is Muktzah just like door, however Tzaruch Iyun as why a regular roof is not Muktzah?

3. Mantling a tented roofing on Shabbos:²⁶³
A. The law:²⁶⁴
Biblical-If it has a handbreadths width on its top:²⁶⁵ [Regarding] a tent which is angled, if it has on its top a consecutive²⁶⁶ roof the width of one handbreadth [which is not slanted at all throughout that handbreadth], or even if it does not have a handbreadth on its top but it contains the width of a handbreadth within less than three handbreadths near its head, being that [all items] less than three handbreadths [apart from each other] are considered attached and it is thus considered as if it has on its top a roofing that is a handbreadth wide, then this is considered a permanent tent if it was made to last²⁶⁷ and one who sets it up on Shabbos is liable for building and one who dismantles it is liable for destroying just like [one who] destroys a complete building.

---

²⁵⁶ Based on 2D above.
²⁵⁷ This is forbidden according to all as stated above in D.
²⁵⁸ As the cover is designated and recognized for that purpose. This is unlike Nitei Gavriel Yom Tov 18:14 which states one must initially be careful in this matter.
²⁵⁹ As it is a recognized cover and is attached through hinges and is hence similar to a folding chair.
²⁶⁰ Piskeiy Teshuvos 315:7; Biur Halacha 315:5 "Kisei" regarding a folding bed
²⁶¹ Pashut, as explained in Halacha 3C in the example of folding chairs.
²⁶² As although ceiling tiles are placed for mere beauty rather than protection, nevertheless since they are placed to be there permanently, they are forbidden due to the building prohibition.
²⁶³ See Piskeiy Teshuvos 315:18
²⁶⁴ Admur 315:15; Michaber 315:8; Shabbos 138
²⁶⁵ Admur ibid; Implication of Michaber ibid; M"B 315:34
²⁶⁶ Meaning that it is a single piece of material that is a handbreadth in width, as will be explained from the second scenario to come.
²⁶⁷ Admur ibid; Rambam 22:27; M"B 315:34; Shaar Hatziyon 315:39; See Nodah Beyehuda Tinyana 30

Rabbinical-If it does not have a handbreadths width on its top:[268] However if it's top does not have a roof [the width of a] handbreadth and [as well] does not have within three handbreadths near its top the width of a handbreadth, then this is considered a temporary tent and one who initially makes this [tent] on Shabbos is exempt [from the Biblical prohibition] although it is Rabbinically forbidden whether to mantle or dismantle it, even if it is not made to last at all.[269]

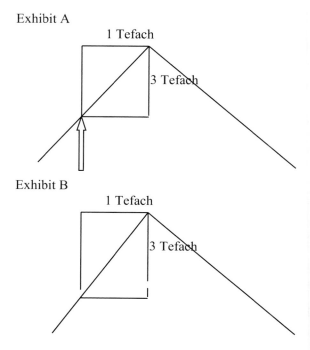

Exhibit A

1 Tefach

3 Tefach

Exhibit B

1 Tefach

3 Tefach

B. Initially draping a sheet and the like over a bar on Shabbos:[270]

[Thus] For example, a folded sheet which is folded over a [horizontal] bar, meaning that half of it is hanging from one side of the bar and half from the other side and both of its ends touch the ground and one enters and sleeps in the shade [that has been formed] between the two ends, then it is forbidden to initially hang it on Shabbos even though it does not have a roof [the width of a] handbreadth and does not have within three handbreadths near its top the width of a handbreadth.[271]

Spreading a sheet over a bar which is designated for this purpose:[272] The bed canopy of a groom[273] which its roof[274] does not have a roof [the width of a] handbreadth and does not have within three handbreadths near its top the width of a handbreadth, since it is prepared for this purpose it is permitted to mantle [the canopy sheet over the rod] and to dismantle it on Shabbos, as long as it does not droop the length of a handbreadth below the [walls of the] bed. [**See below for the full details of this Halacha**]

---

[268] Admur ibid; M"A 315:10; Implication of Michaber ibid; Rambam ibid; Rif; Rabbeinu Chananel; M"B 315:35

Other opinions: There are some Rishonim that hold that such a tent is permitted to be made even initially on Shabbos if it is not meant to last at all. [Rashi; Rosh; brought in P"M 315 A"A 8; M"B 315:35]

[269] Admur ibid; M"B ibid; Biur Halacha "KOl Ohel"

[270] Admur 315:16; Shabbos 138a; Rif; M"B 315:37

[271] The reason: As one is creating walls which act to protect from the sun, and this is an Ohel. [Rashi Shbbos 138a]

[272] Admur 315:18; Michaber 315:10

[273] This refers to a canopy which hangs over a single rod that is supported by a pole in the middle of each end of the bed, similar to a tent. Other bed canopies are supported by four vertical poles which stand on the four corners of the bed. [Rashi Shabbos 138b]

[274] Meaning the horizontal rod that is placed above the bed in order to have the canopy drooped over, forming a tent over the bed.

C. Opening a sheet that was wrapped on a bar from before Shabbos in order to form a tent:[275]

If the material has strings attached which when pulled spread open the tent: [In all cases, even if the bar is not designated for this purpose] if [the sheet] was wrapped on the bar from before Shabbos and it has on its rim strings that are hanging which one pulls at while on the bar in order to spread the sheet to both sides [of the bar], then it is permitted to pull at these strings on Shabbos. [The reason for this is] because since these strings are hanging on it from before Shabbos in order to be pulled at to spread [the sheet], therefore they help [to allow one to be spread it on Shabbos] just like as if it were spread the width of one handbreadth from before Shabbos, in which case by doing so on Shabbos one is only adding to a temporary tent [which is allowed].[276]

Dismantling a tent which was legally mantled on Shabbos:[277] It is likewise permitted to dismantle it from this bar as any tent which is allowed to be mantled and [thus] does not involve [the] building [prohibition], then it likewise does not involve [the] destroying [prohibition] and is [thus] permitted to be dismantled.

[However, this is] with exception to when one adds onto a tent that was [the width of] a handbreadth from before Shabbos, in which case it is only permitted to dismantle the material that was added [on Shabbos] however not the part of the tent that was [already] built from before Shabbos. Despite this, nevertheless it is allowed here [by the sheet case above] to remove the sheet from the bar [on Shabbos] being that here there was never actually a tent the width of a handbreadth from before Shabbos and its only that the strings help [to allow to spread it] just like does having the width of a handbreadth [from before Shabbos].

Spreading the sheets in a case that the bar is a handbreadth wide:[278] The above [allowance to pull at the strings to spread the sheets] however only applies if it does not have a roof [the width of a] handbreadth and does not have within three handbreadths near its top the width of a handbreadth. However, if it does have a roof [the width of a] handbreadth or within three handbreadths near its top the width of a handbreadth, in which case it is a permanent tent, then the strings do not help at all as even to add to a permanent tent is forbidden. [Furthermore] even if this sheet is not meant to last over here as he intends to dismantle it, nevertheless since it is mantled in the same way as a permanent tent, [therefore] the Sages were not lenient by it at all.

The reason for this is because:[279] [The Sages suspected that] one may change his mind and decide to permanently have the sheets remain spread this way, and it thus ends up that he has added a permanent tent [on Shabbos]. They were only lenient to allow one to add to a temporary tent in a case that it is not usual at all to permanently leave it the way that it has been spread, such as by spreading mats over poles or on the ship as written above [in Halacha 2 and 8] as [by these cases] it is not usual at all to permanently leave the mats there the way they have been spread on Shabbos, and the same applies for all similar cases [that it is not usual to permanently spread a roofing there that it is permitted to be added to on Shabbos].

D. Spreading a sheet over the bar of the bed canopy of a groom:[280]

The bed canopy of a groom[281] which its roof[282] does not have a roof [the width of a] handbreadth and does not have within three handbreadths near its top the width of a handbreadth, since it is prepared for this purpose it is permitted to mantle [the canopy sheet over the rod] and to dismantle it on Shabbos, as long as it does not droop the length of a handbreadth below the [walls of the] bed.[283]

---

[275] Admur 315:16; Michaber 315:10; Shabbos 138a
[276] Admur ibid; M"B 315:37
[277] Admur ibid; Michaber 315:10
[278] Admur 315:17; M"A 315:12; M"B 315:37
Other opinions: Some Poskim rule that it is permitted to make the tent by pulling the strings even if it will create a Tefach roof. [P"M 315 M"Z 10 brought in Shaar Hatziyon 315:45]
[279] Admur 315:17
[280] Admur 315:18
[281] This refers to a canopy which hangs over a single rod that is supported by a pole in the middle of each end of the bed, similar to a tent. Other bed canopies are supported by four vertical poles which stand on the four corners of the bed. [Rashi Shabbos 138b]
[282] Meaning the horizontal rod that is placed above the bed in order to have the canopy drooped over, forming a tent over the bed.
[283] Admur ibid; Michaber ibid; Shabbos 138b

The reason for why it may not droop a handbreadth below the bed is:[284] because the canopy is meant to protect one from the sun or from other matters and thus has the status of a roofing on it although [that in actuality it is] without a roof. Thus, [when] it droops the length of a handbreadth below the bed, the bed serves as a roof for the one handbreadth wall [canopy] which now surrounds the bed. Now, although the bed is not made to protect and is thus not considered under the status of a roofing, nevertheless since the one handbreadth wall has the status of a roofing being that it is a part of the canopy which is meant for protection, it thus comes out that there is here a tent with a roof.

The permission to have sheets and tablecloths droop below their surface:[285] However a bed which does not have a canopy, then even though that its sheet which is spread on it droops one handbreadth below the [walls of the] bed on all its sides, [nevertheless] this does not pose a problem, as although that the bed has become a roofing for this one handbreadth wall, there is no Halachic status of a roofing here at all neither on the handbreadth or on the bed.[286] For this reason it is [likewise] permitted to spread a tablecloth over a table initially on Shabbos even if it droops one handbreadth below the table on all its sides.

Summary

Biblically:

A slanted tent [made for sleeping in and the like[287]] is only Biblically prohibited from being initially mantled or dismantled if it contains a top which is at least one handbreadth wide and is permanent. The top area is measured from the very top up to three Tefach down. Thus, if there is one Tefach wide of roofing within three Tefach from the top then it is considered to be one Tefach wide.

Rabbinically:

If the top is less than one handbreadth wide, then it is Rabbinically forbidden to mantel or dismantle this tent even if it is not made to last at all.[288]

Completely permitted to set up a temporary slanted tent if all the following conditions apply:
Scenario A:[289]
  1. The roofing is less than one handbreadth wide on its top and within three Tefach. [see above for definition of top]
And
  2. The tent material was already wrapped around the set-up roofing from before Shabbos,
And
  3. The material has strings which can be pulled and unravel the tent.
And
  4. When done as a canopy over a bed and the like the sheet may not dangle down a handbreadth below the walls of the bed
If all the above is fulfilled, then one may pull at these strings on Shabbos and unravel the tent.

Scenario B:[290]
  1. The roofing is less than one handbreadth wide.
And

---

[284] Admur ibid; Rashi ibid; Rashba; M"B 315:41
[285] Admur ibid; Taz 315:7; M"B 315:41
[286] <u>The reason</u>: The reason for this is because there is no space between the sheet and the bed, and it is hence not an Ohel. [M"B ibid in name of M"A] However from Admur ibid [based on Rashba and Taz] it is implied that the reason is because the bed and the sheet is not meant for protection. The practical ramification would be in a case that one desires to sleep under the bed and place sheets over it in all directions in the form of a tent. [See Taz 315:7-8]
[287] Admur 315:16
[288] Admur 315:15
[289] Admur 315:16
[290] Admur 315:18

2. The roofing is prepared and designated for this purpose.

And

3. When done as a canopy over a bed and the like the sheet may not dangle down a handbreadth below the walls of the bed

In both of the above cases one may likewise completely unravel the material from the roofing.

May one spread a tablecloth over a table if it will drop down a handbreadth below the table?[291]

Yes, as the tablecloth is not set up to serve as a roofing.

May one make a makeshift tent for children to play, such as to place a sheet over two chairs to play under it?

No.

May children spread a sheet over a table in order to make a tent?

No.[292]

May one set up a camping tent on Shabbos?

No.

If one bound the tent to the frame of the tent before Shabbos, may one open and spread it on Shabbos?

If the sheet will hover over a Tefach area within three Tefach from the center frame, then it is forbidden to do so even if one tied it with strings which can be removed and have the material fall on the frame.

If one already made the roof of the tent, and only needs to make the walls: Then if the walls are temporary, some[293] write it is permitted to do so. Vetzaruch Iyun if this will create a Tefach within three Tefach, or will add to an already existing Tefach.[294]

May one spread a sun or rain cover over a baby carriage on Shabbos?[295]

The Poskim[296] rule that it is forbidden to make a tent on Shabbos for protection purposes by placing the material over a surface and having the material then dangle from the two sides, hence making a tent in between. Accordingly, it should remain forbidden to ever place a rain covering over a stroller, as by doing so one is making a tent.[297] However, in truth, since the open hood of a stroller is recognizably there for protection purposes, therefore, adding the plastic material and having it form walls like a tent is simply like adding a temporary hovering to an already established Tefach hovering which is allowed, and hence we don't care if the material now forms a Tefach hovering.[298]

---

[291] Admur 315:18

[292] As one may not make even a temporary tent on Shabbos, and certainly here that the table is a Tefach it is forbidden.

[293] SSH"K 24:16

[294] See Kaf Hachaim 315:61; PT 315:18 footnote 177

[295] Background regarding if doing so is similar to making a tent and should hence be forbidden due to the tent prohibition:

[296] Admur 315:15-18; Michaber 315:8; Shabbos 138

[297] See Piskeiy Teshuvos 315 footnote 99 who implies that indeed if the plastic covering will form a slant of one Tefach within three Tefachim, then it is forbidden

[298] See Tosefes Shabbos 315:18 "Before Shabbos the tent needs to have a tefach opened before Shabbos"; Kaf Hachaim 315:61; Piskeiy Teshuvos 315:8

May one who is sleeping under a table spread a sheet over the table in order to create a tent and block the light? May children play tent on Shabbos?
No.[299]

If the table already had a tablecloth of a Tefach down may one add a sheet to it for the sake of sleeping under it?
This matter requires further analysis.

May one lean a non-Muktzah board on the wall and sleep under it?
Seemingly, it is permitted to do so as this is not similar to a tent at all. Vetzaruch Iyun

---

4. Dismantling a roofing on Shabbos:

The rule:[300] Any tent which is allowed to be mantled and [thus] does not involve [the] building [prohibition], then it likewise does not involve [the] destroying [prohibition] and is [thus] permitted to be dismantled.

Removing a sheet from a bed barred with ropes:[301] If this bed does not have placed on it leather or boards but is rather barred with ropes from above, then if there are three handbreadths between each rope, in which case we do not consider the ropes to be all attached, then it is forbidden to initially spread a sheet over it on Shabbos or place a pillow or blanket on it being that this is similar to making a tent. **Similarly, it is forbidden to remove the lower cloth that is on it being that this is similar to destroying a tent.** [Thus, one may never undo a hovering if it is hovering over a Tefach of space and has walls under it, even it was not made for protection purposes, if the space under is used.[302]]

Removing the cloth covering from the barrel:[303] The same law applies [regarding removing the cloth from the barrel] that it is forbidden to remove [a cloth] covering which covers its entire mouth if it lacks a handbreadth worth of liquid, because it is similar to destroying a tent.

Dismantling the added material to a temporary tent:[304] When one adds onto a tent that was [the width of] a handbreadth from before Shabbos, it is only permitted to dismantle the material that was added [on Shabbos] however not the part of the tent that was [already] built from before Shabbos.

Summary:
Whenever it is forbidden to initially set up a roofing on Shabbos then it is likewise forbidden to take it down.[305] Thus when adding to the handbreadth of a roofing on Shabbos one may only dismantle the added material and not any of the handbreadth material which was set up from before Shabbos.[306]

---

[299] As since the purpose of the Mechitzos of the walls is for protection purposes and it contains more than a Tefach of a top surface, therefore it has the same status as making a tent on Shabbos, which is forbidden. It is also no different than placing a canopy over a Chasans bed which is forbidden if it has a roof of a Tefach.
[300] Admur 315:16; M"A 315:14; M"B 315:38
[301] Admur 315:10; Michaber 315:4
[302] See Shaar Hatziyon 315:31 that from here we see that the prohibition of Setira is more severe than the Issur of Noeh, as one may build this type of bed if the walls were already around before Shabbos [if it is not the size of a barrel] but may not take it apart.
[303] Admur 315:19; Taz 315:11
[304] Admur 315:16

Other opinions: Some Poskim rule that the entire roofing may be dismantled. [Chazon Ish 52:7; SSH"K 24 footnote 31 allows this to be done in stages]
[305] Admur 315:10
[306] Admur 315:16

Q&A

May one dismantle a roofing which was spread from before Shabbos up to a handbreadth of the roofing?

A permanent roofing: Is forbidden according to all.

A temporary roofing: Some Poskim[307] rule that this is permitted.[308] Others[309] rule it is forbidden. The simple implications from Admur appear that he rules stringently.[310]

From the Rav's Desk

Question:

I own a swing set with a canopy like hovering on top to block the sun. The canopy can be moved in different positions, such as horizontal/flat to completely shade from the sun, or upright/vertical, to only block the sun partially. My question is whether I may move it up and down on Shabbos.

Answer:

It is forbidden to create or undo a hovering which was made for protection purposes on Shabbos. Hence, clearly one may not take off the hovering to stop it from blocking the sun, and may not erect it initially on Shabbos so it block the sun. However, here that it is already erected, then there is possibility for allowance, in the following case: If even in its vertical state it still hovers one Tefach [8 centimeters in width] over the swing, then if it was standing in this state before Shabbos it may be further opened to its flat state on Shabbos without issue, and then further closed to its vertical state if desired. However, if it was opened before Shabbos to its full flat state, then seemingly one may not tilt it upwards which will cause some of its flatness to no longer be an Ohel-hovering. If, however, it will always remain a hovering and no part of the materiel will become actually vertical [but just a slanted hovering versus a flat hovering], then seemingly it may be opened and closed without issue, as there is no issue with changing the positions and moving an already established hovering on Shabbos. Practically, I suggest that before Shabbos you open the hovering to its full vertical state, with a single Tefach of stretched hovering, so you can then be allowed on Shabbos to open and close it as needed.

Sources: See Admur 315:1-2; 16 [may not dismantle the part which hovered before Shabbos]; Michaber 315:1-2; Shabbos 125b; Avnei Nezer 211:34 brought in Ketzos Hashulchan 120 footnote 17 [permits dismantling up until Tefach]; Chazon Ish 52:7

5. *Wearing Shabbos hats, sun hats, baseball caps etc. on Shabbos:*

A. Wearing a hat with an extension for protection purposes:[311]

First opinion-Is forbidden if extension is a hard material:[312] A large hat which is placed on one's head in order to shade ones face, to protect it from the sun, or to protect it from flies and any case of the like in which one intention in wearing it is to for it to hover over him to protect him from a certain matter[313], then it is forbidden to wear it on Shabbos, even inside one's house due to the making an "Ohel" prohibition.[314] [This however only applies] if it extends past one's head [the measurement of] one handbreadth [in width]

---

[307] Avnei Nezer 211:34 brought in Ketzos Hashulchan 120 footnote 17. So seems to also be the opinion of the Ketzos Hashulchan himself, [see Piskeiy Teshuvos 315 which plainly brings the Ketzos Hashulchan as following this ruling] although he brings that from the Lashon of Admur "it is only permitted to dismantle the material that was added on Shabbos" it seems that it is forbidden.

[308] The reason: As just like it is permitted to add if there is one Tefach material so too one can take away up until one Tefach of material.

[309] Chazon Ish 52:7

[310] See footnote above in lenient opinion.

[311] Admur 301:48; Michaber 301:40; Shabbos 138b

[312] First opinion in Admur ibid; Michaber ibid

[313] Admur ibid; M"A 301:51; Taz 301:27; M"B 301:152

[314] Admur ibid; Michaber ibid; Tosafus on Gemara ibid

by one handbreadth[315] [in length], (even if [the extension] is only opposite ones face). [Likewise] however this [prohibition] only applies if (this) extending handbreadth is hard and strong and [thus] does not bend over downwards.[316]

If it is a soft bendable material:[317] However if it does bend over downwards, then even if it extends a lot more than a handbreadth around one's entire head, then it is not defined as a "Ohel", and is [thus] permitted.

Spreading a Tallis over one's head:[318] It is therefore permitted to spread the Tallis on one's head even though it extends a lot past ones head, with exception to if it is made from a hard material cloth (called *Grub Green*) [in which case it would be forbidden to wear it on Shabbos for protection purposes]. [Thus, those that avoid wearing the Tallis on their head because of the Ohel prohibition, do not have upon whom to rely in their stringency, and it has no reasoning or source.[319]]

Second Opinion-extension must be as hard as a roof to be forbidden:[320] There are opinions[321] which say that it was only prohibited [to wear a hat with a hard extension] if it is very hard like a roof (in which case it cannot easily be bent [and] therefore it is considered an Ohel. However, if it is merely very hard [but not like a roof] then it is not defined as an "Ohel" and is permitted [to be worn].)

Third opinion-Extension must be flat to be forbidden:[322] There is an opinion[323] which is even furthermore lenient that if [the extension of the hat] is not standing flat but rather is slanted, then it is not defined as an "Ohel" and is permitted [to be worn] even if [the extension] is very hard [like a roof].

The Final Ruling:[324] It is proper[325] to be stringent (in all the above [disputes] that [the extension] be actually drooping below on its own [as opposed to merely slanting, or drooping when applying force], in which case even if he then lifts [the dropping extension] and sets it up flat with his hands, it is Halachically meaningless).

Fourth opinion-Those which are lenient to wear even very hard hats for protection:[326] In those places which are accustomed to be lenient in all cases [to wear felt hats, which have a very hard material extension and would thus be forbidden according to all the above mentioned opinions], even when the person intends [to wear it] as a tent [hovering for protection], one should not protest their actions being that they have upon whom to rely, as there are opinions[327] which completely allow [wearing hats] in all cases, as they hold that there was no decree made here [against wearing this hat] due to [the] making a tent [prohibition] since it is being done in a way of wearing.

B. Wearing a hat with an extension not for protection purposes:[328]

All the above [discussion of prohibition] is only if the person intends [to wear it] for it to hover over him to protect him from something. However, if his intentions are simply to cover his head, then although it inevitably forms a hovering around him, it is Halachically meaningless, as any Ohel/hovering which does not have walls under it contains no prohibition in being made unless ones intentions are to do so to make a tent [i.e. a hovering of protection], as will be explained in chapter 315 [Halacha 9 and 11].

Example-Wearing the accustomed felt hat:[329] It is therefore permitted to wear a large felt[330] hat which is

---

[315] Admur ibid; Michaber ibid writes simply one handbreadth.
[316] Admur ibid; M"B 301:151; Gemara ibid
[317] Admur ibid; M"B 301:151; Gemara ibid
[318] Admur ibid; M"A 301:51; M"B 301:151; Gemara ibid
[319] M"B ibid
[320] Admur ibid; M"A 301:51
[321] Rambam 22:31
[322] Admur ibid; M"A 301:51; M"B 301:152
[323] Sefer Hateruma 254; Hagahos Maimanis
[324] Admur ibid; It seems the M"A ibid rules one may be lenient by hats like the second and third opinion and he hence suggests that even if the hat is as hard as a roof, one can simply bend it down and then it may be worn even for protection purposes.; It is unclear how the M"B himself holds regarding all the leniencies that he recorded.
[325] Lit. good
[326] Admur 301:49; M"A 301:51 in name of Bach; M"B 301:152 in name of Elya Raba
[327] Rashi Shabbos ibid
[328] Admur 301:48; M"A 301:51; Taz 301:27; M"B 301:152
[329] Admur 301:49; Taz 301:27; M"B 301:152

accustomed [apparel] in some places, which [these hats] are called (Brital), even if they contain hard paper which due to this makes it very hard and it stands flat, being that one does not intend [to wear it] as a tent [hovering of protection] but rather in order to cover his head.

It is forbidden to wear a hat on Shabbos even in one's house if all the following conditions apply:
1.   It extends past one's head 1x1 handbreadth. [Such as typical baseball caps].
And
2.   One intends to wear it for protection purposes, such as to provide shade over his face, and not as a mere head covering.
And
3.   The extension is made of a hard material which does not bend down on its own. [If it is as hard as a roof and is flat then it is forbidden according to all. If it is slanted or is not as hard as a roof, then it is disputed, and we are stringent.]
- Those which are lenient to wear hats, despite fulfilling the above conditions, do not need to be protested against doing so as they have upon whom to rely.
- If any of the three conditions are not fulfilled it is permitted to wear such a hat on Shabbos.
- The above only relates to wearing the hat inside one's house or in an area with an Eiruv, regarding wearing it outside by an area without an Eiruv-See chapter 301 Halacha 50.

May one wear a baseball cap on Shabbos?
One may wear it if his intent is not to do so for shade. However, those that are lenient to wear it for shade do not need to be protested.

May one wear a Shabbos hat?
Yes.

May one wear a Shabbos hat if his intent is also for protection from the sun?
This matter requires further analysis.

May one put his Shabbos hat on while sitting in his room in order to protect him from the sun?
No.

May one wear a Tallis over his hat?
Yes.[331] However some[332] are stringent against doing so.

May one place a plastic hat rain cover on a hat on Shabbos?
It is permitted to put on a rain cover onto one's hat on Shabbos and doing so does not pose an Ohel prohibition.[333] This applies whether the cover is special manufactured hat rain cover or one is using a plastic bag. The following will discuss if one may walk with this hat cover in an area without an

---

[330] Felt is a non-woven cloth that is produced by matting, condensing and pressing woolen fibers. While some types of felt are very soft, some are tough enough to form construction materials. Felt can be of any color, and made into any shape or size.
[331] M"A 301:51; M"B 301:152
[332] Brought in M"A ibid; M"B ibid and negated, but so defends the Machatzis Hashekel ibid, stating that so he saw done even by Gedolim.
[333] The reason: As the Ohel prohibition does not apply in a case that there is not a Tefach of space between the cover and the hat. [Admur 315:19; 315:12; 640:10; Michaber 315:13; Rambam 22:23] B) A hovering made to protect an item [in contrast to a human] does not have the status of an Ohel when covering an item less than the size of a barrel. [See Admur 315:19 regarding a barrel]

> Eiruv:
>
> <u>Area without Eiruv:</u>[334] Some Poskim[335] rule it is forbidden to wear a rain cover for a hat in an area without an Eiruv even if the rain cover is manufactured for this purpose.[336] Other Poskim[337] rule it is permitted to wear a rain cover that is manufactured for hats even if one will be walking in an area without an Eiruv.[338] Practically, even those that are lenient are only to do so with a manufactured hat rain cover and not through placing a plastic bag over the hat, in an area without an Eiruv.[339] Those who are careful not to carry even in an area with an Eiruv may be lenient in this regard to wear a hat rain cover.[340]

6. Setting up dividers [makeshift walls] on Shabbos:

A. The prohibition to make a permanent divider:[341]

All the below [to be mentioned allowances in putting up dividers] is only with regards to temporary dividers, however a permanent divider is [Biblically[342]] forbidden in any scenario even if one only does so for mere privacy. [Furthermore] even to add on to [an already existing divider or tent] a permanent addition is forbidden in all scenarios.

Placing up decorative sheets: Nevertheless, it is permitted to hang decorative sheets [on one's wall, as well as separation curtains] even though that they [will be] permanently [placed there, as will be explained in D. See there!][343]

> **What is the definition of a permanent divider?**
>
> It is implied from Admur[344] that a permanent divider is defined as any divider which is meant to remain in its place for a number of days. Vetzaruch Iyun!

B. Setting up a temporary divider for shade, privacy, to prevent cold and similar purposes:[345]

It is permitted to initially make temporary dividers on Shabbos.[346] [Furthermore] even if one makes it in order to protect himself from the sun or the cold it is not considered like a tent because of this. Similarly

---

[334] Piskeiy Teshuvos 301:6 [old] 301:20 [new]

[335] Minchas Yitzchak 3:26; Igros Moshe 1:108-110; Mahariy Shteif 73 and 124; Dvar Yehoshua 2:129; Betzel Hachochmah 2:80; Or Letziyon 2:23-3; Poskim in Piskeiy Teshuvos ibid footnote 144

[336] The reason: As a hat rain cover is not considered a clothing but rather a rain protector, and one hence transgresses carrying an item on Shabbos even when worn. It is thus unlike the allowance brought in Admur 301:11 and 43 which allows wearing one hat on top of another due to the rain, as that case refers to a hat that is wearable during the week even not during rain, unlike our case where the hat is unwearable during non-rain times. It is rather similar to one who wears a cloth over his head to protect his scarf from rain in which case we rule it is considered a Masuiy, as it is not Derech Malbush. [See Admur 301:11]

[337] Chelkas Yaakov 1:99; Har Tzevi 1 Tal Harim Motzi 2; Shevet Halevi 1:61; Divrei Yatziv 1:147; Chesehv Haeifod 1:81 and 2:67; Beir Moshe 2:31; Az Nidbaru 1:71; 4:37; Bris Olam Motzi 10; Tzitz Eliezer 10:23; Tiferes Adam 2:11; SSH"K 18:10 in name of Rav SZ"A regarding Karmalis; Mishneh Halachos 2:72; 6:72; Yabia Omer 5:24; 9:108-146; Poskim in Piskeiy Teshuvos ibid footnote 145

[338] The reason: As one may wear one hat on top of another on Shabbos even simply to protect from rain [Admur 301:11 and 43] and this hat cover is considered a clothing being that it is made to the same fit as a hat and is worn as a Derech Malbush. [Shevet Halevi and Poskim ibid] Likewise, it is also worn to protect the person from rain, in which case we rule one may cover the hat even if it is not a true clothing being that it is worn as a Derech Malbush. [See Admur 301:11]

[339] Piskeiy Teshuvos ibid; See Piskeiy Teshuvos ibid footnote 148 for Poskim who are lenient even in such a case
The reason: As no one walks outside with a plastic bag covering them, and hence it is not considered a Malbush even when used as such. [See Admur 301:43]

[340] Piskeiy Teshuvos ibid footnote 147

[341] Admur 315:6; Beis Yosef 315; M"B 315:6 and 9

[342] Shar Hatziyon 315:6 in name of Peri Megadim

[343] The Chazon Ish however rules that it is never permitted to attach anything permanently due to the building prohibition. [Piskeiy Teshuvah 315:2]

[344] Admur 440:5 rules one cannot make a Mechitza Kavua in front of Chametz on Shabbos or Yom Tov. Now, the Mechitza is only needed until the end of Pesach. Hence, we see, that Kevius can be considered even if one needs it for only a few days. Vetzaruch Iyun!

[345] Admur 315:3; Michaber and Rama 315:1

[346] Admur ibid; Michaber ibid

[it is allowed even] if one made it in order to prevent candles from extinguishing in the wind.[347] It goes without saying that it is allowed to make a divider for mere privacy [purposes] [such as] so that one not sit in a revealed area[348], or such as the dividers which are made during speeches to separate between the men and women, and so too for anything similar to this.[349]

What is the law regarding a slanted divider is it viewed as a divider or as a tent?
Such as to place a plank of wood leaning over a Tzedadin of the tree and sleep under the tree.

C. Setting up temporary dividers to separate domains and thus remove a prohibition:[350]

Setting up the wall for a Sukkah, for a Reshus Hayachid, or to permit marital relations: There is never a case that [making] a temporary divider would be forbidden with exception to if made in order to Halachically legalize the status of a Sukkah as will be explained in chapter 630 [Halacha 12 in Michaber/Rama][351] or [when done] to permit carrying [an object in an otherwise public domain] in the way explained in chapter 362[352] [Halacha 13] or [when done] to remove other prohibitions [from being effective] such as for example one who places a divider the height of ten handbreadths [80 cm] in front of Torah books, [such as] by spreading out a sheet or mat, in order to be allowed to have marital relations in that room or in order to go to the bathroom there, then it is forbidden to make these dividers on Shabbos.[353]

The reason for this restriction is:[354] because in every situation that a divider permits [one to do something] [it is because] it divides that area into its own separate domain, such as [in the case that] it permits one to carry [in the surrounded area] it is because it turns that area into a private domain and separates it from the public domain or Karmalis which encompasses. Similarly, regarding a room with Torah books, [the dividers] divide [the room] into two domains [as] the holy books are [now] in one domain and his marital relations or bathroom use is [being done] in another domain. Thus, since one is making it in order to divide [that area] into its own separate domains, [therefore] this is considered like he is making a tent.

Placing up dividers which separate domains in a case that one does not need to do so in order to remove the prohibition:[355] However, if one does not need [the dividers] to separate the [area] into its own domain then it is allowed to initially make it on Shabbos, even if it [consequently] removes a prohibition. For example one who positions a divider in front of a light in order so he be permitted to have marital relations, [then since] it is not necessary [here] to have separate domains [to permit intercourse] and rather as long as the separation extends above the light in a way that one cannot see the light from the area that he will have intercourse and as long that [the divider] is slightly thick to the point that the light cannot be well seen through the separation, then it is allowed to have intercourse even if [the divider] is not the

---

[347] Admur ibid; Rama ibid; Mordechai

[348] Admur ibid; Rama ibid; Eiruvin 94a; Rashi 125b

[349] Admur ibid; Taz 315:1; Mordechai; M"B 315:5

[350] Admur 315:3; Michaber and Rama 315:1; Rabbeinu Tam Shabbos 125b
Other opinions: Some Rishonim rule that even such dividers are permitted to be made on Shabbos, and there are never any dividers that are forbidden. [Rashi, brought in Shaar Hatziyon 315:12]

[351] Thus, while one may not make the 3rd wall of the Sukkah on Shabbos [Michaber 630:12] he may make a fourth wall. [Rama ibid; Rabbeinu Tam Tosafus Shabbos 125b]

[352] These first two examples are brought in Admur in bid; Michaber ibid; In 365 it explains regarding carrying on Shabbos in a public property that one may not make dividers surrounding him in order to give the surrounded area a status of a Private domain and thus be allowed to carry there.

[353] Admur ibid; Rama ibid

[354] Admur ibid; M"A 315:3; Rabbeinu Tam ibid

[355] Admur ibid; M"A 315:3 in explanation of Rama 315:1; brought in M"B 315:10; M"A ibid in name of Rambam; Rokeiach; Rikanti and Rashi; Taz in 514:2 regarding Yom Tov that one may always make a Mechitza before a candle; Halachos Ketanos 2:206
Other Poskim: Some Poskim rule it is forbidden to create a Mechitza in front of a candle or Sefarim even if one does not need the Mechitza. [Implication of Rama ibid; Elya Raba; Mamar Mordechai; Chemed Moshe; brought in M"B 315:10] The M"B ibid concludes one may be lenient like Admur and the M"A ibid in a case of need.

height of ten handbreadths and thus does not separate [that area] at all into its own domain.[356] Furthermore, [one is allowed to have intercourse even] if [the separation] is not tied on well enough to the point that the wind will not be able to move it, as is required when making a separation in order to separate domains, such as [when having relations in the same room as] Holy Books as was explained in chapter 240 [Halacha 6 in Michaber/Rama]. [Therefore] since one does not need [the dividers] to make a separate domain it is permitted to make it even in a way that it separates the domain, as is the case when [the divider] is higher than ten handbreadths and is tied well. [If, however, one does need the dividers to create a separate domain in order to remove the prohibition, such as if the candlelight is visible above the divider, then it is forbidden to make it on Shabbos.[357]]

Scenario in which it is allowed to place a divider by the Torah books in one's room:[358] The same applies with [making a separation in one's room that contains] Torah Books, that if one hangs the separation across from all the Holy Books in a way that [the books] are not revealed at all[359], in which case one does not need to make [that area into] a separate domain if one has another cover over the Torah books aside from this separation, and thus even if this divider is not ten handbreadth high and is also not tied well and thus does not separate [the area of books into its own] domain at all, nevertheless [it is valid] as this [divider] is no worse than [having] a mere covering [over the books]. It is thus permitted for one to use the bathroom there or even have intercourse if there is another cover on the Torah Books besides for the divider, as there are here two covers [over the books] and it is like a vessel within a vessel. Therefore, it is allowed to place this divider on Shabbos even in a way that will separate [that area into its own] domain since one does not need it to separate the domains. It thus goes without saying that it is allowed to cover the Torah Books with two coverings of clothing being that there is no divider here at all.

D. Adding to an already existing divider:[360]
In all scenarios that it is forbidden to initially place a separation over the Torah Books and the like, it is nevertheless permitted to add to a separation that was placed before Shabbos: [Furthermore] even if the books are revealed from above the divider in which case the divider is not considered a covering, or [if it is but] there is no other covering on the books and one wants to have intercourse and thus needs the separation to be a height of ten handbreadths and be tied as Halachically required in order to make that area into a separate domain, and similarly in any scenario that one wants to make a separation in order to create a separate domain, then it is prohibited to initially do so on Shabbos. However, if it was [already] made from before Shabbos the measurement of a handbreadth then it is allowed to extend it on Shabbos being that adding to a temporary tent is permitted.[361]

[This applies] whether the handbreadth [of the divider] is from top to bottom, such as mats which are wrapped on a [horizontal] bar from before Shabbos and the amount of a handbreadth [of the mat] extends beneath it from before Shabbos, then it is permitted roll it all down on Shabbos and tie it as is Halachically required. [Similarly this also applies] whether this handbreadth [extends] from the side, such as if a divider from the side extended in front of the books the width of a handbreadth then it is allowed to hang sheets if front of [the books] on Shabbos being that the sheets are an addition to a temporary tent.[362]

---

[356] As a divider only has the power to make a domain if it is 10 handbreadths tall and is sturdy enough to not be moved in the wind.
[357] M"A 315:3; M"B 315:10; Rama 315:1 forbids to make a Mechitza before a candle in order to permit Tashmish and the M"A ibid explains this to be the scenario of the prohibition. Vetzaruch Iyun why this clause is omitted by Admur despite the fact he brings the remainder of the ruling of the M"A ibid. Perhaps Admur is of the opinion of the Shlah [recorded in M"B ibid] that if the candle can be seen above the Mechitza, it is forbidden to have relations, and hence according to Admur making a Mechitza before a candle would never be needed as a legal partition, as if the candle can still be seen, it is not valid to permit relations, and if it cannot be seen, it is valid regardless of the creation of the separate domain. However according to the M"A ibid who rules [based on Rama 240:11] that one may have relations using a Tallis if there is a Mechitza, even if the candle is visible then the Mechizt's new domain is Halachically valid and hence cannot be done on Shabbos. Vetzaruch Iyun!
Other opinions: It is implied from some Poskim/Rishonim [brought in M"A ibid and Shaar Hatziyon 315:12] that one may always make a Mechizta in front of a candle even in such a case.
[358] Admur 315:4; M"A 315:3 in explanation of Rama 315:1; brought in M"B 315:10
[359] Meaning that although it does not actually touch the books it nevertheless it blocks one from seeing any of them.
[360] Admur 315:5; Rama 315:1; Mordechai 311
[361] Vetzaruch Iyun if it suffices to have an 8x8 centimeter cube on the floor to be allowed to extend to each direction.
[362] Admur ibid; M"A 315:3 as explained in Levushei Serud

Now, although the divider that extends [to the side] is permanent, [nevertheless] this does not pose a problem as explained in chapter 313 [Halacha 1] that there is only a prohibition [in adding to a tent] when the addition is permanent.

E. Hanging sheets and other items that move in the wind as a separation:

Placing up decorative sheets:[363] It is permitted to hang decorative sheets [on one's wall] even though that they [will be] permanently [placed there] being that they are not meant to serve as separations. [This applies even if the sheet will be attached from all its sides and not move in the wind, and hence have a status of a Halachic divider, nevertheless it is permitted being that it is not serving as a divider.[364]]

Placing door curtains in doorways on Shabbos:[365] Door curtains which [are sheets that are] hung in front of a doorway in substitute for a door, then even though they hang there permanently it is allowed to hang it on Shabbos[366], as since it moves and swings with a common breeze and also does not prevent people from walking through it[367], therefore it is not considered a permanent separation but rather a temporary separation and thus has no prohibition [in being made] when it is not made to remove [a prohibition].[368] For this reason the curtain [Paroches] which is in front of the Holy Ark is allowed to be hung there on Shabbos[369] even if the ark does not have a door and the curtain is thus a fourth divider for the ark, as [the curtain] is a temporary separation and is only made for modesty.[370]

Taking caution to not make a tent in the process:[371] [However the above is only allowed] as long as one is careful when he hangs the curtain and material of the like that it not be folded in a way that it extends a handbreadth towards its width[372] at the time that it is being hung, as [if this occurs then] it comes out that one has made a handbreadth of the roof of a tent.[373] [For this reason, some are careful not to hang a Paroches on Shabbos.[374]]

Hanging a large curtain:[375] Therefore if [one wants to hang] a large curtain it needs to be hung by two people so that it be able to be hung all at once in a way that it won't fold [in the process], however for one [person to hang it alone] is forbidden. [As well] a canopy which has a roof extension sewn and hung around it like [material which surrounds] the rim [of an item], is forbidden to be hung at all on Shabbos, even with ten [people] being that it is impossible to avoid lifting up the rim a little and thus make a temporary tent.[376]

---

[363] Admur 315:6; M"A 315:2; M"B 315:7

Other opinions: The Chazon Ish however rules that it is never permitted to attach anything permanently due to the building prohibition. [Piskeiy Teshuvah 315:2]

[364] Levushei Serud and Machatzis Hashekel on M"A ibid; M"B ibid

[365] Admur 315:7; Rama 315:1; Rebbe Chiya in Shabbos 138a

[366] Admur ibid; Rama ibid; Or Zarua

Other opinions: The Chazon Ish however rules that it is never permitted to attach anything permanently due to the building prohibition. [Piskeiy Teshuvah 315:2]

[367] Lit. those that go and pass and return through that way

[368] Admur ibid; M"A 315:1; M"B 315:6

[369] Admur ibid; Rama ibid

[370] Admur ibid based on Rama and M"A 315:2; M"B 315:7

[371] Admur ibid; Rama ibid; Michaber 315:12; Rambam 22:32;

[372] Meaning that it should not be put up in a way that the curtain will hover a handbreadths worth over the floor, as this is similar to making a tent.

[373] The reason: Regarding the fact that this is Ohel not for protection purposes, which is permitted to make on Shabbos, one can explain that since one is intending to make the Mechitza it therefore gives also the Tefach a status of a Ohel. [M"A 315:18; Shaar Hatziyon 315:52; as explained Admur similarly in 315:18] It is thus unlike the allowance to open a folding chair, where one has no intent to make neither a Mechitza nor a hovering. Regarding why this should be prohibited even though one has no intention to do so, the Mishneh Berurah, in Shaar HaTziyon 315:53 explained it's because it's a Pesik Reisha, or alternatively because this ruling follows the opinion that even if one does not intend to do a prohibition it is forbidden. See there.

[374] M"A 315:19; M"B 315:45

[375] Admur ibid; Michaber ibid

[376] Admur ibid; M"A 315:20; Levushei Serudi ibid; See Biur Halacha 315:12 "Kilah"

Seemingly the rim of the canopy inevitably folds upon lifting up the canopy and thus causes a roof to be made for that moment.

Summary:

It is permitted to set up dividers on Shabbos even for purposes of protection and separation as long as:

    A. One is not doing so for permanent use, with exception to a) items hung up **not** for the sake of making separations, such as a sheet for wall decoration[377], and b) a curtain or sheet which is only attached by its top and thus swings in the wind[378]. These latter two items may be hung even for permanent use. [379]

And

    B. It may not be a separation which has the Halachic definition of a division and thus divides the room into two domains, <u>if</u> through doing so it removes a prohibition that otherwise would be prohibited, such as placing a division of ten handbreadths in front of revealed Torah books that are in one's room in order to allow marital relations.[380]

    If the division extended already a handbreadth from before Shabbos then it is permitted to add it even in such a situation, as long as it is not done for permanent use.[381]

And

    C. The divider will not end up folding the width of a handbreadth over the floor upon setting it up and certainly not after it is set up. Thus, if the divider is a folding material like a sheet, then this precaution must be taken, and if needed must be set up by two people.

Examples:

<u>One is allowed to place a temporary divider in the following cases if condition c) is fulfilled:</u>

1. To use as a Mechitzah between men and women in a Shul.[382]
2. To protect one from the sun or rain.[383]
3. To conceal Torah books which already have one covering over them.[384]
4. To conceal a candle from being seen.[385]
5. For privacy purposes.[386]
6. A curtain which is only attached on its top and thus gets moved in the wind, such as a Paroches for the Aron, or a curtain for a window or doorway, may be put up even for permanent use, as long as condition c) above is fulfilled.[387]
7. To add to a handbreadth of an already existing divider in order to make a separate domain.

It is forbidden to make even temporary dividers in the following cases:

1. To make a private domain in order to permit carrying an object.
2. In front of revealed Torah books, in order to be allowed to have marital relations in that room or in order to go to the bathroom there
3. In order to Halachically legalize the status of a Sukkah.[388]
4. A curtain or sheet that will inevitably fold a handbreadth upon being set up.[389]

---

[377] Admur 315:6

[378] Admur 315:7

[379] So rules also Mishneh Berurah. The Chazon Ish however rules that it is never permitted to attach anything permanently due to the building prohibition. [Piskeiy Teshuvah 315:2]

[380] Admur 315:3

[381] Admur 315:5

[382] Admur 315:3

[383] Admur 315:3

[384] Admur 315:4

[385] Admur 315:3

[386] Admur 315:3

[387] Admur 315:7

[388] Admur 315:3

[389] Admur 315: 7

What is the definition of a divider that divides domains?[390]
It is only considered a divider which has the power to split a domain into two if:
1. It has a height of ten handbreadths.
And
2. Does not move in the wind.

What is the definition of an already made divider?[391]
That it extends a handbreadth from any direction, whether top or side, in front of the area that one wants to divide into a different domain.

May one spread a tablecloth over a table if it will drop down a handbreadth below the table?[392]
Yes, as the tablecloth is not set up to serve as a roofing.

Q&A
May one undo a Tefach hovering of curtain that was folded over a rod?
This matter requires further analysis.

May one set up a temporary divider if it is usually meant to be left as a permanent divider?[393]
No.

May one set up a divider for privacy reasons if it will later serve also to Halachically divide the room?[394]
Yes.

May one undo a divider which served to Halachically divide the room?[395]
If it is still serving a purpose in Halachically dividing the room[396] then it is forbidden to undo it. If it no longer is needed for this purpose then some Poskim[397] have left this matter in question, while others[398] have ruled that it is allowed.

May one open a folded Mechitzah in order to make a Halachic division of a room, such as to enable marital relations?[399]
If it was opened a handbreadth before Shabbos then it may be completely opened. If it was not, then even if when folded its width reaches a handbreadth, nevertheless it may not be opened.[400] However, if it is attached to a wall then it may be opened.[401]

May one open or close a folding wall Mechitzah of a Shul?[402]
Yes.

---

[390] Admur 315:3
[391] Admur 315:5
[392] Admur 315:18
[393] SSH"K 24:27
[394] SSH"K 24:37; Piskeiy Teshuvos 315:3
[395] Piskeiy Teshuvos 315:3
[396] Such as he plans to have marital relations.
[397] Ketzos Hashulchan 120 footnote 27
[398] SSH"K 24:38
[399] Piskeiy Teshuvos 315:3
[400] M"B 315:11 in name of Chayeh Adam
[401] So rules SSH"K 24:35
[402] Piskeiy Teshuvos 315:3

May one close his bedroom closet door in order to permit marital relations [such as if it contains Sefarim]?
Yes, it may be closed even if both doors were left open from before Shabbos, as it is similar to a divider attached to the wall which may be opened and closed.

If a wall decoration or picture tilted out of the way may one straighten it on Shabbos?
Seemingly doing so is permitted, as stated above regarding placing permanent tapestries.

If on Shabbos or Yom Tov the walls blew off due to wind may it be replaced?
No. If however, three walls still remain standing it is permitted to place the fourth wall on with an irregularity [due to Muktzah].

THE LAWS OF TRAPPING AND KILLING ANIMALS, BIRDS AND INSECTS ON SHABBOS

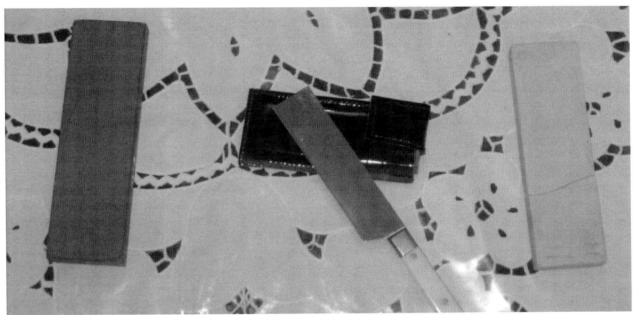

Based on Shulchan Aruch Chapter 316

Translation
Shulchan Aruch Chapter 316

TRANSLATION-CHAPTER 316
Trappings which are forbidden and permitted on Shabbos
25 Halachas

Introduction:
The following chapter will discuss the laws of trapping, killing or injuring creatures on Shabbos. Both trapping and killing or injuring an animal are Principal Shabbos prohibitions. At times it is only Rabbinically forbidden and thus allowed to be done in a scenario of danger. Other times even when Biblically forbidden to be done it is allowed to be done if there is a life-threatening situation.

The laws of Trapping creatures on Shabbos

Halacha 1
The definition of the Biblical and Rabbinical prohibition of trapping:
A Principal Prohibition: Trapping is one of the principals [forbidden] actions [to do on Shabbos], [being] that [it] was done in the [building process for the] Tabernacle [in trapping the] Techashim[1] and Chalozon[2].

A complete form of trapping: One is only liable for [Biblically transgressing] it if the trapped [animal or fish] does not lack any further trapping after this [current] trapping, meaning that he has trapped it to an area where he can easily grab it and one does not need to tell another person to bring a trapping mechanism, and hence one does not need to do any further

An example: Therefore if one chased a bird into a house which is closed or into a roofed shack which is sealed from all sides, and then closed the door before it, or if one chased after an animal until he entered it into a house or into even an unroofed shack or into a garden or courtyard and then closed the door before it, he is [Biblically] liable, as long as that the house or shack is not large enough to the point that one [still] needs to scheme methods of how to grab hold of the bird or animal [that is in there].

[However] so long as the house or shack is large enough to the point that one is not able to reach and grab the bird or animal in a single chase due to it running away from him and he thus needs to chase after it a second time, then they are still [considered to be] lacking being trapped, and one is [thus] Biblically exempt.

Trapping a sparrow: One who traps a sparrow[3] which is a type of bird that dwells in a house just like in a field [meaning that] it knows how to escape [being caught by flying] to all the corners of the house and (it is thus called Drur which means a dwelling as it dwells in all places) one is not liable until he chases it into a tower which it can be trapped in which is a tower that is not very large, and rather [is small enough that] one can grab it without any further schemes.

Trapping a lion: One who traps a lion is not liable until he enters it into a cage that it can be restrained in.

The Rabbinical prohibition of trapping: Anyone who traps into an area where the trapped [animal or bird] is still lacking further trapping then although he is not liable [nevertheless] it is Rabbinically forbidden.

Trapping an animal which needed further trapping: One who traps [an animal or bird] from an area where it was still lacking further trapping there, is liable.

Trapping an animal which did not need further trapping: From an area that the [animal] does not lack any further trapping it is initially allowed to trap it on Yom Tov, although not on Shabbos due to the moving '[Muktzah] prohibition. [In addition] there are those which prohibit this [on Shabbos] also because of a Rabbinical trapping prohibition [which according to them applies even in this case].

---

[1] A type of animal with a unique colored skin
[2] A type of fish which makes blue dye.
[3] The sparrow is the smallest species of birds. They live on branches of trees and spend their time singing. Due to their small size they can live in a house just like in the outside and fly from corner to corner being very difficult to catch. [Mishneh Berurah 1 and Biur Halacha] This translation is based on the modern-day Hebrew term used for this bird and is founded also on the words of the Peri Megadim, brought in the Biur Halacha above.

Halacha 2
Trapping a sick, old, blind, lame, etc animal:

An old, or crippled or exhausted deer: One who traps an item which is not lacking any further trapping, such as for example one trapped a deer which is crippled or old, or week due to exhaustion from doing strenuous activity, and [thus] it is not able to move from where it is, then [although] he is not liable nevertheless it is Rabbinically forbidden.

A sleeping or blind or sick deer: However, one who traps a deer that is sleeping or is blind or is sick [and week] due to a fever that has developed in his body, then he is liable because they are self-trained to escape when they feel the hand of a person, and are thus [considered to be] lacking further trapping.

Halacha 3
Hunting dogs:

On Shabbos: One who instigates a [hunting] dog [to chase] after an animal in order to trap it is exempt [from Biblical liability] but is Rabbinically forbidden.

During the week: [Furthermore] even during the week it is forbidden to trap with dogs[4] because [this symbolizes the actions of a] group of scoffers, and [one who does so] will not merit to participate[5] in the joy of the Leviathan [feast].

Halacha 4
Trapping something which is not commonly trapped being that it serves no use:

Biblically: The Biblical prohibition of trapping something only applies by a species that is [commonly] trapped, which means that it is common for the [people of the] world to trap this species that he is trapping.

For example, [trapping] species of animals and birds and fish [is liable because] it is common for the [people of the] world to trap these species. [6]

However, if he trapped something which is a species that is not [commonly] trapped, such as for example wasps and flies and mosquitoes and the like of which it is not common for [people of] the world to trap these species being that they do not have any use, then even if one happened to trap them for a use, he is exempt [from Biblical liability].

Rabbinically: However, it is Rabbinically forbidden [to do so] even if one wants to trap them for no need at all and rather out of mere casualness. .

Closing a vessel that has flies in it: Therefore, one must be careful not to close a box or cover a vessel which has flies inside it being that they are [consequently] trapped through this covering and closing.

The reason: Now, although one has no intent at all to trap [them], nevertheless [it is forbidden because] it is an inevitable consequence [of one's action, in which the law is that it is forbidden to do even if one does not intend to do so].

Leaving it slightly open: Rather [if one nevertheless still wants to close it] he must place a knife or other item between the cover and the vessel in a way that the [flies] can escape from [inside the vessel] and it will no longer be inevitable [for them to leave].

Other Opinions: [However] there are opinions which are lenient [to allow one to completely close the vessel] in a situation that if one were to open the vessel to take [into one's hand] the flies that in there, then they would escape [before him being able to grab them], as in such a case there is no trapping done at all through this covering.

The Final Ruling-No need to check a vessel before closing it: One may rely on this latter opinion with regards to not being required to be meticulous and check if [the vessel] has flies [in it] [before covering

---

[4] However, the Peri Megadim explains that this only applies when hunting for a hobby. However, one whose occupation involves hunting may use hunting dogs to do so.

[5] Lit. see

[6] It is evident from Halacha 16 that this includes even species which are commonly trapped only because they are harmful, however on such creatures one is only liable for trapping them if he intends on doing so in order to use them, such as for healing and the like.

it]. [Furthermore] even if one sees for certain that there are flies in it suffices for him to chase away those that he sees with his eyes and he does not have to check for any more flies that have perhaps remained. As since there is a doubt as to whether there are any [more flies] in there, it is no longer [considered an] inevitable [consequence of one's actions that he will trap the flies].

Halacha 5
Covering a beehive for protection purposes:
Leaving an escape route available: It is allowed to spread mats over a beehive on a sunny [day] in order [to protect it from] the sun and [on a] rainy [day] in order [to protect it from] the rain as long as one has no intent to trap the bees. As well it must be done in a way that does not inevitably trap them there, such as for example he leaves a hole in the beehive that is not covered by the mats and it is [thus] possible for them to escape through there. Even if it is the hole is small and on the side in which it [thus] is not visible to the bees, [nevertheless] thus does not pose a problem being that he does not intent to trap [them] and it is not inevitable [for them to escape] as it is [still] possible for them to escape through this small side hole and it is not definitive that they will not escape through it.
However, if there is no hole that is [left] uncovered by the mat, then it is forbidden because it is impossible [for them to escape].
The reason: Now, although there are opinions which are lenient regarding [covering a vessel with] flies in a situation that if one were to open the vessel to take [the flies] that are there then they will escape, nevertheless here it [is not allowed because it] is considered a complete trapping for the bees to be trapped in their beehive in a way that that it is not possible for them to escape even though he is not able to take them out from there with his hands.
[The reason for why it is considered a complete trapping is] because the beehive is their [common] place of trapping [in a scenario] that they reside in a beehive, and is [thus] similar to one who traps a lion and enters it into its cage that even though he is not able to take it from there with his hands without having it escape he is [nevertheless] liable because that is its place of trapping.

Halacha 6
Setting up traps on Shabbos, such as mouse traps
Biblically: One who sets up a trap and while doing so an animal entered it, he is liable. However, if it entered into it afterwards then he is exempt [from liability] because at the time that he set it up it is not [yet] known if it will trap or not.
Rabbinically: Nevertheless, it is Rabbinically forbidden and therefore it is forbidden to set up mouse traps on Shabbos.

Halacha 7
Closing the door in front of an animal:
Closed by one person: A deer which entered on its own into a house and someone closed the door in front of it, then even if he did not lock the door with a lock but rather just pressed it closed in a way that the dear is guarded through this that it not be able to escape, then he is liable being that this is its trapping.
Closed by two people: If two people closed it then they are exempt [from liability] as [the rule is that] any action which can be done alone and was done by two people, then they are exempt because it was not done in the usual method that it is done in during the week, as it is not usual at all to for [an action] which can be done alone to be done by two people. [However] if one alone cannot close it and two people closed it then they are liable. If one [of the two] is able to close it alone and the second is not able and they both closed it, then the one that is able is liable and the one that is not able is exempt being that [the one that is not able] is only considered an [unneeded] accomplice to the one that is able, and an [unneeded] accomplice has done a meaningless action. This rule applies for all the [prohibited] actions of Shabbos.

Halacha 8
Locking the closed door of a room which contains an animal:

If the doorway had already been closed by the door after the deer entered the house, whether the door had closed on its own [and] whether one transgressed and closed it, it is permitted to lock it with a lock. As since the deer is already guarded in a way that it cannot escape, it is thus already currently trapped and when one thus locks it with a lock, although he is adding a further means of guarding to the guarding that there is currently, [nevertheless] this is only considered done to guard it from robbers and does not carry with it [the] trapping [prohibition].

Halacha 9
Using one's body to block the exit of a room that contains an animal:

A deer which entered a home and a person [came and] sat by the entrance totally blocking it, which means that there does not remain enough space between himself and the doorpost for the deer to be able to escape through, then he is liable.

Having a second person sit next to the first: [However] it is allowed for another person to [come] sit by the side of this [person] in the unblocked area which is between [the first person] and the doorpost even though that by doing so he is adding further fortification to the fortification provided by the first person.

[Furthermore] even if the first person stood up and left and thus his fortification has been annulled, but the deer is still guarded due to the sitting of the second person, meaning that the now free space between himself and the doorpost, which was the area where the first person sat, is not enough space to allow the deer to escape, nevertheless the second person does not need to get up, and it is thus permitted for him to sit there until after Shabbos and then come take the deer.

The reason for this is: because since at the time that he sat down it was allowed for him to do so being that the deer had been already considered trapped through the sitting of the first person, [therefore] we do not require him to leave after the first person gets up, as he is doing nothing by his [continued] sitting, being that he is only guarding a deer which had already been trapped by the first person.

Sitting next to the first person with intention to trap the deer: [Furthermore] he may even sit near the first person with intent to remain sitting there after the first-person leaves.

Halacha 10
Adding a further trap to an already trapped animal:

The same applies if one had a deer bound up in his house and someone came along and also closed the door in front of it in order to add a [further form of] guarding onto the already existing [form of] guarding, and then afterwards the deer escaped from the ropes, we do not require the person to reopen the door being that at the time that he closed it he was allowed to do so and now he is doing nothing [new].

Trapping an animal unintentionally:

Closing the door of one's house when he does not know of animals inside: Similarly one who locked [the door of] his house in order to guard it [from break ins] without the slightest knowledge that a deer had entered into the house and only afterwards did he find out, then it is permitted for him to leave the entrance locked until after Shabbos with intention to take the deer [after Shabbos], as when he locked his house he was allowed to do so being that he knew of no [existing animals in his home] and now when he discovers this he is not doing anything [new].

Closing the door of one's house when he knows of animals inside: However, if one knows that there is a deer in his house then it is forbidden for him to close the door even if he does not at all intend to trap the deer but rather [just intends] to guard his house [from break ins], as the trapping [which comes as a result of his closing the door] is inevitable.

Halacha 11
Sat by the entrance and unintentionally trapped an animal: Similarly, one who sat by the entrance without knowledge that a deer had entered his house and later discovered this then it is permitted for him to remain sitting there until after Shabbos being that now [upon the discovery] he is not doing anything [new].

A bird which flew into one's cloths trapping itself: Similarly one who had a bird enter under the wing of his clothing and consequently got trapped there, does not need to open for it an escape route and rather may guard it until Shabbos is over.

Halacha 12
Un-trapping an animal on Shabbos
It is allowed for one to open one's house in front of a deer [which is trapped inside] in order for it to run and escape. As well a deer which has entered into a trap one is allowed to release it from its trap on condition that one not move it [being that it is Muktzah].

Halacha 13
The Primary Biblical prohibition:
Slaughtering is one of the principals [forbidden] actions [on Shabbos], [being] that [it] was done in the [building process for the] Tabernacle [in slaughtering the] rams and Techashim[7]. Not only is [the killing form of] slaughtering [included in this principal prohibition] but [also] anyone who takes the soul from any species of animal, bird, fish, and rodent, whether [he did so] by slaughtering it [and] whether by tearing it [open, and] whether by hitting it, he is liable. *Strangling*: One who strangles a creature until it dies is [transgressing] an offshoot of [the prohibited action of] slaughtering.

Removing a fish from water: Therefore, if one took a fish out of a bucket of water, and left it [outside the water] until it died then he is liable for strangulation. [To be liable] one does not have to [leave it out] until it completely dies but rather as soon as it [is left out to the point that] the width of a "Sela" of it has become dry between its fins, then one is liable even if he returns afterwards back into the water, as [once it has been left out for this long] it is no longer able to live. [Furthermore, to be liable one does] not [have to leave it out] until it actually dries but rather even if [it has been left out to the point that] when one touches it with a finger mucus comes out from it and gets pulled out with the finger[8] [he is liable].

Asking a gentile to remove a fish from water: Therefore, one must be careful to not tell a gentile to take out a fish from a barrel of water even if he fears that it will die there [in the water, and thus contaminate the water and cause him a loss [9]].

Halacha 14
Causing a creature to bleed:
The taking of life [prohibition] which one is liable for, is not only when one removes the entire life-force from the creature [i.e. kills it], rather even if one removed [only] a part of its life-force he is liable. For example, one who [injures an animal to the point that he] takes out blood from one of the limbs of the creature then he is liable for taking out life from that area being that blood contains [ones life-force which is] the soul.

Halacha 15
Causing a bruise to a creature:
[Furthermore, he is] not only [held liable] if blood actually comes out [of its skin], but even if one bruised one of the creature's limbs to the point that blood [vessels have been broken and] gathered under the skin [thus causing a "black and blue mark"] then even though [the blood] has not gone out of the skin] he is

---

[7] A type of animal with a unique colored skin
[8] Meaning that it has congealed and thus sticks to the finger and gets stretched out like gum.
[9] Levusheiy Serud

liable being that it is a bruise which will never be replaced. As once the blood [vessels have been broken and] gathered under the skin it can never return back to its place, and it is only that the skin is preventing it from going out, and he is thus liable for taking out the blood of that area.

Bruising an animal and the like: [However] the above only applies to a bruise made in a person or domestic and wild animal or bird or in [any of] the eight rodents mentioned in the Torah (in Parshas Shemini) which are the weasel, the mouse [the toad, the porcupine or hedgehog, the lizard, the snail, and the mole] of which each one of these has skin which prevents the blood from going out.

Bruising an insect: However, one who bruises other creeping creatures and insects is not liable until he removes blood from them. However, if the blood gathered [in its body] and did not leave, then this is a [type of] bruise which will [have the blood] return back to its place, as if the blood had left its area then it would have come out being that it has no skin preventing it[10].

Halacha 16
Removing life-force and trapping is only liable when done for a use of the creature itself:
Killing for self-use: It was already explained in chapter 278 [Halacha 1-2] that there are opinions which say that a Biblical [Shabbos] prohibition only applies if the [forbidden] action was done for its own need, meaning that one needs the actual item to which the action was done to.

What is considered a self-use? Therefore one who removes the life [of a creature] is only liable if he has a need for the body of the creature which had its life-force removed from, or [if he needs] its skin, or he needs the soul which he took out from it, meaning the blood that has left it in order to give it to his dog, or if he bruises a person which is his enemy and he thus desires for blood to come out from him so that he witness revenge on his foes (see Choshen Mishpat chapter 424 [Halacha 2][11]).

Killing to prevent danger: However, one who kills a snake in order to prevent it from injuring him then this is an action done which is not self-needed being that he does not need either the body of the snake or its blood and he is only killing it in order to be saved from injury.

Trapping for self-use versus trapping to prevent injury: Similarly, one who traps is not liable unless he has a need for the actual body of the trapped item. Nevertheless, one who casually traps species of animals, birds, and fish, is liable, as they are generally trapped for need of their body or skin. Similarly, one who casually traps one of the eight rodents mentioned in the Torah is liable as they are generally trapped for need of their skin and not to save oneself from injury being that it is not common for them to injure.

However, one who traps one of the other creeping creatures and insects [which are commonly trapped to prevent injury[12]] is not liable unless he trapped them for a need, such as for a medicine and the like. However if he casually trapped them, then he is exempt [from liability] being that they are generally trapped in order to prevent injury, being that they commonly injure and not for their skin being that they do not have skin, and not for their bodies being that they are inedible and they are not generally [trapped] for medicine unless one explicitly intended [on trapping them] for this, and thus this [trapping] is an action which does not have a self-use being that he has no need for the trapped item itself to which the [forbidden] action [of trapping] is being done to.

---

[10] The Mishneh Berurah 32 explains that since their skin is soft like flesh therefore their blood vessels that have broken are quickly returned to their place. Thus according to this explanation, they do have skin, and it's just a matter of whether their skin is soft or hard.
[11] There it explains that one who injures a person on Shabbos is exempt from paying damages being that he is liable for death.
[12] See Halacha 4

Halacha 17
Initially trapping creeping creatures which can cause injury:

[Furthermore] even initially it is allowed to trap all types of creeping creatures which commonly cause injury, such as snakes and scorpions and the like, even in places where their bite [or sting] is not deadly, and even if they are not currently chasing after him at all, and rather he just suspects that perhaps it may eventually chase after him or after someone else and bite [or sting] him or that perhaps he may not [properly] avoid [stepping on or near] them and they will bite him or perhaps will bite other people which do not know that they have to beware from them. As since one is only trapping them in order to save himself from injury, this is [considered] an action that is not done for its own self use.

The reason: Now, although that any [forbidden] action which is not done for self-use, despite not being liable on, is Rabbinically forbidden, [nevertheless] here the Sages completely permitted it due to chance that one may receive bodily injury [if he were to not be allowed to trap them]. [Furthermore] even according to the opinions which say that an action done not for its own self use one is [also] liable on and [thus according to them it should be prohibited being that] we do not [allow one to] transgress Shabbos through doing a complete Biblical prohibition [just in order to prevent] bodily damage and rather it is only allowed to prevent danger of one life, nevertheless here since one is not trapping them in the normal method but rather just deals with them in order so they not be able to injure, [such as he] covers them with a vessel or surrounds them [with items that prevents them from escaping] or ties them so they not cause harm, therefore the [Sages] permitted one to do so even to creeping creatures which are not at all deadly and rather only cause injury.

Halacha 18
Trapping insects and the like which only cause pain:

[However] all the above is referring to [trapping] creeping creatures which commonly cause injury such as snakes and scorpions, [which may be trapped] even in places that their bite is not deadly being that nevertheless they cause bodily injury with their bite, and the same applies for all creatures of the like. However, anything which does not damage the body but rather just causes it pains alone, such as wasps, and flies, mosquitoes and fleas and the like, then it is forbidden to trap them.

Removing a stinging insect from one's cloths or skin: It is therefore forbidden to take hold of a flea which is on one's clothes, even if it is inside [one's clothes] close to his skin, and even if it is on his skin and has still not stung him it is forbidden to grab it. However, if it is in the midst of stinging him then it is permitted to take hold of it while it is stinging and throw it away.

The reason for why this does not involve the trapping prohibition is: because when one takes hold of it at the time of the stinging he has no intent to trap it and rather is only involving himself with it in order to stop it from stinging him, and [when there is no intent to trap] the [Sages] did not decree [against trapping] even in a case [that doing so is only to prevent] pain alone[13] since [these insects] are items which their species are not commonly trapped [and thus even when trapped with intent it is only Rabbinically forbidden].

The reason this does not involve the Muktzah prohibition: As well, the [Sages] did not decree in a scenario [that involves] pain the prohibition in moving the flea due to it being Muktzah.

Grabbing a wasp in the midst of stinging: Similarly, if a wasp and the like sting him one is allowed to take it with his hands and send it away if it is not possible to fly it away.

Other Opinions: There are opinions[14] which permit to grab the flea even while it is on the inside of his clothes [and not yet on his skin] being that it is able to cause him pain there. [Furthermore] even from his undershirt[15] on the outside it is allowed to grab it since an undershirt is close to the flesh and it is thus possible that the flea will go from there to his flesh and will bite him.

---

[13] Meaning in addition to there not being a decree when there is bodily injury, but even for mere pain there is no decree in such a situation.
[14] The Taz [8]
[15] Based on Taz 8 that he explains there that the "Chaluk" is the shirt closest to the skin while a regular shirt is called something else.

However [even according to this opinion] if the flea is on the person in a way that there is no worry that it may bite him, [such as] that it is on his upper clothes on the outside, then it is forbidden to grab it.

Shaking one's cloths to cause the insect to fall off: Nevertheless, it is [always] permitted to make it fall off of him through shaking [his cloths].

The Final Ruling: The final ruling is that if it is possible for him to easily make the insect fall off of him without [needing to] take it with his hand, then one is to do so even if [the insect] is on the inside of his undershirt. However, if one is wearing long boots which reach to his thighs[16] [or pants] and it is thus difficult[17] for him to shake it away without first grabbing it with his hand then one who relies on the lenient opinion regarding this Rabbinical prohibition has done no harm[18].

Halacha 19
Killing an insect which is in the midst of stinging oneself:
All the above is only regarding [being allowed to] trap the flea, however, to kill it is forbidden according to all opinions even if it's on one's flesh and is in the midst of biting him.

The reason for this is: As due to mere pain [the Sages] only permitted trapping [it] being that it is not a species which is commonly trapped and thus trapping it is not considered a [Biblically forbidden] action at all, however killing it is a complete [Biblically forbidden] action. [Now although] it is not done for its own use in which case there are opinions which say that one is exempt [from liability] on doing so, nevertheless [even according to them] it is Rabbinically forbidden and was not permitted to be done [in order] to prevent mere pain being that its prohibition is rooted in the Biblical [prohibition], meaning if [this same act] were to be done for its own use [in which case it would be Biblically forbidden].

May one squeeze the insect to weaken it? [Furthermore] even to squeeze it with one's fingers to weaken its strength so that it does not return to him is forbidden because of a decree that one may come to kill it. Rather he is to take it in his hand and throw it away.

Halacha 20
The killing of creatures which do not reproduce:
One is only liable for removing life-force on species of creatures which reproduce and are created through [the union of] a male and female, however insects which are created from [the bacteria found in] feces and from spoiled fruits and the like, such as for example worms [that grow] in flesh and like [the] worms which are found in legumes, then one who kills them exempt [from liability].[19]

The reason for this is: because in the Tabernacle the taking of a life was only done to rams, *techashim* and *chalozon* which are [creatures] that reproduce and are born from a [union of] male and female.

Killing creatures which are created from earth: Nevertheless [killing] the flea contains the [Biblical prohibition] of taking a life even though it is created from earth and does not reproduce, because all [creatures] that are created from earth have vitality as if they were created from male and female as initially all creatures were created from earth as it says [in the Torah] "And G-d said let the earth extract....etc.".

Killing lice: What is considered a flea? This is a black insect which jumps. However, the white insect that crawls is called a louse and is permitted to kill it on Shabbos being that it is [created] from sweat.

Killing lice when checking one's clothing for them: However, this [allowance] only refers to when one happens to find a louse on his flesh or [happens to] find it on his clothes. However, one who is [in the

---

[16] Based on Mishneh Berurah 128:16 and the Alter Rebbe there in 128:6
[17] Tzaruch Iyun why wearing long boots should consider it difficult. Perhaps then this is referring to only when the flea has gone inside his pants or boot, in which case it is difficult to shake it off of him entirely.
[18] Lit. has not lost
[19] The Mishneh Berurah adds the following: a) It is nevertheless Rabbinically forbidden [unlike the opinion of the Magid Mishneh brought in the Magen Avraham which holds here that it is completely permitted] and it is only by lice that the Sages completely permitted killing it because it was created from sweat or because it is repugnant.] b) It is only Biblically permitted if it grows while off the tree and after the food has spoiled. However if t grew while on the tree or before the food has spoiled then it is included in the Biblical prohibition.[See Mishneh Berurah and Biur Halacha on Halacha 9]

process of] cleaning his clothing of lice then he may [only] squeeze them with his fingers [without killing them] and throw them (even into water). However, it is forbidden to kill it with his hands as since he is cleaning his clothing of lice, we suspect that he may come to also find fleas and also kill them.

Killing lice when checking one's hair for them: However, when checking one's head [for lice] it is permitted for him to kill the louse with his hands being that fleas are not commonly found on one's head.

Halacha 21
Removing lice from skins:
One may not remove lice from the skins of fox and the like being that [in the process] one removes hair from the skin which contains the sheering prohibition, and although it is done unintentionally, nevertheless it is an inevitable occurrence [and is thus forbidden].

Killing dangerous animals and other dangerous creatures:
Halacha 22
Creatures that definitely have a deadly bite or sting: Any wild animal and crawling creature which bites and definitively kills, such as a lethally venomous snakes and a rabid dog and the like of other dangerous creatures which have a definite deadly bite, then it is allowed to kill them on Shabbos even if they are not chasing after one at all.

The reason for this is: because there is danger of life involved [in refraining from] killing them as they may [come to] kill a Jew, and [the rule is that whenever there is] any possibility [that a] life [will be endangered] then it pushes off Shabbos, [and allows one to do] even a complete Biblically [forbidden] action even according to those opinions which say that even an action which is not done for its own use one is Biblically liable on.

Creatures which only cause bodily injury which are chasing oneself: Other dangerous creatures, even those which definitively do not kill with their bite but rather only damage the body, such as snakes and scorpions in areas that they never kill with their bite [or sting] and rather only damage, and so too any creature of the like, then there are opinions that say that if [these creatures] are running after oneself then it is permitted to kill them according to those who say that any action which done not for its own use is only Rabbinically forbidden.

Their reasoning is: because in a situation that involves bodily injury the [Sages] did not decree [against doing a Rabbinically forbidden action, which includes any action that is not done for its own use].

This case is not similar to the [case of the] flea which is in the midst of stinging one's flesh in which case it is forbidden to kill it, [as] the flea does not cause injury to the body but rather pain alone.

If these creatures are not chasing oneself: However, if [these creatures] are not currently chasing after oneself and it is only that one is worried [that they may do so] in the future, then it is forbidden to kill them in a way that it is blatantly obvious that it was intentionally done. However, it is permitted to trample on it while in the midst of casually walking even if he has intention in doing so in order to kill it, as long as he makes it appear as if he is casually walking and does not intend at all to kill it.

The reason for this is: because since an action which is not done for its own use is only Rabbinically forbidden [therefore it is not forbidden in this case as] the [Sages] did not decree at all against [doing an action even when not for its own use] in a case that involves bodily damage even if there is only mere doubt [as to whether bodily damage will occur]. However, with this [they decreed that] one needs to alter his method of killing them as much as it is possible for him change, which means that he is to make himself appear as if he does not intend to kill them.

Killing creatures which at times can be deadly and at times not that are not chasing after oneself: Furthermore, even those species of animals and crawling creatures which carry a doubt regarding the deadliness of their bite, as at times they can kill and at times they will not kill, then one must altar his method of killing them so long as they are not chasing after him.

Being cautious not to trample on ants and other non-dangerous creatures: However, species of crawling creatures which do not cause injury such as ants and the like, is forbidden to trample them even if one does not intend to kill them [in doing so] but it is inevitable.

[Thus] one must beware of [stepping on] them in areas where they are commonly found.

Other Opinions: [However] according to those opinions which say that even an action which is not done for its own use one is [Biblically] liable on, it was only permitted to kill creatures which are chasing after oneself and to trample on [creatures] casually when they are not chasing after oneself, by those species of animals and crawling creatures which have the possibility of having a deadly bite. However, a creature which never kills with its bite is forbidden to even [casually] trample on it, and even if it is running after oneself, being that one may not desecrate Shabbos with a complete Biblically [forbidden] action in order [to prevent only] bodily damage.

The Final Ruling: The main Halachic opinion is like the former opinion, however nevertheless every meticulous person should be strict upon himself, regarding this [possible] Biblical prohibition in a situation that it is possible [for him to refrain from killing it]. Such as if it is not running after him then he should not trample it if it is possible for him to guard himself from it and to warn others to beware of it.

Halacha 23
Killing spiders:
Those people which kill spiders on Shabbos (that are called *shafin*) need to be rebuked being that [spiders] do not cause bodily damage, and although there is worry that it may fall into ones food [and become lethal[20]], nevertheless [it is forbidden to kill them] as this is not common [to occur], as well as that it is possible to cover the foods, and that also it is only one in a thousand that is lethal in food, and that also even if it did carry a worry of danger [the Sages] only permitted killing it through casually trampling on it.

Trapping domestic animals

Halacha 24
Biblically: Animals and birds which are raised in a person's property, such as one who breeds deer in his house or in his courtyard or geese and chickens and doves, if one trapped them on Shabbos, he is exempt [from liability] being that they are already [considered] trapped.

Wild pigeons which nest in one's property: However, one who traps [wild[21]] pigeons which reside on nests and high surfaces is liable because they are lacking further trapping as when a person comes to take them from their nest, they are trained escape and run away from their nest.

The Rabbinical prohibition in trapping domestic birds and wild natured animals: However, birds which are raised in a house and when they enter into their coop in the evening are easy to be caught, being that they are not able to escape [one's grasp] and run away from there, then even when they are outside their coop they are not considered lacking further trapping being that at night they will go into their coop on their own. However nevertheless it is Rabbinically forbidden to trap them, which means to run after them until they enter into an area in which they are easily caught there. However, to move them with one's hand is forbidden regardless of the trapping prohibition because of [the fact that they are] Muktzah.

However, this is only referring to when [these birds] are in the courtyard or in a house so large that if they had not been raised around humans then they would need to be trapped, meaning that one would need to seek schemes to catch them there and they are thus considered lacking further trapping. For example, if the house is so large that one is not able to catch them with a single chase and [rather must] runs after them until they enter into a room which is not very large, and he then closes the door in front of them [then it is considered that the bird was lacking further trapping].

Cases in which there exist no prohibition in trapping domestic birds: However, if they are in a house which is not very large then they are [considered] already trapped and waiting [and is thus not at all prohibited to be further trapped]. [As well] even if they are in a large house or even if they are in a public domain and one pushed them until they entered into another large house, then there is no trapping

---

[20] Some spiders are lethal when eaten
[21] Meaning that they have not been domestically raised. [Rashi Beitza 24a, and chapter 497 Halacha 16]

[prohibition involved here] at all and it is thus permitted [to even initially be done].

Halacha 25

Domestic calm natured animals: All the above [Rabbinical prohibition to further trap a domestic creature only] refers to wild natured animals[22], and [all] birds, however calm natured animals[23] which are raised in a person's property are permitted to be trapped even from a public domain.

Cats: A cat has the same law as any other wild natured animal and is forbidden to be trapped in ways other than those explained [above in the end of the previous Halacha].

Domestic animals which have rebelled: All the above [allowances to trap domestic animals and birds] only apply if they have not rebelled, however if they have rebelled, [including] even a cow that rebelled and it goes without saying [that it includes] wild natured animals and birds that have rebelled, then one who traps them on Shabbos is liable just like having trapped wild [non-domestic] animals and birds as these [animals and birds which have rebelled will] also not enter into their cage at night.

---

[22] חיות refer to wild animals such as the hart, dear, gazelle and *yachmor*.

[23] בהמות refers to domestic animals such as sheep, cows, and goat.

Compilation of Halachas Summaries and Q&A

Introduction:
The following chapter will discuss the laws of trapping, killing and injuring creatures on Shabbos. Both trapping, killing or injuring an animal are principal Shabbos prohibitions. At times it is only Rabbinically forbidden and thus allowed to be done in a scenario of danger. Other times even when Biblically forbidden to be done it is allowed to be done if there is a life-threatening situation, as will be explained in this chapter.

CHAPTER 1: THE LAWS OF TRAPPING CREATURES ON SHABBOS

1. The Principal Prohibition:[1]
Trapping is one of the principal [forbidden] actions [to do on Shabbos], [being] that [it] was done in the [building process for the] Tabernacle [in trapping the] Techashim[2] and Chilazon[3].[4]

2. The Biblical Prohibition:
The Biblical prohibition of trapping only applies if **all** the below conditions are met:

A. One completely traps the creature:[5]
One is only liable for [Biblically transgressing] it if the trapped [animal or fish] does not lack any further trapping after this [current] trapping[6], meaning that he has trapped it to an area where he can easily grab it and one does not need to tell another person to bring a trapping mechanism[7], and hence one does not need to do any further schemes in order to grab it.[8] If one is not able to reach and grab it in a single chase due to it running away from him and he thus needs to chase after it a second time, then it is still [considered to be] lacking being trapped and one is [thus] Biblically exempt.
Birds and animals:[9] Therefore if one chased a bird into a house which is closed or into a roofed shack which is sealed from all sides, and then closed the door before it, or if one chased after an animal until he entered it into a house or into even an unroofed shack or into a garden or courtyard and then closed the door before it, he is [Biblically] liable, as long as that the house or shack is not large enough to the point that one [still] needs to scheme methods of how to grab hold of the bird or animal [that is in there].
[However] so long as the house or shack is large enough to the point that one is not able to reach and grab the bird or animal in a single chase due to it running away from him and he thus needs to chase after it a second time, then they are still [considered to be] lacking being trapped and one is [thus] Biblically exempt.
Trapping a sparrow: One who traps a sparrow[10] which is a type of bird that dwells in a house just like in a field [meaning that] it knows how to escape [being caught, by flying] to all the corners of the house and (it is thus called Drur which means a dwelling as it dwells in all places) then one is not liable until he chases it into a tower which it can be trapped in which is a tower that is not very large, and rather [is small

---

[1] Admur 316:1; Mishneh Shabbos 73a
[2] A type of animal with a unique colored skin
[3] A type of fish which makes blue dye. [Rashi Shabbos 74b]
[4] As for the reason that trapping a ram is not mentioned, despite it being mentioned in 316:13 regarding the principal Melacha of Shechita, perhaps the reason is because they were considered domestic animals which were raised by many Jews at that time, and there was thus no need to trap them.
[5] Admur 316:1; Michaber 316:1; Mishneh 106b
[6] Admur ibid; Michaber ibid; Mishneh ibid
[7] Admur ibid; See Michaber 497:7; Biur Halacha 316:1 "Sheheim Nitzudim"
[8] Admur ibid; M"A 316:2; M"B 316:4
[9] Admur ibid; Michaber ibid and Shabbos ibid as explained in Taz 316:1; M"A 316:2; M"B 316:1 and 4
[10] The sparrow is one of the smallest species of birds. They live on branches of trees and spend their time singing. Due to their small size they can live in a house just like in the outside and fly from corner to corner being very difficult to catch. [Mishneh Berurah 316:1; Biur Halacha "Hatzad Tzipor Dror] This translation is based on the modern-day Hebrew term used for this bird and is founded also on the words of the Peri Megadim, brought in the Biur Halacha above.

enough that] one can grab it without any further schemes. [However, one who traps it into a house is not liable, even if the house is small and has closed windows and one closed the door.[11] A dove however is considered like a regular bird.]

Trapping a lion:[12] One who traps a lion is not liable until he enters it into a cage that it can be restrained in.

Removing a fish from a river or pool of water:[13] One is exempt from the trapping prohibition if he took out a fish from an area that it was already trapped in and was not lacking any further trapping at all, such as for example [the fish was in a] bucket or barrel (see chapter 497 [Halacha 1][14]). However, if one took it out from an area where it was lacking further trapping, such as for example [taking a fish out from] a river or pool, then even if he immediately returned it into water that is in a vessel, [nevertheless] he is liable for trapping. [Furthermore] even if one did not catch it with his hand at all, but rather simply draw it out of the river with a bucket of water, then he is liable for trapping as when [the fish] is inside a bucket it does not lack any further trapping.[15]

Trapping an animal which needed further trapping:[16] One who traps [an animal or bird] from an area where it was still lacking further trapping there, is liable.

Trapping an animal which did not need further trapping:[17] From an area that the [animal] does not lack any further trapping it is initially allowed to trap it on Yom Tov, although not on Shabbos due to the moving '[Muktzah] prohibition. [In addition] there are those[18] who prohibit this [on Shabbos] also because of a Rabbinical trapping prohibition [which according to them applies even in this case].[19]

B. One traps for self-use as opposed to trapping to prevent injury:[20]

One who traps is not liable unless he has a need for the actual body of the trapped item.[21] Nevertheless one who casually traps species of animals, birds, and fish, is liable, as they are generally trapped for need of their body or skin. Similarly, one who casually traps one of the eight rodents mentioned in the Torah is liable as they are generally trapped for need of their skin and not to save oneself from injury being that it is not common for them to injure.[22]

However, one who traps one of the other creeping creatures [which are commonly trapped to prevent injury[23]] is not liable unless he trapped them for a need, such as for a medicine and the like. However if he casually trapped them, then he is exempt [from liability] being that they are generally trapped in order to prevent injury, being that they commonly injure and not for their skin being that they do not have skin, and not for their bodies being that they are inedible and they are not generally [trapped] for medicine unless one explicitly intended [on trapping them] for this, and thus this [trapping] is an action which does not have a self-use being that he has no need for the trapped item itself to which the [forbidden] action [of trapping] is being done to.

Other Opinions:[24] [However] according to those opinions[25] which say that even an action which is not done for its own use one is [Biblically] liable on, [the same would apply here].

---

[11] M"B 316:1 based on Taz 316:1 and Elya Raba
[12] Admur ibid; M"A 316:2; M"B 316:4; Rambam
[13] Admur 316:13
[14] There it discusses when a fish is considered to be trapped.
[15] Admur ibid; M"A 316:2; M"B 316:4
[16] Admur 316:1; Tosafus Beitza 24a
[17] 316:1; 497:11; Michaber 497:7; Mishneh Beitza 24a
[18] Rama 316:12; Tosafush Shabbos 106b; See Admur 497:11 that plainly rules it is forbidden on Shabbos
[19] The Mishneh Berura [316:55] rules like the 1st opinion that there is no trapping prohibition involved.
[20] Admur 316:16; Michaber 316:8; Mishneh Shabbos 107a as explained in Tosafus [in contrast to Rashi]
[21] Admur ibid; Michaber ibid; Mishneh ibid
[22] Admur ibid; Implication of Michaber; M"A 316:14 based on Ran; Tosafus ibid; M"B 316:28
[23] See C!
[24] Admur 316:17; Michaber ibid
[25] Rambam 1:7; Rebbe Yehuda 105b

If one trapped an animal for playing purposes, is one liable?
No.[26] Thus, one who traps an animal to use it as a pet or for a zoo is not liable. However, some Poskim[27] rule that one is liable in such a case and only when one traps for the sake of a game, and immediately lets the animal free, is not liable.

C. Trapping something which is not commonly trapped being that it serves no use:[28]

The Biblical prohibition of trapping something only applies by a species that is [commonly] trapped, which means that it is common for the [people of the] world to trap this species that he is trapping. For example, [trapping] species of animals and birds and fish [is liable because] it is common for the [people of the] world to trap these species.[29] However, if he trapped something which is a species that is not [commonly] trapped, such as for example wasps and flies and mosquitoes and the like of which it is not common for [people of] the world to trap these species being that they do not have any use, then even if one happened to trap them for a use[30], he is exempt [from Biblical liability].

Are creatures that are commonly trapped simply to prevent injury considered commonly trapped?
Yes.[31]

Are bees considered commonly trapped?[32]
Some rule yes others rule no.

D. The animal is not old or crippled:[33]

An old, or crippled or exhausted deer: One who traps an item which is not lacking any further trapping, such as for example one trapped a deer [or other animal[34]] which is crippled or old [or very young[35]], or weak due to exhaustion from doing strenuous activity[36], and [thus] it is not able to move from where it is, then [although] he is not liable nevertheless it is Rabbinically forbidden.

A sleeping or blind or sick deer: However, one who traps a deer that is sleeping or is blind or is sick [and weak] due to a fever that has developed in his body[37], then he is liable because they are self trained to escape when they feel the hand of a person, and are thus [considered to be] lacking further trapping.

---

[26] M"B 316:33 based on Rambam Shabbos 10:21
[27] Chazon Ish 50:4; SSH"K 27 footnote 117
[28] Admur 316:4; Michaber 316:3; Braisa Shabbos 107a
[29] It is evident from Halacha 16 that this includes even species which are commonly trapped only because they are harmful, however on such creatures one is only liable for trapping them if he intends on doing so in order to use them, such as for healing and the like.
[30] Admur ibid; M"B 316:12; Tosafus; Ritva; Ran; Rashba
[31] Michaber 316:7; M"B 316:26 in name of all Achronim; So is implied from Admur 316:16; Vetzaruch Iyun as to how common is considered common in this regard.
[32] M"B 316:13
[33] Admur 316:2; Michaber 316:2; Shabbos 106b
[34] M"B 316:6 in name of Elya Raba
[35] M"B 316:8
[36] Admur ibid; Taz 316:2; Gemara ibid as explained in Rashi
<u>Other opinions:</u> Some rule that if the animal is sick with fever than one is exempt. [Rabbeinu Chananel in Gemara ibid; implication of Michaber ibid; Gr"a; See Biur Halacha 316:2 "Oh Choleh"]
[37] Admur ibid; Taz 316:2; Gemara ibid as explained in Rashi
<u>Other opinions:</u> Some rule that if the animal is sick with fever than one is exempt. [Rabbeinu Chananel in Gemara ibid; implication of Michaber ibid; Gr"a; See Biur Halacha 316:2 "Oh Choleh"]

E. The trapping was done singlehandedly if possible:[38]

Single person trapped: A deer which entered on its own into a house and someone closed the door in front of it, then even if he did not lock the door with a lock but rather just pressed it closed in a way that the deer is guarded through this that it not be able to escape, then he is liable being that this is its trapping.

Two people trapped together and can be done alone: If two people closed it then they are exempt [from liability] as [the rule is that] any action which can be done alone and was done by two people, then they are exempt because it was not done in the usual method that it is done in during the week, as it is not usual at all to for [an action] which can be done alone to be done by two people.[39]

If it cannot be done alone: [However] if one alone cannot close it and two people closed it then they are liable.

If one of the partners can do it alone:[40] If one [of the two] is able to close it alone and the second is not able and they both closed it, then the one that is able is liable and the one that is not able is exempt being that [the one that is not able] is only considered an [unneeded] accomplice to the one that is able, and an [unneeded] accomplice has done a meaningless action. This rule applies for all the [prohibited] actions of Shabbos.

F. The creature is not one's pet or farm animal:[41]

Animals and birds which are raised in a person's property, such as one who breeds deer in his house or in his courtyard or geese and chickens and doves, then if one trapped them on Shabbos, he is exempt [from liability] being that they are already [considered] trapped.

Wild pigeons which nest in one's property: However one who traps [wild[42]] pigeons which reside on nests and high surfaces is liable because they are lacking further trapping as when a person comes to take them from their nest they are trained to escape and run away from their nest.

Domestic animals which have rebelled:[43] All the above [allowances to trap domestic animals and birds] only apply if they have not rebelled, however if they have rebelled, [including] even a cow that rebelled, and it goes without saying [that it includes] wild natured animals and birds that have rebelled, then one who traps them on Shabbos is liable just like having trapped wild [non-domestic] animals and birds as these [animals and birds which have rebelled will] also, not enter into their cage at night.

G. Form of trapping-Hunting dog or trap:

See below Halacha 4 and Halacha 5!

H. One is trapping them in the normal method:[44]

One is only liable for trapping if he is trapping the creature in the normal method. However, if he rather just deals with them in order so they not be able to injure, [such as he] covers them with a vessel or surrounds them [with items that prevents them from escaping] or ties them so they not cause damage.

---

[38] Admur 316:7; Michaber 316:5; Mishneh Shabbos 106b

[39] Admur ibid based on Rashi 93a; 106b; See Gemara ibid [brought in M"B 316:21] that learns from the verse "Nefesh Achas Techta" that only when a full Melacha is done by one person is one liable.

[40] Admur ibid; M"A 316:10; Rambam 1:16; M"B 316:22

[41] Admur 316:24

[42] Meaning that they have not been domestically raised. [Rashi Beitza 24a, and chapter 497 Halacha 16]

[43] Admur 316:25

[44] Admur 316:17; M"A 316:12; M"B 316:27

Summary of the Biblical Trapping prohibition:
It is only Biblically prohibited to trap a creature on Shabbos if **all** the following seven conditions are met:
1. The animal was previously not fully trapped and one now fully trapped it in a way that he does not need to further trap it.[45]
2. It is a creature which is commonly trapped [irrelevant to the reason why it is commonly trapped[46]].[47]
3. The creature was trapped in order to use its body for a certain purpose, such as to eat or for its skin and the like, or if one casually trapped it but it is a type of creature which is generally trapped for the above purpose.[48]
4. The animal was not old, crippled or exhausted to the point that it could not escape.[49]
5. One is trapping it himself and not through a hunting dog[50], or trap that had already been set up[51].
6. The animal was trapped by a single person, or by two people in a scenario that it required two people to trap.[52]
7. The animal is not a tamed pet or livestock and the like that has not rebelled[53].
8. Trapping in normal way.

Examples:
It is Biblically forbidden to:
1. Remove a fish from a river whether with ones hands or a bucket [or rod].[54]
2. Enter a lion into its cage.[55]
3. Grab a sick animal from outside.[56]
4. Trap a sparrow to an area that it needs no further trapping.[57]

---

3. The Rabbinical prohibition of trapping:

It is Rabbinically forbidden to trap in any of the following cases:

Traps in a way that it still requires further trapping:[58] Anyone who traps into an area where the trapped [animal or bird] is still lacking further trapping then although he is not liable [nevertheless] it is Rabbinically forbidden.

Trapping an animal which did not need further trapping:[59] From an area that the [animal] does not lack any further trapping it is initially allowed to trap it on Yom Tov, although not on Shabbos due to the moving '[Muktzah] prohibition. [In addition] there are those which prohibit this [on Shabbos] also because of a Rabbinical trapping prohibition [which according to them applies even in this case].[60]

---

[45] Admur 316:1
[46] Admur 316:16
[47] Admur 316:4
[48] Admur 316:16
[49] Admur 316:2
[50] Admur 316: 3
[51] Admur 316:6
[52] Admur 316: 7
[53] Admur 316:24-25
[54] Admur 316:13
[55] Admur 316: 1
[56] Admur 316: 2
[57] Admur 316:1
[58] Admur 316:1
[59] Admur 316:1
[60] The Mishneh Berura [316:55] rules like the 1st opinion that there is no trapping prohibition involved.

Trapping a sick, old, blind, lame, etc animal[61]: One who traps an item which is not lacking any further trapping, such as for example one trapped a deer which is crippled or old, or week due to exhaustion from doing strenuous activity, and [thus] it is not able to move from where it is, then [although] he is not liable nevertheless it is Rabbinically forbidden. However, one who traps a deer that is sleeping or is blind or is sick [and weak] due to a fever that has developed in his body, then he is liable because they are self-trained to escape when they feel the hand of a person, and are thus [considered to be] lacking further trapping.

Creature is not commonly trapped:[62] Although the Biblical prohibition of trapping something only applies by a species that is [commonly] trapped[63], while if he trapped something which is a species that is not [commonly] trapped, such as for example wasps and flies and mosquitoes and the like….., he is exempt [from Biblical liability], nevertheless, it is Rabbinically forbidden [to do so] even if one wants to trap them for no need at all and rather out of mere casualness.

One is trapping without intent to make use of the creature[64]: Although any [forbidden] action which is not done for self use one is not liable on, [nevertheless it] is Rabbinically forbidden.

One is unnecessarily trapping with two people:[65] Although when two people trap together they are exempt [from liability] as [the rule is that] any action which can be done alone and was done by two people, then they are exempt….[nevertheless it is Rabbinically forbidden to do so].

Summary-Rabbinically:
It is Rabbinically prohibited to trap a creature on Shabbos even if:
1) One does not fully trap the creature to the point that one can grab it in a single chase.[66]
2) The creature is not commonly trapped being that it does not have a use.[67]
3) One is trapping it out of mere casualness, for no use at all.[68]
4) The animal is exhausted, or old or crippled to the point it cannot escape.[69]
5) One could have trapped it alone and rather did it together with another person.[70]
6) If the animal is already fully trapped, trapping it further is forbidden on Shabbos due to Muktzah, and according to some it also contains a Rabbinical trapping prohibition.[71]

Q&A
May one further trap a fully trapped animal?[72]
Some Poskim[73] rule that it is forbidden to further trap a completely trapped animal due to a Rabbinical trapping prohibition [which according to them applies even in this case].[74]

May one enter a creature from outside a house to inside the house if he leaves the door open, or leaves open another obvious escape route for the creature?
Some Poskim[75] rule that this is completely permitted, and so is implied 316/5. However other

---

[61] Admur 316:2
[62] Admur 316:4
[63] Which means that it is common for the [people of the] world to trap this species that he is trapping. [Ibid]
[64] Admur 316:17
[65] Admur 316:7
[66] Admur 316:1
[67] Admur 316:4
[68] Admur 316:16
[69] Admur 316:2
[70] Admur 316:7
[71] Admur 316:1
[72] Admur 316:1; 497:11; Michaber 497:7; Mishneh Beitza 24a
[73] Rama 316:12; Tosafush Shabbos 106b; See Admur 497:11 that plainly rules it is forbidden on Shabbos
[74] The Mishneh Berura [316:55] rules like the 1st opinion that there is no trapping prohibition involved.
[75] Ketzos Hashulchan 121 footnote 1

Poskim[76] questions as to whether or not this is allowed.

May one trap an animal that is never commonly trapped and can never run away, such as a turtle and ant?

Some Poskim[77] rule that there is no trapping prohibition involved in doing so, as the animal is considered already trapped.[78] However, one may not move the turtle or ant with his hands due to the Muktzah prohibition.

Is there a prohibition involved in trapping humans, such as locking a child in his room, or a lunatic in his room?

There is no trapping prohibition involved in trapping humans.[79] One may thus lock a child in his room if needed[80], and arrest a man on Shabbos who is trying to leave his wife an Aguna.[81] However, there are Poskim[82] who question that perhaps the trapping prohibition applies to a child.[83] Others[84] forbid capturing a lunatic which would otherwise run away from society. In any event, it is forbidden to arrest an individual on Shabbos [unless there is extreme reason to do so] due to the prohibition to bestow punishments on Shabbos, irrelevant of the trapping issue.[85]

May one imprison a man who desires to leave his wife an Aguna?[86]

One may arrest a man on Shabbos who is trying to leave his wife an Aguna.

May one arrest a man who has perpetrated crimes against society, such as robbery, abuse, and bodily injury?[87]

Yes.

---

4. A mouse trap[88] - Setting up a trap mechanism on and before Shabbos:

A. Setting up a trap from before Shabbos to trap on Shabbos:[89]

It is permitted to begin a Melacha on Erev Shabbos close to dark even though one will not be able to finish it while still day, and it will thus consequently become complete on its own on Shabbos. Furthermore, even if it is a situation in which the vessel itself is doing the [entire] Melacha on Shabbos on its own, such as to spread traps for wild animals and birds and fish from before Shabbos, and [thus] having them become trapped on Shabbos, [it is nevertheless permitted] despite the fact that the trap is

---

[76] Mishneh Berurah in Biur Halacha 316:1 "Sheheim"

[77] Rav Shlomo Zalman Aurbach in SSH"K 27 footnote 145

[78] This can hold true even according to the stringent opinion in Admur mentioned above that it is Rabbinically forbidden to trap even an animal that lacks any trapping, as a) They were referring to an animal that in general needs trapping in contrast to here, and b) Perhaps that Rabbinical prohibition only applies by animals that are commonly trapped as opposed to here.

[79] Implication of Admur 339:3, Rama 339:4; Beis Yosef 263; Shivlei Haleket 60 in name of Rav Sharira Gaon in which no trapping prohibition is mentioned for the reason in why it is forbidden to jail a person on Shabbos; Avnei Nezer 189:22 that is no trapping prohibition by an adult however regarding a child he leaves this matter in question; Piskeiy Teshuvos 316:23
Other opinions: Some Poskim question that perhaps there is a trapping prohibition involved in trapping humans. [Makor Chaim 316; See Piskeiy Teshuvos ibid footnote 220]

[80] Tzitz Eliezer 15:41 brought in Piskeiy Teshuvos 316:23

[81] Shvus Yaakov 1:14; Birkeiy Yosef 339:2; Shaareiy Teshuvah 339:3; M"B 339:14; Kaf Hachayim 316:27

[82] Avnei Nezer ibid based on Tosafus Menachos 64a

[83] And accordingly, it would remain forbidden to lock a child in his room. However, Tzitz Eliezer writes that a child is in fear of his parents and is thus in any event already considered like trapped and there is thus no problem in locking him there.

[84] Rav SZ"A in Yesodei Yeshurun, brought in Piskeiy Teshuvos 316:3

[85] Admur 339:3; In Yesodei Yeshurun, in name of Rav SZ"A they mention that arresting a person never involves the trapping prohibition as they do not run away from society to be considered a trapping needed creature.

[86] Shvus Yaakov 1:14; Birkeiy Yosef 339:2; Shaareiy Teshuvah 339:3; M"B 339:14; Kaf Hachaim 316:27

[87] Aruch Hashulchan 339:11; Tzitz Eliezer 11:23

[88] To note that mice are not something which are trapped for their bodies use and may not be commonly trapped, and are thus not included in the Biblical prohibition of trapping even if it gets trapped in the process of setting up the trap.

[89] Admur 252:1

what is doing the action of trapping on Shabbos, being that the metal becomes tied and grabs the bird on Shabbos. Similarly, the booby-trap which they spread [to catch] wild animals to capture them by their feet, in which when the animal touches [the trap] it jumps and attaches itself on its own [against the legs of the animal] and traps it [it is permitted to spread it before Shabbos].

B. Setting up a trap on Shabbos:[90]
Biblically: One who sets up a trap [on Shabbos] and while doing so an animal entered it, he is liable. However, if the animal entered into the trap afterwards, then he is exempt [from liability] because at the time that he set it up it is not [yet] known if it will trap or not.[91]
Rabbinically: Nevertheless, it is Rabbinically forbidden and therefore it is forbidden to set up mouse traps on Shabbos.

Summary- May one set up a trap on and before Shabbos?[92]
Before Shabbos: Is permitted.
On Shabbos: Is forbidden. Doing so involves a Rabbinical prohibition.

Q&A
May one move around a mouse trap from one room to another?
No.

---

5. Hunting dogs:[93]
On Shabbos: One who instigates a [hunting] dog [to chase] after an animal in order to trap it is exempt [from Biblical liability] but is Rabbinically forbidden.[94] [If however the person was also involved in chasing down the animal, then he is liable.[95] Furthermore, some Poskim[96] rule that if it was certain that the dog will be successful in grabbing the animal, then he is liable for trapping even if he was not involved in the Melacha, and is forbidden due to Michameir[97], and if he owns the dog then he is also

---

[90] Admur 316:6; M"A 316:9; Tosafus Shabbos 17b "Porsin"; M"B 252:7;

[91] The reason: As at the time that he set it up it is not [yet] known if it will trap or not. [Admur ibid; M"A ibid; Tosafus ibid; Meaning, that since it is not for certain that the Melacha of trapping will occur, therefore there cannot be any Biblical liability. From here we can learn that whenever its not for sure that a Melacha will happen due to one's actions, then one is exempt even if he desired for it to occur and it did happen.]
The reason one is not exempt due to it being considered Gerama: Based on the above reasoning, it is evident that if one knows for certain that a Melacha will occur, then it is Biblically forbidden even if it is Grama, if one intends for the Melacha to occur. [Yeshuos Yakov ghloss of grandson in end of 334] Alternatively, one can suggest that the above case is not considered Gerama at all, as writes Admur in 265:8 [based on Rabbeinu Chananel and Rabbeinu Tam in Tosafus Shabbos 47b] regarding placing water by a table to extinguish an upcoming fire, that when there is no Hefsek it is not considered Gerama. Alternatively, one can suggest that by Tzeida there is no such thing as Gerama, as this is the entire Melacha. [Chazon Ish 36:1; 38:1]
Other reasons: Some Poskim rule that one is exempt from Biblical liability in the above case because it is a case of mere Gerama when the trapping occurs later on after the trap has been set up, and one is never Biblically liable for Gerama. Accordingly, even a Pesik Reishei of Gerama is only Rabbinical. [Minchas Chinuch Mosach Hashabbos Milachas Tzad p. 99, omitted in Tosafus, M"A and Admur] Alternatively, the reason one is exempt in the above case is because one is only liable by Tzeida if one does so with his actual hands. [Maharam Padua; Rav SZ"A]
The law if one knows for sure that the animal will become trapped: If one knows for sure that the animal will become trapped later on, then some Poskim rule that he is Biblically liable [Implication of Admur ibid, M"A ibid, Tosafus ibid; P"M 316 A"A 9; Minchas Chinuch ibid in opinion of Tosafus ibid; Avnei Nezer 191; Chazon Ish 36:1; 38:1], while other Poskim rule that he is exempt. [Minchas Chinuch ibid]
[92] Halacha 6
[93] Admur 316:3; M"A 316:4 in explanation of Rama 316:2 in name of Kol Bo 31
[94] Ruling of Rama: The Rama ibid rules in name of Kol Bo that one who ends a hunting dog to grab an animal "it's considered trapping." The M"A ibid explains based on the Rambam that when the person was not at all involved in assistance of the trapping then he is Biblically exempt, and hence the meaning of Rama/Kol Bo is "its considered trapping Rabbinically" and so rules Admur ibid. However the Achronim question this interpretation of the M"A ibid being that the wording "it is trapping" implies that it is Biblically forbidden. Hence the M"B [in Biur Halacha "Havei Tzeida"] explains the Rama refers to a case that the person assisted in the trapping in which case he is Biblically liable, as rules the Rambam Shabbos 10:22 rules it is Biblically forbidden and so is implied from Rama 316:2
[95] Rambam 10:22 brought in M"A ibid; Implication of Rama as explained in M"B 316:10 and Biur Halacha "Havei Tzeida"
[96] Avnei Nezer 1:196
[97] See Admur 266:4 that Michamer is forbidden if one does not own the animal

liable for the prohibition of Shevisas Beheima.[98]]

During the week:[99] [Furthermore] even during the week it is forbidden to trap with dogs[100] because [this symbolizes the actions of a] group of scoffers, and [one who does so] will not merit to participate[101] in the joy of the Leviathan [feast].[102]

Summary-May one go hunting with hunting dogs during the week?[103]
No, as this is considered a sport of the scoffers. [Although, for purposes of business there are sources which allow it.[104]]

---

6. Un-trapping an animal on Shabbos:[105]

It is allowed for one to open one's house in front of a deer [which is trapped inside] in order for it to run and escape. As well, a deer which has entered into a trap one is allowed to release it from its trap on condition that one not move it [being that it is Muktzah]. [Furthermore, it is a Mitzvah and obligation to help save an animal from death or pain, even if the animal belongs to Hefker, and even if it belongs to an idol worshiper.[106]]

Summary-May one un-trap an animal on Shabbos?
Yes as long as one does not move it in the process.

Q&A

May one lift up an animal that is stuck in a trap to help it get out?
It is forbidden to lift up the animal being that it is Muktzah.[107] This applies even if the animal is in pain and/or will die as a result.[108] Nonetheless, in the event that the animal is in pain or may die if left in the trap, then one may push it and encourage it to free itself from the trap without actually lifting it.[109] According to all, one may ask a gentile to help release the animal.[110]

May one trap an animal for the sake of helping it, to prevent Tzaar Baalei Chaim?
No, even if the trapping is only Rabbinically forbidden.[111]

---

[98] See Admur 246:7; 266:4; 305:1 that Shevisas Beheima is only forbidden if one owns the animal

[99] Admur ibid; Rama ibid

[100] However, the Peri Megadim explains that this only applies when hunting for a hobby. However, one whose occupation involves hunting may use hunting dogs to do so.

[101] Lit. see

[102] Admur ibid; M"A 316:5; Or Zarua 83:17; M"B 316:11

[103] Halacha 3

[104] Peri Megadim 316

[105] Admur 316:12; M"A 316:11 in name of Maggid Mishneh; M"B 316:25

[106] Admur C.M. Hilchos Ovrei Derachim 4; Rama C.M. 272:9; Baba Metzia 32b

[107] Admur ibid and 308:79 and 305:26

[108] 1st and main opinion in Admur 305:26 regarding pain and death and Stam opinion in Admur 308:79 regarding pain

Other opinions: Some Poskim rule one may even lift the animal to save it from pain and death. [2nd opinion in Admur ibid in parentheses; M"B 305:70; Chazon Ish 52:16]

[109] Admur 308:79

[110] Admur 305:26

[111] This follows the same ruling Muktzah, which is forbidden.

Other opinions: Some Poskim rule one may perform Rabbinical trapping to an animal to save it from pain and death. [Chazon Ish 52:16]

7. One who unintentionally trapped a creature:

Closing the door of one's house when he does not know if an animal's inside:[112] One who locked [the door of] his house in order to guard it [from break ins] without the slightest knowledge that a deer had entered into the house and only afterwards did he find out, then it is permitted for him to leave the entrance locked until after Shabbos with intention to take the deer [after Shabbos], as when he locked his house he was allowed to do so being that he knew of no [existing animals in his home] and now when he discovers this he is not doing anything [new].

Closing the door of one's house when he knows of animals inside: See Halacha 8!

Sat by the entrance and unintentionally trapped an animal:[113] Similarly one who sat by the entrance without knowledge that a deer had entered his house and later discovered this then it is permitted for him to remain sitting there until after Shabbos being that now [upon the discovery] he is not doing anything [new].

A bird which flew into ones clothes trapping itself:[114] Similarly one who had a bird enter under the wing of his clothing and consequently got trapped there, does not need to open for it an escape route and rather may guard it until Shabbos is over. [One may even go into a small room and release the bird there for it to remain trapped until after Shabbos. One may not, however, move the bird with one's hands due to Muktzah.[115]]

Summary-If one unknowingly did an action which trapped a creature must he let it out?[116]
No

Q&A

What is the law if one transgressed and trapped the animal on Shabbos, must it be freed?
If one intended to trap the animal, whether Beshogeg or Bimeizid, then some Poskim[117] rule he is obligated to free it. If he did so Bimeizid he may not benefit from it even after Shabbos.

---

8. Closing the door of one's house when he knows an animal or bird is inside:

A deer which entered on its own into a house and someone closed the door in front of it, then even if he did not lock the door with a lock but rather just pressed it closed in a way that the deer is guarded through this that it not be able to escape, then he is liable being that this is its trapping.[118]

The animal is already trapped:[119] If one had a deer bound up in his house and someone came along and also closed the door in front of it in order to add a [further form of] guarding onto the already existing [form of] guarding, and then afterwards the deer escaped from the ropes, we do not require the person to reopen the door being that at the time that he closed it he was allowed to do so and now he is doing nothing [new].

The animal is not yet trapped but one has no intent to trap:[120] If one knows that there is an [un-trapped] deer in his house then it is forbidden for him to close the door even if he does not at all intend to trap the deer but rather [just intends] to guard his house [from break ins], as the trapping [which comes as a result

---

[112] Admur 316:10; M"A 316:11
[113] Admur 316:11; M"A ibid
[114] Admur 316:11; M"A ibid; Shabbos 107a; M"B 316:25
[115] P"M 316 A"A 11; M"B 316:25
[116] Admur 316:10-11
[117] Biur Halacha 316:6 "Yashav Echad"; So is also implied from Admur 316:8 *"If the doorway had already been closed by the door after the deer entered into the house, whether the door had closed on its own [and] whether **another person** transgressed and closed it, it is permitted to lock it with a lock."*
[118] Admur 316:7; Michaber 316:5; Mishneh Shabbos 106b
[119] Admur 316:10; Ran; M"B 316:23
[120] Admur 316:10; M"A 316:11; Ran; Maggid Mishneh; M"B 316:25
Other opinions: Some Poskim rule it is permitted to close the door if one's intent is not to trap the animal, or even if one's intent is to trap the animal, but one also intends to guard the house. [Rashba brought in M"A ibid; Kneses Hagedola, brought in Machatzis Hashekel] This is not considered a Pesik Reishei according to Rashba, as explained in Shiltei Giborim, and Machatzis Hashekel.

of his closing the door] is inevitable. [This applies even if the animal being trapped is only Rabbinical.[121] However, if it contains two reason for why it is Rabbinical, then some Poskim[122] rule it is permitted, however others rule it is forbidden, and so is implied from Admur. Some Poskim[123] rule one may close the door due to the cold even if it will cause the animal to be trapped, so long as it will not be fully trapped due to this trapping. Vetzaruch Iyun if this allowance applies according to Admur!]

Summary:[124]
One may not close his windows or door even to protect his home from robbers if doing so will trap an animal or bird within his house.

Q&A
May one do an action which will inevitably trap a creature if he does not intend to trap it?[125]
No. For this reason one may not close his windows or door even to protect from robbers if doing so will trap an animal or bird within his house.

May one close the door of his house if he has a mouse, bird, or hornet that entered inside?
If there is another obvious escape route available for the bird or mouse, then doing so is permitted. If not, then it is forbidden.
<u>Closing the door due to the cold:</u> Some Poskim[126] rule one may close the door due to the cold, or to remove other pain[127], even if it will cause the animal to be trapped, so long as it will not be fully trapped due to this trapping. Vetzaruch Iyun if this allowance applies according to Admur!
<u>An uncommonly trapped creature:</u> Some Poskim[128] rule that even if it does not have another escape route, it is permitted to do so **if the animal is not considered commonly trapped**, and one still needs to do further schemes to trap it. Other Poskim[129] however are stringent even in such a case, and so is implied to be the ruling of Admur.[130]

If one has an animal at home that contains a Rabbinical trapping prohibition [such as a pet bird, or cat, or chicken[131]] is it forbidden to ever close the front door once it is opened?[132]
One may open and close the door regularly, even though this will cause the animal to be trapped.[133] Vetzaruch Iyun how this allowance would apply if the animal was out of the home before Shabbos began.

May one close the door or window of the house if there are flies inside?
Yes.[134]

---

[121] So is proven from the case of the flies in a vessel, brought in 316:4, as we hold of Pesik Resishei even by a Rabbinical prohibition. [M"B 316:18] However see Avnei Nezer 193:10 that allows closing the door by a Rabbinical trapping in certain cases.
[122] P"M 316 A"A 4, based on M"A 316:4
[123] M"B 316:5 in name of Chayeh Adam 30:2
[124] Admur 316:10
[125] Admur 316:10
[126] M"B 316:5 in name of Chayeh Adam 30:2; See 276:15 that we are more lenient when it comes to dealing with the cold.
[127] Vetzaruch Iyun if this would include even to prevent robbers.
[128] Rama 316:3; M"A 316:7; P"M 316 A"A 7 and 11; Biur Halacha 316:6 "Yashav Echad"; However from Admur it is implied that we are stringent, as he omits the ruling of the M"A ibid
[129] Levush 316; Kol Bo; brought in Kaf Hachaim 316:24
[130] As Admur omits the word "small" written in the Rama ibid, and rather writes as does the Levush.
[131] Or if the house is very large and one is unable to catch the animal in one chase. [Biur Halacha ibid]
[132] M"A 316:10; P"M 316 A"A 11; Avnei Nezer 193:10; Biur Halacha 316:6 "Vehalacha Lo"; Chikrei Halachos 1:19 [That this applies even according to all the Poskim that argue on the M"A ibid]
[133] <u>The reason:</u> As since the door was originally closed and the animal was originally trapped, one is not considered to be doing a new action of trapping, but rather is simply returning the trapping to the original position, and by a Rabbinical trapping one may be lenient, just as the Sages allowed to return a fire to a pot on Shabbos. [Avnei Nezer ibid]
[134] As flies are not considered any more trapped in the house than out of the house.

9. Locking the **closed** door of a room which contains an animal:[135]

If the doorway had already been closed by the door after the deer entered into the house, whether the door had closed on its own [and] whether another person transgressed and closed it, it is permitted to lock it with a lock. As since the deer is already guarded in a way that it cannot escape, it is thus already currently trapped and when one thus locks it with a lock, although he is adding a further means of guarding to the guarding that there is currently, [nevertheless] this is only considered done to guard it from robbers and does not carry with it [the] trapping [prohibition].

Summary May one lock the closed door of a room that contains an animal?[136]
Yes, even if he is doing so for further security.

---

10. Using one's body to block the exit of a room that contains an animal:[137]

A deer which entered a home and a person [came and] sat by the entrance totally blocking it, which means that there does not remain enough space between himself and the doorpost for the deer to be able to escape through, then he is liable.

Having a second person sit next to the first: [However] it is allowed for another person to [come] sit by the side of this [person] in the unblocked area which is between [the first person] and the doorpost even though that by doing so he is adding further fortification to the fortification provided by the first person.

The law if the first person got up:[138] [Furthermore] even if the first person stood up and left and thus his fortification has been annulled, but the deer is still guarded due to the sitting of the second person, meaning that the now free space between himself and the doorpost, which was the area where the first person sat, is not enough space to allow the deer to escape, nevertheless the second person does not need to get up, and it is thus permitted for him to sit there until after Shabbos and then come take the deer. [However, if the second person moved from the area after the first person got up, it is forbidden for him to return there.[139] Although by a Rabbinical trapping prohibition one may be lenient.[140]]

The reason for this is: because since at the time that he sat down it was allowed for him to do so being that the deer had been already considered trapped through the sitting of the first person, [therefore] we do not require him to leave after the first person gets up, as he is doing nothing by his [continued] sitting, being that he is only guarding a deer which had already been trapped by the first person.

Sitting next to the first person with intention to trap the deer:[141] [Furthermore] he may even sit near the first person with intent to remain sitting there after the first-person leaves.

---

[135] Admur 316:8; Rama 316:5
[136] Admur 316:8
[137] Admur 316:9; Michaber 316:6; Mishneh Shabbos 106b
[138] Admur ibid; Michaber ibid; Gemara ibid
[139] Implication of Admur; Tzemach Tzedek 53; Avnei Nezer 193:10; Tosafus Yom Tov, brought in M"A 316:11; M"B 316:25 in name of many Poskim
Other opinions: Some Poskim rule that once the action of trapping has been done it is permitted to repeat it again, and thus if the first person got up and the second person had to move to let him out, the second person may return there to continue the trapping. [M"A 316:11]
[140] P"M 316 A"A 11; Avnei Nezer 193:10; Biur Halacha 316:6 "Vehalacha Lo"; Chikrei Halachos 1:19 [That this applies even according to all the Poskim that argue on the M"A ibid]
The reason: As since the door was originally closed and the animal was originally trapped, one is not considered to be doing a new action of trapping, but rather is simply returning the trapping to the original position, and by a Rabbinical trapping one may be lenient, just as the Sages allowed to return a fire to a pot on Shabbos. [Avnei Nezer ibid]
[141] Admur ibid; Ramban; M"B 316:24

Summary-May one use one's body to block the exit of a room which contains an animal?[142]
No [even if he does not intend to do so in order to trap it, although if he did so unintentionally, then he does not have to move[143]]

11. Covering a vessel that has flies or other flying insects in it:[144]
One must be careful not to close a box or cover a vessel which has flies inside it, being that they are [consequently] trapped through this covering and closing.

The reason: Now, although one has no intent at all to trap [them], nevertheless [it is forbidden because] it is an inevitable consequence [of one's action, in which the law is that it is forbidden to do even if one does not intend to do so]. [From here we learn that a Pesik Reishei is forbidden even by a Rabbinical prohibition.[145] However if it contains two reason for why it is Rabbinical [i.e. Trei Derabanan], then some Poskim[146] rule it is permitted. However, some Poskim[147] however are stringent even in such a case, and so is implied to be the ruling of Admur.[148] Some Poskim[149] rule we are only lenient by Trei Derabanan when it is not beneficial for the person [i.e. Lo Nicha Lei].]

Leaving it slightly open:[150] Rather [if one nevertheless still wants to close it] he must place a knife or other item between the cover and the vessel in a way that the [flies] can escape from [inside the vessel] and it will no longer be inevitable [for them to leave].

Other Opinions:[151] [However] there are opinions[152] who are lenient [to allow one to completely close the vessel] in a situation that if one were to open the vessel to take [into ones hand] the flies that in there, then they would escape [before him being able to grab them], as in such a case there is no trapping done at all through this covering.

The Final Ruling-No need to check a vessel before closing it:[153] One may rely on this latter opinion with regards to not being required to be meticulous and check if [the vessel] has flies [in it] [before covering it]. [Furthermore] even if one sees for certain that there are flies in it, it suffices for him to chase away those that he sees with his eyes and he does not have to check for any more flies that have perhaps remained. As since there is a doubt as to whether there are any [more flies] in there, it is no longer

---

[142] Halacha 9
[143] Halacha 10-11
[144] Admur 316:4; 1st and Stam opinion in Rama 316:3
[145] M"A 314:5; 316:9; Taz 315:3; M"B 316:17 regarding bees

Other opinions: Some Poskim rule we are lenient to permit a Pesik Reishei by a Rabbinical prohibition. [Terumos Hadeshen, brought in M"A 314:5; Shaar Hatziyon 316:21; See Beis Yosef brought in Taz 316:3; Admur 314:3 regarding bees]
[146] P"M 316 A"A 4, based on M"A 316:4; M"B 316:15
[147] Levush 316; Kol Bor; brought in Kaf Hachaim 316:24
[148] As Admur omits the word "small" written in the Rama ibid, and rather writes as does the Levush.
[149] Shaar Hatziyon 337:2
[150] Admur ibid; Tur; Kol Bo; Mordechai; Levush; M"B 316:14
[151] Admur ibid; 2nd opinion in Rama ibid
[152] Tur 316
[153] Admur ibid; Taz 316:4; M"B 316:16

Other opinions: Some Poskim rule completely like the first opinion. [M"A 316:8; Bach]
Opinion of Taz/M"B: The ruling of Admur ibid is based on Taz ibid, albite with slight differences. The Taz 316:3 novelizes that a Safek Pesik Reishei is permitted, and hence in 316:4 he rules by the case of flies, which is only a Rabbinical trapping, one may be lenient if he is not certain that there are flies. The M"B ibid likewise accepts this ruling, as brought in Biur Halacha 316:3 "Vilachen." It is evident however that even the Taz does not accept this novelty of Safek Pesik Reishei in all cases, as in 316:4 he uses this novelty to permit an action especially by a Rabbinical prohibition, however by a Biblical prohibition perhaps he would be stringent. However, the Biur Halacha ibid explains that one may be lenient even by a Biblical prohibition according to the Taz. Regarding how this differentiates from Admur's ruling-see next.
Ruling of Admur by Safek Pesik Reishei: Admur rules that Safek Pesik Reishei is forbidden, just as is any Biblical prohibition, and in any case that there is a Safek that perhaps one's actions will certainly cause the Issur, then it is forbidden. A Safek only permits a Pesik Reishei [and makes it no longer be considered a Pesik Reishei] if there is doubt as to whether the physical action done at that very moment is of enough quality to cause the Issur. [Kuntrus Achron 277:1; See first explanation in Biur Halacha ibid] Thus in this case as well since perhaps there are flies inside, and one's actions will certainly cause the Issur, it is a Safek Pesik Reishei, and thus Admur rules that only because of the lenient opinion of the Tur can one be lenient in this case, and so is seemingly his understanding of the Taz. However, the M"B in Biur Halacha ibid seems to understand the Taz is completely lenient by Safek Pesik Reishei, irrelevant to the lenient opinion of the Tur.

[considered an] inevitable [consequence of one's actions that he will trap the flies].[154]

Summary-May one cover a vessel if there are insects, such as flies inside it?[155]
No. He must either a) rid it of all the flies and other insects that are currently visible to him, although he does not need to search it for any more insects. Or b) leave it slightly open to the point that the bugs can fly out.
Must one search a vessel for bugs prior to closing it?[156] No.

Q&A
May one cover a vessel if it is very large?
Some Poskim[157] rule it is permitted to close a large vessel that contain flying insects if it is so large that one is unable to grab the insect in a single grab.[158] Other Poskim[159] however are stringent even in such a case, and so is implied to be the ruling of Admur.[160]

May one open the fridge if he has doubt whether the light is on?[161]
No.

May one ask a friend to open the fridge if he knows the light is on?[162]
No.

---

12. Covering a beehive in order to protect it from damage:[163]

Leaving an escape route available: It is allowed to spread mats over a beehive on a sunny [day] in order [to protect it from] the sun and [on a] rainy [day] in order [to protect it from] the rain, as long as one has no intent to trap the bees. As well it must be done in a way that does not inevitably trap them there, such as for example he leaves a hole in the beehive that is not covered by the mats and it is [thus] possible for them to escape through there.[164] Even if the hole is small and on the side in which it [thus] is not visible to the bees, [nevertheless] this does not pose a problem, being that he does not intent to trap [them], and it is not inevitable [for them to escape], as it is [still] possible for them to escape through this small side hole and it is not definitive that they will not escape through it.[165] However if there is no hole that is [left] uncovered by the mat, then it is forbidden because it is impossible [for them to escape].
The reason:[166] Now, although there are opinions which are lenient regarding [covering a vessel with] flies in a situation that if one were to open the vessel to take [the flies] that are there then they will escape,

---

[154] Although in general a Safek Pesik Reishei is ruled stringently like a Pesik Reishei, as ruled in many cases [such as 277:1; see Kuntrus Achron 277:1 for a list of cases and explanation], in this case since there is another lenient opinion, therefore one may be lenient not to check.
[155] Admur 316:4
[156] Admur 316:4
[157] Rama 316:3; M"A 316:7; P"M 316 A"A 7 and 11; M"B 316:15; Biur Halacha 316:6 "Vehalach Lo"
[158] The reason: As in such a case it is a Pesik Resihei of two Derabanan's which is permitted to be done. [P"M ibid]
[159] Levush 316; Kol Bo; brought in Kaf Hachaim 316:24
[160] As Admur omits the word "small" written in the Rama ibid, and rather writes as does the Levush.
[161] Based on Admur 271:1, and 316:4 as explained above
Other opinions: Some rule that according to the Taz 316:3-4 one may be lenient. [See Biur Halacha 316:4 "Vilachen"; SSH"K 10:15 Footnote 42]
[162] Based on Admur 271:1, and 3
16:4 as explained above
Other opinions: Some rule that according to the Taz 316:3-4 one may be lenient. [See Biur Halacha 316:4 "Vilachen"; SSH"K 10:15 Footnote 42]
[163] Admur 316:5; Michaber 316:4; Braisa Shabbos 43a; Beitza 36b
[164] Admur ibid; Michaber ibid; Tosafus Beitza ibid
[165] Admur ibid; M"A 316:9; Tosafus ibid; M"B 316:18 that this applies according to Rebbe Shimon
If one does intend to trap them: If one intends to trap the bees then it does not help unless one leaves an obvious escape route available for the insect. [Biur Halacha 316:4 "Ubilvad Shelo"; Implication oif Admur ibid "being that he does not intent to trap [them], and it is not inevitable"]
[166] Admur ibid; Beis Yosef

nevertheless here it [is not allowed because it] is considered a complete trapping for the bees to be trapped in their beehive in a way that that it is not possible for them to escape even though he is not able to take them out from there with his hands. [The reason for why it is considered a complete trapping is] because the beehive is their [common] place of trapping [in a scenario] that they reside in a beehive, and is [thus] similar to one who traps a lion and enters it into its cage that even though he is not able to take it from there with his hands without having it escape he is [nevertheless] liable because that is its place of trapping.

Summary-May one cover a beehive with a cloth in order to protect it from rain and the like?[167]
Only if he leaves at least one hole uncovered through which it is possible for them to escape through. However, when done in order to trap the bees it is forbidden even with a hole left uncovered.

---

13. Trapping pets and farm animals:[168]
A. The Biblical Prohibition-Trapping rebellious pets and farm animals:
Animals and birds which are raised in a person's property, such as one who breeds deer in his house or in his courtyard, or geese and chickens and doves, then if one trapped them on Shabbos, he is exempt [from liability] being that they are already [considered] trapped.[169]
Animals that rebelled:[170] However, all the above only apply if they have not rebelled, however if they have rebelled, [including] even a cow that rebelled, and it goes without saying [that it includes] wild natured animals and birds that have rebelled, then one who traps them on Shabbos is liable just like having trapped wild [non-domestic] animals and birds as these [animals and birds which have rebelled will] too, do not enter into their cage at night. [An animal is considered to have rebelled if it does not return to its cage at night and rather sleep in the wild and requires schemes to be caught.[171]]
Wild pigeons which nest in one's property:[172] One who traps [wild[173]] pigeons which reside on nests and high surfaces is liable because they are lacking further trapping as when a person comes to take them from their nest they are trained to escape and run away from their nest.

B. The Rabbinical prohibition- Trapping domestic birds [and wild natured animals[174]]:[175]
Birds which are raised in a house and when they enter into their coop in the evening are easy to be caught, being that they are not able to escape [ones grasp] and run away from there, then even when they are outside their coop they are not considered lacking further trapping being that at night they will go into their coop on their own. However nevertheless it is Rabbinically forbidden to trap them, which means to run after them until they enter into an area in which they are easily caught there. However, to move them with one's hand is forbidden regardless of the trapping prohibition because of [the fact that they are] Muktzah.
However, this is only referring to when [these birds] are in the courtyard or in a house so large that if they

---

[167] Admur 316:5
[168] Admur 316:24-25; Michaber 316:12; Mishneh Shabbos 107
[169] Admur 316:24; Mishneh ibid
[170] Admur 316:25; Rama ibid [Michaber simply states "forbidden" and does not state "liable". The word liable is added by the Rama ibid]
Other opinions: Some Poskim rule that trapping rebellious animals is only Rabbinically forbidden. [Implication of Michaber ibid; M"B 316:56 as explains Gr"a] However see M"B 316:60 that even the Michaber agrees it is Biblically forbidden if they have rebelled to the point that they do not return to their cage at night. Vetzaruch Iyun.
[171] M"B 316:59-60
[172] Admur 316:24; Shabbos ibid
[173] Meaning that they have not been domestically raised. [Rashi Beitza 24a, and chapter 497 Halacha 16]
[174] From 316:25 it is evident that the following Halacha includes wild animals as well.
[175] Admur 316:24; Rama ibid; Rif; Rambam; Ramban; Ravan; Aguda; Rokeiach; M"B 316:57 and Biur Halacha "Veyeish" in anme of many Rishonim
Other opinions: Some Poskim rule it is permitted to trap all pet animals that are not rebellious. [Michaber ibid as rules Hagahos Maimanis; explained in Shaar Hatziyon 316:81 as explains Gr"a]

had not been raised around humans then they would need to be trapped, meaning that one would need to seek schemes to catch them there and they are thus considered lacking further trapping. For example, if the house is so large that one is not able to catch them with a single chase and [rather must] runs after them until they enter into a room which is not very large, and he then closes the door in front of them [then it is considered that the bird was lacking further trapping].

Helping a chicken enter back into its coop:[176] However, it is permitted to push the chicken from its back with ones hands in order so it enter [back] into its coop if it ran away from it.[177]

C. Trapping pet birds [or wild natured animals] from an already trapped area:[178]
However, if they are in a house which is not very large then they are [considered] already trapped and waiting [and is thus not at all prohibited to be further trapped].

D. Trapping pet birds or wild natured animals from one large area to another large area:[179]
[As well] even if they are in a large house or even if they are in a public domain and one pushed them until they entered into another large house, then there is no trapping [prohibition involved here] at all and it is thus permitted [to even initially be done].

E. Trapping calm natured pets and farm animals:[180]
All the above [Rabbinical prohibition to further trap a domestic creature only] refers to wild natured animals[181], and [all] birds; however calm natured animals[182] which are raised in a person's property are permitted to be trapped even from a public domain.

F. Trapping pet cats:[183]
A cat has the same law as any other wild natured animal and is forbidden to be trapped in ways other than those explained [above in C and D].

Summary
Biblically:
It is only Biblically forbidden to trap pets and raised animals if they have rebelled against their master and will not enter on their own into their sleeping quarters at night.

Rabbinically:
It is Rabbinically forbidden to further trap all home raised **birds and wild natured animals** that are trapped in a large room in which they could not be caught with a single chase.

It is permitted to trap a pet or house raised animal in the following conditions:
  1. The animal has not rebelled against its owner.
And
  2. It is a calm natured animal such as a cow.

---

[176] Admur 308:79; M"A 316:26 in name of Aguda permits only to push the chicken until it enters into a large house, however not its coop and so writes M"B 316:57

[177] Does this allowance apply even if the coop is small? If the coop is small, then seemingly this should be forbidden, as rules the M"A and M"B ibid and brought in Admur 316:24. However from the fact Admur here did not stipulate that the coop be large it implies that the allowance applies to any size coop. Hence, perhaps one can answer that Admur here only allows one to help the chicken enter and not that he pushes him actually into the coop. Vetzaruch Iyun.

[178] Admur 316:24; Michaber ibid; M"B 316:55

[179] Admur 316:24; M"A 316:26 in name of Aguda; M"B 316:57 as explained in Biur Halacha 316:12 "Veyeish Omrim"

[180] Admur 316:25; Rama ibid as explained in M"A 316:26; M"B 316:59

[181] חיות refer to wild animals such as the hart, dear, gazelle and *yachmor*.

[182] בהמות refers to domestic animals such as sheep, cows, and goat.

[183] Admur 316:25; Rama ibid

Or

3. All pets may be brought from one large area to another large area and from an area where they can be grasped with a single chase into a smaller area.

Q&A

Are new pets that are not yet trained and tamed considered a Rabbinical or Biblical trapping prohibition?[184]

They contain a Biblical trapping prohibition, just as animals that have rebelled.

If one has a pet at home that contains a Rabbinical trapping prohibition [such as a bird, or cat, or chicken] is it forbidden to ever close the front door once it is opened?[185]

One may open and close the door regularly, even though this will cause the animal to be trapped.[186] However seemingly one may only be lenient if his intent is not to trap the animal, or if in any event the pet cannot be grabbed in one chase if the door is closed.[187]

May one stand in the way of a pet animal to prevent it from running out of the house?[188]

Yes.

If one tamed a wild animal to follow his every order, can he further trap that animal on Shabbos?[189]

In such a case it is similar to domestic livestock and does not contain a trapping prohibition.

Is commanding a pet to go to its cage considered trapping it?

Seemingly not.[190]

May one push a chicken back into its coop, or a bird back into its cage?

No.[191] Although one may push it until it reaches its coop and then let it enter on its own.[192] Some Poskim[193] however rule one may enter a tamed bird into its cage in order to prevent it from doing damage to the home.

If a parakeet lands on one's arm may one bring it to the cage and have it walk in?[194]

Yes.

May one close the cage of a bird or dog after it entered inside the cage?[195]

No, doing so is forbidden. However, if the room is small and thus even if the dog, bird, were to leave the cage it could be caught in a single chase, then it is permitted to be done.

---

[184] Admur 497:11; M"B 316:60; Biur Halacha "Chaya Veof" in name of Masaas Binyamin

[185] M"A 316:10; P"M 316 A"A 11; Avnei Nezer 193:10; Biur Halacha 316:6 "Vehalach Lo"; Chikrei Halachos 1:19 [That this applies even according to all the Poskim that argue on the M"A ibid]

[186] The reason: As since the door was originally closed and the animal was originally trapped, one is not considered to be doing a new action of trapping, but rather is simply returning the trapping to the original position, and by a Rabbinical trapping one may be lenient, just as the Sages allowed to return a fire to a pot on Shabbos. [Avnei Nezer ibid]

[187] See Biur Halacha ibid

[188] M"B 316:57 in name of Chayeh Adam

[189] See M"B 316:57 in name of Chayeh Adam regarding a very tamed chicken that never runs away that it does not have the trapping prohibition.

[190] So is implied from 308:79 that when it enters into the trapped area on its own accord then it is not considered trapping.

[191] M"B 316:58

[192] Admur 308:79

[193] M"B ibid; Biur Halacha "Latzud"

The reason: As it is Trei Derabanan in a case of loss, and is hence permitted.

[194] Admur 308:79 regarding pushing a chicken until it goes [on its own] into its coop.

[195] Biur Halacha 316:12 "Deassur"

May one trap a pet scorpion which escaped its cage?
Had its stinger removed: No, unless its bite can cause bodily damage.
Did not have its stinger removed: May be trapped and casually killed.

May one trap a chicken and the like if it is running away and one is in fear that it may get stolen?[196]
One may ask a gentile to do so. Likewise, one is not required to protest against children who do so.

May one chase a dog back into one's home?
This follows the same ruling as above regarding a chicken, that one may push the dog from its back with one's hands in order so it enter back into the home, although one may not actually push it into the house, unless the house is also large, and it is not considered trapped inside. However, in a case of loss one may even have the dog chased into a small house through a gentile.

14. Trapping to prevent injury:[197]
A. Initially trapping creeping creatures which can cause bodily injury [in contrast to mere pain]:[198]
Even initially, it is allowed to trap all types of creeping creatures which commonly cause injury, such as snakes and scorpions and the like, even in places where their bite [or sting] is not deadly[199], and even if they are not currently chasing after him at all[200], and rather he just suspects that perhaps it may eventually chase after him or after someone else and bite [or sting] him or that perhaps he may not [properly] avoid [stepping on or near] them and they will bite him or perhaps will bite other people which do not know that they have to beware from them.
The reason:[201] As since one is only trapping them in order to save himself from injury, this is [considered] an action that is not done for its own self use. Now, although that any [forbidden] action which is not done for self use despite not being liable on, is Rabbinically forbidden, [nevertheless] here the Sages completely permitted it due to chance that one may receive bodily injury [if he were to not be allowed to trap them]. [Furthermore] even according to the opinions which say that an action done not for its own self use one is [also] liable on and [thus according to them it should be prohibited being that] we do not [allow one to] transgress Shabbos through doing a complete Biblical prohibition [just in order to prevent] bodily damage and rather is only allowed to prevent danger of one's life, nevertheless here since one is not trapping them in the normal method but rather just deals with them in order so they not be able to injure, [such as he] covers them with a vessel or surrounds them [with items that prevents them from escaping] or ties them so they not cause damage, therefore the [Sages] permitted one to do so even to creeping creatures which are not at all deadly and rather only cause injury.[202]
How to trap them:[203] One covers them with a vessel or surrounds them [with items that prevents them from escaping] or ties them so they do not cause damage.
Charming snakes and scorpions to prevent injury:[204] One may charm[205] snakes and scorpions on Shabbos

---

[196] M"A 316:26 in name of Aguda; M"B 316:57 in name of Chayeh Adam
[197] Admur 316:17-18; Michaber 316:7, 9; Shabbos 107b
[198] Admur 316:17; Michaber 316:7; Shabbos ibid
[199] Admur ibid; M"A 316:12; Rambam 10:25; M"B 316:27
Other opinions: Some Poskim rule that if the creature is not lethal then one may not capture it. [Maggid Mishneh, brought in Machatzis Hashekel; Shaar Hatziyon 316:38]
[200] Admur ibid; M"B ibid
[201] Admur ibid; M"A ibid; M"B ibid
[202] However it is not permitted under the basis that it is not common to trap these creatures and is hence only Rabbiniclaly forbidden, as a number of these creatures are in truth commonly trapped to prevent injury. [Michaber 316:7; M"B 316:37 in name of all Achronim; So is implied from Admur 316-317]
[203] Admur ibid; M"B 316:27
Other opinions: Some Poskim write it is best not to cover the creature, as doing so is considered the common way of trapping. [Nehar Shalom brought in Shaar Hatziyon 316:39]
[204] Admur 328:50; Michaber 328:45; Sanhedrin 101a

so they do not cause injury even if they are not pursuing oneself, and doing so does not contain the trapping prohibition even according to those opinions which hold liable one who does an action that is not needed for itself.

B. Trapping insects and the like which only cause pain:[206]
[However] all the above is referring to [trapping] creeping creatures which commonly cause injury such as snakes and scorpions, [which may be trapped] even in places that their bite is not deadly being that nevertheless they cause bodily injury with their bite, and the same applies for all creatures of the like. However, anything which does not damage the body but rather just causes it pain alone, such as wasps[207], and flies, mosquitoes and fleas and the like, then it is forbidden to trap them.

Removing a stinging insect from one's cloths or skin-First Opinion:[208] It is therefore forbidden to take hold of a flea which is on ones clothes, even if it is inside [ones clothes] close to his skin, and even if it is on his skin and has still not stung him it is forbidden to grab it.

Other Opinions: There are opinions[209] which permit to grab the flea even while it is on the inside of his clothes [and not yet on his skin] being that it is able to cause him pain there. [Furthermore] even from his undershirt[210] on the outside it is allowed to grab it since an undershirt is close to the flesh and it is thus possible that the flea will go from there to his flesh and will bite him. [Regarding the reason that this is allowed-see C and the reason mentioned there!]

However [even according to this opinion] if the flea is on the person in a way that there is no worry that it may bite him, [such as] that it is on his upper clothes on the outside, then it is forbidden to grab it.

Shaking one's cloths to caused the insect to fall off: Nevertheless it is [always] permitted to make it fall off of him through shaking [his cloths].

The Final Ruling:[211] The final ruling is that if it is possible for him to easily make it fall off of him without [needing to] take it with his hand, then one is to do so even if [the insect] is on the inside of his undershirt. However, if one is wearing long boots [which reach to his thighs[212], or pants] and it is thus difficult[213] for him to shake it away without first grabbing it with his hand then one who relies on the lenient opinion regarding this Rabbinical prohibition has done no harm.[214]

The prohibition to kill or squish an insect which is in the midst of stinging oneself:[215] The above allowance is only with regards to lifting the insect off oneself, however, to kill it is forbidden according to all opinions even if it's on ones flesh and is in the midst of biting him. ....[Furthermore] even to squeeze it with ones fingers to weaken its strength so that it not return to him is forbidden because of a decree that one may come to kill it. Rather he is to take it in his hand and throw it away. [See Chapter 2 Halacha 7 for the reason behind this prohibition]

---

[205] Snake charming is the practice of apparently hypnotizing a snake by simply playing an instrument. A typical performance may also include handling the snakes or performing other seemingly dangerous acts, as well as other street performance staples, like juggling and sleight of hand. This practice is most common in India, though other Asian nations such as Pakistan, Bangladesh, Sri Lanka, Thailand, and Malaysia are also home to performers, as are the North African countries of Egypt, Morocco and Tunisia. Seemingly playing an instrument is allowed on Shabbos in order to restrain a dangerous snake, just like it is allowed to trap them, which is also a Rabbinical prohibition.
[206] Admur 316:18; Michaber 316:9; Rambam 10:24
[207] Admur ibid; Rambam ibid; See also Biur Halacha 316:8 "O Stam"
Other Opinions: In SSH"K 25 footnote 7 they write that based on the Mishneh Berura 316:46 which differentiates between lots of pain and a small amount of pain, there may be room for one to be allowed to trap a wasp if its sting gives him tremendous pain. However clearly according to Admur one may not be lenient.
[208] Admur ibid; Michaber ibid as explained in M"A 316:18 and Taz 316:8; M"B 316:37
[209] Beis Yosef in opinion of Rashi and Rashba and Ran and Tosafus; brought in M"A 316:18 and Taz 316:8; and so concludes Taz
[210] Based on Taz ibid that he explains there that the "Chaluk" is the shirt closest to the skin while a regular shirt is called something else.
[211] Admur ibid; Taz ibid; implication of M"B 316:35; However see Shaar Hatziyon 316:63 that writes one is initially to be stringent.
[212] Based on Mishneh Berurah 128:16 and the Alter Rebbe there in 128:6
[213] Tzaruch Iyun why wearing long boots should consider it difficult. Perhaps then this is referring to only when the flea has gone inside his pants or boot, in which case it is difficult to shake it off of him entirely.
[214] Lit. has not lost
[215] Admur 316:19; Michaber and Rama ibid

C. Removing an insect that is in the midst of stinging:[216]

If a flea is in the midst of stinging oneself then it is permitted to take hold of it while it is stinging and to throw it away.

The reason for why this does not involve the trapping prohibition is: because when one takes hold of it at the time of the stinging he has no intent to trap it and rather is only involving himself with it in order to stop it from stinging him, and [when there is no intent to trap] the [Sages] did not decree [against trapping] even in a case [that doing so is only to prevent] pain alone[217] since [these insects] are items which their species are not commonly trapped [and thus even when trapped with intent it is only Rabbinically forbidden].

The reason this does not involve the Muktzah prohibition: As well, the [Sages] did not decree in a scenario [that involves] pain the prohibition in moving the flea due to it being Muktzah.

Grabbing a wasp in the midst of stinging: Similarly if a wasp and the like stings him one is allowed to take it with his hands and send it away if it is not possible to brush it away.

The prohibition to kill or squish an insect which is in the midst of stinging oneself:[218] It is only permitted to trap a flea which is in the midst of biting oneself, however to kill it is forbidden according to all opinions even if it's on ones flesh and is in the midst of biting him............ [Furthermore] even to squeeze it with ones fingers to weaken its strength so that it not return to him is forbidden because of a decree that one may come to kill it. Rather he is to take it in his hand and throw it away. [See Chapter 2 Halacha 7 for the reason behind this prohibition].

Summary

The Sages allowed one to trap creatures which pose a threat in the following scenarios:

1. Causes bodily injury: It is permitted to trap for sake of protection all creatures which can cause bodily injury [as opposed to mere pain] even if they are not chasing after oneself. It is forbidden to trap them for other purposes.

2. Only causes pain but is on one's inner clothing or skin: It is forbidden to trap even for protection in a case that they do not cause bodily injury even if they cause pain.[219] However, if a [non-deadly or bodily injuring] insect is in ones inner clothing [the one that touches his skin] or on ones actual skin but not yet in midst of a bite then if it is difficult to brush the insect away one may be lenient to pick it up with his fingers and throw it away. However there are opinions which are stringent.

3. Insect is in the midst of a bite or sting: If the insect is in the midst of a sting or bite then if it cannot easily be brushed off, according to all opinions one may grab it with his hands and throw it.

Being careful to not kill the insect upon lifting it: However when doing so it is forbidden to even squeeze the insect in the process as he may come to kill it which is forbidden in all cases, even if the insect is in the midst of a sting.

If insect is on outer clothing: If the insect is on his outer clothing then one may not pick it up and must rather suffice with brushing or shaking it away.[220]

Examples:
One may trap in order to prevent danger:
1. Scorpions
2. Snakes

---

[216] Admur 316:18; Michaber ibid; Tosafus Shabbos 107b

[217] Meaning in addition to there not being a decree when there is bodily injury, but even for mere pain there is no decree in such a situation.

[218] Admur 316:19; Michaber and Rama ibid

[219] Admur 316:17

[220] Admur 316:18 and 19

One may not trap [unless condition 2/3 is fulfilled]:

- Wasps[221]

Q&A

May a wasp be trapped when in the presence of an infant?
Some Poskim[222] rule that they may even be killed when near an infant, as their sting can be lethal. However seemingly this no longer applies today, and they thus may not be trapped.

May one trap an insect which he is allergic to?
If one knows that he is allergic to a certain insect sting, and he could get from it a lethal allergic reaction [not just mere pain] then one may trap it and even kill it on Shabbos.

May one trap a wasp or bee if he is unsure if he is allergic?
Seemingly one may not do so as is implied from the ruling regarding spiders in 316/23 that there being a chance that an insect is deadly is not a good enough reason to allow killing it.

May one trap a snake if he is unsure if it is poisonous?
Seemingly, yes.

May one trap a hornet which is disturbing ones Shabbos meal?
Allergies: If there are any people which are allergic to their sting then it may be trapped or killed.
No allergies: Then it may not be trapped.[223]

May one trap a typical spider?[224]
No. A typical spider does not bite.

May one trap a tarantula?[225]
A typical tarantula bite causes mere pain, similar to a bee sting, and hence may not be trapped on Shabbos unless it is in the process of biting, or is close to one's skin and one cannot shake it off.

---

[221] Admur 316:17
Other Opinions: In SSH"K 25 footnote 7 they write that based on the Mishneh Berura 316:46 which differentiates between lots of pain and a small amount of pain, there may be room for one to be allowed to trap a wasp if its sting gives him tremendous pain. However clearly according to Admur one may not be lenient.
[222] SSH"K 25:1
[223] Advice: Try using the end of a broom to latch it on the broom and then take it outside.
[224] See 316:23
[225] Despite their often threatening appearance and reputation, no tarantula has been known to have a bite that is deadly to humans. In general, the effects of the bites of all kinds of tarantula are not well known. While the bites of many species are known to be no worse than a wasp sting, accounts of bites by some species are reported to be very painful and to produce intense spasms that may recur over a period of several days; the venom by the African tarantula *Pelinobius muticus* also causes strong hallucinations. In all cases, it is prudent to seek medical aid. Because other proteins are included when a toxin is injected, some individuals may suffer severe symptoms due to an allergic reaction rather than to the venom. Such allergic effects can be life-threatening.

General Summary:

It is only permitted to trap on Shabbos in the following cases:

1. A calm natured pet or farm animal which has not rebelled.
2. A wild natured pet which has not rebelled may be brought from one large area to another large area and from an area where they can be grasped with a single chase into a smaller area.
3. Trapping creatures to prevent bodily injury to oneself [as opposed to mere pain].
4. Grasping gently an insect in the midst of a bite or sting, or that is on one's skin and one cannot remove it in any other way.

CHAPTER 2: KILLING OR INJURING CREATURES ON SHABBOS

1. The Primary Melacha that was in the Tabernacle-Slaughtering:[1]
Slaughtering is one of the principal [forbidden] actions [on Shabbos], [being] that [it] was done in the [building process for the] Tabernacle [in slaughtering the] rams and Techashim[2].[3]

2. The Biblical Prohibitions included in the above principal Melacha:
A. Killing in forms other than slaughtering:[4]
Not only is slaughtering [included in this principal prohibition] but [also] anyone who takes the soul from any species of animal, bird, fish, and rodent, whether [he did so] by slaughtering it [and] whether by tearing it [open, and] whether by hitting it, he is liable.

Strangling: One who strangles a creature until it dies is [transgressing] an offshoot of [the prohibited action of] slaughtering. [As will be explained in Halacha 5 regarding removing fish from water to the point that it can no longer live.]

B. Injuring a creature:
❖ *Causing a creature to bleed:[5]*
The taking of life [prohibition] which one is liable for, is not only when one removes the entire life-force from the creature [i.e. kills it], rather even if one removed [only] a part of its life-force he is liable. For example, one who [injures an animal to the point that he] takes out blood from one of the limbs of the creature then he is liable for taking out life from that area being that blood contains [ones life-force which is] the soul.

Scratching a pimple/boil on Shabbos:[6] It is forbidden to scratch a boil [on Shabbos] as doing so removes blood and contains the prohibition of inflicting a wound.

❖ *Causing a bruise to a creature:[7]*
[Furthermore, he is] not only [held liable] if blood actually comes out [of its skin], but even if one bruised one of the creatures limbs to the point that blood [vessels have been broken and] gathered under the skin [thus causing a "black and blue mark"] then even though [the blood] has not gone out [of the skin] he is liable being that it is a bruise which will never be replaced. As once the blood [vessels have been broken and] gathered under the skin it can never return back to its place, and its only that the skin is preventing it from going out, and he is thus liable for taking out the blood of that area.

Bruising an animal and the like: [However] the above only applies to a bruise made in a person or domestic and wild animal or bird[8] or in [any of] the eight rodents mentioned in the Torah (in Parshas Shemini) which are the weasel, the mouse [the toad, the porcupine or hedgehog, the lizard, the snail, and the mole] of which each one of these has skin which prevents the blood from going out.

---

[1] Admur 316:13; Mishneh Shabbos 73a
[2] A type of animal with a unique colored skin
[3] Admur ibid; Smag 65
The Chilazon: Tzaruch Iyun as for why the Chilazon was not mentioned here, despite it being mentioned in 316:1 regarding trapping, and in 316:20 regarding learning the source that all the animals killed must be from male and female union. Perhaps though one can say that only those animals which are actually slaughtered are considered a Melacha in the legal sense, as an action must be done to actually kill them. This is in contrast to a fish which merely needs to be removed from the water, and no action of killing need be done.
[4] Admur 316:13; M"B 316:38
[5] Admur 316:14; Michaber 316:8; Mishneh Shabbos 107a; Rashi and other Rishonim on Chulin 46a and Shabbos 107a; M"A 316:14 in name of majority of Mefarshim; Levush 316:8; Yerushalmi 7:2; Rabbeinu Tam Kesubos 5b; M"B 316:29; Biur Halacha 316:8 "Hachovel" in name of majority of Rishonim including: Rashi; Ramban; Rashba; Ritva; Meiri
Other opinions: Some Poskim rule the prohibition of bruising a creature, and causing its blood to spill, is not due to Shechita, but due to the prohibition of Dush/Mifarek. [Rambam Shabbos 8:7 brought in M"A and M"B ibid] Others rule it is due to dyeing. [brought in M"A ibid]
Prohibition of Mifareik: See Admur 328:54 who implies that making a wound it contains both the prohibition of Chovel and Mifareik.
[6] Admur 328:33
[7] Admur 316:15; Michaber 316:8; Braisa Shabbos 107b; Vetzaruch Iyun how causing a bruise is Biblically forbidden according to the opinion who exempts a Melacha Sheyno Tzericha Legufo, as how is a bruise ever Legufo, as explained in C?
[8] Admur ibid; M"B 316:30

Bruising an insect: However, one who bruises other creeping creatures and insects is not liable until he removes blood from them. However, if the blood gathered [in its body] and did not leave, then this is a [type of] bruise which will [have the blood] return back to its place, as if the blood had left its area then it would have come out being that it has no skin preventing it.[9]

Disciplining children on Shabbos:

It is permitted to discipline or punish children on Shabbos.[10] One may thus lock a child in his room for disciplinary purposes.[11] Nonetheless, it is possibly even Biblically forbidden to hit or spank a child if doing so can cause a bruise to the child.[12] Furthermore, it is not in the spirit of Shabbos to show anger or fury, or give punishment even for the sake of Chinuch, as learned from the reason why the Torah prohibited a Beis Din from giving punishment on Shabbos. The Torah desired that Shabbos be a day of rest for all, even those who deserve punishment, and hence one is to abstain from punishing or showing any anger on Shabbos to the utmost extreme.[13]

C. Killing or injuring not for a use of the creature itself:[14]

Killing for self-use: It was already explained in chapter 278 [Halacha 1-2] that there are opinions who say that a Biblical [Shabbos] prohibition only applies if the [forbidden] action was done for its own need, meaning that one needs the actual item to which the action was done to.

What is considered a self-use? Therefore one who removes the life [of a creature] is only liable if he has a need for the body of the creature which had its life-force removed from, or [if he needs] its skin, or he needs the soul which he took out from it, meaning the blood that has left it in order to give it to his dog, or if he bruises a person which is his enemy and he thus desires for blood to come out from him so that he witness revenge on his foes[15] (see Choshen Mishpat chapter 424 [Halacha 2][16]). [Likewise one is liable if he makes a bruise in an animal for the sake of weakening it in order to capture it, or because one is angry at his friend and hence injures his animal.[17]] However, one who kills a snake in order to prevent it from injuring him then this is an action done which is not self-needed being that he does not need either the

---

[9] Mishneh Berurah 316:32 explains that since their skin is soft like flesh therefore their blood vessels that have broken are quickly returned to their place. Thus according to this explanation, they do have skin, and it's just a matter of whether their skin is soft or hard.

[10] Setimas Hapoksim as the above prohibition is only in reference to a Beis Din, or community, punishing or incarcerating an individual, and not to a parent who does so for educational purposes.

[11] Tzitz Eliezer 15:41 brought in Piskeiy Teshuvos 316:23

The trapping prohibition: There is no trapping prohibition involved in trapping humans. [Setimas Hapoksim in 339; Piskeiy Teshuvos 316:23] One may thus lock a child in his room if needed. [Tzitz Eliezer 15:41 brought in Piskeiy Teshuvos 316:23]

Other opinions: Some Poskim question that perhaps the trapping prohibition applies to a child. [Avnei Nezer 189:22 based on Tosafus Menachos 64a]

[12] Some Poskim suggest that perhaps giving lashes is Biblically forbidden because it may cause a wound, which is a Biblical prohibition, and is thus included in the Biblical prohibition against giving punishment. [Rambam 24:7 as explained in M"A ibid; M"A 278:1 in name of Turei Even 40 and Rashal regarding a fight that this applies even according to Rebbe Shimon who holds Eino Tzarich Legufa is exempt; P"M 339 A"A 3] However, in truth, perhaps it is only a Rabbinical prohibition, as it is a Melacha She'eiyno Tzarich Legufa and one has no intent to make a wound. [see Machatzis Hashekel on M"A ibid that he has no intent to make a wound; P"M ibid that the above Biblical prohibition only applies according to opinion of Eino Tzarich Legufa Chayav; Admur 316:16]

[13] Piskeiy Teshuvos 339:7

[14] Admur 316:16; See also M"B 316:30 which deals with the issue of Mikalkel, which is not dealt with here in Admur.

The three levels of a destructive Melacha: There are three levels involved in a destructive Mealcha. 1) Melacha Htazricha Legufa, which means that one is doing the destruction for the sake of using the destroyed parts for a certain purpose [i.e. to use the blood for one's dog]. In such a case one is liable according to all. 2) Melacha Sheiyno Tzricha Legufa, which means that one has no need for the actual parts of the destroyed item, although the action was done for some other external purpose. [i.e. Killed creature to prevent damage] In such a case it is disputed as to if one is liable. 3) Mikalkel, this means that one has no need at all for the Melacha, and it serves no gain or purpose, even external. In such a case one is exempt according to all, although it is Rabbinically forbidden.

[15] Admur ibid; M"A 278:1 in name of Rashal; See also M"A 316:15

Other opinions: The Raavad and Rambam dispute whether one is liable for injuring an enemy and causing his blood to spill. [M"A 316:15; M"B 316:30] It seems from Admur ibid that in a case that one receives pleasure from seeing the actual blood, then it is considered Melacha Legufa according to all, and one is hence liable even according to the Raavad.

[16] There it explains that one who injures a person on Shabbos is exempt from paying damages being that he is liable for death.

[17] See M"A 316:15; M"B 316:31; Shaar Hatziyon 316:48; Biur Halacha 316:8 "Vehachovel"

body of the snake or its blood and he is only killing it in order to be saved from injury.[18]

Releasing blood for medical purposes:[19] One who has a tooth ache which causes him such pain that his entire body feels sick (is allowed to transgress Shabbos through a gentile) [and] may tell the gentile to remove [the tooth]. (And according to those opinions which say that any action which is not done for its own use is only Rabbinically forbidden then it is permitted to remove [the tooth] through a gentile even if the entire person's body has not become sick [so long as it is more than a mere ache] as was explained [in Halacha 328/20])

D. The killing of creatures which do not reproduce-Fleas and Lice:[20]

One is only liable for removing life-force on species of creatures which reproduce and are created through [the union of] a male and female, [as will be explained below in Halacha 4]........ Nevertheless [killing] the flea contains the [Biblical prohibition] of taking a life even though it is created from earth and does not reproduce, because all [creatures] that are created from earth have vitality as if they were created from male and female, as initially all creatures were created from earth as it says [in the Torah] "And G-d said let the earth extract....etc.".

Summary of the Biblical prohibition of killing a creature:

It is a Biblical prohibition to kill or remove blood from any creature.[21] Included in this is strangling a creature, such as taking a fish out of the water to the point that it can no longer live.

However, it is only Biblically prohibited to do the above if:

1. The creature was killed or bruised in order to use its body for a certain purpose, such as to eat or for its skin and the like. [or if one casually killed it and it is a type of creature which is generally killed for the above purpose].[22]

   And

2. The creature reproduces and is thus not a spontaneous generation, with exception to if it is created from earth in which case it too is included in the Biblical prohibition.[23]

May one cause a bruise [black and blue mark] to a creature?[24]

Any creature which has skin, which includes all animals, and birds, one is Biblically liable for forming a bruise on them. However, by creeping creatures and insects which do not have skin one is not liable until blood actually leaves their body.

Matters that are forbidden to be done due to the causing an injury prohibition:

1. Taking blood
2. Insulin injections [Rabbinical as is not Letzorech Gufo]
3. Removing a bee during a sting if it will cause bleeding. [Rabbinical as is not Letzorech Gufo]
4. Removing a splinter or stinger if it will cause bleeding. [Rabbinical as is not Letzorech Gufo]
5. Brushing teeth if it will cause bleeding gums. [Rabbinical as is not Letzorech Gufo]

---

[18] What's the difference between the two cases of killing for the sake of preventing injury versus killing an enemy, as also in the former case one is quenching his fear by killing the creature, and is also accomplishing that the creature does not hurt him, so it also has a purpose and should be considered Legufa. Also, if someone hits and injures someone in self-defense is that considered Legufa? Vetzaruch Iyun!

[19] Admur 328:3; Mamar Mordechia, brought in M"B 316:30

Other opinions: Some Poskim rule that removing a tooth for medical purposes [or doing any bruise for medical purposes] is considered a Melacha Shetzricha Legufa. [M"A 316:15; 328:3; P"M; Chayeh Adam; M"B 316:30]

[20] Admur 316:20; Shabbos 107b; Michaber 316:9

[21] Admur 316:14

[22] Admur 316:16

[23] Admur 316:20

[24] Admur 316:15

3. The Rabbinical prohibition
Rabbinically forbidden to kill even not for a self-use:[25] Any [forbidden] action which is not done for self-use is despite not being liable on, is Rabbinically forbidden [with exception to when done to prevent danger as will be explained].

Summary-The Rabbinical prohibition:
It is Rabbinically prohibited to kill or injure a creature when done not in order to use its body or blood.

---

4. The killing of creatures which do not reproduce-Fleas and Lice:[26]
One is only liable for removing life-force on species of creatures which reproduce and are created through [the union of] a male and female, however insects which are created from [the bacteria found in] feces and from spoiled fruits and the like, such as for example worms [that grow] in flesh and like [the] worms which are found in legumes, then one who kills them exempt [from liability].[27]
The reason for this is:[28] because in the Tabernacle the taking of a life was only done to rams, *techashim* and *chilazon* which are [creatures] that reproduce and are born from a [union of] male and female.
Killing creatures which are created from earth:[29] Nevertheless [killing] the flea contains the [Biblical prohibition] of taking a life even though it is created from earth and does not reproduce, because all [creatures] that are created from earth have vitality as if they were created from male and female, as initially all creatures were created from earth as it says [in the Torah] "And G-d said let the earth extract....etc.".[30]
Killing lice:[31] What is considered a flea? This is a black insect which jumps. However, the white insect that crawls is called lice and is permitted to kill it on Shabbos being that it is [created] from sweat.
Killing lice when checking one's clothing for them:[32] However this [allowance] only refers to when one happens to find a lice on his flesh or [happens to] find it on his clothes. However, one who is [in the process of] cleaning his clothing of lice then he may [only] squeeze them with his fingers [without killing them] and throw them (even into water[33]). However, it is forbidden to kill it with his hands as since he is cleaning his clothing of lice, we suspect that he may come to also find fleas and also kill them.
Killing lice when checking one's hair for them:[34] However, when checking one's head [for lice] it is permitted for him to kill the lice with his hands being that fleas are not commonly found on one's head.
Removing lice from skins:[35] One may not remove lice form the skins of fox and the like being that [in the process] one removes hair from the skin which contains the sheering prohibition, and although it is done

---

[25] Admur 316:17
[26] Admur 316:20; Shabbos 12a and 107b; Michaber 316:9
Other opinions: The Gemara ibid brings the opinion of Rebbe Eliezer and Beis Shamaiy that one is liable on all creatures, even if it does not reproduce.
[27] Admur ibid; M"A 316:20; Rambam 11:2
The Mishneh Berurah adds the following: a) It is nevertheless Rabbinically forbidden [unlike the opinion of the Magid Mishneh brought in the Magen Avraham which holds here that it is completely permitted] and it is only by lice that the Sages completely permitted killing it because it was created from sweat or because it is repugnant.] b) It is only Biblically permitted if it grows while off the tree and after the food has spoiled. However, if it grew while on the tree or before the food has spoiled then it is included in the Biblical prohibition. [See Mishneh Berurah and Biur Halacha on Halacha 9] See Q&A below
[28] Admur ibid; Gemara ibid; M"B 316:38
[29] Admur ibid; Gemara ibid; Michaber ibid
[30] Admur ibid; Ran M"B ibid
[31] Admur ibid; Shabbos ibid; Michaber ibid
[32] Admur ibid; Michaber ibid; Rosh 1:29
Other opinions: Some Poskim rule it is permitted to check and kill lice even of clothing. [Rashi; Ramban; Ran; Ritva, Chaim Tzanzer, Elya Raba, brought in Biur Halacha 316:9 "Lo Yehargem"]
[33] Admur ibid [parentheses in original, in Mareh Mekomos of Admur it says "See Rosh Vetzaruch Iyun Gadol"; See Ketzos Hashulchan 122 footnote 6]; M"A 316:21; M"B 316:42; See Elya Raba; Chaim Tzanzer brought in Biur Halacha 316 "Lo Yehargeim"
Other opinions: Some Poskim rule one may not throw the lice in the water. [Elya Raba 316, brought in P"M 316 A"A 21]
[34] Admur ibid; Michaber ibid
[35] Admur 316:21; M"A 316:21

unintentionally, nevertheless it is an inevitable occurrence [and is thus forbidden].

Summary:[36]
The general rule: It is only Biblically forbidden to kill creatures which were born from a male and female union, or which were spontaneously created from earth such as fleas. However, killing a spontaneous creation not created from earth does not contain a Biblical prohibition [However regarding if doing so contains a Rabbinical prohibition, see Q&A.]

May one kill lice? Yes, as lice reproduce through sweat and not through male and female union. [See Q&A 3]

May one check someone's hair for lice on Shabbos? Yes, and one may also kill them in the process. [However, he may not do so using a lice comb being that it pulls out hair in the process.[37]]

May one check clothing for lice on Shabbos? Yes, although he may not kill them with his hands upon doing so. As well, it is Biblically forbidden to remove lice from animal skins.

May one kill fleas? No, as they are created from earth which has the equivalent life-force to having been created through a male and female.

May one kill worms that grow in meat and inside legumes? One is not Biblically liable for doing so [although it is Rabbinically forbidden to do so according to some opinions as will be explained below in the Q&A.]

Q&A
May one kill insects that are born from waste but have ability to reproduce through male and female?[38]
It is disputed amongst Rishonim whether it is possible for creatures that were not created from male and female have ability to reproduce.[39] Practically, such insects are included within the Biblical prohibition.[40]

May one today kill lice even though we see with our own eyes that it lays eggs?
The vast majority of Halachic authorities[41], including the Lubavitcher Rebbe[42], rule that the laws of the Torah are not negotiable, and thus once the ruling has been given that lice are permitted be killed

---

[36] Admur 316:20

[37] Admur 303:27

[38] Biur Halacha 316:9 "Mutar"

[39] The Rambam in Sefer Hamitzvos Lo Sasei 178 holds that so long as the insect was not created from spoiled waste, such as insects created in fruits of a tree, then it can reproduce. The Ramban however in his Hasagos Shiresh 9 argues that such an insect can never reproduce.

[40] Opinion of Admur: In the beginning of 316:20 Admur states that only if the creature is both created by a male and female and also reproduces do we say one is liable. This implies that if t either does not reproduce, or was not created by a male and female [even if it does reproduce] then he is not liable. However, In the middle of 316:20 Admur writes "Nevertheless [killing] the flea contains the [Biblical prohibition] of taking a life even though it is created from earth and does not reproduce" hence implying that only if the creature is both created spontaneously and does not reproduce, do we say it is exempt. Vetzaruch Iyun

[41] Rav Dessler in Michtav Eliyahu vol. 4 page 355, Opinion of Rav Yehuda Bril brought in Pachad Yitzchak "Tzeida", and many other Poskim listed in Yalkut Yosef Vol. 4 chapter 316.

[42] Brought in Sharreiy Emunah chapter 43
There the Rebbe states the following rules regarding scientific studies that contradict the teachings of Torah:
1) Science is based on theories and not facts, and thus one cannot distort or change the simple interpretation of the words of our Sages which are the words of the Living G-d which states the absolute truth, based on conclusions developed from un-provable and merely theoretical hypothesis of a human.
2) However, when science has come to a conclusion based on an absolutely provable fact then within the allegorical sections of the Talmud there is room to interpret the sayings in deviation of their simple meaning.
3) However, when it comes to the legal aspects of the Torah then there is no room for deviation at all from its simple meaning, irrelevant to what scientific study has proven with human intellect, and thus the Halacha is to be taken literally for all matters. Regarding this specific issue the Rebbe there states that he has thoroughly investigated the topic of spontaneous generation while in Paris with the greatest professors in this field, and although there are studies which have showed that creatures which in the past were believed to have generated spontaneously in truth were reproduced through male and female, nevertheless they have no conclusive evidence that such a concept does not exist. Furthermore, there are many biologists which firmly believe that organisms can be created from inanimate items.

being that they are born from sweat, this is the final ruling both for leniency and stringency irrelevant to what scientists and biologists may say. However, there are opinions[43] which say that in light of the scientific and biological discovery that lice reproduce, it is proper to be stringent and not kill the lice today. [See note[44]]

May one kill insects that were created from rotting fruits and meat?
Although doing so does not contain a Biblical prohibition as stated above, there is discussion as to whether it contains a Rabbinical prohibition. Some Poskim[45] rule that doing so is permitted, just like lice. Others[46] rule that it is Rabbinically forbidden, and so is implied from Admur.[47]

May one kill insects that have grown within fruits prior to them having spoiled?
If they grew on the fruits while attached to the tree then it is forbidden to kill them.[48] Others[49] go on to further say that even if they grew when detached, but prior to spoilage of the fruit, they are forbidden to be killed.[50] It is possible to learn this way in Admur as well.[51]

5. Removing a fish from water:[52]
One who strangles a creature until it dies is [transgressing] an offshoot of [the prohibited action of] slaughtering. Therefore, if one took a fish out of a bucket of water, and left it [outside the water] until it died then he is liable for strangulation. [To be liable], one does not have to [leave it out] until it completely dies but rather as soon as it [is left out to the point that] the width of a "Sela" of it has become dry between its fins, then one is liable even if he returns afterwards back into the water, as [once it has been left out for this long] it is no longer able to live. [Furthermore, to be liable one does] not [have to leave it out] until it actually dries but rather even if [it has been left out to the point that] when one touches it with a finger mucus comes out from it and gets pulled out with the finger[53] [he is liable].
Asking a gentile to remove a fish from water: Therefore, one must be careful to not tell a gentile to take out a fish from a barrel of water even if he fears that it will die there[54] [in the water, and thus contaminate the water and cause him a loss[55]].

[43] Pachad Yitzchak 10 "Tzeida" p. 21; Sheivet Hakehasy, brought in Piskeiy Teshuvos 316 and Yalkut Yosef ibid
[44] Authors personal thoughts:
A question on the first opinion: If science has today "proven" that lice are reproduced through male and female then why do we not simply say that this is not the species of lice referred to by the Sages, and thus there is no contradiction and it is thus forbidden to kill the species of lice that does reproduce.
A. Seemingly the answer to this question is that tradition-which is as authentic as Halacha- has it that these lice are the same lice referred to always and thus there is no room for compromise.
A question on the dissenting opinions and their scientific facts: To my knowledge studies have not proven that sweat does not take a pivotal role in the development and growth process of the egg while in the mother lice and after it has been laid. Perhaps then this is the meaning behind the saying of the Sages that the lice are created from sweat, and there is thus no proven contradiction to the saying of the Sages. If so there is no room at all to be stringent against the ruling of the Sages of all generations.
[45] Magen Avraham 316:20, based on Magid Mishna on Rambam 11:2
[46] Mishneh Berurah 316:41, based on Lechem Mishna ibid, and so is brought in Peri Megadim A"A 20.
[47] From fact a) omits the clear ruling of Magen Avraham that it is permitted. B) simply states that one is exempt as opposed to permitted as he writes by lice.
[48] Magen Avraham 316:20, however, see Peri Megadim ibid that questions this saying either way it should still be permitted being that the insects were not created from the earth. However, the Biur Halacha negates this proving clearly that insects which were grown within a fruit when attached are considered grown from the earth.
[49] Biur Halacha Leharga
[50] As all bugs that are created from fruit prior to deterioration are able to have offspring. [Biur Halacha ibid]
[51] From the fact that Admur mentions the wording of the Rambam which only mentions the allowance by spoiled fruits, and completely omits the ruling of the M"A that allows it when detached. Perhaps this is coming to teach that even when detached it is forbidden so long as the fruit has not yet spoiled.
[52] Admur 316:13; M"A 316:17; M"B 316:33
[53] Meaning that it has congealed and thus sticks to the finger and gets stretched out like gum.
[54] The reason it is not permitted due to Pesik Reishei: As Amira Lenachri was only permitted by a Pesik Reishei in which the Melacha is the result of the inevitable occurrence of a second action, such as to remove the pot from the coals which will cause the coals to fall. If, however, the Pesik Reishei is a result of the actual action performed by the gentile, then it is forbidden to ask a gentile.
[55] Levusheiy Serud

Removing a fish from a river or pool of water: All the above is referring to when he took out the fish from an area that it was already trapped in and was not lacking any further trapping at all, such as for example [the fish was in a] bucket or barrel (see chapter 497 [Halacha 1][56]). However, if one took it out from an area where it was lacking further trapping, such as for example [taking a fish out from] a river or pool, then even if he immediately returned it into water that is in a vessel, [nevertheless] he is liable for trapping. [Furthermore] even if one did not catch it with his hand at all, but rather simply draw it out of the river with a bucket of water, then he is liable for trapping as when [the fish] is inside a bucket it does not lack any further trapping.

Summary:
It is a Biblical prohibition to strange a creature, such as taking a fish out of the water to the point that it can no longer live.

Q&A

May one ask a gentile to remove a fish for him from a bucket of water?[57]
No.

May one remove a fish from a bucket of water and then replace it right away into other waters prior to its drying?[58]
No, due to Muktzah. However, one may ask a gentile to do so [or remove it with a Shinui].

---

6. Killing dangerous animals and creatures:[59]
A. Creatures that definitely have a deadly bite or sting:[60]
Any wild animal and crawling creature which bites and definitively kills, such as a lethally venomous snakes and a rabid dog and the like of other dangerous creatures which have a definite deadly bite, then it is allowed to kill them on Shabbos even if they are not chasing after one at all [and even if they are running away from him[61]]. [One may even search for the creature to kill it if it is found in an area that people are commonly found in.[62]]
The reason for this is: because there is danger of life involved [in refraining from] killing them as they may [come to] kill a Jew, and [the rule is that whenever there is] any possibility [that a] life [will be endangered] then it pushes off Shabbos, [and allows one to do] even a complete Biblically [forbidden] action even according to those opinions which say that even an action which is not done for its own use one is Biblically liable on.

---

[56] There it discusses when a fish is considered to be trapped.
[57] Admur 316:13
[58] See M"B 316:33
[59] Admur 316:22; Michaber 316:10; Shabbos 121b
[60] Admur ibid; Michaber ibid; Shabbos ibid
[61] M"B 316:45 in name of Peri Megadim
[62] Shaar Hatziyon 316:72

B. Creatures which are not deadly but cause bodily injury [in contrast to mere pain[63]]:

❖ *First Opinion:[64]*

If the creature is chasing oneself: Other dangerous creatures, even those which definitily do not kill with their bite but rather only damage the body[65], such as snakes and scorpions in areas that they never kill with their bite [or sting] and rather only damage, and so too any creature of the like, then there are opinions who say that if [these creatures] are chasing him then it is permitted to kill them according to those who say that any action which done not for its own use is only Rabbinically forbidden. [**Regarding insects and the like which only cause mere pain-see next Halacha 7-9!**]

Their reasoning is:[66] because in a situation that involves bodily injury the [Sages] did not decree [against doing a Rabbinically forbidden action, which includes any action that is not done for its own use]. This case is not similar to the [case of the] flea which is in the midst of stinging ones flesh in which case it is forbidden to kill it, [as] the flea does not cause injury to the body but rather pain alone.

If these creatures are not chasing oneself: However, if [these creatures] are not currently chasing after him and it is only that one is worried [that they may do so] in the future, then it is forbidden to kill them in a way that it is blatantly obvious that it was intentionally done. However, it is permitted to trample on it while in the midst of casually walking even if he has intention in doing so in order to kill it, as long as he makes it appear as if he is casually walking and does not intend at all to kill it.

The reason for this is:[67] because since an action which is not done for its own use is only Rabbinically forbidden [therefore it is not forbidden in this case as] the [Sages] did not decree at all against [doing an action even when not for its own use] in a case that involves bodily damage even if there is only mere doubt [as to whether bodily damage will occur]. However, in this case [that they are not chasing him] one needs to alter his method of killing them as much as it is possible for him change, which means that he is to make himself appear as if he does not intend to kill them.

❖ *Other Opinions:[68]*

[However] according to those opinions[69] which say that even an action which is not done for its own use one is [Biblically] liable on, it was only permitted to kill creatures which are chasing after him and to trample on [creatures] casually when they are not chasing after him, by those species of animals and crawling creatures which have the possibility of having a deadly bite. However, a creature which never kills with its bite is forbidden to even [casually] trample on it, and even if it is running after oneself, being that one may not desecrate Shabbos with a complete Biblically [forbidden] action in order [to prevent only] bodily damage.

❖ *The Final Ruling:[70]*

The main Halachic opinion is like the former opinion[71], however nevertheless every meticulous person should be strict upon himself, regarding this [possible] Biblical prohibition, in a situation that it is possible [for him to refrain from killing it]. Such as if it is not running after him then he should not trample it if it is possible for him to guard himself from it and to warn others to beware of it.

---

[63] See Halacha 7

[64] Admur ibid; Michaber 316:10; Shabbos ibid in opinion of Rav Katina, as explained in Tosafus Beratzin

[65] Admur ibid; implication of Michaber ibid; Mordechai 402

[66] Admur ibid; M"B 316:44

[67] Admur ibid; M"B 316:48

[68] Admur ibid; Tosafus Shabbos ibid; Kesef Mishneh; M"A 316:23; M"B 316:44

[69] Rambam and Rebbe Yehuda

[70] Admur ibid; See Shabbos ibid *"The spirit of the Chassidim are not pleasant with those that kill Mazikin, and the spirit of the Sages is not pleasant with these Chassidim";* Vetzaruch Iyun if one can trap it versus killing it, if he must do so to avoid a potential Biblical prohibition?
Ruling of M"B: In 334:85 and 340:1 the M"B rules that the main opinion follows the lenient opinion.

[71] See also 334:29; Kuntrus Achron 275:2

C. Killing creatures which at times can be deadly and at times not that are not chasing after him:[72]
Even by those species of animals and crawling creatures which carry a doubt regarding the deadliness of their bite, as at times they can kill and at times they will not kill, one must alter his method of killing them so long as they are not chasing after him. [Thus, one may only kill them if they are not chasing him by stepping over them while he is casually walking as explained above in B under the first opinion.]

Summary:
One may kill creatures which pose danger in the following scenarios:
1. If the creature is definitely lethally dangerous, [which means that their bite always kills] then one may kill it in any form [in order to neutralize the threat], even if it is not chasing after a person.[73]
2. If the creature is not definitively lethally dangerous but at times it can be lethal and at times not then it is permitted to kill them if either a) they are chasing after oneself, or it is not chasing after oneself but b) one kills it by stepping on it in a way that he makes it appear as if he were in the midst of a casual walk, and it thus appears to the bystander that he did so unintentionally.
3. Creatures which never kill but can cause bodily injury [as opposed to just mere pain] then if they are chasing oneself, they may be killed in any way. If they are not chasing after oneself, then one is allowed to kill them through casually walking on them, as explained above, although with these creatures, if it is possible to guard oneself from them as well as to warn others, then every meticulous person should refrain from killing them.
    In short: One may always kill a creature that is chasing after oneself if it causes bodily damage as opposed to mere pain. If it is not chasing after oneself then one is to kill it casually, with exception to a case that the creature never poses danger to life, in which case one is only to kill it if he and others cannot beware from it.

A scorpion sting:[74]
Is dangerous and one may desecrate Shabbos for it. A known cure is to capture the scorpion, kill it and fry it and then place it on the wound. This thus may be done even on Shabbos.

If one finds a snake on Shabbos and is unsure as to its level of danger, may he kill it?
Seemingly yes. Vetzaruch Iyun!

If a snake is hissing at a person is it considered as if it is chasing after him?[75]
Yes.

---

7. *The prohibition to kill insects which cause mere pain even in the midst of a bite:*[76]
It is permitted to only trap a flea which is in the midst of biting oneself, however, to kill it is forbidden according to all opinions even if it's on one's flesh and is in the midst of biting him.
The reason for this is: As due to mere pain [the Sages] only permitted trapping [it] being that it is not a species which is commonly trapped and thus trapping it is not considered a [Biblically forbidden] action at all, however killing it is a complete [Biblically forbidden] action. [Now although] it is not done for its own use in which case there are opinions which say that one is exempt [from liability] on doing so, nevertheless [even according to them] it is Rabbinically forbidden and was not permitted to be done [in order] to prevent mere pain being that its prohibition is rooted in the Biblical [prohibition], meaning if

---

[72] Admur ibid; Implication of Ramban and Rashba
[73] Admur 316:22
[74] Admur 328:6, Ketzos Hashulchan 137 footnote 1. See also chapter 316
[75] Biur Halacha
[76] Admur 316:19; Michaber 316:9; Beis Yosef; M"B 316:44; Biur Halacha 316:9 "Veassur Lehargo"

[this same act] were to be done for its own use [in which case it would be Biblically forbidden].

May one squeeze the insect to weaken it?[77] [Furthermore] even to squeeze it with one's fingers to weaken its strength so that it not return to him is forbidden because of a decree that one may come to kill it. Rather he is to take it in his hand and throw it away.

Summary:
It is forbidden to squeeze an insect, even if it is in the midst of a bite, as he may come to kill it which is forbidden in all cases, even if the insect is in the midst of a sting.

---

8. Killing spiders:[78]

Those people who kill spiders on Shabbos (that are called *shafin*) need to be rebuked being that [spiders] do not cause bodily damage, and although there is worry that it may fall into ones food [and become lethal[79]], nevertheless [it is forbidden to kill them] as this is not common [to occur], as well as that it is possible to cover the foods, and that also it is only one in a thousand that is lethal in food. Furthermore, even if it did carry a worry of danger [the Sages] only permitted killing it through casually trampling on it.

May one kill spiders?[80]
No, they are not deadly and do not cause bodily harm.

Q&A

May one kill a tarantula?[81]
If the tarantula causes bodily damage, then it may be killed following the rules mentioned above. If it does not cause bodily damage, and merely causes great pain then it may not be killed.

May one remove cobwebs on Shabbos?[82]
Some Poskim[83] imply that it is permitted to break cobwebs on Shabbos, and doing so does not involve the Muktzah or destroying prohibition, or any other prohibition. Other Poskim[84], however,

---

[77] Admur ibid; Michaber ibid; Biur Halacha 316:9 "Lo Yimalelenu"
Other opinions: Some Poskim rule one may squeeze the insect to weaken it. [Elya Raba, brought in Biur Halacha ibid]
[78] Admur 316:23
Other opinions: Some Poskim rule one may casually kill a spider on Shabbos. [P"M] The Biur Halacha ibid negates his opinion.
[79] Some spiders are lethal when eaten
[80] Admur 316:23
[81] Despite their often-threatening appearance and reputation, no tarantula has been known to have a bite that is deadly to humans. In general, the effects of the bites of all kinds of tarantula are not well known. While the bites of many species are known to be no worse than a wasp sting, accounts of bites by some species are reported to be very painful and to produce intense spasms that may recur over a period of several days; the venom by the African tarantula *Pelinobius muticus* also causes strong hallucinations. In all cases, it is prudent to seek medical aid. Because other proteins are included when a toxin is injected, some individuals may suffer severe symptoms due to an allergic reaction rather than to the venom. Such allergic effects can be life-threatening.
[82] See Piskeiy Teshuvos 250:9
[83] Implication of Leket Yosher "*One time a spiders web was made on the faucet and he [the Terumas Hadeshen] said that it is permitted to break it on Shabbos.*" [Nonetheless, it is still possible to interpret the allowance only to a vessel, such as a faucet, and not to a wall. However, the Betzeil Hachachmah 5:18 and Rav SZ"A in SSH"K 23 footnote 34 clearly rule that there is no destroying or Toleish prohibition involved by cobwebs, and hence when this is joined with the opinion of the Leket Yosher that it also does not contain a Muktzah prohibition, then it is allowed in all cases to be removed or broken on Shabbos]; See Admur 328:53 [based on 1st opinion in Michaber 328:48; Rokeaich 70; Kol Bo 31] that one may treat a bleeding wound through wrapping a spiders web around it, thus proving that it is not Muktzah. See, however, Tehila Ledavid 328:79 that for the sake of relieving pain, the Sages permitted the moving of Muktzah. However, from Leket Yosher ibid, it is implied that it is permitted even not for the sake of relieving pain, as well as that no such allowance is recorded in Admur regarding Muktzah, and on the contrary, he explicitly mentions the Muktzah prohibition even in a case of pain. [See Admur 308:56 regarding placing raw cloth materials on a wound and 328:51 regarding eye pain] Thus, one must conclude that according to the Poskim ibid, cobwebs are not Muktzah on Shabbos. On the other hand, perhaps one can establish the case to be referring to cobwebs that were already prepared before Shabbos. Vetzaruch Iyun.
[84] Mor Uketzia 328; Tehila Ledavid 328:79; Pesach HaDvir 328:11; See Kaf Hachaim 328:270; Orchos Chaim Spinka 328:36

rule that cobwebs are considered Muktzah, just like earth and twigs and other waste. Accordingly, they may only be removed on Shabbos with an irregularity/Shinuiy [such as using ones elbow or feet].[85] Alternatively, if they have become repulsive to oneself, or to the guests in the room, then they may be removed even regularly.[86] Other Poskim[87], however, rule that one is to completely avoid breaking or removing cobwebs that are attached to a wall altogether, as perhaps doing so transgresses the "uprooting an item from its place of growth" prohibition, or other prohibition. Practically, one may be lenient in a time of need to move the cobwebs in the method stated above.[88] Nevertheless, in all cases one must beware not to kill the spider in the process.[89]

9. *Being cautious not to trample on ants and other non-dangerous creatures*:[90]

Species of crawling creatures which do not cause injury such as ants and the like, is forbidden to trample them even if one does not intend to kill them [in doing so] but it is inevitable. [Thus] one must beware of [stepping on] them in areas where they are commonly found.

May one step on ants while walking?[91]
This is forbidden being that they will inevitably be killed, and thus one must take caution when walking near areas which he knows contains insects.

General Summary
It is only allowed to kill a creature if:
1. It is a spontaneous creation not created from earth such as lice. [However, regarding other spontaneous creatures, see Q&A above] [92]
Or
2. One is doing so to prevent himself from danger as was explained in Halacha 6-See there.

Practical Q&A
May one spray pesticide in his house if insects have become a nuisance to him?[93]
Some Poskim[94] rule it is forbidden to spray pesticide, as in addition to it being Muktzah being that it is not edible[95], and that it initially creates a repulsive area of dead insects which one will then move, it also inevitably kills insects while spraying and is thus forbidden. Other Poskim[96], however, rule it is allowed to spray in a different direction then the bugs, as long as one leaves a door or window open, as in such a case it is no longer inevitable to kill them.[97] According to this opinion, it is permitted to spray it on one's clothing and does not contain the prohibition of "making a new smell" being that it is

---

[85] Betzeil Hachachmah 5:18; Regarding the allowance of moving Muktzah with a Shinuiy-See: Admur 308:15; 311:15; 276:9-10; 266:19

[86] SSH"K 23 footnote 34 in name of Rav SZ"A; Beir Moshe 37; In such a case they may be removed even normally, as then they are considered a Graf Shel Reiy. [SSH"K 23 footnote 34 in name of Rav SZ"A]

[87] Yifei Laleiv 328:3 leaves this matter in question as to if its considered a prohibition of removing an item from its place of growth; Kaf Hachaim 328:270; SSH"K 23:9

[88] Betzeil Hachachmah ibid and Rav SZ"A ibid both argue that this prohibition does not at all apply; Piskeiy Teshuvos 250:9

[89] See Admur 316:23; M"A 316:23; M"B 316:48; Biur Halacha "Veafilu"

[90] Admur 316:22; M"B 316:48; Elya Zuta 316:18 in name of Issur Viheter 58

[91] Admur 316:22

[92] Admur 316:20

[93] Piskeiy Teshuvos 316

[94] Ketzos Hashulchan 122 note 11, and other Poskim

[95] So rules also Shvus Yaakov 2:45

[96] Bear Moshe 2:23

[97] There he explains that from the letter of the law it is permitted to spray it even if the insects have nowhere to escape, so long as one does not directly spray it on them, as in case of pain one may be lenient by a mere Grama by a case of pain.

not made to give a new smell.

May one place poison on the floor to kill roaches and mice on Shabbos?
Some Poskim[98] rule that one may not do so, as although this form of killing is only a "Grama" nevertheless as said above the poison is Muktzah. However other Poskim[99] rule that it is permitted. However, regarding a trap-see above Chapter 1 Halacha 4

May one place on himself a spray that has a bad smell and will cause the insects to leave?[100]
If doing so will not kill any insects, then it is allowed. One may likewise smear the substance on his body.

If there are insects in one's toilet may he flush it on Shabbos after using it?[101]
If not doing so will cause a repulsive situation for people, then one may flush it.[102]

May one wash bugs off of a fruit or vegetable?[103]
One may do so even initially in order to eat right away, as it is considered like peeling off the peel of a food which is allowed to be done in close proximately to the meal.[104] To note however that it is forbidden to wash the bugs off with salt water or vinegar and other liquids which kill the insects, due to the killing prohibition on Shabbos.[105]

May a Mosquito zapper be turned on before Shabbos?
Yes.

---

[98] Ketzos Hashulchan 122 footnote 11, as rules Shvus Yaakov 2:45
[99] Beir Moshe 2:23
[100] Ketzos Hashulchan chapter 138 footnote 31
[101] Minchas Yitzchak 10:27; Sheivet Halevy 7:94; Piskeiy Teshuvos 316,
[102] The reason: based on the fact that anyways flushing the insects together with the feces is an indirect act which one has no intention to do and is thus allowed in pressing times.
[103] Shabbos Kihalacha Vol. 2 p. 134-136
[104] So rules Ketzos Hashulchan 125 footnote 16
[105] Shabbos Kihalacha Vol. 2 p. 199

Compilation-Killing and/or trapping stinging insects such as mosquitoes, bees, wasps, hornets and the like, on Shabbos:

*Skip to B and summary for the quick answer!

A. Background:[1]

Under normal conditions, it is forbidden to kill or trap any living creature on Shabbos.[2] In certain circumstances doing so contains a Biblical prohibition, while in others it contains a merely Rabbinical prohibition.[3] This prohibition applies even to covering a flying insect which can escape as soon as the cover is lifted.[4] However, in cases where the living creature poses a threat to a human, then certain leniencies are given which allow one to trap or even kill the creature. These allowances depend on the level of existing threat posed by the creature, whether one's desire is to trap it or kill it, and as well on the method in which one desires to perform the trapping or killing. Practically, the general rule is as follows [the practical ruling in regarding flying stinging insects is brought in B]:

*The rule for **trapping** creatures which pose human threat*: It is permitted to trap any living creature on Shabbos which poses a threat of bodily injury, such as a snake, scorpion, [wild dog, brown recluse spiders, black widow spiders and the like]. This applies even if their bite is not deadly.[5] One covers them with a vessel or surrounds them [with items that prevents them from escaping] or ties them so they not cause damage.[6] However, a creature which does not pose a threat of bodily injury, is forbidden to be trapped on Shabbos even if its bite or sting causes pain.[7] [Seemingly, the difference between bodily injury

---

[1] See Admur 316:1 and 13-22; Piskeiy Teshuvos 316:12

[2] Admur 316:1 regarding trapping, 316:13 regarding killing; Michaber 316:1 regarding trapping, 316:8 regarding killing; Mishneh Shabbos 73a

[3] Trapping: It is only Biblically prohibited to trap a creature on Shabbos if all the following seven conditions are met: 1) The animal was previously not fully trapped and one now fully trapped it in a way that he does not need to further trap it. [Admur 316:1] 2) It is a creature which is commonly trapped [irrelevant to the reason why it is commonly trapped]. [Admur 316:16] 3) The creature was trapped in order to use its body for a certain purpose, such as to eat or for its skin and the like, or if one casually trapped it but it is a type of creature which is generally trapped for the above purpose. [Admur 316:16] 4) The animal was not old, crippled or exhausted to the point that it could not escape. [Admur 316:2] 5) One is trapping it himself and not through a hunting dog, or trap that had already been set up. [Admur 316:6] 6) The animal was trapped by a single person, or by two people in a scenario that it required two people to trap. [Admur 316:7] 7) The animal is not a tamed pet or livestock and the like that has not rebelled. [Admur 316:24-25] 8) One is trapping them in the normal method. [Admur 316:17; M"A 316:12; M"B 316:27]

Killing: It is only Biblically prohibited to kill a creature on Shabbos if the following two conditions are met: 1) The creature was killed or bruised in order to use its body for a certain purpose, such as to eat or for its skin and the like. [or if one casually killed it and it is a type of creature which is generally killed for the above purpose]. 2) The creature reproduces and is thus not a spontaneous generation, with exception to if it is created from earth in which case it too is included in the Biblical prohibition.

[4] Admur 316:4 *"One must be careful not to close a box or cover a vessel which has flies inside it, being that they are [consequently] trapped through this covering and closing."*; Rama 316:3; Taz 316:4; M"B 316:16

Other Opinions: There are opinions who are lenient [to allow one to completely close the vessel] in a situation that if one were to open the vessel to take [into ones hand] the flies that in there, then they would escape [before him being able to grab them], as in such a case there is no trapping done at all through this covering. [Tur 316, brought in Admur and Poskim ibid]

[5] Admur 316:17 *"Even initially it is allowed to trap all types of creeping creatures which commonly cause injury, such as snakes and scorpions and the like, even in places where their bite [or sting] is not deadly, and even if they are not currently chasing after him at all , and rather he just suspects that perhaps it may eventually chase after him or after someone else and bite [or sting] him or that perhaps he may not [properly] avoid [stepping on or near] them and they will bite him or perhaps will bite other people which do not know that they have to beware from them."*; Michaber 316:7, 9; Rambam 10:25; Shabbos 107b

The reason: As since one is only trapping them in order to save himself from injury, this is [considered] an action that is not done for its own self use. Now, although that any [forbidden] action which is not done for self-use despite not being liable on, is Rabbinically forbidden, [nevertheless] here the Sages completely permitted it due to chance that one may receive bodily injury [if he were to not be allowed to trap them]. [Furthermore] even according to the opinions which say that an action done not for its own self use one is [also] liable on and [thus according to them it should be prohibited being that] we do not [allow one to] transgress Shabbos through doing a complete Biblical prohibition [just in order to prevent] bodily damage and rather is only allowed to prevent danger of one's life, nevertheless here since one is not trapping them in the normal method but rather just deals with them in order so they not be able to injure, [such as he] covers them with a vessel or surrounds them [with items that prevents them from escaping] or ties them so they not cause damage, therefore the [Sages] permitted one to do so even to creeping creatures which are not at all deadly and rather only cause injury. [Admur ibid; M"A 316:12; M"B 316:27]

Other opinions: Some Poskim rule that if the creature is not lethal then one may not capture it. [Maggid Mishneh, brought in Machatzis Hashekel; Shaar Hatziyon 316:38]

[6] Admur ibid; M"B 316:27

Other opinions: Some Poskim write it is best not to cover the creature, as doing so is considered the common way of trapping. [Nehar Shalom brought in Shaar Hatziyon 316:39]

[7] Admur 316:18 *"[However] all the above is referring to [trapping] creeping creatures which commonly cause injury such as snakes and scorpions, [which may be trapped] even in places that their bite is not deadly being that nevertheless they cause bodily injury with their bite, and*

and mere pain is that bodily injury causes a painful injury to the body **which takes time to recover**, while mere pain refers to a temporary and mild pain which goes away on its own after a few days. It, however, is not measured by the amount of pain caused at the time of the sting, and so long as its effects are not long lasting, it is not defined as posing a threat of bodily injury.[8]]

*The rule for **killing** creatures which pose human threat*: It is permitted, and at times encouraged, to kill any living creature on Shabbos, which poses threat to human life. This law splits to four cases: **Case 1**: If the creature is definitely lethally dangerous, [which means that their bite always kills] then one may kill it in any form [in order to neutralize the threat], even if it is not chasing after a person.[9] **Case 2:** If the creature is not definitively lethally dangerous but at times it can be lethal and at times not, then it is permitted to kill them if either **a)** the creature is chasing after oneself, or it is not chasing after oneself but **b)** one kills it by stepping on it in a way that he makes it appear as if he were in the midst of a casual walk, and it thus appears to the bystander that he did so unintentionally.[10] **Case 3:** Creatures which never kill but can cause bodily injury [as opposed to just mere pain], then if they are chasing after a person, they may be killed in any way.[11] If they are not chasing after oneself, then one is allowed to kill them through casually walking on them[12], as explained above, although with these creatures, if it is possible to guard

---

the same applies for all creatures of the like. However, anything which does not damage the body but rather just causes it pain alone, such as wasps, and flies, mosquitoes and fleas and the like, then it is forbidden to trap them."; Michaber 316:9; Rambam 10:24
[8] Implication of Admur ibid
Other Opinions: Some Poskim differentiate between a lot of pain versus mild pain, saying that if a sting can cause a lot of pain then one may trap the creature even if it does not formally leave a long-standing injury. [Mishneh Berura 316:46]
[9] Admur 316:22 "*Any wild animal and crawling creature which bites and definitively kills, such as a lethally venomous snakes and a rabid dog and the like of other dangerous creatures which have a definite deadly bite, then it is allowed to kill them on Shabbos even if they are not chasing after one at all [and even if they are running away from him]*"; Michaber 316:10; Shabbos 121b
The reason: The reason for this is because there is danger of life involved [in refraining from] killing them as they may [come to] kill a Jew, and [the rule is that whenever there is] any possibility [that a] life [will be endangered] then it pushes off Shabbos, [and allows one to do] even a complete Biblically [forbidden] action even according to those opinions which say that even an action which is not done for its own use one is Biblically liable on. [Admur ibid]
[10] Admur ibid "*Even by those species of animals and crawling creatures which carry a doubt regarding the deadliness of their bite, as at times they can kill and at times they will not kill, one must alter his method of killing them so long as they are not chasing after him.*"; Implication of Ramban and Rashba; This applies according to both opinions in Admur ibid [brought in next footnotes]
[11] 1st opinion and final ruling in Admur ibid "*Other dangerous creatures, even those which definitely do not kill with their bite but rather only damage the body , such as snakes and scorpions in areas that they never kill with their bite [or sting] and rather only damage, and so too any creature of the like, then there are opinions that say that if [these creatures] are running after oneself then it is permitted to kill them according to those who say that any action which done not for its own use is only Rabbinically forbidden..... The main Halachic opinion is like the former opinion*"; Michaber 316:10; Shabbos ibid in opinion of Rav Katina, as explained in Tosafus Beratzin
The reason: Their reasoning is because in a situation that involves bodily injury the [Sages] did not decree [against doing a Rabbinically forbidden action, which includes any action that is not done for its own use]. This case is not similar to the [case of the] flea which is in the midst of stinging ones flesh in which case it is forbidden to kill it, [as] the flea does not cause injury to the body but rather pain alone. [Admur ibid; M"B 316:44]
Other opinions in Admur: According to those opinions [Rambam and Rebbe Yehuda] who say that even an action which is not done for its own use one is [Biblically] liable on, it was only permitted to kill creatures which are chasing after oneself and to trample on [creatures] casually when they are not chasing after oneself, by those species of animals and crawling creatures which have the possibility of having a deadly bite. However, a creature which never kills with its bite is forbidden to even [casually] trample on it, and even if it is running after oneself, being that one may not desecrate Shabbos with a complete Biblically [forbidden] action in order [to prevent only] bodily damage. [2nd opinion in Admur ibid; Tosafus Shabbos ibid; Kesef Mishneh; M"A 316:23; M"B 316:44] The main Halachic opinion is like the former opinion. [Admur ibid; See also 334:29; Kuntrus Achron 275:2; M"B 334:85 and 340:1]
[12] 1st and main opinion in Admur ibid "*However if [these creatures] are not currently chasing after oneself and it is only that one is worried [that they may do so] in the future, then it is forbidden to kill them in a way that it is blatantly obvious that it was intentionally done. However it is permitted to trample on it while in the midst of casually walking even if he has intention in doing so in order to kill it, as long as he makes it appear as if he is casually walking and does not intend at all to kill it.*"; Michaber 316:10; Shabbos ibid in opinion of Rav Katina, as explained in Tosafus Beratzin
The reason: The reason for this is because since an action which is not done for its own use is only Rabbinically forbidden [therefore it is not forbidden in this case as] the [Sages] did not decree at all against [doing an action even when not for its own use] in a case that involves bodily damage even if there is only mere doubt [as to whether bodily damage will occur]. However, in this case [that they are not chasing oneself] one needs to alter his method of killing them as much as it is possible for him change, which means that he is to make himself appear as if he does not intend to kill them. [Admur ibid; M"B 316:48]
Other opinions in Admur: See other opinions in previous footnote

oneself from them as well as to warn others, then every meticulous person should refrain from killing them.[13]

The law if the insect is on ones body, or in the midst of a sting: If an insect which contains a painful bite or sting is on one's inner clothing that touches his skin, or on one's actual skin [but not yet in the midst of a sting], then if it is difficult to brush the insect away, one may choose to be lenient like those opinions who permit one to pick it up with his fingers and throw it away.[14] If, however, the insect is already in the midst of a sting, then according to all it is permitted to take hold of it while it is stinging and to throw it away.[15] In the above cases, it is only permitted to grab the insect and throw it away, however to kill it, or even injure it, is forbidden according to all.[16]

B. The practical ruling by flying insects which sting:[17]
Under normal circumstances, it is forbidden to kill, or even trap, stinging flying insects such as **mosquitoes, bees, wasps, hornets, yellowjackets**, and the like, even if one's intent of doing so is to prevent a sting. This prohibition applies even to simply covering the insect with a cup and the like.[18] [However, if one is allergic to the sting, then it may be trapped, and even killed if necessary [see

---

[13] Final ruling in Admur ibid *"The main Halachic opinion is like the former opinion, however nevertheless every meticulous person should be strict upon himself, regarding this [possible] Biblical prohibition, in a situation that it is possible [for him to refrain from killing it]. Such as if it is not running after him then he should not trample it if it is possible for him to guard himself from it and to warn others to beware of it."*

[14] Admur ibid *"There are opinions who permit to grab the flea even while it is on the inside of his clothes [and not yet on his skin] being that it is able to cause him pain there. [Furthermore] even from his undershirt on the outside it is allowed to grab it since an undershirt is close to the flesh and it is thus possible that the flea will go from there to his flesh and will bite him. However [even according to this opinion] if the flea is on the person in a way that there is no worry that it may bite him, [such as] that it is on his upper clothes on the outside, then it is forbidden to grab it. The final ruling is that if it is possible for him to easily make it fall off of him without [needing to] take it with his hand, then one is to do so even if [the insect] is on the inside of his undershirt. However if one is wearing long boots [which reach to his thighs, or pants] and it is thus difficult for him to shake it away without first grabbing it with his hand then one who relies on the lenient opinion regarding this Rabbinical prohibition has done no harm."* Taz ibid; implication of M"B 316:35; However see Shaar Hatziyon 316:63 that writes one is initially to be stringent.
Other opinions: Some Poskim rule that it is forbidden to take hold of a flea which is on ones clothes, even if it is inside [ones clothes] close to his skin, and even if it is on his skin and has still not stung him it is forbidden to grab it. [1st and Stam opinion in Admur ibid; Michaber ibid as explained in M"A 316:18 and Taz 316:8; M"B 316:37]

[15] Admur 316:18; Michaber 316:9; Tosafus Shabbos 107b
The reason it does not involve the trapping prohibition is: The reason it does not involve the trapping prohibition is because when one takes hold of it at the time of the stinging he has no intent to trap it and rather is only involving himself with it in order to stop it from stinging him, and [when there is no intent to trap] the [Sages] did not decree [against trapping] even in a case [that doing so is only to prevent] pain alone since [these insects] are items which their species are not commonly trapped [and thus even when trapped with intent it is only Rabbinically forbidden]. [Admur ibid]
The reason it does not involve the Muktzah prohibition: The [Sages] did not decree in a scenario [that involves] pain the prohibition in moving the flea due to it being Muktzah. [Admur ibid]

[16] Admur 316:19 *"It is only permitted to trap a flea which is in the midst of biting oneself, however to kill it is forbidden according to all opinions even if it's on one's flesh and is in the midst of biting him. [Furthermore] even to squeeze it with ones fingers to weaken its strength so that it not return to him is forbidden because of a decree that one may come to kill it. Rather he is to take it in his hand and throw it away."* Michaber and Rama 316:9; Beis Yosef; M"B 316:44; Biur Halacha 316:9 "Veassur Lehargo"
The reason: As due to mere pain [the Sages] only permitted trapping [it] being that it is not a species which is commonly trapped and thus trapping it is not considered a [Biblically forbidden] action at all, however killing it is a complete [Biblically forbidden] action. [Now although] it is not done for its own use in which case there are opinions which say that one is exempt [from liability] on doing so, nevertheless [even according to them] it is Rabbinically forbidden and was not permitted to be done [in order] to prevent mere pain being that its prohibition is rooted in the Biblical [prohibition], meaning if [this same act] were to be done for its own use [in which case it would be Biblically forbidden]. [Admur ibid]
Other opinions: Some Poskim rule one may squeeze the insect to weaken it. [Elya Raba, brought in Biur Halacha ibid]

[17] Admur 316:18 *"However, anything which does not damage the body but rather just causes it pain alone, **such as wasps, and flies, mosquitoes and fleas** and the like, then it is forbidden to trap them."*; Rambam 10:24; See also Biur Halacha 316:8 "O Stam"; Piskeiy Teshuvos 316:12
Other Opinions: Some Poskim differentiate between a lot of pain versus mild pain, saying that if a sting can cause a lot of pain then one may trap the creature even if it does not formally leave a long-standing injury. [Mishneh Berura 316:46; See Kaf Hachaim 316:78; Ketzos Hashulchan 121 footnote 20] Accordingly, some deduce based on this that there is room to allow trapping a wasp on Shabbos if its sting gives him tremendous pain. [SSH"K 25 footnote 7] However, clearly according to Admur one may not be lenient.

[18] Admur 316:4 *"One must be careful not to close a box or cover a vessel which has flies inside it, being that they are [consequently] trapped through this covering and closing."*; Rama 316:3; Taz 316:4; M"B 316:16
Other Opinions: There are opinions who are lenient [to allow one to completely close the vessel] in a situation that if one were to open the vessel to take [into ones hand] the flies that in there, then they would escape [before him being able to grab them], as in such a case there is no trapping done at all through this covering. [Tur 316, brought in Admur and Poskim ibid]

footnote].[19] If one is not aware of an allergy, it may not be trapped or killed, even if he is uncertain as to whether he is allergic due to never having been stung.[20] It may not be trapped or killed even if a baby is in the room, unless one is aware of a specific sensitivity the baby has towards the sting.[21] If the insect is carrying a possibly deadly disease, as has become common for mosquitoes of certain regions, then it may be trapped and even killed.[22] Some Poskim[23] permit trapping the insect if it causing panic and hysteria in the vicinity, even if its sting does not pose a real danger of injury to anyone present. This especially applies if there is a young child who is in a state of panic due to the insect.[24] Practically, in a real time of need such as the above, seemingly there is room to be lenient to trapping the insect by covering it with a cup and the like and then transferring it outside, letting it free.[25]]

The law if the insect is in the midst of a sting:[26] If a wasp and the like is already in the midst of a sting, one is allowed to take it with his hands and send it away if it is not possible to brush it away, as explained in A.

Summary:
It is forbidden to trap or kill mosquitoes, bees, wasps, hornets and the like unless any of the following apply:
1. One is allergic to the sting, to the point that it will cause him bodily injury, or possible death.
2. The insect is possibly carrying a potential disease.
3. Some Poskim permit trapping the insect if it is causing panic and hysteria in the vicinity.

---

[19] Piskeiy Teshuvos 316:12; If one is deadly allergic, then it may even be killed. [Admur 316:22] If one is not deadly allergic, but is allergic enough for it to cause bodily injury, then it may be trapped [Admur 316:18]. They however may not be killed even in such a case unless they are chasing after oneself. Even if they are not chasing oneself, one may be lenient to step on them casually without notice to others, although some are stringent. [See Admur 316:22; Piskeiy Teshuvos 316 footnote 107

[20] Seemingly one may not do so as is implied from the ruling regarding spiders in Admur 316:23 that there being a chance that an insect is deadly is not a good enough reason to allow killing it.

[21] Some Poskim rule that bees and the like may even be killed when near an infant, as their sting can be lethal. [SSH"K 25:1] However, seemingly this no longer applies today, and they thus may not be trapped. [See various medical professional websites who state there is no greater inherent danger for a baby to get a sting, versus an adult. They provide general instructions for homecare if a sting occurs and there is no need to visit the emergency room or doctor, unless allergic signs become apparent.]

[22] Pashut based on Admur 316:22; Piskeiy Teshuvos 316:12 footnote 95; SSH"K 25 footnote 3

[23] Piskeiy Teshuvos 316:12 footnote 107 and 115 in name of Rav Elyashiv and Rav Karelitz

[24] See Admur 328:15 regarding a child locked in a room

[25] See Admur 316:4 that there are opinions [Tur 316] who permit one to trap an insect in a situation that if one were to open the vessel the insect would escape, and Admur and the Poskim ibid relay on this opinion to permit a Safek Pesik Reishei. Seemingly the same would apply here in a case of panic or hysteria that one would be allowed to rely on this opinion. Vetzaruch Iyun!

[26] Admur ibid

THE LAWS OF TYING AND UNTYING KNOTS ON SHABBOS

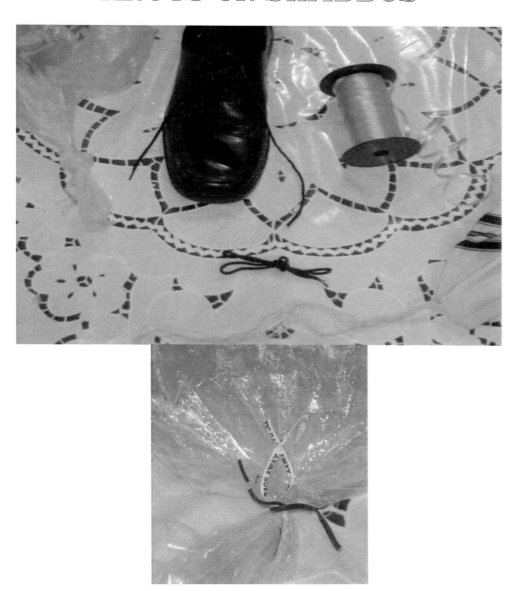

Shulchan Aruch Chapter 317

Translation
Shulchan Aruch Chapter 317

TRANSLATION CHAPTER 317
Laws of tying and making bows on Shabbos.
11 Halachos

Introduction:
The following chapter will discuss when one may tie a knot on Shabbos. Doing so involves at times a Biblical prohibition, at others a Rabbinical prohibition, and at others is completely allowed. This is dependent on the type of knot being made and the length of time it is meant to last for.

The rules of making and untying knots on Shabbos

Halacha 1
The Principal Prohibition: Tying and untying are amongst the principal [forbidden] actions being that in the [process of building the] Tabernacle the fishermen for the *chilazon* would tie and untie their nets. As all nets are made of many knots and these knots are permanent, and at times [the fishermen] would need to remove a rope from one net and add it to another net and [he would thus] untie it from [the first net] and [then] tie it [on the second net], [and thus we see that there existed both tying and untying in the works done for the Tabernacle].

What is considered a permanent knot? [However] Biblically one is only liable [on making] a permanent knot which is made to last forever, which means that he ties it with intention that it remain [tied] so long as it is able to exist and so long that he does not need to untie it.

The reason for this definition: Now, although it is possible that he [may] need to untie it in a [very] short time and will thus untie it, nevertheless since when he ties it he does not set a date in his mind for when he will un-tie it, and it is [thus] possible that it will remain [tied] forever, [therefore] it is considered a permanent knot, and one is liable on tying it and on untying it.

The Rabbinical definition of a permanent knot: However, if he sets in his mind a designated time in which he will then certainly untie it, then even if this [designated time] is in a very long time [from now], it is not Biblically considered [a] permanent [knot] and he is [thus] exempt [from liability] whether upon tying it or untying it. However, Rabbinically this is also considered [a] permanent [knot] being that it is designated to last a certain amount of time and it is thus [Rabbinically] forbidden to tie or untie.

Knots that are meant to be untied on the same day that they are made: However if it is not designated to last at all but rather to be untied the same day [that it was tied], such as knots of clothing and shoes of which when one places them on in the morning they are tied and when he removes them in the evening comes they are untied, then it is allowed to tie and untie it on Shabbos.

Torah Scholars who intend to not untie their shoes and clothes that night: However, if one intends to not untie them that day, such as for example Torah Scholars that learn at night and do not remove their shoes and clothes at night, then it is forbidden for them to tie it on the morning of Shabbos if they intend to not untie them in the evening. Similarly, it is forbidden to untie them on Shabbos if when he tied them on one of the days of the week he intended to not untie it immediately that coming night.

Tying their shoes and clothing on Shabbos without any intention: However, if [the Torah Scholars] do not have any intention at all when they tie them, and rather they tie them casually, then they are allowed to tie them on Shabbos. [Furthermore] even if afterwards he [ends up] not untying it that night [and rather only unties it] after some time it is not considered due to this [even] a [Rabbinical] permanent knot being that at the time of tying it, it was not for certain that it would not be untied on the night after Shabbos, being that at times even the Torah Scholars remove their shoes at night prior to lying down.

Untying knots of cloths made without intention: Similarly, it is allowed to untie it on Shabbos if one had tied it casually [without intention to leave overnight] even if it was tied a long time before Shabbos and was not untied in-between.

Knots that are always made to not be untied the next day: However, knots that are always for certain left [tied] for a certain amount of time and it is never usual to untie it that same day, it is forbidden to tie them on Shabbos even casually or to untie them.

Other Opinions: [However] there are opinions which say that any knot which is not made to last seven days is not considered a permanent knot even Rabbinically and it is [thus] allowed to tie it and untie it on Shabbos. [Furthermore] even if most of the time it is common to tie it to last for seven days and only at times does one also untie it within seven days, such as for example a Torah Scholar which the majority of the time only removes his shoes and clothes from one Shabbos to the next Shabbos and it is thus found that their knots are left tied for seven days, although at times he does untie it within seven days, then it is not considered a permanent knot unless one has in mind while tying it to not untie it until after seven [days]. However when he casually ties them [without any intention] then it is not considered permanent unless it is common for him to always leave it [tied] for seven days, such as for example the strings used to tie the neck of a cloak, then for a person for whom it is never common to untie it [within 7 days] but rather only when he changes the cloak from Shabbos to Shabbos, then it is forbidden [for him] to tie it and untie it on Shabbos.

The Final Ruling: The final ruling is that one is to be stringent like the first opinion [to only allow to tie or untie a knot which is made to untie the day it is made] unless one is in great need [to tie or untie it], in which case one may be lenient to do so through a gentile.

Halacha 2
Other Opinions:[1]

Biblical liability is only applicable by professional knots: There are opinions which say that one is [never] Biblically liable even on a knot that is meant to last forever unless it has been professionally done, which means that it is a strong and tough knot similar to the knots that the professionals make during their work, such as the knots of the straps for shoes and sandals which the strap makers tie at the time of making them, and the same applies for all similar cases. However, one who ties a permanent knot which is not professionally done is exempt [from liability].

For example, a strap broke and one tied it [or a] rope tore and one tied it, or one tied a rope to a bucket or one tied an animal leash [to an animal] and so too all cases [of knots] similar to these knots which are made by amateurs [then] any person who ties them permanently is exempt [from liability].

Rabbinical prohibition by amateur knots made to last even temporarily: Nevertheless, it is Rabbinically forbidden [to tie such knots] even if it is not made to last forever but rather only for a set period of time as explained [above, meaning for more than one day according to the stringent opinion, and 7 days according to the lenient opinion].

Rabbinical prohibition to ever tie or untie a professional knot: However, a knot which is done professionally, even if it not made to last at all but rather to be untied that same day, is Rabbinically forbidden to tie or untie on Shabbos, due to a decree [that if this were to be allowed then one may come to make also] a professional knot that is meant to last forever of which one is Biblically liable on.

Other opinions-No difference between professional and amateur: [However] there are other opinions[2] that say there is no difference at all between a professionally made and amateur made [knots], as even on an amateur knot one is Biblically liable if made for it to permanently last, and if [a knot] is designated to not last at all [then] in a situation that it is [thus] allowed to make an amateur knot it is also allowed to make a professional knot.

The Final Ruling: One is to be strict like the first opinion.

Making and untying a double knot on Shabbos: [For this reason that we rule stringently] we are therefore accustomed to be careful not to tie or untie any knot which is a double knot one on top the other even if made [with intent] to undo on that same day.[3]

The reason is: because we are not experts as to which knots are considered professional of which are

---

[1] Rif, Rambam and Michaber
[2] Rosh, Rashi, Tur and Rama
[3] However, the Shareiy Teshuvah 1 brings from the Bircheiy Yosef that their custom is to allow tying a double knot to undo that day as it is considered an amateur knot, and its only a minority opinion which argues this.

[thus] forbidden to tie and untie even if not made to last at all, and [thus] any strong knot which is very tightly tied there is doubt that perhaps this is considered a professional [knot], and [thus since] a double knot is also a strong knot [therefore we are stringent].

Untying a double knot in a scenario that involves pain: Nevertheless in a scenario [that involves] pain one need not be strict regarding [the dispute of the] Rabbinical [prohibition] and one is [thus] allowed to untie it if [the knot] is not made to last at all in a way that it would for certain be allowed to be done [if it were an] amateur [knot], being that according to the latter opinion it is allowed even if it is a professional [knot].

Halacha 3
A bow knot and a single knot
A bow made on top of a single knot: The above only refers to [a double knot made of] two knots one of top of the other, however by one knot and a bow on top of it there is no doubt at all [that it is not considered] a professional knot and it is thus allowed to tie and untie in any case that it is not designated to last at all[4].

Making a single knot: [As well] if it is only a single knot without a bow on top of it, then it is not considered a knot at all and is allowed to be tied and untied even if made to last forever. [However] all this refers to tying two things together, however if one makes a knot using the single end of a rope or thread or string then it has the same law as a double knot for all matters.

Halacha 4
Making a knot for the sake of a Mitzvah
A knot which is not Biblically considered a permanent knot but rather only Rabbinically is allowed to be tied for the sake of a Mitzvah, such as to make a knot in order to measure one of the Torah required measurements[5], and even to tie a professional knot is allowed if it is impossible to measure it otherwise.

Specific examples of knots that are permitted and forbidden to be made and undone

Halacha 5
Inserting straps into clothing:
Inserting the straps of a shoe and sandal into its hole: If the straps of shoes and sandals have come out [of the hole that they were fastened into] it is permitted to return them to their place as long as one does not make a knot at the end of the strap so it does not escape from the hole, being that [such a knot] is a permanent knot.

However [even this] only [is allowed] in places that it is not common to tie such a knot [at the end of the strap]. However, in those places that are accustomed to make this knot then it is forbidden [for them] to even reinsert [the straps] due to a decree that they may come to tie it.

To do this for the first time on Shabbos: Furthermore, even in those places that are not accustomed [to make such knots] it was only permitted to reinsert [the straps after having come out of their hole], however by a new shoe [which never yet had its straps fastened] it is forbidden to insert the strap on Shabbos being that doing so is fixing a vessel.

To reinsert into a narrow hole: Furthermore, even reinserting the strap was only permitted by a wide hole which it can be inserted into without effort, however if the hole is narrow to the point that one needs effort to enter the strap into it then it is not considered like he is reinserting it but rather like he is doing so for the first time and is [thus] forbidden due to that it is fixing a vessel.

Inserting straps into pants: The same applies by the straps of pants. However, belts are allowed to be initially inserted into pants on Shabbos being that he does not nullify it there and it is [rather] made to constantly insert and remove, [and] therefore it does not pose a problem of fixing a vessel. However, it is

[4] Meaning to undo that same day, So rules also Mishneh Berurah 19.
[5] Back then measuring was done through a rope have knots made on the various parts of the rope which represent different measurements.

forbidden to enter a string into the [pants] being that he nullifies it there.

Halacha 6
Undoing the knot of a collar[6]:
Made by the launderer: [It is allowed] to untie the collar [of a shirt] from the knot that the launderer knotted as it is not considered a permanent knot being that majority of times it is opened the day that it was made, immediately after the laundering.

Made by the tailor: However, it may not be opened for its first time[7] being that this is [considered] fixing a vessel and one is [thus] liable [in doing so] on [the] "Finishing touch" [prohibition]. However, he is not liable for [the] tearing [prohibition] unless he [tears it] with intent to re-sew as was explained in chapter 302 [Halacha 4].

Cutting the sewing and knot of the tailor: [Furthermore] even if the collar had already been opened [after being made] but a professional [tailor] returned and sewed [the two sides of the collar] together in the way done by professionals, or if the professional tied it [in a way] that one is unable to untie it, then it is forbidden to cut the strings. However, this [prohibition to cut an undoable knot] only refers to a knot tied by the professional prior to having finished making the clothing, being that then the cutting of the strings of this knot involves the [prohibition of doing a] "Finishing touch". As this finalizes the work needed to be done to the clothing being that through doing so the clothing is now fit to be worn, while until this was done it was never yet fit to be worn, [and it is thus forbidden as] any [action] done which is the finishing stroke [of the making of the vessel] contains [the prohibition of] "Finishing Touch" as was explained in chapter 302 [Halacha 5]

Cutting the knot of the launderer: However other knots which were tied after the clothing had finished having its work done to it, such as the knots of the laundering or the strings of a cloak which have been tied and one is not able to undo, [then] it is permitted to cut them. Nevertheless, even so one may not be lenient [to cut it] in front of an ignoramus, and rather should do it privately.

By a knot made to last 7 days: If one is accustomed to only cut the strings [of the collar knot] upon changing the cloak from Shabbos to Shabbos, then it is forbidden to cut [the strings of the knot] just like it is forbidden to undo it [as explained in Halacha 1].

Halacha 7
Cutting and tearing sewn threads:
However, the above only refers to a knot made by the launderer, however if the launderer sewed the collar [together], as well as [a case that] a pair of shoes that have been sewed together in the way that is done by professionals, it is forbidden to cut them or to tear them from each other.

The reason for this is: because by sewing there is no difference whether it was made to last or not to last, and destroying it always contains [the] tearing [prohibition]. Now, although one who tears is not liable unless done on condition to re-sew it [afterwards] nevertheless it is Rabbinically forbidden in all scenarios [even when destroyed without intent to re-sew].

Other Opinions: [However] there are opinions which allow tearing or cutting sewing that was not made to last.

The Final Ruling: The main Halachic opinion is like the latter opinion, although nevertheless one should not be lenient in front of an ignoramus.

Halacha 8
Tying a rope or thread to the bucket of a pit
One may tie a bucket to the mouth of a pit with a thread or sash and the like of materials which one does not [plan] to nullify there. However, one may not do so with a rope being that he will nullify it there and it

---

[6] Back then it was the custom for the launderers to tie the collars with a knot in order to have it be shaped. The question here thus is if such a knot may be undone on Shabbos.

[7] Meaning that if one had just bought this shirt from the tailor then one may not undo the collar knot on Shabbos.

is [thus] a permanent knot being that the bucket is constantly hanging and tied there. [Furthermore] even with a woven rope[8] which is of importance and will not be nullified there it is forbidden [to tie with] due to a decree [that one may come to use also] other ropes.

However, this only refers to buckets that are designated for the pit, however our buckets which are not designated for the pit [and will thus eventually be removed from the pit for another use[9]] [tying a rope on it] is not considered a permanent knot and it is [thus] permitted to tie to it even other ropes as long as the knot is not done professionally. [As if it is professionally done] it is forbidden to be done even if it is not made to last as was explained above [in Halacha 2]

Halacha 9
Tying a rope to block the passageway for an animal
One may tie a rope in front of a cow in the width of the passageway in order to prevent it from leaving being that [such a knot] is not made to last as it is meant to be constantly untied in order take the animal out to be given to drink.

Furthermore, even to tie on Shabbos the two ends of a rope on the two posts of the doorway which were not at all tied to the doorway from before Shabbos is allowed, as we do not suspect that one may nullify one end [of the rope] that it be tied there forever and he will only let the animal out through untying the second end of the rope, being that at times he will undo one end and at times the other end [and there will thus never be one end nullified there].

However, if in truth one does nullify one end [there] then it is forbidden.

Halacha 10
Knots which are at times made permanently.
Any knot which at times one retracts his initial intentions and decides to nullify it there forever, then even if [one] now wants to make it without intent to nullify it there, it is forbidden [to make it] because he may change his mind and decide to nullify it there.

Tying a rope to a cow and its trough: Therefore, it is forbidden to take a rope and tie [one end of] it to a trough and [the other end to] a cow, because perhaps when one will wish to remove the cow from there he will always untie only one of [the rope's] ends and leave the second [knot of the second end] there permanently and it will [thus] be a permanent knot.

Woven ropes: However, this only refers to other [non-woven] ropes, however with a woven rope it is allowed [to tie it] being that one will not nullify it there. There is no decree made here against a woven rope due to [that one may come to use] other ropes being that even by other ropes it is not common that one will nullify one end to be there forever, and rather he will at times undo end and at time the other end.

Tying the rope of a cow to its trough or vice versa: All the above is referring to tying a rope on Shabbos onto [both] the trough and the cow, however if it was already tied to the trough and one wants to tie it now to the cow or if it was tied to the cow and he now wants to tie it to the trough, then it is allowed to be done with any rope, as if he will come to nullify one of its knots to stay there permanently one can assume that the same knot which was already tied will [be the one that he will decide to nullify and] leave tied there forever.

Halacha 11
Weaving and unraveling ropes and wicks:
Biblically: One who weaves ropes of any type of material is liable for [the] tying [prohibition]. The amount [needed to be tied] to be Biblically liable is to the point that the rope can last with its weaving without needing to be tied at its end, in which case the work done to it is lasting.

Rabbinically: However, Rabbinically it is forbidden to [weave it] any amount.

Unraveling: Similarly, one who separates a wick is liable for untying and its measurement is like that of

---

[8] This refers to a rope which is not usual to be used to draw water with. [Rashi Pesachim 11a]
[9] Mishneh Berurah 28. This applies even if one plans to leave the bucket there for more than one day. [Biur Halacha]

one who weaves it[10], although [this liability is only applicable] as long as he did not intend to destroy [the wick], as all those that destroy are Biblically exempt although it is Rabbinically forbidden to be done.

---

[10] Meaning that if the wick could have lasted without needing a knot at its end then one who undoes it is liable.

Compilation of Halachas Summaries and Q&A

COMPILATION OF HALACHAS

Introduction:
The following chapter will discuss when and when not one may tie a knot on Shabbos. Doing so involves at times a Biblical prohibition, at others a Rabbinical prohibition, and at others is completely allowed. This is dependent on many factors. This is dependent on the amount of time the knot is meant to last for and the form of the knot, as will be explained.

The rules of making and untying knots on Shabbos

1. The Biblical prohibition of making a permanent knot:

The Principal Prohibition that was in the Mishkan:[11] Tying and untying are amongst the principal [forbidden] actions[12], being that in the [process of building the] Tabernacle, the fishermen for the *chilazon* would tie and untie their nets.[13] As all nets are made of many knots and these knots are permanent, and at times [the fishermen] would need to remove a rope from one net and add it to another net and [he would thus] untie it from [the first net] and [then] tie it [on the second net], [and thus we see that there existed both tying and untying in the works done for the Tabernacle].[14]

One is only liable on a permanent knot? Biblically one is only liable [on making] a permanent knot[15] [called a Kesher Shel Kayama] which is made to last forever[16], which means that he ties it with intention that it remain [tied] as long as it is able to exist and as long that he does not need to untie it.[17]

If one changed his mind to undo the knot: Now, although it is possible that he [may] need to untie it in a [very] short time and will thus untie it, nevertheless since when he ties it he does not set a date in his mind for when he will un-tie it, and it is [thus] possible that it will remain [tied] forever, [therefore] it is considered a permanent knot, and one is liable on tying it and on untying it. However, if one sets in his mind a designated time in which he will then certainly untie the knot, then even if this [designated time] is in a very long time [from now], it is not Biblically considered [a] permanent [knot] and he is [thus] exempt [from liability] whether upon tying it or untying it.

First Opinion-Biblical liability is only applicable by professional knots:[18] There are opinions[19] which say that one is [never] Biblically liable even on a knot that is meant to last forever unless it has been professionally done, which means that it is a strong and tough knot similar to the knots that the professionals make during their work[20], such as the knots of the straps for shoes and sandals which the

---

[11] Admur 317:1; Shabbos 73a and 74b
[12] Admur ibid; Mishneh Shabbos 73a
[13] Admur ibid; Rava in Shabbos 74b
Other opinions: The Gemara ibid gives two other options of the Av Melacha a) The tying of the ropes of the tapestries to the pegs of the Mishkan. 2) The tying of torn threads in the process of making the tapestries. The Gemara asks on each Melacha stating that the tying of ropes to the pegs is not a Kesher Shel Kayama, as it was untied each time the Mishkan moved. Likewise, the tying of the threads of the sewing only contains the tying Melacha and not the untying Melacha and hence cannot serve as the source for the Av Melacha. Vetzaruch Iyun why we don't learn the Av Melacha from the pegs, and simply learn that even a Kesher that is not Shel Kayama is Biblically forbidden?
[14] Admur ibid; Rashi Shabbos ibid
[15] Admur ibid; Michaber 317:1; Mishneh Shabbos 113a
[16] Admur ibid; Taz 317:1; M"A 317:1; Tur and Beis Yosef 317; Rashi 11b; M"B 317:1
Other opinions: Some Poskim rule that it is considered a permanent knot if it is made to last over a month, or over half a year or a year. [Beis Yosef 317 in one explanation of Rashi, brought in M"A 317:1; Rabbeinu Yerucham 14:12; See P"M 317 A"A 1]
[17] The reason: The reason why the Torah only prohibited a permanent knot is because only then is a true connection and unity made, and thus if one plans to undo the knot, even in a very long time, it is no longer a true unity and hence it is not a Melacha at all. For this reason there is no prohibition of "Chetzi Shiur" in making a knot to last for only some time. [Likkutei Sichos 14:16-17]
[18] Admur 317:2
[19] Rif 41b; Rambam [Shabbos 10:1] and Michaber 317:1
[20] So rules Taz. However, see Biur Halacha which learns that a professional knot is defined as a knot which will not be undone on its own, even if it can be undone with a single hand. The Nafka Mina between these two opinions is regarding making a loose double knot to untie on the same day, to which according to Admur would be permitted as opposed to in accordance to the Mishneh Berurah.

strap makers tie at the time of making them, and the same applies for all similar cases. However, one who ties a permanent knot which is not professionally done is exempt [from liability]. For example, a strap broke and one tied it, [or a] rope tore and one tied it, or one tied a rope to a bucket or one tied an animal leash [to an animal] and so too all cases [of knots] similar to these knots which are made by amateurs [then] any person who ties them permanently is exempt [from liability].

Second Opinion -No difference between a professional and amateur knot:[21] Some opinions[22] rule that there is no difference at all between a professionally made and amateur made [knot], as even on an amateur knot one is Biblically liable if made to permanently last, and if [a knot] is designated to not last at all [then] in a situation that it is [thus] allowed to make an amateur knot then it is also allowed to make a professional knot.

Q&A

What is the law of a knot that was tied without any specific intent?

Seemingly, we follow the general intent of this knot, and thus if it is always commonly left to be tied forever, or until one changes his mind to untie it, then he is liable.[23] If, however, it is at times common and at times is not common, then Tzaruch Iyun if he is liable.[24] If however it is always common to untie the knot, then he is not liable.

What is the law of a knot that was tied with intent to undo and one then changed his mind to leave it forever?[25]

In a case that it is not common to leave this knot there forever then there is never a Biblical prohibition involved.[26] Vetzaruch Iyun if there is a Biblical prohibition involved in a case that it is common, or even always common, to at times leave it tied forever in this position.[27]

Is a knot that can be undone with one hand considered a Maaseh Uman or Hedyot?[28]

From some Poskim[29] it is understood that it is considered a Maaseh Hedyot, and is hence subject to the dispute mentioned above in regards to its Biblcial status.[30] However, some Poskim[31] rule it is considered a Maaseh Uman even if it can be undone with one hand, so long as it last forever and will not untie on its own.

---

[21] Admur 317:2

[22] Rosh 15:1, Rashi, Tur; Rama 317:1

[23] So is implied from Admur 317 1 "Now, although it is possible that he [may] need to untie it in a [very] short time and will thus untie it, nevertheless since **when he ties it he does not set a date in his mind for when he will un-tie it, and it is [thus] possible that it will remain [tied] forever**"; Likewise this is implied from the ruling brought next regarding the Rabbinical prohibition: "However knots that **are always for certain left [tied] for a certain amount** of time and **it is never usual** to untie it that same day, then it is forbidden to tie them on Shabbos even casually or to untie them."; So is also implied from 316 [Michaber 316:8; Admur 316:?] regarding the trapping prohibition that we follow the general intent of the trapping in regards to defining it as Melacha Shetzricha Legufo.

[24] From the wording of Admur ibid it is implied that he is liable even in such a case as "**when he ties it he does not set a date in his mind for when he will un-tie it, and it is [thus] possible that it will remain [tied] forever**"; On the other hand, in the continuation of 317:1 regarding the Rabbinical prohibition he rules that if at times it is untied within the week or within the day, then it may be tied Setam. Vetzaruch Iyun!

[25] Based on Admur 317:10

[26] So is clearly implied from 317:1, and 317:10 and many other Halachos

[27] From the fact we make a decree against tying such a knot that is commonly left forever even with intent to undo it seems that it is a Biblical prohibition to change one's mind, however see P"M 317 A"A 20 which implies it is not a Biblical prohibition as he states "One can say it is forbidden, but one is not liable for a Chatas"

[28] See Mishneh Shabbos 111b; Biur Halacha 317:1 "Hakosher"

[29] Taz 317:1; Admur ibid "unless it has been professionally done, which means that it is a **strong and tough knot** similar to the knots that the professionals make during their work"

[30] According to this approach it ends up that the Rambam; Rif and Michaber rule like Rebbe Meir in the Mishneh Shabbos 111b which states "any knot that can be undone with one hand one is exempt", Vetzaruch Iyun as the Poskim explain that the Chachamim argue on Rebbe Meir and we rule like Chachamim, hence one must say that even according to the Rambam/Rif/Michaber, a one hand knot is considered a Maaseh Uman. Vetzaruch Iyun. [Biur Halacha ibid]

[31] M"B 317:1; Biur Halacha 317:1 "Hakosher"; This ruling is due to the fact that we do not rule like Rebbe Meir, as explained in the previous footnote, and one must hence conclude that even according to the Rambam/Rif/Michaber it is defined as a Maaseh Uman.

Is it Biblically forbidden to untie a knot when done without intent to re-tie?[32]

This matter is disputed amongst Rishonim.[33] Practically one is liable.[34] Thus a permanent knot may never be untied on Shabbos even through a gentile, even in a case of need.

May an amateur permanent knot be tied or untied by a gentile in times of need?[35]

No.[36]

2. The Rabbinical prohibition of making a knot and the knots which are permitted to be tied and untied:[37]

A. The Rabbinical definition of a permanent knot:

If one sets in his mind a designated time in which he will then certainly untie the knot, then even if this [designated time] is in a very long time [from now], it is not Biblically considered [a] permanent [knot] and he is [thus] exempt [from liability] whether upon tying it or untying it. However, Rabbinically this is also considered [a] permanent [knot] being that it is designated to last a certain amount of time and it is thus [Rabbinically] forbidden to tie or untie. [This Rabbinical prohibition applies according to all opinions, even regarding an amateur knot.[38]]

Knots that are meant to be untied on the same day that they are made:[39] However if it is not designated to last at all but rather to be untied the same day [that it was tied], such as knots of clothing and shoes of which when one places them on in the morning they are tied and when he removes them in the evening comes they are untied, then one is allowed to tie and untie it on Shabbos.

Torah Scholars who intend to not untie their shoes and clothes that night:[40] However if one intends to not untie them that day, such as for example Torah Scholars that learn at night and do not remove their shoes and clothes at night, then it is forbidden for them to tie it on the morning of Shabbos if they intend to not untie them in the evening. Similarly, it is forbidden to untie them on Shabbos if when he tied them on one of the days of the week he intended to not untie it **immediately** that coming night.

Tying their shoes and clothes on Shabbos without any intention:[41] However if [the Torah Scholars] do not have any intention at all when they tie them, and rather they tie them casually, then they are allowed to tie them on Shabbos. [Furthermore] even if afterwards he [ends up] not untying it that night [and rather only unties it] **after some time** it is not considered due to this [even] a [Rabbinical] permanent knot being that at the time of tying it, it was not for certain that it would not be untied on the night after Shabbos, being that at times even the Torah Scholars remove their shoes at night prior to lying down.

Untying knots of clothes made without intention:[42] Similarly it is allowed to untie it on Shabbos if one had tied it casually [without intention to leave overnight] even if it was tied a long time before Shabbos and was not untied in-between.

---

[32] Biur Halacha 317:1 "Dino Kemo"

[33] Some Rishonim hold it is Biblically forbidden even if performed without intent to retie. [Rashi in Shabbos 74b; brought in Tosafus Shabbos 71a] Other Rishonim however rule that it is only Biblically forbidden if one unties with intent to retie. [Rosh; Rabbeinu Chananel, brought in Tosafus ibid]

[34] Vetzaruch Iyun as in the Mishkan such knots were made with intent to re-tie?

[35] Peri Megadim 317 M"Z 5

[36] As this matter is disputed whether it contains a Biblical prohibition. This applies even if one were to hold that a Biblical doubt is only Rabbinical, as it nevertheless has a Torah root. [ibid]

[37] Admur 317:1

[38] Admur 317:2; Shiltei Giborim 41a in the opinion of Rif and Rambam; Hagahos Maimanis 4; Implication of Taz 317:1; Implication of Beis Yosef 317; Kaf Hachaim 317:16; Ketzos Hashulchan 123 footnote 3
Other opinions: Some Poskim rule that if an amateur knot is not made to last forever, then it may be tied and untied according to the Rif and Rambam. [Implication of Michaber 317:1; Implication of Rif and Rambam; P"M 317 M"Z 1; Machatzis Hashekel 317:14; M"B 317:5; Biur Halacha 317:1 "Sheyno Shel Kayama"]

[39] Admur ibid; first opinion in Rama 317:1; Kol Bo and Hagahos Maimanis

[40] Admur ibid; Taz 317:2; Sefer Hateruma 243 in name of Riy; Shabbos 112a regarding the shoes of "Derabanan" as explained in Rashi there

[41] Admur ibid; Taz ibid

[42] Admur ibid based on Taz ibid

317

Knots that are always made to not be untied the next day:[43] However knots that are always for certain left [tied] for a certain amount of time and it is never usual to untie it that same day, then it is forbidden to tie them on Shabbos even casually or to untie them.

Other Opinions:[44] [However] there are opinions which say that any knot which is not made to last seven days is not considered a permanent knot even Rabbinically and it is [thus] allowed to tie it and untie it on Shabbos. [Furthermore] even if most of the time it is common to tie it to last for seven days and only at times does one also untie it within seven days, such as for example a Torah Scholar which the majority of the time only removes his shoes and clothes from one Shabbos to the next Shabbos and it is thus found that their knots are left tied for seven days, although at times he does untie it within seven days, then it is not considered a permanent knot unless one has in mind while tying it to not untie it until after seven [days]. However when he casually ties them [without any intention] then it is not considered permanent unless it is common for him to always leave it [tied] for seven days, such as for example the strings used to tie the neck of a cloak, then for a person for whom it is never common to untie it [within 7 days] but rather only when he changes the cloak from Shabbos to Shabbos, then it is forbidden [for him] to tie it and untie it on Shabbos.

The Final Ruling:[45] The final ruling is that one is to be stringent like the first opinion [to only allow to tie or untie a knot which is made to untie the day it is made] unless one is in great need [to tie or untie it], in which case one may be lenient to do so through a gentile.[46]

What is the definition of a knot that is meant to be untied within the same day?
Some Poskim[47] rule it means that it is meant to be untied within 24 hours. However, from Admur[48] it is implied that it must be undone that same day, "immediately at night", and hence if it was tied Shabbos morning it must be untied immediately by Motzei Shabbos. Vetzaruch Iyun.

May one ask a gentile to untie a temporary knot in a time of need?
Even if the knot is meant to last for more than 7 days, it is allowed to be done.[49] However it requires further analysis if this applies even according to Admur/Taz.[50] Some Poskim[51] rule that in a time of great need one may ask a gentile to untie any Rabbinical knot, which is defined as any knot that is not

---

[43] Admur ibid; Taz 317:1
[44] Admur ibid; 2nd opinion in Rama ibid; Mordechaiy 386
[45] Admur ibid; Taz 317:5
Ruling of the M"B: The M"B does not give an explicit arbitration egaridng this dispute, however it is impleid from various areas that he is stringent as ruels Admur ibiud [see M"B 317:21, 29] although in a time of need he justifies those that desire to be lenient. [Biur Halacha 317:4 "Sheiynam"]
[46] Brought in Taz 317:5, as is always the ruling regarding a Shevus Deshvus, that in a time of need one may be lenient. [Levushei Serud on Taz, as is explained in 307]. Vetzaruch Iyun as to what is the novelty here of stating this allowance if it is a general rule in all Rabbinical cases. Furthermore, it can be implied from here that only in a case that the knot is made to be undone within 7 days is it permitted in a case of need to ask a gentile. If however it is meant to be undone past 7 days then it would be forbidden to even ask a gentile. Vetzaruch Iyun as for what reason would this be any different than any other Rabbinical prohibition, which the rule is that one is allowed to do it through a gentile in times of need. Perhaps however one can say that the above rule only applies by a new Rabbinical decree made against coming to do something else. However if it is a Rabbinical prohibition due to a redefinition of the Biblical law, as is the case here with regards to the definition of "permanent knot", then it receives the same severity as does a Biblical prohibition, and may not be done through a gentile. [see Peri Megadim M"Z 317:5 which suggests a similar differentiation; This is also similar to Admur's ruling in Hilchos Pesach of the Rabbinical prohibition of Baal Yerah, that the sages invalidated the Bittul, and thus consequently the prohibition of Baal Yerah remains] Thus accordingly, in a case that it is Rabbinically forbidden to make a knot according to all, which for more than 7 days, then it may not be undone at all through a gentile. Vetzaruch Iyun.
[47] P"M 317 A"A 2; M"B 317:6; Ketzos Hashulchan 123 footnote 2
[48] "Similarly, it is forbidden to untie them on Shabbos if when he tied them on one of the days of the week, he intended to not untie it **immediately** that coming night. However, if [the Torah Scholars] do not have any intention at all when they tie them, and rather they tie them casually, then they are allowed to tie them on Shabbos. [Furthermore] even if afterwards he [ends up] not untying it that night [and rather only unties it] **after some time** it is not considered due to this [even] a [Rabbinical] permanent knot being that at the time of tying it, it was not for certain that it would not be untied on the night after Shabbos, being that at times even the Torah Scholars remove their shoes at night prior to lying down.
[49] Levushei Serud on Taz 317:5, as is ruled in 307
[50] See footnote above which dealt with this issue.
[51] M"B 317:3

meant to last forever, even if it is a strong knot.

B. May one make a professional knot to last one day or an amateur knot to last many days?[52]

First Opinion[53]- *Rabbinical prohibition by amateur knots made to last even temporarily, and by all professional knots*: It is Rabbinically forbidden [to tie even amateur knots] even if it is not made to last forever but rather only for a set period of time as explained [above, meaning for more than one day according to the stringent opinion, and 7 days according to the lenient opinion].[54] However a knot which is done professionally, even if it not made to last at all but rather to be untied that same day, is Rabbinically forbidden to tie or untie on Shabbos, due to a decree [that if this were to be allowed then one may come to make also] a professional knot that is meant to last forever of which one is Biblically liable on.[55]

Second Opinion[56]-*No difference between a professional and amateur knot*: There are other opinions[57] that say there is no difference at all between a professionally made and amateur made [knots], as even on an amateur knot one is Biblically liable if made for it to permanently last, and if [a knot] is designated to not last at all [then] in a situation that it is [thus] allowed to make an amateur knot it is also allowed to make a professional knot.[58]

The Final Ruling:[59] One is to be strict like the first opinion [and it is thus forbidden to tie or untie professional knots in all cases].

C. Knots which are at times left permanently:[60]

Any knot which at times one retracts his initial intentions and decides to nullify it there forever, then even if [one] now wants to make it without intent to nullify it there, it is [Rabbinically[61]] forbidden [to make it] because he may change his mind and decide to nullify it there.[62]

Tying a rope to a cow and its trough: Therefore, it is forbidden to take a rope and tie [one end of] it to a trough and [the other end to] a cow, because perhaps when one will wish to remove the cow from there, he will always untie only one of [the ropes] ends and leave the second [knot of the second end] there permanently and it will [thus] be a permanent knot.

Woven ropes: However, this only refers to other [non-woven] ropes, however with a woven rope it is allowed [to tie it] being that one will not nullify it there. There is no decree made here against a woven rope due to [that one may come to use] other ropes being that even by other ropes it is not common that one will nullify one end to be there forever, and rather he will at times undo one end and at time the other end.

Tying the rope of a cow to its trough or vice versa: All the above is referring to tying a rope on Shabbos onto [both] the trough and the cow, however if it was already tied to the trough and one wants to tie it

---

[52] Admur 317:2

[53] This opinion is the same opinion mentioned above by the Biblical prohibition.

[54] Admur ibid; Shiltei Giborim 41a in the opinion of Rif and Rambam; Implication of Taz 317:1; Kaf Hachaim 317:16

Other opinions: Some Poskim rule that if an amateur knot is not made to last forever, then it may be tied and untied according to the Rif and Rambam. [Implication of Michaber 317:1; Implication of Rif and Rambam; P"M 317 M"Z 1; Machatzis Hashekel 317:14; M"B 317:5; Biur Halacha 317:1 "Sheiyno Shel Kayama"]

[55] Admur ibid; Rif 41b; Rambam [Shabbos 10:1] and Michaber 317:1

[56] This opinion is the same opinion mentioned above by the Biblical prohibition.

[57] Rosh, Rashi, Tur and Rama

[58] Admur ibid; Taz 317:1; M"B 317 Hakdama

[59] Admur ibid; Rama ibid rules like Michaber in this matter

[60] Admur 317:10; M"A 317:20; Kol Bo 31; Yireim 274; Beis Yosef; M"B 317:34

[61] Implication of Admur; M"B 317:34 in name of Yireim; implication of all Poskim brought in Biur Halacha 317 1 "Hakosher"

Other opinions: The Biur Halacha ibid suggests that perhaps when the common custom is to leave such a knot to last forever then it is Biblcially forbidden to make it even if the person makes it with intent to untie

[62] Vetzrauch Iyun if he does in fact nullify it there if he now transgresses a Biblical prohibition. From the fact we make this decree it seems that it is a Biblical prohibition, however see P"M 317 A"A 20 which implies it is not a Biblical prohibition as he states "One can say it is forbidden, but one is not liable for a Chatas"

now to the cow or if it was tied to the cow and he now wants to tie it to the trough, then it is allowed to be done with any rope, as if he will come to nullify one of its knots to stay there permanently one can assume that the same knot which was already tied will [be the one that he will decide to nullify and] leave tied there forever.

3. Tying and untying a double knot on Shabbos:[63]
[Due to that we rule stringently in the above dispute to prohibit tying and untying professional knots in all cases] we are therefore accustomed to be careful not to tie or untie any knot which is a double knot one on top the other even if made [in order] to undo on that same day. [See Q&A]

The reason is: because we are not experts as to which knots are considered professional of which are [thus] forbidden to tie and untie even if not made to last at all, and [thus] any strong knot which is very tightly tied there is doubt that perhaps this is considered a professional [knot][64], and [thus since] a double knot is also a strong knot [therefore we are stringent].

Untying a double knot in a scenario that involves pain:[65] Nevertheless in a scenario [that involves] pain one need not be strict regarding [the dispute of the] Rabbinical [prohibition] and one is [thus] allowed to untie it if [the knot] is not made to last at all in a way that it would for certain be allowed to be done [if it were an] amateur [knot], being that according to the latter opinion it is allowed even if it is certainly a professional [knot]. [See Q&A regarding tying a bandage on a wound]

Q&A

May one tie or untie a loose double knot?
Yes. If it was tied to undo that day it may be untied, as a knot can only be considered a professional knot when it is strong and tight.[66] However, the Misheneh Berurah[67] learns that so long as it will not be undone on its own, even if it can be undone with one hand, then [knot] is considered a professional knot.

Does the above allowance of pain apply to all professional knots and to all Rabbinical knots?[68]
No. The above allowance in a case of pain only applies to a double knot which is a doubtful professional knot, and only if it is not meant to last for 24 hours. It does not apply to any other professional knot, or an amateur knot that is meant to last more than one day.[69]

---

[63] Admur 317:2; Rama 317:1; Shiltei Giborim 41b
Other opinions: The Shareiy Teshuvah 317:1 brings from the Bircheiy Yosef 317:1 that their custom is to allow tying a double knot to undo that day as it is considered an amateur knot, and it's only a minority opinion which argues on this, and their opinion is nullified. However, the Kaf Hachaim 317:23 explains the Birkeiy Yosef to refer to a type of double knot that is not very tight.
[64] Admur ibid; M"A 317:4; Shiltei Giborim ibid; M"B 317:14
[65] Admur ibid; Rama ibid
[66] Ketzos Hashulchan 123 footnote 4; Kaf Hachayim 317:22-23 based on 317: 2
[67] Admur 317:1-see Biur Halacha there,
So too seems to learn the Kitzur Shulchan Aruch who prohibits double knotting a scarf.
[68] Ketzos Hashulchan 123 footnote 5; Implication of Chayeh Adam 26; Kalkeles Shabbos
Other opinions: The Karban Nesanel on the Rosh Shabbos "Eilu Kesharim" writes that according to the Rama all Rabbinical knots may be untied in a case of pain. [See Ketzos Hashulchan ibid]
[69] Ketzos Hashulchan 123 footnote 5 learns that this allowance to undo a knot in a case of pain only applies to a double knot, being that there is doubt as to whether it at all is considered professional. However, by a knot that is certainly professional, then despite that this too is disputed whether it is Rabbinically forbidden when made to last less than one day, nevertheless one is to be stringent even in a case of pain. This is also implied from the ending wording of Admur "being that according to the latter opinion it is allowed even if it is certainly a professional [knot]." Thus, implying that his allowance was only referring to the last case mentioned which involved a double knot which is a questionable professional knot.

4. A bow knot and a single knot:[70]

A bow made on top of a single knot:[71] The above only refers to [a double knot made of] two knots one of top of the other, however by one knot and a bow on top of it there is no doubt at all [that it is not considered] a professional knot and it is thus allowed to tie and untie in any case that it is not designated to last at all[72]. [See Q&A]

May one make a bow on top of a bow?[73] Yes, it may be done even with intent to never undo.

Making a single knot: A single knot without a bow on top of it, is not considered a knot at all and is allowed to be tied and untied even if made to last forever.[74] [See Q&A] [However] all this refers to tying two things together, however if one makes a knot using the single end of a rope or thread or string then it has the same law as a double knot for all matters.[75]

May one make a single bow to last forever?[76]
Yes.

What is the law of a slip knot?
This matter requires further analysis.

---

5. Making a knot for the sake of a Mitzvah:[77]

A knot which is not Biblically considered a permanent knot but rather only Rabbinically is allowed to be tied for the sake of a Mitzvah, such as to make a knot in order to measure one of the Torah required measurements.[78] Even to tie a professional knot is allowed if it is impossible to measure it otherwise.[79]

6. Examples of Cases:

A. Untying the rope that secures a cover to its vessel:[80]

Seals that are on vessels, such as a chest of drawers, box and portable tower which have their covering tied to them with a rope, it is permitted to cut the rope even with a knife or undo [the rope even] through taking apart its threads[81], in order to open [the box] to remove its content.

Undoing its knot: It goes without saying that it is allowed to undo the knot as it is not a permanent knot being that it is meant to be constantly removed.

---

[70] Admur 317:3
[71] Admur ibid; Rama 317:5; Iggur 465; Shiltei Giborim 41b
[72] Meaning to undo that same day, So rules Shiltei Giborim ibid; Taz 317:7; M"A 317:15; Mishneh Berurah 317:29.
[73] Admur 651:6; Mishneh Berurah 317:29
[74] Admur ibid; M"A 317:20; Hagahos Maimanis 10:10; Yireim 274
[75] Admur ibid; Rama 317:1; Semag
[76] Michaber 317:5; Ruled in Ketzos Hashulchan 123:4. In footnote 11 he leaves it with a Tzaruch Iyun why the Alter Rebbe did not mention this here.
[77] Admur 317:4; Michaber 317:1; Mishneh Shabbos 157a as rules the Rambam and Tur; M"B 317:13; Shaar Hatziyon 317:6
Other opinions: Some Poskim rule that according to Rashi [on Mishneh ibid] and Tosafus it is forbidden to tie a Rabbinical knot even for the sake of a Mitzvah. [Beis Meir, brought in M"B 317:13]
[78] Back then measuring was done through a rope have knots made on the various parts of the rope which represent different measurements.
The reason: The reason specifically by the laws of Kosher the Sages were lenient to permit tying for the sake of a Miztvah is because the Rabbinical prohibition is not due to a decree that one may come to do an Issur, but rather being it is similar to the Biblical Melacha, and for this reason we are stringent. [See Likkutei Sichos 14 p. 15]
[79] Admur ibid; M"A 317:3; M"B 317:12
[80] Admur 314:17
[81] As opposed to untying the actual knot, which will explained below.

B. Untying the knot of a collar:[82]

Made by the launderer: [It is allowed] to untie the collar [of a shirt] from the knot that the launderer knotted as it is not considered a permanent knot being that majority of times it is opened the day that it was done, immediately after the laundering.

Made by the tailor: However, it may not be opened for its first time[83] being that this is [considered] fixing a vessel and one is [thus] liable [in doing so] on [the] "Finishing touch" [prohibition]. However, he is not liable for [the] tearing [prohibition] unless he [tears it] with intent to re-sew as was explained in chapter 302 [Halacha 4].

C. Tying a Lulav:[84]

One may not tie a Lulav on Yom Tov with a double knot or bow over a knot. Rather one is to make a bow over a bow.[85]

D. Tying a rope or thread to the bucket of a pit:[86]

One may tie a bucket to the mouth of a pit with a thread or sash and the like of materials which one does not [plan] to nullify there. However, one may not do so with a rope being that he will nullify it there and it is [thus] a permanent knot being that the bucket is constantly hanging and tied there. [Furthermore] even with a woven rope[87] which is of importance and will not be nullified there it is forbidden [to tie with] due to a decree [that one may come to use also] other ropes.

However, this only refers to buckets that are designated for the pit, however our buckets which are not designated for the pit [and will thus eventually be removed from the pit for another use[88]] [tying a rope on it] is not considered a permanent knot and it is [thus] permitted to tie to it even other ropes as long as the knot is not done professionally. [As if it is professionally done] it is forbidden to be done even if it is not made to last as was explained above [in Halacha 2]

E. Tying a rope to block the passageway for an animal:[89]

One may a tie rope in front of a cow in the width of the passageway in order to prevent it from leaving being that [such a knot] is not made to last as it is meant to be constantly untied in order take the animal out to be given to drink.

Furthermore, even to tie on Shabbos the two ends of a rope on the two posts of the doorway which were not at all tied to the doorway from before Shabbos is allowed, as we do not suspect that one may nullify one end [of the rope] that it be tied there forever and he will only let the animal out through untying the second end of the rope, being that at times he will undo one end and at times the other end [and there will thus never be one end nullified there].

However, if in truth one does nullify one end [there] then it is forbidden.

---

[82] Admur 317:6

Back then it was the custom for the launderers to tie the collars with a knot in order to have it be shaped. The question here thus is if such a knot may be undone on Shabbos.

[83] Meaning that if one had just bought this shirt from the tailor then one may not undo the collar knot on Shabbos.

[84] Admur 651:6; Michaber 651:1; Sukkah 33b and Rashi there; M"B 317:29

[85] The reason: As one never plans to undo the knot from the Lulav, and it is thus considered made to last forever. [Admur ibid based on Rashi ibid] Vetzaruch Iyun why one cannot simply make a Kesher Hedyot with intent to undo that day.

[86] Admur 317:8

[87] This refers to a rope which is not usual to be used to draw water with. [Rashi Pesachim 11a]

[88] Mishneh Berurah 317:28. This applies even if one plans to leave the bucket there for more than one day. [Biur Halacha]

[89] Admur 317:9

Summary

Biblically:

It is only Biblically prohibited to tie or untie a knot if:

1) At the time of making, it one plans to let the knot remain tied for as long as it can possibly last and does not plan to ever untie it.[90]

2) According to some opinions there must also be fulfilled: That the knot is strong and tough similar to the knots that professionals make in their labor.[91]

Rabbinically:

It is Rabbinically forbidden to tie or untie any knot that:

1) Is made in a professional manner even if not meant to last at all [even in a scenario that involves pain].[92]

Or

2) Is meant to last temporarily, meaning that one has in mind a set time by when he will undo the knot, and this set time is past 24 hours from when the knot has been made.

Or

3) The knot is a type of knot that is at times left to last forever, then it is forbidden to tie it.[93]

Permitted:

It is permitted to tie and untie any knot which is:

1) Any knot which is only Rabbinically forbidden to tie and untie [i.e. any knot which one has a set date to untie] may be tied <u>for the sake of a Mitzvah</u>.[94]

Or

2) If not needed for the sake of a Mitzvah, then it is permitted if <u>all</u> the following conditions are fulfilled:

    A. The knot is not meant to last for 24 hours. In time of need if it is meant to last for 24 hours, but for less than 7 days, then one may tie or untie it through a gentile[95]

    And

    B. It is not a professional knot.

    And

    C. The knot is never usually left to last forever.[96]

    And

    D. It is not the first time that this knot is being open or is but does not make a finishing touch to the vessel. If it does then it is forbidden due to Fixing a vessel.[97]

---

[90] Admur 317:1
[91] Admur 317:2
[92] Admur 317:2
[93] Admur 317:10
[94] Admur 317:4
[95] Admur 317:1
[96] Admur 317:10
[97] Admur 317:6

What is considered a professionally made knot?[98]

Any strong knot which is tightly tied there is doubt that perhaps it is considered a professional knot.

<u>Double knots:</u> Therefore [strong] double knots are forbidden to be tied or untied unless in a case of pain when made to not last 24 hours.[99]

<u>A bow on top of a single knot:</u> Is considered an amateur knot and is allowed to be tied and untied with intention to undo that day.[100]

<u>May one make a bow on top of a bow?[101]</u> Yes, it may be done even with intent to never undo.

<u>A single knot made with two ends:</u> Is not considered a knot at all and may thus be tied and untied even if meant to last forever.[102]

<u>A single knot made with one end:</u> Has the same law as a double knot for all matters.[103]

What is the law if one does not have any intent upon tying an amateur knot regarding when to untie it?
When making an amateur knot must one have in mind to undo it within 24 hours?[104]

If the knot is a type of knot which is at times opened within 24 hours, and certainly if it is meant to constantly be opened, then there is no need for one to intend upon tying it on Shabbos, to open it within 24 hours. Furthermore, he is not even obligated to open it within 24 hours. Nevertheless, it is forbidden to specifically have in mind to undo it after 24 hours. Thus, it is only remains permitted to make the knot in such a case if one has no intent on when he will untie it. If, however, the knot is never commonly opened within 24 hours, then it is forbidden to be casually tied [unless one has intention to untie it within the same day].

May one untie an amateur knot which was made without any specific intent regarding when to be untied?[105]

If it is a type of knot that one at times unties within 24 hours, and certainly if it is meant to constantly be opened, then he may untie it even if when it was made it was made without any intention of when to untie. This applies even if many days past since the knot was made. However, if made with intention to untie past 24 hours, or it is a knot that is never untied within 24 hours, then it is prohibited to untie.

Q&A on professional knots
Definition of Maaseh Hedyot-What is the law of a knot that can be undone with one hand?[106]

All knots that are forbidden to be untied, may not be untied even if one can do so with one hand. However, seemingly, if the knot can be untied with one hand due too it being a weak knot, then it is not defined as Maaaseh Uman and hence may be untied if it is meant to be opened that day.[107] However, according to some Poskim[108] even in such a case the knot can be defined as Maaseh Uman if it is strong enough to last forever and will not untie on its own.

---

[98] Admur 317:2
[99] Admur 317:2
[100] Admur 317:3
[101] Admur 651:6; Mishneh Berurah 317:29
[102] Admur 317:3
[103] Admur 317:3
[104] Admur 317:2
[105] Admur 317:1-2
[106] See Biur Halacha 317:1 "Hakosher"
[107] As in such a case it is not a strong knot,m and is hence not a Mashe Uman, as rules the Taz and Admru ibid
[108] M"B 317:1 and Biur Halacha ibid

If a professional knot occurred on its own, like strings became tangled and formed a double knot, or a bow over a knot became a double knot, may one open it on Shabbos?[109]

It may only be undone if:

1. [By the latter case, only if one did not have intention to undo the bow after that day], and
2. The current knot is not tied tightly. [Some Poskim[110] however rule it may even be done if tied tightly.]
   or
3. Is tied tightly but is a case that involves pain.

If ones Tzitzis became tied onto another person's Tzitzis, may it be undone?

According to above answer it may only be undone if the knot is not tight.

If one's shoes became tied in a double knot and he cannot remove them may he undo the knot?[111]

Even if the knot is tight one may undo it, as in a case of pain we allow to untie double knots.

Q&A on temporary knots

May one make a knot which is usually not undone that day if he intends to undo it that day?
Yes.[112]

May a knot with a bow on top be made on a disposable bag or the like which one plans to throw out and never actually undo?
Some Poskim[113] rule doing so is forbidden. Others[114] rule that it is allowed to be done, as throwing out an item is equivalent to untying it.

May one tie a Gartel to a Sefer Torah?
Some Poskim[115] rule that when it is done in a way that one makes a bow over a knot then it may only be done to undo that day, such as to undo by Mincha. If, however, one will not be using the Sefer Torah until Monday or later, as is the case when reading after Mincha, then doing so is forbidden.[116]

---

[109] Ketzos Hashulchan 123 footnote 11 in explanation of Chayeh Adam, brought in Mishneh Berurah 317:23
Background:
The Chayeh Adam, brought in Mishneh Berurah [317:23] as well as in the Ketzos Hashulchan [chapter 123 footnote 11], writes that if one usually ties a bow [over a single knot] and accidentally tied a knot [over the single knot thus forming a double knot] then it has the same law as a knot made with intention to undo that same day. However, the Ketzos Hashulchan ibid explains this to mean that only if it was not tied strongly and is thus not a professional knot may it be untied. Alternatively, even if tied strongly it may be untied in a scenario of pain. [However, this is only referring to a double knot, which is questionable as to whether it is considered professional or not. However, by another type of strong knot which is for certain a professional knot then even in a case of pain seemingly untying it would be forbidden, as explained above. Vetzaruch Iyun Gadol as according to this explanation of the Ketzos Hashulchan there has been no novelty said in the words of the Chayeh Adam, as it has the same exact law as one who intentionally tied a double knot, of which if strong may not be undone unless in a case of pain and if lose may be undone?] The Chazon Ish 52:17 however explains that the allowance applies even by a tight double knot being that avoiding a double knot is a mere stringency, and hence in a case that it occurred without intent one may be lenient.
[110] Chazon Ish 52:17 in explanation of M"B ibid
[111] Mishneh Halachos 3:38
[112] So is implied from Admur 317:1: *However knots that are always for certain left [tied] for a certain amount of time and it is never usual to untie it that same day, then it is forbidden to tie them on Shabbos even casually or to untie them.*
[113] See Maharil Diskin Kuntrus Achron 5:35; Rav SZ"A in SSH"K 35 footnote 63, brought in Piskeiy Teshuvos 317 footnote 24
Opinion of Admur: It can be implied from Admur 651:6 [and Rashi Sukkah 33b] which considers the knot of a Lulav **made to never be undone**, even though after Sukkos it has no use, that throwing out is not considered like destroying. However, see Tzitz Eliezer 15:17 which explains that possibly one keeps a Lulav to inherit to his children. Vetzaruch Iyun.
[114] Minchas Yitzchak 8:27; Tzitz Eliezer 15:17; In Minchas Yitzchak 8:27 he brings that Rav SZ"A ruled to him that when the item is thrown out it is considered destroyed, and thus should be allowed, and is brought by Rav SZ"A himself in Tikkunim Umiluim of SSH"K.
[115] Minchas Shabbos 80; Minchas Yitzchak 8:19; Beir Moshe quoted in Piskeiy Teshuvos 317 footnote 19; Mentioned in Betzeil Hachachma 3:112.
The reason: Seemingly they do not permit this on the basis that it is being done for the sake of a Mitzvah being that it is possible to not tie it at all.
[116] As rules Admur in 317:1 that it is only permitted to make even an amateur knot when doing so to undo that day.

Rather one is to fasten the ends into the binding. Other Poskim[117] however defend the worldly custom in making a bow over a knot even when the scroll will not be opened that day.[118] Regarding making a double knot see footnote.[119]

Untying the Gartel: If the Gartel of a Sefer Torah has been tied in a way that is forbidden to undo on Shabbos, such as a double knot or a bow over a knot, then it is likewise disputed whether it may be untied. Some Poskim[120] rule that if another Torah scroll is available then one is to take it out. Others[121] however rule that there is no need to return the Sefer Torah and remove another one, and one may thus undo the knot even if it is a double knot.[122]

If one took out the Sefer Torah and found that it was tied with a double knot may it be undone?
See above regarding the dispute. The Ketzos Hashulchan[123] rules that one may untie it and does not need to take out another scroll.

May one tighten his Tzitzis on Shabbos?
No and does so it is possibly a Biblical prohibition.[124] [One must be especially careful regarding a new pair of Tzitzis of which it is very common for the upper not to become loose, and hence care must be taken not to tighten it on Shabbos.]

Is one to check his Tallis on Shabbos?[125]
One is required to check the validity of the Tzitzis also on Shabbos, and so is the widespread custom.[126] [Upon checking the Tzitzis strings on Shabbos, one is to hold the upper knot of the Tzitzis and then check each string, in order to prevent tightening that knot on Shabbos.[127]]

---

[117] *Ketzos Hashulchan* 123 footnote 9; *Shut Mahrshag* 60 although in his conclusion he suggests to be stringent although not to protest against those which are lenient. *Rav SZ"A* in SSH"K 15 footnote 178 says the custom is to be lenient.

[118] The reason: Doing so is considered an honor for the Sefer Torah, and any knot which is only Rabbinically forbidden is allowed to be done for a Mitzvah. However, it is honorable to merely stick the endings into the binding was suggested above. [ibid] This is also implied from the ruling of Admur in chapter 651:6 that Admur rules that by a Lulav such a knot may not be made because one never plans to untie it. Thus, implying that if done to eventually untie is allowed because doing so is a Mitzvah. [so learns also Ketzos Hashulchan ibid; Shut Maharshag ibid]

[119] On the one hand one can claim that according to all it would be forbidden when done with intent to undo that day as since one can tie it in a permitted way which is by making a bow over a knot, it is no longer considered a need for a Mitzvah. If, however, it is done after Mincha, to be undone 2 days later, then since whatever knot one makes is the same Rabbinical prohibition, which may be done for the sake of a Mitzvah then there is no difference in regards to which knot one makes, and so rules Shut Maharshag 1:60 that one is not to protest over one who makes a double knot.

[120] Kaf Hachaim in name of Ruach Chayim, brought in Ketzos Hashulchan ibid; following the above mentioned Poskim which are stringent regarding tying the Gartel on Shabbos. However, if no other Sefer Torah is available then obviously according to all one may untie it, as it is for the need of a Mitzvah.

[121] Ketzos Hashulchan ibid

[122] As one is doing so for the sake of a Mitzvah.

[123] 123 footnote 9

[124] Ketzos Hashulchan 123 footnote 4. However if done to untie that day then even to make the entire Tzitzis initially is only Rabinically forbidden. Now although one is doing so for the sake of a Mitzvah, nevertheless this was only allowed by an item that is normally eventually untied while by Tzitzis we suspect that he may leave it there forever. [Peri Megadim 317 A"A 20 brought in Ketzos Hashulchan 123 note 9] See however Biur Halacha 317:1 "Hakosher" that learns it is Biblically forbidden even if intended to undo that same day.

[125] Admur 8:13 in Kuntrus Achron 2; See also 275:1; Bach 8; Implication of Rama 13:2; M"A 13:5; 275:3 in name of Mateh Moshe and Rashal; Mamar Mordechai 8:9; Ben Ish Chaiy Bereishis 3; Kaf Hachaim 8:36; M"B 8:20 and 13:7 that so is implied from M"A ibid; Daas Torah 8:9 that so is implied from Taz 13:3; Mate Efraim 584:17

Other opinions: Some Poskim rule one is not required to check the Tzitzis on Shabbos unless one has another Tallis available. [Beis Yaakov 84 as explained in Admur ibid; Koheles Shlomo brought in Kaf Hachaim ibid] As on Shabbos, if one does not have another Tallis available he will anyways be allowed to wear the Tallis. [Biur Halacha below] Admur in Kuntrus Achron ibid negates this opinion, as nevertheless one must check in order to save himself from a blessing in vain. Some Poskim record that the world is not accustomed to check the Tzitzis on Shabbos. [M"B ibid; Siach Yitzchak 4 that so was custom of Kesav Sofer; Rabbanim in Piskei Teshuvos 13 footnote 18] However Admur ibid records that the custom is to do so.

Ruling of M"B: In M"B 13:7 he writes that although from the Poskim ibid it is proven that one should check the Tzitzis even on Shabbos, nevertheless the custom is to not do so. The M"B in Biur Halacha 13:2 "Kodem Sheyeitzei" writes that one is to check the Tzitzis on Erev Shabbos for the sake of Shabbos. If one did not do so then he is to check it at home prior to going to Shul with the Tzitzis. If the Tzitzis is already in Shul then according to the M"A there is no longer a need to check, although according to the Taz one is still to check. [ibid]

[126] So writes Admur ibid in Kuntrus Achron; The M"B ibid however concludes that the custom of the world is not to check the Tzitzis on Shabbos. See Ketzos Hashulchan 7 footnote 21

Is one to separate the strings of his Tallis also on Shabbos prior to the blessing?
Some Poskim[128] rule one may not separate the strings on Shabbos, [even if they are loosely entangled].[129] Others[130] however rule that one may separate [loosely] entangled strings on Shabbos. Practically one is to do so[131] although one must beware not to untangle any strong knots that may have formed, and also not to tighten the top knot of the Tzitzis which commonly becomes loose.[132] [Upon checking the Tzitzis strings on Shabbos, one is to hold the upper knot of the Tzitzis and then check each string, in order to prevent tightening that knot on Shabbos.[133]] If however this is a new Tallis and it is the first time one is wearing it, then one is not to separate the strings at all on Shabbos, and is rather to do so on Erev Shabbos.[134]

May one make a tie on Shabbos?[135]
If not made in way of a double knot [or any type of tight knot] then it is allowed when done to untie within 24 hours. If the tie was made before Shabbos in a double knot, then the other side of the tie may nevertheless be loosened and tightened.

May one tie a scarf around his neck, or a tichel on one's hair?
It is best to do so with a bow over a knot. However, there are Poskim[136] which allow one to make even a double knot as long as the double knot is not tight. Other Poskim[137] however forbid a double knot. In all cases, neither a double knot nor a bow knot, may be done with intent to undo the next day [past 24 hours]. Thus, those women that do not undo their Tichel knots may not make any form of knot on their Tichel on Shabbos, even a bow knot.[138]

May one tie a bandage onto a wound?[139]
One is to do so through making a bow over a single knot, and not through a double knot, as doing so may involve the tying prohibition. If, however, it is not possible to make a single knot with a bow then if one is in pain one may make a double knot with intent to remove that day[140], or at the very least in a time of need within seven days.[141]

6. Inserting straps into clothing:
See "The Laws of Building and Destroying" Chapter 1 Halacha 2E!

---

[127] Kovetz Oholei Lubavitch 3:5 that the Rebbe showed a young married student this order of checking on Shabbos. [printed in Shulchan Menachem 1:40]
[128] Gan Hamelech 65; Kesher Gudal 2:3; Shalmei Tzibur 29; Shesilei Zeisim 8:13; Chesed Lealafim 8:8; Shaareiy Teshuvah 8:8; Kisei Eliyahu 8:5; Ben Ish Chaiy Bereishis 3; Kaf Hachaim 8:30; Artzos Hachaim 8:7
[129] The reason: This is forbidden due to a possible Shabbos prohibition of fixing a vessel. [ibid]
[130] Implication of Mateh Moshe 443; Kneses Hagedola 281:4; Kisei Eliyahu; Yifei Laleiv 8:16; Chayeh Adam 8:17; Mamar Mordechai 8:9; brought in Kaf Hachaim ibid; Shulchan Hatahor 8:5; Halichos Shlomo 3:5; Yabia Omer 5:3
[131] So is implied from Admur 8:13 in Kuntrus Achron 2
[132] See Shulchan Aruch chapter 317 for the laws of tying and untying on Shabbos; Ketzos Hashulchan 123 foonote 4; SSH"K 15:7; Az Nidbaru 3:22; Toldas Shmuel Kosher 9; Piskeiy Teshuvos 13 footnote 17
[133] Kovetz Ohalei Lubavitch 3:5 that so showed the Rebbe to a young married student the order of checking on Shabbos. [printed in Shulchan menachem 1:40]
[134] See Poskim ibid of lenient opinion that when the strings are being untangled for the first time it is possibly Tikkun Mana. [Mamar Mordechai ibid in his explanation of the Gan Hamaelech]
[135] SSH"K 15:58
[136] Ketzos Hashulchan 123 footnote 4; brought also in Shaareiy Teshuvah in name of Birkeiy Yosef;
[137] Kitzur Shulchan Aruch; and so would seem from the Mishneh Berurah definition of a Maaseh Uman as stated in the previous Q&A.
[138] SSH"K 15:54
[139] Piskeiy Teshuvah 328:21, see also Tzitz Eliezer ibid which writes that a bow knot is to be made.
[140] However there in Piskeiy Teshuvos he writes "if the bandage is a type which is meant to be removed that day". However, based on chapter 317:1 -2 it makes no difference if the bandage usually is made to last more than one day so long as ones intent is for it to last less than one day.
[141] So is implied from Admur 317:1-2. Vetzaruch Iyun as there Admur only permits for a gentile.

7. Cutting a knot:[142]

Cutting the sewing and knot of the tailor: Even if a collar had already been opened [after being made] but a professional [tailor] returned and sewed [the two sides of the collar] together in the way done by professionals, or if the professional tied it [in a way] that one is unable to untie it, then it is forbidden to cut the strings. However, this [prohibition to cut an undoable knot] only refers to a knot tied by the professional prior to having finished making the clothing, being that then the cutting of the strings of this knot involves the [prohibition of doing a] "Finishing touch." As this finalizes the work needed to be done to the clothing being that through doing so the clothing is now fit to be worn, while until this was done it was never yet fit to be worn, [and it is thus forbidden as] any [action] done which is the finishing stroke [of the making of the vessel] contains [the prohibition of] "Finishing Touch" as was explained in chapter 302 [Halacha 5]

Cutting the knot of the launderer:[143] However other knots which were tied after the clothing had finished having its work done to it, such as the knots of the laundering or the strings of a cloak which have been tied and one is not able to undo, [then] it is permitted to cut them. Nevertheless, even so one may not be lenient [to cut it] in front of an ignoramus, and rather should do it privately.

By a knot made to last 7 days:[144] If one is accustomed to only cut the strings [of the collar knot] upon changing the cloak from Shabbos to Shabbos, then it is forbidden to cut [the strings of the knot] just like it is forbidden to undo it [as explained in Halacha 1]. [However, some Poskim[145] rule that this prohibition only applies if one plans to continue using the string for knots. If, however, one breaks it in a destructive manner to throw it in the garbage and not reuse, then it is permitted to break through the string even if it is made of a knot that is forbidden to be undone, just as we permit one to break through a wicker basket that contains figs.]

Summary-Cutting the strings of a knot:[146]

Anytime it is permitted to open a knot on Shabbos one is likewise permitted to cut it. However, one may not be lenient to cut it in front of an ignoramus, and rather should do it privately. [As well in a case that the rope attaches an item to the ground then the rope may not be torn even if one is allowed to untie the knot being that doing so involves the destroying prohibition.[147]] Anytime that the knot is forbidden to be undone, it is likewise forbidden to be cut.

---

8. Cutting and tearing sewn threads:[148]

See "The Laws of cutting and Tearing" Prohibition #1 Halacha 4!

9. Weaving and unraveling ropes and wicks:[149]

Biblically: One who weaves ropes of any type of material is liable for [the] tying [prohibition]. The amount [needed to be tied] to be Biblically liable is to the point that the rope can last with its weaving without needing to be tied at its end, in which case the work done to it is lasting.

Rabbinically: However, Rabbinically it is forbidden to [weave it] any amount.

Unraveling: Similarly, one who separates a wick is liable for untying and its measurement is like that of one who weaves it[150], although [this liability is only applicable] as long as he did not intend to destroy

---

[142] Admur 317:6; Michaber 317:3
[143] Admur ibid; M"A 317:11 in name of Rashal; M"B 317:23
[144] Admur ibid; M"B ibid; based on M"A ibid
[145] Chazon Ish 51:13; 52:17; Piskeiy Teshuvos 317:3
[146] Admur 317:6
[147] Admur 314:19
[148] Admur 317:7
[149] Admur 317:11; M"A 317:20; M"B 317:34
[150] Meaning that if the wick could have lasted without needing a knot at its end then one who undoes it is liable.

[the wick], as all those that destroy are Biblically exempt although it is Rabbinically forbidden to be done.

Summary-Weaving and unraveling ropes and wicks:[151]

Biblically: It is Biblically forbidden to ravel threads together to the point that they can last without needing to be tied at their ends.

Rabbinically: It is Rabbinically forbidden to ravel threads in any situation.

Unraveling: It is forbidden to unravel all ropes and wicks and the like. However, one who does so is only Biblically liable if a) The rope would have been Biblically forbidden to make and b) One made it with intent to rewind the rope.

Q&A

May one wind or unwind twist-ties on Shabbos?[152]

Some Poskim[153] rule it is forbidden to do so. However, there are authorities[154] which defend the widespread custom to allow doing so on the basis that here one has no true intent to make the twist tie into a rope.

---

[151] Admur 317:11

[152] Piskeiy Teshuvos 317:6

[153] SSH"K 9:13 writes that tying or untying twist-ties is forbidden on Shabbos if done strongly due to that this is similar to raveling threads together into a rope, which is forbidden due to the tying prohibition. It is therefore likewise forbidden to undo.

[154] Sheivet Halevy brought in Piskeiy Teshuvos ibid

THE LAWS OF BORER

**Separating, Peeling,
And Filtering on Shabbos**

Shulchan Aruch Chapter 319

TRANSLATION-SHULCHAN ARUCH CHAPTER 319

Chapter 319
The Laws of separating [items] on Shabbos
29 Halachos

<u>Part 1: Separating items within mixtures</u>

Introduction:
The following section will deal with the laws of separating foods and other items from amongst other foods and items, such as separating cucumbers from tomatoes in a salad, or a white shirt from amongst other shirts. Doing so in certain cases *involve the Borer/separating prohibition, as will be explained in this section.*

Halacha 1
Removing the waste from the food: Separating is one of the principal [Shabbos prohibited] actions, as in the Tabernacle they would separate the waste from the herbs [used for the dyes[1]] and therefore anyone who separates waste from food even with one's hand and even in order to eat right away, is liable.
Removing the food from the waste- Using a Sieve and Sifter: However one who separates food from waste in order to eat the food right away is not liable unless he separated it with a sieve or sifter which is its common form of sifting.
Using a Knon and plate: However, if one separated it with a *Knon*[2] or a plate[3] then he is Biblically exempt [from liability] although it is Rabbinically forbidden to be done due to a decree [that one may come to use] a sieve and sifter.
Separating with ones hands: [However] to separate the food with ones hands in order to eat right away is allowed.
The reason that this is allowed is: because to remove food from amongst waste in order to eat right away is not at all similar to any [forbidden form of] work being that doing so is the normal form of eating, as it is impossible to eat the entire mixture, [eating] the food together with the waste, and the Torah only prohibited [separating food from waste while eating when] using its designated vessel [to separate it] which is a sieve and sifter.
The reason for why removing the waste is forbidden: However, to remove the waste [from the food] is not [considered done in] the normal framework of eating but is rather [considered] preparing the food so it be fit to eat which is a complete [Biblically prohibited] act. Therefore, even if [the mixture contains] a lot more food than waste and there is greater bother in having to separate the food, nevertheless one may not separate the waste even in order to eat [the food] straight away.

The ruling of the Alter Rebbe in the Siddur:
Avoid eating shelled nuts/seeds on Shabbos:
It is proper[4] to avoid eating almonds and nuts on Shabbos unless they have been removed from their shells from before Shabbos.
The reason for this is: because, although even when the nut/fruit remains totally or partially in its shell [on Shabbos] it is permitted to remove its shell with ones hands and does not contain [a] separating bad from good [prohibition], nevertheless after the fruit has been removed if there remains a piece of the shell

---

[1] The curtains and roofing in the Tabernacle were made of dyed skins. The dye was made by boiling different herbs. Prior to the boiling they would separate the mixed waste from amongst the herbs. The Melacha of Borer does not refer to the separating of waste done to the herbs of the incense as only those Melachas which were done in the process of building the Tabernacle are counted as part of the 39 Melachas, and not Melachas done once the Tabernacle was built. [Rav Ovadia Bartenura Mishnayos Shabbos 7:1]
[2] This refers to a wooden tube which is wide on top and narrow on bottom. Places the legumes in from the wide part and then shakes off its peels and the legumes fallout from the narrow bottom while the peels remain inside. [Rash in Shabbos 74a]
[3] Mishneh Berurah 2
[4] Lit. good

amongst the pieces of fruit/nut or amongst whole nuts, then if one removes [that shell] from there he is liable for a sin offering [if done unintentionally] and stoning [if done intentionally] for [transgressing the prohibition of] separating waste from food. Rather one must separate the fruit/nut from amongst the shells and may not touch the shells at all.

Furthermore [in additional reason to avoid nuts] even if the shells are bunched up alone without having any mixture of fruit [of the nuts] amongst them, [nevertheless] there [still remains] a great prohibition in moving them due to that they are Muktzah, as is known.

And [since] it is difficult to beware from all the above [prohibitions, therefore it should be avoided.]

Halacha 2
Separating the food in order to eat later on
As well one who separates food from waste without intent to eat it right away but rather to leave it to be eaten later on, even [later on] that day, then it is [considered] like he had separated [the food to place it in] storage and he is liable.

The reason for this is: because it is not applicable here to say that what he did was within the context of eating being that he is not eating it right away.

Halacha 3
What is the definition of "right away"?
The definition of "Right away" is [that the separation is done] very close to the meal, however if one does not plan to eat for a while, then it is forbidden [to separate at that time]. However so long as [one wishes to do the separation] close to the meal it is permitted for him to separate for the need of that entire meal even if [the meal itself] will be prolonged for some time.

Separating for the need of others: [Furthermore] even if other people are dining with him, he is allowed to separate for the need of everyone.

If there are left-over's after the meal: If there are remains after the meal from what had been separated [nevertheless] this does not pose any problem being that when it was separated it was done permissively.

Intentionally separating more than needed prior to the meal: However one may not conspire regarding this [and intentionally separate more food than needed prior to the meal so he have what to eat later on].

Halacha 4
Separating unwanted food from wanted food
Edible food from edible food of same species: There is only a prohibition of separating when one separates waste [i.e. inedible parts] from the food or vice versa. However, if one separates food from food, even if he only wishes to eat one of them while the second one he wants to take and throw out, [nevertheless this unwanted food] is not considered waste due to this since it is [nevertheless] fit to be eaten. Therefore, it is allowed to separate it from the food which one wishes to eat and doing so does not contain [the prohibition] of separating waste from food.

Edible food from food that is only edible in pressing times: [However] if [the unwanted food] is only fit to be eaten in a pressing time then even though it is not considered actual waste and there is [thus] no Biblical prohibition in separating it, nevertheless it is Rabbinically forbidden [to separate it] just like is the law by actual waste.

Therefore, it is forbidden to remove the rotten leaves from the vegetable (called lettuce) even if they are fit to be eaten in times of need. Rather one is to separate the vegetable from the leaves, which is [separating] the food from the waste.

Waiting until after Shul to separate: [As well] one must be careful to not separate them until after [the congregation] leaves Shul in order so [it be separated] actually close to the meal, in which case it is then allowed to separate as much as one needs to eat for that meal.

Halacha 5

Edible food from edible food of different species: However, the above allowance to separate food from food only refers to when both foods are all the same species. However, if one had in front of him two different types of foods which are mixed together and he wishes to separate [in order] to eat one of them right away and to place the second [food] aside to be eaten later on, then that species [of food] which one wishes to eat right away is considered the food while the other [species of] food is considered like the waste. Therefore, one must separate with his hands that [food] which he wishes to eat right away from amongst the other [food], thus [separating] the food from the waste and not vice versa. If one separates it and sets it aside to be eaten later on, even [later on] that day, he is liable.

Halacha 6
Two species of fish: Two species of fish are considered two species of foods and it is [thus] forbidden to separate [them even] by hand unless [one separates] that species which he wants to eat right away and [he is] not [separating it] from [prior to the coming] meal for [the need of the next] meal.
Separating a large species from amongst a small species: [Furthermore,] even if one of the species are large and thus each species is [easily] recognizable and it is hence possible that there is no separating [prohibition] involved here at all, nevertheless one may not be lenient being that [doing so] is in question of being liable for a sin offering [meaning that it is questionable if this is a Biblical prohibition, and thus one must be stringent].
Separating large pieces from small pieces: However as long as [the mixture] is of a single species, then even though one separates large pieces from small pieces [nevertheless] this is not [Halachically] considered separating at all being that the entire [mixture] is fit to be eaten, and there is thus no waste [in the mixture]. [It is therefore] allowed to separate from it in any way that he wishes[5] and even in order to eat it later on that day [meaning while it is still Shabbos[6]].
[Furthermore] even if the [mixture] contains two different species and one [wishes to] separate from amongst both of them together the large pieces from the small pieces, it is allowed since one is not separating one species from another.

Halacha 7
Separating lupine beans from their flowers and shells
One who separates lupine beans[7] from their waste is liable.
The reason for this is: because their waste sweetens them when they are boiled together, otherwise [the seeds] remain very bitter, therefore [the seeds] are considered the waste and the waste which sweeten them are considered the food, and it is thus found that one has separated waste from amongst food, and is [thus] liable even if he separates with his hand in order to eat it right away.

Halacha 8
Separating vessels from waste and from amongst other types of vessels
Just like there is a prohibition of separating food [from waste] so too there is also [a prohibition in separating] other items from amongst their waste, or [in separating] one type of item which is mixed with another type of item.
Example: For example, if one had in front of him two types of vessels which are mixed together and one wants to select one type from amongst another type in order to use it, then this item [which he wishes to take now] is considered like food and the other item is considered like waste and one thus is required to remove the food from the waste and not vice versa, even in a case that one of the items is larger than the other and is [thus easily] recognizable on its own. As well one is required to separate to use right away as was explained regarding [separating from a mixture which contains] two types of food.

---

[5] Meaning even to separate the unwanted food from the wanted food.
[6] As otherwise this is considered preparing on Shabbos for after Shabbos which is forbidden.
[7] Lupines are a type of legume. Their flowers are produced in dense or open whorls on an erect spike, each flower 1-2 cm long, with a typical pea flower shape with an upper 'standard', two lateral 'wings' and two lower petals fused as a 'keel'. The fruit is a pod containing several seeds.

<u>Part 2: The laws of Mifarek [separating grains and legumes from their peels and stalks]</u>

Introduction:
The following section will deal with peeling shells/peels off of foods such as nuts and beans in a pod and the like. Doing so in addition to involving the Borer restrictions[8], as well at times involves a prohibition of Mifarek, which is to detach an item from another item, as will be explained below.

Halacha 9
Rubbing seeds out from their stalks and pods:
Doing so with an irregularity: One may not extract seeds from stalks in the same method used during the week, which is to rub the stalks within the palms of one's hands in order so the seeds fallout from it. Rather he must rub them with a slight irregularity using the tips of his fingers.
The reason this is allowed: Now, although by doing so he separates the seeds from the stalks with his hands, and one who separates [seed from a stalk] with his hands is [liable for transgressing] an offshoot of the threshing prohibition which is done using a vessel, as was explained in chapter 305 [Halacha 28], nevertheless [here] since he is separating it irregularly in order to eat (right away) it is permitted.
It was not decreed against doing so due to that one may come to separate [the seeds] as regularly done, being that even one who separates them in the usual method is also only considered to be doing so irregularly being that he does not take the food and actually remove it with his hands [from the stalks] but rather just rubs the stalk and causes the grains to fall and [this method] is usually only done with a vessel that is designated for threshing. However nevertheless it is Rabbinically forbidden [to separate by rubbing it with one's hands], although when this too is done with an irregularity they made no decree against doing so.
Other Opinions: [However] there are opinions which are stringent to not sort at all [the seeds out from] stalks of grains or from pods of legumes even using the tips of one's fingers.
Rubbing off the shell of nuts: Therefore [according to this latter opinion] it is forbidden to rub out the Luz nuts[9] or large nuts from within their upper green shell which covers over their thick and hard shell, even with the tips of one's fingers.
The Final Ruling: It is proper[10] to be stringent [to not rub off the shell] being that one can anyways break it open and eat it without needing to separate [the shell][11]. [However according to Siddur rubbing is forbidden under all circumstances].
To peel off the thin peel of nuts, grains and legumes: However, it is permitted to break [the shell] and then peel off the thin peel that is on the fruit which is under the hard shell which is broken, as the separating prohibition is only applicable by the top shell.
Similarly, it is permitted to peel [the chaffs of] grains and legumes which have been removed from their stalks and pods from before Shabbos, although one must be careful to only peel as much as he needs to eat right away and not for what he will need to eat later on as will be explained in chapter 321 [Halacha 19[12]]
Peeling off the pods from legumes: However (according to all opinions) it is forbidden to peel the pods on Shabbos and remove the legumes from within them (with ones hands as doing so is [Halachically considered] actually separating [which is forbidden]).
Moist pods: However [the populace of] the world is accustomed to allow this to be done and there are opinions which seek merit [to justify] their actions [saying] that since the stalks are still moist and thus

---

[8] Based on Rama in end of chapter 321 Halacha 19, and alluded to in Admur here in Halacha 9. [see Shabbos Kihalacha Vol 2 page 290]
[9] This refers to almonds which when small are sweet and when they ripen become bitter. [Likuteiy Sichos 33 Matos]
[10] Lit. Good
[11] It seems that this is only referring to nuts, being that the shell can be cracked, however by pods being that the only option is to rub them, then doing so would be allowed with an irregularity according to the final ruling of Admur, and so is implied also from chapter 321 Halacha 1.
[12] In Rama, the end of the chapter was not printed in the Alter Rebbe's Shulchan Aruch. There he explained that one may not peel onions and garlic to eat later on.

the pods themselves are still edible, it is thus like one is simply separating food from food which does not contain the detaching prohibition as explained in chapter 305 [Halacha 28].

Inedible-dry-pods: However, those legumes which their pods are not edible there contains no permission at all to remove the legumes from within them on Shabbos unless the legumes are not at all attached to their pods, having been detached from them before Shabbos and it is rather simply sitting [loosely] within [the pod]. In such a case it is permitted to remove [as many legumes from the pod] as he wishes to eat right away, however he may not do so to eat later on due to the separating prohibition.

The ruling of Admur in the Siddur:
Not to eat legumes that are still in their pods on Shabbos:
[One] needs to be very careful not to eat on Shabbos beans, whether raw or cooked, which are still in their pods.

The reason for this is: because being that their pods are not edible removing them contains the Mifarek/detaching prohibition according to all opinions, which is an offshoot of the threshing prohibition which one is liable for a sin offering and stoning Heaven Forbid.

Now, although the beans have already [become] detached [inside] from their pod through the cooking process and are thus no longer attached to it [nevertheless the above Mifarek prohibition still applies].

Sesame seeds: The same restriction applies also towards sesame seeds.

Legumes with edible pods: A meticulous person should be stringent upon himself also with regards to the species of legumes called (Arbes) when they are still attached to their pods, even though their pods are also edible, as [separating the seeds from the pods] is not clearly allowed.

Halacha 10
Shaking off the thin peel from the grains:
If one had kernels which were removed from before Shabbos from their stalks and are still mixed with their chaff[13] they may not be sifted [out] with a Kenon or plate due to a decree that one may come to sift them with a sieve and sifter in which case one is liable.

[Furthermore] even to do so with two hands, meaning to shake them from one hand to another in order to separate [the grains] from their thin peel [is forbidden]. Rather one is to sift them using a single hand placing into it all his strength in order to differ from the method that is used during the week (and thus not come to sift in a sifter).

Halacha 11
Placing food with its waste into water in order to remove the waste:
Food and waste which are mixed [together] is forbidden to be placed into water in order for the waste to sink to the bottom, as is the case if the waste is earth, or [so the waste] float to the top as is the case [if the waste] is straw.

Similarly, *Karshinin*[14] may not be soaked in water in order so their waste float to the top, and as well one may not rub it with his hands to remove the waste as doing so is similar to [the] separating [prohibition].[15]

However, one may place them in a sieve even though the waste [might[16]] fall through the holes of the sieve and it is thus found that [the waste] becomes separated on its own.

---

[13] Chaff is the inedible, dry, scaly protective casings of the seeds of cereal grain, or similar fine, dry, scaly plant material such as scaly parts of flowers, or finely chopped straw. In agriculture chaff is used as livestock fodder, or is a waste material ploughed into the soil or burnt. The process of loosening the chaff from the grain is called *threshing*, and separating the loose chaff from the grain is called *winnowing* – traditionally done by tossing grain up into lightly blowing wind, dividing it from the lighter chaff, which is blown aside. This process typically utilizes a broad, plate-shaped basket, or similar receptacle for holding and collecting the winnowed grain as it comes back down. Chaff should not be confused with bran, which is finer, scaly material forming part of the grain itself.

[14] Possible this refers to the horse been which is similar to the broad been and is used for horse fodder.

[15] Some hold that this is not considered the way of eating and is thus forbidden. Others hold that it is like separating the waste from the good.

[16] Based on Chapter 324 Halacha 1 where Admur writes "that at times the food falls". So concludes the Ketzos Hashulchan 131 footnote 17, and Shabbos Kihalacha Vol. 2 page 356. Thus if it is for certain that the waste will fall through, then it is forbidden. This cannot be proven from

Supplement from chapter 321 Rama Halacha 19[17]:
Peeling foods:
It is forbidden to peel garlic and onions [as well as other foods such as apples and nuts[18]] which one [peels] to set aside [from being eaten right away, due to that this contains a separating prohibition[19]]. However [to peel them] in order to eat right away is allowed.
Throwing out the pit of foods:[20] [Contains the separating prohibition and thus may only be done in order to eat the food right away.]

Part 3: Miraked-Filtering wine, water and other liquids on Shabbos

Introduction:
The following section will deal with the laws of separating through using a filter. In addition to the problems of Borer that are sometimes applicable as will be explained, the prohibition of Miraked may likewise apply, amongst other prohibitions.
In essence the prohibitions of Borer and Miraked are really one and the same, being that they are both a separating prohibition. The difference between Miraked and Borer is only with regards to the form of separation.
Borer is considered separating from a solid mixture using a sifter to sift out the waste and have the food remain above. Meraked is a prohibition of sifting a solid mixture and having the food fall out and the waste remain above.
Regarding a liquid mixture Admur in Halacha 12 rules that straining it and having the sediment remain above may be Borer or Miraked. Thus by liquid mixtures it is unclear as to which prohibition applies.
The reason why this action of separating was split to two different prohibitions is because these were two distinct actions done in the Mishkan and thus were given two different names of prohibition.[21]

Halacha 12
Using a strainer
Wine with sediment: One who filters dregs [of wine], meaning that he filters it through a strainer, [has done an] offshoot of [the] separating [prohibition to separate] food from its waste using a sifter and sieve, or [has done] an offshoot of [the] Sifting/Miraked [prohibition] and is liable.
Water through dregs- winey water: However, if one had placed dregs in the strainer from before Shabbos then it is permitted to pour water over it in order so the water become more [clean and] clear.

Halacha 13
Clear wine and water in a strainer: Water or wine which are clear are permitted to be filtered through a filter in order so they become even more clear, or even in order [to remove] the sediment that floats on top of the wine or [to filter out] small twigs that have fallen into it[22].
The reason that this is allowed: This is not considered like separating being that [the wine and water] are still drinkable to majority of people even without this filtration.

Halacha 21 where Admur rules that placing mustard with barn in the strainer is forbidden being that there it is discussing having the bran [waste] remain above and the mustard fall out, which contains a Meraked prohibition, while here it refers to having the waste fall out on its own, which does not contain a Miraked prohibition as will explained in the introduction to the next section.
[17] The end of this chapter does not appear in the Alter Rebbe's Shulchan Aruch and we have thus brought the rulings of the Rama and Mishneh Berurah as a supplement for those omissions.
[18] Mishneh Berurah 84
[19] Mishneh Berurah 83
[20] Mishneh Berurah 84
[21] Based on Shabbos Kehalacha Vol 2 page 342
[22] Today this permission no longer applies being that majority of people today are particular not to drink wine with twigs until it is filtered, being that today it is very uncommon for wine to include twigs. [Ketzos Hashulchan 125 footnote 28. Shabbos Kehalacha Vol 2 page 348]

Filtering with a cloth:

White liquids: However, with a cloth it is forbidden to filter the water or white wine and the like [of other liquids] due to the whitening prohibition, being that soaking a cloth is considered laundering it.

The reason why there is no whitening prohibition involved by a strainer: However, a strainer is made for this purpose and one thus does not care to squeeze [out the liquid which it absorbs] and as well does not care to whiten it at all, therefore its whitening does not pose a problem to prohibit soaking it in liquid due to this even according to those opinions which say that the soaking of a cloth is [considered] laundering it.

Colored liquids: However red wine or beer or other liquids which do not whiten of which we do not suspect that one may come to squeeze [a cloth soaked in these liquids] as explained there [in chapter 320 Halacha 21] then it is permitted to strain it with a cloth even if [the liquids] are slightly murky to the point that most people would not drink them without filtration.

The reason that filtering even murky colored liquids in a cloth is allowed is: because since nevertheless it is possible to push oneself to drink these liquids, [filtering them] is therefore not considered actually separating, and was [thus] allowed to be done through an irregularity, such as by using a cloth.

Other Opinions: [However] there are opinions which prohibit [filtering even with a cloth] in this scenario [that the colored liquids are slightly murky].

The Final Ruling: It is proper[23] to suspect for this latter opinion.

If the colored liquids are very murky: However, if the [colored liquids] are completely murky to the point that it is not possible to drink them in this state, or [in a case that] they have sediment [in them] then it is forbidden to [filter them] even using a cloth.

Halacha 14

Filtering pre-fermented wine: Wine that has just been pressed, so long as it remains within its primary fermentation [process][24] one may mix a barrel of it together with its dregs and may place it even inside a strainer.

The reason for this is because: so long as the wine is still within its [primary] fermentation the wine has not yet separated well from its dregs and thus the entire [mixture of the] wine [with its dregs] is considered one food, and there is [thus] no [prohibition] of separating food from its waste involved here. Furthermore [there is no problem of separating here because] the wine is fit to be drunk even without filtration, and this is commonly done during the times of its pressing when all wines are murky and majority of people drink it the way it is without filtering it.

Filtering vinegar: The same applies with vinegar, which is likewise common to use even when it is still slightly thick, that it is permitted to filter it. However, if [the vinegar] is very thick and is not fit at all [to be used] without filtering then it is forbidden to filter it even with a cloth.

Filtering almond milk: Similarly, the milk of crushed almonds [which were made] before Shabbos is permitted to be filtered being that it is able to be drunk without filtering.

Halacha 15
Indenting the cloth to intake the liquid

Upon filtering with a cloth slightly murky [colored] liquids one must beware to not make an indent within the cloth in order for it to intake the liquid. Rather one is to pour the liquid on to it and let it form an indentation on its own in order to differ from the way this is done during the week.[25]

---

[23] Lit. Good

[24] With red wines, the must is pressed after the primary fermentation, which separates the skins and other solid matter from the liquid. Thus during the primary fermentation, the dregs still remain with the wine.

[25] This restriction only applies to when straining a) murky liquids b) with a cloth. However by clear liquids even by a strainer it is allowed to make an indentation for the liquid to fall in. [Ketzos Hashulchan 125:13 footnote 33, Mishneh Berurah 45, Shabbos Kihalacha Vol 2 p. 354]

Halacha 16
An Egyptian basket
Any liquid which is permitted to filter with a cloth is permitted to be filtered with an Egyptian basket[26] as long as one does not lift the basket from the bottom of the lower vessel [in which one is filtering into] the height of a handbreadth, in order to differ from the way this is done during the week.

However, that vessel which is made like a sieve which is used to filter, since it is designated for this purpose, it has the same laws as does a filter[27] which is that one may only filter with it clear liquids which do not have dregs as explained [above in Halacha 12].

Halacha 17
Placing twigs into the opening of a bottle:
A vessel into which one empties the wine from the barrel may not have strongly inserted into its opening twigs and reeds, as this is similar to a filter.

The reason: Now, although it's not an actual filter being that dregs still pass through it, nevertheless since there are twigs and dirt which do not bypass it is thus similar to a filter.

However, if [in the barrel] there is clear wine which does not contain sediment and rather only thin splinters, then it is permitted to filter it even using an actual strainer as explained above [in Halacha 13].

Pouring from one vessel to another

Introduction:
The following section will deal with the laws separating through spilling from a vessel. The rulings brought below from the Alter Rebbe's Shulchan Aruch differ entirely from the rulings brought below from the Alter Rebbe's Siddur [by Halacha 24]. For this reason, it is incumbent to read the summary to understand the final ruling in what one is to do.

Halacha 18
When one wants to eat the food being poured out
May pour up until the stream stops if does not plan to eat right away: It is permitted to gently pour [food or liquid] from one vessel into another in order so the residue and dregs remain on the bottom of the vessel [being poured from].

However, one must be careful once the stream [being poured] has stopped and small trickles begin to drip out from the last remainder [of food that is] amongst the waste, then one must stop [pouring] and leave [that remainder of food] together with the waste.

The reason for this is because: if one were to not do so, then these last drops prove [to all] that [his true intentions in this pouring] were to separate [the food from the waste]. However, during the initial pouring when the waste is not yet recognizable, then he has done no separation.

Gathering the fat off from the surface of milk: Therefore, it is permitted to gather from above the fat which floats on the surface of milk[28] (called cream) and when one reaches near the actual milk he is to leave some of the fat still [on the surface] together with the milk.

Doing the above is only allowed if needed for Shabbos: However [doing the above is only allowed] if one needs the fat [or other poured food] for that day [meaning for Shabbos], as if one does not need to use it [for Shabbos] then it is forbidden [to do so as] it is forbidden to trouble oneself [to do an action] on Shabbos for [the use of] a weekday.

---

[26] This refers to a basket made of different willows and papyrus plant [Rama]

[27] This vessel is not actually considered a filter being that it does not hold back the dregs of the wine. Nevertheless since it filters out twigs and filth therefore it has the same status as does a filter. [M"B 52]

[28] Upon standing for 12 to 24 hours, fresh milk has a tendency to separate into a high-fat cream layer on top of a larger, low-fat milk layer. The cream is often sold as a separate product with its own uses; today the separation of the cream from the milk is usually accomplished rapidly in centrifugal cream separators. The fat globules rise to the top of a container of milk because fat is less dense than water.

In a case of loss may have a gentile do it even for a weekday: However, if one suspects that [the fat may perhaps] lose [its substance] or spoil [if he were to not separate it now] then it is permitted for him to remove it through a gentile.

The reason for this is: because the prohibition to trouble oneself and prepare on Shabbos for a weekday is a Shvus [which is a] Rabbinical prohibition, and in cases of loss it is permitted to ask a gentile [to do an action for oneself] with regards to all [actions that are] Rabbinical prohibitions, as was explained in chapter 307 [Halacha 12].[29]

If one wants to eat right away: [However] if one wants to eat the [fat] right away, then [it is permitted to remove all the fat and] he does not need to have remain any [of the fat] together with the milk.

Similarly one who pours liquid from one vessel to another [in order to eat the liquid being poured right away] is not required to stop [pouring] once it begins to trickle drops [of the liquid].

The reason for this is: because it is permitted to separate food or liquid from amongst residue in any case that one plans to eat or drink it right away so long as he does not separate it through using a vessel but rather does so with his hands as was explained [above in Halacha 1].

The definition of using hands to separate: Now, although here he is [separating through] pouring from one vessel to another [and thus is not doing the separation with his hands], nevertheless [it is permitted since] the core of the separation is being done through ones hands, and it is only considered that one is separating with a vessel when one separates using a cloth or basket and the like.

Halacha 19
When one wants to eat the food remaining in the pot
However, fat which floats on the surface of food is forbidden to be entirely poured out even when done in order to eat the food right away.

The reason for this is: because [the fat and the food] are two types of food [in which case we say] that food which one plans to eat right away is considered the "food" while the other is considered the waste, and [thus] upon pouring out the fat which one does not want to eat it is considered like separating waste from food [which is forbidden].

Halacha 20
Tilting a barrel of wine in order to pour it out: It is permitted to [tilt] a barrel [by] elevating [one side of it] over an item in order so that the wine pour out of it well.

Now, although that through this wine is also poured out from amongst the sediment, [nevertheless] this is not considered like separating so long as [he has not poured out so much to the point that] drops have not yet begun to trickle from amongst the sediment as explained [in Halacha 18].

Placing water into wine sediment in order to absorb taste: Similarly, it is allowed to place water on top of sediment that is in a barrel in order for it to absorb the taste of the wine and doing so does not contain the separating [prohibition], although [this may only be done] to drink from it that day [while still Shabbos].

Miscellaneous scenarios of filtering/separating foods:

Halacha 21
Filtering mustard from bran:
One may not filter mustard from its bran even though [the bran itself] is also edible and the bran is [thus] not waste at all and hence does not contain [in separating it] the Biblical separating prohibition, as [nevertheless] it is Rabbinically forbidden being that appears like one is separating food from its waste being that one filters it in order to eat the mustard and throw out the bran.

Filtering an egg yolk into the mustard: However, if one placed the mustard into the strainer from before Shabbos [and thus filtered it out from the bran] then it is permitted to place an egg into [the strainer] in order to [have the yolk fall through the strainer and] give color to the mustard that has been filtered through it.

---

[29] To note however that there it was only permitted in a case of great loss, and not any case of loss. The difference is that here the prohibition is not an actual Shvus and thus is permitted even without great loss.

The reason: Now, although the yolk falls out [through the holes of the strainer] together with the mustard while the white which is [all] connected remains above with the waste, [nevertheless] this does not appear like separating food from waste being that both the yolk and the white are foods and he is not filtering the yolk from the white because he desires to eat the yolk and not the white, but rather because the yolk helps give color to the mustard as opposed to the white.

Now, although he [eventually] throws out the white together with the waste and eats the yolk together with the mustard, nevertheless since the filtering [of the yolk] is not done for eating but rather to give color, it [therefore] does not appear like separating food from waste being that in truth they are both the same type of food.

Halacha 22
Separating food parts which come from the same food:
By eggs: [Furthermore] even if one were to filter [the yolk] for the purpose of eating it, it would only be forbidden in this case [which involves an egg] being that although the white is considered a food nevertheless it is not edible in its current state, as well as that it is common to throw it out together with the waste and thus appears like waste in comparison to the yolk which is eaten the way it is together with the mustard, and would [thus be] Rabbinically forbidden [to separate in order to eat].

By other foods: However, in other scenarios [involving different parts of the same food] there would be no prohibition at all, even Rabbinically, in separating [one part of the food from another part] of the same food. Meaning that one may even separate small pieces from slightly large pieces, even if he throws the small pieces to the ground, as they nevertheless do not appear like waste due to this since they are edible and are commonly eaten.

Halacha 23
Filtering water from insects
Filtering it prior to drinking: Water which contains worms that are forbidden to be eaten in accordance to what is explained in Yorah Deah chapter 84 [Halacha 1-3], is forbidden to be filtered even using a cloth as it is impossible to drink it without filtering it being that he may swallow one of the worms.

Filtering it while drinking: However, it is permitted to drink it through a napkin.

The reason for this is: because the separating and filtering prohibition only applies when one is mending [the food] prior to eating or drinking it in order so it be able to be eaten or drank [afterwards] as doing so is a form of an [individual] action [of separating], however when holding back the waste upon drinking in order so it not enter into ones mouth is not similar to an action [of separating] and is [thus] permitted.

The reason that doing the above does not contain a laundering prohibition: Doing so is not forbidden due to [the law] that the soaking of a cloth is considered laundering and neither due to a decree that one may come to squeeze it, being that there is only a small amount [of cloth] which is soaking in the water [as it is only] the size of the opening of his mouth, and by a small amount there is no worry [regarding the above] as explained in chapter 302 [Halacha 21].[30]

Other Opinions: However according to the [dissenting opinion] there which prohibits [soaking in water] even a small amount [of cloth] due to [the law] that the soaking of a cloth is considered laundering, here too [according to their opinion doing the above] would be forbidden.

The Final Ruling: It was already explained there [in chapter 302] that every meticulous person should be stringent upon himself when possible.

---

[30] There the following is explained: There is a dispute whether placing a minute amount of water on a cloth is forbidden. The first opinion holds that it is always permitted by a clean and white cloth, even when done intentionally to launder being since it is already clean laundering is inapplicable, and thus the only suspicion in such a case is that one may come to squeeze out the water and by a small amount of water this suspicion does not apply. The second opinion holds that it is always forbidden due to that even the soaking of a white cloth is itself considered laundering and is thus forbidden in all cases even when done not for the intent of laundering being that the laundering is an inevitable occurrence. A third opinion then holds that in truth the second opinion only forbids even a minute amount of water in a case that one intends to launder, however if one does not intend to launder, such as when using it to filter, then even according to them it is allowed. Thus according to two of the three opinions mentioned there it is permitted to filter through a cloth when the cloth is placed in ones mouth and the like.

Halacha 24
Removing a fly from ones soup or cup of juice:
If a fly fell into a cup one may not remove only the fly from the cup being that doing so is equivalent to separating waste from food which is forbidden to be done even in order to eat right away. Rather one is to remove also some of the liquid together with the fly being that when one does so it does not appear like one is separating at all, as explained above (Halacha 14 [in the Michaber, and Halacha 18 above in the Alter Rebbe[31]]).

The opinion of Admur in the Siddur:
Introduction: The following are a number of warnings and statements to remove stumbling blocks and common and frequent inadvertent [acts done on Shabbos] which according to many of the greatest of the Rishonim doing so involves a prohibition of Kares and Sekilah when done intentionally and a sin offering for when done unintentionally, may G-d atone for us.

Removing a fly from ones soup: One may not rely on the customary permission granted that if a fly or other waste falls into ones cup or plate then one removes it together with a spoon and takes out with the fly some liquid etc, as doing so is questionable if it contains a sin offering liability and a prohibition of Sekilah G-d forbid.

Thus the only solution that remains is to pour out from the cup until the waste comes out from it.

Blowing the fly: One may not blow on [the waste] with his mouth until it is blown out,[32] although he may blow it to bring it nearer to the wall of the cup and then tilt it and pour from it until the waste comes out.

The reason that tilting it out is allowed: As since the removal of the waste is being done through him holding the cup of liquid in his hand and tilting it with his hand this is considered separating food from waste which is permitted to be done in order to drink it immediately.

The same applies if [the fly] fell into a plate with gravy, and even with fat that floats on the surface of the gravy, one may not throw it out through a spoon taking with it some of the liquid as this is similar to removing waste from food which one is liable on.

Catalyzing milk and beverages on Shabbos:

Halacha 25
Making cheese on Shabbos
Making the curd: One who curds [milk], in which he takes milk and places a stomach [or other enzyme] into it in order to curd it[33], is liable for separating because he has separated the curd from the milk.

Placing the curd into a strainer: Similarly, if one places the curd into an elastic vessel[34] and the whey drips from inside it then this is an offshoot of separating food from waste through using a sieve and sifter and one is thus liable.

The reason: Now, although the curd and the milk are both a single species of food and there is [thus] no waste [here] at all, nevertheless since they are liquid substances which mix well which he is [now] separating, therefore this contains the separating [prohibition] just like one who is separating food from waste.

---

[31] Shabbos Kehalacha Vol 2 page 243 note 288. There he explains that the Alter Rebbe himself never wrote this "Halacha 14" and it was rather written by the printers. In the new Shulchan Aruch of Admur they omitted this all together.

[32] Doing so is prohibited due to the Melacha of Zoreh [winnowing] and not Borer.

[33] Cheese is made by separating the milk into solid curds and liquid whey. Usually this is done by acidifying (souring) the milk and adding rennet. The acidification can be accomplished directly by the addition of an acid like vinegar These starter bacteria convert milk sugars into lactic acid. Most cheeses are made with starter bacteria from the *Lactococci,Lactobacilli,* or *Streptococci* families.

[34] This refers to a vessel made of material that can be stretched out do to having tiny holes in it, and thus allows the milk to drip out. Similar to a plastic bag.

Halacha 26
Making hard cheese
If one solidified [curd] and turned it into cheese he is liable for building.

The reason for this is: because anyone who gathers parts [of an item] to each other and bonds them together until they become a single substance has [transgressed] an offshoot of [the] building [prohibition].

Halacha 27
Removing seeds and nuts from honey:
One may place sesame and nuts into honey, although he may not [gather them[35] and] separate them with his hands [as doing so is considered separating[36]].

Halacha 28
Catalyzing beverages on Shabbos
It is forbidden to place dregs into beverages in order to catalyze it even though [the liquid] is already fit to be drunk on Shabbos being that through doing so one causes the dregs of the liquid itself to sink to the bottom of the vessel and it is an offshoot of separating similar to one who curds milk.

Halacha 29
Spitting into the wind
One who spits in the wind and the wind scatters the saliva is liable for the winnowing prohibition.

Other Opinions: However according to those opinions which say that any action done which is not for its own use one is exempt, so too here he is exempt [from winnowing]. However, it is Rabbinically forbidden even if he does not intend to winnow, so long as the occurrence [of its scattering] is inevitable.

---

[35] Mishneh Berurah on 319:66
[36] Mishneh Berurah on 340:11

Compilation of Halachos
Summaries and Q&A

CHAPTER 1: THE GENERAL LAWS OF BORER

Introduction:
The following section will deal with the laws of separating foods and items from amongst other foods and items, such as separating cucumbers from tomatoes in a salad, or a white shirt from amongst other colored shirts. Doing so in certain cases involves the Borer/separating prohibition. The laws of Borer are one of the more difficult subjects in Hilchos Shabbos[1], and due to this many of its laws are unknown to the masses which lead to people desecrating Shabbos.[2]

General Rule:
The general rule is the following: Any form of separating which is determined as a form of preparation for the food to be eaten, is forbidden to be done, while when done in the process of eating the food, is allowed to be done. The Sages defined which forms are considered a preparation and which are considered the form of eating. The following section below will explain which mixtures are defined as actual mixtures and thus receive the separating restrictions which will be explained in Halachas 1-2. Any mixture which is not defined as a mixture in this regard does not contain any separating restrictions being that the pieces are already considered separated.

What is the definition of a "mixture" to which the regulations of Borer apply?

1. How close to each other must the pieces be, and are the most outer pieces considered mixed?
A. If a mixture has scattered do the Borer restrictions still apply?[3]
A mixture of foods which became scattered to the point that people would not consider them to be actually mixed together do not have the Borer restrictions apply to them being that they are not considered mixed. Thus, if one placed a spoon of vegetable salad on his plate and the pieces of vegetables scattered from each other to the point that one would not define them as being mixed, one would be allowed to remove even the species that he does not want from his plate. However, see next question regarding if one may purposely cause the mixture to disperse in order to then be allowed to separate the unwanted pieces.

B. May one purposely cause a mixture to become scattered in order so it lose its mixture definition and then be allowed to separate from it the unwanted parts?[4]
This is allowed to be done even initially.[5] However it is initially proper for one to have another person do the separating rather than the person who caused the mixture to become scattered.[6] In a time of need one may rely on the lenient opinions and allow the person who scattered it to then subsequently do the separating.[7]

C. If two pieces are sitting side by side are they considered mixed?[8]
No, a piece is only considered mixed if the piece which one desires to remove is sitting between, and close by, to two other pieces.[9] As well if the piece is sitting between other pieces but at a distance to the point that one would not consider this a mixture then the Borer regulations do not apply, as explained

---

[1] Sefer Hazichronos of Rav Abuhav
[2] M"B 319 Hakdama
[3] Shabbos Kihalacha Vol. 2 P. 108; Maor Hashabbos 1:8-2 in name of Rav SZ"A; Rav Wozner in Kovetz Mibeis Levy 6-1
[4] Shabbos 74a; Igros Moshe 4:74-11; SSH"K 3 footnote 6 in name of Rav SZ"A; Shabbos Kihalacha Vol. 2 P. 108
[5] Igros Moshe ibid based on Gemara ibid
[6] Rav SZ"A ibid
[7] Shabbos Kehalacha ibid
[8] Shabbos Kihalacha Vol. 2 P. 108
[9] Ketzos Hashulchan 125 footnote 14

above. Thus if one has one pear sitting near one orange Borer does not apply.

D. Are the outer pieces of a side by side mixture subject to the Borer restrictions?[10]
The most outer pieces which are not surrounded at all on their outer side by any other part of the mixture are not subject to the Borer restrictions.[11] However with regards to a mixture where the items sit one on top of another, see below. [Thus, if one has a vegetable platter with sliced onions on the outskirts of the platter and the other vegetables on the inner part of the platter, the onions may be removed without restriction.]

E. If one has a basket of fruits and on the bottom lies a rotten fruit which he wants to separate does the Borer restriction apply?[12]
One may remove without restriction all the fruits which are not in direct contact with the rotten fruit. However, the fruits that are in contact with it, and certainly the rotten fruit itself is subject to the Borer restrictions.

F. May one remove empty bottles from a table which contains full bottles?[13]
One may do so without restriction even if the empty bottles are touching the full bottles.[14]

G. Do the Borer restrictions apply to removing bottles from a box which contains various bottles of juice or empty bottles?[15]
Yes.[16]

2. Are two pieces of food which are lying on top of each other considered mixed?[17]
A. The Rule:
If they are a) not stuck to each other and b) are each individually recognizable to the point that they are not considered mixed in people's eyes: they are not defined as mixed and do not contain the separating restrictions.
> For example: One may remove a carrot from on top of Gefilte fish, or a cherry from on top of a cake or ice cream.
> As well if one has a basket of different fruits then the most upper fruits which have no other fruit on top of them are not subject to the Borer restrictions.

If the pieces are stuck to each other, such as the cream that lies on top of cake, then the Borer restrictions apply, and one thus may not remove the cream from on the cake unless he plans to eat the cream right away.
If the pieces are not stuck to each other but are not individually recognizable and are thus considered mixed in people's eyes then if one desires to reach the lower item and he has no interest to use the upper item at all, then he may remove the upper item even if he plans to use the lower item at a later time. However, if one is interested also in the upper item, such as to use it later on that day or the next day, then all the separating restrictions apply and one may thus only remove that item which he wants, with his hands, in order to use right away.[18]

---

[10] Shabbos Kihalacha Vol. 2 P. 110
[11] As explained in the previous answer that Borer only applies when the piece which one wants to remove is sitting between two other pieces.
[12] Shabbos Kihalacha Vol. 2 P. 110
[13] Shabbos Kihalacha Vol. 2 P. 110
[14] Being that they are all individually recognizable they are not considered to be mixed, as well as that one is removing the empty bottles in order to make room on the table and not in order to separate. [However regarding full bottles, such as taking certain flavors out from ones freezer, the laws of Borer do apply, as explained in Halacha 5-Q&A there!]
[15] Shabbos Kihalacha Vol. 2 P. 110
[16] As in this case the removing of the empty bottles benefit the box.
[17] Shabbos Kihalacha Vol. 2 p. 110, and 201-206
[18] So rules the M"B in 319 Biur Halacha "Lechol Miyad"

> For example: A box of index cards in which one needs to find one card, one may search through the cards in order to use the needed card right away.

B. Removing insects from on top of fruits:[19]

Based on the above, if an insect is stuck onto a fruit removing it retains all the separating restrictions, and thus is only allowed to remove it in close proximity to the meal. If it is not stuck to the fruit, then one may remove it without restriction being that it is not considered mixed.[20] Regarding washing the bugs off, see Halacha 1D Q&A there. For further elaboration on this topic, see next chapter under the section of peeling fruits.

3. Mixtures of a solid within a liquid:[21]

Small solids:[22] Small solids retain all the Borer restrictions with regards to removing them from liquid or vice versa. Thus, separating small pieces of onion, chicken, vegetables from soup contains the Borer restrictions. Likewise, removing a fly or hair from a liquid contains the Borer restrictions.

Large solids:[23] Solid pieces, which are large and thus individually recognizable from amongst the liquid, are not considered a mixture with the liquid and the Borer restrictions thus do not apply. However, this only applies if the solid that one wants to remove is not mixed with other solids, as in such a case, if one desires to select one solid from amongst another, the Borer restrictions would apply, as the solids are considered a mixture with each other, irrelevant of the liquid. Examples:

> Vegetable or chicken soup: One may remove a Matzah ball, large piece of potato or large piece of meat from soup without following the Borer restrictions so long as there is only one species of solid within the soup.[24] Alternatively, if one desires to remove all the solids from the soup, then if all the solids are large, one may remove it from the soup without Borer restrictions.

> One may remove a hardboiled egg from within water.

> One may remove a tea bag from tea. However, one must use a spoon to do so in order to prevent any dripping of tea from the bag back into one's cup.

> One may remove a rice bag from amongst the *chulent* [although according to some Poskim one is to do so in a way that the gravy from within the bag does not drip into the *chulent* in the process of removing it, such as through removing it with a spoon.]

Cans?[25] Regarding removing the solid from the liquid inside of a can, If the food that is within the can is in small enough pieces to be defined as mixed together with the liquid, then the separating restrictions apply. However, if the liquid only contains large solid foods, then it is not defined as mixed with the liquid and thus none of the separating restrictions apply.

> Canned **whole** pickles/sardines/eggplant: Are not defined as mixed and thus may have their liquid removed in any which way.

> Canned **cut pieces** of pickles/sardines/eggplant: Are defined as mixed and thus retain all the separating restrictions explained.

> Canned olives: Are defined as mixed and thus retain all the separating restrictions.

> Canned Tuna: Is defined as mixed and thus retains all the separating restrictions.

May one pour out the oil from a sardine can?[26] So long as the sardines are whole one may do so as this is not considered a mixture. However, if the sardines are cut to pieces this would not be allowed. Thus,

---

[19] Shabbos Kihalacha Vol. 2 p. 198

[20] As well removing it does not pose a problem of Muktzah being that a) It is insignificant, and b) it is a Graf Shel Reiy

[21] See Shevisas Hashabbos Borer 18; Ketzos Hashulchan 125 footnote 14 and 126 footnote 19; Az Nidbaru 4:21; Shabbos Kihalacha Vol. 2 p. 211; Piskeiy Teshuvos 319:17; Nishmas Adam 179

[22] So is proven from Admur 319:24; Admur in Siddur; Taz 319:13; 506:3; M"B 319:61 and all Poskim who discuss the methods of removing a fly from a soup in a way that will not transgress the Borer restrictions.

[23] Shevisas Hashabbos Borer 18; Ketzos Hashulchan 125 footnote 14 and 126 footnote 19; Az Nidbaru 4:21; Shabbos Kihalacha Vol. 2 p. 211; Piskeiy Teshuvos 319:17; Nishmas Adam 179; See however Kaneh Bosem 3:19 regaridng pickels in a can

[24] Meaning, that they are the only solids in the liquid. Such as soup which contains only Matzah balls, or only potatoes, and cases of the like.

[25] Shabbos Kehalacha Vol. 2 p. 212

[26] Shabbos Kehalacha Vol. 2 p. 212

by tuna cans all the Borer restrictions apply being that the oil/water and tuna are considered mixed.

1. The Biblical prohibition of separating:[27]
A. The General Law:

Intro: It is Biblically forbidden to separate any mixture which was defined above as a mixture by either a) removing the bad from the good, or b) using an instrument designated for separating or c) doing so for a later use.

The Av Melacha-Removing the waste from the food:[28] Separating is one of the principal [Shabbos prohibited] actions[29], as in the Tabernacle they would separate the waste from the herbs [used for the dyes[30]] and therefore anyone who separates waste from food, even with one hand[31], and even in order to eat right away, is liable.[32]

The reason for why removing the waste is forbidden: The removing of the waste [from the food] is not [considered done in] the normal framework of eating [which is permitted to be done as will be explained below] but is rather [considered] preparing the food so it be fit to eat which is a complete [Biblically prohibited] act.

Removing waste from food when the waste is the minority:[33] Therefore even if [the mixture contains] a lot more food than waste and there is greater bother in having to separate the food, nevertheless one may not separate the waste even in order to eat [the food] straight away.

Removing the food from the waste- Using a Sieve and Sifter:[34] As well, one who separates food from waste with a sieve or sifter is Biblically liable even if one did so in order to eat the food right away.

The reason for this is: because using a sieve or sifter is the common form of sifting food [and is thus not considered a form of eating but rather a form of preparation].

Separating the food in order to eat later on:[35] As well one who separates food from waste without intent to eat it right away but rather to leave it to be eaten later on, even [later on] that day, then it is [considered] like he had separated [the food to place it in] storage and he is liable.

The reason for this is:[36] because it is not applicable here to say that what he did was within the context of eating being that he is not eating it right away.

Summary-The Biblical prohibition:
It is Biblically forbidden to separate in any one of the following ways:
1. Bad from good.
2. For later use.

---

[27] Admur 319:1
[28] Admur ibid; Michaber 319:4
[29] Admur ibid; Mishnah Shabbos 73a
[30] The curtains and roofing in the Tabernacle were made of dyed skins. The dye was made by boiling different herbs. Prior to the boiling they would separate the mixed waste from amongst the herbs. The Melacha of Borer does not refer to the separating of waste done to the herbs of the incense as only those Melachas which were done in the process of building the Tabernacle are counted as part of the 39 Melachas, and not Melachas done once the Tabernacle was built. [Rav Ovadia Bartenura Mishnayos Shabbos 7:1]
[31] Admur ibid; Michaber ibid; See M"B 319:17 regarding the novelty of this ruling
The novelty: In Michaber 319:7 and Admur 319:10 it states that one may shake Pesoles out from food using one hand as doing so is aconsidreed a Shinui, and hence the novelty here is that picking out Pesoles with one's hand is forbidden being that doing so is not a Shinui. [M"B ibid]
[32] Admur ibid; Michaber 319:1
[33] Admur ibid; Rama 319:4; Beis Yosef 319 based on Rambam
Other opinions: This is opposed to the ruling of the Tur 319 which holds that in such a case one is allowed to remove the waste rather than the food as doing so is the way of eating. Admur and others however limit this ruling only to Yom Tov and not on Shabbos. [See Shabbos Kihalacha Vol. 2 p. 141]
Opinion of Michaber: The Michaber agrees with the ruling of the Rama ibid, as is implied from the fact that he did not mention any allowance in his rulings regarding majority food. [Biuur Halacha 319:1 "Haborer"]
[34] Admur ibid; Michaber 319:1
[35] Admur 319:2; Michaber 319:2
[36] Admur 319:2

> 3. With a utensil designated for separating.

B. Removing the bad/waste together with some of the good/food:

The opinion of Admur in the Shulchan Aruch:[37] It is permitted to remove from food which has waste in it, the waste together with some of the food, such as [using a spoon to] remove a fly from a cup together with some of the liquid, being that then it does not appear like one is separating at all.[38] [From here one can learn that it is permitted to remove the waste together with some of the food, and the Borer prohibition only applies when one removes the waste alone from the food. However, some Poskim[39] limit this allowance to only specific cases. Admur in the Siddur completely negates this allowance, as explained next.]

The opinion of Admur in the Siddur:[40] One may not rely on the customary permission granted that if there is waste in one's food[41] then one removes it together with some of the food etc, as doing so is questionable of containing a sin offering liability and a prohibition of Sekilah G-d forbid.[42] [Accordingly, it is forbidden to remove the waste even together with some of the food, and the Borer prohibition applies even in such a case.[43] Practically, we rule like the Siddur.[44]]

Summary:
It is forbidden to separate the bad even when one takes with it some of the good.

Q&A
Practically, what is one to do if a fly or other waste fell into one's food?
If a fly or hair or any other waste or unwanted food fell into one's soup, tea, coffee, drink, plate of food, it does not help to remove the fly/waste together with the food. By a plate of food, one is to eat around the area of waste, and leave the waste positioned in its place. In a drink/soup one may pour out the fly together with some of the soup.

If one will separate only some of the bad together with good and will thus still leave some of the bad with the mixture do the Borer regulations still apply?[45]
This is Rabbinically forbidden to be done in all cases that separating would involve a Chatas obligation.[46]

---

[37] Admur 319:24; Taz 319:13 and 506:3; Beir Heiytiv 319:19; Ben Ish Chaiy Beshalach 12; Chayeh Adam 16:2; M"B 319:61; Kaf Hachaim 319:42; Even Yisarel 9:25
[38] The reason: Seemingly, the reason is because when one removes the bad together with the good, it is not recognizable that one has selected bad from good, and it is thus permitted.
[39] However from the ruling of Peri Megadim 319 M"Z 13 [brought in Q&A] it implies that this Heter to remove the bad with the good only applies in certain scenarios.
[40] Admur in Siddur; Kaf Hachaim ibid concludes it is best to be stringent like Admur in Siddur; Chazon Ish 53 questions ruling of Taz ibid; See Piskeiy Teshuvos 319:44
[41] Such as a fly or fat over gravy, one may not remove the fat or fly together with some gravy. [ibid]
[42] The reason: The reason that Admur retracted his ruling from the SH"A is because since ones main intent is to remove the inedible and the good that is removed is only in order to allow him to remove the fly, therefore the good is nullified to the bad and it is considered that he is removing solely the bad from the good. [Ketzos Hashulchan 125 footnote 17; See P"M 319 A"A 15; Chazon Ish 53]
[43] So learns Ketzos Hashulchan ibid; See P"M 319 A"A 15
[44] Shaar Hakolel 1:1; Likkutei Sichos 11 p. 246; Introduction of the Rebbe to the Shulchan Aruch Harav; See Divrei Nechmia 21; Kaf Hachaim and Piskeiy Teshuvos ibid conclude it is best to be stringent
The reason: Whenever there is a difference in ruling between the Siddur and the Shulchan Aruch one is to follow the rulings of the Siddur. The reason for this is because the Siddur was written later than the Shulchan Aruch and hence represents the final ruling of Admur in the given subject. [ibid]
[45] Shabbos Kehalacha Vol. 2 p. 93
[46] Peri Megadim 319 M"Z 13; Aruch Hashulchan 319

Compilation-How to remove dirt [i.e. dust, hair lash, insect] from your food on Shabbos:

Background: It is Biblically forbidden to separate waste from the food on Shabbos.[47] This prohibition is called Borer. This prohibition applies even if the waste is the minority of the food.[48] Any item which one does not desire to eat right away and is of a different substance than the remaining food is defined as waste in this regard.[49] Accordingly, the question is asked as to how one is to separate dirt from one's food on Shabbos without transgressing the Borer prohibition.

The law: It is Biblically forbidden to remove the dirt from the food, as explained above.[50] However, some Poskim[51] rule that this only applies if one removes the dirt by itself, without removing any of the food together with it. However, if one removes the waste together with some of the food, such as [using a spoon to] remove a fly from a cup together with some of the liquid, then it is permitted to be done.[52] However, other Poskim[53] negate this allowance and rule that it is forbidden to remove the waste even together with some of the food, and the Borer prohibition applies even in such a case. Practically, although many are accustomed to being lenient[54], one is to be stringent like the latter opinion[55], and so is the ruling followed by Chabad Chassidim.[56] Accordingly, the only remaining option for removing the dirt from one's food on Shabbos is to eat around the area of waste, and leave the waste positioned in its place. Once one has concluded eating around the waste, and it is no longer considered mixed with other foods, he may wipe it entirely off the plate. If the dirt is floating in a liquid, such as a drink or soup then another available option is to blow the waste to the side of the cup and then pour out the dirt together with some of the liquid.[57]

---

[47] Admur 319:1; Michaber 319:4

The reason: The reason for why removing the waste is forbidden is because the removing of the waste [from the food] is not [considered done in] the normal framework of eating [which is permitted to be done as will be explained below] but is rather [considered] preparing the food so it be fit to eat which is a complete [Biblically prohibited] act. [Admur ibid]

[48] Admur ibid; Rama 319:4; Beis Yosef 319 based on Rambam

Other opinions: This is opposed to the ruling of the Tur 319 which holds that in such a case one is allowed to remove the waste rather than the food as doing so is the way of eating. Admur and others however limit this ruling only to Yom Tov and not on Shabbos. [See Shabbos Kihalacha Vol. 2 p. 141]

Opinion of Michaber: The Michaber agrees with the ruling of the Rama ibid, as is implied from the fact that he did not mention any allowance in his rulings regarding majority food. [Biur Halacha 319:1 "Haborer"]

[49] Admur 319:5; Michaber 319:3

[50] Admur 319:24 *"If a fly fell into a cup one may not remove only the fly from the cup being that doing so is equivalent to separating waste from food which is forbidden to be done even in order to eat right away."*; Taz 319:13; All Poskim in next footnote

[51] Admur 319:24 [unlike his ruling in the Siddur]; Taz 319:13 and 506:3; Beir Heiytiv 319:19; Ben Ish Chaiy Beshalach 12; Chayeh Adam 16:2; M"B 319:61; Kaf Hachaim 319:42; Even Yisrael 9:25

[52] The reason: Being that then it does not appear like one is separating at all. [Admur ibid] Seemingly, the reason is because when one removes the bad together with the good, it is not recognizable that one has selected bad from good, and it is thus permitted.

[53] Admur in Siddur [unlike his ruling in 319:24] *"One may not rely on the customary permission granted that if there is waste in ones food then one removes it together with some of the food etc, as doing so is questionable of containing a sin offering liability and a prohibition of Sekilah G-d forbid."*; Peri Megadim 319 M"Z 13 implies that this Heter to remove the bad with the good only applies in certain scenarios, as explained below; Kaf Hachaim ibid concludes it is best to be stringent like Admur in Siddur; Chazon Ish 53 questions ruling of Taz ibid; See Piskeiy Teshuvos 319:44

Opinion of Peri Megadim: Peri Megadim 319 M"Z 13 implies that only if one separates only some of the bad together with good, and will thus still leave some of the bad with the mixture, is one not liable for Borer, however if one separates the entire bad, then he is liable for Borer even if he removes some of the good. Furthermore, he implies that even if one leaves some of the bad with the good, and removes the bad with some of the good, it is only permitted in a case that if one were to remove the entire bad from the good he would not be Biblically liable, otherwise, it remains Rabbinically forbidden."

[54] As testified by Admur in Siddur ibid

[55] As concludes Kaf Hachaim ibid

[56] Shaar Hakolel 1:1; Likkutei Sichos 11 p. 246; Introduction of the Rebbe to the Shulchan Aruch Harav; See Divrei Nechmia 21; Kaf Hachaim and Piskeiy Teshuvos ibid conclude it is best to be stringent

The reason: Whenever there is a difference in ruling between the Siddur and the Shulchan Aruch one is to follow the rulings of the Siddur. The reason for this is because the Siddur was written later than the Shulchan Aruch and hence represents the final ruling of Admur in the given subject. [ibid]

[57] Admur in Siddur ibid *"One may not rely on the customary permission granted that if a fly or other waste falls into ones cup or plate then one removes it together with a spoon and takes out with it some liquid etc, as doing so is questionable of containing a sin offering liability and a prohibition of Sekilah G-d forbid.* **Thus, the only solution that remains is to pour out from the cup until the waste comes out from it.** *One may not blow on [the waste] with his mouth until it is blown out, although he may blow it to bring it nearer to the wall of the cup and then tilt it and pour from it until the waste comes out."*

The reason that tilting it out is allowed: As since the removal of the waste is being done through him holding the cup of liquid in his hand and tilting it with his hand this is considered separating food from waste which is permitted to be done in order to drink it immediately. [Admur in

Summary:
If dirt fell into one's food, the only option for removing the dirt from one's food on Shabbos is to eat around the area of dirt, and leave the dirt positioned in its place. Once one has concluded eating around the dirt, and it is no longer considered mixed with other foods, he may wipe it entirely off the plate. If the dirt is floating in a liquid, such as a drink or soup then another available option is to blow the waste to the side of the cup and then pour out the dirt together with some of the liquid.

C. May one blow away waste from amongst food?

- *The Siddur:*
  One may not blow on [the waste] with his mouth until it is blown out of the food.[58] **[See Q&A]**

Q&A

May one blow the nut shells and chaff away from a grouping of opened nuts, as is common with opened peanuts which have their chaff [the brown thin shelling] mixed with them?[59]

This is forbidden being that blowing away the bad is considered like separating it with one's hands.

D. May one soak food with its waste in water in order to separate and remove the waste:[60]

Food and waste which are mixed [together] is forbidden to be placed into water in order for the waste to sink to the bottom, as is the case if the waste is earth, or [so the waste] float to the top as is the case [if the waste] is straw. Similarly, *Karshinin*[61] may not be soaked in water in order so their waste float to the top, and as well one may not rub it with his hands [while it is in the water[62]] so the waste float up as doing so is similar to [the] separating [prohibition].[63] **[See Q&A]**

However, one may place them in a sieve even though the waste [might[64]] fall through the holes of the sieve and it is thus found that [the waste] becomes separated on its own. [One may not however place the *Karshinin* in the sieve with specific intent that it possibly be filtered from its waste.[65]]

Rinsing off waste from foods: **See Q&A**

Siddur ibid]

[58] Doing so is prohibited due to the Melacha of Zoreh [winnowing] and not Borer.

[59] Shabbos Kehalacha Vol. 2 p. 98

[60] Admur 319:11; Michaber 319:8

[61] Possible this refers to the horse been which is similar to the broad been and is used for horse fodder.

[62] So is evident from the wording of Admur "to cause to float" hence implying the Karshinin are currently in the water. If however they are taken out of the water, then rubbing the waste off is forbidden due to the Mifareik prohibition and not due to Borer. In any event it can be derived from here that merely rinsing a food [in contrast to soaking] is not forbidden due to Borer when done with intent to eat right away, while soaking it is forbidden due to Borer. Hence by foods which the Mifareik prohibition is not applicable, one may rinse off their waste with intent to eat the food right away. The reason for the differentiation is because soaking a food is considered *Derech Borer* while rinsing it is considered *Derech Achila*. See Q&A! [Ketzos Hashulchan 146 p. 109; Igleiy Tal Borer 16; Shabbos Kehalacha 2 p. 132]

[63] The reason: Some hold that this is not considered the way of eating and is thus forbidden. Others hold that it is like separating the waste from the good. [P"M 319 M"Z 5] Others hold it is a decree due to that one may come to do so with a vessel, and therefore the word similar was used. [Ketzos Hashulchan 146 footnote 50-10]

Why the word "similar": See P"M 319 M"Z 5 that perhaps is a Shinui and not Biblical; Biur Halacha 319 "Dehaveh Lei Keborer" that it is Biblical and so is the wording in Rashi "Borer"

[64] Based on 324:1 where Admur writes regarding placing straw in a sieve that it is allowed although "that at times the food falls, as one has no intent to do so and it is not an inevitable occurrence." So concludes the Ketzos Hashulchan 131 footnote 17, and Shabbos Kihalacha Vol 2 page 356. Thus if it is for certain that the waste will fall through, then it is forbidden. This cannot be proven from Halacha 21 where Admur rules that placing mustard with barn in the strainer is forbidden being that there it is discussing having the bran [waste] remain above and the mustard fall out, which contains a Meraked prohibition, while here it refers to having the waste fall out on its own, which does not contain a Miraked prohibition as will explained in the introduction to the next section.

[65] Admur 324:1 regarding straw. As when one intends to do a certain Melacha, even if it is not inevitable, it is forbidden to be done.

Summary: Separating waste from food through soaking the mixture in water:[66]
Is forbidden to be done due to the separating prohibition [even when done to eat right away].

Q&A on soaking foods in water:
May one soak foods in order to remove waste that majority of people are not particular to wash off?[67]
If the person himself is not always particular about this then he may wash it off in all cases, as the waste is not considered waste.[68]

If the food was already within the water from before Shabbos may one rub the waste off on Shabbos?[69]
No.[70] However see next Q&A!

May one soak a fruit or vegetable in order to remove the pesticide, bugs, or dirt that is stuck on the fruit or vegetable?[71]
If it is not possible to remove the dirt through simply rinsing the fruit/vegetable,[72] then one may pour water over it numerous times until it is clean. If this too does not suffice, then one may soak the fruit or vegetable in water. If this too does not suffice one may even scrub them in the water.[73] This allowance especially applies to washing off pesticide which is not even visible. It is however forbidden to soak a group of fruits or vegetables together with their waste as will be explained next. In all cases it is forbidden to wash the fruit or vegetable for later use.

May one use a Shabbos sponge to scrub off the dirt from a fruit?
This matter requires further analysis.

May one soak a basket of small fruits such as blueberries or grapes in water?[74]
If the grapes or blueberries contain stems which will float to the top, doing so is forbidden.[75] If, however, they are clean of stems and one merely desires to wash off the dirt stuck onto the fruits, then doing so is allowed for right away use if it is not possible to rinse them by pouring water over them.

May one soak lettuce in water?
If it is not possible to clean it of the waste through rinsing, then it is permitted to soak it in water for right away use. It is forbidden to add soap to the water, as will be explained below.

---

[66] Admur 319:11
[67] Shabbos Kehalacha Vol. 2 p. 131; Ketzos Hashulchan 146 footnote 50-10
[68] This is similar to the law by small pieces of bark in one's wine which is considered nullified to the wine if one is not particular against drinking it, as will be explained in chapter 3 in the laws of filtering. [Ketzos Hashulchan 146 p. 116] This does not contradict the notion that Borer applies even by two edible foods of different species, as there one cannot say that one species is nullified to another. However here, waste which people pay no attention to is nullified to the food. [Rav SZ"A in SSH"K 3 footnote 156]
[69] Shabbos Kehalacha Vol. 2 p. 132
[70] As rules Admur above regarding the Karshinin "*and as well one may not rub it with his hands so the waste float up*". See footnote there!
[71] Ketzos Hashulchan 146 footnote 50-10; Shabbos Kihalacha Vol. 2 p. 134
[72] As is the case by all small fruits such as grapes and berries. However if the grapes have stems which will float up, then this is forbidden. See next Q&A!
[73] So rules Ketzos Hashulchan 146 footnote 50-10 as he explains that the above prohibition in truth only applies to the case of Karshinim [and other mixtures of the like] being that if one were to filter it with a sieve it would carry a Biblical prohibition being that it is common to do so, as opposed to the removal of dirt from fruits and the like. This is proven form the fact that in 318 it ruled without dispute that one may soak salted fish in water and it does not contain an issue of Borer.
[74] Ketzos Hashulchan 146 p. 117
[75] As this is directly similar to the prohibition written above by Admur.

Q&A on Washing/Rinsing off waste from food:
May one wash off waste from foods that majority of people are not particular to wash off?[76]
If the person himself is not always particular about this then one may wash it off in all cases, as the waste is not considered waste.

May one rinse away the waste from a mixture of food and waste? [77]
This has the same laws as soaking them which is forbidden.

May one wash off the pesticide, bugs, or dirt which is stuck on a fruit or vegetable?[78]
One may do so even initially in order to eat right away, as it is considered like peeling off the peel of a food which is allowed to be done in close proximately to the meal.[79] To note however that it is forbidden to wash the bugs off with salt water or vinegar and other liquids which kill the insects, due to the killing prohibition.[80]

May one use soap and the like to wash foods:[81]
Foods which majority of people eat without rinsing then if the person himself is also not always particular to wash this food, it may be washed with soap according to all. However, if one is particular to wash it with soap then it is disputed in the Poskim as to whether it is allowed[82]. Thus, one should not do so unless there is great need for it.

May one rinse fruits inside of a strainer?
See Halacha 4 Q&A

May one pour fruits that are within water into a strainer in order to strain the water?
See Halacha 4 Q&A

General Q&A
May one separate the bad from the good using a Shinui/irregularity?[83]
It is forbidden to separate the bad from the good even through using an irregularity, such as through using ones left hand. According to some opinions[84] doing so with one's left hand involves a Biblical transgression, while according to others[85] it is only a Rabbinical transgression, as is the general rule of doing Melacha with a Shinuiy that it is only Rabbinical.

If one will not separate all the bad from the good or vice versa, and thus will still be left with a mixture of some bad and good do the Borer regulations still apply?[86]
This is Rabbinically forbidden to be done in all cases that separating would involve a Chatas obligation.[87]

---

[76] Shabbos Kehalacha Vol. 2 p. 131
[77] Shabbos Kehalacha Vol. 2 p. 134
[78] Shabbos Kehalacha Vol. 2 p. 134-136
[79] So rules Ketzos Hashulchan 125 footnote 16; 146 p. 116
[80] Shabbos Kehalacha Vol. 2 p. 199
[81] Shabbos Kehalacha Vol. 2 p. 136
[82] The Ketzos Hashulchan [146 footnote 50] debates whether this is allowed and concludes that despite the reasons to allow it he refrains from doing so being that it appears like a belittling of Shabbos and a mundane act. On the other hand the Chazon Ish clearly rules that it is allowed, and so seems to be the opinion of Rav SZ"A. In SSH"K [note 54] they rule that it is allowed.
[83] Shabbos Kehalacha Vol. 2 p. 91. Minchas Yitzchak 5:38
[84] Chayeh Adam brought in M"B 340:22 [towards end] "Every Melacha that one uses his left hand he is Biblically liable with exception to the Melacha of writing."
[85] Shevisas Hashabbos- Borer.
[86] Shabbos Kehalacha Vol. 2 p. 93
[87] Peri Megadim M"Z 13, Aruch Hashulchan

What is the law if one accidently did Borer on Shabbos, may the food still be eaten?[88]

It is permitted to be eaten on Shabbos if done accidently or without knowledge of the prohibition.[89] However there are opinions[90] that are stringent to prohibit the food.

If one accidently [without intent] removed the waste from the mixture does he need to replace it back into the mixture?[91]

Examples:
1. One accidentally grabbed a rotten fruit from amongst a pile of fruits.
2. One accidentally removed an onion from his salad instead of a tomato.
3. One has a pile of blackberries and raspberries and he wants to eat the raspberry and accidently removed a blackberry.

The Law: In a case that the fruit which was taken out is rotten [Example 1] then one does not need to replace the fruit back into the pile. However, in a case that the food is fully edible and one simply accidently removed the wrong species of food [Example 2-3], then he must replace the food into the mixture as otherwise this appears like Borer.[92] One should not eat the food rather than placing it back. However, there are Poskim[93] that require one to return the Pesoles in all cases.

Intentionally removed the Pesoles: In all cases that one intended to remove the Pesoles or unwanted food, according to all he is not required to return it as the act of prohibited Borer has already been performed and complete.

May one remove waste from waste, such as to remove peels of Kedushas Shevias away from other waste?[94]

One may only remove waste from waste if he has no intent in using either of the items for any purpose, neither now or later on. Thus, one may remove Kedushas Sheviis peels from amongst regular peels in order to place the regular ones in the garbage and the Kedushas Shevias in a separate bag for it to rot. However, if one intends to use one of the items for a purpose then the full Borer restrictions apply.

May one separate recyclable items on Shabbos?[95]

It is permitted to do so.

May one separate bottles with a return policy from other bottles that are to be discarded?

No.

May one separate for the purpose of verifying whether or not he has a certain item or not?[96]

For example: One desires to eat tomatoes tomorrow by his meal, may he check through his vegetable drawer, removing vegetables, to see if there are tomatoes on the bottom.

Although there are certain Poskim[97] which allow this if finding the object will cause him current

---

[88] Biur Halacha 319:1 "Haborer" in name of Gr"a; Ketzos Hashulchan 129 footnote 5; Teshuvos Vehanhagos 2:185

[89] The reason: As although in general we rule that by all Biblical prohibitions done by mistake it is forbidden for all until after Shabbos, nevertheless here being that Borer is so common to be done to food if this were true then it should have been mentioned. As well as that one's actions is not his source of benefit being that he could have separated it in a permitted way. As well as that here there is no reason to decree Atu Meizid being that one can anyways do so in a permitted way. [Poskim ibid]

[90] P"M 319 brought in Biur Halacha ibid

[91] Shabbos Kehalacha Vol. 2 p. 97, and 194; SSH"K 3 footnote 11 in name of Rav SZ"a

[92] The reason: Perhaps the reason is because by Pesoles everyone sees that he did an Issur already and returning the Pesoles will not change anything. However, by food it will only be recognizable to others that he did Borer if he throws it out and hence he is to return it.

[93] Shevisas Hashabbos Borer 3 footnote 10; See Ketzos Hashulchan 125 footnote 47

[94] Shabbos Kehalacha Vol. 2 p. 138; P"M 319 M"Z 12; Biur Halacha 319:3 "Hayu Lefanav"

[95] Shabbos Kehalacha Vol. 2 p. 138

[96] Shabbos Kehalacha Vol. 2 p. 168

[97] Shulchan Shlomo

satisfaction, nevertheless one should not practically rely on this opinion.

A Chassidic perspective

<u>The meaning behind Borer</u>: Every food that we eat contains in it Divine sparks of G-dliness of which is explained in the Kabalistic and Chassidic teachings to have fallen within the foods during the destruction of the supernal world of Tohu. Through eating foods and then serving G-d with the strength that one benefited from those foods one elevates those Divine sparks back to their source in G-dliness. This service of elevation however only applies during the weekdays. On Shabbos all physicality is elevated to its source and is thus not of need of refinement. This is why Borer is forbidden on Shabbos.

---

2. *Cases which contain the Borer prohibition:*

A. Making cheese on Shabbos:[98]

Making the curd:[99] One who curds [milk], in which he takes milk and places a stomach [or other enzyme] into it in order to curd[100] it, is liable for separating because he has separated the curd from the milk.

Placing the curd into a strainer: Similarly, if one places the curd into an elastic vessel[101] and the whey drips from inside it then this is an offshoot of separating food from waste through using a sieve and sifter and one is thus liable.

The reason: Now, although the curd and the milk are both a single species of food and there is [thus] no waste [here] at all, nevertheless since they are liquid substances which mix well which he is [now] separating, therefore this contains the separating [prohibition] just like one who is separating food from waste.

Making hard cheese:[102] If one solidified [curd] and turned it into cheese he is liable for building.

The reason for this is:[103] because anyone who gathers parts [of an item] to each other and bonds them together until they become a single substance has [transgressed] an offshoot of [the] building [prohibition].

Q&A

May one place lemon into milk on Shabbos to turn it into cheese?[104]
No.

May one place milk in a hot area on Shabbos in order to turn it into cheese?[105]
No.

---

[98] Admur 319:25; Michaber 319:17

[99] Admur ibid; M"A 39:18; M"B 319:62

[100] Cheese is made by separating the milk into solid curds and liquid whey. Usually this is done by acidifying (souring) the milk and adding rennet. The acidification can be accomplished directly by the addition of an acid like vinegar These starter bacteria convert milk sugars into lactic acid. Most cheeses are made with starter bacteria from the *Lactococci*, *Lactobacilli*, or *Streptococci* families.

[101] This refers to a vessel made of material that can be stretched out do to having tiny holes in it, and thus allows the milk to drip out. Similar to a plastic bag.

[102] Admur 319:26; M"A 319:18; M"B 319:63; Shabbos 95b; Vetzaruch Iyun if making Tofu or Halva into a block also transgresses the Boneh prohibition

[103] Admur 319:26

[104] Shabbos Kehalacha Vol. 2 p. 176

[105] M"B 319:60; Shabbos Kehalacha Vol. 2 p. 176

B. Removing seeds and nuts from honey:[106]
One may place sesame and nuts into honey, although he may not [press them[107] and thus] separate them [from the honey] with his hands [as doing so is considered separating.[108] Accordingly, it may be done for immediate use.[109] Alternatively, doing so is considered Kneading and is forbidden to be done even for right away use.[110] However, according to all to simply remove a seed or nut from the honey would be permitted for right away use.]

C. Catalyzing beverages on Shabbos:[111]
It is forbidden to place dregs into beverages in order to catalyze it even though [the liquid] is already fit to be drunk on Shabbos being that through doing so one causes the dregs of the liquid itself to sink to the bottom of the vessel and it is an offshoot of separating similar to one who curds milk.

3. The Rabbinical prohibition of Separating:[112]
Using a Knon and plate: If one separated the food from the waste with a *Knon*[113] or a plate[114] then he is Biblically exempt [from liability] although it is Rabbinically forbidden to be done due to a decree [that one may come to use] a sieve and sifter. [The same applies for any irregular Borer utensil, that it is only Rabbinically forbidden to be used, while a regular Borer utensil is Biblically forbidden.]
Separating an egg yolk from its white: See Halacha 6

Q&A

May one use a garlic tube peeler?
No.

---

4. The permitted method of separating:[115]
Separating the food from the waste with ones hands to eat immediately: It is permitted to separate food, as opposed to the waste, with ones hands in order to eat right away. [Regarding the definition of right away, see the next Halacha. Regarding separating food from other foods- see Halacha 6.]
The reason that this is allowed is: because to remove food from amongst waste in order to eat right away is not at all similar to any [forbidden form of] work being that doing so is the normal form of eating, as it is impossible to eat the entire mixture, [eating] the food together with the waste, and the Torah only prohibited doing so [separating food from waste while eating when] using its designated vessel [to separate it] which is a sieve and sifter. [See Q&A]

---

[106] Admur 319:27; Michaber 319:17; 340:11
[107] Mishneh Berurah on 319:66; 340:39; Literally "Michabeitz"
[108] Mishneh Berurah on 340:39
[109] M"B 319:64
[110] M"B ibid based on M"A from Tosefta
[111] Admur 319:29; M"A 319:28
[112] Admur 319:1
[113] This refers to a wooden tube which is wide on top and narrow on bottom. One places the legumes in from the wide part and then shakes off its peels and the legumes fallout from the narrow bottom while the peels remain inside. Nevertheless, this item is only Rabbinically forbidden as it is not the commonly used item for Borer, and is hence considered a Shinuiy, which makes the Melacha only Rabbinical. [Rashi in Shabbos 74a; M"B 319:2] Vetzaruch Iyun as to why a Knon is only Rabbinical, is it because it is considered 1) a shinuiy, or 2) is not a manufacturers choice vessel, or 3) it has other usages and is not designated for separating per say.
[114] Mishneh Berurah 2
[115] Admur 319:1

Summary: The permitted method of separating
It is permitted to separate if <u>all</u> the following three conditions are fulfilled:
1. One removes the good from the bad
2. One removes it to eat right away.
3. One removes it using his hand.

Q&A on the definition of what is considered waste/unwanted
May one for whom a certain food is considered inedible separate it for one for whom that food is considered edible, such as to separate the unwanted onions of a salad in order to give them to an onion lover?[116]
Yes, so long as he is doing so for that person to eat right away.

May one separate inedible items from food if his intent is to use that item for a certain purpose, such as to remove the bone of a fish in order to use as a toothpick, or to remove a bone to give to a pet dog to eat?[117]
This is allowed to be done for right away use being that since he desires to use it, it therefore is not considered waste.

May one remove the waste/food that he does not want with intent to eat some of it or use it, in order to retroactively allow the separating?[118]
No. One may only separate that which he truly desires, and it does not help to eat from it if he truly desires to separate it from that which he truly wants to eat.

If one does not want to remove the wanted food from a certain vessel, such as that he desires to serve the food in this vessel, how then is he to separate the wanted from the unwanted?[119]
He is to pour the entire dish into another vessel and then remove the wanted food into the original vessel in order to eat right away.

Regarding separating bad with good and removing waste from waste, See above Halacha 1C and General Q&A.
Q&A on what is considered separating "using ones hands"
May one use his hand to strain food for right away use?[120]
No, as this is not considered the way of eating, and it is thus equivalent to using a strainer. [See Chapter 3 Halacha 1 Q&A]

May one separate the food using a fork or spoon and the like?[121]
<u>To remove a food from amongst other solids</u>: Yes. Cutlery may be used to remove a food from a mixture on Shabbos in order to use right away.[122] Any item which is not designated for separating is

---

[116] Shabbos Kehalacha Vol. 2 p. 128; SSH"K 3 footnote 13
[117] Shabbos Kehalacha Vol. 2 p. 128 and 130
[118] Shabbos Kehalacha Vol. 2 p. 129; See Meor Hashabbos 3:40-1; Mishmeres Hashabbos 319:14-5
[119] Shabbos Kehalacha Vol. 2 p. 130
[120] Shabbos Kehalacha Vol. 2 p. 381
[121] Shabbos Kehalacha Vol. 2 p. 148-150 and p. 236
[122] Ketzos Hashulchan 125 footnote 24; Chayeh Adam in Nishmas Adam 82:2
So, rules Ketzos Hashulchan 125 footnote 24 based on an inference from the Alter Rebbe in the Shulchan Aruch [However see Ketzos Hashulchan 129 footnote 3 where he differentiates between a dry food of which it is usual to separate it with one's hands and thus a spoon may not be used, and between a wet food which is usually separated with a utensil so one does not get dirty.]
So rules also: Minchas Yitzchak 1:76, Igros Moshe, Chazon Ish and other Poskim.
<u>Opinion of M"B</u>: In 319:62 the M"B rules a spoon may not be used to gather the fat above milk even if one plans to eat it immediately. However, in 319:66 he contradicts himself and rules a spoon may be used. The Chazon Ish answers this by saying the case of cream on top of milk was an

considered like one's hand and is allowed to be used even in a scenario which using a fork or spoon is unusual and is thus recognizably done for the separating purpose.[123] Thus although it is not usual to eat pieces of chicken or meat with a spoon, nevertheless one may separate them using a spoon with intent to eat them right away.

<u>Using the fork to remove a food from amongst liquids:</u>[124] If one's intent in removing the solid is to separate it from the liquid then its laws are equivalent to those of a strainer spoon- See Q&A below. **Using a spoon to remove a food from amongst liquids- See next Question.**

May one separate a solid from a liquid through lifting the solid with a spoon and tilting it against the wall of the pot, thereby draining the liquid and keeping leverage of the solid?[125]
There are Poskim which prohibit this from being done due to doubt that this may be considered like separating with a vessel, as the spoon together with the walls of the pot may be considered a vessel.

May one separate through tilting a cup or can and spilling out the wanted or unwanted?
Doing so does not pose a problem of separating with a vessel as it is like one is separating with one's hand. Nevertheless, due to the Borer restrictions this is only allowed in specific scenarios as will be explained in Halacha 7, see there at length.

May one use a nutcracker to crack nuts, thus separating them from their shell?[126]
This is allowed in scenarios that the breaking of the shells do not separate the food completely from the shells, but rather just breaks them thus giving one the ability to separate the fruit. However, in cases that the actual fruit falls out from the shells and is thus fully separated, it is not allowed.

Regarding separating through blowing away the waste, soaking it, rinsing it, See above Halacha 1.

Q&A on separating through using a strainer

Figure 1: Straining bowl

Figure 2: Straining utensil

---

exception being that the spoon helps for the actual separation, while in 66 it is allowed as it is used simply so one does not dirty himself. So concludes also Minchas Yitzchak ibid. See Shabbos Kehalacha P. 148-149
[123] However, see previous footnote regarding ruling of Ketzos Hashulchan.
[124] Shabbos Kehalacha Vol. 2 p. 359
[125] Shabbos Kehalacha Vol. 2 p. 359; SSH"K 3 footnote 159 in name of Rav SZ"A; Shulchan Shlomo footnote 48
[126] Shabbos Kehalacha Vol. 2 p. 151

May one use a strainer spoon [a spoon with small holes made to strain the liquid of the food removed] on Shabbos to remove a food which is within liquid?[127]

No. Such a vessel is considered designated for separation and is thus forbidden to be used to separate any food from liquid if the solid and liquid are designated as mixed. [See Introduction above and Q&A there for the definition of mixed with regards to soup and the like.]

May one use a strainer spoon if no other spoon is available? One is to be stringent to not use a strainer spoon [in cases designated as mixed] even if no other spoon is available and one simply desires to use it due to lack of choice and not in order to separate.[128] However, there are Poskim[129] that are lenient in this matter if in truth one does not desire to separate between the food and gravy.

If a pot contains a strainer in its upper part into which the solids are placed into and it then cooks in the liquid, may one remove this strainer with solids from amongst the liquid on Shabbos?[130]

This has the same laws and limitations as does using a strainer spoon, see above.

May one pour fruits that are within water into a strainer in order to strain the water?[131]

Those fruits which are small and are thus considered mixed with the water, such as blueberries and the like, may not be poured into a strainer. However, large fruits, such as apples and the like, may be poured into a strainer being that they are too big to be considered mixed with the water and thus do not contain the separating restrictions.

May one pour from a tea pot that has a strainer on its tip to prevent the leaves from falling in the cup?

See Halacha 7 Q&A there.

List of practical Q&A cases in which it is allowed to remove the waste from the food

May one remove a tea bag from one's cup of tea or does this pose a separating prohibition?[132]

Yes.[133] However, there are some Poskim[134] which leave this matter in question.

How is one to remove it? According, to some Poskim[135] one may only remove the tea bag with a spoon being that otherwise tea will drip out of the bag into the cup, which may pose a filtering prohibition, as one has in effect filtered liquid from the tea bag. According to other Poskim[136], however, so long as one does not intend to have the bag drip tea into the cup there is no problem in removing it with one's hands even though that it will in truth drip tea into the cup.

Shaking the tea bag within the tea:[137] It is permitted to lift the tea bag up and down within the tea in order to extract better taste from the tea bag. *See Chapter 3 Halacha 1 in Q&A that it is a dispute in Poskim.*

Regarding if one may squeeze a tea bag while in the cup and other laws relating to separation with regards to tea, see chapter 3 Halacha 1 and Q&A there. Regarding if one may pour the liquid out from the cup, leaving the tea bag inside- see Halacha 7 Q&A there.

---

[127] Shabbos Kehalacha Vol. 2 p. 151; p. 355-359; Shevet Hlaevi 8:58
[128] Shabbos Kehalacha 14:20
[129] Rav SZ"A brought in Shulchan Shlomo 319:20
[130] Shabbos Kehalacha Vol. 2 p. 357
[131] Shabbos Kehalacha Vol. 2 p. 358
[132] Shabbos Kehalacha Vol. 2 p. 371
[133] This is allowed being that a large item is not considered mixed together with a liquid that it is in, as explained in the introduction Q&A.
[134] Minchas Yitzchak 4:99-2
[135] Minchas Yitzchak ibid; Sheivet Halevy 8:58; SSH"K 3 footnote 171 in name of Rav SZ"A
[136] Shabbos Kehalacha ibid based on SSH"K 3 footnote 125
[137] See Shabbos Kehalacha 2 p. 370

May one remove a bag of rice from ones Chulent?[138]
Yes.[139] However, according to some Poskim[140] one should only remove it with a spoon in order to prevent any of the gravy that is absorbed in the bag from dripping back into the chulent and thus posing a straining prohibition. Nevertheless, those which are lenient in this have upon whom to rely.[141]

May one remove bones from fish, or must he remove the fish from the bones?[142]
Small bones: It is permitted for one to remove the small bones that are within fish being that doing so is the form of eating.[143] However, one should only do so immediately prior to placing the piece of fish in his mouth as opposed to preparing it prior to the meal [despite that this is still defined as "right away"].[144]
Large bones: Are forbidden to be removed from the fish. Rather one must remove the fish from the bone, such as by holding on to the bone and then sliding off the fish.[145]
Bones that have already been removed from the fish: Are forbidden to be removed from amongst the fish even if they are small, as this is no longer the normal way of eating.

May one remove bones from meat, or must he remove the meat from the bones?[146]
One may not remove the bones from the meat and may only remove the meat from the bones directly prior to the meal.[147] This applies as well even if the bones contain marrow as nevertheless the bone and the meat are considered two different foods. However, if one desires to suck the marrow as well as eat the meat then obviously one may remove the bone from the meat. [However, if one does not desire to eat the meat right away but rather only the marrow then there are Poskim[148] which write that one may not remove the bone from the meat, or the meat from the bone. Nevertheless, in a time of need there is no need to be stringent in this.]

May one remove skin from chicken/meat/fish?[149]
One may do so immediately prior to the meal.[150]

May one pluck a feather from his piece of chicken?[151]
This matter is disputed amongst Poskim.[152] The dispute applies even if one intends to eat the chicken

---

[138] Shabbos Kehalacha Vol. 2 p. 382
[139] This is allowed being that a large item is not considered mixed together with a liquid that it is in, as explained in the introduction Q&A. [Shabbos Kehalacha 12:19] [Vetzaruch Iyun Gadol on this ruling as there are other foods in the Chulent from which he is doing Borer to?]
[140] See Minchas Yitzchak ibid; Sheivet Halevy 8:58; SSH"K 3 footnote 171 in name of Rav SZ"A
[141] This case is even more lenient then the removing of tea from ones cup as here one is anyway interested in eating the rice with the chulent and thus is not benefiting at all from the dripping of the gravy. This is opposed to the case of tea in which one has no interest in the leaves but does in the liquid that is absorbed in it.
[142] Shabbos Kehalacha Vol. 2 p. 227
[143] So rules the Tzemach Tzedek in his Piskeiy Dinim on this chapter, and so concludes the Ketzos Hashulchan [125:16] as the final ruling and so rule other Poskim.
Other Poskim: There are opinions which rule stringently in a case one is able to remove the bones in his mouth. Nevertheless, according to all it is permitted to separate the bones from within the fish for the need of children. [Igros Moshe 4:74; Minchas Yitzchak 1:75; Shabbos Kehalacha Vol. 2 p. 227]
[144] So rules Ketzos Hashulchan 125 footnote 44, and other Poskim.
[145] So rules Mamar Murdechaiy, Biur Halacha and so implies the Ketzos Hashulchan
[146] Shabbos Kihalacha Vol. 2 p. 227; See Biur Halacha 319:4 "Metoch"; Piskeiy Teshuvos 319:8; Chazon Ish 54:3
[147] As meat bones are large and it is thus not the normal way of eating to remove the bones from the meat as is the case by the small bones which are within fish.
[148] Rav SZ"A SSH"K 3 footnote 13
[149] Shabbos Kehalacha Vol. 2 p. 229
[150] Although in SSH"K [3:30] [as well as Igros Moshe Orach Chayim 4 chapter 74 Borer 8] they rule that one may remove it even not for right away use being that both the chicken and skin are viewed as the same species of foods being that majority of people do eat the skin, nevertheless one should be stringent in this being that a) today many people do not eat the skin and b) even if the case were that majority of people eat it nevertheless there are people which are stringent.
[151] Shabbos Kihalacha Vol. 2 p. 229

right away after removing the feathers, due to a question of whether this involves the "Shearing" prohibition. Practically one should initially avoid removing feathers from chicken[153], [although those that do so have upon whom to rely if they eat the chicken right away[154]]. This prohibition certainly applies if one desires to remove the feathers in order to make the chicken more presentable to the guests in which case one must take great care not to remove those feathers.

For later use: According to all it is forbidden to remove the feathers for later use due to the Borer restrictions.[155]

May one remove the pit of a fruit, or must he remove the fruit from the pit?[156]

The rule: Those fruits which it is the common way to remove the pit from the fruit and then eat the fruit one is allowed to remove the pit immediately prior to eating the fruit. Those fruits which the common way is not to remove the pit from the fruit but rather to eat the fruit with the pit and spit out the pit or to eat around the pit, then it is forbidden to remove the pit from the fruit, and one may only remove the fruit from the pit for right away use.

Examples:

- Peaches, Plums:[157] If it is common for one to remove the pit from the fruit, then one may do so prior to eating.
- Apricot: Since the pit is anyways loose within the fruit one is to shake out the pit rather then remove it with his hands.
- Melon/Watermelon:[158] One is to shake out whatever seeds are able to fall out through shaking and may then remove the remaining seeds from within the melon, whether with his hands or with a spoon in order to eat the melon right away.
- Using special instrument to remove pits: Is forbidden even by those fruits which may have their pits removed as one may only separate with his hands. Thus, one may not use olive pitters on Shabbos.

Laws of Muktzah: Removing the pit from those fruits which are allowed to have their pits removed as explained above does not pose a Muktzah prohibition.[159] Nevertheless once the pit has been placed down it is now Muktzah and may only be moved in a case that moving Muktzah is allowed.

May one shake inedible seeds/pits out from fruits/vegetables?[160]

One may do so according to all opinions in order to eat the food right away. Thus, one may shake a pit out from a date, or the seeds of a watermelon out of a slice in order to eat the date/watermelon right away.

Does removing food labels from food, such as from bakery bread, contain the separating restrictions?[161]

Yes. Thus, one may only remove it immediately prior to eating the food.[162] If one desires to remove

---

[152] The stringent opinion: Is brought in Ketzos Hashulchan 143 footnote 1 in name of the Yeshuos Chachma, and so plainly rules SSH"K 3:30.
The lenient opinions: The Ketzos Hashulchan [ibid] says that the world is not accustomed to be stringent in this and he goes on to be Melamed Zechus bringing four different reasons for why removing feathers of cooked chicken does not contain a prohibition of "Shearing", and he thus concludes that one should "leave the Jews to do so". So rules also that it is allowed: Shut Har Tzevi, Yalkut Yosef, Igros Moshe.
[153] So rules Rav Farkash ibid, however the Ketzos Hashulchan rules that the world is lenient in this, and so rules Piskeiy Teshuvos [340:2].
[154] Ketzos Hashulchan 143 footnote 1
[155] As this is similar to the removing of the skin or peel of a fruit which is only allowed to be done prior to the meal. [Piskeiy Teshuvos 340:2]
[156] Shabbos Kehalacha Vol. 2 p. 232; See also Ketzos Hashulchan 125:16 and footnote 43 in name of Tzemach Tzedek that one may remove the pit from the date
[157] P"M 321 A"A 30; M"B 321:84 and Shaar Hatziyon 321:99 in name of Peri Megadim regarding plums; Ketzos Hashulchan 125:16 in name of P"M ibid
[158] So rules Ketzos Hashulchan 125 footnote 43 in name of Ben Ish Chaiy; Kaf Hachayim 319:47
[159] So rules Ketzos Hashulchan 125 footnote 43
[160] Ashel Avraham Tinyana 319; Shabbos Kehalacha Vol. 2 p. 122
[161] Shabbos Kehalacha Vol. 2 p. 239
[162] It is allowed to remove the label, which is the unwanted, as is the law with regards to peeling fruits and the like, that the fruits may be peeled

the label a while before the meal then he is to cut with it a recognizable piece of the bread/food.

<u>Note:</u> When removing the label, one must take extra care not to cut the letters written on the label.

Does removing baking paper from cake, Kishkeh, Kugel, hotdogs, and the like contain the separating restrictions?[163]

Yes. Thus, one may only remove it immediately prior to eating the food.[164]

Does the removing of candy wrappers contain the separating restrictions?[165]

<u>If the wrapper is not stuck onto the candy,</u> then one may remove the wrapper without restriction as doing so is similar to removing an item from a box. Nevertheless, if one has many candies which he desires to remove from their wrapping then he should only do so in close proximity to their consumption.

<u>If the candy is stuck onto the wrapper</u> then it is similar to peeling a fruit which may only be done in close proximity to eating it.[166]

Is the wrapper and cork on a wine bottle considered mixed with the bottle and only be allowed to be removed for right away use?

No, as the wrapper is not glued to the bottle, and neither is the cork.

May one remove a rotten/wormy part of fruit/vegetable in order to eat the rest of the fruit/vegetable?[167]

Majority of Poskim[168] allow one to cut it off so long as he plans to eat the fruit right away. Nevertheless, it is best for one to cut part of the fruit itself together with the rotten part as doing so adds to the leniency. One may not remove the rotten part of the fruit simply in order so the fruit not continue to rot, and he be able to eat it later on.

May one remove a worm or other bug from a fruit/vegetable?[169]

<u>Inside the fruit</u>: If the worm is inside the fruit than one may remove it so long as he plans to eat the fruit right away.

<u>On the surface of the fruit/vegetables</u>: If the insect is on the surface of the fruit then it depends. If the insect is not stuck onto the fruit then one may remove it without restriction as in such a case there is no "mixture" of good and bad, as explained above in the introduction. If the insect is stuck onto the fruit, then one may only remove it with intent to eat right away. Nevertheless, it is best in such a case to shake the insect off rather than lift it with one's hands. If this is not possible, then one may even remove it with one's hands.[170]

---

immediately prior to eating it.

[163] Shabbos Kehalacha Vol. 2 p. 239

[164] It is allowed to remove the paper, which is the unwanted, as is the law with regards to peeling fruits and the like, that the fruits may be peeled immediately prior to eating it.

[165] Shabbos Kehalacha Vol. 2 p. 239

[166] So rules Rav SZ"A

[167] Shabbos Kehalacha Vol. 2 p. 195-197

[168] Mahrahm Kazis p. 163; Orchos Chaim Spinka 319:2; Minchas Yitzchak 5:38-2

<u>Other opinions</u>: Some Poskim rule it is forbidden to do so. [Nishmas Shabbos 112]

[169] Shabbos Kehalacha Vol. 2 p. 198

[170] Removing it does not pose a problem of Muktzah being that a) It is insignificant, and b) it is a Graf Shel Reiy

5. What is the definition of separating to eat "right away?"[171]

The definition of "Right away" is [that the separation is done] very close to the meal[172], however if one does not plan to eat for a while, it is forbidden [to separate it at that time].

Waiting until after Shul to begin to separate the foods for the meal:[173] One must be careful to not separate foods until after [the congregation] leaves Shul[174] in order so [it be separated] truly close to the meal, in which case it is then allowed to separate as much as one needs to eat for that meal. [**See Q&A**]

Separating for a meal which will last a long time:[175] So long as [one wishes to do the separation] close to the meal it is permitted for him to separate for the need of that entire meal even if [the meal itself] will be prolonged for some time.

Separating for the need of others:[176] [Furthermore] even if other people are dining with him[177] he is allowed to separate for the need of everyone. [**See Q&A**]

If there are left-over's after the meal:[178] If there are remains after the meal from what had been separated [nevertheless] this does not pose any problem being that when it was separated it was done permissively. [**See Q&A**]

Intentionally separating more than needed prior to the meal:[179] However, one may not conspire regarding this [and intentionally separate more food than needed prior to the meal so he has what to eat later on].

May one remove the food and place it in a basket and the like for the purpose of eating right away?[180]

One whose fruits have [fallen and] into pebbles and dust, may gather them one at a time [in order to eat right away]. However, he may not place them into a basket or box. [**See Q&A regarding if this ruling applies to other cases other than fruits**]

The reason for this is so he does not do a mundane act [which resembles Borer[181]].

Q&A On The Definition of Right Away

If one requires a lot of time in advance to prepare for the meal and do the required separations, how long in advance may he begin preparing for the meal?[182]

One may begin the meal preparations as much time prior to the meal as is needed in order to start the meal at the required time. Thus, if one desires to begin the meal at 1:00 and it takes about 1 hour to separate and thus prepare all the meal preparations, then one may begin the preparations starting from 12:00, irrelevant to if Shul ends later than 12:00, and may thus separate all that requires separation within this hour. [**See Q&A 3**] This ruling applies likewise to Shalosh Seudos even if one plans to continue the meal past the night. One may never begin the separations within more time prior to the meal then is actually needed for one to do all the preparations [i.e. in the example prior to 12:00].

---

[171] Admur 319:3; Michaber 319:3; Rama 319:1
[172] See Rama 319:1 "For the need of the meal that he will be eating immediately."
[173] Admur 319:4; M"A 321:15; M"B 321:45
[174] See Q&A 1 that this only applies if one will be able to finish all the preparations by the time the husband returns from Shul and is ready to eat. Otherwise one may obviously begin the preparations as much time as needed prior to the meal.
[175] Admur ibid; M"B 319:4
[176] Admur ibid; Rama 319:1
[177] Must one be dining with them in order to permit Borer for others? Some Poskim rule it is not neccessary to dine with them, and Borer may always be performed for others to eat right away. [Birkeiy Yosef 319; M"B 319:6 based on Tosafus and Darkei Moshe 319] Other Poskim however rule it may only be done for others if he is also participating in the meal. [See Kaf Hachaim 319:12] Practically some rule it is best to eat some of the food when doing Borer for others in order for it to be permitted according to all. [Kaf Hachaim ibid] Others however rule one may even initially lenient. [M"B ibid; see Shabbos Kehalacha 12 footnote 9 p. 96 for an analysis on this subject, and on the wording of Admur ibid]
[178] Admur ibid; Levush 319:2; M"B 319:5
[179] Admur ibid; M"B 319:5
[180] Admur 335:5
[181] Ketzos Hashulchan 146 p. 98 number 2
[182] Shabbos Kehalacha Vol. 2 p. 158

May one be lenient to separate within one hour before the meal even if he does not require a full hour to do the separations?[183]

Although there are Poskim[184] who are lenient to allow Boer to be done within one hour prior to the meal, nevertheless one is not to rely on this opinion.

May one begin separating prior to the meal more time than is needed if he will not be able to separate right before the meal?[185]

For example, if a guest is eating over someone's house and desires to bring with him a salad for the meal, then if the meal will not begin immediately upon the guest entering the house, it is forbidden to do forms of separation while making the salad being that it is not considered done directly prior to the meal. However, if the meal will begin right away upon one's arrival then it is permitted to separate for that meal even though his walking to the meal is an interval between the separation and the meal. Although when doing so one may not make any other diversions in his walk.

Other examples of the above scenario: The meal will begin at 1:00 and the mother needs to visit someone at 12:30, she may not begin the Borer preparations prior to leaving so the meal can begin when she returns. Similarly, a maid may not separate for the need of the meal more time prior to the meal then is needed even if she wants to rid herself already of the job.

When doing many preparations for the meal are the separating preparations to be pushed off to the very end so it be as close to the meal as possible, or may one do so even in the beginning of the required preparations?[186]

For example, if one needs to make a salad, may he only peel and add in the onions after cutting all the other vegetables, or may he do so even to begin with. One may do so even to begin with.

May one separate a food in more time prior to the meal than needed, if the food will be better tasting if separated at this time?[187] *Such as to peel garlic hours before the meal and soak it in Techina so the Techina absorbs the taste.*

This is allowed to be done as it is included in "the way of eating". However, there are opinions which are stringent and forbid to do separations in such a way just so the food taste better if it were possible to do so from before Shabbos without having the food spoil. Thus, according to all it would be allowed to remove frozen pastries or cold drinks [from the fridge[188]] from amongst other foods/bottles much time prior to the meal so they defrost on time, as if one were to remove them from before Shabbos, they would become stale/warm. As well in the opposite case, if one desires to separate a food from amongst other foods and enter it into the fridge so it be cold for the meal, this may be done.

Should one estimate prior to the meal how much food will be eaten and thus how much separation needs to be done or may he separate without limit so long as he intends on doing so for this meal?[189]

One should only separate as much as he estimates will need to be eaten by the meal.

Does the regulation of "Right away" apply also when separating food that one desires to eat from food which he does not desire to eat?

See Halacha 6

---

[183] Shabbos Kehalacha Vol. 2 p. 152-153
[184] Iglei Tal Borer 319:9; Ben Ish Chaiy; Az Nidbaru 6:72-5 writes 30 minutes
[185] Shabbos Kehalacha Vol. 2 p. 159
[186] See Shabbos Kehalacha Vol. 2 p. 161-163
[187] Shabbos Kehalacha Vol. 2 p. 163-164; SSH"K 3 footnote 200
[188] Regarding frozen drinks-See "The laws of Melting snow ice and other materials"
[189] Shabbos Kehalacha Vol. 2 p. 164

May one separate many foods for later use if he will take a bite of each individual food right away?[190]

No.

May one separate fruits from amongst rotten fruits to prevent them from spoiling faster?[191]

One may only separate the fruits if he plans to eat or use them right away.

If one has a mixture of different spices may he separate from it a specific spice for immediate use?[192]

Although there are opinions[193] which are stringent against allowing this to be done one may be lenient to do so

May one separate clothing or a Sefer to take with him upon leaving the house even though he does not plan to wear it or read it until later on?[194]

No, as its use is not being done right away.

May one separate prior to going to sleep medicines [which may be taken on Shabbos] in order so he can take them as soon as he awakes in middle of the night?

No.

Q&A on Leftovers

May one intentionally not eat some of the separated food during the meal in order to save it for another meal?[195]

According to all it is forbidden to separate before the meal with this intention. The question however arises in a case that before the meal one intended on eating all the food during the meal and now wants to change his mind.

This matter is disputed amongst Poskim. According to some Poskim[196] one may not do so. Thus, according to them it is only permitted to leave leftovers if one does not feel like eating any more food and not solely in order to save it for another meal. However other Poskim[197] are lenient to allow one to intentionally leave it over for the next meal. Seemingly in a case of need one may rely on the lenient opinion.[198]

Q&A on Separating for others

May one separate the good with his hands solely for others to eat right away, not having himself partake in the food?[199]

This is permitted.[200] Although there are opinions[201] who have written that it is proper for one to be stringent to partake in some of the food that he has separated for others.

---

[190] Shabbos Kehalacha Vol. 2 p. 170

[191] Shabbos Kehalacha Vol. 2 p. 168

[192] Shabbos Kehalacha Vol. 2 p. 143 Biurim 10

[193] Igleiy Tal Tochen 11

The reason: His reasoning is that since one is merely using the spices to place in another food and not to eat them immediately, the allowance of separating "within the eating process" does not apply. His proof is from 321:7 regarding spices that it is forbidden to cut them small even for immeditae use.

[194] Shabbos Kehalacha Vol. 2 p. 169

[195] Shabbos Kehalacha Vol. 2 p. 164

[196] So rules Shut Rav Poalim 1:12 in the opinion of Admur. This follows a compromise with the opinion of the Beis Yosef 319 which holds that one may never leave leftovers.

[197] Peri Megadim 319 M"Z 2 brought in Shaar Hatziyon 319:5

[198] As the M"B in Shaar Hatziyon ibid comments on the ruling of the Peri Megadim ibid that it requires analysis to to verify the source of this ruling of the P"M. [Shabbos Kehalacha ibid]

[199] Shabbos Kihalacha Vol. 2 p. 96

[200] So rules M"B 319:6, and so rules Rav Farkash.

[201] The conclusion of the Kaf Hachaim 319:12

May one separate good with his hands for the sake of animals to eat right away?²⁰²
Yes.²⁰³

May one's separation for the meal include also people which will only be arriving for the meal much later than its initial time?²⁰⁴
This is only allowed if the people will arrive before the end of the meal. However, if they will be arriving after the meals conclusion then it is not allowed for the one doing the separation to separate extra food for them.

May one separate more food than needed for the sake of having a large portion on the table and thus have his guests feel at ease in taking however much they want?²⁰⁵
Yes.²⁰⁶

May one separate foods for the honor of his guests even if he knows that they will not be eating those foods?²⁰⁷
Yes.²⁰⁸

May one separate foods on behalf of giving a snack for guests to take on their way out even though they may not eat it until later on?
Yes.²⁰⁹

May one separate foods for kids despite the lack of knowledge of how much they will eat of the food, if not at all?²¹⁰
This may be done, although one who is stringent²¹¹ to make sure that they finish all that was prepared for them has upon what to be stringent for.

May one separate food for the need of lending to a neighbor even though the neighbor does not plan to eat it right away?²¹²
If the neighbor will be leaving one's house immediately after receiving the separated item, then one may do so even if the neighbor will not be using it right away.²¹³ If the borrower will be staying for some time in one's house then one is to give it to him only before he leaves.

Does this restriction against placing the selected food into a basket apply to other foods as well or only to fruits that have fallen into earth?²¹⁴
From the letter of the law, it does not apply to any situation other than the one listed above, and thus so long as one plans to eat the selected item right away he may place it anywhere he wishes.²¹⁵

---

²⁰² P"M 319 M"Z 5; Biur Halacha 319:1 "Kdei"; Shabbos Kihalacha Vol. 2 p. 96 and p. 141
²⁰³ <u>The proof:</u> As so is ruled regarding the Melacha of Tochein [cutting small] that it may be done for right away use even for the sake of chickens. [M"A 321; Admur 321:10]
²⁰⁴ Shabbos Kihalacha Vol. 2 p. 156
²⁰⁵ Shabbos Kihalacha Vol. 2 p. 156; Ketzos Hashulchan 125 footnote 40; Rav Poalim 1:12; Ben Ish Chaiy Bishalach 3
²⁰⁶ So rules
²⁰⁷ Shabbos Kihalacha Vol. 2 p. 156
²⁰⁸ As the honor which he gives them in having the food prepared for them is in it of itself a useful purpose which is met during the meal.
²⁰⁹ As the honor which he gives them in having the food prepared for them is in it of itself a useful purpose which is met as soon as he gives them the food.
²¹⁰ Shabbos Kihalacha Vol. 2 p. 167
²¹¹ As so rules the ??? in name of the Rashba regarding one who did Borer for chickens that he must stand over them to verify that they eat the food right away.
²¹² Shabbos Kehalacha Vol. 2 p. 168
²¹³ As the purpose, which is the lending, is achieved for the person separating it as soon as the borrower leaves the house.
²¹⁴ Shabbos Kehalacha 12:45
²¹⁵ So rules the Beis Yosef and Tosefas Rid, and so rules Rav Farkash proving that this too is the opinion of Admur.

However, there are opinions[216] which are stringent in this with regards to all cases to restrict one from placing the selected food in one's pocket or designated basket even if he plans to eat it right away. Nevertheless, even according to them it is allowed to place the food on the eating table or one's plate and he does not have to literally place it his mouth directly following the separation.

6. Does the Borer restrictions apply when separating edible foods from amongst edible foods?
A. Edible food from edible food of same species:[217]
There is only a prohibition of separating when one separates waste [i.e. inedible parts] from the food or vice versa. However, if one separates food from food [of the same species], even if he utterly only wishes to eat one of them while the second one he wants to take and throw out, [nevertheless this unwanted food] is not considered waste due to this since it is [nevertheless] fit to be eaten. Therefore, it is allowed to separate it from the food which one wishes to eat and doing so does not contain [the prohibition] of separating waste from food. [**See Q&A**]
Separating large pieces from small pieces:[218] As long as [the mixture] is of a single species, then even though one separates large pieces from small pieces [nevertheless] this is not [Halachically] considered separating at all being that the entire [mixture] is fit to be eaten, and there is thus no waste [in the mixture]. [It is therefore] allowed to separate from it in any way that he wishes[219] and even in order to eat it later on that day [meaning while it is still Shabbos[220]]. [**See Q&A**]
Edible food from food of same species that is only edible in pressing times:[221] If [the unwanted food] is only fit to be eaten in a pressing time then even though it is not considered actual waste and there is [thus] no Biblical prohibition in separating it, nevertheless it is Rabbinically forbidden [to separate it] just like is the law by actual waste. [**See Q&A**]
Removing the rotten lettuce leaves:[222] Therefore it is forbidden to remove the rotten leaves from the vegetable (called lettuce) even if they are fit to be eaten in times of need. Rather one is to separate the vegetable from the leaves, which is [separating] the food from the waste. [**See Q&A regarding if this restriction applies even when the leaves are still attached to the stem!**]
If a same species mixture contains parts which are Halachically forbidden to eat may one nevertheless remove the forbidden part?[223] It is permitted to remove the forbidden parts of the meat of an animal on Yom Tov even if one was able to do so before Yom Tov [and the same applies for any other case **see Q&A**].
The reason for this is because:[224] removing the forbidden parts of the meat is not a complete Melacha as although one is separating food from food, this poses no Halachic meaning being that it is all one species, and it is only that the Torah has forbidden it from being eaten. Now, the prohibition of Borer only applies when one is separating two species of foods from each other or is separating waste from food which is considered like two species.
If the species contains two different parts such as an egg white and yolk:[225] To separate the yolk of an egg

---

[216] So rules the Igleiy Tal, brought in Ketzos Hashulchan 125 footnote 8
[217] Admur 319:4; Rama 319:3; Terumos Hadeshen 57
Other opinions: Some Poskim rule the prohibition of Borer applies even by a mixture of the same species of food. [Taz 319:2] Practically we do not rule like this opinion. [M"B 319:15; omitted in Admur ibid]
[218] Admur 319:6; Rama ibid
[219] Meaning even to separate the unwanted food from the wanted food.
[220] As otherwise this is considered preparing on Shabbos for after Shabbos which is forbidden.
[221] Admur 319:4; M"A 319:3; M"B 319:15
[222] Admur 319:4; Rama 319:1
[223] Admur 500:18; M"A 500:12; Peri Chadash 500:6; Iglei Tal Borer 21; M"B 500:29
Other opinion: Some Poskim rule the Borer restrictions apply by a mixture of Kosher and non-Kosher foods even if they are the same species. [SSH"K 3:28 footnote 100 in name of Rishonim and Achronim; Vetzaruch Iyun on the Ketzos Hashulchan end of 125 which seems to imply that two Lulavim of two different people on Sukkos would be considered Borer on the first day of Sukkos when one cannot fulfill his obligation with another person's Lulav. See Shabbos Kehalacha Vol. 2 p. 102.]
[224] Admur 500:18
[225] Admur 319:22; See 319:15; M"A 319:16; M"B 319:58; Shabbos Kehalacha p. 187

from its white for the purpose of eating it contains all the separating restrictions. Nevertheless, this ruling would only apply in this case [which involves an egg] being that although the white is considered a food nevertheless it is not edible in its current state, as well as that it is common to throw it out together with the waste and thus appears like waste in comparison to the yolk which is eaten the way it is together with the mustard [or other food], and would [thus be] Rabbinically[226] forbidden [to separate in order to eat]. [See Q&A] However in other scenarios [involving different parts of the same food] there would be no prohibition at all, even Rabbinically, in separating [one part of the food from another part] of the same food. Meaning that one may even separate small pieces from slightly large pieces, even if he throws the small pieces to the ground, as they nevertheless do not appear like waste due to this since they are edible and are commonly eaten.

If the two different parts of the same species are liquid substances and combine well:[227] If one places the curd of milk into an elastic vessel[228] and the whey drips from inside it then this is an offshoot of separating food from waste through using a sieve and sifter and one is thus liable.

The reason: Now, although the curd and the milk are both a single species of food and there is [thus] no waste [here] at all, nevertheless since they are liquid substances which mix well which he is [now] separating, therefore this contains the separating [prohibition] just like one who is separating food from waste. [**Regarding turning milk to cheese on Shabbos- See Halacha 2 above. Regarding removing the fat off the surface of milk-See Halacha 8**]

B. Edible food from edible food of different species:[229]

However, the above allowance to separate food from food only refers to when both foods are all the same species. However if one had in front of him two different types of foods which are mixed together and he wishes to separate [in order] to eat one of them right away and to place the second [food] aside to be eaten later on, then that species [of food] which one wishes to eat right away is considered the food while the other [species of] food is considered like the waste.[230] Therefore one must separate with his hands that [food] which he wishes to eat right away from amongst the other [food], thus [separating] the food from the waste and not vice versa. If one separates it and sets it aside to be eaten later on, even [later on] that day, he is liable. [See Q&A]

Two species of fish:[231] Two species of fish are considered two species of foods and it is [thus] forbidden to separate [even] by hand unless [one separates] that species which he wants to eat right away and [he is] not [separating it] from [prior to the coming] meal for [the need of the next] meal.

*Separating a large **species** from amongst a small species*:[232] [Furthermore,] even if one of the species are large and thus each species is [easily] recognizable and it is hence possible that there is no separating [prohibition] involved here at all, nevertheless one may not be lenient being that [doing so] is in question of being liable for a sin offering [meaning that it is questionable if this is a Biblical prohibition, and thus one must be stringent].

*Separating large **pieces** of both species from amongst small pieces*:[233] If the [mixture] contains two

---

[226] This follows the ruling of the Magen Avraham [319:16] as well as Taz [319:12] and Olas Shabbos that the white and yolk are considered one food, and it is only Rabbinically that one may not separate without restriction. However, the Mishneh Berurah [319:58] rules that it is considered two different foods and thus it Biblically retains all the separating restrictions. The difference between these two opinions would be that if one desires to use both the white and yolk according to the opinion of Admur and others one would be allowed to use a designated vessel to separate, as when one desires also the white the Rabbinical decree no longer applies. However according to the M"B all the separating regulations would still apply and thus a designated vessel may not be used to separate. [Shabbos Kihalacha Vol. 2 p. 187]
[227] Admur 319:25
[228] This refers to a vessel made of material that can be stretched out do to having tiny holes in it, and thus allows the milk to drip out. Similar to a plastic bag.
[229] Admur 319:5; Michaber 319:3
[230] Admur ibid; M"A 319:?; M"B 319:12; Biur Halacha ibid "Umaniach"
Other opinions: Some Poskim rule that there is no Pesoles in this mixture and one may hence remove whichever food he wants so long as he eats one of the foods right away. [Mamar Mordechai and Megilas Sefer brought in Biur Halacha ibid in opinion of Rambam and so may also be the opinion of Michaber]
[231] Admur 319:6
[232] Admur 319:6; Rama 319:3; Terumos Hadeshen 57
[233] Admur 319:6; Rama 319:3; Terumos Hadeshen 57

different species and one [wishes to] separate from amongst both of them together the large pieces from the small pieces, then it is allowed since one is not separating one species from another. [**See Q&A**]
May one separate large and small bread/Matzah crumbs from each other without restriction?[234] No. All the separating restrictions apply, as anything which is as small as flour which is together with a slightly large crumb receives the same status as a mixture of two different species.

Summary-Separating from mixtures which contain edible foods:

The same species of foods, and the entire mixture is equally edible/useable:
There are no separating restrictions involved in separating food from food of the same species and level of edibility. Thus, one may separate big pieces from small pieces or vice versa.
Regarding a food which contains two different parts, such as an egg which has a white and yolk, then if one wishes to eat one of them and throw out the other then if the food which one wishes to throw out is commonly thrown out despite it being edible, all the Borer restrictions Rabbinically apply. However, if both parts of the food are commonly eaten then no Borer restrictions apply[235], unless it is a food which in essence contains two united parts, such as curd and whey of milk which are joined together, then separating one from the other does contain a separating prohibition.[236]

A mixture which contains the same species of foods but some of the mixture is only edible in pressing times:
Such as the withered leaves of lettuce.
It Rabbinically contains all the separating restrictions mentioned above.

A mixture containing two different species of food:
A mixture containing two different species of food, such as two different types of fish[237], even if one is large and the other small, contains all the Borer restrictions mentioned above.[238]

Q&A regarding the definition of a same species mixture and a different species mixture?

The Rule:[239]
Any two foods which have the same name, taste and use are defined as being the same species. If either the name, taste or use is different than it is considered a different species.

Examples of foods which are considered two different species and retain all separating restrictions:
1. Two different types of fish either in name or taste.
2. Stuffed fish with plain fish: Two fish from the same species but one is stuffed while the other is not.
3. Candies which have different tastes or has the same taste but different color.
4. Cooked with roasted:[240] A cooked piece of fish/meat with a fried piece of fish/meat, even if they are from the same piece of fish/meat.
5. Cooked with raw: A cooked/fried piece of fish/meat with a raw piece of fish/meat.
6. Meat with liver or other parts of the cow.

---

[234] Admur in 504:6; Shabbos Kehalacha Vol. 2 p. 181
[235] Admur 319:21-22
[236] Admur 319:25
[237] Admur 319:6
[238] Admur 319: 6 However if one of the species is large while the other is small then it is only questionable as to whether the separating prohibitions apply, although nevertheless one must be stringent.
[239] See Shabbos Kehalacha 2:182-188
[240] M"B 319:15

7. <u>Meat with bones</u> even if the bone has marrow.
8. <u>Meat with chicken.</u>
9. Different types of meats or poultry. [241]
10. <u>Hot with cold</u>: A hot piece of meat with a cold piece of meat of the same species is considered like two different species.
11. <u>Cookies</u>: Cookies of different types which have different tastes, such as honey cookies with butterscotch cookies.
12. <u>Bread</u>: breads which have different appearance or taste such as white and whole wheat.
13. <u>Fruits</u>: Red grapes/plums/apples with yellow grapes/plums/apples. As well sweet fruits with sour fruits of the same species[242], or even if both fruits are sweet and same color but have a different taste of sweetness, as is common with different types of grapes, they are considered two different species.
14. <u>Nuts:</u> A mixture of different types of almonds, or of whole nuts with crushed nuts [designated for baking etc] even if they are of the same species.
15. <u>Sugar</u>: Ground sugar with sugar cubicles. As well regular sugar with powdered sugar [used to place on cakes].
16. <u>Cutlery</u>: Bowls of different size or depth are considered two different species.
17. <u>Keys</u>: Of different doors are considered two different species.
18. <u>Clothing:</u>[243] Shabbos with weekday clothing, or clothing of two different people [which are particular not to use each other's clothes] are considered two different species even if they are the same article of clothing.
19. <u>Books</u>: See Halacha 12 below
20. <u>Egg white and yolk</u>: See above Halacha.
For further cases and examples see Q&A below!

May one separate a piece of fish with many bones from other pieces of that same fish?[244]
Yes.

May one separate the different parts of the chicken from each other without restriction, such as to separate a thigh from a breast?[245]
There are opinions[246] which hold that the upper and lower parts of the chicken are considered two different species and therefore retain all the separating restrictions. According to others[247] however it has the status of one species.

May one separate different sized diapers without restriction?[248]
Depends. If all the diapers in the mixture are useable for the child, then yes. If only a certain size is useable then it has the same status as separating good from bad, and has all the separating restrictions apply.
<u>Regarding separating diapers of different thickness, such as is common in a mixture of different brands of diapers</u>: Some[249] rule that it contains all the separating restrictions. However, Rav Farkash rules that if the difference in thickness was not manufactured intentionally to be used for different purposes, then one may separate without restriction. However, if it was done intentionally, so the

---

[241] M"B 319:15
[242] P"M 319 brought in M"B 319:15 leaves this matter in doubt
[243] See M"B 319:15
[244] Shabbos Kehalacha Vol. 2 p. 176
[245] Shabbos Kehalacha Vol. 2 p. 184
[246] So rules Rav SZ"A in Maor Hashabbos 3:40-3; Binyan Shalom Borer p. 7
[247] Ayel Meshulash 3:8
[248] Shabbos Kehalacha Vol. 2 p. 180
[249] SSH"K 3:1

thicker ones can be used at night to intake more liquid, then it has all the separating restrictions.

May one separate sesame seeds from on top of Challah?
One may only do so for right away use.

May one separate the cream off one's piece of cake?[250]
If he does not want to eat the cream: Only if a) one leaves a recognizable sliver of cream on the cakes surface and thus does not totally remove all the cream. Or b) One slices off a recognizable portion of the surface of the cake together with the cream that is on it.
If he wants to eat the cream or to give it to someone else to eat: Then so long as one plans to eat it right away the cream may be removed without restriction.

May one scrape off a dip from one's bread?
Has the same laws as removing cream from on top of cake, see above.

May one separate burnt pieces of fish and the like from the other fully edible pieces of fish?[251]
No.

May one cut off the burnt part of a pastry?[252]
Although from the letter of the law it is permitted to do so prior to eating, nevertheless Lechatchila one should cut together with it part of the edible side of the pastry.

May one separate fruits which have rotten parts on them from fully edible fruits of the same species?[253]
If the fruit is rotten and spoiled to the point that they are only considered edible in pressing times, then it is forbidden. If, however, only a minute amount of the fruit is spoiled to the point that people will regularly just cut off the spoiled part and eat the rest, it is allowed.

May one remove rotten grapes from a vine?[254]
No.

Q&A on separating from same species foods which contain a forbidden part
May one remove the Kefula area of a Matzah on Pesach or does this pose a problem of Borer?[255]
It may be removed, as explained with regards to removing the forbidden parts off meat.

May one pour out the foam of a drink[256]**?**[257]
Yes, as explained above that forbidden parts of the same food do not contain the Borer restrictions.

May one separate whole Matzahs from broken Matzahs?[258]
Yes.[259]

---

[250] Shabbos Kehalacha Vol. 2 p. 235
[251] M"B 319:15; Shabbos Kehalacha Vol. 2 p. 178
[252] Shabbos Kehalacha Vol. 2 p. 235
[253] Shabbos Kehalacha Vol. 2 p. 178-179; Rav SZ"A 3 footnote 63
[254] Shabbos Kehalacha Vol. 2 p. 316
[255] Shabbos Kehalacha Vol. 2 p. 104
[256] The foam of a drink is forbidden to be drank as stated in Hilchos Shemiras Haguf Vehanefesh Halacha 9
"One who drinks the foam that come on the surface of a beverage can lead to Ririn which comes from the nose, and one who blows it with his mouth can lead to a difficulty in the head, and one who pushes it to the side can lead to poverty."
[257] Shabbos Kehalacha Vol. 2 p. 102
[258] Shabbos Kehalacha Vol. 2 p. 104-105
[259] To note however that the SSH"K rules that this is forbidden being that according to them if one item is forbidden and one is permitted they are considered like two different species despite the fact that they are all from the same species. This however does not follow the ruling of Admur and others as explained above in Halacha 6 that a prohibited part is not considered another species in the case of removal of forbidden fats. This

---

May one separate without restriction the yolk from the white or vice versa if he also plans to eat the white?[260]

Yes.

Q&A that relate directly to the Halachas inside

May one separate the large pieces of all the species in a mixture and in the process place the large pieces of each species separately?[261]

For example, one has a vegetable salad and desires to remove all the large pieces of vegetables from the small pieces. May one remove all the large tomatoes and put them on one side and then all the large cucumbers and place them on another side?

This may not be done as in the end of the day one has still separated one species from another which is forbidden. Thus, when doing so the large pieces of all species must remain mixed.

May one separate from within the same species even with a vessel?[262]

Yes.[263]

May one separate from within the same species the big pieces from the small in order to give them to two different people, the big pieces to one person and the small to another? What is the law if the pieces belong to two different people?[264]

The Borer restrictions do not apply.[265]

Does the restriction of separating bad lettuce leaves apply even when the rotten leaves are still attached to the lettuce head?[266]

The above law that one may only remove the good leaves from the bad only refers to when the leaves have already been cut up. However, when the leaves are still attached to the lettuce head one may remove the bad leaves from the lettuce head immediately prior to the meal, as is the law with regards to peeling any peel off an item.[267]

General Q&A on Separating from amongst different species.

If one does not care to eat either food until later on, at which time he will eat them both at that time, may he separate them now?[268]

This matter is disputed in the Poskim.[269] Practically it seems that one is to be stringent.

---

is also the opinion of the Magen Avraham and Mishneh Berurah. Vetzaruch Iyun on the Ketzos Hashulchan end of 125 which seems to imply that two Lulavim of two different people on Sukkos would be considered Borer on the first day of Sukkos when one cannot fulfill his obligation with another person's Lulav. See Shabbos Kehalacha Vol. 2 p. 102.

[260] Shabbos Kehalacha Vol. 2 p. 187 footnote 167 based on Admur 319:22; M"A 319:16

Other opinions: Some Poskim rule the egg and white are in truth considred two different foods and hence it would be forbidden to separate one from the other without fulfilling the Borer conditions. [M"B 319:58]

[261] Shabbos Kehalacha Vol. 2 p. 176; Rav SZ"A in SSH"K 3 footnote 68

[262] Tehila Ledavid 319:5; Shabbos Kehalacha Vol. 2 p. 174

Other opinions: Some Poskim leave this matter in question. [P"M 319 M"Z 2; A"A 5]

[263] So is evident from the wording of Admur in the case of straining eggs.

[264] Shabbos Kehalacha Vol. 2 p. 102

[265] So rules Rav S"Z Aurbauch in Shulchan Shlomo 319:6-10, thus coming to a conclusion of the doubt he raised in SSH"K [3 footnote 62].

[266] Shabbos Kehalacha Vol. 2 p. 233

[267] Peri Megadim 319 M"Z 3; Kaf Hachaim 319:15; Ben Ish Chaiy Beshalach 6; Biur Halacha 319:1 "Min Haalim Hameupashim"

Other opinions: Some Poskim rule one is required to remove the inner leaves from the lettuce and may not remove the outer leaves. [Mamar Mordechai; See Tehila Ledavid 319:4]

[268] Shabbos Kehalacha Vol. 2 p. 188

[269] Some Poskim rule it is permitted, or questionable. [P"M 319 M"Z 2 and 12] Others rule it is forbidden. [Biur Halacha "Hayu Lefanav"]

If one desires to eat both foods during the meal, but desires to eat one prior to the other, do the separating restrictions apply?[270]

➢ For example: If one desires to serve for the current course soup without the vegetables, and for the next course plans to serve the vegetables, may one separate the two without the separating restrictions, or may he only separate the soup [what he currently wants] from the vegetables?

There are some codifiers[271] who rule as follows: If one also desires to serve the vegetables without any soup, then the separating restrictions do not apply, and one may even remove the vegetables from the soup even though he is currently only interested in the soup for the coming course and the vegetables will only be served in a later course. However, if one does not care to separate the vegetables from the soup and only cares to separate the soup from the vegetables then the separating restrictions apply, and one may only separate that food which he now wants.

Other Codifiers[272] however rule that since both foods are to be eaten in the same meal, it therefore poses no separating restrictions.

If one is interested in both foods right away may he separate them with a designated vessel?[273]

➢ For example, if one has soup and would like to serve the liquid separately from the vegetables which he will also serve, may he use a strainer to remove the vegetables?

This matter is disputed amongst Poskim. Practically one is to be stringent.

Does the condition of "Right away" apply when separating to different types of food?[274]

Some Poskim[275] rule that the law of "right away" differs between mixtures of foods and mixtures of food with waste. By mixtures food with waste, one may only separate right before the meal. However, by mixtures of different foods one may separate even 4-5 hours prior to the upcoming meal, and the prohibition is only to separate before the previous meal for the need of the next meal. Practically however one is to be stringent and follow all the regulations explained in the previous Halacha with regards to separating the food for right away use.[276] Although in a case of great need one may be lenient to separate the wanted food within an hour before the meal.

---

[270] Shabbos Kehalacha Vol. 2 p. 192

[271] Brought in name of Rav Moshe Feinstein in an English book on Hilchos Shabbos p. 155 footnote 148; Az Nidbaru 1:79:42 leaves this question in doubt, and so is brought in Shulchan Shlomo 319:4-3 in the name of Rav SZ"A that he was in doubt regarding this question. However see next footnote that others bring that Rav SZ"A ruled leniently in this

[272] Sheivet Halevy in Kovetz Mibeis Levy 6:3; Rav SZ"A as brought in Migilas Sefer, and so leans Rav Farkash.

[273] Shabbos Kehalacha Vol. 2 p. 191

[274] Shabbos Kehalacha Vol. 2 p. 172

[275] Beis Yosef 319 in opinion of Rambam; brought in Magen Avraham 319:6; So rules also Aruch Hashulchan 319:15

[276] Tosefes Shabbos; Maaseh Rokeiach; M"B 319:16; Biur Halacha "Shebirer Shacharis"; Machatzis Hashekel 319:7 in the opinion of Rama and so seems to be the opinion of Admur; Ben Ish Chaiy Beshalach 2

7. Pouring food or waste out from a vessel:[277]

Important Note 1: *The following Halacha will deal with the laws of separating through spilling from a vessel. At times the separating prohibition applies as will be explained. The rulings brought below from the Alter Rebbe's Shulchan Aruch differ entirely from the rulings brought below from the Alter Rebbe's Siddur. For this reason, it is incumbent to read the summary below to understand the final ruling in what one is to do. The basic discrepancy between the Shulchan Aruch and the Siddur, **as is understood by majority of codifiers**[278], is with regards to what is considered the item being separated when one pours. Is the item being poured out being separated or is the item which remains in the cup considered to have been separated. Now, being that it is always forbidden to separate the bad from the good this question plays a pivotal role in regards to when one may separate through pouring. If one says that the item being poured is being separated then one may never pour out the bad, but may pour out the good to eat right away. However, if the item which remains is what is being separated then one may pour out the bad but not the good.*

Important Note 2*: The following laws of whether or not one is allowed to separate liquid from solid through pouring only apply to those foods which are small enough to be defined as mixed together with their liquids. However, if the liquid only contains large solid foods, then it is not defined as mixed with the liquid and thus none of the separating restrictions apply, as explained in the Q&A to the Introduction, See There!*

❖ **The Opinion of Admur in the Shulchan Aruch**
When one wants to eat the food being poured out:[279]

May pour up until the stream stops if does not plan to eat that which is being poured right away:[280] It is permitted to gently pour [food or liquid] from one vessel into another in order so the residue and dregs remain on the bottom of the vessel [being poured from]. However, one must be careful once the stream [being poured] has stopped and small trickles begin to drip out from the last remainder [of food that is] amongst the waste, then one must stop [pouring] and leave [that remainder of food] together with the waste.

The reason for this is because:[281] if one were to not do so, then these last drops prove [to all] that [his true intentions in this pouring] were to separate [the food from the waste]. However, during the initial pouring when the waste is not yet recognizable, then he has done no separation.

Pouring up to when the stream stops is only allowed if needed for Shabbos:[282] However [doing the above is only allowed] if one needs the fat [or other poured food] for that day [meaning for Shabbos], as if one does not need to use it [for Shabbos] then it is forbidden [to do so as] it is forbidden to trouble oneself [to do an action] on Shabbos for [the use of] a weekday.

In a case of loss may have a gentile do it even for a weekday: However, if one suspects that [the fat may perhaps] lose [its substance] or spoil [if he were to not separate it now] then it is permitted for him to remove it through a gentile.

The reason for this is: because the prohibition to trouble oneself and prepare on Shabbos for a weekday is a Shvus [which is a] Rabbinical prohibition, and in cases of loss it is permitted to ask a gentile [to do an action for oneself] with regards to all [actions that are] Rabbinical prohibitions, as was explained in chapter 307 [Halacha 12].[283]

---

[277] Admur 319:18-20; Michaber 319:14
[278] So explains and rules: SHU"T Divreiy Nechemia 21, Ketzos Hashulchan 125:9 and footnote 21; Iglei Tal Borer 5; Chayeh Adam 16:9; Sefer Oar LeTziyon. As opposed to the ruling of Rav Farkash in Shabbos Kehalacha in which he understands that there is no dispute between the Siddur and Shulchan Aruch as will be explained within the footnotes of the summary see there.
[279] 319:18
[280] Admur 319:18; Michaber 319:14
[281] Admur 319:18; Michaber 319:14
[282] Admur ibid; M"A 510:13; Tosefes Shabbos 319:28
[283] To note however that there it was only permitted in a case of great loss, and not any case of loss. The difference is that here the prohibition is not an actual Shvus and thus is permitted even without great loss.

If one wants to eat that which is being poured right away:[284] One who pours liquid from one vessel to another [in order to eat the liquid being poured right away] is not required to stop [pouring] once it begins to trickle drops [of the liquid].

The reason for this is: because it is permitted to separate food or liquid from amongst residue in any case that one plans to eat or drink it right away so long as he does not separate it through using a vessel but rather does so with his hands as was explained [above in Halacha 4].

The definition of using hands to separate:[285] Now, although here he is [separating through] pouring from one vessel to another [and thus is not doing the separation with his hands], nevertheless [it is permitted since] the core of the separation is being done through one's hands, and it is only considered that one is separating with a vessel when one separates using a cloth or basket and the like.

Tilting a barrel of wine in order to pour it out:[286] It is permitted to [tilt] a barrel [by] elevating [one side of it] over an item in order so that the wine pour out of it well. Now, although that through this, wine is also poured out from amongst the sediment, [nevertheless] this is not considered like separating so long as [he has not poured out so much to the point that] drops have not yet begun to trickle from amongst the sediment as explained above.

When one wants to eat the food remaining in the pot:[287]

Fat which floats on the surface of food is forbidden to be entirely poured out even when done in order to eat the food right away. [**See Q&A 1**]

The reason for this is: because [the fat and the food] are two types of food [in which case we say] that food which one plans to eat right away is considered the "food" while the other is considered the waste, and [thus] upon pouring out the fat which one does not want to eat it is considered like separating waste from food [which is forbidden].

❖ **The opinion of Admur in the Siddur:[288]**

Removing a fly from ones soup: The only solution that remains is to pour out from the cup until the waste comes out from it.

The reason that tilting it out is allowed: As since the removal of the waste is being done through him holding the cup of liquid in his hand and tilting it with his hand this is considered separating food from waste which is permitted to be done in order to drink it immediately.

---

[284] Admur ibid; M"A 319:15; M"B 319:55
[285] Admur ibid based on M"A ibid; M"B ibid
[286] Admur 319:20
[287] Admur 319:19; M"A 319:15
[288] Divreiy Nechemia 21; Ketzos Hashulchan 125:9 and footnote 21; Iglei Tal Borer 5; Chayeh Adam 16:9, brought in Shaar Hatziyon 319:44; Oar LeTziyon 2:31-10.

Summary: Pouring a substance from a pot of food, whether one wishes to pour out the food or the waste:[289]

Based on the rulings in the Siddur and the Shulchan Aruch:

<u>Before it begins to trickle out</u>: One is allowed to pour one food from another food without the separating restrictions up to the point that the item being poured out begins to trickle out from the item that remains [see Q&A for the exact definition]. Thus, one may do so even to eat later on, on Shabbos. It however may not be done in order to eat during the week as is always the law regarding preparing on Shabbos for after Shabbos.[290]

<u>When it begins to trickle out</u>: Once the food being poured begins to trickle out then if one wants to eat what is being poured it is forbidden to continue pouring [**see footnote**][291] even in order to eat that food right away. Furthermore, even if one wants to eat that which will remain in the pot and thus wants pour out what he does not want, nevertheless one is to be stringent to not continue pouring, even if he desires to eat the remaining food right away. [**see footnote**][292] This however is with exception to when the food being poured out is inedible and is being poured out through the food that he desires to eat right away, such as tilting a cup and having the fly spill out together with the liquid.

<u>Note</u>: **The above restrictions only apply by liquids which are defined as "mixed" with the foods that are in them, such as that the solids are small. However, if the liquid only contains large solid foods, then it is not defined as mixed with the liquid and thus none of the separating restrictions apply, as explained in the Q&A to the Introduction, See there for examples!**

Q&A of the above Halacha with regards to vegetable soup:

Note: In all cases that one plans to eat both the liquid and vegetables during the meal then the Borer restrictions do not apply according to many opinions [see Halacha 6 Q&A "Desires to eat both foods right away"]. Thus, according to those opinions, the laws mentioned below only apply to cases that one does not plan to eat the liquid or the vegetables at all during that meal.[293]

May one pour out small vegetables from soup in order to eat the vegetables right away [and not eat the soup that meal]?

Based on the ruling in the Siddur this is forbidden even if one desires to eat the vegetables right away [and according to Rav Farkash's understanding when done to eat right away it is a mere stringency to

---

[289] The following summary which takes into account the major difference of opinion between the Alter Rebbe in the Siddur and in his Shulchan Aruch is based on the summarizations and rulings of the Ketzos Hashulchan chapter 125 Halachas 8-11, and footnotes there, as well as partially on Shabbos Kehalacha Vol 2 pages 113-122. To note however that there are differences between the final conclusion of the Ketzos Hashulchan and Shabbos Kehalacha as will be explained in the relevant footnotes.

The following is the summary based on solely the Alter Rebbe's Shulchan Aruch:

Pouring out the food that one wants to eat, leaving the waste on the bottom: [Halacha 18] Is allowed to be done without the separating restrictions up to the point where the food being poured out begins to trickle out from the waste. Thus, one may do so even to eat later on, on Shabbos. Although it may not be done to eat by the weekday as is always the law regarding preparing on Shabbos for the week. Once it begins to trickle out it may only be poured out in order to eat right away, being that all the separating restriction then begin to apply.

Pouring out the waste from the food leaving the food on the bottom: [Halacha 19] Is only allowed to be done up to the point that drops of the waste begin to trickle out from the food, even if one plans to eat it right away.

[290] Admur 319:18 regarding pouring out food and 19 regarding pouring out waste.

[291] Based on the ruling in Siddur, as is understood by the Ketzos Hashulchan and others. However, in Shabbos Kehalacha Vol. 2 p. 121 Rav Farkash rules simply that "one who desires to be stringent should never pour out the good" and not that doing so is forbidden. This is due to the fact that he explains there that in truth even according to the Siddur, Admur holds that the food being poured is considered to be that which is being separated. See there for a further analysis on this subject.

[292] To suspect for the ruling in Shulchan Aruch 319:18. So rules the Ketzos Hashulchan in 125 footnote 25, despite the ruling in the Siddur in which this is allowed. To note however that Rav Farkash in Shabbos Kehalacha Vol 2 p. 121 rules that it is forbidden [and not just a mere stringency] to pour out that which one does not want, as according to his view even according to Admur in the Siddur that which is being poured is considered to be that which is being separated. For a further analysis on this subject see Shabbos Kihalacha there.

[293] Vetzaruch Iyun on all cases below as since both the foods are eaten together by majority of people, perhaps it should not contain a prohibition- See Ketzos Hashulchan 125 footnote 21 who writes this logic regarding pouring water from coffee all the way until end. [See Shevisas Hashabbos Borer footnote 25; and Tal Oros; Ketzos Hashulchan chapter 125 footnote 28, [although there he concludes with a Tzaruch Iyun due to that he brings also the opinions which allow this.]; Tehila Ledavid; and Rav Farkash in Shabbos Kehalacha Vol 2 page 348-349

avoid doing so]. If, however, one also pours out liquid together with the vegetables seemingly this is allowed.[294] With regards to large vegetables, see Introduction above that they do not contain the Borer restrictions.

May one pour out small vegetables from soup in order to eat the soup right away?
One should be stringent not to do so due to the ruling in Shulchan Aruch [and according to Rav Farkash's understanding this is forbidden even according to the Siddur]. If, however, one also pours out liquid together with the vegetables seemingly this is allowed.[295]

May one pour the liquid out from the soup in order to eat the liquid right away, having the vegetables remain in the pot?
If the vegetables are floating on the top of the soup then this is forbidden based on the ruling of the Siddur [and according to Rav Farkash's understanding when done to eat right away it is a mere stringency to avoid doing so].
If the vegetables are on the bottom of the pot then it is permitted according to all to pour out soup to the point that the liquid begins to drip out from amongst the vegetables.

May one pour the liquid out from the soup or chulent in order to eat the vegetables/chulent which will remain in the pot?
If the vegetables are floating on the top of the soup: This has the same law as Q2.
If the vegetables are on the bottom of the pot: It is permitted according to all to pour out soup to the point that the liquid begins to drip out from amongst the vegetables.

May one pour out the soup from the vegetables if he wants the soup and another wants the vegetables?
Seemingly this should have the same ruling as the above Q&A.

May one spill the liquid out of a canned food, such as oil from a tuna can and the like?[296]
The rule: If the food that is within the can is in small enough pieces to be defined as mixed together with the liquid, then the separating restrictions [written in the summary] apply. However, if the liquid only contains large solid foods, then it is not defined as mixed with the liquid and thus none of the separating restrictions apply, as explained in the Q&A to the Introduction, See There!
Examples:
- Canned **whole** pickles/sardines/eggplant: Are not defined as mixed and thus may have their liquid removed in any which way.
- Canned **cut pieces** of pickles/sardines/eggplant: Are defined as mixed and thus retain all the separating restrictions explained.
- Canned olives: Are defined as mixed and thus retain all the separating restrictions explained.
- Canned Tuna: Is defined as mixed and thus retains all the separating restrictions explained.
- ➢ In cases that the separating restrictions apply one may never partially open the can, or puncture a hole in it and then drain out the liquid through it by turning the can over. However, to open the can and spill out the liquid by tilting it, is allowed so long as the solids are sunk to the bottom and thus the liquid is floating on top, and even this is only allowed until the point that the liquid begins to trickle as explained in Q 4.

---

[294] See Q&A 5
[295] See Q&A 5
[296] Shabbos Kehalacha Vol 2 p. 360

May one spill out the unwanted fat that is on the surface of soup or cholent?[297]
One may do so by spilling it out together with some of the soup, or through leaving a nice amount still on the surface of the soup/chulent. However, one should be stringent not to spill it out entirely due to the ruling in Shulchan Aruch [and according to Rav Farkash's understanding this is forbidden even according to the Siddur].

May one spill out the whey that is on the surface of a yogurt or cream cheese?[298]
One should be stringent not to do so due to the ruling in Shulchan Aruch [and according to Rav Farkash's understanding this is forbidden even according to the Siddur]. Regarding removing the whey with a spoon, see Halacha 8.

May one tilt out the liquid of a pot through holding back the food with a spoon?[299]
No.

May one pour from a tea pot that has a strainer on its top to prevent the leaves from falling in the cup?[300]
It is permitted to pour tea up to the bottom of the pot where the tea is mixed with the leaves.[301] To pour out the tea past this point[302] many Poskim[303] permit doing so [even according to the ruling of Admur in the Siddur which views that which is left in the pot as that which is separated, and thus should ideally be prohibited[304]].[305] However others[306] rule that one is to be stringent. In any event, when relying on the lenient opinions he should only do so for right away use[307].

May one pour tea out of the cup which contains the tea bag?[308]
Yes, this may be done according to all.[309] Regarding other questions which relate to tea, see chapter 3 Halacha 1 Q&A.

May one pour coffee out of a cup that contains Turkish coffee on the bottom?
The custom is to be lenient to allow pouring the coffee out even from the bottom area that is mixed with the Turkish coffee.[310] However some Poskim[311] are stringent to forbid doing so.

---

[297] Shabbos Kehalacha Vol. 2 p. 121
[298] Shabbos Kehalacha Vol. 2 p. 121
[299] Shabbos Kehalacha Vol. 2 p. 151
[300] See Shabbos Kehalacha Vol. 2 p. 368; Piskeiy Teshuvos 319:38
[301] As is always the rule regarding pouring one thing from another, as the fact that there is a strainer on the top of the pot does not make a difference in this regard.
[302] The problems faced in doing so is that a) one is separating with a vessel [the strainer that is attached to the top of the kettle] and b) According to Admur in Siddur one is separating the bad from the good.
[303] Shevisas Shabbos Borer 29 and 49 is Milameid Zechus, although brings from Rav Zonenfeld to be initially stringent; Chazon Ish 53, Ketzos Hashulchan 125 footnote 21; Rav SZ"A in SSH"K 3 footnote 125; Shabbos Kehalacha ibid
[304] So is proven from the fact that the Ketzos Hashulchan which rules like Admur in the Siddur rules that it is allowed in our case for the reasons mentioned in the previous footnote; See Shabbos Kehalacha ibid Biurim 7 that it is similar to pealing a fruit which is allowed even though one is removing the Pesoles from the food, being that doing so is Derech Achila.
[305] The reason: The problems mentioned in the previous footnote are answered in the following ways according to the lenient opinions: a) The tea leaves are fit to be drank together with the liquid [by most people] and thus it is permitted to strain the liquid from it, as is explained in the laws of straining. [Shevisas Hashabbos ibid; Ketzos Hashulchan ibid] b) One does not intend to separate the leaves from the tea but rather just to drink the tea. [Ketzos Hashulchan ibid; Chazon Ish ibid] c) A vessel which is designated to separate for only right away use, as is a kettle, is not included in the separating restrictions. [Rav SZ"A in SSH"K ibid].
[306] Ben Ish Chaiy Beshalach 2:18; Kaf Hachaim 319:113 in name of Beis Menucha; Bris Olam Borer 40; Az Nidbaru 1:23; Sheivet Halevi 1:84; Minchas Yitzchak 7:23; Or Letziyon 1:27; Yechaveh Daas 2:51Rav SZ"A in Shulchan Shlomo 319:32
[307] So rules Rav Farkash, as then one can also join in the reason of Rav SZ"A mentioned in the previous footnotes.
[308] Shabbos Kehalacha Vol. 2 p. 372
[309] As a tea bag is not defined as mixed when within water. However one may not pour to the very end to the point that liquid drains from the actual tea bag, as this poses a possible filtering prohibition, as explained in Halacha 4 Q&A with regards to removing the tea bag from the cup and having it drip into the cup.
[310] Shevisas Hashabbos Borer footnote 29; Ketzos Hashulchan 125 footnote 21
The reason: The problems mentioned in the previous footnote are answered in the following ways according to the lenient opinions: a) The tea leaves and coffee are fit to be drank together with the liquid [by most people] and thus it is permitted to strain the liquid from it, as is explained in

---

How much fat is one required to leave on the surface when removing the fat due to desiring only the food that is under?[312]

It is not enough to simply leave a mere sliver of fat which in any case would be very difficult to actually separate from the food [without taking the food with it], rather one must leave over a recognizable amount, enough of an amount that it could technically be easily removed from the milk.

---

8. Removing the fat off from the surface of milk and all cases of the like such as removing dirt from food:[313]

If one desires the milk and not the fat: As was explained in the previous Halacha with regards to pouring out unwanted liquid from a food, similarly it is permitted to gather[314] [some of] the fat which floats on the surface of milk[315] (called cream) and when one reaches near the actual milk, he is to leave some of the fat still [on the surface] together with the milk[316]. [**See Q&A**]

If one desires to eat the fat right away: [However] if one wants to eat the [fat] right away, then [it is permitted to remove all the fat and] he does not need to have remain any [of the fat] together with the milk.

The reason for this is: because it is permitted to separate food or liquid from amongst the residue in any case that one plans to eat or drink it right away so long as he does not separate it through using a vessel but rather does so with his hands as was explained [above in Halacha 4]. [**See Q&A**]

Ruling of Siddur-Removing fat together with some liquid: Regarding fat that floats on the surface of the gravy, one may not throw it out through a spoon taking with it some of the liquid as this is similar to removing waste from food which one is liable on.

Summary: Gathering the top layer off the surface of a food in order to eat that layer:[317]

To remove fat that is on the surface of milk is permitted to be done to eat anytime on Shabbos [whether one plans to eat the fat on Shabbos or to eat the milk under the fat] up to the area of the surface that is in direct contact with the milk/food under it. The area of fat however that is in direct contact with the milk

---

the laws of straining. [Shevisas Hashabbos; ibid; Ketzos Hashulchan ibid] b) One does not intend to separate the leaves from the tea but rather just to drink the tea. [Ketzos Hashulchan ibid]

[311] Chayeh Adam 16; Sheivet Haleivy, and others brought in Kaf Hachayim 319:113

[312] So rules the Ketzos Hashulchan [125 footnote 24]

[313] Admur 319:18; M"A 510:13; M"B 319:62

[314] The term used by Admur seems to imply it is permitted to gather using a spoon.

[315] Upon standing for 12 to 24 hours, fresh milk has a tendency to separate into a high-fat cream layer on top of a larger, low-fat milk layer. The cream is often sold as a separate product with its own uses; today the separation of the cream from the milk is usually accomplished rapidly in centrifugal cream. The fat globules rise to the top of a container of milk because fat is less dense than water.

[316] According to Admur above in the previous Halacha one must leave some of the fat together with the milk even if he plans to immediately drink the milk and this is not similar to the peeling of a fruit which is allowed to be done prior to eating it. [This opposes the opinion of the Igleiy Tal which allows one to remove it immediately prior to eating it.] See Shabbos Kehalacha Vol. 2 p. 237

[317] Admur 319:18

has all the separating prohibitions and thus may only be removed to be eaten right away.[318]

Q&A

How much fat is one required to leave upon the surface when removing the fat due to desiring only the milk?[319]

It is not enough to simply leave a mere sliver of fat which in any case would be very difficult to actually separate from the milk [without taking the milk with it], rather one must leave over a recognizable amount, enough of an amount that it could technically be easily removed from the milk.[320]

May one remove the entire fat together with some of the milk if he desires to get rid of the fat and drink the milk?[321]

According to the opinion of Admur in the Siddur this is forbidden to be done.[322]

May one use a spoon to remove the fat?[323]

Whatever amount of fat is permitted to be removed [dependent on whether one desires the fat or the milk] may be removed with a spoon, as explained above in Halacha 4 Q&A that using a spoon is equivalent to using one's hands.[324]

May one remove dirt/waste from the surface of a food, such as on top of cream cheese and the like?

Doing so is only permitted through pouring out the dirt together with some of the cheese.

May one remove whip cream from on top of pudding?

The area of cream that is in direct contact with the milk has all the separating prohibitions applicable and thus may only be removed to be eaten right away.[325]

---

[318] This applies even according to the Siddur being that here we are not discussing pouring the fat out but rather gathering it with ones hand and the like, of which the Siddur never argued on.

[319] Shabbos Kehalacha Vol. 2 p. 236

[320] So rules the Ketzos Hashulchan [125 footnote 24] with regards to how much fat one is allowed to pour out of the dish. The same thus applies here when removing fat from the surface.

[321] Shabbos Kehalacha Vol. 2 p. 237

[322] As rules Admur regarding removing the fly together with some of the liquid. [See Ketzos Hashulchan 125 footnote 24]
However the M"B rules that this is allowed.

[323] Ketzos Hashulchan 125 footnote 24; Chayeh Adam in Nishmas Ada, 82:2; Shabbos Kehalacha Vol. 2 p. 236

[324] So rules the Ketzos Hashulchan 125 footnote 24 based on an inference from the Alter Rebbe in the Shulchan Aruch on the word "Liklot" that he uses.
Opinion of M"B: In 319:62 the M"B rules a spoon may not be used to gather the fat above milk even if one plans to eat it immediately. In Shaar Hatziyon 319:58 he explains this to also be the opinion of Admur. However, in 319:66 he contradicts himself and rules a spoon may be used. The Chazon Ish answers this by saying the case of cream on top of milk was an exception being that the spoon helps for the actual separation, while in 66 it is allowed as it is used simply so one does not dirty himself. So, concludes also Minchas Yitzchak 1:76. See Shabbos Kehalacha P. 148-149

[325] This applies even according to the Siddur being that here we are not discussing pouring the fat out but rather gathering it with one's hand and the like, of which the Siddur never argued on.

9. Removing a fly or other waste from ones soup or cup of juice:

Note: The explanation behind the differences between the rulings of the Shulchan Aruch and the Siddur with regards to pouring out in-edibles have already been discussed in Halacha 7, see there. As well the difference of rulings with regards to if one may remove some of the bad with the good was already discussed in Halacha 1b. See there.

A. The opinion of Admur in the Shulchan Aruch:[326]

If a fly fell into a cup one may not remove only the fly from the cup being that doing so is equivalent to separating waste from food which is forbidden to be done even in order to eat right away. Rather, one is to remove also some of the liquid together with the fly being that when one does so it does not appear like one is separating at all[327], as explained above (Halacha 14 [in the Michaber, and Halacha 18 above in the Alter Rebbe[328]]).

B. The opinion of Admur in the Siddur:

Introduction: The following are a number of warnings and statements to remove stumbling blocks and common and frequent inadvertent [acts done on Shabbos] which according to many of the greatest of the Rishonim doing so involves a prohibition of Kares and Sekilah when done intentionally and a sin offering for when done unintentionally, may G-d atone for us.

Removing a fly from ones soup: One may not rely on the customary permission granted that if a fly or other waste falls into ones cup or plate then one removes it together with a spoon and takes out with it some liquid etc, as doing so is questionable of containing a sin offering liability and a prohibition of Sekilah G-d forbid. Thus, the only solution that remains is to pour out from the cup until the waste comes out from it.

Blowing the fly: One may not blow on [the waste] with his mouth until it is blown out[329], although he may blow it to bring it nearer to the wall of the cup and then tilt it and pour from it until the waste comes out. **[See Q&A]**

The reason that tilting it out is allowed: As since the removal of the waste is being done through him holding the cup of liquid in his hand and tilting it with his hand this is considered separating food from waste which is permitted to be done in order to drink it immediately.

Removing fat from a dish: The same applies if [the fly] fell into a plate with gravy, and even with fat that floats on the surface of the gravy, one may not throw it out through a spoon taking with it some of the liquid as this is similar to removing waste from food which one is liable on.

Summary-Removing a fly and the like from one's food:[330]
One may blow the fly/insect/dirt to the side of the cup and then pour it out, by tilting the cup, together with some of the liquid. This however may only be done in order to drink its content right away. It is forbidden to remove the fly if he plans to eat the food later on. One may not remove the fly with a spoon even if he takes some of the liquid out together with it. As well he may not blow it out.

---

[326] Admur 319:24; Taz 319:13; 506:3; M"B 319:61

[327] And thus one may do so even with intent to eat later on

[328] Shabbos Kehalacha Vol 2 page 243 note 288. There he explains that the Alter Rebbe himself never wrote this "Halacha 14" and it was rather written by the printers. In the new Shulchan Aruch of Admur they omitted this all together.

[329] Doing so is prohibited due to the Melacha of Zoreh [winnowing] and not Borer.

[330] Based on the Siddur.

 However according to the Shulchan Aruch Halacha 24 it is permitted to remove through using a spoon and taking out a bit of liquid together with it.

Q&A

May one hold onto the cup with one hand and place the spoon under the fly with the other hand, and then pull away the cup?
Some[331] write that one may do so. Practically, one is not to do so.[332]

May one remove pieces of cork from one's wine on Shabbos?
See Q&A in the filtering chapter.

May one move the fly or other waste to the side of the cup using one's hand or spoon?[333]
No. This may only be done through blowing on it, as moving it with a spoon or finger involves the Muktzah prohibition.[334]

May one blow the waste to the side even if it is covering the surface of the food to the point that it is impossible to drink it without blowing it to the side?[335]
No. The permission to blow the waste to the side only applies when one would in any event be able to manage to drink the liquid even without blowing it to the side.[336] However if this is not the case then it is forbidden to blow it to the side at all, and rather one may only pour it out as it is together with some of the liquid in order to drink right away.

May one splash away the dirt that floats on the surface of a Mikvah?[337]
One may do so even with his hands in order to allow himself to immerse in a clear area of the water. This applies even if the dirt covers over the entire Mikveh and one thus would not desire to immerse without splashing the dirt away.[338] Some[339] however write that it is nevertheless proper to take care to splash the dirt away to the sides together with a lot of water.

May one remove the dirt from the Mikveh using with his hands?
No.[340] However some[341] suggest that one may be lenient to remove the dirt from the Mikveh using his hands. Practically, it is forbidden to do so.[342]

May one use a vessel to discard the dirt from the Mikveh, if he does so together with some of the water?
No.[343] However some[344] rule one may be lenient to do so if he respells part of that water back into the

---

[331] Piskeiy Teshuvos 319:44 footnote 351 in name of Imrei Emes and Toras Yekusiel
[332] As according to Admur whatever is left in your hand is considered what you took, and so here it would be considered that you took both the Pesoles from the food and the food from the Pesoles, which is forbidden.
[333] Shabbos Kehalacha Vol. 2 p. 240
[334] So infers the Ketzos Hashulchan 125 footnote 18 from the Alter Rebbe above in the Siddur.
[335] Shabbos Kehalacha Vol. 2 p. 240
[336] So rules Peri Megadim
[337] Ketzos Hashulchan 146 footnote 35; Shabbos Kehalacha Vol. 2 p. 242; Piskeiy Teshuvos 319:45
[338] So is implied from Ketzos Hashulchan and so rules Shabbos Kehalacha ibid.
Other Poskim: Some Poskim rule that if there is a lot of filth blocking the entire water then it is considered Borer even to splash the water to another side. [P"M 339 A"A 14] See however Ketzos Hashulchan ibid that brings many reasons why in this case one may be lenient even according to the P"M ibid
[339] Chelkas Yaakov ibid, brought in the Ketzos Hashulchan ibid, and so rules Shabbos Kehalacha ibid that it is proper to do so as this strengthens the allowance even more, although it is not required from the letter of the law. However, the Ketzos Hashulchan himself sides that there is no need at all to do so.
[340] P"M 339 A"A 14
[341] Piskeiy Teshuvos ibid footnote 359 based on that a) Some Poskim rule there is no Borer by floating objects. [Mahriytiz brought in Beir Heiytiv 319; Tal Oros 31; Iglei Tal Borer 6:5; Ketzos Hashulchan ibid] And b) The water is useable even with the dirt. Furthermore, another reason for allowance is because it is similar to peeling an item which is Derech Achila, so too removing the dirt from the water is Derech Achila, as there is no other way to clean the water. [This is in contrast to a fly in a cup in which one has the option to remove the liquid or the fly.]
[342] Ass all Poskim ibid that do not record this option and we do not rule like the Maharititz, and people are initially Makpid against the dirt.
[343] Based on Siddur Admur
[344] Vayaan Yosef 139; Piskeiy Teshuvos 319:45

Mikveh.

May one use a pool net to remove dirt from a Mikveh or pool on Shabbos?[345]
No. Doing is forbidden due to the Borer prohibition.

---

10. May one remove fruits etc that have fallen into pebbles and dirt, from the floor?[346]
One whose fruits have [fallen] into pebbles and dust, may be gathered one at a time in order to eat [right away[347]]. However, he may not place them into a basket or box.
The reason for this is so he does not do a mundane act [which resembles Borer[348]].

11. Separating vessels from waste and from amongst other types of vessels:[349]
Just like there is a prohibition of separating food [from waste] so too there is also [a prohibition in separating] other items from amongst their waste, or [in separating] one type of item which is mixed with another type of item.
Example: For example, if one had in front of him two types of vessels which are mixed together and one wants to select one type from amongst another type in order to use it, then this item [which he wishes to take now] is considered like food and the other item is considered like waste and one thus is required to remove the food from the waste and not vice versa, even in a case that one of the items is larger than the other and is [thus easily] recognizable on its own. As well one is required to separate it to use it right away as was explained regarding [separating from a mixture which contains] two types of food.
Washing dirt from vessels:[350] One may wash vessels for the need of that day, such as if there still remains a meal which one desires to eat with the use of these vessels, then one may wash it even immediately after the current meal.[351]

Summary: The Borer restrictions explained above apply equally to:
1) A mixture of a vessel or other item together with waste.[352]
2) A mixture of two different types of vessels/items[353] [even if one is large and the other small[354] such as a mixture of clothing or books and the like].

---

[345] See Ketzos Hashulchan 146 footnote 35; Piskeiy Teshuvos 319:45 footnote 359
[346] Admur 335:5
[347] Shabbos Kehalacha 14:45
[348] Ketzos Hashulchan 146 p. 98 number 2
[349] Admur 319:8; Taz 319:12 based on Rashi 74b; Tosefes Shabbos 319:14; Chayeh Adam 16:5; M"B 319:15
Background: Prior to the Taz the Poskim do not mention any case of Borer that relate to vessels. All the examples and cases mentioned of Borer, both in the Gemara Shabbos 74a, Rambam and Tur Shulchan Aruch, only relate to foods. This leads one to think that the laws of Borer do not apply to vessels. The Taz ibid finds a further proof for this from a Tosafus ibid. However, there is one source in the Rishonim that stick out and point towards there being a prohibition of Borer even by vessels. This source is the words of Rashi on the Gemara 74b that states that the making of an earthenware vessel can involve 7 sin offerings. Rashi learns that one of the sin offerings is due to a Borer transgression of separating between large pieces of pottery and small ones. The Taz ibid concludes based on this that there is a prohibition of Borer also by vessels, and so is concluded in Admur ibid and all the other Achronim that came afterwards.
Vessels that are all individually recognizable: Some Poskim rule that the above law of Borer by vessels does not apply by a mixture of vessels that are individually recognizable such as clothing, books and silverware and plates. However, most Poskim rule that the laws of Borer apply even in such cases. See Q&A!
[350] Admur 323:6; Michaber 323:6; M"B 323:27
[351] Q. Why does this not contain a prohibition of Borer as does washing off dirt from lettuce and the like?
[352] Admur 319:8
[353] Admur 319:8
[354] Admur 319:6 However if one of the species is large while the other is small then it is only questionable as to whether the separating prohibitions apply, although nevertheless one must be stringent.

Q&A

May one separate paper with words of Torah from mundane papers in order to throw out the pile of mundane papers and place the Torah papers in genizah?[355]

Yes, so long as doing so is not for a weekday need.[356] One however may not do so in order to prevent disgrace to the Torah papers, such as in a case that the Torah papers are mixed with dirty objects, as in such a case the Borer restrictions apply.

May one separate recycling items on Shabbos?[357]

Yes, so long as doing so is not for the need of the weekday.

The laws of Borer which pertain to clothing:[358]

The definition of a mixture to which the Borer restrictions apply:[359]

A mixture of different articles of clothing: A mixture of different articles of clothing [i.e. clothing which serve different purposes], such as socks with undergarments is considered a mixture to which the Borer restrictions apply. Thus, if one has a pile of laundry all the separating restrictions apply in separating the different articles of clothing. It is thus only permitted to remove an article of clothing which one desires to use right away.

A mixture of the same article of clothing, such as a mixture of shirts, does not have the Borer restrictions apply unless a) they are of different colors and one specifically desires to now remove a specific color from the mixture. In such a case all the Borer restrictions would apply. Or b) they are of different sizes and only a specific size fits.

Two articles of clothing of which one is sitting on top of the other is not considered a mixture and does not contain the Borer restrictions, as is always the rule that two items do not have the definition of a mixture. Thus, one may remove the clothing that are sitting on top of a lower clothing in order to reach that lower clothing.[360] However this only applies if one does not also desire to use the upper clothing. However, if one also desires to use the upper clothing then all the separating restrictions apply in removing it and it thus may only be removed to use right away.

Word of advice: In any situation that the mixture of clothing contains the separating restrictions one can have another person take the entire bundle of clothing and throw them up in the air thus having them separate from each other, nullifying their mixed status. One may then go and choose whichever clothing he desires. Initially one should refrain from throwing up the clothing himself and rather have someone else do it for him.

May one remove clothing from his closet or drawer in order to reach a specific clothing?

One is permitted to move the clothing aside having the clothing remain within the drawer/closet[361], so long as he plans to use the requested clothing right away. However, to remove the clothing from the drawer for the purpose of searching for the requested clothing is dependent on how the clothing are mixed. If the clothing is simply sitting one on top of the other then if one is uninterested at all in the upper clothing, the separating restrictions do not apply. If one is also interested in the upper clothing, then all the separating restrictions apply. If the clothing is mixed up [not one on top of the other] then initially one may only remove those clothing that he is interested in using right away. However, in a case that it is not possible to find the requested clothing without removing the other clothing then one

---

[355] Shabbos Kehalacha Vol. 2 p. 138-139

[356] As since he is not interested in using any of the papers at all it is similar to separating two foods of which one is not interested in eating either one at any future time which is allowed.

[357] Shabbos Kehalacha Vol. 2 p. 138, see previous footnote for the reason

[358] Shabbos Kehalacha Vol. 2 p. 206-211

[359] Shabbos Kehalacha Vol. 2 p. 206-211

[360] Based on M"B 319:15; Az Nidbaru 7:31; Piskeiy Teshuvos 319 footnote 33; See in length Shabbos Kehalacha chapter 12 footnote 188

[361] As doing so is similar to moving the fly in ones cup towards the side of the cup which is allowed. [Ketzos Hashulchan 125, last footnote]

386

may do so although taking care to replace the clothing back afterwards.

May one remove clothing from a mixture for later use if he will not have the ability to separate the clothing right away prior to the use? Such as may one separate his sweater from a mixture of clothing prior to leaving the house even though he does not plan on using it until later on at night when it becomes cold?[362]

If the clothing is defined as mixed [as explained above] then doing so is forbidden being one is taking the sweater for later use. Furthermore, even if one plans to wear the clothing now in order to give it a right away use, it remains forbidden being that in truth he has no current need for the sweater. Thus, the only remaining advice in such a case is for one to have someone else throw the mixture of clothing up in the air, having the clothing separate from each other and then take the sweater.

May one separate clothing from a mixture on Friday night to have it prepared to be worn the next day on Shabbos?[363]

If the clothing is defined as mixed [See above] then doing so is forbidden.

If clothing is sitting on top of each other on a clothing hanger may one remove the upper clothing in order to reach the lower clothing?

One may do so[364] although it is best to return the unwanted clothing back onto the hook after removing the clothing which one desires.[365]

May one remove dirt/crumbs and the like from ones shtreimal or Sheitel?[366]

If the crumb is simply sitting on top of the shtreimal/Sheitel and is not stuck inside it then one may remove it in any way he desires.[367] If, however, the crumb is stuck within the hair of the shtreimal/Sheitel then it is best to shake the dirt/crumb out of the shtreimal/Sheitel <u>immediately prior to using it</u>[368] rather than remove it with one's hands. Nevertheless, if needed one may remove it with one's hands[369] although taking caution not to remove any of the hairs in the process.

May one shake dust and the like off a hat, Sheitel?[370]

It is best to do so in close proximity to their use.

The laws of Borer which pertain to eating utensils:

May one remove the eating utensils from their drawer in order to set up the table much time prior to the meal?[371]

If this is being done in order to currently have a nice table setting, it is allowed in all cases, even if the utensils are mixed with each other.[372] If however this is not the intent and one simply desires to currently set the table so he does not have to do so later on, then if the utensils are mixed, such as forks with knives and the like, it is forbidden to separate them from each other, and one thus must delay the setting of the table until immediately prior to the meal. However, if the utensils are each in their set area, such

---

[362] Shabbos Kehalacha Vol. 2 p. 209

[363] Shabbos Kehalacha Vol. 2 p. 208

[364] So rules the M"B 319:15

[365] So rules the Ketzos Hashulchan 125

[366] Shabbos Kehalacha Vol. 2 p. 123, and 211

[367] As in such a case the crumb is not considered mixed with the Sheitel/shtreimal.

[368] Thus, keeping to all the separating restrictions, removing the good from the bad for right away use.

[369] As there are opinions which hold that the separating restrictions do not at all apply in such a case as a) it is merely considered cleaning a cloth which does not contain the separating restrictions [Rav SZ"A] and b) If the hair is made of real hair then it is considered like an attached item to which the separating restrictions do not apply.

[370] Shabbos Kehalacha Vol. 2 p. 123

[371] Shabbos Kehalacha Vol. 2 P. 212

[372] Rav SZ"A in letter in Maor Hashabbos 1:8-2

as the forks with the forks etc, then since the utensils are not considered mixed one may set the table whatever time he wishes. Nevertheless, care must be taken not to place the different utensils in his hand at the same time, thus mixing them in his hand in the process, as if they become mixed in his hand all the separating restrictions would now apply and one would not be allowed to set the table unless it is right before the start of the meal. Thus, one should set up each utensil individually.

If the utensils are mixed may one only remove the exact number of utensils prior to the meal?[373]
Yes. If one knows the exact number of utensils that he will need then he may not separate extra utensils, as doing so is equivalent to separating for no use which is forbidden.

May one remove a utensil from the mixture for the purpose of using it to save his spot on the table, or as a separation between a man and his wife?[374]
Yes.

May one separate the Milk utensils from the meat utensils and the like?[375]
If the mixture is of the same utensils, such as dairy spoons which are mixed with meat spoons then one may separate them without restriction, as previously explained in Halacha 6. [376]

May one remove the dirty utensils from the table in order to clean the table?[377]
If the dirty utensils are mixed together with clean utensils [as mixed was defined in the Introduction of this chapter-see there] doing so is forbidden being that one is removing the bad from the good. Rather one is to remove the clean utensils from the table and may then remove the dirty utensils.

May one remove the dirty fish plate from on top of the meat plate if one will not be eating meat right away?
Yes, as they are not defined as mixed.

After the meal may one remove the utensils from amongst the waste that is on the table?[378]
If the vessels are mixed with the food wastes in a way that is defined as mixed [as explained in the introduction to this chapter] then it is forbidden to remove the utensils from the waste unless one plans to use it right away. Included in this is if one desires to wash the utensils clean at this time so he can use them or to prevent the food from drying on it or to prevent insects from gathering. If one has no need for the utensils then one should shake the utensils away from the waste, so they no longer be defined as mixed, and then remove them.

May one remove a fork/spoon/knife that fell into a liquid?[379]
Yes, one may do so without restriction being that it is not defined as mixed as explained in the Introduction in the Q&A there.

---

[373] Shabbos Kehalacha Vol. 2 P. 212
[374] Shabbos Kehalacha Vol. 2 P. 212
[375] Shabbos Kehalacha Vol. 2 P. 212
[376] Other Opinions: To note however that the SSH"K rules that this is forbidden being that according to them if one item is forbidden and one is permitted they are considered like two different species despite the fact that they are all from the same species. This however does not follow the ruling of Admur and others as explained above in Halacha 6 that a prohibited part is not considered another species in the case of removal of forbidden fats. This is also the opinion of the Magen Avraham and Mishneh Berurah. Vetzaruch Iyun on the Ketzos Hashulchan which seems to imply that two Lulavim of two different people on Sukkos would be considered Borer on the first day of Sukkos when one cannot fulfill his obligation with another person's Lulav. See Shabbos Kihalacha Vol. 2 p. 102.
[377] Shabbos Kehalacha Vol. 2 P. 213
[378] Shabbos Kehalacha Vol. 2 P. 213
[379] Shabbos Kehalacha Vol. 2 p. 363

If a vessel fell into the garbage may one remove it from the garbage without restriction?[380]
One may only remove it if he plans to use it right away such as if he plans to wash it.

May one sort out the utensils, each one with its kind, to place them in the dish washer so they are ready for after Shabbos?[381]
No. This is forbidden because of the separating prohibition.

May one sort out the utensils in order to wash them separately?[382]
No unless a) one has a need to wash them now, such as he plans to use them now or he desires to wash them to prevent flies from coming and the like. And b) It is easier for him to wash each type of utensil separately.

May one sort out the utensils in order to dry them separately or place them away each one in their set spot?[383]
If it is easier to dry each type of utensil separate from the other type, then this is allowed. If not, then one may either a) as he washes or dries each individual utensil, he places down each type of utensil separate from the other. Or b) One may have another person spread out the mixture of utensils in a way that they are no longer defined as mixed.

Avoiding Borer when cleaning table:
When cleaning a table, one must be careful to avoid transgressing the Borer prohibition when separating items.

The laws of Borer which pertain to keys:[384]
Are keys in a key chain defined as mixed and thereby retain the separating restrictions?
If there are three or more keys in a keychain then all the middle keys, which are defined as all the keys besides for the outer most key of both sides, are defined as mixed and thus retain the separating restrictions. Thus, one may only remove or take hold of any of the middle keys for a right away use. If there are only two keys on the keychain then no separating restrictions apply.

May one separate one of the middle keys not for a right away use if he is simply holding on to it without removing it from the key chain?
The separating restrictions apply even if one does not actually remove any of the middle keys from the key chain but simply takes hold of it, and thus separates it from the other keys, while it still remains attached to the key chain.

What is one to do if he needs to remove a middle key from the key chain to take with him when he leaves the house, so he be able to open the door when he returns, but does not need to lock the door now upon him leaving, such as if people are still awake in the home?
The only choice he has is to have another person scatter all the keys from each other, so they no longer be defined as mixed and then take the key that he needs.

The laws of Borer which pertain to books:[385]
Does the Borer prohibition by vessels pertain also to a mixture of Sefarim?
Some Poskim[386] rule the laws of Borer do not pertain to Sefarim.

---

[380] Shabbos Kehalacha Vol. 2 P. 214
[381] Shabbos Kehalacha Vol. 2 P. 214
[382] Shabbos Kehalacha Vol. 2 P. 214
[383] Shabbos Kehalacha Vol. 2 P. 214
[384] Shabbos Kehalacha Vol. 2 p. 216-217
[385] Shabbos Kehalacha Vol. 2 p. 219-223

What is defined as a mixture of two different types of books?

As explained many times above the separating restrictions only apply by a) two different items which are b) defined as mixed. The following is the definition of the above two conditions as they relate to books.

Two different types: Regarding books any two books which are of different topic, even if they share the same name, or are of the same topic but have different features, such as different Nuschaos of Sidurim or different types of Chumashim containing different commentaries, then they are defined as two different types.

Books of the same exact topic but are simply of different prints and fonts are disputed whether they are considered like two different types of books. Practically one may be lenient so long as one type of font is not meant to be used only by children and the like.

Books of the same exact topic or even print but some are new while others are worn out are only considered two different types of books if the old print is so worn out that it is only useable in pressing situations.

The definition of a mixture: Books are only defined as mixed if they are sitting one on top of the other. Books which are sitting next to each other on a bookshelf, one next to the other, are not defined as mixed and one may thus remove any book from the shelf even not for right away use.[387] Books which are lying next to each other on a table, as is common in Shuls are not defined as mixed and one may thus remove whichever book he desires from the table even not for right away use.

Word of Advice: Whenever books are defined as mixed and one desires to separate them not for a right away use one may have another person [if not practical then even the same person may do so] separate all the books throughout the table in a way that they are no longer sitting on top of each other and then gather whichever book he desires. However, it only helps to separate the books by tilting the pile in a way that they all fall on a different spot of the table, however, to remove each book from the pile and place it down separately does not help as this action itself is considered separating.

May one gather all the Chumashim or Siddurim from the tables of the Shul in order to place them in their set place on the shelves?

Any book which does not have another type of book lying on top of it may be removed from the table without restriction. Those books which have other types of books piled on top of them are forbidden to be removed from amongst the mixture. Thus, the only way to go about it is to have another person [or oneself if another person is not available] separate all the books throughout the table through tilting the pile in a way that they are no longer sitting on top of each other and then gather whichever book he desires.

Regarding if one may remove one book at a time from the pile, see the next question.

If one has a pile of different books may he remove one book at a time and place it in its set place on the shelf?

If one would in any event take one book at a time due to weight purposes or the like, then once the book is in his hands, he may place it in its correct area on the shelf. However, to specifically take one book at a time in order to place each one in its set place is forbidden.

If one has a pile of different books and desires to organize them on the shelf does it help if one looks into each book after separating it in order to be considered a right away use?

Regarding doing so for one or two books perhaps this would be allowed. However, for many books doing so is questionable being that it appears to all that one is not really interested in reading the book

---

[386] Aruch Hashulchan 319:8 in 1st explanation; Mahrshag 1:37 and 54; Beir Moshe 6:68; Tzitz Eliezer 12:35

[387] Rav SZ"A 3 footnote 197; The reason for this is, as explained Rav SZ"A, because each individual book placed on a shelf is considered of importance and is not defined in people's eyes as a mixture.

and is simply doing so for separating which thus makes it forbidden.

If a pile of papers from a folder got mixed up may one separate them from each other in order to organize them?
Only if one plans to now read these papers.

The laws of Borer that pertain to a mixture of toys/cards/games/etc.[388]

- Chess: The separation of the black pieces from the white pieces, or one type of piece from another, such as a king from a pawn, retains all the separating restrictions and thus may only be done for right away use.
- Cards:[389] One may separate the same types of cards for a right away purpose. One may not do so for the purpose of putting the cards away in an orderly fashion.
- Puzzles: Do not contain a separating prohibition in the separation of the pieces in order to make the puzzle. Nevertheless, one should never make a puzzle on Shabbos as doing so involves putting together words or pictures which is forbidden due to the writing prohibition. Nevertheless, children which play with puzzles on Shabbos do not need to be protested against.
- Games which the separating is their goal of play: Such as games which the purpose is to have all the pieces together in their set seemingly is forbidden to play, as when the separation of the piece is also the purpose of the separation it is not considered a right away use.
- Rubikube/Hungarian cube: Playing with a Hungarian cube and arranging the colors in order does not involve the Borer prohibition, and is thus permitted to play on Shabbos. [390]

Summary
The cases which contain the separating prohibition:
1. A mixture of food and waste, such as pits and shells with seeds and food.[391]
2. A mixture containing two different species of food[392], such as two different types of fish[393], even if one is large and the other small[394].
3. A mixture of a vessel or other item together with waste.[395]
4. A mixture of two different types of vessels/items[396] [even if one is large and the other small[397] such as a mixture of clothing or books and the like].
5. A mixture which contains the same species of foods but some of the mixture is only edible in pressing times, such as the withered leaves of lettuce. Such a mixture Rabbinically contains all the separating restrictions mentioned below.[398]
6. Peeling off peels and shells of fruits/nuts.[399]

---

[388] Shabbos Kehalacha Vol. 2 p. 223-226
[389] To note that the playing of poker cards and the like is greatly spoken against by Rav Levi Yitzchak of Berditchiv being that they contain much impurity. One should thus guard himself from ever playing with them even during the week.
[390] As one is not separating from item from another, but rather arranging the order of the item itself.
[391] Admur 319:1
[392] Admur 319:5
[393] Admur 319:6
[394] Admur 319:6 However if one of the species is large while the other is small then it is only questionable as to whether the separating prohibitions apply, although nevertheless one must be stringent.
[395] Admur 319:8
[396] Admur 319:8
[397] Admur 319:6 However if one of the species is large while the other is small then it is only questionable as to whether the separating prohibitions apply, although nevertheless one must be stringent.
[398] Admur 319:4
[399] Based on Rama in end of chapter 321, and alluded to in Admur here in Halacha 9. [see Shabbos Kihalacha Vol 2 page 290]

The separating restrictions that apply to all the above-mentioned cases:[400]

It is Biblically forbidden to separate in the above cases in any of the following ways:

1. One separates the bad, which is defined as the food/item that one does not want right now, from the good which is defined as what one wants right now.
   Or
2. Separates even the good but using a vessel designated for separation such as a sieve or sifter.[401]
   Or
3. Separates the good from bad with his hands but with intent to eat later on.[402]

It is Rabbinically forbidden to separate:

Good from bad to use right away using a vessel that is not professionally used for sifting.[403]

It is permitted to separate with the fulfillment of all the following three conditions:

1. One does so with intent to eat right away, which is defined as right before the start of the meal [after the conclusion of services in Shul[404]]. One may only separate enough to eat for the people participating in the meal, and not for leftovers for after the meal[405].
   And
2. One separates the food, which is defined as the item that one wishes to eat, from the waste which is defined as the item that one does not wish to eat.[406]
   And
3. One does so using his hands, and not a vessel.[407]

Separating through placing the mixture in a sieve and having the waste fallout from the holes:
See below in the section dealing with sifting.

---

[400] Admur 319:1
[401] Admur 319:1
[402] Admur 319:2
[403] Admur 319:1
[404] Admur 319:4
[405] Admur 319:2-3
[406] Admur 319:1
[407] Admur 319:1

CHAPTER 2: THE LAWS OF MIFAREK [SEPARATING GRAINS AND LEGUMES FROM THEIR PEELS AND STALKS] AND PEELING FRUITS AND VEGETABLES

Halacha 1. Rubbing and peeling shells/stalks/pods off from nuts/seeds/beans on Shabbos:

Halacha 2. Peeling fruits and vegetables

Introduction:

The following section will deal with peeling shells/peels off of foods such as removing the pods/shells of nuts and beans and removing the peels of fruits and the like. Doing so in addition to involving the Borer restrictions[1], as well at times involves a prohibition of Mifarek or Dash, which is to detach an item from another item. The Mifarek prohibition is an offshoot of the Dash prohibition, and when it applies there is no permission at all to peel the item on Shabbos, even when done for right away use. This is opposed to the Borer prohibition which contains a leniency that it is always permitted to remove the good from the bad for right away use. Thus, whenever the Mifarek prohibition applies the food may not be eaten on Shabbos.

---

1. Rubbing and peeling shells/stalks/pods off from nuts/seeds/beans on Shabbos:

Note: In these laws there are various discrepancies between the rulings of the Shulchan Aruch and that of the Siddur. Although both rulings have been brought below, it is incumbent upon the reader to read the summary to know how we practically rule, taking into account all the rulings of the Siddur, which is the final say in these matters.

❖ ***The rulings of Admur in the Shulchan Aruch[2]:***

Rubbing:

First opinion-It is allowed to do so with an irregularity:[3] One may not extract seeds from stalks in the same method used during the week, which is to rub the stalks within the palms of one's hands in order so the seeds fall out from it. Rather he must rub them with a slight[4] irregularity using the tips of his fingers.

The reason this is allowed: Now, although by doing so he separates the seeds from the stalks with his hands, and one who separates [seed from a stalk] with his hands is [liable for transgressing] an offshoot of the threshing prohibition which is done using a vessel, as was explained in chapter 305 [Halacha 28], nevertheless [here] since he is separating it irregularly in order to eat (right away) it is permitted.[5]

It was not decreed against doing so due to that one may come to separate [the seeds] as regularly done, being that even one who separates them in the usual method is also only considered to be doing so irregularly being that he does not take the food and actually remove it with his hands [from the stalks] but rather just rubs the stalk and causes the grains to fall and [this method] is usually only done with a vessel that is designated for threshing. However nevertheless it is Rabbinically forbidden [to separate by rubbing it with ones hands], although when this too is done with an irregularity they made no decree against doing so.

Other Opinions:[6] [However] there are opinions[7] which are stringent to not sort at all [the seeds out from] stalks of grains or from pods of legumes even using the tips of one's fingers.

---

[1] Based on Rama in end of chapter 321 Halacha 19, and alluded to in Admur here in Halacha 9. [see Shabbos Kihalacha Vol 2 page 290]

[2] Admur 319:9; Michaber 319:6

[3] Admur ibid; Michaber ibid

[4] There are two ways of reading these words "Bishinuiy Me'at". It can either mean as written above "with a slight irregularity" or it can mean "a small amount", meaning that one may only rub a small amount of stalks. The M"B 319:21 rules [based on Gamara and Olas Shabbos] like the latter, that it means a small amount at a time. Vetzaruch Iyun in Admur.

[5] Admur ibid; Rama ibid

[6] Admur ibid; Rama ibid

[7] Mordechai and Ran

Rubbing off the green shell of nuts:[8] Therefore [according to this latter opinion] it is forbidden to rub out the Luz nuts[9] or large nuts from within their upper green shell which covers over their thick and hard shell, even with the tips of one's fingers.[10]

The Final Ruling:[11] It is proper[12] to be stringent [to not rub off the shell] being that one can anyways break it open and eat it without needing to separate [the shell][13]. [However according to the Siddur rubbing is forbidden under all circumstances]. [**See Q&A**]

❖ *Peeling:*

To peel off the thin peel of nuts, grains and legumes:[14] It is permitted to break [the shell] and then peel off the thin peel that is on the fruit which is under the hard shell which is broken, as the Mifarek/detaching prohibition is only applicable by the top [greenish] shell. [**See Q&A 7-8**]

Similarly, it is permitted to peel [the chaffs off] grains and legumes which have been removed from their stalks and pods from before Shabbos, although one must be careful to only peel as much as he needs to eat right away and not for what he will need to eat later on as will be explained in chapter 321 [Halacha 19[15]]

[Regarding if one may shake off the thin peels from amongst the grains in a case that they have already been peeled off and are now sitting together with the grains- see Chapter 3.]

Peeling off the pods from legumes:[16] However (according to all opinions) it is forbidden to peel the pods on Shabbos and remove the legumes from within them (with ones hands as doing so is [Halachically considered] actually Mifarek/detaching [which is forbidden]).

Moist pods:[17] However [the populace of] the world is accustomed to allow this to be done and there are opinions which seek merit [to justify] their actions [saying] that since the stalks are still moist and thus the pods themselves are still edible, it is thus like one is simply separating food from food which does not contain the detaching prohibition as explained in chapter 305 [Halacha 28].

Inedible-dry-pods:[18] However those legumes which their pods are not edible there contains no permission at all to remove the legumes from within them on Shabbos unless the legumes are not at all attached to their pods, having been detached from them before Shabbos and it is rather simply sitting [loosely] within [the pod]. In such a case it is permitted to remove [as many legumes from the pod] as he wishes to eat right away, however he may not do so to eat later on due to the separating prohibition.

❖ *The ruling of Admur in the Siddur:*
Not to eat legumes that are still in their pods on Shabbos:

Inedible pods: [One] needs to be very careful not to eat on Shabbos beans, whether raw or cooked, which are still in their [inedible[19]] pods. [**See Q&A**]

The reason for this is: because being that their pods are not edible, removing them contains the Mifarek/detaching prohibition according to all opinions, which is an offshoot of the threshing prohibition which one is liable for a sin offering and stoning Heaven Forbid.

---

[8] Admur ibid; Rama ibid

[9] This refers to almonds which when small are sweet and when they ripen become bitter. [Likuteiy Sichos 33 page Matos]

[10] The upper green shell usually is removed in the field or by the distributer and is thus usually not seen on the nut by the time it reaches the consumer. However, there are times during the year that fresh original nuts are sold still in their green shell and thus due care must be taken not to remove the upper green shell through rubbing it.

[11] Admur ibid; Rama ibid

[12] Lit. Good

[13] It seems that this is referring to nuts, being that the shell can be cracked, however by pods being that the only option is to rub them, then doing so would be allowed with an irregularity according to the final ruling of Admur, and so is implied also from chapter 321 Halacha 1.

[14] Admur ibid; Olas Shabbos 319:14; M"A 319:8 and 321:30; M"B 319:22; See P"M 320 A"A 1; Rav Akiva Eiger 319:6; Shevet Halevi 1:81 which question why there is no Mifarek prohibition relevant by the outer shell.

[15] In Rama, the end of the chapter was not printed in the Alter Rebbe's Shulchan Aruch. There he explained that one may not peel onions and garlic to eat later on.

[16] Admur ibid; Taz 319:4; M"A 319:8

[17] Admur ibid; M"A 319:8; Elya Zuta 319:5; M"B 319:21

[18] Admur ibid; Taz 319:4

[19] So is evident from below in which the case of edible pods is mentioned with different laws.

The above applies even if the beans have detached from their pods: Now, although the beans have already [become] detached [inside] from their pod through the cooking process and are thus no longer attached to it [nevertheless the above Mifarek prohibition still applies].[20]

Sesame seeds: The same restriction applies also towards sesame seeds.

Legumes with edible pods: A meticulous person should be stringent upon himself also with regards to the species of legumes called (Arbes[21]) when they are still attached to their pods, even though their pods are also edible, as [separating the seeds from the pods] is not clearly allowed.

Avoid eating shelled nuts/seeds on Shabbos:
It is proper[22] to avoid eating almonds and nuts on Shabbos unless they have been removed from their shells from before Shabbos. [**See Q&A**]

The reason for this is: because, although even when the nut/fruit remains totally or partially in its shell [on Shabbos] it is permitted to remove its shell with ones hands and does not contain [a] separating bad from good [prohibition], nevertheless after the fruit has been removed if there remains a piece of the shell amongst the pieces of fruit/nut or amongst whole nuts, then if one removes [that shell] from there he is liable for a sin offering [if done unintentionally] and stoning [if done intentionally] for [transgressing the prohibition of] separating waste from food. Rather one must separate the fruit/nut from amongst the shells and may not touch the shells at all.

Furthermore [in additional reason to avoid nuts] even if the shells are bunched up alone without having any mixture of fruit [of the nuts] amongst them, [nevertheless] there [still remains] a great prohibition in moving them due to that they are Muktzah, as is known. And [since] it is difficult to beware from all the above [prohibitions, therefore it should be avoided.]

Summary

Pods of legumes and stalks of grains:
Rubbing off the pods and stalks of grains and legumes:[23] If the pods are inedible then it is completely forbidden to rub them off [due to the threshing prohibition] even if they were cooked, and thus the legumes have already separated within the pod. If the pods are edible, then a meticulous person should avoid eating them even in such a case.

Peeling off the pods of legumes:
Pods that are inedible: Is forbidden due to Mifarek according to all[24], even if the beans were separated from the pods from before Shabbos.[25]
Pods that are edible: The custom is to be lenient to peel off the pod[26], although a meticulous person should avoid eating them even in such a case.[27] [Nevertheless, if the beans have detached from their pods then seemingly according to all one may be lenient.]
Peeling off the thin peel of nuts, legumes and grains:[28] Does not contain any Mifarek prohibition, although contains the separating restrictions and thus may only be peeled directly prior to the meal.

---

[20] So rules also M"B in Biur Halacha 6 "Bishinui", as opposed to the ruling of Admur in the SH"A.
[21] This term is used today to refer to chickpeas
[22] Lit. good
[23] Siddur.
However in the Shulchan Aruch 319:9 Admur rules that merely "It is proper to be stringent to not rub them even with an irregularity", which is with using the tips of one's fingers, even though that there are opinions which permit doing so in order to eat right away. However, to rub them without an irregularity is forbidden according to all opinions even in the Shulchan Aruch.
[24] Admur 319:9 and Siddur
[25] Siddur
However according to the Shulchan Aruch 319:9, if the beans have been separated from the pods from before Shabbos then there is no Mifarek prohibition involved, although one must beware of all the separating restrictions explained above
[26] Admur 319:9 Regarding whether or not the restrictions of Borer apply too in this case. Rav Farkash in chapter 13 page 318 [see Biurim 6] sides that it is permitted being that it is simply like removing food from food. So rules also the Ketzos Hashulchan [126 footnote 3] and Peri Megadim.
[27] Siddur
[28] Admur 319:9

Nuts with shells:

Avoid eating nuts/seeds on Shabbos:[29] It is proper to avoid eating them unless they have been shelled before Shabbos and are thus no longer mixed in with their shells. In the event that one eats nuts with shells on Shabbos the following are the laws involved in removing its shell:

Rubbing off the upper green shell:[30] It is forbidden to be done even with the tips of one's fingers due to the threshing prohibition and rather one must crack it open.

Peeling off the upper green shell:[31] Is forbidden due to the Mifarek prohibition.

Peeling off the thin peel of nuts, legumes, and grains:[32] Does not contain any Mifarek prohibition, although contains all the separating restrictions, and thus may only be peeled directly prior to the meal.

Q&A

Does the Mifarek prohibition also apply to pods which are grown with intent to be marketed together with their pods?

If the pods are grown with intent to be marketed together with their pods then some Poskim[33] rule the Mifarek prohibition does not apply, although if the pod is inedible then all the Borer prohibitions would still apply. See next question. Other Poskim[34] however are stringent even in such a case. [It is implied from Admur that he learns like the former opinion that permits it.[35]]

May one peel off the pods of beans, peas, green beans?[36]

Legumes which are grown with intent to be marketed without their pods: If the pods are inedible then they may not be removed, due to the Mifarek prohibition, even if the beans have already become detached from within the pods.[37] If the pods are edible then from the letter of the law the pods may be removed without restriction and do not contain either the Mifarek or Borer prohibitions. However, as Admur concludes in the Siddur a meticulous person is to be stringent even in such a case.

Pods which are grown with intent to be marketed while still within their pods: Such as green beans and Okra and the like, then if the pod is also edible, it contains neither a Mifarek or Borer prohibition. If the pod is inedible then although it does not contain a Mifarek prohibition, nevertheless it contains all the Borer restrictions and thus may only be peeled off right before the meal.[38]

May one cut the pod and remove the beans?[39]

No.

May one remove corn from the cob on Shabbos?[40]

To remove the kernels from the root in the cob is disputed amongst the Poskim. Some hold[41] that doing

---

[29] Siddur

[30] Siddur

However according to the Shulchan Aruch: It is proper[30] to be stringent to not rub off the shell being that one can anyways break it open and then eat it without needing to separate the shell.

[31] Admur 319:9

[32] Admur 319:9

[33] Ketzos Hashulchan 126 footnote 5 and 8 based on Iglei Tal 2:3 and Chayeh Adam 14; Shabbos Kehalacha Vol. 2 p. 320; See Minchas Yitzchak 3:32 and Shevet Halevi 1:81 that mention such a logic. The Shevet Halevi ibid however negates this differentiation.

[34] Shevet Halevi 1:81 based on P"M 320 A"A 1; Rav Akiva Eiger 319:6; See also Ketzos Hashulchan 126 footnote 8 which leaves this matter in a Tzaruch Iyun.

[35] Admur 319:9 which writes that there is no Mifarek prohibition relevant by the inner shell, hence forcing the conclusion of the Ketzos Hashuclhan ibid, unlike the question of the P"M ibid. So also explained the Shevet Halevi ibid in Admur.

[36] Shabbos Kehalacha Vol. 2 p. 316-320

[37] This follows the ruling of the Siddur, however according Admur in the SHU"A [Halacha 9] it is permitted in a case that the legumes have detached from within from their pod.

[38] Based on Ketzos Hashulchan 126 footnote 4

[39] So is implied from Admur 319:9 which forbids peeling the pod and then removing the beans with one's hands.

[40] Shabbos Kehalacha Vol. 2 p. 321-322

[41] Tehila Ledavid 319:9 based on P"M 3109 M"Z 4 and 320 A"A 1; Mahrsham in Orchos Chaim 319 and Daas Torah

so does not contain the Mifarek prohibition[42] [although one must guard the Borer restrictions in doing so]. Others hold[43] that it does contain the Mifarek restrictions and thus cannot be done at all.

<u>To cut the kernels off the cob without removing the root from the cob:</u> Since one only cuts off the upper part of the kernel, it does not contain the Mifarek prohibition although does contain the Borer restrictions and thus may only be done in close proximity to the meal.

<u>To eat the kernels while on the cob:</u> Is permitted according to all.

May one remove dates from its stalk?[44]

Some Poskim[45] rule this is forbidden to be done even in order to eat right away.[46] Other Poskim[47] rule it is permitted.[48]

May one remove bananas from the stalk or grapes from their vine?[49]

One may only do so immediately prior to the meal.[50]

May one break open the shells of a nut using a vessel which is specified for that purpose, such as a nutcracker?[51]

Depends on the nut. If it is a type of nut, such as a hazel nut, which upon having its shell cracked will have the nut fall out and thus be completely separated from the shell, then all the separating restrictions apply and one may not use a designated vessel in order to break it. However, nuts which even after breaking still need to be separated from their shell, then one may use even a specified vessel to break it open.

May one use a hammer to break open the nut?[52]

Yes, as a hammer is Muktzah Machamas Issur which may be used for a permitted purpose on Shabbos.

Once the shell has been cracked may one remove it from around the nut or must he remove the nut from out of the shell?[53]

When the nut remains totally or partially in its shell it is permitted to remove its shell with one's hands and does not contain [a] separating bad from good [prohibition], [despite that by doing so one is removing the bad from the good, being that this is equivalent to peeling a fruit.] Nevertheless, after the fruit has been removed if there remains a piece of the shell amongst the pieces of fruit/nut or amongst

---

[42] The reason: Being that it is only covered from its inner side as opposed to its outer side, and according to them only a food which is covered from both sides contains the Mifarek prohibition.

[43] Iglei Tal; Shevisas Shabbos [Dash 5] leaves this as a Tzaruch Iyun. The Ketzos Hashulchan [126:5 footnote 11] goes into depth on the sides of the doubt and rules that one is to be stringent out of doubt based on the words of the Shevisas Shabbos.

[44] Ketzos Hashulchan 126:5

[45] Ketzos Hashulchan ibid based on Iglei Tal and Shevisas Hashabbos ibid

[46] This is forbidden due to the Mifarek prohibition, as it is the common way to verse remove the stalk of dates from the tree and then cut the dates off the stalks and send them to storage. This is directly similar to threshing. Others however argue that threshing only applies to fruits which are concealed within their stalks, as are grains, and not by revealed fruits. [see Ketzos Hashulchan ibid footnote 9]

[47] Peri Megadim A"A 320

[48] Others argue that threshing only applies to fruits which are concealed within their stalks, as are grains, and not by revealed fruits. [see Ketzos Hashulchan ibid footnote 9]

[49] Ketzos Hashulchan 126 footnote 10-11; Shabbos Kihalacha Vol. 2 p. 316;

[50] Some Poskim [Iglei Tal unlike Peri Megadim A"A 320] rule that the "Dosh" "Threshing" prohibition applies equally to items which are removed from their stalk even if the fruits are revealed. Meaning that not only by concealed fruits such as legumes in their pods does the prohibition apply, but also by all foods which are attached to a stalk. Nevertheless, even according to them it is only forbidden when done in order to store, or eat later on, as is the form of Melacha of threshing that it is done for storage purposes. If however it is done to eat right away then it is allowed according to all, as this is not like Dash at all. Thus, one may remove bananas from their stalk, and grapes from their vines to eat right away. However, this is only by fruits which it is common to eat the food soon after removing it from its stalk. If however it is common to store the fruits after removing them from their stalk then they have the same law as does removing dates, in which some rule it is forbidden even to do in order to eat right away due to the threshing prohibition. [see Ketzos Hashulchan ibid footnote 9-10]

[51] Shabbos Kehalacha Vol. 2 p. 307

[52] Shabbos Kehalacha Vol. 2 p. 307

[53] Siddur of Admur; M"B 319:24 in name of M"A unlike the implication in the P"M which is stringent

whole nuts, then if one removes [that shell] from there he is liable for a sin offering [if done unintentionally] and stoning [if done intentionally] for [transgressing the prohibition of] separating waste from food. Rather one must separate the fruit/nut from amongst the shells and may not touch the shells at all.

May one peel off the outer shells of peanuts?[54]

Some[55] have forbidden doing so being that they consider this to be under the prohibition of Mifarek.[56] Many others[57] however have permitted this so long as it is done right before the meal and so is the general custom.[58] In any event those which are stringent like Admur in the Siddur not to eat nuts with shells on Shabbos also avoid eating peanuts that have not been shelled before Shabbos.

May one peel off the outer peel of garlic [the peel which contains within it all the cloves] and take apart the cloves from each other on Shabbos?[59]

Being that there are opinions[60] which hold that removing the outer shell may contain the Mifarek prohibition therefore one is to remove this peel and separate the cloves from before Shabbos. If one did not do so from before Shabbos, then he is to rub off the outer shell using the tips of his fingers which is an irregularity.[61] However Rav Farkash suggests that prior to resorting to this option[62] one should try to remove the clove together with its outer peel and then remove the garlic from both the outer and inner peel without separating between the inner and outer peel.

According to Admur in the Siddur may one eat sunflower seeds on Shabbos?[63]

If they are still in their shell certainly one is to avoid eating them on Shabbos for the reasons mentioned in the Siddur.

---

[54] Shabbos Kehalacha Vol. 2 p. 313

[55] Sheivet Halevy 1:81; 79-2; 3:42; Chelkas Yaakov 133 writes to be stringent

[56] The reason: As it is similar to the most outer green shell of the almond which is forbidden to remove due to Mifarek. [Shevet Halevi ibid] Now although it is permitted to break open the almond even with the green shell, this is because the green shell does not peel off and rather remains attached to the hard shell. Thus, one has not performed Mifarek to the outer shell, which is to remove it from its area of growth as is done in the field. However in this case it is being removed from its area of growth through breaking it and is hence forbidden due to the Mifarek prohibition.

[57] Maharshag 2:108; Minchas Yitzchak 3:32; Bear Moshe 38

[58] The reason: As peanuts are grown to also be marketed with tehri shells and hence are not relevant to the Izzur of Mifarek, as explained above. [See also Ketzos Hashulchan 126 footnote 5 and 8 based on Iglei Tal 2:3 and Chayeh Adam 14; Shabbos Kehalacha Vol. 2 p. 320; See Minchas Yitzchak ibid and Shevet Halevi 1:81 that mention such a logic. The Shevet Halevi ibid however negates this differentiation, and brings proofs against it; See also Ketzos Hashulchan 126 footnote 8 which leaves this matter in a Tzaruch Iyun.]

[59] Shabbos Kehalacha Vol. 2 p. 313-315

[60] Peri Megadim 319 A"A 8

[61] So rules Ketzos Hashulchan 126 footnote 8

[62] This is because based on Admur in the Siddur it seems that he rules like the stringent opinion above that it is forbidden to peel even using an irregularity such as using the tips of one's fingers.

[63] Shabbos Kehalacha Vol. 2 p. 313

2. Peeling fruits and vegetables:[64]

It is forbidden to peel garlic and onions [as well as other foods such as apples and nuts[65]] which one [peels with intent] to set aside [from being eaten right away, due to that this contains a separating prohibition[66]]. However [to peel them] in order to eat right away is allowed.[67] [**See Q&A 1-13**]

Summary-Does peeling fruits and vegetables contain the Separating prohibition?[68]

❖ The Summary takes into account that which is explained in the Q&A below-see there!

If the food is eaten by most people together with its peel: According to some Poskim[69] it may be peeled without the separating restrictions. Thus, it may be peeled to eat later on and may be peeled using a peeler. However other Poskim[70] hold that it does contain the separating prohibition and thus may not be peeled with a peeler, and may only be peeled to eat right away.

The Final Ruling: Rav Farkash rules that one who wishes to be stringent like all the opinions should always apply the separating prohibition to anything being peeled.

If the food is not eaten by most people together with its peel: Then according to all opinions, the separating restrictions apply and thus it may not be peeled using a peeler or any other designated vessel, and may only be peeled in order to eat right away.

Do the Borer restrictions [i.e. to peel for a right away use] apply even when peeling fruits/vegetables which are edible with their peel?[71]

If the food is not eaten by most people together with its peel such as carrots and the like: Then according to all opinions, the separating restrictions apply even to a person which usually always eats this fruit/vegetable with its peel, and thus it may not be peeled using a peeler or any other designated vessel, and may only be done in order to eat right away.

If the food is eaten by most people together with its peel such as cucumbers [in some places], apples, tomatoes, pears, apricots, plum, peaches: According to many Poskim[72] it may be peeled without the separating restrictions and thus may be peeled to eat later on and may be peeled using a peeler. [Regarding if the person peeling it is someone who cannot eat the food with the peel due to it being disgusting to him and the like then some hold[73] that even according to this opinion it is proper to be

---

[64] Rama 321:19 [The end of chapter 321 does not appear in the Alter Rebbe's Shulchan Aruch and we have thus brought the rulings of the Rama and Mishneh Berurah as a supplement for those omissions.] This law is also recorded in: Admur 319:9; M"B 319:22 and 24

Admur 319:9: Similarly it is permitted to peel [the chaffs off] grains and legumes which have been removed from their stalks and pods from before Shabbos, although one must be careful to only peel as much as *he needs to eat right away and not for what he will need to eat later on as will be explained in chapter 321* [Halacha 19] …..However those legumes which their pods are not edible there contains no permission at all to remove the legumes from within them on Shabbos unless the legumes are not at all attached to their pods, having been detached from them before Shabbos and it is rather simply sitting [loosely] within [the pod]. *In such a case it is permitted to remove [as many legumes from the pod] as he wishes to eat right away, however he may not do so to eat later on due to the separating prohibition.*

[65] Mishneh Berurah 321:84

[66] Mishneh Berurah 321:83

[67] Rama ibid

The reason one may peel off the Pesoles: The reason that this does not contradict the condition that one may not remove the waste from the food and rather must remove the food from the waste is because a) It is impossible in this case to remove the food from the waste, and thus here the removal of the waste from the food is what is considered the way of eating and not the opposite. [Ketzos Hashulchan 147 page 107; See also M"B 321:84, Shaar Hatziyon 321:99 and Biur Halacha 321:19 "Liklof" for a similar explanation; See Shabbos Kehalacha 13 Biurim 1; Piskeiy Teshuvos 321:33] b) Because according to Admur in the Siddur that which is being held in ones hand is considered that which is being separated, and thus here in truth the fruit is being separated from the peel when one peels it. [Tehila Ledavid and Divreiy Nechemiah] See Shabbos Kehalacha Vol. 2 p. 291 c) Because the peels are not considered Pesoles until they are removed. [Ketzos Hashulchan 126 footnote 8 in parethesese]

[68] See Shabbos Kihalacha Vol. 2 pages 299-307

[69] Peri Megadim 321 A"A 30; Iglei Tal Borer 12; Ketzos Hashulchan 125:16 in name of Iglei Tal Borer; Shaar Hatziyon 321:97 in name of P"M; SSH"K; See Mahrshag 1:47

[70] Magen Avraham 321:99 regarding apples; Mishneh Berurah 321:84 [however see Shaar Hatziyon ibid]; Igros Moshe 4:74-8, and others rule that even so it does contain the separating prohibition.

[71] Shabbos Kihalacha Vol. 2 p. 299-307

[72] Peri Megadim 321 A"A 30, brought in Shaar Hatziyon 321:97; Iglei Tal Borer 6:12; Shevisas Hashabbos Borer 24 and footnote 45; Kaf Hachaim 321:141; Ketzos Hashulchan 125:16 [see however Ketzos Hashulchan 126 footnote 19]; SSH"K 3:34

[73] Rav Farkash in Shabbos Kihalacha Vol 2 p. 300. However in SSH"K they rule plainly that even such a person may peel it without restriction

stringent and follow all the separating restrictions.] Other Poskim[74] hold that it does contain the separating prohibition and thus may not be peeled with a peeler, and may only be peeled to eat right away.[75]

The Final Ruling: Practically, those who are stringent are doing a proper act, although those who are lenient have upon whom to rely, and each person is to ask his Rav.[76] In a case that one is pressured to peel using a peeler, such as when one has a lot of fruits/vegetables to peel, or in a case that one is pressured to peel the fruits a while prior to the meal, such as in a case that one must leave ones house now and will only return when the meal will commence, then although one may be lenient like the latter opinions, nevertheless it is proper to also cut off part of the actual fruit together with the peel.[77]

In any case whenever one chooses to be lenient to follow the latter opinions one must know that in truth the selected fruit/vegetable is eaten with its peel by most people. Thus, cucumbers for example must be verified in each area if it is in truth eaten with its peel by most people.

May one peel off the outer peel of garlic [the peel which contains within it all the cloves] and take apart the cloves from each other on Shabbos?
See above Halacha 1 Q&A 8!

May one remove dates from its stalk?[78]
See above.

May one remove bananas from the stalk or grapes from their vine?[79]
See above.

May one remove the stems from fruits and vegetables?[80]
Yes, although this may only be done immediately prior to the meal.

May one peel fruits/vegetables which do not contain the separating restriction even for the need of after Shabbos?
No, this is forbidden as it is always forbidden to prepare on Shabbos for a weekday.

May one use a peeler to peel fruits and vegetables on Shabbos?[81]
Whenever the peeling of the fruit/vegetable contains the separating restriction [as explained in the summary above] it is forbidden to peel them using a peeler even if he plans peel them in close proximity to the meal.[82] Thus according to all Poskim it is forbidden to use a peeler to remove peels that are not eaten by majority of people. However, those peels that majority of people eat, are permitted to be peeled using a peeler according to those Poskim[83] who rule that such peels do not contain a Borer

---

[74] M"A 321:19 regarding apples; Elya Raba 321:30; Tosefes Shabbos 321:41; M"B 321:84; Orchos Chaim 319:22 in name of Meorei Or; Igros Moshe 4:74 Borer 8; Az Nidbaru 9:10; Chut Shani 25:7

[75] The reason: As these Poskim hold that the separating prohibition applies to even edible peels and thus when peeling it one must abide by all Borer restrictions, which include not peeling it with a peeler, and even when using a knife, to only do it for right away use. The reason that even edible peels contain the Borer restriction is because when the are peeled off, they are generally thrown out, and hence have a status of Pesoles when one comes to peel it. [Piskeiy Teshuvos 321:34]

[76] Minchas Shabbos 80:69 that it is proper to be stringent when possible, and so concludes: Shabbos Kehalacha ibid; Piskeiy Teshuvos 321:34-35 that it is bets to be stringent when possible, although one who is leninet has upon whom to rely; Michzei Eliyahu 1:51-52; Teshuvos Vehanhagos 1:208

Ruling of Rav Farkash in Shabbos Kehalacha ibid: Rav Farkash rules that one who wishes to be stringent like all opinions [which he rules one initially is to do], is to always apply the separating prohibition to anything being peeled.

[77] Shabbos Kehalacha 13:9; Piskeiy Teshuvos 321:34

[78] Ketzos Hashulchan 126:5

[79] Ketzos Hashulchan 126 footnote 10-11; Shabbos Kihalacha Vol. 2 p. 316;

[80] Shabbos Kehalacha Vol. 2 p. 316

[81] Shabbos Kehalacha Vol. 2 p. 294

[82] Being that a peeler is a designated item for separating and negates the required condition of separating with ones hands.

[83] Ketzos Hashulchan 125 :16

prohibition, as explained above.

May one use a peeler to peel fruits and vegetables on Shabbos?[84]

Inedible peels:[85] Those fruits and vegetable which majority of people do not eat together with the peel, and it is rather removed and discarded prior to eating, according to all opinions, it is [Biblically[86]] forbidden to use a peeler to remove the peel on Shabbos.[87] This applies even if one intends to do so in order to eat the food right away.

Edible peels: Those fruits and vegetables which majority of people eat together with the peel, some Poskim[88] rule it is forbidden to be peeled using a peeler, and rather may only be peeled with a knife for right away use.[89] Other Poskim[90] however rule it may be peeled using a peeler, and may even be peeled for later use on Shabbos.[91] Practically, those who are stringent are doing a proper act, although those who are lenient have upon whom to rely, and each person is to ask his Rav.[92] [Whenever one chooses to be lenient like the latter opinions one must know in truth that the selected fruit/vegetable is eaten with its peel by majority of people. Thus, cucumbers for example must be verified in each area if it is in truth eaten with its peel by majority of people, as explained next.]

Examples of fruits/vegetables and their peel status: According to the lenient opinion, it is permitted to peel with the help of a peeler apples, tomatoes, pears, apricots, plums, peaches using a peeler. According to all, it is forbidden to peel with a peeler a carrot, orange, grapefruit, Kiwi. The permissibility to peel cucumbers with a peeler is dependent on one's countries eating habits; if the majority of people are accustomed to eat the cucumber with the peel, then according to the lenient opinion, it may be peeled using a peeler, while if the majority of people remove the peel then it is forbidden to use a peeler according to all.[93]

One who is particular to never eat the peel: If a person is particular to always peel a certain fruit/vegetable, despite it being eaten by majority of people, some Poskim[94] rule that even according to the lenient opinion, one must abide by the Borer restrictions and may not peel it using a peeler and may only peel it for right away use. Other Poskim[95] however rule that it is permitted for him to use a peeler even in such a case.

One who is never particular to remove the peel:[96] All fruits and vegetables that majority of people do

---

[84] See Shabbos Kehalacha Vol. 2 p. 294 and 299-307; Piskeiy Teshuvos 321:34-35
[85] Iglei Tal Borer 6; Ketzos Hashulchan 125:16; Piskeiy Teshuvos 321:35
[86] As a peeler is the normal vessel used to remove the peel from a fruit/vegetable and hence is similar to a sieve and sifter, which is Biblically forbidden to be used. [See Admur 319:1; M"B 319:2; Rashi Shabbos 74a]
[87] The reason: As a peeler is a designated item for separating and negates the required condition of separating with one's hands. [ibid]
[88] M"A 321:19 regarding apples; Elya Raba 321:30; Tosefes Shabbos 321:41; M"B 321:84; Orchos Chaim 319:22 in name of Meorei Or; Igros Moshe 4:74 Borer 8; Az Nidbaru 9:10; Chut Shani 25:7
[89] The reason: As these Poskim hold that the separating prohibition applies to even edible peels and thus when peeling it one must abide by all Borer restrictions, which include not peeling it with a peeler, and even when using a knife, to only do it for right away use. The reason that even edible peels contain the Borer restriction is because when the are peeled off, they are generally thrown out, and hence have a status of Pesoles when one comes to peel it. [Piskeiy Teshuvos 321:34]
[90] Peri Megadim 321 A"A 30, brought in Shaar Hatziyon 321:97; Iglei Tal Borer 6:12; Shevisas Hashabbos Borer 24 and footnote 45; Kaf Hachaim 321:141; Ketzos Hashulchan 125:16 [see however Ketzos Hashulchan 126 footnote 19]; SSH"K 3:34
[91] The reason: As according to these Poskim edible peels do not contain a Borer prohibition, as explained above, and hence there is no need to abide by the Borer conditions which restricts one from using a Borer instrument and requires the peeling to be done for right away use. Regarding if the peeler contains an Issur of Muktzah or Uvdin Dechol-see Piskeiy Teshuvos 321:35 footnote 373-374
[92] Minchas Shabbos 80:69 that it is proper to be stringent when possible, and so concludes: Shabbos Kehalacha ibid; Piskeiy Teshuvos 321:34-35 that it is bets to be stringent when possible, although one who is leninet has upon whom to rely; Michzei Eliyahu 1:51-52; Teshuvos Vehanhagos 1:208
Ruling of Rav Farkash in Shabbos Kehalacha ibid: Rav Farkash rules that one who wishes to be stringent like all opinions [which he rules one initially is to do], is to always apply the separating prohibition to anything being peeled. In a case that one is pressured to peel using a peeler, such as when one has a lot of fruits:vegetables to peel, or in a case that one is pressured to peel the fruits a while prior to the meal, such as in a case that one must leave one's house now and will only return when the meal will commence, then although one may be lenient like the latter opinions, nevertheless it is proper to also cut off part of the actual fruit together with the peel. [Shabbos Kehalacha 13:9; Piskeiy Teshuvos 321:34]
[93] See SSH"K 3:34; Shabbos Kehalacha ibid; Piskeiy Teshuvos ibid footnote 363
[94] Shabbos Kihalacha Vol 2 13 Biurim 2 [p. 300] writes it is proper to be stringent and follow all the separating restrictions. Orchos Shabbos 3:40
[95] SSH"K 3 footnote 88; See Piskeiy Teshuvos 321 footnote 363
[96] Piskeiy Teshuvos 321 footnote 363

not eat with the peel must abide by all Borer restrictions even if the person eating it is personally accustomed to eat the fruit/vegetable with the peel. Thus, it may not be peeled using a peeler or any other designated vessel, and may only be done in order to eat right away.

<u>Pesach</u>: Those who are particular not to eat peels on Pesach, and hence peel all their produce, seemingly may still abide by the leniency of using the peeler on Shabbos Pesach for peels that are generally eaten by majority of people, if they are accustomed to follow the lenient opinion during the other Shabbosim of the year.[97]

May one use a knife to peel fruits and vegetables?[98]
Yes. So long as one peels the food immediately prior to the meal one may use a knife to peel.

If one only desires to eat part of the fruit is he nevertheless allowed to peel the entire fruit?[99]
Rav SZ"A leaves this matter in doubt as to whether one may peel the entire fruit, as is the way of eating, or if he may only peel the area which he plans to eat.

May one peel many fruits and vegetables with intent to eat later on if he takes a bite from each fruit/vegetable right away?[100]
No as it is obvious that one plans to leave it for later on and the peeling is thus not done in the way of eating.

May one peel many fruits/vegetables for later on if he leaves the peels together with the fruits/vegetables?[101]
Such as if one has many carrots in a bowl may he peel them for later use if he leaves the peels within the bowl together with the carrots?
One may do so if he peels the food within the bowl without removing the food, as in such a case the peel in essence never separates from the fruit. However, one may not do so if he lifts the fruit/vegetable out of the bowl as when he peels it in such a state the peel has already separated from the fruit for a non-immediate use and what will it help now to replace it back in the bowl.

May one peel right before the meal more fruits than needed for the purpose of making his guests feel comfortable in taking as much as they want?[102]
Yes, as since one is doing it in order so the guests feel more at ease, he is receiving this immediate benefit from the separation, and does not need to also benefit from them eating it in order to consider it to have been done for an immediate use. [For other examples of when one may separate/peel for a guest, see Chapter 1 Halacha 5 Q&A there.]

May one peel a fruit for a child to take with him upon leaving the house even though the child will not be eating it until later on?[103]
No. This includes even if one decides to eat some of the fruit before leaving being that one's main intention is to peel it for later on.

---

[97] <u>The reason</u>: As the peel itself is still viewed as a food, and it is simply due to its Chametz contingency that people avoid it, and not because they suddenly view the actual peel as Chametz or inedible. Accordingly, at the very most they are removing the bad [Chametz] with the good [the peel] of which many Poskim rule is permitted, and hence the leniency would still apply according to the lenient opinion.
[98] Shabbos Kehalacha Vol 2 p. 295
[99] Shabbos Kehalacha Vol. 2 p. 294; Rav SZ"A in Maor Hashabbos 3:40 footnote 62
[100] Shabbos Kehalacha Vol. 2 p. 296
[101] Shabbos Kehalacha Vol. 2 p. 296
[102] Shabbos Kehalacha Vol. 2 p. 297
[103] Shabbos Kehalacha Vol. 2 p. 298

May one peel fruits in order to make a fruit compote many hours prior to the meal in order so it extract and absorb taste into and from the salad?[104]
Yes.

May one remove a rotten/wormy part of fruit/vegetable in order to eat the rest of the fruit/vegetable?[105]
Majority of Poskim allow one to cut it off so long as he plans to eat the fruit right away. Nevertheless, it is best for one to cut a part of the fruit itself together with the rotten part, as doing so adds to the leniency. One may not remove the rotten part of the fruit simply in order so the fruit not continue to rot, and he be able to eat it later on.

May one remove good fruits from amongst rotten ones to prevent them from rotting?
No. See Halacha 6 Q&A there

May one remove a worm or other bug from a fruit/vegetable?[106]
Inside the fruit: If the worm is inside the fruit than one may remove it so long as he plans to eat the fruit right away.
On the surface of the fruit/vegetables: If the insect is on the surface of the fruit then it depends. If the insect is not stuck onto the fruit then one may remove it without restriction as in such a case there is no "mixture" of good and bad, as explained above in chapter 1 the Q&A under the introduction. If the insect is stuck onto the fruit, then one may only remove it with intent to eat right away. Nevertheless, it is best in such a case to shake the insect off rather than lift it with one's hands. If this is not possible, then one may even remove it with one's hands.[107]

May one peel fruits that are generally not peeled but rather quartered together with their peel, such as oranges, lemons and the like?
See Piskeiy Teshuvos 321/33.

Regarding removing the skin off fish/chicken, removing the pit from a fruit, removing labels from bread or baking paper from baked goods see Chapter 1 Halacha 4 Q&A there.
Regarding washing off dirt from a fruit/vegetable, see Chapter 1 Halacha 1d Q&A there.

---

[104] Shabbos Kehalacha Vol. 2 p. 299
[105] Shabbos Kehalacha
[106] Shabbos Kehalacha Vol. 2 p. 198
[107] Removing it does not pose a problem of Muktzah being that a) It is insignificant, and b) it is a Graf Shel Reiy

CHAPTER 3: MIRAKED-FILTERING WINE, WATER AND OTHER LIQUIDS ON SHABBOS

Introduction:[1]
The following section will deal with the laws of separating through using a filter. In addition to the problems of Borer that are sometimes applicable as will be explained, the prohibition of Miraked may likewise apply, amongst other prohibitions. In essence the prohibitions of Borer and Miraked are really one and the same, being that they are both a separating prohibition. The difference between Miraked and Borer is only with regards to the form of separation. Borer is considered separating from a solid mixture using a sifter to sift out the waste and have the food remain above. Meraked is a prohibition of sifting a solid mixture and having the food fall out and the waste remain above.[2] Regarding a liquid mixture Admur in 319/12[3] rules that straining it and having the sediment remain above may be Borer or Miraked. Thus, by liquid mixtures it is unclear as to which prohibition applies.[4] The reason why this action of separating was split to two different prohibitions is because these were two distinct actions done in the Mishkan and thus were given two different names of prohibition.[5]

1. *Filtering liquids with a filter/strainer:*[6]
Wine with sediment and cases of the like:[7] One who filters dregs [of wine], meaning that he filters [wine which contains dregs] through a strainer, [has done an] offshoot of [the] separating [prohibition which is to separate] food from its waste using a sifter and sieve, or [has done] an offshoot of [the] Sifting/Miraked [prohibition] and is liable. **[See Q&A 1]**

Filtering wine with sediment by placing twigs into the opening of the bottle:[8] A vessel into which one empties the wine from the barrel may not have strongly inserted into its opening twigs and reeds, as this is similar to a filter.

The reason:[9] Now, although it's not an actual filter being that dregs still pass through it, nevertheless since there are twigs and dirt which do not bypass it is thus similar to a filter. However, if [in the barrel] there is clear wine which does not contain sediment and rather only thin splinters, then it is permitted to filter it even using an actual strainer as will be explained next.

Clear wine and clear water in a strainer:[10] Water or wine which are clear are permitted to be filtered through a filter in order so they become even more clear[11], or even in order [to remove] the sediment that floats on top of the wine or [to filter out] small twigs that have fallen into it.[12] **[See Q&A]**

---

[1] See Gemara Shabbos 73b; 138a; Iglei Tal Zoreh 2-3; Miraked 1; Shevisas Hashabbos Zoreh 2; Toldos Shmuel Zoreh; Tehila Ledavid 319:21; Biur Halacha 319:8 "Meshameres"; Shabbos Kehalacha Vol 2 page 342

[2] Rashi Shabbos 138a; See Shevisas Shabbos ibid; Shabbos Kehalacha ibid

[3] Gemara Shabbos 138a; 138a; So rules also Rambam 8:11; Biur Halacha 319:8 "Meshameres"; Tehila Ledavid 319:21; Shabbos Kehalacha Vol 2 page 342

[4] The reason: The Gemara Shabbos 138a brings a dispute between Rabah and Rebbe Zeira as to which Melacha applies. The Biur Halacha ibid explains that this dispute is only relevant by wine as one does not do an action to the filter, and the filtering happens on its own as one pours the wine through it. However, when one shakes a sifter to separate the waste from the food, then when the food falls below, such as when sifting flour, all agree that the Melacha is Miraked.

[5] Gemara Shabbos 73b; Shabbos Kehalacha Vol 2 page 342

[6] Gemara Shabbos 139b; Michaber 319:9-13 and 16; Admur 319:12-17

[7] Admur 319:12; Michaber 319:9; Gemara Shabbos 138a; So rules also Rambam 8:11; See Biur Halacha 319:8 "Meshameres"; Tehila Ledavid 319:21; Shabbos Kehalacha Vol 2 page 342

[8] Admur 319:17; Michaber 319:13; Gemara Shabbos 139b

[9] Admur ibid; M"B 319:51-52

[10] Admur 319:13; Michaber 319:9; Shabbos 139b

Other opinions: Some Poskim rule one may never use a filter on Shabbos even if the liquid is clear and fit to be drunk by majority of people. [Rambam 8 brought in Michaber 319:10] Practically we do not rule like this opinion. [M"B 319:41; Admur omitted this opinion]

[11] Michaber ibid

[12] Rama ibid

The reason that this is allowed:[13] This is not considered like separating being that [the wine and water] are still drinkable to majority[14] of people even without this filtration. [**See Q&A**]

The reason why there is no whitening prohibition involved by a strainer:[15] Since a strainer is made for this purpose of having liquids pass through it thus one does not care to squeeze [out the liquid which it absorbs] and as well does not care to whiten it at all, therefore its whitening does not pose a problem to prohibit soaking it in liquid due to this even according to those opinions which say that the soaking of a cloth is [considered] laundering it.

Filtering water through a filter which contains dregs of wine:[16] If one had placed dregs in the strainer from before Shabbos then it is permitted to pour water over it in order so the water become more [clean and] clear. [**See Q&A on tea**]

Filtering pre-fermented wine:[17] Wine that has just been pressed, so long as it remains within its primary fermentation [stage][18], one may mix a barrel of it together with its dregs and may place it even inside a strainer.

The reason for this is because: so long as the wine is still within its [primary] fermentation the wine has not yet separated well from its dregs and thus the entire [mixture of the] wine [with its dregs] is considered one food, and there is [thus] no [prohibition] of separating food from its waste involved here. Furthermore [there is no problem of separating here because] the wine is fit to be drunk even without filtration, and this is commonly done during the times of its pressing when all wines are murky, and majority of people drink it the way it is without filtering it.

Filtering vinegar:[19] The same applies with vinegar, which is likewise common to use even when it is still slightly thick, that it is permitted to filter it. However, if [the vinegar] is very thick and is not fit at all [to be used] without filtering then it is forbidden to filter it even with a cloth.

Filtering almond milk:[20] Similarly the milk of crushed almonds [which were made] before Shabbos is permitted to be filtered being that it is able to be drunk without filtering.

Placing milk curd into a strainer:[21] If one places the curd into an elastic vessel[22] and the whey drips from inside it then this is an offshoot of separating food from waste through using a sieve and sifter and one is thus liable.

The reason: Now, although the curd and the milk are both a single species of food and there is [thus] no waste [here] at all, nevertheless since they are liquid substances which mix well which he is [now] separating, therefore this contains the separating [prohibition] just like one who is separating food from

---

The ruling today: Today this permission no longer applies being that majority of people today are particular not to drink wine with twigs until it is filtered, being that today it is very uncommon for wine to include twigs. [Ketzos Hashulchan 125 footnote 28; Shabbos Kehalacha Vol 2 page 348]

[13] Admur 319:13; Rama 319:10 "because it is fit to drink regardless of the twigs"

[14] Admur ibid; Ran; Rashba; Beis Yosef; first opinion in M"B 319:34; Tzemach Tzedek Yoreh Deah 45;Shabbos Kehalacha 2 p. 346
Other opinions: Some Poskim rule it must be fit for drinking to all people. [Bach brought in M"B 319:10; See Tzemach Tzedek ibid]

[15] Admur 319:13

[16] Admur 319:12; Michaber 319:9

Must the coffee be placed in the strainer on Shabbos? No. [Piskeiy Teshuvos ibid footnote 274] Now, although Admur in 319:12 discusses a cases in which the dregs were placed in the strainer from before Shabbos, this is only because dregs are naturally mixed with wine, and it is forbidden to filter dregs on Shabbos. However, placing dry coffee powder onto a strainer causes no filtering to take place and is hence permitted even on Shabbos. [See Admur 315:14 and 319:12]

Is there a prohibition of Ohel in covering the vessel with the strainer: No. [See Admur 315:19-20; Piskeiy Teshuvos ibid footnote 274] Now, although Admur 315:14 and Michaber 315:9 rules it is forbidden to set up a strainer on Shabbos due to the Ohel prohibition, this only applies to a strainer that contains wine dregs inside of it, being that it is forbidden to strain it on Shabbos, and hence one who sets it up on Shabbos is doing a mundane act and belittling Shabbos. However, if the strainer does not contain wine dregs, then it is permitted to set it up on Shabbos [Admur 315:14; M"A 319:18] even over a vessel, so long as it is not the size of a barrel. [Admur 315:19]. See however Taz 315:9 "It is forbidden due to the vessel under it." who implies the prohibition would apply to ever placing it over a vessel due to Ohel. Vetzaruch Iyun

[17] Admur 319:14

[18] With red wines, the must is pressed after the primary fermentation, which separates the skins and other solid matter from the liquid. Thus, during the primary fermentation, the dregs still remain with the wine.

[19] Admur 319:14; Taz 319:10

[20] Admur 319:14; M"A 319:12; M"B 319:34

[21] Admur 319:25; M"A 39:18; M"B 319:62

[22] This refers to a vessel made of material that can be stretched out do to having tiny holes in it, and thus allows the milk to drip out. Similar to a plastic bag.

waste.

Summary- Filtering liquid using a strainer [or any item designated to filter²³]:²⁴
If the liquid is drinkable in its current state to majority of people, then it is allowed to be filtered, [even if it contains pieces of food or dregs such as almond milk and wine that is in its first stage of fermentation²⁵]. If it is not drinkable to majority of people in its current state then it is Biblically forbidden to filter.

Placing a filter on the lid of a bottle and pouring through it:
Has all the filtering restrictions mentioned by a filter even if it does not help to filter out all of the sediment.²⁶

Q&A
May one filter murky liquids, which are not drinkable to majority of people, for the purpose of washing dishes and the like?²⁷
Even though that for washing dishes the water is perfectly useable even without being filtered, nevertheless it is forbidden to filter it in a filter. However, if the water is mixed with soap or other ingredient which has made it no longer drinkable, then it may be filtered so long as it is fit for washing even without filtering it.

May one today filter wine that contains small twigs even though today such an occurrence is uncommon?²⁸
No. Being that today such an occurrence is uncommon, most likely people would be particular to filter it out and thus doing so would be forbidden on Shabbos.²⁹

May one filter cork pieces out from wine on Shabbos?³⁰
Using a strainer to filter it: Depends. If the pieces are small in size and in amount, then majority of people are not particular to drink it in an unfiltered state, and it is allowed to be filtered if the person himself is also not particular against ever drinking the wine together with these small pieces. However, if the pieces are large, or are many, or one is particular to never drink wine with cork pieces, then it is forbidden to be filtered.
Removing the pieces with one's hand: In all cases that it is forbidden to filter the pieces it is likewise forbidden to remove them with one's hands. Regarding cases that it is permitted to filter the wine then: There are opinions³¹ which forbid doing so.³² Others³³ however permit this to be done being that anyways people drink it in this state, and thus it is not considered separating bad from good.
Pouring the cork pieces out together with some wine: Is permitted according to all.

---

²³ Admur 319:16. Shabbos Kihalacha Vol 2 page 345
²⁴ Admur 319:12-13
²⁵ Admur 319:14
²⁶ Admur 319:17
²⁷ Shabbos Kihalacha Vol. 2 p. 349
²⁸ Shabbos Kehalacha Vol. 2 p. 348
²⁹ Ketzos Hashulchan 125 footnote 28
³⁰ Shabbos Kehalacha Vol 2 page 348-349
³¹ Ketzos Hashulchan chapter 125 footnote 28, [although there he concludes with a Tzaruch Iyun due to that he brings also the opinions which allow this.]; Tehila Ledavid; and Rav Farkash in Shabbos Kehalacha Vol 2 page 348-349.
³² The reason: As the laws of filtering are different than that of separating, as by filtering it is not clearly evident that one desires to separate the pieces as perhaps he just wants clearer wine, while when separating the pieces with ones hands this is clearly evident, and is forbidden as here one is clearly separating the bad from the good.
³³ Shevisas Hashabbos Borer footnote 25; and Tal Oros

May one who is particular to never drink unfiltered water filter it on Shabbos if it is drinkable by majority of people?[34]

If the water is slightly recognizably dirty, but nevertheless majority of people will drink from it then: It is nevertheless forbidden for one who is always particular, to filter it on Shabbos.[35] [**See next two questions**]

If the water is clean: If the water is clean and one thus simply desires to make it clearer, then it is allowed for one to filter it even if he is always particular against drinking it.[36] Nevertheless there are opinions[37] who are stringent even in such a case to prohibit a person which is always particular from filtering it. Thus, according to those opinions, people which are particular to only drink filtered water must prepare filtered water from before Shabbos. If one does not yet know the state of the water, such as water which enters directly from the tab into a filter, then it has the same status as clear water.[38]

May a person which is not particular against drinking unfiltered water filter water for one who is particular in doing so and may thus not filter it?[39]

There is an opinion[40] which leans to be lenient to allow one to filter for his particular friend although he concludes that he has not relied on this viewpoint to actually allow it to be done. [Thus, in pressing situations, one should seek a Rav to see if one can rely on this side for leniency.]

May one who is particular to only drink filtered water, filter water for one who is not particular to do so?[41]

One may not be lenient to do so.[42]

May one use a Brita filter on Shabbos to filter water?[43]

If majority of people drink this water in its current unfiltered state, and the person which desires to filter it also does not mind to drink it in its current unfiltered state[44] and just wants to filter it so it be even more clean from any possible waste, then it may be filtered. Regarding if the person who wishes to filter it is particular to never drink this water in its unfiltered state- see Q&A 4 above.

If majority of people filter this water due to a problem with the water, then it is always forbidden to filter it on Shabbos. Thus, water that has been infected with bugs or contaminated with sand and the like which may only be drunk after being filtered, it may not be filtered on Shabbos and one must thus prepare from before Shabbos enough water for Shabbos. *Regarding if the water is clear and no change is seen in the water through filtering-See Q&A 4 above!*

May one use the tab filter contained in all faucets on Shabbos or does this pose a filtering prohibition and thus must be removed before Shabbos?[45]

Yes, one may use it on Shabbos being that the water is fit to be drunk by majority of people in its current state without being filtered [see footnote for additional reason[46]]. Regarding if the person who

---

[34] Shabbos Kehalacha Vol. 2 p. 347 and 361 footnote 52

[35] So rules Peri Megadim 319 M"Z 6; brought in Ketzos Hashulchan 125 footnote 28

[36] So concludes Shabbos Kehalacha p. 361 based on ruling of Rav SZ"A 3 footnote 163 regarding Pesach cloth of which the allowance to use it is due to that one is not certain that it contains Chameitz, and Minchas Yitzchak 7:23, Ketzos Hashulchan 125 footnote 37 and others that by waste which is only questionable if contained within the liquid, the separating prohibition does not apply. So is also implied from the Lashon of the Peri Megadim which is the source for the stringency which mentions "water that has small twigs" in his case of a particular type of person.

[37] Poskim brought in Orchos Shabbos, mentioned in Shabbos Kehalacha ibid footnote 52

[38] Ketzos Hashulchan 125 footnote 37

[39] Shabbos Kehalacha page Vol. 2 347

[40] Shut Maharahm Shik

[41] Shabbos Kehalacha Vol 2 page 347

[42] Rav SZ"A questions whether this is allowed or not and concludes with a Tzaruch Iyun.

[43] Shabbos Kehalacha Vol. 2 P. 346-347

[44] So rules the Peri Megadim in M"Z 6

[45] Shabbos Kehalacha Vol. 2 p. 363

[46] This is in addition to the allowance of the Minchas Yitzchak [7:23] regarding using a cloth that is attached to the faucet being that since one uses the cloth for all waters which come from the sink, including washing and the like, therefore even the water used for drinking is not

wishes to filter it is particular to never drink this water in its unfiltered state- see Q 4 above and footnote below.[47] Regarding if the water is not fit for majority of people [and will become fit through passing through this filter] - see above mentioned footnotes that according to the Minchas Yitzchak this would be allowed. See also the next question.

If the only available water is undrinkable, such as it contains sand or worms and thus must be filtered, is there any way to filter it on Shabbos?[48]
It is forbidden to take the water and pour it through any type of filter unless one is doing so in the process of drinking, as will be explained in Halacha 4-See there.
Using a filter that is attached to the sink: However one may use a filter that is attached to the spout of the faucet and thus have the water automatically get filtered as it leaves the faucet.[49] [This however does not include filters which have a tube leading into the spout of the faucet of which one has an option to ether have the water come through the filter or come through the faucet, as in such a case the filter is only used for drinking water which negates the basis for the allowance of a sink attached filter, as explained in the footnotes of the previous question.] Even when attached to the spout, ideally it is best not to use a non-cloth filter [**see footnote[50]**] and rather a designated cloth filter is to be used. **See Halacha 2 and Q&A there for further details in when a cloth filter is allowed**.

May one pour a liquid which contains solids into the drain of the sink if the drain has a filter [as do most sink drains]?[51]
If both the liquid and solid are waste: Such as leftovers, then this is allowed.[52]
If the solid is not waste: Such as that a ring fell into a mixture and one desires to find the ring by placing it down the filter of the drain, then it is forbidden.

May one use a spoon with holes to remove a solid out from a liquid, such as vegetables from soup?
As already explained in Chapter 1 Halacha 4 Q&A there, in all cases that the solid and liquid are designated as mixed [see Introduction to chapter 1 and Q&A there] it is forbidden to remove any solid from the liquid using a straining spoon being that doing so is considered separating with a vessel which is Biblically forbidden. With regards to if one desires to eat both the liquid and solid right away but separately see Halacha 6 Q&A there.

May one filter fruit pulp out from one's fruit drink?[53]
If majority of people drink this juice together with its pulp, **and** the person who desires to filter it also does not usually mind to drink it together with its pulp[54], then it may be filtered.
However, if the person who wishes to filter it is particular to never drink this juice without first filtering the pulp **or** even if he is not particular but majority of people filter out the pulp, then it is always forbidden to filter it on Shabbos. Thus, such juice one is not allowed to pour into a cup through a pitcher which has a screen on its top which withholds the pulp.

---

considered problematic. To note however that not all accept this argument [See Ketzos Hashulchan 125:37 end from which it is proven that he did not hold of this Heter]. The ramification between this reason and the one mentioned above is in a case that in truth the water is not fit to be drunk by majority of people, in which according to the Minchas Yitzchak one would be able to use it. See next note.
[47] According to the Minchas Yitzchak mentioned in the previous footnote this would be allowed regardless of what was explained in Q 4 being that the filter placed in the faucet is used for also washing and the like.
[48] Shabbos Kehalacha Vol. 2 p. 362
[49] Minchas Yitzchak 7:23
[50] So writes Minchas Yitzchak, and so concludes Rav Farkash, in order so one do the filtering with an irregularity. Nevertheless from the letter of the law the Minchas Yitzchak rules that even a metal filter is allowed when attached to the spout of the faucet being that it is also filtering the non-drinking water.
[51] Shabbos Kehalacha Vol. 2 p. 362
[52] So rules Rav SZ"A in SSH"K 12 footnote 47; Igros Moshe 4:74-4; Tzitz Eliezer 7:12
[53] Shabbos Kihalacha Vol. 2 p. 375
[54] So rules the Peri Megadim in M"Z 6

<u>For a baby</u>: According to the above it is forbidden to filter the pulp out of juice in order to give to a baby to drink if one is filtering it due to choking hazard for the baby, as the baby is considered like a person which is always particular to filter the juice. However, there is no problem to filter it simply in order to prevent the bottle hole from getting stuffed.

May one filter liquid baby cereal from their lumpy parts?[55]

If majority of people are not particular to filter out the lumps, and the person who desires to filter it also does not usually mind to drink it together with the lumps[56], then it may be filtered. If the person is particular, then it is best for him to filter it using a cloth rather than a standard filter even though the latter is also valid from the letter of the law.

<u>For a baby</u>: Some Poskim hold that so long as the lumps are able to be eaten by an older baby, then one may filter it for any age baby. However even so it is best to do so through a cloth. There is no problem to filter it in order to prevent the bottle hole from getting stuffed.

May one sift foods that are fot to be eaten by majority of people in their natural state, as is the law by liquid?

Seemingly no, as this law was only said by liquids for the reason that by liquids the filtering happens as soon as one enters the liquid inside and it is not very recognizable that one has done Borer. This is opposed to foods in which one must shake the sifter in order to sift it.

May one filter the fat out from milk?[57]

<u>The layer of fat which covers the top of the milk</u>: Is forbidden to be filtered being that most people today do not drink the milk with this fat.

<u>Small pieces of fat</u>: If one is not always particular to filter it then it has the same law as slightly murky liquids which may not be filtered through a filter but may be filtered with a cloth- see Halacha 2 Summary. If one is always particular to filter it then he should be stringent.

May one use a saltshaker if there are pieces of hardened salt or rice inside?[58]

See Halacha 5 Q&A!

Q&A regarding tea bags:

May one use a tea pot that has a strainer on its tip to prevent the leaves from falling into the cup?[59]

It is permitted to pour the tea from this pot until one reaches the liquid on the bottom of the pot where the tea is mixed with the tea leaves.[60] Regarding if one may pour out the tea past this point[61] many Poskim[62] allow doing so. [This applies even according to the ruling of Admur in the Siddur which

---

[55] Shabbos Kihalacha Vol. 2 p. 376
[56] So rules the Peri Megadim in M"Z 6
[57] Shabbos Kihalacha Vol. 2 p. 377
[58] Shabbos Kihalacha Vol. 2 p. 380
[59] Shabbos Kihalacha Vol. 2 p. 368

[60] <u>The reason</u>: As is always the rule regarding pouring one thing from another, as the fact that there is a strainer on the top of the pot does not make a difference in this regard.

[61] The problems faced in doing so is that a) one is separating with a vessel [the strainer that is attached to the top of the kettle] and b) According to Admur in the Siddur one is separating the bad from the good, as the Pesoles-tea leaves-is what remains in one's hands, and hence seemingly may not be done even for right away use.

[62] Shevisas Hashabbos Borer footnote 29; Ketzos Hashulchan 125 footnote 21; Chazon Ish brought in SSH"K 3; Rav SZ"A in SSH"K 3 footnote 125

<u>The reason</u>: The problems mentioned in the previous footnote are answered in the following ways according to the lenient opinions: a) The tea leaves are fit to be drank together with the liquid [by most people] and thus it is permitted to strain the liquid from it, as is explained in the laws of straining. [Shevisas Hashabbos ibid; Ketzos Hashulchan ibid] b) One does not intend to separate the leaves from the tea but rather just to drink the tea. [Ketzos Hashulchan ibid] c) A vessel which is designated to separate for only right away use, as is a kettle, is not included in the separating restrictions. [Rav SZ"A in SSH"K ibid].

views that the food which is left in the pot is considered that which is separated, and thus should ideally be prohibited[63]]. However, others[64] rule that one is to be stringent. In any event when relying on the lenient opinions he should only do so for right away use.[65]

May one use a coffee cup with a strainer inside that prevents the ground coffee from spilling out?
This matter follows the same ruling as above.

May one pour coffee out of a cup that contains Turkish coffee on the bottom?
The custom is to be lenient to allow pouring the coffee out even from the bottom area that is mixed with the Turkish coffee.[66] However some Poskim[67] are stringent to forbid doing so.

May one use tea bags on Shabbos?[68]
Yes. This does not pose a filtering prohibition, despite the fact that while the bag is in the liquid the liquid is being filtered through the herbs in the bag, absorbing the taste of the tea bag.[69]

May one shake the tea bag while inside the liquid in order to dissipate more tea essence?[70]
This matter is disputed amongst the Poskim.[71] Seemingly one may be lenient to do so for right away use.[72]

May one remove the tea bag from the tea?
See chapter 1 Halacha 4 Q&A there.

May one pour the tea out from the cup, leaving the tea bag inside?
See Chapter 1 Halacha 7 Q&A there.

May one remove a sliced lemon from one's tea?[73]
Yes, as large items are not defined as "mixed" with liquid. Regarding if initially it is allowed to place lemon into liquid on Shabbos, see "The laws of Cooking" chapter 1 towards the end.

May one use his hand to strain food for right away use?[74]
No as this is not considered the way of eating, and it is thus equivalent to using a strainer. However, see Halacha 6 below and the footnote to the Q&A there.

---

[63] Shabbos Kehalacha ibid and So is proven from the fact that the Ketzos Hashulchan which rules like Admur in the Siddur rules that it is allowed in our case for the reasons mentioned in the previous footnote.
[64] Chayeh Adam 16; Sheivet Haleivy 1:84; Poskim brought in Kaf Hachaim 319:113
[65] So rules Rav Farkash, as then one can also join in the reason of Rav SZ"A mentioned in the previous footnotes.
[66] Shevisas Hashabbos Borer footnote 29; Ketzos Hashulchan 125 footnote 21
The reason: The problems mentioned in the previous footnote are answered in the following ways according to the lenient opinions: a) The tea leaves and coffee are fit to be drank together with the liquid [by most people] and thus it is permitted to strain the liquid from it, as is explained in the laws of straining. [Shevisas Hashabbos; ibid; Ketzos Hashulchan ibid] b) One does not intend to separate the leaves from the tea but rather just to drink the tea. [Ketzos Hashulchan ibid]
[67] Chayeh Adam 16; Sheivet Haleivy 1:84; Poskim brought in Kaf Hachaim 319:113
[68] Shabbos Kehalacha Vol. 2 p. 370
[69] So rules Minchas Yitzchak 4:99-2
This is because this is similar to the case of filtering water through a filter that contains dregs of wine which is allowed despite the fact that the water is mixing in with the dregs and then becoming filtered out.
[70] Shabbos Kehalacha Vol. 2 p. 370
[71] Seemingly according to the Minchas Yitzchak [ibid] this would be allowed. However others have argued on this -See Shabbos Kihalacha ibid
[72] Thus relying also on the allowance of Rav SZ"A that any vessel used for only right away use does not contain a filtering prohibition.
[73] Shabbos Kehalacha Vol. 2 p. 374
[74] Shabbos Kehalacha Vol. 2 p. 381

Compilation-Making Turkish/ground coffee beverage on Shabbos:

Ground coffee is made through roasting and then grinding the coffee bean. It does not dissolve like instant coffee and has never before been cooked in water. This is in contrast with instant coffee which is made from dehydrated water that had ground coffee cooked in it, and thus dissolves when it reaches contact with liquid. The fact that ground coffee has never before been cooked and does not dissolve raises the Halachic question of whether one may make this coffee beverage on Shabbos using hot water, and whether one may filter the water from the undissolved ground coffee. Making the beverage using hot water can fall under the cooking prohibition, while filtering may fall under the Border prohibition. We will now analyze both of these aspects:

Filtering the coffee liquid from the ground powder:

The general rule: The Borer prohibition of filtering liquids only applies towards liquids that contain solids which people are not accustomed to eating. However, if the solid material that is found in the liquid is consumable by majority[75] of people together with the liquid, then the liquid may be filtered.[76] This, however, only applies to one who is not always particular to filter the liquid from the solid. If, however, one is always particular to avoid drinking the liquid with this solid, then it is forbidden for him to filter it on Shabbos even if it is drinkable by majority of people.[77] Practically, many people [especially in the army] drink their coffee drink together with the ground coffee [i.e. cowboy coffee, mud, Turkish coffee] and are not particular to filter it. Other's however are particular to always filter their ground coffee, and it is unclear as to which group is in the majority. Using this information, we will now analyze the different forms of filtration available and their practical law:

Pouring the coffee liquid into another cup, having the ground coffee remain on bottom of the original cup: It is permitted to pour the coffee liquid out from the cup without any restriction so long as one leaves some amount of liquid remaining above the ground coffee that remains on bottom.[78] To pour coffee past this point, and completely separate all the coffee liquid from the ground coffee is permitted according to most Poskim[79] if done to drink right away. However, according to Admur in his Siddur this matter is under several grounds of debate even if one intends to drink the coffee right away and is hence better to be avoided.[80] However, those who are lenient have upon whom to rely especially if they will be drinking the coffee right away and are not always particular to filter it.[81]

---

[75] Admur 319:13; Ran; Rashba; Beis Yosef; first opinion in M"B 319:34; Tzemach Tzedek Yoreh Deah 45; Shabbos Kehalacha 2 p. 346
Other opinions: Some Poskim rule it must be fit for drinking to all people. [Bach brought in M"B 319:10; See Tzemach Tzedek ibid]

[76] See Admur 319:13 *"Water or wine which are clear are permitted to be filtered through a filter in order so they become even more clear, or even in order [to remove] the sediment that floats on top of the wine or [to filter out] small twigs that have fallen into it. This is not considered like separating being that [the wine and water] are still drinkable to majority of people even without this filtration"*; Rama 319:10 *"because it is fit to drink regardless of the twigs"*; Michaber 319:9; Shabbos 139b
Other opinions: Some Poskim rule one may never use a filter on Shabbos even if the liquid is clear and fit to be drunk by majority of people. [Rambam 8, brought in Michaber 319:10] Practically, we do not rule like this opinion. [M"B 319:41; Admur omitted this opinion]

[77] See Peri Megadim 319 M"Z 6, brought in Ketzos Hashulchan 125 footnote 28 and Biur Halacha 319 "Hoil"; Maharam Shick 134; Shabbos Kehalacha Vol. 2 p. 347 and 361 footnote 52; Piskeiy Teshuvos 319:33

[78] Admur 319:18; *"It is permitted to gently pour [food or liquid] from one vessel into another in order so the residue and dregs remain on the bottom of the vessel [being poured from]. However, one must be careful once the stream [being poured] has stopped and small trickles begin to drip out from the last remainder [of food that is] amongst the waste, then one must stop [pouring] and leave [that remainder of food] together with the waste. The reason for this is because if one were to not do so, then these last drops prove [to all] that [his true intentions in this pouring] were to separate [the food from the waste]. However, during the initial pouring when the waste is not yet recognizable, then he has done no separation."*; Michaber 319:14; Kaf Hachaim 319:113 regarding tea and all mixtures

[79] Admur 319:18; M"A 319:15; M"B 319:55; Kaf Hachaim 319:113

[80] The reason: As a) perhaps coffee is not considered drunk by majority of people with its ground powder and hence contains the Borer restrictions. [Chayeh Adam 16, brought in Ketzos Hashulchan 125 footnote 21] b) According to many Poskim, Admur in his Siddur rules that when one pours liquid from a cup it is considered that one is removing the solid which remains in the cup from the light, and if forbidden due to the Borer restriction against removing bad from good. [see next footnote]

[81] Arguments to permit: 1) Perhaps coffee is considered edible by majority of people together with its ground powder, and hence has no filtering/Borer prohibition. [Ketzos Hashulchan 125 footnote 21] 2) If he pours to drink the coffee right away, many Poskim rule it is considered like taking the food from the waste which is permitted for right away use. [Admur 319:18; M"A 319:15; M"B 319:55; Kaf Hachaim 319:113] Now, although Admur in the Siddur seemingly retracted from this view [Divreiy Nechemia 21; Ketzos Hashulchan 125:9 and footnote 21; Iglei Tal Borer 5; Chayeh Adam 16:9, brought in Shaar Hatziyon 319:44; Oar LeTziyon 2:31-10.], those who are lenient, especially in light of the first argument, have upon whom to rely. [See Shabbos Kehalacha Vol 2 pages 113-122]

Pouring the coffee using a French press strainer and the like:[82] It is permitted to pour the coffee liquid out from the French press without any restriction, so long as one leaves some amount of liquid remaining above the strainer that rests on bottom.[83] To pour coffee past this point, and completely separate all the coffee liquid from the ground coffee which is below the strainer, is debated amongst the Poskim. Some Poskim[84] rule it is forbidden to do so, as coffee powder is not edible by majority of people, and it is forbidden to separate using a strainer. Other Poskim[85], however, justify the custom to be lenient to allow filtering the coffee liquid even from the bottom area of the strainer, under several grounds.[86] Practically, it is best to avoid pouring out all the liquid and one should rather stop pouring as soon as one reaches the area of liquid that is above the strainer/coffee powder, in which case it is permitted according to all. This especially applies to one who is always particular to filter his ground coffee, in which case he is certainly to avoid pouring out all the coffee liquid.[87]

Pouring hot water into a coffee strainer which contains ground coffee:[88] It is permitted to place ground coffee into a strainer and then pour water [from a Keli Sheiyni or onwards] onto it, thus having the water pass through the ground coffee and strainer. [This applies even if the water will take some time to pass through the strainer.[89] However, one may not pour coffee liquid that is already mixed with the ground coffee through a strainer in order to strain the ground coffee.[90] This especially applies if one is always particular to strain it, in which case it is certainly forbidden to do so, as stated above. Likewise, even when pouring the water onto the ground coffee which is in the strainer, one is to beware of the following: a) Not to do any action to help the water strain faster or better, such as not to shake it, mix it using a finger or a vessel.[91] B) If the strainer is sitting inside the liquid, one is to remove it using a spoon and the like to avoid any drops from falling into the coffee after it is removed.[92]]

Summary:
It is permitted to make a hot beverage of ground/Turkish coffee on Shabbos through using a Keli Shelishi or Iruiy Keli Sheiyni.

Pouring from a cup and French press: One may likewise filter the coffee liquid from the ground coffee powder through pouring the liquid into another cup, although making sure to stop pouring as soon as one reaches the area in which the liquid is mixed with the coffee powder. This allowance applies even if one is using a French press. However, it is best not pour the coffee liquid out once it reaches the

---

[82] See Shabbos Kihalacha Vol. 2 p. 368; Piskeiy Teshuvos 319:37

[83] See sources previous footnotes

[84] Chayeh Adam 16, brought in Ketzos Hashulchan 125 footnote 21; Beis Menucha 48; Ben Ish Chaiy Beshalach 2:18; Kaf Hachaim 319:113; Shevet Halevy 1:84; Bris Olam Borer 40; Az Nidbaru 1:23; See Piskeiy Teshuvos 319:37

[85] Shevisas Hashabbos Borer footnote 29 and 49 regarding tea questions the allowance but then concludes that so is the custom; Ketzos Hashulchan 125 footnote 21 regarding also coffee; Chazon Ish 53; Rav SZ"A in SSH"K 3 footnote 125; See Minchas Yitzchak 7:23; Or Letziyon 1:27; Yechaveh Daas 2:51; Piskeiy Teshuvos 319:37

[86] The reason: As a) As [most] people are not particular against consuming some of the ground coffee together with the liquid and it is thus permitted to strain the liquid from it. [Shevisas Hashabbos ibid; Ketzos Hashulchan ibid] b) In any even the coffee powder goes to the bottom and is hence not considered to be strained. [Ketzos Hashulchan ibid] c) One does not intend to separate the coffee liquid from the coffee powder but rather just to drink the coffee. [Ketzos Hashulchan ibid; Chazon Ish ibid] d) A vessel which is designated to separate for only right away use, as is a kettle, is not included in the separating restrictions. [Rav SZ"A in SSH"K ibid].

[87] See Peri Megadim 319 M"Z 6; brought in Ketzos Hashulchan 125 footnote 28; Shabbos Kehalacha Vol. 2 p. 347 and 361 footnote 52

[88] See Admur 319:12, Michaber 319:9 and Mishneh Shabbos 139b *"If one had placed dregs in the strainer from before Shabbos then it is permitted to pour water over it in order so the water become more [clean and] clear."*; Shabbos Kehalalacha 14:36 and Biurim 8; SSH"K 3:64; Piskeiy Teshuvos 319:32 that from here we can learn the allowance to pour water onto coffee that is in a strainer; Minchas Yitzchak 4:99-2 and Shabbos Kehalacha Vol. 2 p. 370

Must the coffee be placed in the strainer on Shabbos? No. [See Piskeiy Teshuvos ibid footnote 274]

Is there a prohibition of Ohel in covering the vessel with the strainer: No. [See Admur Admur 315:19-20; Piskeiy Teshuvos ibid]

[89] Pashut. The Poskim do not differentiate in this matter, and this is in fact the Yesod for allowing using tea bags on Shabbos. [See Shabbos Kehalaha ibid in Biurim]

[90] This case is even more severe than the case of a French press, as the only logic of allowance that remains in this case is that coffee powder is edible to majority of people, which is under debate.

[91] Minchas Yitzchak 4:99; Shevet Halevi 8:58; Piskeiy Teshuvos ibid; See however See Shabbos Kehalacha 2 p. 370

[92] Minchas Yitzchak 4:99-2; Sheivet Halevy 8:58; SSH"K 3 footnote 171 in name of Rav SZ"A; See however Shabbos Kehalacha Vol. 2 p. 371 based on SSH"K 3 footnote 125

level area of the ground coffee/strainer, even if one plans to drink it right away.

Pouring through a strainer: Certainly, one should not pour the coffee liquid directly through a strainer in order to filter the ground coffee. One may however pour hot Keli Sheiyni water into a strainer that contains ground coffee and have the liquid drip into one's cup. One, however, should beware not to shake the strainer and is to remove it from the liquid using a spoon.

2. Filtering liquids with a cloth:[93]

White liquids: It is forbidden to filter water or white wine[94] and the like [of other liquids], using a [non-designated- **See Q&A 1**] cloth, due to the whitening prohibition, being that soaking a cloth is considered laundering.[95]

The reason why there is no whitening prohibition involved by a strainer as opposed to by a cloth:[96] [A typical cloth which is not designated to be used as a strainer does contain a laundering prohibition with clear liquids being that one is particular that the cloth not be wet and thus may come to squeeze it or intend to whiten it.] However, a strainer is made for this purpose and one thus does not care to squeeze [out the liquid which it absorbs] and as well does not care to whiten it at all, therefore its whitening does not pose a problem to prohibit soaking it in liquid due to this even according to those opinions which say that the soaking of a cloth is [considered] laundering it.

Colored liquids:[97] However red wine or beer or other liquids which do not whiten of which we do not suspect that one may come to squeeze [a cloth soaked in these liquids] as explained there [in chapter 320 Halacha 21], then it is permitted to strain it with a cloth even if [the liquids] are slightly murky[98] to the point that most people would not drink them without filtration. [See Q&A]

The reason that filtering even murky colored liquids in a cloth is allowed is: because since nevertheless it is possible to push oneself to drink these liquids, [filtering them] is therefore not considered actually separating, and was [thus] allowed to be done through an irregularity, such as by using a cloth. [**See Q&A**]

Other Opinion with regards to colored but murky liquids: [However] there are opinions[99] who prohibit [filtering even with a cloth] in this scenario [that the colored liquids are slightly murky].

The Final Ruling:[100] It is proper[101] to suspect for this latter opinion.

If the colored liquids are very murky: However if the [colored liquids] are completely murky to the point that it is not possible to drink them in this state, or [in a case that] they have sediment [within them] then it is forbidden to [filter them] even using a cloth, according to all.

A. Not to indent the cloth to intake the liquid:[102]

Upon filtering with a cloth slightly **murky**[103] [colored] liquids one must beware to not make an indent within the cloth in order for it to intake the liquid. Rather one is to pour the liquid on to it and let it form an indentation on its own in order to differ from the way this is done during the week.[104] [**See Q&A**]

---

[93] Admur319:13; Michaber 319:10
[94] Admur ibid and 320:21 and 24; Taz 319:2; Yireim brought in Shaar Hatziyon 319:29; See M"B 319:38
Other opinions: The Elya Raba rules that it is permitted to filter white wine as it does not contain the laundering prohibition as is applicable by water. [brought in M"B ibid]
[95] This follows the second opinion [Tosafus 121] in 302:21, however according to the first opinion [M"A and Gr"a] there the prohibition is because one may come to squeeze the cloth. [See Admur 302:21; M"B 319:37]
[96] Admur ibid; M"B 319:37
[97] Admur ibid; Michaber ibid
[98] Admur ibid; Taz 319:9; M"A 319:12; M"B 319:42 in name of Ran and Rashba; Kaf Hachaim 319:88
[99] Rambam brought in Michaber 319:10; Admur ibid
[100] Admur ibid; M"B 319:42
[101] Lit. Good
[102] Admur319:15; Michaber 319:11; M"B 319:45-46
[103] Admur ibid; M"B 319:45
[104] This restriction only applies to when straining a) murky liquids b) with a cloth. However, by clear liquids even by a strainer it is allowed to make an indentation for the liquid to fall in. [Ketzos Hashulchan 125:13 footnote 33, Mishneh Berurah 319:45, Shabbos Kihalacha Vol 2 p. 354]

B. Sifting with an Egyptian basket:[105]

Any liquid which is permitted to filter with a cloth is permitted to be filtered with an Egyptian basket[106] as long as one does not lift the basket from the bottom of the lower vessel [in which one is filtering into] the height of a handbreadth, in order to differ from the way this is done during the week. However, that vessel which is made like a sieve which is used to filter, since it is designated for this purpose, it has the same laws as does a filter[107] which is that one may only filter with it clear liquids which do not have dregs.

Summary- Filtering with a cloth:

Note: The summary takes into account the crucial clarification which is discussed in Q&A 1 with regards to a designated cloth.

A cloth designated to be used to filter:[108] It is allowed for one to filter in a designated cloth any liquid, even white, even if it is a bit murky to the point that most people would not drink it in its current state [although in such a case one may not make an indentation in the cloth and may only simply pour the liquid into it]. Nevertheless, it is proper to be stringent to not filter liquids that are a bit murky to the point that majority of people will not drink them.

However, if the liquids are completely murky to the point that it is not possible to drink them in this state, or in a case that they have sediment within them then it is forbidden to filter them even using a cloth.

A cloth that is not designated to be used for a filter:[109] All white liquids are forbidden to be filtered through such a cloth due to the laundering prohibition. Colored liquids however do not have a laundering prohibition and are thus allowed to be filtered in all cases that it is allowed to filter with a designated cloth, as explained above. [Nevertheless, according to some filtering colored liquids may pose a dyeing prohibition- See Q&A below]

Q&A

May one filter water with a cloth that is designated to be used for the purpose of filtering?[110]

Yes. In such a case it has the same status as does a filter.[111]

May one who is particular to never drink a certain unfiltered liquid filter it on Shabbos with a designated cloth?[112]

If the water is slightly recognizably dirty, but nevertheless majority of people will drink from it then: It is forbidden to filter it on Shabbos.[113] Thus those people who are particular to only drink filtered water must prepare water from before Shabbos if the water is slightly dirty. However, if one would be willing to drink the liquid unfiltered in a pressing situation then it is permitted for him to filter it **with a cloth** [however not with a filter, as explained above in Halacha 1 Q&A there.]

If the water is clean: and one thus simply desires to make it clearer, then it is allowed for one to filter it even if he is always particular against drinking it without filtering it.[114] Nevertheless there are opinions which are stringent even in such a case to prohibit a person which is always particular to filter the water from filtering it on Shabbos. Thus, according to those opinions people which are particular to only drink

---

[105] Admur319:16; Michaber 319:12

[106] This refers to a basket made of different willows and papyrus plant [Rama]

[107] This vessel is not actually considered a filter being that it does not hold back the dregs of the wine. Nevertheless, since it filters out twigs and filth therefore it has the same status as does a filter. [See M"B 319:52]

[108] Based on Halacha 13 and so rules Ketzos Hashulchan 125 footnote 30, and Shabbos Kehalacha Vol. 2 page 350

[109] Admur319:13

[110] M"B 319:36-37; Ketzos Hashulchan 125 footnote 30; Shabbos Kehalacha Vol. 2 page 350

[111] Being that once it is designated for that purpose, we no longer suspect of the laundering prohibition, as explained in the Alter Rebbe's reasoning behind why a filter does not contain the laundering prohibition with clear liquids.

[112] Shabbos Kehalacha Vol. 2 p. 351

[113] So rules Peri Megadim 319 M"Z 6

[114] Based on ruling of Rav SZ"A regarding Pesach cloth, and Minchas Yitzchak 7:23, Ketzos Hashulchan and others that by waste that is not recognizable the separating prohibition does not apply. So is also implied from the Lashon of the Peri Megadim which is the source for the stringency which mentions "water that has small twigs" in his case of a particular type of person.

filtered water must prepare water from before Shabbos. If one does not yet know the state of the water, such as water which enters directly from the tab into a filter, then it has the same status as clear water.[115]

Does filtering colored liquids through a cloth contain the dyeing prohibition?[116]
There exists different explanations to this query. The following are those opinions:
Tehila Ledavid:[117] The dyeing prohibition only applies to cloths that are common to be dyed and by them one should be stringent. However, cloths which are not normally dyed there is no suspicion for dyeing, and it is allowed. Thus, here that Admur allows the filtering of colored liquids through cloths it is referring only to using cloths that are not commonly dyed and thus do not contain the dyeing prohibition.
Ketzos Hashulchan[118] explains that perhaps the dyeing prohibition only applies by very red wine, although by light red wine it does not, and thus those areas where Admur stated that it is allowed is because he is referring to light red wine. He then concludes that one who wants to do according to all opinions, should use a designated cloth for filtering the wine.
Rabbi Farkash:[119] Argues on the above two answers and rather explains: According to Admur, he learns like those Rishonim that learn that wine [and other fruit juices] are never considered to dye a cloth but rather its color dirties a cloth, and thus it is never applicable to the prohibition of dyeing. It is however applicable to strawberries and the like which can be used for dyeing.
Conclusion: One who wants to follow all opinions, should use a designated cloth for filtering the wine.

May one filter semi-murky liquids with a cloth that is designated to be used for the purpose of filtering?[120]
Yes. This is despite the fact that a designated cloth has the same ruling as a filter, as explained in Q&A 1.

If the city water is undrinkable, such as it has sand in it or worms and thus must be filtered, is there any way to do this on Shabbos?[121]
If there is no other water available one may attach a cloth, which is designated only for filtering, to the sink faucet and use it to filter the water for both drinking **and washing.** One should only filter the water for right away use.[122]
It is forbidden to use an undesignated cloth for the filtering, and as well even a designated cloth may only be used when attached to the sink faucet.

Does this restriction of not making an indentation apply as well to non-murky liquids?[123]
This restriction only applies to when straining murky liquids. However, by clear liquids it is allowed to make an indentation for the liquid to fall in.

---

[115] Ketzos Hashulchan 125 footnote 37
[116] Shabbos Kehalacha Vol. 2 page 352 and 384
[117] Admur319:16
[118] chapter 146 Badei Hashulchan 14 number 13
[119] Shabbos Kehalacha Vol. 2 page 352 and 384
[120] Ketzos Hashulchan 125 footnote 30, and Shabbos Kehalacha Vol. 2 page 350
[121] Shabbos Kehalacha Vol. 2 p. 362
[122] This is in based on the Minchas Yitzchak [7:23] which allows using a cloth that is attached to the faucet being that since one uses the cloth for all waters which come from the sink, including washing and the like, therefore even the water used for drinking is not considered problematic. To note however that not all accept this argument [See Ketzos Hashulchan 125:37 end from which it is proven that he did not hold of this Heter].
[123] Ketzos Hashulchan 125:13 footnote 33, Mishneh Berurah 45, Shabbos Kihalacha Vol 2 p. 354]

3. Filtering insects from water:[124]
Filtering it prior to drinking: Water which contains worms that are forbidden to be eaten, as explained in Yorah Deah chapter 84 [Halacha 1-3], is forbidden to be filtered even using a cloth, as it is impossible to drink it without filtering it being that he may swallow one of the worms.
Filtering it while drinking: see next Halacha

Summary- Water which must Halachicly be filtered from worms and the like:[125]
Is forbidden to filter on Shabbos, unless one does so through placing a filter on the opening of his mouth and then pours the water through it, as will be explained.

Q&A

If the only available water is undrinkable, such as it contains sand or worms and thus must be filtered, is there any way to filter it on Shabbos?[126]
It is forbidden to take the water and pour it through any type of filter unless one is doing so in the process of drinking, as will be explained in Halacha 4-See there.
<u>Using a filter that is attached to the sink</u>: However one may use a filter that is attached to the spout of the faucet and thus have the water automatically get filtered as it leaves the faucet.[127] [This however does not include filters which have a tube leading into the spout of the faucet of which one has an option to ether have the water come through the filter or come through the faucet, as in such a case the filter is only used for drinking water which negates the basis for the allowance of a sink attached filter, as explained in the footnotes of the previous question.] Even when attached to the spout, ideally it is best not to use a non-cloth filter [**see footnote[128]**] and rather a designated cloth filter is to be used. **See Halacha 2 and Q&A there for further details in when a cloth filter is allowed.**

---

4. Filtering undrinkable liquids within the process of drinking:[129]
Filtering wormy water while drinking: It is permitted to drink it through a cloth napkin [such as by placing it on one's mouth and then pouring the water through it, or by placing the napkin on the opening of the bottle and drinking directly from the opening].
The reason for this is: because the separating and filtering prohibition only applies when one is mending [the food] prior to eating or drinking it in order so it be able to be eaten or drank [afterwards] as doing so is a form of an [individual] action [of separating], however when holding back the waste upon drinking in order so it not enter into ones mouth is not similar to an action [of separating] and is [thus] permitted.
The reason that doing the above does not contain a laundering prohibition: Doing so is not forbidden due to [the law] that the soaking of a cloth is considered laundering and neither due to a decree that one may come to squeeze it, being that there is only a small amount [of cloth] which is soaking in the water [as it is only] the size of the opening of his mouth, and by a small amount there is no worry [regarding the above] as explained in chapter 302 [Halacha 21].[130]

---

[124] 319:23; see Michaber 319:16 that implies it is generally forbidden to filter insects
<u>Other opinions</u>: Some Poskim rule that insects are forbidden to be filtered due to being repulsive [Pesoles] and not do to being forbidden. Hence those worms that are small and are not repulsive are not forbidden. [Nishmas Adam 16:5; See Ketzos Hashulchan 125 footnote 37; Kaf Hachaim 319] From Admuyr however it is evident that doing so is forbidden as the insects are not Kosher and hence contain a Borer restriction. [Ketzos Hashulchan ibid]
[125] 319:23
[126] Shabbos Kehalacha Vol. 2 p. 362
[127] Minchas Yitzchak 7:23
[128] So writes Minchas Yitzchak, and so concludes Rav Farkash, in order so one do the filtering with an irregularity. Nevertheless from the letter of the law the Minchas Yitzchak rules that even a metal filter is allowed when attached to the spout of the faucet being that it is also filtering the non-drinking water.
[129] 319:23
[130] There the following is explained: There is a dispute whether placing a minute amount of water on a cloth is forbidden. The first opinion holds that it is always permitted by a clean and white cloth, even when done intentionally to launder being since it is already clean laundering is inapplicable, and thus the only suspicion in such a case is that one may come to squeeze out the water and by a small amount of water this

Other Opinions: However according to the [dissenting] opinion there which prohibits [soaking in water] even a small amount [of cloth] due to [the law] that the soaking of [even a brightly clean/white[131]] cloth is considered laundering [as although one does not intend to launder it, nevertheless this is an inevitable occurrence[132]], here too [according to their opinion filtering water that contains worms through a cloth napkin] would be forbidden [even though only a small amount of the napkin is getting wet, which is the area that is placed by the mouth[133]].

The Final Ruling: It was already explained there [in chapter 302] that every meticulous person should be stringent upon himself when possible. [**See Q&A**]

In chapter 302/21 Admur stated this ruling as follows: One need not protest against those which are lenient [to filter through a cloth when placed by one's mouth] as according to the first opinion this is permitted in all cases [even when done with intent to launder], however every G-d fearing Jew is to be stringent upon himself not to enter into a questionable Biblical prohibition.

Summary-Filtering a liquid in the midst of drinking it:[134]

Placing a filter on the opening of one's mouth and then pouring in the liquid, is permitted under all circumstances, even if the liquid is undrinkable in its current state. It is allowed even if one is using an undesignated white cloth. However, every meticulous and G-d fearing person should avoid, when possible, filtering white liquids when using an **undesignated** cloth [**see Q&A**], due to opinions which rule doing so contains a laundering prohibition.

Q&A

Practically is only a "meticulous" person to avoid being lenient or every G-d fearing person?

In Rav Farkash's summaries[135] he seems to side that one is to be stringent and that only in a time of need may one be lenient. However, the Ketzos Hashulchan[136] does not seem to accept this being that he simply rules that "it is allowed and a meticulous person is to be stringent" thus implying that one may be lenient if he so wishes.

Need one be stringent when filtering water with a cloth that is designated to be used for the purpose of filtering?[137]

No.[138]

Is there any difference in the above laws if the cloth is colored or white or if made of wool or linen?

There is no difference.

---

suspicion does not apply. The second opinion holds that it is always forbidden due to that even the soaking of a white cloth is itself considered laundering and is thus forbidden in all cases even when done not for the intent of laundering being that the laundering is an inevitable occurrence. A third opinion then holds that in truth the second opinion only forbids even a minute amount of water in a case that one intends to launder, however if one does not intend to launder, such as when using it to filter, then even according to them it is allowed.

Thus, according to two of the three opinions mentioned there it is permitted to filter through a cloth when the cloth is placed in one's mouth and the like.

[131] Admur 302:21
[132] Admur 302:21
[133] Admur 302:21
[134] Admur 319:23
[135] Shabbos Kehalacha Vol. 2 p. 364
[136] 125:15
[137] Ketzos Hashulchan 125 footnote 30, and Shabbos Kehalacha Vol. 2 page 350
[138] In such a case it has the same status as does a filter, being that once it is designated for that purpose we no longer suspect of the laundering prohibition, as explained in the Alter Rebbe's reasoning behind why a filter does not contain the laundering prohibition with clear liquids.

May one who follows the lenient opinion filter even through a dirty cloth that is placed by ones mouth?[139]
One should try to do so only with a very clean white cloth being that in such a case there is not much suspicion the cloth will whiten further.[140]

May one use his shirt sleeve as a filter?[141]
Many Poskim[142] have written against doing so even if one places the sleeve against his mouth, as there is worry one may come to squeeze his sleeve from the absorbed liquid.

May one who is stringent nevertheless filter colored liquid through a cloth while drinking?[143]
Yes. This is allowed according to all as by colored liquids the laundering prohibition does not apply.

May one drink a liquid that contains solids through a bottle which filters out the solids?[144]
Yes. This may be used according to all being that there is no laundering prohibition applicable here.

May one use a filtering straw on Shabbos to drink liquids which need filtering?[145]
If the filter is positioned in the area of the straw that enters one mouth, then this is permitted to be used according to all. However, if the filter is on the lower part of the straw then this matter is questionable. Practically in such a case one is to be stringent although one who is lenient has upon whom to rely.

5. Filtering solid food parts which come from the same food:

The general rule:[146] In scenarios others than those listed below [which involve different parts of the **same food**] there would be no prohibition at all, even Rabbinically, in separating [one part of the food from another part] of the same food. Meaning that one may even filter small pieces from slightly large pieces, even if he throws the small pieces to the ground, as they nevertheless do not appear like waste due to this since they are edible and are commonly eaten. [**However to filter out a solid of a different food is forbidden in all cases. Regarding the definition of a same food mixture- see Chapter 1 Halacha 6.**]

Filtering mustard from bran:[147] One may not filter mustard from its bran even though [the bran itself] is also edible and the bran is [thus] not waste at all and [thus] does not contain [in separating it] the Biblical separating prohibition, as [nevertheless] it is Rabbinically forbidden being that appears like one is separating food from its waste being that one filters it in order to eat the mustard and throw out the bran.

Filtering an egg yolk from its white in order to color the mustard[148]**:** However if one placed the mustard into the strainer from before Shabbos [and thus filtered it out from the bran] then it is permitted to place an egg into [the strainer] in order to [have the yolk fall through the strainer and] give color to the mustard that has been filtered through it.

The reason: Now, although the yolk falls out [through the holes of the strainer] together with the mustard while the white which is [all] connected remains above with the waste, [nevertheless] this does not appear like separating food from waste being that both the yolk and the white are foods and he is not filtering the yolk from the white because he desires to eat the yolk and not the white, but rather because the yolk helps give color to the mustard as opposed to the white.

---

[139] Ketzos Hashulchan 125:15
[140] So rules Tzemach Tzedek .
[141] Shabbos Kehalacha Vol. 2 p. 364
[142] Chayeh Adam; Ketzos Hashulchan; Kitzur SHU"A; M"B 319:60
[143] Ketzos Hashulchan 125:15
[144] Shabbos Kehalacha Vol. 2 p. 365
[145] Shabbos Kehalacha Vol. 2 p. 365-356
[146] Admur319:22
[147] Admur319:21
[148] Admur319:21

Now, although he [eventually] throws out the white together with the waste and eats the yolk together with the mustard, nevertheless since the filtering [of the yolk] is not done for eating but rather to give color, it [therefore] does not appear like separating food from waste being that in truth they are both the same type of food.

Filtering the egg yolk from the white in order to eat it:[149] Even if one were to filter [the yolk] for the purpose of eating it, it would only be forbidden in this case [which involves an egg] being that although the white is considered a food nevertheless it is not edible in its current state, as well as that it is common to throw it out together with the waste and thus appears like waste in comparison to the yolk which is eaten the way it is together with the mustard, and would [thus be] Rabbinically forbidden [to separate in order to eat].

Separating foods through placing the mixture in a sieve and having the waste fallout from the holes:
Filtering out the waste of Karshinin: [150] One may place *Karshinin*[151] which is mixed with waste into a sieve even though the waste [might[152]] fall through the holes of the sieve and it is thus found that [the waste] becomes separated on its own.

Summary:

Filtering foods of the same species:[153]
If both are commonly eaten, then there is no separating prohibition involved. If one is commonly throw out, then it has the same laws as eggs mentioned below. To filter out a solid of a different type food is forbidden in all cases. Regarding the definition of a same food mixture- see Chapter 1 Halacha 6.

Filtering mustard from bran:[154]
Is Rabbinically forbidden to be done, being that one plans to throw out the bran and it thus appears like food and waste.

Filtering egg yolk from the white:[155]
Is permitted to be done if one only needs to use the egg yolk to give color to a food. However, if one is doing so in order to eat the yolk and throw out the white then it is Rabbinically forbidden to filter it being that it appears as if one is separating good from bad using a vessel, [being that it is common to throw out the white[156]].

Separating foods through placing the mixture in a sieve and having the waste fallout from the holes:
Is permitted to be done[157] [if it is not inevitable that the waste will be sifted out. However, if it is inevitable, then it is not allowed[158].]

---

[149] Admur319:22
[150] Admur319:11
[151] Possible this refers to the horse been which is similar to the broad been and is used for horse fodder.
[152] Based on Chapter 324 Halacha 1 where Admur writes "that at times the food falls". So concludes the Ketzos Hashulchan 131 footnote 17, and Shabbos Kihalacha Vol 2 page 356. Thus if it is for certain that the waste will fall through, then it is forbidden. This cannot be proven from Halacha 21 where Admur rules that placing mustard with barn in the strainer is forbidden being that there it is discussing having the bran [waste] remain above and the mustard fall out, which contains a Meraked prohibition, while here it refers to having the waste fall out on its own, which does not contain a Miraked prohibition as will explained in the introduction to the next section.
[153] Admur319:22
[154] Admur319:21
[155] Admur319:21
[156] Admur319:22
[157] Halacha 11
[158] See footnote there on Halacha 11

Q&A on sifting:
May one sift foods that are fit to be eaten by majority of people in their natural state, as is the law by liquid?
Seemingly no, as this law was only said by liquids for the reason that by liquids the filtering happens as soon as one enters the liquid inside and it is not very recognizable that one has done Borer. This is opposed to foods in which one must shake the sifter in order to sift it.

May one sift flour on Shabbos?[159]
In addition to the Muktzah prohibition doing so is forbidden also due to Miraked.

May one sift Matzah flour, baby formula and the like on Shabbos?[160]
Sifting it from waste: Although it is not Muktzah, if one desires to sift it in order to remove waste it is forbidden due to the Miraked prohibition.
Sifting it in order to spread onto food: If the flour has already been sifted and one does not need to remove any waste from it but simply desires to sift it for other intentions, such as in order to properly spread the Matzah meal on a food, then one may do so. However, this may only be done if either a) one is using a sifter of the same sized holes to filter the Matzah meal or b) is using an even smaller holed sifter but the Matzah meal does not contain any waste at all which needs to be filtered.
Sifting to remove thick pieces: If the Matzah meal and the like has already been sifted and completely clean of any waste and one desires to filter it in order to remove the thicker flour of Matzah meal from the thinner flour then one may do so with an irregularity[161] such as by sifting it onto the table if one normally does so into a vessel, or vice versa if one usually does it onto a table. However even this is only allowed if the thicker pieces are themselves not very large and are thus still defined as flour, however if the pieces are large enough to be considered crumbs, sifting them is forbidden due to the Miraked prohibition.

May one use a saltshaker if there are pieces of hardened salt or rice inside?[162]
Hardened salt: This is allowed if one is not particular to throw the hardened piece to the trash, and does not mind using it, such as by crushing it and placing it in food. If one is particular against using it and thus throws it out, then the saltshaker should not be used.
Rice: Such a saltshaker is forbidden to be used on Shabbos as people are particular against having the rice fall into their food.[163] Nevertheless there is an opinion[164] which permits using it. Regarding Muktzah, there is no issue involved despite that in general rice is Muktzah, being that the rice was placed in before Shabbos and was thus designated for this use.

---

6. Shaking waste off from foods:
Shaking off the thin peel from the grains:[165] If one had kernels which were removed from before Shabbos from their stalks and are still mixed with their chaff[166] they may not be sifted [out] with a Kenon or plate

---

[159] Shabbos Kihalacha Vol. 2 p. 343
[160] Shabbos Kihalacha Vol. 2 p. 343-345
[161] This is required due to that otherwise it is considered a mundane act.
[162] Shabbos Kihalacha Vol. 2 p. 380
[163] So rules Rav Farkash and so rules Rav SZ"A in SSH"K 3 footnote 179. However, he later retracts this ruling as explained next.
[164] Rav SZ"A in supplements to SSH"K ibid; Otzros HaShabbos Breira footnote 156
The reason: As a saltshaker is meant for immediate use and by vessles meant for immediate use we do not forbid filtering through them. [RSZ"A ibid] Shabbos Kehalacha ibid negates this ruling for numerous reasons, as a) Stating that vessels meant for immediate use do not contain a Borer prohibition is a great novelty that is contradicted in Poskim and b) a salt shaker is many times not sued for immediate use.
[165] Admur 319:10; Michaber 319:7
[166] Chaff is the inedible, dry, scaly protective casings of the seeds of cereal grain, or similar fine, dry, scaly plant material such as scaly parts of flowers, or finely chopped straw. In agriculture chaff is used as livestock fodder, or is a waste material ploughed into the soil or burnt. The process of loosening the chaff from the grain is called *threshing*, and separating the loose chaff from the grain is called *winnowing* – traditionally done by tossing grain up into lightly blowing wind, dividing it from the lighter chaff, which is blown aside. This process typically utilizes a

due to a decree that one may come to sift them with a sieve and sifter in which case one is liable. [Furthermore] even to do so with two hands, meaning to shake them from one hand to another in order to separate [the grains] from their thin peel [is forbidden]. Rather one is to sift them using a single hand placing into it all his strength in order to differ from the method that is used during the week (and thus not come to sift in a sifter). [See Q&A]

Summary-Shaking off the grains in order to remove their thin peels:[167]
Is forbidden to be done with a vessel, or even through shaking from one hand to another. Rather it may only be done through shaking it strongly in one hand, [and even then one may only do so to eat right away].

Q&A
May one use his hand to sift food for right away use by spreading the fingers slightly apart and pouring the mixture over his hand?[168]
No as this is not considered the way of eating, and it is thus equivalent to using a strainer.[169]

May one shake grapes/peanuts/berries from hand to hand in order to get rid of the peels and stems?
No.

---

broad, plate-shaped basket, or similar receptacle for holding and collecting the winnowed grain as it comes back down. Chaff should not be confused with bran, which is finer, scaly material forming part of the grain itself.
[167] Halacha 10
[168] Shabbos Kihalacha Vol. 2 p. 381
[169] Vetzaruch Iyun how this differs from the case mentioned in Admur in which one sifts the waste out from the grains through shaking them in ones hands?

THE LAWS OF ZOREH/WINNOWING

1. Scattering items by throwing them into the wind
A. The prohibition[2762]

First opinion-Is always liable: One who throws something into the wind and the wind scatters it, is always[2763] liable for the winnowing prohibition.[2764]

Second Opinion-Only if intends to scatter: However according to those opinions which say that any action done which is not for its own use one is exempt on, so too here he is exempt [from winnowing in a case where he does not care for the scattering of the item] although it is Rabbinically forbidden even if he does not intend to do so long as the occurrence [of scattering] is inevitable.

Third Opinion-Only if intends to retrieve part of the scattered item after scattering it: Biblically one may crumble bread and throw it into the wind, as Zorah is only an Av Melacha when throwing kernels in order to separate the peel from it, as this is considered Borer (food from the wastes [psoles]) (wastes from the food[2765]), however when one throws all of the food into the wind, there is no Biblical prohibition.[2766] [However Rabbinically this is forbidden to be done.[2767]]
See Footnote for Final ruling[2768]

B. Spitting into the wind:[2769]

One who spits in the wind and the wind scatters the saliva is liable for the winnowing prohibition.[2770]

Other Opinions: However according to those opinions which say that any action done which is not for its own use one is exempt on, so too here he is exempt [from winnowing]. However, it is Rabbinically forbidden even if he does not intend to winnow, so long as the occurrence [of its

---

[2762] There is no single Halacha in Admur which mentions these opinions together, they were rather allocated from the two cases below [B AND C] in which Admur makes mention of these opinions.

[2763] Even if he does not care for the fact that it will become scattered.

[2764] This ruling follows the Yerushalmi [49a], [as opposed to the later ruling which follows the Bavli] that even scattering items not for the sake of separating contains the winnowing prohibition. They as well rule like the opinion which holds that one is liable even for an action which is not done for its own use.

[2765] It is unclear what Admur is saying by placing both scenarios in parentheses.

[2766] This opinion follows the ruling of the Bavli, as Admur writes in the Kuntrus Achron [446:3] that "Crumbling [a food] and then throwing it into the wind does not contain a Biblical prohibition in accordance to our Talmud [Bavli] which equates the Winnowing prohibition to that of separating, and so rules also the Rambam." The previous opinion however follows the ruling of the Yerushalmi. The Igleiy Tal as well as many other Achronim rule like this opinion. The Magen Avraham rules to suspect for the opinion of the Yerushalmi as a mere stringency. [Ketzos Hashulchan 146 footnote 13]

[2767] So is implied from fact Admur only mentions "Biblically", and so rules Ketzos Hashulchan 146 footnote 13-see there! See as well 446:6 "If it is possible to destroy it by throwing it into the toilet, or sea then one should not burn it, or throw it into the wind, in order so he diminish the desecration of Yom Tov." Which implies that it is nevertheless Rabbinically forbidden.
The Ketzos Hashulchan explains that it is Rabbinically forbidden due to that it appears like winnowing.

[2768] See B and Footnote there where we conclude that the first opinion is the main Halachic opinion in opposition to the third opinion here. However, regarding the second opinion, since we rule that "any action done which is not for its own use one is exempt on" therefore that opinion would hold true over the first opinion which holds that one is liable even for an action which is not done for its own use. Thus, in conclusion one would only be liable for the winnowing prohibition when scattering the item for a use of its own. Nevertheless, it would be Rabbinically forbidden to do so in all cases.

[2769] Admur 319:29

[2770] As for the reason that Admur here did not make mention of the dissenting opinion brought in 446:5 [mentioned in C], The Ketzos Hashulchan [146 footnote 13] explains that one must conclude that there was some Kuntrus Achron here which must have gotten lost, as it is impeccable to say that here Admur rules completely like the Yerushalmi and does not even make mention of the opinion of the Bavli which is the opinion mentioned in 446. [Nevertheless, perhaps from the fact that here within the text Admur did not bring the dissenting opinion of the Bavli despite him having mentioned it earlier in the laws of Pesach [which were printed first], and it is only a chance that here there is a Kuntrus Achron on this, it seems clear that practically Admur rules the opinion of the Yerushalmi as the main Halachic opinion.]

scattering] is inevitable. [This opinion is the main Halachic opinion, as explained in Final ruling in A] [**See footnote for opinion of M"B²⁷⁷¹**] [**See Q&A**]

C. Crumbling bread and throwing it into the wind:²⁷⁷²

First Opinion: Biblically one may crumble bread [on Pesach] and throw it into the wind, as Zorah is only an Av Melacha when throwing kernels in order to separate the peel from it, as this is considered Borer (food from the wastes [psoles]) (wastes from the food²⁷⁷³), however when he throws all of the food into the wind, there is no Biblical prohibition.

Second Opinion:²⁷⁷⁴ There are opinions which say that throwing the crumbs in the wind is a complete Biblical Melacha, as explained in the above Halacha regarding spitting.²⁷⁷⁵

Summary:
Although there is dispute with regards to in which cases scattering an item through throwing it in the wind contains a Biblical prohibition, according to all it remains Rabbinically forbidden to do so. One may thus not spit or throw breadcrumbs into the wind on Shabbos.

Q&A

Does the Winnowing prohibition apply only if the wind will scatter the thrown item to many pieces or even if it simply carries the item, having it remain a single unit?²⁷⁷⁶
This matter is disputed between the commentators on the Yerushalmi [49b].²⁷⁷⁷ Practically one is to be stringent in this matter, as so seems to be the logical definition of winnowing.

If the wind will not scatter the saliva but simply carry it along, is it nevertheless forbidden?
Yes- See above.

May one spit into the wind if having it carried in the wind is against his will, such as that he is spitting in a direction that the wind will throw the saliva back at him?²⁷⁷⁸
Yes, one may spit in such a situation. The reason is because in such a case it is considered an inevitable act which one desires not to occur, of which we rule that it is allowed to be done by a Rabbinical prohibition.²⁷⁷⁹

May one spit into the air if it is indefinite whether or not the wind will in truth take the saliva with it?²⁷⁸⁰
Yes, as in such a case it is not inevitable that one will transgress the scattering prohibition [which by saliva is anyways only Rabbinical, as explained] and is therefore allowed.

---

²⁷⁷¹ The above ruling of Admur follows the Rama in which it is forbidden to spit into the wind and it is just a dispute with regards to whether this is a Biblical or Rabbinical prohibit. Many Achronim follow this ruling. However the M"B [319:67] rules [based on Rav Akivah Eigar] that the world is not accustomed to be careful in this being that a) one has not intent to scatter the saliva as well as b) doing so is not the normal way of winnowing. [See Ketzos Hashulchan 146 footnote 13]
²⁷⁷² Admur 446:5
²⁷⁷³ It is unclear to me what Admur is saying by placing both scenarios in parentheses.
²⁷⁷⁴ Admur 446:6
²⁷⁷⁵ With regards to why Admur did not make mention here of the opinion in 319:29 that it is only Rabbinically forbidden due to that one is only liable for a transgression if it was done for a need of itself [Legufo], explains the Ketzos Hashulchan [146 footnote 13] that throwing chameitz into the wind on Pesach is considered for its own need, being that it is forbidden to own chameitz on Pesach.
²⁷⁷⁶ Ketzos Hashulchan 146 footnote 13
²⁷⁷⁷ The Karban Nesanal explains that only when the item is scattered into many pieces is it considered winnowing. However, the Pnei Moshe does not make mention of this and simply writes that having the wind take it away is liable for winnowing.
²⁷⁷⁸ Ketzos Hashulchan 146 footnote 13
²⁷⁷⁹ So concludes Ketzos Hashulchan based on that even by the Av Melacha of winnowing which is to throw kernels into the wind to fly away their shaft, of which the wind is not separating the shaft, being that it was already separating through the threshing process, and the wind simply causes the shaft to fly away.
²⁷⁸⁰ Ketzos Hashulchan 146 footnote 13

May one throw pieces of paper or other scatter-able materials into the wind?[2781]
No, being that the wind scatters them it is forbidden to do so, just as is the law by saliva. Furthermore, one may not even throw a single piece of paper or other item into the wind.[2782]

May one spray a can into the air even though the content is being scattered or does this contain a Zoreh prohibition?[2783]
Yes, one may spray a can, as it is not the wind that is scattering it but rather the air pressure in the can.

Questions for further analysis
May one throw a paper plane into the wind on Shabbos?

May one fly a kite on Shabbos?

May one enter water into a fan and have the wind spread the water?

May one play with a water gun while it is windy outside?

[2781] Ketzos Hashulchan 146:6
[2782] Ketzos Hashulchan 146 footnote 13
[2783] Minchas Yitzchak 6:26

THE LAWS OF MIFAREIK- SQUEEZING LIQUIDS ON SHABBOS

Shulchan Aruch Chapter 320

Translation
Shulchan Aruch Chapter 320
Halacha's 1-15

TRANSLATION-CHAPTER 320
Laws of squeezing on Shabbos
Contains 28 Halachos

Introduction:

The following chapter will deal with the laws of squeezing liquids out of solids on Shabbos. Squeezing liquid from a solid involves the Mifarek prohibition and is thus only permitted to be done in certain scenarios. The first section will deal with the laws of squeezing from fruits/vegetables for purposes of drinking the liquid. The second section will deal with squeezing them in order to season a food. The third section will deal with squeezing liquids out from cooked or pickled fruits and vegetables. The fourth section will deal with the laws of melting ice, snow, and salt. According to some this does contain the Mifarek prohibition but rather a Rabbinical prohibition of Nolad. According to others however this was Rabbinically prohibited due to that one may come to squeeze fruits and transgress the Mifarek prohibition. The fifth section will deal with the laws of squeezing liquids out from cloth. Doing so in addition to containing the Mifarek prohibition as well contains at times the laundering prohibition.

Part 1: the laws of squeezing from fruits/vegetables for purposes of drinking the liquid.

Halacha 1
Squeezing fruits on Shabbos
Biblically

Olives and grapes: One who squeezes olives in order to take out oil, or grapes in order to take out wine is liable due to that he has detached the juice from the fruit, and it was already explained in chapter 305 [Halacha 28] that anyone who detaches food or juice from the area where it was absorbed in has [transgressed] an offshoot of [the] threshing [prohibition].

Other fruits: However other fruits are Biblically allowed to be squeezed to take out their juice.

The reason for this is: because fruit juices do not have the status of a liquid with exception to what comes out of olives and grapes alone. Rather they have a status of food on them and [squeezing them out] is like separating food from food which does not contain the prohibition of squeezing, as explained there [in chapter 305].

Rabbinically:

Fruits which are squeezed for juice when there are plenty of them: However, Rabbinically it is forbidden to squeeze even strawberries and pomegranates.

The reason for this is: due to there being segment of people which have a large number of strawberries and pomegranates and they squeeze them for their juice just like [is done with] olives and grapes, and if other people also had such a large amount of [these fruits] then they too would be accustomed to squeeze it for its juice. Therefore, anyone who squeezes them for the sake of its juice these thoughts of his help give [the juice] a liquid status Rabbinically, as we do not claim that [the persons thoughts of using the fruits for juice] is nullified in face of the [intended use of this fruit by the] populace.

Pears and other fruits: Similarly, those pears (that we call *brenis*) which are common to squeeze for their juice in certain places, is forbidden to squeeze on Shabbos for the entire [populace of the] world, because it is possible that if the entire world had as much of these [pears] as the other places do, then they too would squeeze the pears for their juice. The same law applies for all fruits of the sort.

Other Fruits that are never squeezed for juice even when they have a lot of the fruit: However [all] other fruits which is not common for [people of] the world to squeeze for their juice, to drink their liquids to quench their thirst or for pleasure, even if they have a lot of them, then even if they are commonly squeezed for medicine they do not have the status of juice due to this even Rabbinically and is [thus] allowed to be squeezed on Shabbos, as it is like separating food from food.

Now although that this person who wants to squeeze them intends to do so for their juice, nevertheless his intentions are nullified in face of the [common practice] worldwide.

431

Fruits which are squeezed for juice in one's area but not in others: Nevertheless in any area where the custom is to squeeze a certain fruit for its juice then its laws in that area are the same as the laws of strawberries and pomegranates and is thus forbidden to squeeze it in those places for their juice, because the intent of this [person] that wants to squeeze it is not nullified [to the world custom] since all the people of his area do this during the week. However other places are allowed to squeeze them since they are not accustomed to squeeze them for their juice even if they have a lot of the [fruit].

Other Opinions[1]: [However] there are opinions which say that all fruits are Rabbinically forbidden to squeeze for the sake of their juice, as since the person squeezing it intends to do so in order drink the juice to quench his thirst or for pleasure (or even for healing) therefore they are Rabbinically considered [the status of] juice, and we do not say that his intentions are nullified in face of the worldly custom.

Squeezing in order to flavor food: (However if his intention [in squeezing] is in order to give flavor to a food then it is allowed [even according to this opinion] as will be explained in Halacha 7 and 10).

Squeezing in order to sweeten the fruit: However, if one is squeezing it simply to sweeten the fruit and not for its juice then it is allowed [to be done] by all other fruits [which the custom of the world is not to squeeze even when they have plentiful of it]. [Furthermore] even if one drinks the juice which is squeezed it is allowed being that one did not have intent to squeeze it for its juices.

[However the above law is] with exception to strawberries and pomegranates and the like (of fruits which a segment of people which have a large amount of them squeeze them for their juice just like olives and grapes, and if there were to be this amount of these fruits by other people they too would commonly squeeze them for their juice) in which case [the Sages made it] forbidden to squeeze them even in order to merely sweeten [the fruit] due to a decree that one may come to also squeeze them for their juices (as do those people which have plenty of [this fruit]).

The Final Ruling: Likewise, the custom in many places is to be stringent [like this latter opinion] although the main Halachic opinion is like the first opinion. Nevertheless, in a place where the custom is to be stringent one may not do differently.[2]

Halacha 2
To suck the juice out from fruits:

First Opinion: The above however only applies to squeezing, however, to suck out the juice from the fruit with one's mouth there are opinions whom allow one to do so even by olives and grapes because this is not the regular form of squeezing and one's intent is [thus] nullified to that of the rest of people.

Second Opinion: However, there are opinions which say that nevertheless it is Rabbinically forbidden [to do so] just like [the Sages] forbade one to nurse with his mouth from an animal even though he is removing [the milk] in an irregular method, as will be explained in chapter 328 [Halacha 40].

An additional reason for 2nd opinion: In addition [sucking juice from olives and grapes] is [still] questionable regarding if one is liable for a sin offering [on doing so] as perhaps [sucking] is not considered [squeezing in] an irregular way as is nursing from an animal being that nursing [from an animal] is a complete irregularity as it is never common to nurse [from it] but rather to milk it. However sucking fruit is not such a great irregularity being that it is at times common to do so.

[Furthermore] even fruits which are [only] Rabbinically forbidden to be squeezed are forbidden to suck from as is done by olives and grapes, because the Sages did not make differentiations within their decree.

To suck on meat [according to 2nd opinion]: The same law applies when placing bread in wine or meat in soup that it is forbidden to suck them even though there is only a Rabbinical prohibition involved in squeezing them.

Sucking on sugar cane [according to 2nd opinion]: Therefore, it is forbidden to suck on sugarcane due to that it has the same laws as strawberries and pomegranates and fruits of the like.

The final ruling: The custom is to be lenient [to] even [suck] olives and grapes like the first opinion. [Although] one who is stringent [to avoid sucking] even bread and meat will be blessed.

---

[1] Bach
[2] So rules Magen Avraham and Mishneh Berurah [8].

However by other fruits³, excluding olives and grapes, one may be lenient because there is [another] aspect [involved] to [allow one to] be lenient with the sucking of fruit being that one can say that doing so is within the norm of eating and so long as something is done in a way of eating it is not at all similar to a [forbidden] action and even the Sages did not make a decree in such cases as explained in chapter 319 [Halacha 1] regarding separating food from waste.⁴

Halacha 3
Juice which flowed on their own from fruits on Shabbos
From grapes and olives: Liquids which flowed out on Shabbos on their own from olives and grapes are forbidden [to be eaten] until evening [i.e. after Shabbos] due to a decree that one may come to squeeze them with his hands in order to drink them today [on Shabbos] if [these liquids] were to be permitted. [Furthermore] even if the olives and grapes [from which the juice flowed from] are designated to be eaten [and not squeezed] [nevertheless] we suspect that one may change his mind to squeeze it for its juices just like is common for majority of olives and grapes.
From other fruits: However, juice which has flowed from strawberries and pomegranates and the like then if they are designated to be eaten then the liquid is permitted, as we do not suspect that one may change his mind to [use them] for juice. However, if they are designated for their juice then the juice is forbidden.

Halacha 4
If the grapes and olives were crushed from before Shabbos: Olives and grapes which were crushed from before Shabbos, the juice which comes out from them on Shabbos is allowed [to be drank] for the reasons explained in chapter 252 [Halacha 14].
If the grapes were in a vat of wine: [Furthermore] even if they had not been crushed from before Shabbos, if there is wine in the vats that the grapes are inside of, then even though the grapes break open on Shabbos inside the vat and more wine comes out [from them into the vat], [nevertheless] one is allowed to drink from this vat on Shabbos, because every little bit of wine which comes out of the grapes on Shabbos becomes nullified in 60 times the wine that was already in the vat [from before Shabbos].
The reason that the wine is not considered a Davar Sheyeish Lo Matirin: Now, although this wine [which flowed on Shabbos] is considered an item which will eventually become permitted [in which case it should never be nullified until then] being that after Shabbos it will be permitted without any nullification [needed], nevertheless since this wine that came out on Shabbos was never recognizable prior to it being mixed [into the vat] and it [thus] never had the status of wine on it (look in Yorah Deah chapter 123 regarding when juice from a grape receives a status of wine) [therefore] it does not receive the status of an item which will eventually become permitted [without needing nullification] until after it already became nullified [within the wine that it seeped into], and [the Sages] only said that something which will eventually become permitted is not nullified in a case that the prohibition was initially visible and it already then received a status of something which will eventually become permitted and then afterwards got mixed [into another food].
If one placed the grapes into the vat on Shabbos: [Furthermore] even if one placed whole grapes into the vat on Shabbos and they then broke open [and seeped wine] on that day into the wine [that was already in the vat], it is permitted to drink wine from the vat for the above mentioned reason.
However, it is initially forbidden to place whole grapes into wine on Shabbos in order so they split open and ooze their wine [into the vat] due to the prohibition of squeezing, as although he is not squeezing it actually with his hands nevertheless it is Rabbinically prohibited [to cause it to be squeezed].⁵

---
³ See footnote by the summary of this Halacha for the difficulties presented in the wording here.
⁴ According to the Mishneh Berurah it is only proper to be stringent regarding olives and grapes and not regarding other fruits.
⁵ So rules the Taz. However the Magen Avraham and Chayeh Adam and Mishneh Berurah [14] rule that it is allowed to be done even initially.

Halacha 5
Grape seeds and skins: Grape seeds and skin which had water placed on them in order to make grape-skin wine, it is permitted to draw [wine] out from these [seeds and skins, into the water] and then drink it. Furthermore, even if one had not placed water [onto them] and the wine squeezes and flows out on its own, it is permitted to drink it being that it already was broken up before Shabbos.

Part 2: Squeezing juice into food [and liquid[6]]:
Halacha 6
Fruits which are edible the way they are:
Squeezing grapes directly into food: It is permissible to squeeze a cluster of grapes into a pot of food in order to give better [taste] (see chapter 505 [Halacha 2][7]) to the food.
The reason for this is: because all liquid that enters into food is considered like food and does not have a status of liquid at all, and thus it is as if one is separating food from food.
Squeezing grapes into an empty bowl and then into food: However, if it is not [being currently squeezed into] food then it is forbidden to squeeze it [even if one plans to mix food into it later on].
The Reason: Now, although one plans eventually to mix food into it and it is for this reason that he is now squeezing this wine into [the vessel], in order to use it to enhance and sweeten the food that he will eventually eat with this wine and it is thus liquid which is entered into food which is considered like food, nevertheless since at the time of squeezing the wine there is not yet any food [which is mixing into it] and it is not evident at all that it is for this purpose of enhancing the food [for which he is squeezing the wine], therefore it is Rabbinically forbidden.

Halacha 7
Other fruits which some areas squeeze for Juice: The above law applies [as well to] strawberries and pomegranates and other similar fruits.
Other fruits which are never commonly squeezed anywhere: However other fruits, even according to those which forbid squeezing them for their juices, nevertheless if one is only squeezing them in order to season the food with their liquid then it is allowed even if there is no food currently within the vessel that he is now squeezing them into.
The reason for this is: because at the time of the squeezing it is known to all that he is squeezing them in order to sweeten the food and not in order to drink their juice being that it is not at all common to squeeze these [fruits] for juice.

Halacha 8
Squeezing fruits that are not fit to be eaten into food:
However, the above is only referring to fruits which are fit to be eaten however fruits which are not fit to be eaten are forbidden to be squeezed according to all opinions even into food.
The reason for this is: because when one squeezes food which is not fit for eating he is not separating food from food but rather is [separating] food from waste which contains [the prohibition of] "detaching" as was explained in chapter 305 [Halacha 28]. [It is] also [forbidden] because of [the prohibition of] separating food from amongst waste even if he wants to eat it right away, as [the Sages] only permitted to separate food from waste with ones hands in order to eat right away because so is the form of eating, to take the food with his hands from the waste and eat it and [it is thus] not similar to [forbidden] work, however to squeeze and then eat is not a form of eating but is a form of work.

---

[6] See end of Halacha 10 regarding squeezing into liquids.
[7] There it is explained that squeezing into food is only allowed if the liquid will become completely absorbed into the food. If not then it is forbidden.

Halacha 9

Unripe grapes: Likewise, it is forbidden to squeeze unripe grapes, which are [all] grapes which have not yet reach the [the size of] a white been, even into foods because these [grapes] are inedible, and are thus considered like waste in relation to the wine which is squeezed out from it. Now, because we do not know the size of the white been it is forbidden to squeeze grapes into food until they are fit to be eaten by majority of people.

Other Opinions: [However] there is an opinion which permits squeezing unripe grapes into food (and it goes without saying that they permit this to be done to other fruits which are not fit to be eaten, and even to squeeze them for their juice is permitted according to those who permit this with other fruits [which are edible]).

The Final Ruling: One is to be stringent like the former opinion.[8]

Halacha 10

Apples and lemons: Apples have the same law as other fruits [which are not commonly squeezed anywhere]. [Furthermore] even lemons do not have the same laws as strawberries and pomegranates, but rather like other fruits. [Therefore they] are allowed to be squeezed for the need of their juices even for the sake of drinking [the juice, as opposed to using it for other purposes,] according to those opinions which permit [doing so to fruits that are never squeezed for their juice]. According to those opinions who forbid [squeezing any fruit for the sake of drinking their juice] it is at the very least allowed to squeeze them for the need of food, meaning in order to flavor the food with their liquids and the like.

The Reason: Now, although that in those places that there are plenty of these fruits, they [are accustomed to] squeeze them for their juices, [nevertheless] they do not receive the same laws as strawberries and pomegranates just because of this even in those places [that squeeze them]. [The reason for this is] because they do not squeeze their liquid for the sake of drinking it but rather for the sake of using for [flavoring] food. [Furthermore,] even if they are accustomed to squeeze the [juice] into water in order to drink, it is allowed since it is not common to drink them plain [in their concentrated state].

Squeezing fruits into a liquid: Nevertheless according to those opinions which forbid to squeeze [any] fruit for the sake of drinking their liquids, then it is forbidden to squeeze on Shabbos lemons or other fruits into water or other liquids in order to drink, as [the Sages] only said that juices which enter into foods are considered like food [and are thus allowed to be squeezed into them] and not [juices that enter] into liquid.

Part 3: Squeezing juice out of pickles and other foods saturated with external liquids:

Halacha 11

Not for the sake of adding the liquid into food:

For the sake of their liquids: All this refers to fresh ripe lemons, however those that are pickled in salt and vinegar or in salt water, as well as other fruits and vegetable which are pickled as well as those which are cooked are forbidden according to all opinions to be squeezed for their liquids.

In order to enhance the food being squeezed: Rather [they are] only [allowed to be squeezed] for their own need in order to prepare them to be eaten through doing this, in which case doing so is not prohibited due to "detaching" since one does not at all need the item being detached, which is their juice.

The above is only a Rabbinical prohibition: [Furthermore] if one [transgressed and] squeezed [the above foods] for their liquids he is not Biblically liable because even though the liquids were fully fledged liquids prior to becoming absorbed into the [foods], such as [occurs] if one pickled or cooked them in water or wine and vinegar and the like of other liquids, nevertheless since now they are being squeezed from food they have the same status as food and it is thus like separating food from food. Nevertheless, it is Rabbinically forbidden to squeeze them for the sake of their liquid since they were fully fledged liquids prior to this.

---

[8] The Michaber brings two opinions on this matter regarding inedible grapes, the latter-stringent- opinion being like that of Rabeinu Tam. The Magen Avraham, Tosefes Shabbos, and Mishneh Berurah[21] all rule like the latter opinion in Michaber, like the ruling here by Admur.

However raw fruits since their squeezed liquids never had upon them the status of liquids [prior to the squeezing] therefore it is allowed to squeeze them according to those opinions which permit doing so.

Halacha 12
Squeezing cooked and pickled foods into food:
It is permitted to squeeze pickled and cooked [foods] for the sake of their liquids into a pot of food in order to enhance it. However, if the pot does not yet have food in it then it is forbidden to squeeze into it even though one will eventually mix food into it, as was explained above [in Halacha 6]

Halacha 13
Squeezing into a creamy dip:
It is permitted to squeeze [fruits and pickled foods] into Muryas[9] because it is considered a food however into liquids it is forbidden to squeeze them.

Halacha 14
Squeezing fish:
One who [wishes to] squeeze fish for its gravy has the same laws as squeezing pickled and cooked [foods] for the sake of their juices.

Halacha 15
Squeezing out the food part of a fruit or cooked food
Apples or other cooked fruits are allowed to be squeezed in order to remove from it all of its content because he is squeezing out all the food from it and is not [doing so] in order to take out its liquid.

❖ **For the Translation of Halachos 16-20 See the next section "The Laws of Nolad"**

Part 2: Wetting and squeezing cloths on Shabbos
Halacha 21
Spreading a cloth over an open bottle;
Over a bottle of clear liquid: It is forbidden to spread a cloth over a barrel of water in order to cover it, as it may get wet from the water and one will then come to squeeze it and be liable for [the] whitening [prohibition].

A cloth designated for covering: However, a cloth which is designated to be used to spread over the [opening of the barrel] is permitted [to be spread] being that one has no care to squeeze it if it gets wet as it is designated for this purpose.

Over a bottle of colored liquid: However, it is permitted to spread a cloth over a barrel of red wine or of oil or beer and other beverages of the sort [which are not clear]. Furthermore, it is even permitted to initially soak the cloths in these liquids with one's hands such as to filter colored liquids over this cloth.

The reason for this is: because the [prohibition of] whitening only applies with water and white wine and the like.

Squeezing cloths that have become wet with colored liquids: Nevertheless, even cloths which have been soaked in liquids which do not whiten, it is forbidden to squeeze them due to the prohibition of "detaching" which is an offshoot of [the] threshing [prohibition] just as squeezing fruits is prohibited because of "detaching". However, one is only liable on this squeezing if he needs the liquids being squeezed from the cloth, however if one does not need the liquids squeezed out from the cloth and is only doing so in order to clean the cloth, then this is not similar to threshing at all, as by threshing one needs the grains that he is detaching from the stalks. Therefore, this squeezing does not contain a Biblical prohibition but rather a Rabbinical.

---
[9] A creamy dip made from fish fat.

The reason that we do not decree that one may come to squeeze cloths wet from colored liquids: Therefore the [Sages] did not decree against soaking a cloth in liquids which do not whiten due to a decree that one may come to squeeze it and be liable for "detaching", as one is only liable if he needs the liquids being squeezed of which there is no remote suspicion [here] that one may squeeze the cloth for the sake of the liquids that will come out from it being that [these liquids] are not of any significance and it is not at all common to do this.

Halacha 22
Inserting a wet cloth into the opening of a bottle
It is forbidden to insert [wet[10]] Mochin [i.e. any soft material] into the opening of a bottle which contains [even colored[11]] liquid[12].

The reason for this is because: one may come to squeeze [the material] as through inserting it one will squeeze the liquid that is absorbed in the material into the bottle.

Now although one has no intention to do so, nevertheless [since] it is an inevitable occurrence when one inserts it tightly [therefore it is forbidden].

Inserting it lightly: Therefore the [Sages even] prohibited inserting it lightly due to that one may come to insert it strongly.

Halacha 23
Using a sponge to clean
With a handle: A [dish] sponge which has a handle of leather [or other non-absorbent material] which one uses to hold on to it, may be used to clean with [as through using the handle nothing squeezes out from the sponge].

Without a handle: If it does not have [a handle] then it may not be used to clean with as when one holds it in his hands it squeezes in between his fingers, and although this is done unintentionally [nevertheless it is forbidden because] it is an inevitable occurrence.

Other Opinions in why with a handle is allowed: [However] there is an opinion which says that even if [the sponge] has a handle it is impossible to clean with the sponge without squeezing it and nevertheless it is permitted as since the squeezing is being done through the [pressing of] the handle it is [therefore] not [Halachically] considered squeezing and is rather like emptying water from a flask which does not contain [the] "detaching" [prohibition].

However, when it does not have a handle in which case it gets squeezed in the area that he holds it with his hand, then it is forbidden.

Halacha 24
Plugging the hole of a barrel with a pipe and wet cloth on Shabbos
A drain pipe which one inserts into a hole in the wall of a barrel from which the wine is removed from, and [before doing so] one wraps around the drain pipe a piece of cloth or thin residue of flax[13] with which he [uses to fully] plug up the whole in the barrel[14], it is forbidden to plug [the hole of the barrel with this pipe] on Shabbos even if the barrel contains red wine or other [colored] liquids which do not whiten as through plugging it one squeezes out the liquid absorbed in the cloth, and this is an inevitable occurrence. Now although the squeezed liquid is going to waste nevertheless it is Rabbinically forbidden as explained above [in Halacha 21].

---

[10] Mishneh Berurah 44, and so is evident from the Alter Rebbe here.

[11] Mishneh Berurah 44

[12] The Mishneh Berurah rules that this is not to be taken literally, as it is forbidden even if the bottle does not contain liquid, and liquid was only mentioned for the reader to deduce that the material had previously become wet from it.

[13] When flax is pressed there are small pieces of residue which fall from it.

[14] Meaning in order so no liquid leak out from the hole where the pipe has been inserted one wraps cloth around the area of the pipe being inserted thus closing up any possibility of leakage.

Other Opinions: [However] there are opinions which say that so long as the liquid is going to waste then there is only a Rabbinical prohibition involved if one has intention to squeeze it, however so long as he does not intend to [squeeze] it, even if this is an inevitable occurrence, it is permitted.

Their reasoning is: because the squeezing [of this cloth] gives one no satisfaction being that one has no benefit from it, and it was only made forbidden to insert Mochin into the opening of the bottle even though he has no intent to squeeze it because the liquid that is being squeezed out from the Mochin enters into the bottle and one benefits from this squeezing. However, the liquids that are squeezed from the cloth that surrounds the pipe go to waste if there is no vessel under them, and there is thus nothing to benefit from it for him.

The Main Halachic Opinion: The main Halachic opinion is like the former opinion, as [we ruled above in Halacha 23 that] a sponge that does not have a handle may not be used to clean with even though he has no intention to squeeze [liquid out] and the liquid which is squeezed from the sponge goes to waste.

The Custom: Nevertheless, [despite the above reasoning] the world is accustomed to allow plugging up with [a pipe that has] cloth [surrounding it] on Shabbos.

The justification of the custom: There are those opinions which have learned justification for [this custom] as since the pipe has a long extension past the cloth and no hand touches the cloth [in the process of inserting and removing the pipe] then even though there is liquid being squeezed out of the cloth it is [nevertheless] permitted [to insert/remove] the pipe just like is the ruling by a sponge which has a handle according to the opinion [there] which says that even if liquid is squeezed out from it, it is allowed [to be used] as it is similar to emptying a flask of its water.

According to this reasoning even if there is a vessel under the pipe which intakes the liquid squeezed from the cloth it is permitted [to be inserted/removed].

The Final Ruling: Due to there being many opinions which argue on the above justification therefore one should accustom [those which allow inserting and removing the pipe] that there should not be a vessel under the pipe. [This should be done] in order so the squeezed liquid go to waste, and thus [have one] rely upon the [leniency mentioned by] the second opinion that was explained [above]. Now although this opinion is not the main Halachic opinion, [nevertheless it is allowed to rely on them] as there are opinions which entirely permit to even intentionally squeeze [liquid out from a cloth] so long as the liquid goes to waste.

As well [they should be careful that] the pipe extend out from the cloth in order to also join this leniency [mentioned in the justification].

The above may be done even by a barrel of white wine: (There is no need to worry of the prohibition of whitening [in inserting/removing the pipe with the] flax residue and pieces of cloth which surrounds the pipe even if it is white wine which whitens, because [these cloths] are meant to get wet [and dirty] and one does not care to whiten it at all as was written in chapter 319 [Halacha 13] regarding a strainer).

Halacha 25
Plugging up the hole of a leaking pipe

One may plug up a [leaking] pipe with cloths and any other moveable materials in order so that the water [from the pipe] not flood one's food and vessels.

The reason for this allowance is: as one does not care if a little bit of water trickles out from the hole [in the pipe] and therefore he will not come to insert it strongly and will not come to inevitably squeeze [water out from the cloth].

Compilation of Halachas Summaries and Q&A

CHAPTER 1: THE LAWS OF SQUEEZING JUICE FROM FRUITS/VEGETABLES ON SHABBOS

Introduction:
The following chapter will deal with the laws of squeezing liquids out of solids on Shabbos. Squeezing liquid from a fruit or vegetable involves the Mifarek prohibition which is an offshoot of the threshing prohibition and is thus only permitted to be done in certain scenarios.

The following are the main Halachas of the first chapter.
The first and second Halacha will deal with the laws of squeezing from fruits/vegetables for purposes of drinking the liquid. The third Halacha will deal with squeezing them in order to season a food. The seventh Halacha will deal with squeezing liquids out from cooked or pickled fruits and vegetables.

The Melacha of Dash

A. The Av Melacha of Dash:[1]
Threshing [the act of industrially separating grains from their stalk, such as by stomping on a threshing floor of wheat stalks] is one of the Av Melacha, a principal Melacha, that was performed in the Mishkan. [In the Mishkan this was performed with the dyes, as the dyes were extracted from seeds that were removed from stalks.]

B. The Tolda/subcategories of Dash:[2]
Whoever separates food or drink from the area in which it was covered is performing a Tolda, a subcategory, of the Dash prohibition. The reason for this is because the Av Melacha of Dash involves loosening the grains from the stalk.

C. Examples:
- One who milks an animal is liable for Dash, as he has separated the milk from the utter.[3]
- One who removes beans from their pods.[4]
- Squeezing liquid out of olives and grapes.[5]
- Squeezing liquid from a cloth.[6]
- A woman who squeezes milk from her breasts.[7]

---

[1] Admur 305:28; Mishneh Shabbos 73a
[2] Admur 305:28; 320:1; 319:9
[3] Admur 305:28
[4] Admur 319:9 and Siddur
[5] Admur 320:1
[6] Admur 320:22
[7] Admur 328:44

1. The Biblical prohibition in squeezing fruits on Shabbos:
A. Edible Fruits:[8]
Olives and grapes: One who squeezes olives in order to take out oil, or grapes in order to take out wine is liable[9] due to that he has detached the juice from the fruit[10], and it was already explained in chapter 305 [Halacha 28] that anyone who detaches food or juice from the area where it was absorbed in, has [transgressed] an offshoot of [the] threshing [prohibition].

Other fruits:[11] However other [edible[12]] fruits are Biblically allowed to be squeezed to take out their juice. *The reason for this is*:[13] because fruit juices do not have the status of a liquid with exception to what comes out of olives and grapes alone [as explained in Admur 158/4-5[14]]. Rather they have a status of food on them and [squeezing them out] is like separating food from food which does not contain the prohibition of squeezing, as explained there [in chapter 305].

Are fruits other than grapes and olives considered Biblically forbidden today if they are commonly squeezed, just as are olives and grapes?[15]

Approximately 90% of cultivated olives are used for oil making; 70% of cultivated grapes are used for wine and 70% of oranges are used for juice. 90% of Florida oranges are juiced. The question is hence asked whether juicing oranges and other citrus fruits today would fall under the Biblical prohibition just like olives. The answer is as follows:

Some Poskim[16] rule that in today's times all commonly juiced citrus fruits are Biblically forbidden just as olives and grapes. Others[17] however rule that it remains Rabbinically forbidden, and so is implied to be the opinion of Admur.[18]

Is there a Borer prohibition involved in squeezing fruits?[19]

No, as the fruit and its juice are Min Bemino, the same species, to which the Borer restrictions do not apply.

---

[8] Admur 320:1
[9] Admur ibid; Braisa 145a; Rambam 8:10; M"B 320:1
[10] Admur ibid; Rambam ibid; Rashi 143a
[11] Admur ibid; M"A 320:1; Shabbos 145a
Other opinions: According to Tosafus and Rabbeinu Chananel, Rebbe Yochanun rules other fruits are also Biblcially forbidden. [Brought in Tzemach Tzedek Shabbos 22; Shabbos Kehalacha 2:404]
[12] Regarding inedible fruits refer to Halacha 2D regarding if squeezing them contains a Biblical prohibition.
[13] Admur ibid; Ran 61a; Rashba 145a; Rosh; Tzemach Tzedek 58
Ruling of Rashi: Rashi 145a states that the reason why other fruits are only Rabbinical is because they are not commonly squeezed. This reason is not recorded in Admur ibid, Some explain this reason of Rashi to be a different opinion than the Ran. [P"M 320 A"A Hakdama] Others explain that Rashis commentary is complimentary to that of the Ran, and it is due to the fact that the squeezing is not common, that its liquid is not considered liquid, as states the Ran. [Iglei Tal Dash 16; Rashba ibid] It is clear from Admur 252 Kuntrus Achron 12 that Rashi and the Ran are stating two different reasons. The practical ramification is regarding fruits today that are commonly squeezed.
[14] Michaber 158:4; Mishneh Terumos 11:2; Machshirin 6:4; There it is explained that only seven liquids are considerd Mashkeh according to Torah law of receiving impurity 1. Water 2. Wine 3) Olive oil; 4)Milk 5) Dew; 6) Honey; 7) Blood
[15] See Shabbos Kehalacha 2 pp. 388-393
[16] Based on Rashi ibid and Rashba ibid that mention "not commonly juiced" as part of their reason; Chazon Ish 33:5; Mishmeres Shabbos 1:41
[17] Ketzos Hashulchan 126 footnote 14; Rav SZ"A and Shevet Halevi, brought in Shabbos Kehalacha ibid; Shabbos Kehalacha p. 393 concludes that we follow this opinion
[18] As Admur omits the wording of Rashi in 320:1 and in 252 Kuntrus Achron 12 he explains that Rashi and Ran are arguing.
[19] M"A 319:16; Iglei Tal Borer 10:5; Ketzos Hashulchan 126 footnote 19; See Minchas Yitzchak 1:75-4; Shabbos Kehalacha 15:1 in Biurim [p. 388]
Opinion of Admur: It is proven from Admur 320:8 [and M"A 320:7] that there is no Borer oprohibition involved in squeezing fruits, as if there was then it would be forbidden to squeeze any fruit on Shabbos, irrelevant of the Mifarek prohibition, due to that it is considered Borer Derech Melacha, as expaliend Admur ibid. [Ketzos Hashulchan ibid]
Other opinions: Some Poskim rule that squeezing fruits involves the Borer prohibition and hence may only be done [even by the permitted fruits] a) for right away use and b) without using a vessel. [See P"M 320 A"A Hakdama; Ketzos Hashulchan ibid writes that even according to the M"A in 321:30, it is forbidden to squeeze even permitted fruoits for right away use, just as he rules regarding peeling.]

B. Inedible fruits:

First Opinion:[20] The above is only referring to fruits which are fit to be eaten, however fruits which are not fit to be eaten are forbidden to be squeezed according to all opinions[21] even into food [and certainly not in order to drink their juice].

The reason for this is:[22] because when one squeezes food which is not fit for eating he is not separating food from food but rather is [separating] food from waste which contains [the prohibition of] "detaching" as was explained in chapter 305 [Halacha 28].[23] It is also forbidden because of [the prohibition of] separating food from amongst waste[24], even if he wants to eat it right away[25], as [the Sages] only permitted to separate food from waste with ones hands in order to eat right away being that it is the form of eating to take the food with his hands from the waste and eat it, and [it is thus] not similar to [forbidden] work, however to squeeze and then eat is not a form of eating but is a form of work.[26]

Second Opinion:[27] There is an opinion[28] which permits squeezing unripe grapes into food (and it goes without saying that they permit this to be done to other fruits which are not fit to be eaten, and even to squeeze them for their juice is permitted according to those who permit this with other fruits [which are edible]). [This lenient opinion however only applies by grapes that are ripe enough to be eaten in a time of need, however if the fruit is completely inedible, then all agree that it contains the Borer [and perhaps also Mifarek] prohibition.[29]]

The Final Ruling:[30] One is to be stringent like the former opinion [even if the fruit is edible in a time of need, and if it is completely inedible, then it is Biblically forbidden according to all[31]].

---

[20] Admur 320:8; Michaber 320:5 in name of Rabbeinu Tam; M"A 320:7

[21] Meaning even according to the opinion which holds that fruits which are not commonly squeezed may be squeezed for their juice.

[22] Admur 320:8; based on M"A 320:7

[23] Admur ibid as is implied from M"A ibid; Biur Halacha 320:5 "Lechol"; See Admur 305:28 that even regarding milking a cow there is no Biblical Mifarek prohibition when squeezing into food. Hence it remains to be understood, why here Admur writes there is a Mifarek prohibition. The Tehila Ledavid 320:6 explains that in truth an animal is not considered real Pesoles, and hence it is only Rabbinical when squeezed into food. However, an inedible fruit is real Pesoles, and hence is Biblical Mifarek even into food. See Shabbos Kehalacha 15 footnote 80 [p. 443]

Other opinions: It is understood from the Taz and Olas Shabbos [brought in next footnote] that they do not hold there is a Mifarek prohibition when squeezing into food, and the only prohibition involved is Borer.

[24] Admur ibid; Tur 320, brought in name of Rabbeinu Tam

[25] Admur ibid; M"A 320:7; Conclusion of M"B 320:20 and Biur Halacha "Lechol"

Other Poskim: Some Poskim rule it is permitted to squeeze inedible fruits into food if one plans to eat it right away. [Olas Shabbos 320; Taz 320:4; Elya Raba 320:?] The M"B ibid concludes to be stringent like the M"A ibid; Admur, although one who is lenient does not need to be protested.

The reason: The M"A ibid severely negates this opinion, as there is no allowance to do a Melacha for right away use. Admur ibid understands the M"A ibid that there are two reasons why one may not squeeze for right away use, as 1) The prohibition here is due to Mifarek, and by Mifarek there is no allowance to squeeze for right away use. [so learns also Biur Halacha ibid as impleid in P"M 320 A"A 7] and 2) As even Borer was only allowed when done as Derech Achila, and here it is considered Derech Melacha.

[26] Admur ibid, based on M"A ibid

[27] Admur 320:9; Michaber 320:5

[28] Tur in name of Semag in name of Rabbeinu Yosef

[29] Tehila Ledavid 320:6, as explained in M"A 319:16, and implied from Admur here which only brings this lenient opinion in 320:9 regarding Boser, and not in 320:18 regarding the general rule of all fruits; See also M"B 320:19

The reason: As everyone agrees it is Borer to separate food from waste.

[30] Admur 320:9; M"B 320:21 , see Shaar Hatziyon 320:24; The Michaber ibid brings two opinions on this matter regarding inedible grapes, the latter-stringent- opinion being like that of Rabeinu Tam. The Michaber does not give a final ruling on this matter.

[31] Previous footnote

C. Grapes and olives which have already been crushed:[32]
It is Rabbinically forbidden to squeeze juice out of grapes and olives even if they have been crushed from before Shabbos and have juice flowing out from them.

Summary-The Biblical prohibition in squeezing fruits on Shabbos:[33]
Edible foods: The Biblical prohibition of squeezing juice from a solid is the Mifarek/detaching prohibition which is an offshoot of the threshing prohibition. It applies to squeezing juice from grapes and olives. It does not apply to squeezing the juice from any other edible foods.
Inedible foods: Regarding squeezing juice from inedible foods, it is disputed if it contains a Biblical prohibition or is even initially allowed. Practically one is to be stringent.

The Rabbinical prohibition of squeezing fruits and the cases in which it is permitted even initially

2. Squeezing edible fruits on Shabbos for the purpose of drinking their juice:
A. Strawberries, pomegranates and all fruits which are squeezed when there are plenty of them:[34]
Rabbinically it is forbidden to squeeze even strawberries and pomegranates in order to drink their liquid.[35] *The reason for this is:*[36] due to there being segment of people which have a large amount of strawberries and pomegranates and they squeeze them for their juice just like [is done with] olives and grapes [**See Q&A**], and if other people also had such a large amount of [these fruits] then they too would be accustomed to squeeze it for its juice. Therefore, anyone who squeezes them for the sake of its juice these thoughts of his help give [the juice] a liquid status Rabbinically, as we do not claim that [the persons thoughts of using the fruits for juice] is nullified in face of the [intended use of this fruit by the] populace. *Pears and other fruits:*[37] Similarly those pears (that we call *brenis*) which are common to squeeze for their juice in certain places, is forbidden to squeeze on Shabbos for the entire [populace of the] world, because it is possible that if the entire world had as much of these [pears] as the other places do, then they too would squeeze the pears for their juice. The same law applies for all fruits of the sort.

B. Edible fruits that are never squeezed for juice even when they have a lot of the fruit:[38]
❖ *First Opinion:*[39]
All other [**edible**] fruits which are not common for [people of] the world to squeeze for their juice, to drink their liquids to quench their thirst or for pleasure, even if they have a lot of them, then even if they are commonly squeezed for medicine[40] they do not have the status of juice due to this even Rabbinically and is [thus] allowed to be squeezed on Shabbos, as it is like separating food from food. Now although that this person who wants to squeeze them intends to do so for their juice, nevertheless his intentions are

---

[32] Admur 252:14
[33] Halacha 1
[34] Admur 320:1; Mishneh Shabbos 143b
[35] Admur ibid; Michaber 320:1; Shabbos 143b; Rif 60; Rambam 21:12; Rosh 22:2
[36] Admur ibid; M"A 320:1; M"B 320:5; Rambam ibid
Decree due to grapes and olives: The Poskim write that the reason the Sages decreed against strawberries and the like is because since many people squeeze them similar to grapes and olives, then people may come to squeeze grapes and olives. [Rambam 21:12; Aruch Hashulchan 320:11; M"B ibid] Vetzaruch Iyun why according to this reason one must resort to the concept that the juice of these fruits have a Rabbinical status of juice. Vetzaruch Iyun if this reason is negating the reason brought in Admur ibid.
[37] Admur ibid; M"A ibid; brought in M"B 320:8
Other opinions: The Rama 320:1 implies that by other fruits, it is only prohibited to squeeze them in the locality that they are commonly squeezed, while in other localities it is permitted. [M"A ibid; M"B ibid] Admur ibid based on M"A ibid explains the Rama to refer to a case in which the other cities do not squeeze it even when there is a lot of fruits. See Tehila Ledavid 320:1
[38] Admur 320:1
[39] 1st opinion in Admur; Michaber 320:1; Rif ibid; Rambam ibid; Rosh ibid
[40] Admur ibid; Rama ibid; Beis Yosef

nullified in face of the [common practice] worldwide.[41]

Fruits which are squeezed for juice in ones area but not in others:[42] Nevertheless in any area where the custom is to squeeze a certain fruit for its juice then its laws in that area are the same as the laws of strawberries and pomegranates and is thus forbidden to squeeze it in those places for their juice, because the intent of this [person] that wants to squeeze it is not nullified [to the world custom] since all the people of his area do this during the week. However other places are allowed to squeeze them since they are not accustomed to squeeze them for their juice even if they have a lot of the [fruit].

❖ *Second Opinion:*[43]
There are opinions which say that all fruits are Rabbinically forbidden to squeeze for the sake of their juice, as since the person squeezing it intends to do so in order drink the juice to quench his thirst or for pleasure (or even for healing[44]) therefore they are Rabbinically considered [the status of] juice, and we do not say that his intentions are nullified in face of the worldly custom. (However, if ones intention [in squeezing] is in order to give flavor to a food then it is allowed [according to all opinions] as will be explained in Halacha 3B).

❖ *The Final Ruling:*
The custom in many places is to be stringent[45] [like this latter opinion] although the main Halachic opinion is like the first opinion. Nevertheless, in a place where the custom is to be stringent one may not do differently.[46] [Practically, there is no known place today that is particular like the stringent opinion to never squeeze a fruit to drink its juice even if it is never commonly squeezed.[47]]

C. Fruits which are commonly squeezed but which their juices are not commonly drunk plain:[48]

Apples and lemons: Apples have the same law as other fruits [which are not commonly squeezed anywhere].[49] [Furthermore] even lemons do not have the same laws as strawberries and pomegranates, but rather like other fruits. [Therefore they] are allowed to be squeezed for the need of their juices even for the sake of drinking [the juice, as opposed to using it for other purposes,] according to those opinions which permit [doing so to fruits that are never squeezed for their juice].[50] According to those opinions who forbid [squeezing any fruit for the sake of drinking their juice] it is at the very least allowed squeezing them for the need of food, meaning in order to flavor the food with their liquids and the like.[51]

---

[41] Admur ibid; M"A 320:1; M"B 320:7; Ramban 144; Rashba; See Biur Halacha 320:1 "Mutar" in length that brings many Rishonim who hold of this ruling and understanding; The Michaber ibid does not state for what purpose one may squeeze the fruits and hence it can be understood either way, as in truth understand the second opinion brought next.

[42] Admur ibid based on Rama 320:1 and M"A ibid and so concludes M"B in Biur Halacha 320:1 "Ubemakom"; See Tehila Ledavid 320:1

[43] 2nd opinion in Admur ibid; Rashi 144b; Tosafus; Hagahos Semak; Taz 320:1; Bach 320; based on Shabbos 144b "Like Rav Chisda that since they squeeze the fruit for its juice it is considered juice for them"

[44] See Shabbos Kehalacha 15 Biurim 4

[45] Admur ibid; Bach 320; Elya Zuta 320:1

[46] Admur ibid; Magen Avraham 320:1; Mishneh Berurah 320:8; See Biur Halacha 320:1 "Mutar" in length that brings many proofs for this ruling and understanding

[47] So rules the Ketzos Hashulchan 126 [footnote 20] and other Poskim; Shabbos Kihalacha Vol. 2 p. 401;

[48] Admur 320:10

[49] Admur ibid; Taz 320:5

Other opinions-Final ruling today: Other Poskim rule it is forbidden to squeeze apples for juice and so is the ruling today being that it is common to squeeze apples for juice. [Mishneh Berurah 320:9 in name of Chayeh Adam; Biur Halacha "Dino"; Rav Farkash in Vol. 2 p. 392] Although Admur rules like the Taz that apples are permitted to be squeezed, nevertheless this was back then when apples were never commonly squeezed to drink their juice plain. However today that this is done, then certainly they too agree that it is forbidden.

[50] Admur ibid; Michaber 320:6; Teshuvas Rosh 22:2; Taz 320:5

Other opinions: The Yaavetz in Mor Uketzia 320, as well as the Tzemach Tzedek Shabbos 60 bring many arguments against this leniency of lemons, and thus side to forbid it; So rules M"B 320:22 in name of Chayeh Adam; Kitzur SHU"A 80:12; Ketzos Hashulchan 126:11 footnote 25; Shabbos Kehalacha Vol. 2 p. 404

Sephardi custom: The Michaber ibid is lenient to allow squeezing lemons as explained above. Many Sephardi Poskim agree with this ruling and negate the arguments of the Mor Uketzia. [See Yalkut Yosef 320:18; Shabbos Kehalacha 2 p. 405]

[51] Admur ibid; M"A 320:1; See Taz 320:5

Lit. "Letavel Bo Es Hamachal" this can also be translated as "in order to dip the food into it", Vetzrauch Iyun. The practical ramification is regarding if one may squeeze pure lemon juice into an empty bowl for the sake of later using for seasoning. Practically, so is implied as otherwise

[See Q&A regarding the ruling today if one may squeeze lemon]

The Reason:[52] Now, although that in those places that there are plenty of these fruits, they [are accustomed to] squeeze them for their juices, [nevertheless] they do not receive the same laws as strawberries and pomegranates just because of this, even in those places [that squeeze them]. [The reason for this is] because they do not squeeze their liquid for the sake of drinking it but rather for the sake of using for [flavoring] food. [Furthermore,] even if they are accustomed to squeeze the [juice] into water in order to drink, it is allowed since it is not common to drink them plain [in their concentrated state].[53]

D. Squeezing juice from inedible fruits:

The above is only referring to fruits which are fit to be eaten however fruits which are not fit to be eaten are forbidden to be squeezed according to all opinions[54] even into food [and certainly not in order to drink their juice].

See above Halacha 1B.

Summary-Squeezing fruits for the purpose of drinking their juice:

1. The Rabbinical prohibition:

It is Rabbinically forbidden to squeeze juice from fruits in the following cases:

-Fruits which are commonly squeezed for their juice[55] when one possesses much of that fruit: It is Rabbinically forbidden to squeeze them anywhere in the world.

-Fruits which are not commonly squeezed for juices even when possessing much of them but in ones city it is common to do so: Then it is Rabbinically forbidden to be squeezed in that city. Regarding other cities, this will be explained below under the permitted cases.

Fruits which are not currently edible.[56] Are [possibly Biblically] forbidden to be squeezed even into food, and certainly not in order to drink, no matter what type of fruit it is.

2. The Permitted cases:

All **edible** fruits which are not commonly squeezed for their juice throughout the world [**see below for definition**] even when possessing much of them, and are not squeezed in one's city, may be squeezed on Shabbos even for their juice. However, in an area where people are stringent to not squeeze any fruits for their juice, one may not change from their custom and may thus not squeeze juice to drink even for medicinal purposes.[57] [Practically, there is no known place today that is

---

what would be the novelty according to the stringent opinion? Also so is explicitly written in the Beis Yosef in name of Shivlei Haleket that one may squeeze it into an empty bowl for the sake of seasoning. Thus, in conclusion according to all opinions it is permitted to squeeze "other fruits" into an empty bowl for the sake of seasoning foods. So concludes also Shabbos Kehalacha 2:404 footnote 22, and that this applies to lemons even today.

[52] Admur ibid; M"A 320:8; Rosh ibid; M"B 320:22

[53] There are two possible explanations given in Beis Yosef, brought in M"B 320:22: A) It is permitted because one does not drink the juice plain; b) It is permitted because one squeezes the juice directly into water. According to the second reason if it is accustomed to squeeze into an empty bowl and then into liquid, then even lemons would be forbidden, and thus today since the custom is to squeeze lemons into empty vessels, and then to mix them with water, it is forbidden to squeeze lemons on Shabbos. [M"B ibid in name of Chayeh Adam] However according to the first reason mentioned, even today it would remain permitted. Admur and M"A ibid record both aspects, as on the one hand they write "squeezing into liquid" as requires the 2nd reason, and on the other hand they conclude "since the juice is not drunk plain", as writes the first reason. Vetzaruch Iyun which is their main reason?! See Ketzos Hashulchan 126 footnote 25 who in the end concludes that even according to Admur one should be stringent today, as perhaps Admur holds of the 2nd reason; However, see Shabbos Kehalacha 15 Biurim 7 that proofs that they only hold of the 1st reason and hence even today it is permitted to squeeze lemons in their opinion, however practically we are stringent like the Tzemach Tzedek as stated above.

[54] Meaning even according to the opinion which holds that fruits which are not commonly squeezed may be squeezed for their juice. However as mentioned above in 1B there is an opinion which rules that squeezing inedible foods has the same law as edible foods. Admur ruled that one is to be stringent.

[55] See 3 for the definition

[56] Admur 320:8

[57] See Ketzos Hashulchan 126 footnote 20. And Shabbos Kehalacha Vol 2 page 400.

particular like the stringent opinion to never squeeze a fruit to drink its juice even if it is never commonly squeezed.[58]]

3. The definition of "squeezed for its juice"[59]:
The rule: Only fruits which are 1) commonly squeezed in order to drink their juice plain <u>and</u> 2) are drank in order to quench one's thirst, or for mere pleasure, are defined as "squeezed for their juice".
<u>Juice which is not commonly drunk in its concentrated form</u>: If a fruit is not commonly squeezed to drink its juice in its concentrated state even when there is plentiful of it, then even if it is commonly squeezed to season foods, or to be used as concentrate, and have liquid added to them, nevertheless it has a definition of a fruit that is <u>not</u> commonly squeezed.
<u>Juice which is commonly drunk as medicine[60]</u>: A fruit which is not commonly squeezed to drink its juice to quench one's thirst or for mere pleasure but rather to drink as medicine has a definition of a fruit which is <u>not</u> commonly squeezed.

<u>Final Summary-It is only permitted to squeeze fruits for their juice if the following 4 conditions are met:</u>
1) The fruit is edible in its current raw state.
2) The fruit is not commonly squeezed for its juice by people around the world even if they were to have plentiful of it.
3) The fruit is not accustomed to be squeezed for its juice in one's city.
4) It is not the custom in one's city to be stringent and always prohibit the squeezing of fruits even when all the above conditions are met.

Q&A
May one squeeze fruits for medicinal purposes if the fruit is customarily squeezed for juice?
Seemingly it is forbidden to squeeze it even for medicinal purposes, being that its juice has a status of liquid to the rest of the world. Vetzaruch Iyun.[61]

May one squeeze juice out from crushed fruits:[62]
<u>Grapes and olives</u>: Doing so is Rabbinically forbidden.

If one is unsure whether a certain fruit is commonly squeezed to drink its juice, when there is plenty of that fruit available, is it still forbidden to squeeze it due to doubt?[63]
No. A fruit only is prohibited to be squeezed if one knows for certain that there are places which squeeze the fruit when there is plenty of it.

If in one's city a fruit is not squeezed for its juice despite there being plentiful of it, may one squeeze the juice on Shabbos even if the rest of the world does squeeze it for juice?[64]

58 So rules the Ketzos Hashulchan 126 [footnote 20] and other Poskim; Shabbos Kihalacha Vol. 2 p. 401
59 Admur 320:10
60 Admur 320:1
61 On the one hand it is implied from Admur and Poskim that it is forbidden to squeeze pomegranates and strawberries for any purpose of drink, even for medicinal purposes, being that its juice has a status of liquid. On the other hand from Admur and Rama ibid that rule if the custom of the world is to squeeze for the sake of medicine, its juice is not considered liquid and hence it is permitted to be squeezed for juice on Shabbos [according to the lenient opinion]. Furthermore, Admur only explicitly writes that squeezing for medicine is forbidden in the second stringent opinion, and even that he leaves in parentheses. Vetzaruch Iyun! [See Shabbos Kehalacha 15 Biurim 4]
62 Admur 252:14
63 Shabbos Kehalacha Vol. 2 p. 392
64 Shabbos Kehalacha Vol. 2 p. 394

Yes.[65] However this is only applies if they do not sell these juices in stores of that city, as will be explained next.

If a fruit is only squeezed for its juice within factories and then sold in one's city, while in one's private home they do not squeeze it for its juice even when there is plenty of it, is it nevertheless considered commonly squeezed and thus forbidden to squeeze on Shabbos?[66]
Yes. So long as the fruits are commonly squeezed in factories and bought by the populace they are considered commonly squeezed. **As a result of this, being that today many different fruits are squeezed in different parts of the world and their juice is then sold in ones city, all the fruits of these juices are forbidden to be squeezed.**

Practically which fruits today are forbidden to squeeze?[67]
In truth, today majority of fruits are forbidden to squeeze, as majority of fruits are commonly squeezed to drink their juice somewhere in the world and are then sold in one's city for drinking [see previous Q&A].[68]
The following is a partial list of fruits that are forbidden to be squeezed on Shabbos in order to drink their juice, being that they are commonly squeezed for juice when they are in plentiful. This list is not all inclusive and may include other fruits as well.
1. Apples:[69] Today, apples are forbidden to be squeezed for their juice.[70]
2. Citric fruits such as oranges/grapefruit:[71] Are forbidden to be squeezed on Shabbos for their juice being that they are commonly squeezed in today's times in order to drink their juice.
3. Lemons:[72] One may not squeez them for their juice. Regarding if one may squeeze lemons into water or food, see Halacha 3 Q&A there.
4. Mangos
5. Pears
6. Peach
7. Pomegranate
8. Strawberries
9. Pineapple
10. Grape

---

[65] The reason: As the prohibition of squeezing commonly squeezed fruits is only due to the fact that we say perhaps if there were to be plenty of a given fruit in one's city then they too would drink its juice. Thus, here where it is clearly evident that despite their abundance they do not drink its juice, therefore it is allowed.
[66] M"B 320:8 based on M"A 320:1; Shabbos Kehalacha Vol. 2 p. 393-394
[67] Shabbos Kehalacha Vol. 2 p. 392-394
[68] Shabbos Kehalacha Vol. 2 p. 393
[69] So rules Mishneh Berurah in Biur Halacha based on Chayeh Adam. And so rules Rav Farkash in Vol. 2 p. 392
[70] Although Admur rules like the Taz that apples are permitted to be squeezed, nevertheless this was back then when apples were never commonly squeezed to drink their juice plain. However today that this is done, then certainly they too agree that it is forbidden.
[71] Ketzos Hashulchan 126:6
[72] Tzemach Tzedek Shabbos 60 bring many arguments against this leniency of lemons, and thus side to forbid it; M"B 320:22 in name of Chayeh Adam; Kitzur SHU"A 80:12; Ketzos Hashulchan 126:11 footnote 25; Shabbos Kehalacha Vol. 2 p. 404; Yaavetz in Mor Uketzia 320
Background: Although lemons are not considered fruits that are commonly squeezed to drink their juice plain and thus from the letter of the law may be squeezed even for their juice, nevertheless today one is to be stringent regarding lemons like those opinions who forbid squeezing them. So rules Ketzos Hashulchan 126 footnote 25. The Yaavetz, as well as the Tzemach Tzedek bring many arguments against the leniency of lemons, and thus side to forbid it.
Ruling of Admur today by lemons: There are two possible explanations given in Beis Yosef, brought in M"B 320:22, for why lemons are permitted to squeeze: A) It is permitted because one does not drink the juice plain; b) It is permitted because one squeezes the juice directly into water. According to the second reason if it is accustomed to squeeze into an empty bowl and then into liquid, then even lemons would be forbidden, and thus today since the custom is to squeeze lemons into empty vessels, and then to mix them with water, it is forbidden to squeeze lemons on Shabbos. [M"B ibid in name of Chayeh Adam] However according to the first reason mentioned, even today it would remain permitted. Admur and M"A ibid record both aspects, as on the one hand they write "squeezing into liquid" as requires the 2nd reason, and on the other hand they conclude "since the juice is not drunk plain", as writes the first reason. Veztaruch Iyun which is their main reason?! See Ketzos Hashulchan 126 footnote 25 who in the end concludes that even accoridng to Admur one should be stringent today, as perhaps Admur holds of the 2nd reason; However see Shabbos Kehalacha 15 Biurim 7 that proofs that they only hold of the 1st reason and hence even today it is permitted to squeeze lemons in their opinion, however practically we are stringent like the Tzemach Tzedek as stated above.

11. Kiwi
12. Carrot
13. Watermelon, cantaloupe, honey dew, apricot, seemingly are not commonly juiced but they are juiced in juice stores and hence perhaps are forbidden to be squeezed.

May one squeeze the permitted fruits in order to drink their juice later on and may one use a vessel?
Yes.[73] However some Poskim[74] rule one may only squeeze it for right away use and may not use a vessel.

May one use a juicer to squeeze fruits that are permitted to be squeezed?[75]
No. It is only permitted to do so using one's hands, being that using a specified vessel is a mundane act which defiles the sanctity of Shabbos.[76]

May one use a spoon to eat a fruit that may not be squeezed, such as a grapefruit?[77]
Being that doing so causes juice to be squeezed out from the fruit this poses a problem of squeezing, and carries the following laws.
-Intends to drink the juice: If at the time of using the spoon one intends to drink the juice which squeezes out, then it is forbidden according to all opinions to eat the fruit with a spoon, being that this is exactly similar to initially squeezing a fruit for its juice.[78]
-Does not intend to drink the juice: If, however, one does not have any intent to squeeze out juice and tries his best not to do so then there are Poskim[79] which have been lenient to allow one to use a spoon even though it is impossible to completely avoid the squeezing of any juice. Nevertheless, even in this case it is proper to be stringent being that the squeezing is inevitable.[80]

May one cut a fruit which may not be squeezed, if in the process juice will squeeze out, as is common with citric fruits?[81]
If the juice that is squeezed out will go to waste it is allowed.[82] This applies whether the juice goes directly to waste, such as when cutting directly on the counter, or if he plans to throw it out, such as when one is cutting on a plate.[83] If, however, one intends to drink the juice, it is forbidden to cut it.
May one drink the juice?[84] Even if the fruit was cut without intent to drink the juice, one may not change his mind and later decide to drink it.[85]
May one cut up a fruit salad and add the juice that will be squeezed in the process, into the fruit salad?
See Halacha 3 Q&A

---

[73] No such restrictions are mentioned in Shulchan Aruch. This is based on all the following Poskim who real there is no Borer prohibition involved: M"A 319:16; Iglei Tal Borer 10:5; Ketzos Hashulchan 126 footnote 19; See Minchas Yitzchak 1:75-4; Shabbos Kehalacha 15:1 in Biurim [p. 388]

[74] P"M 320 A"A Pesicha; Ketzos Hashulchan 126 footnote 19 writes that even according to the M"A in 321:30, it is forbidden to squeeze even permitted fruits for right away use, just as he rules regarding peeling.

[75] Shabbos Kehalacha Vol. 2 p. 396

[76] So rules Ketzos Hashulchan 126 footnote 19

[77] Shabbos Kehalacha Vol. 2 p. 408-410

[78] So rules Ketzos Hashulchan 126 footnote 14, SSH"K 5:12, Yalkut Yosef

[79] Rav SZ"A in SSH"K 5:12

[80] It's said that Rav SZ"A later retracted the ruling in SSH"K due to reasons of Psik Reisha Velo Yamus.

[81] Shabbos Kehalacha 15:17; See Piskeiy Teshuvos 320:3; Article of Rav Braun on Halacha2go

[82] See Taz 320:7; Admur 320:17; Minchas Yitzchak 4:99-2 in explanation of Tiferes Yisrael; Koveitz Mibeis Levi 8:20

[83] Koveitz Mibeis Levi ibid; Shabbos Kehalacha ibid Biurim 9

[84] Implication of Admur 320:11 regarding squeezing pickles to better its taste, as rules Tzemach Tzedek Piskei Dinim 320 and Ketzos Hashulchan 126 footnote 26; Shabbos Kehalacha ibid; Piskeiy Teshuvos 320 footnote 35 and 320:11 in opinion of Admur
Other opinions: Some Poskim rule one may drink the juice of the fruit. [Piskeiy Teshuvos ibid]

[85] See Shabbos Kehalacha ibid for the explanation

May one cut a lemon over one's tea having its liquid fall into the tea?[86]
See Halacha 3 Q&A

May one squeeze out the juice of a fruit for no need at all but rather simply out of habit or the like?[87]
If doing so does not benefit the fruit and the juice will go to waste, then many Poskim are lenient to allow it by all fruits other than grapes and olives. However, the Tzemach Tzedek along with other Poskim forbid this.

If a food will only become edible due the squeezing may it nevertheless be squeezed?[88]
No, as this poses a Borer prohibition. This may not be done in any cases, whether with intent to squeeze the liquid into food or to sweeten it.[89]

3. Squeezing juice into food and liquid:
A. Squeezing ripe grapes into food [as opposed to liquid]:[90]
Squeezing grapes directly into food: It is permitted to squeeze a cluster of grapes into a pot that contains food in order to give better [taste] (see chapter 505 [Halacha 2][91]) to the food.
The reason for this is:[92] because all liquid that enters into food is considered like food and does not have a status of liquid at all, and thus it is as if one is separating food from food.
Squeezing grapes into an empty bowl and then into food:[93] However if it is not [being currently squeezed into] food then it is forbidden to squeeze it even if one plans to mix food into it later on[94].
The reason:[95] Now, although one plans eventually to mix food into it and it is for this reason that he is now squeezing this wine into [the vessel], in order to use it to enhance and sweeten the food that he will eventually eat with this wine and it is thus liquid which is entered into food which is considered like food, nevertheless since at the time of squeezing the wine there is not yet any food [which is mixing into it] and it is not evident at all that it is for this purpose of enhancing the food [for which he is squeezing the wine], therefore it is Rabbinically forbidden.[96]

---

[86] Shabbos Kehalacha 7:18
[87] Shabbos Kehalacha Vol. 2 p. 418; Biurim 10 and Tosefes Biur 15
[88] Shabbos Kehalacha Vol. 2 p. 446
[89] So rules Tehila Ledavid 320:14
[90] Admur 320:6; Michaber 320:4; Shmuel in Shabbos 144a; see also 305:28 regarding squeezing milk from a cow
Other opinions: Some Poskim rule it is forbidden to squeeze forbidden fruits even into other foods, and it retains its full Biblical or Rabbinical prohibition as squeezing in order to drink the juice. [Michaber and Rama 320:7 in name of Rabbeinu Chananeil in Shabbos 125a in explanation of Rebbe Yochanan ibid; Rabbeinu Chananel concludes "We do not rule like Shmuel neither by Shabbos or Yom Tov and rather we rule like Rebbe Yochanan, and so we have received from our teachers"; The Biur Halacha 320:7 "Rabbeinu Channanel" learns that even Rabbeinu Chananel is only stringent regarding olives and grapes, while regarding other fruits he would agree that it is even initially permitted to squeeze into food. Other Poskim however learn Rabbeinu Chananel to argue even in such a case-see there.] Practically we do not rule like this opinion. [Admur ibid omits it completely from his Shulchan Aruch; Michaber 320:4 omitted it (however see Biur Halacha ibid); M"B 320:17 and 30] Nevertheless some Poskim conclude that one who is stringent is blessed. [M"B ibid; Teshuvas Harosh brought in Beis Yosef; Mishkanos Yaakov 112] According to the M"B ibid it is only relevant to be stringent against squeezing grapes and olives and not regarding other fruits. [See Biur Halacha ibid] According to Admur and other Poskim there is no need to be stringent even regarding olives and grapes and they do not record any blessing for doing so. [See Shabbos Kehalacha 15 footnote 55]
[91] There it is explained that squeezing into food is only allowed if the liquid will become completely absorbed into the food. If not then it is forbidden. To note however that this is referring to a case that one is mainly interested in the juice and not the food. If, however, one is interested in seasoning the food, then one may squeeze as much as necessary even if it will not become absorbed within it.
[92] Admur ibid; 305:28 regarding squeezing milk from a cow; Michaber ibid
[93] Admur ibid; Michaber ibid; Shmuel Gemara ibid "However not into a plate"
[94] Admur ibid; M"A 320:1; M"B 320:18
[95] Admur ibid based partially on Rashi and Levush 320:4
[96] Admur ibid; Radbaz 686; Peri Megadim, brought in Shaar Hatziyon 320:23
Other opinions: Some Poskim rule it is Biblically forbidden. [Derisha and Rambam brought in M"B 320:18 and Biur Halacha 320:4 "Assur"] Seemingly their reason is because they hold that in order for the juice to receive a food status it must actually mix with the food and immediately becomes part of it.

❖ *Regarding unripe grapes- see D below.*

B. Squeezing all other fruits which are edible in their raw state into foods:

❖ *Important note: Regarding the definition of commonly squeezed fruits- See Halacha 2 and Q&A there!*

Fruits which are commonly squeezed for Juice:[97] The above law mentioned by grapes applies [as well to] strawberries and pomegranates and other similar fruits that are commonly squeezed for juice when they are in plentiful.

Other fruits which are never commonly squeezed anywhere:[98] However other fruits which are not commonly squeezed for their juice even when there are plentiful of them, then even according to those opinions which forbid to squeeze them for their juices, nevertheless if one is only squeezing them in order to season the food with their liquid then it is allowed even if there is no food currently within the vessel that he is now squeezing them into.

The reason for this is:[99] because at the time of the squeezing it is known to all that he is squeezing them in order to sweeten the food and not in order to drink their juice being that it is not at all common to squeeze these [fruits] for juice.

Apples and lemons:[100] As explained above in Halacha 2C apples and lemons have the same law as fruits which are not commonly squeezed anywhere. Therefore, they are allowed to be squeezed according to all opinions [in an empty bowl[101]] for the need of food, meaning in order to flavor the food with their liquids and the like.[102]

Important note: Regarding how much juice is allowed to be squeezed into a food- See Q&A below!

C. Squeezing fruits that are not fit to be eaten in their current state, into food:
See Halacha 1!

Summary: It is disputed if one may squeeze inedible fruits into food on Shabbos. Practically one is to be stringent, as according to some opinions doing so is Biblically prohibited due to Mifarek and Borer. [Furthermore, if the fruit is not edible at all, even in a time of need, it is Biblically forbidden according to all due to Borer to squeeze it even into food.]

---

[97] 320:7; Shaar Hatziyon 320:23 in name of Peir Megadim
[98] 320:7; M"A 320:1; M"B 3208
[99] Admur 320:7
[100] Admur 320:10
[101] Beis Yosef in name of Shiveliy Haleket; Shabbos Kehalacha 15 footnote 22; see next footnote
[102] Lit. "Letavel Bo Es Hamachal" this can also be translated as "in order to dip the food into it", Vetzaruch Iyun. The practical ramification is regarding if one may squeeze pure lemon juice into an empty bowl for the sake of later using for seasoning. Practically, it is implied that one may do so as otherwise what would be the novelty according to the stringent opinion? Also so is explicitly written in the Beis Yosef in name of Shivlei Haleket that one may squeeze it into an empty bowl for the sake of seasoning. Thus, in conclusion according to all opinions it is permitted to squeeze "other fruits" into an empty bowl for the sake of seasoning foods. Nevertheless, seemingly this only applies according to those that hold that lemons are not considered a commonly squeezed fruit, however according to those that argue on Admur [and so we rule today] and consider it a commonly squeezed fruit, perhaps it would be forbidden to squeeze lemons into an empty vessel. Practically, in SSH"K 5:5 they rule it is forbidden to do so. However Shabbos Kehalacha 2:404 footnote 22\ rule it is permitted to so, and that this applies to lemons even today.

D. Squeezing fruits into a liquid:[103]

According to those opinions which forbid to squeeze [any] fruit for the sake of drinking their liquids, then it is forbidden to squeeze on Shabbos lemons or [any] other fruits into water or other liquids in order to drink. [**See Q&A**] [However, according to the lenient opinion, although it is permitted to squeeze uncommonly juiced fruits even to drink their juice, nevertheless it certainly remains forbidden to squeeze commonly juiced fruits even into liquids.[104] Hence according to the custom today to forbid squeezing lemons for juice, it is forbidden to squeeze it even into water.[105]]

The Reason: As [the Sages] only said that juices which enter into foods are considered like food [and are thus allowed to be squeezed into them] and not [juices that enter] into liquid.

E. Squeezing into a creamy dip:[106]

It is permitted to squeeze [fruits and pickled foods] into Muryas[107] because it is considered food however into liquids it is forbidden to squeeze them as explained above. [**See Q&A**]

Summary of squeezing fruits into food and liquid

Fruits that are currently edible:

Directly into food:[108] All fruits, even grapes and olives, are permitted to be squeezed directly into foods.

Into an empty vessel, which will then be poured into food:[109] Is Rabbinically forbidden to be done to all fruits which are commonly squeezed to drink their juice upon having much of them available.

Fruits which are not commonly squeezed to drink their juice even when one has much of them available are permitted according to all opinions to be squeezed into an empty vessel with intent to place into food. [**Thus, today that almost all fruits have a status that they are squeezed to drink their juice, are forbidden to be squeezed into an empty bowl.[110]**]

Directly into liquids:[111] Has the same laws as one who is squeezing them to drink their juice plain, and thus is only permitted by fruits that are never commonly squeezed for their juice, and only in places that are not accustomed against squeezing these types of fruits for their juice on Shabbos, as explained above in Halacha 2.

---

[103] 320:10; M"A 320:10; Biur Halacha 320:4 "Haba Lechol" in name of Elya Raba 320:4

Other opinions: Some Poskim rule that even according to the stringent opinion it is permitted to squeeze "lemons and other fruits" into liquids. [Taz 320:5] As this is similar to squeezing the fruit for the sake of sweetening it. [P"M 320 M"Z 5] However this only refers to fruits that are not commonly squeezed, and hence require Achashvei to make them forbidden. However, those fruits that are commonly squeezed for their juice, and are hence forbidden according to all to be squeezed for their liquids, then it is likewise forbidden even according to the Taz to squeeze them into juice. [P"M ibid]

[104] Implication of Admur ibid [even though he only mentions the prohibition of squeezing into liquid in the second, stringent opinion]; Admur 320:13; M"A 320:10; M"B 320:28; Biur Halacha 320:4 "Haba Lechol" in name of Elya Raba 320:4; This ruling applies even according to the Taz 320:5, as explained in P"M 320 M"Z 5.

[105] M"B 320:22; This may apply even according to the Taz ibid as perhaps he holds of the second reason in Beis Yosef as the main reason for allowing to squeeze lemons into liquid. See M"B ibid

[106] Admur 320:13; M"A 320:10; M"B 320:28

[107] A creamy dip made from fish fat.

[108] Admur 320:6

[109] Admur 320:6-7

[110] See 320:2 Q&A 4

[111] Admur 320:10

A creamy dip:[112] Has the same status as food and not liquid.

Fruits which are not currently edible:[113]
Are forbidden to be squeezed even into food no matter what type of fruit it is.

Q&A
May one squeeze fruits that are permitted to be squeezed using a juicer?[114]
No. It is only permitted to do so using one's hands, being that using a specified vessel is a mundane act which defiles the sanctity of Shabbos.[115]

How much juice may one squeeze into a food?[116]
One desires to use it to season the food: One may squeeze as much juice as needed in order to give taste to the dish.
One desires an excess amount of juice for other purposes:[117] If one desires to squeeze juice onto food to season the food and also in order to have an access of liquid to drink then it is only permitted to squeeze the excess amount of liquid if either a) **majority** of the juice is being used to give taste to the dish or b) Majority of the juice is not giving taste but **majority** will become absorbed within the food and thus not be separately recognizable. Thus, it is forbidden to place small amount of food in a bowl and then squeeze into it a large enough amount of juice that the liquid is separately recognizable from the food.

May one squeeze juice onto food if his main intent is to drink the juice and not to season the food?
If majority[118] of the squeezed juice will be absorbed in the food, it is permitted to do so.[119]

May one squeeze lemon into his food?[120]
Yes, as is true of all fruits.

May one squeeze juice, such as orange or lemon juice, onto sugar?
If one is doing so in order to eat the sugar which has now been saturated with lemon juice, it is

[112] Admur 320:13
[113] Admur 320:8
[114] Shabbos Kehalacha Vol. 2 p. 396
[115] So rules Ketzos Hashulchan 126 footnote 19
[116] Shabbos Kehalacha Vol. 2 p. 432-433, 439
[117] Mamar Mordechai 505:2; Peri Megadim 505 M"Z 2 based on Taz 505:2; Tzemach Tzedek 25; Panim Meiros 1:85; M"B 505:5-6; Kaf Hachaim 505:10; See Admur 505:2; Michaber 505:1
Other Poskim: Some Poskim rule that one may not squeeze any excess amount of juice even if majority is being used for the food. [Chayeh Adam brought in Shaar Hatziyon 505:6]
[118] Mamar Mordechai 505:2; Peri Megadim 505 M"Z 2 based on Taz 505:2; Tzemach Tzedek 25; Panim Meiros 1:85; M"B 505:5-6; Kaf Hachaim 505:10
Other Poskim: Some Poskim rule that one may not squeeze any excess amount of juice even if majority is being used for the food. [Chayeh Adam brought in Shaar Hatziyon 505:6]
[119] Admur 505:2; Michaber 505:1
[120] Shabbos Kehalacha Vol. 2 p. 404-406; p. 441

allowed. However, if one plans to enter the sugar into a drink, then it is forbidden.[121] This applies even to lemons, and thus one may not squeeze lemons onto sugar if his intent is to then take the sugar with the lemon juice and add it to a drink.[122] However some Poskim[123] are lenient in this matter.

May one squeeze lemon into his tea on Shabbos?[124]
The custom today is to forbid squeezing lemon even into a Keli[125] Shelishi, or even into cold tea, as explained in Halacha 2 Q&A that we are today stringent to not squeeze lemons in order to drink their juice. [However according to the Sephardim this is allowed even today so long as this does not pose a problem of cooking. However, one who is stringent is blessed.[126]]

Regarding placing a sliced lemon in one's hot tea on Shabbos- see The Laws of Cooking Chapter 1 Halacha 14 Q&A, as well as the Final summary of that Chapter.

May one cut a lemon over one's tea having its liquid fall into the tea?[127]
No.

May one rub his hands on lemon in order to remove stains from his hands?[128]
If the lemon still contains juice it is forbidden. If it no longer contains any juice, then it is permitted. It is therefore permitted to rub one's hands on a lemon peel.

May one squeeze into food the juice of a peel, such as a lemon peel or orange peel?[129]
Yes, [although it is best to do so only right before the meal in order to avoid the Borer prohibition according to all[130]].

May one cut a fruit salad despite the fact that juice will be squeezed in the process, and eventually eaten?
If the juice adds flavor to the fruit salad, as is almost always the case, then it may done. If it does not add taste to the salad then it may only be done if majority of the juice will get absorbed into the fruit. Otherwise, it is forbidden to cut such a fruit on Shabbos with intent to drink its juice.
Must the juice enter directly into the salad bowl? Tzaruch Iyun!

If a food will only become edible due the squeezing may it nevertheless be squeezed?[131]
No, as this contains a Borer prohibition. This may not be done in any case, whether with intent to squeeze the liquid into food or to sweeten it.[132]

---

[121] All Poskim in next footnote; Igros Moshe 4:16; 5:24 that this applies even according to M"B 320:6 and those Poskim that are lenient by lemon [brought next]; Shabbos Kehalacha Vol. 2 p. 441

[122] Tzemach Tzedek Shabbos 22; Ketzos Hashulchan 126 footnote 25; Chayeh Adam 14:4; Yabia Omer 8:36; Chazon Ish 56:7; Shabbos Kehalacha Vol. 2 p. 406

[123] Radbaz 1:10; Mishneh Berurah 320:22; Machzikeiy Bracha 320:2; Ben Ish Chaiy Yisro 2:5

[124] Shabbos Kehalacha Vol. 2 p. 404

[125] Shabbos Kehalacha Vol. 2 p. 441

[126] So rules Yalkut Yosef 320:18; Shabbos Kehalacha 2 p. 405, based on the Beis Yosef after bringing many proofs that it is allowed.

[127] Shabbos Kehalacha 7:18

[128] Kneses Hagedola 320:5; Elya Raba 320:16; Peri Chadash 326 Likkutim; Lev Chaim 2:58; Shabbos Kehalacha Vol. 2 p. 408
Other opinions: The SSH"K 14:17 rules that it is forbidden to ever rub lemon or a lemon peel as juice will always squeeze out.

[129] Shabbos Kehalacha Vol. 2 p. 444

[130] So rules Ketzos Hashulchan 126 Footnote 19

[131] Shabbos Kehalacha Vol. 2 p. 446

[132] So rules Tehila Ledavid 320:14

Q&A

May one squeeze juice into a food that also contains liquid, such as gravy or vegetable soup?[133]

By a dish which its main aspect is the solid foods that are in it, such as chicken with gravy or soup with a large amount of vegetables and little liquid: It is allowed if done in order to give taste to the solid.

By a dish which its main aspect is the liquid, such as a large amount of soup with little vegetables: It is forbidden even if done to give taste to the vegetables.

What is the definition of a liquid? How thin must the fluid be?[134]

If the substance is thick to the point that while drinking it one commonly uses his tongue to help swallow it down then it is defined as a solid and may be squeezed into. If, however, it is smooth enough to be drunk without help from ones tongue then it has the same status as does liquid and is forbidden to squeeze fruits into it.[135]

May one squeeze juice into a very liquidly dip, such as Italian dressing?[136]

If it is a liquid which is known that is not meant to be drunk but rather to dip bread or other foods into, then it is allowed being that the dip is considered like food. However even in such a case it is only allowed if the liquid was originally a solid and was then squeezed out, as is the case with Italian dressing. However, if the dip was always a liquid, such as the water that received taste from a chicken and then became gravy then it is forbidden, as the gravy is viewed as a liquid.

Olive oil: Tzaruch Iyun Gadol as Olive oil is one of the seven liquids Min Hatorah, and is a liquid from a sold, so how can one consider olive oil as food and allow squeezing into it?

May one squeeze juice into a thick liquidly substance which is not meant for dips, such as fruit or vegetable puree?[137]

This depends on how thick the substance is as was explained in Q&A above- See There!

May one squeeze juice into a melted fatty substance which will eventually congeal?[138]

If one plans to eat the food while it remains a fluid then this is certainly forbidden by those fruits that may not be squeezed to drink their juice. However, if one plans to only eat it later after it already congeals then its law requires further analysis.[139]

---

4. Squeezing in order to sweeten the fruit:[140]

Important note: Regarding the definition of commonly squeezed fruits- See Halacha 2 and Q&A there!

By fruits that are not commonly squeezed for their juice even when in plentiful: If one is squeezing a fruit simply to sweeten the fruit and not for its juice then it is allowed [to be done **according to all opinions**] by all fruits other than strawberries, pomegranates and the like [of fruits which the custom of the world is to squeeze when they have plentiful of it, as will be explained below].

May one drink the squeezed juice? [Furthermore] even if one drinks the juice which is squeezed it is allowed being that one did not have intent to squeeze it for its juices.

The law by fruits which are commonly squeezed for their juice:[141] However by strawberries and

---

[133] Shabbos Kehalacha Vol. 2 p. 434
[134] Shabbos Kehalacha Vol. 2 p. 436
[135] This definition is based on the definition of Admur in the Laws of blessings with regards to when a flour drink becomes Shehakol. [See 208:8]
[136] Shabbos Kehalacha Vol. 2 p. 434-436
[137] Shabbos Kehalacha Vol. 2 p. 436
[138] Shabbos Kehalacha Vol. 2 p. 441
[139] So rules Ketzos Hashulchan 126 footnote 25
[140] Admur 320:1; Taz 320:1
[141] Admur ibid; Taz 320:1 as explained in P"M 320 M"Z 1; So rule regarding olives and grapes: M"A 320:9; M"B 320:24

pomegranates and the like (of fruits which a segment of people which have a large amount of them squeeze them for their juice just like olives and grapes, and if there were to be this amount of these fruits by other people they too would commonly squeeze them for their juice) then [the Sages made it] forbidden to squeeze them even in order to merely sweeten [the fruit] due to a decree that one may come to also squeeze them for their juices (as do those people which have plenty of [this fruit]). [**See Q&A if this ruling applies according to all opinions**]

Summary- Squeezing fruits in order to sweeten the fruit:
Edible fruits which are not commonly squeezed by the world for their juice even when possessing much of them, and are not squeezed in one's city [see Halacha 2 and Q&A there], are allowed according to all to be squeezed in all places in order to sweeten the fruit, even if one decides to also drink the juice. [Regarding fruits which are commonly squeezed-see Q&A]

Q&A
Does the restriction against squeezing fruits [which are commonly squeezed] in order to sweeten them apply also according to the opinion which holds that fruits that are not commonly squeezed may be squeezed to drink their juice?[142]
The Alter Rebbe brings this Halacha regarding squeezing to sweeten in continuation of the stringent opinion which holds that one may never squeeze any fruit to drink its juice. It is thus unclear according to Admur what the ruling in this would be according to the lenient opinion, which is the opinion that we rule according to.
The following is the ruling in Poskim: It is forbidden to squeeze olives and grapes even in order to sweeten the fruit.[143] Some Poskim[144] rule this prohibition applies also to strawberries and pomegranates and all fruits that are forbidden to squeeze for their juice. Other Poskim[145] rule it is permitted to squeeze all other fruits in order to sweeten them.
Practically the following is the ruling of Rav Farkash: By grapes, olives, and all other fruits which are mainly grown for their juice it is forbidden according to all. By other fruits that are commonly squeezed to drink their juice, but this is not their main purpose, one is to be stringent unless it is a case of need in which case one may squeeze it while having its liquid go to waste.

May one squeeze out the juice of a fruit for no need at all but rather simply out of habit or the like?[146]
See Halacha 2 Q&A there.

If a food will only become edible due the squeezing may it nevertheless be squeezed?[147]
No, as this poses a Borer prohibition. This may not be done in any case, whether with intent to squeeze the liquid into food or to sweeten it.[148]

---

[142] Shabbos Kehalacha Vol. 2 p. 415
[143] M"A 320:9; M"B 320:24
[144] Tzemach Tzedek Chidushim Shabbos 22; Tehila Ledavid 320:4 leaves this matter in question
[145] Taz 320:1 as explained in P"M 320 M"Z 1 and A"A 9; Implication of M"B [and M"A] ibid
The reason: As only by olives and grapes which are meant to be squeezed does the prohibition apply. [P"M ibid]
[146] Shabbos Kehalacha Vol. 2 p. 420
[147] Shabbos Kehalacha Vol. 2 p. 446
[148] So rules Tehila Ledavid 320:14

5. To suck the juice out from fruits:[149]

First Opinion: The above however only applies to squeezing, however, to suck out the juice from the fruit with one's mouth there are opinions[150] which allow one to do so even by olives and grapes because this is not the regular form of squeezing and one's intent is [thus] nullified to that of the rest of people.[151]

Second Opinion: However, there are opinions[152] which say that nevertheless it is Rabbinically forbidden [to do so] just like [the Sages] forbade one to nurse with his mouth from an animal even though he is removing [the milk] in an irregular method, as will be explained in chapter 328 [Halacha 40].[153]

An additional reason for 2nd opinion:[154] In addition [sucking juice from olives and grapes] is [still] questionable regarding if one is liable for a sin offering [on doing so] as perhaps [sucking] is not considered [squeezing in] an irregular way as is nursing from an animal being that nursing [from an animal] is a complete irregularity as it is never common to nurse [from it] but rather to milk it. However sucking fruit is not such a great irregularity being that it is at times common to do so.

Sucking on other fruits [according to 2nd opinion]:[155] Even fruits which are [only] Rabbinically forbidden to be squeezed are forbidden to suck from as is done by olives and grapes, because the Sages did not make differentiations within their decree.

To suck on meat [according to 2nd opinion]:[156] The same law applies when placing bread in wine or meat in soup that it is forbidden to suck them even though there is only a Rabbinical prohibition involved in squeezing them.

Sucking on sugar cane [according to 2nd opinion]:[157] Therefore it is forbidden to suck on sugarcane due to that it has the same laws as strawberries and pomegranates and fruits of the like.

The final ruling: The custom is to be lenient [to] even [suck] olives and grapes like the first opinion.[158] [Although] one who is stringent [to avoid sucking] even bread and meat will be blessed.[159] However by other fruits[160], excluding olives and grapes, one may be lenient[161] because there is [another] aspect [involved] to [allow one to] be lenient with the sucking of fruit being that one can say that doing so is within the norm of eating and so long as something is done in a way of eating it is not at all similar to a [forbidden] action and even the Sages did not make a decree in such cases as explained in chapter 319 [Halacha 1] regarding separating food from waste.

---

[149] Admur 320:2; Rama 320:1

[150] 1st opinion in Rama ibid; Shivlei Haleket 90; Haittur

[151] Admur ibid; Shivlei Haleket ibid; M"B 320:10; Thus although the Sages forbade one to suckle on the utter of an animal, nevertheless here since it is such a great irregularity, it is allowed. [M"B ibid in name of M"A 320:2 and P"M 320 A"A 2] Vetzaruch Iyun why this is not simply permitted due to Derech Achila, just as we permit Borer and the like?

[152] 2nd opinion in Rama ibid; Hagahos Maimanis in name of Yireim; Yireim 274

[153] Admur ibid; M"B 320:12

[154] Admur ibid; Hagahos Maimanis in name of Yireim; Taz 320:2

[155] Admur ibid based on Beis Yosef; Rama ibid; M"B 20:12

[156] Admur ibid; M"A 320:4; Hagahos Maimanis in name of Yireim

[157] Admur ibid; Beis Yosef according to Yireim

[158] Admur ibid; Taz 320:2 [rules like first opinion and says so is custom; Elya Raba 320:3

[159] Admur ibid

Other Opinions: Some Poskim rule that there is only a matter to be stringent regarding grapes and olives and not regarding other items. [M"B 320:12 in name of Elya Raba]

[160] See footnote by the summary of this Halacha for the difficulties presented in the wording here.

[161] Admur ibid; Olas Shabbos 320:9; Elya Zuta 320:2

Proper understanding of the final ruling of Admur: It is unclear from the wording of Admur in Halacha 2 regarding how the final ruling is with regards to fruits, as after mentioning that the custom is to be lenient by everything and there is room to be stringent even by bread he mentions that "however by other fruits one may be lenient except for olives and grapes". On what part of the ruling is this statement going on? Some [Shabbos Kehalacha Vol. 2 p 448] understand this to mean that only by olives and grapes and bread and meat is there a blessing for being stringent while by other fruits there is no blessing as there is no need to be stringent at all. Others [Ketzos Hashulchan 126:13] however seem to learn that while one may be lenient by all foods, there is room to be stringent by all foods, including other fruits and one who does so is blessed. An alternative explanation is that one is to be stringent by olives and grapes, [as rules the Elya Raba and M"B ibid] while by all other foods one may be lenient, especially being that this is the way of eating, although one who is stringent by all other foods, including other fruits, is blessed. Vetzaruch Iyun. Practically, it seems from the wording of Admur that the following is the final ruling that one is to practice: One is to be stringent by grapes and olives. There is no need to be stringent by other fruits. One is encouraged to be stringent by bread and meat. Vetzaruch Iyun.

Summary-To suck out the juice with ones mouth:[162]

The custom is to be lenient to allow one to suck the juices of even grapes and olives. However, it is proper to be stringent against sucking grapes and olives[163] and one who is stringent to not suck the juice of even soaked bread and meat will be blessed. It is unclear from the wording of Admur if one is encouraged with a blessing to be stringent also by other fruits or not.

Q&A

May one who chooses to be stringent suck sugar cubes which have been dipped in tea or the like?[164]

One is to be stringent to avoid placing the cube partially in his mouth and then suck it. However once the cube is already fully in his mouth he may be lenient to suck it.

May one who is stringent, suck a fruit/food when the entire food is already in his mouth?[165]

Ketzos Hashulchan:[166] One should not do so by those fruits which are mainly juice, such as a grape. However, by those fruits which are mainly solids, and one also sucks out and eats the solids, this is allowed.

Mishneh Berurah:[167] There is no need to be stringent at all when one places the entire fruit/food in his mouth and then sucks its juice.

May one suck out liquid that is absorbed in a cloth?[168]

One should not be lenient to do so, although seemingly for a Bris in which it is accustomed that the infant sucks some wine from a cotton ball this is allowed.

6. Juice which flowed on its own from fruits on Shabbos:

A. From grapes and olives:

Forbidden to be drunk on Shabbos:[169] Liquids which flowed out on Shabbos on their own from olives and grapes are forbidden[170] [to be eaten] until evening[171] [i.e. after Shabbos] due to a decree that one may come to squeeze them with his hands in order to drink them today [on Shabbos] if [these liquids] were to be permitted.[172] [Furthermore] even if the olives and grapes [from which the juice flowed from] are designated to be eaten [and not squeezed] [nevertheless it is forbidden to drink the juice that flowed on its own as] we suspect that one may change his mind to squeeze it for its juices just like is common for majority of olives and grapes.[173]

If the grapes and olives were crushed from before Shabbos:[174] Olives and grapes which were crushed from before Shabbos, the juice which comes out from them on Shabbos is allowed [to be drunk] for the reasons explained in chapter 252 [Halacha 14]. [However, this only applies if one began crushing the grapes and olives a while before the commencing of Shabbos, to the point that by the time Shabbos began the grapes and olives were already crushed[175]. If however one began crushing the grapes and olives right

---

[162] Admur 320:2
[163] As rules Elya Raba and M"B 320:12 and so can be understood from Admur that one should not be lenient at all by olives and grapes.
[164] Shabbos Kehalacha Vol. 2 p. 448
[165] Shabbos Kehalacha Vol. 2 p. 448
[166] Ketzos Hashulchan 126 footnote 28
[167] M"B 320:12 as is implied from P"M 320 M"Z 2
[168] Shabbos Kehalacha Vol. 2 p. 452
[169] Admur 320:3; Michaber 320:1; Shabbos 143b
[170] Admur ibid; Michaber ibid; Mishneh ibid
[171] Admur ibid; Rashi Beitza 3a
[172] Admur ibid; Rashi on Mishneh ibid; M"B 320:3
[173] Admur ibid; Michaber ibid; Gemara ibid
[174] Admur 320:4; Michaber 320:2; See Biur Halacha 320:2 "Shenisrasku"
[175] The reason: The reason for the allowance in such a case is because even if one were to come to squeeze these olives and grapes on Shabbos, which is the suspicion behind the prohibition, he would not transgress a Biblical decree being that the fruits are already crushed and their liquids

before Shabbos began, such as he placed a heavy board on top of them right before Shabbos, then their liquids remain forbidden to be eaten on Shabbos.[176]]

If the grapes were in a vat of wine:[177] [Furthermore] even if they had not been crushed from before Shabbos, if there is wine in the vats that the grapes are inside of, then even though the grapes break open on Shabbos inside the vat and more wine comes out [from them into the vat], [nevertheless] one is allowed to drink from this vat on Shabbos, because every little bit[178] of wine which comes out of the grapes on Shabbos becomes nullified against 60[179] times the wine that was already in the vat [from before Shabbos]. [If however the grapes were outside of the vat and its juice flowed into the wine that is in the vat, then the entire barrel of wine is forbidden until after Shabbos.[180] If however the wine flowed into water, or another liquid then it is nullified in majority. Furthermore, even if there is majority of wine in the end it is not considered Muktzah [although seemingly is forbidden to be drunk].[181] Vetzaruch Iyun if this applies even if the grapes are in the water and seeping wine into it.[182]]

The reason that the wine is not considered a Davar Sheyeish Lo Matirin:[183] Now, although this wine [which flowed on Shabbos] is considered an item which will eventually become permitted [in which case it should never be nullified until then] being that after Shabbos it will be permitted without any nullification [needed], nevertheless since this wine that came out on Shabbos was never recognizable prior to it being mixed [into the vat] and it [thus] never had the status of wine on it (look in Yorah Deah chapter 123 regarding when juice from a grape receives a status of wine) [therefore] it does not receive the status of an item which will eventually become permitted [without needing nullification] until after it already became nullified [within the wine that it seeped into], and [the Sages] only said that something which will eventually become permitted is not nullified in a case that the prohibition was initially visible and it already then received a status of something which will eventually become permitted and then afterwards got mixed [into another food].

If one placed the grapes into the vat on Shabbos:[184] [Furthermore] even if one placed whole grapes into

---

would flow regardless. Thus by squeezing them one is merely hastening the process, of which doing so is only a Rabbinical prohibition. [252:14; M"B 320:13]

[176] As we suspect one may come to squeeze them on Shabbos, in which case doing so involves a Biblical prohibition being that they had not at all been crushed from before Shabbos.[ibid]

[177] Admur 320:4; Michaber 320:2; Sefer Hateruma 223; Smag 65; Semak 281

[178] This teaches us that every drop of wine is nullified in 60x and one does not need to have a total of 60x in the wine before Shabbos versus all the wine that will flow, as by each drop we apply Kama Kama Batul. [Avnei Nezer Y.D. 225; Shabbos Kehalacha 16 Biurim 8 p. 20] To note however that in 335:4 Admur implies that in order <u>to drink</u> the wine we require a total of [60x-see Shach Y.D. 134:4] of wine from Erev Shabbos [and only regarding Muktzah do we say Kama Kama Batul]. This contradicts the ruling here. However perhaps however one can say there is a difference between if the wine drips into the water [in which we do not apply Kama Kama Batul] or is inside the vat and dripping straight into the wine, in which case we do apply Kama Kama Batul, Vetzaruch Iyun. [See Shabbos Kehalacha ibid]

<u>Other opinions:</u> Some Poskim rule we do not apply the rule of Kama Kama Batul and one thus requires 60x in total. [P"M 320 M"Z 3]

[179] Admur ibid; P"M 320 M"Z 3; M"B 320:14

<u>The reason:</u> As this is considered a mixture of Lech Belach of Min Bemino of which we rule that one requires 60x Rabbinically. [P"M ibid; See Admur 447:61]

<u>Do we say Kama Kama Batil:</u> In Yoreh Deah 134:1 there is a concept that although Yayin Nesech is never nullified in other wine, nevertheless if it fell into the Kosher wine [as opposed to the Kosher wine falling into it] every drop of the Yayin Nesech is nullified. Vetzaruch Iyun why we don't apply this rule here as well, and why we require 60x. See Admur 335:4 that if the wine drips into water it is nullified because there is no DSL"M by Eino Mino and we apply the rule of Kama Kama Batul, thus why don't we apply the same rule here as this wine is not a DSL"M and hence why don't we say Kama Kama Batul, and not require Bittul?!!!. The answer is that a) here too we apply Kama Kama Batul and thus only initially does each individual drop of the wine in the vat to have 60x against it, however one does not require 60x versus the total wine that came out on Shabbos, as explained above. However, in 335:4 Admur implies that we do require majority:60x of wine from Erev Shabbos even when we say Kama Kama Batul and only regarding Muktzah are we lenient to not require even majority. See previous footnote.

[180] M"B 320:14; Sefer Hateruma 223 as is understood from reason of Admur brought next

<u>Why we don't say Kama Kama Batil:</u> In Yoreh Deah 134:1 there is a concept that although Yayin Nesech is never nullified in Kosher wine, nevertheless if it fell into the Kosher wine [as opposed to the Kosher wine falling into it] every drop of the Yayin Nesech is nullified. However, by a DSL"M we do not apply the rule of Kama Kama Batul. [See Admur 334:4 that if the wine drips into water it is nullified because there is no DSL"M by Eino Mino and we apply the rule of Kama Kama Batul, if however, it fell into Mino then it is not nullified. Hence we see we do not apply the concept of Kama Kama Batul in a case of DSL"M.]

[181] Admur 334:4; M"A 334:4

[182] As here Admur rules one requires 60x even by Min Bemino and hence certainly one should require 60x by Min Beino Mino. However, in 334:4 Admur explicitly rules that majority suffices and even minority suffices regarding Muktzah.

[183] Admur 320:4; M"A 320:5; M"B 320:14; See also Rama Yoreh Deah 102:4; Shach 102:12; Taz 102:11; 507:2; M"A 507:3; Admur 507:3; 445:8

[184] Admur 320:4; Taz 320:3

the vat on Shabbos and they then broke open [and seeped wine] on that day into the wine [that was already in the vat], it is permitted to drink wine from the vat for the above mentioned reason.[185] However it is initially forbidden to place whole grapes into wine on Shabbos in order so they split open and ooze their wine [into the vat] due to the prohibition of squeezing, as although he is not squeezing it actually with his hands nevertheless it is Rabbinically prohibited [to cause it to be squeezed].[186]

Grape seeds and skins[187]: Grape seeds and skin which had water placed on them in order to make grape-skin, wine it is permitted to draw[188] [wine] out from these [seeds and skins, into the water] and then drink it.

Furthermore, even if one had not placed water [onto them] and the wine squeezes and flows out on its own, it is permitted to drink it being that it already was broken up before Shabbos.

B. From other fruits:[189]
Juice which has flowed from strawberries and pomegranates and the like then if they are designated to be eaten then the liquid is permitted, as we do not suspect that one may change his mind to [use them] for juice. However if they are designated for their juice then the juice is forbidden.

Summary-Juice which flowed on their own from fruits on Shabbos[190]
- *From grapes and olives*:
  Are forbidden [to be eaten] until after Shabbos, unless:
  1) The grapes/olives were crushed from before Shabbos
     Or
  2) They are in a vat of wine or oil
  The juices of grape seeds and skins that have flowed on their own are allowed.

- *From other fruits*:
  If the fruits are designated to be eaten, then the liquid is permitted. If they are designated for their juice, then it has the same law as grapes and olives.

---

7. Squeezing juice out of pickles and other foods saturated with external liquids:
A. Squeezing out the liquid for the sake of drinking their liquids:[191]
Fruits and vegetables that are pickled in salt and vinegar, or in salt water, as well as those which are cooked, are forbidden according to all opinions to be squeezed for their liquids.

The above is only a Rabbinical prohibition:[192] If one [transgressed and] squeezed [the above foods] for their liquids he is not Biblically liable[193] because even though the liquids were fully fledged liquids prior to becoming absorbed into the [foods], such as [occurs] if one pickled or cooked them in water or wine and vinegar and the like of other liquids, nevertheless since now they are being squeezed from food they have the same status as food and it is thus like separating food from food. Nevertheless, it is Rabbinically forbidden to squeeze them for the sake of their liquid since they were fully fledged liquids prior to this. However raw fruits [that are not commonly squeezed to drink their juice] since their squeezed liquids

---

Other opinions: Some Poskim rule it is even initially permitted to place the grapes intop the wine barrel in order so they seep wine into the vat. [M"A 320:5 in name of Bach; Elya Raba; Chayeh Adam; M"B 320:14]
[185] Admur ibid; Taz ibid and all Poskim in next footnote
[186] So rules the Taz. However the Magen Avraham and Chayeh Adam and Mishneh Berurah [14] rule that it is allowed to be done even initially.
[187] Admur 320:5
[188] What does this mean? May one squeeze them? In next Halacha it is explained that it is forbidden to squeeze absorbed liquids.
[189] Admur 320:3; Michaber 320:1; Gemara ibid
[190] Admur 320:3-5
[191] Admur 320:11; Michaber 320:7; Shmuel in Shabbos 145a
[192] Admur ibid; M"A 320:9, 12; M"B 320:29; Riy in Tosafus Kesubos 6a
[193] Admur ibid; Shmuel in Gemara ibid

never had upon them the status of liquids [prior to the squeezing] therefore it is allowed to squeeze them according to those opinions which permit doing so.

Squeezing fish:[194] One who [wishes to] squeeze fish for its gravy has the same laws as squeezing pickled and cooked [foods] for the sake of their juices which is forbidden. [Some Poskim[195] however learn this only applies towards pickled or cooked fish, however the natural gravy of the fish may be squeezed out even to drink, just as is the law regarding other fruits.]

Q&A
May juice which had been directly squeezed into a food be then squeezed out of that food?[196]
- *For example: One squeezed lemon juice into his fruit salad and then desires to squeeze it out after it having absorbed the taste?*

This is allowed to be done as since the juice which was squeezed into it never received a liquid status it therefore does not receive the same status as pickles and the like which contain juice that was previously defined as liquid. Nevertheless, it is proper to only rely on this in a time of need. [Vetzaruch Iyun Gadol as it is forbidden to squeeze the natural juices of the fruits in the salad, irrelevant of the juice it absorbed!]

B. Squeezing out the liquid for the sake of enhancing the food being squeezed:[197]
One is allowed to squeeze pickles and the like for their own need, in order to prepare them to be eaten through doing this, [such as to making it taste better through doing so].

The reason for this allowance:[198] This case is not prohibited due to "detaching" since one does not at all need the item being detached, which is their juice.[199]

Q&A
When squeezing out liquid in order to enhance the food may one squeeze the liquid into an empty vessel and then drink it?[200]
The Poskim[201] rule one may squeeze the liquid even into an empty vessel. Furthermore, some Poskim[202] rule that according to this opinion one may even later decide to drink it. Others[203] rule it is forbidden to drink the liquid. Furthermore, it is implied according to this opinion that it is forbidden to even squeeze the juice into an empty vessel and it must rather go directly to waste.[204] From Admur here it is implied like this latter opinion that one may not drink the liquid[205] and also must squeeze it in a way it goes directly to waste and not into an empty vessel[206], even if one plans to later throw it out.[207] Practically, one is not even to squeeze the liquid into a plate but rather he is to squeeze it in an area that it will go directly to waste.

---

[194] Admur 320:14; Michaber 320:8; Abayey Shabbos 145a
[195] Implication of M"A 320:12; P"M 320 A"A 12; M"B 320:31
[196] Shabbos Kehalacha Vol. 2 p. 440
[197] Admur 320:11; Michaber 320:7; Shabbos 145a
[198] Admur ibid; Rashi ibid; M"A 320:9
[199] Seemingly these items are not considered commonly squeezed and hence it is allowed to squeeze them to sweeten according to all, just as we rule by fruits that are not commonly squeezed.
[200] Shabbos Kehalacha Vol. 2 p. 424
[201] Michaber 320:7; M"B 320:24
[202] Tehila Ledavid 320:8; SSH"K 5:5; As rules Admur in 320:1
[203] Tzemach Tzedek in Piskei Dinim 320; Nishmas Adam 14 brought in Tehila Ledavid; Ketzos Hashulchan 126 footnote 26
[204] Shabbos Kehalacha Vol. 2 p. 424 [see there Biurim 13 and Tosefes Biur 20] based on Tzemach Tzedek in Piskei Dinim 320; Nishmas Adam 14 brought in Tehila Ledavid; Ketzos Hashulchan 126 footnote 26
[205] As he clearly rights in his reason "Since one does not need the liquid **at all**". The words "at all" is in addition to the wording of the M"A ibid
[206] As Admur completely omits this allowance of the Michaber.
[207] So learns Shabbos Kehalacha 15:23 and so is implied from Ketzos Hashulchan ibid

Why does squeezing liquid out from a food not contain the Borer/separating prohibition?[208]

As the food and liquid that is absorbed in it are considered one food to which the separating restrictions do not apply as explained in The Laws of Borer Chapter 1.

If a food will only become edible due the squeezing may it nevertheless be squeezed?[209]

No, as this poses a Borer prohibition. This may not be done in any cases, whether with intent to squeeze the liquid into food or to sweeten it.[210]

May one squeeze liquid out from his challah if it fell into liquid?

Seemingly yes as it is in order to enhance the food.

Practically, may one squeeze out the oil from a Sufganiya/Latke?[211]

If he is doing so in order to enhance the food and make it more edible, then it is allowed. This includes if he is doing so due to that the oil absorbed in the food bothers him.[212] However if one desires to use the liquid for other purposes then it is forbidden.[213] As well to do so for no reason at all is to be avoided, as explained above.

If one is doing so in order to both enhance the food and reuse the liquid, then see above Q&A where this matter is disputed, with the Tzemach Tzedek ruling that it is forbidden.

May one squeeze out the oil from eggplant or vinegar from cucumber salad?[214]

Has the same laws squeezing oil from Sufganiyot, as explained above.

May one squeeze out the juice of a fruit for no need at all but rather simply out of habit or the like?[215]

See Halacha 2 Q&A there

C. Squeezing cooked and pickled foods into food:[216]

It is permitted to squeeze pickled and cooked [foods] for the sake of their liquids into a pot of food in order to enhance the food.[217]

If the pot is empty:[218] However if the pot does not yet have food in it then it is forbidden to squeeze into it even though one will eventually mix food into it, as was explained above [in Halacha 3]

Squeezing into a liquid or a creamy dip:[219] It is permitted to squeeze [fruits and pickled foods] into

---

[208] Ketzos Hashulchan 126 Footnote 19

[209] Shabbos Kehalacha Vol. 2 p. 446

[210] So rules Tehila Ledavid 320:14

[211] Shabbos Kehalacha Vol. 2 p. 425

[212] M"B 320:25 in name of Derisha regarding Lokshun

[213] However, the Chayeh Adam rules that oil is considered food, and it is hence permitted to squeeze it out even for a use, as one may separate a food from a food. [brought in M"B 320:25]

[214] Shabbos Kehalacha Vol. 2 p. 426

[215] Shabbos Kehalacha Vol. 2 p. 420

[216] Admur 320:12; Michaber 320:7; Tosafus Shabbos 145a

Other opinions: Some Poskim rule it is forbidden to squeeze cooked and pickled foods for the sake of their liquids even if one squeezes into other foods, and doing so contains a Biblical prohibition. [Michaber 320:7 in name of Rabbeinu Chananeil in Shabbos 125a in explanation of Rebbe Yochanan ibid; Rabbeinu Chananel concludes "We do not rule like Shmuel neither by Shabbos or Yom Tov and rather we rule like Rebbe Yochanan, and so we have received from our teachers"] Practically we do not rule like this opinion. [Admur ibid omits it completely from his Shulchan Aruch; Michaber 320:4 omitted it (however see Biur Halacha ibid); M"B 320:17 and 30] Nevertheless some Poskim conclude that one who is stringent is blessed. [M"B ibid; Teshuvas Harosh brought in Beis Yosef; Mishkanos Yaakov 112] According to Admur there is no need to be stringent at all. [See Shabbos Kehalacha 15 footnote 55]

[217] However the M"B [30] rules that one who is stringent to avoid squeezing these types of liquids even into food is to be praised.

[218] Admur ibid; Michaber ibid

[219] Admur 320:13; M"A 320:10; M"B 320:28

Muryas[220] because it is considered a food however into liquids it is forbidden to squeeze them.[221]

Important Note: Regarding the definition of food and liquid and how much juice may be squeezed into a

D. Squeezing out the food part of a fruit or cooked food:[222]
Apples or other cooked fruits are allowed to be squeezed in order to remove from it all of its content because he is squeezing out all the food from it and is not [doing so] in order to take out its liquid.

Summary: Squeezing juice out of pickles and other foods saturated with external liquids:
Squeezing them in order to drink the liquid:[223] Is Rabbinically forbidden
In order to enhance the food being squeezed:[224] Permitted.
In order to place into food:[225] It is permitted to squeeze it directly into food. However, to squeeze it into an empty vessel is forbidden even if one plans to place it into food.
Squeezing out the entire content of the food:[226] Such as to squeeze out cooked apples from their peel is allowed.

---

8. Pumping and squeezing breast milk on Shabbos:[227]
Into a cup and the like: A woman may not squeeze milk from her breasts into a cup or into a pot in order to nurse [the milk] to her child. [**See Q&A regarding if the child refuses to nurse and there is danger involved**]
The reason for this is: because one who milks into a vessel is completely detaching [the milk from its source] and is liable for the threshing prohibition. It was only permitted to do a Biblical prohibition in a case of life-threatening danger [and not simply to feed a child].
Trickling milk in order to stimulate her child to nurse: However, it is permitted for a woman to squeeze out some milk [and have it trickle down her skin and the like[228]] in order to stimulate the child to take hold of her breast and nurse. [However, she may not squeeze the milk into his mouth in order to stimulate him -**See Q&A below**]
The reason for this is because: as since this milk [that is squeezed] is going to waste it does not contain a Biblical "detaching" prohibition, but rather a Rabbinical prohibition as explained above, and for the need of a child [the Sages] did not apply their decree.
Squirting milk onto one who is spellbound: It is forbidden to squirt milk onto one who has been overtaken by an evil spell, as he is not in any danger and is not in great pain for us to rescind for him a Rabbinical prohibition to be done through a Jew, as [opposed to] what was permitted by one who has heart ache and the like. See chapter 330 [Halacha 9].

---

[220] A creamy dip made from fish fat.
[221] Admur 320:13; 320:10; M"A 320:10; M"B 320:28; Biur Halacha 320:4 "Haba Lechol" in name of Elya Raba 320:4
Other opinions: Some Poskim rule that even according to the stringent opinion it is permitted to squeeze "lemons and other fruits" into liquids. [Taz 320:5] As this is similar to squeezing the fruit for the sake of sweetening it. [P"M 320 M"Z 5] However this only refers to fruits that are not commonly squeezed, and hence require Achashvei to make them forbidden. However, those fruits that are commonly squeezed for their juice, and are hence forbidden according to all to be squeezed for their liquids, then it is likewise forbidden even according to the Taz to squeeze them into juice. [P"M ibid]
[222] Admur 320:15; Taz 320:5
[223] Admur 320:11
[224] Admur 320:11
[225] Admur 320:12
[226] Admur 320:15
[227] Admur 328:41
Nolad: See 305:31 regarding milk of an animal that it is forbidden on Shabbos due to Nolad/Muktzah Vetzaruch Iyun why no mention of this is recorded here!
[228] See reason and footnote below.

Is it permitted for a woman to squeeze out milk from her breast to relieve pain?[229] Even a child which is for certain an eighth month [child], which is [therefore] forbidden to move according to all, his mother may bend over him and nurse him due to the pain of the milk. Similarly, she herself may remove with her hands the milk which is causing her pain. **[See Q&A regarding using a pump]**

The reason for this allowance is: as since this milk is going to waste it does not contain the [Biblical] detaching prohibition but rather [only] the Rabbinical prohibition, and due to her pain they did not decree [against removing it].

Summary-Pumping breast milk on Shabbos:
Is forbidden to be done into a vessel due to the Biblical detaching prohibition. However, it is permitted for a woman to squeeze out some milk and have it trickle down her skin in order to stimulate her child to take hold of her breast and nurse. As well it is permitted for her to squeeze milk from her breast onto the ground in order to relieve breast pain caused by the milk.

Q&A
May a woman pump milk out to feed her baby if he refuses to suck from the breast?[230]
If there is nothing else available for the child to eat [such as formula] and there is thus possible danger involved then she may pump out less than a Grogeres[231] worth of milk at a time and feed him it, and then pump out another Grogeres worth and feed him it. She may not pump out more milk until the child is fed the previous milk that was pumped.

May one squeeze the milk into the baby's mouth to stimulate it to eat?[232]
No! One may **not** squirt the milk into the mouth of the baby as in such a case it is not going to waste and thus squeezing it contains a Biblical prohibition. **[See footnote for opinion of M"B**[233]**]**

May a woman use a pump to release milk in order to relieve breast pain?[234]
If plans to store this milk: If the pump contains a bottle which will store the milk, then it is forbidden to be done if she plans to use the milk.
If plans to throw out the milk: If she plans to throw out the milk from the bottle then some Poskim[235] rule it is nevertheless forbidden. Others[236] however rule that this is allowed to be done. The Ketzos Hashulchan[237] rules that one may be lenient like these opinions to pump out less than a Grogeres[238] worth of milk at a time and then spill it out prior to pumping again.[239]
If the milk goes directly to waste from the pump: It is allowed according to all opinions to use a pump to release the milk, in order to relieve pain, if the pump squeezes out the milk directly onto the floor or garbage.

---

[229] Admur 330:9
[230] Har Tzevi 201
[231] A Grogeres is 19.2 milliliters [Shiurei Torah 3:17], thus one is to squeeze less than this amount at a time.
[232] Ketzos Hashulchan 138 footnote 30
[233] This is unlike the understanding of the Mishneh Berurah [112] based on the Shevulay Haleket that one may squirt into the baby's mouth. In the Sharreiy Tziyon the Mishneh Berurah queries how come this is allowed. According to the Alter Rebbe the query does not apply as in truth it is not allowed.
[234] Piskeiy Teshuvos 330:8
[235] Bris Olam
[236] Avnei Nezer 47
[237] 138 footnote 30
[238] A Grogeres is 19.2 milliliters [Shiurei Torah 3:17], thus one is to squeeze less than this amount at a time.
[239] As one is only liable for the Detaching prohibition if he pumps the minimum measurement of a Grogeres.

9. Squeezing milk of animal:
See Chapter 305 Halacha 28

10. Sucking the milk from an animal:[240]
As a cure for heart pain: One who is moaning from heart pain of which his treatment is to suckle with his mouth from [the breast of] an animal, is permitted to suckle on Shabbos.

The Reason: As doing so is [merely] detaching in an irregular manner as it is not common to suckle milk [from the animal breast] with one's mouth but rather to milk it into a vessel and drink from it, therefore there is no Biblical prohibition involved in this nursing but rather merely Rabbinical and in a case of pain [the Sages] did not make their decree.

Due to hunger: However, this allowance only applies to one with heart pain however one who is merely hungry it is forbidden for him to nurse from an animal on Shabbos.

However, on Yom Tov it is permitted to nurse [from it] (if it is impossible to milk it through a gentile and also if he does not have food into which he can milk into).

Summary-Sucking the milk from an animal:
One who is moaning from heart pain of which his treatment is to suckle with his mouth from an animal, is permitted to suckle on Shabbos. However, one who is merely hungry is forbidden to nurse from an animal on Shabbos due to a Rabbinical detaching prohibition. However, on Yom Tov it is permitted to nurse from it (if it is impossible to milk it through a gentile and also if he does not have food into which he can milk into).

---

[240] Admur 328:40

CHAPTER 2: SQUEEZING LIQUID FROM CLOTHS ON SHABBOS

Introduction:
This chapter deals with the laws of squeezing liquids out from cloth. Doing so in addition to containing the Mifarek prohibition as well contains at times the laundering prohibition. Regarding the laundering prohibition, only those laws that relate to squeezing out liquid from a cloth will be mentioned. There will IY"H be a separate section which will deal with the laundering laws in their full length.

---

1. Squeezing cloths that have become wet:[1]

The laundering prohibition: One who squeezes a cloth [which had absorbed clear/white liquids] until its liquids come out is considered as if he has laundered clothing and is thus liable for [the] whitening [prohibition].[2] However, if it had absorbed red wine or beer or other liquids which do not whiten, then there contains no laundering prohibition in squeezing out these liquids.[3]

The Mifarek prohibition: Even cloths which have been soaked in liquids which do not whiten [i.e. have been soaked in colored liquids], are forbidden to be squeezed.

The reason:[4] The reason for this restriction is due to the prohibition of "detaching" which is an offshoot of [the] threshing [prohibition] just as squeezing fruits is prohibited because of "detaching".

If one does not need the liquid:[5] However one is only liable on this squeezing if he needs the liquids being squeezed from the cloth, however if one does not need the liquids squeezed out from the cloth and is only doing so in order to clean the cloth, then this is not similar to threshing at all, as by threshing one needs the grains that he is detaching from the stalks, and therefore this squeezing does not contain a Biblical prohibition but rather a Rabbinical.

Cloth designated for getting wet:[6] (There is no need to worry of the prohibition of whitening [in inserting/removing the pipe with the] flax residue and pieces of cloth which surrounds the pipe even if it is white wine which whitens, because [these cloths] are meant to get wet [and dirty] and one does not care to whiten it at all as was written in chapter 319 [Halacha 13] regarding a strainer).

---

[1] Admur 320:21
[2] Admur 301:56
[3] Admur 320:21; 301:59; 319:13; M"A 319:11; Taz 320:12; Rabbeinu Tam in Sefer Hayashar; Tosafus Beitza 30a; Kesubos 6a; Shabbos 111b; Rashba; Rivash; Rav Hamaggid; Implication of Michaber 320:18; Biur Halacha 320:18 "Yeish Mi Shematir"
Other opinions: Some Poskim rule there is no difference between water and other liquids, and one is Biblically liable for Milabein on the squeezing of all liquids [Ran brought in Taz 320:12; Riy brought in Tosafus Shabbos ibid; Rambam 2:11; See Beis Yosef 320; Avnei Nezer 158:12; Biur Halacha ibid]
[4] Admur ibid; M"A 320:23; Riy; Mordechai; Ran
Other opinions: Some Rishonim rule there is no prohibition, even Rabbinically, if the liquid goes to waist. [Rashba brought in Maggid Mishneh; Rivash in opinion of Rabbeinu Tam; brought in Admur end of 320:24-we do not rule like this opinion]
[5] Admur ibid; Rabbeinu Tam Kesubos ibid; Beitza 30a
[6] Admur ibid parentheses in original
Other opinions: Some Poskim rule that the entire case here is referring to a barrel of red wine, as by water or white wine there is a prohibition of Milabein and all Poskim would agree that there is a Biblical prohibition even if the liquid is going to waste and one uses a handle to squeeze it. [M"B 320:55; Biur Halacha 320:18 "Yeish Mi Shematir"]
Is there a prohibition of Milabein involved in causing a Shemtah to squeeze its water while using it for cleaning? According to Admur it seems there is no prohibition while according to the M"B ibid it seems there is a prohibition.

Squeezing liquid out of a cloth:[7]

A. Biblically:

No need for the squeezed liquid: It is forbidden to squeeze a <u>white</u> liquid out of a cloth due to the laundering prohibition.

One needs the squeezed liquid: It is forbidden to squeeze even colored liquids out of a cloth due to the Mifareik/detaching prohibition.

B. Rabbinically:

It is forbidden to squeeze even a colored liquid out of a cloth even if one does not need the liquid.

---

2. _Spreading a cloth over an open bottle:_[8]

Over a bottle of clear liquid: It is forbidden to spread a cloth over a barrel of water[9] in order to cover it, as it may get wet from the water and one will then come to squeeze it and be liable for [the] whitening [prohibition].[10] [One may also not place a wet vessel on top of the cloth.[11]]

A cloth designated for covering: However, a cloth which is designated to be used to spread over the [opening of the barrel] is permitted [to be spread] being that one has no care to squeeze it if it gets wet as it is designated for this purpose.

Over a bottle of colored liquid:[12] However it is permitted to spread a cloth over a barrel of red wine or of oil or beer and other beverages of the sort [which are not clear].

Initially dipping a cloth in colored liquids:[13] Furthermore, it is even permitted to initially soak the cloths in these liquids with one's hands such as to filter colored liquids over this cloth.

The reason for this is:[14] because the [prohibition of] whitening only applies with water and white wine[15] and the like.

The reason that we do not decree against initially soaking the cloth in even colored liquids due to that one may come to squeeze it: Therefore the [Sages] did not decree against soaking a cloth in liquids which do not whiten due to a decree that one may come to squeeze it and be liable for "detaching", as one is only liable if he needs the liquids being squeezed, of which there is no remote suspicion [here] that one may squeeze the cloth for the sake of the liquids that will come out from it being that [these liquids] are not of any significance and it is not at all common to do this.

Spreading a cloth over an open bottle:

A bottle containing white liquid: Is Rabbinically forbidden to be covered unless the cloth is designated for this purpose in which case it is allowed.

A bottle containing colored liquid: Is permitted to be covered.

---

[7] Halacha 21

[8] Admur 320:21; Michaber 320:15; Shabbos 48a

[9] Admur ibid; Rashi ibid; Rambam; Rabbeinu Yerucham; M"B 320:42

[10] Admur ibid; Rambam 22:25; M"B 320:42 in name of Rebbe Akiva Eiger

[11] This is the original case in the Michaber ibid and Shabbos ibid

[12] Admur ibid; M"A 319:11; 510:16; Tosafus Beitza 30a

[13] Admur ibid and 319:13 and 301:59; See M"A ibid; Tosafus ibid; Smag 65

[14] Admur 320:21; 301:59; 319:13; M"A 319:11; Taz 320:12; Rabbeinu Tam in Sefer Hayashar; Tosafus Beitza 30a; Shabbos 111b; Rashba; Rivash; Rav Hamaggid; Implication of Michaber 320:18; Biur Halacha 320:18 "Yeish Mi Shematir"

Other opinions: Some Poskim rule there is no difference between water and other liquids, and one is Biblically laible for Milabein on the squeezing of all liquids [Ran brought in Taz 320:12; Riy brought in Tosafus Shabbos ibid; Rmabam 2:11; See Beis Yosef 320; Avnei Nezer 158:12; Biur Halacha ibid]

[15] Admur ibid; Taz 320:12

3. Doing an action with a cloth which may cause liquid to squeeze out:

A. Inserting a wet cloth into the opening of a bottle:[16]

It is forbidden to insert [wet[17]] Mochin [i.e. any soft material] into the opening of a bottle which contains liquid.[18] [This applies even if the cloth is wet due to colored liquids, and even if the cloth is designated for this purpose.[19]]

The reason for this is because:[20] one may come to squeeze [the material], as through inserting it one will squeeze the liquid that is absorbed in the material into the bottle. Now, although one has no intention to do so, nevertheless [since] it is an inevitable occurrence when one inserts it tightly [therefore it is forbidden].

Inserting it lightly:[21] Therefore the [Sages even] prohibited inserting it lightly due to that one may come to insert it strongly.

B. Plugging up the hole of a leaking pipe:[22]

One may plug up a [leaking] pipe with cloths and any other moveable materials in order so that the water [from the pipe] not flood one's food and vessels.

The reason for this allowance is: as one does not care if a little bit of water trickles out from the hole [in the pipe] and therefore he will not come to insert it strongly and will not come to inevitably squeeze [water out from the cloth].

C. Using a sponge to clean:[23]

With a handle: A [dish] sponge which has a handle of leather [or other non-absorbent material] which one uses to hold on to it, may be used to clean with [as through using the handle one is able to clean without anything squeezing out from the bottom of the sponge[24]].

Without a handle: If it does not have [a handle] then it may not be used to clean with as when one holds it in his hands it squeezes in between his fingers[25], and although this is done unintentionally [nevertheless it is forbidden because] it is an inevitable occurrence.[26]

Other Opinions in why with a handle is allowed: [However] there is an opinion[27] which says that even if [the sponge] has a handle it is impossible to clean with the sponge without squeezing it and nevertheless it is permitted as since the squeezing is being done through the [pressing of] the handle it is [therefore] not [Halachically] considered squeezing and is rather like emptying water from a flask which does not contain [the] "detaching" [prohibition].

However, when it does not have a handle in which case it gets squeezed in the area that he holds it with his hand, then it is forbidden.

Cleaning a spill of liquid with intent of having the liquid drip back into its vessel:[28] It is forbidden to clean a spill of liquid with any cloth or sponge if one plans to drip the absorbed liquid from the cloth back into its vessel.[29] This prohibition applies even if one only desires to clean and save only part of the spill for use on Shabbos.

---

[16] 320:22; Michaber 320:16; Rava in Shabbos 141a

[17] Mishneh Berurah 320:44, and so is evident from the Alter Rebbe in reason here.

[18] The Mishneh Berurah 320:44 and Biur Halacha "Lihadek" rules that this is not to be taken literally, as it is forbidden even if the bottle does not contain liquid, and liquid was only mentioned for the reader to deduce that the material had previously become wet from it.

[19] Mishneh Berurah 320:44

[20] Admur ibid; Mordechai; M"B 320:44

[21] Admur ibid; See Kuntrus Achron 277:1; Gemara ibid; Shaar Hatziyon 320:49 in name of Tosefes Shabbos

[22] 320:25; M"A 320:23; Rambam; Tosefta Eiruvin 8:5

[23] 320:23; Michaber 320:17; Mishneh Shabbos 143a

[24] Rashi and Rambam 22:15, brought in M"B 320:46

[25] Admur ibid; Rashi ibid; Rambam 22:15; M"B 320:47

[26] Admur ibid; Rashi ibid; Rambam 22:15; M"A 320: ; Biur Hagr"a; M"B 320:47-48

[27] Raavad ibid, brought in M"A 320:19; M"B 320:46

[28] 335:1

[29] This applies even if the sponge contains a handle and thus it is not inevitable that one will squeeze liquid upon holding the cloth. The reason for this prohibition is because it is considered a mundane act and a desecration of Shabbos. Furthermore, there is suspicion that if one were allowed to clean the spill and drip out the absorbed liquid as he does during the week he may come to intentionally squeeze out the liquid. [ibid]

Practically, may one use a sponge with a handle if it will inevitably cause liquid to come out?
No. One may only use it gently in a way that it will not squeeze out liquid from its bottom.[30]

Which forms of sponges may be used to wash the dishes?
Regular sponge: It is forbidden to use a sponge on Shabbos due to the squeezing prohibition.[31] This applies even if the sponge has a handle.
Synthetic sponges and steel wool:[32] Some Poskim[33] rule all forms of synthetic or steel wool sponges are forbidden to be used due to it being a mundane act, and due to the squeezing prohibition. Others[34] however permit using synthetic [or metal[35]] sponges which have their threads visibly spread apart from each other, as in such a case using them does not involve the squeezing prohibition. However they forbid using steel wool[36], and any sponge which has its threads close to each other. Others[37] question that perhaps it is permitted to use all types of synthetic or metal sponges[38]. Practically they rule one is not to be lenient by closely knitted sponges. Others[39] rule that even those sponges which are permitted to be used, may only be used it if the sponge is designated specifically for Shabbos.

---

[30] The dispute behind the reason that it is allowed to use a sponge with a handle: The reason this is allowed is because when using a handle to clean with nothing squeezes out from the sponge in the process. [However] there is an opinion which says that even if [the sponge] has a handle it is impossible to clean with the sponge without squeezing it and nevertheless it is permitted as since the squeezing is being done through the [pressing of] the handle it is [therefore] not [Halachically] considered squeezing and is rather like emptying water from a flask which does not contain [the] "detaching" [prohibition]. However, when it does not have a handle in which case it gets squeezed in the area that he holds it with his hand, then it is forbidden. [ibid]
The practical ramification between these two reasons is in a case that liquid will certainly be squeezed from the sponge. Thus, whether one may apply strength when using a sponge with a handle to clean the liquid, and inevitably cause the liquid to spill, is subject to the above dispute.
Practically: It is implied that Admur rules mainly like the first opinion mentioned there that using a handle is only allowed due to it not being an inevitable occurrence. If however one sees the squeezing is inevitable, then it once again becomes prohibited. [So is evident from 320:24 that we do not hold of the 2nd opinion above as the final Halacha, as Admur does not simply allow inserting a barrel pipe with a cloth due to this reason, but adds that one must also make sure the liquid goes to waste. In the words of Admur 320:24: "As many argue on their words". Vetzaruch Iyun if these words are going on the opinion of Raavad that even if it squeezes out it is allowed, or if it's going on opinion of the Melamdim Zechus. Furthermore, Tzaruch Iyun on if one can truly derive anything from the Barza case to a regular sponge case, as seemingly Admur learns that a Barza does not have the same status as a handle of the sponge and that's why the Heter is not so clear, however by an actual handle of a sponge perhaps Admur would be lenient even if the liquid does not go to waste, and certainly if it does. Vetzaruch Iyun. I later however found in Shabbos Kehalacha Vol. 3 p. 211-212 a similar conclusion that it is evident from Admur that one may only use a sponge with a handle if it does not inevitably cause squeezing. He deduces this also from Ketzos Hashulchan [133-end] that a toothbrush, despite it having a handle, is forbidden to be used due to it causing inevitable squeezing.
[31] 320:23
[32] There are three possible issues discussed in Poskim regarding these forms of sponges: Squeezing and Uvdin Dechol may apply by all sponges and in addition Mimacheik may also apply by steel wool.
[33] Ketzos Hashulchan 146 footnote 33; Minchas Yitzchak 3:49; Beir Moshe 1:34
The Ketzos Hashulchan ibid prohibits it due to both reasons. The Minchas Yitzchak states that steel wool is forbidden being that it contains a Rabbinical squeezing prohibition similar to hair. Beir Moshe 1:34 states that although doing so does not involve a squeezing prohibition [certainly not by the thick stranded steel wool] it is perhaps forbidden due to Uvdin Dechol. Nevertheless he does not rule this way conclusively and hence leaves room for it being allowed.
[34] SSH"K 12:10; Cheishev Haeifod 2:149 [however see below that he rules the sponge must be designated.]
Beir Moshe ibid in previous footnote rules that possibly no prohibition of squeezing is involved even by closely netted sponges of synthetic or metal materials, although it may be forbidden by all sponges due to Uvdin Dechol. Practically he concludes that by closely knitted sponges it is forbidden, while by others it is unclear due to Uvdin Dechol. SSH"K argues that there is no precedence to claim that there is an issue of Uvdin Dechol involved.
[35] According to this opinion if the metal sponge visibly has its strands distanced from each other then it is permitted to be used. [Piskeiy Teshuvos 323:4]
[36] Due to the Mimacheik prohibition, as ruled similarly regarding silver in 323:11 [SSH"K ibid] However it is clear from Beir Moshe:Ketzos Hashulchan ibid that he does not hold of this. Nevertheless, the Beir Moshe concludes not to use the steel wool on plates which one will have to scrub them for a while.
[37] Beir Moshe ibid
[38] Even with steel wool [so long as one does not rub very thoroughly], and even if the strands are close together. [ibid]
[39] Cheishev Haeifod 2:149; Minchas Yitzchak 3:50 regarding a sponge with a handle.

D. Plugging the hole of a barrel with a pipe and wet cloth on Shabbos:[40]

A drain pipe which one inserts into a hole in the wall of a barrel from which the wine is removed from, and [before doing so] one wraps around the drain pipe a piece of cloth or thin residue of flax[41] with which he [uses to fully] plug up the hole in the barrel[42], it is forbidden to plug [the hole of the barrel with this pipe] on Shabbos even if the barrel contains red wine or other [colored] liquids which do not whiten as through plugging it one squeezes out the liquid absorbed in the cloth, and this is an inevitable occurrence. Now although the squeezed liquid is going to waste nevertheless it is Rabbinically forbidden as explained above [in Halacha A].[43]

Other Opinions: [However] there are opinions[44] who say that so long as the liquid is going to waste then there is only a Rabbinical prohibition involved if one has intention to squeeze it, however so long as he does not intend to [squeeze] it, even if this is an inevitable occurrence, it is permitted. [If however the liquid does not go to waste, such as one places a vessel under it, then it is Bibclailly forbidden even according to this opinion.[45]]

Their reasoning is: because the squeezing [of this cloth] gives one no satisfaction being that one has no benefit from it, and it was only made forbidden to insert Mochin into the opening of the bottle even though he has no intent to squeeze it because the liquid that is being squeezed out from the Mochin enters into the bottle and one benefits from this squeezing. However, the liquids that are squeezed from the cloth that surrounds the pipe go to waste if there is no vessel under them, and there is thus nothing to benefit from it for him.

The Main Halachic Opinion:[46] The main Halachic opinion is like the former opinion, as [we ruled above in Halacha B that] a sponge that does not have a handle may not be used to clean with even though he has no intention to squeeze [liquid out] and the liquid which is squeezed from the sponge goes to waste.

The Custom:[47] Nevertheless, [despite the above reasoning] the world is accustomed to allowing plugging up with [a pipe that has] cloth [surrounding it] on Shabbos.

The justification of the custom:[48] There are those opinions which have learned justification for [this custom] as since the pipe has a long extension past the cloth and no hand touches the cloth [in the process of inserting and removing the pipe] then even though there is liquid being squeezed out of the cloth it is [nevertheless] permitted [to insert/remove] the pipe just like is the ruling by a sponge which has a handle according to the opinion [there] which says that even if liquid is squeezed out from it, it is allowed [to be used] as it is similar to emptying a flask of its water. According to this reasoning even if there is a vessel under the pipe which intakes the liquid squeezed from the cloth it is permitted [to be inserted/removed].

The Final Ruling:[49] Due to there being many opinions which argue on the above justification therefore one should accustom [those which allow inserting and removing the pipe] that there should not be a vessel under the pipe. [This should be done] in order so the squeezed liquid go to waste, and thus [have one] rely upon the [leniency mentioned by] the second opinion that was explained [above]. Now although this opinion is not the main Halachic opinion, [nevertheless it is allowed to rely on them] as there are opinions[50] which entirely permit to even intentionally squeeze [liquid out from a cloth] so long as the liquid goes to waste. As well [they should be careful that] the pipe extend out from the cloth in order to

[40] Admur 320:24; Michaber 320:18; Rav in Shabbos 111a
[41] When flax is pressed there are small pieces of residue which fall from it.
[42] Meaning in order so no liquid leak out from the hole where the pipe has been inserted one wraps cloth around the area of the pipe being inserted thus closing up any possibility of leakage.
[43] Admur ibid; 2nd opinion in Michaber ibid; Riy; Mordechai; Tosafus 103a; Rosh 12:1
[44] Aruch Erech Sever, brought in Tosafus 103a; 1st opinion in Michaber
[45] M"B 320:52
[46] Admur ibid; implication of Michaber ibid
Opinion of Michaber by Pesik Resihei of Derabana: From this Halacha we see the Michaber rules there is a prohibition of Pesik Resihei by a Rabbinical prohibition even if Lo Nicha Lei. Vetzrauch Iyun as in 314:1 the Michaber rules by a Rabbinical case that one may do a Pesik Resihei. Veztaruch Iyun Gadol!
[47] Admur ibid; Michaber ibid
[48] Admur ibid; Michaber ibid; Kol Bo 31
[49] Admur ibid; Michaber ibid
[50] Rashba brought in Maggid Mishneh; Rivash in opinion of Rabbeinu Tam

also join this leniency [mentioned in the justification].

The above may be done even by a barrel of white wine:[51] (There is no need to worry of the prohibition of whitening [in inserting/removing the pipe with the] flax residue and pieces of cloth which surrounds the pipe even if it is white wine which whitens, because [these cloths] are meant to get wet [and dirty] and one does not care to whiten it at all as was written in chapter 319 [Halacha 13] regarding a strainer).

E. Using towel to dry the inside of cup:[52]
It is forbidden to dry a wet cup with a cloth [or tissue or napkin[53]] on Shabbos.[54] This applies whether the cup is wet due to water, wine or other beverages.[55] This prohibition applies even against using a cloth which one is not particular against getting wet [such as a towel which is designated for drying]. [This prohibition applies by all cups, whether wide or narrow; whether a Kiddush cup, coffee cup or shot glass.[56] It also applies irrelevant of how wet the cup is.[57] However some Poskim[58] learn it only applies to narrow cups, such as a shot glass. Likewise, some Poskim[59] rule one may be lenient to dry the cup if one shakes the water out of the cup beforehand and it hence only contains a few drops. Some Poskim[60] even allow drying with a cloth that is not designated for drying. Practically, those that are lenient to dry wide cups [such as a Kiddush cup and the like] should shake the water out beforehand.[61]]

---

[51] Admur ibid parentheses in original

Other opinions: Some Poskim rule that the entire case here is referring to a barrel of red wine, as by water or white wine there is a prohibition of Milabein and all Poskim would agree that there is a Biblical prohibition even if the liquid is going to waste and one uses a handle to squeeze it. [M"B 320:55; Biur Halacha 320:18 "Yeish Mi Shematir"]

Is there a prohibition of Milabein involved in causing a Shemtah to squeeze its water while using it for cleaning? According to Admur it seems there is no prohibition while according to the M"B ibid it seems there is a prohibition.

[52] Admur 302:12; Michaber 302:12; Tashbatz 28; Mahram 511; Rabbeinu Yerucham 12:13

[53] See Az Nidbaru 7:9; However according to the Igros Moshe 2:70 this would be allowed

[54] The reason: As since the cup is narrow, it is not possible to avoid the cloth from squeezing out some of the water which it absorbed while drying it, and it is thus Rabbinically forbidden [due to the squeezing/Mifarek prohibition] even by liquids that do not contain a laundering prohibition. [Admur ibid; M"A 302:27 in his second answer; M"B 302:60]

Other opinions: Some Poskim rule the reason for this prohibition is due to the laundering prohibition, and hence it is only prohibited by water or white wine, and only when using a cloth that is not designated for drying. [1st answer in M"A ibid; M"B 320:58] Some Poskim rule the custom is to be lenient to allow drying cups. [Ridbaz 1:213, brought in Birkeiy Yosef 302:89; M"B 302:59; See Biur Halacha "Mishum" that this applies even by narrow cups]

[55] Meaning that the prohibition applies even if the cup has a liquid to which the laundering prohibition is unapplicable. [ibid]

[56] Implication of Admur ibid and Michaber and M"A ibid which do not differentiate between the size of the cup; See Minchas Shabbos 80:129 and Misgeres Hashulchan 80:74 that negate limiting the prohibition to cups with narrow tops being the Poskim above did not differentiate in this; See Az Nidbaru 3:20 that tea and coffee cups should also be considered narrow cups although the custom is to be lenient; See Toras Hamelachos 13 Melaben

The reason: Seemingly the reason for this is because all cups are considered narrow enough to cause squeezing when drying its ends at the bottom. However, a bowl or pot is wide enough to be dried without causing any squeezing.

[57] Implication of Admur ibid and Michaber ibid which do not differentiate between the wetness of the cup; Biur Halacha "Mishum" only allows to be lenient in a time of need if one shakes out the water

[58] SSH"K 12:22 footnote 61 [new]; See Kitzur SHU"A 80:34 "or other vessels that have a narrow opening"

[59] Or Letziyon 2:24-7; Az Nidbaru ibid that those that are lenient to dry coffee cups and the like should first shake out the water; Biur Halacha ibid is lenient to allow drying even a narrow cup in a time of need if one first shakes out the water.

[60] See M"A 302:27; M"B 302:59 which implies according to the Radbaz one may use even a non-designated cloth as there will not be inevitable squeezing, and the laundering prohibition does not apply when drying an item. Admur records a dispute in this matter in 302:21 and 319:23 and concludes that a G-d fearing Jew is to be stringent.

[61] Az Nidbaru ibid

May one dry his Kiddush cup after rinsing it prior to Kiddush?
Based on the above, one is not to dry his Kiddush cup after rinsing it. Nevertheless, those which are lenient to shake out the water from Kiddush cup and then dry it have upon whom to rely, as stated above.[62]

Drying dishes:
One may dry dishes on Shabbos as normal.[63] If the towel has become wet to the point of Tofeiach Al Menas Lehatfiach then it may no longer be used to dry.[64]

F. Using a wet towel on Shabbos and Yom Kippur:[65]
From the letter of the law, it is permitted to soak a cloth in water on Erev Yom Kippur and remove it from the water before Yom Kippur, and let it dry out until it no longer contains [enough water] to get another item wet enough to get something else wet, and he may then wipe his face, hands, and legs with it in order to cool off. Even though he is not doing so in order to remove dirt but rather to receive pleasure, nevertheless it is permitted from the letter of the law [to do so], being that [the towel] is dry from the water, as is explained in chapter 554 regarding Tishe Beav. Nevertheless, on Yom Kippur one is to be stringent being that if one were to clean himself with a cloth that was not dried from its water, it would contain a Biblical prohibition due to squeezing. Therefore, one is to be stringent even by a [cloth which was] dry from the water which was on it from before Yom Kippur, due to a decree that perhaps it will not dry well and one will clean with it and come to squeeze.
May one use a towel on Shabbos if it was wet before Shabbos? Yes, as one would never transgress a Biblical prohibition even if he came to squeeze it.

4. Squeezing hair:
See the laws of bathing!

Summary:
A. Doing an action which will inevitably cause liquid to squeeze out, if one has no intent to do so:[66]
Is forbidden to be done even if the liquid is going to waste. However, the world is accustomed to be lenient to allow this to be done if a) the liquid is going to waste, and b) the pressing of the liquid is being done through a handle and not through the direct pressing of the cloth.

B. Using a sponge to clean a liquid:
<u>Without a handle:</u>[67] Is forbidden for any liquid because one will come to inevitably squeeze.
<u>With a handle:</u> Is permitted because a) the liquid will not definitely be squeezed out, or will definitely be squeezed[68] but b) the liquid is going to waste and is being squeezed through the handle[69]. [Thus

---

[62] <u>The Rebbe's custom:</u> Rabbi Groner related to me that the Rebbe dried his Kiddush cup by the weekly farbrengen only after the cup had been rinsed and already dried. The reason the Rebbe preceded to dry the already dried cup is based on that the Rebbe desired to personally clean his cup, and one can use a napkin in place of water. [See Kaf Hachaim 183:5]
[63] See M"B 302:59
[64] See Admur 613:16
[65] Admur 613:16; Rama 613:9
[66] Admur 320:24
[67] Admur 320:23
[68] Admur 320:23
[69] Admur 320:24

regarding cleaning a spill, if one has a sponge or cloth[70] that is attached to a handle then one may hold it by the handle and gently[71] clean the spill.[72] If however even when using the handle one sees that it causes inevitable squeezing from the cloth then one is not to use it.[73]]

C. Inserting a wet cloth into the opening of a bottle:[74]

Is forbidden to be inserted even lightly no matter what kind of cloth it is or from what it is wet from, being that if one were to insert it strongly it would inevitably squeeze liquid into the bottle.

Q&A

Does the squeezing prohibition apply to a napkin or tissue?
Yes.[75] However some Poskim[76] rule it does not apply.[77]

May one clean a spill using napkins or tissues?[78]
It is permitted to place the tissue or napkin onto the spill.[79] However one may not rub the napkin or tissue around the spill. However, some Poskim[80] allow doing so.[81] Practically one is not to be lenient.[82]

May one clean a dry table/counter using a wet cloth?[83]
No, as one will inevitably cause water to squeeze out. This applies even if the cloth is only slightly wet.

---

[70] This refers to a cloth that does not involve a laundering prohibition in wetting it as explained above.

[71] This is based on that which is explained in the next footnote

[72] Admur 320:23; SSH"K 12 footnote 37

The dispute behind the reason that it is allowed to use a sponge with a handle: The reason this is allowed is because when using a handle to clean with nothing squeezes out from the sponge in the process. [However] there is an opinion which says that even if [the sponge] has a handle it is impossible to clean with the sponge without squeezing it and nevertheless it is permitted as since the squeezing is being done through the [pressing of] the handle it is [therefore] not [Halachically] considered squeezing and is rather like emptying water from a flask which does not contain [the] "detaching" [prohibition]. However, when it does not have a handle in which case it gets squeezed in the area that he holds it with his hand, then it is forbidden. [ibid]

The practical ramification between these two reasons is in a case that liquid will certainly be squeezed from the sponge. Thus, whether one may apply strength when using a sponge with a handle to clean the liquid, and inevitably cause the liquid to spill, is subject to the above dispute.

Practically: It is implied that Admur rules mainly like the first opinion mentioned there that using a handle is only allowed due to it not being an inevitable occurrence. If, however, one sees the squeezing is inevitable, then it once again becomes prohibited. [So is evident from 320:24 that we do not hold of the 2nd opinion above as the final Halacha, as Admur does not simply allow inserting a barrel pipe with a cloth due to this reason, but adds that one must also make sure the liquid goes to waste. In the words of Admur 320:24: "As many argue on their words". Vetzaruch Iyun if these words are going on the opinion of Raavad that even if it squeezes out is allowed, or if it's going on opinion of the Melamdim Zechus. Furthermore, Tzaruch Iyun on if one can truly derive anything from the Barza case to a regular sponge case, as seemingly Admur learns that a Barza does not have the same status as a handle of the sponge and that's why the Heter is not so clear, however by an actual handle of a sponge perhaps Admur would be lenient even if the liquid does not go to waste, and certainly if it does. Vetzaruch Iyun. I later however found in Shabbos Kehalacha Vol. 3 p. 211-212 a similar conclusion that it is evident from Admur that one may only use a sponge with a handle if it does not inevitably cause squeezing. He deduces this also from Ketzos Hashulchan [133-end] that a toothbrush, despite it having a handle, is forbidden to be used due to it causing inevitable squeezing.

[73] Shabbos Kehalacha ibid; Based on what was explained in the previous footnote: If the liquid will not be going to waste then certainly one may not do so. ["As many argue on the lenient opinion"-320:24] If the liquid is going to waste, then it seems from Michaber/Admur that initially even so one should not do so although those which are lenient have upon what to rely. [As Admur/Michaber rule by the Barza case that it should not be done and it is only that we are Melameid Zechus on those that do. However, Tzaruch Iyun on if one can truly derive anything from the Barza case to a regular sponge case, as seemingly Admur learns that a Barza does not have the same status as a handle of the sponge and that's why the Heter is not so clear, however by an actual handle of a sponge perhaps Admur would be lenient even if the liquid does not go to waste, and certainly if it does. Vetzaruch Iyun.] See M"B 320:55; SSH"K 12 footnote 37; Minchas Yitzchak 3:50

[74] Admur 320:22

[75] See Az Nidbaru 7:9 which argues on many points of the leniency of the Igros Moshe.

[76] Igros Moshe 2:70

[77] As he claims there is no concept of Sechita [squeezing] by tissue and paper, as it is not truly an absorbent material.

[78] Piskeiy Teshuvos 302:10

[79] As they are designated for this purpose

[80] Igros Moshe 2:70

[81] As he claims there is no concept of Sechita [squeezing] by tissue and paper, as it is not truly an absorbent material.

[82] See Az Nidbaru 7:9 which argues on many points of the leniency of the Igros Moshe.

[83] SSH"K 12:40

May one clean a wet counter or table [that does not contain an absorbent tablecloth] using a dry cloth?[84]
No. Only synthetic material may be used as using an absorbent material to press against the counter/table will inevitably cause liquid to squeeze out which is forbidden.

May one soak up a spill on Shabbos by placing on it a cloth napkin/tissue/rag?[85]
Any cloth [even if dirty] which is designated for cleaning spills [such as a paper napkin, tissue, or rag] may be placed over a spill of any liquid including water, and have it absorb the liquid on its own. However, one may not rub the cloth around the spill in a way that will apply pressure to the cloth and cause it to squeeze out some of its absorbed liquid. It may only be moved around the spill in a gentle manner. A cloth which is not designated for cleaning spills [such as a cloth napkin, or undershirt and the like] may only be used to clean spills of colored liquids [which do not contain a dyeing prohibition]. However, to cover spills of clear or white liquids, such as water, is forbidden.[86] In all the above scenarios one must beware to avoid squeezing liquid from the cloth in the process of cleaning the spill, and certainly may not squeeze it afterwards. As well it is forbidden to clean the spill for a purpose of using the absorbed liquid after Shabbos.

May one move a wet rag or napkin that was used to clean a spill?
If there is a dry area left on the cloth it is permitted to be lifted and moved from that area.[87] If, however, the entire cloth is soaking wet, it is forbidden to move it as doing so will inevitably cause liquid to squeeze out.[88] Seemingly, in such a case it is permitted to move the cloth through placing a knife under it and lifting it up as it is not certain that this will cause squeezing. According to some Poskim[89] one may always move a wet tissue or napkin and there is no need to suspect for the squeezing prohibition.

May one tie his shoes if the laces are wet, as occurs often in a Mikveh?[90]
If the top of the lace is covered with plastic, or the top area is not wet, then it is permitted to be tied from that area.

May one walk with wet shoes and socks if doing so will cause water to squeeze out?[91]
Yes.[92] One may even initially walk in them even though water gets squeezed in the process. Nevertheless, some Tzaddikim[93] were stringent in this matter, as a Midas Chassidus.

---

[84] SSH"K 12:40
[85] Admur 319:13; 320:21; SSH"K 12:38
[86] Admur 302:20; 319:13; 320:21
The reason: If the cloth is not designated for this purpose of cleaning spills it is forbidden to soak it in clear liquids due to the laundering prohibition. As if one intends to soak it in the liquid in order to whiten the cloth he would be liable for laundering. Likewise, if one would proceed to squeeze the liquid out from the cloth he would be liable for laundering. Hence it is forbidden to use such cloths to clean clear liquid spills. However, if the cloth is designated for this purpose then there is no reason to suspect one may place it on the spill for laundering purposes or come to squeeze the liquid out, as this is the entire purpose of the cloth. [319:13; 320:21]
[87] As if there is an area that is not wet it is similar to a sponge with a handle which is allowed to be used being that no water will squeeze out from the area he is holding on to. [320:23] So is also proven from Admur 301:59 [Rama 301:46; M"B 301:172] that it is permitted to lift wet clothing if there is no suspicion one will come to squeeze. In our case there is no suspicion one will come to squeeze the rag or tissue being they are designated for this purpose of cleaning. [see 301:59]
[88] This is similar to a sponge that does not have a handle which is forbidden to even lift due to inevitably causing squeezing. [320:22] One must thus establish the case in Admur 301:59 to be discussing even if there is a dry area of the cloth. However, if the entire cloth is soaked without any area, then it is forbidden to be lifted with one's fingers due to the squeezing prohibition.
[89] Igros Moshe 2:70
[90] See Piskeiy Teshuvos 302 footnote 218; Orchos Shabbos 1 13:15; Maor Hashabbos 4 in end in letter of Rav Fisher
[91] Ashel Avraham Butchach 614:4; Minchas Shabbos 80:131; and Kuntrus Achron 7; Piskeiy Teshuvos 301:56 footnote 391; So is proven from Setimas HaPoskim who allow entering a river on Yom Kippur to visit one's Rebbe. See???
[92] The reason: As a) The custom is to be lenient to allow squeezing with an item [i.e. one's shoes] when one does not intend to squeeze. B) Even according to the stringent opinion, this is considered an irregular way of squeezing and is hence more lenient. [Poskim ibid]
[93] See Tiferes Beis David p. 35 in name of Shinover Rav; Orchos Rabbeinu 1:133

May one step on a wet rag, or other wet item, if stepping on it will make it squeeze out water?[94]
It is best to avoid stepping on it, if it is possible to circumvent the wet rag. However, from the letter of the law, one may be lenient to step on it while walking even if water gets squeezed out in the process.[95] One may certainly do so if it is not possible to walkaround it. One may never step on it specifically for the sake of squeezing.

May one wipe the liquid off a wet tablecloth using a knife and the like?[96]
One may only do so lightly, without pressing against the cloth so as not to cause liquid to squeeze out of it.

May one use baby wipes on Shabbos?
Some Poskim[97] prohibit them from being used due to a suspicion of squeezing. However other Poskim[98] permit using baby wipes. Practically, according to Admur if the baby wipes are usually wet to the point of Tofeiach Al Menas Lehatfiach, they may not be used even if dry. If however they are usually less wet than Tofeiach Al Menas Lehatfiach then they may be used even if they are not completely dry.[99]
Baby wipe was left out or left open and dried:
Scented baby wipes: Some Poskim[100] rule that good scents may be used to remove bad smells, even according to those [such as Admur] that hold of a prohibition on placing a scent on one's skin.

---

[94] Lehoros Nasan 1:16; Divrei Shalom 4:226; Rivivos Efraim 3:236; See Piskeiy Teshuvos 301 footnote 391

[95] The reason: As a) The custom is to be lenient to allow squeezing with an item [i.e. one's shoes] when one does not intend to squeeze. B) Even according to the stringent opinion, this is considered an irregular way of squeezing and is hence more lenient. [See Poskim ibid regarding wet socks]

[96] M"B 320:55; Biur Halacha 320:18 "Yeish Lehanhigam"; SSH"K 12:37; See Taz 320:12 that allows using a knife by other liquids to squeeze out the liquid from the cloth. Admur completely omits this case.

[97] Minchas Yitzchak 10:25, in name of also other Rabbanim.

[98] SSH"K 14:33 in name of Rav SZ"A, Rav Wozner allows it for babies only. The Piskeiy Teshuvos [327:1] and SSH"K learns that the foundation for the allowance is from the M"B/Magen Avraham in 613:9 which allow one to dry his legs/hands :feet from before Shabbos and then use it on Shabbos to clean his eyes. However, Tzaruch Iyun on this as baby wipes may have a lot more water absorbed in them than the above-mentioned towel used to dry only ones hands/feet and face.

[99] Based on Rama 613:9 and Admur 613:16 which rule one may not place a clothe that was wet before Shabbos on one's body even if it is now dry, due to worry of squeezing. Admur ibid adds that a) From the letter of the law if the cloth is not wet to the point of Tofeiach Al Menas Lehatfiach then it does not have a Sechita prohibition and b) The worry is only in a case that the squeezed liquid is not going to waist, and hence it is a Biblical Sechita prohibition. To note that Admur here omits the ruling of the Magen Avraham [brought in previous footnote, which serves as the source for the ruling of the lenient opinions] that if one wiped his hands/legs/face with a towel before Shabbos one may use them for his eyes on Shabbos. Seemingly Admur omitted this ruling being it is already included in his mentioned rule that if it contains enough water before Shabbos to be "Tofeaich Al Minas Lehatfiach" then it may not be used, and if it does not then it may. From all the above we learn: a) When you clean yourself with a damp cloth it automatically causes squeezing. b) One may not use a cloth that was wet before Shabbos even if it is now dry, if one's purpose is to benefit from the squeezed liquid. C) One may clean himself with an item that is damp, but not Tofeiach Al Menas Lehatfiach, if one has no benefit from the squeezed liquid, or it was never this wet before Shabbos. From all this we can deduce that by baby wipes the main issue is the amount of normal wetness that it contains. If it is normally wet Tofeiach Al Menas Lehatfiach, then it may not be used even when dry, just as is the law here in 613:16 and if it is not normally this wet then it may be used.

[100] Beir Moshe 1:34 [based on Sheilas Yaavetz] rules that good smells may always be applied in order to remove bad odors, and so rules Piskeiy Teshuvah [327:1, 328:26]. SSH"K [ibid] also rules leniently in this, although to note that they hold [unlike Admur] there is never a prohibition to place good smells on one's skin.

THE LAWS OF NOLAD

Melting and freezing snow, ice, gravy, soap, and fat

Based on Shulchan Aruch Chapter 320

TRANSLATION-SHULCHAN ARUCH CHAPTER 320 HALACHAS 16-20

Melting snow and ice

Halacha 16

Crushing ice with ones hands: Snow and hail and all matters of the like are forbidden to crush with ones hands, meaning to break them into little pieces, in order so they dissolve into water.

The reason for this is: because doing so is similar to a [forbidden] action [as it appears like] he is creating these waters.

Placing ice into a glass of liquid: Nevertheless, one may place it into a glass of wine or water during the summer in order to cool down [the drink] into which [the ice] melts on its own, and one need not worry [that doing so transgresses any prohibition.

Placing the ice near a source of heat: Likewise, it is permitted to place them in the sun or opposite a bonfire in an area where it cannot become hot to the point of Yad Soledes, and they dissolve there on their own.

Other Opinions: [However] there are opinions which say that [the Sages] only permitted to place [the ice] into a cup [of liquid] being that the dissolved water [from the ice] is not recognizable on its own and is rather mixed into the wine or water that is in the cup. However, when the dissolved liquid is recognizable on its own then it is forbidden [to drink this water] even if it already melted, due to the reason explained in chapter 318 [Halacha 25][1].

The Final Ruling: It was already explained there [in chapter 318 Halacha 27] that the main Halachic opinion is like the first opinion [here] although that the custom is to initially be stringent [to not melt the ice by placing it near a source of heat, unless it is a time of need].

Halacha 17
Breaking a piece off from the ice:
It was only forbidden [to crush the ice] when one's intention to crush it is so that it melts. However, it is permitted to break a piece off from it even if through doing so a small amount of water will flow from it.

The reason for this is: because this [melting] is only a small amount and is not given any consideration, as well as that one does not have intention [to melt it] and it is not considered an inevitable occurrence and furthermore [because] the [melted water] will be going to waste.

The reason for why we do not decree against doing so: ([Since the melted ice is going to waste], it is thus not at all similar to squeezing fruits designated to be juiced in which the squeezed juices are not going to waste, and therefore there is no reason to decree [against breaking a piece of ice] because [one may come to then squeeze fruits for their juice]).

Halacha 18
Breaking ice in order to get to the water which is underneath it
By a vessel: It is allowed to break ice [which is covering the water of a vessel] in order to draw water from underneath it as he is not creating water by doing so.

The reason that there is no destroying prohibition involved in this: [As well] there is no [destroying] prohibition involved at all in breaking the ice as anything that is detached [from the ground] which is not a vessel there is no prohibition at all involved in breaking and detaching it, as explained in chapter 314 [Halacha 12].

By a river: However, by a river or a well since the ice is attached to the ground it is forbidden to break it.

---

[1] There it is explained that the flow of fat is similar to the flow of juice from olives on Shabbos which is forbidden.

Halacha 19
Dissolving a material into water not for purposes of drinking it:

Salt: One must beware from rubbing one's hands with salt being that the salt dissolves on ones hands.

Washing with salt water: However, it is permitted to place water onto salt and wash ones hands with it even though that the salt dissolves there on its own, as long as one does not rub his hands.

Washing with icy water: [Although] in the winter one needs [to try] to not wash his hands at all with water that has snow or ice, as [congealed water] is more easily dissolved then is salt. If one does wash his hands with them he must beware to not press it against his hands in order so he not actively dissolve the ice.

Other Opinions: [However] other opinions say that so long as the melted [substance] is not individually recognizable and rather mixes into another substance, then even if one crushes it with one's hands it is permitted.

Therefore, it is permitted to wash ones hands and rub them with water that contains snow and ice or salt even though he crushes and dissolves them with his hands, being that they mix into the water that is on his hands. Similarly, it is permitted to even to crush with ones hands pieces of ice and snow in order so it melt and flow into a cup of wine or water.

Their reasoning is: because [in their view] the reason behind the prohibition to crush with one hands [pieces of snow and ice] is due to a decree that one may come to squeeze fruits which are designated to be juiced, being that snow and ice are designated [also] for their liquids, [thus here] since they are being mixed into other liquids [the Sages] did not make a decree as doing so is not similar to squeezing fruits designated to be juiced in which the juice squeezed is recognizable on its own.

The Final Ruling: One is to be stringent like the former opinion.

Halacha 20

Not to urinate on snow: Due to the above [stringency] there is an opinion which [says that one should] beware from urinating into snow, as a result of the urine the snow melts and it is like one is melting it with his hands which is forbidden according to the first opinion despite that the melted [snow] is not individually recognizable (and as well is going to waste).

Stepping on snow: However, it is permitted to step on snow with ones feet being that it is possible that doing so will not melt and dissolve it, and thus even if it does [end up] melting and dissolving [since] it is done unintentionally it is [therefore] permitted being that it is not an inevitable occurrence.

Other Opinions: [However] there is an opinion which says that even if one's shoes are wet in which case it will for certain melt the snow [that he steps on] [nevertheless] it is permitted.

Likewise, [this opinion says that] it is permitted to urinate onto snow.

Their reasoning is: because this is something which is not possible to avoid doing during the winter when the entire earth is filled with snow and therefore the Sages did not make any decree against doing so.

The Final Ruling: (It is proper to be stringent in an instance that one can easily avoid doing so.)

❖ **For the Translation of Halachas 21-25 please refer back to the previous section "The Laws of Squeezing"**

❖ **For the Translation of Halachas 26-28 please refer to the next section "The Laws of Dyeing"**

COMPILATION OF HALACHAS SUMMARIES AND Q&A

The Laws Of Crushing & Melting Ice

The Term Nolad:

The term Nolad generally refers to the Mukztah prohibition associated with items recreated on Shabbos. This term however is also used to refer to the prohibition against melting foods on Shabbos.[1] In Admur, this prohibition is called Molid.[2] The use of the term Nolad throughout this section refers to the prohibition of melting foods and not to the Muktzah prohibition.

1. Crushing and breaking ice/snow with one's body:

A. Crushing a piece of snow or ice with one's hands:[3]

Snow and hail and all matters of the like are forbidden to crush with one's hands, meaning to break them into little pieces, in order so they dissolve into water.

The reason for this is:[4] because doing so is similar to a [forbidden] action [as it appears like] he is creating these waters. [In 318/25 Admur similarly states: "because [through doing so] one is creating [a new substance] on Shabbos which is similar to a [Biblically] forbidden action being that he is creating this water." This prohibition is formally known as Molid.[5] Others[6] however learn that the prohibition is due to the prohibition of Nolad, which is Muktzah. Others[7] however rule the reason behind this prohibition is due to a decree that one may come to squeeze fruits which are designated to be juiced, being that snow and ice are designated [also] for their liquids.]

Example:

- If one froze a bottle of water or juice, it is forbidden to smash the bottle in order to break the ice and drink the liquid.

---

[1] See Rama 326:10 "Due to Nolad"; Sefer Haterumah 235 "Nolad"

[2] See Admur 318:25 and 326:10; Rashi Shabbos 51b

[3] 320:16; Michaber 320:9; Shabbos 51b

[4] Admur ibid and 318:25 "He is Molid"; Taz 320:7; Rashi Gemara ibid "The reason is because he is Molid Beshabbos"; Sefer Hateruma 234-235 "Because of Nolad" as understood by Rosh 4:13; brought in M"B 320:33

The ruling of the Sefer Hateruma: Some Rishonim learn the Sefer Hateruma to be agreeing with the reason of Rashi, and that the reason is because of Molid, and the word Nolad in the Sefer Hateruma means Molid. [Rosh 4:13] Others however understand the Sefer Hateruma to be giving an alternative reason behind the prohibition, and that Nolad and Molid are two different concepts, and that Nolad refers to the Muktzah prohibition. [Ramban 51b; Rashba 51b; brought in Shaar Hatziyon 320:35; M"B 318:105] It is implied from Admur 318:25 like the Rosh, that he holds the Sefer Haterumos term Nolad refers to Molid Davar Chadash.

[5] Rashi ibid; Admur 318:25

[6] Sefer Hateruma ibid as understood by Ramban 51b and Rashba 51b; brought in M"B 320:33 and 318:105; See Rama 326:10

Opinion of Admur in Sefer Hateruma: Admur does not mention the term Nolad anywhere in the Halachos dealing with this prohibition. Furthermore, when explaining the opinion of the Sefer Hateruma in 318:25 regarding the prohibition to place fat near the sun he writes the reason is due to Molid. Hence, we clearly see that Admur interprets Nolad as Molid and not as Muktzah.

[7] Opinion in Admur 320:19 [brought in Halacha 1B], as well as 326:10 [brought in Halacha 4]; M"A 320:13; Ramban 51b; Rashba 51b; Implication of Rambam Shabbos 21:12 brought in Maggid Mishneh; brought in M"B 320:33; Vetzaruch Iyun as to why this reason was omitted here, in 320:16, which is the Halacha dealing with the reason behind the prohibition. Perhaps this is because in truth Admur holds that the main reason behind the prohibition is "Nolad" and as he himself rules in both Halachas mentioned above that one is to be stringent like the opinion which holds of the "Nolad" reason. Regarding why Admur in 318:25 mentions this reason to explain why the melted substance is forbidden, see below Halacha 4 in the footnotes.

May one Bedieved benefit from the liquid if he broke the ice?
If he melted it BeMeizid then it is forbidden for all on Shabbos to benefit from it, and permitted for all immediately after Shabbos.[8] If he did so BeShogeg then is dependent on the dispute in ice that melted near sun. Now although there we rule that Bedieved one may be lenient, perhaps in a case of transgression we are stringent. Vetzaruch Iyun.

May one melt ice or other foods within the process of eating?
Yes.[9] There is thus no Shabbos prohibition involved in eating ices or ice cubes, or ice cream on Shabbos even if doing so will cause it to melt.

B. Washing with icy or salty water/Crushing ice in a way that it melts directly into water:[10]

Washing with salt water: One must beware from rubbing one's hands with salt being that the salt dissolves on ones hands.[11] However it is permitted to place water onto salt and wash ones hands with it even though that the salt dissolves there on its own, as long as one does not rub his hands.[12]

Washing with icy water:[13] In the winter one needs [to try] to not wash his hands at all with water that has snow or ice [even if one will not rub his hands[14]], as [congealed water] is more easily dissolved then is salt. If one does wash his hands with them[15] he must beware to not press it against his hands in order so he not actively dissolve the ice.

Other Opinions:[16] [However] other opinions say that so long as the melted [substance] is not individually recognizable and rather mixes into another substance, then even if one crushes it with one's hands it is permitted. Therefore, it is permitted to wash ones hands and rub them with water that contains snow and ice or salt even though he crushes and dissolves them with his hands, being that they mix into the water that is on his hands. Similarly, it is permitted to even to crush with ones hands pieces of ice and snow in order so it melt and flow into a cup of wine or water.

Their reasoning is:[17] because [in their view] the reason behind the prohibition to crush with one hands [pieces of snow and ice] is due to a decree that one may come to squeeze fruits which are designated to be juiced, being that snow and ice are designated [also] for their liquids, [thus here] since they are being mixed into other liquids [the Sages] did not make a decree as doing so is not similar to squeezing fruits designated to be juiced in which the juice squeezed is recognizable on its own.

The Final Ruling:[18] One is to be stringent like the former opinion.

---

[8] Admur 339:7; Mishneh Terumos 2:3

[9] Setimas Haposkim; We have never heard of such a prohibition, or even stringency, not to eat foods that melt in the mouth. This is because it is Derech Achila and is thus not a Melacha. So is also inferred from the Poskim which write only that one may not turn water into ice using one's **hands**, hence implying that the decree only applies when done with one's body, not within the process of eating. See also 320:2 that it is disputed if one may enter the grape into his mouth and suck and the main opinion rules it is permitted, although one who is stringent is blessed. Vetzaruch Iyun as for the reason why here no such stringency applies. Perhaps however eating a meltable food is the only way of eating and is hence the Derech Achila whole a grape can be eaten and not sucked, and hence when one sucks it can be more compared to a Melacha. Vetzaruch Iyun!

[10] Admur 320:19; Michaber 320:12; Rosh

[11] Admur ibid; Michaber 320:12; Sefer Hateruma 235

[12] Admur ibid; Taz 320:9; M"B 320:38

[13] Admur ibid; Michaber 320:11; Rosh and Tosafus 51b

[14] So is evident from Admur ibid, as washing with salt water is only permitted if one does not rub his hands and here Admur is saying we are more stringent by icy water and do not wash with it at all.

[15] As the lenient opinions [brought next] allow

[16] 2nd opinion in Admur ibid; M"A 320:13 and 16; M"B 320:34; Tosefta; Ramban ibid; Rashba ibid; Ran; Maggid Mishneh 21:13

[17] Rishonim ibid

[18] Admur ibid; Michaber ibid; Biur Halacha 320:11 "Yizaher"; Shaar Hatziyon 318:146 "It is proper to initially be stringent"; So is evident also from Michaber 320:13-14 and the fact the Poskim don't argue on the ruling on the basis that it melts into liquid. [Shaar Hatziyon ibid; See Ketzos Hashulchan 126 footnote 2 and 14]; Rav Poalim 3:14

Breaking/crushing ice/snow with ones hand:
To melt it: Is forbidden to break ice into small pieces in order so that it melt[19], even inside of liquid.[20]

Q&A
May one crush a piece of ice that is in ones cup of water or juice?[21]
No, as explained in Halacha 1B.

May one melt ice if the resultant water will anyways go to waste, such as to throw ice cubes in ones sink?
See Halacha 4 Q&A there!

May one pour water onto ice/salt/sugar and other dissolvable items?
See Halacha 2 Q&A there!

May one mix the ice cube or other dissolvable item in his drink using a spoon or the like?[22]
See Halacha 2 Q&A there!

C. Breaking a piece off from ice:[23]
It was only forbidden [to crush the ice] when one's intention to crush it is so that it melts. However, it is permitted to break a piece off from it even if through doing so a small amount of water will flow from it. *The reason for this is:* because this [melting] is only a small amount and is not given any consideration[24], as well as that one does not have intention [to melt it][25] and it is not considered an inevitable occurrence[26] and furthermore [because] the [melted water] will be going to waste.[27]

---

[19] Admur 320:16
[20] Admur 320:19
[21] Ketzos Hashulchan 127:1
[22] So is implied from Ketzos Hashulchan 127 footnote 2. See also SSH"K 10:2 and footnote there.
[23] Admur 320:17; Taz 320:7; M"B 320:32
[24] Admur ibid; Beis Yosef 320; omitted in Taz and M"B ibid; To note however that everyone agrees that the Rosh holds one may not urinate on snow even though one has no intent and it goes to waste and hence certainly this reason is necessary even according to the Taz and M"B ibid Vetzrauch Iyun as for what reason they did not mention it.
[25] Admur ibid; Taz 320:7; Beis Yosef ibid; M"B 320:32
[26] Admur ibid; omitted in Taz, Beis Yosef ibid, M"B; To note that in Michaber 320:14 and Admur 320:20 we explicitly rule that not having intent to melt does not suffice [if it is a Pesik Resihei], and hence it is forbidden to urinate on snow according to the Machmirim. However see M"B 320:36 and 39 which seems to accept that the reason of "no intent" can suffice [even if it is a Pesik Reishei] according to the Makilim regarding urinating on snow.
[27] Admur ibid; Taz ibid; Beis Yosef ibid; M"B 320:32
Are all three reasons required? See Shabbos Kehalacha vol. 3 17 footnote 84 and Tosefes Biur p. 157 that one does not require all three reasons. The Meor Hashabbos 3:13-98 writes that perhaps we require all three reasons and hence one cannot learn any allowance to other cases of a "small amount" unless all three reasons apply. **Reason of "A small amount"**: In 318:26 it states that one may place fat near the sun if only a small amount will melt. Hence, we see a small amount is not significant. However perhaps here that one is doing so with his hands it is more stringent and this reason alone does not suffice. Likewise, perhaps this reason only helps according to the Rishonim that hold of "Molid Davar Chadash" while according to those that hole of "Atu Sechitas Peiros" then even a Davar Muat is forbidden, as where do we ever see in the laws of Sechitas Peiros that one may squeeze a small amount? [See Shabbos Kehalacha vol. 3 17 footnote 84 and Tosefes Biur p. 157 that the reason of "a small amount" suffices as Admur rules in 318:26. Vetzaruch Iyun as explained above that there is a difference in case.] **Reason of not Pesik Reishei and no intent**: In other areas in Shulchan Aruch it is ruled that this reason alone suffices. [Shabbos Kehalacha ibid] Regarding if no intent but is Pesik Reishei-see previous footnote. **Reason of "going to waste"**: In 320:20 Admur explicitly writes that it alone does not suffice according to the opinion [Rashi] that holds the reason of Molid, and thus holds one may not urinate on snow even though the snow melts into the urine [and is permitted according to the Rishonim that hold of Sechitas Peiros]. So is also implied from the fact that Admur in parentheses in the reason troubles himself to explain why if it goes to waste it is permitted according to the Rishon of Sechitas Peiros and does not explain whether this suffices according to the Rishonim of Molid. [So explicitly writes Tehila Ledavid 320:15] **Does reason 1 and 2 suffice:** If only a little will melt and one has no intent, seemingly it would still be forbidden if it does not go to waste, due to the decree of Sechitas Peiros according to Ramban/Rashba. Hence one may not pour water into a cup with ice. So rules Piskeiy Teshuvos 320, however Shabbos Kehalacha is lenient. **Does reason 1 and 3 suffice**: Tzaruch Iyun if the melting is a small amount and will go to waste it is permitted even though it is a Pesik Reishei and hence the 2nd reason is not relevant. The ramification would be in a case that one desires to wash his hands over ice cubes. Shabbos Kehalacha 17:29 rules leniently. **Does reason 2 and 3 suffice**: If the melting is not a small amount but one has no intent and will not go to waste, it does not

The reason for why we do not decree against doing so:[28] ([Since the melted ice is going to waste], it is thus not at all similar to squeezing fruits designated to be juiced in which the squeezed juices are not going to waste, and therefore there is no reason to decree [against breaking a piece of ice] because [one may come to then squeeze fruits for their juice]).

D. Breaking ice in order to get to the water which is underneath it:[29]

By a vessel:[30] It is allowed to break ice [which is covering the water of a vessel] in order to draw water from underneath it as he is not creating water by doing so.[31]

The reason that there is no destroying prohibition involved in this:[32] [As well] there is no [destroying] prohibition involved at all in breaking the ice as anything that is detached [from the ground] which is not a vessel there is no prohibition at all involved in breaking and detaching it, as explained in chapter 314 [Halacha 12].

By a river:[33] However by a river or a well since the ice is attached to the ground it is forbidden to break it.

E. Urinating on snow:[34]

Due to the above [stringency in 1B] there is a Posek[35] who was careful not to urinate into snow as a result of the urine the snow melts and this is like one is melting it with his hands which is forbidden according to the first opinion despite that the melted [snow] is not individually recognizable[36] (and as well is going to waste[37]).

Other Opinions: [However] there is an opinion[38] who says that….. it is permitted to urinate onto snow.

Their reasoning is:[39] because this is something which is not possible to avoid doing during the winter when the entire earth is filled with snow and therefore the Sages did not make any decree against doing so.

suffice, as is proven from Michaber 320:14 that brings the Rosh who rules one may not urinate on snow even though one has no intent and it goes to waste. Thus, one may not open the sink with a strong current onto ice even if he has no intent and it will go to waste. Vetzaruch Iyun as for why the Taz and M"B ibid omitted the reason of "small amount" [hence implying it is not necessary] if they too agree to this ruling of the Rosh.

[28] Admur ibid; See previous footnote that this reason only suffices according to the Rashba/Ramban and not according to Rashi.

[29] Admur 320:18

[30] Admur ibid; Michaber 320:10; Tur in name of Avi Haezri

[31] Admur ibid; Taz 320:8; Vetzaruch Iyun as in the previous Halacha we assumed that breaking a piece of ice does cause water to melt, thus what is the difference between here and there?
Other reasons: Some write the reason is because one does not have intent for the water to melt. [Gr"a 320:10; M"B 320:36] Vetzaruch Iyun as in Michaber 320:14 regarding the prohibition of urinating on snow it is clear that even if one does not have intyent to melt it is nevertheless forbidden.

[32] Admur ibid; Mamar Mordechaiy, brought in Shaar Hatziyon 320:39
Other reasons: Some Poskim write the reason it is permitted is because it is similar to the Heter to break a barrel to get to the food that is inside. [M"A 320:15 in name of Mordechai] The M"B ibid negates this reason as being superfluous, and so is apparent from Admur ibid

[33] Admur ibid; M"A 320:15; P"M 320 A"A 15; Chasam Sofer 89; Nishmas Shabbos 257; Yad Eliyahu; Ben Ish Chaiy 2 Yisro 10; Shulchan Atzei Shitim; Chesed Lealafim; See Ketzos Hashulchan 127 footnote 11; Shabbos Kehalacha 17:34
Other opinions: Some Poskim rule there is never building or destroying prohibition by ice even if it is attached to the ground. [Even Haozer 363; Kneses Yisrael; Mamar Mordechaiy; Tosefes Shabbos; Elya Raba; Machatizs Hashekel] The Mishneh Berura 320:36 concludes one may be lenient if there is a Shabbos need.
Breaking ice in time of need-Tevila:Netilas Yadayim; thirsty: Some of the above Poskim [that rule like Admur ibid] rule one may be lenient in a time of need such as for Tevilas Mitzvah. [Ben Ish Chaiy ibid; Kaf Hachaim 320:5; Shabbos Kehalacha 17:35]
Is the above prohibition Biblical or Rabbinical: The Poskim ibid do not write whether the above is Biblically or Rabbinically forbidden, and whether the prohibition is Soser or Boneh. The P"M writes it is Boneh, as one is Mitaken the floor. If the prohibition is Soser, it is certainly only Rabbinically forbidden being that one does not intend to rebuild it.

[34] Admur 320:20; Michaber 320:14

[35] Rosh brought in Tur; Michaber ibid

[36] Admur ibid; M"A 320:17

[37] From here we learn that the fact the melted liquid goes to waste does not suffice to permit the action of melting, and hence in 320:17 the reason of "goes to waste" was only used in combination of other reasons. This follows the ruling of Rashi [who the Rosh evidently rules according to] that the entire prohibition against melting is due to Molid Davar Chadash and hence going to waste does not make it permitted. This follows the first opinion in 320:19, the previous Halacha. However according to the opinion of the Rashba/Ramban [which is the second opinion in the previous Halacha], if it goes to waste it is permitted. Hence, according to the Rashba/Ramban there are two reasons here to permit urinating on snow, as it mixes with water and goes to waste. [See Tehila Ledavid 320:15]

[38] Mahram Merothenberg brought in Tur; Michaber ibid; Tashbatz 65

[39] Admur ibid; Taz 320:11

The Final Ruling:[40] (It is proper to be stringent in an instance that one can easily avoid doing so.)

F. Stepping on snow:[41]
However, it is permitted to step on snow with ones feet being that it is possible that doing so will not melt and dissolve it, and thus even if it does [end up] melting and dissolving [since] it is done unintentionally it is [therefore] permitted being that it is not an inevitable occurrence.[42]

Other Opinions: [However] there is an opinion[43] which says that even if one's shoes are wet in which case it will for certain melt the snow [that he steps on] [nevertheless] it is permitted. Likewise, [this opinion says that] it is permitted to urinate onto snow.

Their reasoning is:[44] because this is something which is not possible to avoid doing during the winter when the entire earth is filled with snow and therefore the Sages did not make any decree against doing so.

The Final Ruling:[45] (It is proper to be stringent in an instance that one can easily avoid doing so.)

General Summary
Breaking/crushing ice/snow with one's hand:
To melt it: Is forbidden to break ice into small pieces in order so that it melt[46], even inside of liquid.[47]

To use it: However, to break off a piece of ice [to use] is permitted even though doing so will cause some of it to melt, being that one has no intention to melt it and only a small amount is melted.[48]

To get the water under it: To break the ice that has frozen over a liquid in a vessel is permitted, although to break ice on the ground is forbidden due to the "destroying" prohibition. [See footnote for other Opinions[49]]

To wash one's hands with it:[50] Is forbidden. Thus, one is to avoid washing one's hands with icy water even if he will not rub his hands. If one does so he must beware not to press the ice against his hands in order not to actively dissolve it.

Urinating on snow/ice:[51]
It is proper to be stringent to avoid urinating on snow or ice in an instance that this can easily be avoided. If it is not easily avoidable then one may urinate on it even though it will melt the snow/ice in the process.

Stepping on snow/ice:[52]
With dry shoes is permitted.

---

[40] Admur ibid; Rashal on Tur; Bach 320; Shelah Shabbos Neir Mitzvah; Elya Zuta 320:8; M"B 320:40; Kitzur SHU"A 80
If the urine will become absorbed within the snow: Some Poskim rule that if the urine will become completely absorbed in the snow then it is permitted to do so, being the liquid is not recognizable. [Ashel Avraham Butchach 320; See Shabbos Kehalacha 17:57 who negates this matter being the Poskim did not mention any such leniency.]
[41] Admur 320:20; Michaber 320:13; Tur in name of Mahrahm Merothenberg and the Rosh
[42] Admur ibid; Tur in name of Rosh, brought in Taz 320:11; Levush 320:11
[43] Taz 320:10
[44] Admur ibid; Taz ibid based on Tur; Brought in M"B 320:39
Other reasons: Some Poskim rule the reason is because one does not have any intent to melt the ice through doing so. [M"B 320:39 in name of Tosefes Shabbos; See Shabbos Kehalacha 17 footnote 147]
[45] Admur ibid; See Shabbos Kehalacha 17 footnote 145
[46] Admur 320:16
[47] Admur 320:19
[48] Admur 320:17
[49] Admur 320:18; So rules the Magen Avraham that ice attached to the ground has a building and destroying prohibition. However, there are Poskim [Mamar Mordechaiy; Tosefes Shabbos; Elya Raba] which rule that there is never building or destroying prohibition by ice, and so rules the Mishneh Berura [320:36] if there is a Shabbos need.
[50] Admur 320:19
[51] Admur 320:20
[52] Admur 320:20

With wet shoes it is proper to be stringent to avoid doing so in an instance that this can easily be avoided.

Q&A

May one crush a piece of ice that is in one's cup of water or juice?[53]
No, as explained in Halacha 1B.

May one break the surface of ice of a drink that has begun to freeze?
Yes.

May one break pieces of ice from one's ice tray in order to place it in his drink?[54]
Yes.

May one pour some water onto an ice tray to help break the ice?[55]
Yes, as this is similar to breaking a piece of ice which is allowed due to that it only melts a minute amount as well as that the excess liquid goes to waste.

May one break the surface of ice that is over a very large barrel?[56]
If the barrel is large enough to hold 40 Seah then it has the same status as ice which is attached to the ground which may not be broken.

May one remove an item that has become frozen to a freezer or fridge?
If the fridge/freezer can hold 40 Seah, then seemingly it is forbidden to do so.

May an item which has frozen onto one's windowsill or other area attached to one's house be removed?[57]
If the bottom of the item is frozen stuck to the windowsill or other part of the house, then one may not remove the item from there on Shabbos, as this is similar to breaking the ice that covers a well, which is forbidden.

May one remove the sheets of ice that have frozen on one's windows?[58]
No, as this is similar to breaking ice that covers a well which is forbidden to be done.

May one break icicles from one's roof?
No.

May one melt ice if the resultant water will anyways go to waste, such as to throw ice cubes in ones sink?
See Halacha 4 Q&A there!

May one pour water onto ice/salt/sugar and other dissolvable items?
See Halacha 2 Q&A there!

---

[53] Ketzos Hashulchan 127:1
[54] Ketzos Hashulchan 127 footnote 11 Minchas Shabbos
[55] Az Nidbaru 6:5; Vetzaruch Iyun according to Admur who writes that the reason of permission of no intent is because it is not a Pesik Resihei, while here it is a Pesik Reishei.
[56] Ketzos Hashulchan 127 footnote 11
[57] Ketzos Hashulchan 127 footnote 11
[58] Ketzos Hashulchan 127 Footnote 12

Q&A on snow from later Poskim

May one purposely step on snow for the fun of it on Shabbos?[59]

If one's feet are wet, or the ground is wet, and doing so will inevitably cause the snow to melt then it is forbidden to do so.

Is snow Muktzah?[60]

Snow retains the same law as rainwater, and is thus not Muktzah, even if it fell on Shabbos, if it is useable for eating or drinking [of even an animal[61]], or bathing, as stated above by rainwater. However, some Poskim[62] rule that snow that fell on Shabbos is Mukztah due to Nolad.

May one sweep snow or ice away from his lawn?[63]

Place without Eiruv: It is forbidden for a Jew to move the ice or snow four Amos even if it is not attached to the ground. It is permitted to move it for a space of less than four Amos, if the ice/snow is not attached to the ground as explained next. Whether one may ask a gentile to move the snow-see next!

Place with Eiruv or moving less than four Amos: If the snow or ice is attached to the ground then it is forbidden to break it due to the destroying prohibition.[64] If it is not attached to the ground then it may be moved.[65] In a time of great need, such as due to worry of falling and injury, many Poskim[66] are lenient to allow one to move the ice even if it is attached to the ground. Nevertheless, if possible, one should do so through a gentile.

Asking a gentile:[67] It is permitted to ask a gentile to sweep away the snow or ice in order to prevent injury. This applies even if there is no Eiruv and the ice is attached to the ground.[68]

May one spread salt on snow?[69]

It is permitted to spread salt on snow or ice in order to prevent people from slipping.[70] If possible, however, one should only do so in private, or through a gentile due to Maaras Ayin.[71] [It is, however, initially forbidden to do so for no need at all, such as people anyways do not walk through that area.[72]]

---

[59] Makor Chaim 320:13; Shabbos Kehalacha 3:59
[60] Rav SZ"A in SSH"K 16:44 footnote 110; Beir Moshe 6:30; Har Tzevi Kuntrus of 39 Melachos "Soser", and so is implied from other Poskim who deal with the question of making snowballs on Shabbos.
[61] M"B 338:30
[62] Igros Moshe 5:22-37; The Peri Megadim Introduction to Hilchos Yom Tov 29 rules that snow that fell on Shabbos is considered Muktzah due to Nolad Gamur. The Beir Moshe ibid questions this ruling, bringing many proofs against it.
[63] See Shabbos Kehalacha 17:66
[64] This follows the ruling of Admur 320:18; Shabbos Kehalacha 17:66; However according to those Poskim which rule that doing so does not involve a destroying prohibition, then it is permitted to be done in a place with an Eiruv. So rules Mishneh Halachos 4:45; Piskeiy Teshuvos 338:13.
[65] Seemingly it may be moved even if it is dirty being that it is a Geraf Shel Reiy
[66] See Ben Ish Chaiy ibid; Kaf Hachaim 320:65; Shabbos Kehalacha 17:35 that allow this in a time of need, even though they hold of the opinion that breaking ice attached to the ground involves Soser. The Ben Ish Chaiy ibid rules that in such a case one may rely on the lenient opinion. However, the Kaf Hachaim ibid writes that perhaps in a case of pain all agree that the Sages did not make their decree. Nevertheless, from the simple implication of Admur that rules like the M"A that doing so is forbidden it seems that this allowance does not exist even in a time of need, just like any other prohibition. This is unlike Shabbos Kehalacha ibid.
[67] Shabbos Kehalacha ibid
[68] As it is permitted to perform a Shevus Deshvus in a case of a great need, and breaking the ice as well as carrying today in a Karmalis is only a Rabbinical prohibition. [However, in places like Manhattan that it is considered a Biblical domain according to many Poskim, seemingly one may not ask the gentile to clear the path in a way that he will move the snow or ice four Amos.]
[69] Beir Moshe 1:28; SSH"K 25 footnote 49; Shabbos Kehalacha 3 17:61
[70] The reason: As this is similar to placing ice near a fire which is permitted to be done in a time of need, as explained in Halacha D. [Shabbos Kehalacha ibid footnote 158] The Beir Moshe ibid also deals with the aspect of "Mashveh Gumos" in regards to spreading salt on the ice [See Admur end of 313], however he negates this matter completely. To note that according to science, salt does not heat up the ice but simply lowers its freezing temperature from 0 celsius to -10 celsius.
If the ice is attached to the ground: It requires further analysis if this would be allowed according to Admur which holds there is a destroying prohibition by ice attached to the ground. Vetzaruch Iyun as in this case he is not actually breaking anything but rather simply causing it to melt. Vetzaruch Iyun
[71] Beir Moshe ibid; Shabbos Kehalacha ibid
[72] Pashut, as we are initially stringent against placing ice near the fire

May one pour water on the ice in order to melt it and prevent slipping?
Some[73] write that it is permitted to do so.[74]

May one make snowballs and snow men?
Making snowballs on Shabbos does not transgress the Molid prohibition.[75] Nevertheless, some Poskim[76] rule it is forbidden to make snow balls on Shabbos.[77]
Children: Some Poskim[78] rule that by children below nine years old one may be lenient to allow them to make snowballs in an area where there is an Eiruv. If however there is no Eiruv then every child above Chinuch is forbidden to throw snowballs. Other Poskim[79] rule it is proper to refrain all children [which have reached the age of Chinuch] from making snowballs on Shabbos.
Snow man:[80] In all cases it is forbidden for even children [above the age of Chinuch] to make snowmen and the like.

Eating an "Igloo" ["otter pops" popsicle in plastic wrapper] on Shabbos:[81]
Opening the Igloo: Some Poskim[82] rule that the hole in the Ices is to be torn with one's mouth and not with a vessel.[83] One must be careful not to tear it in an area that contains letters or pictures.
Erasing letters:[84] One must be careful to avoid sucking on the Igloo in a way that the letters will be erased. If the erasing of the letters will inevitably occur then it is forbidden to eat it on Shabbos. However, one may give it to a child below the age of Chinuch.
Crushing the ice: It is forbidden to crush the ice that is inside the wrapper due to the melting [Nolad] prohibition. However, one may chew on the section of the igloo that is in his mouth as doing so is the form of eating. One however may not do so with intent to melt the ice and remove it to eat later on.
Freezing the igloo on Shabbos:[85] One is to be stringent to avoid doing so.

---

[73] Shabbos Kehalacha 3 17:62; Nishmas Shabbos Sechita 246

[74] The reason: As in a time of need one may rely on the lenient opinion [Rashba/Ramban] that rules it is permitted to even actively melt ice if it mixes with the water and is not individually recognizable. [see above Halacha B] and it is precisely for this reason that their opinion was recorded in Admur ibid and other Poskim, to allow one to be lenient in a time of need. [Shabbos Kehalacha ibid footnote 160]

[75] Shabbos Kehalacha ibid; Nishmas Shabbos 320:249
The reason: As all the reasons for permitting breaking ice on Shabbos is likewise relevant here.

[76] Makor Chaim [Chavos Yair] 320:9; Shabbos Kehalacha Vol. 3 17:67; SSH"K 16:44; Beir Moshe 6:30

[77] The reason: Some Poskim rule that doing so is forbidden due to the building prohibition. [Makor Chaim ibid; SSH"K 16:44] Other Poskim argue that doing so contains no building prohibition being that it does not contain the building characteristics and does not last at all. [Beir Moshe 6:30] However the Beir Moshe concludes that it is nevertheless forbidden being that doing so causes snow to melt, which is forbidden. [Vetzaruch Iyun Gadol as from Admur [320:16 -18] who writes that the prohibition is only when one intends to use the melted water, while by a snowball there is no intent for it to melt at all. Furthermore, the source of the Beir Moshe from 320:19 itself is dealing with crushing snow together within water when washing, and one thus certainly cares about having more melted water.]

[78] Beir Moshe ibid

[79] Shabbos Kehalacha ibid; In footnote 167 he writes that in truth there seems to be no reason to prohibit making snowballs, however he nullifies his opinion in face of the Makor Chaim which explicitly chastises those that make lads that make snowballs on Shabbos and throw them at each other.

[80] Beir Moshe ibid; Shabbos Kehalacha ibid

[81] See Shabbos Kehalacha Vol. 3 17:52-55

[82] Shabbos Kehalacha 17 footnote 131; See Meor Hashabbos 13 footnote 105

[83] As perhaps since the size and form of the hole made is of benefit to the eater, perhaps it is considered a "nice hole" which is forbidden due to Tikkun Keli. [314:1]

[84] See Volume 3 "The Laws of Writing and Erasing"

[85] See end of the section.

2. Placing ice into a glass of liquid:[86]

One may place ice into a glass of wine or water during the summer in order to cool down [the drink] into which [the ice] melts on its own. One need not worry [that doing so transgresses any prohibition].[87] *Regarding crushing the ice while it is in the cup of liquid –See above Halacha 1B! Regarding pouring water onto the ice- See Q&A!*

Placing ice into a glass of liquid to melt:

It is permitted to place ice into liquid. [Although to crush it inside the liquid, or into the liquid is forbidden, as explained above in Halacha 1B].

Q&A

How much ice can be added to the water? Does one need to have 60x or majority of water in the cup when one puts the ice inside?[88]

Some[89] write one does not even require majority and one can hence add as much ice as he desires. Others[90] however write that majority is required. Others[91] write it even requires 60x. Practically, one may follow the first opinion.[92]

May one pour liquid onto the ice in one's cup?

It is forbidden to pour the liquid onto the ice being that doing so causes it to melt.[93] However there are Poskim[94] that rule one is permitted to do so if only a small amount of the ice will melt due to the

---

[86] Admur 320:16; Michaber 320:9; Shabbos 51b

[87] The reason: Some say the reason is because one has not done any actions with his hands [Opinion in Admur 318:27; 320:16; M"B 320:34; Michaber 318:16; Ramban Shabbos 51b; Implication of Rambam Shabbos 21:12 brought in Maggid Mishneh; Smag; Smak; Rabbeinu Yerucham] Others say the reason is because the liquid is entering directly into the water and is hence not recognizable on its own. [Admur 318:26; 320:16 and 19; M"B 320:34] Admur rules mainly like the first reason although states the custom is to be stringent like the second reason. The practical ramification is regarding whether one may place an ice cube in the sun for it to melt, as explained in Halacha 3.

[88] See Shabbos Kehalacha 17 Biurim 25 [p. 89]

[89] Implication of Admur and all Poskim which do not mention that Bittul is required; Betzeil Hachochmah 2:26; Shivilei David 20:1; Shabbos Kehalacha 17 Biurim 25 [p. 89] and 16 Biurim 8 [p. 19-24] that every melted drop is individually nullified in 60x [explained next].

If there was originally 60x in the water: See Shabbos Kehalacha 17 Biurim 25 [p. 89] and 16 Biurim 8 [p. 19-24] that every melted drop is individually nullified in 60x, and we say Kama Kama Batul, even by wine [as is implied from Admur 320:4 and rules Peri Chadash in Y.D. 99], and certainly here. As for why by 305:32 Admur requires a total majority and we don't say Kama Kama Batul-see there that he does not have an answer to this contradiction, and suggests perhaps the milk enters in one shot into the utter and even initially there isn't majority. Vetzaruch Iyun Gadol on his novelty. As for why in 335:4 Admur implies that we need 60x in total with exception to Muktzah, and we don't apply Kama Kama Batul if one wants to drink the wine, he answers that there must be a difference between if the liquid is recognizable before it mixes in [in which case we require 60x total as ruels in 335:4] versus if the liquid mixes straight into the other liquid in which case we say Kama Kama is Batul in 60x, as implied from 320:4.

Must one initially have majority or 60x versus the first drop: From the fact Admur here does not mention any level of Bittul [unlike 320:4 and 305:32] implies that even initially Bittul is not required. Perhaps the reason for this is because there is no prohibition here at all that needs nullification, as since the drop is not recognizable, it is not considered Molid, and it is likewise not similar to Sechitas Peiros as explains Admur here in 320:19. Thus there is no Issur here at all when it enters on its own into liquid, and therefore no Bittul is required even originally. This explains why here Admur makes no mention of majority or 60x Bittul. However, in 320:4 he mentions 60x being that juice that flowed on Shabbos is a real Issur and needs regular Bittul of 60x. Likewise in 305:32 Admur mentions majority being that the milk is Muktzah due to Nolad, and hence requires majority. Vetzaruch Iyun.

[90] Implication of Admur 305:32 regarding milk in utter of cow, that majority is required [Betzeil Hachochmah ibid; Divrei Yatziv 159] However see previous footnote that one cannot learn from here anything as it is a case of Muktzah-Nolad. Perhaps also this can be implied from the added wording of Admur in 320:16 "One may place ice into a glass of wine or water **during the summer in order to cool down [the drink]** into which [the ice] melts on its own." As usually when one desires to cool off a drink there is majority water inside. On the other hand, perhaps the novelty in these words is that although the drink is hot, and will melt the ice cube, one may nevertheless do so.

Reason why by grapes in vat 60x is required: As the juice of the grapes is a Rabbinical prohibition, and hence requires 60x. However, Nolad is more lenient and hence only requires majority. [Betzeil Hachochmah ibid; Divrei Yatziv ibid in answer of question of Iglei Tal Dash 17:83]

[91] Rosh Yosef [of Peri Megadim] Shabbos 51a; Implication of Admur 320:4, P"M 320 M"Z 3, M"B 320:14 regarding grapes in a wine vat that 60x is required; Peri Hagan; However see previous footnote that one cannot learn from here anything as it is a case of actual Issur of juice that flowed on Shabbos.

[92] As is implied from Setimas Haposkim, and we answered the contradictions in Admur in each area as for why he required majority or 60x.

[93] Piskeiy Teshuvos 320:5; And it is thus similar to urinating on ice which is to be avoided. See Ketzos Hashulchan 127 Footnote 14 that implies it is only allowed by sugar/salt and not buy ice; Furthermore, perhaps we require all three reasons mentioned in 320:17 to be allowed to melt with an action. See Meor Hashabbos 3:13-98; Shabbos Kehalacha vol. 3 17 footnote 84 and Tosefes Biur p. 157. See next footnotes.

[94] Minchas Shay 320:9; Shabbos Kehalacha Vol. 3 17:28 [p. 71] regarding gravy and 17:50 [p. 94] regarding ice cubes.

pouring.[95] Practically it is best to always place the water in first and then the ice cube.[96]

May one enter instant coffee into water?[97]
Yes. Nevertheless, it is best to place the coffee into the water rather than place the water onto the coffee. Some are stringent to prepare coffee essence from before Shabbos and thus avoid any suspicion of prohibition.[98] Nevertheless, if one did not do so he may do it on Shabbos itself.[99]

May one pour water onto salt/sugar and other dissolvable items?[100]
Yes, as they are hard and do not dissolve through the pouring and thus are not similar to the case of urinating on ice.[101] Seemingly one may even pour hot water from a Keli Sheiny onto these substances as the amount that it will melt is only slight.[102]

May one mix the ice cube in his drink using a spoon or the like?[103]
No, as by doing so one is actively causing the ice to melt which is similar to washing one's hands with icy water of which one is to be stringent against doing so.

May one place a dissolvable item such as sugar and instant coffee into liquid and then mix it with a spoon so it dissolves?[104]
Yes.[105]

May one place soap into a cup of liquid and have it dissolve and then use that to wash ones hands?
Yes. See below Halacha 4 Q&A there!

---

[95] As he learns that the reason of "small amount" in 320:17 suffices to allow an action of melting to be done [as in truth rules Admur in 318:25]. See also Ketzos Hashulchan 127 footnote 14 that uses "a very small amount" to permit pouring even hot water onto sugar and salt, although he implies that he agrees it is forbidden to pour the water over ice, seemingly due to that it melts a lot more than just a small amount. Vetzaruch Iyun as Admur troubles himself to explain that the reason we do not make a decree is because the water is going to waste and is hence not similar to juice of fruits. Hence the implication from Admur is that without this condition fulfilled we cannot allow it to be done.

[96] Shabbos Kehalacha Vol. 3 17:50 [p. 94]

[97] Rav SZ"A in SSH"K 12 footnote 14; Shabbos Kehalacha Vol. 3 17:86; Vol. 1 p. 266; See Igros Moshe 4:74 Lash 1

[98] Shabbos Kehalacha Vol. 1 p. 266

[99] So is evident from all Poskim which have never written of such a prohibition and some [SSH"K] have even allowed placing instant coffee into a Keli Sheiyni. So is implied also from Shabbos Kihalacha ibid.

[100] Ketzos Hashulchan 127 footnote 14

[101] So is evident from Admur 320:19 that writes "However **it is permitted to pour water onto salt** and wash one's hands with it"

[102] So is evident from the fact the Poskim do not discuss the issue of Nolad when discussing the laws of cooking involved in pouring from a Keli Rishon or Sheiyni onto sugar. [Ketzos Hashulchan ibid]

[103] So is implied from Ketzos Hashulchan 127 footnote 2. See also SSH"K 10:2 and footnote there.

[104] Ketzos Hashulchan 127 Footnote 2; Shevisas Hashabbos Dash 56; Rav Poalim 3:14; Shabbos Kehalacha 33 17:83

[105] Seemingly doing so should be forbidden just like it is forbidden to crush ice with one's hands even into a liquid. Nevertheless, the custom is to permit doing so, due to the fact it is not really the mixing of the spoon which dissolves the sugar but really the liquid, and the mixing only quickens the job. [ibid]

3. Placing a frozen/congealed item in an area where it will melt on its own:

Important Note: In all scenarios below, it is forbidden due to the cooking restrictions to place the item in an area where it can reach Yad Soledes. The below discussion is only with regards to if melting the item to less than Yad Soledes contains a Nolad prohibition. See "The Laws of Cooking" for further reference on the cooking prohibition!

A. Placing congealed fat in an area where it will melt:[106]

Note: This Halacha was already fully discussed in "The Laws of Cooking" Halacha 8. See there for the full discussion on this topic.

❖ **The First Opinion:[107]**

Foods which are filled with pieces of congealed fat [whether of meat or fish[108]] are forbidden to be heated up even at a distance from the fire which is even in a place where [the food will] not [be able to get heated top the point of] Yad Soledes.[109]

The reason for the above restriction is:[110] because the congealed fat that is inside [the food] melts [in the heat] and doing so is similar to [one] crushing a piece of ice in order to liquefy it, in which case the Sages prohibited [one from doing so] being that [through doing so] one is creating [a new substance] on Shabbos which is similar to a forbidden action being that he is creating this water [from the ice] as will be explained in the next Halacha regarding placing ice near a source of heat. This same decree applies as well to dissolving fat.

The law if the fat will melt into the food and will thus not be recognizable:[111] However the above [prohibition to melt the fat] only refers to when so much fat has melted that it oozes out [of the pastry], and is its own substance. [Meaning] that it is not mixed into any other food and is [thus] recognizable on its own. However if it has been left such a great distance [from the fire] that not enough fat will melt for it to ooze out [of the pastry], and rather only a slight amount of it will melt and will get absorbed into the pastry itself and [will thus] not be visible on its own, then it is allowed to [be placed there] even initially just like it is allowed to place a piece of ice in a cup of wine despite that the ice will melt into it, being that [the melted water] will get mixed and nullified within the wine in the cup, and is [thus] not a separate substance as was explained above.

Melting congealed fat on top of legumes:[112] According to all opinions it is permitted to place fat that has congealed on top of hot legumes and flour as long as one does not break [the fat] apart with one's hands, and rather simply places [the fat] on top of them or into them letting it melt on its own, being that [the fat] that melts is not [recognizable as] its own substance and rather becomes absorbed within the food.

If a small amount is recognizable:[113] [Furthermore] even if a small amount of [the fat] does flow out [of the pastry or legumes] and is [recognizable as] a substance of its own, [nevertheless] since it is a small amount it is not given any [Halachic] importance and is permitted.

Heating up fatty meat:[114] Therefore it is allowed to heat up on Shabbos a piece of fatty meat even though some of [its fat] will flow being that [what will flow] is [only] a small amount [of fat].

Melting congealed fat on top of a hot roast:[115] It is questionable whether one may place congealed fat on top of a hot roast in order for it to dissolve on its own, as since the melted fat does not get absorbed into

---

[106] Based on Chapter 318. See "The Laws of Cooking" Halacha 8 for the full discussion on this topic.
[107] 1st opinion in Admur ibid; 2nd opinion in Admur 320:16; Rama 318:16; Sefer Haterumah 235; Ran in name of Sefer Haterumah; Rosh chapter 4 in name of Sefer Hateruma
[108] Machatzis Hashekel 318:42
[109] Admur 318:25
[110] Admur 318:25; Sefer Haterumah ibid
Other opinions: Some Poskim write it is forbidden due to Nolad. [Sefer Haterumah ibid; M"A 318:42; M"B 318:105] It is unclear however if they refer to Nolad of Mukztah or Molid.
[111] Admur 318:26; M"A 318:40; Sefer Haterumah ibid; M"B 318:105
[112] Admur 318:28; Derisha 318:6; Elya Zuta 318:17; M"B 318:118
[113] Admur 318:26; Taz 318:21; Beis Yosef according to Sefer Haterumos; M"B 318:105
[114] Admur 318:26; Taz 318:21; Bies Yosef according to Sefer Haterumos; M"B 318:105
[115] Admur 318:28; M"A 318:45

the meat but rather floats on its surface it therefore can be compared to a pot [of soup or stew] which its fat has congealed of which the custom is to be initially stringent.

Heating up soup or stew:[116] However it is forbidden to heat up a pot [of stew or soup], which its fat has congealed, even by an area that [it will] not [reach] Yad Soledes, even if there is a lot of gravy inside [the pot] and the fat will thus dissolve into the gravy, as nevertheless the fat will float on its surface and be [recognizable as a] separate substance.

Melting fat in the sun:[117] In all cases that it is forbidden to heat up a food with congealed fat [it is] even [forbidden] to do so by leaving it in the sun.

If the fat melted on Shabbos it may not be eaten:[118] If [the fat] already [melted] then the fat that had melted on Shabbos is forbidden [to be eaten]. [This however only applies if one transgressed Molid in the process.[119]]

The reason for this is:[120] as this is the law with juice that has flowed on Shabbos from fruits that are designated to be used for juice which are forbidden [to be drunk] due to a decree that [if this were to be allowed then] one may come to squeeze the fruits on Shabbos [in order to make juice] being that these [fruits] are designated for this purpose as will be explained there [in chapter 320 Halacha 3]. This [suspicion] likewise applies to this fat [that has melted on Shabbos] as since it is common for [the fat] to be liquidly and transparent therefore when it is congealed it is similar to fruits that are designated to be juiced, of which the juice that flows from it on Shabbos is forbidden until night [i.e. after Shabbos].

❖ **The Second Opinion:**[121]

However, there are opinions which argue on all this and say that there is no prohibition at all in melting fat through placing it in a hot area, as the [Sages] only prohibited breaking [and thus dissolving] a piece of ice with one's hands, however, to let it dissolve on its own there is no decree [against doing so].[122]

Other opinions: Some Poskim are lenient to allow placing precooked fat on hot roast and that doing so does not contain a Nolad prohibition. [M"B 318:118 based on Elya Raba]

[116] Admur 318:26; Rama 318:16; M"B 318:105
[117] Admur 318:25 and Admur 320:16; Taz 318:21; Beis Yosef; M"B 318:105
[118] Admur 318:25; M"A 318:42; 320:14
[119] So can be learned from fact Admur permits even Lechatchila to place the food near an oven that will be turned on by a gentile. See P"M 318 A"A 42 and Iglei Tal Dash 36:12; However according to those that hold of the reason of Nolad-Muktzah, seemingly this would not help. Vetzaruch Iyun. See Shabbos Kehalacha 3 17:3 and 29
[120] Admur ibid; Ran 51b in answer of question of Ramban against Sefer Hateruma

The source of this ruling: The reason mentioned here [in Admur based on Ran] is in truth an alternative reason against the prohibition of melting ice, and is the reason of the Ramban 51b and Rashba 51b and Rambam ibid which argue that melting ice is not forbidden due to Nolad or Molid but rather due to Sechitas Peiros. The fact Admur uses this reason to explain why the melted substance is forbidden aggravates a number of questions: 1) The M"A ibid states the reason it is forbidden is because of Nolad and Admur himself stated earlier this is the reason for the prohibition to initially do so. Why then is Admur here mentioning a different reason for why it is forbidden Bedieved? Furthermore, those that hold [Ramban; Rambam] of the reason of "coming to squeeze fruits" in truth is the second opinion mentioned next which holds it is even initially permitetd to place the fat near the sun to melt, and hence how can their reason now be used against them to prohibit even Bedieved?!!!! Perhaps the explanation is as follows: Just as we see the Sages forbade the juice of fruits that flowed on their own due to that one may come to squeeze them and transgress Mifarek, simiallry the fat that melts on its ownis forbidden due to that one may come to melt the fat with ones hands and transgress Molid! Thus in truth Admur does not hold at all of the reason of the Ramban and Rashba and just uses the concept to explain why here it would be forbidden. To note that the Rashba ibid does not explicitly rule that one may melt the fat near the sun and only the Ramban and Maggid Mishneh mention it, even though they all hold of the same reason.

Other opinions: Some Poskim write the reason behind the prohibition is due to Nolad. [M"A ibid and in 320:14] This follows the understanding of the Ramban 51b and Rashba 51b in the Sefer Hateruma 235 that Nolad is a Mukztah prohibition, and is different than the concept of Molid brought in Rashi. See P"M 318 A"A 42 and Panim Meiros 1:84 which explains the M"A ibid is in truth giving two reasons behind the prohibition, one being Nolad [as rules the Sefer Hateruma] and the second being Sechitas Peiros.

[121] Admur 318:27; Michaber 318:16; 320:9; Ramban Shabbos 51b; Implication of Rambam Shabbos 21:12 brought in Maggid Mishneh; Smag; Smak; Rabbeinu Yerucham

[122] The reason: As the prohibition against melting foods on Shabbos is only when done actively, such as with one's hands and the like. This is just like is the prohibition against squeezing juice on Shabbos which is only forbidden when done actively, and the entire reason for prohibitiong melting items on Shabbos is due to the prohibition of squeezing fruits, and it hence intakes all its leniencies. Now, although juice that flowed from fruits on Shabbos is forbidden to be drunk, even though no action was done, this only applies by fruits that are designated for drinking their juice. However, fruits that are designated for eating do not have this prohibition apply, and hence here too, that the fat and ice are meant for eating, the prohibition does not apply. [Ramban ibid, brought in Ran 51b; To note however that Admur omits any explanation or reason for the lenient opinion both in 318:27 and in 320:16. Vetzaruch Iyun Gadol why Admur omits their reason, despite bringing their reason in 320:19 and 326:10 regarding a different dispute that these opinions have. Could it possibly be that Admur holds of a different reason according to the lenient opinion? Vetzrauch Iyun]

❖ *The Final Ruling in Shulchan Aruch:*[123]
Concerning the final ruling the custom is to initially be stringent like the first opinion[124] although once the fat has already melted one may be lenient like the second opinion.[125] [Furthermore] even initially[126] one may rely on the second opinion in a time of need, being that this is the main Halachic opinion.[127]

Placing the fat on top of a heater that is not yet lit:[128] As well one may be lenient to place pastries filled with fat onto a heater before it is lit and have it consequently melt when the gentile lights the heater.

The reason for this is:[129] because [in this scenario] even regarding the cooking prohibition, [meaning if one were to place there] a food which has a cooking prohibition applicable to it, [cooking it] would not contain a Biblical prohibition but rather only a Rabbinical [prohibition] if he places it there prior to the gentile lighting the fire of the oven as explained in chapter 253 Halacha 27]. Thus, here since there are opinions which completely permit [one to place even near an active fire] one may at the very least be lenient regarding placing it there before the oven is lit.

Doing it through a gentile, and not in front of an ignoramus: Nevertheless, one should not be lenient in front of an uneducated Jew, and one should do so through a gentile.

Summary-Placing congealed fat in an area where it will melt:
In all scenarios below it is forbidden due to the cooking restrictions to place the item in an area where it can reach Yad Soledes.

If only a minute amount of the melted substance is recognizable outside of the solid food, such as the fat of meat, and certainly if it is completely absorbed within the solid food and is not individually recognizable at all, it is permitted. If, however, there is a lot of recognizable melted substance flowing out of the food then initially, if there is no pressing need to do so, it may not be heated even below Yad Soledes, even in direct sun light. However, in times of need it may be heated to below Yad Soledes. As well as it may be placed by a gentile, not in the presence of an ignoramus Jew, on top of a heating surface that will eventually be turned on by a gentile.

In any event, Bedieved that one went head and melted it to below Yad Soledes without the above allowances it is nevertheless permitted to be eaten on Shabbos.

Examples:[130] One may place butter or margarine onto hot lentils and rice and the like of foods that will absorb the melted butter, if it will not reach the point of Yad Soledes. One may not place margarine, or fat onto a hot piece of meat [or potato] if it will not reach Yad Soledes.

---

[123] Admur 318:27; 320:16; Rama 318:16
[124] Admur ibid; Rama ibid
[125] Admur ibid; M"A 318:42; M"B 318:106
[126] Admur ibid; M"B ibid
[127] Admur ibid; Rama ibid
[128] Admur ibid; M"A 318:42; M"B 318:106
[129] Admur ibid; M"A ibid; M"B ibid

Why no Issur due to Nolad? Taruch Iyun as according to the Machmir opinion even Bedieved the liquid is forbidden due to that it is similar to the flow of juice, and hence based on this there should be no differentiation whether it is defrosted near a flame or on its own, or through a gentile. [P"M 318 A"A 42 and Iglei Tal Dash 36:12] Perhaps one can answer [according to Admur] that the prohibition of Bedieved only applies when one transgressed the Lechatchila, such as one did an action to cause it to melt, however if one did not do an action, such as the gentile turned on the flame, then even the Sefer Hateruma agrees it is permitted Bedieved. However according to those that hold of the reason of Nolad-Muktzah, seemingly this would not help. Vetzaruch Iyun. See Shabbos Kehalacha 3 17:3 and 29;

Can one learn from here that according to all one may cause an itme to melt in room temperature: No, as perhaps only here, since ones action did not do any melting at all [and only the gentile did so] is it permitted, however to bring the food to room temperature is forbidden. A proof for this perhaps can be brought from the fact Admur does not write the reason behind the allowance to have the gentile turn it on because the Jew did no action and it is not considered Molid according to any opinion, but rather simply because even by Bishul some opinions are lenient. This implies that even though one did not do an action, it is forbidden according to the Machmirim, and it is only due to that a gentile is doing the entire action that we are lenient.
[130] Admur 318:28

Q&A

May one melt congealed chicken, meat or fish gravy near a flame or in the sun?[131]

It may never be melted in an area which will reach Yad Soledes. If it will not be able to reach Yad Soledes then if there will be a nice amount of melted liquid which is apparent, it is forbidden. If, however, it will become absorbed into the food and thus not be very evident, it is permitted.

Melting foods that are eaten in their congealed state:

Some Poskim[132] permit melting gravy which is accustomed to be eaten even when congealed.[133] Thus, one may melt Gala [Calfs foot jell], fish gravy and ice cream on Shabbos. Practically however, one is to be stringent unless in a time of need.[134]

May one melt ice cream on Shabbos?

Some Poskim[135] rule it is permitted to do so being it is considered like a food and not like a liquid and thus does not contain a Nolad prohibition. Practically however, one is to be stringent unless in a time of need.[136]

May one melt foods that cannot be eaten in their frozen state, in a time of need?

Some Poskim[137] rule that frozen foods, such as gravy, which can never be eaten in their frozen state may not be defrosted on Shabbos according to all opinions, and hence there is no allowance to place them near a fire even in a time of need. Practically, one may be lenient in this matter.[138]

B. Placing plain ice in an area where it will melt on its own:[139]

Note: The two opinions below as well as the final ruling follows the same opinions and ruling of the previous case of melting fat. Here it is brought in reference to melting ice.

First Opinion:[140] It is permitted to place them in the sun or opposite a bonfire in an area where it cannot become hot to the point of Yad Soledes, and they dissolve there on their own.[141]

Other Opinions:[142] [However] there are opinion[143] which say that [the Sages] only permitted to place [the ice] into a cup [of liquid] being that the dissolved water [from the ice] is not recognizable on its own and is rather mixed into the wine or water that is in the cup. However, when the dissolved liquid is recognizable on its own then it is forbidden [to drink this water] even if it already melted, due to the reason explained in Halacha 3A.[144]

The Final Ruling: It was already explained in the previous Halacha that the main Halachic opinion is like the first opinion [here] although that the custom is to initially be stringent [to not melt the ice by placing it near a source of heat, unless it is a time of need. As well it may be done by a gentile not in the presence of an ignoramus on top of a heating surface which he will eventually turn on].

---

[131] Based on a 318:25-27. So rules Rav Farkash in Shabbos Kehalacha 4:14 without bringing any lenient opinion.

[132] Bris Olam 71; SSH"K 1:37 [43 in new] in name of Rav SZ"A; Az Nidbaru 3:8

[133] The reason: As even by fruits we only decree against the juice that flowed on its own in a case that the fruits are designated to be juiced, and hence the nentir reason of the stringent opinion is not applicable here. [ibid] Vetzaruch Iyun, as this only explains why Bedieved the jucie is permitted, however Lechatchila it should still remain forbidden to squeeze it due to Molid Davar Chadash.

[134] Shabbos Kehalacha 3 17:19 based on Machatzis Hashekel 318:42 which prohibits melting fish fat

[135] SSH"K 10:7

[136] Shabbos Kehalacha 3 17:19

[137] P"M 318 A"A 40

[138] Shabbos Kehalacha 3 17:20

[139] Admur 320:16; brought also in 318:25-27 regaridng fat

[140] Admur ibid; opinion in 318:27; Michaber 318:16; 320:9; Ramban Shabbos 51b; Implication of Rambam Shabbos 21:12 brought in Maggid Mishneh; Smag; Smak; Rabbeinu Yerucham

[141] The reason: See A in footnotes.

[142] Admur ibid; opinion in 318:25; M"A 320:14; M"B 320:35; Rama 318:16 regarding fat

[143] Sefer Haterumah 235; Ran in name of Sefer Haterumah; Rosh chapter 4 in name of Sefer Haterumah

[144] There it is explained that the flow of fat is similar to the flow of juice from olives on Shabbos which is forbidden. See A in footnotes

Summary-Placing ice in an area where it will melt on its own:[145]
In all scenarios below it is forbidden due to the cooking restrictions to place the item in an area near a flame where it can reach Yad Soledes.
May only be done: a) in times of need, or b) through a gentile, not in the presence of an ignoramus Jew, on top of a heating surface that will eventually be turned on by a gentile. In any event, Bedieved that one went ahead and melted it to below Yad Soledes without the above allowances it is nevertheless permitted to drink on Shabbos.[146]

Q&A

May one melt a frozen baby bottle in the sun or near heat in an area that it will not reach Yad Soledes?[147]
Yes.[148]

May one cause an item to melt by removing it from the freezer, if he does not place it near the fire or sun?
Some Poskim[149] rule it permitted to cause items to melt by removing it from the freezer so long as one does not place it near the sun or fire.[150] Other Poskim[151] rule it is initially forbidden to do so, just as one

---

[145] Based on 320:16 and Chapter 318 Halacha 27

[146] So is implied from Admur above. However in SSH"K 10:3 he writes in the name of Rav SZ"A that ice is different than fat and one should try to initially be stringent to avoid using the liquid even Bedieved. This however clearly does not seem to be the opinion of Admur, being that he equates the final ruling by melted ice to that of melted fat of which one need only initially be stringent.

[147] Shabbos Kehalacha Vol. 1 p. 212

[148] Although Admur rules that one is to be stringent due to Nolad, nevertheless since the needs of a child are considered a great need, therefore when there is need to do so it is allowed.

[149] Sheivet Halevy 7:40; Az Nidbaru 6:3 and 34; 10:10; Tzitz Eliezer 6:34-30; Divrei Yatziv 159; Shabbos Kehalacha 3 17:3 and 27
The Sheivet Halevy differentiates between placing something by a fire and the like or by room temperature saying that only when doing an actual action of placing it by a fire or room temperature is melting forbidden even in accordance to the stringent opinion. Vetzaruch Iyun why placing it near the sun or fire is any more of an action then removing it from a colder climate [the freezer] to a warmer climate [ones room]. Furthermore, he brings there a proof for this differentiation from the Halacha that one may place fat near an oven which will be turned on by a gentile, thus showing that only when the Jew does an action is it problematic. The proof for this is as follows: According to the Machmirim who even forbid the food Bedieved, it makes no difference whether an action was done or not, as some hold the reason for the prohibition according to the Machmirim is due to Nolad [Rama; M"A and M"B] and Admur holds that it is forbidden even bedieved being it is similar to juice of fruits that flowed on Shabbos. Hence, why are we lenient to permit having a gentile turn on the oven if the result is the same result. From here the above Poskim prove that we must conclude that when no melting action has been done, it is permitted according to all, and hence here too it is permitted. However, Tzaruch Iyun on this as well, being that in that case the Jews action could never make it melt, while here bringing it room temperature is itself enough to make it melt, the same way placing it near a fire is enough to make it melt, and hence perhaps in this case the Sefer Hateruma would hold it is forbidden even Bedieved, even though one did not place it near a flame. A proof for this perhaps can be brought from the fact Admur does not write the reason behind the allowance to have the gentile turn it on is because the Jew did no action and it is not considered Molid according to any opinion, but rather simply because even by Bishul some opinions are lenient. This implies that even though one did not do an action, it is forbidden according to the Machmirim, and it is only due to that a gentile is doing the entire action that we are lenient.

[150] The reason: The Sheivet Halevy differentiates between placing something by a fire and the like or by room temperature saying that only when doing an actual action of placing it by a fire or room temperature is melting forbidden even in accordance to the stringent opinion. Vetzaruch Iyun why placing it near the sun or fire is any more of an action then removing it from a colder climate [the freezer] to a warmer climate [one's room]. Furthermore, he brings there a proof for this differentiation from the Halacha that one may place fat near an oven which will be turned on by a gentile, thus showing that only when the Jew does an action is it problematic. The proof for this is as follows: According to the Machmirim who even forbid the food Bedieved, it makes no difference whether an action was done or not, as some hold the reason for the prohibition according to the Machmirim is due to Nolad [Rama; M"A and M"B] and Admur holds that it is forbidden even bedieved being it is similar to juice of fruits that flowed on Shabbos. Hence, why are we lenient to permit having a gentile turn on the oven if the result is the same result. From here the above Poskim prove that we must conclude that when no melting action has been done, it is permitted according to all, and hence here too it is permitted. However, Tzaruch Iyun on this as well, being that in that case the Jews action could never make it melt, while here bringing it room temperature is itself enough to make it melt, the same way placing it near a fire is enough to make it melt, and hence perhaps in this case the Sefer Hateruma would hold it is forbidden even Bedieved, even though one did not place it near a flame. A proof for this perhaps can be brought from the fact Admur does not write the reason behind the allowance to have the gentile turn it on is because the Jew did no action and it is not considered Molid according to any opinion, but rather simply because even by Bishul some opinions are lenient. This implies that even though one did not do an action, it is forbidden according to the Machmirim, and it is only due to that a gentile is doing the entire action that we are lenient.

[151] SSH"K 10:3; 1:74, as is the simple Halacha ruled by Admur that one may not cause frozen water to melt. [320:16] Rav SZ"A as brought in Mioreiy Hashabbos.

may not place it near the sun or fire.[152] Seemingly, according to Admur one is to be stringent.[153]

May one defrost a frozen bottle of water, soda or juice by removing it from the freezer, if he does not place it near the fire?

Completely frozen: Bottles of water/soda/juices which are completely frozen may not be defrosted on Shabbos due to Nolad, unless in a case of need, as explained in the summary above. This applies even if one does not place them near the sun or fire.[154] However some Poskim[155] permit to defrost all items, including frozen bottles so long as one does not place it near the sun or fire. [Seemingly according to Admur one is to be stringent[156]]. Furthermore, some Poskim[157] allow defrosting liquids of significance [such as milk and wine] even near the sun.[158] Practically however, one is not to rely on this opinion, and is to follow the same ruling as all frozen liquids.[159]

Partially frozen: It is permitted according to all to be placed even in the sun, or by a non-Yad Soledes area near the fire.[160]

May one place ice cubes in his cup with the intent of having it melt and then drink its water?

No[161], although in a time of need one may be lenient to do so.[162] However there are Poskim[163] which rule that this is always allowed so long as one does not place it near a fire or near the sun.

May one place ice cubes on top of bottles of soda and the like in order to cool them down?[164]

Yes, as the resultant water will anyways go to waste. It is thus similar to breaking off a piece of ice which is allowed due to that the melted water which is resulted from the breaking goes to waste, as explained in Halacha 1D.[165]

---

[152] The reason: As the fact is you brought the ice to a higher temperature, and the Mahchmirim prohibit even Bedieved due to fruits that flowed on Shabbos or due to Nolad of Mukztah. No proof can be brought from the case of having the gentile turn on the oven as there no action was done at all, and perhaps in that case the Sefer Hateruma agrees that bedieved it is permitted.

[153] As according to the opinion which holds that the melting prohibition is due to that it is similar to the flow of juice, based on this there should be no differentiation whether it is defrosted near a flame or on its own. Vetzaruch Iyun, as if so then why did Admur permit placing it near the unlit oven and then having the gentile turn it on. [As asks the P"M 318 A"A 42 and Iglei Tal Dash 36:12] Perhaps one can answer [according to Admur] that the prohibition of Bedieved only applies when one transgressed the Lechatchila, such as one did an action to cause it to melt, however if one did not transgress the Lechatchila, such as the gentile turned on the flame, then even the Sefer Hateruma agrees it is permitted Bedieved. However according to those that hold of the reason of Nolad-Muktzah, seemingly this would not help. Veztaruch Iyun. See previous footnotes.

[154] SSH"K 10:3; 1:74, as is the simple Halacha ruled by Admur that one may not cause frozen water to melt. [320:16] Rav SZ"A as brought in Mioreiy Hashabbos.

[155] Sheivet Halevy 7:40; Az Nidbaru 10:10; Tzitz Eliezer 6:34-30;

[156] As according to the opinion which holds that the melting prohibition is due to that it is similar to the flow of juice, based on this there should be no differentiation whether it is defrosted near a flame or on its own.

[157] SSH"K 10:5 in name of Rav SZ"A; Maor Hashabbos 13:44 in name of RSZ"A allows to defrost even juices near the sun

[158] Milk and other foods which are not eaten in their frozen state are not considered Nolad as since they are not eaten in their frozen state they are considered by people as liquids as opposed to solids even when they are frozen, and it is thus not considered a new change. Only water which is not a Chashuv item is not considered a liquid when frozen. [Rav SZ"A ibid footnote 15]

[159] Shabbos Kehalacha 3 17:51; Nishmas Shabbos Sechita 237; Emek Hateshuvah 47

The reason: As the Poskim explicitly rule that wine may not be defrosted. [Elya Raba 318:36; M"B 318:105] Furthermore, the above reason to differentiate only follows those that hold the prohibition is due to Sechitas Peiros while those that hold the prohibition is Nolad Davar Chadash, seemingly it should be forbidden, as it still appears like a new item.

[160] The reason: As it is permitted to place ice in warm water being the melted ice is not recognizable.

[161] SSH"K 10:3; 1:74 as is the simple implication in Shulchan Aruch 320:16

[162] As rules Admur in 320:16 that in times of need one may be lenient to follow the opinion which permits doing so.

[163] See previous Q&A

[164] SSH"K 10:1

[165] Vetzaruch Iyun as there Admur mentions three reasons why it is allowed and perhaps the reason of that it goes to waste it itself not enough. However in the parentheses when explaining why it is not similar to squeezing fruits Admur only mentions the reason that it goes to waste. Vetzaruch Iyun.

May one place ice cubes in a serving tray for the meal despite the fact that they will melt?[166]
Yes, as one has no intent to drink the melted water but rather only to use the ice and it is thus similar to throwing ice in ones sink which is allowed due to that the liquid will be going to waste.[167]

May one throw out his leftover ice cubes into the kitchen sink despite the fact that they will melt?
According to those Poskim that allow placing ice outside the fridge, if it is not near a flame or the sun, then it is permitted to do so in this case as well. Furthermore, some[168] write that according to all it is permitted in this case being that the resultant water is going to waste. However seemingly according to Admur one is not to be lenient in this matter.[169] According to all however one may take the ice from one area of melting and place it in another area, such as from one's table to the sink. It is only forbidden to take it from the freezer and place it into the sink.

May one wash his hands in a sink that contains ice, such as discarded ice cubes?[170]
Yes.[171]

May one open the faucet if the water stream will directly fall on the ice cubes in the sink?[172]
No.[173]

May one defrost frozen foods that do not turn into liquids on Shabbos, such as defrosting a frozen bottle of soda?[174]
Frozen foods that do not change form upon being defrosted, such as cooked meat [as raw meat is Muktzah], bread, may be defrosted in order to be eaten on Shabbos.[175]

May one defrost frozen milk?
Some Poskim[176] write it is permitted to defrost frozen milk on Shabbos.[177] Practically however, one is not to rely on this opinion, and is to follow the same ruling as all frozen liquids.[178]

---

[166] Piskeiy Teshuvos 320 footnote 22

[167] If however one does plan to use the melted water then this is dependent on the above mentioned dispute in the previous two questions. In any event even in such a case, according to all one may first place water in the bowl and then place the ice cubes in it.

[168] SSH"K 10:1

[169] As a) It is implied from Admur that there is no difference between placing the ice near the sun or in any area in which it does not melt. B) The reason of going to waste does not suffice according to the opinion of Rashi, as explained above in Halacha 1C and Tehila Ledavid 320:15

[170] Shabbos Kehalacha Vol. 3 17:29 [p. 72]; Meor Hashabbos 13:61

[171] As only a small amount will melt and it will be going to waste and one has no intent to do so. [320:17] Seemingly this is not comparable to urine which comes as a hard stream and hence melts more than a small amount.

[172] Shabbos Kehalacha Vol. 3 17:29 [p. 72]; See Meor Hashabbos 13:61 footnote 162

[173] As a lot more than a small amount will melt due to the stream and it is hence similar to urinating on snow.

[174] SSH"K 10:5 in name of Rav SZ"A

[175] The reason: Meat and bread are not Nolad being that their state has never changed. It however may not be deforsted for use of after Shabbos being that it is forbidden to do any preparations on Shabbos for after Shabbos.]

[176] SSH"K 10:5 in name of Rav SZ"A; Maor Hashabbos 13:44 in name of RSZ"A allows to deforst even juices near the sun

[177] Milk and other foods which are not eaten in their frozen state are not considered Nolad as since they are not eaten in their frozen state they are considered by people as liquids as opposed to solids even when they are frozen, and it is thus not considered a new change. Only water which is not a Chashuv item is not considered a liquid when frozen. [Rav SZ"A ibid footnote 15]

[178] Shabbos Kehalacha 3 17:51; Nishmas Shabbos Sechita 237; Emek Hateshuvah 47
The reason: As the Poskim explicitly rule that wine may not be defrosted. [Elya Raba 318:36; M"B 318:105] Furthermore, the above reason to differentiate only follows those that hold the prohibition is due to Sechitas Peiros while those that hold the prohibition is Nolad Davar Chadash, seemingly it should be forbidden, as it still appears like a new item.

Compilation-May one serve ice cubes in a serving bowl on Shabbos?

It is forbidden to actively melt ice on Shabbos through crushing it and the like.[179] It is disputed whether it is permitted to inactively cause ice to melt, such as through placing it near a heat source, such as the sun.[180] Practically, the custom is to be stringent, unless it is a time of need.[181] A further dispute is added when one is simply removing the ice from its cold environment, such as the freezer and is simply placing it in room temperature.[182] Nonetheless, in a case that one has no intended use of the resultant water that will melt as a result, and one plans to simply throw it out, then it is permitted to inactively cause the ice to melt through placing it in room temperature.[183] Accordingly, there is no prohibition involved in preparing a serving bowl of ice to serve at one's meal so long as one does not plan to make use of the resultant water that melted from the ice.[184] There is no need to first add water to the ice tray, although doing so certainly adds to the allowance.[185] If, however, one does plan to use the melted water such as to drink and the like, then whether it is permitted to serve the ice in a serving bowl is subject to the above mentioned dispute regarding removing ice from its cold environment. In any event, even in such a case, it is permitted to do so if one first places some water in the bowl and then places the ice cubes into it.[186]

Summary:

It is permitted to have a serving bowl of ice cubes at one's meal so long as one does not plan to make use of the resultant water that will melt from the ice. If one does plan to use the melted water such as to drink and the like, then one is to first place some water in the bowl and then places the ice cubes in it.

---

4. Washing ones hands with salt/ soap/fats:[187]

It is forbidden to wash one's hands in salt[188] and certainly with soap[189] or other fats.

The reason for this is: because [the material] dissolves in one's hand and is as if one has created a new substance on Shabbos which resembles a forbidden action, as was explained above in Halacha 1 that it is forbidden to crush snow and hail for this reason. [This prohibition is referred to as Molid.]

Other Opinions:[190] [However] according to those which [held there] that the reason for the prohibition of crushing snow and hail is because of a decree made [to safeguard one from coming to] squeeze fruits which are designated for their juices, and snow and hail are likewise designated for their liquids as was explained there [in 320/19], [then according to them] soap and other fat which are not designated as liquids are permitted to be [even] initially crushed.[191]

The Final Ruling: One is to be stringent like the former opinion. [The custom of all Israel is to be

---

[179] Admur 320:16; Michaber 320:9; Shabbos 51b
[180] See both opinions in Admur 320:16; brought also in 318:25-27 regarding melting fat; See Michaber [lenient] and Rama [stringent] 318:16; 320:9
[181] Admur 318:27; 320:16; Rama 318:16
[182] The following Poskim are lenient: Sheivet Halevy 7:40; Az Nidbaru 6:3 and 34; 10:10; Tzitz Eliezer 6:34-30; Divrei Yatziv 159; Shabbos Kehalacha 3 17:3 and 27. The following Poskim are stringent: SSH"K 10:3; 1:74, as is the simple Halacha ruled by Admur that one may not cause frozen water to melt. [320:16] Rav SZ"A as brought in Mioreiy Hashabbos.
[183] SSH"K 10:1; Piskeiy Teshuvos 320 footnote 22 [old] 320:13-14 [new]
The reason: As the melting prohibition does not apply in a case that the melted item will be going to waste and one does not have intent to melt it. [See Admur 320:17; Taz 320:7; M"B 320:32; Meor Hashabbos 3:13-98; Shabbos Kehalacha vol. 3 17 footnote 84 and Tosefes Biur p. 157]
[184] As one has no intent to drink the melted water but rather only to use the ice and it is thus similar to throwing ice in ones sink which is allowed due to that the liquid will be going to waste
[185] See Admur 320:16; Michaber 320:9; Shabbos 51b
[186] See Admur 320:16; Michaber 320:9; Shabbos 51b; Piskeiy Teshuvos 320 footnote 152
[187] Admur 326:10; Rama 326:10; Tur; Iggur 486; Baal Hateruma 235
[188] Brought also in 320:19; Michaber 320:12; Rosh
[189] Admur ibid; Rama ibid; Binyamin Zeev 278 [206]
[190] Admur ibid; M"A 326:11; Shiltei Giborim; M"B 326:30
[191] Seemingly according to this opinion it is permitted to melt soap and fat even not into water. However, salt would remain forbidden to rub and dissolve without water according to all. See 320:19

stringent against using soap on Shabbos.[192]]

Summary of using soap:[193]

Has the same status as ice [stated above in Halacha 1-3], and thus although the soap may be placed in water to dissolve it may not be dissolved with one's hands. Nevertheless, one may place salt in water and wash with it, so long as he does not rub his hands in the process.

Q&A

Does washing one's hands with a bar of soap contain the smoothening prohibition [Mimacheik] and would thus be prohibited according to all?[194]

Some Poskim[195] rule that the Biblical Mimacheik/smoothening prohibition applies to soft soap and thus using it is forbidden according to all opinions. The[196] however, Other Poskim[197] however argue that there is no smoothening prohibition applicable in such a case for variety of reasons [see footnote[198]]. In any event the custom is not to wash at all with a bar of soap, as explained above that we are stringent like the opinion which holds that doing so involves a Molid prohibition.

Does washing one's hands with a bar of soap which contains engraved lettering contain the "erasing" prohibition?[199]

The Ketzos Hashulchan leaves this matter in doubt[200] although in any event the custom is not to wash at all with a bar of soap as explained above.

May one place soap into a cup of liquid and have it dissolve and then use that to wash ones hands?[201]

Yes, as doing so is similar to placing ice in ones drink which is allowed. Furthermore, some[202] write one may even mix the soap into the water through shaking the vessel. However, some are stringent to only enter the bar of soap into the water from before Shabbos.[203] **See below regarding scented soaps.**

May one wash his hands with liquid soap?

Liquid soap may be used on Shabbos.[204] This includes even if the soap is slightly thick to the point that

---

[192] M"B 320:30
[193] Admur 320:19 and chapter 326 Halacha 10
[194] Based mainly on Ketzos Hashulchan 146 footnote 32
[195] M"B in name of Tiferes Yisrael, brought in Ketzos Hashulchan 127 footnote 13; 146 footnote 32 [Vetzaruch Iyun from his later ruling brought in footnote below. One must say that he retracted his ruling.]; Igros Moshe 1:113
[196]
[197] Ketzos Hashulchan 146 footnote 32; SSH"K 14 footnote 49, in name of RSZ"A and others.
[198] A) It's a Melacha which is not needed for itself [Eino Tzarich Legufa] being that the source of the Memacheik prohibition is by smoothening the skin of an animal which benefits the skin. This is opposed to here where the smoothening of the soap does not benefit the soap but rather is done for the person to use the dissolved layer. B) Since the inevitable smoothening of the soap serves no benefit, as it makes no difference to oneself whether it is smooth or not, it is therefore allowed to be done even Rabbinically, as by Mimacheik if one has no intent to benefit the item from the smoothening than it is not considered a Melacha at all, similar to the ruling regarding pouring cold water into a plastic cup [brought in "The Laws of Cooking Halacha 1 Q&A there!] C) It is done in a way of its normal use, and just like we say regarding food prohibitions that when done in its way of eating it is allowed, the same applies by soap when used in the midst of bathing.
[199] Ketzos Hashulchan 146 footnote 32
[200] As the Magen Avraham concludes with a Tzarich Iyun regarding the stringency of Avraham Halevy by engraved letters. [ibid] Now although Admur rules in 458:8 that engraved letters are forbidden to be broken, nevertheless see Ketzos Hashulchan 144 footnote 3 that this is only forbidden when one breaks it and then eats it, if however, one breaks it within the process of eating it is allowed. Thus, perhaps here too there is room to question whether erasing the letters in the process of using the soap is truly forbidden.
[201] Ketzos Hashulchan 127 footnote 13
[202] SSH"K 14:16 as explained above in Halacha 2 Q&A there, based on Ketzos Hashulchan 127 Footnote 2.
[203] Ketzos Hashulchan 146 footnote 32 [page 58]; Aruch Hashulchan 326:11
[204] Ketzos Hashulchan 146 footnote 32; 138 footnote 31 regarding toothpaste; Aruch Hashulchan 326:11; SSH"K 14:16 footnote 49; Shabbos Kehalacha Volume 3 17:73
The reason: As it is already a liquid and the bubbles that it creates have no significance. [ibid]

it cannot be poured like actual liquid but is rather more like a pasty substance.[205] [However there is an opinion[206] who is stringent against using liquid soap even when the soap is thin like water due to the smoothening prohibition. However, if one adds water to the soap, and it has thus already been dissolved with water, then it is permitted to be used according to all.[207]] Practically, the custom is to avoid using thick liquid soap on Shabbos [and rather to mix it with water from before Shabbos].[208] [If one did not do so before Shabbos, he may nevertheless do so on Shabbos.[209]]
See below regarding scented soaps.

May one wash his hands with scented soaps?
See "The Laws of Molid Reiach".[210]

May one use a toilet that contains toilet soap?
One is to avoid using all forms of toilet soaps on Shabbos.[211] Thus, one is to remove the soap from the toilet before Shabbos. If one did not do so it is permitted to remove the soap on Shabbos, although some are stringent to remove it with an irregularity.[212] Some Poskim[213] however rule it is permitted to use such soaps in cases of discomfort. Some Poskim[214] rule it is only forbidden to use toilet soaps if one intends that the soap color the water or that it release a good smell. If however one does not have intent for this to occur then one may use toilet soaps even if they color the water and release good smell.
Urinating away from the soap:[215] In all cases it is permitted to urinate in a toilet that contains toilet soap so long as one does not urinate directly onto the soap. The above question of prohibition only relates to the flushing of the toilet.
Is the soap Muktzah?[216] Toilet soap is considered Muktzah Machmas Issur. Some Poskim[217] however

---

[205] Implication of Ketzos Hashulchan ibid; Shabbos Kehalacha ibid
[206] Igros Moshe 1:113
[207] So rules Az Nidbaru 1:16 brought in Piskeiy Teshuvos 326:8
[208] Shabbos Kehalacha Vol. 3 17:73
[209] The reason: As there is no prohibition of Molid in liquifying soap, as explained above regarding bubbles, and thus the entire remaining issue is Mimacheik, which is avoided once the soap is liquified. Furthermore, the Poskim rule that one may place even hard soap in a cup of water for it to make soap water on Shabbos, however one may not shake it. [See Ketzos Hashulchan 127 footnote 13; SSH"K 14:16 as explained above in Halacha 2 Q&A there, based on Ketzos Hashulchan 127 Footnote 2]
[210] Seemingly it is forbidden as this case is no different than the case mentioned there of washing ones hands with scented water in which although the main intent is not for the scent, nevertheless since one does also intend in absorbing it, it is thereby forbidden. However perhaps it is considered similar to one who desires to remove a bad smell, in which case some Poskim permit it. See there!
[211] Orach Yisrael 35
Background of the prohibition:
The use of toilet soaps may involve any of the following three prohibitions: *Molid Reiach; Nolad and Tzoveia [dyeing]*
1. *Prohibition of Nolad*: Seemingly it is forbidden to use toilet soaps due to the Nolad prohibition being that one is melting the solid soap thru flushing the toilet [which is similar to urinating on snow which was viewed as if one is melting the snow with one's hands]. Thus, even using unscented and non-colored toilet soaps would be problematic. [Orach Yisrael 35 rules based on this reason that initially it is forbidden o use toilet soaps unless it is a case of Shaas Hadchak] However there are Poskim which rule that there is no issue of Nolad with toilet soaps as it is only a minute amount which melts, and that itself is through an indirect action. [Shabbos Kehalacha Vol. 3 17:80]
2. *Prohibition of Tzoveia*: If the toilet soap releases a color into the water, then it may not be used due to the dyeing prohibition. [SSH"K 23:14] However some Poskim allow its use if one has no interest at all in the coloring of the water. [Shabbos Kehalacha Vol. 3 17:80]
3. *Prohibition of creating a new smell*: The prohibition of Molid Reiach does not apply even when using a scented toilet soap. [Practically although Poskim [Sharreiy Teshuvah and Mishneh Berurah in 128:6; Minchas Yitzchak 6:26] rule it is forbidden to create a good smell in water, nevertheless it is allowed to absorb a good smell into the toilet water as the good smell is simply there to remove bad odor. [Beir Moshe 1:34 rules that good smells may always be applied in order to remove bad odors, and so rules Piskeiy Teshuvos [327:1, 328:26] Other Poskim however rule it is only allowed if one has no intent to create a good smell within the water. [Shabbos Kehalacha Vol. 3 17:80]
[212] See below and Shabbos Kehalacha Vol. 3 17 footnote 196 for a discussion on the Muktzah status of the soap.
[213] Orach Yisrael 35; Shabbos Kehalacha ibid, there he extends the leniency to even toilet soaps that dye the water.
In Sefer Orach Yisrael 35 he rules that one may be lenient to use such soaps if lack of doing so will cause bad odors and distress, as he rules that in a Shaas Hadchak one may be lenient like the opinion which holds that melting soaps and fats do not contain a Nolad prohibition. Furthermore, he rules that if one forgot to remove it before Shabbos then it may be used on Shabbos being that it is Muktzah and is forbidden to remove and thus this case too is a Shaas Hadchak. Vetzaruch Iyun according to Admur why he rules by melting fats near fire that one is to be stringent unless it is a Shaas Hadchak while here by soaps he plainly rules that one is to be stringent [implying even in Shaas Hadchak].
[214] Shabbos Kehalacha ibid
[215] Shabbos Kehalacha Vol. 3 17:81
[216] Shabbos Kehalacha Vol. 3 17 footnote 196
[217] Igros Moshe 5

consider it Muktzah Machmas Chisaron Kis. According to this latter opinion one may not enter or remove the toilet soap from the toilet on Shabbos due to the Muktzah prohibition. It is however permitted to move it with an irregularity.

General Q&A on Nolad

May one make seltzer water on Shabbos?
Doing so is not forbidden due to the Nolad prohibition[218], however may encounter other prohibitions. Practically, Some Poskim[219] rule it is permitted. However other Poskim[220] rule that it is forbidden due to other prohibitions.[221]

Question:
Hi. Is it permitted on Shabbos to make seltzer using SodaStream with the non-electric model?

Answer:
While this matter is under debate amongst the Poskim with some claiming that it transgresses the rabbinical Nolad prohibition, as well as other possible prohibitions [i.e. Tikkun Keli] especially if one needs to assemble the cylinder to it on Shabbos. Practically, the vast majority of Poskim rule that is permitted to be used on Shabbos to make soda water and many even permit attaching the cylinder to it on Shabbos [being that it is made for constant entrance and removal and is thus similar to the cover of a bottle]. Nonetheless, I would suggest that the best thing is to make it before Shabbos and certainly not to attach the cylinder on Shabbos. Although if the cylinder is already attached and one forgot to make the soda water before Shabbos than he may be lenient to make it on Shabbos, and those who even attach a new cylinder to it on Shabbos have upon whom to rely, although those who are stringent not to attach a new cylinder and not to even make soda water on Shabbos, are blessed.

Sources: See Ketzos Hashulchan 130 footnote 12 and 146 footnote 32; Minchas Yitzchak 4:122 although it is best to do so from before Shabbos [9:33]; SSH"K 11:35 in name of Rav SZ"A; Yabia Omer 3:21 who also permits the attaching of the cylinder; See Maharsham 3:140; 6:33; Bris Olam Ofeh 91; Chelkas Yaakov 3:168; Tzitz Eliezer 7:24; 20:13; See list of all Poskim who are stringent and lenient in Piskeiy Teshuvos 320:15 footnote 163 and 313 footnote 99 regarding attaching the cylinder

May one blow bubbles on Shabbos?[222]
Blowing bubbles on Shabbos enters into the question of whether it transgresses the Molid prohibition due to it changing the form of the water into foam. Practically, the mainstream approach follows that it does not contain a Molid prohibition, and therefore children may blow bubbles on Shabbos.[223]

---

[218] Ketzos Hashulchan 146 footnote 32; However, see Maharsham 6:33 that one may not do so on Yom Tov due to Molid.
[219] Ketzos Hashulchan 130 footnote 12 and 146 footnote 32; Minchas Yitzchak 4:122 although it is best to do so from before Shabbos [9:33]; SSH"K 11:35 in name of Rav SZ"A; Yabia Omer 3:21; See Mahrsham 3:140
[220] See Ketzos Hashulchan ibid; Bris Olam Ofeh 91; Chelkas Yaakov 3:168; Tzitz Eliezer 7:24; 20:13
[221] Such as Boneh:Tikkun Keli upon screwing the gas canister into mechanisim.
[222] See SSH"K 16:30; Shabbos Kehalacha Vol. 3 17:79; Piskeiy Teshuvos 326:13 footnote 161
[223] Evident from Ketzos Hashulchan 146:32; SSH"K ibid in name of Rav SH"Z Aurbauch; Shabbos Kehalacha ibid; Piskeiy Teshuvos ibid although writes that initially one should not instruct children to do so and it is just that if they do so they do not have to be protested
The reason: Although it is forbidden on Shabbos to change the form of an item, such as to turn ice into water, due to the Molid/Nolad prohibition, nevertheless the Poskim rule that the formation of foam/bubbles that becomes created when using soap to wash hands/dishes does not fall under this prohibition as the foam has no real substance, and does not last at all. [So rules Ketzos Hashulchan 146 footnote 32; Tzitz Eliezer 6:34; -14; in length; Beir Moshe 8:247; SSH"K ibid in name of Rav SZ"A; Piskeiy Teshuvos ibid; However some are stringent in this: See Ginas Veradim [Halevi] O.C. Klall 3:14 regarding hard soap; Shevisas Hashabbos Dash 61; Az Nidbaru 10:16] For this reason, also the placing of toothpaste on one's teeth [without a tooth brush] does not consist of a Nolad prohibition, even though it creates foam in the process, as the foam has no substance. [Ketzos Hashulchan 138 footnote 31]. Accordingly, it would be permitted here as well to blow bubbles, being that the bubbles hold no substance and do not last. However, Tzaruch Iyun, as in the case of blowing bubbles one has intent to create the foam and it is thus unlike the case discussed above in the Poskim regarding soap bubbles, in which case one has no intent for them to be made. [see Shabbos Kehalacha ibid; Piskeiy Teshuvos ibid] Nevertheless, it is clear that the Ketzos Hashulchan 146 footnote 32 learns it is permitted even a case that one intends to

However, it is best for adults to abstain from doing so.[224] Furthermore, some Poskim[225] rule that even children who have reached the age of Chinuch are to avoid blowing bubbles on Shabbos.[226]

May one shake milk on Shabbos in order to form foam from the milk, as is common for drinking cappuccino.
Yes.[227] However seemingly those Poskim[228] that are stringent regarding making bubbles would be stringent in this matter as well.

May one use a spray can of whip cream and the like?
Some[229] write it is forbidden to do so due to Nolad.

Q&A on Freezing foods/liquid on Shabbos
May one make ice cubes, or freeze drinks on Shabbos?[230]
Many Poskim[231] rule it is permitted to do so even initially, and so is the widespread custom.[232] Others Poskim[233] however rule it is forbidden to do so.[234] Others[235] rule one may only do so in a time of need.[236] Practically, it is proper to avoid doing so unless there is great need for this to be done.[237] So is also the implied opinion of Admur.[238]

---

make the bubbles, as he also explains that it is permitted to make seltzer for this reason, even though one certainly has intent to create the bubbles.

[224] SSH"K ibid; Shabbos Kehalacha ibid
The reason: As one intends to make the bubble and it is hence unlike the case discussed regarding soap bubbles in which case one has no intent for them to be made. [SSH"K ibid; Piskeiy Teshuvos ibid]
[225] Shraga Hameir 7:44; Koveitz Mibeiys Halevy 6:44 in name of Rav Shmuel Wozner and Nishmas Shabbos 250, brought in Shabbos Kehalacha ibid footnote 192
[226] The reason: As nevertheless, one has intent to make the bubbles and it is hence similar to Molid Davar Chadash. [ibid]
[227] The reason: Seemingly it is permitted to do so being that foam has no real substance and hence does not constitute the Nolad prohibition. This is similar to the foam of liquid soap which is not considered Nolad. [As rules Ketzos Hashulchan 146 footnote 32; SSH"K 14:16 footnote 49] It is likewise similar to the foam of toothpaste which is not considered Nolad. [Ketzos Hashulchan 138 footnote 31]. It is likewise similar to blowing bubbles which is not considered Nolad. [SSH"K 16:30; Shabbos Kehalacha Vol. 3 17:79] However Tzaruch Iyun as here one has intent to make the foam unlike the case discussed regarding soap bubbles in which case one has no intent for them to be made. [see Shabbos Kehalacha ibid] Nevertheless, it is clear the Ketzos Hashulchan 146 footnote 32 learns it is permitted even in such a case that one intends to make the bubbles, as he also explains that it is permitted to make seltzer for this reason.
[228] Koveitz Mibeis Levi; Nishmas Shabbos 250, brought in Shabbos Kehalacha ibid
The reason: As nevertheless, one has intent to make the bubbles and it is hence similar to Molid Davar Chadash. [Shabbos Kehalacha ibid footnote 192]
[229] Maor Hashabbos 13:60 brought in Shabbos Kehalacha 3 17:78 [p. 117]; Piskeiy Teshuvos 326 footnote 161; 321 footnote 330; See there that perhaps one can allow it on the basis that the person is simply pressing the button to expel the content, and is not actually creating it with his hands. See also Orchos Shabbos 15:28 that permits it.
[230] SSH"K 10:4; Piskeiy Teshuvos 320:4
[231] Shevisas Hashabbos Choshev 2; Toras Shabbos 318:10; Mahrshag 2:103; Nishmas Shabbos Sechita 251; Chelkas Yaakov 2:98; 3:113; Rav SZ"A in SSH"K 10 footnote 14 [in new] and Maor Hashabbos 1; Beir Moshe 2:25-26, 6:11; Vayaan Yosef 20; Shearim Hametzuyanim Behalacha 80:18; Tzitz Eliezer 6:34 and 8:12; Lehoros Nasan 1:17; Az Nidbaru 7:7; 10:12; Or Letziyon 2:32; Shabbos Kehalacha 17:93 that so is the accepted ruling; Betzeil Hachachmah 2:25 rules that if one's entire intent is to re-melt the ice and then drink it then it is permitted, thus by ice cubes it would be permitted, although by ices forbidden.
[232] The reason: As it is not considered Boneh as it is food that is not meant to last, and is not similar to Sechitas Peiros, and is not Molid Davar Chadash in an active form, and is also not Nolad of Muktzah. [ibid]
[233] Pesach Hadvir 325:1, brought in Shevisas Hashabbos Choshev 2; Doveiv Meisharim 1:55
[234] The reason: This is forbidden due to Boneh [Pesach Dvir ibid] and Nolad. [Pesach Dvir ibid; Dovev Meisharim ibid] This form of Nolad is forbidden according to all opinions, even according to the Ramban, and is forbidden even Bedieved. [Doveiv Meisharim ibid]
[235] Minchas Yitzchak 8:24; Shevet Halevi 3:55; Mishneh Halachas 4:48; SSH"K ibid
[236] The reason: As it is only forbidden according to the Sefer Haterumah, of which the Rama rules one may be lenient in a time of need. [ibid]
[237] So is the final ruling in SSH"K ibid, as well as in Mishneh Halachas. It is permitted to do so in a case of need as this is similar to placing ice in an area where it will melt which Admur rules may be done in a case of need. This is in contrast to the Doveiv Meisharim which rules that even in time of need it is forbidden, and the ice is Muktzah as all opinions agree by freezing that it has a Nolad prohibition, and it was only regarding melting that the dispute was brought. However, many Poskim argue on this and say it retains the same dispute. [See Piskeiy Teshuvos ibid footnote 14]
[238] As Admur rules the reason behind the opinion of the Sefer Haterumah is due to Molid Davar Chadash, and hence this is applicable also by freezing. However just as we are lenient to place the fat near the sun in a time of need, so too here one can be lenient.

May one place a bottle in the freezer so it becomes cold as opposed to freeze?[239]
Yes, this is permitted even according to the stringent opinions mentioned above.[240]

May one place liquids in the freezer before Shabbos having them freeze over Shabbos?[241]
This is permitted according to all opinions.

May one place solid foods in the freezer on Shabbos?[242]
It is permitted to freeze solid foods which are normally not eaten in their frozen state. One may thus freeze cooked meat, milk and other items which are edible when not frozen.
Note: One must beware not to move any Muktzah foods while placing foods into the freezer on Shabbos.

May one freeze a liquidly food in order so it not spoil?[243]
Yes, as this is considered a time of need in which one may be lenient.

May one enter foods with gravy into the fridge/freezer despite that they will congeal?
Some Poskim[244] rule this is allowed since they are also eaten in their congealed state there is no Nolad prohibition involved.

May one place liquids in the freezer prior to the freezer turning on?
Yes.[245] However some Poskim[246] are stringent even in such a case.

Regarding if one may defrost frozen foods/liquids on Shabbos- See Halacha 3B Q&A there!

May one freeze ice cream on Shabbos?
Some Poskim[247] rule this is allowed as ice cream is considered like a food and not like a liquid and thus does not contain a Nolad prohibition. Practically however, those that avoid freezing foods on Shabbos are to be stringent unless in a time of need.[248]

May one melt ice cream on Shabbos?[249]
Yes, as ice cream is considered like a food and not like a liquid and thus does not contain a Nolad prohibition. Nevertheless, this may only be done with intent to eat on Shabbos.

Q&A on Yom Tov
Is melting fat or ice on Yom Tov forbidden due to the Nolad prohibition which applies on Yom Tov?
Some Poskim[250] rule that all forms of Nolad are forbidden on Yom Tov and therefore it is forbidden to

---

[239] Az Nidbaru 10:8
[240] As although it may begin to freeze a little before one remembers to remove it, nevertheless since the entire prohibition of freezing items is itself only stringency, therefore here it is allowed.
[241] Chelkas Yaakov 2:98
[242] SSH"K 10:5
[243] Minchas Yitzchak 8:24
[244] Piskeiy Teshuvos 320:4
[245] Shabbos Kehalacha 17:96
The reason: As Admur permits placing the fat near the oven that will be truned on by the gentile.
[246] According to Dovev Meisharim ibid one is to be stringnet even in such a case.
[247] SSH"K 10:7
[248] See Shabbos Kehalacha 3 17:19 based on Machatzis Hashekel 318:42 which prohibits melting fish fat, and the same would apply to freezing, for those that are stringent not to freeze on Shabbos
[249] SSH"K 10:8
[250] Shut Mahrsham 6:33; Doveiv Meisharim 1:55; Shevet Hakihasi 3:170

melt fat or ice on Yom Tov as their own individual substance. However, to melt them into another substance is permitted being that it is not recognizable as Nolad. Other Poskim[251] rule that such a form of Nolad is permitted, and thus one may melt ice and fat on Yom Tov. It is implied from Admur[252] that it is permitted to melt ice and fat on Yom Tov, as the prohibition of Molid on Yom Tov was not made applicable to foods.[253] Some[254] write that nevertheless, regarding melting ice it is proper to be stringent.

May one make ice cubes, freeze ice cream and the like on Yom Tov?
It is permitted to freeze water to make ice cubes and freeze ice cream on Yom Tov[255], and so is the ruling according to Admur.[256] However, there are Poskim[257] which are stringent due to the prohibition of Nolad/Muktzah.[258]

May one make ice cream on Yom Tov?
Some Poskim[259] rule that this is allowed[260], although using an irregularity[261]. Other Poskim[262] rule that it is forbidden due to the Boneh prohibition which applies equally on Yom Tov.

---

[251] SSH"K 12 footnote 29 in name of Rav SZ"A based on Admur and M"A brought in next footnote; Nitei Gavriel Yom Tov 17:7; Piskeiy Teshuvos 495 footnote 48; See however for later retractions of Rav SZ"A in the Miluim for SSH"K as well as Meor Hashabbos that he forbids melting ice on Yom Tov and only melting fat is permitted. So also rules Shabbos Kehalacha 17:114 that regarding ice it is proper to be stringent.
[252] 511:7 and Kuntrus Achron 511:1; M"A 511:10
Background:
Admur ibid deals with the prohibition against making new smells in an item on Shabbos which is forbidden due to Molid Davar Chadash. Admur ibid states "Although all the Melachos were permitted for the sake of food, nevertheless making a new smell is not such a need for the food and is not something desired by all people....however even to make a new smell is permitted if his main intent is not to do so, but rather to give good taste." From here it is implied that by foods there is no prohibition against melting them being it is a real need for the food and is desired by all people.
[253] The reason: As all matters that relate to Ochel Nefesh are permitted on Yom Tov. [see Admur ibid]
[254] See later retractions of Rav SZ"A in the Miluim for SSH"K as well as Meor Hashabbos that he forbids melting ice on Yom Tov and only melting fat is permitted. So also rules Shabbos Kehalacha 17:114 that regarding ice it is proper to be stringent.
[255] 511:7 and Kuntrus Achron 511:1; M"A 511:10
[255] So rules Chelkas Yaakov 2:98; Piskeiy Teshuvos 495:10; Shabbos Kehalacha 17:117
As a) Nolad does not apply by food on Yom Tov. [Admur in previous question]; b) According to many Poskim making ice on Shabbos is not clearly a problem of Nolad and thus they allow it to be done in times of need, thus here by Yom Tov where it is even questionable whether Nolad applies to foods at all one may be lenient.
[256] As Admur rules [511:7] that Molid does not apply to foods on Yom Tov and Admur does not hold of the concept of Nolad:Mukztah by melting foods.
[257] Doveiv Meisharim 1:55; Nitei Gavriel 17:8
[258] This follows the ruling of the Sefer Hateruma as is understood by some Rishonim. According to Admur however which rules like the Rosh that even the Sefer Hateruma does not hold of Nolad due to Muktzah, then certainly on Yom Tov it is permitted to freeze, as according to Admur Molid does not apply on Yom Tov.
[259] SSH"K 10:6
[260] As kneading is permitted to be done on Yom Tov.
[261] As anything which could have been done before Yom Tov without having its taste or quality diminished may only be done on Yom Tov with an irregularity. [Rama 495:1 Admur 495:5, and so rules M"A and M"B] Vetzaruch Iyun Gadol on SSH"K ibid which did not mention that an irregularity is needed. As well Tzaruch Iyun on Piskeiy Teshuvos which adds that an irregularity is needed if one had time to do it before Yom Tov, as it is ruled [Admur 495:6; M"B 495:10] that only in a case of "Ones" may one do it on Yom Tov without an irregularity. However if no "Ones" occurred, even if one forgot to do it before Yom Tov, it may only be done on Yom Tov with an irregularity.
[262] Piskeiy Teshuvos 495 footnote 52 based on the many Poskim which rule that making ice cream contains a Boneh prohibition which is equally forbidden on Yom Tov.

Compilation-May one wash his hands with liquid soap on Shabbos?
A. The Issues:
Using liquid soaps on Shabbos touch upon the following three issues.
1. The prohibition of Molid Davar Chadash [i.e. melting or dissolving].[263]
2. The Mimacheik/Mimareiach [i.e. smoothening] prohibition.[264]
3. The Molid Reiach prohibition [i.e. making a new smell].[265]

B. The law by unscented liquid soaps:
Unscented liquid soap may be used on Shabbos.[266] Doing so does not consist of a Molid prohibition or a Mimchaeik prohibition, or of any other prohibition.[267] This includes even if the soap is slightly thick to the point that it cannot be poured like actual liquid but is rather more like a pasty substance.[268] [However there is an opinion[269] who is stringent against using liquid soap even when the soap is thin like water due to the smoothening prohibition. However, if one adds water to the soap, and it has thus already been dissolved with water, then it is permitted to be used according to all.[270]] Practically, the custom is to avoid using thick liquid soap on Shabbos [and rather to mix it with water from before Shabbos].[271] [If one did not do so before Shabbos, he may nevertheless do so on Shabbos.[272]]

C. Scented liquid soaps?[273]
It is forbidden for one to wash his hands with scented water, as although the main intent is not for the scent but rather for the cleanliness, nevertheless one also intends in having his hands absorb the good scent and it is hence forbidden to do so.[274] [Accordingly, it is forbidden to wash ones hands with scented

---

[263] See regarding the prohibition of using a bar of soap: Admur 326:10; Rama 326:10; Tur; Iggur 486; Baal Hateruma 235
[264] See Admur 314:21; 327:1; 328:28; M"A 316:24, Levushei Serud on M"A; M"B 316:49; Ketzos Hashulchan 146 footnote 32
[265] See C!
[266] Ketzos Hashulchan 146 footnote 32; 138 footnote 31 regarding toothpaste; Aruch Hashulchan 326:11; SSH"K 14:16 footnote 49; Shabbos Kehalacha Volume 3 17:73
[267] The reason: As it is already a liquid and the bubbles that it creates have no significance. [ibid]
[268] Implication of Ketzos Hashulchan ibid; Shabbos Kehalacha ibid
[269] Igros Moshe 1:113
[270] So rules Az Nidbaru 1:16 brought in Piskeiy Teshuvos 326:8
[271] Shabbos Kehalacha Vol. 3 17:73
[272] The reason: As there is no prohibition of Molid in liquifying soap, as explained above regarding bubbles, and thus the entire remaining issue is Mimacheik, which is avoided once the soap is liquified. Furthermore, the Poskim rule that one may place even hard soap in a cup of water for it to make soap water on Shabbos, however one may not shake it. [See Ketzos Hashulchan 127 footnote 13; SSH"K 14:16 as explained above in Halacha 2 Q&A there, based on Ketzos Hashulchan 127 Footnote 2]
[273] Admur 511:7; Taz 511:8; Halachos Ketanos 1:19; Ben Ish Chaiy 2 Tetzaveh 11; Rav Poalim 2:51; Shoel Umeishiv Tinyana 2:7; Minchas Yitzchak 6:26 [see below in opinion of M"B]; Poskim in Kaf Hachaim 128:44 and 511:44 and so concludes the Kaf Hachaim ibid; Magen Avraham 511:11; 128:8 prohibits placing the secnt into the water, although he does not mention if this prohibition applies even if the scent was placed from before Shabbos.
Background: This ruling of Admur follows the ruling of the Taz which hold that the prohibition to create a new smell applies as well to skin. The Magen Avraham 511 [as well as Magen Avraham in 128:6]
Other Opinions: Some Poskim rule the prohibition of Molid Reiach does not to one's skin being the smell does not last, and it is hence permitted to place perfume/cologne on the body on Shabbos. Thus, if one placed the perfume in the water from before Yom Tov it may be used. [Chacham Tzevi 92; Elya Raba 128:8; Ginas Veradim 3:16; Nechpah Bakesef 4; Shaareiy Teshuvah 511:4; Mishneh Berurah 128:23 and so is implied from 511:28; Beir Moshe 1:34 rules one may be lenient by skin, although one who is stringent is blessed; SSH"K 14:32 rules leniently that perfume may be applied anywhere on one's body, as learns the Chacham Tzevi, as brought in M"B] These opinions can draw proof for their ruling from Michaber 327:1 and 328:36 in which the Michaber allows smearing rose oil on the body, and cheing scented gum in the mouth. Admur and the Poskim ibid however elarn that the scnted oil is permitted because one has no intent for the scent, while the gum is permitted because its intent is only to remove the bad smell.
According to the M"B may one add smells to other parts of one's body other than the hands? In M"B 128:23 he rules that one may be lenient like the Chacham Tzevi and Elyah Raba that one may wash hands with perfume water. However the Minchas Yitzchak 6:26 explains that the M"B himself only allows this to be done to ones hands and not to the rest of one's body, as perfume on ones hands rubs off quicker then on the rest of the body. To note however that the Minchas Yitzchak himself there leans to be stringent like Admur and the other Gedolei Haposkim which prohibit perfume on any part of the body. However Rav SZ"A [brought in SSH"K 14 footnote 92, and so they rule in Halacha 32] learns that the M"B permits applying perfume to any part of one's body.
Placing perfume on one's hair: Is forbidden according to all opinions being that hair is considered like clothing to which all agree there is a prohibition of Molid Reiach. [Piskeiy Teshuvos 327:1, see Minchas Yitzchak ibid.]
[274] The reason: The reason for this is because they intend to create a new smell on the hands of the Kohanim. Now, although the scented oil is placed into the water from before Yom Tov, nevertheless [this is forbidden] being that on Yom Tov when the Kohanim rinse their hands they are

soaps, if one also intends that his hands absorb the good smell, and accordingly it is best to avoid washing hands with scented soaps on Shabbos as it is difficult to ascertain that one has no intent to absorb the good scent into his hands.[275] However, if in truth one has no intent at all to create a good smell on his hands and is using it simply for cleanliness purposes, then it may be used.[276] Furthermore, some Poskim[277] rule that if one's intent of using the scented soap is to remove a bad smell from his hands, then it is permitted to be used even if one intends to benefit from the good smell, being that its purpose is to get rid of the bad smell.

Summary:

It is permitted to use liquid soap on Shabbos, although the custom is to liquify it with water before Shabbos, or to liquify on Shabbos before use if this was not done before Shabbos. Ideally, one should use only unscented soap to wash his hands, although if unscented soap is not available, then scented soap may be used so long as one does not intend at all to place the scent on his hands but simply to clean them.

---

creating a new smell on their hands, and they benefit from this smell, and it is pleasant for them and they intend to do so , therefore they are to refrain from doing so.

[275] See Shabbos Kehalacha Vol. 3 18:4 footnote 13 that it is very difficult to ascertain that one truly has no intent to absorb the smell.

[276] Shabbos Kehalacha ibid; See the following Poskim that it is permitted to do an action that causes a smell to enter into an item if one does not have any intention to do so: Admur 327:1; 511:7; Michaber 327:1; Mishneh Shabbos 111; Rashal Beitza 2:34; Taz 511:8; implication of M"A 511:10; Kuntrus Achron 511:1 based on proof from many Rishonim [Ramban; Ran; Rosh; Rif]; Neziros Shimshon; Mamar Mordechai; So rule regarding rose oil, that it may be smeared for pleasure purposes, thus proving that it does not contain a prohibition of creating a new smell if that is not one's intent: Admur 327:1; Michaber 327:1; Mishneh Shabbos 111

The reason: As Holadas Reiach is a light prohibition and is hence permitted if one does not have intent to do so. [Machatzis Hashekel 658:2 in explanation of Rashal; Implication of Admur in Kuntrus Achron ibid] Others however explain the reason is because these Poskim rule one may be lenient by a Pesik Reishei of a Rabbinical prohibition, and especially if Lo Nicha Lei. [P"M 321 M"Z 7 and 511 M"Z 8; Chemed Moshe; Nehar Shalom; Shaar Hatziyon 658:6; as rules Terumos Hadeshen, brought in M"A 314:5; Shaar Hatziyon 316:21; See Beis Yosef brought in Taz 316:3; Admur 314:3 regarding bees] This however is incorrect as Admur rules stringently regarding Pesik Resihei Delo Nicha Lei even by a Rabbinical prohibition, as brought in 316:4 and 320:24]

[277] Beir Moshe 1:34 rules that good smells may always be applied in order to remove bad odors, and so rules Piskeiy Teshuvos [327:1, 328:26] Shabbos Kehalacha Vol. 3 18:6

THE LAWS OF MOLID REIACH
Applying perfume; cologne; Deodorant; air fresheners on Shabbos

1. Molid Reiach-The laws of placing perfume and the like onto objects/clothing and one's skin:

A. Smoking fruits on Yom Tov over incense:[1]

In order to absorb a good taste:[2] Even to smoke fruits is only permitted when one's intent is only for the fruits to absorb the taste of the incense and thus become better to be eaten.

In order to absorb a good smell:[3] However it is forbidden to smoke the fruits in order so they absorb the smell of the incense and upon eating them one will then benefit from their good smell.

The reason for this prohibition is: because it is [Rabbinically[4]] forbidden to create a smell on Yom Tov[5] [or Shabbos] within an item that did not contain that smell [prior], as one who creates a new substance is similar to one who does a new [forbidden] action.[6] Now, although all forbidden actions are permitted [on Yom Tov] for the sake of eating, nevertheless [here it is forbidden as] the absorption of the smell [into the fruits] is not needed so much for the sake of eating and is not an equal necessity for all. It was thus only permitted to smoke fruits when one's intent is not for the fruits to absorb the smell of the incense but rather to benefit their taste and hence be better to be eaten. Now, although in such a case the new smell will anyways inevitably become absorbed in the fruits, nevertheless since his (main[7]) intent is not for the new smell, therefore the Sages did not decree against doing so.[8]

B. Absorbing a good smell into a cloth:

Through crushing spices into the cloth:[9] One may not place the pepper into a cloth and crush it with a knife [by pounding its handle] on top of it, as doing so creates a smell in the cloth [which is prohibited to do on Shabbos] **even though one does not have any intent to do so**[10] [as is written in chapter 511 [Halacha 7, which is brought next].

Through simply leaving the spices in the cloth:[11] [Based on that which was explained above regarding

---

[1] Admur 511:7

[2] Admur ibid and 511:4; Michaber 511:4; Shmuel in Beitza 22b

[3] Admur ibid and Kuntrus Achron 511:1; Implication of Michaber ibid; M"A 511:10 and 128:8 and 510:11 regarding water; Taz 511:8 regarding water; Milchamos 12b; Ran 12b; Raba Beitza 23a according to Shita Mekubetzes ibid

Background: The Gemara Beitza 23a and Rama in 511:4 state it is forbidden to enter perfume into a cloth, due to the prohibition of Molid Reiach. Admur and the above Poskim extend this ruling even to foods, as in his opinion, as rule the above Poskim, the prohibition of Holadas Reiach applies even to foods. In Kuntrus Achron ibid Admur lengthens to prove this opinion and negates the opinion of the Chacham Tzvi brought next.

Other opinions: Some Poskim rule that the prohibition of Molid Reiach does not apply to foods at all. [Implication of Rashi Beitza 23a; Chacham Tzvi 92 [brought in Shaareiy Teshuvah 511:4]; Rav Yehuda Beitza 23a according to Shita Mekubetzes ibid, brought in Kuntrus Achron ibid; see Eliya Raba 128:8]

[4] Rashi and M"B in coming footnotes

[5] Admur ibid; Rama 511:4; Beitza 23a

[6] Admur ibid; Rashi 23a; M"B 511:27; Sheilas Yaavatz 1:42; See Shabbos Kehalacha 17 Biurim 2

It is not forbidden due to the Melacha of making the Shemen Hamishcha in the Mishkan as only those Melachos which are connected with the building of the Mishkan were used to derive the 39 Melachos. [Sheilas Yaavatz 42]

Tikkun Keli: See M"B 658:7 and Kaf Hachaim 658:6 who record the reason for the prohibition of Molid Reiach is due to Tikkun Keli. Seemingly however this is the same reason as stated in Rashi ibid.

[7] See C and footnote there!

[8] Admur ibid; Rashal 2:34; Taz 511:8; M"A 511:10; Kuntrus Achron 511:1 based on proof from many Rishonim.

Other opinions: Some Poskim rule it is forbidden to create a smell in an item even if one does not intend to do so. [Implication of Rama 658:2; Maharil; Rokeiach; and so rules M"A 658:2; P"M 511 A"A 11; M"B 658:7 is lenient in a time of need] As for why according to these opinions it is permitted to enter scent into fruits for the sake of adding taste, see Admur in Kuntrus Achron ibid who explains that they hold the reason it is permitted is because it is considered Ochel Nefesh, s explained Rashi in Shabbos ibid]

[9] Admur 321:7; Taz 321:7

[10] Seemingly the reason why here Admur rules that even when one has no intent to absorb the smell it is forbidden is because here a real action [crushing] is being done which causes the smell to get absorbed and thus we are stringent even when one does not intend to do so. However, in the previous case of smoking fruits, as well as in the next case of simply placing the spices into the cloth, since no action is being done, it therefore is only prohibited when one intends to do so. [So explains Rav Yisrael Labkowski in Kinnus Torah 18 p. 50. See there from page 44 and on for an analysis on this entire subject of the contradiction of Admur in Hilchos Shabbos and Yom Tov]. To note that the Taz himself writes the same contradiction as Admur, of which many Achronim [Peri Megadim; M"B 321:25] explain that the Taz retracted his earlier ruling in Shabbos. This however cannot be the explanation for here in Admur as a) Admur already saw the contradiction in the Taz prior to writing the SH"A, and b) Admur himself writes here in Shabbos "as explained in 511", thus it is not possible that it can contradict 511. See however Shabbos Kehalacha Vol. 3 p. 168 for an analysis on this subject, and how he learns it is a contradiction in Admur and that we rule leniently.

[11] Admur 511:7; Rashal Beitza 2:34; Taz 511:8; implication of M"A 511:10; Kuntrus Achron 511:1 based on proof from many Rishonim [Ramban; Ran; Rosh; Rif]; Neziros Shimshon; Mamar Mordechai

The reason: As Holadas Reiach is a light prohibition and is hence permitted if one does not have intent to do so. [Machatzis Hashekel 658:2 in explanation of Rashal; Implication of Admur in Kuntrus Achron ibid] Others however explain the reason is because these Poskim rule one may

fruits,] it is permitted to place a species of incense into a cloth if one's intent is not to create a new smell within that cloth. However, if he does intend to do so it is forbidden.

Adding more of a smell into a cloth which already absorbed the smell before Shabbos:[12] If a cloth already had a certain incense placed onto it in a way that its smell absorbed into the cloth from before Yom Tov [or Shabbos], then it is permitted to place on it on Yom Tov [or Shabbos] more of this species of incense in order to increase the smell of this spice into the cloth. However, it is forbidden to place into it another species of incense as he is creating a new smell in the cloth on Yom Tov [or Shabbos].

C. Placing scents into liquids and washing hands with scented liquids:[13]

Those few places which place scented oil into the water, with which the Kohanim wash their hands with prior to going to say the Priestly blessing, are doing a matter that is against Halacha.

The reason for this is: because they intend to create a new smell on the hands of the Kohanim. Now, although the scented oil is placed into the water from before Yom Tov, nevertheless [this is forbidden] being that on Yom Tov when the Kohanim rinse their hands they are creating a new smell on their hands, and they benefit from this smell, and it is pleasant for them and they intend to do so[14], therefore they are to refrain from doing so. **[See Q&A regarding using scented soaps]**

---

be lenient by a Pesik Reishei of a Rabbinical prohibition, and especially if Lo Nicha Lei. [P"M 321 M"Z 7 and 511 M"Z 8; Chemed Moshe; Nehar Shalom; Shaar Hatziyon 658:6; as rules Terumos Hadeshen, brought in M"A 314:5; Shaar Hatziyon 316:21; See Beis Yosef brought in Taz 316:3; Admur 314:3 regarding bees] This however is incorrect as Admur rules stringently regarding Pesik Reishei Delo Nicha Lei even by a Rabbinical prohibition, as brought in 316:4 and 320:24]

The ruling of the Gemara and Rama in 511:4: The Gemara Beitza 23a rules one may not place a cup of incense on clothing due to the prohibition of Molid Reiach, and so rules Rama ibid. They do not differentiate between whether one intended to do so or not.

Other opinions: Some Poskim rule it is forbidden to create a smell in clothing even if one does not intend to do so, and it is hence forbidden to place spices on clothing. [Implication of Rama 658:2; Maharil; Rokeiach 219 as explains M"A 658:2 and Admur in Kuntrus Achron 511:1; Implication of Rashi Beitza 23a as brings Admur ibid; and so rules M"A 658:2; Elya Raba 658:3; P"M 511 A"A 11; Chayeh Adam 141:20; Kitzur SHU"A 137:7; Moed Lekol Chaiy 23:46; M"B 658:7 and Kaf Hachaim 658:8 are lenient in a time of need] The reason this opinion is stringent is because we hold that Pesik Reishei is forbidden even by a Rabbinical prohibition. [Chemed Moshe; Nehar Shalom; Shaar Hatziyon 658:6; As rules Admur 316:4; M"A 314:5; 316:9; Taz 315:3; M"B 316:17 regarding bees]

Is the stringent opinion Machmir regarding adding smell to fruits; removing bad smells: The stringent opinion is lenient in both of these matters which are ruled in the Michaber without argument. Seemingly, the reason is because they hold that there is no prohibition of Holadas Reiach when it is in the way of eating, or for the need of food, and perhaps they hold the Sages were lenient to remove bad smells due to Kavod Habriyos. However, seemingly according to the stringent opinion it would be forbidden to cut a lemon or use scented soaps even if one does not intend to have the scent on his hands, according to those Poskim that forbid Holadas Reiach by the body. Vetzrauch Iyun.

[12] Admur 511:7; Beitza 23a regarding rubbing a myrtle; Admur's learning in M"A 511:11 and 658:2 regarding an Esrog; Rav SZ"A 15 footnote 237; See Machatzis Hashekel 658:2; Shabbos Kehalacha 18:2 Biurim 1; Implication of Rashi Beitza ibid

Other opinions: Some Poskim rule one may not add more smell to an item even if it already contains that same smell. [Implication of M"A 511:11; M"B 511:26; SSH"K 15:77; Beir Moshe 1:34; See Shabbos Kehalacha ibid]

[13] Admur 511:7; Taz 511:8; Halachos Ketanos 1:19; Ben Ish Chaiy 2 Tetzaveh 11; Rav Poalim 2:51; Shoel Umeishiv Tinyana 2:7; Minchas Yitzchak 6:26 [see below in opinion of M"B]; Poskim in Kaf Hachaim 128:44 and 511:44 and so concludes the Kaf Hachaim ibid; Magen Avraham 511:11; 128:8 prohibits placing the secnt into the water, although he does not mention if this prohibition applies even if the scent was placed from before Shabbos.

Background: This ruling of Admur follows the ruling of the Taz which hold that the prohibition to create a new smell applies as well to skin. The Magen Avraham 511 [as well as Magen Avraham in 128:6]

Other Opinions: Some Poskim rule the prohibition of Molid Reiach does not to one's skin being the smell does not last, and it is hence permitted to place perfume/cologne on the body on Shabbos. Thus, if one placed the perfume in the water from before Yom Tov it may be used. [Chacham Tzevi 92; Elya Raba 128:8; Ginas Veradim 3:16; Nechpah Bakesef 4; Shaareiy Teshuvah 511:4; Mishneh Berurah 128:23 and so is implied from 511:28; Beir Moshe 1:34 rules one may be lenient by skin, although one who is stringent is blessed; SSH"K 14:32 rules leniently that perfume may be applied anywhere on one's body, as learns the Chacham Tzevi, as brought in M"B] These opinions can draw proof for their ruling from Michaber 327:1 and 328:36 in which the Michaber allows smearing rose oil on the body, and chewing scented gum in the mouth. Admur and the Poskim ibid however learn that the scented oil is permitted because one has no intent for the scent, while the gum is permitted because its intent is only to remove the bad smell.

According to the M"B may one add smells to other parts of one's body other than the hands? In M"B 128:23 he rules that one may be lenient like the Chacham Tzevi and Elyah Raba that one may wash hands with perfume water. However the Minchas Yitzchak 6:26 explains that the M"B himself only allows this to be done to ones hands and not to the rest of one's body, as perfume on ones hands rubs off quicker then on the rest of the body. To note however that the Minchas Yitzchak himself there leans to be stringent like Admur and the other Gedolei Haposkim which prohibit perfume on any part of the body. However Rav SZ"A [brought in SSH"K 14 footnote 92, and so they rule in Halacha 32] learns that the M"B permits applying perfume to any part of one's body.

Placing perfume on one's hair: Is forbidden according to all opinions being that hair is considered like clothing to which all agree there is a prohibition of Molid Reiach. [Piskeiy Teshuvos 327:1, see Minchas Yitzchak ibid.]

[14] Vetzaruch Iyun as for certain their main intent is to do the Mitzvah and not to absorb the smell, and above Admur mentioned in parentheses that absorbing the smell into the fruits is allowed when ones main intent is not for the smell.

D. Removing mouth odor:[15]

One may not chew a species of resin called Mastichi[16] and may not rub a drug on one's teeth when one's intention in doing so is for healing purposes. However, if he is only doing so to [remove foul] odor from his mouth, then it is allowed [to rub an herb or chew the gum].[17] [**See Q&A regarding mouthwash**]

E. Fragranced oil:[118]

One is allowed to smear (plain) oil [on one's hip], although not rose oil[19] because it is very expensive and is not commonly found and [thus] it is only common to oil [one's body] with it for healing [purposes]. [Although] if one is found in a place where rose oil is commonly available and it is common for people to smear it not for healing [purposes] then it is permitted to smear it for even healing [purposes].[20] *[See Q&A regarding using scented oils]*

---

[15] Admur 328:42; Michaber 328:36; Tosefta brought in Rif and Rambam

[16] This is a type of resin with a pleasant smell which comes out of a tree. [Mishneh Berurah 114]

[17] The reason: Some Poskim suggest that the reason for this allowance is because there is no prohibition in creating a new smell on a body, as rules the Chacham Tzvi, and this law hence serves as a proof for his opinion. [Rav Poalim 2:51] Other Poskim however negate this proof and explain the reason is because one has no intent to create a good smell but rather to get rid of the bad smell and so one must conclude according to Admur and all the Poskim who rule that creating a new smell on the body is forbidden on Shabbos. [Sheilas Yaavatz 1:42; Beir Moshe 1:34] The Beir Moshe 1:34 rules based on this law that good smells may always be applied in order to remove bad odors, and so rules Piskeiy Teshuvos [327:1, 328:26]. Vetzaruch Iyun as perhaps in truth the prohibition of Moild Reiach does not apply at all to ones mouth and it is only due to this that it is permitted.

[18] 327:1; Michaber 327:1; Mishneh Shabbos 111

[19] Rose oil, is the essential oil extracted from the petals of various types of rose. *Rose ottos* are extracted through steam distillation, while *rose absolutes* are obtained through solvent extraction or supercritical carbon dioxide extraction, with the absolute being used more commonly in perfumery. Even with their high price and the advent of organic synthesis, rose oils are still perhaps the most widely used essential oil in perfumery.

[20] Vetzaruch Iyun Gadol how using rose oil does not transgress a prohibition of "creating a smell" on Shabbos, as explained in "Molid Reiach". One must thus conclude that using such oil is only allowed if one does not intend at all to create a new smell on his body, in which case it is allowed to be smeared, as explained there. However, if one also intends on creating the smell on his body, then doing this would be forbidden. Vetzaruch Iyun why Admur who holds of the prohibition of creating new smells on the body, does not make issue of this here in this Halacha. Furthermore, to note there are those [see Piskeiy Teshuvos 327:1] which use this ruling regarding rose oil [which is sourced in the Michaber] to say that there is no prohibition at all to create scents on ones skin. [So rules Chacham Tzevi 92, as opposed to the Taz, Magen Avraham and Admur in chapter 511 which prohibit.] It is thus on the one hand not understood why Admur here did not emphasize the limitation to that it is only allowed when not intended at all for smell, as well as on the other hand one cannot infer from this ruling here the opinion of the Michaber, the same way one cannot infer from here the ruling of Admur of which he makes clear in 511 that he does hold of a prohibition.

Compilation-Molid Reiach:

It is forbidden to enter a good scent into an item on Shabbos or Yom Tov.

Clothing:[21] The above prohibition applies to clothing. It is thus forbidden to enter a good scent into a clothing on Shabbos or Yom Tov. Due to this one may not place perfume on a clothing on Shabbos or Yom Tov.[22]

Food:[23] The above prohibition applies even to foods. It is thus forbidden to enter a good scent into a food on Shabbos or Yom Tov, for simply the sake of giving the food a good smell. Due to this one may not place perfume into washing water on Shabbos or Yom Tov. One may however enter good scents into the food when one's true intent is to enhance the foods taste.

Body:[24] The above prohibition applies even to one's body. It is thus forbidden to enter a good scent onto one's skin Shabbos or Yom Tov. Due to this one may not place perfume or cologne on his/her body on Shabbos or Yom Tov.

Unintentionally:[25] It is permitted to do an action that causes a smell to enter into an item if one does not

---

[21] Admur 511:7 and 321:7; Rama 511:4; Beitza 23a

[22] See Shabbos Kehalacha 18 which states that doing so can also constitute a prohibition of Laundering.

[23] Admur 511:7 and Kuntrus Achron 511:1; Implication of Michaber ibid; M"A 511:10 and 128:8 and 510:11 regarding water; Taz 511:8 regarding water; Milchamos 12b; Ran 12b; Raba Beitza 23a according to Shita Mekubetzes ibid; Ginas Veradim 3:16; Nechpah Bakesef 4; Shoel Umeishiv Tinyana 2:7; M"B 511:28]
Background: The Gemara Beitza 23a and Rama in 511:4 state it is forbidden to enter perfume into a cloth, due to the prohibition of Molid Reiach. Admur and the above Poskim extend this ruling even to foods, as in his opinion, as rule the above Poskim, the prohibition of Holadas Reiach applies even to foods. In kuntrus Achron ibid Admur lengthens to prove this opinion and negates the opinion of the Chacham Tzvi brought next.
Other opinions: Some Poskim rule that the prohibition of Molid Reiach does not apply to foods at all. [Implication of Rashi Beitza 23a; Chacham Tzevi 92 [brought in Shaareiy Teshuvah 511:4]; Rav Yehuda Beitza 23a according to Shita Mekubetzes ibid, brought in Kuntrus Achron ibid; see Eliya Raba 128:8]

[24] Admur 511:7; Taz 511:8; Halachos Ketanos 1:19; Ben Ish Chaiy 2 Tetzaveh 11; Rav Poalim 2:51; Shoel Umeishiv Tinyana 2:7; Minchas Yitzchak 6:26 [see below in opinion of M"B]; Poskim in Kaf Hachaim 128:44 and 511:44 and so concludes the Kaf Hachaim ibid; Magen Avraham 511:11; 128:8 prohibits placing the scent into the water, although he does not mention if this prohibition applies even if the scent was placed from before Shabbos.
Background: This ruling of Admur follows the ruling of the Taz which hold that the prohibition to create a new smell applies as well to skin. The Magen Avraham 511 [as well as Magen Avraham in 128:6]
Other Opinions: Some Poskim rule the prohibition of Molid Reiach does not to one's skin being the smell does not last, and it is hence permitted to place perfume/cologne on the body on Shabbos. Thus, if one placed the perfume in the water from before Yom Tov it may be used. [Chacham Tzevi 92; Elya Raba 128:8; Ginas Veradim 3:16; Nechpah Bakesef 4; Shaareiy Teshuvah 511:4; Mishneh Berurah 128:23 and so is implied from 511:28; Beir Moshe 1:34 rules one may be lenient by skin, although one who is stringent is blessed; SSH"K 14:32 rules leniently that perfume may be applied anywhere on one's body, as learns the Chacham Tzevi, as brought in M"B] These opinions can draw proof for their ruling from Michaber 327:1 and 328:36 in which the Michaber allows smearing rose oil on the body, and chewing scented gum in the mouth. Admur and the Poskim ibid however learn that the scented oil is permitted because one has no intent for the scent, while the gum is permitted because its intent is only to remove the bad smell.
According to the M"B may one add smells to other parts of one's body other than the hands? In M"B 128:23 he rules that one may be lenient like the Chacham Tzevi and Elyah Raba that one may wash hands with perfume water. However the Minchas Yitzchak 6:26 explains that the M"B himself only allows this to be done to ones hands and not to the rest of one's body, as perfume on ones hands rubs off quicker than on the rest of the body. To note however that the Minchas Yitzchak himself there leans to be stringent like Admur and the other Gedolei Haposkim which prohibit perfume on any part of the body. However Rav SZ"A [brought in SSH"K 14 footnote 92, and so they rule in Halacha 32] learns that the M"B permits applying perfume to any part of one's body.
Placing perfume on one's hair: Is forbidden according to all opinions being that hair is considered like clothing to which all agree there is a prohibition of Molid Reiach. [Piskeiy Teshuvos 327:1, see Minchas Yitzchak ibid.]

[25] Admur 511:7; Rashal Beitza 2:34; Taz 511:8; implication of M"A 511:10; Kuntrus Achron 511:1 based on proof from many Rishonim [Ramban; Ran; Rosh; Rif]; Neziros Shimshon; Mamar Mordechai; So rule regarding rose oil, that it may be smeared for pleasure purposes, thus proving that it does not contain a prohibition of creating a new smell if that is not one's intent: Admur 327:1; Michaber 327:1; Mishneh Shabbos 111
The reason: As Holadas Reiach is a light prohibition and is hence permitted if one does not have intent to do so. [Machatzis Hashekel 658:2 in explanation of Rashal; Implication of Admur in Kuntrus Achron ibid] Others however explain the reason is because these Poskim rule one may be lenient by a Pesik Reishei of a Rabbinical prohibition, and especially if Lo Nicha Lei. [P"M 321 M"Z 7 and 511 M"Z 8; Chemed Moshe; Nehar Shalom; Shaar Hatziyon 658:6; as rules Terumos Hadeshen, brought in M"A 314:5; Shaar Hatziyon 316:21; See Beis Yosef brought in Taz 316:3; Admur 314:3 regarding bees] This however is incorrect as Admur rules stringently regarding Pesik Resihei Delo Nicha Lei even by a Rabbinical prohibition, as brought in 316:4 and 320:24]
The ruling of the Gemara and Rama in 511:4: The Gemara Beitza 23a rules one may not place a cup of incense on clothing due to the prohibition of Molid Reiach, and so rules Rama ibid. They do not differentiate between whether one intended to do so or not.
Other opinions: Some Poskim rule it is forbidden to create a smell in clothing even if one does not intend to do so, and it is hence forbidden to place spices on clothing. [Implication of Rama 658:2; Maharil; Rokeiach 219 as explains M"A 658:2 and Admur in Kuntrus Achron 511:1; Implication of Rashi Beitza 23a as brings Admur ibid; and so rules M"A 658:2; Elya Raba 658:3; P"M 511 A"A 11; Chayeh Adam 141:20; Kitzur SHU"A 137:7; Moed Lekol Chaiy 23:46; M"B 658:7 and Kaf Hachaim 658:8 are lenient in a time of need] The reason this opinion is

have any intention to do so. Thus, one may add a scent to fruits if the intent is to benefit the taste of the food. Likewise, one may place spices on a cloth if he does not have intent to create a new smell on the cloth. Likewise, one may smear rose oil on one's skin for pleasure purposes.[26] [Some[27] however learn that it is forbidden to do an action which causes the smell to penetrate the item, even unintentionally, such as to crush the spices into the cloth. Others[28] however learn this is allowed.] If however one also intends to create this new smell on the item through doing the action, then it is forbidden to do so. Thus, it is forbidden to wash one's hands with scented liquids, even if one intends simply to clean his hands, if he also intends to create a good smell on them.

Adding more scent:[29] It is permitted to add to an existing scent on Shabbos and Yom Tov. Hence, if a cloth, or one's body, already had a certain scent placed on it before Yom Tov [or Shabbos], it is permitted to add on Yom Tov [or Shabbos] more of this same scent in order to increase its smell. It is forbidden however to place a different scent onto the garment/body.[30] [Likewise, if the old scent has completely disappeared from the garment/body, then it is forbidden to add more scent to it on Shabbos/Yom Tov even if it is the same scent that used to be on this item.[31]]

Summary-Scenting items/clothing/skin on Shabbos
It is forbidden to initially place any scent onto any item or object on Shabbos or Yom Tov, whether it be food, clothing, or one's body. In the following two cases however doing so is allowed:
1) To add to a scent that was already placed into the item from before Shabbos is allowed so long as [the item still retains the scent that was originally placed in and] one adds more of the same scent.
2) If the absorbing of the scent into the item is done unintentionally, and one's true intent is to achieve something else and it's just that the absorbing of the smell is inevitable, then if one does not actively cause the smell to enter the item, such as one simply places the incense over the item, then it is allowed. If, however, one actively causes the smell to absorb, such as crushing the incense over the item, then even in such a case it is forbidden.[32]

Q&A
Does the prohibition of Molid Reiach apply to foods?[33]
Yes, if one's intent is for the food to receive good smell.

Does the prohibition of Molid Reiach apply to one's body/skin?
Yes.

---

stringent is because we hold that Pesik Reishei is forbidden even by a Rabbinical prohibition. [Chemed Moshe; Nehar Shalom; Shaar Hatziyon 658:6; As rules Admur 316:4; M"A 314:5; 316:9; Taz 315:3; M"B 316:17 regarding bees]
Is the stringent opinion Machmir regarding adding smell to fruits; removing bad smells: The stringent opinion is lenient in both of these matters which are ruled in the Michaber without argument. Seemingly, the reason is because they hold that there is no prohibition of Holadas Reiach when it is in the way of eating, or for the need of food, and perhaps they hold the Sages were lenient to remove bad smells due to Kavod Habriyos. However, seemingly according to the stringent opinion it would be forbidden to cut a lemon or use scented soaps even if one does not intend to have the scent on his hands, according to those Poskim that forbid Holadas Reiach by the body. Vetzrauch Iyun.
[26] See Admur 327:1; Michaber 327:1; Mishneh Shabbos 111
[27] Kinnus Torah 18 p. 50 as rules Admur 321:7; Taz 321:7
[28] Shabbos Kehalacha Vol. 3 p. 168 that Admur and Taz in 511:7 retracted this ruling
[29] Admur 511:7; Beitza 23a regarding rubbing a myrtle; Admur's learning in M"A 511:11 and 658:2 regarding an Esrog; Rav SZ"A 15 footnote 237; See Machatzis Hashekel 658:2; Shabbos Kehalacha 18:2 Biurim 1; Implication of Rashi Beitza ibid
Other opinions: Some Poskim rule one may not add more smell to an item even if it already contains that same smell. [Implication of M"A 511:11; M"B 511:26; SSH"K 15:77; Beir Moshe 1:34; See Shabbos Kehalacha ibid]
[30] The reason: As he is creating a new smell in the cloth on Yom Tov [or Shabbos]. [ibid]
[31] Pashut!
[32] This summary is based on the answer to the contradiction between 321:7 and 511:7 explained in the prior footnotes. See however Shabbos Kehalacha Vol. 3 p. 168 for an analysis on this subject, and how he learns it is a contradiction in Admur and that we rule leniently.
[33]

Does the prohibition of Holadas Reiach apply to the air?[34]
No. It is permitted to create new smells in the air on Shabbos.

Does the prohibition of Pesik Reishei apply by Molid Reiach?
No. Hence, if one does not intend to make a new smell it is permitted.

May one place an Esrog on top of a cloth on Shabbos/Yom Tov?
It is forbidden to place an Esrog on top of a cloth on Shabbos/Yom Tov due to the prohibition of Molid Reiach.[35] This however only applies if one intends to create a new smell on the garment, while if one does not intend to create a new smell then doing so is permitted.[36]

May one place spices into food on Shabbos if doing so gives it a good smell?[37]
One may do so if his main intent is to give the food a good taste and not necessarily for the smell. If, however, one intends to do so for the smell, then it is forbidden to add the spices on Yom Tov/Sabbos.

May one spray perfume or cologne onto his/her body or clothing on Shabbos?[38]
It is forbidden to apply perfume or cologne onto one's skin unless he had already placed this same perfume on from before Shabbos and it still retains some of its smell.

May one place a good smell if his intent is to get rid of a bad smell?[39]
Yes.

May one apply deodorant on Shabbos:
Spray/liquid deodorant: Yes.[40] However some Poskim[41] limit this allowance only to if one does not intend to create a good smell on his skin, and is simply doing so to prevent bad smell. Thus, they rule if one has a non-scent deodorant available which properly prevents bad smell, then he may not use a scented deodorant if he currently does not smell bad.
Stick deodorant: No.[42]

May one wash his hands with scented soaps?
Bar of soap: May not be used regardless due to the Nolad prohibition.[43]
Liquid soap: Seemingly this is forbidden, as it is no different than the case mentioned above of washing ones hands with scented water in which although the main intent is not for the scent, nevertheless one does also intend in absorbing it.[44] Nevertheless perhaps this is similar to applying deodorant to remove

---

[34] Beir Heiytiv 511:5 in name of Rashal; M"B 511:23
[35] Rama 658:2 in name of Maharil; Rokeiach; M"A 658:2
[36] Admur 511:7 and Kuntrus Achron 511:1; Rashal 2:34 [brought in M"A ibid]; Taz 511:8; implication of M"A 511:10 [unlike his ruling in 658:2-see Kuntrus Achron ibid that he retracted his ruling]
Other opinions: Some Poskim rule it is forbidden to place the Esrog on a garment even if one does not intend to create a new smell. [Implication of Rama 658:2; Maharil; Rokeiach; M"A 658:2]
[37] Admur 511:7 Kuntrus Achron 1
[38] Based on Admur above. However see footnote above [in C] regarding the other opinions which allow to create smell on skin
[39] 328:42; Michaber 328:36; Tosefta brought in Rif and Rambam; Sheilas Yaavetz 1:42; Beir Moshe 1:34; Piskeiy Teshuvos 327:1, 328:26.
[40] Beir Moshe 1:34 rules that good smells may always be applied in order to remove bad odors, and so rules Piskeiy Teshuvos [327:1, 328:26]. This is based on Sheleis Yaavetz 1:42 on the law ruled in SH"A Michaber:Admur that one may use good odors to remove bad breath.
[41] Shabbos Kehalacha 18:8
[42] As even if one placed it from before Shabbos using it on Shabbos perhaps involves the smoothening prohibition. However based on Ketzos Hashulchan [146 footnote 32] this should be permitted as it does not involve smoothening. Nevertheless according to all it is the custom to not allow to use it on Shabbos.
[43] See "The Laws of Bathing" Halacha 10
[44] See Shabbos Kehalacha Vol. 3 18:4 footnote 13 that it is very difficult to ascertain that one truly has no intent to absorb the smell.

bad smells in which Poskim[45] rule it is allowed to be done. In any event, if one has no intent at all to create a good smell, it may be used.[46]

May one use scented oil in cases in which it is allowed to smear it on Shabbos [as explained in "The Laws of oiling Skin"]?
Seemingly if one is intending to also create a new smell on his skin in addition to the smearing of oil, it is forbidden to do on Shabbos.[47] However if one has no intent at all to create a new smell on him, it is allowed.

May one place scented oil on his skin or on a tissue for the sake of smelling it, as is common for some people to do on Yom Kippur?
No. However one may place an item in his hands, including scented oil, if his intent is to use his hands to hold the oil while he smells it and not in order to create a smell on the hand on his hand for future smelling.[48]

May one spray air freshener in his room or bathroom?[49]
Yes. There is no prohibition of Mild Reicha[50], or of Zoreh involved in doing so.[51] One may thus spray air freshener into the air without limitation. However, one may not spray it onto an object and the like unless one's intent is to get rid of bad smells.[52]

May one use a toilet that contains scented toilet soap?
See "The Laws of Crushing & Melting Ice" Halacha 4 Q&A

May one use mouthwash to remove bad odor?[53]
Yes, this is permitted.

May one place a good smelling powder or spray on his feet?
When doing so in order to remove bad smell then it has the same law as does spray deodorant [mentioned above] in which there are Poskim which allow it.[54] However if the powder has healing powers then it is forbidden [to be placed on feet which require healing] due to the healing prohibition.

Men using cologne during the week:[55]
It is improper for a Torah scholar to place cologne.

---

[45] Beir Moshe 1:34 rules that good smells may always be applied in order to remove bad odors, and so rules Piskeiy Teshuvos [327:1, 328:26] Shabbos Kehalacha Vol. 3 18:6
[46] Shabbos Kehalacha ibid
[47] As one is intending to create a new smell which is forbidden to do on Shabbos and it is thus no different than the case mentioned above of washing ones hands with scented water in which although the main intent is not for the scent, nevertheless one does also intend in absorbing it.
[48] Rav Poalim 2:51; Kaf Hachaim 128:44
[49] Beir Moshe 1:34; Shabbos Kehalacha 3 18:15-16; See also Minchas Yitzchak 6:26 who was asked this question amongst others although he does not seem to answer this particular point.
[50] The reason: As one is not creating a new smell on any object and it is permitted to cause a smell to be created within the air. [Beir Heiytiv 511:5 in name of Rashal; M"B 511:23; Shabbos Kehalacha ibid], as well as that one is doing so in order to repel the bad smells.
[51] Minchas Yitzchak 6:26; Shabbos Kehalacha ibid footnote 32
The reason: As it is not the wind that is scattering it but rather the air pressure in the can. [ibid]
[52] Shabbos Kehalacha ibid
[53] Piskeiy Teshuvos 328:26 based on 328:42; Beir Moshe 1:34
[54] Beir Moshe 1:34; Piskeiy Teshuvah 328:26
[55] Rambam Deios 5:9; Beir Sarim 6:58

THE PROHIBITION OF DYEING
Dyeing clothing, food and applying makeup on Shabbos

Shulchan Aruch Chapter 320

TRANSLATION-CHAPTER 320 HALACHA'S 26-28

Halacha 26
Dyeing foods
One is permitted to place turmeric in food and there is no need to worry [that doing so] is [transgressing the] coloring [prohibition] as there is no coloring [prohibition involved] in [dyeing] food.

Halacha 27
Getting pigment on clothes, food and skin
Wiping stained hands on a cloth: One who eats strawberries or other fruits which have a dyeing pigment needs to be careful not to touch with his stained hands his clothing or a [non designated] cloth due to the prohibition of dyeing.

Now, although when doing so one [has no intention to dye, but] is actually ruining the cloth, and whenever one does an action on Shabbos in a way of damage, he has not Biblically transgressed, nevertheless it is forbidden to be done Rabbinically.

Other Opinions: [However] there are those which are lenient [to allow this to be done] being that [wiping one's dirty hands on the cloth] is only a form of dirtying it [rather than dyeing it], and thus it is not [even] considered to be [Rabbinical] dyeing at all.

The Final Ruling: One is to be stringent [even when wiping one's hands on a white cloth] and certainly when one wipes on a red cloth, of which [dirtying it with the fruit pigment] is not considered to be damaging the cloth at all. [See summary and Q&A below for the ruling regarding other colors.]

Getting pigment on one's bread: However, if one dyes his bread with the pigment of fruits there is no problem involved being that there is no [prohibition of] coloring by foods.

Dirtying one's skin with pigment: As well there is no problem involved at all in [dirtying] one's hands and face with the pigment, as [the] coloring [prohibition] only applies towards an item which is commonly dyed.

Applying makeup: It was only made forbidden for a woman to apply makeup on her face due to the coloring [prohibition], as was explained in Chapter 303 [Halacha 25[1]], due to that this is commonly done on woman.

Applying eyeliner: As well to apply eyeliner was prohibited whether for a man or woman due to the coloring prohibition, being that this is commonly done.

Kuntras Achron in chapter 302:
Cloths that are designated specifically for wiping on: May be used for wiping ones colored hands, and is not a problem of dyeing, as we only say there is a problem of dyeing when it is not in a way of wiping, or it is but is done to a random cloth.[2]

Halacha 28
Dye which does not last
Biblically: There is only a Biblical prohibition [involved in dyeing] when dyeing with a permanent dye, however a dye which will not last at all, such as one who placed vermillion [a bright red pigment], or rouge[3] on metal and copper and [thus] dyed it, is not liable because one is only coloring it temporarily and is thus not dyeing anything.

Rabbinically: Nevertheless, doing so is Rabbinically forbidden.

---

[1] In Michaber Rama
[2] Kuntrus Achron in 302
[3] Reddish makeup for cheeks

COMPILATION OF HALACHAS SUMMARIES AND Q&A

1. The Prohibition of dyeing clothing and other objects:[4]
A. The dye is lasting:
Biblically: There is only a Biblical prohibition [involved in dyeing] when dyeing with a permanent dye, however a dye which will not last at all[5], such as one who placed vermillion [a bright red pigment], or rouge[6] on metal and copper and [thus] dyed it, is not liable because one is only coloring it temporarily and is thus not dyeing anything.
Rabbinically: Nevertheless, doing so is Rabbinically forbidden.

Summary:
Permanent dye: Is Biblically forbidden [when done with intention to dye[7]].
Temporary dye: Is Rabbinically forbidden.

Invisible ink:
Is seemingly Biblically forbidden to use as a dye, as it will last for at least some time until it becomes invisible.

Placing shaded plastic on a table or window:
Is permitted as this is not considered dyeing at all.

Eating on plate that will get it dyed:
Is permitted if one has no intent to dye. If, however, one intends to dye the plate, even temporarily, then it is forbidden to do so. Thus, one may not smear beets out of casualness in order to make the surface of his plate red.

B. Hastening the dyeing of a product and adding dye:
Mixing a pot that contains wool and dye:[8] It is Biblically forbidden to mix a pot of wool with dye, even if the dye has been fully cooked before Shabbos[9], and the wool has received the dye[10], due to the dyeing prohibition.[11] [From here we can learn that it is forbidden to a) Hasten the dyeing of a product, and b) Thicken the dye of a product.]

---

[4] Admur 320:28; M"A 320:25; Rambam 9:13; Machatzis Hashekel 320:24; M"B 320:59
Av Melacha: The Av Melacha of dyeing in the Mishkan was with the dyeing of the tapestries and curtains used for the Mishkan's walls and tent.
[5] This implies that if the dye will last some time, or some of the ink will penetrate and remain, then it is Biblically forbidden even though it will not last forever, and so is implied from the fact the Poskim rule that dyeing the human body is Rabbinical only because it is skin and not because it will not last forever.
[6] Reddish makeup for cheeks
[7] As is understood from Halacha 3 below.
[8] Admur 252:2 and 318:30 in parentheses; Michaber 318:18; M"A 318:43; Taz 318:22; M"B 252:5 and 318:116; Regarding why in Admur 318:30 he writes the "dyeing prohibition" in parentheses-see "The reason"
[9] Admur 252:2
[10] Admur 318:30; Michaber ibid
[11] The reason: As the mixing causes the dye to become more absorbed into the wool. [Admur 252:2; 2nd answer in Rosh; M"B 318:116] Alternatively, the reason is because constant mixing is part of the dyeing process, in order to prevent the wool from burning. [Admur 318:30; Ran, brought in M"B 318:116] Alternatively, mixing a hot pot of dye is forbidden due to the cooking prohibition, as dye is never fully cooked. [Rosh in 1st answer, brought in Taz ibid; Shaar Hatziyon 318:138] The practical ramification is regarding whether one may mix a pot of dye that is fully cooked, even if there is no wool inside. [Shaar Hatziyon ibid] Based on all this it is understood why Admur placed his ruling in 318:30 in parentheses, as there are opinions that say the prohibition is due to cooking. As for why Admur mentions two different reasons in 252:2 and 318:30, as well as only in 318:30 he places the ruling in parentheses, seemingly the explanation is as follows: In 352:2 the case is discussing that the wool has not yet fully absorbed the dye, and hence according to all there is a dyeing prohibition involved. However, in 318:30 in which the wool has fully absorbed the dye, Admur states the reason is because it is "the way of the dyers to prevent the item from burning", however in this matter he was in question and hence placed the ruling of "due to the dyeing prohibition" in parentheses.

C. Making dye on Shabbos:[12]
It is forbidden to make dye on Shabbos, such as by soaking pigment in water, [due to the dyeing prohibition[13], or alternatively due to the kneading prohibition[14].]

2. Pesik Resihei by dyeing-Wiping stained hands on a cloth:[15]

As explained in Halacha 1, dyeing clothing contains a Biblical prohibition when done with a permanent dye and a Rabbinical prohibition when done with a temporary dye. The following law will discuss if one may wipe his colored hands on a cloth in order to clean them, having no intent at all to dye the cloth in doing so.

First Opinion:[16] One who eats strawberries or other fruits which have a dyeing pigment needs to be careful to not touch with his stained hands his clothing or a [non designated] cloth due to the prohibition of dyeing.

The reason: Now, although when doing so one [has no intention to dye, but] is actually ruining the cloth, and whenever one does an action on Shabbos in a way of damage, he has not Biblically transgressed, nevertheless it is forbidden to be done Rabbinically.[17] [This is because a cloth is common to be dyed, and if one would clean his hands on the cloth for dyeing purposes, he would transgress Biblically. Thus, although now he is doing it in order to clean his hands in a destructive manner, nevertheless, since it is similar to the actual Melacha, therefore it is Rabbinically forbidden.[18] The above Poskim follow the ruling that it is forbidden to perform a Pesik Resihei on Shabbos even if it is not Nicha Lei.[19]]

Other Opinions:[20] [However] there are those[21] who are lenient [to allow this to be done] being that [wiping one's dirty hands on the cloth] is only a form of dirtying it [rather than dyeing it], and thus it is not [even] considered to be [Rabbinical] dyeing at all.

The Final Ruling:[22] One is to be stringent [even when wiping one's hands on a white cloth] and certainly when one wipes on a red cloth, of which [dirtying it with the fruit pigment] is not considered to be damaging the cloth at all.[23] [**See summary and Q&A below for the ruling regarding other colors, such as wine.**]

Clothes that are designated specifically for wiping on:[24] Clothes that are designated for wiping may be used to clean one's colored hands. Doing so is not prohibited due to the dyeing prohibition, as the dyeing prohibition only applies when one is intentionally doing so for the purpose of dyeing, or when done to a non-designated cloth which is common to dye.[25]

---

[12] Magen Avraham 320:25 brought in Mishneh Berurah 320:59; 252:1; Michaber and Admur 252:1 that doing so is only permitted from before Shabbos.

[13] As rules Rambam 9; Opinion of Rebbe Yossi Bar Rebbe Yehudah in Shabbos 18a, and so rules Michaber in Shulchan Aruch [321:14] that there is no kneading prohibition involved in simply adding water to kneading material.

[14] As rules Raavad based on Rebbe Yehudah Hanassi Shabbos ibid that there is a kneading prohibition involved even in simply adding water to kneading material; brought in M"A ibid and M"B ibid

[15] 320:27

[16] First opinion in Admur ibid; "Yeish Mi Sheomer" in Michaber 320:20; Shibulei Haleket 86; Yireim 274; Rokeiach 70; Kol Bo 31; Maharam Rikanti 123

[17] Admur ibid; M"A 328:52; Yireim ibid; Rikanti ibid; M"B 320:57

[18] Kuntrus Achron 302:1

[19] M"B 320:57

[20] 2nd opinion in Admur ibid; brought in M"A 320:24; M"B 320:59

[21] Igor 484; Darkei Moshe 2; Radbaz 131; Chacham Tzevi

[22] Admur ibid; M"A 320:24-25; Michaber 328:48; To note that in Admur 328:54 [brought in Halacha 3 below] Admur plainly rules like the stringent opinion regarding wiping blood on a cloth and does not even make mention of the lenient opinion mentioned here.
Other Poskim: Some Poskim rule one may be lenient in a time of need. [Elya Raba; Machatzis Hashekel; Chayeh Adam; M"B 320:59 and 328:146]

[23] Admur ibid; 328:53; M"A 320:25; 328:52; M"B 320:57

[24] Kuntrus Achron 302:1; See 319:13; 320:21; M"A 319:11; Ketzos Hashulchan 136 footnote 11; SSH"K 14:19; Piskeiy Teshuvos 320:11 based on Admur Kuntrus Achron 302; Shabbos Kehalacha Vol. 3 20:20 [p. 295]
Other opinions: Some Poskim rule it does not suffice to designate a garment for this purpose, and only by an item which people do not care to dye does the allowance apply. [Avnei Nezer 175, brought in Ketzos Hashulchan 136 footnote 11]

[25] The reason: Seemingly, the reason why a designated cloth helps is because it is evident to all that one is not doing an act of dyeing [or laundering] when using it to clean his hands [or strain liquid through] and it is hence not similar to the Melacha at all. If, however, the cloth is not designated for this purpose, then it appears as if one is doing an act of dyeing, or laundering, and is hence at least Rabbinically forbidden.

Summary- Dyeing Clothing:

<u>Clothes designated for wiping:</u> One may wipe ones dirty/colored hands on cloths designated for wiping.

<u>However, by cloths not designated for wiping</u> then it depends on what color one is wiping off. If it is a dyeing color like of strawberries and pomegranates, it is not allowed irrelevant of the color of the cloth. [However, if it is a dirty color, like of red wine, R. Farkash rules it is always allowed. However, Ketzos Hashulchan rules that by very red wine it is not allowed. Tehilah Ledavid holds that all wine is only allowed to be wipes on clothes not made to be dyed].[26]

Q&A

Must one today be careful not to touch his shirt with dyed hands, even though we no longer dye clothing today at home?

Yes. However, some[27] write that this is no longer necessary to be careful in this matter today as our clothing are never commonly dyed at home, and hence according to all opinions one may wipe his hands on all colored clothing.

May one who wet his hands with red wine use clothing to dry them?[28]

Some Poskim[29] rule one may do so without restriction on towels and clothing that are not commonly dyed. Others[30] rule it is only allowed by light red wine, as opposed to dark red wine. Others[31] rule one may wipe wine from one's hands on any clothing as wine is not a dyeing agent.

Must one be careful when drinking wine that it does not spill on one's shirt and the like?

If the wine is very red, then one is to be careful in this matter, as stated above regarding strawberries. One is likewise to be careful not to touch his shirt with his wet hands after making Kiddush on this wine.

May one clean a spill of wine using a cloth?

If the cloth is designated for this purpose, then it may be sued irrelevant of the color of the wine. If the

---

Alternatively, the reason is because once the cloth has been designated for this purpose it is no longer common to dye it at all, and hence there is no need to decree against dyeing if one has no intent to do so. If, however, one intends to dye it or launder it, then certainly it is forbidden to do on Shabbos even if one designated the cloth for this purpose. It is only that when it is done Derech Lichluch, and no intent to dye, and is not common to dye that we permit it. The practical ramification would be regarding a urine test sticks, and baby diapers that change color, as explained in Q&A at end of chapter!

[26] This is based on what is explained in the Q&A below.

[27] Piskeiy Teshuvos 320:26 based on Admur in Kuntrus Achron ibid

[28] Based on the above that one is to be stringent when wiping off stains, seemingly the same applies regarding red wine, that one should not wipe it on a cloth and should rather wash it off.

However, from other rulings of Admur it appears that by wine this is allowed, and thus it remains to be understood why it does not fall under the same ruling as above, that one is to be stringent not to wipe his hands. The following are the cases that Admur allows it to be done:

In 319:13 Admur allows one to use a random cloth for filtering red wine and beer and does not mention any problem of that it dyes the cloth and is therefore forbidden. [although Lechatchila it is proper ["tov"] for one to suspect for the stringent opinion that it is a problem of Borer, although according to all there is no problem of dyeing.] Similarly, in 301:59 Admur rules that one may even Lechatchilah place a cloth into red wine and beer, such as when he is doing it to filter the liquid. Similarly, in 320:21 Admur rules the same as above.

<u>Answers that were given for the above question:</u>

The Tehila Ledavid 319:16: In 319 and 301 Admur is referring to cloths which are not normally dyed and thus by them there is no suspicion for dyeing, and it is allowed, while by here 320 Admur is referring to cloths that are common to be dyed and by them one should be stringent.

The Ketzos Hashulchan [146 Badei Hashulchan 14 number 13] explains that perhaps by very red wine it has the same problem as by strawberries, although by light red wine it does not, and thus those areas where Admur stated that it is allowed is because he is referring to light red wine. He then concludes that one who wants to do according to all opinions, should use a designated cloth for filtering the wine, as explained above from the Kuntrus Achron.

Rabbi Farkash [Shabbos Kihalacha Vol. 2 page 352 and 384]: Argues on the above two answers and rather explains: According to Admur, he learns like those Rishonim that learn that by wine [and other fruit juices] its color is never considered able to dye a cloth but rather its color dirties a cloth, and thus it is never applicable to the Issur of dyeing, as opposed to strawberries and the like which can be used for dyeing, and thus even when used to dirty a cloth, like to wipe ones hands, we still prohibit it Rabbinically.

[29] Tehila Ledavid 319:16

[30] Ketzos Hashulchan 146 Badei Hashulchan 16 number 13

[31] Shabbos Kihalacha Vol. 2 page 352 and 384

cloth is not designated for this purpose, then it may not be used if the wine is white due to the laundering prohibition, and if the wine is very red it may not be used due to the dyeing prohibition. If, however, the wine is rose color, it may be used.

May one use a tissue or napkin to wipe his stained hands?[32]
Yes, this may be done even if his hands are stained with a strawberry color.[33]
<u>Cloth napkin</u>: A cloth napkin may be used to clean one's stained hands, being that it is designated for this purpose.

May one filter red wine through a cloth?
See "The laws of Separating" Chapter 3!

May one use Q-tips on Shabbos?
This is allowed.[34]

3. *Treating a bleeding wound on Shabbos:*[35]
Placing a [non-designated] cloth on a wound:[36] It is forbidden to place a garment on a wound that is bleeding.
The Reason:[37] The reason for this is because the blood will dye it. Now, although one is ruining [the cloth in this dyeing, as he is simply staining it] nevertheless it is Rabbinically forbidden [to be done].[38]
A red cloth:[39] It is certainly [prohibited to place on the bleeding wound] a red garment, being that one is fixing it [by dyeing it with its natural red color].
Squeeze out the blood:[40] It is not allowed for one to squeeze out the blood from the wound prior [to placing the cloth on it] as doing so contains the wounding prohibition as explained in 328 [Halacha 33].
Wrapping spider webs around it:[41] Thus how is one to treat a bleeding wound? One is to wrap around it spiders web and cover with it all the blood and the entire wound and afterwards wrap a rag around it.
Other Opinions: There are opinions which question [whether it is allowed] and prohibit wrapping [the wound in] spider webs being that they have healing powers.
Rinsing off the blood and then applying the bandage:[42] Rather [according to this latter opinion] one is to rinse [off the wound] in water or wine [prior to applying bandage to it] in order to remove the blood which is on the wound and afterwards [one may] wrap on it a rag. [**See Q&A regarding if this may be done if one knows that it will still continue to bleed after bandaging it.**]
The Final Ruling:[43] It is proper[44] to suspect for this latter opinion [to rinse off the blood rather than use a

---

[32] SSH"K 14:19; Piskeiy Teshuvos 320:11 based on Admur Kuntrus Achron 302; Shabbos Kehalacha Vol. 3 20:20 [p. 295]
This is unlike the ruling of Rav Farkash in Tahara Kehalacha 10:28 which rules that tissues should not be used as they are not specifically designated for this purpose. Vetzaruch Iyun Gadol from where he understood that they must be designated for a specific form of wiping, as opposed to general wiping. In Shabbos Kehalacha ibid he clearly contradicts himself.
[33] As they are designated for wiping, and thus do not contain a dyeing prohibition.
[34] As it is no different than one using tissues after the bathroom.
[35] Admur 328:53
[36] Admur ibid; Michaber 328:48; Shibulei Haleket 86; Yireim 274; Vetzaruch Iyun why here Admur only brings the stringent opinion brought in Halacha 3 regarding wiping stained hands on a cloth, while there in Halacha 2 he also brings a lenient opinion. In any event, the final ruling remains as explained there in Halacha 3, like the stringent opinion.
Other Poskim: Some Poskim rule one may be lenient in a time of need. [Elya Raba; Machatzis Hashekel; Chayeh Adam; M"B 320:59 and 328:146]
[37] Admur ibid; M"A 328:52; Yireim 274; Maharam Rikanti 123
[38] Vetzaruch Iyun why here Admur only brings the stringent opinion brought in Halacha 3 regarding wiping stained hands on a cloth, while there in Halacha 3 he also brings a lenient opinion. In any event the final ruling remains as explained there in Halacha 3, like the stringent opinion.
[39] Admur ibid; M"A ibid
[40] Admur ibid; Michaber ibid; Mishneh Eiruvin 103b; Shivlei Haleket
[41] Admur ibid; Michaber ibid; Rokeiach 70; Kol Bo 31
[42] Admur ibid; Michaber ibid; Shibulei Haleket 86
[43] Admur ibid; implication of Michaber ibid; Main opinion is like first opinion-so rules Malbushei Yom Tov 328:48; Elya Zuta 328:30
[44] Lit. good

spiders web], although the main Halachic ruling follows the first opinion.

Clothes that are designated specifically for wiping on:[45] Clothes that are designated for wiping may be used to clean a bloody wound. Doing so is not prohibited due to the dyeing prohibition, as the dyeing prohibition only applies when one is intentionally doing so for the purpose of dyeing, or when done to a non-designated cloth which is common to dye.

Cleaning the blood of a wound:[46]

Is forbidden to be done with any cloth, irrelevant of color, which is not designated for that purpose due to the dyeing prohibition. If thus there are no pre-designated cloths available, one is to rinse it off with water and then place the cloth on it prior to it beginning to bleed.

Q&A

May a woman use a pad on Shabbos or do a Bedika?[47]

Yes.[48]

May a bandage be used over a bleeding wound?

Yes, as bandages are designated for this purpose.

May one place a tissue or napkin on the wound?[49]

Yes.[50]

May one wrap a towel over a bleeding wound?

Seemingly one may not do so as towels are not meant to be used to dry colored liquids but rather to dry water on. Vetzaruch Iyun.

May one use a cloth to clean or catch the blood?[51]

Although it is permitted to have marital relations for the first time on Friday night, even if she is a Besula, nevertheless, one must be careful not to use an undesignated towel or other undesignated cloth to clean the blood.[52] This applies irrelevant of color, whether the cloth is white or red.[53] Rather, one is

---

[45] Kuntrus Achron 302:1; See 319:13; 320:21; M"A 319:11

Other opinions: Some Poskim rule it does not suffice to designate a garment for this purpose, and only by an item which people do not care to dye does the allowance apply. [Avnei Nezer 175, brought in Ketzos Hashulchan 136 footnote 11]

[46] 328:53 and Kuntress Achron 3011

[47] Admur Kuntrus Achron 302:1; See also Avnei Nezer 175; Ketzos Hashulchan 136 footnote 11; Lehoros Nasan 8:73; Michzeh Eliyahu 65; Hisorerus Teshuvah 166; Tzitzi Eliezer 18:14; Piskeiy Teshuvos 320:26 footnote 292 and 294

[48] The reason: As it is designated for this purpose. [Admur ibid] Other Poskim however rule the reason is because the staining is a mere Grama. [Avnei Nezer 175; See Ketzos Hashulchan 136 footnote 11]

[49] SSH"K 14:19; Piskeiy Teshuvos 320:11 based on Admur Kuntrus Achron 302 Shabbos Kehalacha Vol. 3 20:20 [p. 295]

This is unlike the ruling of Rav Farkash in Tahara Kehalacha 10:28 and chapter 15 p. 506 which rules that tissues should not be used as they are not specifically designated for this purpose. Vetzaruch Iyun Gadol from where he understood that they must be designated for a specific form of wiping, as opposed to general wiping. In Shabbos Kehalacha ibid he clearly contradicts himself.

[50] As they are designated for wiping, and thus do not contain a dyeing prohibition.

[51] See Piskeiy Teshuvos 280:6; 328:48; Tzitz Eliezer 18:14; SSH"K 14:19; Piskeiy Teshuvos 320:11; Shabbos Kehalacha Vol. 3 20:20 [p. 295]; Tahara Kehalacha 10:28 and chapter 15 p. 506

[52] See 1st and main opinion in Admur 320:27; Stam opinion in 328:53; "Yeish Mi Sheomer" in Michaber 320:20; 328:48; Shibulei Haleket 86; Yireim 274; Rokeiach 70; Kol Bo 31; Maharam Rikanti 123; M"A 320:25; 328:52; M"B 320:57; Rav Massas, brought in Tzitz Eliezer ibid, that certainly it is forbidden to wipe the Dam Besulin with a cloth on Shabbos

The reason: Although when doing so one [has no intention to dye, but] is actually ruining the cloth, and whenever one does an action on Shabbos in a way of damage, he has not Biblically transgressed, nevertheless it is forbidden to be done Rabbinically. [Admur ibid]

Other Opinions: Some Poskim rule that it is permitted to wipe the blood on Shabbos being that [wiping one's dirty hands on the cloth] is only a form of dirtying it [rather than dyeing it], and thus it is not [even] considered to be [Rabbinical] dyeing at all. [2nd opinion in Admur ibid, brought in M"A 320:24 and M"B 320:59; Igor 484; Darkei Moshe 2; Radbaz 131; Chacham Tzevi Likkutim in end of Sefer 5 that so is implication of Kesubos 7b that one may wipe the Dam Besulin on Shabbos; Shoel Umeishiv Basra 2:7; Pekudas Elazar O.C. 280] Some Poskim rule one may be lenient in a time of need. [Elya Raba; Machatzis Hashekel; Chayeh Adam; M"B 320:59 and 328:146] Some Poskim rule that wiping the blood of a Besula is always considered a time of need, and may hence always be done even initially. [Tzitz Eliezer ibid; Piskeiy Teshuvos 280:6]

[53] Admur ibid and ibid; M"A ibid

to use a towel that is designated for this purpose.[54] One may use tissues or napkins for this purpose.[55] One may not use the sheets to clean the blood.

Must the couple place a designated towel under her during the intercourse, to prevent the blood from hitting the sheet?[56] No. They may use regular sheets.

One who has cleaned a wound from blood, may he place on it a cloth even though he knows that it will eventually continue to bleed?[57]
Some Poskim[58] require that it be cleaned until the blood stops secreting. Others[59] however rule that once the wound is clean one may put a cloth on it.[60] Practically, it is best to designate garment for this purpose, and hence avoid the issue altogether.[61]

4. Dyeing foods:[62]

One is permitted to place turmeric in food and there is no need to worry [that doing so] is [transgressing the] coloring [prohibition] as there is no coloring [prohibition involved] in [dyeing] food.
Getting pigment on one's bread:[63] If one dyes his bread with the pigment of fruits, such as strawberries and pomegranates, there is no problem involved being that there is no [prohibition of] coloring by foods.

Summary – Dyeing Foods:
This summary is based on various important clarifications that were gleaned from the Q&A below!
Without any intent to dye the food-simply for the sake of the taste:[64] Foods do not contain a dyeing

---

[54] Kuntrus Achron 302:1; See 319:13; 320:21; M"A 319:11; Ketzos Hashulchan 136 footnote 11; SSH"K 14:19; Piskeiy Teshuvos 320:11 based on Admur Kuntrus Achron 302; Shabbos Kehalacha Vol. 3 20:20 [p. 295]; Tzitz Eliezer ibid 7
Other opinions: Some Poskim rule it does not suffice to designate a garment for this purpose, and only by an item which people do not care to dye does the allowance apply. [Avnei Nezer 175, brought in Ketzos Hashulchan 136 footnote 11]
[55] SSH"K 14:19; Piskeiy Teshuvos 320:11 based on Admur Kuntrus Achron 302; Shabbos Kehalacha Vol. 3 20:20 [p. 295]; This is unlike the ruling of Rav Farkash in Tahara Kehalacha 10:28 and chapter 15 p. 506 which rules that tissues should not be used as they are not specifically designated for this purpose. Vetzaruch Iyun Gadol from where he understood that they must be designated for a specific form of wiping, as opposed to general wiping. In Shabbos Kehalacha ibid he clearly contradicts himself.
[56] There is no mention in Poskim regarding this matter, and hence seemingly it is permitted to have relations on the sheet even though it will cause it to be stained, as this is a mere Grama, and is hence not similar to wiping stained hands on a cloth. It is likewise not a Pesik Resihei that the blood will hit the sheet, as perhaps there will not be any blood at all, and perhaps it will not reach the sheet. This is similar to drinking red wine on a tablecloth, in which case there is no prohibition involved even though it is possible and common for some wine to spill on the tablecloth. Upashut!
[57] Ketzos Hashulchan chapter 136 footnote 11
[58] Machatzis Hashekel 328:54
[59] Avnei Nezer 175
[60] As even if it later bleeds this is only Grama and is allowed, and so seems to be the opinion of the Poskim.
[61] Ketzos Hashulchan ibid
[62] Admur 320:26; Michaber 320:19; Shibulei Haleket 86 in name of Yireim
Other opinions: Some Poskim rule the prohibition of dyeing applies even to foods. [Tosafus Rid Shabbos 75a [as explained in in Avnei Nezer 173], based on Shabbos ibid that there is a dyeing prohibition involved in slaughtering [However see Ketzos Hashulchan 136 footnote 7]; Chayeh Adam 24:5 and Nishmas Adam 24:3, brought in Biur Halacha 320:19 "Litein Karkum" leaves this matter in question; Ginas Veradim 3:9 regarding liquids; Darkei Moshe 320:2 in name of Avraham Mintz regarding liquids; Avnei Nezer 173 concludes it is proper to be stringent like the Tosafus Rid against the Michaber]
Why is there a dyeing prohibition involved in slaughtering an animal if an animal is food? According to the Michaber and Poskim ibid this is because a) This neck area that is dyed during slaughtering is forbidden to be eaten and one's intent is to sell the meat and therefore it is forbidden. [Chacham Tzvi 92, brought in Avnei Nezer 173] b) Because one is dyeing the skin of the neck, and this skin is not food. [Or Zarua, brought in Avnei Nezer ibid and Biur Halacha ibid]
[63] Admur 320:27; Michaber 320:20; Shibulei Haleket 86 in name of Yireim
[64] Admur 320:26; Michaber 320:19; Shibulei Haleket 86 in name of Yireim
Other opinions: Some Poskim rule the prohibition of dyeing applies even to foods. [Tosafus Rid Shabbos 75a, based on Shabbos ibid that there is a dyeing prohibition involved in slaughtering; Chayeh Adam 24:5 and Nishmas Adam 24:3, brought in Biur Halacha 320:19 "Litein Karkum" leaves this matter in question; Ginas Veradim 3:9 regarding liquids; Darkei Moshe 320:2 in name of Avraham Mintz regarding liquids; Avnei Nezer 173 concludes it is proper to be stringent like the Tosafus Rid against the Michaber]
Why is there a dyeing prohibition involved in slaughtering an animal if an animal is food? According to the Michaber and Poskim ibid this is because a) This neck area that is dyed during slaughtering is forbidden to be eaten and one's intent is to sell the meat and therefore it is forbidden.

prohibition [when one does not intend to dye the food but simply to give taste]. Thus, one may add a spice to his food even if it will dye or color his food in the process. [This however is regarding foods. Regarding liquids however this matter is disputed in Poskim. Some Poskim[65] rule the dyeing prohibition does not apply to liquids. Other Poskim[66] however rule the dyeing prohibition applies to liquids. Some Poskim[67] rule however that one may add the water to the dyed liquids but not the dyed liquid to the water.[68] Practically, according to the Shulchan Aruch and Alter Rebbe doing so is completely permitted without restriction when doing so to drink that day.[69]]

With intent to to dye and to add taste: Some Poskim[70] rule it is permitted to be done in such a case.[71] Others[72] however rule one may not dye the foods. Practically one may be lenient.[73]

With intent to dye and not to add taste, but with intent to eat the dyed food: Some Poskim[74] rule it is permitted to do so even in such a case.[75] Other Poskim[76] rule it is forbidden to add the dye to it on Shabbos. Practically, some[77] rule one is to be stringent if there is no benefit for the eating of the food, although one may be lenient if there is benefit for the eating of the food.

With intent to dye and not in order to eat food:[78] Dyeing a food for non-eating purposes contains a Dyeing prohibition.

Q&A on dyeing liquids
May one dye water or other liquids?[79]
  ➤ Example: May one mix concentrated juice with water? May one enter a tea bag or tea essence into his water?

[Chacham Tzvi 92, brought in Avnei Nezer 173] b) Because one is dyeing the skin of the neck, and this skin is not food. [Or Zarua, brought in Avnei Nezer ibid and Biur Halacha ibid]

[65] Michaber 320:19 and Admur 320:26 regarding adding Turmeric into a liquid dish; Darkei Moshe 320:2 in name of Yireim; Tal Oros 48; Chacham Tzevi 92; P"M 320 A"A 25 and 321 A"A 24, M"B 320:56; Aruch Hashulchan 320:7; Ketzos Hashulchan 146 footnolte 16-12; Sheivet Halevi 9:71; SSH"K 11 footnote 158; Yabia Omer 2:20; Piskeiy Teshuvos 320:24

[66] Avraham of Mintz, brought in Darkei Moshe ibid; Ginas Veradim 3:9 [brought in Rav Poalim 2:3 and Shaareiy Teshuvah 318:4]; Minchas Shabbos 80:152; Chesed Lealafim 320:6; Ben Ish Chaiy Pekudei 2:3; Rav Poalim 3:11; Lev Chaim 3:78; Halef Lecha Shlomo 136; Kaf Hachaim 320:113 and 116; Shabbos Kehalacha 20:3

[67] Chesed Lealafim 320:6; Ben Ish Chaiy Pekudei 3; Rav Poalim 2:11; Kaf Hachaim 320:117; Mishneh Berurah in Shaar HaTziyon 318:65; This follows their interpretation of the stringent opinion brought in Ginas Veradim and Darkei Moshe; However see Ketzos Hashulchan 146 footnote 16-12 that according to the Poskim ibid it is forbidden even in this fashion.

[68] The reason: As when adding the dye to the water it is evident to all the color change of the water in the glass, when however, adding water to the dye this is not evident at all. [Rav Poalim ibid; See Ketzos Hashulchan ibid who negates this understanding]

[69] Ketzos Hashulchan ibid; Ketzos Hashulchan ibid; Sheivet Halevi 9:71; SSH"K 11 footnote 158; Yabia Omer 2:20; Piskeiy Teshuvos 320:24; However, for the next day is forbidden according to all as one may not trouble himself on Shabbos for the week.
Ruling of M"B: The M"B 320:56 rules one may pour red wine into white wine. However, in Shaar Hatziyon ibid he writes it is best to pour in the opposite way. See Piskeiy Teshuvos 320 footnote 271!

[70] Peri Megadim 320 A.A. 25 brought in M"B 320:56; Aruch Hashulchan 320:7; Ketzos Hashulchan 146 footnote 16-11 [however see footnote 15-1]; Chasam Sofer Shabbos 75; Or Letziyon 1:29; Yechaveh Daas 6:23; Tzitz Eliezer 14:47; Sheivet Halevi 9:71; Yabia Omer 2:20; SSH"K 11 footnote 158 in name of Rav SZ"A regarding Petel

[71] The reason: As there is no dyeing prohibition by foods at all, even if one does so for the purpose of the dye. [ibid]

[72] Possible way of learning Nishmas Adam brought in M"B ibid and ruled in Kitzur SHU"A 80:42 [See Piskeiy Teshuvos 320 footnote 273]; See Shabbos Kehalacha ibid footnote 17 which learns this opinion from Sheilas Yaavetz 1:42; Peri Megadim 318; Shoel Umeishiv 2:7; Rav Poalim 3:11

[73] Shabbos Kehalacha ibid; Piskeiy Teshuvos 320:24; As no mention of this is made in Shulchan Aruch when it states that one may add dye to his foods.

[74] P"M 320 A"A 25 [brought in M"B 320:56]; Aruch Hashulchan 320:7; Ketzos Hashulchan 146 footnote 16-11 [however see footnote 15-1]; Chasam Sofer Shabbos 75; Or Letziyon 1:29; Yechaveh Daas 6:23; Tzitz Eliezer 14:47

[75] The reason: As there is no dyeing prohibition by foods at all, even if one does so for the purpose of the dye. [ibid]

[76] Ben Ish Chaiy Pekudei 2:3; Nishmas Adam brought in M"B ibid; Kitzur SHU"A 80:42; Kaf Hachaim 320:116; Beir Moseh 8:23-15; Mishnas Yosef 7:77; Bris Olam Tzoveia 12; Piskeiy Teshuvos 320:24; See Shabbos Kehalacha ibid footnote 17 which learns this opinion from Sheilas Yaavetz 1:42; Peri Megadim 318; Shoel Umeishiv 2:7; SSH"K 11 footnote 158000

[77] Shabbos Kehalacha ibid; Piskeiy Teshuvos ibid

[78] P"M 320 A"A 25; Ben Ish Chaiy Pekudei 2:3; M"B 320:56; Ketzos Hashulchan 146:8; Nishmas Adam brought in M"B ibid; Beir Moseh 8:23-15; Mishnas Yosef 7:77; Bris Olam Tzoveia 12; Kaf Hachaim 320:116; Many Poskim in Piskeiy Teshuvos 320:25 footnote 279; See Shabbos Kehalacha ibid footnote 17 which learns this opinion from Sheilas Yaavetz 1:42; Peri Megadim 318; Shoel Umeishiv 2:7; Shabbos Kehalacha vol. 3 20:4 based on Poskim in previous footnote; Piskeiy Teshuvos 320:25
Other Opinions: The Chacham Tzevi 92 rules that the dyeing prohibition does not apply to foods or liquids that are fit for consumption even if one is doing so for non-eating purposes.

[79] Shaar HaTziyon 318:65

It is permitted to dye water on Shabbos for purposes of drinking, just as it is permitted to dye other foods on Shabbos.[80] One may thus place red wine into white wine.[81] However some Poskim[82] rule the dyeing prohibition applies to liquids and one is hence not to place a dyeing color into liquids.[83] Some Poskim[84] rule however that one may add the water to the dyed liquids but not the dyed liquid to the water.[85] Practically, according to the Shulchan Aruch and Alter Rebbe doing so is completely permitted without restriction when doing so to drink that day.[86]

Q&A on dyeing for food purposes but to also add color
May one add dye to foods if he intends to both give it taste and to color the food?[87]
➢ Example: One desires to add cumin to his soup in order to make it yellow and also in order to give it taste? One desires to mix concentrated juice with water in order to add color and taste?
Some Poskim[88] rule it is permitted to be done in such a case.[89] Others[90] however rule one may not dye the foods. Practically, one may be lenient.[91]

Q&A on dyeing for purpose of color but plans to eat the food
May one dye foods that he plans to eat if his entire intent is to color the food?[92]
➢ Example 1: One desires to give a child to drink red colored water, and thus desires to add red pigment to the water?
➢ Example 2: One desires to add food coloring or dye to a drink or food in order to impress guests.
Some Poskim[93] rule it is permitted to do so even in such a case.[94] Other Poskim[95] rule it is forbidden to add the dye to it on Shabbos.[96] Practically, some[97] rule one is to be stringent in case 2 being there is no benefit for the eating of the food in this case, although one may be lenient in case 1 where there is

---

[80] Michaber 320:19 and Admur 320:26 regarding adding Turmeric into a liquid dish; Darkei Moshe 320:2 in name of Yireim; Tal Oros 48; Chacham Tzevi 92; P"M 320 A"A 25 and 321 A"A 24 M"B 320:56; Aruch Hashulchan 320:7; Ketzos Hashulchan 146 footnolte 16-12; Sheivet Halevi 9:71; SSH"K 11 footnote 158; Yabia Omer 2:20; Piskeiy Teshuvos 320:24

[81] Darkei Moshe ibid; P"M 320 A"A 25; M"B ibid; Sheivet Halevi 9:71; SSH"K 11 footnote 158

[82] Avraham of Mintz, brought in Darkei Moshe ibid; Ginas Veradim 3:9 [brought in Shaareiy Teshuvah 318:4 and Rav Poalim 2:3]; Minchas Shabbos 80:152; Chesed Lealafim 320:6; Ben Ish Chaiy Pekudei 2:3; Rav Poalim 3:11; Lev Chaim 1:78; Halef Lecha Shlomo 136; Kaf Hachaim 320:113 and 116; Beir Moshe 8:24-17

[83] <u>The reason:</u> As it is Biblically forbidden to create dye on Shabbos, and entering a dyed food into liquid is similar to making a dye. [Rav Poalim ibid; Ben Ish Chaiy ibid]

[84] Chesed Lealafim 320:6; Ben Ish Chaiy Pekudei 3; Rav Poalim 2:3; Kaf Hachaim 320:117; Mishneh Berurah in Shaar HaTziyon 318:65; Beir Moshe ibid; This follows their interpretation of the stringent opinion ibid brought in Ginas Veradim and Darkei Moshe; However, see Ketzos Hashulchan 146 footnolte 16-12 that according to the Poskim ibid it is forbidden even in this fashion.

[85] <u>The reason:</u> As when adding the dye to the water it is evident to all the color change of the water in the glass, when however, adding water to the dye this is not evident at all. [Rav Poalim ibid; See Ketzos Hashulchan ibid who negates this understanding]

[86] Ketzos Hashulchan ibid; Sheivet Halevi 9:71; SSH"K 11 footnote 158; Yabia Omer 2:20; Piskeiy Teshuvos 320:24
However, for the next day is forbidden according to all as one may not trouble himself on Shabbos for the week.
<u>Ruling of M"B:</u> The M"B 320:56 rules one may pour red wine into white wine. However, in Shaar Hatziyon ibid he writes it is best to pour in the opposite way. See Piskeiy Teshuvos 320 footnote 271!

[87] Shabbos Kehalacha Vol. 3 20:7-9; Piskeiy Teshuvos 320:24

[88] Peri Megadim 320 A.A. 25 brought in M"B 320:56; Aruch Hashulchan 320:7; Ketzos Hashulchan 146 footnote 16-11 [however see footnote 15-1]; Chasam Sofer Shabbos 75; Or Letziyon 1:29; Yechaveh Daas 6:23; Tzitz Eliezer 14:47; Sheivet Halevi 9:71; Yabia Omer 2:20; SSH"K 11 footnote 158

[89] <u>The reason:</u> As there is no dyeing prohibition by foods at all, even if one does so for the purpose of the dye. [ibid]

[90] Possible way of learning Nishmas Adam brought in M"B ibid and ruled in Kitzur SHU"A 80:42 [See Piskeiy teshuvos 320 footnote 273]; See Shabbos Kehalacha ibid footnote 17 which learns this opinion from Sheilas Yaavetz 1:42; Peri Megadim 318; Shoel Umeishiv 2:7; Rav Poalim 3:11

[91] Shabbos Kehalacha ibid; Piskeiy Teshuvos 320:24; As no mention of this is made in Shulchan Aruch when it states that one may add dye to his foods.

[92] Shabbos Kehalacha Vol. 3 20:8-9

[93] P"M 320 A"A 25 [brought in M"B 320:56]; Aruch Hashulchan 320:7; Ketzos Hashulchan 146 footnote 16-11 [however see footnote 15-1]; Chasam Sofer Shabbos 75; Or Letziyon 1:29; Yechaveh Daas 6:23; Tzitz Eliezer 14:47

[94] <u>The reason:</u> As there is no dyeing prohibition by foods at all, even if one does so for the purpose of the dye. [ibid]

[95] Ben Ish Chaiy Pekudei 2:3; Nishmas Adam brought in M"B ibid; Kitzur SHU"A 80:42; Kaf Hachaim 320:116; Beir Moseh 8:23-15; Mishnas Yosef 7:77; Bris Olam Tzoveia 12; Piskeiy Teshuvos 320:24; See Shabbos Kehalacha ibid footnote 17 which learns this opinion from Sheilas Yaavetz 1:42; Peri Megadim 318; Shoel Umeishiv 2:7; SSH"K 11 footnote 158

[96] It is possible that there Poskim prohibit that if the dye does not add taste or benefit to the food then

[97] Shabbos Kehalacha ibid; Piskeiy Teshuvos ibid

benefit for the eating of the food.

May one mix red wine with white wine at the night of the Seder?
This matter follows the same dispute as the previous Q&A.[98] Practically, one may do so[99], although it is best to pour in the red wine first and then pour in the white wine.[100]

Q&A on dyeing for non-food purposes

May one dye foods for non-eating purposes?[101]
No. Dyeing a food for non-eating purposes contains a Dyeing prohibition.

May one on Shabbos place food coloring into foods or liquids that are planned to be sold?[102]
No. Doing so contains the dyeing prohibition.[103]

May one add dye to water that is in a vase?[104]
No.

May one dye toilet water using toilet soaps?
It is forbidden to do so if one intends to dye the water in the process.[105]

---

[98] Piskeiy Teshuvos 320 footnote 276

[99] Shevet Halevi 10:56

[100] Shabbos Kehalacha 20:10

[101] P"M 320 A"A 25; Ben Ish Chaiy Pekudei 2:3; M"B 320:56; Ketzos Hashulchan 146:8; Nishmas Adam brought in M"B ibid; Beir Moshe 8:23-15; Mishnas Yosef 7:77; Bris Olam Tzoveia 12; Kaf Hachaim 320:116; Many Poskim in Piskeiy Teshuvos 320:25 footnote 279; See Shabbos Kehalacha ibid footnote 17 which learns this opinion from Sheilas Yaavetz 1:42; Peri Megadim 318; Shoel Umeishiv 2:7; Shabbos Kehalacha vol. 3 20:4 based on Poskim in next footnote; Piskeiy Teshuvos 320:25
Other Opinions: The Chacham Tzevi 92 rules that the dyeing prohibition does not apply to foods or liquids that are fit for consumption even if one is doing so for non-eating purposes.

[102] Peri Megadim 320 A.A. 25; M"B 320:56; Ketzos Hashulchan 146:8; Shabbos Kehalacha vol. 3 20:6
Other Opinions: According to the Chacham Tzevi ibid this would be permitted.

[103] The reason for this prohibition is due to that the dyeing of food is only permitted when it is done for eating purposes. However, when it is done for non-eating purposes then it is the Melacha of dyeing. [See P"M ibid; Shabbos Kehalacha ibid footnote 13]

[104] Peri Megadim ibid; Ben Ish Chaiy Pekudei 2:3; Shabbos Kehalacha vol. 3 20:6 based on Poskim in previous footnotes.
Other Opinions: The Chacham Tzevi 92 rules that the dyeing prohibition does not apply to foods or liquids that are fit for consumption even if one is doing so for non-eating purposes.

[105] If one has no intent to dye the water at all, then see Piskeiy Teshuvos 321:25 in name of many Poskim; Shabbos Kehalacha; M"B Dirsshu p. 768 in name of SSH"K 24:14 that is assur.

5. Dyeing one's skin with pigment/Applying makeup:[106]

In the process of eating:[107] There is no problem involved at all in [**dirtying**] one's hands and face with the pigment of the food that he is eating, as [the] coloring [prohibition] only applies towards an item which is commonly dyed. [This applies for both a man and woman.[108] Nevertheless, it is proper to eat strawberries with a fork.[109]]

Applying makeup:[110] It was prohibited for a woman to apply makeup on her face due to the coloring [prohibition], as was explained in Chapter 303 [Halacha 25[111]], due to that this is commonly done on woman.[112]

Applying eyeliner:[113] As well to apply eyeliner was prohibited whether for a man or woman due to the coloring prohibition, being that this is commonly done.

Summary- Dyeing Skin:
To dye areas of skin that are commonly dyed is Rabbinically forbidden. Thus, one may not apply makeup. To dye other areas is allowed. Thus, one may eat fruits that have pigment, despite getting the coloring on one's skin.

Q&A
The Mimacheik prohibition applicable with makeup:
In addition to the dyeing prohibition associated with using makeup on Shabbos, the prohibition of Mimacheik may also be applicable. Some Poskim[114] rule the Mimacheik prohibition applies by all hard substances that are smeared. Others[115] rule that the Mimacheik prohibition does not apply. Possibly however the Molid prohibition would apply according to all.[116]

May a woman apply nail polish or lip stick on Shabbos?[117]
No. In addition to containing a dyeing prohibition it may also contain the Mimacheik/Smearing prohibition.

---

[106] Admur 320:27
[107] Admur ibid; M"A 320:25; Yireim ibid; Shibulei Haleket ibid; M"B 320:58
[108] Shaar Hatziyon 303:79; Ketzos Hashulchan 146 footnote 19
Shaar HaTziyon 303:65; Ketzos Hashulchan 146 footnote 19
The reason: The Ketzos Hashulchan ibid offers 6 reasons as to why this is permitted, despite the fact we rule that by women it is Derech Tzevia to dye the face, and amongst these reasons is that: 1) It is done is a way of Derech Achila, the way of eating. 2) It is done in an irregular way- Keliacher Yad. The Shaar Hatziyon ibid states the reason is because it is not common to dye the lips. Vetzaruch Iyun Gadol, as certainly women dye the lips. Furthermore, even if one were to learn the intent of the Shaar Hatziyon that it is not common to dye using fruits, nevertheless since it is common to dye the face it should nevertheless be forbidden, just as we rule regarding cleaning the hands on a cloth. [Ketzos Hashulchan ibid; Shabbos Kehalacha ibid]
[109] Ketzos Hashulchan 146:9
[110] Admur ibid; Michaber 303:25; Mishneh Shabbos 94b; 95a
Biblical or Rabbinical? The dyeing of human skin is only Rabbinically forbidden as the prohibition of dyeing does not apply to skin. [Implication of Michaber ibid and Admur ibid; M"A 303:19; Olas Shabbos 303:19; M"B 303:79; Chachamim in Mishneh ibid; Rambam 20; See Biur Halacha 303:25 "Mishum Tzoveia"; Kaf Hachaim 303:115] However some Poskim rule it is Biblically forbidden. [Elya Raba 303:40 in name of Rishonim who rule like Rebbe Eliezer in Mishneh ibid; Yireim, brought in Nishmas Adam; Semag; Ran; Ravan; See Biur Halacha ibid and Kaf Hachaim ibid]. From the above one can learn that the fact that a dye may not last a long time is not a reason to not be Biblically forbidden.
Dyeing the face of a friend: Some Poskim rule that, according to all opinions, one who dyes the face of his friend transgresses a Biblical prohibition. [Elya Raba ibid based on Shabbos 95a] Others argue that according to those who hold dyeing of skin is Rabbinical, agree it is Rabbinical even in such a case. [Biur Halacha ibid; Kaf Hachaim 320:115]
[111] In Michaber/Rama
[112] Admur ibid; M"A 303:19; 320:25; M"B 303:79; 320:58; Yireim ibid brought in Shibulei Haleket
[113] Admur ibid; Michaber ibid; Shabbos 95a
[114] M"B 327:20; Igros Moshe 1:114; 5:27; Piskeiy Teshuvos 303:14; See Shabbos Kehalacha 18 footnote 48
[115] Ketzos Hashulchan 146 footnote 20
[116] Shabbos Kehalacha ibid
[117] Ketzos Hashulchan page 31 footnote 20

May a woman use white and clear makeup/nail polish/lipstick?
The prohibition against applying makeup and nail polish applies even if the nail polish or lipstick is of a white color[118], or even a clear color that simply makes the lips shine.[119] However some Poskim[120] are lenient if it does not have a color and simply shines the skin. In all cases, it is forbidden to use lipstick due to the smearing prohibition, irrelevant of the color.

May a woman apply powdered makeup ["foundation"] to her face on Shabbos?[121]
Has makeup on face:[122] If the woman had put on makeup on her face from before Shabbos and now desires to apply face powder to it then this is forbidden according to all being that the powder clings on to the makeup and enhances its color.[123]
No makeup on face-White powder: If, however, the woman does not have makeup on her face, then this matter is disputed amongst Poskim. Many Poskim[124] rule it is allowed to be done being that so long as the powder does not stick on to one's skin [as does a paste] it is not defined as a dye. However, some Poskim[125] rule it is forbidden.
No makeup on face-Other color powders: Some Poskim[126] rule all powdered makeup may be used, irrelevent of color, so long as there isn't any really makeup on the face, and the powder does not contain oil and hence does not stick to the face. Other Poskim[127] however rule that colored powder is forbidden in use in all cases. If the powder contains oil, or other sticking substance which makes it last on the face, then it is forbidden according to all to be used on Shabbos.[128]

Shabbos makeup:[129]
Shabbos makeup is colored powder that is applied to the face, and is subject to the dispute mentioned above. Hence, even those powders that contain a Hashgacha, are only permitted according to the lenient opinion above. The Hashgacha must ensure that the powder does not contain any oil or other sticking substance which would render the powder forbidden even according to the lenient opinion.

May a woman use powdered makeup [i.e. Shabbos makeup] on Shabbos?
It is forbidden for a woman to apply makeup on Shabbos due to the dyeing [prohibition].[130] Nonetheless, the Poskim debate whether this prohibition applies to all forms of coloring that one places on their face, or if it only applies to makeup that sticks to the face. This dispute created a

---

[118] Kaf Hachaim 303:113; See Beir Moshe 8:25
[119] SSH"K 14:57-58 in name of Rav SZ"A regarding a clear color that makes the skin shine; Shabbos Kehalacha 18:18; Piskeiy Teshuvos 303:14
[120] Ateres Moshe 94 brought in Piskeiy Teshuvos ibid; See Shabbos Kehalacha ibid
[121] SSH"K 14:59
[122] Ketzos Hashulchan 146 footnote 20
[123] Ketzos Hashulchan 146 footnote 20
[124] Ketzos Hashulchan 146 footnote 20; Igros Moshe 1:114; 5:27; Maharam Brisk 1:23; Yabia Omer 6:37; Ateres Moshe 95; Beir Moshe 8:25; Shevet Halevi 6:33; Piskeiy Teshuvos 303:14
[125] Rav SZ"A brought in SSHK 14 footnote 158; Beis Yisrael 1:56
[126] Ketzos Hashulchan 146 footnote 20; Yabia Omer 6:37; Igros Moshe 1:114; 5:27; Shabbos Kehalacha 18:22 [Volume 3 page 175]
[127] Maharam Brisk 1:23; Ateres Moshe 95; Beir Moshe 8:25; Shevet Halevi 6:33; Rav SZ"A brought in SSHK 14 footnote 158; Beis Yisrael 1:56; Piskeiy Teshuvos 303:14
[128] Igros Moshe 5:27
[129] Igros Moshe ibid
[130] Admur 320:27; Michaber 303:25; Mishneh Shabbos 94b; 95a; M"A 303:19; 320:25; M"B 303:79; 320:58; Yireim ibid brought in Shibulei Haleket
Biblical or Rabbinical? The dyeing of human skin is only Rabbinically forbidden as the prohibition of dyeing does not apply to skin. [Implication of Michaber ibid and Admur ibid; M"A 303:19; Olas Shabbos 303:19; M"B 303:79; Chachamim in Mishneh ibid; Rambam 20; See Biur Halacha 303:25 "Mishum Tzoveia"; Kaf Hachaim 303:115] However some Poskim rule it is Biblically forbidden. [Elya Raba 303:40 in name of Rishonim who rule like Rebbe Eliezer in Mishneh ibid; Yireim, brought in Nishmas Adam; Semag; Ran; Ravan; See Biur Halacha ibid and Kaf Hachaim ibid]. From the above one can learn that the fact that a dye may not last a long time is not a reason to not be Biblically forbidden.
Dyeing the face of a friend: Some Poskim rule that, according to all opinions, one who dyes the face of his friend transgresses a Biblical prohibition. [Elya Raba ibid based on Shabbos 95a] Others argue that according to those who hold dyeing of skin is Rabbinical, agree it is Rabbinical even in such a case. [Biur Halacha ibid; Kaf Hachaim 320:115]

debate regarding using powdered makeup on Shabbos. The following are the opinions in Poskim: Many Poskim[131] rule that one may apply white powder [foundation] to the face, so long as it does not stick on to one's skin [as does a paste], as in such a case it is not defined as a dye.[132] Furthermore, some Poskim[133] add that all powdered makeup may be used, irrelevant of color, so long as it does not stick to the face, as explained above.[134] Practically, this means that there isn't any makeup on the face, and one's face is not wet or oily, and that the powder does not contain oil and hence will not stick to the face. If the powder contains oil, or other sticking substance which makes it last on the face, then it is forbidden according to all to be used on Shabbos.[135] Other Poskim[136] however rule that colored powder is forbidden in use in all cases, even if it will not stick to the face, and only white powdered makeup is allowed, when it does not stick to the face.[137] Furthermore, some Poskim[138] rule it is forbidden to use any type of powdered makeup, whether white or colored, even if it will not stick to the skin, due to the dyeing prohibition. Practically, one is to discuss with his Rav for a final ruling, although in general, the leaning approach is to be stringent.

Applying the powder to makeup placed before Shabbos:[139] Even according to the lenient opinion, if the woman put on makeup on her face from before Shabbos and now desires to apply face powder to it, then it is forbidden to do so according to all, being that the powder clings on to the makeup and enhances its color.[140]

Practically, may I use Shabbos makeup that has a Hechsher? Shabbos makeup is colored powder that is applied to the face, and fall under the above dispute as to their validity. Hence, even those powders that contain a Hashgacha, are only permitted according to the lenient opinion above, and are forbidden according to the stringent opinion. Accordingly, there is no such thing as Kosher Shabbos makeup that is Mehadrin, and abides by all opinions. The purpose of the Hashgacha is to ensure that the powder does not contain any oil or other sticking substance which would render the powder forbidden even according to the lenient opinion. Practically, before making using Shabbos makeup, even if it has a Hechsher, one is to contact their Rav. Certainly, one should not use a powder that does not contain a Hashgacha, as it may contain oil-based ingredients that make it stick to the face, and are forbidden according to all.

Other matters to beware: Those who are lenient to use Shabbos approved makeup, must beware of the following matters: 1) Not to mix the colored powders.[141] 2) One's face is dry, not oily, and clean from

---

[131] Ketzos Hashulchan 146 footnote 20; Igros Moshe 1:114; 5:27; Maharam Brisk 1:23; Yabia Omer 6:37; Ateres Moshe 95; Beir Moshe 8:25; Shevet Halevi 6:33; Piskeiy Teshuvos 303:14

[132] The reason: Some Poskim rule that the prohibition against applying makeup does not apply regarding a white color. [Beir Moshe 8:25; Shevet Halevi ibid] In addition, some of the above Poskim rule that even if white does pose a problem of dyeing in such a case it is permitted to do so, as the powder does not stick to the face as does a regular dye and is thus not similar at all to the dyeing prohibition. Thus, although it technically does cause the face to be dyed, since it is not in the same manner as regular dyeing it remains permitted, as we do not find that the Sages decreed against this form of dyeing in any area, and we cannot create new decrees on our own. [Ketzos Hashulchan ibid]

[133] Ketzos Hashulchan 146 footnote 20; Yabia Omer 6:37; Igros Moshe 1:114; 5:27; Shabbos Kehalacha 18:22 [Volume 3 page 178]

[134] The reason: As the powder does not stick to the face as does a regular dye and is thus not similar at all to the dyeing prohibition. Thus, although it technically does cause the face to be dyed, since it is not in the same manner as regular dyeing it remains permitted, as we do not find that the Sages decreed against this form of dyeing in any area, and we cannot create new decrees on our own. [Ketzos Hashulchan ibid] Others however suggest that the reason makeup is allowed is because the dye does not last on the face at all, and only when the dye lasts, is it considered a prohibited form of dyeing. [Igros Moshe ibid] This latter explanation, however, is most difficult to accept, as the Sages explicitly decreed against dyeing even if it does not last at all. [See Admur 320:28; M"A 320:25; Rambam 9:13; Machatzis Hashekel 320:24; M"B 320:59] In addition, what would determine the difference between lasting makeup, and temporary makeup, when in truth all makeup disappears with time.

[135] Igros Moshe 5:27

[136] Maharam Brisk 1:23; Ateres Moshe 95; Beir Moshe 8:25; Shevet Halevi 6:33; Rav SZ"A brought in SSHK 14 footnote 158; Beis Yisrael 1:56; Piskeiy Teshuvos 303:14

[137] The reason: As there is no difference between whether the powder sticks to the face or does not stick to the face, and we find no source to differentiate on this matter. Likewise, it is clearly ruled that even temporary dye that does not last at all is nevertheless Rabbinically forbidden. [Poskim ibid]

[138] Rav SZ"A brought in SSHK 14 footnote 158; Beis Yisrael 1:56

[139] Ketzos Hashulchan 146 footnote 20

[140] Ketzos Hashulchan 146 footnote 20

[141] The reason: Due to the prohibition against making dye. [Magen Avraham 320:25 brought in Mishneh Berurah 320:59; 252:1; Michaber and Admur 252:1 that doing so is only permitted from before Shabbos.]

makeup, in order so the powder does not stick. 3) It is best for the powder to be loosened before Shabbos.[142] 4) It is permitted to use the designated brush, or any other designated item [such as a designated Q-tip], in order to apply the makeup.[143] It may also be applied using the fingers.

May one apply cream to their face on Shabbos?[144]
No, this contains the Mimacheik prohibition.

May one smear Dead sea mud on their face on Shabbos?
No.

May a man apply makeup?[145]
All makeup that is common for a man to put on, is forbidden to be placed on Shabbos. If however it is uncommon for a man to put on this makeup, then doing so is permitted. However, some Poskim[146] are stringent even in such a case. In all cases, even during the weekday, it is forbidden for a man to apply makeup for beauty purposes, due to the prohibition of Lo Silbash.[147]

Q&A on Pesik Reshei
Does the prohibition of Pesik Reshei apply towards dyeing the body?[148]
Yes.

May one pat a towel on one's face if doing so will leave a red color on the face?[149]
It is permitted for a man to do so in all circumstances, being it is not common for a man to dye his face. However, a woman may not do so even if she has no intent to dye her face, being it is common for her to dye her face.

May one eat a food that dyes the lips red?[150]
It is permitted for a woman to eat fruits and the like which leave a red pigment on her lips so long as this is not her intent.[151] If, however, she intends to dye her lips red, then doing so is forbidden due to the dying prohibition.[152] It is permitted for a man to eat these foods in all cases, [so long as he does not intend to dye his lips for beauty purposes].[153]

May one eat colored ices if he intends to dye his lips?[154]
It is forbidden for a woman, [or female child who is above the age of Chinuch], to do so. [It is permitted for a man, or male child to do so, so long as he is not intending to do so for beauty

---

[142] The reason: The avoid the question of Tochein:grinding. [See Ketzos Hashulchan 129 footnote 15]
[143] As predesignated items, for the sake of getting dirty with a pigment, do not contain the dyeing prohibition. [See Kuntrus Achron 302:1]
[144] SSH"K 14:60
[145] See Admur 320:27; M"A 303:19; M"B 303:79; Ketzos Hashulchan 146 footnote 20 based on Admur Kuntrus Achron 302:1
[146] Kalkeles Shabbos Tzoveia [brought in Ketzos Hashulchan ibid]; Beis Yisrael 57; Piskeiy Teshuvos 303:14
[147] Ketzos Hashulchan ibid; Piskeiy Teshuvos ibid
[148] M"B 303:79 based on Tosefta; Implication of M"A 320:25; Admur 320:27; Ketzos Hashulchan 146 footnote 19
[149] M"B 303:79
[150] Shabbos Kehalacha Vol. 3 20:17-18; Piskeiy Teshuvos 303:14; Yabi Omer 6:37
[151] Shaar HaTziyon 303:65; Ketzos Hashulchan 146 footnote 19
The reason: The Ketzos Hashulchan ibid offers 6 reasons as to why this is permitted, despite the fact we rule that by women it is Derech Tzevia to dye the face, and amongst these reasons is that: 1) It is done is a way of Derech Achila, the way of eating. 2) It is done in an irregular way-Keliacher Yad. The Shaar Hatziyon ibid states the reason is because it is not common to dye the lips. Vetzaruch Iyun Gadol, as certainly women dye the lips. Furthermore, even if one were to learn the intent of the Shaar Hatziyon that it is not common to dye using fruits, nevertheless since it is common to dye the face it should nevertheless be forbidden, just as we rule regarding cleaning the hands on a cloth. [Ketzos Hashulchan ibid; Shabbos Kehalacha ibid]
[152] Piskeiy Teshuvos ibid; Shabbos Kehalacha ibid
[153] See Admur 320:27; M"A 303:19; M"B 303:79; Ketzos Hashulchan 146 footnote 20 based on Admur Kuntrus Achron 302:1
The reason: As it is not common for a man to dye his body.
[154] Piskeiy Teshuvos ibid; Shabbos Kehalacha ibid

purposes.]

Q&A on removing makeup

May one remove dye from an item on Shabbos?

The Melacha of dyeing in the Mishkan does not contain an opposite Melacha against erasing the dye. Likewise, in the Talmud and Shulchan Aruch, we do not find any attribution of a prohibition against erasing dye on Shabbos. Nevertheless, the later Poskim question whether the erasing of dye contains the erasing prohibition, which corresponds to the writing prohibition on Shabbos. Many Poskim[155] rule it is forbidden to erase dye from the skin due to the erasing prohibition. Other Poskim[156] rule it is permitted to erase dye from one's skin and practically so is the custom.[157]

May one wash ink blotches off his skin?[158]

Many Poskim[159] rule it is forbidden to erase dye from the skin due to the erasing prohibition. According to these Poskim one must be careful when washing hands to avoid erasing the ink, and is to bind a cloth around the hand prior to washing it. Other Poskim[160] however rule ink or paint blotches may be washed off one's skin and so is the worldly custom.[161] [However according to all one must avoid wiping the ink on a towel and the like due to a dying prohibition.[162]]

May one remove makeup from the face on Shabbos?[163]

This matter is relevant to the same dispute in Poskim regarding erasing ink blotches from one's skin, in which the custom is to be lenient. Nevertheless, some[164] write one is to be stringent not to remove makeup on Shabbos even according to the lenient opinion mentioned above. Practically, those who are lenient have upon whom to rely.[165]

---

[155] Chayeh Adam [Laws of Netilas Yadayim] 40:8; Minchas Shabbos 80:199; Peri Haaretz 2:4; Ikkarei Dinim 14:70; Kaf Hachaim [Falagi] 30:57; Vayaan Avraham 31; Ben Ish Chaiy Pekudeiy 2:1; Tal Oros p. 334
[156] Ketzos Hashulchan 144 footnote 10; Kaf Hachayim 161:27 in name of Pischeiy Teshuvah; Meged Yehuda 2; Minchas Shlomo 2:10; Beir Moshe 8:25; SSH"K 14 footnote 83 in name of Rav SZ"A; Piskeiy Teshuvos 340:5
[157] The reason: Since the blotches of ink was not the Melacha in Mishkan and since the skin is not an area of writing and thus one is not fixing the area for writing by erasing the ink, the Sages therefore did not prohibit erasing ink from one's skin. This can be proven from fact a) One may wash off the pomegranate and strawberry dye from his hands and it does not involve a erasing prohibition. And b) One may clean a spill of an item off a table and doing so does not involve an erasing prohibition. Therefore, since it is embarrassing to walk around with dirty hands and it is as well a Mitzvah to dry one's hands after washing for bread and the like, one should not protest those that are lenient in this. [Ketzos Hasulchan ibid]
[158] See Ketzos Hashulchan 144 footnote 10; Piskeiy Teshuvos 340:3
[159] Chayeh Adam [Laws of Netilas Yadayim] 40:8; Minchas Shabbos 80:199; Peri Haaretz 2:4; Ikkarei Dinim 14:70; Kaf Hachaim [Falagi] 30:57; Vayaan Avraham 31; Ben Ish Chaiy Pekudeiy 2:1; Tal Oros p. 334
[160] Ketzos Hashulchan 144 footnote 10; Kaf Hachayim 161:27 in name of Pischeiy Teshuvah; Meged Yehuda 2; Minchas Shlomo 2:10; Beir Moshe 8:25; SSH"K 14 footnote 83 in name of Rav SZ"A; Piskeiy Teshuvos 340:5
[161] The reason: Since the blotches of ink was not the Melacha in Mishkan and since the skin is not an area of writing and thus one is not fixing the area for writing by erasing the ink, the Sages therefore did not prohibit erasing ink from one's skin. This can be proven from fact a) One may wash off the pomegranate and strawberry dye from his hands and it does not involve a erasing prohibition. And b) One may clean a spill of an item off a table and doing so does not involve an erasing prohibition. Therefore, since it is embarrassing to walk around with dirty hands and it is as well a Mitzvah to dry one's hands after washing for bread and the like, one should not protest those that are lenient in this. So rules also Kaf Hachaim 161:27
[162] Kaf Hachaim 340
[163] SSH"K 14:61; Orchos Shabbos 15:85 in name of many Poskim; Based on 320:27 that one may wash off the pomegranate and strawberry dye from his hands and it does not involve a erasing prohibition.
[164] Piskeiy Teshuvos 340:5; SSH"K 14:66 writes initially to remove the nail polish with a gentile, if a gentile is available; So rules also Shabbos Kehalacha 18:27 [Volume 3 p. 179] that one may only remove the nail polish in times of great need, such as to go to Mikveh; See also Ketzos Hashulchan ibid which concludes "since it is shameful to walk with stained hands, one is not to protest against those that are lenient"
The reason: This case is more severe than the case of removing ink blotches from the skin, as in this case one intends to eventually redye the skin after removing the makeup, and it is similar to the Biblical prohibition against erasing with intent to write.
[165] Beir Moshe 8:25 rules one may remove makeup on Shabbos prior to Mikveh; See SSH"K ibid; Orchos Shabbos 15 footnote 85; Shabbos Kehalacha footnote 55
The reason: As although one intends to eventually redye the skin after removing the makeup, and it is similar to the Biblical prohibition against erasing with intent to write, nevertheless, we rule that erasing dye from the skin is not relevnt at all to the erasing prohibition, and there is no prohibition of erasing dye which corresponds to the prohibition of dyeing, and hence there is no source in Halacha to prohibit this [ibid]

May one remove nail polish on Shabbos?[166]

This matter is relevant to the same dispute in Poskim regarding erasing ink blotches from one's skin, in which the custom is to be lenient. Nevertheless, some[167] write one is to be stringent not to remove nail polish on Shabbos even according to the lenient opinion mentioned above. Practically, those who are lenient have upon whom to rely.[168]

If a woman forgot to remove her nail polish from her nails before Shabbos, may she do so on Shabbos in order to immerse in a Mikveh?

Some Poskim[169] rule she is allowed to remove the nail polish herself, following the lenient opinion stated above. Others[170] rule that she should ask a gentile to remove it for her, and only in the event that a gentile is not available may she do so herself. Others[171] rule that if the polish is complete on all the nails, it is better to immerse with the polished nails then to remove it on Shabbos.[172] If, however, the polish has begun coming off, then she should ask a gentile to remove it. If no gentile is available, she may remove it herself. Others[173] write it is best for her to push off her immersion until the next night. [When removing the nail polish, one may use nail polish remover, although she may not soak a cotton ball in the liquid. She may however rub the polish off using a dry cotton ball.[174]]

General Q&A

May one take a suntan on Shabbos?

This matter is disputed amongst Poskim. Some Poskim[175] rule that it is forbidden even when done for mere pleasure.[176] Other Poskim[177], however, rule that it is allowed when done for mere pleasure[178], and is done in private, and one has no intent to tan his skin. However, according to others[179], it is even allowed if he intends to tan the skin being that he himself is not adding any dye.

---

[166] SSH"K 14:61

[167] Piskeiy Teshuvos 340:5; SSH"K 14:66 writes initially to remove the nail polish with a gentile, if a gentile is available; So rules also Shabbos Kehalacha 18:27 [Volume 3 p. 179] that one may only remove the nail polish in times of great need, such as to go to Mikveh.
The reason: This case is more severe than the case of removing ink blotches from the skin, as in this case one intends to eventually redye the skin after removing the makeup, and it is similar to the Biblical prohibition against erasing with intent to write.

[168] Beir Moshe 8:25 rules one may remove makeup on Shabbos prior to Mikveh; See SSH"K ibid; Orchos Shabbos 15 footnote 85; Shabbos Kehalacha footnote 55
The reason: As although one intends to eventually redye the skin after removing the makeup, and it is similar to the Biblical prohibition against erasing with intent to write, nevertheless, we rule that erasing dye from the skin is not relevnt at all to the erasing prohibition, and there is no prohibition of erasing dye which corresponds to the prohibition of dyeing, and hence there is no source in Halacha to prohibit this [ibid]

[169] Yesod Yeshurun brought in Piskeiy Teshuvos 340 footnote 7; Beir Moshe 8:25 rules one may remove makeup on Shabbos prior to Mikveh; See SSH"K ibid; Orchos Shabbos 15 footnote 85; Shabbos Kehalacha footnote 55

[170] SSH"K 14:66; Ateres Moshe 1:94; Piskeiy Teshuvos 340:5

[171] Taharah Kehalacha 15:79 p. 505 based on Rav SZ"A; However see what he writes in Shabbos Kehalacha 18:27 [vol. 3 p. 179]

[172] As RSZ"A questions whether removing nail polish is similar to erasing with intent to write, as she does have in mind to repaint it later on.

[173] Pischeiy Daas in name of Rav Elyashiv, brought in Piskeiy Teshuvos 340:5

[174] As dyeing is not relevant to cotton balls as they are designated for this purpose to become dirty and be discarded. It is hence similar to all items which are designated specifically for a dirty use which does not contain the dying prohibition. This follows the ruling written in "The Laws of Dyeing" regarding using a tissue to clean a wound, which is allowed based that it is designated for this purpose. [Admur Kuntrus Achron 302; SSH"K 14:19; Piskeiy Teshuvos 320:11] This ruling is unlike the ruling of Rav Farkash in Taharah Kehalacha ibid which prohibits the use of a cotton ball in all cases. Vetzaruch Iyun Gadol on his opinion.

[175] Minchas Yitzchak 5:32; See Michaber regarding dough making face red

[176] Due to a dyeing prohibition, and a possible pain afflicting prohibition [if it is very hot], and it being a degrading act which does not keep with the spirit of Shabbos, and it may come to cause one to smear creams on him. If done for healing, then it is also forbidden due to a healing prohibition as one may come to try to heal himself with herbs. [Minchas Yitzchak ibid-Vetzaruch Iyun Gadol as since people sunbathes for mere pleasure, thus the healing is not recognizable and should be allowed.]

[177] Az Nidbaru 2:30

[178] As if done for healing, it is questionable whether it contains the healing prohibition.

[179] SSH"K 18 footnote 70

May one take a urine or saliva test on Shabbos if doing so involves using a stick that will change color due to the urine/saliva?

Some Poskim[180] rule it is permitted to be used.[181] Other Poskim[182] rule it is forbidden to do so.[183] Practically, one is to be stringent in this matter, unless it is a case of need, or illness.[184] It is best to do so in a form of Grama, in which the urine does not directly hit the stick but rather flows off an item [such as the toilet] and then hits the stick.[185]

May one use eyeglasses that darken in the sun?[186]
Yes.[187]

May one use baby cups and plates that change color when hot food is placed on it?
Yes.[188] However, some[189] write one is to be stringent in such a case.

May one use a heat detector[190] that changes color to detect fever on Shabbos?
Yes.[191] However, some[192] write one is to be stringent in such a case.

May one use diapers that have urine indicators[193] that change color upon becoming wet?
Yes.[194] However, some[195] write one is to be stringent in such a case.

---

[180] Shearim Hametzuyanim Behalacha 91; Beir Moshe 8:24; Tzitz Eliezer 10:25; SSH"K 33:20

[181] The reason: As the stick is designated for this purpose and is thus not commonly dyed, as rules Admur in Kuntrus Achron 302:1. [SSH"K ibid; Shearim Hametzuyanim ibid] As the change of color is due to chemicals, and is hence not similar to dyeing at all. [Beir Moshe ibid]

[182] Michzeh Eliyahu 1:65; Nishmas Hashabbos 290; See Rav SZ"A ibid

[183] The reason: Being one is interested in having the stick change color, and is hence as if he is intending to dye it in which case being desiganetd does not help at all. [ibid]

[184] Piskeiy Teshuvos 320:27

[185] Rav SZ"A ibid

[186] Igros Moshe 3:45; Betzeil Hachochmah 4:4; Beir Moshe 6:46; Kinyan Torah 3:39; Tzitz Eliezer 14:31; 20:14; Mishneh Halachos 8:44; Shevet Halevi 4:23; Yechaveh Daas 2:47; SSH"K 18:18; Michzeh Eliyahu 1:65; Piskeiy Teshuvos 320:28

[187] The reason: As one has not done any act of dyeing here at all, as the change of color is internal, and the change of color happens on its own without any real action, and the color does not last at all and changes back to its original color right away. [Poskim ibid; SSH"K ibid footnote 70]

[188] Based on Poskim ibid that permit using eye-glasses that change color

[189] Piskeiy Teshuvos 320:28 being that in this case one is doing an action that causes the change of color.

[190] This is a strip that is placed on the forehead to detect fever. It changes color to show if there is fever.

[191] Based on Poskim ibid that permit using eye-glasses that change color and so writes SSH"K 40:2 footnote 9

[192] Piskeiy Teshuvos 320:28 being that in this case one is doing an action that causes the change of color.

[193] The product includes a material on the outside front of the diaper/training pant that allows color to be seen thru it from outside the diaper. Behind this material will be litmus paper or a color changing ink. Behind this litmus paper or color changing ink will be the urine absorbing material. The intent being that when the urine has sufficiently passed the layer of urine absorbing material and makes contact with the litmus paper or color changing ink a reaction will occur that will change the color of the litmus paper or the color changing ink. This color change would be visible from outside the diaper indicating that the diaper has been soiled.

[194] Based on Poskim ibid that permit using urine tests sticks that change color due to the reasons mentioned above. Furthermore, even according to the stringent opinion, in this case it is permitted as the ends of a child have the status of a bedridden person [see 328:22], as well as that it is permitted to give a child below Chinuch an item even if the child will do a Melacha with the item [see Admur 343:9-10], and hence certainly here it should be permitted.

[195] Piskeiy Teshuvos 320:28 being that in this case one is doing an action that causes the change of color.

THE LAWS OF TANNING SKINS AND SALTING FOODS ON SHABBOS

Shulchan Aruch Chapter 321

Translation
Shulchan Aruch Chapter 321
Halachas 1-6

TRANSLATION-CHAPTER 321

Laws of detaching food from the ground, grinding, fixing food, working leather and kneading.

Contains 16 Halachos

Halacha 1
Using bundles of herbs on Shabbos:

Avoiding Muktzah: Bundles of madder[1], hyssop, and thyme[2] which were collected in order to dry out and be used for firewood, may not be used on Shabbos [because of Muktzah].

If they were collected to be used as animal fodder, or even if they were collected without any specific intent, then they are considered collected for animal fodder and it is permitted to use them.

Avoiding other prohibitions: [In such a case that the bundles are not Muktzah] one may cut off [a piece of the herbs] with one's hands in order to eat[3], although he may not [cut it] using a utensil as is done normally during the week.[4]

One may rub the pods with the tips of his fingers in order to [free up and] eat internal seeds, although he may not use his entire hand as is normally done during the week, [being that doing so is a problem of threshing as explained in chapter 319 Halacha 9. However, in the Siddur Admur rules that one may nor rub the pods off under any circumstance, see 319 there.]

The Tanning and Salting prohibition

Introduction:

The following chapter will deal with the laws of salting foods and items on Shabbos. Salting skins contains a prohibition of tanning. As an offshoot of this prohibition, some hold it was decreed as well not to pickle and salt food in certain ways. Others however hold that the decree against food has nothing to do with the tanning prohibition but rather was decreed due to that it appears like cooking.

Halacha 2

The Biblical prohibition: One who tans skin is [transgressing one of] the principal prohibited actions being that in the [building process of the] Tabernacle they would tan the skins of the *techashim* and rams. One who salts the skin is liable for [the prohibition of] tanning being that salting is one of the necessary components in the tanning [of leather].

However, one who salts raw meat, even if he salts it increasingly in order so that it last for a long time and not get spoiled [in the interim], is not liable being that there is no Biblical prohibition of tanning foods.

The Rabbinical prohibition of salting meat: However, there is a Rabbinical [prohibition of] tanning food and therefore it is forbidden to salt raw meat, even with intent to eat it raw on Shabbos (if it had still not yet been salted in order to kosher it from its blood).

The reason for this prohibition is: because salt helps raw meat (which has not been previously salted) to soften it and prepare it and make it ready to eat and is [thus] similar to tanning.

Salting for preservation: It goes without saying that it is forbidden to salt [meat] in order so it stay preserved and not spoil, even if [not doing so] will cause a great financial loss, and even if had been already salted and koshered from its blood.

This law as well applies for other items [and foods], that it is forbidden to salt them on Shabbos in order to preserve them even in a case of great financial loss.

---

[1] A perennial plant with a fleshy red root.
[2] These are all different types of herbs.
[3] The Mishneh Berurah explains that the food is partially edible also for humans.
[4] Tzaruch Iyun why cutting it using a vessel is prohibited and what difference is there in cutting these foods and cutting other foods which is allowed with a vessel!

Halacha 3
Making salt water on Shabbos:
For pickling foods: Similarly, it is forbidden to make heavy salt water [on Shabbos] or other liquids heavily salted in order to place [these liquids] into pickled foods, meaning [to place them in] vegetables or other foods which are pickled to be preserved (even if one plans to eat from them right away in which case he is not troubling himself for only a weekday purpose)

The reason for this is: ([as] nevertheless) since he is pickling them to preserve it is similar to tanning in which the salt preserves them.

Other opinions regarding the reason: [However] there are opinions which say that pickling is forbidden [not because of the tanning prohibition but] because it is Rabbinically considered cooking.

For dipping foods into: even to make salt water or other salted liquids not [in order to use] for pickling, but rather in order to dip ones bread into and to place it into a dish is forbidden to make a lot of it at a time, which is defined as making in one time enough for dipping for two meals, rather [one may] only [make] a small amount enough for dipping for one meal.

Their reason: (is because when one makes a lot [at one time] it appears that he is doing so for pickling)

The condition that it must be made to eat right away: [Furthermore] even when making it for [only] one meal one is only allowed to make it in close proximately to the meal [in which one plans to dip in it], however [it is] not [allowed to be made] from [before] one meal for the need of another meal.[5]

The reason for this is: because it is forbidden to salt any item which one does not plans to eat right away as will be explained [in Halacha 4].

One who places oil in the dish prior to the salt: [Furthermore] even if one places oil into [the dish] in between the placing of the water and the placing of the salt into it[6] [in which case] the salt will not mix in well with the water and [the oil thus] weakens its strength of being strong salt water, nevertheless it is forbidden.[7]

Salt water made of 2/3rds salt: If one places 2/3rds salt and 1/3rd water or other liquid, then it is forbidden to make even a small amount of it for the purpose of dipping in the upcoming meal.

The reason for this is: being that it appears like one is making the Muryus gravy to pickle fish, as it is common to make Muryus in this way, [thus it is forbidden to make it as] it is forbidden to pickle on Shabbos due to the tanning or cooking prohibition as was explained.

Halacha 4
Salting foods which salt helps to change their natural state:
Not to salt more than one piece at a time: Any item which salt helps to change its natural state, [such as] to soften it or harden it or remove its bitterness and other [changes] of the like, such as for example radish or onion or garlic and the like of other spicy foods which when they are left in salt they secrete and remove their bitterness and become hard, as well as beans and lentils which were cooked with their peel of which salt softens their hardness which they have as a result of their peel, as well as species of raw cucumbers (called *ugerkis*) of which the salt helps them, as well as all other things which are commonly pickled, it is forbidden to salt more than one piece at a time in order to eat it right away.

The reason for this is because: as when one salts two pieces together and certainly [when he salts] more [than two pieces] it appears like one is pickling pickled foods.

Not to salt for a later use: [Furthermore] even one piece of radish and the like is forbidden to dip into salt and leave it [with the salt] for a long time in order so its sharpness dissipate through it secreting moisture, being that doing so is similar to tanning.

Dipping many pieces individually to eat right away: However, it is permitted to dip even a few pieces [when dipping] each one individually and one places it in front of him in order to them eat right away,

---

[5] This follows the ruling of the Magen Avraham. However, the Mishneh Berurah [11] based on other Poskim rules that it is allowed to be made even for later on.
[6] Meaning that prior to placing salt into the dish one places oil into it.
[7] However, the Mishneh Berurah [10] rules that one may be lenient if the oil is placed in prior to placing in the salt.

one after the other without much delay. Even if the [pieces] remain a small amount of time [in their salt prior to being eaten] and they [thus] secrete some moisture [nevertheless] this poses no problem so long as that they do not remain a long time [with their salt] even [when planning to eat them] within the same meal. [Meaning] for example [if] from the beginning of the meal to the end [of the meal there is enough time] for [the salted food] to secrete a lot of moisture [then it is forbidden to delay eating it until the end of the meal] because doing so is similar to tanning which is forbidden [to do] with even only one piece [of food].

Other Opinions: [However] there are opinions which say that it is forbidden to leave [the food] in salt at all even for a small amount of time, [and] even [when it is] only a single piece. Therefore [according to this view] it is forbidden to dip two pieces [in salt even] one after the other and then place them in front of him to eat immediately one after the other being that until one [finishes] eating the first piece the second piece remains in the salt. [Thus] it is only permitted to dip a single piece and then eat it right away.

The Final Ruling: The custom is like this latter opinion and so is the law with regards to any [food] which salt benefits.

The reason behind why one may not salt more than one piece at a time according to the 2nd opinion: According to the latter opinion the reason that [the Sages] prohibited to salt a few pieces at the same time is not because it appears like [one is] pickling pickled [foods], but rather is because that until one [finishes] eating the first [piece] the second piece remained in the salt, and since the salt benefits it this is similar to tanning.

Salting many pieces at the same time and then immediately adding vinegar or oil: Therefore [according to the latter opinion] that which [people are] accustomed [on Shabbos] to cut a radish very thin and then place it on a plate and salt it and then pour on it vinegar involves no prohibition even though that this is similar to salting many pieces together which [we said above] is forbidden [to be done] even to eat right away, [as] nevertheless since [the radish pieces] do not remain at all alone with the salt, as one immediately pours on it vinegar and other species, it is [therefore] not similar to tanning. Certainly [this allowance applies] if one pours oil on it being that oil weakens the strength of the salt.

Nevertheless, one must beware to pour the oil or vinegar [on the salted pieces] immediately after salting it [and doing so may not be delayed]. However that which some [people] are accustomed to make a vegetable (called *lettuce*) in which they first salt the vegetable on its own and then leave it this way and drain the water that comes out from it and then [only] afterwards mix it with oil and vinegar, doing so is a complete prohibition and is more similar to tanning [than when it is not left at all alone its salt] being that he delays until [the food] absorbs the salt well.

Halacha 5
Salting foods which salt only helps to give taste:
Any item [or food] which salt does not help to change its nature and rather only gives it taste, such as for example [salted] egg and [pre-salted[8]] meat is [only] forbidden to salt when done in order to leave it for another meal.

Other opinion: [However] there is an opinion which says that if there is any reason that it is better to salt [the food] now as opposed to salting it later on in proximity to the meal, such as if now [the food] is slightly hot[9] and will [thus] absorb the salt much better [if it were to be salted now] then there is no prohibition involved in doing so.

The Final Ruling: (One may rely on their words to be lenient in a [dispute over a] Rabbinical prohibition if one needs to do so[10]).

---

[8] Meaning meat that had been already salted to remove its blood, as otherwise it is forbidden even when done to eat right away as explained in Halacha 2

[9] Perhaps Admur mentions only slightly hot as if it were Yad Soledes than it is proper to not place salt on it at all, even in a Keli Sheiyni. [Ketzos Hashulchan 128 footnote 7]

[10] From the Ketzos Hashulchan [128:4] it seems that he learned this "need so" to mean that it will soften the meat. However, this does not seem to be the simple meaning of Admur, as if so then saying "needs so" is superfluous being that the arguing opinion itself only holds that when one needs so it is allowed.

Halacha 6

Edible vegetables: It is permitted to water detached vegetables in order so they do not shrivel, as since these vegetables are fit to be eaten today [on Shabbos] it is [therefore] allowed to water them just as it is [similarly] allowed to move them.

Inedible vegetables: However, if they are not fit to be eaten today [on Shabbos] in which case they are forbidden to be moved [because of Muktzah] it is [also] forbidden to water them.

Rinsing raw meat in order to eat after Shabbos: Therefore, it is forbidden to rinse meat which had not been [previously] salted which its third day [after being slaughtered] falls on Shabbos in order to prevent it from becoming forbidden to be cooked[11].

The reason for this is: because [the meat] is forbidden to be moved [is Muktzah] if it is hard meat that is not fit to be chewed [in its raw state] as was explained in chapter 308 [Halacha 68].

[Furthermore] even if [the meat] is soft and is fit to chew [in its raw state] one may not be lenient [to rinse it] as since he does not want to eat it today, rinsing it involves the prohibition of doing [an action which entails] effort on Shabbos for [the need of] a weekday.

The reason why watering the vegetables is not considered preparing for a weekday while rinsing meat is: [Rinsing the meat] is not similar to [watering] vegetables [which is allowed] being that they are fit today to be eaten by any person and it is thus not at all evident that one is [doing an action that entails] effort on Shabbos for the [need of a] weekday being that he may eat these [vegetables] today. However raw meat which is only fit to be chewed by a well minded person[12] as well as that [even by these people] it is not common to chew it raw and it is rather cooked, it is [therefore] recognizable [that when one rinses it] one is doing [an action which entails] effort on Shabbos for the [need of a] weekday.

Having a gentile rinse the meat: [Furthermore] even [to rinse the meat] through a gentile one may not be lenient, as although [the Sages] allowed in a scenario of a great financial loss to do anything through a gentile which is only a Rabbinical prohibition, as explained in chapter 307, nevertheless here it does not entail such a great loss if one were to not rinse it, being that he is [still] able to eat it roasted.

❖ **For Translation of Halachas 7-16 please refer to the next section "The Laws of Grinding and Mashing"**

---

[11] Meat which has not been salted or rinsed for three days becomes prohibited in being cooked even if one were to later salt it being that after three days the blood no longer comes out fully through salting, and is thus only permitted to be roasted. Thus the scenario here is that one desires to rinse the meat in order to prevent this law of taking affect.

[12] Meaning that the thought of eating it does not bother him.

COMPILATION OF HALACHAS-
SUMMARIES AND Q&A

Introduction:
The following chapter will deal with the laws of salting foods and items on Shabbos. Salting skins contains a prohibition of tanning. As an offshoot of this prohibition, some hold it was decreed as well not to pickle and salt food in certain ways. Others however hold that the decree against food has nothing to do with the tanning prohibition but rather was decreed due to that it appears like cooking.

---

1. The Biblical prohibition - Tanning and salting skins:[13]

The principal prohibition-Tanning skin:[14] One who tans skin is [transgressing one of] the principal prohibited actions being that in the [building process of the] Tabernacle they would tan the skins of the *techashim* and rams.

The prohibition of salting skin:[15] One who salts the skin is liable for [the prohibition of] tanning being that salting is one of the necessary components in the tanning [of leather].

No Biblical prohibition by foods:[16] However one who salts raw meat, even if he salts it increasingly in order so that it last for a long time and not get spoiled [in the interim], is not liable being that there is no Biblical prohibition of tanning foods.

Salting Fat:[17] It is Biblically forbidden to salt Cheilev/forbidden fats on Shabbos or Yom Tov [for the sake of preservation[18]], and one who does so is liable for the Miabeid/tanning prohibition.[19]

Summary- The Biblical Prohibition:[20]
The Biblical prohibition applies only to salting and tanning skins and forbidden fats, as opposed to meat or foods.

---

2. The Rabbinical prohibition- Salting foods:
For a general summary see 2D!
Although Biblically the prohibition of tanning does not apply to foods, nevertheless Rabbinically the prohibition of tanning applies food.[21]

A. Salting raw meat [which is edible by some in its raw state[22]] in order to soften it:[23]
Meat which has not yet been salted for blood:[24] There is a Rabbinical [prohibition of] tanning food and

---

[13] Admur 321:2
[14] Admur ibid; Mishnhe 73a
[15] Admur ibid; M"B 321:8; Shabbos 75b
Background:
The Mishneh ibid lists salting and Tanning as two of the Av Melachos. The Gemara ibid asks why they were listed as two if they are really one and the same. The Gemara answered that in truth they are one Av Melacha and one must enter a different one in its place.
Is salting a Tolda of Miabeid? It is implied that although Tanning is the Av Melacha, nevertheless salting is part of this Av Melacha and is not considered a Tolda.
[16] Admur ibid; M"A 321:7; M"B 320:8; Rambam 11; Rava Shabbos 75b; See Toras Hamelachos 28 p. 64
Other opinions in Gemara and Rishonim: Raba Bar Rav Huna holds that there is a Biblical prohibition to salt meat for the sake of preservation. Some Rishonim hold like this opinion. [Tosafus Rid 75b, brought in Avnei Nezer 173; Rashba, brought in M"A ibid]
[17] Admur 499:9; M"A 499:7; Ran 5b; Implication of Michaber 499:4 as explained in Machatzis Hashekel ibid; M"B 499:13
[18] M"B ibid
[19] The reason: Although it was explained above from 321:2 that the prohibition of Miabeis does not apply to foods, nevertheless, an item that is not a complete food, such as forbidden fats, one is liable due to Miabeid if he salts them.
[20] Halacha 2
[21] Admur 321:2; Tosafus Shabbos 75b; Smag 65
Other opinions: Some Rishonim hold there is no prohibition at all in salting foods even Rabbinically. [See Toras Hamelachos]-recheck if correct.
[22] Otherwise, the meat is Muktzah, as will IY"H be explained in the Laws of Muktzah.
[23] Admur 321:2

therefore it is forbidden to salt raw meat, even with intent to eat it raw on Shabbos (if it had still not yet been salted in order to kosher it from its blood[25]). [If, however, the meat was already slated for its blood, then one may salt it on Shabbos if he plans to eat it that day.[26]]

The reason for this prohibition is:[27] because salt helps raw meat (which has not been previously salted[28]) to soften it and prepare it and make it ready to eat and is [thus] similar to tanning.

Meat which has already been salted for blood: See D below

Summary:[29]
It is forbidden to salt raw meat even in order to eat the meat on Shabbos, if it had never yet been salted for its blood. Regarding meat that has been previously salted, see next case.

Q&A

May one salt raw fish such as Sushi?
No. It is forbidden to salt raw fish on Shabbos just like it is forbidden to salt raw meat.[30] This applies even if the fish is edible such as in a sushi dish. This however only applies to fish which the salt helps to soften it and prepare it and make it ready to eat and is [thus] similar to tanning. If, however, one is salting the fish simply to give it taste, then it may be done right before the meal, but only if one adds oil and the like to the sushi prior to the salting, as explained above.[31]

B. Salting in order to preserve:[32]

Salting raw meat for preservation:[33] It goes without saying that it is forbidden to salt [meat] in order so it stay preserved and not spoil, even if [not doing so] will cause a great financial loss, and even if it had been already salted and koshered from its blood.

Salting other foods for preservation:[34] This law as well applies for other items [and foods], that it is forbidden to salt them on Shabbos in order to preserve them even in a case of great financial loss.

Summary-Salting a food in order to preserve it:[35]
All foods are forbidden to be salted for preservation purposes, even if not doing so will cause great financial loss.

---

[24] Admur ibid; M"A 321:7; M"B 321:21; Tosafus Chulin 14a; Rosh 1:19

[25] Admur ibid; Tosafus ibid

[26] Admur ibid based on parentheses, in his understanding of the M"A and Rosh, and Tosafus ibid that the prohibition is only regarding a case of where it was not yet salted for blood; So also rules Elya Raba 321:9 in name of Rabbeinu Yerucham that it is permitted to salt raw or cooked meat on Shabbos if one plans to eat it that day.
Other opinions: Some Poskim rule it is forbidden to salt raw meat and fish on Shabbos in all cases, even if it was already salted for its blood. [Implication of M"A and M"B ibid; See P"M 321 A"A 7]

[27] Admur ibid; M"A ibid; Ran Chulin 5a; M"B ibid

[28] See previous footnotes; If however the meat was previously salted, then the salt does not help.

[29] Halacha 2

[30] M"A 321:7; M"B 321:21; omitted in Admur ibid; See there Biurim 18 that this law of raw fish was omitted by Admur because fish is Muktzah

[31] Shabbos Kehalacha Vol. 3 20:42

[32] Admur 321:2

[33] Admur ibid; M"A 321:7; M"B 321:21; Shibulei Haleket 88; Beis Yosef
Other opinions: Some Poskim rule it is permitted to salt raw meat on Shabbos in order to prevent a monetary loss. [Elya Raba 321:9 in implication of Shibulei Haleket]

[34] Admur ibid

[35] Halacha 4

C. Pickling foods on Shabbos:[36]

Similarly, it is forbidden to place heavily salted water or other liquids[37] [such as vinegar or wine[38]] into vegetables or other foods which are pickled to be preserved (even if one plans to eat from them right away[39] in which case he is not troubling himself for only a weekday purpose) [**See Q&A regarding vinegar**]

The reason for this is:[40] ([as] nevertheless) since he is pickling them to preserve, it is similar to tanning in which the salt preserves them.

Other opinions regarding the reason:[41] [However] there are opinions[42] which say that pickling is forbidden [not because of the tanning prohibition but] because it is Rabbinically[43] considered cooking.

Dipping foods in salt water: One may dip foods into salt water for taste, following the regulations explained in Halacha D-E regarding salting foods for taste.

Summary-Salting a food in order to preserve it:[44]
It is forbidden to pickle foods in salt water.

Q&A
May one pickle foods that are not normally pickled?
Salt water:[45] One may not allow a food to sit in salt water for even less than Shiur Kevisha, unless it is a food that salt does not help to change its form, as explained in Halacha E. Regarding if these foods that salt does not help to change its form, may be left for more than Shiur Kevisha, see Q&A below regarding vinegar that it is disputed as to whether one may leave uncommonly pickled foods in vinegar. Vetzaruch Iyun if the lenient opinion would be lenient even regarding salt water.
Vinegar: See next Q&A! Ketzos Hashulchan 321

Q&A on vinegar and other non-salt pickling agents
May one pickle foods in vinegar, or other non-salt pickling agent, on Shabbos?
Many Poskim[46] rule it is forbidden to pickle foods even in vinegar on Shabbos, even if one plans to eat it on Shabbos. Some Poskim[47] however rule it is permitted to pickle foods in vinegar on Shabbos [if one plans to eat it on Shabbos]. Practically, one is to be stringent.[48] Some Poskim[49] arbitrate that it is

---

[36] Admur 321:3; Michaber 321:2; Mishneh Shabbos 108b and Braisa there
[37] Admur ibid; M"A 321:3; M"B 321:8; Smak 281:17
[38] M"B ibid
[39] This implies that he plans to only eat some of them and leave some more left soaking in the liquid. So is also evident from the reasoning.
[40] Admur 321:3; Michaber ibid; Tur; Rashi; Levush 321:2; M"B 321:9
[41] Admur 321:3, brought in Michaber 321:3, Taz 321:3; M"B 321:15; Vetzaruch Iyun as in 321:2 the Michaber wrote the reason is due to that it is similar to tanning, which is reason brought by the Tur? See P"M 321 M"Z 3 which explains that regarding pickling the Michaber felt the reason of "similar to tanning" is more appropriate, while regarding salting he felt the reason of "cooking" is more appropriate.
Practical ramification between the reason of the Rambam and Rashi: The practical ramification between the reasons is if one may place foods into vinegar, as according to the Rambam it is forbidden while according to the Tur perhaps it is permitted. [P"M ibid based on Taz 321:3; See Toras Hamelachos Miabeid p. 69] Regarding how we rule in this dispute-see Q&A!
[42] Rambam 22:10
[43] Admur ibid; P"M Y.D. 105 M"Z 1; Chochmas Adam 58:1; Iglei Tal Ofeh 61; M"B 321:16;
Other opinions: Some learn that according to the Rambam there is a Biblcial cooking prohibition involved in pickling foods. [Perisha 321:4; Mor Uketzia 320; Pleisy 105:2; Nodah Beyehuda Kama Y.D. 26; See Sdei Chemed Chaf Klal 43]
[44] Halacha 4
[45] Although it is implied from Admur and Michaber ibid that is allowed, in truth it should be no better than the limitations to salt vegetables on Shabbos brought in Admur 321:4; See Kaf Hachaim 321:12, Piskeiy Teshuvos 321:1 and footnote 69
[46] Taz 321:3 regarding adding wine to vinegar that according to Rambam is forbidden; P"M 321 M"Z 3 and A"A 7 that so applies according to Rambam being it appears like cooking; Aruch Hashulchan 321:34; Ketzos Hashulchan 128 footnote 8; M"B 321:15; Piskeiy Teshuvos 321:6; Shabbos Kehalacha 20 Biurim 11
[47] M"A 321:7 regarding raw meat, as explained in P"M 321 A"A 7 that he holds unlike Rambam that there is no prohibition of Kevisha by vinegar; To note that Admur omitted both this ruling of the M"A ibid and of the Taz ibid Vetzaruch Iyun as to what is his opinion. See 321:4 that he allows adding vinegar to the food.
[48] As all Poskim brought in previous footnotes, and many other Poskim who discuss different cases of pickling involving vinegar.
[49] Ketzos Hashulchan 128 footnote 2 and 8 in explanation of M"A ibid

permitted to pickle in vinegar foods that are not normally pickled, and only those foods that are normally pickled are forbidden. Others[50] however rule one is to be stringent by all foods.

May one place liquid into vinegar on Shabbos in order to create more vinegar?
Some Poskim[51] rule it is forbidden to do so. Others[52] however rule it is permitted to do so. If one is doing so in order to weaken the vinegar, then it is allowed according to all.[53]

May one add vinegar to a salad on Shabbos?[54]
Yes. One may add a small amount of vinegar to the salad.

How long must the food remain in the mixture for it to be considered pickling?[55]
It must remain for 24 hours, unless the liquid is very strong, in which case it can pickle in 18 minutes. See next Q&A regarding if one may pickle the food for less than this amount of time.

May one leave the food in the pickling juice for less than Shiur Kevisha?
Salt water:[56] One may not allow the food to sit in the salt water for even less than Shiur Kevisha, unless it is a food that salt does not help to change its form, as explained in Halacha E. It is permitted to dip all foods in salt water, following the limitations explained in Halacha D-E!
Vinegar: Some Poskim[57] rule if the vinegar is strong then one may not leave a commonly pickled food in it even for a short amount of time, less than Shiur Kevisha, as it appears like one is pickling it. Other Poskim[58] rule one may leave all foods in vinegar [for less than Shiur Kevisha[59]], if one does so during the actual meal. From other Poskim[60] it is implied that it is completely permitted to leave all foods in vinegar for less than Shiur Kevisha.

May one enter foods into water if it will remain for 24 hours?
Yes[61], so long as he will eat some of this food on Shabbos, and it is hence not considered that he is troubling himself on Shabbos for a weekday.[62]

May one pickle foods if he adds oil to the pickling liquid?
See M"B 321:10 for a dispute.

May one return pickled foods into the vinegar or brine?[63]
➤ Example: One removed olives and pickles from the jar. May he return the leftovers to the brine after the meal?
Yes. It is permitted to return pickled foods to their vinegar or brine on Shabbos. This however only applies if the food has completed its pickling process. If, however, it is still within the process of pickling it may not be returned.

---

[50] Piskeiy Teshuvos 321 footnote 66
[51] Taz 321:3 based on Rambam; M"B 321:15; Yad Ahron [brought in M"B ibid] rules it is forbidden only due to Uvdin Dechol
[52] Implication of Admur who omits this ruling of Taz; Aruch Hashulchan 321:34; Toras Shabbos 321:7; See Piskeiy Teshuvos 321:5
[53] M"B ibid
[54] Admur 321:4 regarding adding vinegar to salted salad; See Piskeiy Teshuvos 321:4; Shabbos Kehalacha 20:32
[55] See Piskeiy Teshuvos 321:6; Shabbos Kehalacha 20:35 Biurim 16
[56] See Admur ibid which implies that only when left for Shiur Kevisha is it forbidden, however in truth it should be no better than the limitations to salt vegetables on Shabbos brought in Admur 321:4; See Aruch Hashulchan 321:34; Kaf Hachaim 321:12, Piskeiy Teshuvos 321:1 and footnote 69
[57] Ketzos Hashulchan 128 footnote 8
[58] Makor Chaim 321; Aruch Hashulchan 321:34; Conclusion of Shabbos Kehalacha ibid; See Piskeiy Teshuvos 321:6;
[59] Piskeiy Tehsuvos 321 footnote 69
[60] Taz 321:3; P"M 321 M"Z 3; M"B 321:15; Shabbos Kehalacha ibid rules leniently, although says is best to do so for only that meal
[61] Daas Torah 321; Piskeiy Teshuvos 321 footnote 66; See M"B 320:14 and 336:51 regarding soaking raisins in water.
[62] As implies Admur ibid in parentheses; See Shabbos Kehalacha 20 Biurim 15
[63] Rav Poalim 1:15; Chelkas Yaakov 1:137; Shabbos Kehalacha Vol. 3 20:37-38; Piskeiy Teshuvos 321:6

May one return an already pickled food to a different pickling mixture?
➢ Example: One removed herring or olives and pickles from a saltwater mixture. May he then place it into vinegar?
Some[64] rule it is permitted to do so. Others[65] rule it is forbidden.

May one pickle an already cooked food?[66]
No.[67] This applies whether in salt water or vinegar.

D. Salting foods which salt helps to change their natural state, or are commonly pickled, in order to eat on Shabbos:[68]
Regarding placing food in salt water-See 2B! Regarding salting raw meat-See above 2A. The following laws refer placing salt on all other foods.

❖ *First Opinion:[69]*

Not to salt more than one piece at a time: Any item which salt helps to change its natural state[70], [such as] to soften[71] it or harden[72] it or remove its bitterness and other [changes] of the like, such as for example radish[73] or onion or garlic[74] and the like of other spicy foods which when they are left in salt they secrete and remove their bitterness and become hard[75], as well as beans and lentils[76] which were cooked with their peel of which salt softens their hardness which they have as a result of their peel[77] [**See Q&A**], as well as species of raw cucumbers (called *ugerkis*) of which the salt helps them[78], as well as all other things which are commonly pickled[79], it is forbidden to salt more than one[80] piece at a time [even] in order to eat it right away.

The reason for this is because: as when one salts two pieces together and certainly [when he salts] more [than two pieces] it appears like one is <u>pickling pickled foods[81]</u> [which itself is forbidden due to cooking[82], or do due it being similar to tanning[83]]. [Regarding the reason behind the prohibition of

---

[64] Minchas Shabbos 80:35
[65] Poskim in Piskeiy Teshuvos 321:6 footnote 74
[66] See Ketzos Hashulchan 128 footnote 2
[67] <u>The reason</u>: Regarding salt water it is forbidden due to the Miabeid prohibition according to Rashi, and even according to the Rambam it is nevertheless not allowed even in vinegar as possibly the Sages did not make any differentiation in their decree against salting foods. Alternatively, pickling a precooked food is similar to roasting after cooking which is not allowed, as pickling is a different form of cooking than is cooking.
[68] Admur 321:4; Michaber 321:3-6; Shabbos 108b
[69] Stam in Admur; Michaber 321:3; Rambam
[70] Admur ibid Taz ibid
[71] Admur ibid; Taz 321:6
[72] Admur ibid; Rashi ibid
[73] Admur ibid; Michaber 321:3; Shabbos ibid; See Shabbos Kehalacha 20 footnote 69 regarding radishes of today which are not very sharp, although he nevertheless concludes to be stringent.
[74] Admur ibid; Taz 321:2; M"B 321:13
[75] Admur ibid; Taz 321:1; M"A 321:7; M"B 321:13
<u>Must all these conditions be fulfilled for it to be forbidden?</u> See Ketzos Hashulchan 128 footnote 2; Shabbos Kehalacha 20 Biurim 5
[76] Admur ibid; Michaber ibid; Tur in name of Rabbeinu Peretz
[77] Admur ibid; Taz 321:6; M"B 321:22
[78] Admur ibid; M"A ibid; M"B ibid
[79] Admur ibid; Taz 321:5 according to Rambam; M"A 321:7
<u>Foods that are not normally pickeled</u>: Some Poskim rule that foods which are not normally pickled may be salted on Shabbos regularly as is the law with eggs and cooked meat. [P"M 321 M"Z 2; M"B 321:13; Rav SZ"A SSH"K 11:2; See M"A 321:7; Taz 321:5 that according to Rambam if it is not commonly pickled it is permitted; Shabbos Kehalacha 20:33] Admur ibid does not hold of this opinion as is clear from the fact that he differentiates between foods that are commonly pickled and all foods that salt helps to change, and so rules Nehar Shalom 321:2; Kaf Hachaim 321:17; implication of M"B 321:18
[80] Admur ibid; Rashi ibid "3-4 pieces"; Michaber ibid "One may not salt 4-5 pieces at a time but is rather to dip each one individually"; See Piskeiy Teshuvos 321 footnote 26 that 4-5 is Lav Davka and he means as writes Admur ibid
[81] Admur ibid; Michaber ibid; Rambam ibid
[82] Michaber ibid; Rambam ibid, omitted by Admur ibid

pickling-See Halacha 3A!]

Not to salt for a later use:[84] [Furthermore] even one piece of radish and the like is forbidden to dip into salt and leave it [with the salt] for a long time in order so its sharpness dissipate through it secreting moisture, being that doing so is similar to <u>tanning</u>.

Dipping many pieces individually to eat right away:[85] However it is permitted to dip even a few pieces [when dipping] each one individually and one places it in front of him in order to them eat right away, one after the other without much delay. Even if the [pieces] remain a small amount of time [in their salt prior to being eaten] and they [thus] secrete some moisture [nevertheless] this poses no problem so long as that they do not remain a long time [with their salt] even [when planning to eat them] within the same meal [as nevertheless it does not appear like pickling[86]]. [Meaning] for example [if] from the beginning of the meal to the end [of the meal there is enough time] for [the salted food] to secrete a lot of moisture [then it is forbidden to delay eating it until the end of the meal] because doing so is similar to tanning which is forbidden [to do] with even only one piece [of food].

❖ *Other Opinions:*

[However] there are opinions[87] which say that it is forbidden to leave [the food] in salt at all even for a small amount of time, [and] even [when it is] only a single piece. Therefore [according to this view] it is forbidden to dip two pieces [in salt even] one after the other and then place them in front of him to eat immediately one after the other being that until one [finishes] eating the first piece the second piece remains in the salt. [Thus] it is only permitted to dip a single piece and then eat it right away.

The reason behind why one may not salt more than one piece at a time according to the 2nd opinion:[88] According to the latter opinion the reason that [the Sages] prohibited to salt a few pieces at the same time is not because it appears like [one is] pickling pickled [foods], but rather is because that until one [finishes] eating the first [piece] the second piece remained in the salt and since the salt benefits it, this is similar to tanning. [**See Q&A**]

Salting many pieces at the same time and then immediately adding vinegar or oil:[89] Therefore [based on the latter opinion] that which [people are] accustomed [on Shabbos] to cut a radish very thin[90] and then place it on a plate and salt it and then pour on it vinegar involves no prohibition even though that this is similar to salting many pieces together which [we said above] is forbidden [to be done] even to eat right away, [as] nevertheless since [the radish pieces] do not remain at all alone with the salt, as one immediately pours on it vinegar and other species, it is [therefore] not similar to tanning. Certainly [this allowance applies] if one pours oil on it being that oil weakens the strength of the salt.[91] [**See Q&A regarding how close to the meal this must be done**]

Nevertheless one must beware to pour the oil or vinegar [on the salted pieces] immediately after salting it [and doing so may not be delayed].[92] However that which some [people] are accustomed to make a vegetable (called *lettuce*) in which they first salt the vegetable on its own and then leave it this way and drain the water that comes out from it and then [only] afterwards mix it with oil and vinegar, doing so is a complete prohibition and is more similar to tanning [than when it is not left at all alone its salt] being that he delays until [the food] absorbs the salt well.[93] [**See Q&A**]

---

[83] Admur 321:3; Tur; M"B 321:14

[84] Admur ibid; Taz 321:1; Terumos Hadeshen 1:55

[85] Admur ibid; Opinion in Michaber 321:4; Terumos Hadeshen in name of Or Zarua; Taz 321:1; M"B 321:14 and 17 and 20; This opinion is based on the reason of the Rambam behind the prohibition against salting, as explained in Bach 321 and M"A 321:6 and Admur ibid that there is no suspicion of pickling when salting individually.

[86] M"B 321:19; see M"A 321:6

[87] M"A 321:6; Raavan 352; Elya Raba 321:6; Bach; M"B 321:14; based on reason of Rashi behind the prohibition

[88] Admur ibid; M"A ibid

[89] Admur ibid; Taz 321:1; M"A 321:6; M"B 321:14; Shiltei Giborim; Rashi ibid; Regarding why pouring vinegar is not considered like pickling-see Shabbos Kehalacha 20 Biurim 11

[90] This is allowed to be done in close proximity to the meal as will be explained in "The laws of Grinding".

[91] See story of Chofetz Chaim mentioned in Q&A in the footnote there!

[92] Admur ibid; Shaar Hatziyon 321:15

[93] Admur ibid; Taz ibid; M"B 321:14

❖ *The Final Ruling:*[94]

The custom is like this latter opinion [that one may not delay the eating of the salted food at all] and so is the law with regards to any [food] which salt benefits. [**See Q&A**]

Summary- Salting foods which salt helps to change their natural state:[95]

All foods which salt helps to soften it or harden it or remove its bitterness and other changes of the like, which includes all foods which are commonly pickled, may only be salted one piece at a time, and must be eaten immediately. It is thus forbidden to salt another piece prior to eating the first piece as doing so delays the eating of the first piece.

Examples of foods which salt helps change and are included in above restriction: Radishes, Onion, Garlic, Beans and Lentils that were cooked in their peels, cucumbers, lettuce.

Adding oil or vinegar to the food:[96] However, if one immediately adds oil or vinegar to the food after salting, [and certainly if one did so even before the salting] then it is permitted to salt even many pieces at the same time [and they may even be eaten later on, on Shabbos, although one must do so in close proximity to the meal.] [**See Q&A**]

Salting salad on Shabbos:[97]

All foods which salt helps to change its natural state[98], [such as] to soften[99] it or harden[100] it or remove its bitterness and other [changes] of the like, which includes all foods which are commonly pickled, may only be salted one piece at a time[101], and must be eaten immediately.[102] It is thus forbidden to salt another piece prior to eating the first piece, as doing so delays the eating of the first piece. Amongst foods included in the above category are: radish[103] or onion or garlic[104], beans and lentils[105] that were cooked in their peels, cucumbers, lettuce. Accordingly, it would be forbidden to salt a salad on Shabbos being that doing so transgresses both of the conditions, as it involves salting more than one piece of food at a time and one does not eat the salted food immediately. There is however one method available in which it is permitted to salt a salad on Shabbos, and that is through adding oil or vinegar to the food either before, or immediately after the salting. If one adds oil or vinegar to the food immediately after salting, then it is permitted to salt even many pieces at the same time and they may even be eaten later on, on Shabbos, although one must do so in close proximity to the meal.[106]

---

[94] Admur ibid; M"A 321:6; Bach 321; M"B 321:20; Kaf Hachaim 321:26

Ruling of Michaber: The Michaber does not mention the stringent opinion here although only brings the lenient opinion in 321:4 as "There is an opinion". The M"B ibid seems to learn the Michaber is lenient, although the Kaf Hachaim ibid concludes to be stringent. [See Shabbos Kehalacha 20:29]

[95] Admur 321:4

[96] Admur 321:4

[97] Admur 321:4; Michaber 321:3-6; Shabbos 108b

[98] Admur ibid Taz ibid

[99] Admur ibid; Taz 321:6

[100] Admur ibid; Rashi ibid

[101] Stam opinion in Admur; Michaber 321:3; Rambam

The reason: The reason for this is because when one salts two pieces together and certainly [when he salts] more [than two pieces] it appears like one is pickling pickled foods [which itself is forbidden due to cooking, or do due it being similar to tanning].

[102] 2nd opinion in Admur ibid; M"A 321:6; Raavan 352; Elya Raba 321:6; Bach; M"B 321:14; based on reason of Rashi behind the prohibition

The reason: According to the 2nd opinion the reason that [the Sages] prohibited to salt a few pieces at the same time is not because it appears like [one is] pickling pickled [foods], but rather is because that until one [finishes] eating the first [piece] the second piece remained in the salt and since the salt benefits it, this is similar to tanning.

[103] Admur ibid; Michaber 321:3; Shabbos ibid; See Shabbos Kehalacha 20 footnote 69 regarding radishes of today which are not evry sharp, although he nevertheless concludes to be stringent.

[104] Admur ibid; Taz 321:2; M"B 321:13

[105] Admur ibid; Michaber ibid; Tur in name of Rabbeinu Peretz

[106] Admur ibid; Taz 321:1; M"A 321:6; M"B 321:14; Shiltei Giborim; Rashi ibid; Regarding why pouring vinegar is not considered like pickling- see Shabbos Kehalacha 20 Biurim 11

The reason: Even though salting many pieces together is forbidden [to be done] even to eat right away, nevertheless since [the pieces] do not remain at all alone with the salt, as one immediately pours on it vinegar and other species, it is [therefore] not similar to tanning. [ibid]

Q&A

Canned fruits and vegetables:[107]

All canned foods that are not pickled in their packaging process, are not included in the definition of commonly pickled foods, and only those foods that are commonly preserved in pickling agents, such as salt and vinegar are included in this prohibition.

May one sprinkle salt onto the foods rather than dip the foods into the salt?

Yes.[108] However some Poskim[109] rule one may only dip the foods into the salt and not sprinkle them on top.

If the reason behind the prohibition to salt more than one food at a time is due to that it appears like pickling which itself is prohibited according to some due to that it appears like cooking, why may one therefore not be lenient to salt already cooked foods, after all there is no cooking after cooking?[110]

The reason that this is nevertheless not allowed is possibly because the Sages did not make any differentiation in their decree against salting foods. Alternatively, pickling a precooked food is similar to roasting after cooking which is not allowed, as pickling is a different form of cooking than is cooking.[111]

May one salt an already salted food?[112]

If the food was already fully salted, it is permitted to add salt to it on Shabbos. If, however, adding more salt will help in changing the food, then doing so is forbidden.

May one ask a gentile to salt one's foods on Shabbos?[113]

This follows the same ruling as all Rabbinical prohibitions in which it is forbidden to ask a gentile to perform them. Thus, it is forbidden to ask a gentile maid to add salt to one's food unless one also tells her to add oil right away. One may however ask a gentile to make a salad, which includes slating it and dressing it, and she can decide to do it in whatever order she chooses, whether to first place the dressing and then the salt, or first the slat and then sometime later the dressing, and one is not required to protest her actions. Nevertheless, one may note explicitly ask her to delay the placing of the dressing on the salad after the salting.

Q&A on salting more than one at a time

May one also be lenient like the second opinion, or must one be stringent like both opinions?[114]

Seemingly the custom is only to be stringent like the second opinion with regards to prohibit the salting of even two foods one after the other. However, with regards to leniencies which derive from the view of the second opinion [see the next question], seemingly one is to be stringent as holds the first opinion.

---

[107] Piskeiy Teshuvos footnote 24

[108] Taz 321:1; P"M 321 M"Z 4; See Piskeiy Teshuvos 321 footnote 25; Shabbos Kehalacha 20:30

[109] Menorah Hatehorah 321:8

[110] Ketzos Hashulchan 128 footnote 2

[111] [An alternative reason: The second opinion here argues on the fact that salting was prohibited due to pickling and rather holds that it was prohibited due to tanning, and this is the main opinion. As well even regarding the pickling prohibition some hold that it itself is due to a decree against tanning and not because it appears like cooking. Thus the concept of no cooking after cooking is irrelevant according to these opinions and it is thus prohibited to salt a food even if previously cooked. Vetzaruch Iyun as to why the Ketzos Hashulchan ignores this reason and accepts simply that the salting decree is because it appears like cooking.]

[112] Piskeiy Teshuvos footnote 21; See regarding Pickling: Rav Poalim 1:15; Chelkas Yaakov 1:137; Shabbos Kehalacha Vol. 3 20:37-38; Piskeiy Teshuvos 321:6

[113] See Admur 307:16; 276:10; Minchas Yitzchak 1:109-2; Piskeiy Teshuvos 321:3

[114] Ketzos Hashulchan 128 footnote 3

May one salt more than one food at a time if he plans to eat both of them at the same time?

No.[115] However, some Poskim[116] rule there is room to be lenient, although practically it is proper to be stringent.[117]

May one salt more than one bean at a time and the like of other foods which are usually eaten many at one time?[118]

Yes.[119] However this may only be done to an amount of beans which he will be eating immediately within one mouthful. It is forbidden to salt more than one mouthful worth of the bean or other food of the like.

Q&A on adding oil

Should one add the oil before the salt or may he add the salt and then the oil?[120]

The custom is to allow placing the salt first and then the oil, as written in Poskim ibid.[121] However it is proper to first place the oil and then the salt.[122]

May one be lenient to salt many foods and then add oil to it immediately even according to the first opinion, and if not then may one today practically be lenient in the above?[123]

There is room to question whether this would be allowed according to the first opinion. Practically although there is certainly room to be lenient even according to the first opinion[124], it is proper to be stringent to place in the oil prior to placing in the salt in which case this is permitted according to all without question.

Is the placing of oil and salt on one's food only allowed to be done in proximity to the upcoming meal?

Some Poskim[125] rule it is only allowed to be done prior to the current meal and may not be done for the sake of the next meal.[126] However some[127] write it may be done for even later use.

---

[115] Implication of Taz 321:1 and M"A 321:6; P"M 321 M"Z 1 regarding sprinkiling salt; M"B 321:14 in name of Taz and other Achronim; implication of Terumos Hadeshen; Shabbos Kehalacha 20:28; Biurim 9; Piskeiy Teshuvos 321:2 footnote 28

[116] Conclusion of Ketzos Hashulchan 128 footnote 3; See Shabbos Kehalacha 20 Biurim 9; Piskeiy Teshuvos 321:2 footnote 28

[117] Seemingly this is allowed according to the second opinion mentioned above as is evident from the radish example brought by Admur. However according to the first reason [the Rambam's reason] there is room to question whether this would be allowed as on the one hand perhaps they view the actual salting of more than one food at a time as appearing like pickling, irrelevant to whether or not one plans to eat them together. However, on the other hand perhaps as so long as the salted foods do not delay at all from being eaten, then perhaps even according to the Rambam this would be allowed as it does not appear like pickling. [Ketzos Hashulchan ibid]

[118] Ketzos Hashulchan 128 footnote 2; Ben Ish Chaiy Bo 2:14; Peulas Tzaddik 2:48; Kaf Hachaim 321:28; Piskeiy teshuvos 321:2; See Shabbos Kehalacha 20 footnote 72

[119] This may be done according to all, as one does not commonly eat one single bean at a time, but rather many at one time and it thus does not appear like one is tanning/pickling. Although this may only be done to an amount of beans which he will be eating immediately within one mouthful. It is forbidden to salt more than one mouthful worth of the bean or other food of the like.

[120] Ketzos Hashulchan 128 footnote 3 and 5; Menorah Hatehorah 321:6; Piskeiy Teshuvos 321:4; See Shaareiy Teshuvah 321:1 in name of Shvus Yaakov that "if one first places the oil, it is permitted"; See however Shabbos Kehalacha 20:31 and Biurim 12 and Tosefes Biur that there is no need to first place the oil, as is the simple implication of Admur ibid

[121] So is wording in Shiltei Giborim; M"A 321:6; Admur ibid; M"B ibid; However see Shaareiy Teshuvah ibid in name of Shvus Yaakov which says to first place in the oil, although in truth in the Svus Yaakov the word first is omitted.

[122] The reason: As perhaps if one were to place the salt first he may come to forget to place in the oil immediately after. [Ketzos Hashulchan ibid 5] As well this should be done being that according all opinions when the oil is placed first there is no question of a prohibition, as will be explained in the next Q&A, and it is better to do an act that will go in accordance to all. [Ketzos Hashulchan ibid 3] As well some Poskim explicitly write to place the oil first. [Shaareiy Teshuvah 321:1]

[123] Ketzos Hashulchan 128 footnote 3

[124] As explained in the previous question in the footnote there. To note however that from the wording of Admur above in the radish case it strongly implies that this is only permitted according to the second opinion. On the other hand, it is difficult to accept that we would be lenient against the first opinion which is the opinion of the Rambam which is plainly ruled by the Michaber and Rama. It therefore would seem that even according to the Rambam's opinion this would be allowed, as explained in the previous footnote. Vetzaruch Iyun! [Ketzos Hashulchan 128 footnote 3]

[125] Ketzos Hashulchan 128 footnote 4

[126] As this is no different than salting foods which salt only helps to give taste of which is only allowed to be done prior to the current meal and may not be done for the sake of the next meal. [See next Halacha "D" and Q&A there with regards to how close to the meal this must be done!] As for the reason that this was not mentioned by Admur, perhaps he relied on the fact that the reader understood that since the case is discussing

What liquids may be added to the salad to nullify its salt?[128]
All liquids are valid, including lemon juice and water.

How much salt may one add to the food that will have liquid placed on it?[129]
One may not add a lot of salt, as this will turn the liquid into salt water.

How much vinegar may one add to the food that has salt on it?[130]
One may not add a lot of vinegar, as this will consider the foods as Kavush.

Q&A on other spices
May one place sugar [or other spices] on fruits or vegetables without restriction?[131]
Some Poskim[132] rule that those foods which are commonly preserved using sugar or sugar water [such as canned peaches and other canned fruits[133]; dried fruits, and fruits used in jams[134]] are not to have sugar placed on them in a way it appears like one is preserving them.[135] However, foods that are not normally pickled would be allowed to be sugared according to all. Other Poskim[136] however rule there is no salting prohibition relevant to, even to foods that are commonly preserved in sugar. Even according to the stringent opinion, one may sprinkle a small amount of sugar onto even many foods for the sake of mere taste, and is not required to follow the limitations of one piece at a time and to eat it right away.[137] It is only forbidden to spread a large amount of sugar in a way that it appears one is preserving it.

May one sugar his grapefruit on Shabbos?[138]
Yes, as grapefruit is not commonly pickled.

May one place pepper on foods without restriction?[139]
Yes, as doing so does not involve either pickling or tanning.

---

cutting the radish thin, it can only be discussing a situation that one is doing so prior to the current meal, as otherwise this poses a grinding prohibition, as will be explained in "The laws of Grinding". [Ketzos Hashulchan 128 footnote 4]
[127] Shabbos Kehalacha 20:32; Piskeiy Teshuvos 321:4; based on Shvus Yaakov 2:14
[128] Piskeiy teshuvos 321:4; Shabbos Kehalacha Tosefes Biur 20:7; However see P"M 321 A"A 7 that implies water is not valid. See Shabbos Kehalacha ibid
[129] Menorah Hatehorah 321:6; Piskeiy Teshuvos 321:4; See Shabbos Kehalacha 20:32
[130] Piskeiy Teshuvos 321:4; Shabbos Kehalacha 20:32
[131] See Ketzos Hashulchan 128 footnote 2; Shabbos Kehalacha 20:46; Piskeiy Teshuvos 321:3
[132] Makor Chaim 321:3; Ketzos Hashulchan 128 footnote 2; Rav SZ"A in SSH"K 11 footnote 1; Shabbos Kehalacha 20:46; Piskeiy Teshuvos 321:3 and Poskim in footnote 37; See Or Letziyon 2:33-1
[133] Shabbos Kehalacha ibid
[134] Piskeiy Teshuvos ibid footnote 39
[135] The reason: This matter is dependent on the disputed reason behind the salting prohibition; whether it is forbidden due to tanning or pickling. According to the second reason mentioned above that salting is prohibited due to a tanning prohibition, sugaring a food would be allowed as it neither serves to soften or to preserve the food, nor is it used in the tanning process. However, according to the first reason mentioned above [the Rambam's reason] behind the salting prohibition that it is due to pickling, than sugar too would be prohibited to place on foods that are normally pickled, just as is the law with salt, unless it is done in the permitted way mentioned by salt. [Ketzos Hashulchan ibid]
Does sugar help remove blood from food? This matter is disputed in Poskim. See "A Semicha Aid for learning the Laws of Melicha" Chapter 69:7 in Q&A!
[136] See Shabbos Kehalacha ibid Biurim 22
[137] Piskeiy Teshuvos ibid; However, see Shabbos Kehalacha ibid who rules one is to follow all the restrictions mentioned by salt, and is hence not to sugar more than one piece at a time, and is to eat it right away.
The reason: As the concept of Miabeid does not apply to sugar, and it is hence similar to the ruling regarding vinegar that it may be sprinkled on food during the meal. [See ibid footnote 40
[138] Shabbos Kehalacha Vol. 2 p. 408, Yalkut Yosef
[139] See Ketzos Hashulchan 128 footnote 2

May one add preservatives to foods on Shabbos?[140]
No.

If one salted a food that salt helps change their natural state on Shabbos without adding oil/vinegar to it may one still eat it on Shabbos?[141]

If this was done unintentionally, such as he forgot to place oil in it right away, or he was not aware that salting involves a prohibition, then the food may be eaten.[142] If it was done despite knowledge of the prohibition, and one advertently delayed placing in oil, then it may not be eaten by anyone until Motzei Shabbos.[143] [See "The laws of Cooking" chapter 2 Q&A there!] In all cases, if one has oil, vinegar or other liquid available, he is to immediately pour it into the salted food in order to avoid it coming to a transgression. [Alternatively, one can rinse the salt off the food if he plans to eat the food right away.]

E. Salting foods which salt only helps to give taste and are not commonly pickled:[144]

Any item [or food] which salt does not help to change its nature and rather only gives it taste[145] [and is also not commonly pickled[146], See previous Halacha 3C for exact definition], such as for example [a cooked[147]] egg[148] and [pre-salted[149] cooked[150] or even raw[151]] meat is [permitted to be salted[152] although nevertheless it is] forbidden to salt when done in order to leave it[153] for another meal.[154]

Other opinion: [However] there is an opinion[155] which says that if there is any reason that it is better to salt [the food] now as opposed to salting it later on in proximity to the meal, such as if now [the food] is slightly hot[156] and will [thus] absorb the salt much better [if it were to be salted now] then there is no

---

[140] Piskeiy Teshuvos 321:3; Toras Hamelachos Miabeid 81; See Piskeiy Teshuvos footnote 41 for other opinions
[141] Ketzos Hashulchan 128 footnote 5; Shabbos Kehalacha 20:54; Piskeiy Teshuvos 321:3
[142] Implication of 339:7; 405:9; Gr"a; Chayeh Adam; M"B 318:3 and in Biur Halacha "Hamivashel"; and is implied from Admur in the Halacha here that the fine only applies to a Biblical prohibition. [Ketzos Hashulchan 124 footnote 2]
Other opinions: Some Poskim rule that a Rabbinical transgression has the same law as a Rabbinical transgression. [P"M 318 brought in Biur Halacha ibid; Ketzos Hashulchan 124]
Story with Chofetz Chaim: There is a story told of the Chofetz Chaim [told over by Rav Shmuel Chaim Kublanken, who was eating by the Chofetz Chaim to the author of the Ketzos Hashulchan] that he forgot and accidently salted radishes prior to adding oil to it [which is possibly forbidden according to the reason of the Rambam, as well perhaps he did not have oil] and when he remembered he pushed the radishes away and avoided eating them. Nevertheless, one must say that this was a mere stringency of the Chofetz Chaim in order to follow those opinions [Peri Megadim] which are also stringent by Rabbinical prohibitions to forbid the food. This however is not the actual Halachic ruling. As well one must say that the Chofetz Chaim added some liquid to the radishes as otherwise he would in truth have transgressed the salting prohibition according to the second opinion. [Ketzos Hashulchan 128 footnote 5]
[143] Based on the general rule of Meizid by Dirabanan on Shabbos as brought in 339:7; Mishneh Terumos 2:3
[144] 321:5; Michaber 321:5; Shibulei Haleket in name of Geonim
[145] Admur ibid; Taz 321:5; See M"B 321:18
[146] Admur 321:4; M"B 321:18; Kaf Hachaim 321:18
[147] Michaber 321:5
[148] Admur ibid; Michaber 321:3 and 5; Shabbos 108b
[149] Meaning meat that had been already salted to remove its blood, as otherwise it is forbidden even when done to eat right away as explained in Halacha 2. Vetzaruch Iyun as even pre-salted meat can be salted for preservation and salt helps change its form to harden it, thus perhaps in truth it refers to cooked meat, Vetzaruch Iyun.
[150] Michaber 321:5
[151] Based on Admur 321:2 in parentheses [brought above in 2A], and the fact he omits the Michaber's wording of "**cooked** meat"
[152] See new printing of Shulchan Aruch Admur 321:5 that so is the correct reading of text in Admur; Kuntrus Hashulchan ibid
[153] Admur ibid; Michaber ibid; Shibulei Haleket ibid
[154] Admur ibid; M"A 321:7; M"B 321:21
The reason: As even by these foods, if they are left a long time in the salt, it is similar to Miabeid/tanning. [M"B 321:21 in name of Levush and Mamar Mordechai; Panim Meiros, brought in Shaareiy Teshuvah 321:9] Alternatively, the reason is because although there is no similarity to Miabeid by such foods, the Sages did not allow one to trouble himself on Shabbos if he does not need to benefit from the action at this time. [Taz 321:5]
[155] Taz 321:5
Other opinions: Some Poskim rule it is always permitted to salt it even for the need of the next meal, so long as one plans to eat the food on Shabbos. [Elya Raba 321 and implication of Gr"a, brought in M"B 321:21] Some conclude that one may be lenient to salt the food for another meal, if it will be eaten in close proximity of the first meal. [M"B ibid based on P"M 321]
[156] Perhaps Admur mentions only slightly hot as if it were Yad Soledes than it is proper to not place salt on it at all, even in a Keli Sheiyni. [Ketzos Hashulchan 128 footnote 7]

prohibition involved in doing so.

The Final Ruling:[157] (One may rely on their words to be lenient in a [dispute over a] Rabbinical prohibition if one needs to do so[158]).

Summary-Salting foods which salt only helps to give taste:
Is permitted to be done for the need of the coming meal. However, for the need of a later meal is forbidden to salt it, unless there is need to do so such as salting it now benefits the food more than salting it prior to the meal.

Q&A

May one salt his food even much time prior to beginning the upcoming meal?[159]
No. It may only be done in close proximity to the meal.[160]

May one salt a dip on Friday night if he will also be eating from it the next day?
Seemingly this is allowed.

List of foods and their regulations:
- Radish:[161] Follows regulations brought in C.
- Onion:[162] Follows regulations brought in C.
- Garlic:[163] Follows regulations brought in C.
- Beans and lentils: Beans and lentils of today may be salted without regulation, so long as it is done in proximity to the meal. This applies even if they were cooked with their peel.[164]
- Cucumbers:[165] Follows regulations brought in C.
- Lettuce: Follows regulations brought in C.
- Cooked meat: Follows regulations brought in D.
- Tomatoes: Requires further analysis.[166]
- Avocado: Follows regulations brought in D.
- Cooked fruits and vegetables: Follows regulations brought in D.
- Mixed vegetables:[167]

Practical questions based on above

May one place vinegar into his cucumber salad on Shabbos?
See above Halacha 2B Q&A.

---

[157] Admur ibid; Mishneh Berurah 321:2121

[158] From the Ketzos Hashulchan [128:4] it seems that he learned this "need so" to mean that it will soften the meat. However, this does not seem to be the simple meaning of Admur, as if so then saying "needs so" is superfluous being that the arguing opinion itself only holds that when one needs so it is allowed.

[159] Ketzos Hashulchan 128 footnote 9; Shabbos Kehalacha 20
Other opinions: Some conclude that one may be lenient to salt the food for another meal, if it will be eaten in close proximity of the first meal. [M"B ibid based on P"M 321]

[160] The Ketzos Hashulchan [based on Magen Avraham] rules that this may not be done. Rather it is only allowed to be salted right before the meal, as is the law with regards to Borer, that it may only be done right before the meal.

[161] Admur 321:4

[162] Admur 321:4

[163] Admur 321:4

[164] See Piskeiy Teshuvos 321:8

[165] Admur 321:4; See SSH"K 11 footnote 6; Shabbos Kehalacha 20:33

[166] See SSH"K 11:2 that it is allowed to be salted without restriction so long as it is done prior to the upcoming meal, just like eggs; Shabbos Kehalacha 20:33 that is lenient in time of need; See Piskeiy Teshuvos 321:2 that is stringent by all vegetables.

[167] See Piskeiy Teshuvos 321:2 footnote 32

May one add salt to his cooked meat or chulent?
Yes, although this may only be done in close proximity to his meal.

May one add salt to a tomato salad?
If the salad also contains onions then it has the same ruling as does a vegetable salad, which requires oil for this to be allowed. If however it is just plain tomatoes, or tomatoes with another vegetable which salt only adds to it taste, then it is allowed to be done close to the meal.

May one add salt to his vegetable salad prior to the meal?
If the salad contains cucumbers, lettuce, or onions then this may only be done if one has already added oil to the salad or plans to do so immediately after salting it. In all cases it may only be done in close proximity to the meal.

General Summary- The Rabbinical prohibition of Salting:
Salting a food in order to preserve it[168]:
All foods are forbidden to salt in order to preserve, even if not doing so will cause great financial loss.

Salting a food in order to eat on Shabbos:
<u>All foods which salt helps to change their natural state:</u>[169] Such as to soften it or harden it or remove its bitterness and other changes of the like, which includes all foods which are commonly pickled, may only be salted one piece at a time, and must be eaten immediately. It is thus forbidden to salt another piece prior to eating the first piece as doing so delays the eating of the first piece.
<u>Examples of foods which salt helps change and are included in above restriction:</u> Radishes, Onion, Garlic, Beans and Lentils that were cooked in their peels, cucumbers.
<u>Adding oil or vinegar to the food:</u>[170] However if one immediately adds oil or vinegar to the food after salting, [and certainly if one did so even before the salting] then it is permitted to salt even many pieces at the same time [and they may even be eaten later on, on Shabbos.]
<u>Meat:</u>[171] It is forbidden to salt raw meat even in order to eat it on Shabbos if it had never yet been salted for its blood. Regarding meat that has been previously salted, see next case.
<u>Salting foods which salt only helps to give taste:</u>[172] Is permitted to be done for the need of the coming meal. However for the need of a later meal it is forbidden to salt it, unless there is need to do so and salting it now is better for the food then salting it only prior to the meal.

---

3. Making salt water on Shabbos:[173]
A. For pickling foods:[174]
It is forbidden to make heavy salt water [on Shabbos] or other heavily salted liquids[175] in order to place [these liquids] into pickled foods, meaning [to place them in] vegetables or other foods which are pickled to be preserved (even if one plans to eat from them right away[176] in which case he is not troubling himself for only a weekday purpose)
The reason for this is: See above Halacha 2B!

---

[168] Admur 321:4
[169] Admur 321:4
[170] Admur 321:4
[171] Admur 321:2
[172] Admur 321:5
[173] Admur 321:3; Michaber 321:2; Shabbos 108b
[174] Admur 321:3; Michaber 321:2; Mishneh Shabbos 108b and Braisa there
[175] Admur ibid; M"A 321:3; M"B 321:8; Smak 281:17
[176] This implies that he plans to only eat some of them and leave some more left soaking in the liquid. So is also evident from the reasoning

B. For dipping foods into:

Enough for that meal:[177] Even to make salt water or other salted liquids not [in order to use] for pickling, but rather in order to dip ones bread into and to place it into a dish is forbidden to make a lot of it at a time[178], which is defined as making in one time enough for dipping for two meals, rather [one may] only [make] a small amount enough to for dipping for one meal.[179]

Their reason:[180] (is because when one makes a lot [at one time] it appears that he is doing so for pickling)

The condition that it must be made to eat right away:[181] [Furthermore] even when making it for [only] one meal one is only allowed to make it in close proximately to the meal [in which one plans to dip in it], however [it is] not [allowed to be made] from [before] one meal for the need of another meal. [**See Q&A**]

The reason for this is: because it is forbidden to salt any item which one does not plan to eat right away as explained in Halacha 321/5 [2D].

One who places oil in the dish prior to the salt:[182] [Furthermore] even if one places oil into [the dish] in between the placing of the water and the placing of the salt into it[183] [in which case] the salt will not mix in well with the water and [the oil thus] weakens its strength of being strong salt water, nevertheless it is forbidden.

Salt water made of 2/3rds salt:[184] If one places 2/3rds salt and 1/3rd water or other liquid, then it is forbidden to make even a small amount of it for the purpose of dipping in the upcoming meal. [**See Q&A regarding making sugar water**]

The reason for this is:[185] being that it appears like one is making the Muryus gravy to pickle fish, as it is common to make Muryus in this way, [thus it is forbidden to make as] it is forbidden to pickle on Shabbos due to the tanning or cooking prohibition as was explained.

Summary-Making salt water or other salty liquids on Shabbos:[186]

For pickling: Is Rabbinically forbidden to be done for pickling purposes.

For dipping foods: When done for dipping it may only be done if all the following three conditions are met:

A. One does so right before the meal. [See Q&A]
   And
B. One makes just enough to dip for that meal.
   And
C. One has a ratio of salt that is less than 2/3.

These restrictions apply even if one places oil into the dish prior to placing the salt.

---

[177] See Admur 473:19

[178] Admur ibid; Implication of Michaber ibid; M"A 321:4; Olas Shabbos 321:1; Taz 473:3; Chok Yaakov 473:13; Elya Raba 321 brought in M"B 321:8

Other opinions: Some Poskim rule one may make as much salt water as he desires. [Tosefes Shabbos, brought in M"B ibid]

[179] Admur ibid; M"A 321:4; Olas Shabbos 321:1; The Mishneh Berurah in 321:11 is not arguing on this ruling; See Ketzos Hashulchan 128 footnote 9 which questions this ruling of the Mishneh Berurah.] Vetzaruch Iyun if this means one can make enough of an amount to last two meals, or if one can only make enough for one meal, although it may be made even prior to the previous meal.

[180] Admur ibid; M"B 321:8

[181] Admur ibid; M"A 321:4 based on Ran; Ben Ish Chaiy Bo 2:19; Kaf Hachaim 321:11

Other opinions: Some Poskim rule one may make a small amount of salt water even for the need of another meal, so long as one plans to eat from it on Shabbos. [Elyah Raba 321:3 in name of many Rishonim; Nehar Shalom; Mishneh Berurah 321:11; Biur Halacha "Aval; See Ketzos Hashulchan 128 footnote 9 which questions this ruling of the Mishneh Berurah.]

[182] Admur ibid; M"A 321:4, brought in M"B 321:10

Other opinions: Some Poskim rule one may that if the oil is placed in prior to placing in the salt, then it is permitted to be made without restriction. [Olas Shabbos; Tosefes Shabbos; Mishneh Berurah 321:10]

[183] Meaning that prior to placing salt into the dish one places oil into it.

[184] Admur ibid; Michaber ibid; Shabbos ibid

[185] Admur ibid; M"B 321:12 in name of Rambam and Levush

[186] Halacha 3

Q&A

According to Admur may one make salt water even much time prior to beginning the upcoming meal?[187]

No. The wording of "from one meal to another meal" written by Admur is not exact, as Admur already stated [above in Halacha 2 C] that it is forbidden to salt anything if one does not plan to eat it right away. Thus, even for the upcoming meal salt water may only be made in close proximity to it.

If one has 100 guests for his Seder meal that falls on Shabbos, may he prepare three liters of salt water on behalf of all 100 guests?[188]

Some Poskim[189] rule it is permitted to do so. Other Poskim[190] rule it is forbidden to do so.

May one make sugar water on Shabbos with two thirds being sugar?[191]

Some Poskim rule it is forbidden. Practically this matter requires further analysis.

---

[187] Ketzos Hashulchan 128 footnote 9
[188] See Shabbos Kehalacha 20 Biurim 27; Piskeiy Teshuvos 321 footnote 7
[189] Pnei Shabbos 321:7-3 based on Olas Shabbos 321:1
[190] Toras Shabbos 321:4
[191] Ketzos Hashulchan 128 footnote 10

Compilation-Salting salad on Shabbos:[192]

All foods which salt helps to change its natural state[193], [such as] to soften[194] it or harden[195] it or remove its bitterness and other [changes] of the like, which includes all foods which are commonly pickled, may only be salted one piece at a time[196], and must be eaten immediately.[197] It is thus forbidden to salt another piece prior to eating the first piece, as doing so delays the eating of the first piece. Amongst foods included in the above category are: radish[198] or onion or garlic[199], beans and lentils[200] that were cooked in their peels, cucumbers, lettuce. Accordingly, it would be forbidden to salt a salad on Shabbos being that doing so transgresses both of the conditions, as it involves salting more than one piece of food at a time and one does not eat the salted food immediately. There is however one method available in which it is permitted to salt a salad on Shabbos, and that is through adding oil or vinegar to the food either before, or immediately after the salting. If one adds oil or vinegar to the food immediately after salting, then it is permitted to salt even many pieces at the same time and they may even be eaten later on, on Shabbos, although one must do so in close proximity to the meal.[201]

---

[192] Admur 321:4; Michaber 321/3-6; Shabbos 108b

[193] Admur ibid Taz ibid

[194] Admur ibid; Taz 321/6

[195] Admur ibid; Rashi ibid

[196] Stam opinion in Admur; Michaber 321/3; Rambam

The reason: The reason for this is because when one salts two pieces together and certainly [when he salts] more [than two pieces] it appears like one is pickling pickled foods [which itself is forbidden due to cooking, or do due it being similar to tanning].

[197] 2nd opinion in Admur ibid; M"A 321/6; Raavan 352; Elya Raba 321/6; Bach; M"B 321/14; based on reason of Rashi behind the prohibition

The reason: According to the 2nd opinion the reason that [the Sages] prohibited to salt a few pieces at the same time is not because it appears like [one is] pickling pickled [foods], but rather is because that until one [finishes] eating the first [piece] the second piece remained in the salt and since the salt benefits it, this is similar to tanning.

[198] Admur ibid; Michaber 321/3; Shabbos ibid; See Shabbos Kehalacha 20 footnote 69 regarding radishes of today which are not very sharp, although he nevertheless concludes to be stringent.

[199] Admur ibid; Taz 321/2; M"B 321/13

[200] Admur ibid; Michaber ibid; Tur in name of Rabbeinu Peretz

[201] Admur ibid; Taz 321/1; M"A 321/6; M"B 321/14; Shiltei Giborim; Rashi ibid; Regarding why pouring vinegar is not considered like pickling- see Shabbos Kehalacha 20 Biurim 11

The reason: Even though salting many pieces together is forbidden [to be done] even to eat right away, nevertheless since [the pieces] do not remain at all alone with the salt, as one immediately pours on it vinegar and other species, it is [therefore] not similar to tanning. [ibid]

THE LAWS OF CRUSHING, GRINDING, MASHING AND CUTTING FOODS ON SHABBOS

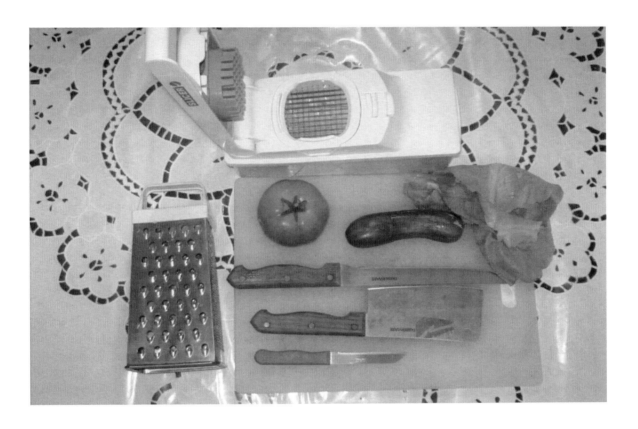

Shulchan Aruch Chapter 321

TRANSLATION-SHULCHAN ARUCH 321 HALACHAS 7-15

Introduction:
The following section will deal with the laws of grinding on Shabbos. Grinding is one of the Biblical Shabbos prohibitions. Different foods contain different laws regarding if and how they may be grinded.

Halacha 7
Crushing spices:
Crushing with a great variation: One who needs to crush peppers [or other spices] and the like in order to place them into food on Shabbos is allowed to crush them with a great variation from the way it is done during the week, such as [to crush it] with the handle of a knife and the like. [This is allowed] even if [crushing] a lot at a time.
However, one may not crush the peppers using a pestle[1]. [This applies] even if it is not made of stone as is [the] common [use] during the week, but rather is made of wood and the like.
Crushing in a plate: There are opinions which say that one is likewise required to crush the spices in a plate and the like, as opposed to a mortar[2] even if one is grinding it with the handle of a knife and the like.
[As well] one may not place the pepper into a cloth and crush it with a knife [by pounding its handle] on top of it, as doing so creates a smell in the cloth [which is prohibited to do on Shabbos] even though one does not have any intent to do so as is written in chapter 511 [Halacha 7].
Other Opinions: [However] other opinions permit to crush spices inside a mortar.
The Final Ruling: (It is proper[3] to be stringent in a situation that doing so is possible).
To cut spices with a knife: However, it is forbidden to cut [the pepper] with a knife [into small pieces[4]] even in order to eat immediately.[5]
The above law applies for all spices which are commonly only eaten when mixed [with other foods].

Halacha 8
Cutting foods which do not grow from the ground, into small pieces:
However any food which is fit to be eaten the way it is [without needing further preparation] and does not grow on the ground, in which case its species does not contain the concept of grinding at all, such as cooked or roasted meat or cheese and the like, then it is permitted to cut it very thin even [when done] not in order to eat right away, being that there is no grinding [prohibition] by [these] foods.
Hard Cheese: [Furthermore] even very hard cheese is allowed [to be cut small] being that it is [still] possible to be chewed, albeit with difficulty, and [thus] has a status of [a readily edible] food upon it.
If a person cannot chew: [Furthermore] it is allowed to be cut even by a person who cannot chew.
With what items may one cut it? [It is allowed to be cut] whether with a knife or with an ax or a chisel as although these are vessels designated for prohibited use it is allowed to move them in order to use [for a permitted purpose] as explained in chapter 308 [Halacha 12].
A Grater: However, it is forbidden to grate it very thin with a dented grater which has sharp teeth (that is called *Riv Eizin* [grating iron] in Yiddish) even in order to eat right away.
The reason for this is: as since the vessel is designated for this use, doing so is considered a weekday action as is crushing spices with a pestle and mortar.
Other cutting vessels: This law applies for any other vessel that is designated for this use of cutting small.

Halacha 9
Raw Meat
However [soft] raw meat, since it is only fit for the strong[6] minded which are willing to chew it in an irregular way [meaning while still raw], [therefore] it does not have the status of food on it for this matter and [the] grinding [prohibition] is applicable to it. Therefore, it is forbidden to cut it very thin to [feed] the birds.
The reason that it being fit for dog does not render it the status of food: Now, although it is fit for dogs [to eat,

---

[1] A pestle is an object made for crushing and grinding
[2] This refers to a grinding bowl.
[3] Lit. Good
[4] Mishneh Berurah 25 and Ketzos Hashulchan 129:2. Vetzaruch Iyun why Admur did not write this.
[5] However, in the Shaareiy Tziyon he permits even cutting it small when done to eat right away.
[6] Lit. well. Meaning that the thought does not disgust them.

nevertheless] it does not receive the status of food due to this being that it is not designated [to be given] to dogs but rather for people or for birds due to its value[7], and for them [the meat] is not fit [to be chewed] without this cutting [and is thus not considered to be food yet at this stage].

Halacha 10
Grinding foods that grow from the ground
All the above refers to food that does not grow from the ground, however any food that grows from the ground, even if it is food that can be readily eaten[8] has [the] grinding [prohibition] apply to it.

The reason for this is: because amongst these species [of foods are] foods that are ground, which refers to grains and legumes.

Vegetables and Fruits: Therefore, it is forbidden to cut a vegetable very small in order to eat it, and so too [it is forbidden to cut very small] dried dates and carobs for old people. If one does cut them very small, he is liable for grinding.

Crumbling bread: However, it is permitted to crumble bread very small for chickens and doing so does not involve the grinding prohibition.

The reason for this is: because the grain from which the bread was made had already been previously ground and there is no [prohibition to] grind a previously ground [food].

Cutting small with intent to eat right away: [However] all this refers to when one cuts [the food] and leaves it [there] not planning to eat it right away but rather to eat later on. However, it is permitted to [even initially] cut [food] very small in order to eat it right away or for others to eat right away or for chickens to eat right away.

The reason for this allowance is: because [the Torah] did not forbid a person to eat his food in big or small pieces and thus [we see that] it is the way of eating to eat also small pieces and anything that is done in a way of eating carries no prohibition as was explained in chapter 319 [Halacha 1] regarding separating food from its waste in order to eat it right away that it does not contain any prohibition since this is the way of eating. It is allowed to do so even initially.

Other Opinions: There are opinions which question this allowance [to cut small when intending to eat it right away].

The Final Ruling: It is proper to suspect for this latter opinion and be careful to cut the vegetable (which is called lettuce) into slightly large pieces as then according to all opinion there is no grinding prohibition involved. However, in our provinces it is the custom to cut radish very very small, as well as onion, and they have upon whom to [Halachically] rely. Nevertheless, at the very least they must beware to not begin to cut them until after [the men] leave the Shul being that it may only be done in actual proximity to the meal as was explained in chapter 319 [Halacha 4] regarding separating [food from its waste].

Halacha 11
Grinding food with a grinder
All the above [allowance] is only with regards to cutting [food] very small using a knife, however, to grind [the food] with a pestle, even if made of wood, is forbidden even if done to eat immediately.

[Furthermore] even food that is readily able to be eaten [in its current state] such as dry figs and carobs for old people, as well as garlic and lepidium[9] and the like of foods which are [commonly] ground are forbidden to be ground even in order to eat immediately.

Crushing with an irregularity: However, it is permitted to crush them with a great irregularity such as with using a wooden pot ladle or with the handle of a knife and the like as was explained [above in Halacha 7] regarding spices.

Halacha 12
Grinding salt with a grinder and cutting it with a knife
One may not grind salt with a pestle even if it is made of wood and rather it is required for him to grind with a great irregularity such as to grind it with the handle of a knife or a wooden pot ladle.

Cutting it with a knife: However, it is forbidden to cut it very small with a knife.

The reason for this is: (because since [salt] is only fit to be eaten when mixed into other foods it therefore has the same laws as do spices and is not comparable to meat and cheese even though it too does not grow on the ground

[7] Lit. importance
[8] Lit. complete food
[9] *Lepidium* is a genus of plants in the mustard family Brassicaceae. It includes about 175 species found worldwide, including cress and pepperweed; additional common names include peppercress, peppergrass, and pepperwort.

just as they do not.)

Thick pieces of cooked salt: However, this [prohibition to cut small] only applies with salt that is initially thick. However, salt which was initially thin which was then cooked and became [thick] pieces is permitted to be cut very thin with a knife just as is permitted by bread being that there is no [prohibition to] grind a previously ground [food].

Halacha 13
Grinding food with one's teeth for later use
Food [that has a grinding prohibition] which one does not wish to eat [himself] (or to feed to a child) right away is forbidden for him to chew with his teeth due to the grinding prohibition.

Laws dealing with honeycombs.

Halacha 14
Removing honey from honeycomb
Honeycomb which has been detached from the hive from before Shabbos is forbidden to be crushed in order to remove their honey as doing so is separating food from waste, meaning [that he is separating] the honey which is edible from the wax, which is inedible, and contains the *"Mifarek"* [detaching] prohibition, as well as the separating of food from waste [prohibition].

This applies even if one is removing the honey in order to eat right away as explained in chapter 320 [Halacha 8].

If the honey seeped out from the comb on Shabbos: [Furthermore] even if the honey seeped out on its own it is forbidden [to be eaten] until evening [after Shabbos] due to a decree that one may come to crush it with one's hands in order to eat it today [on Shabbos].

However, if the combs had been crushed from before Shabbos then the honey which seeps out from it on Shabbos is permitted as is the law with grapes and olives which had been crushed from before Shabbos [and had liquid flow from them on Shabbos] as was explained there [in Chapter 320 Halacha 4] and in chapter 252 [Halacha 14].

Eating the honey that is on the surface of the combs: However, it is permitted to eat the honey which is stuck around the surface of the combs even if the [combs] had not been crushed from before Shabbos.

Halacha 15
Removing honeycombs from their hives:
It is Rabbinically forbidden to remove honey from a hive on Shabbos being that doing so resembles the prohibition of *"Toleish"* [detaching items from the ground].

If the comb was detached from before Shabbos: However, this only refers to when the combs are [still] attached to the hive as then [removing the honey] appears like one is detaching an item from its source of growth. However, if [the combs] were detached from the hive from before Shabbos and were left this way [loose] inside [the hive] then it is permitted to remove the [comb] and eat the honey that is attached around its surface.

If the comb was crushed from before Shabbos: Furthermore, even if the comb is attached to the hive but was crushed within the hive from before Shabbos and the honey is floating inside the hive then it is permitted to remove it and eat it.

❖ **For Translation of Halacha 16 please refer to the next section "The Laws of Kneading"**

COMPILATION OF HALACHOS SUMMARIES AND Q&A

Introduction:
The following section will deal with the laws of grinding on Shabbos. Different foods have different laws regarding if and how they may be grinded.

The Av Melacha:
Grinding was one of the principal actions done in the Mishkan[10], as in the Mishkan they would grind the herbs to use to make dye.[11]

Toldos:[12] The following actions are a subcategory of this principal prohibition: Cutting a vegetable very thin, cutting wood into very thin pieces in order to use to ignite a fire or in order to make a vessel, one who crumbles a thick piece of dirt in order to make a use with the crumbs.

When does the prohibition apply?

Nonfoods:
According to all, the grinding prohibition applies to non-food products[13], such as grinding wood[14], or earth[15] and the like. This applies even if the product does not grow from the ground.[16]

Foods:
Some Poskim[17] rule the Grinding prohibition does not apply to foods. Other Poskim[18] rule it only applies to foods that one plans to cook. Other Poskim[19] rule it applies to even raw foods. The Shulchan Aruch rules like the latter opinion.

Foods that do not grow from the ground:
Some Poskim[20] rule the Grinding prohibition does not apply to foods that do not grow from the ground.[21] Other Poskim[22] rule the Grinding prohibition applies even towards foods that do not grow from the ground. The Shulchan Aruch rules like the former opinion.

In proximity to the meal:
Some Poskim[23] rule foods may be cut small in proximity to the meals. Other Poskim[24] rule it may not be cut small in proximity to the meals. It is disputed as to when this allowance applies even according to the lenient opinion.[25]

---

[10] Mishneh Shabbos 73a

[11] Rashi 49b and ibid

[12] Iglei Tal Tochein 3; Ketzos Hashulchan 129 footnote 1

[13] See Toras Hamelachos Tochein 1-4

[14] Shabbos 74b; Admur 314:16; M"A 314:14; Taz 501:2

[15] Admur 302:17; P"M 321 M"Z 10; Iglei Tal Dash 7:8

[16] This applies even according to the Terumos Hadeshen; See Tehila Ledavid 321:12 that by non-food products one is liable even if it does not grow on the ground; Iglei Tal Dash 7:7 that earth is similar to the dyes and one is hence liable.

[17] Tosafus 74a; Rabbeinu Chananel and Rosh; brought in M"B 321:31]

[18] Rambam 21:18 as explained in Beis Yosef 321

[19] Rashbam; Hagahos Maimanis; Semag; Ran; Mordechai; Yireim and Rashba

[20] Terumos Hadeshen 57

[21] The reason: As we rule regarding Meameir that it only applies to Gidulei Karka, and the same applies to Techina. [ibid]

[22] Shiltei Giborim 32 in Rif]; Rivash 184; Nishmas Adam 17:2; Kaf Hachaim 321:52; Chazon Ish 57

[23] Admur ibid; Rama 321:12; Rashba and Ran; See Ketzos Hashulchan 129 footnote 3 which learns that the same laws which apply to allow one to do Borer apply here as well, as by both cases the permission is based on that it is done in the way of eating. Thus, to grate vegetables using a designated vessel for grating would contain a Biblical prohibition according to all, just as is the law by Borer.

[24] M"A 321; In name of Shiltei Giborim; M"B 321:45

[25] Some Poskim rule it does not apply to spices, or to crushing in a regular way. [Admur] Others rule it does apply. [M"B]

If one does not need the item:[26]
The grinding prohibition only applies when one needs to use the ground item.

Grinding with Shinuiy:
See Halacha 1A

Grinding with hands:
See Q&A below.

---

1. Grinding foods:

A. Crushing spices:[27]

[One who grinds pepper and other spices in a grinder in its normal method transgresses the Biblical Grinding prohibition. This applies even if he ground only one kernel.[28]]

Crushing with the handle of a knife:[29] One who needs to crush peppers and the like in order to place them into food on Shabbos[30] is allowed to crush them with a great[31] variation from the way it is done during the week, such as [to crush it] with the handle of a knife and the like [such as the bottom of a plate[32]], even if [crushing] a lot at a time.[33]

Crushing with a pestle:[34] However one may not crush them using a pestle[35], even if it is not made of stone as is common [to use] during the week but rather is made of wood and the like.[36] [This applies even if one plans to eat the spices right away.[37]]

Crushing in a plate: There are opinions[38] who say that one is likewise required to crush the spices in a plate and the like, as opposed to a mortar[39], even if one is grinding it with the handle of a knife and the like.[40]

Crushing spices into a cloth:[41] One may not place the pepper into a cloth and crush it with a knife [by pounding its handle] on top of it, as doing so creates a smell in the cloth [which is prohibited to do on

---

[26] Admur 302:17
[27] Admur 321:7; Michaber 321:7; Shabbos 141a as rules Rava
[28] M"B 321:23; Rambam Shabbos 21:20
[29] Admur ibid; Michaber ibid; Rava in Shabbos ibid
Other Poskim: Some Poskim rule that today we should not crush at all on Shabbos even with a great irregularity, as we are no longer experts in how to do so and one may break the plate. [Birkeiy Yosef 321:2 in Shiyurei Bracha in name of Maharash] Practically, we do not hold of this opinion. [Kaf Hachaim 321:41]
[30] This implies that one does not need to do so immediately prior to the meal, but rather so long as he plans to eat from it on Shabbos it suffices, unlike the law by cutting small, as will be explained. So also rules M"B 321:24 in name of Peri Megadim 321 M"Z 7.
Other opinions: Some Poskim rule one may only crush the spice in close proximity to the meal. [Olas Shabbos 321:6; Iglei Tal Tochein 12; Aruch Hashulchan 321:12; Kaf Hachaim 321:37]
[31] Admur ibid; M"A 321:9; Shibulei Haleket 92 in name of Rabbeinu Yeshaya, brought in Beis Yosef 321
The reason why in this case we permit a Shinuiy? The reason for this is because one is doing a great Shinuiy. However, with a regular Shinuiy, it remains Rabbinically forbidden as is the law by all other Melachos, that it is Rabbinically forbidden to perform even with a Shinuiy. [Shibulei Haleket ibid]
[32] M"A 321:9; M"B 321:25
[33] See previous footnotes that from here it is evident that one is not required to the crushing .
[34] Admur ibid; Shibulei Haleket ibid; brought also in Michaber 321:8 and Admur 321:11 regarding salt
[35] A pestle is an object made for crushing and grinding
[36] The reason: As although this is considered an irregularity, it is not considered a great irregularity. [implication of Admur, see also M"B 321:26]
[37] Admur 321:11 regarding foods that grow from the ground; Admur ibid regarding cutting spices with a knife that it is forbidden even for right away use; Ketzos Hashulchan 129:2 footnote 9; M"B 321:26
[38] First opinion in Admur ibid; implication of Michaber 321:7 and his ruling in Beis Yosef; Implication of Rambam 21:20; Taz 321:7; Elya Raba; Mateh Yehuda; Gr"a; M"B 321:25
[39] This refers to a grinding bowl.
[40] The reason: This is forbidden as one is required to use two Shinuyim. [Beis Yosef 321, brought in Machatzis Hashekel 321:9; implication of wording of Admur] Alternatively, it is due to it appearing as a mundane act. [Taz ibid; Olas Shabbos 321; M"B 321:25]
[41] Admur 321:7; Taz 321:7; The following Poskim rule it is always forbidden to cause a garment to receive a smell even if one does not have intent to do so: Implication of Rama 658:2; Maharil; Rokeiach 219 as explains M"A 658:2 and Admur in Kuntrus Achron 511:1; Implication of Rashi Beitza 23a as brings Admur ibid; and so rules M"A 658:2; Elya Raba 658:3; P"M 511 A"A 11; Chayeh Adam 141:20; Kitzur SHU"A 137:7; Moed Lekol Chaiy 23:46; M"B 658:7 and Kaf Hachaim 658:8 are lenient in a time of need.

Shabbos] even though one does not have any intent to do so[42] [as is written in chapter 511 [Halacha 7, which is brought next].

Other Opinions: [However] other opinions[43] permit to crush spices inside a mortar.

The Final Ruling:[44] (It is proper[45] to be stringent in a situation that doing so is possible).

Grinding salt:[46] One may not grind salt with a pestle even if made of wood and rather is required to use a great irregularity such as to grind it with the handle of a knife or a wooden pot ladle.[47] [It is forbidden to use a regular grinder even if the salt was initially thin and only became a thick piece through cooking.[48] It is however permitted to use an instrument that is not regularly used for grinding, such as a hammer, to grind such salt.[49]] [**See Q&A regarding crumbling a thick piece of salt/spice/sugar with ones hands!**]

The reason for this is:[50] (because since [salt] is only fit to be eaten when mixed into other foods it therefore has the same laws as do spices and is not comparable to meat and cheese even though it too does not derive from growing on the ground just like they.)[51]

Summary:
All spices are Biblically forbidden to be ground in their regular way, even in order to eat right away. It is permitted to grind them with a great irregularity, such as using the back of a knife and the like. One is not to grind them into a mortar if one has a plate or other vessel available.

Q&A
When crushing a spice with a great irregularity must one do so in close proximity to the meal?
No, it is permitted to be done so long as one is doing so to eat on Shabbos.[52] However, some Poskim[53] are stringent in this matter.

May one crush spices in their regular way if he does so for right away use?[54]
No, it remains Biblically forbidden to do so.[55]

---

[42] Seemingly the reason why here Admur rules that even when one has no intent to absorb the smell it is forbidden is because here a real action [crushing] is being done which causes the smell to get absorbed and thus we are stringent even when one does not intend to do so. However, in the case of smoking fruits, as well as in the case of simply placing the spices into the cloth, since no action is being done, it therefore is only prohibited when one intends to do so. [So explains Rav Yisrael Labkowski in Kinnus Torah 18 p. 50. See there from page 44 and on for an analysis on this entire subject of the contradiction of Admur in Hilchos Shabbos and Yom Tov]. To note that the Taz himself writes the same contradiction as Admur, of which many Achronim [Peri Megadim; M"B 321:25] explain that the Taz retracted his earlier ruling in Shabbos. This however cannot be the explanation for here in Admur as a) Admur already saw the contradiction in the Taz prior to writing the SH"A, and b) Admur himself writes here in Shabbos "as explained in 511", thus it is not possible that it can contradict 511. See however Shabbos Kehalacha Vol. 3 p. 168 for an analysis on this subject, and how he learns it is a contradiction in Admur and that we rule leniently.

[43] Second opinion in Admur ibid; M"A 321:9; Iggur 488 in name of a lenient opinion

[44] Admur ibid; Implication of Rivash 184

[45] Lit. Good

[46] Admur 321:12; Michaber 321:8; Tosefta 15:13

[47] The reason it is forbidden even though it does not grow from the ground: This [prohibition to cut salt to small pieces] only applies with salt that was initially thick. However, salt which was initially thin and was then cooked and became [thick] pieces is permitted to be cut very thin with a knife just as it is permitted to do so by bread being that there is no [prohibition to] grind a previously ground [food].

[48] Olas Shabbos 321:9; M"B 321:30; Iglei Tal; Shevisas Hashabbos; Tehila Ledavid 321:9; Ketzos Hashulchan 129 footnote 15 and 17
The reason: This is due to it being a mundane act. [Olas Shabbos ibid; Ketzos Hashulchan ibid] If the lump is a result of moisture bringing the pieces together there is no grinding prohibition involved being that the salt was already crushed in the past. However, by rock salt, which is an original block of salt, crushing it contains the grinding prohibitions. [321:12]

[49] Implication of Rama 321:8 that one may use a grinder of wood for such salt, and seemingly the reason is because a) It is not a designated instrument and hence does not pose a prohibition of Uvdin Dechol, b) There is no grinding after grinding, and hence a great irregularity is not required.

[50] Admur 321:12

[51] In other words: Although salt does not grow on the ground, nevertheless it contains a grinding prohibition being that it is used as a spice. [See Ketzos Hashulchan 129 footnote 12]

[52] Peri Megadim 321 M"Z 7; M"B 321:24; Ketzos Hashulchan 129 footnote 8; and so is implied from Admur 321:7 "*One who needs to crush peppers and the like in order to place them into food on Shabbos*" that one does not need to do so immediately prior to the meal, but rather so long as he plans to eat from it on Shabbos it suffices, unlike the law by cutting small, as will be explained.

[53] Olas Shabbos 321:6; Iglei Tal Tochein 12; Aruch Hashulchan 321:12; Kaf Hachaim 321:37

[54] Admur ibid regarding cutting spices with a knife that it is forbidden even for right away use; Ketzos Hashulchan 129:2 footnote 9; P"M 321 M"Z 10; M"B 321:26

Q&A on grinding vessels

May one use a spice crusher[56] to sprinkle salt or pepper?
No.[57]

May one use a grinder with an irregularity, such as to crush using the opposite side?[58]
No.

May one crush spices using a hammer?[59]
Seemingly it is forbidden to do so due to it not being a great irregularity and is similar to a wooden pestle. It is forbidden to do so even for right away use.[60]

May one grind on top of a grinding plate and the like?
One is not to do so if one has a plate or other vessel available, as rules Admur ibid regarding a mortar.

Q&A on grinding with hands

May one crumble a lump of salt or spice with his hands?[61]
Yes.[62] However, this only applies by foods that are not regularly ground with one's hands, while those that are regularly ground with ones hands, are forbidden to be ground using one's fingers.[63] However by vegetables, one may do so for right away use.[64] However, by spices seemingly it is forbidden even for right away use.[65]

May one crumble a spice with his hands in order to smell it?
Some Poskim[66] rule one may use his fingers to crush a spice that has never been ground in order to

---

[55] The reason: As it is forbidden to grind using an instrument that is designated for grinding. [M"B ibid] Alternatively, the reason is because this does not appear like Derech Achila. [P"M ibid]

[56] black and white pepper used in spice crushers.

[57] It is forbidden to do so even by salt, as this grinder is a vessel designated for this purpose and hence using it is considered a mundane act. [321:8] It is Biblically forbidden to use it to crush black pepper. Also, rock salt is Biblical

[58] Zivcheiy Tzedek 20; Rav Poalim 2:42

[59] See 308:6: A chisel that is used to crush spices, in areas that one is careful not to use it for any other purpose in order so it not get dirty, is [considered under the category of] Muktzah Machamas Chisaron Kis. However, in places that people are not particular [against using it for other purposes] then it is permitted to move it in order to use it or in order to use the space that it under it, just like [is the law by] all other vessels which are designated for a purpose that is prohibited to do on Shabbos, as will be explained.

[60] As rules Admur 321:7 and 11 and P"M 321 M"Z 10 regarding cutting spices for right away use and using a wooden pestle on foods for right away use and seemingly the same would apply here; However, from the M"B 321:26 it is implied that so long as the vessel is not desiganetd for crushing, it may be used for right away use. Piskeiy Teshuvos 321:9 allows doing so right before the meal.

[61] See Ketzos Hashulchan 129 footnote 15

[62] Shibuleiy Haleket Shabbos 92; Rashal Beitza 4:7; Elya Raba 321:12; M"B 321:29 in name of regarding salt and spices; Ketzos Hashulchan 129 footnote 15

The reason: The reason it is allowed is because using one's fingers is considered a great irregularity. [ibid] Hence it would be allowed even if the spice or salt has never yet been crushed, such as rock salt, which is an original block of salt, as doing so is considered a great irregularity.

[63] Tehila Ledavid 321:10; Shevisas Shabbos Tochein 6; P"M 321 A"A 2; Shabbos Kehalacha 21:45; Piskeiy Teshuvos 321:9

The reason: This is based on fact that the Rashba discusses the allowance of crumbling bread based on that there is no grinding after grinding, and not due to it being a great irregularity, and so writes Michaber 302:7 that crumbling mud with ones hands is prohibited due to Tochein. So brings the Tehila Ledavid 321:10 and Shevisas Shabbos Tochein 6, and so writes P"M 321 A"A 2 regarding grinding the Silka with one's hands, and one hence must conclude that by those foods of which it is common to grind using the hands it is forbidden to do so.

[64] P"M ibid; Shabbos Kehalacha ibid; Piskeiy Teshuvos ibid

[65] As rules Admur 321:7 regarding cutting spices.

[66] Birkeiy Yosef 321:1

smell it right away. Other Poskim[67] however rule one may not crumble with his fingers a thick piece of spice which has never yet been crushed in order to smell.[68]

If it was already ground: See next Q&A!

May one crumble a thick piece of snuff with his hands in order to smell it?[69]

Yes.[70] However some Poskim[71] forbid doing so.[72]

Q&A on types of spices

May one grind sugar cubes?

Some Poskim[73] rule that sugar cubes do not contain the grinding prohibition, and hence do not require a great irregularity when ground.[74] Other Poskim[75] rule sugar cubes contain the grinding prohibition and hence may only be ground using a great irregularity.[76] Practically, one may be lenient[77], although a G-d fearing Jew is to be stringent.[78] According to all, one may not grind it with vessels which are designated for grinding/crushing, due to it being a mundane act.[79]

Grinding a crystal of sugar: Is forbidden, as explained in the Q&A in end of this Halacha.

Sugar candy: One is to be stringent to avoid grinding candy, unless one uses a great irregularity.

Chocolate: One is to be stringent to avoid grinding chocolate, unless one uses a great irregularity.

May one break up a glob of coffee or cocoa powder?

Yes, it may be done even in the regular way, however without using a vessel that is designated for this purpose.

---

[67] Iglei Tal, brought in Ketzos Hashulchan 129 footnote 15

[68] Vetzaruch Iyun why should this be any different than salt? I could not find the source inside the Iglei Tal to see his reasoning although perhaps one can suggest it is forbidden to do so when smelling spices as we do not view crushing spices with one's fingers in order to smell as a great irregularity but rather as the common way of smelling. This is opposed to crushing salt with one's finger which is certainly always a great irregularity. Vetzaruch Iyun.

[69] Ketzos Hashulchan 129 footnote 15; Minchas Shabbos

[70] As it was previously ground and thus no longer contains a grounding prohibition. [So rules Minchas Shabbos and so sides Ketzos Hashulchan 129 footnote 16 that it is not similar to crushing dried mud which is forbidden, as this prohibition only applies by items such as earth and not to items which grow from the ground.]

[71] Tiferes Yisrael brought in Ketzos Hashulchan ibid

[72] His reasoning is because it is similar to crushing dried mud which is forbidden. The Ketzos Hashulchan ibid however negates this similarity stating the above law by dry mud does not apply by items that have grown on the ground. As with regards to why it should not be permitted due to it having already been ground this is because perhaps this is similar to that which is explained below regarding grinding sugar cubes in which there are Poskim which say that although it was previously ground since it has become hard the grinding prohibition remains, and this leniency of previously ground foods only apply by consistencies such as that of bread.

[73] Peri Megadim 321 M"Z 10; M"B 321:30; Ketzos Hashulchan 129: 4and footnote 16; SSH"K 6:11

[74] The reason: Sugar has the same status as cooked lumps of salt which does not contain a grinding prohibition, as salt was previously small pieces and only becomes one piece through the cooking. [ibid] The Ketzos Hashulchan ibid sides like the Peri Megadim that there is no grinding prohibition by sugar. He negates the source of the Shevisas Shabbos saying the prohibition by earthenware does not apply by items that have grown on the ground.

[75] Shevisas Shabbos Tochein 43; Ben Ish Chaiy Mishpatim 7 and Tiferes Yisrael one is do one irregularity in the crushing of it; See Poskim in Piskeiy Teshuvos 321 footnote 122

[76] The reason: The Shevisas Shabbos [Tochein 43] rules the grinding prohibition does apply by sugar cubes. His reasoning is because this rule that grinding does not apply by previously ground items was only said by bread since it is a soft food, however by other items which become hard like sugar the grinding prohibition remains. His proof is from the fact all agree grinding applies by earthenware even though it was previously ground. The Tiferes Yisrael rules that in any event one must do one irregularity in the crushing of it.

[77] As rules Ketzos Hashulchan ibid; SSH"K ibid

[78] Chofetz Chaium in Nidchei Yisrael 39:1; Chazon Ish 60:1; Shabbos Kehalacha 21:58;

[79] Using vessels designated for crushing is always forbidden by all types of food due to it being a mundane act. [Admur 321:8]

B. Grinding foods that do not grow from the ground:[80]

Any food which is fit to be eaten the way it is [without needing to be mixed with other foods[81]] and does not grow on the ground, its species does not contain the concept of grinding at all and is permitted to be done (even for later use[82]). [**See Q&A regarding how one is allowed to grind it**]

Examples of such foods:[83] Such as cooked or roasted meat or cheese. [This applies even if the roasted meat is not edible to all people, so long as it is edible to majority of people.[84]]

Raw Meat:[85] However [soft] raw meat, since it is only fit for the strong[86] minded which are willing to chew it in an irregular way [meaning while still raw], [therefore] it does not have the status of food on it for this matter and [the] grinding [prohibition] is applicable to it.[87] Therefore, it is forbidden to cut it very thin to [feed] the birds.

The reason that it being fit for dog does not render it the status of food:[88] Now, although it is fit for dogs [nevertheless] it does not receive the status of food just for this being that it is not designated [to be given] to dogs but rather for people or for birds due to its value[89], and for them [the meat] is not fit [to be chewed] without this cutting [and is thus not considered to be food yet at this stage].

Hard cheese:[90] [Furthermore] even very hard cheese is allowed [to be cut small] being that it is [still] possible to be chewed, albeit with difficulty, and [thus] has a status of [a readily edible] food upon it. ([Furthermore] it is allowed to be cut even by a person who cannot chew.[91])

Nieveila meat: [It is however permitted to cut Treif meat into very small pieces to feed the birds even later on Shabbos.[92]]

What items may be used to grind with? May graters and the like be used?[93]

A knife/chisel/ax: [It is allowed to be cut] whether with a knife or with an ax or a chisel as although these are vessels designated for prohibited use it is allowed to move them in order to use [for a permitted purpose] as explained in chapter 308 [Halacha 12].

A Grater:[94] It is forbidden to grate the cheese [or any food, including bread[95]], even one that does not grow on the ground, very thin with a dented grater which has sharp teeth (that is called *Riv Eizin* [grating

---

[80] Admur 321:8; Terumos Hadeshen 27; Implication of Michaber 321:9; M"A 321:10; M"B 321:31
Other opinions: Some Poskim rule the Grinding prohibition applies towards meat, being the animal feeds off the ground. [brought in M"B 321:31] Some Poskim rule the Biblical Grinding prohibition applies even towards foods that do not grow from the ground. [Shiltei Giborim 32 in Rif; Rivash 184; Nishmas Adam 17:2; brought in Kaf Hachaim 321:52; Chazon Ish 57; Piskeiy Teshuvos 321:12] Some Poskim rule a Rabbinical grinding prohibition applies towards foods that do not grow from the ground. [Beis Yosef 340; P"M 321 M"Z 10; Tehila Ledavid 321:7; Iglei Tal Tochein 21; Shut Rebbe Akiva Eigar 21 leaves this matter in question]
Ruling of Admur/Rama in 504: It is forbidden to use a grater to grate cheese on Yom Tov unless one uses a Shinui. [Rama 504:3; Admur 504:5 based on Rivash 184] Although it is permitted to use a grater to grate bread, as there is no grating prohibition by bread. [Rama ibid; Admur 504:6] Vetzaruch Iyun as by cheese as well there is no prohibition of grinding, being it does not grow on the ground, thus why is the law by cheese any different than the law by bread. Furthermore, from the wording of the Rama and Admur ibid it implies they are saying there is a grinding prohibition by cheese, and they even reference to the Rivash ibid who is one of the Rishonim who argue and rule the prohibition of grinding applies by all foods, even cheese. See P"M 504 M"Z 1; Piskeiy Teshuvos 504 footnote 19 for suggested answers. Vetzaruch Iyun!
[81] Meaning it is not a spice.
[82] Admur ibid; M"B 321:31
[83] Admur ibid; Michaber ibid regarding meat; Tosafus Shabbos 74
[84] M"A 321:10
[85] Admur 321:9; Rama 321:9; Terumos Hadeshen 27 or 56; M"A 321:10; M"B 321:33
Other Poskim: Some Poskim rule it is permitted to cut the meat small even in such a case as we never hold there is a grinding prohibition by foods that do not grow from the ground. [Taz 321:9; 324:4; Gr"a, brought in M"B 321:34] The proof for this is from the fact we rule in 324:7 that one may cut Niveila meat for a dog if it is not edible in its current state. [Taz 324:4] The other Poskim however explain that the above allowance in 324:7 is regarding cutting the Niveila meat to large pieces and not to small pieces. [See M"A 324:5; M"B 321:35; 324:20]
[86] Lit. well. Meaning that the thought does not disgust them.
[87] Admur ibid; M"A ibid; Terumos Hadeshen ibid
[88] Admur 321:9
[89] Lit. importance
[90] Admur 321:8; M"A 321:12; M"B 321:36
[91] Admur ibid; See M"A 321:10
[92] Biur Halacha 324:7 "Veayin Leil"; Ketzos Hashulchan 131 footnote 12
[93] Admur 321:8; Michaber 321:10; Rivash
[94] Admur 321:8; Michaber 321:10; Rivash 184; M"B 321:30 regarding cooked salt
[95] Biur Halacha 321:12 "Lifarer"; Ketzos Hashulchan 129 footnote 17; Iglei Tal; Shevisas Hashabbos Tochein 15; See Shabbos Kehalacha 21 Biurim 24

iron] in Yiddish*)* even in order to eat right away.[96]

The reason for this is:[97] as since the vessel is designated for this use, doing so is considered a mundane action, as is crushing spices with a pestle and mortar. [However, with regards to foods that grow from the ground, this is Biblically forbidden to be used even if done to eat immediately.[98]]

Other cutting vessels: This law applies for any other vessel that is designated for this use of cutting small.

Summary:

All foods which do not grow on the ground and are currently edible, and is not used as a spice is permitted to be ground in their common form, even for later use. Nevertheless, it is forbidden to use a vessel which is specifically designated for grinding for this purpose.

Q&A

Must the above foods be ground for right away use?

No. However some Poskim[99] rule one is to do so for right away use.

May one grind without restriction foods that do not grow on the ground, or foods that have already been ground [such as bread]?[100]

Although doing so certainly does not contain a grinding prohibition, nevertheless, it remains prohibited to use any utensil which is designated for grinding, as doing so is a mundane act which is forbidden to do on Shabbos, just as is the law with regards to using a grater to cut items small, as explained above.

Examples of utensils which are designated for grinding and thus may never be used on Shabbos:[101]

1. Mincer, including a garlic mincer. [Using a garlic mincer to grind garlic on Shabbos would entail a Biblical grinding prohibition.]
2. Mortar
3. Grater
4. Pepper mill
5. Grinding hammer
6. Mashing instrument

C. Grinding foods that grow from the ground:[102]

All the above refers to food that does not grow from the ground, however any food that grows from the ground, even if it is food that can be readily eaten[103], has [the] grinding [prohibition] apply to it.[104] Thus it is forbidden to grind [the food] with a pestle, even if [the pestle is] made of wood, [and] even if done to eat immediately.[105]

The reason for this is:[106] because amongst species [of foods which grow on the ground are] foods that are ground, such as grains and legumes. [**See Q&A regarding foods that are not commonly ground**]

---

[96] Admur ibid; M"B 321:36

[97] Admur ibid; M"A 321:12; Rivash ibid; M"B 321:36

[98] Rivash 184; Ketzos Hashulchan 129 footnote 6 [see also footnote 3 and 4]; M"B 321:45; Biur Halacha "Midei Dehavei"

The reason: It is Biblically forbidden to use any grinding designated vessel for foods which have a grinding prohibition, even if done to eat right away, as using such vessels is not the way of eating but rather the way of working. This is in addition to it being due a mundane act. [ibid]

[99] See Shiltei Giborim 32 in Rif]; Rivash 184; Nishmas Adam 17:2; Kaf Hachaim 321:52; Chazon Ish 57; Piskeiy Teshuvos 321:12

[100] Ketzos Hashulchan 129 footnote 17, SSH"K 6:2

[101] SSH"K 6:2; Piskeiy Teshuvos 321:9 and 13; Shabbos Kehalacha 21:16-21 footnote 49; Ketzos Hashulchan 129 footnote 6

[102] Admur 321:10-11; Michaber 321:12; Shabbos 74

[103] Lit. complete food

[104] 321:10; Yireim 274; Hagahos Maimanis 21:Ayin; Or Zarua 2:60; Terumos Hadeshen 56; M"A 321:10; M"B 321:38

[105] 321:11; Rivash 184; See M"B 321:26

[106] 321:10; Terumos Hadeshen 56; See M"B 321:39

Grinding foods which are currently edible in order to eat right away:[107] [Furthermore] even food that is readily able to be eaten [in its current state] such as dry figs and carobs for old people[108], as well as garlic and lepidium and the like of foods which are [commonly] ground are [Biblically[109]] forbidden to be ground even in order to eat immediately.

Crushing with an irregularity:[110] It is permitted to crush them with a great irregularity such as with using a wooden pot ladle or with the handle of a knife and the like as was explained [above in Halacha 1A] regarding spices.

Crumbling bread:[111] It is permitted to crumble bread very small for chickens [for even later use[112]] and doing so does not involve the grinding prohibition. [See Q&A] [It is however forbidden to grate the bread using a grater and other designated vessel of the like, due to Uvdin Dechol.[113]],

The reason for this is: because the grain from which the bread was made had already been previously ground and there is no [prohibition to] grind a previously ground [food]. [In certain cases, however, the grinding prohibition applies even to an already ground item.[114] It is forbidden to grind dry mud with one's hands due to the grinding prohibition, despite the fact that the earth has already been ground.[115] Likewise, one who grinds metal is liable for grinding, despite the fact that metal must be melted in order to be made.[116] Likewise one who grinds earthenware is liable for grinding despite the fact that it was made of earth which is ground.[117] Some Poskim[118] explain that the above rule is only applicable to foods, while non-food items retain the grinding prohibition even when previously ground. Others[119] however rule that it applies even by non-food products. Others[120] explain that only when human hands caused the regrouping of the grinded item, do we say there is no grinding after grinding, and not when this occurred naturally. Others[121] rule that it only applies to Gidulei Karka and not to Karka. Others[122] rule it only applies if the item did not become hardened, however if it became hardened then it retains the grinding prohibition. Other Poskim[123] however negate this ruling. Others[124] rule it only applies to an item that turned into crumbs, while items that simply melted and liquified and then became solids, the grinding prohibition applies.[125]

---

[107] Admur 321:11

[108] May one grind foods that are edible in their current state? Some Poskim rule it is permitted to do so. [M"A 321:14] However from Admur ibid it is implied that it is forbidden even in such a case [Ketzos Hashulchan 129 footnote 6], and so rules M"B 321:39 based on Olas Shabbos.

[109] Rivash 184; Ketzos Hashulchan 129 footnote 6 [see also footnote 3 and 4]; M"B 321:45; Biur Halacha "Midei Dehavei"

The reason: It is Biblically forbidden to use any grinding designated vessel for foods which have a grinding prohibition, even if done to eat right away, as using such vessels is not the way of eating but rather the way of working. This is in addition to it being due a mundane act. [ibid]

[110] Admur 321:11

[111] Admur 321:10; 504:6; Rama 321:12; 504:3 regarding Matzos; Rashbam in Hagahos Maimanis 21 Ayin; Ran Perek Klal Gadol; Smag 65; Mordechai 365; Maharil; See also Admur 446:5-6 regarding destroying Chameitz on Shabbos:Yom Tov by crumbling it into the wind

Other Poskim: Some Poskim rule that there is grinding after grinding [Mishneh Lamelech on Rambam 1:3 in Hilchos Chameitz Umatazah; opinion in Ran; Implication of Rashba 4:75 as he only allows grinding bread for right away use; implication of Termuos Hadeshen brought in Beis Yosef; See Shabbos Kehalacha 21 Biurim 22] Some Poskim conclude that one is to be stringent like this opinion. [Nishmas Adam 17:3, brought in Kaf Hachaim 321:74; Maharshag 2:54; See Arugos Habosem 80 Tochein 1; Chofetz Chaim in Nidchei Yisrael 39 Tochein 2; Letters of Chazon Ish 60:1; The Michaber does not mention this allowance in his Shulchan Aruch; See Ben Ish Chaiy Mishpatim 2:7; Piskeiy Teshuvos 321:11 footnote 122]

[112] M"B 321:40

[113] Biur Halacha 321:12 "Lifarer"; Ketzos Hashulchan 129 footnote 17; Iglei Tal; Shevisas Hashabbos Tochein 15; See Shabbos Kehalacha 21 Biurim 24

Ruling on Yom Tov: It is permitted to use a grater to grate bread on Yom Tov. [Rama 504:3; Admur 504:6] Vetzaruch Iyun why this is not forbidden due to Uvdin Dechol. See P"M 504 M"Z 1; Piskeiy Teshuvos 504 footnote 19 for suggested answers. Vetzaruch Iyun!

[114] For a Likkut in this matter: See Shabbos Kehalacha 21 Biurim 23; Piskeiy Teshuvos 321:11

[115] Admur 302:17; Michaber 302:7; Beitza 7b; See Hagahos Rav Akiva Eiger 302

[116] Rambam 8:15

[117] Yerushalmi 7:2

[118] First explanation in Tal Oros p. 33; Wording of Maharil, brought in Rama 504:7

[119] Ben Ish Chaiy Mishpatim 2:7

[120] Second explanation in Tal Oros p. 33

[121] Iglei Tal Tochein 9-10

[122] Shevisas Hashabbos Tocehin 7

[123] Peri Megadim 321 M"Z 10; M"B 321:30; Ketzos Hashulchan 129:3; SSH"K 6:11

[124] Ketzos Hashulchan 129 footnote 16

[125] This explains why cheese is not exempt due to it having already been ground, in its milks tate.

Summary:
All foods which grow on the ground are Biblically forbidden to be ground in their regular way, even in order to eat right away. It is permitted to grind them with a great irregularity, such as using the back of a knife. It is permitted to grind foods which have been previously ground, such as bread.

Q&A
May one grind without restriction foods which grow from the earth which are <u>not</u> commonly ground?[126]
No. All foods which grow from the ground are forbidden to be ground without a great irregularity, even if the food is not commonly ground.[127] The term "that are commonly ground" used by Admur is simply used due to that this is what is usually ground. It however does not come to exclude other foods that are not commonly ground.

Mushrooms:[128]
Some Poskim[129] rule it is not considered Gidulei Karka. Other Poskim[130] rule it is considered Gidulei Karka.

May one crumble peels of nuts with one's hands:[131]
Seemingly it is permitted to do so as it is considered a great irregularity.

Q&A on "No Grinding after Grinding"
May one grind foods which are already very small?[132]
One is to only do so with a great irregularity, as is the law by all foods. Some[133] write it is only Rabbinically forbidden to grind these items regularly. Others write it is Biblically forbidden to grind these items regularly. Others[134] write it is only forbidden to grind these items regularly if by doing so one enhances the food.

May one grind sugar cubes?
Some Poskim[135] rule that sugar cubes do not contain the grinding prohibition, and hence do not require a great irregularity when ground.[136] Other Poskim[137] rule sugar cubes contain the grinding prohibition and hence may only be ground using a great irregularity.[138] Practically, one may be lenient[139], although a G-d fearing Jew is to be stringent.[140] According to all one may not grind it with

---

[126] Ketzos Hashulchan 129 footnote 6
[127] This is because a) doing so contains a grinding prohibition and b) using the regular tools to grind is a mundane act. [Ketzos Hashulchan ibid]
[128] Shabbos Kehalacha 21 footnote 39 p. 454
[129] Rosh Yosef Shabbos 75
[130] Iglei Tal Dash 24:3
[131] Pisekiy Teshuvos 321 Footnote
[132] Iglei Tal Tochein 5:15; See Ketzos Hashulchan 129 footnote 16; Piskeiy Teshuvos 321:11; Shabbos Kehalacha 21:61; Minchas Shlomo 2:6-2
[133] Iglei Tal ibid
[134] Shabbos Kehalacha ibid
[135] Peri Megadim 321 M"Z 10; M"B 321:30; Ketzos Hashulchan 129:3; SSH"K 6:11
[136] The reason: Sugar has the same status as cooked lumps of salt which does not contain a grinding prohibition, as salt was previously small pieces and only becomes one piece through the cooking. [ibid] The Ketzos Hashulchan ibid sides like the Peri Megadim that there is no grinding prohibition by sugar. He negates the source of the Shevisas Shabbos saying the prohibition by earthenware does not apply by items that have grown on the ground.
[137] Shevisas Shabbos Tochein 43; Ben Ish Chaiy Mishpatim 7 and Tiferes Yisrael one is do one irregularity in the crushing of it; See Poskim in Piskeiy Teshuvos 321 footnote 122
[138] The reason: The Shevisas Shabbos [Tochein 43] rules the grinding prohibition does apply by sugar cubes. His reasoning is because this rule that grinding does not apply by previously ground items was only said by bread since it is a soft food, however by other items which become hard like sugar the grinding prohibition remains. His proof is from the fact all agree grinding applies by earthenware even though it was previously ground. The Tiferes Yisrael rules that in any event one must do one irregularity in the crushing of it.
[139] As rules Ketzos Hashulchan ibid; SSH"K ibid
[140] Chofetz Chaim in Nidchei Yisrael 39:1; Chazon Ish 60:1; Shabbos Kehalacha 21:58; Piskeiy Teshuvos 321:11

vessels which are designated for grinding/crushing, due to it being a mundane act.[141]

May one grind bread/crackers/Matzah and other foods of the like which have been ground in their process of preparation?[142]
Yes, one may do so with any utensil that is not specifically designated for grinding.

Question:
Is one allowed to crush Doritos or other types of chips into his salad on Shabbos. Basically, I love eating my salad together with crushed Doritos and would like to know if it is permitted for me to do on Shabbos as well?

Answer:
It is permitted to be done to all previously ground chips, such as Doritos which is made from ground corn, and is thus similar to a cracker, as the grinding prohibition does not apply to foods already previously ground. However, chips and snacks that are made from whole pieces of fruit or vegetable retain the grinding prohibition, and hence it would be forbidden to grind regular whole potato chips into one's salad due to the grinding prohibition unless it is done with the great irregularity, such as using the back of a knife to smash it. However, potato chips made from ground potato flour, would not retain a grinding prohibition, just like Doritos. However, according to some opinions, even by whole chips it nonetheless remains permitted to crush the chips using one's hand directly prior to eating the salad. According to this approach, it would also be permitted to stomp on the potato chip bag using one's fists or feet until everything is crushed to put into one's salad right away for it to be eaten right away. [With one's feet one can argue that it may be done even for later use being that is considered a great irregularity.]

Sources: **see regarding the general grinding prohibition**: *Admur 321:10-11; Michaber 321:12; Shabbos 74;* **see regarding the allowance to grind pre-ground products**: *Admur 321:10; 504:6; Rama 321:12; 504:3 regarding Matzos; Rashbam in Hagahos Maimanis 21:Ayin; Ran Perek Klal Gadol; Smag 65; Mordechai 365; Maharil; See also Admur 446:5-6 regarding destroying Chameitz on Shabbos:Yom Tov by crumbling it into the wind* **See regarding crushing with one's hands and its status regarding vegetables that are eaten right away**: *Tehila Ledavid 321:10; Shevisas Shabbos Tochein 6; P"M 321 A"A 2; Shabbos Kehalacha 21:45; Piskeiy Teshuvos 321:9*

Sugar candy:[143]
One is to be stringent to avoid grinding candy, unless one uses a great irregularity.[144]

Chocolate:[145]
One is to be stringent to avoid grinding chocolate, unless one uses a great irregularity.

Medicine capsules:[146]
One is to be stringent to avoid grinding medicine, unless one uses a great irregularity. However, some[147] write it is permitted to do so.

---

[141] Using vessels designated for crushing is always forbidden by all types of food due to it being a mundane act. [Admur 321:8]
[142] SSH"K 6:11
[143] See Shabbos Kehalacha 21:59; Ketzos Hashulchan 129 footnote 16; Piskeiy Teshuvos 321:11 in footnote 121
[144] Although the above foods were previously ground, nevertheless they now have a new existence, as they went from a liquid to a solid, and is hence not similar to the allowance of regrinding bread.
[145] Orchos Shabbos 5:21; Shabbos Kehalacha 21:59; See Ketzos Hashulchan 129 footnote 16; Piskeiy Teshuvos 321:11 in footnote 121
[146] Piskeiy Teshuvos 321 footnote 124; Shabbos Kehalacha 21:65
[147] SSH"K 33:4

D. Grinding food with one's teeth for later use:[148]

Food [which grows on the ground] which one does not wish to eat [himself], (or to feed to a child[149]) right away[150] is forbidden to chew with his teeth due to the grinding prohibition.[151]

Q&A

May one chew a food and later spit it out?[152]
If one is doing so in order to taste the food then it is permitted, as only when one does so purely for the sake of grinding is it it forbidden.[153]

May one who chewed a food and realized it is spoiled, spit it out?
Yes.[154]

May one chew tobacco leaves and spit it out?
Yes.[155]

General summary-Crushing/grinding foods:[156]

❖ *The summary takes into account that which is explained in the Q&A!*
<u>Using utensils designated for grinding</u>: Is forbidden by all foods.[157]
<u>Using utensils which are not designated for grinding and in a way that is not usually done during the week[158]</u>: Is permitted by all foods so long as one is doing so in order to eat the food on Shabbos.[159]
<u>Using utensils which are not designated for grinding but are commonly used to grind with</u>: Is only permitted by foods which do not contain the grinding prohibition. [i.e. Do not grow on the ground and are not a spice, and are edible in their current state {not raw meat}].
<u>Grinding food with one's teeth[160]</u>: Is forbidden to be done to eat at a later time [by those foods which contain a grinding prohibition]. It is permitted though to chew it to feed a child immediately.

List of conditions required for an item to be free of the grinding prohibition:
All three conditions are required if the item has not been previously ground.

1. Is not a spice.
2. Does not grow on the earth.
3. Is fit to be eaten in its current state without being cut.

---

[148] Admur 321:13; M"A 321:12; M"B 321:36; Based on Rashi 133
<u>Other opinions</u>: Some Poskim rule there is never any grinding prohibition relevant to one's teeth. [Aruch Hashulchan 321:43]
[149] Admur ibid; M"B ibid; The novelty here is that even though one will be removing it from his mouth it is permitted to do so.
<u>Other opinions</u>: Some Poskim rule one is not to remove the food at all from his mouth, even in order to eat right away. [Piskeiy Teshuvos 321 footnote 109 in name of Arugos Bosem 1:80 and Chazon Ish 57]
[150] Admur ibid; Omitted in M"A and M"B ibid
[151] This is not considered an absolute Shinuiy, and is hence not permitted
[152] M"B 321:36; Shabbos Kehalacha 21:5; However see Piskeiy Teshuvos 321 footnote 109 in name of Arugos Bosem 1:80 and Chazon Ish 57
[153] <u>The reason</u>: Seemingly the reason is because this is considered Derech Achila, even if he later spits it out, and only when one takes the food out and later plans to eat it do we rule that his action was grinding and not Derech Achila.
[154] This follows the same ruling, and reasoning as stated above.
[155] This follows the same ruling, and reasoning as stated above.
[156] Halacha 7, 11 and 12
[157] This is forbidden even foods which do not grow on the ground and thus do not contain a grinding prohibition, due to it being a mundane act. [See Q&A] As well, spices and foods which grow on the ground contain a grinding prohibition in doing so, in addition to the prohibition of doing a mundane act.
[158] Such as to crush with the handle of a knife and the like.
[159] Since doing so is considered a great irregularity from its usually way, it is therefore permitted by all foods so long as one is doing so in order to eat the food on Shabbos. If these conditions are fulfilled, then it is allowed to crush even a lot of the food at a time.
[160] Halacha 13

Laws relating to mashing foods on Shabbos[161]

May one mash foods on Shabbos?

A. Is mashing defined as Grinding?

Some Poskim[162] rule that mashing has the same status as grinding with a grinder and thus may only be done with a great irregularity by foods which contain the grinding prohibition. Other Poskim[163] however rule that mashing is not defined as grinding at all.[164] Practically, one is to be stringent.[165]

B. In proximity to meal:

It is forbidden to mash the foods in their regular way even in close proximity to the meal.[166] However some Poskim[167] are lenient in this matter.[168] Practically, one is to be stringent.[169]

C. Using an instrument designated for mashing:[170]

By all foods, one may never use an instrument which is designated for mashing due to a mundane act prohibition, as was explained regarding grinding.

D. May one mash foods using a fork or spoon? Is mashing with a spoon/fork considered an irregularity?

Spoons:

Either side of a spoon may be used to mash all foods.[171] However some Poskim[172] rule one may not use the front of a spoon or the front of any other cutlery for foods which contain the grinding prohibition as doing so is not defined as an irregularity.[173]

Forks:[174]

Those foods which have a grinding prohibition [i.e. grow on ground or are spices] may only be mashed with the back of the fork as opposed to the teeth.[175] The back of the fork however may be

[161] See Piskeiy Teshuvos 321:15; Shabbos Kehalacha 21:35-43
[162] Chazon Ish 57; SSH"K 6:1
[163] Tehila Ledevaid 252:12; Ketzos Hashulchan 130 footnote 19 [regarding mashing bananas]; Igros Moshe 4:74-4; Ateres Moshe 1:103
[164] The reason: The Ketzos Hashulchan ibid and Igros Moshe ibid rule regarding mashing bananas that it does not contain the mashing prohibition being that the food does not break into small pieces, and rather remains one glob, and thus does not consist of grinding. This is opposed to garlic which when mashed turns into small pieces and would thus contain the grinding prohibition. As well it seems from there that even if the grinding prohibition would apply, he holds that mashing is similar to cutting and is hence permitted to be done in close proximity to the meal. This understanding of mashing would defer greatly from the understanding of SSH"K in that mashing has a status of cutting and not crushing. Vetzaruch Iyun.
[165] Conclusion of Shabbos Kehalacha ibid; Piskeiy Teshuvos ibid footnote 174; However, see Shabbos Kehalacha ibid that even the Chazon Ish is only stringent in a case that the food turns into small pieces which remain connect, and not if it simply goes from hard to soft.
[166] Chazon Ish ibid; Shevet Halevi 1:86; 7:92; Az Nidbaru 2:1
The reason: As mashing is considered Derech Melacha even when done in proximity to the meal, just as we ruled regarding using a grinder, and is not similar to cutting with a knife in proximity to the meal, which is considered Derech Achila. [ibid]
[167] Ketzos Hashulchan 130 footnote 19; Yechaveh Daas 5:27; Igros Moshe 4:74-4; SSH"K 6 footnote 21 in name of Rav SZ"A that so holds Gr"a; Rivash 184 that according to Rashba one may even use a vessel so long as it is not designated for grinding; Shevisas Hashabbos Tochein 12
[168] The reason: The Ketzos Hashulchan ibid writes that even if the grinding prohibition would apply to bananas, he holds that mashing is similar to cutting and is hence permitted to be done in close proximity to the meal. This understanding of mashing would defer greatly from the understanding of SSH"K in that mashing has a status of grinding and not cutting. Vetzaruch Iyun.
[169] Conclusion of Shabbos Kehalacha ibid; Piskeiy Teshuvos ibid footnote 174
[170] Piskeiy Teshuvos 321:15
[171] SSH"K 6:8 in name of Rav SZ"A footnote 21; Shabbos Kehalacha 21:36; See Piskeiy Teshuvos 321 footnote 171
[172] Chazon Ish 57; Az Nidbaru 9:11 and so rules Piskeiy Teshuvos 321:15 and footnote 99 and 171
[173] They hold one is not to novelize forms of crushing that was not mentioned in the Talmud, and that using the front of a spoon is not defined as a great irregularity.
[174] SSH"K 6:14; Shabbos Kehalacha 21:36; See Piskeiy Teshuvos 321 footnote 171
[175] Being that using the teeth of the fork is the normal way of mashing during the week, which contains a grinding prohibition on Shabbos.
To note however from Ketzos Hashulchan 130 footnote 19 who implies [regarding mashing bananas with a spoon] that so long as one does not use a vessel which is designated for grinding, then it may be used to mash in order to eat right away. This would thus imply that it is always permitted to use even the teeth of a fork by any food being that it is not designated specifically for grinding so long as one desires to eat the food right away.

used as it is considered a great irregularity. Foods that do not have a grinding prohibition [i.e. Foods which do not grow on the ground and are not spices] may be mashed with either side of the fork.

Knives:

One may use either side of a knife to mash a food if doing so is considered an irregular method. One may not mash and spread a hard piece of avocado and the like with the front part of the knife as doing so is considered the regular method.[176] Some Poskim[177] rule one may not use the front of a knife for foods which contain the grinding prohibition as doing so is not defined as an irregularity.

<u>Back of plate or cup</u>:[178] Is considered an irregularity.

Q&A

When mashing a food in the irregular ways mentioned above must one do so immediately prior to the meal?[179]

No, it may be done any time so long as one plans to eat the food on Shabbos. This applies even by foods which do contain a grinding prohibition.[180] When mashing in the regular form then according to some Poskim one may do so in close proximity to the meal, while according to others it is completely forbidden, as explained in B.

List of foods that can be mashed with the teeth of a fork:

- Meat
- Chicken
- Cheese
- Eggs
- All Cooked soft vegetables
- Very ripe and soft avocado or banana or other fruit

May one mash eggs/meat/chicken using the teeth of a fork?[181]

Yes, as these foods do not contain a grinding prohibition.

E. Soft foods:[182]

If the food is very soft, then at times the grinding prohibition does not apply. See Q&A below regarding different cases of this sort, and what is defined as mashing with an irregularity, which may be done to all foods as explained above.

Q&A

May one mash and spread banana or avocado on bread using the teeth of a fork?[183]

If the fruit is so soft that if part were to be held in one's hand the other part would fall off, then it is

---

[176] See Piskeiy Teshuvos 321:9 and 15 that consideres the front part of the knife not to be a Shiynuiy.

[177] Chazon Ish; Az Nidbaru 9:11 and so rules Piskeiy Teshuvos 321:9 and 15

[178] M"A 321:9; M"B 321:25

[179] Piskeiy Teshuvos 321:9 in letter Beis and Gimel

[180] Being that it is similar to crushing with a great irregularity which is not required to be done immediately prior to the meal, as explained in Halacha 1A. [Peri Megadim 321 M"Z 7; M"B 321:24; Ketzos Hashulchan 129 footnote 8; and so is implied from Admur 321:7 *"One who needs to crush peppers and the like in order to place them into food on Shabbos"* that one does not need to do so immediately prior to the meal, but rather so long as he plans to eat from it on Shabbos it suffices, unlike the law by cutting small, as will be explained.]

Nevertheless, from Ketzos Hashulchan 130 footnote 19 [regarding crushing bananas with a spoon] it is implied that it is required to be done immediately prior to the meal as is the law regarding cutting a food small. Perhaps however he learns that mashing bananas with a spoon is not considered an irregularity and that mashing has a status of cutting and not crushing, and is thus allowed to be done immediately before the meal. Vetzaruch Iyun.

[181] SSH"K 6:14

[182] Tiferes Yisrael Tochein; Tehila Ledavid 321:20; 252:14; Shevisas Hashabbos Tochein 11; Igros Moshe 4:74 Tochein 5; SSH"K 6:7; Piskeiy Teshuvos 321:15

[183] SSH"K 6:7

already defined as mashed and thus may be mashed with any utensil that is not designated for grinding.[184] If the fruit is not soft to this point mashing it regularly [with the teeth of a fork] contains the grinding prohibition.[185]

May one mash cooked fruits and vegetables using the teeth of a fork?[186]

If the food is very soft and easily mashed[187], it is allowed to mash it using any utensil which is not specifically designated for mashing [such as he may use the teeth of a fork].[188] One may thus spread jam or cooked apples onto his bread on Shabbos. Furthermore, some Poskim[189] are lenient by cooked foods even if they are not very soft.

May one mash the foods in his chulent using the front of his fork?[190]

Yes, this may be done so long as the foods are cooked and soft, as explained in the previous Q&A!

❖ ***Regarding adding liquids to a mashed food- see" The Laws of Kneading"!***

---

[184] Regarding if one may spread the avocado and the like on the bread in order to make it look fancier-See "Misc Shabbos Laws"

[185] So rules SSH"K ibid. Vetzaruch Iyun from Ketzos Hashulchan 130 footnote 19, which implies that mashing bananas and the like never contains a grinding prohibition. As well it seems from there that even if the grinding prohibition would apply, he holds that mashing is similar to cutting and is hence permitted to be done in close proximity to the meal according to some.

[186] SSH"K 6:10 in name of Rav SZ"A; Ketzos Hashulchan 129 footnote 21; Igros Moshe 4:74

[187] Some write even if the food is slightly soft it may be mashed. [Tiferes Yisrael Tochein brought in Piskeiy Teshuvos 321:13; In however SSH"K ibid and Ketzos Hashulchan ibid they both state the Tiferes Yisrael is stringent. Vetzaruch Iyun.]

[188] As since they are very soft they are already defined as mashed and do not contain a grinding prohibition. [One can bring a proof to this from Michaber 321:19 2 which allows finishing the crushing of the cooked bran and Magen Avraham 321:29 which rules that one may spread [cooked-M"B] apples onto bread. Thus, we see he learns that there is no mashing prohibition by cooked foods.

[189] Tiferes Yisrael Tochein brought in Piskeiy Teshuvos 321:13 and 15 [In however SSH"K ibid and Ketzos Hashulchan ibid they both state the Tiferes Yisrael is stringent. Vetzaruch Iyun.]; Chazon Ish 58:9; Aruch Hashulchan 321:39; Iglei Tal Tochein 21; See Igros Moshe 4:74 Tochein; Az Nidbaru 5:11; Piskeiy Teshuvos 321:15 footnote 179]

[190] Aruch Hashulchan 321:39

2. Cutting foods to small pieces:

The cutting of foods to very small pieces [Dak Dak] is included in the Melacha of grinding.[191] The following laws will discuss as to which foods this prohibition applies:

What is the definition of cutting small?[192]

If it is cut small to the point that it is similar to a ground product, one is liable for grinding. If however it is cut slightly larger than this, one is not liable, although it is still forbidden to do so.[193] There is no known measurement for what is defined as small, and one must thus always be very careful to cut the pieces largely in order to avoid the prohibition.[194] Some Poskim[195] however rule that cutting small is defined as cutting it to whatever size one usually cuts it to during the week, while cutting large is defined as slightly larger than one's normal size of cutting. Others[196] rule that so long as the food is not cut small enough to the point it does not require chewing top be eaten, it is not defined as small.

Strips: Some Poskim[197] rule cutting very thin is equivalent to cutting into very small pieces, even if the slices remain long. Other Poskim[198] however rule that it is not considered grinding.

Slices: Some Poskim[199] rule that cutting a food into slices, such as cutting a cucumber into round slices, is not considered grinding even if it is cut very thin, even according to the stringent opinion above. Others[200] however rule it is considered grinding according to the above strict opinion.

A. To cut spices with a knife:

Spices other than salt:[201] It is forbidden to cut pepper with a knife [into small pieces[202]] even in order to eat immediately.[203] The above law applies for all spices which are commonly only eaten when mixed [with other foods]. [See Q&A]

Cutting salt with a knife:[204] It is forbidden to cut salt very small with a knife.

The reason for this is:[205] (because since [salt] is only fit to be eaten when mixed into other foods it therefore has the same laws as do spices and is not comparable to meat and cheese even though it too does not derive from growing on the ground just like they.)[206]

Thick pieces of cooked salt:[207] This [prohibition to cut salt to small pieces] only applies with salt that was initially thick. However, salt which was initially thin and was then cooked and became [thick] pieces is permitted to be cut very thin with a knife just as it is permitted to do so by bread being that there is no [prohibition to] grind a previously ground [food].

---

[191] Shabbos 74a "Parim Silka" as explained in Rashi; Michaber 321:12; Rama 321:9; Admur 321:10; See Tur 321 that it is not actual Tochein but is similar to Tochein

[192] See Piskeiy Teshuvos 321 footnote 151; Shabbos Kehalacha 21 footnote 40 and 56

[193] Biur Halacha 321:12 "Hamichateich"

[194] Yireim brought in Biur Halacha ibid

[195] Az Nidbaru 12:22

[196] Minchas Shlomo 1:91-13; Peas Sadcha 1:38; Or Letziyon 2:47-25

[197] Tzemach Tzedek in Mishnayis Shabbos 7 based on Shabbos 74b; Ketzos Hashulchan 129 footnote 2; Shabbos Kehalacha 21:29

[198] Igros Moshe 4:74-Tochein 3; Minchas Shlomo 1:91-13; and so rules plainly Piskeiy Teshuvos 321:4 [14]

[199] Shabbos Kehalacha 21:29; Piskeiy Teshuvos 321:14; Orchos Shabbos 5:3-4; See also Igros Moshe 4:74;

[200] Dvar Halacha 5:4, brought in Shabbos Kehalacha ibid footnote 67

[201] Admur 321:7; M"A 321:9; M"B 321:25

[202] Mishneh Berurah 321:25 and Ketzos Hashulchan 129:2. Vetzaruch Iyun why Admur omitted this point

[203] Admur ibid; based on implication of Rambam 21:18; P"M 321 M"Z 10; Iglei Tal 11; Tehila Ledavid 321:8; Kaf Hachaim 321:48
The reason: This is forbidden due to it not being Derech Achila, as spices are not eaten directly and are rather placed into foods. [P"M ibid]
Other opinions: Some Poskim rule it is permitted to cut spices small when done to eat right away. [Shaar Tziyon 321:30] Other Poskim leave this matter in question. [Peri Megadim and Elyah Raba]

[204] Admur 321:12; Rama 321:8; M"B 321:27

[205] Admur 321:12

[206] In other words: Although salt does not grow on the ground, nevertheless it contains a grinding prohibition being that it is used as a spice. [See Ketzos Hashulchan 129 footnote 12]

[207] Admur 321:12; Rama 321:8; Kol Bo; M"B 321:30

Summary of cutting foods that are only used to season foods:
Spices and salt may not be cut to very small pieces even in order to eat right away.

Q&A
May one cut fresh jalapeño peppers to small pieces in order to eat right away?[208]
Yes.[209] However dried hot peppers may never be cut into small pieces.[210]

Is a cinnamon stick considered a spice or a food?[211]
Seemingly it is considered a spice and thus may not be cut small even in order to eat right away.[212]

May one grate horse radish, or cut it very small?[213]
No. It is forbidden to do so even in order to eat right away.[214] One may not even grate it using a knife. Thus, it is only permitted to cut it to large pieces.

Are onions and garlic considered spices?[215]
Onions:[216] No, as stated explicitly by Admur below in Halacha C-See there for their ruling!
Garlic: No, as at times it is eaten plain. They thus have the same law as all foods which grow on the ground, as explained in Halacha C below- See there!

May one cut sugar cubes into small pieces [i.e. Is sugar considered a spice]?[217]
One may cut sugar cubes into small pieces even for non-immediate use so long as one plans to eat it on Shabbos.[218] Nevertheless some Poskim[219] rule that sugar cubes do contain a grinding prohibition[220], and therefore in their opinion it is best to be stringent and only do so for right away use[221], in which case it is allowed according to all[222].

---

[208] Ketzos Hashulchan 129 footnote 12

[209] As since today many people eat them while still fresh, prior to them drying up and becoming very spicy, they therefore do not have the status of a spice and rather have the same status as foods that grow on the ground, of which there is a dispute as to whether they may be cut small for immediate use. [ibid]

[210] As they are never usually eaten plain and thus have the status of a spice. [ibid]

[211] Ketzos Hashulchan 129 footnote 13

[212] It used to be that cinnamon sticks were eaten plain, and it is for this reason that Admur rules in the laws of blessings [Seder Birchas Hanehnin 6:19] that its blessing is "Hadama". However today since eating the sticks are unheard of, perhaps it has lost its food status and is only considered a spice and thus today may not be cut small even if one will eat them right away. [ibid]

[213] Admur 504:4; M"A 504:7; Ketzos Hashulchan 129 footnote 13

[214] As it is never eaten plain and is thus considered a spice. [ibid]

[215] Ketzos Hashulchan 129 footnote 14-regarding garlic

[216] Vetzaruch Iyun as in 318:11 Admur rules that onions

[217] Ketzos Hashulchan 129:4 footnote 16

[218] M"B 321:30; Ketzos Hashulchan 129 footnote 16, and Peri Megadim 321 M"Z 10
Sugar cubes do not contain the grinding prohibition as there is no grinding after grinding. It is similar to pieces of salt which have been cooked and turned into solid pieces which do not contain the grinding restrictions. [Ketzos Hashulchan 129 footnote 16, M"B and Peri Megadim 321 M"Z 10.]

[219] Shevisas Shabbos Tochein 16

[220] His reasoning is because this rule that grinding does not apply by previously ground items was only said by bread since it is a soft food, however other items which become hard like sugar the grinding prohibition remains. His proof is from the fact all agree grinding applies by earthenware even though it was previously ground.
The Ketzos Hashulchan 129:3 sides like the Peri Megadim that there is no grinding prohibition by sugar. He negates the source of the Shevisas Shabbos saying the above law by earthenware does not apply by items that have grown on the ground.

[221] Aside for the Ketzos Hashulchan's argument that sugar does not contain the grinding prohibition, he further argues that even if it does using a knife to cut it is considered a great irregularity and hence allowed. Thus, in his opinion there is no need to be stringent at all to cut it for right away use, even under the basis that it contains the grinding prohibition.

[222] Sugar is not considered a spice as it is edible on its own and hence may be cut for right away use. [Ketzos Hashulchan ibid]

B. Cutting into small pieces foods that do not grow from the ground:[223]

Any food which is fit to be eaten in its current form [without needing to be mixed with other foods] and does not grow on the ground, of which its species does not contain the concept of grinding at all, such as cooked or roasted meat[224] or cheese and the like, then it is permitted to cut it very thin (even [when done] not in order to eat right away[225]), being that there is no grinding [prohibition] by foods.[226]

Hard Cheese:[227] [Furthermore] even very hard cheese is allowed [to be cut small] being that it is [still] possible to be chewed, albeit with difficulty, and [thus] has a status of [a readily edible] food upon it.

If a person cannot chew:[228] ([Furthermore] it is allowed to be cut even by a person who cannot chew.)

Raw Meat:[229] However [soft] raw meat, since it is only fit for the strong[230] minded which are willing to chew it in an irregular way [meaning while still raw], [therefore] it does not have the status of food on it for this matter and [the] grinding [prohibition] is applicable to it. Therefore, it is forbidden to cut [Kosher[231]] raw meat very thin to [feed] the birds [unless one does so to feed them right away.[232] It is however permitted to cut Treif meat into very small pieces to feed the birds even later on Shabbos.[233]]

The reason that it being fit for dog does not render it the status of food:[234] Now, although it is fit for dogs [nevertheless] it does not receive the status of food due to this being it is not designated [to be given] to dogs but rather for people or for birds due to its value[235], and for them [the meat] is not fit [to be chewed] without this cutting. [Thus, the food is not yet considered to be food at this stage.]

Summary:

Foods that do not grow on the ground which are edible in their current state:[236] Do not have the grinding prohibition and may be cut even small.

Foods that do not grow on the ground which are inedible in their current state:[237] Such as raw meat contains the grinding prohibition and thus is forbidden to be cut very small.

❖ The above is only with regard to using a regular knife and vessels of the like which are not designated for cutting small. Regarding vessels which are designated for cutting small-See Halacha D!

---

[223] Admur 321:8; M"A 321:10; M"B 321:31

Other opinions: Some Poskim rule the Grinding prohibition applies towards meat, being the animal feeds off the ground. [brought in M"B 321:31] Some Poskim rule the Biblical Grinding prohibition applies even towards foods that do not grow from the ground. [Shiltei Giborim 32 in Rif; Rivash 184; Nishmas Adam 17:2; brought in Kaf Hachaim 321:52; Chazon Ish 57; Piskiey Teshuvos 321:12] Some Poskim rule a Rabbinical grinding prohibition applies towards foods that do not grow from the ground. [Beis Yosef 340; P"M 321 M"Z 10; Tehila Ledavid 321:7; Iglei Tal Tochein 21; Shut Rebbe Akiva Eigar 21 leaves this matter in question]]

[224] Admur ibid; Michaber 321:9; Tosafus Shabbos 74

[225] Admur ibid; M"B 321:31

[226] See M"A 321:10 and M"B 321:31 that since there are opinions [Tosafus and Rosh] that rule there is no grinding prohibition by foods, therefore we are lenient like the Terumos Hadeshen to say there is no grinding prohibition by foods that don't grow from the ground.

[227] Admur 321:8; M"A 321:12; M"B 321:36

[228] Admur ibid; See M"A 321:10

[229] Admur 321:9

[230] Lit. well. Meaning that the thought does not disgust them.

[231] Ketzos Hashulchan 131:3; Biur Halacha 324:7 "Veayin Leil"

[232] As concludes Admur in next Halacha 321:10 [brought in C]; So rules M"B 321:33; Biur Halacha 321:9 "Veinan"; Ketzos Hashulchan 131:3

Other opinions: Some Poskim leave this matter in question. [P"M 321, brought in Biur Halahca ibid]

[233] Biur Halacha 324:7 "Veayin Leil"; Ketzos Hashulchan 131 footnote 12

[234] Admur 321:9

[235] Lit. importance

[236] Halacha 8

[237] Halacha 9

C. Cutting into small pieces foods that grow from the ground:[238]
All the above refers to food that does not grow from the ground, however any food that grows from the ground, even if it is food that can be readily eaten[239] has [the] grinding [prohibition] apply to it.
The reason for this is: because amongst these species [of foods are] foods that are ground, such as grains and legumes.
Vegetables and Fruits:[240] Therefore it is forbidden to cut a vegetable very small in order to eat it, and so too [it is forbidden to cut very small] dried dates and carobs for old[241] people, and if one does cut them very small then he is liable for grinding.
Crumbling and cutting bread: It is permitted to crumble bread very small for chickens and doing so does not involve the grinding prohibition. [It is likewise permitted to cut bread to small pieces.[242]]
The reason for this is: because the grain from which the bread was made had already been previously ground and there is no [prohibition to] grind a previously ground [food].
Cutting small with intent to eat right away:[243] [However] all this refers to when one cuts [the food] and leaves it [there] not planning to eat it right away but rather to eat later on. However, it is permitted to [even initially] cut [food] very small in order to eat it right away or for others to eat right away[244] or for chickens to eat right away.[245]
The reason for this allowance is:[246] because [the Torah] did not forbid a person to eat his food in big or small pieces and thus [we see that] it is the way of eating to eat also small pieces and anything that is done in a way of eating carries no prohibition as was explained in chapter 319 [Halacha 1] regarding separating food from its waste in order to eat it right away that it does not contain any prohibition since this is the way of eating and it is allowed to even initially do so.[247]
Other Opinions: There are opinions[248] which question this allowance [to cut small when intending to eat it right away].
The Final Ruling:[249] It is proper to suspect for this latter opinion and be careful to cut the vegetable (which is called lettuce) into slightly large pieces as then according to all opinion there is no grinding prohibition involved. However, in our provinces it is the custom to cut radish very very small as well as onion and they have upon whom to rely on [Halachically]. Nevertheless, at the very least they must beware to not begin to cut them until after [the men] leave the Shul being that it may only be done in actual proximity to the meal as was explained in chapter 319 [Halacha 4] regarding separating [food from its waste]. [**See Q&A regarding if when cutting large one may do so even much time prior to the meal!**]

Summary of cutting foods that grow on the ground
Foods which have never before been grinded small:[250] Such as all fruits and vegetables, is Biblically forbidden to cut small in order to eat later on. Regarding cutting them to eat right away it is disputed if doing so is forbidden, and it is proper to be stringent to cut the pieces slightly large. Nevertheless, those

---

[238] Admur 321:10
[239] Lit. complete food
[240] Admur ibid; Michaber 321:12
[241] See M"A; Biur Halacha 321:12 "Lifnei Zekeinim"
[242] Admur 321:12; Rama 321:8 as expalined in M"B 321:30 and Olas Shabbos
[243] Admur ibid; Rama 321:12; Rashba 4:75; Ran 32b
[244] Admur ibid; Beis Yosef; M"B 321:43
[245] Admur ibid; M"A 321:15; M"B 321:44
[246] Admur ibid; M"A ibid; M"B 321:44
The reason one may use a knife for this purpose even though one may nopt use a vessel for Borer: This is because a knife is considered Derech Achila regarding cutting, just as using the hands is cosndiered Derech Achila regarding Boroer. [Biur Halacha 321:12 "Midi Dihavei"]
[247] See Ketzos Hashulchan 129 footnote 3 which learns that the same laws which apply to allow one to do Borer apply here as well, as by both cases the permission is based on that it is done in the way of eating. Thus to grate vegetables using a designated vessel for grating would contain a Biblical prohibition according to all, just as is the law by Borer.
[248] M"A 321:15 In name of Shiltei Giborim; M"B 321:45
[249] Admur ibid; M"A ibid; Beis Yosef; M"B 321:45
[250] Admur 321:10

communities which are accustomed to be lenient have upon whom to rely, so long as they do so right before the meal. [See "The Laws of Borer" Halacha 4 regarding the exact definition of "right away"]
Foods which have been already ground:[251] Such as bread of which its grains were already grinded to flower, and precooked salt which had dissolved and the reformed a block, is allowed to be cut small even to eat later on.

Q&A

When cutting the food slightly large may one do so even much time prior to the meal?
Some Poskim[252] rule that even when cutting to slightly large pieces it must be done in close proximity to the meal. However, from Admur ibid it is implied that when cutting to slightly large pieces he may do so whenever he wishes so long as he intends to eat the food on Shabbos.[253]

What is the definition of cutting small?
Some opinions[254] rule cutting small is defined as cutting it to whatever size one usually cuts it to. Thus, cutting it slightly larger would mean to cut it larger than one usually would cut it during the week.
Others[255] however rule that there is no known measurement for what is defined as small, and one must thus always be careful to cut the pieces slightly large.

May one cut a fruit/vegetable to very thin slices [long but thin]?
Some Poskim[256] rule that it is forbidden to do so as cutting very thin is equivalent to cutting into very small pieces, even if the slices remain long.[257] Other Poskim[258] however rule that this is permitted to be done.

If one transgressed and cut fruits/vegetables into small pieces not in close proximity to the meal, may the food still be eaten?[259]
Advertently[260]:[261] If one advertently cut the food into small pieces much time prior to the meal it is forbidden to eat the food.[262]
Inadvertently: If it was done inadvertently [such as one forgot about the prohibition and the like] it is permitted to eat the food.[263] However some Poskim[264] are stringent in this matter.
Transgressed and mashed food in regular way: Permitetd as many Poskim rule there is no prohibition involved at all.
Trangressed and crushed spices in regular way: Seemingly is forbidden according to all even if done inadvertently. Vetzaruch Iyun

---

[251] Admur 321:10 and 12
[252] Beis Yosef 321; Biur Halacha 321:12 "Hamechateich"; SSH"K ; Shabbos Kehalacha 21:23
[253] See Shabbos Kehalacha 21:23 footnote 57
[254] Az Nidbaru 12:22
[255] Yireim brought in Biur Halacha 321 "Hamichateich"
[256] Ketzos Hashulchan 129 footnote 2
[257] So rules Tzemach Tzedek in Mishnayis Shabbos
[258] Igros Moshe 4:74-Tochein 3; Minchas Shlomo 91:13; and so rules plainly Piskeiy Teshuvos 321:4
[259] Ketzos Hashulchan 129 footnote 5; M"B 321:45
[260] This means one did so despite having knowledge of the prohibition.
[261] Based on the general rule of Meizid by Dirabanan on Shabbos as brought in 339:7; Mishneh Terumos 2:3
[262] Just as is the rule with all Shabbos transgressions which are done intentionally. [See "Laws of Cooking" Chapter 2].
[263] Ketzos Hashulchan 129 footnote 5; Aruch Hashulchan 321:9; Shevisas Hashabbos Tochein 5; Piskeiy Teshuvos 321:14
The reason: The reason for this is because a) there are opinions [Rambam] which hold that the Biblical grinding prohibition only applies if one plans to cook the grinded food. And b) Since here one is allowed to cut thinly prior to the meal, there is no worry that if we allow the inadvertent sinner to eat the food then people will do it advertently and say that it was inadvertent, as they could simply do it near the meal. [Ketzos Hashulchan 129 footnote 5]
[264] Chayeh Adam 17:2; M"B 321:45; Levushei Mordechai Telisa 167

D. What items may be used to cut with? May graters and the like be used? [265]

A knife/chisel/ax:[266] [It is allowed to be cut] whether with a knife or with an ax or a chisel as although these are vessels designated for prohibited use it is allowed to move them in order to use [for a permitted purpose] as explained in chapter 308 [Halacha 12].

A Grater:[267] It is forbidden to grate the cheese [or any food, including bread[268]], even one that does not grow on the ground, very thin with a dented grater which has sharp teeth (that is called *Riv Eizin* [grating iron] in Yiddish) even in order to eat right away.[269]

The reason for this is:[270] as since the vessel is designated for this use, doing so is considered a mundane action, as is crushing spices with a pestle and mortar. [However, with regards to foods that grow from the ground this is Biblically forbidden to be used even if done to eat immediately.[271]]

Other cutting vessels:[272] This law applies for any other vessel that is designated for this use of cutting small.

Using a grater or other instruments made for cutting items small:[273]

It is forbidden to grate <u>any food</u> very thin with a grater, or with any vessel made to cut items small, even in order to eat right away.

Examples of utensils which are designated for grinding and thus may never be used on Shabbos:[274]

- Mincer, including a garlic mincer. [Using a garlic mincer to grind garlic on Shabbos would entail a Biblical grinding prohibition.]
- Mortar
- Grater
- Pepper mill
- Vegetable chopper[275] [a set of blades which revolve around an axis and cut the food placed in them into small pieces.]

Q&A

May one use a knife which is specifically made for cutting small?

Some Poskim[276] rule it is forbidden to use such a knife at all, even with foods that do not have a grinding prohibition, and even in close proximity to the meal.[277] Other Poskim[278] however rule it is permitted to use such vessels. Practically, one is avoid using it on Shabbos.

---

[265] Admur 321:8; Michaber 321:10; Rivash
[266] Admur ibid; Mishneh Shabbos 122b; M"A 321:12; M"B 321:36
[267] Admur 321:8; Michaber 321:10; Rivash 184; M"B 321:30 regarding cooked salt
[268] Biur Halacha 321:12 "Lifarer"; Ketzos Hashulchan 129 footnote 17; Iglei Tal; Shevisas Hashabbos Tochein 15; See Shabbos Kehalacha 21 Biurim 24
[269] Admur ibid; M"B 321:36
[270] Admur ibid; M"A 321:12; Rivash ibid; M"B 321:36
[271] Rivash 184; Ketzos Hashulchan 129 footnote 6 [see also footnote 3 and 4]; M"B 321:45; Biur Halacha "Midei Dehavei"
The reason: It is Biblically forbidden to use any grinding designated vessel for foods which have a grinding prohibition, even if done to eat right away, as using such vessels is not the way of eating but rather the way of working. This is in addition to it being due a mundane act. [ibid]
[272] Admur ibid; M"A ibid; M"B ibid
[273] Halacha 8
[274] SSH"K 6:2
[275] Piskeiy Teshuvos 321:13; Shabbos Kehalacha 321:17
[276] M"B 321:45; Biur Halacha 321:12 "Midi Dihavei"; SSH"K 6:2; Piskeiy Teshuvos 321:13; Shabbos Kehalacha 21:17
[277] The reason: This is due to Uvdin Dechol, and if one uses it with foods that have a grinding prohibition, then it is likewise forbidden due to grinding, even if done in proximity to the meal, being that also Borer is forbidden when done with a vessel that is designated for this purpose, even if done in proximity to the meal. [M"B and Biur Halacha ibid]
[278] Aruch Hashulchan 321:9; Igros Moshe 4:74-1; See Shabbos Kehalacha ibid footnote 50

May one use an egg slicer on Shabbos to cut eggs?[279]

Yes. However, some Poskim[280] are stringent in this matter.

May one use a bread machine to slice bread on Shabbos?[281]

If doing so does not involve electricity it is allowed. One may even adjust the blades to fit the sizes of the slices that he desires. However, some Poskim[282] are stringent in this matter.

May one use the above vessels to grind the item to large pieces?

Some Poskim[283] rule it is permitted to do so. Some[284] write one may not use a vegetable chopper even with its large set of blades due to that it is also at times used with its small set of blades, and hence contains Uvdin Dechol.

May one use a vegetable chopper with a large set of blades?

Some Poskim[285] rule it is permitted to do so. Some[286] write one may not use a vegetable chopper even with its large set of blades due to that it is also at times used with its small set of blades, and hence contains Uvdin Dechol. If, however, the chopper has only a single set of large blades, it is permitted to be used for all foods, being it does not cut into small pieces.[287] However some Poskim[288] are stringent in this matter.

E. Cutting nonfood items into very small pieces:[289]

Even if one is not meticulous on the sizes, if he cuts [wood] into very thin pieces in order to light up a fire [with them], then he is liable for [the] grinding [prohibition].

Practical Summary-Cutting foods to small pieces:

Foods may only be cut small if either:

    A. They have already been previously ground,

        or

    B. Have never been previously ground but do not grow on the ground, and are edible in their current state, and are not used as a spice. [Those that are accustomed to cut very small those foods that grow from the ground and are not a spice have upon whom to rely if they do so right before the meal. However, it is best to be stringent to cut the pieces slightly large. According to all it is forbidden to cut such foods much time prior to the meal.]

    ➢ In all cases they may only be cut using vessels that are not designated for cutting small.

---

[279] Igros Moshe 4:74-4; Koveitz Mibeis Levi 8:16; SSH"K 6:3; Piskeiy Teshuvos 321:13; Shabbos Kehalacha 321:20
[280] Beir Moshe 1:38; Mishneh Halachos 5:53
[281] SHH"K 6:11
[282] Beir Moshe 1:38; Mishneh Halachos 5:53
[283] Igros Moshe 4:74-4
[284] Piskeiy Teshuvos 321 footnote 142
[285] Igros Moshe 4:74-4
[286] Piskeiy Teshuvos 321 footnote 142
[287] See Igros Moshe 4:74-4; Koveitz Mibeis Levi 8:16; SSH"K 6:3; Piskeiy Teshuvos 321:13; Shabbos Kehalacha 321:20
[288] Beir Moshe 1:38; Mishneh Halachos 5:53
[289] Admur 314:16

THE LAWS OF KNEADING

Shulchan Aruch Chapter 321 Halacha 16

TRANSLATION OF 321/16

Halacha 16

Kneading is one of the principal Shabbos prohibited actions.

[Two opinions exist regarding the definition of kneading, and the mixtures which are considered kneaded.]

The first opinion:

The Biblical definition of kneading: One does not Biblically transgress kneading by placing water into flour alone, but rather must knead them together as is done during the week.

Mixtures that are not allowed to be kneaded Biblically: One only Biblically transgresses kneading with materials which are kneadable, such as [adding water to] flour or earth used for bricks of a building. However, ash and course sand and crushed grain and parched flour and the like are not kneadable materials, and thus one who kneads them [with water] does not transgress a Biblical prohibition.

Rabbinical prohibitions:

Roasted flour: Nevertheless, it is Rabbinically forbidden to knead a lot of roasted flour [into a thick batter[4156]], as this may lead one to come to knead non-roasted flour and he will transgress a Biblical prohibition.

However, one is allowed to knead the roasted flour little by little as this is considered a change from the way it is normally done during the week [and one will thus not come to forget and also knead regular flour]. (Furthermore, even if he kneads it into a thick and course mixture and thus appears like kneading [nevertheless] it is permitted being that he is kneading with an irregularity.)

Thick flour/Shesisa: However, grains which have not yet grown a third [of their growth] and have been roasted, and then ground thickly, having structure like sand, being called *shetisa*, may be kneaded with vinegar and the like even a lot at a time so long as one kneads it into a thin batter.

However [to knead it into] a thick batter is forbidden [to do a lot at a time even if one does so with an irregularity] as it appears like kneading. (However, if kneaded a little at a time it is permitted [to be made even into a thick batter] as was explained by roasted [flour].)

Even [when kneading] a thin batter, when making a lot at a time, one must do so slightly differently than the way it is normally done [as will be explained now].

The definition of a "different way than usual" when making a lot at a time[4157]: [This depends on how the mixture is normally made in one's area]. If in one's areas during the week the custom is that the vinegar is placed first [and then the flour is placed], then [on Shabbos] one first places the flour/shesisa [in the bowl] and then afterwards places the vinegar.

In a place they are accustomed to place the flour first [and then the vinegar], on Shabbos one first places the vinegar in [and then the flour].

The second opinion:

There are those which argue on all the above and hold that:

Mixtures that are Biblically not allowed to be kneaded: There is no difference between materials which are kneadable and materials which are not kneadable, and by all the materials one is Biblically liable by simply placing water into them or one of the other liquids and fruits juices [when making a thick batter as will be explained below].

The Biblical definition of kneading: [One Biblically transgresses kneading by even just placing water or another liquid or fruit juice into any material] even if one does not knead them at all, as the placing of the water is itself the kneading. However [this only applies if the amount of liquid placed will make a thick batter of the material, however] by a thin batter there is no Biblical Prohibition of kneading at all.

[4156] Ketzos Hashulchan 130:2. However when kneading it to a thin mixture it is allowed, as stated in the second opinion below.

[4157] However, when making it little by little, then this itself is considered an irregularity, as explained above.

Rabinically Forbidden and Totally permitted: However, Rabbinically [even a thin batter is forbidden from being made] unless it is done differently than the way it is normally done as was explained above, in which case the sages permitted it to be done if it is needed on Shabbos, whether the material is kneadable and whether the material is not kneadable.

Thus, both roasted flour and *Shesisa* are forbidden to have liquid placed in them on Shabbos even if one does so in a different way than is normally done, unless it is made into a thin batter. In such a case the thin batter may be done in a different way than normal, such as to first places the flour/shesisa in the bowl and then place the vinegar in an area that this is different than usual, or the opposite in a place that the opposite is considered a different way [as explained above].

Kneading a lot at a time: When placing the [material] in an irregular way it is permitted to knead even a lot at a time being that it is being made into a thin batter.

If water was placed in the mixture from before Shabbos: However, a thick batter is forbidden [to be made] in all circumstances due to it is considered kneading, unless one already placed the liquid [in the flour and the like] from before Shabbos in which case it is permitted [according to this opinion] to knead it on Shabbos [little by little] whether with roasted flour or with Shesisa.

If water was kneaded into the mixture from before Shabbos: [Even] according to the first opinion mustard which one kneaded from before Shabbos is allowed to be mixed with liquids the next day [on Shabbos] whether by hand or with a spoon[4158]. One may have honey placed in it so long as one does not mix it strongly and rather mixes it little by little [I.e. slowly][4159].

Supplement
The remainder of this Halacha was lost from the text. The following is the Final Ruling of Admur in Chapter 324 Halacha 3

The Final Ruling: One should be stringent like the second opinion, and so is the custom [to not place water into even un-kneadable material in a way that if mixed will knead into a thick mixture, even with an irregularity. Although to make a thin batter is permitted to make even with kneadable materials as long as one does so with an irregularity[4160].]

Translation 324/3
Kneading course flour for animals on Shabbos:
Biblically: It was already explained in chapter 321 [Halacha 16] that coarse grain is not a kneadable product and if it is kneaded on Shabbos there are opinions which say that he is Biblically exempt [from the transgression].

Rabbinically: Nevertheless, it is Rabbinically forbidden to knead coarse grain for an animal or chickens as is done during the week, and rather one must implore in irregularity [in the kneading process].

The definition of an irregularity is: Such as to knead it little by little as was explained there, or even a lot at a time although taking care to not mix it with one's hands after placing the water in it as is the usual way that one mixes it during the week. Rather one is to mix it with a large serving spoon or a stick which contains a horizontal piece of wood on it, even many times until it mixes well. This is considered an irregularity since he is not mixing it with his hands and is not circling the spoon or wooden stick in its usual form as done during the week, but rather is mixing it by pushing it horizontally and vertically; therefore, this is considered a complete irregularity.

It is as well permitted to pour it from vessel to vessel until it mixes well.

[4158] However, the Ketzos Hashulchan brings from the Mishneh
[4159] This is required because even further kneading a material that was kneaded before Shabbos is Rabbinically forbidden unless done with an irregularity. [Ketzos Hashulchan 130 footnote 13]
[4160] Based on Ketzos Hashulchan 130:2

Mixing a lot at a time: It is permitted to mix the course flour in this method even a lot at a time, in accordance to the amount that his animals need, and separates the mixture into many different vessels and places it in front of each animal.

[However] according to the opinion which holds that one who kneads course flour is Biblically liable even by simply placing water into it, without kneading it, as [they hold] that the placing of the water is defined as kneading, as was explained there, then it is forbidden to place water into course flour on Shabbos even using an irregularity, unless the water was placed in from before Shabbos in which case kneading it on Shabbos does not contain a Biblical prohibition but rather a Rabbinical prohibition, which was permitted through making it with an irregularity in this form explained above.

It was already explained there that one is to be stringent like the latter opinion and so is the custom.

Chapter 473 Halacha 34
How to make Charoses on Shabbos:

[The Charoses may be made on Yom Tov, with exception to] when Yom Tov falls on Shabbos, [in which case] one must make it before Shabbos. If one forgot to do so, he may make it on Shabbos [into a very thin batter[4161]] with an irregularity, which is defined as first place the wine in the vessel and then the Charoses, and to mix it with one's hand or with the vessel itself, through shaking it.

[4161] See above Halacha 16. So also rules Ketzos Hashulchan 130 footnote 9, and explained that this is what Admur meant when saying to look in chapter 321. So rules also the Mishneh Berurah 321:64

COMPILATION OF HALACHAS SUMMARIES AND Q&A

Introduction:

Kneading is one of the Biblically forbidden Shabbos labors. There is a dispute dating back to the Talmud, which is likewise disputed in the codifiers, as to what constitutes kneading and as to which materials are forbidden to be kneaded. The rule is that we are stringent like all opinions.[4162] It is incumbent for the learner to read the summary being that many details regarding the final Halacha are based on rulings mentioned in other places of Admur, as the current Halacha was partially omitted. The summary is based on the noted Sefer "Ketzos Hashulchan."

Definition of Lash:

The Melacha of Lash only becomes applicable if the following conditions are fulfilled. If these conditions are not fulfilled, then the prohibition does not apply.

1. One is uniting two substances together. Mixing a single substance into itself is not defined as Lash and is permitted. See Halacha 1 Q&A regarding if mixing a single food into its natural liquid is defined as Lash [dispute] and whether mixing two pieces of the same food is defined as lash [dispute]
2. The two substances are united with each other through moisture, and stick and bond to form one item.[4163]
3. Whether one of the substances must be a liquid and the second a solid, or even if both are solids or creams-see Q&A [dispute].

The three types of materials:[4164]

1. Bar Gibul: Biblical material according to all.
2. Eino Bar Gibul: Biblical material according to many; Rabbinical material according to some
3. No attachment: No prohibition at all.

The three types of kneading results:[4165]

1. Belila Ava: Biblical according to all.
2. Belila Raka: Rabbinical according to some
3. Very Raka: No prohibition at all.

Kneading is one of the principal Shabbos prohibited actions that was done in the Mishkan.[4166] [Two opinions exist regarding what is the definition of kneading, and what mixtures are considered to be kneaded.]

[4162] Ketzos Hashulchan 130 footnote 1

[4163] Michaber 340:12; SSH"K 8:4; Shabbos Kehalacha 22:4

[4164] See Piskeiy Teshuvos 321:18

[4165] See Piskeiy Teshuvos 321:18

[4166] 321:16; Shabbos 73a; M"B 321:50; This Melacha occurred with the dyes in the Mishkan [Rashi ibid] However some write it occurred with the Menachos and Chavitim. [Yerushalmi, recorded in Iglei Tal Lash]

1. The definition of kneading: The liquid-Placing liquid in a food or mixing it in?[4167]

First opinion:[4168] One does <u>not</u> Biblically transgress kneading by placing water [**See Q&A regarding other liquids**] into flour alone, but rather one must knead them together as is done during the week.[4169] [This applies whether the material is defined as kneadable or un-kneadable material.[4170] Nevertheless, even according to this opinion, there is a Rabbinical prohibition to add water to kneadable materials, and it is only permitted to do so to un-kneadable materials.[4171]]

Second Opinion:[4172] [One Biblically transgresses kneading by even just placing water or another liquid or fruit juice into any material] even if one does not knead them at all, as the placing of the water is itself the kneading.[4173] However [this only applies to if the amount of liquid placed will make a thick batter of the material however] by a thin batter there is no Biblical Prohibition of kneading at all.

The Final Ruling:[4174] One should be stringent like the second opinion, and so is the custom. [As well, in cases that the second opinion is lenient, we are stringent like the first opinion.[4175]]

Placing sesame seeds into liquids on Shabbos: One who places flax or sesame seeds into water and the like is liable for kneading [**according to all opinions**[4176]] being that they [the water and the seed] mix and stick to each other.[4177] However one may place sesame and nuts into honey [**See Q&A regarding mixing it**], although he may not [gather them[4178] and] separate them with his hands [as doing so is considered separating[4179]].[4180]

Washing oneself with bran:[4181] It is permitted to wash one's hands with bran on Shabbos[4182] being that [although] doing so involves kneading [it is considered done] with an irregularity.[4183]

[4167] Admur 321:16

[4168] Admur ibid; Rebbe Yossi Bar Rebbe Yehudah in Shabbos 18a, Rambam 21:33; Rif 67; Rosh 24:3; Razah; Ramban; Ran; Or Zarua; Rokeiach; Michaber 321:14 which allows kneading with Shinuiy items that are not Bar Gibul, hence proving he holds like Rebbe Yossi and Rambam [M"A 321:18; P"M 321 A"A 18] Michaber 324:3; See M"B 321:50 and Shaar Hatziyon ibid

Chiyuv only on Grogeres of flour: According to this opinion the Shiur Chiyuv for Lash is a Grogeres of the material, without taking the liquid into the Shiur. [Iglei Tal Lash 9; Avnei Nezer 125; See Mosach Hashabbos Mitzvah 32:10]

[4169] The reason: As the Lash prohibition is against uniting the pieces of the material to each other and not against uniting the water ingredient with the flour ingredient. [Iglei Tal Lash 9:12-13]

[4170] Admur ibid that according to this opinion one does not transgress at all by non-Bar Gibul material even if he kneads it; Rambam 21:33; Rif 67; Rashi; See Shabbos 18a

Other opinions by material that is not kneadable-Not Bar Gibul: Some Poskim rule that the above leniency of Rebbe Yossi applies only if the material is kneadable material, such as flour, while if it is not kneadable material, then even Rebbe Yossi agrees it is forbidden to even place water. [Tosafus 18a; Rosh Beitza 4; Raavad ibud; Ramban 156a; Rashba 156a; brought in M"A 321:19; M"B 321:50; This opinion is not mentioned in Michaber or Admur ibid-see P"M 321 A"A 19; Shabbos Kehalacha 22 Biurim 13]

[4171] P"M 321 A"A 19; Biur Halacha 324:3 "Ein Govlin"; M"B 321:57; Iglei Tal Lash 9:20; Maggid Mishneh on Rambam ibid

[4172] Admur ibid; Michaber 321:16 and 324:3 in name of Yeish Omrim; Rebbe Yehudah Hanassi in Shabbos ibid; Sefer Haterumah 220; Yireim [Eliezer of Mitz; Semag 65; Smak 281; Hagahos Maimanis; See M"B ibid and Shaar Hatziyon ibid

Un-kneadable materials: Some Poskim rule that the above leniency of Rebbe Yossi applies only if the material is kneadable material, such as flour, while if it is not kneadable material, then even Rebbe Yossi agrees it is forbidden to even place water. [Tosafus 18a; Rosh Beitza 4; Raavad ibid; Ramban 156a; Rashba 156a; brought in M"A 321:19; M"B 321:50; This opinion is not mentioned in Michaber or Admur ibid-see P"M 321 A"A 19; Shabbos Kehalacha 22 Biurim 13]

Chiyuv only on Grogeres of dough: According to this opinion the Shiur Chiyuv for Lash is a Grogeres of dough, thus taking the liquid into the Shiur. [Iglei Tal Lash 9; Avnei Nezer 125; See Mosach Hashabbos Mitzvah 32:10]

[4173] The reason: As the Lash prohibition is against uniting the water ingredient with the flour ingredient, and this is accomplished by merely adding the water to the flour. [Iglei Tal Lash 9:12-13]

[4174] Admur 324:3; Darkei Moshe 324:1; Bach 324; Rama 321:16 and 324:3; M"A 321:19 regarding non-Bar Gibul;

[4175] See Next Halacha Q&A there! See below Q&A for an example of such a case where the second opinion would be lenient.

[4176] Meaning even according to the first opinion mentioned above one is liable in such a case, as stated explicitly in Rambam that one is liable for kneading in such a case despite that he himself rules like the first opinion.

The reason: As by these foods the final result of a united item is achieved simply through adding water even without any kneading in the process. [See P"M 321 M"Z 12; Iglei Tal Lash 9:18; See Shabbos Kehalacha 22:27 for a thorough discussion on this matter]

[4177] Admur 340:16; Michaber 340:12; Rambam 8; Zevachim 94b

[4178] Mishneh Berurah on 319:66

[4179] Mishneh Berurah on 340:39, as well as doing so contains the kneading prohibition [Ketzos Hashulchan 130 footnote 18]

[4180] Admur 319:27; Michaber 319:17 and 340:11; See Shabbos Kehalacha 22:27

[4181] Admur 326:9

[4182] Admur ibid; Michaber 326:10; Mordechai Remez 325

[4183] Admur ibid; Rama 326:10

The reason this is allowed:[4184] Now, although one is to be stringent not to knead on Shabbos [a thick mixture even] with an irregularity unless one placed the water in the mixture from before Shabbos as was explained in chapter 321 [Halacha 16], nevertheless here since he is not actually placing water into the bran and rather is merely taking the bran with wet hands it is permitted according to all [opinions].

Summary:
Any mixture which contains the kneading prohibition is forbidden to have the liquid placed inside the mixture, even if one does not plan to mix it.

Q&A

Are we also stringent like the first opinion in cases that there is a kneading prohibition only according to their opinion?[4185]
Yes. We are stringent like both opinions. For an example of a case where the first opinion is strict over the second opinion- See Q&A below, and footnote there!

May one place kneadable food into liquid [as opposed to liquid into food] according to the second opinion?[4186]
No, it makes no difference which ingredient one places first.

May one place sesame seeds/almonds and the like into honey on Shabbos?[4187]
One may place <u>whole</u> almonds/sesame into honey, although one may <u>not</u> knead them into the honey. Ground sesame or almonds may not ever be placed into honey.

May one place moist sushi on sesame seeds?
If this will cause the sesame seeds to stick to each other, it is forbidden to do so due to kneading. If however it is a mere coating which is spread apart, or there is not enough liquid on the sushi to cause the sesame to stick, it is permitted.

May one pour milk into cereal?[4188]
<u>Leaving the cereal in the milk until it becomes a glob</u>: Doing so is forbidden due to the above law.

May one touch a food that has a kneading prohibition with wet hands?
Yes, as stated above regarding bran.
<u>Dish detergent</u>:[4189] May be used with a large amount of water, so as not to transgress the kneading prohibition. Likewise, one may rub it onto the dishes using wet hands and then wash it off.

Adding a lot of water to the mixture:
Is permitted if it is like a drink, as this is not considered Lash according to any opinion.

[4184] Admur ibid; M"A 326:10; M"B 326:28; See Biur Halacha 326:9 "Lirchotz Yadav"
[4185] Ketzos Hashulchan 130 footnote 1 and 8
[4186] Iglei Tal Lash 9:18; Ketzos Hashulchan 130 footnote 2
[4187] Ketzos Hashulchan 130:5 and footnote 17 and 18
[4188] Shabbos Kehalacha 22:57; Nishmas Shabbos p. 343; Piskeiy Teshuvos 321:28-6
[4189] Piskeiy Teshuvos 323:5

General Q&A on the definition of kneading

The ingredients that contain Lash

Does kneading a single ingredient into itself without any liquid contain a kneading prohibition?[4190]

The kneading prohibition only applies when one kneads two substances into each other to join and they become one substance. It does not apply when kneading a single food into itself. Nevertheless, one must beware that he does not transgress a grinding prohibition in the process, as explained in "The laws of grinding".

Does mashing a banana and the like contain a kneading prohibition?[4191]

No. Nevertheless mashing contains a grinding prohibition and may only be done in ways explained in "The laws of Grinding"-See There!

Is mixing two dry solids together defined as Lash?[4192]
No.

May one mix sugar with cocoa powder?[4193]

So long as no water is added this is allowed as the substances do not stick to each other and is thus not considered kneading.

Is mixing two solids or semi-liquids together defined as Lash if they unite and become one?[4194]

<u>Dough with dough/bread with bread</u>: Some Poskim[4195] rule the kneading prohibition does not apply in such a case Other Poskim[4196] however question that perhaps the kneading prohibition applies even in such a case.

<u>Semi-liquids such as cheese with honey</u>: Some Poskim[4197] rule the kneading prohibition does not apply in such a case. Other Poskim[4198] however question that perhaps the kneading prohibition applies even in such a case.

Does the kneading prohibition also apply when adding liquids other than water into a mixture?[4199]

Yes. It applies by all liquidly substances such as oil, honey, soy sauce, cream cheese, butter,

---

[4190] Tehila Ledavid 321:29; 252:46 "Mashing a single food does not contain Lash or Tochein, as the food was a single substance and has remained a single substance"; SSH"K 8:3; See Chazon Ish 58:9; Igros Moshe 4:74 Tochein 2; Shevisas Hashabbos Hakdama Lash 8:6-9; Shabbos Kehalacha 22:6-7

<u>Other opinions</u>: However some opinions are stringent in this matter. [Bris Olam Lash]

[4191] SSH"K 8:3

[4192] Michaber 340:12; SSH"K 8:4; Shabbos Kehalacha 22:4

[4193] SSH"K 8:5

[4194] Shabbos Kehalacha 22:49; Piskeiy Teshuvos 321:24-25

[4195] Shevisas Hashabbos Lash 8-9 as one is not uniting two different species of foods; Orchos Shabbos 6:20; Nishmas Shabbos 321:306; Igros Moshe 4:74-13; Chut Hashani 13:2 as the kneading prohibition only applies when mixing a liquid with many solids to join and become one solid.

[4196] Rav SZ"A 8 footnote 13 as perhaps the prohibition applies anytime one unites two pieces together through moisture.

[4197] Orchos Shabbos 6:20; Nishmas Shabbos 321:306; Igros Moshe 4:74-13; Chut Hashani 13:2 as the kneading prohibition only applies when mixing a liquid with many solids to join and become one solid; See Ketzos Hashulchan 130 footnote 12 regarding lentils.

[4198] Shevisas Hashabbos Lash 11; Rav SZ"A 8 footnote 13 as perhaps the prohibition applies anytime one unites two pieces together through moisture.

[4199] Admur 321:16 in second opinion "water or one of the other liquids or fruit juice"; M"B 321:50; Ketzos Hashulchan 130:1 and SSH"K 8:1

<u>Other opinions</u>: Some Poskim rule the kneading prohibition only applies with the seven liquids that contract Tuma.

fruit juices.

Does the kneading prohibition apply against mixing a foods own liquids into that food?

- Ground garlic:[4200] For example ground garlic which has secreted liquids may one mix that liquid into the garlic on Shabbos? If the garlic was ground on Shabbos in a permitted way it is forbidden to mix in its extracted liquids on Shabbos.[4201] If however one crushed the garlic before Shabbos, it is permitted to knead in the liquid on Shabbos using an irregularity, such as one's finger or doing slowly with a spoon.[4202]
- Peanut oil:[4203] It is permitted to slowly mix with a spoon[4204] oil which floats on top of peanut butter into the peanut butter.[4205]
- Tuna oil: May one mix tuna with its oil? One may mix the oil into the tuna with an irregularity[4206], doing so slowly even with a spoon.[4207]

If adding liquid to the food will thin it out, as is common to occur when adding liquid to certain pastes, such as peanut butter, is there a kneading prohibition involved?

Some Poskim[4208] rule that if the material was not kneaded before Shabbos with an external liquid [as opposed to its own moisture] then it is forbidden to do so. Other Poskim[4209] rule it is permitted to do so. Practically, one is to be stringent in this matter.[4210]

[4200] Ketzos Hashulchan 130:3 footnote 8 in name of Igleiy Tal

[4201] This matter follows the same dispute as mentioned above.
According to the first opinion mentioned, doing so is considered kneading and is thus forbidden. The reason for this is because according to the first opinion the prohibition of kneading is simply to join two items into one, which is accomplished even when kneading food with its own liquid. However according to the second opinion doing so is not considered kneading and would thus be permitted. The reason for this is because they hold that the main aspect of kneading is the adding of ingredients, and here no ingredients were added, as the food naturally came with it.
The final ruling: As was explained above we are stringent like both opinions, and thus this may not be done.

[4202] M"B 321:62 in the name of the Magen Avraham 321:22 that when mixing in the original liquid that was placed before Shabbos a spoon may be used even according to the Rama.

[4203] So rules SSH"K 8:7

[4204] M"B [62] in the name of the Magen Avraham [22] that when mixing in the original liquid that was placed before Shabbos a spoon may be used even according to the Rama.

[4205] This is allowed to be done being that the butter is considered to have been kneaded from before Shabbos with its oil of which some still remains within the mixture, of which the law is that one may add its liquid to it on Shabbos, as will be explained in Halacha 5. [SSH"K ibid]
Adding in other liquids: SSH"K ibid allows one to add other liquids as well to the peanut butter based on their understanding [in Biur Halacha 321 Yachol Learvo"] that adding liquid is allowed when one intends to make a food thinner as, kneading only applies when one desires to thicken the food. Vetzaruch Iyun Gadol from what will be explained in Practical Q&A, as well as in Halacha 5 Q&A, that the mixing of a foods own liquid before Shabbos does not consider it mixed, and thus there would remain no allowance to enter other liquids into the peanut butter. Furthermore the ruling there in Biur Halacha is referring to adding water to an already kneaded food as then one destroys the kneading that was already done, and does not apply when a food was never yet kneaded. This is in addition to that SSH"K contradict themselves later regarding Tehina, that one may not add liquids to it. See also Ketzos Hashulchan 130 footnote 19 which brings up such a logic that thinning a food is not considered kneading, although he concludes one may not rely on this as we see even by radishes the Taz was stringent to require a Shinui.
Despite the above to enter the peanut oil into the butter would be allowed even in accordance to the ruling there as according to both opinions there once the oil has been mixed into it before Shabbos, entering back its own oil is not problematic-see there!

[4206] As the oil was already placed within the tuna from before Shabbos, and tuna is not a kneadable material. [See Halacha 4 and Q&A there]

[4207] M"B [62] in the name of the Magen Avraham [22] that when mixing in the original liquid that was placed before Shabbos a spoon may be used even according to the Rama.

[4208] Ketzos Hashulchan 130 footnote 19; SSH"K regarding Techina however see SSH"K 8:7 who allows adding other liquids to the food even if it was not mixed with external liquid before Shabbos; See Tehila Ledavid 321:21 that so is ruling according to Rebbe Yehuda, brought in Michaber 321:16; Piskeiy Teshuvos 321:25
Background:
SSH"K ibid allows one to add other liquids as well to the peanut butter based on their understanding [in Biur Halacha 321 Yachol Learvo"] that adding liquid is allowed when one intends to make a food thinner as, kneading only applies when one desires to thicken the food. Vetzaruch Iyun Gadol from what will be explained in Practical Q&A, as well as in Halacha 5 Q&A, that the mixing of a foods own liquid before Shabbos does not consider it mixed, and thus there would remain no allowance to enter other liquids into the peanut butter. Furthermore the ruling there in Biur Halacha is referring to adding water to an already kneaded food as then one destroys the kneading that was already done, and does not apply when a food was never yet kneaded. This is in addition to that SSH"K contradict themselves later regarding Tehina, that one may not add liquids to it. See also Ketzos Hashulchan 130 footnote 19 which

Does the kneading prohibition apply to foods which do not grow from the ground?
Some Poskim[4211] rule it applies even to foods that do not grow on the ground, such as fish and meat and eggs. Other Poskim[4212] rule it does not apply to foods that do not grow on the ground.

Does the kneading prohibition apply to non-foods?[4213]
Yes.

Does the Lisha prohibition apply to baked foods?
Some Poskim[4214] rule that according to some[4215] opinions the Biblical kneading prohibition does not apply to baked or cooked foods.[4216] Nevertheless, even according to this opinion it remains Rabbinically forbidden to do so, and thus may only be done with the irregularities listed by the Sages.[4217] Practically, even baked products must follow the regular kneading rules and hence may only be made into a thin mixture following the irregularities listed by the Sages.[4218] This applies even if the baked product was previously kneaded with water prior to the baking.[4219]

What mixtures of soilds with liquids are defined as kneading?[4220]
The kneading prohibition only applies when the two substances are being mixed in a way that they join and stick to each other forming one entity, as is the case with dough which is a mixture of flour and water, or with cooked oatmeal. Thus, whenever solids are large enough to prevent this form of unity in their mixture, and it is rather that the liquid coats over the solids, or that the solids are submerged within the liquids, then it is allowed.

May one knead food right before a meal, as is allowed with Borer and cutting food small?[4221]
Doing so right before the meal does not make the laws any more lenient. This is unlike the laws of Borer and cutting food small which may be done right before a meal with certain conditions, as explained in their sections.

---

brings up such a logic that thinning a food is not considered kneading, although he concludes one may not rely on this as we see even by radishes the Taz was stringent to require a Shinui. Despite the above to enter the peanut oil into the butter would be allowed even in accordance to the ruling there as according to both opinions there once the oil has been mixed into it before Shabbos, entering back its own oil is not problematic-see there!
[4209] Or Letziyon 2:33-7; Many Rabbanim including Yalkut Yosef; Rav Avraham Yosef; Rav Dov Lior; as the liquid simply dilutes the food and does not make its pieces stick together; See Michaber 321:15 as explained in P"M 321 M"Z 13 [brought in M"B 321:? and Biur Halacha ibid] that if a food was previously kneaded with its own juice it is permitted to be kneaded on Shabbos with a Shinuiy.
[4210] SSH"K 8:? regarding techina; Shabbos Kehalacha 22:60 footnote 60
[4211] Igros Moshe 4:74 Lash 13; Shevet Halevi 4:32; Piskeiy Teshuvos 321:17; See Tehila Ledavid 321:25
[4212] Halef Lecha Shlomo 139; Tzitzis Eliezer 11:36; See Tehila Ledavid 321:25
[4213] Shabbos 18a "One who mixes earth with water…"; Rambam 8:16; Shabbos Kehalacha 22 footnote 5
[4214] Biur Halacha 321:14 "Shema Yavo" in opinion of Tosafus
[4215] Tosafus Shabbos 18a; Vetzaruch Iyun if this would apply likewise according to the opinion of the Rambam. However certainly it would not apply according to the opinion of Rebbe Yehuda, as he prohibits to kenad roasted flour even with the irregularities, as brought in Shabbos 155b.
[4216] The reason: As the food is ready to be eaten in its current state, and hence adding water to it is not considered part of the Melacha of Lisha but rather as part of the eating process. [ibid]
[4217] Biur Halacha ibid
[4218] As according to Rebbe Yehuda baked products retain the Biblcial prohibition, and initially we are stringent like the opinion of Rebbe Yehuda.
[4219] Taz 321:11; Tehila Ledavid ibid; Iglei Tal ibid; Har Tzevi ibid; Ketzos Hashulchan 130 footnote 12
[4220] Taz 321:12 in name of Bach regarding lettuce; Ketzos Hashulchan 130:6 footnote 19; Shevisas Hashabbos Pesicha 20; SSH"K 8:4; Piskeiy Teshuvos 321:27
[4221] Magen Avraham 321:24; M"B 321:66; Ketzos Hashulchan 130 footnote 7; SSH"K 8:2

May one knead on Yom Tov?
It is permitted to knead on Yom Tov as one regularly does during the week.[4222] However if it is a type of food which is better in quality when kneaded before Yom Tov one may only do so on Yom Tov using an irregularity.[4223]

---

2. The definition of kneading: The solid-The mixtures that are not allowed to be kneaded:[4224]

A. First opinion:

Biblically:[4225] One only Biblically transgresses kneading with materials which are kneadable, such as flour or earth used for bricks of a building. However, ash and course sand and crushed grain and parched flour and the like are not kneadable materials, and thus one who kneads them does not transgress a Biblical prohibition.

Rabbinically-Roasted flour:[4226] It is Rabbinically forbidden to knead a lot of roasted flour [into a thick batter[4227]], as this may lead one to come to knead non-roasted flour and he will transgress a Biblical prohibition.

Kneading thick batter of Rabbinical solids a small amount at a time:[4228] However one is allowed to knead the roasted flour little by little as this is considered a change from the way it is normally done during the week [and one will thus not come to forget and also knead regular flour]. (Furthermore, even if he kneads it into a thick and course mixture and thus appears like kneading [nevertheless] it is permitted being that he is kneading with an irregularity.[4229])

Kneading Thick flour/Shesisa a lot at a time into a thin batter: Grains which have not yet grown a third [of their growth] and have been roasted, and then ground thickly, having structure like sand, and is called *shetisa*, may be kneaded with vinegar and the like even a lot at a time so long as one kneads it into a thin batter. However [to knead it into] a thick batter is forbidden [to do a lot at a time even if one does it with an irregularity] as it appears like kneading. (However, if kneaded a little at a time it is permitted [to be made even into a thick batter] as was explained by roasted [flour]).

A thin batter: Even [when kneading] a thin batter, when making a lot at a time one must do so slightly differently than the way it is normally done.

The definition of a "different way than usual": See Halacha 3

B. The second opinion:

There are those which argue on the above and hold that:

Biblically:[4230] There is no difference between materials which are kneadable and materials which

---

[4222] 495:5; SSH"K 8 in side note; Piskeiy Teshuvos 506:1

[4223] Admur rules in 495:5 that all the Melachos which are not done for many days worth, like Kneading, may be done on Yom Tov. Nevertheless, it may only be done with an irregularity, unless it was not done on Erev Yom Tov due to *Onness*, or due to it not being as fresh if it were to be done then, in which case it's permitted to do regularly on Yom Tov. In general foods which are kneaded taste better when kneaded that day as opposed to the day before. Hence Admur rules there is no implied that kneading may always be done regularly on Yom Tov. So is also implied from chapter 473 Halacha 34 that Admur does not mention any regulations regarding kneading the charoses on Yom Tov that does not fall on Shabbos. Nevertheless, in the event one is making a food that is better kneaded the day before, such as making homemade pasta, then the above ruling would apply that an irregularity is needed. [Piskeiy Teshuvos ibid]

[4224] 321:16

[4225] Admur ibid; Michaber 321:14 and 324:3; Rambam 21:33; Rashi Beitza 32b; Rif Beitza 18; Rav Yosef in Shabbos 18a according to Rebbe Yossi there is no prohibition by placing water in the dye; and Shabbos 155b that according to Rebbe Yossi one may place water in Morson, and may knead Kali with a Shinuiy; See M"B 321:50 and Shaar Hatziyon ibid

[4226] Admur ibid; Michaber 321:14; Rambam 21:33

[4227] Ketzos Hashulchan 130:2; However, when kneading it to a thin mixture it is allowed, as stated in the second opinion below.

[4228] Admur ibid; Michaber 321:14; Rav Chisda Shabbos 156a

[4229] Admur ibid; Bach; Taz 321:11; Elya Raba; M"A 321:18; M"B 321:54

[4230] Admur ibid; Michaber 321:16 and 324:3 in name of Yeish Omrim; Rebbe Yehudah Hanassi in Shabbos 18a and 155b; Sefer Haterumah 220; Yireim [Eliezer of Mitz]; Semag 65; Smak 281; Hagahos Maimanis; [The previous Poskim rule like Rebbe Yehuda. The following Poskim who generally rule like Rebbe Yossi over Rebbe Yehuda in the previous dispute, in this case rule that this ruling applies even according to Rebbe Yossi] Tosafus 18a and Beitza 32b; Rosh Beitza 4; Raavad ibid; Ramban 156a; Rashba 156a; See M"A 321:19; M"B 321:50; Abayey in Shabbos 18a according to Rebbe Yossi there is no prohibition by placing water in the dye;

are not kneadable, and by all the materials one is Biblically liable by simply placing water into them or one of the other liquids and fruits juices [when making a thick batter as will be explained below].

Rabbinically forbidden and totally permitted:[4231] However [the above only applies if the amount of liquid placed will make a thick batter of the material, however] by a thin batter there is no Biblical Prohibition of kneading at all. However, Rabbinically [even a thin batter is forbidden from being made] unless it is done differently than the way it is normally done as was explained above, in which case the sages permitted it to be done if it is needed on Shabbos, whether the material is kneadable and whether the material is not kneadable. Thus both roasted flour and *Shesisa* are forbidden to have liquid placed in them on Shabbos even if one does so in a different way than is normally done, unless it is made into a thin batter in which case it may be done in a different way than normal, such as to first places the flour/shesisa in the bowl and then place the vinegar in an area that this is different than usual, or the opposite in a place that the opposite is considered a different way [as will be explained in Halacha 3].[4232]

Kneading a lot at a time: When placing the [material] in an irregular way it is permitted to knead even a lot at a time being that it is being made into a thin batter.

A thick batter:[4233] However to make a thick batter is forbidden in all circumstances due to that it is considered kneading.

C. The Final Ruling:
The remainder of the above quoted Halacha was lost from the text. The following is the Final Ruling of Admur in Chapter 324 Halacha 3

The Final Ruling: One should be stringent like the second opinion, and so is the custom [to not place water into even un-knead able material in a way that if mixed will knead into a thick mixture, even with an irregularity. Although to make a thin batter is permitted to make even with kneadable materials as long as one does so with an irregularity[4234].]

See Q&A below regarding the definition of a thin mixture!

Summary-Placing water into food/material on Shabbos:

First Opinion: Some opinions rule that Biblical kneading only applies by kneadable materials like flour or cement. Non-kneadable materials are only Rabbinically prohibited, and if done with an irregularity, which is defined as kneading a little at a time, it is allowed to be made even into a thick mixture. Furthermore, they rule it only applies when one actually kneads the kneadable material with liquid, and does not apply when merely placing water into it without

---

brought in M"A 321:19; M"B 321:50; This opinion is not mentioned in Michaber or Admur ibid-see P"M 321 A"A 19; Shabbos Kehalacha 22 Biurim 13]

Does this ruling apply even according to Rebbe Yossi: Everyone agrees that the Lash prohibition applies even to non-Bar Gibbbul according to Rebbe Yehuda. It is disputed however in the Rishonim in whether this applies even according to Rebbe Yossi. The following Poskim rule that it applies even according to Rebbe Yossi: Tosafus 18a and Beitza 32b; Rosh Beitza 4; Raavad ibid; Ramban 156a; Rashba 156a; See M"A 321:19; M"B 321:50; Abayey in Shabbos 18a according to Rebbe Yossi there is no prohibition by placing water in the dye; brought in M"A 321:19; M"B 321:50; This opinion is not mentioned in Michaber or Admur ibid-see P"M 321 A"A 19; Shabbos Kehalacha 22 Biurim 13]

[4231] Admur ibid; Shabbos 156a; Terumos Hadeshen 53; M"A 321:24; Taz 321:12; M"B 321:66; Shaar Hatziyon 321:63

Opinion of Rama and Sefer Hateruma: From this ruling of Admur and Poskim ibid we learn that a) There is never an allowance to make a thick batter according to this opinion, even if one does so with a Shinuiy. B) Even a thin batter is only allowed with a Shinuiy. However, some Poskim understand the Rama 321:16 to rule that one may make even a thick batter with a Shinuiy [even according to this opinion]. [Taz 321:12] The Taz ibid asks this question on the Rama and concludes that one should make it only into a thin batter. However, other Poskim [M"A ibid; Admur ibid; M"B ibid] explain that in truth the intent of the Rama is only to make it into a thin batter and not a thick batter. [See P"M 321 M"Z 12; A"A 24; M"B 321:66]

[4232] The M"B [52] however rules that by roasted flour one may knead it little by little being that he holds that we do not apply the kneading prohibition by cooked foods. See Halacha 5 Q&A!

[4233] Admur ibid; Shabbos 156a; Terumos Hadeshen 53; M"A 321:24; Taz 321:12; M"B 321:66; Shaar Hatziyon 321:63

[4234] Based on Ketzos Hashulchan 130:2

kneading it.

<u>Second Opinion:</u> Others rule that Biblical kneading applies by all materials, even un-kneadable, and even if one just places water in it without actually kneading.

<u>Thin batters:</u> According to all kneading is only Biblically prohibited when the mixture is made into a thick mixture. If made into a thin batter, it is only Rabbinically prohibited and if done with an irregularity it is permitted to be done even a lot at a time.

❖ <u>The Final Ruling:</u>
We are stringent like the latter opinion and thus one may only knead liquid with material [whether knead- able or not] into a thin batter and only with an irregularity. As well one may not even simply place water into a mixture, even if he does not plan to mix it, if this will create a thick batter. Regarding the definition of an "irregularity"- See Halacha 4! Regarding adding more water to an already kneaded food-See Halacha 4.

Q&A
What is the definition of Bar Gibbul and Eino Bar Gibbul?
See Piskeiy Teshuvos chapter 321.

When permitted to knead, must one do so right before the meal?
No.[4235] However one who is stringent to do so has upon whom to base his stringency on.[4236]

Q&A on thick mixture
May one be lenient like the first opinion in a time of need to make a thick batter of un-kneadable material using a Shinuiy?[4237]
Yes, one may be lenient like the first opinion in a case that kneading the food before Shabbos would cause it to be ruined.[4238]

If mixing liquid into a food before Shabbos will ruin that food, is there room to be lenient like the first opinion to make it into a thick mixture on Shabbos?[4239]
If doing so before Shabbos would ruin the food, or make it less appetizing [even if refrigerated[4240]], than one may be lenient like the first opinion mentioned above which allows kneading into a thick mixture, with an irregularity[4241] foods which are not knead-able, such as bananas and radishes. Foods which are kneadable are forbidden to be kneaded according to all.[4242] [In all cases where one cannot knead the mixture before Shabbos it is preferable to place the liquid in the food from before Shabbos without kneading it, and then knead it on Shabbos.[4243] If, however, this too will ruin the food then one may do as stated above.[4244]]

[4235] Mishneh Berurah 321:66 based on Magen Avraham 321:24; so is implied from Admur that states that one may do even a lot at a time.
[4236] As according to the Rashba adding liquid to a food on Shabbos contains the "Make Bipatish/Finishing Touch" prohibition unless done right before the meal. See Ketzos Hashulchan 130 footnote 12
[4237] Taz 321:12; M"B 321:68 and Shaar Hatziyon 321:84; Shabbos Kehalacha 22:26 Biurim 13
[4238] The reason: As we mainly rule like Rebbe Yossi and like the Rambam's opinion in Rebbe Yossi, and it is only that we are stringent like Rebbe Yehuda and like the other Rishonim in Rebbe Yossi. [See Taz and Shabbos Kehalacha ibid]
[4239] Taz 321:12; Ketzos Hashulchan 130:6 footnote 19; SSH"K 8:11; Piskeiy Teshuvos 321:20; Shabbos Kehalacha 22:26
[4240] See Shabbos Kehalacha ibid footnote 85
[4241] Regarding the type of irregularity required, Admur brings in the first opinion that when one makes the thick batter of un-kneadable material a little at a time it is considered an irregularity. Later when he mentions kneading a thin batter he mentions the changes of the order of which food to enter, and changing in the mixing method. Vetzaruch Iyun regarding the difference of these two forms of irregularities and as in truth which irregularity should be used when being lenient to make a thick batter. In SSH"K ibid they mention doing the latter irregularity which is ruled to do for a thin batter. See Igros Moshe 4:74 Lash for a summary of the different forms of irregularities.
[4242] Piskeiy Teshuvos ibid; Shabbos Kehalacha ibid; Vetzaruch Iyun Gadol that the SSH"K does not limit this allowance only to a case that the mixture is of a non-knead-able substance!
[4243] SSH"K 8:10; Shabos Kehalacha ibid; Piskeiy Teshuvos ibid
The reason: As in this case it would be allowed according to all as will be explained in Halacha 5 –See summary there!

If one forgot to knead a food before Shabbos may he be lenient like the first opinion mentioned to make a thick mixture using an irregularity?[4245]
No.[4246]

May one ask a gentile to make a thick batter of un-keadable material?[4247]
Yes, one may ask the gentile to do so using the irregularities that the Sages required.[4248] This may be done even if it does not involve a time of need. It is however forbidden to do so with a kneadable substance.

Q&A on thin mixture
What is the definition of a thin mixture?[4249]
Some Poskim[4250] rule that it is only considered a thick mixture if made as thick as dough, while anything less than this is considered a thin mixture. Others[4251] suggest that it must be drinkable to be considered a thin mixture. Other Poskim[4252] conclude that making a mixture thinner [i.e. more watery] then it usually is made, is considered a thin mixture and may be done with an irregularity, however to make it in its normal thickness is a thick mixture and is forbidden.

Very watery mixture:[4253] If the mixture is made so thin that it can be drunk, then according to all this would be considered a thin mixture and does not even contain the concept of kneading, [unless this is the normal way that the mixture is made, such as regarding cement].

When making a thin mixture must one place all the liquid into the food simultaneously or may one place it in a little at a time?[4254]
One must place all the liquid in simultaneously.[4255]

If the adding of liquid to a certain food will at first thicken it and only after further mixing of water will it thin it out, may one make it into a thin mixture on Shabbos?[4256]
No. Thus one may not make Tehina on Shabbos into a thick mixture even if he plans to eventually thin it out with more liquid as nevertheless in the interim it thickens due to the liquids added.

[4244] SSH"K 8:10; Shabos Kehalacha ibid; Piskeiy Teshuvos ibid

[4245] Piskeiy Teshuvos 321 footnote 230

[4246] If the mixture is a kneadable substance this is forbidden according to all. If the mixture is not a kneadable substance then Tzaruch Iyun, as on the one hand why should this be any different than the previous Q&A of which we allow to knead on Shabbos if it could not have been done before Shabbos. On the other hand from Admur this does not seem to be the case, as Admur rules that the custom is to be stringent like the second opinion, as well as that regarding Charoses 473:34, as learns Ketzos Hashulchan [See Halacha 6] and M"B, one may only make the Charoses into a thin batter, and there it is discussing that one forgot to do so before Shabbos. Vetzaruch Iyun Gadol on SSH"K [8:11] which rules that even a thick batter may be made with an irregularity if one forgot to do so before Shabbos, and footnotes to the M"B regarding Charoses when the M"B himself rules as stated above that one may only be lenient to make it into a thin batter! [Piskeiy Teshuvos ibid]

[4247] Chayeh Adam 19:1; M"B 324:11; Shabbos Kehalacha 22:26; Piskeiy Teshuvos 321:20 [See there that he permits to to have the gentile place the water in on Shabbos and then have the Jew mix it with a Shinuiy-Vetzrauch Iyun Gadol, as according to Rebbe Yossi, when the Jew starts mixing it he transgresses!]

[4248] As it is permitted to ask a gentile to perform an action that is forbidden to a Jew only due to stringency. [See ??]

[4249] See Ketzos Hashulchan ibid; Chazon Ish 58:9; Piskeiy Teshuvos 321:18; Shabbos Kehalacha 22:20

[4250] Shvisas Hashabbos; Chazon Ish 58:9; Shevet Halevi 7:105; Piskeiy Teshuvos 321:18; Shabbos Kehalacha 22:20 The Chazon Ish ibid rules that the definition of a thin mixture is so long as it is thick and flowy, thus implying that a thick mixture is when it is so thick that it does not flow.

[4251] See Ketzos Hashulchan ibid in name of Shevisas Hashabbos

[4252] Ketzos Hashulchan 130 footnote 3; See Shevet Halevi 7:105

[4253] Ketzos Hashulchan 130 footnote 3; Chazon Ish 58:9

[4254] Ketzos Hashulchan 130 footnote 4, SSH"K 8:9

[4255] As otherwise during the interval of which only some of the liquid has been placed the mixture is considered a thick mixture which is forbidden to be done.

[4256] SSH"K 8:26

May one place a small amount of hot water onto food powder in order to melt it, and then place a lot of water inside?
One may not do so, unless it will turn into a thin batter with this water and is done in the irregularities stated by the Sages.

When making a drink using dissolvable powders must one do so with an irregularity?[4257]
If the powder will dissolve immediately upon adding the liquid to it, it is allowed to be made without any irregularities. [However according to some, doing so would involve a Nolad prohibition, and thus although one is allowed to be lenient, it is proper if possible to prepare this mixture from before Shabbos.[4258]]
If the powder does not dissolve right away: If the powder will not dissolve right away then if it will become a semi thick mixture in the interim of it dissolving into the liquid, some[4259] write that it may only be made with the mentioned irregularities. Others[4260] however write that it may be made regularly even in such a case.

May one make a protein shake?
There are many recipes for protein shakes, and hence the Halacha would depend on the type of shake one is making. One may not make the shake into a thick batter if using oatmeal or other grain, and must do so with the mentioned irregularities when making it into a thin batter. When using a thick liquid, such as honey, syrup, eggs, thick whey protein and the like one is to avoid mixing the liquids together very quickly.

3. The definition of an "irregularity":[4261]
The Sages permitted for one to knead a Rabbinical kneading mixture if one uses certain irregularities in the kneading process. One may thus knead all materials into a thin batter, using these irregularities. Likewise, in a time of need one may even make a thick batter of un-kneadable materials, using these irregularities. The following law will discuss the details of these irregularities, and which one's are valid, and how many of them are required to permit kneading a Rabbinical mixture on Shabbos:
There are four different irregularities mentioned in the Gemara and Shulchan Aruch:
1. Kneading a little at a time.
2. Switching order of the foods.
3. Mixing with a finger or the back of a spoon or fork.
4. Making vertical and horizontal strokes with a spoon.

A. Mixing a little at a time:
Kneading a very small amount at a time is defined as a valid form of irregularity.[4262] It is a valid irregularity both for thick batters [which is permitted with un-kneadable materials in a time of need] and thin batters.[4263] One who uses this form of irregularity is not required to perform any of the other forms of irregularities mentioned below.[4264]

[4257] SSH"K 8:18; Piskeiy Teshuvos 321:28-1; Shabbos Kehalacha 22:37
[4258] As rules Rav Farkash with regards to instant coffee. See The laws of cooking Halacha 12 Q&A there!
[4259] SSH"K 8:18
[4260] Rav SZ"A in SSH"K 8 footnote 61; Igros Moshe 4:74-1; Menuchas Ahava 2:9 footnote 52; Otzros Hashabbos 22; Shabbos Kehalacha 22:37
[4261] Admur 321:16; 324:3; 473:34; Michaber 321:14-16; 324:3; Shabbos 156a; See Igros Moshe 4:74 Lash 9 and Shabbos Kehalacha 22:14 for a summary and explanation behind the different forms of irregularities.
[4262] Admur 321:16 and 324:3 and Michaber 321:14 and Shabbos ibid regarding a thick batter of roasted flour;
[4263] Derisha 321:3; Tehila Ledavid 321:22 and 25; Piskeiy Teshuvos 321:21; Shabbos Kehalacha 22:19
[4264] Derisha 321:3; Tehila Ledavid 321:22 and 25; Piskeiy Teshuvos 321:21; Shabbos Kehalacha 22:19

Q&A
What is the definition of a little at a time?[4265]
One is to make a smaller amount than usual[4266], and it is to be made to eat right away.[4267]
Some[4268] write one may make as much as one desires for the need of that meal. Practically, it is
best to only make a small amount to enter right away into one's mouth[4269], or alternatively to
make a recognizably smaller amount than usual to be eaten right away.[4270]

B. Changing the order of how the food and liquid are usually placed in:[4271]

Changing the order of how the food is normally kneaded is considered a valid form of irregularity
for the mixing of thin batters [and thick batters of unkneadable materials in a time of need[4272]].
[This irregularity is referred to as "Mi Techila".[4273] It however does not suffice to perform this
irregularity alone, and in addition, one must also perform one of the irregularities to be
enumerated in C.[4274] The above requirement of irregularities only applies when making a lot of
kneaded food simultaneously, one however who does only a very small amount at a time is not
required to perform any of these irregularities, as explained in A.[4275]]

Other opinions: Some Poskim rule that in addition to this irregularity, one must also do the irregularity of changing the form of mixing. [Aruch Hashulchan 321:20; See Biur Halacha "Shema"]
To note however that this form of change was only required if one were to make a lot at a time. If, however, one were to make a little at a time, then that itself [the fact that he is only making a little at a time] is considered an irregularity. [See Halacha 2A above, as well as 324:3 in the first opinion] Vetzaruch Iyun why this option of making a little at a time was not mentioned in the second opinion [neither here nor in 324:3] as well as with regards to Charoses [brought below Halacha 5]. As well Tzaruch Iyun why this option of irregularity was not mentioned either by the Ketzos Hashulchan or SSH"K. Seemingly this option does not hold true in accordance to the second opinion as it only helps when making an item into a thick batter, which is always forbidden according to the second opinion, Vetzaruch Iyun. See Igros Moshe 4:74 Lash for a summary of the different forms of irregularities.
[4265] Shabbos Kehalacha 22:23; Piskeiy Teshuvos 321:20 footnote 224
[4266] Implication of Admur 324:3 which defines "Meat Meat" as a Shinuiy, and hence if he makes the same amount as normally done, how would this be a Shinuiy; Piskeiy Teshuvos ibid; Shabbos Kehalacha ibid; Orchos Shabbos 6 p. 234; See M"B 321:54 that the Poskim did not define the Shiur of "Meat Meat" and that even if it has a Shiur of Grogeres; See Biur Halacha 321 "Shema"
[4267] Biur Halacha "Shema"; Piskeiy Teshuvos ibid; Shabbos Kehalacha ibid
[4268] Tehila Ledavid 321:25
[4269] Shabbos Kehalacha ibid; Piskeiy Teshuvos ibid
[4270] Shabbos Kehalacha ibid
[4271] Admur 321:16; Michaber 321:14; Shabbos ibid
Roasted flour: Some Poskim rule that the irregularity of Mi Techila is invalid for roasted flour, even when making it onto a thin mixture, and the only allowance is to do so in a form of little by little. [Rambam brought in Tehila Ledavid 321:24]
[4272]
Regarding the type of irregularity required, Admur brings in the first opinion that when one makes the thick batter of un-kneadable material a little at a time it is considered an irregularity. Later when he mentions kneading a thin batter he mentions the changes of the order of which food to enter, and changing in the mixing method. Vetzaruch Iyun regarding the difference of these two forms of irregularities and as in truth which irregularity should be used when being lenient to make a thick batter. In SSH"K 8:11 they mention doing the later irregularity which is ruled to do for a thin batter. See Igros Moshe 4:74 Lash for a summary of the different forms of irregularities.
[4273] Tehila Ledavid 321:19; Shabbos Kehalacha 22 Biurim 7
[4274] Admur 473:34 regarding making Charoses; Rama 321:16; M"A 321:24; Taz 321:12; Terumos Hadeshen 53 brought in Beis Yosef 321; Or Zarua, brought in Biur Halacha "Veyeish Omrim"; Mordechai, brought in Beis Yosef; M"B 321:57 and 68; Ketzos Hashulchan 130:3 and footnote 9; Kaf Hachaim 321:111; Shabbos Kehalacha 22:14-Biurim 7; Piskeiy Teshuvos 321:21; Toras Hamelachos Lash 16
The reason: As one is required to perform a Shinuiy according to the Lisha definition of both Rebbe Yehuda and Rebbe Yossi, in both the placing of the liquid and the actual kneading. [Terumos Hadeshen ibid; See Iglei Tal Lash 30:14] Alternatively, the reason is because it is forbidden to mix the mixture very forcefully, and hence one requires an irregularity in the actual mixing so he not come to mix it strongly. [Or Zarua as explained in Chazon Ish ibid] Alternatively, the reason is because it is not considered such an irregularity to simply place the foods in the opposite order. [Igros Moshe 4:74 Lash 9]
Other opinions: Some Poskim rule it suffices to use the irregularity of Mi Techila, and one is not required to also change the way of mixing. [Derisha; Chazon Ish 58:5, See Shabbos Kehalacha ibid in Biurim; To note that Admur in 321:16 only mentions this Shinuiy and makes no mention of making a Shinuiy in the mixing, however in 473:34 he mentions both Shinuyim]
Shesisa and Matzah flour: Some Poskim write that Shesisa, and Matzah flour, this irregularity alone suffices. [Michaber ibid; Iglei Tal ibid; Igros Moshe 4:74 Lash 9; Shabbos Kehalacha ibid]
[4275] This form of change was only required if one were to make a lot at a time. If, however, one were to make a little at a time, then that itself [the fact that he is only making a little at a time] is considered an irregularity. [See Halacha A above]

How does one do a change of order:[4276] [This depends on how the mixture is normally made in one's area]. If in one's areas during the week the custom is that the vinegar is placed first [and then the flour is placed], then [on Shabbos] one first places the flour [in the bowl] and afterwards places the vinegar. In a place that they are accustomed that the flour be placed first [and then the vinegar], on Shabbos one first places the vinegar in [and then the flour]. [See Q&A]

Q&A

What does one do if he does not know the order of which a certain mixture is mixed?
Some Poskim[4277] rule if one does not know what the custom is he is to first place in the food and then the liquid. Other Poskim[4278] however rule if one does not know the custom then he is not allowed to knead the mixture.

If one desires to squeeze lemon juice onto avocado dip, may he first place in the food and then squeeze the lemon?
Some[4279] write it is permitted to do so. Others[4280] write that doing so is forbidden.

C. Changing the form of mixing:

Mixing the food in an irregular manner is defined as an irregularity for the mixing of thin batters [and thick batters of un-kneadable materials in a time of need[4281]].[4282] It however does not suffice to perform this irregularity alone, and in addition, one must also perform the irregularity explained in B of "Mi Techila", changing the order of how the liquid is placed in the vessel.[4283]

Mixing slowly:[4284] Mixing the mixture in a slower pace than usual does not suffice as a valid irregularity, and rather one must use one of the irregularities enumerated below.

[4276] 321:16; Rama 321:16
[4277] Terumos Hadeshen 53; Chok Yaakov 473:26; Elya Raba 321:20; Tosefes Shabbos 321:30; P"M 321 M"Z 12; Mishneh Berurah 321:57; Ketzos Hashulchan 130:2; Shabbos Kehalacha 22:14 footnote 42; Piskeiy Teshuvos 321:21; See Iglei Tal 30:15
[4278] Taz 321:11; Aruch Hashulchan 321:20; Chazon Ish 58:1; Igros Moshe 4:74; See Iglei Tal Lash 30:15 and Bris Olam Lash; See Piskeiy Teshuvos ibid footnote 234 that when making a thin batter one may be lenient even according to the Chazon Ish in this case, as it suffices to make the irregularity of the form of mixing.
[4279] SSH"K 8:17; Piskeiy Teshuvos 321 footnote 233
[4280] Ketzos Hashulchan 130 footnote 19
[4281] Michaber 324:3 and Admur 324:3 mentions this irregularity regarding Morsan; Menorah Hatehorah 321:34; Piskeiy Teshuvos 321:20 footnote 226; Shabbos Kehalacha 22:24
Other opinions: Some Poskim rule that in addition to this irregularity, one must also do the irregularity of "little by little" when mixing thick batters. [Aruch Hashulchan 321:20; See Biur Halacha "Shema"]
[4282] Admur 324:3; Michaber and Rama 316:15-16; 324:3; Shabbos ibid
[4283] Admur 473:34 regarding making Charoses; Rama 321:16; M"A 321:24; Taz 321:12; Terumos Hadeshen 53 brought in Beis Yosef 321; Or Zarua, brought in Biur Halacha "Veyeish Omrim"; Mordechai, brought in Beis Yosef; M"B 321:57 and 68; Ketzos Hashulchan 130:3 and footnote 9; Kaf Hachaim 321:111; Shabbos Kehalacha 22:14-Biurim 7; Piskeiy Teshuvos 321:21; Toras Hamelachos Lash 16
The reason: As one is required to perform a Shinuiy according to the Lisha definition of both Rebbe Yehuda and Rebbe Yossi, in both the placing of the liquid and the actual kneading. [Terumos Hadeshen ibid; See Iglei Tal Lash 30:14] Alternatively, the reason is because it is forbidden to mix the mixture very forcefully, and hence one requires an irregularity in the actual mixing so he not come to mix it strongly. [Or Zarua as explained in Chazon Ish ibid] Alternatively, the reason is because it is not considered such an irregularity to simply place the foods in the opposite order. [Igros Moshe 4:74 Lash 9]
Other opinions: Some Poskim rule it suffices to use the irregularity of Mi Techila, and one is not required to also change the way of mixing. [Derisha, See Chazon Ish 58:5, See Shabbos Kehalacha ibid in Biurim; To note that Admur in 321:16 only mentions this Shinuiy and makes no mention of making a Shinuiy in the mixing, however in 473:34 he mentions both Shinuyim]
Shesisa and Matzah flour: Some Poskim write that Shesisa, and Matzah flour do not require this irregularity and the irregularity of Mi Techila suffices. [Michaber 321:14 based on Rishonim; Iglei Tal ibid; Igros Moshe 4:74 Lash 9; Shabbos Kehalacha ibid]
[4284] Rama 321:16; Or Zarua; Mordechai; M"B 321:62-64; Implication of Admur 473:34; Ketzos Hashulchan 130 footnote 13; Shabbos Kehalacha 22:15; Regarding why Admur 321:16 writes that a spoon may be used by the case of mustard, see next Halacha and the footnote there!
Other opinions: Some Poskim rule it suffices to mix the items slower than usual. [Michaber 321:15-16; See M"B 321:58 and Biur Halacha "Yachol"; See Shabbos Kehalacha ibid footnote 46; Vetzaruch Iyun on Piskeiy Teshuvos 321:21 who rules like the Michaber when the Rama clearly argues]

Using a finger:[4285] Mixing with the finger is a valid method of irregularity.

Shesi Vaereiv:[4286] Mixing in a form of Shesi Vaeirev is a valid method of irregularity. [This means that one is to make alternative strokes vertical and horizontal as opposed to in circular motion.] One may use even a regular vessel when doing this method.[4287] It is permitted to make as many strokes as one desires in this method, [moving the vessel many times vertically and then many times horizontally] until it mixes well.[4288] [He is to remove the spoon between changing directions from horizontal to vertical or vice versa.[4289] From the letter of the law however removing the spoon between each stroke is unnecessary so long as he is careful not to make a circular motion with the spoon.[4290]]

Mixing the vessel:[4291] Shaking the vessel which contains the mixture until the mixture is kneaded is defined as a valid method of irregularity.

Pouring from one vessel to another:[4292] Pouring the mixture from one vessel to another until it mixes well[4293] is defined as a valid method of irregularity.

Summary-The definition of an irregularity:

Although it is permitted to knead a thin batter one is required to make **two** changes[4294] from the normal way one kneads during the week. These are:

A. <u>Changing the order of ingredients.</u> If in ones areas during the week the custom is that the liquid is placed first and then the food is placed, on Shabbos one first places the food and afterwards places the liquid. If the custom is vice versa, on Shabbos one first places in the liquid and then the food[4295].

B. <u>Changing the mixing method</u>: In addition to the above, one may not blend the mixture with a spoon. One is rather to do so with his hands or through shaking the vessel [or through pouring the food from one vessel to another] until it mixes in.

Q&A

May one use an irregular vessel to mix the ingredients?[4296]

➤ Example: May one use a knife, the back of a spoon or fork, to mix the mixture?

It is allowed to use an irregular item, such as a knife to mix the ingredients, although one may not mix the ingredients in a fast pace. Likewise, one may use a common vessel in an irregular

---

[4285] Admur 473:34; Rama 321:16; Or Zarua; Mordechai
[4286] Admur 324:3 and Michaber 324:3 regarding Morson; Shabbos ibid; Piskeiy Teshuvos 321:21 and Shabbos Kehalacha 22:18 footnote 56 that this irregularity is valid regarding all mixtures
[4287] The reason: This is considered an irregularity since he is not mixing it with his hands and is not circling the spoon or wooden stick in its usual form as done during the week, but rather is mixing it by pushing it horizontally and vertically; therefore, this is considered a complete irregularity. [Admur ibid]
[4288] Admur ibid; Beis Yosef 324 in name of Rif and Rambam; Bach
Other opinions: Some Poskim rule one may not make more than one stroke in this method. [Rashi Shabbos ibid; Tur; See however Peulas Tzaddik 3:160 and Shabbos Kehalacha 22 footnote 58 that this means that one is not to move the vessel more than one stroke at a time, meaning one-time Shesi and one-time Arev, however one may repeat the Shesi and Arev many times.]
[4289] Chazon Ish 58:6; Shevet Halevi 6:86-6; Shabbos Kehalacha 7:61; 22:18; Bris Olam; Piskeiy Teshuvos 321:21
The reason: The reason for this requirement is so one not come to make a circular motion accidently when mixing.
[4290] Igros Moshe 4:74 Lash 10; See Shabbos Kehalacha ibid footnote 57
[4291] Admur 324:3; 473:34; Shabbos ibid; Taz 321:12; Terumos Hadeshen 53; M"B 321:57 and 63; Shabbos Kehalacha 22:17; Piskeiy Teshuvos ibid
[4292] Admur 324:3; Michaber 324:3; Rambam 21:34; Shabbos Kehalacha 22:17; Piskeiy Teshuvos ibid
[4293] Admur ibid; See Igros Moshe ibid; Shabbos Kehalacha ibid footnote 53
[4294] Admur 473:34; Rama 321:16
Other Opinions: Chazon Ish 58:5 rules by a thin batter one is only required to make one change from the way it is done during the week, such as to place the ingredients in differently, although he may mix it normally with a spoon.
[4295] Above Halacha 16
[4296] Igros Moshe 4:74 Lash 11; Minchas Yitzchak 1:74; Piskeiy Teshuvos 321:21; See Shabbos Kehalacha 22 Biurim 10 that this irregularity only helps in certain cases.
Ruling of Taz: The Taz 321:11 rules it does not help to mix using a knife. Perhaps however this refers to a case in which using a knife is the regular method. See Poskim ibid

way, such as the back of a spoon or fork.

If one is unable to mix the mixture together using his fingers or bowl may he use a spoon?[4297]

Yes. Although he is to do so by making alternative strokes vertical and horizontal as opposed to in circular motion.[4298] Likewise, he is to remove the spoon between each stroke.[4299] From the letter of the law however removing the spoon between each stroke is unnecessary so long as he is careful not to make a circular motion with the spoon.[4300]

May one mix a baby's bottle by shaking it?[4301]

No.

May one blend the mixture quickly when using his hands to mix?

Tzaruch Iyun.[4302]

4. May one knead a food which was already kneaded?[4303]

A food or material that was already kneaded does not contain a kneading prohibition to be re-kneaded[4304] unless the food has now become dry[4305], or if further kneading will benefit the food to make it into a thick batter.[4306] Even in a case that the kneading prohibition does not apply, one must still perform the kneading with certain irregularities, as will be explained. The following law in the Shulchan Aruch deals with two cases: 1) kneading a food on Shabbos that was not kneaded before Shabbos but had liquid placed into it, and 2) Kneading a food on Shabbos that was kneaded before Shabbos and one is now kneading in more liquid to make it thinner.

[4297] SSH"K 8:9 based on ruling in 324:3: *One may knead even a lot at a time although taking care to not mix it with ones hands after placing the water in it as is the usual way that one mixes it during the week. Rather one is to mix it with a large serving spoon or a stick which contains a horizontal piece of wood on it, even many times until it mixes well. This is considered an irregularity since he is not mixing it with his hands and is not circling the spoon or wooden stick in its usual form as done during the week, but rather is mixing it by pushing it horizontally and vertically; therefore this is considered a complete irregularity.*

[4298] Seemingly Rav Farkash learns that this may be done even initially, as he rules regarding kneading egg salad with oil that it may be mixed in this method. There he mentions it is proper to remove the spoon in between each stroke. [Shabbos Kehalacha 7:61] Nevertheless in Piskeiy Teshuvos 321:9 he learns this method is only to be done in a time of need.

[4299] Shabbos Kehalacha 7:61 and so questions Chazon Ish and so rules Bris Olam. The reason for this requirement is so one not come to make a circular motion accidently when mixing.

[4300] Igros Moshe 4:74 Lash 10

[4301] Piskeiy Teshuvos 321 footnote 239; Shabbos Kehalacha 22:39

[4302] On the one hand Admur writes in Halacha 5 below that when adding liquid to the mustard one may only mix in slowly. However regarding Charoses he does not make mention of this. On the one hand one can explain that by Charoses he relied on what he already explained in this chapter, although this is difficult to accept being that he does make mention of the other forms of irregularity so why would he omit this one. As well the end of the case regarding mustard is discussing using a spoon to mix, and perhaps the ending of "not to mix quickly" is going on when a spoon is used. As well it seems unlikely that 3 irregularities would be required. It is also implied from all Poskim which mention using the finger and do not limit this to being done slowly, that it is allowed. On the other hand, from Chazon Ish 58:5 it is implied that one may not mix it quickly even when using an irregular vessel, and so implies Shabbos Kehalacha 22:15.

[4303] 321:16; Michaber 321:15-16; Sefer Hateruma; See Shabbos Kehalacha 22:32-35 and Biurim 17 for all the below points to be mentioned.

[4304] Admur and Michaber 321:15 as explained in Biur Halacha 321:15 "Yachol Learbavo"; Toras Shabbos 321:22; Har Tzevi Lash 2; Maharsham 7:7; Tehila Ledavid 321:20; Iglei Tal Lash 14; See Ketzos Hashulchan 130 footnote 1 and footnote 6
Rabbinical prohibition: Some Poskim rule that there is nevertheless a Rabbinical prohibition involved in doing Lisha, and hence it may only be done with the Shinuyim recorded here. [Ketzos Hashulchan 130 footnote 6; Arugas Habosem 80:9]

[4305] Taz 321:11; Tehila Ledavid ibid; Iglei Tal ibid; Har Tzevi ibid; Ketzos Hashulchan 130 footnote 12

[4306] Biur Halacha 321:14 "Ein Megablin"; Ketzos Hashulchan ibid
Other opinions: Some Poskim rule that even in such a case the kneading prohibition does not apply. [Iglei Tal Lash 6 brought in Ketzos Hashulchan ibid; Chazon Ish 58:5; see Har Tzevi 1:193]

A. If water was simply placed in the mixture from before Shabbos, but was not kneaded into it:[4307]

To make a thick batter is forbidden in all circumstances [according to the second opinion] due to that it is considered kneading unless one already placed the liquid [in the flour and the like] from before Shabbos in which case [according to the second opinion mentioned above] it is permitted to knead it on Shabbos (little by little[4308] [or through another irregularity[4309] such as using one's finger[4310]]) whether with roasted flour or with Shesisa.[4311] The reason for this is because if the water was placed in from before Shabbos, kneading it on Shabbos does not contain a Biblical prohibition but rather a Rabbinical[4312] prohibition, which was permitted through making it with an irregularity in the form explained above.[4313] [The above law refers to an un-kneadable material.[4314] However if it is a kneadable material then some Poskim[4315] rule that according to the first opinion mentioned in Halacha 1, it is Biblically forbidden to knead it into a thick batter even if the water was placed in before Shabbos. Furthermore, some Poskim[4316] rule that if it is a kneadable material then it is Biblically forbidden to knead into a thick batter even according to the second opinion mentioned here. Practically we are stringent like all opinions in this matter, and hence one may not knead kneadable material into a thick batter even if liquid was placed into before Shabbos.[4317] However regarding un-kneadable material, if the liquid was placed into it

---

[4307] 321:16 and 324:3; Michaber 321:15-16; Sefer Hateruma

[4308] Seemingly this means to do so slowly, as brought in Michaber 321:15 and M"B 321:62; This would be permitted even with a spoon. [Magen Avraham 321:21; M"B 321:62 that when mixing in the original liquid that was placed before Shabbos a spoon may be used even according to the Rama.] Vetzaruch Iyun from Admur; See Biur Halacha 321:15 "Veyeish Omrim"

[4309] Admur 324:3

[4310] M"B 321:64

[4311] Admur 321:16

[4312] From here we can learn that kneading an already kneaded item still contains a Rabbinical kneading prohibition, and hence requires the mixing irregularities mentioned above. [Ketzos Hashulchan 130 footnote 13]

[4313] Admur 324:3

The reason: As according to this opinion, placing the water into the material already considers the mixture to have been kneaded, and hence one is not doing any extra act through mixing it. [M"B 321:64] Furthermore, by un-kneadable materials, there is no further action that can be done as the entering of the water accomplishes the entire kneading. [See Biur Halacha 321:14 "Ein Megablin"] However according to the former opinion that only actually kneading the water is considered kneading, than it is only allowed to be done with un-kneadable material, as explained above, and even then only with an irregularity, which is defined as kneading it with one's hand, or by shaking the bowl. However, kneadable material is forbidden to initially knead on Shabbos into a thick batter even with an irregularity.

[4314] Morson is an un-kneadable material, see also Ketzos Hashulchan 130 footnote 11 that mustard is an un-kneadable material

[4315] See Biur Halacha 321:15 "Yachol Learvo" and Shabbos Kehalacha Tosefes Biur 22:10; The Biur Halacha ibid states that in this matter [of liquid placed in before Shabbos] the opinion of Rebbe Yossi and Rambam is stricter than the opinion of Rebbe Yehuda and Sefer Hateruma.

The reason: As according to the first opinion it is only considered kneading when one kneads the water into the material and hence if one does so on Shabbos to a kneadable material he Biblically transgresses irrelevent of whether the water was placed into the material before Shabbos, and it is hence forbidden to initially knead it on Shabbos even with an irregularity. [See Biur Halacha ibid]

Other opinions: Some Poskim rule that if liquid was placed before Shabbos then according to Rebbe Yossi there is no prohibition to further knead it even by kneadable material, as even in his opinion the prohibition is only when one performs both steps of adding the water and mixing it. [Iglei Tal Lash 2 brought in Ketzos Hashulchan 130 footnote 12; See Shabbos Kehalacha Tosefes Biur 22:10] Nevertheless this opinion holds that according to Rebbe Yehuda there is a Biblical prohibition involved by kneadable materials according to Rebbe Yehuda, as brought next. Hence, according to all approaches, there is one opinion [either Rebbe Yehuda or Rebbe Yossi] that holds there remains a Biblical prohibition to knead the water into kneadable material. The practical ramifications between who holds of this opinion is regarding if one may be lenient in a time of need, as rules Rebbe Yossi. [see coming footnotes]

[4316] Biur Halacha 321:14 "Ein Megablim" based on Yerushalmi; Iglei Tal Lash 4, brought in Ketzos Hashulchan 130 footnote 12; Implication of Admur in Rebbe Yehuda which writes "

The reason: Even according to Rebbe [second opinion] the above Poskim rule that there a Biblical prohibition to knead a kneadable material mixture that had the liquid placed in it before Shabbos, but was not kneaded. The reason for this is because the kneading process is not complete until the liquid is actually kneaded into the food and thus even according to Rebbe there is a Biblical prohibition involved to knead the mixture together. However, by un-kneadable material there is no further action that can be done through the kneading, as the entering of the water accomplishes the entire kneading. [See Biur Halacha 321:14 "Ein Megablim" based on Yerushalmi; Iglei Tal Lash 4, brought in Ketzos Hashulchan 130 footnote 12]

Other opinions: Other Poskim rule that there is no Biblical prohibition involved in further kneading it according to Rebbe even by kneadable materials. [Chazon Ish 58:5; See Shabbos Kehalacha Tosefes Biur 22:10]

[4317] Ketzos Hashulchan 130 footnote 1 and 12

In a time of need: Some Poskim rule that in a time of need one may knead even kneadable material on Shabbos if liquid was placed into it before Shabbos. [Ketzos Hashulchan 130 footnote 12] This is based on the Iglei Tal Lash 2 which rules that according to Rebbe

before Shabbos then all opinions agree that it is permitted to knead it on Shabbos into a thick batter using the stated mixing irregularities.[4318] It is permitted to even add more liquid to this food on Shabbos, and mix it in with the stated irregularities.[4319] However in such a case one may not use a spoon to mix it[4320], while when mixing in the original liquid some Poskim[4321] rule one may use a spoon to mix it slowly.]

B. If water was kneaded into the mixture from before Shabbos:[4322]

[Even] according to the first opinion, mustard [or any other material, whether kneadable or not kneadable] which one kneaded [with liquid[4323]] from before Shabbos is allowed to be mixed with liquids the next day [on Shabbos] whether by hand or with a spoon[4324] and have honey or [or any other liquid[4325]] placed in it so long as one does not mix it strongly and rather mixes it little by little [i.e. slowly][4326].[4327] [**See Q&A**] [One may knead it with liquid on Shabbos even into a thick

---

Yossi there is no Biblical prohibition involved in doing so, and in a time of need one may be lenient like Rebbe Yossi over Rebbe Yehuda, as rules the Taz 321:12. However according to the other opinions [Biur Halacha ibid] which rule that according to Rebbe Yossi there remains a Biblical prohibition against doing so, then it is forbidden to do so even in a time of need, as we do not rule like Rebbe Yehuda in a time of need. Practically, one is to be stringent in this matter. [Sheveit Halevi 3:50; See Piskeiy Teshuvos 321:19; See Shabbos Kehalacha Tosefes Biur 22:10]

[4318] If the material is not a kneadable material, then there is no Biblical prohibition in mixing it in according to Rebbe or Rebbe Yossi [Chazon Ish 58:5], being that its complete form of kneading has already been accomplished according to Rebbe, and according to Rebbe Yossi there is never a Biblical prohibition in kneading un-kneadable materials. However according to Rebbe Yossi there is still a Rabbinical prohibition involved in doing so, being in his opinion the Sages decreed against kneading un-kneadable products and this product has never yet been kneaded, and it hence must be done with the irregularities. [See Biur Halacha 321:15 "Yachol Learbavo"; Ketzos Hashulchan 130 footnote 12; Shabbos Kehalacha Tosefes Biur 22:10] Furthermore, even according to Rebbe there is a Rabbinical prohibition involved in doing so being Rabbinically it is forbidden to re-knead a food that was kneaded before Shabbos, and hence in conclusion according to all one must perform the kneading of this liquid through the above-mentioned irregularities. [See Admur 324:3; Ketzos Hashulchan 130 footnote 13]
Why one is not required to perform the irregularity of Mi Techila according to Rebbe Yossi? Seemingly the reason for this is because the liquid was already entered into the food and hence this irregularity is no longer relevant. Furthermore, perhaps in such a case everyone agrees that one irregularity suffices.

[4319] M"B 321:64

[4320] M"B ibid; Ketzos Hashulchan 130:3 and footnote 13
Other opinions: However, the Igleiy Tal argues and allows to mix it slowly with a spoon even in such a case.

[4321] Magen Avraham 321:21; M"B 321:62 that when mixing in the original liquid that was placed before Shabbos a spoon may be used even according to the Rama. Vetzaruch Iyun from Admur 324:2; See Biur Halacha 321:15 "Veyeish Omrim" who questions this ruling

[4322] 321:16; Michaber 321:15 regarding mustard and 321:16 regarding Shiclim/Lepidum and garlic; Shabbos 140a regarding all three

[4323] Biur Halacha 321:15 "Yachol Learbavo"; This means that it was kneaded with liquid from before Shabbos, and it is hence permitted to add water to it on Shabbos being there is no kneading after kneading as it simply makes the food liquidier like a drink. [Biur Halacha 321:15 "Yachol Learbavo"]
Other opinions-Kneaded with its own liquid: Some Poskim rule that according to Rebbe Yossi/Rambam [first opinion] it is permitted to knead the mustard on Shabbos even if it was not kneaded before Shabbos with other liquids, and simply with its own moisture. [Taz 321:14; P"M 321 M"Z 13; Elya Raba brought in M"B 321:58; See Biur Halacha ibid] Perhaps this is because it is made into a thin batter, or perhaps it is because mustard is not Bar Gibbul. However, the simple implication of this ruling is that even a thick batter is permitted, and hence one must establish that it is not Bar Gibbul, and for it to apply according to all opinions in Rebbe Yossi one must say it was fully kneaded before Shabbos with other liquids. Furthermore, even by a thin batter we require it to be done with the irregularities stated by the Sages, as brought in Michaber 321:14 and hence one must establish the case to refer to a pre-kneaded food. [Biur Halacha ibid] Alternatively however one can explain that the above Poskim learn in the Michaber that a food that was kneaded with its own juice is considered fully kneaded, and there is no kneading after kneading. [See Tehila Ledavid 321:21] Howevre it is clear that the M"B does not accept this opinion

[4324] The Ketzos Hashulchan [130 footnote 9 and 13] brings from the Mishneh Berurah [321:62 and 64] that one may only use one's fingers to mix it. This follows the ruling of Admur regarding Charoses, brought in the next Halacha. Apparently, the reason why here Admur writes that a spoon may be used is because he is following the ruling of the Michaber at this point in the text, which allows a spoon to be used. However, in the remaining part of the text, which was lost, perhaps Admur brought down the Rama which forbids its use. This would explain why there is no contradiction between the ruling of Admur here and the ruling by Charoses. Alternatively, however one can explain that Admur holds that only when one is adding liquid for the first time, as is the case by Charoses, a spoon may not be used, although when simply adding more liquid on Shabbos, as is the case here, then perhaps a spoon can be used. [See Ketzos ibid in name of Iglei Tal] Practically the Mishneh Berurah [321:64] and Ketzos Hashulchan 130 footnote 13 rule the Rama's ruling to not use a spoon applies equally by both cases.

[4325] So is proven from the fact Admur mentions above "with liquids..........honey..........".

[4326] This is required because even further kneading a material that was kneaded before Shabbos is Rabbinically forbidden unless done with an irregularity. [Ketzos Hashulchan 130 footnote 13]

batter[4328], and may enter the liquid into it in the regular order followed during the week. Practically however, one may not use a spoon to mix it.[4329] Likewise, the above only applies to a product that is still moist on Shabbos due to the liquid that was mixed in. If, however, the product has dried, such as it was baked after the kneading on Erev Shabbos, then the kneading prohibition fully applies to this product, and it may only be made into a thin batter following the irregularities required by the Sages.[4330]]

Summary:

One did not knead the added water before Shabbos: By un-kneadable materials one may mix with an irregularity the liquid that was added before Shabbos into the material even if one will make a thick batter. It is to be mixed slowly [and a spoon may be used for this mixing[4331]]. One may also add liquid to it and make it into a thick batter [although if one is adding more liquid to it, then a spoon may not be used, and one thus needs to mix it with his hands[4332]]. However, by kneadable materials one is to be stringent not to knead it at all into a thick batter [even in a time of need[4333]].[4334]

If one kneaded the water into the food before Shabbos: If the food was kneaded before Shabbos [and still remains moist] then according to all one may add water or any other liquid[4335] to the food on Shabbos and knead it with one's fingers [as opposed to with a spoon[4336]] even if it will be a thick batter. [This applies even by a kneadable material.[4337] However, the above only applies to a product that is still moist on Shabbos due to the liquid that was mixed in. If however the product has dried, such as it was baked after the kneading on Erev Shabbos, then the kneading prohibition fully applies to this product, and it may only be made into a thin batter following the irregularities required by the Sages.]

Q&A

How much liquid must be added to a food before Shabbos to consider it previously kneaded?

It does not suffice to add/knead a few mere drops into the food before Shabbos.[4338] However it suffices to put/knead in a small amount of liquid.[4339]

Other opinions: Some Poskim rule that a previously kneaded food does not require an irregularity upon being kneaded. [So rule regarding cooked foods-Beis Yosef in name of Teshuvos HaRambam; Taz 321:14; brought also in M"A 321:28] Practically, the Poskim negate this opinion. [M"A 321:28; Bach; Elya Raba 321:28; Chayeh Adam 20:21; Kaf Hachaim 321:134]

[4327] The reason: As there is no Lisha after Lisha. [See Toras Shabbos 321:22; Har Tzevi Lash 2; Maharsham 7:7; Tehila Ledavid 321:20; Iglei Tal Lash 14] Alternatively, the reason is because this is not considered Lisha at all but rather a dilution, as Lisha is only when one causes solids to stick together through the adding of liquid and here the opposite is accomplished. [Biur Halacha 321:15 "Yachol"]

[4328] Ketzos Hashulchan 130:3 as is evident from Admur 321:16 in the second opinion

[4329] Mishneh Berurah 321:62 and 64; Ketzos Hashulchan 130 footnote 9 and 13

[4330] Taz 321:11; Tehila Ledavid ibid; Iglei Tal ibid; Har Tzevi ibid; Ketzos Hashulchan 130 footnote 12

[4331] Magen Avraham 321:21; M"B 321:62 that when mixing in the original liquid that was placed before Shabbos a spoon may be used even according to the Rama. Vetzaruch Iyun from Admur 324:2; See Biur Halacha 321:15 "Veyeish Omrim" who questions this ruling

[4332] M"B 321:64; Ketzos Hashulchan 130:3 and footnote 13

[4333] Explained in previous footnotes

[4334] Biur Halacha "Ein Megablin" according to Rebbe Yehuda and "Yachol Learbo" according to Rebbe Yossi; Igleiy Tal Lash 14 according to Rebbe Yehuda

The explanation: See previous footnotes that a) According to Biur Halacha this is Biblically forbidden according to Rebbe Yossi and b) According to some Poskim this is Biblically forbidden [also, or only] according to Rebbe Yehuda.

[4335] So is proven from the fact Admur mentions above "with liquids...........honey..........".

[4336] Ketzos Hashulchan 130:3 and footnote 13. See explanation in previous footnote.

[4337] So seems logical from the above ruling by mustard, even though mustard is not necessarily considered kneadable material, and so rules SS"K Chapter 20 Halacha 7.

[4338] M"A 321:23; Taz 321:13 based on Terumos Hadeshen; Elya Raba 321; M"B 321:65; Ketzos Hashulchan 130 footnote 11

[4339] Taz ibid; M"B ibid; Biur Halacha 321:15 "Davka" that so agrees also M"A ibid

Other opinions: Some Poskim rule that it does not suffice to put in a small amount. [Beir Heiytiv 321:20 in M"A ibid] The Biur Halacha ibid argues on this understanding

Definition of small amount:[4340] One needs to add enough liquid so that the entire food became wet due to it, and that it be enough to make the food pasty enough to be used as a dip. If water was placed in but was not enough to turn the food from a solid into a dip, it is forbidden to add liquid to it on Shabbos [unless made into a thin batter with an irregularity]. Nevertheless if a few drops sufficed to turning it into a dip, then this too would be considered already kneaded.[4341]

May one add more food into a mixture that was kneaded before Shabbos in order to thicken it?[4342]
No, as by doing so one is kneading that added substance which was not previously kneaded.

May one mix a foods own liquids into the food if it becomes one unit?
Some Poskim[4343] rule it is permitted to do so. Other Poskim[4344] rule it is forbidden to do so. Practically, one is to be stringent.[4345] However this only applies if the food was not kneaded with this liquid before Shabbos.[4346]

- Ground garlic: If ground garlic secreted liquids the following is the law regarding if one may mix that liquid into the garlic on Shabbos. If the garlic was ground on Shabbos in a permitted way it is forbidden to mix in its extracted liquids on Shabbos.[4347] If, however, one crushed the garlic before Shabbos, it is permitted to knead in the liquid on Shabbos using an irregularity, [such as one's finger or doing slowly with a spoon[4348]].

- Peanut or Tehina oil:[4349] It is permitted to slowly mix with a spoon[4350] oil which floats on top of peanut butter into the peanut butter.[4351]

[4340] Ketzos Hashulchan 130 footnote 11; See also Iglei Tal 14; Shevisas Hashabbos Lash 2; Chazon Ish 58:5; Piskeiy Teshuvos 321:25
[4341] Ketzos Hashulchan 130 footnote 12
[4342] SSH"K 8:7
[4343] Chazon Ish 58:8-9; Shevisas Hashabbos Lash 8-9; Igros Moshe 4:74 Lash 2; Everyone agrees that according to the second opinion doing so is not considered kneading and would thus be permitted. The reason for this is because they hold that the main aspect of kneading is the adding of ingredients, and here no ingredients were added, as the food naturally came with it.
[4344] Tehila Ledavid 321:21 and 29; Ketzos Hashulchan 130:3 footnote 8 in name of Igleiy Tal 30 that according to the first opinion mentioned, doing so is considered kneading and is thus forbidden. The reason for this is because according to the first opinion the prohibition of kneading is simply to join two items into one, which is accomplished even when kneading food with its own liquid. However according to the second opinion doing so is not considered kneading and would thus be permitted. The reason for this is because they hold that the main aspect of kneading is the adding of ingredients, and here no ingredients were added, as the food naturally came with it. The final ruling: As was explained above we are stringent like both opinions, and thus this may not be done.
[4345] Piskeiy Teshuvos 321:24
[4346] SSH"K 8:7
[4347] Tehila Ledavid 321:21 and 29; Ketzos Hashulchan 130:3 footnote 8 in name of Igleiy Tal
[4348] M"B 321:62 in the name of the Magen Avraham 321:22 that when mixing in the original liquid that was placed before Shabbos a spoon may be used even according to the Rama.
[4349] So rules SSH"K 8:7
[4350] M"B [62] in the name of the Magen Avraham [22] that when mixing in the original liquid that was placed before Shabbos a spoon may be used even according to the Rama.
[4351] This is allowed to be done being that the butter is considered to have been kneaded from before Shabbos with its oil of which some still remains within the mixture, of which the law is that one may add its liquid to it on Shabbos, as will be explained in Halacha 5. [SSH"K ibid]
Adding in other liquids: SSH"K ibid allows one to add other liquids as well to the peanut butter based on their understanding [in Biur Halacha 321 Yachol Learvo"] that adding liquid is allowed when one intends to make a food thinner as, kneading only applies when one desires to thicken the food. Vetzaruch Iyun Gadol from what will be explained in Practical Q&A, as well as in Halacha 5 Q&A, that the mixing of a foods own liquid before Shabbos does not consider it mixed, and thus there would remain no allowance to enter other liquids into the peanut butter. Furthermore, the ruling there in Biur Halacha is referring to adding water to an already kneaded food as then one destroys the kneading that was already done, and does not apply when a food was never yet kneaded. This is in addition to that SSH"K contradict themselves later regarding Tehina, that one may not add liquids to it. See also Ketzos Hashulchan 130 footnote 19 which brings up such a logic that thinning a food is not considered kneading, although he concludes one may not rely on this as we see even by radishes the Taz was stringent to require a Shinui. Despite the above to enter the peanut oil into the butter would be allowed even in accordance to the ruling there as according to both opinions there once the oil has been mixed into it before Shabbos, entering back its own oil is not problematic-see there!

- Tuna oil: May one mix tuna with its oil? One may mix the oil into the tuna with an irregularity[4352], doing so slowly even with a spoon.[4353]

May one add liquid on Shabbos to a mixture which was previously kneaded with only its own liquids?[4354]

➤ Example: Tehina or peanut butter which was mixed before Shabbos with their oil. Ground garlic which was mixed with its own secreted liquid before Shabbos. May one add water to it on Shabbos?

Some Poskim[4355] rule is forbidden to be done on Shabbos [unless made into a thin batter with an irregularity]. Other Poskim[4356] rule it is permitted to be done on Shabbos. Practically one is to be stringent.[4357]

Regarding if one may knead a foods own liquid into the food on Shabbos, such as mixing the peanut butter oil into the peanut butter-See previous Q&A there!

May one add liquid to one's dip which was kneaded with liquid before Shabbos if it is now dry?[4358]

No[4359] [unless made into a thin batter with an irregularity].

Q&A on baked foods
Does the Lisha prohibition apply to baked foods?
Some Poskim[4360] rule that according to some[4361] opinions the Biblical kneading prohibition

---

[4352] As the oil was already placed within the tuna from before Shabbos, and tuna is not a kneadable material. [See Halacha 4 and Q&A there]

[4353] M"B [62] in the name of the Magen Avraham [22] that when mixing in the original liquid that was placed before Shabbos a spoon may be used even according to the Rama.

[4354] Ketzos Hashulchan 130:3 footnote 8 in name of Igleiy Tal; So rules also Chazon Ish 58:8-9. Vetzaruch Iyun Gadol on the SSH"K 8:7 which permits adding liquid to peanut butter on the basis that it had already been kneaded with its oil, even in a case that the oil is floating. Vetzaruch Iyun Gadol.

[4355] Tehila Ledavid 321:21 and Ketzos Hashulchan 130:3 footnote 8 in name of Igleiy Tal 30 that so is ruling according to Rebbe Yehuda, brought in Michaber 321:16; Implication of Biur Halacha 321 "Yachol Learbevo" which negates the explanation of P"M 321 M"Z 13 and implies that by Bar Gibul, even according to Rebbe Yossi there would be a prohibition in doing so; So rules also Chazon Ish 58:8-9; SSH"K regarding Techina however see SSH"K 8:7 who allows adding other liquids to the food even if it was not mixed with external liquid before Shabbos; See Piskeiy Teshuvos 321:25
The reason: This matter follows the same dispute as mentioned above [in Halacha 1]. According to the first opinion mentioned the mixture is already considered kneaded, and thus adding liquid is allowed. As according to the first opinion the prohibition of kneading is simply to join two items into one, which is accomplished even when kneading food with its own liquid. However according to the second opinion the mixture is not considered previously kneaded unless it was kneaded with a substance other than its own. As they hold that the main aspect of kneading is the adding of ingredients, and here no ingredients were added, as the food naturally came with it. Therefore, according to them in the above cases remain forbidden to add water on Shabbos to the mixture. The final ruling: As was explained above we are stringent like both opinions, and thus this may not be done [unless made into a thin batter with an irregularity]. To note that if the food is Bar Gibul, then according to some Poskim this would be forbidden even according to Rebbe Yossi, as explained above from M"B.

[4356] Tehila Ledavid 321:21 that so is ruling of first opinion in Michaber 321:15 as explained in P"M 321 M"Z 13 [brought in M"B 321 and Biur Halacha ibid] that if the mustard was kneaded with its juice before Shabbos it may be kneaded even into a thick mixture on Shabbos with a Shinuiy; The following Poskim rule it is permitted if the liquid simply dilutes the food and does not make its pieces stick together: Or Letziyon 2:33-7 and many Rabbanim regarding Techina including Yalkut Yosef; Rav Avraham Yosef; Rav Dov Lior; See Biur Halacha "Yachol learvo" and SSH"K 8:7 for similar logic that by diluting there is no prohibition. To note however that the Biur Halacha ibid clearly refers to a food that was kneaded with a separate liquid before Shabbos, in which case diluting it is permitted, as Ein lash after lash. Likewise, according to Rebbe Yehuda that the Melacha is to join the liquid with the soild then here too it would be forbidden.

[4357] SSH"K 8 regarding Techina; Shabbos Kehalacha 22:60 footnote 60 as we are initially stringent like the opinion of Rebbe Yehuda

[4358] Ketzos Hashulchan 130 footnote 12

[4359] As this is similar to dough which has been turned into bread which contains a kneading prohibition as explained.

[4360] Biur Halacha 321:14 "Shema Yavo" in opinion of Tosafus

[4361] This refers to the opinion of Tosafus Shabbos 18a in Rebbe Yossi which is part of the 2nd opinion in Admur ibid; Vetzaruch Iyun if this would apply likewise according to the opinion of the Rambam, which is the first opinion in Admur ibid. However certainly it would not apply according to the opinion of Rebbe Yehuda [2nd opinion in Admur ibid], as he prohibits to knead roasted flour even with the irregularities, as brought in Shabbos 155b and Admur ibid.

does not apply to baked or cooked foods.[4362] Nevertheless, even according to this opinion it remains Rabbinically forbidden to do so, and thus may only be done with the irregularities listed by the Sages.[4363] Practically, even baked products must follow the regular kneading rules and hence may only be made into a thin mixture following the irregularities listed by the Sages.[4364] This applies even if the baked product was previously kneaded with water prior to the baking.[4365]

May one knead an already kneaded item that has now become a solid, such as bread/crackers and the like?[4366]
No. The kneading prohibition applies even to a kneaded baked item. Thus, one may not add water/wine/oil to bread and then knead it with one's hands, unless done in a way permitted above [i.e. a thin batter with an irregularity].

May one dip a piece of bread in soup or a biscuit in tea/coffee?[4367]
One is allowed to dip a piece of bread in the soup.[4368] Nevertheless, one may not knead the bread together with the liquid [unless making it into a thin batter, using an irregularity]

May one break his bread/biscuits into pieces and place them into his soup/tea?[4369]
This may only be done without restriction if one places in large pieces of bread or crackers which will float above the liquid. If, however, one desires to mix them together, or is placing in small pieces of bread or crackers, it may only be done mixture will be kneaded into thin batter, using an irregularity.

Q&A on cooked foods
Does the Lisha prohibition apply to cooked foods?[4370]
Some Poskim[4371] rule that the kneading prohibition does not apply to cooked foods and does not even require an irregularity upon being kneaded.[4372] Other Poskim[4373] rule that it applies to cooked foods and hence one may only knead it [even into a thick batter[4374]] using a Shinuiy. Practically, if the cooked dish contains many small pieces which stick to each other,

---

[4362] The reason: As the food is ready to be eaten in its current state, and hence adding water to it is not considered part of the Melacha of Lisha but rather as part of the eating process. [ibid]
[4363] Biur Halacha ibid
[4364] As according to Rebbe Yehuda baked products retain the Biblical prohibition [as seen from Shabbos 155b and Admur 321:16 regarding roasted flour], and initially we are stringent like the opinion of Rebbe Yehuda.
[4365] Taz 321:11; Tehila Ledavid ibid; Iglei Tal ibid; Har Tzevi ibid; Ketzos Hashulchan 130 footnote 12
[4366] Ketzos Hashulchan 130 footnote 1 and 6
[4367] Ketzos Hashulchan 130 footnote 6
[4368] Doing so does not constitute kneading according to any opinion.
[4369] Ketzos Hashulchan 130 footnote 6; See also Chazon Ish 58:7 and Biur Halacha 321:12 "Lefareir Lechem"
[4370] See Shabbos Kehalacha 22:12-13; Piskeiy Teshuvos 321:23
[4371] Beis Yosef 321 in name of Teshuvos HaRambam brought also in M"A 321:28; Taz 321:14; Orchos Shabbos 6:13
Opinion of Michaber: The Michaber 321:19 permits to knead/mix a dish that came off the fire. It is however disputed amongst the Poskim here as to whether one must follow the kneading restrictions or not.
Opinion of Biur Halacha: The Biur Halacha 321:14 "Shema Yavo" states that that according to the opinion of Tosafus the Biblical kneading prohibition does not apply to cooked or baked foods. The reason for this is because the food is ready to be eaten in its current state, and hence adding water to it is not considered part of the Melacha of Lisha but rather as part of the eating process. Nevertheless, even according to this opinion it remains Rabbinically forbidden to do so, and thus may only be done with the irregularities listed by the Sages. Furthermore, according to Rebbe Yehuda baked products retain the Biblical prohibition, as he prohibits to knead roasted flour even with the irregularities, as brought in Shabbos 155b and Admur 321:16, and initially we are stringent like the opinion of Rebbe Yehuda. Practically, it seems that even according to the above novelty of the Biur Halacha he holds that cooked products must follow the regular kneading rules and hence may only be made into a thin mixture following the irregularities listed by the Sages.
[4372] The reason: As the food is ready to be eaten in its current state, and hence adding water to it is not considered part of the Melacha of Lisha but rather as part of the eating process. [ibid]
[4373] M"A 321:28; Bach; Elya Raba 321:28; Chayeh Adam 20:21; Kaf Hachaim 321:134
[4374] The above Poskim that argue on the above opinion only rule that a Shinuiy is required, however do not require it to be made into a thin batter. Simply speaking, the reason for this is because we are discussing a food that had water placed in it before Shabbos [as it was cooked in water] and is of un-kneadable material, and hence according to all may be made into a thick batter using a Shinuiy.

such as cooked rice and the like, then it may be kneaded without a Shinuiy even into a thick batter even if the food is dry.[4375] Furthermore, there are opinions[4376] which permit kneading without a Shinuiy all cooked foods which are now soft and easily mash-able even if the pieces are currently not sticking together and will become a thick batter due to the kneading.[4377] Other Poskim[4378] argue on this conclusion.

May one add liquid to a cooked dish on Shabbos if doing so will make it into a thick batter?

This follows the same answer as above, and hence if the food is not currently a single unit, it should be done with an irregularity.

May one knead gravy into mashed potatoes?

Yes, as the potatoes have already been kneaded with water when cooked.

May one add soup to his rice/lentils/chulent if doing so will make it into a thick batter?[4379]

Yes, this may be done even if the food is dry, as explained in Halacha 5 Q&A.

5. *How to make Charoses on Yom Tov which falls on Shabbos:*[4380]

Making it before Shabbos: [The Charoses may be made on Yom Tov in its regular fashion, with exception to] when Yom Tov falls on Shabbos, [in which case] one must make it before Shabbos.

If one forgot to make it before Shabbos: If one forgot to make the Charoses before Shabbos, he may make it on Shabbos [into a thin batter[4381]] with an irregularity, which is defined as first place the wine in the vessel and then the Charoses, and to mix it with one's hand or through shaking the vessel.

6. *Kneading course flour for animal fodder:*[4382]

A. First Opinion:

Biblically: It was already explained in chapter 321 [Halacha 16] that coarse grain is not a knead-able product and if it is kneaded on Shabbos there are opinions which say that he is Biblically exempt [from the transgression].

[4375] Ketzos Hashulchan 130 footnote 12 regarding lentils, Chazon Ish 58:9

The reason: As the food is already considered kneaded, as it is currently a thick mixture which sticks to each other and is ready to be eaten, and thus the adding of liquid does not change its state of food.

[4376] SSH"K 8:19, based on Chazon Ish 58:9 which writes that the same way that cooking a food removes its grinding restrictions it similarly removes its kneading restrictions. Nevertheless, the Chazon Ish limits this to case that the food is still moist. If however the food is now dry, he too agrees that it is forbidden; However based on the M"B in Biur Halacha "Shema Yavo" on Halacha 14, which writes that by cooked foods the kneading prohibition does not apply as adding liquid is considered the way of eating, then even if the food is now dry the prohibition would not apply. See previous footnotes regarding this matter.

The opinion of Admur regarding a dry food: He for certain does not hold of the M"B allowance to knead dry cooked foods, as stated regarding roasted flour which Admur rules according to the second opinion contains the kneading prohibition and thus may only be made into a thin batter. However regarding moist/soft cooked foods it is unclear what Admur would hold. From the Ketzos Hashulchan however it seems clear that he would not allow it, as he limits the allowance to add liquid to cooked dishes to cases where the particles of the food stick together and form a glob, such as in rice, and thus excludes kneading single cooked food into liquid.

[4377] As they say that cooked, soft foods do not contain the kneading prohibition and thus one may add liquid to them and knead the liquid into it even into a thick batter, using the regular methods.

[4378] Shabbos Kehalacha ibid; Piskeiy Teshuvos ibid

[4379] Ketzos Hashulchan 130 footnote 12

[4380] 473:34; M"B 321:68; Shabbos Kehalacha 22:80

[4381] Mishneh Berurah 321:64; Peri Megadim 321 M"Z 23; Igros Moshe 4:74 Lash; So also rules Ketzos Hashulchan 130 footnote 9, and explained that this is what Admur meant when saying to look in chapter 321. See above Halacha 2

[4382] Admur 324:3

Rabbinically: Nevertheless, it is Rabbinically forbidden to knead coarse grain for an animal or chickens as is done during the week, and rather one must implore in irregularity [in the kneading process].

The definition of an irregularity is: Such as to knead it little by little as was explained there, or even a lot at a time although taking care to not mix it with one's hands after placing the water in it as is the usual way that one mixes it during the week. Rather one is to mix it with a large serving spoon or a stick which contains a horizontal piece of wood on it, even many times until it mixes well. This is considered an irregularity since he is not mixing it with his hands and is not circling the spoon or wooden stick in its usual form as done during the week, but rather is mixing it by pushing it horizontally and vertically; therefore, this is considered a complete irregularity.

It is as well permitted to pour it from vessel to vessel until it mixes well.

Mixing a lot at a time: It is permitted to mix the course flour in this method even a lot at a time, in accordance with the amount that his animals need, and separates the mixture into many different vessels and places it in front of each animal.

B. Second Opinion:

[However] according to the opinion which holds that one who kneads course flour is Biblically liable even by simply placing water into it, without kneading it, as [they hold] that the placing of the water is defined as kneading, as was explained there, then it is forbidden to place water into course flour on Shabbos even using an irregularity, unless the water was placed in from before Shabbos in which case kneading it on Shabbos does not contain a Biblical prohibition but rather a Rabbinical prohibition, which was permitted through making it with an irregularity in this form explained above.

C. Final Ruling

It was already explained there that one is to be stringent like the latter opinion and so is the custom.

Practical Q&A

May one make instant foods through mixing water and a powder together, such as instant mashed potatoes/porridge/rice?[4383]

All instant food powders such as mashed potato mix, and the like, which are only edible when mixed with water may not be made on Shabbos into a thick mixture. However, one may make it into a thin mixture together with the required irregularities, as defined above. [However, there are Poskim[4384] which prohibit making instant potato mix even into a thin batter under the basis that they nevertheless stick to each other.]

May one make oatmeal on Shabbos?

It is forbidden to make it into a thick batter even using cold water. However, one may make it into a thin mixture using an irregularity, as defined above. In all cases one may not use hot water even of a Keli Shelishi due to the cooking prohibition.[4385]

[4383] Piskeiy Teshuvos 321:8; See Shabbos Kehalacha 22:78

[4384] Igros Moshe 4:74 Lash 12; Shabbos Kehalacha 22:78; Shmiras Shabbos Kihilchasa chapter 8 Halacha 25, in the name of the Chazon Ish [Orach Chayim 56:9]. Vetzaruch Iyun Gadol as why here even a thin batter is prohibited. Even the Mishneh Berurah himself [chapter 337:52], to whom they mention in the footnote only says that to make it thick is forbidden, as well as in all cases the food somewhat sticks together, and under what basis can one prohibit it?

[4385] Shabbos Kehalacha p. 73

May one make instant pudding or Jell-O?[4386]

No.[4387] It is however permitted to make it very liquidly to the point it can be drunk, and will not congeal in the interim.[4388]

May one make Tehina on Shabbos?

Adding water to pure Tehina:[4389] It is forbidden to make a normal texture of Tehina by placing water to pure Tehina, if the Tehina did not have water mixed into to it before Shabbos.[4390] It is however permitted to add a large amount of water [simultaneously-not drop by drop] to the Tehina and make it into a thin batter [i.e. a thinner mixture than usual[4391]], provided one does so with the two forms of irregularities. [One is to 1) Place the ingredients together in opposite order and 2) not mix the batter in a way that is usually done with a spoon or fork.] Some Poskim[4392] however rule it is permitted to make Tehina regularly on Shabbos, even if the mixture will not be thinner than usual. [Practically, one is not to make Tehina on Shabbos unless he follows the regulations mentioned above which are 1) Thinner batter than usual and 2) Place the ingredients together in opposite order and 3) Not mix the batter in a way that is usually done with a spoon or fork.]

Adding more water to a Tehina dip: If water was mixed into the Tehina from before Shabbos and one now desires to make it thinner, it is allowed to be done so long as the Tehina will not thicken in the interim. Nevertheless, one may only mix the water using one's hands rather than a spoon, or use another form of irregularity.

Thickening it: If the Tehina is too liquidly, it remains forbidden [according to the main opinion above] to add any Tehina or other food to the mixture to make it thicker [unless the final batter will still be thinner than the way it is made during the week, and one uses the above two forms of irregularities].

May one make an egg salad with mayonnaise on Shabbos?

Some[4393] rule it is forbidden to be made on Shabbos.[4394] Others[4395] rule it may be done on

---

[4386] Beir Moshe 6:45; Sheivet Halevy 7:41

[4387] As doing so forms a thick mixture which is forbidden to be done on Shabbos. Furthermore, some prohibit doing so due to Nolad.

[4388] See Igros Moshe 4:74 Lash 12 which allows making pudding into a thin batter.

[4389] SSH"K [new edition]; Shabbos Kehalacha 22:60; Piskeiy Teshuvos 321:27-7 and footnote 270; And so is the ruling according to Tehila Ledavid 321:21 and Ketzos Hashulchan 130:3 footnote 8 in name of Igleiy Tal 30 that so is ruling according to Rebbe Yehuda, brought in Michaber 321:16; Implication of Biur Halacha 321 "Yachol Learbevo" which negates the explanation of P"M 321 M"Z 13 and implies that by Bar Gibul, even according to Rebbe Yossi there would be a prohibition in doing so; So rules also Chazon Ish 58:8-9; however see SSH"K 8:7 who allows adding other liquids to the food even if it was not mixed with external liquid before Shabbos; See Piskeiy Teshuvos 321:25

[4390] The reason: This matter follows the same dispute as mentioned above [in Halacha 1]. According to the first opinion mentioned the mixture is already considered kneaded, and thus adding liquid is allowed. As according to the first opinion the prohibition of kneading is simply to join two items into one, which is accomplished even when kneading food with its own liquid. However according to the second opinion the mixture is not considered previously kneaded unless it was kneaded with a substance other than its own. As they hold that the main aspect of kneading is the adding of ingredients, and here no ingredients were added, as the food naturally came with it. Therefore, according to them in the above cases remain forbidden to add water on Shabbos to the mixture. The final ruling: As was explained above we are stringent like both opinions, and thus this may not be done [unless made into a thin batter with an irregularity]. To note that when the food is Bar Gibul [as is the case with Tehina], then according to some Poskim this would be forbidden even according to Rebbe Yossi, as explained above from M"B.

[4391] See above Q&A regarding the definition of a thin batter.

[4392] Or Letziyon 2:33-7; Many Rabbanim including Yalkut Yosef; Rav Avraham Yosef; Rav Dov Lior; Tehila Ledavid 321:21 that so is ruling of first opinion in Michaber 321:15 as explained in P"M 321 M"Z 13 [brought in M"B 321:? and Biur Halacha ibid] that if the mustard was kneaded with its juice before Shabbos it may be kneaded even into a thick mixture on Shabbos with a Shinuiy.
The reason: As the Melacha of Lash is only when one connects pieces together and not when one dilutes a food.

[4393] Shabbos Kehalacha 22:70

[4394] As it is forbidden to make a thick batter on Shabbos.

[4395] Nishmas Shabbos 321:305; Orchos Shabbos 6:18 footnote 46; Shabbos Kehalacha 7:61

Shabbos. Practically, one may do so using an irregularity.[4396] Thus he is to first place in the mayonnaise and then the eggs, as well as he is to mix it [using his fingers or by shaking the bowl, and if this is not possible then he may] with a spoon back and forth and opposed to in a circular motion. It is preferable to remove the spoon between each time.

May one mix mayonnaise into tuna fish on Shabbos?

This follows same status as egg salad in which some Poskim[4397] prohibit making it on Shabbos, while others[4398] rule it is permitted.

May one mix mayonnaise into eggplant to make Chatzilim?

This follows the same ruling as stated above regarding egg salad in which some Poskim[4399] prohibit making it on Shabbos, while others[4400] rule it is permitted.

May one mix mayonnaise with tuna or eggs on Shabbos?

Some[4401] rule it is forbidden to be made on Shabbos.[4402] Others[4403] rule it may be done on Shabbos.[4404] [Practically, one may do so using an irregularity.[4405] Thus he is to first place in the mayonnaise and then the tuna/eggs, as well as he is to mix it [using his fingers or by shaking the bowl, and if this is not possible then he may] with a spoon back and forth and opposed to in a circular motion. It is preferable to remove the spoon between each time. The above only refers to mixing mayonnaise with small pieces of egg or tuna and hence making it into a single lump. However, if the piece of the egg or tuna are chunky, and hence do not form a single lump, it is permitted to be mixed according to all, even without an irregularity.]

May one mix mayonnaise into eggplant to make Chatzilim?

This follows same status as egg salad in which some Poskim[4406] prohibit making it on Shabbos, while others[4407] rule it is permitted. [Practically, it is best to only do so before Shabbos.[4408]]

[4396] Although a thick mixture is made since this is un-kneadable material [which according to the first opinion may always be made with an irregularity] and it is unclear if this form of mixture contains at all a kneading prohibition [as the food is cooked, and had water placed in it before Shabbos through the cooking], we are thus lenient [like the first opinion] to allow making it on Shabbos.

[4397] Shabbos Kehalacha 22:70

[4398] Nishmas Shabbos 321:305; Orchos Shabbos 6:18 footnote 46; ; So I saw ruled in the name of Rav Shternbuch
The leniencies of tuna is that it is unclear if it is at all a material which contains a kneading prohibition. Furthermore, all tuna comes with either water or oil, and is hence considered kneaded before Shabbos to which one may add more liquids on Shabbos. [See above Halacha 4 Q&A]

[4399] Shabbos Kehalacha 22:3

[4400] Nishmas Shabbos 321:305; Orchos Shabbos 6:18 footnote 46; ; So I saw ruled in the name of Rav Shternbuch
The leniencies of tuna is that it is unclear if it is at all a material which contains a kneading prohibition. Furthermore, all tuna comes with either water or oil, and is hence considered kneaded before Shabbos to which one may add more liquids on Shabbos. [See above Halacha 4 Q&A]

[4401] Shabbos Kehalacha 22:70

[4402] The reason: As it is forbidden to make a thick batter on Shabbos due to the kneading prohibition.

[4403] Nishmas Shabbos 321:305; Orchos Shabbos 6:18 footnote 46; Shabbos Kehalacha 7:61; So I saw ruled in the name of Rav Shternbuch

[4404] The reason: As from their understanding, there is no prohibition of mixing mayonaise with a solid on Shabbos even in accordance to Rebbe Yehuda, and therefore, since the mixture is Eino Bar Gibul, it does not transgress the laws of kneading at all. [See Shabbos Kehalacha ibid]

[4405] The reason: Although a thick mixture is made, since this is un-kneadable material [which according to the first opinion may always be made with an irregularity] and the food is cooked, and had water placed in it before Shabbos through the cooking, therefore even according to the opinion of Rebbe Yehuda, there is no kneading prohibition involved. This certainly applies with tuna that was in a can in which it actually sat in liquid, and hence whether according to Rebbe Yehuda, or Rebbe Yossi, it is permitted to be kneaded, as according to Rebbe Yehuda it was already pre-kneaded, and according to Rebbe Yossi it is Eino Bar Gibul which may always be kneaded with an irregularity. [See Admur 324:3]

[4406] Shabbos Kehalacha 22:70

[4407] Nishmas Shabbos 321:305; Orchos Shabbos 6:18 footnote 46

[4408] The reason: As we are initially stringent like the opinion who holds it is forbidden to knead even Eino Bar Gibbul, and here there is no added Heter of it being pre-kneaded, as it is not cooked in other liquids.

Does mashing a banana and the like contain a kneading prohibition?[4409]
No –See above Halacha 1 Q&A. Nevertheless, mashing contains a grinding prohibition and may only be done in ways explained in "The laws of Grinding"-See There!

May one knead liquid into a mashed banana?[4410]
The Ketzos Hashulchan allows this to be done with an irregularity for the reason that doing so before Shabbos would ruin the banana, and thus in such a case one may be lenient like the first opinion mentioned above which allows kneading with an irregularity foods which are not knead-able. The Chazon Ish[4411] however rules that liquid may not be added to bananas.

Q&A on mixture not defined as kneading
When making a bottle for an infant from milk powder must it be made with the required irregularities?[4412]
If the milk powder will dissolve immediately upon adding the liquid to it, then it is allowed to be made without any irregularities[4413] [although according to some doing so would involve a Nolad prohibition, and thus although one may be lenient it is proper if possible, to prepare this mixture from before Shabbos.[4414]]
However, if the powder will not dissolve right away and will become a semi thick mixture in the interim of it dissolving into the liquid, then it may only be made with the above-mentioned irregularities.[4415] Others[4416] however rule even in such a case one may do so in the normal way.
Due to the cooking prohibition, one is only to use water from a Keli Shelishi, or water which is poured from a Keli Sheiyni.

When adding liquid into cocoa powder and the like must one do so with an irregularity?[4417]
See above Q&A.

May one mix mayonnaise/oil/honey into cut fruits/vegetables and foods of the like?[4418]
Cut large: The kneading prohibition only applies when the two substances are being mixed in a way that they join and stick to each other forming one entity, as is the case with dough which is a mixture of flour and water, or with cooked oatmeal. Thus, whenever solids are large enough to prevent this form of unity in their mixture, and it is rather that the liquid cotes over the solids, or that the solids are submerged within the liquids, then it is allowed. One may thus pour oil over his vegetable salad and cases of the like.

[4409] SSH"K 8:3
[4410] Ketzos Hashulchan 130 footnote 19 and SSH"K 8:14; Shabbos Kehalacha 22:41
[4411] 58:9
[4412] SSH"K 8:18
[4413] As it does not resemble in any way the concept of kneading, as explained in Halacha 2 in Q&A there with regards to the definition of a thin batter. It is only when there is some thickness to a mixture that it is within the kneading requirements of an irregularity
[4414] As rules Rav Farkash with regards to instant coffee. See The laws of cooking Halacha 12 Q&A there!
[4415] Vetzaruch Iyun how this case is any different than any case in which the added liquid at first thickens the food and only after further mixing does it thin it out, of which was explained in Halacha 3 Q&A that it is forbidden to do so. Perhaps however the difference is that here one has no intent to knead the powder but to dissolve it and thus it is considered a Pisek Reishe, of which we are lenient in being that anyways according to one opinion this is always allowed with an irregularity. However, by cases where one intends to knead the food, then although his intent is to make it into a thin batter nevertheless since it becoming a thick batter also serves his use, it is not allowed. See SSH"K 8 footnote 61.
[4416] Igros Moshe 4:74 Lash 1
[4417] See SSH"K 18 and 24 and footnote 56. Vetzaruch Iyun why they did not mention explicitly that if it does not dissolve right away an irregularity is to be used, as they wrote by milk powder.
[4418] Taz 321:12 in name of Bach regarding lettuce; Ketzos Hashulchan 130:6 footnote 19; Shevisas Hashabbos Pesicha 20; SSH"K 8:4; Piskeiy Teshuvos 321:27

Cut small: However, if the pieces are cut small enough that the addition of the liquid will combine and unite with the solids to form one food then this is forbidden [unless made into a thin batter using an irregularity]. [**See footnote for explanation and for a list of vegetables which may be allowed even if cut small[4419]**]

Cooked fruits/vegetables:[4420] There are opinions which say that cooked foods which are now soft and easily mash-able do not contain the kneading prohibition and thus one may add liquid to them and knead the liquid into it even into a thick batter, using the regular methods. According to them one may thus add any liquid to mashed potatoes, or to cut pieces of cooked potatoes even if doing so makes it into a thick batter.

Q&A on mixing two semi solids together

Is mixing two solids or semi-liquids together defined as Lash if they unite and become one?[4421]

Dough with dough/bread with bread: Some Poskim[4422] rule the kneading prohibition does not apply in such a case Other Poskim[4423] however question that perhaps the kneading prohibition applies even in such a case.

Semi-liquids such as cheese with honey: Some Poskim[4424] rule the kneading prohibition does not apply in such a case Other Poskim[4425] however question that perhaps the kneading prohibition applies even in such a case.

May one mix sugar with cocoa powder?[4426]
So long as no water is added this is allowed as the substances do not stick to each other and is thus not considered kneading.

May one combine honey with cream cheese?
Some rule[4427] this may not be done as it will be made into a thick mixture. Others[4428] however question this prohibition.[4429]

[4419] This ruling is based on Taz 321:12 which rules that the allowance to cut vegetables small and then add liquid to them is only in accordance to the first opinion being that vegetables are not a knead-able food however according to the second opinion this would be forbidden, [unless made into a thin batter with an irregularity]. Thus, since we rule like the stringent opinion it would be forbidden for us to make a thick mixture of radish. Nevertheless, many are accustomed to be lenient by radishes even if they are cut small. The Taz there writes the reason for this being due to that if one were to make the mixture before Shabbos its taste would be ruined, and it was therefore allowed to do so on Shabbos with an irregularity, relying on the first opinion above. The Ketzos Hashulchan [ibid] as well suggests that perhaps the reason for this leniency by radishes is because the concept of kneading only applies by foods which will stick together to the liquid, such as garlic and the like. However solid vegetables, even when very small, which will not form a real combination with a liquid would be allowed to be mixed even into a thick batter. In any event this is certainly not the opinion of the Taz which mentions explicitly the case of radishes as a case of kneading. The Ketzos Hashulchan [ibid], based on the Taz and Shevisas Hashabbos, rules that by radishes one may be lenient however not by horseradish/beats or any vegetable which secrets a juice which will cause the mixture to stick.
[4420] SSH"K 8:19-See above Halacha 5 Q&A
[4421] Shabbos Kehalacha 22:49; Piskeiy Teshuvos 321:24-25
[4422] Shevisas Hashabbos Lash 8-9 as one is not uniting two different species of foods; Orchos Shabbos 6:20; Nishmas Shabbos 321:306; Igros Moshe 4:74-13; Chut Hashani 13:2 as the kneading prohibition only applies when mixing a liquid with many solids to join and become one soild.
[4423] Rav SZ"A 8 footnote 13 as perhaps the prohibition applies anytime one unites two pieces together through moisture.
[4424] Orchos Shabbos 6:20; Nishmas Shabbos 321:306; Igros Moshe 4:74-13; Chut Hashani 13:2 as the kneading prohibition only applies when mixing a liquid with many soilds to join and become one soild.
[4425] Shevisas Hashabbos Lash 11; Rav SZ"A 8 footnote 13 as perhaps the prohibition applies anytime one unites two pieces together through moisture.
[4426] SSH"K 8:5
[4427] SSH"K 8:13
[4428] Rav Avraham Elyashvili
[4429] As in their opinion these kneading only applies by a solid with a liquid and not by two semi-liquids. Perhaps however there is difference between whether the cream cheese and honey is thick or thin.

May one make thousand island dressing on Shabbos? May one mix mayonnaise with ketchup?
This is dependent on the same dispute mentioned above. According to the lenient opinion above, this is allowed to be done[4430] so long as one mixes the ingredients slowly. However, according to the ruling of the stringent opinion above, seemingly in their opinion here too it would be forbidden.

May one combine two different yogurts, or yogurt with soft cheese?[4431]
Some rule[4432] this may be done so long as one makes it into a thin batter using the mentioned irregularities.
Others[4433] however rule this may be done without restriction.[4434]

May one mix Chumus with Tehina?
This is dependent on the same dispute mentioned above. However, the Chumus and Tehina have water in them, and are considered pre-kneaded, and hence seemingly have greater room for leniency.

May one mix the fruit on bottom of a yogurt?
Yes, however according to the stringent opinion it should be done with an irregularity.

May one break biscuits into his yogurt?
This may be done so long as either a) the biscuits are broken to slightly large pieces [as opposed to crumbs] or b) the biscuits are broken small but the mixture will form a thin batter and is done with an irregularity.

May one add sugar to soft cheese or yogurt?[4435]
One may not add sugar to soft cheese as doing say may thicken the mixture and turn it into a thick batter. However, one may add it into yogurt, being that it makes it thinner.

May one combine cocoa powder with butter or margarine?[4436]
No as doing so forms a thick mixture.

If one transgressed and kneaded a food on Shabbos may the food be eaten?[4437]
Bimeizid: Forbidden until after Shabbos.
Beshogeg: If one transgressed a Biblical kneading prohibition according to all opinions, such as one made a thick batter of kneadable material, then the food is forbidden in benefit until after Shabbos for all people. If, however, only a Rabbinical prohibition was transgressed, such as one made a thin batter without the irregularities required by the Sages, then it is permitted to be eaten by all on Shabbos. If one made a thick batter of un-kneadable material, in which there is a dispute as to whether one transgressed Biblically or Rabbinically, one may be lenient to eat the food on Shabbos.[4438]

[4430] As ketchup with mayonnaise are both semi liquids and thus are not subject to kneading which is with a liquid and a solid.
[4431] SSH"K 8:12
[4432] SSH"K 8:12
[4433] Igros Moshe 4:74 Lash; Rav Avraham Elyashvili mentioned in Rav Gadasi's Hilchos Shabbos
[4434] As in their opinion these kneading only applies by a solid with a liquid and not by two semi-liquids.
[4435] SSH"K 8:16
[4436] SSH"K 8:17
[4437] Biur Halacha 321:16 "Aval Beshabbos"; Shabbos Kehalacha 22:28
[4438] Biur Halacha ibid in name of Elya Raba

May one pour liquid or urinate onto earth?[4439]

Loose earth:[4440] Even if doing so does not contain a planting prohibition[4441] doing so is forbidden due to the kneading prohibition.[4442] [However, if there is no other area to urinate then one may be lenient to do so.[4443]]

Hard earth:[4444] It is permitted to pour water or urinate over hard earth if doing so does not contain a planting prohibition.

May one pour liquid or urinate onto Sand/Ash:[4445]

It is forbidden to urinate or pour liquids over sand, ash and all items of the like. [Thus, children that have reached the age of Chinuch are to be prevented from playing with sand and water on Shabbos.[4446]]

In a time of need: If there is no other area to urinate then one may be lenient to do so.[4447]

May one pour liquid or urinate onto mud?[4448]

Very liquidy mud: If the mud is very liquidly, like a mud puddle than this is allowed.

Thick mud: If the mud is still slightly thick, it is forbidden to be done due to the kneading prohibition.[4449]

Hard and dry mud: Even if the mud is hard and dry it is forbidden to urinate on it, as the mud will soften due to the urine.[4450]

Time of need: Some Poskim[4451] rule that in a time of need one may urinate on the mud if the mud does not belong to him.[4452]

May one spit into a vessel or area which contains sand/dirt?[4453]

It is proper to avoid doing so[4454] although there is much room to side that this is allowed to be

[4439] Ketzos Hashulchan 130:8
[4440] M"A 321:19 regarding mud; P"M 321 A"A 19; M"B 321:57; Ketzos Hashulchan ibid
[4441] See Admur 336:9; The Laws of Shabbos Volume 3 "Plants trees and Garden produce" that urinating on earth is from the letter of the law not prohibited due to the sowing, and that earth which is not designated for sowing and is not near plants or trees does not contain the sowing prohibition even with water.
[4442] The reason: This is Biblically forbidden according to Rebbe Yehuda, and is Rabbinically forbidden according to Rebbe Yossi. [ibid]
[4443] Beis Meir brought in M"B 321:57; Implication of M"A ibid which motions the reader to Michaber 320:14 which brings a dispute if one may urinate on snow, and regarding that dispute Admur rules that in a time of need one may do so, and here too seemingly it is allowed as the main ruling is like Rebbe Yossi that there is no prohibition until one actually kneads the liquid. [See P"M 321 A"A 19]
[4444] Ketzos Hashulchan ibid; Aruch Hashulchan 321:25; Chazon Ish 58:8
[4445] P"M ibid; M"B ibid; Ketzos Hashulchan ibid
[4446] SSH"K 16:4
[4447] Beis Meir brought in M"B 321:57; Implication of M"A ibid which motions the reader to Michaber 320:14 which brings a dispute if one may urinate on snow, and regarding that dispute Admur rules that in a time of need one may do so, and here too seemingly it is allowed as the main ruling is like the Rambam in the opinion of Rebbe Yossi that there is no prohibition until one actually kneads the liquid, and that there is no prohibition by Eino Bar Gibul. [See P"M 321 A"A 19]
[4448] Ketzos Hashulchan 130:8
The reason there is no allowance due to the rule of "Ewin Lash Acchar Lash": As the mud still requires more water for its kneading or the mud is hard and dried, hence entering into the Lash prohibition. [Ketzos Hashulchan ibid footnote 3; Shevisas Hashabbos Lash 6]
[4449] The reason: This is Biblically forbidden according to Rebbe Yehuda, and is Rabbinically forbidden according to Rebbe Yossi. [ibid]
[4450] Peri Megadim 321 A"A 19 leaves this matter in question being that the mud eventually melts due to the liquid; brought in M"B 321:57 and Shaareiy Tziyon 321:66
[4451] M"B 321:57; Beis Meir brought in M"B ibid permits in all cases in a time of need
[4452] The reason: As this is considered a Piseik Reisha Delo Nicha Lei on which one may be lenient in a time of need. [ibid] To note however that Admur rules stringently regarding Pesik Resihei Delo Nicha Lei even by a Rabbinical prohibition, as brought in 316:4 and 320:24]
[4453] Ketzos Hashulchan 130:8 footnote 22
[4454] The Peri Megadim ibid [brought in M"B ibid] leaves this matter in question due to the following reason: According to the second opinion mentioned above, even entering liquid into a non-kneadable material constitutes a Biblical kneading prohibition, and thus perhaps there is no room to permit the spitting. On the other hand perhaps in this case one can be leniently as he has no intent to knead the material with his saliva, and it's a case of "Pisek Reshei Dilo Nicha Lei". [P"M ibid]

done[4455], and so rule some Poskim[4456].

May one cover liquid [such as urine] with sand/dirt?[4457]
One may only do so with a large ratio of dirt/sand over water to the point that the mixture will not form a knead-able substance.

Beating an egg:[4458]
It is forbidden to beat an egg[4459] quickly in a bowl on Shabbos.[4460] Rather, one is to mix it slowly with a spoon.[4461]

May one mix two liquids into each other?[4462]
Yes, doing so does not resemble kneading at all.[4463] Nevertheless, it is forbidden to mix very quickly with a spoon, or other utensil, thick liquids into thin liquids[4464], such as to mix an egg into wine.[4465] It is however permitted to mix two thin liquids very quickly, such as lemon juice and water and cases of the like. Seemingly when mixing concentrated juice or oil into water one is to be stringent to do so slowly.[4466]

Mixing sugar and water quickly:[4467] When mixing two items of which one is not recognizable within the other, such as mixing sugar into water, it is permitted to mix them together quickly with a spoon.

Mixing salad dressing: One may not mix salad dressing very quickly using a spoon if it contains a thick liquid, such as oil with lemon juice. He is rather to mix it slowly.

[4455] So rules Ketzos Hashulchan based on that a) spitting is an irregularity and thus only Rabbinical. B) The amount that can be mixed is less than the Biblical amount needed to transgress kneading. C) Naturally saliva does not sink into material but rather floats over it.
[4456] Beis Meir, brought in M"B ibid
[4457] Chayeh Adam; M"B 321:57; Ketzos Hashulchan 130:8
[4458] M"A 321:24; M"B 321:68; Shabbos 109a
[4459] Other opinions: Some Poskim rule it is permitted to beat a single egg and the prohibition only applies to more than one egg at a time. [Tiferes Yisrael Ofeh 11]
[4460] The reason: Being that this appears like one plans to cook it on Shabbos. [M"A ibid; Rashi ibid] Doing so is forbidden due to Uvdin Dechol. Others rule the reason is because doing so is considered kneading. [Peri Megadim 321 A"A 24] According to the first reason the prohibition is limited only to eggs. According to the second reason the prohibition extends to all matters, as states M"A ibid in name of Hagahos Maimanis 22 and P"M ibid. [Machatzis Hashekel ibid]
[4461] Ketzos Hashulchan 130:7; Chayeh Adam 20:21
[4462] Based on Magen Avraham 321:24 as explained in Ketzos Hashulchan 130:7 footnote 20
[4463] In Yoreh Deah 266:3 the Michaber rules that wine must be mixed with oil from before Shabbos, and so rules Admur in 331:1. The reason for it being forbidden is not because of a kneading prohibition but because doing so was considered a medicine, and it is forbidden to make a medicine on Shabbos. [So writes Admur there]
[4464] So seems evident from all sources listed regarding this law that the prohibition is only applicable when mixing a thick liquid into thin. [See Ketzos Hashulchan ibid; Chayeh Adam 20:21; Peri Megadim A"A 321:24 "As it appears like kneading when making thick"] However to mix two liquids into each other very quickly there is no restriction. This is also implied in the meaning of "Litrof" to beat rather than simply mix. Now, although the Magen Avraham 321:24 brings from the Hagahos Maimanis that one may not mix Zirga wine very quickly. It is unclear as what this wine consists of, and perhaps in truth it does consist of two items of which one is thick and the other thin. [See Beir Yaakov 321 which explains this to be the case]. Furthermore, although the M"A concludes "and so it seems from the Hagahos Maimanis that it is forbidden to beat **all matters**" perhaps this is only coming to include other thick liquids similar to eggs, and is not coming to include all liquids. [See Machatzis Hashekel that this is coming to exclude the opinion of Rashi which rules the prohibition against beating is only by eggs as it appears one is doing so for cooking purposes.] As for the reason it is forbidden to beat two liquids very quickly perhaps this is because it is considered a troublesome act [as writes M"A 321:25 regarding making "Yaynomalin"]. Accordingly, it would be permitted to mix two thin liquids, as doing so involves no trouble at all.
[4465] Magen Avraham 321:24-25
The reason: As for the reason it is forbidden to beat two liquids very quickly perhaps this is because it is considered a troublesome act [as writes M"A 321:25 regarding making "Yaynomalin"]. Alternatively, the reason is because doing so is considered kneading. [Peri Megadim 321 A"A 24] Accordingly, it would be permitted to mix two thin liquids, as doing so involves no trouble at all and is not similar to kneading.
[4466] As the definition of a thick liquid brought above is unclear. Vetzaruch Iyun.
[4467] Ketzos Hashulchan ibid.

May one mix a batch of lemon aid or other juice very quickly with a spoon?
Yes. See above Halacha 1 Q&A.

May one make mayonnaise on Shabbos?[4468]
No.[4469]

May one ice cream on Shabbos?[4470]
No.[4471] This applies even if one makes it into a very thin batter.[4472]

May one whip cream on Shabbos?[4473]
No.[4474]

May one use a whip cream or confetti spray can on Shabbos?
No, due to Molid.

[4468] Tzitz Eliezer 12:32; SSH"K 11 footnote 128

[4469] The reason: As it is forbidden to beat an egg on Shabbos. [Magen Avraham 321:24]

[4470] Betzeil Hachachmah 2:26; Piskeiy Teshuvos 321:30

Other opinions: Some write it is permitted to make ice cream on Shabbos. [SSH"K 10:6]

[4471] This is forbidden due to it being similar to making "Yaynmulin" which is a mixture of wine pepper and oil, of which it is forbidden to beet and then strain due to it being a great trouble. [See Magen Avraham 321:25; Michaber 321:17; Mishneh Shabbos 139b] Alternatively, the reason is because doing so is considered kneading. [Peri Megadim 321 A"A 24; Chemed Moshe 321:6; Biur Hlaacha 321:15 "Yachol"] It is likewise forbidden due to Nolad-forming a new matter on Shabbos. [SSH"K ibid]

[4472] As the prohibition is not due to kneading. In truth however making ice cream into a thick batter would certainly transgress also the kneading prohibition.

[4473] SSH"K 11:31 in name of Rav SZ"A; Piskeiy Teshuvos 321:30

[4474] This is forbidden due to it being similar to making "Yaynmulin" which is a mixture of wine pepper and oil, of which it is forbidden to beet and then strain due to it being a great trouble. [See Magen Avraham 321:25; Michaber 321:17; Mishneh Shabbos 139b] Alternatively, the reason is because doing so is considered kneading. [Peri Megadim 321 A"A 24; Chemed Moshe 321:6; Biur Hlaacha 321:15 "Yachol"] It is likewise forbidden due to Nolad-forming a new matter on Shabbos. [SSH"K ibid]

SHULCHANARUCHHARAV.COM MEMBERS BENEFITS

Choose a subscription plan today and gain access to extra features, including access to our full Audio Shiurim database with over 1500 classes, original source sheets behind the laws, PDF downloads of articles, and much more!

Subscription level	Monthly Payment	Help support a Torah Institution	PDF download of article	10% off purchase of all titles	Access all audio Shiurim	Free copy of annual publication	Access Sources Database	Request Source Sheets	Access Courses
Silver	$18	YES	YES	YES	YES	✖	✖	✖	✖
Gold	$36	YES	YES	YES	YES	YES	✖	✖	✖
Platinum	$54	YES	YES	YES	YES	YES	YES	✖	✖
Sapphire	$100	YES	YES	YES	YES	YES	YES	Four monthly*	✖
Diamond	$150	YES	YES	YES	YES	YES	YES	Eight monthly*	One course per year

*Source sheet requests are dependent on their availability in our personal database

How to subscribe:
- See the following link: https://shulchanaruchharav.com/product/support-subscription/

Membership level Features
PDF downloads [starting from silver]:
- Our online articles on http://shulchanaruchharav.com/ contain a special PDF download option available to all site members and subscribers who are logged in. This allows you to be able to publish, and save or print, a PDF style format of the article for easier reading and for you to keep for your record.
- This feature is only available if you are logged into the website using your username and password. You will receive a username and password after your subscription. If you have lost your username or password, or never received one to begin with, then please contact us to receive it.
- Also, to note, the PDF feature is not available in all articles and it depends on its length. Due to technical limitations, the PDF feature cannot publish into a PDF, articles that have very long HTML pages and thus the above feature is limited only to the short articles which is the bulk of the articles on the website.

10% off all purchases[starting from silver]:
- All members and subscribers can receive a 10% discount on all their book purchases done through our website through entering the discount code in the shopping cart towards the end of the purchase.
- You will receive the code in your confirmation email after your subscription.
- Please save this code for all your future purchases. In case you forget it, you can always request it from us.

Access all our audio Shiurim[starting from silver]:
- Our exciting new feature which is now available for all members is access to our database of recorded Shiurim, which includes over 1,500 recorded classes. While many of the classes are already publicly available for free on our various outlets, such as our website, YouTube, Vimeo, and Podbean, there are many classes which have

never been published and are available in our personal database which we are now extending access to all members. In addition, the classes are all organized under their specific topic and hence you will have a much easier time accessing them and searching for a specific Shiur. Likewise, you are able to download the entire library and listen to it at your leisure without Internet connection. These are benefits not available to the public through our already established outlets.

- The classes consist of all our previous Daily Halacha audios that have featured on the Daily Halacha email and Whatsapp for the past seven years, organized according to topic. They likewise include recordings of public classes that have been given over the years on various subjects, such as the weekly Parsha, Farbrengens, and other events. In addition, our entire Hebrew collection of classes on the laws of Shabbos is likewise available for those who are Hebrew friendly. There are also recordings for various courses that we have taught, such as the Shabbos kitchen, and Meat and Milk for women, and various Semicha courses that are likewise available.
- We will give you access to your email to the folder after your subscription is processed.
- If you choose to download the classes, or the entire folder, which you may, it is strictly for your own personal use and may not be shared with others. If others would like to benefit from it then they should either look for our free public options on the various outlets mentioned above, or become a member just like you.
- Subscribers must commit to remain a member for a full year to merit this benefit.

Free copy of our publications [starting from Gold]:
- All members and subscribers from **gold** level and above are sent a free copy of all new titles that are published in their year of membership.
- If you change your address, please update us right away and especially after a new publication is advertised so that we can send it to the correct address.

Access database of our sources [starting from Platinum]:
- All members and subscribers from **platinum** level and above will be given access to a special OneDrive folder that will hold a database of source sheets for various topics and Halachos.
- This new feature is without doubt one of our most prized and most beneficial for all those who are interested in further researching a given law or subject, without taking the time in searching for all the original sources. In this feature we give applicable members access to files which contain both full articles on various subjects, as well as original photocopies of many of the sources used to write the article.
- Mainly, this feature will include the photocopied sources behind the articles that feature in the daily Halacha. The source sheets will be archived in the relevant folder of their topic. Additional source sheets will also feature in this database, and with time this will become a very large database of source sheets with a photocopy of original sources.
- This feature is perfect for Rabbis, teachers, Magidei Shiurim, etc, for them to be able to prepare a class using the original sources, and even make photocopies to distribute to the participants.

Request source sheets [starting from Sapphire]:

- Members and subscribers from **sapphire** level and above will be able to request a limited amount of source sheets per month on topics that are not found in our database. For example, if a subscriber of sapphire level and above desires to do research on a certain topic, or give a class on a certain subject, and it is not already available in the above-mentioned database, then he may send us a request for sources on the subject, and based on availability in our private personal database, we will arrange it to be sent to the person requesting it.

- Providing source sheets for topics requested is dependent on current availability in our private database and the amount of time required to research the subject. We also reserve the right to reject providing sources on a certain subject based on our discretion. To note, that we already have over 25,000 source sheets in our private database on myriads of subjects that simply require restructuring to be made available upon request.

- The number of requests per month is limited to four monthly requests for a sapphire member and eight monthly requests for a diamond member.

Access courses [Diamond]:

- Members and subscribers from **diamond** level and above will be able to request free enrollment in one of our available courses.

- Members are limited to one course per year and must finish their previous course prior to choosing another course the next year.

Our other Sefarim available on shulchanaruchharav.com, Amazon.com and selected book stores

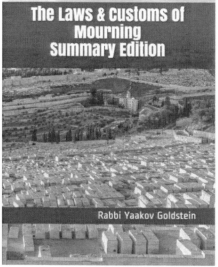

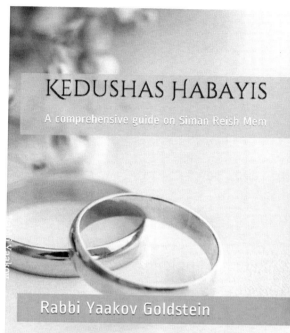

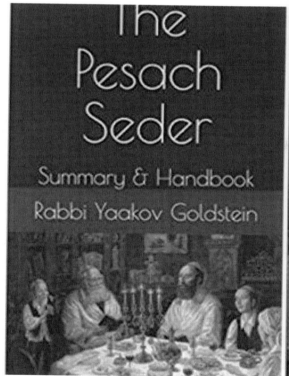

היה קורא פרק שני ברכות   יז.

ולא פריה ורביה ולא משא ומתן ולא קנאה ולא שנאה ולא תחרות אלא צדיקים יושבין ועטרותיהם
בראשיהם ונהנים מזיו השכינה שנאמר יויחזו את האלהים ויאכלו וישתו: גדולה הבטחה שהבטיחן
הקב"ה לנשים יותר מן האנשים שנא' ינשים שאננות קומנה שמענה קולי בנות בוטחות האזנה אמרתי
א"ל רב לר' חייא נשים במאי זכיין "באקרויי בנייהו לבי כנישתא ובאתנויי גברייהו בי רבנן ונטרין לגברייהו
עד דאתו מבי רבנן. כי הוו מפטרי רבנן מבי ר' אמי ואמרי לה מבי ר' חנינא אמרי ליה הכי עולמך תראה בחייך
ואחריתך לחיי העולם הבא ותקותך לדור דורים לבך יהגה תבונה פיך ידבר חכמות ולשונך ירחיש רננות
עפעפיך יישירו נגדך עיניך יאירו במאור תורה ופניך יזהירו כזוהר הרקיע שפתותיך יביעו דעת וכליותיך

Rav said to Rav Chiya

*"With what do women receive merit [of learning Torah]? Through escorting
their children to the Talmud Torah, and assisting their husbands in learning
Torah, and waiting for their husbands to return from the Beis Midrash"*

*This Sefer is dedicated to my dear wife whose continuous support and
sharing of joint goals in spreading Torah and Judaism have allowed this
Sefer to become a reality.*

*May Hashem grant her and our children much
success and blessing in all their endeavors*

שיינא שרה ליבא בת חיה ראשא

&

מושקא פריידא
שניאור זלמן
דבורה לאה
נחמה דינה
מנוחה רחל
חנה
שטערנא מרים
שלום דובער
חוה אסתר
בתשבע
יהודית שמחה

Made in United States
North Haven, CT
17 July 2022

21473729R00352